More information about this series at http://www.springer.com/series/7412

T0188927

Lecture Notes in Computer Science 9913

Commenced Publication in 1973
Founding and Former Series Editors:
Gerhard Goos, Juris Hartmanis, and Jan van Leeuwen

Gang Hua · Hervé Jégou (Eds.)

Computer Vision – ECCV 2016 Workshops

Amsterdam, The Netherlands, October 8–10 and 15–16, 2016
Proceedings, Part I

 Springer

Editors
Gang Hua
Microsoft Research Asia
Beijing
China

Hervé Jégou
Facebook AI Research (FAIR)
Menlo Park, CA
USA

ISSN 0302-9743   ISSN 1611-3349   (electronic)
Lecture Notes in Computer Science
ISBN 978-3-319-46603-3   ISBN 978-3-319-46604-0   (eBook)
DOI 10.1007/978-3-319-46604-0

Library of Congress Control Number: 2016951693

LNCS Sublibrary: SL6 – Image Processing, Computer Vision, Pattern Recognition, and Graphics

Printed on acid-free paper

This Springer imprint is published by Springer Nature
The registered company is Springer International Publishing AG Switzerland

Foreword

Welcome to the proceedings of the 2016 edition of the European Conference on Computer Vision held in Amsterdam! It is safe to say that the European Conference on Computer Vision is one of the top conferences in computer vision. It is good to reiterate the history of the conference to see the broad base the conference has built in the 13 editions. First held in 1990 in Antibes (France), it was followed by subsequent conferences in Santa Margherita Ligure (Italy) in 1992, Stockholm (Sweden) in 1994, Cambridge (UK) in 1996, Freiburg (Germany) in 1998, Dublin (Ireland) in 2000, Copenhagen (Denmark) in 2002, Prague (Czech Republic) in 2004, Graz (Austria) in 2006, Marseille (France) in 2008, Heraklion (Greece) in 2010, Florence (Italy) in 2012, and Zürich (Switzerland) in 2014.

For the 14th edition, many people worked hard to provide attendees with a most warm welcome while enjoying the best science. The Program Committee, Bastian Leibe, Jiri Matas, Nicu Sebe, and Max Welling, did an excellent job. Apart from the scientific program, the workshops were selected and handled by Hervé Jégou and Gang Hua, and the tutorials by Jacob Verbeek and Rita Cucchiara. Thanks for the great job. The coordination with the subsequent ACM Multimedia offered an opportunity to expand the tutorials with an additional invited session, offered by the University of Amsterdam and organized together with the help of ACM Multimedia.

Of the many people who worked hard as local organizers, we would like to single out Martine de Wit of the UvA Conference Office, who delicately and efficiently organized the main body. Also the local organizers Hamdi Dibeklioglu, Efstratios Gavves, Jan van Gemert, Thomas Mensink, and Mihir Jain had their hands full. As a venue, we chose the Royal Theatre Carré located on the canals of the Amstel River in downtown Amsterdam. Space in Amsterdam is sparse, so it was a little tighter than usual. The university lent us their downtown campuses for the tutorials and the workshops. A relatively new thing was the industry and the sponsors for which Ronald Poppe and Peter de With did a great job, while Andy Bagdanov and John Schavemaker arranged the demos. Michael Wilkinson took care to make Yom Kippur as comfortable as possible for those for whom it is an important day. We thank Marc Pollefeys, Alberto del Bimbo, and Virginie Mes for their advice and help behind the scenes. We thank all the anonymous volunteers for their hard and precise work. We also thank our generous sponsors. Their support is an essential part of the program. It is good to see such a level of industrial interest in what our community is doing!

Amsterdam does not need any introduction. Please emerge yourself but do not drown in it, have a nice time.

October 2016

Theo Gevers
Arnold Smeulders

Preface

It is our great pleasure to present the workshop proceedings of the 14th European Conference on Computer Vision, which was held during October 8–16, 2016, in Amsterdam, The Netherlands. We were delighted that the main conference of ECCV 2016 was accompanied by 26 workshops. The workshop proceedings are presented in multiple Springer LNCS volumes.

This year, the 2016 ACM International Conference on Multimedia was collocated with ECCV 2016. As a synergistic arrangement, four out of the 26 ECCV workshops, whose topics are of interest to both the computer vision and multimedia communities, were held together with selected 2016 ACM Multimedia workshops.

We received 44 workshop proposals on a broad set of topics related to computer vision. The high quality of the proposals made the selection process rather difficult. Owing to space limitation, 27 proposals were accepted, among which two proposals were merged to form a single workshop due to overlapping themes.

The final 26 workshops complemented the main conference program well. The workshop topics present a good orchestration of new trends and traditional issues, as well as fundamental technologies and novel applications. We would like to thank all the workshop organizers for their unreserved efforts to make the workshop sessions a great success.

October 2016

Hervé Jégou
Gang Hua

Organization

General Chairs

Theo Gevers   University of Amsterdam, The Netherlands
Arnold Smeulders   University of Amsterdam, The Netherlands

Program Committee Co-chairs

Bastian Leibe   RWTH Aachen, Germany
Jiri Matas   Czech Technical University, Czech Republic
Nicu Sebe   University of Trento, Italy
Max Welling   University of Amsterdam, The Netherlands

Honorary Chair

Jan Koenderink   Delft University of Technology, The Netherlands
     and KU Leuven, Belgium

Advisory Program Chair

Luc van Gool   ETH Zurich, Switzerland

Advisory Workshop Chair

Josef Kittler   University of Surrey, UK

Advisory Conference Chair

Alberto del Bimbo   University of Florence, Italy

Local Arrangements Chairs

Hamdi Dibeklioglu   Delft University of Technology, The Netherlands
Efstratios Gavves   University of Amsterdam, The Netherlands
Jan van Gemert   Delft University of Technology, The Netherlands
Thomas Mensink   University of Amsterdam, The Netherlands
Michael Wilkinson   University of Groningen, The Netherlands

Workshop Chairs

Hervé Jégou   Facebook AI Research, USA
Gang Hua   Microsoft Research Asia, China

Tutorial Chairs

Jacob Verbeek   Inria Grenoble, France
Rita Cucchiara   University of Modena and Reggio Emilia, Italy

Poster Chairs

Jasper Uijlings   University of Edinburgh, UK
Roberto Valenti   Sightcorp, The Netherlands

Publication Chairs

Albert Ali Salah   Boğaziçi University, Turkey
Robby T. Tan   Yale-NUS College and National University
                           of Singapore, Singapore

Video Chair

Mihir Jain   University of Amsterdam, The Netherlands

Demo Chairs

John Schavemaker   Twnkls, The Netherlands
Andy Bagdanov   University of Florence, Italy

Social Media Chair

Efstratios Gavves   University of Amsterdam, The Netherlands

Industrial Liaison Chairs

Ronald Poppe   Utrecht University, The Netherlands
Peter de With   Eindhoven University of Technology, The Netherlands

Conference Coordinator, Accommodation, and Finance

Conference Office
Martine de Wit   University of Amsterdam, The Netherlands
Melanie Venverloo   University of Amsterdam, The Netherlands
Niels Klein   University of Amsterdam, The Netherlands

Workshop Organizers

W01 — Datasets and Performance Analysis in Early Vision

Michael Goesele	TU Darmstadt, Germany
Bernd Jähne	Heidelberg University, Germany
Katrin Honauer	Heidelberg University, Germany
Michael Waechter	TU Darmstadt, Germany

W02 — Visual Analysis of Sketches

Yi-Zhe Song	Queen Mary University of London, UK
John Collomosse	University of Surrey, UK
Metin Sezgin	Koç University, Turkey
James Z. Wang	The Pennsylvania State University, USA

W03 — Biological and Artificial Vision

Kandan Ramakrishnan	University of Amsterdam, The Netherlands
Radoslaw M. Cichy	Free University Berlin, Germany
Sennay Ghebreab	University of Amsterdam, The Netherlands
H. Steven Scholte	University of Amsterdam, The Netherlands
Arnold W.M. Smeulders	University of Amsterdam, The Netherlands

W04 — Brave New Ideas For Motion Representations

Efstratios Gavves	University of Amsterdam, The Netherlands
Basura Fernando	The Australian National University, Australia
Jan van Gemert	Delft University of Technology, The Netherlands

W05 — Joint ImageNet and MS COCO Visual Recognition Challenge

Workshop Wei Liu	The University of North Carolina at Chapel Hill, USA
Genevieve Patterson	Brown University, USA
M. Ronchi	California Institute of Technology, USA
Yin Cui	Cornell Tech, USA
Tsung-Yi Lin	Cornell Tech, USA
Larry Zitnick	Facebook AI Research, USA
Piotr Dollár	Facebook AI Research, USA
Olga Russakovsky	Carnegie Mellon University, USA
Jia Deng	University of Michigan, USA
Fei–Fei Li	Stanford University, USA
Alexander C. Berg	The University of North Carolina at Chapel Hill, USA

W06 — Geometry Meets Deep Learning

Emanuele Rodolà	Università della Svizzera Italiana, Switzerland
Jonathan Masci	Università della Svizzera Italiana, Switzerland
Pierre Vandergheynst	Ecole Polytechnique Fédérale de Lausanne, Switzerland

Sanja Fidler   University of Toronto, Canada
Xiaowei Zhou   University of Pennsylvania, USA
Kostas Daniilidis   University of Pennsylvania, USA

W07 — Action and Anticipation for Visual Learning

Dinesh Jayaraman   University of Texas at Austin, USA
Kristen Grauman   University of Texas at Austin, USA
Sergey Levine   University of Washington, USA

W08 — Computer Vision for Road Scene Understanding and Autonomous Driving

Jose Alvarez   NICTA, Australia
Mathieu Salzmann   Ecole Polytechnique Fédérale de Lausanne,
                                    Switzerland
Lars Petersson   NICTA, Australia
Fredrik Kahl   Chalmers University of Technology, Sweden
Bart Nabbe   Faraday Future, USA

W09 — Challenge on Automatic Personality Analysis

Sergio Escalera   Computer Vision Center (UAB) and University
                                    of Barcelona, Spain
Xavier Baró   Universitat Oberta de Catalunya and Computer Vision
                                    Center (UAB), Spain
Isabelle Guyon   Université Paris-Saclay, France, and ChaLearn, USA
Hugo Jair Escalante   INAOE, Mexico
Víctor Ponce López   Computer Vision Center (UAB) and University
                                    of Barcelona, Spain

W10 — BioImage Computing

Patrick Bouthemy   Inria Research Institute, Switzerland
Fred Hamprecht   Heidelberg University, Germany
Erik Meijering   Erasmus University Medical Center, The Netherlands
Thierry Pécot   Inria, France
Pietro Perona   California Institute of Technology, USA
Carsten Rother   TU Dresden, Germany

W11 — Benchmarking Multi-Target Tracking: MOTChallenge

Laura Leal-Taixé   TU Munich, Germany
Anton Milan   University of Adelaide, Australia
Konrad Schindler   ETH Zürich, Switzerland
Daniel Cremers   TU Munich, Germany
Ian Reid   University of Adelaide, Australia
Stefan Roth   TU Darmstadt, Germany

W12 — Assistive Computer Vision and Robotics

Giovanni Maria Farinella	University of Catania, Italy
Marco Leo	CNR – Institute of Applied Sciences and Intelligent Systems, Italy
Gerard G. Medioni	University of Southern California, USA
Mohan Trivedi	University of California, San Diego, USA

W13 — Transferring and Adapting Source Knowledge in Computer Vision

Wen Li	ETH Zürich, Switzerland
Tatiana Tommasi	University of North Carolina at Chapel Hill, USA
Francesco Orabona	Yahoo Research, NY, USA
David Vázquez	CVC and Universitat Autònoma de Barcelona, Spain
Antonio M. López	CVC and Universitat Autònoma de Barcelona, Spain
Jiaolong Xu	CVC and Universitat Autònoma de Barcelona, Spain
Hugo Larochelle	Twitter Cortex, USA

W14 — Recovering 6D Object Pose

Tae-Kyun Kim	Imperial College London, UK
Jiri Matas	Czech Technical University, Czech Republic
Vincent Lepetit	Technical University Graz, Germany
Carsten Rother	Technical University Dresden, Germany
Ales Leonardis	University of Birmingham, UK
Krzysztof Wallas	Poznan University of Technology, Poland
Carsten Steger	MVTec GmbH, Germany
Rigas Kouskouridas	Imperial College London, UK

W15 — Robust Reading

Dimosthenis Karatzas	CVC and Universitat Autònoma de Barcelona, Spain
Masakazu Iwamura	Osaka Prefecture University, Japan
Jiri Matas	Czech Technical University, Czech Republic
Pramod Sankar Kompalli	Flipkart.com, India
Faisal Shafait	National University of Sciences and Technology, Pakistan

W16 — 3D Face Alignment in the Wild and Challenge

Jeffrey Cohn	Carnegie Mellon University and University of Pittsburgh, USA
Laszlo Jeni	Carnegie Mellon University, USA
Nicu Sebe	University of Trento, Italy
Sergey Tulyakov	University of Trento, Italy
Lijun Yin	Binghamton University, USA

W17 — Egocentric Perception, Interaction, and Computing

Giuseppe Serra	University of Modena and Reggio Emilia, Italy
Rita Cucchiara	University of Modena and Reggio Emilia, Italy
Walterio Mayol-Cuevas	University of Bristol, UK
Andreas Bulling	Max Planck Institute for Informatics, Germany
Dima Damen	University of Bristol, UK

W18 — Local Features: State of the Art, Open Problems, and Performance Evaluation

Jiri Matas	Czech Technical University, Czech Republic
Krystian Mikolajczyk	Imperial College London, UK
Tinne Tuytelaars	KU Leuven, Belgium
Andrea Vedaldi	University of Oxford, UK
Vassileios Balntas	Imperial College London, UK
Karel Lenc	University of Oxford, UK

W19 — Crowd Understanding

François Brémond	Inria Sophia Antipolis, France
Vít Líbal	Honeywell ACS Global Labs Prague, Czech Republic
Andrea Cavallaro	Queen Mary University of London, UK
Tomas Pajdla	Czech Technical University, Czech Republic
Petr Palatka	Neovision, Czech Republic
Jana Trojanova	Honeywell ACS Global Labs Prague, Czech Republic

W20 — Video Segmentation

Thomas Brox	University of Freiburg, Germany
Katerina Fragkiadaki	Google Research, USA
Fabio Galasso	OSRAM GmbH, Germany
Fuxin Li	Oregon State University, USA
James M. Rehg	Georgia Institute of Technology, USA
Bernt Schiele	Max Planck Institute Informatics and Saarland University, Germany
Michael Ying Yang	University of Twente, The Netherlands

W21 — The Visual Object Tracking Challenge Workshop

Matej Kristan	University of Ljubljana, Slovenia
Aleš Leonardis	University of Birmingham, UK
Jiri Matas	Czech Technical University in Prague, Czech Republic
Michael Felsberg	Linköping University, Sweden
Roman Pflugfelder	Austrian Institute of Technology, Austria

W22 — Web-Scale Vision and Social Media

Lamberto Ballan	Stanford University, USA

Marco Bertini   University of Florence, Italy
Thomas Mensink   University of Amsterdam, The Netherlands

W23 — Computer Vision for Audio visual Media

Jean-Charles Bazin   Disney Research, USA
Zhengyou Zhang   Microsoft Research, USA
Wilmot Li   Adobe Research, USA

W24 — Computer Vision for Art Analysis

Joao Paulo Costeira   Instituto Superior Técnico, Portugal
Gustavo Carneiro   University of Adelaide, Australia
Alessio Del Bue   Istituto Italiano di Tecnologia (IIT), Italy
Ahmed Elgammal   Rutgers University, USA
Peter Hall   University of Bath, UK
Ann-Sophie Lehmann   University of Groningen, The Netherlands
Hans Brandhorst   Iconclass and Arkyves, The Netherlands
Emily L. Spratt   Princeton University, USA

W25 — Virtual/Augmented Reality for Visual Artificial Intelligence

Antonio M. López   CVC and Universitat Autònoma de Barcelona, Spain
Adrien Gaidon   Xerox Research Center Europe (XRCE), France
German Ros   CVC and Universitat Autònoma de Barcelona, Spain
Eleonora Vig   German Aerospace Center (DLR), Germany
David Vázquez   CVC and Universitat Autònoma de Barcelona, Spain
Hao Su   Stanford University, USA
Florent Perronnin   Facebook AI Research (FAIR), France

W26 — Joint Workshop on Storytelling with Images and Videos and Large-Scale Movie Description and Understanding Challenge

Gunhee Kim   Seoul National University, South Korea
Leonid Sigal   Disney Research Pittsburgh, USA
Kristen Grauman   University of Texas at Austin, USA
Tamara Berg   University of North Carolina at Chapel Hill, USA
Anna Rohrbach   Max Planck Institute for Informatics, Germany
Atousa Torabi   Disney Research Pittsburgh, USA
Tegan Maharaj   École Polytechnique de Montréal, Canada
Marcus Rohrbach   University of California, Berkeley, USA
Christopher Pal   École Polytechnique de Montréal, Canada
Aaron Courville   Université de Montréal, Canada
Bernt Schiele   Max Planck Institute for Informatics, Germany

Contents – Part I

W10 – BioImage Computing

W22 – Web–scale Vision and Social Media

W24 – Computer Vision for Art Analysis

W02 – Visual Analysis of Sketches

Preface

Welcome to the 1st Workshop on Visual Analysis of Sketches (VASE'16), held in conjunction with ECCV'16, Amsterdam, the Netherlands.

With the proliferation of touchscreens, sketching has become a much easier undertaking for many – we can sketch on phones, tablets and even watches. Research on sketches has consequently flourished in recent years, both in terms of the number of publications and their quality (e.g., Best Demo in ICCV'15 and Best Science Paper in BMVC'15). The objective of this workshop is to bring together researchers exploring the parsing, matching, recognising and understanding of human-generated sketches with a view to consolidating insights and encouraging cross-fertilisation of ideas.

The Computer Vision community in particular is increasingly interested in understanding the medium of sketch, which represents a salient abstraction of visual content. Recently, papers on visual sketch analysis have appeared in BMVC (2013–16), CVPR (2014–16), ECCV (2014–15) exploring a wide spectrum of work from probabilistic and deformable models to the application of contemporary deep learning approaches to sketch. This pursuit is also shared by a diverse range of research areas, including cognitive science, human computer interaction, computer graphics, machine learning and biometrics.

The ultimate purpose of this workshop is therefore to create a common ground for researchers within the computer vision community to showcase their research on human sketch analysis and trigger consolidated discussions towards the future of sketch related research.

We would like to thank the workshop chairs of ECCV'16 for giving us the opportunity to run the first sketch-specific workshop in a major computer vision conference, and we would also like to thank the two keynote speakers Changhu Wang and James Hays, and all authors who contributed towards paper submissions. We look forward to welcoming you in Amsterdam.

October 2016

Yi-Zhe Song
John Collomosse
Metin Sezgin
James Z. Wang

Preface

Welcome to the 1st Workshop on Visual Analysis of Sketches (VASE) as ICPR 2016, in conjunction with ICPR 2016, Amsterdam, the Netherlands.

Face Recognition from Multiple Stylistic Sketches: Scenarios, Datasets, and Evaluation

Chunlei Peng, Nannan Wang$^{(\boxtimes)}$, Xinbo Gao, and Jie Li

State Key Laboratory of Integrated Services Networks,
Xidian University, Xi'an, China
clp.xidian@gmail.com, nnwang@xidian.edu.cn,
{xbgao,leejie}@mail.xidian.edu.cn

Abstract. Matching a face sketch against mug shots, which plays an important role in law enforcement and security, is an interesting and challenging topic in face recognition community. Although great progress has been made in recent years, main focus is the face recognition based on SINGLE sketch in existing studies. In this paper, we present a fundamental study of face recognition from multiple stylistic sketches. Three specific scenarios with corresponding datasets are carefully introduced to mimic real-world situations: (1) recognition from multiple hand-drawn sketches; (2) recognition from hand-drawn sketch and composite sketches; (3) recognition from multiple composite sketches. We further provide the evaluation protocols and several benchmarks on these proposed scenarios. Finally, we discuss the plenty of challenges and possible future directions that worth to be further investigated. All the materials will be publicly available online (Available at http://chunleipeng.com/ FRMSketches.html.) for comparisons and further study of this problem.

Keywords: Face recognition · Viewed sketch · Composite sketch · Fusion

1 Introduction

In criminal investigation, face sketch recognition is an essential technique for real-world situations when the photo of the suspect is unavailable or is captured under poor quality. A face sketch is usually generated by the forensic artist [40] or facial composite software [10] based on the information provided by an eyewitness, victim, or poor quality surveillance videos. The sketch is the only clue to identify the suspect. Due to the large domain gap between face sketches and photos, face recognition from a probe sketch remains a challenging and prevalent topic in the community.

The technique of matching a face sketch against photos has been extensively studied in recent years. Existing approaches can be generally classified into four categories based on the types of sketches used: hand-drawn viewed sketch [36,40], hand-drawn semi-forensic sketch [5,25], hand-drawn forensic sketch [15,16,30], and software-generated composite sketch [10]. Early study mainly focuses on

© Springer International Publishing Switzerland 2016
G. Hua and H. Jégou (Eds.): ECCV 2016 Workshops, Part I, LNCS 9913, pp. 3–18, 2016.
DOI: 10.1007/978-3-319-46604-0_1

viewed sketch, which is drawn by viewing the photo directly. Because the viewed sketch is relatively reliable for identifying the subject, saturated performance [7,29–31,41,42] has been achieved on the viewed sketch benchmark (CUHK face sketch database, CUFS [40]). However, face sketches are usually unreliable in real-world situations due to the domain gap caused by perceptual bias, descriptive bias, and generating bias [24,25]. In order to better understand face sketch recognition in real-worlds, semi-forensic sketch is introduced recently, which is drawn based on the recall of the artist after viewing the photo a few minutes ago. Models trained on semi-forensic sketches have shown their possibility to improve face sketch recognition in practice [5,25]. Forensic sketch is drawn by a forensic artist according to the description of an eyewitness or victim. Forensic sketch recognition is relatively a far from being well studied and solved problem because of the unreliability of forensic sketch. Software-generated composite sketch is widely used in many law enforcement agencies [10]. This is because it is more convenient and efficient to generate a composite sketch by using software than training a skilled forensic artist. However, the composite sketch is composed of isolated facial components. Combining these components to form a face image introduces additional bias than drawing a forensic sketch with pencil in a continuous way. This just makes matching composite sketch with photo being one of the most challenging problems.

Despite the extensive studies on matching a face sketch against photos, they mainly focus on SINGLE sketch based face recognition. However, single sketch can be unreliable in real-world situations[1] according to psychology study [6,24]. Sometimes this unreliability could be at heightened risk for false identification[2]. Researchers have noticed the unreliability of single sketch in recent years. Nejati et al. [24] carefully analyzed the existing biases in matching sketch with photo, and proposed a two-step bias modeling framework. Ouyang et al. [26] introduced the fusion of attributes with low-level features to deal with the cross-modal gap. However, these approaches still cannot cope with the defect of relying on single sketch. In forensic investigations multiple sources of information is available about the suspect [4,9], such as verbal descriptions provided by multiple witnesses or victims, or information obtained from both the verbal description and poor quality surveillance video tracks. These clues can be used to generate multiple face sketches and figure the suspect in different ways with complementary information. Even if there is only one version of description about the suspect, multiple forensic artists can be invited to generate hand-drawn sketches under different styles [8], or multiple software tools can be exploited to generate different stylistic composite sketches [22]. The combination usage of both hand-drawn sketches and composite sketches does exist in real-world cases. The usage of multiple stylistic sketches can be helpful in improving the recognition performance, which has not been rigorously defined and evaluated in the community.

---

[1] http://www.nbcnews.com/news/crime-courts/dying-art-forensic-sketch-artists-face-digital-future-n41421.

[2] http://www.scientificamerican.com/article/do-the-eyes-have-it.

This paper presents a study of face recognition from multiple stylistic sketches. To the best of our knowledge, this is the first study on this essential problem. According to different generation procedures, *i.e.* hand-drawn sketch and software-generated composite sketch, we define three specific scenarios with corresponding datasets and protocols: (1) recognition from multiple hand-drawn sketches drawn by different artists; (2) recognition from a hand-drawn sketch and multiple composite sketches produced by different software tools; (3) recognition from multiple composite sketches from different software tools. We further provide several baseline performances of these three scenarios under pre-defined evaluation protocols. After that we discuss the challenges and possible directions that worth to be investigated in the future, thus making a good start point for research on face recognition from multiple stylistic sketches. All the related materials can be downloaded online (the website will be available after the blind review process) to boost further study on this problem.

In this paper, we make the following three contributions. (1) We present a fundamental study of face recognition from multiple stylistic sketches, and three specific scenarios with corresponding datasets are carefully defined to mimic real-world situations; (2) we provide the evaluation protocols and several benchmarks to address these scenarios, which opens new possibilities of research and further experiments for the benefit of face sketch recognition community; (3) significant challenges and several possible research directions are discussed, which can stimulate future research on this topic.

The remainder of this paper is organized as follows. We first describe related face sketch datasets and representative face sketch recognition methods in Sect. 2. We then define the problem of face recognition from multiple stylistic sketches and three specific scenarios in Sect. 3. Baseline approaches evaluated on the proposed scenarios are introduced in Sect. 4. Evaluations are given in Sect. 5. Conclusion and promising directions are presented in Sect. 6.

2   Related Work

2.1   Face Sketch Recognition

We briefly review representative face sketch recognition methods in this subsection. Existing approaches can be generally classified into four categories based on the types of sketches used: hand-drawn viewed sketch, hand-drawn semi-forensic sketch, hand-drawn forensic sketch, and software-generated composite sketch.

Face sketch recognition started from the seminal work of face sketch synthesis based recognition [36]. Representative approaches include the eigentransformation algorithm [36], the locally linear embedding approach [18], the Markov random field (MRF) based method [40] and a series of improved Markov networks based photo-sketch synthesis methods [29,31,38,44]. However, most of the synthesis-based approaches mainly focused on viewed sketches except for the multiple representations based method [31] evaluated on forensic sketch-photo synthesis and recognition. Later common space projection based approaches were exploited for face sketch recognition. Representative approaches include the partial least squares (PLS) based method [34] and the multi-view discriminant analysis (MvDA) method [14]. Researchers also attempted to design modality-invariant feature descriptor for viewed sketch recognition, such as the coupled information-theoretic encoding (CITE) based face descriptor [42] and the local radon binary pattern (LRBP) [7].

Bhatt et al. [5] firstly introduced the semi-forensic sketches for performance evaluation and bridging the gap between viewed sketches and forensic sketches. They proposed a multiscale circular Weber's local descriptor (MCWLD) and mimetically optimized χ^2 distance for face sketch recognition. Recently, Ouyang et al. [25] proposed a memory-aware approach with the corresponding memory gap database. The 1 hour-sketch and 24 hour-sketch in [25] are two types of semi-forensic sketches, which were proven to be helpful for forensic sketch recognition.

The first study to face recognition based on forensic sketch was proposed by [13]. Klare et al. proposed a series of frameworks for matching forensic sketches to mug shot photos [15,16]. They further designed the FaceSketchID system [17] for face sketch recognition. Peng et al. [30] proposed a graphical representation based method recently. Notice that [15,17,30] evaluated their recognition algorithms on multiple types of sketches respectively including viewed sketches, forensic sketches and composite sketches.

A number of software-generated composite sketch recognition methods were proposed. Han et al. [22] firstly proposed a component based approach considering the fact that composite sketches are generated through combining facial components in software tools. Mittal et al. proposed a transfer-learning based deep learning approach [23] for composite sketch recognition.

There are several works involved multiple stylistic sketches. Zhang et al. [43] studied the fusion of sketches drawn by different artists and compared the performances of humans and a principal component analysis (PCA)-based algorithm. However, the dataset and protocols used in [43] is not available, and they merely used PCA-based algorithm. Gao et al. [8] evaluate their sparse representation based face sketch-photo synthesis method on the VIPSL dataset. Multiple stylistic sketches were involved for training, but only single sketch was utilized during the test procedure. In this paper, we assume that multiple stylistic sketches can still be available in test and real-world scenarios. Recently Mittal et al. [22] proposed composite sketch recognition using saliency and attribute feedback. Multiple stylistic composite sketches were combined for improving the matching performance. Their experiments showed the latent capacity of face recognition from multiple stylistic sketches. However, they merely involved multiple composite sketches and ignored other styles of sketches like hand-drawn sketches. On the other hand, they merely evaluated three fusion strategies (score-level, rank-level and decision-level) and other strategies, e.g. pixel-level and feature-level, were ignored. In this paper, we will conduct extensive evaluations on a variety of baselines with all protocols publicly available for further experiments on face recognition from multiple stylistic sketches.

Table 1. Summary of existing face sketch datasets.

Dataset	Photo	Sketch	Description	Sources of photos
CUFS [40]	606	606	Hand-drawn viewed sketch	CUHK student database, AR [20], and XM2VTS [21]
CUFSF [42]	1,194	1,194	Hand-drawn viewed sketch	FERET [32]
IIIT-D Viewed [5]	238	238	Hand-drawn viewed sketch	FG-NET [1], LFW [12], IIIT-D student & Staff
IIIT-D Semi-Forensic [5]	140	140	Hand-drawn semi-forensic sketch	Same with IIIT-D Viewed database
IIIT-D Forensic [5]	190	190	Hand-drawn forensic sketch	Lois Gibson [9], Karen Taylor [37], and Internet
PRIP-HDC [17]	47	47	Hand-drawn forensic sketch	Internet
PRIP-VSGC [17]	123	123	Software-generated composite sketch	AR [20]
E-PRIP [23]	123	123	Software-generated composite sketch	AR [20]
Memory Gap Database [25]	100	400	Hand-drawn sketch	Internet (mugshots.com)
VIPSL [8]	200	1,000	Hand-drawn viewed sketch	FERET [32], FRAVG2D [33] Indian Face Database [2]

2.2   Face Sketch Datasets

We summarize existing face sketch datasets as shown in Table 1. CUHK face sketch database (CUFS) [40] and CUHK face sketch FERET database (CUFSF) [42] are two publicly available benchmarks provided by the multimedia lab in the Chinese University of Hong Kong (CUHK). These two benchmarks have contributed to the great progress in both face sketch synthesis [39] and face sketch recognition [30] in recent years. Saturated performances have been achieved [27] on these two viewed sketch databases due to the sketches in CUFS and CUFSF are captured under relatively controlled conditions. IIIT Delhi image analysis and biometrics lab published a more challenging IIIT-D Sketch database, which is composed of three types of sketches, namely IIIT-D viewed, IIIT-D semi-forensic, and IIIT-D forensic sketches. The IIIT-D semi-forensic sketches are introduced to bridge the large gap between viewed sketches and forensic sketches. With the great progress on viewed sketches, researchers begin to focus on more challenging real-world scenarios, such as hand-drawn forensic sketches and software-generated composite sketches. Because forensic sketches usually come from real-world criminal investigations, it is quite difficult to obtain a large scale dataset of forensic sketches. Existing methods often use images from two scanned textbooks [9,37] and other Internet sources. Biometrics research group in Michigan State University published their 47 forensic sketch pairs from the Internet [17]. Considering the fact that law enforcement agencies are now using software tools to generate composite sketches, two software-generated composite sketch datasets PRIP Viewed Software-Generated Composite dataset (PRIP-VSGC) [17] and extended PRIP (E-PRIP) [23] are created. Both the two composite sketch datasets utilized the same 123 photos from the AR dataset [20], and create composites using two kinds of software named Identi-Kit[3] and FACES[4] respectively. Recently a memory gap database[5] was released to investigate the effects of forgetting process and communication process in face sketch recognition. There are 100 subjects in this database, and each subject has four types of sketches drawn after different times of delay. There is another VIPSL dataset [8] which also contain multiple styles of sketches per subject. There are 200 face photos in the VIPSL database, and five sketches are drawn by five different artists for each photo. As shown in Table 1, in several datasets there are multiple stylistic sketches per person, like the memory gap dataset and the VIPSL dataset. There are also several datasets whose photos come from the same source. For example, the AR dataset is the photo source of CUFS, PRIP-VSGC, and E-PRIP. These datasets provide fundamental resources for our study of face recognition from multiple stylistic sketches.

3   Face Recognition from Multiple Stylistic Sketches

3.1   Overview

In this section, we provide an overview of face recognition from multiple stylistic sketches. As motivated in Sect. 1, we aim to present a fundamental study of face recognition from multiple stylistic sketches. Considering there are a variety of styles of sketches, we specify three scenarios as follows:

(1) **Scenario-MHS:** recognition from multiple hand-drawn sketches drawn by different artists;
(2) **Scenario-MHCS:** recognition from a hand-drawn sketch and multiple composite sketches produced by different software tools;
(3) **Scenario-MCS:** recognition from multiple composite sketches from different software tools.

Illustrations of these three scenarios are shown in Fig. 1. We will provide detailed explanations and corresponding dataset settings later in this section. The specific protocols will be introduced in the experimental setup section.

---

[3] http://www.identikit.net/.

[4] http://www.iqbiometrix.com/.

[5] Because this dataset is relatively new, it is still unavailable currently.

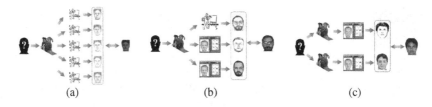

Fig. 1. Illustrations of the proposed three scenarios of face recognition from multiple stylistic sketches. (a) Scenario-MHS; (b) Scenario-MHCS; (c) Scenario-MCS. Note that the composite software symbols come from FACES, and some other symbols come from the Internet.

3.2 Scenario-MHS

In this scenario, we consider the situations in which multiple hand-drawn sketches per subject can be available. For example, there are circumstances that multiple witnesses may be interviewed to help produce hand-drawn sketches. Because these witnesses experienced the incident together, their descriptions about the subject will share common information. But each person has his own way of face perception and face description. Therefore, there is complementary information among these different sketches. Another circumstance is when both the witness and surveillance video tracks are available. Multiple sketches can also be drawn based on these different information sources respectively. Even if there is only one clue about the suspect, law enforcement agencies can invite multiple artists to drawn sketches respectively. The artists have different drawing skills and experience, thus multiple stylistic sketches can be obtained.

In order to evaluate this multiple hand-drawn sketches scenario, we adopt the VIPSL dataset[6] [8]. This dataset consists of 200 photos and 1,000 sketches. For each subject, 5 different styles of sketches are drawn by 5 different artists. The photo come from different face databases. There are different skin colors, background colors, and lighting variations in photos of this dataset, and the sketches are drawn with shape exaggeration. Because the sketches are drawn by different artists, there are different styles of sketches in VIPSL, which is appropriate to mimic this scenario. Examples of the sketches utilized in Scenario-MHS are shown in Fig. 2.

3.3 Scenario-MHCS

This scenario involves both hand-drawn sketches and software-generated composite sketches. More and more law enforcement agencies are using software tools to create composite sketch. Considering the fact that it usually spends years to train a forensic artist, it only takes a few hours to get used to composite-generation software. Therefore, besides the forensic artist, law enforcement agencies can exploit software tools in criminal investigation as well. Furthermore,

---

[6] The VIPSL dataset is available at: http://www.ihitworld.com/index.php/vipsl-database.

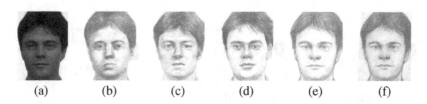

(a)   (b)   (c)   (d)   (e)   (f)

Fig. 2. Examples of the photo and the sketches used in Scenario-MHS. (a): Photo of a subject. (b–f): Five hand-drawn sketches of (a) from five artists.

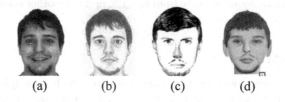

(a)   (b)   (c)   (d)

Fig. 3. Examples of the photo and the sketches used in Scenario-MHCS. (a): Photo of a suspect. (b): Hand-drawn sketch of (a). (c)–(d): Two composite sketches of (a).

there exist imperfect communications of the memory of witness [25] when the witness describes the suspect. But the witness can create the composite sketch by himself, thus skip the communication bias.

We utilize part of the CUFS dataset (sketches drawn based on the AR dataset), the PRIP-VSGC dataset, and E-PRIP dataset to simulate this scenario. There are 123 photos from the AR dataset. Because the hand-drawn sketches in CUFS are created strictly based on the AR photos, the sketches and photos in CUFS have exactly the same facial contour, shading, and even hairstyle. This is impossible in real-world conditions. In order to mimic real-world scenario, we randomly replace the photos with another photo of the same identity in the AR dataset. 123 hand-drawn sketches corresponding to the AR identities are used here. The composite sketches in PRIP-VSGC and E-PRIP were created by two different software. Example images used in this scenario are shown in Fig. 3. It can be seen that the hand-drawn sketch contains more texture information, while the contour information in the composite sketch is more distinct. Therefore, there is complementary information in these different stylistic sketches which is favorable to the recognition task.

3.4   Scenario-MCS

According to our conversations with law enforcement agencies, there are many agencies that do not have forensic artists. In contrast, composite-generation software is easier to be obtained. This scenario only involves software-generated composite sketches. In this scenario, multiple witnesses can create multiple composite sketches to figure out the suspect in their memory. Multiple software tools can also be utilized for composite sketch generation. Because the styles of

Table 2. Statistics of the proposed three scenarios.

Scenario name	Photo	Hand-drawn sketch	Software-generated composite sketch
Scenario-MHS	200	1,000	0
Scenario-MHCS	123	123	246
Scenario-MCS	123	0	246

facial components are different in these software tools, the obtained composite sketches vary a lot. This complementary information can be useful for identifying the suspect.

We utilize the PRIP-VSGC dataset and E-PRIP dataset in this scenario. The photos used are the same with Sect. 3.3. For each photo, there are two corresponding composite sketches respectively. Examples are shown in Fig. 3(a), (c), and (d).

Table 2 presents the general statistics of the proposed three scenarios.

4   Baseline Approaches

4.1   Baseline Face Recognition Approaches

To give a benchmark for future comparisons under the settings on aforementioned datasets in above three scenarios, we have conducted experiments using three baseline face recognition algorithms.

(1) **Basic LBP-based face recognition:** We implemented the face recognition algorithm based on Local Binary Pattern (LBP) based texture feature [35]. We modify the original strategy in [35] by replacing LBP with a multi-scale version. There is no training procedure in this method.
(2) **Fisherface:** We then utilize the supervised algorithm Fisherface [3] as baseline approach. We implemented the Fisherface with part of the codes available online[7]. Within class whitening is added to improve the performance.
(3) **VGG-Face:** A convolutional neural networks (CNNs) based face recognition algorithm is further taken as the baseline. We use the pre-trained model VGG-Face [28] available in the MATLAB toolbox MatConvNet. Because the face sketch datasets are relatively small, it is impossible to train a ConvNet from scratch. It is not practical to fine-tune through the network which may lead to overfitting. We therefore utilize the high-level features in the Convnet as deep features. In our experiments, removing the last three fully connected layers can achieve the best performance of 99 % accuracy on CUFS with cosine distance as the similarity metric.

---

[7] http://www.cad.zju.edu.cn/home/dengcai/Data/DimensionReduction.html.

4.2   Baseline Fusion Approaches

We present the fusion techniques used in this paper at five possible levels: pixel level, feature level, score level, rank level, and decision level. The L2 normalization will be used if needed in these fusion approaches.

(1) Pixel level fusion using average summation (**PL-AS**): Pixel level image fusion simply fuses the raw data at pixel level. A simple geometry alignment based on centers of two eyes is pre-processed on the face images. We then average the pixel intensities at the same location of multiple stylistic sketches as the PL-AS result. Experiments show that this kind of fusion significantly improves the performance of hand-drawn sketches, which will be discussed later.

(2) Feature level fusion using feature concatenation (**FL-FC**): The feature descriptors are extracted on these different stylistic sketches. As these features are independent with each other, it is reasonable to simply concatenate them together to form a long vector. This new vector can then be used for recognition.

(3) Score level fusion using equal-weighted sum rule (**SL-SR**): Each sketch provides a matching score with the photo gallery using the face recognition algorithms introduced above. These scores can then be combined through an equal-weighted summation to exploit the complementary information among sketches.

  We further evaluate switching the equal-weighted sum rule with product rule, abbreviate to **SL-PR**, in this paper. Kernel based fusion strategy also shows effective performance. We therefore add two more score level fusion techniques utilizing two-class SVM and one-class SVM, abbreviating as **SL-TSVM** and **SL-OSVM** respectively.

(4) Rank level fusion using highest rank rule (**RL-HR**): In recognition systems, the ranked lists from multiple stylistic sketches can be fused at the rank level by selecting the highest rank among candidates. There is another rank level fusion technique, namely Borda count method [11], in which the sum of the ranks from multiple identification systems is taken as the final rank list. We abbreviate this strategy as **RL-BC** in this paper.

(5) Decision level fusion using majority voting (**DL-MV**): Each recognition system makes its own decision, and a majority vote strategy can then be applied to generate the final decision.

  We adopt these simple fusion techniques to evaluate the proposed three scenarios. Researchers are invited to submit their own algorithms and experimental results on these scenarios later (after the review process).

5   Experiments

5.1   Experimental Setup

All the face images used in this paper are firstly pre-processed by a simple geometry alignment based on the centers of two eyes and cropped to 200×250.

Fig. 4. Examples faces used in this paper: VIPSL photos with enlarged gallery (left) and AR photos with enlarged gallery (right).

The images are divided into patches of size 20×20 with 10 pixels overlapping. In the basic LBP-based face recognition baseline, multi-scale LBP feature is extracted on each patch by concatenating LBP feature descriptors with radius of 1, 3, 5, 7. Therefore, each face image yields a 107,616-D LBP-based feature for recognition. In the Fisherface baseline, 128-D scale invariant feature transform (SIFT) feature [19] is extracted on each image patch, thus leads to a 58,368-D SIFT feature for recognition. In the VGG-Face baseline, after removing the last three fully connected layers, each face image generates a 25,088-D deep feature.

In order to report unbiased performances, we define two views for each scenario. View 1 is used for parameter tuning and view 2 is used for algorithm evaluation. In view 2, protocols of 10 random partitions of dataset are provided and the average performances are reported. We follow the same partition ratio as [15]. For scenario-MHS, 133 subjects are used for training and 67 subjects are left for testing. For scenario-MHCS and scenario-MCS, 82 and 41 subjects are selected for training and testing respectively. The lists of image names are generated randomly, which will be available online.

In order to present results that can better mimic real-world criminal investigation scenarios, we construct an enlarged gallery set of 10,000 subjects. This enlarged gallery is composed of subjects from four sources: FERET [32] (2,437 subjects), XM2VTS [21] (1,180 subjects), MORPH (3,383 subjects), and LFW [12] (3,000 subjects). The face images in the first three datasets are captured under relatively controlled conditions similar to VIPSL and AR. The subjects from LFW are added to increase the diversity of the enlarged gallery. We have shown two groups of example faces in Fig. 4. The left three columns of faces in Fig. 4(a) and (b) are selected from VIPSL photos and AR photos, while the rest are from the enlarged gallery. It can be seen that the quality of these photos are similar, thus the enlarged gallery can affect the performances and help present results closer to real-world scenarios.

Given the experimental settings introduced, we present experimental results under identification scenario[8]. We first present the face recognition performances

---

[8] Due to the limitation of paper length, we only present the identification results in this paper. Verification performances will be released online later.

from single stylistic sketch in Table 3. The five styles of hand-drawn sketches in VIPSL are named style-A, style-B, style-C, style-D, and style-E respectively. For AR photos, the hand-drawn sketches from CUFS are named viewed, while the two styles of composite sketches are called PRIP and EPRIP in this paper. It can be seen that face recognition from the hand-drawn sketches in VIPSL is a relatively easy task, but the rank-1 accuracy can still be improved. Recognition from the composite sketches in AR is very difficult, with very low rank-1 accuracy. We expect this task to be improved by fusion of multiple stylistic sketches.

Table 3. Face recognition accuracies from single stylistic sketch on view 2 of each dataset. (accuracy±std, %)

Dataset	Basic LBP Rank 1	Basic LBP Rank 50	Fisherface Rank 1	Fisherface Rank 50	VGG-Face Rank 1	VGG-Face Rank 50
VIPSL Style-A	49.10 ± 5.47	86.87 ± 3.78	68.36 ± 4.49	96.57 ± 1.87	60.60 ± 3.24	100 ± 0
VIPSL Style-B	45.07 ± 4.44	85.97 ± 2.13	66.27 ± 4.05	97.76 ± 1.06	58.21 ± 2.73	98.36 ± 1.31
VIPSL Style-C	65.67 ± 5.67	97.46 ± 1.42	72.39 ± 2.25	99.55 ± 0.72	59.10 ± 3.16	99.85 ± 0.47
VIPSL Style-D	55.82 ± 4.46	92.69 ± 3.26	71.94 ± 6.20	99.40 ± 0.77	64.18 ± 4.16	100 ± 0
VIPSL Style-E	55.07 ± 6.47	92.54 ± 2.73	75.52 ± 4.83	98.66 ± 1.31	62.24 ± 5.67	100 ± 0
AR Viewed	28.05 ± 6.11	67.56 ± 5.52	58.78 ± 6.13	88.05 ± 4.80	77.07 ± 6.52	96.83 ± 2.31
AR PRIP	3.41 ± 3.49	18.78 ± 5.75	1.46 ± 1.26	10.00 ± 4.22	0.49 ± 1.03	23.90 ± 4.71
AR EPRIP	4.63 ± 2.92	30.10 ± 7.16	1.46 ± 2.36	19.76 ± 7.49	5.12 ± 2.43	46.59 ± 7.75

5.2   Experimental Results

We first evaluate the baseline approaches in scenario-MHS. Figure 5 shows results of the baseline fusion approaches based on three recognition algorithms (Basic LBP-based face recognition, Fisherface, and VGG-Face). Comparing with the performance of recognition from single stylistic sketch in Table 3, fusion of information from multiple stylistic sketches can improve the accuracy. An interesting phenomenon is that pixel level fusion (PL-AS) yields excellent performance in this scenario. This may be because the sketches in scenario-MHS are all hand-drawn viewed sketches. The usage of pixel level fusion technique can be further investigated in the future.

Figure 6 demonstrates the results of baseline approaches in scenario-MHCS. Because this scenario contains both hand-drawn sketches from CUFS and composite sketches from PRIP-VSGC and EPRIP, it is harder than scenario-MHS. From Fig. 6 we can find that score level fusion techniques can achieve better results, while decision level fusion technique (DL-MV) performs poor. This is because there are two styles of composite sketches, whose recognition performances are poor in single sketch scenario as shown in Table 3. They usually takes the majority during voting, thus contributes to the poor performance of DL-MV.

We finally present the baseline performances in scenario-MCS, as shown in Fig. 7. This is the most difficult scenario among the three proposed in this paper.

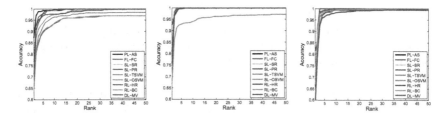

Fig. 5. Recognition performances of using basic LBP (left), Fisherface (middle), and VGG-Face (right) in scenario-MHS.

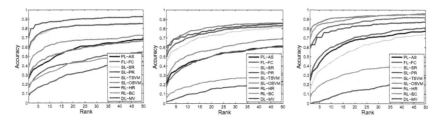

Fig. 6. Recognition performances of using basic LBP (left), Fisherface (middle), and VGG-Face (right) in scenario-MHCS.

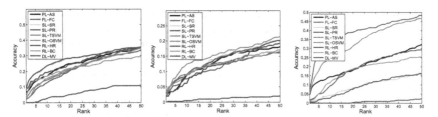

Fig. 7. Recognition performances of using basic LBP (left), Fisherface (middle), and VGG-Face (right) in scenario-MCS.

The Decision level fusion technique (DL-MV) failed to help improve this scenario. Score level fusion techniques achieve better results than other fusion methods, but their performances are still unsatisfying. It remains an unsolved problem of recognition from multiple stylistic sketches in scenario-MCS.

6   Conclusion and Future Directions

This paper presents a fundamental study of face recognition from multiple stylistic sketches. Three scenarios with different degrees of difficulty are proposed to mimic real-world situations. We also describe the corresponding dataset, evaluation protocols and several benchmarks to help illustrate these scenarios. More importantly, preliminary experimental results demonstrate the great challenges of this problem. There are also several interesting findings in the experiments.

For example, pixel level fusion of multiple hand-drawn sketches reveals exciting performance, which is rarely exploited before. However, none of the baseline fusion approaches introduced in this paper can achieve satisfying recognition performance from multiple composite sketches. This remains an open issue for further research.

In the future, we intend to add more baseline approaches into this problem, such as the kernel prototype similarities based method [15] and the graphical representation approach [30]. While we have tried the VGG-face model as the deep learning feature, we merely explored the simplest way. Future research of exploiting deep learning technique to deal with this problem is preferred.

Acknowledgement. This work was supported in part by the National Natural Science Foundation of China (under Grant 61432014, 61501339, and 61671339), in part by the Fundamental Research Funds for the Central Universities (under Grant XJS15049, and JB160104), in part by the China Post-Doctoral Science Foundation under Grant 2015M580818 and Grant 2016T90893 and in part by the Shaanxi Province Post-Doctoral Science Foundation.

References

1. FG-NET. http://www-prima.inrialpes.fr/FGnet/
2. Indian Face Database.http://vis-www.cs.umass.edu/~vidit/IndianFaceDatabase/
3. Belhumeur, P., Hespanda, J., Kiregeman, D.: Eigenfaces vs. fisherfaces: recognition using class specific linear projection. IEEE TPAMI **19**(7), 711–720 (1997)
4. Best-Rowden, L., Han, H., Otto, C., Klare, B., Jain, A.: Unconstrained face recognition: identifying a person of interest from a media collection. IEEE TIFS **9**(12), 2144–2157 (2014)
5. Bhatt, H., Bharadwaj, S., Singh, R., Vatsa, M.: Memetically optimized MCWLD for matching sketches with digital face images. IEEE TIFS **7**(5), 1522–1535 (2012)
6. Frowd, C.: Eyewitnesses and the use and application of cognitive theory. Introduction to applied psychology (2011)
7. Galoogahi, H., Sim, T.: Face sketch recognition by local radon binary pattern. In: ICIP, pp. 1837–1840 (2012)
8. Gao, X., Wang, N., Tao, D., Li, X.: Face sketch-photo synthesis and retrieval using sparse representation. IEEE TCSVT **22**, 1213–1226 (2012)
9. Gibson, L.: Forensic Art Essentials: A Manual for Law Enforcement Artists. Academic Press, Waltham (2010)
10. Han, H., Klare, B., Bonnen, K., Jain, A.: Matching composite sketches to face photos: a component-based approach. IEEE TIFS **8**(1), 191–204 (2013)
11. Ho, T., Hull, J., Srihari, S.: Decision combination in multiple classifier systems. IEEE TPAMI **16**(1), 66–75 (1994)
12. Huang, G.B., Ramesh, M., Berg, T., Learned-Miller, E.: Labeled faces in the wild: A database for studying face recognition in unconstrained environments. Technical report. 07–49, University of Massachusetts, Amherst (2007)
13. Uhl Jr., R.G., da Victoria Lobo., N.: A framework for recognizing a facial image from a police sketch. In: CVPR, pp. 586–593 (1996)

14. Kan, M., Shan, S., Zhang, H., Lao, S., Chen, X.: Multi-view discriminant analysis. In: Fitzgibbon, A., Lazebnik, S., Perona, P., Sato, Y., Schmid, C. (eds.) ECCV 2012. LNCS, vol. 7572, pp. 808–821. Springer, Heidelberg (2012). doi:10.1007/978-3-642-33718-5_58

15. Klare, B., Jain, A.: Heterogeneous face recognition using kernel prototype similarities. IEEE TPAMI **35**(6), 1410–1422 (2013)

16. Klare, B., Li, Z., Jain, A.: Matching forensic sketches to mug shot photos. IEEE TPAMI **33**, 639–646 (2011)

17. Klum, S., Han, H., Klare, B., Jain, A.K.: The FaceSketchID system: matching facial composites to mugshots. IEEE TIFS **9**(12), 2248–2263 (2014)

18. Liu, Q., Tang, X., Jin, H., Lu, H., Ma, S.: A nonlinear approach for face sketch synthesis and recognition. In: CVPR, pp. 1005–1010 (2005)

19. Lowe, D.: Distinctive image features from scale-invariant key-points. IJCV **60**(2), 91–110 (2004)

20. Martinez, A., Benavente, R.: The AR face database. Technical report 24, CVC, Barcelona, Spain, June 1998

21. Messer, K., Matas, J., Kittler, J., Luettin, J., Maitre, G.: XM2VTSDB: the extended M2VTS database. In: AVBPA, Washington, DC, USA, pp. 72–77, April 1999

22. Mittal, P., Jain, A., Goswami, G., Vatsa, M., Singh, R.: Composite sketch recognition using saliency and attribute feedback. Inf. Fusion **33**, 86–99 (2017)

23. Mittal, P., Vatsa, M., Singh, R.: Composite sketch recognition via deep network-A transfer learning approach. In: ICB (2015)

24. Nejati, H., Zhang, L., Sim, T.: Eyewitness face sketch recognition based on two-step bias modeling. In: Wilson, R., Hancock, E., Bors, A., Smith, W. (eds.) CAIP 2013. LNCS, vol. 8048, pp. 26–33. Springer, Heidelberg (2013). doi:10.1007/978-3-642-40246-3_4

25. Ouyang, S., Hospedales, T., Song, Y., Li, X.: ForgetMeNot: memory-aware forensic facial sketch matching. In: CVPR

26. Ouyang, S., Hospedales, T., Song, Y.-Z., Li, X.: Cross-modal face matching: beyond viewed sketches. In: Cremers, D., Reid, I., Saito, H., Yang, M.-H. (eds.) ACCV 2014. LNCS, vol. 9004, pp. 210–225. Springer, Heidelberg (2015). doi:10.1007/978-3-319-16808-1_15

27. Ouyang, S., Hospedales, T., Song, Y.Z., Li, X.: A survey on heterogeneous face recognition: Sketch, infra-red, 3d and low-resolution (2014). http://arxiv.org/abs/1409.5114

28. Parkhi, O.M., Vedaldi, A., Zisserman, A.: Deep face recognition. In: BMVC (2015)

29. Peng, C., Gao, X., Wang, N., Li, J.: Superpixel-based face sketch-photo synthesis. IEEE TCSVT (2015)

30. Peng, C., Gao, X., Wang, N., Li, J.: Graphical representation for heterogeneous face recognition. IEEE TPAMI (2016)

31. Peng, C., Gao, X., Wang, N., Tao, D., Li, X., Li, J.: Multiple representations-based face sketch-photo synthesis. IEEE TNNLS (2015)

32. Phillips, P., Moon, H., Rizvi, S., Rauss, P.: The FERET evaluation methodology for face recognition algorithms. IEEE TPAMI **22**(10), 1090–1104 (2000)

33. Serrano, A., de Diego, I., Conde, C., Cabello, E., Shen, L., Bai, L.: Influence of wavelet frequency and orientation in an SVM based parallel Gabor PCA face verification system. In: IDEAL, pp. 219–228 (2007)

34. Sharma, A., Jacobs, D.: Bypass synthesis: PLS for face recognition with pose, low-resolution and sketch. In: CVPR, pp. 593–600 (2011)

35. Ahonen, T., Hadid, A., Pietikäinen, M.: Face description with local binarypatterns: application to face recognition. IEEE TPAMI **28**(12), 2037–2041 (2006)
36. Tang, X., Wang, X.: Face photo recognition using sketch. In: ICIP, pp. 257–260, September 2002
37. Taylor, K.: Forensic Art and Illustration. CRC Press, Boca Raton (2001)
38. Wang, N., Tao, D., Gao, X., Li, X., Li, J.: Transductive face sketch-photo synthesis. IEEE TNNLS **24**(9), 1364–1376 (2013)
39. Wang, N., Tao, D., Gao, X., Li, X., Li, J.: A comprehensive survey to face hallucination. IJCV **31**(1), 9–30 (2014)
40. Wang, X., Tang, X.: Face photo-sketch synthesis and recognition. IEEE TPAMI **31**(11), 1955–1967 (2009)
41. Zhang, S., Gao, X., Wang, N., Li, J., Zhang, M.: Face sketch synthesis via sparse representation-based greedy search. IEEE TIP **24**(8), 2466–2477 (2015)
42. Zhang, W., Wang, X., Tang, X.: Coupled information-theoretic encoding for face photo-sketch recognition. In: CVPR, pp. 513–520 (2011)
43. Zhang, Y., McCullough, C., Sullins, J., Ross, C.: Hand-drawn face sketch recognition by humans and a pca-based algorithm for forensic applications. IEEE TSMC-Part A **40**(3), 475–485 (2010)
44. Zhou, H., Kuang, Z., Wong, K.: Markov weight fields for face sketch synthesis. In: CVPR, pp. 1091–1097 (2012)

Instance-Level Coupled Subspace Learning for Fine-Grained Sketch-Based Image Retrieval

Peng Xu[1], Qiyue Yin[2], Yonggang Qi[1], Yi-Zhe Song[3],
Zhanyu Ma[1(✉)], Liang Wang[2], and Jun Guo[1]

[1] Pattern Recognition and Intelligent System Laboratory,
Beijing University of Posts and Telecommunications, Beijing, China
{peng.xu,qiyg,mazhanyu,guojun}@bupt.edu.cn
[2] National Lab of Pattern Recognition, Institute of Automation,
Chinese Academy of Sciences, Beijing, China
{qyyin,wangliang}@nlpr.ia.ac.cn
[3] SketchX Lab, School of Electronic Engineering and Computer Science,
Queen Mary University of London, London, UK
yizhe.song@qmul.ac.uk

Abstract. Fine-grained sketch-based image retrieval (FG-SBIR) is a newly emerged topic in computer vision. The problem is challenging because in addition to bridging the sketch-photo domain gap, it also asks for instance-level discrimination within object categories. Most prior approaches focused on feature engineering and fine-grained ranking, yet neglected an important and central problem: how to establish a fine-grained cross-domain feature space to conduct retrieval. In this paper, for the first time we formulate a cross-domain framework specifically designed for the task of FG-SBIR that simultaneously conducts instance-level retrieval and attribute prediction. Different to conventional photo-text cross-domain frameworks that performs transfer on category-level data, our joint multi-view space uniquely learns from the instance-level pair-wise annotations of sketch and photo. More specifically, we propose a joint view selection and attribute subspace learning algorithm to learn domain projection matrices for photo and sketch, respectively. It follows that visual attributes can be extracted from such matrices through projection to build a coupled semantic space to conduct retrieval. Experimental results on two recently released fine-grained photo-sketch datasets show that the proposed method is able to perform at a level close to those of deep models, while removing the need for extensive manual annotations.

Keywords: Fine-grained SBIR · Attribute supervision · Attribute prediction · Multi-view domain adaptation

1 Introduction

Sketch-based image retrieval (SBIR) is traditionally casted into a classification problem, and most prior art evaluates retrieval performance at category-level.

© Springer International Publishing Switzerland 2016
G. Hua and H. Jégou (Eds.): ECCV 2016 Workshops, Part I, LNCS 9913, pp. 19–34, 2016.
DOI: 10.1007/978-3-319-46604-0_2

[1,2,4,8,13,14,16,17,19,24], i.e. given a query sketch, the goal is to discover photos with the same class label. However, it was recently argued [12,28] that SBIR is more reasonable to be conducted at a fine-grained level, where instead of conducting retrieval across object categories, it focuses on finding similar photos to the query sketch within specific categories. By specifically exploring the unique fine-grained visual characteristics captured in human sketches, fine-grained SBIR is likely to transform the traditional landscape of image retrieval by introducing a new form of user interaction that underpins the ubiquitous commercial adoption of SBIR technology.

Shared with conventional category-level SBIR, the core problem of fine-grained SBIR lies with that of cross-domain, that is sketches and photos are from inherently heterogeneous domains. This domain difference can be summarized into two main gaps: (i) the visual modality gap, i.e., sketches are coarse line drawings with plain white background and photos are made of dense color pixels on textured background, and (ii) the semantic gap, i.e., free-hand sketches are highly abstract and iconic, whereas photos are pixel-perfect depictions of the visual world. The problem is further made difficult for fine-grained SBIR since *fine-grained* correspondence between sketch and photo is difficult to establish especially given the abstract and iconic nature of free-hand sketches. It is therefore important for any fine-grained SBIR framework to not only seek a fine-grained metric, but also learn a joint semantic space to effectively model the domain gap.

Prior work on fine-grained SBIR either focused on feature engineering [12] or learning a fine-grained feature space [28]. There has been a largely neglected problem of addressing the cross-domain gap per sa. Majority of work ease the domain gap by first converting images to edgemaps, and conduct further comparisons by treating the extracted edgemaps as somewhat "good" sketches. For example, Yu et al. employed Sketch-a-Net [29] that is specifically designed to parse sketches for both photo and sketch branches in their triplet ranking network. However, sketches and photos are fundamentally different: photos closely follow natural image statistics and are taken by cameras, yet sketches are drawn from visual memory and produced by hand. In this work, for the first time, we explicitly model the cross-domain gap between photo and sketch by jointly learning a coupled semantic embedding using fine-grained visual attributes.

Parallel to traversing the photo-sketch domain gap, the modality gap between text and photo has been widely studied in recent years [6,9,10,15,18,26,27]. In essence, the goal of cross-modal techniques is to shorten the semantic gap between text and photo through projecting the inherently different domains into a common subspace and consequently perform matching. Although many were shown to able to effectively traverse the cross-domain gap, they only conduct transfer at category-level or domain-level, rendering them unsuitable for fine-grained retrieval where instance-level differences are sought after instead. Our cross-domain model on the other hand learns from instance-level sketch-photo pairs, resulting in a subspace that is not only domain-independent, but also fine-grained.

In this paper, we present a novel subspace learning method for FG-SBIR based on attribute supervision and view selection. Our framework performs joint attribute regressions for sketch and photo modalities, which is able to select relevant and discriminative feature views from coupled sketch-photo spaces simultaneously. The goal is to project sketch and photo features into coupled attribute spaces. Meanwhile, such space is also capable of predicting attributes by multiplying the learned projection matrices. Specifically, our objective function consists of three parts: (i) coupled supervised linear regression, (ii) coupled group norms of all projection matrices, and (iii) a Frobenius norm regularization. The coupled supervised linear regressions take advantage of the rich attribute information to learn local feature-wise relationships at an abstract level. The group norms of the projection matrices play the role of simultaneous and joint view selection among multi-view features. The Frobenius norm regularization can bridge the gap between sketch-photo attribute spaces. Accordingly, an efficient algorithm is derived to solve the proposed optimization problem. Experimental results on two fine-grained image-sketch datasets demonstrate that the proposed method outperforms the state-of-the-art shallow approaches and its performance is even close to the deep models.

The main contributions of our work are as follows:

1. We propose for the first time an unified cross-domain framework of FG-SBIR.
2. We study how fine-grained visual attributes can be useful to construct a fine-grained and domain-independent joint feature space.
3. We introduce an efficient algorithm to solve the challenging non-smooth optimization problem.
4. The proposed method outperforms state-of-the-art shallow models and offers comparable performance against deep alternatives on two recently released fine-grained photo-sketch datasets.

2 Related Work

SBIR vs. Fine-Grained SBIR. Traditional sketch-based retrieval tasks usually focus on global visual similarities and high-level semantics. As a result, retrieval is often performed coarsely at category-level. In contrast, fine-grained retrieval paradigms concentrate on subtle visual and semantic descriptions of objects. As shown in Fig. 1, most SBIR work can be broadly summarized into four categories according to the level of detail they operate on: (i) *Category-level retrieval* aims to examine objects on category-level [4,8,19], e.g., shoes against chairs; (ii) *Subclass-level retrieval* differentiate objects on within-class category level, e.g., shoes are classified into three subcategories according to their general usage; (iii) *Part-level retrieval* finds objects according to the subtle part properties [11], e.g. four high-heel shoes are marked out according to the properties of heel and boot; (iv) For *fine-grained instance-level retrieval* [12,28], the sketch shoe and two high-heel sandals become the nearest neighbors on the basis of similarities on the heel, body, and toe. Our proposed fine-grained SBIR model is able to generalize to all four variations, and we offer experimental comparisons for each later in Sect. 4.

Towards Fine-Grained SBIR. Li et al. [12] first proposed fine-grained SBIR (FG-SBIR) but limited their study to pose variations only and the cross-domain gap is only traversed holistically by matching coarse graph structures. Yu et al. [28] further extended the definition of fine-grained and proposed a new dataset of sketch-photo pairs with detailed triplet annotation. They developed a deep triplet-ranking network to learn a fine-grained feature metric, however avoided addressing the cross-domain gap by converting photos to edgemaps prior to training and testing. The very recent work of Li et al. [11] remains the single work that specifically tackled the cross-domain nature of the problem, where they used three-view Canonical Correlation Analysis (CCA) to fuse fine-grained visual attributes and low-level features. However, they did not learn a joint feature space since CCA is only conducted independently on each domain. Moreover, it required separately trained set of attribute detectors at testing time, making it less generalizable to other datasets. In this paper, we follow Li et al. [11] in using fine-grained attributes to traverse different domains, but explicitly learn a joint fine-grained space to conduct retrieval. Once learned, this attribute-driven space is also able to perform implicit attribute detection without additional training.

Cross-Modal Retrieval. Broadly speaking, cross-modal retrieval involves two main tasks: measure of relevance and coupled feature selection [26]. The challenge of cross-modal matching is therefore finding a semantic feature space that can withstand modal variation at an abstract level. Most cross-modal methods can be classified into three main categories: probabilistic models [9,18], metric learning approaches [15,27] and subspace learning methods [6,10]. Probabilistic approaches aim to model the joint distribution of multi-modal data in order to learn their correlation [18]. Metric learning methods set out to compute appropriate distance metrics between different modalities [27]. Subspace learning approaches map multi-modal data into a common subspace to conduct matching [26]. Among these categories of cross-modal techniques, subspace learning methods [3,20,22,26] have gained state-of-the-art results in recent years. All aforementioned cross-domain models can not work with instance-level

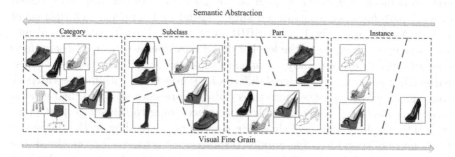

Fig. 1. Retrievals based on different level of grains. The top arrow from right to left denotes the enhanced semantic abstraction. The bottom arrow from left to right indicates increasing fine-grained level.

annotations (e.g., sketch-photo pairs), largely limiting their applicability for fine-grained retrieval. Our proposed model is however specifically designed to mine a joint subspace where cross-domain comparisons can be performed at a fine-grained level.

3   Fine-Grained SBIR via Attribute Supervision and View Selection

In this section, we introduce our framework for FG-SBIR based on attribute supervision and view selection. An effective algorithm is also presented to solve the proposed objective function.

3.1   Notations

Matrices and column vectors will be consistently denoted as bold uppercase letters and bold lowercase letters, respectively. Given a matrix $\mathbf{M} \in \mathbb{R}^{m \times n}$, we express its i-th row as $\mathbf{M}^i$ and j-th column as $\mathbf{M}_j$.

The Frobenius norm of the matrix $\mathbf{M}$ is defined as

$$\|\mathbf{M}\|_F = \sqrt{\sum_{i=1}^{m} \|\mathbf{M}^i\|_2^2}. \tag{1}$$

The Group ℓ_1-norm (G_1-norm) of the matrix $\mathbf{M}$ is defined as

$$\|\mathbf{M}\|_{G_1} = \sum_{i=1}^{n} \sum_{j=1}^{k} \|\mathbf{m}_i^j\|_2, \tag{2}$$

where $\mathbf{m}_i^j$ is the j-th segment vector in the i-th column of $\mathbf{M}$.

3.2   Problem Formulation

Suppose there are n pairs of photo and sketch, which are denoted as $\mathbf{P} = [\mathbf{p}_1, \mathbf{p}_2, ..., \mathbf{p}_n] \in \Re^{d^p \times n}$ and $\mathbf{S} = [\mathbf{s}_1, \mathbf{s}_2, ..., \mathbf{s}_n] \in \Re^{d^s \times n}$, respectively. As illustrated in Fig. 2, $\mathbf{p}_i \in \Re^{d^p}$ is formed by stacking features from all the k^p views, and the feature for each view j is a d_j^p dimensional vector, i.e. $d^p = \sum_{j=1}^{k^p} d_j^p$, similarly so for each element $\mathbf{s}_i$ in $\mathbf{S}$. The features used for different views can be low-level features (e.g., HOG), or those extracted from deep networks, (e.g., [28]). Each photo-sketch pair $\{\mathbf{p}_i, \mathbf{s}_i\}$ represents the same object. Let $\mathbf{A}_p = [\mathbf{a}_1^p, \mathbf{a}_2^p, ..., \mathbf{a}_n^p]^T \in \Re^{n \times u}$ denotes the attribute label matrix of the photo samples and u is the number of photo attribute. Similarly, $\mathbf{A}_s = [\mathbf{a}_1^s, \mathbf{a}_2^s, ..., \mathbf{a}_n^s]^T \in \Re^{n \times v}$ denotes the attribute label matrix of the sketch samples and v is the number of sketch attribute.

As previously discussed, SBIR and FG-SBIR generally belong to the task of cross-modal retrieval. Recently, many cross-modal approaches

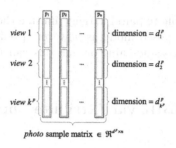

Fig. 2. Illustration of the photo sample matrix, **P**.

[3, 7, 20, 22, 23, 26, 30] have achieved satisfying results on matching photo and text. Yet, all of them evaluated retrieval results on category-level by calculating the mean average precision (MAP) [21]. More specifically, given multi-modal sample matrices $\mathbf{X}_a$, $\mathbf{X}_b$, and class label matrix $\mathbf{Y}$, we can summarize a framework for supervised cross-modal subspace learning:

$$\min_{\mathbf{W}_a, \mathbf{W}_b} \|\mathbf{X}_a^T \mathbf{W}_a - \mathbf{Y}\|_F^2 + \|\mathbf{X}_b^T \mathbf{W}_b - \mathbf{Y}\|_F^2 + \Omega, \tag{3}$$

where $\mathbf{W}_a$ and $\mathbf{W}_b$ are the projection matrices and Ω is some form of constraint.

In this paper, we would like to conduct FG-SBIR in the visual attribute spaces. It follows that Eq. (3) naturally inspires us to project sketch and photo into a common attribute subspace as shown in Fig. 3(a). However, it would otherwise be difficult to define or annotate a desired common space and give it a clear semantic interpretation like the low dimensional class label matrix Y used in usual cross-modal frameworks. Motivated by several unsupervised cross-modal subspace learning methods [3, 20, 22, 23], we propose to map sketch and photo data into two intermediate and isomorphic spaces U^S and U^P that have a natural correspondence. This means that U^S and U^P are approximation versions for each other in the ideal case. It follows that we can establish invertible mappings as follows:

$$\Re^{d^p} \rightleftarrows U^P \rightleftarrows U^S \rightleftarrows \Re^{d^s}. \tag{4}$$

The photo attribute space $\Re^u$ itself can potentially be directly used as its intermediate space U^P as shown in Fig. 3(b). For constructing the intermediate space of sketch U^S, the following can be adopted to approach U^P:

$$U^P \longleftarrow \mathbf{A}_s \mathbf{T}_s, \quad U^P \longleftarrow \mathbf{A}_p \mathbf{T}_p. \tag{5}$$

where $\mathbf{T}_s$ and $\mathbf{T}_p$ are the transformation matrices for sketch sample attribute matrix $\mathbf{A}_s$ and photo sample attribute matrix $\mathbf{A}_p$, respectively. Mathematically, we have $\min_{\mathbf{T}_s} \|\mathbf{A}_p - \mathbf{A}_s \mathbf{T}_s\|_F^2$, and $\min_{\mathbf{T}_p} \|\mathbf{A}_p - \mathbf{A}_p \mathbf{T}_p\|_F^2$.

An important point to note here is that as a result of the abstract nature sketches, they are often harder to interpret, resulting in a higher degree of noise in human attribute annotation when compared with photos. Hence the sketch sample attribute matrix $\mathbf{A}_s$ often loses information and is stuck in sparsity and low rank. For these reasons, in practice, we opt to the following to approach U^P: $\min_{\mathbf{T}_p} \|\mathbf{A}_p - \mathbf{A}_p\mathbf{T}_p\|_F^2$, whose optimization process starts from $\mathbf{A}_p$.

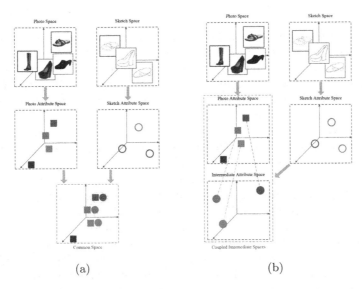

(a)   (b)

Fig. 3. Schematic comparison of conventional common-space learning (a), and the proposed coupled space learning (b)

Our goal is to learn two projection matrices $\mathbf{W}_p$ and $\mathbf{W}_s$ jointly to map the associated data pairs into coupled intermediate spaces denoted by the corresponding attribute labels, subject to that the distance should be small if they belong to the same object. Therefore, the proposed objective function is formulated as follows:

$$J = \min_{\mathbf{W}_p, \mathbf{W}_s, \mathbf{T}} \|\mathbf{P}^T\mathbf{W}_p - \mathbf{A}_p\|_F^2 + \|\mathbf{S}^T\mathbf{W}_s - \mathbf{A}_p\mathbf{T}\|_F^2$$
$$+ \lambda_1(\|\mathbf{W}_p\|_{G_1} + \|\mathbf{W}_s\|_{G_1}) + \lambda_2\|\mathbf{A}_p - \mathbf{A}_p\mathbf{T}\|_F^2 , \tag{6}$$

where $\mathbf{W}_p \in \Re^{d^p \times u}$ and $\mathbf{W}_s \in \Re^{d^s \times u}$ are the projection matrices for coupled photo and sketch spaces, respectively. $\mathbf{W}_p$ is a matrix which consist of weights for features from each individual view over u different attributes. And $\mathbf{W}_p$ can be re-written as:

$$\mathbf{W}_p = \begin{bmatrix} (\mathbf{w}_1^p)^1 & (\mathbf{w}_2^p)^1 & \cdots & (\mathbf{w}_u^p)^1 \\ (\mathbf{w}_1^p)^2 & (\mathbf{w}_2^p)^2 & \cdots & (\mathbf{w}_u^p)^2 \\ \vdots & \vdots & \ddots & \vdots \\ (\mathbf{w}_1^p)^{k^p} & (\mathbf{w}_2^p)^{k^p} & \cdots & (\mathbf{w}_u^p)^{k^p} \end{bmatrix}, \tag{7}$$

where $(\mathbf{w}_x^p)^y \in \Re^{d_y^p}$ is a weighting vector contains the weights for all features in the y-th view of p (photo) sample with respect to the x-th attribute. $\mathbf{T} \in \Re^{u \times u}$ is a conversion matrix.

Similarly:

$$\mathbf{W}_s = \begin{bmatrix} (\mathbf{w}_1^s)^1 & (\mathbf{w}_2^s)^1 & \cdots & (\mathbf{w}_v^s)^1 \\ (\mathbf{w}_1^s)^2 & (\mathbf{w}_2^s)^2 & \cdots & (\mathbf{w}_v^s)^2 \\ \vdots & \vdots & \ddots & \vdots \\ (\mathbf{w}_1^s)^{k^s} & (\mathbf{w}_2^s)^{k^s} & \cdots & (\mathbf{w}_v^s)^{k^s} \end{bmatrix}. \tag{8}$$

We want to present sketch data in an approximate space of the photo attribute space. By minimizing the projected residuals with respect to attribute information, we can preliminarily shorten the gap between the coupled intermediate spaces. And we can minimize the term $\lambda_2 \|\mathbf{A}_p - \mathbf{A}_p\mathbf{T}\|_F^2$ to learn the relationship $\mathbf{T}$ between the coupled attribute intermediate spaces. $\mathbf{T}$ contains the attribute mappings across U^S and U^P.

$\mathbf{W}_p$ and $\mathbf{W}_s$ are able to learn the weight vector for each single view feature, such that the feature-wise importance corresponding to a certain attribute in the intermediate spaces can be captured. However, the multi-view features interactions are extremely complicated, i.e., inhibition, promotion or competition depending on differnet cases. To solve this problem, motivated by [25], a Group ℓ_1-norm (G_1-norm) is utilized, i.e., the second part of Eq. (6).

According to the effectiveness of paired Group ℓ_1-norms upon $\mathbf{W}_p$ and $\mathbf{W}_s$, inside each column of these two projection matrices, the weight vectors for multi-view features are organized under the ℓ_1-norm framework. The view-wise relationships of ℓ_1-norm enforces the structured sparsity among different views. If certain view of features does not own enough contribution or discrimination for certain attribute, the corresponding weight vector of this view will be assigned with zeros, and vice versa. Within each column inside photo or sketch modality, the local interrelations among views are captured by Group ℓ_1-norm regularizer.

More importantly, our objective function optimizes the Group ℓ_1-norm regularizers of $\mathbf{W}_p$ and $\mathbf{W}_s$ simultaneously. Therefore, multi-modal data is fully integrated and equally taken into account to complete more reasonable view selection without unnecessary information loss. All the weight vectors for all the views are organized under the ℓ_1-norm framework. Hence the global relationships among all the views are also captured by the coupled Group ℓ_1-norm regularizers:

$$\|\mathbf{W}_p\|_{G_1} + \|\mathbf{W}_s\|_{G_1} = \sum_{i=1}^{u}\sum_{j=1}^{k^P} \|(\mathbf{w}_p)_i^j\|_2 + \sum_{i=1}^{u}\sum_{j=1}^{k^s} \|(\mathbf{w}_s)_i^j\|_2$$
$$= \sum_{i=1}^{u}\Big(\sum_{j=1}^{k^P} \|(\mathbf{w}_p)_i^j\|_2 + \sum_{j=1}^{k^s} \|(\mathbf{w}_s)_i^j\|_2\Big). \tag{9}$$

In summary, the residual terms based on the attribute labels use the semantic information to preliminarily shorten the gaps between photo-sketch pairs across the coupled intermediate spaces. Next the Group ℓ_1-norm terms captured the local interrelations of multi-view features inside photo or sketch and the global relationships of data pairs crossing photo and sketch modalities. Finally the Frobenius norm term enforces the accuracy of attribute space transition.

3.3   Solving for Non-smooth Optimization

The designed objective function contains the non-smooth regularization terms of Group ℓ_1-norm, which is difficult to solve by general methods. The unknown quantities of our objective function are $\mathbf{W}_p$, $\mathbf{W}_s$, and $\mathbf{T}$. Fortunately, our objective function has no constraint conditions. We can use the variable separation approach to derive an alternative iterative algorithm to solve it.

Take the derivative of the objective J with respect to $(\mathbf{W}_p)_i$ $(1 \leq i \leq u)$, we have[1]

$$\frac{\partial J}{\partial(\mathbf{W}_p)_i} = 2\mathbf{P}\mathbf{P}^T(\mathbf{W}_p)_i - 2\mathbf{P}(\mathbf{A}_p)_i + \lambda_1 \mathbf{D}_p^i(\mathbf{W}_p)_i, \tag{10}$$

where $\mathbf{D}_p^i$ is a block diagonal matrix with the j-th diagonal block as $\frac{1}{2\|(\mathbf{W}_p)_i^j\|_2}\mathbf{I}_j$, $\mathbf{I}_j$ is an identity matrix with the same size as d_j^p, $(\mathbf{W}_p)_i^j$ is the j-th segment of $(\mathbf{W}_p)_i$ and includes the weighting vector for the features in the j-th view of photo sample matrix. Set $\frac{\partial J}{\partial(\mathbf{W}_p)_i} = 0$, we can get

$$(\mathbf{W}_p)_i = (2\mathbf{P}\mathbf{P}^T + \lambda_1 \mathbf{D}_p^i)^{-1}(2\mathbf{P}(\mathbf{A}_p)_i). \tag{11}$$

Similarly, we can obtain $(\mathbf{W}_s)_i$ as

$$(\mathbf{W}_s)_i = (2\mathbf{S}\mathbf{S}^T + \lambda_1 \mathbf{D}_s^i)^{-1}(2\mathbf{S}\mathbf{A}_P(\mathbf{T})_i). \tag{12}$$

Take the derivative of the objective J with respect to $(\mathbf{T})_i$ $(1 \leq i \leq u)$, and set $\frac{\partial J}{\partial(\mathbf{T})_i} = 0$, we can get

$$(\mathbf{T})_i = (\mathbf{A}_p^T\mathbf{A}_p + \lambda_2 \mathbf{A}_p^T\mathbf{A}_p)^{-1}(\mathbf{A}_p^T\mathbf{S}^T(\mathbf{W}_s)_i + \lambda_2 \mathbf{A}_p^T(\mathbf{A}_p)_i). \tag{13}$$

Note that $\mathbf{D}_p^i$ $(1 \leq i \leq u)$ and $\mathbf{D}_s^i$ $(1 \leq i \leq u)$ are dependent on $\mathbf{W}_p$ and $\mathbf{W}_s$, respectively. We can optimize them alternatively and iteratively until convergence. During each optimization step of $\mathbf{W}_p$, $\mathbf{W}_s$, and $\mathbf{T}$, both of them are obtained column by column.

The whole algorithm is summarized in Algorithm 1.

4   Experimental Results and Discussions

In this section, we describe how to apply the proposed approach for a fine-grained sketch-based image retrieval task on two recently released fine-grained image-sketch datasets [28].

---

[1] When $\|(\mathbf{W}_p)_i^j\|_2 = 0$, (6) is not differentiable. Following [5], a small perturbation can be introduced to smooth the j-th diagonal block of $\mathbf{D}_p^i$ as $\frac{1}{2\sqrt{\|(\mathbf{W}_p)_i^j\|_2^2 + \zeta}}\mathbf{I}_j$.
Similarly, when $\|(\mathbf{W}_s)_i^j\|_2 = 0$, the j-th diagonal block of $\mathbf{D}_s^i$ can be regularized as $\frac{1}{2\sqrt{\|(\mathbf{W}_s)_i^j\|_2^2 + \zeta}}\mathbf{I}_j$. We set $\zeta = 1.0000e - 8$ in our following experiments.

Algorithm 1. An efficient iterative algorithm to solve the optimization problem in Eq. (6).

Input: $P = [\mathbf{p}_1, \mathbf{p}_2, ..., \mathbf{p}_n] \in \Re^{d^p \times n}$, $S = [\mathbf{s}_1, \mathbf{s}_2, ..., \mathbf{s}_n] \in \Re^{d^s \times n}$,
$\quad A_p = [\mathbf{a}_1^p, \mathbf{a}_2^p, ..., \mathbf{a}_n^p]^T \in \Re^{n \times u}$.

1. *Set $t = 0$.*
Initialize $(W_p)_t$, $(W_s)_t$ by solving $\min_{W_p} \|P^T W_p - A_p\|_F^2$ and $\min_{W_s} \|S^T W_s - A_p T\|_F^2$ respectively.
Initialize $(T)_t$.
while not converge **do**
$\quad$ 2. *Calculate the block diagonal matrices $(D_p^i)_{t+1}$ $(1 \leqslant i \leqslant u)$ and $(D_s^i)_{t+1}$ $(1 \leqslant i \leqslant u)$,*
$\quad\quad$ *where the j-th diagonal block of $(D_p^i)_{t+1}$ is $\dfrac{1}{2\|((W_p)_i^j)_t\|_2} I_j$*
$\quad\quad$ *and the j-th diagonal block of $(D_s^i)_{t+1}$ is $\dfrac{1}{2\|((W_s)_i^j)_t\|_2} I_j$.*
$\quad$ 3. *For each $(W_p)_i$ $(1 \leqslant i \leqslant u)$,*
$\quad\quad ((W_p)_i)_{t+1} \leftarrow (2PP^T + \lambda_1(D_p^i)_{t+1})^{-1}(2P(A_p)_i)$.
$\quad$ 4. *For each $(W_s)_i$ $(1 \leqslant i \leqslant u)$,*
$\quad\quad ((W_s)_i)_{t+1} \leftarrow (2SS^T + \lambda_1(D_s^i)_{t+1})^{-1}(2SA_p(T_i)_t)$.
$\quad$ 5. *For each $(T)_i$ $(1 \leqslant i \leqslant u)$,*
$\quad\quad (T_i)_{t+1} \leftarrow (A_p^T A_p + \lambda_2 A_p^T A_p)^{-1}(A_p^T S^T((W_s)_i)_{t+1} + \lambda_2 A_p^T(A_p)_i)$.
$\quad$ 6. $t \leftarrow t + 1$.
end while
Output: $W_p \in \Re^{d^p \times u}$, $W_s \in \Re^{d^s \times u}$, and $T \in \Re^{u \times u}$.

4.1 Experimental Settings

Datasets: In the experiment, two newly released fine-grained SBIR dataset [28] for shoe and chair are utilized. Specifically, there are 419 pairs of photo-sketch samples in the shoe dataset, and 297 pairs of photo-sketch instances in the chair dataset. Attribute annotations are also available for both categories. Taking shoe for example, each shoe is divided into several parts, i.e., toe cap, body, vamp, hell, etc. For each shoe part, a list of part-specific binary attributes are defined. For example, the 1st dimension of shoe attribute denotes whether the toe cap is round or not. For a full list of attributes, please refer to [28] instead. It however worth noting that although visual attributes are shared semantic concepts (i.e., toe cap, shoe heel, chair arm, etc.), corresponding photo and sketch attributes for the same shoe do not necessarily agree. This is due to (i) attribute annotations for photos and sketches were conducted independently, and (ii) sketches are often too abstract and iconic to vividly depict certain attributes.

Features: HOG and fc7 Deep [28] are served as features in our experiments. The dimension of HOG is reduced to 210 and 160 for shoe and chair via Principal Component Analysis (PCA), respectively. fc7 Deep is obtained by using the well trained modal provided by [28]. We ran the FG-SBIR experiments for 30 times, and for each time we randomly selected 304/200 pairs of shoe/chair samples for training and took the rest samples for testing.

Evaluation Metric: We follow the same metric used in [11,28] for evaluation, i.e., given a query sketch, "*acc.@K*", which is the percentage of relevant photos ranked in the top K results offered by our proposed method.

4.2 Influence of Visual Attributes

To investigate the effect of visual attributes on retrieval result, we choose different sets of attributes as labels for training. More specifically, (i) we divide shoe/chair datasets into three/six subclasses, respectively, (ii) we then select 10d, 15d, 21d from the original shoe attribute to form new supervision labels; for the chair dataset, the selected dimensions are 5d, 10d, and 15d, and finally (iii) we evaluate the retrieval performances on instance-level. Here, two-view feature via concatenating HOG and $fc7$ deep features is used.

Experiments on each setting are repeated for 30 times, where training and testing data are selected randomly each time. The average retrieval results are reported in Tables 1 and 2, where we provide retrieval accuracies of @ $K = 1$, 5, 10. Corresponding plots are also provided in the Fig. 4.

From results on the shoe dataset, we can observe that accuracy on subclass labels is the lowest as expected. The reason is that the subclass labels are a coarse semantic concept and they can not sufficiently capture discriminative visual cues. Furthermore, we discover that attributes with varying dimensions influence the retrieval results dramatically: the more attributes used, the better the results. However, for results on chair (Table 2 and Fig. 4(b)), it is observed that the performance of 5d attribute is worse than that of subclass label. The reason is two-fold: (i) the chair attributes introduced by [28] are not overly discriminative (as we also conclude later in Sect. 4.3), and (ii) the dimensionality of 5d is too low to form a discriminative feature representation.

In summary, we can conclude that: (i) attribute labels can be effectively used as supervision information in FG-SBIR; (ii) the dimensionality of the attribute is strongly connected to the capacity of the fine-grained space and has clear effect on retrieval accuracy.

Table 1. Instance-level retrieval accuracies using various attributes on the shoe dataset.

	Subclass label	10d attribute	15d attribute	21d attribute
@ $K = 1$	10.23 %	19.71 %	26.12 %	34.78 %
@ $K = 5$	35.65 %	46.06 %	57.74 %	64.49 %
@ $K = 10$	53.07 %	65.30 %	74.20 %	79.41 %

4.3 Results of FG-SBIR

Competitors: We mainly benchmark against the very recent deep triplet model proposed in [28]. In addition, we also introduce two shallow variants of our model for comparison:

Table 2. Instance-level retrieval accuracies using various attributes on the chair dataset.

	Subclass label	5d attribute	10d attribute	15d attribute
@ $K = 1$	14.78 %	14.12 %	27.04 %	36.40 %
@ $K = 5$	44.57 %	38.42 %	59.76 %	66.01 %
@ $K = 10$	63.78 %	52.37 %	75.81 %	84.54 %

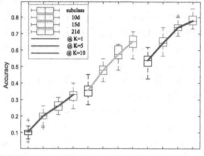

(a) Instance-level retrieval accuracies using various attributes on the shoe dataset

(b) Instance-level retrieval accuracies using various attributes on the chair dataset

Fig. 4. Instance-level accuracies. The bold lines colored red, green, and blue denote the retrieval accuracies @ $K = 1$, 5, 10 respectively. In (a), the boxes colored black, green, blue, and red denote the results obtained by different supervision labels: subclass, 10d attribute, 15d attribute, 21d attribute. In (b), the boxes colored black, green, blue, and red denote the results obtained by different supervision labels: subclass, 5d attribute, 10d attribute, 15d attribute. For each box, the central mark is the median. The top and bottom edges of the box are the 75th and 25th percentiles, respectively. The outliers are marked individually. (Color figure online)

Deep triplet-ranking: Representing current state-of-the-art for FB-SBIR, the authors [28] develop a deep triplet ranking network with a data augmentation and staged pre-training strategy to address the problem of insufficient training data. We use it for comparison on both the shoe and chair dataset.

A_s model: In Sect. 3, we have illustrated that sketch sample attribute matrix A_s is usually excessively sparse and low-rank. This is likely to lead to inaccurate computation results, and exactly optimizing for A_sT_s that approximate A_p might not be feasible. In order to verify this, we design the following model for verification and comparison:

$$J_2 = \min_{W_p, W_s, T_s} \|P^T W_p - A_p\|_F^2 + \|S^T W_s - A_s T_s\|_F^2$$
$$+ \lambda_1(\|W_p\|_{G_1} + \|W_s\|_{G_1}) + \lambda_2\|A_p - A_s T_s\|_F^2 , \tag{14}$$

where T_s is the transformation matrices for sketch sample attribute matrix A_s. In the following experiments, we denote this method as "A_s model".

F model: In order to verify the benefits of multi-view features, we introduce models using single-view features for comparison. In Eq. (6), the physical significance of the Group norm terms is view selection. If we set the coefficients of Group norms in Eq. (6) as zero when we use single-view features, and the projection matrices $\mathbf{W}_p$ and $\mathbf{W}_s$ will lose all the constraints. In this case, our model can be adjusted as:

$$J_3 = \min_{\mathbf{W}_p, \mathbf{W}_s, \mathbf{T}} \|\mathbf{P}^T \mathbf{W}_p - \mathbf{A}_p\|_F^2 + \|\mathbf{S}^T \mathbf{W}_s - \mathbf{A}_p \mathbf{T}\|_F^2$$
$$+ \lambda_1 (\|\mathbf{W}_p\|_F + \|\mathbf{W}_s\|_F) + \lambda_2 \|\mathbf{A}_p - \mathbf{A}_p \mathbf{T}\|_F^2 . \tag{15}$$

In the following experiments, we denote this method as "F model". A_s model and F model qualify for shallow model baselines, which are derived from some state-of-the-art shallow cross-modal subspace learning methods elaborated for image-text matching.

Results and Discussion: Results are shown in Table 3. Overall, it can be observed that, on the shoe dataset, our model using concatenation of HOG and $fc7$ deep feature offers the best among all the shallow variants and closely resembles the performance of deep triplet-ranking [28], i.e. 34.78 % vs 39.13 % for top 1 and 84.54 % vs 87.83 % for top 10. It is promising to notice that shallow cross-modal method tailored for FG-SBIR is able to deliver retrieval performances close to that of deep models where ample training data and extensive user annotations are required. However, on chairs, our model performed considerably worse than [28], scoring only 36.40 % vs 69.07 % for top 1 and 84.54 % vs 97.04 % for top 10. This phenomenon is largely explained by the lack of discriminative power of chair attributes, which was also highlighted as part of previous set of experiments (Sect. 4.2). We believe redesigning a better set of attributes for chairs would help to boost retrieval performance, but would leave as future work.

In addition, results also show that our model is better than using the single-view feature by "F model", i.e. F model (HOG) and F model (fc7 Deep), and deep feature fc7 Deep is proven to be better than HOG on the FG-SBIR task. It is interesting that when CCA is applied to fuse HOG and fc7 Deep, i.e. F model (HOG&fc7 Deep+2View-CCA), it leads to worse performance when compared against single-view models. The reason is that CCA might result in information loss when fusing features from different modalities. In contrast, our model is capable of keep the properties of the original multi-view features as much as possible via joint view selection. Moreover, in Table 3, we can observe that the experimental results of "A_s model (HOG&fc7 Deep)" on the shoe and the chair datasets are much worse than "Our model (HOG&fc7 Deep)". It indicates that it is more reasonable to use the photo attribute space as the coupled intermediate space for both photo and sketch. In other words, sketch attribute space might suffer from data sparsity and low-rank of attribute matrix $\mathbf{A}_s$, which leads to inefficiency of the model.

Computational Complexity: Average running time of our Matlab code on a 3.30 GHz Desktop PC with 16 GB RAM, across 30 experiments conducted on the shoe/chair datasets, are 0.87 s and 0.39 s, respectively.

Table 3. Experimental results comparisons.

	Shoe		Chair	
	acc.@1	acc.@10	acc.@1	acc.@10
Deep triplet-ranking (fc7 Deep) [28]	39.13 %	87.83 %	69.07 %	97.04 %
F model (HOG)	3.04 %	31.33 %	7.22 %	42.92 %
F model (fc7 Deep)	30.43 %	77.91 %	35.77 %	80.98 %
F model (HOG&fc7 Deep+2View-CCA)	6.96 %	28.19 %	29.00 %	70.15 %
A_s model (HOG&fc7 Deep)	7.48 %	56.52 %	24.99 %	74.64 %
Our model (HOG&fc7 Deep)	34.78 %	79.41 %	36.40 %	84.54 %

5   Conclusion

In this paper, for the first time, we proposed an unified cross-domain framework for fine-grained sketch-based image retrieval. Our model not only learns a domain-independent subspace to conduct retrieval, but also ensures effective fine-grained comparisons at the same time. Different to traditional text-photo cross-domain methods that works only on category-level, it uniquely learns from pair-wise sketch-photo data, therefore constructing a coupled space that is fitting for fine-grained retrieval. Once learned the model can also be used to predict attributes without the need for explicit training of attribute classifiers. Experiments on the latest fine-grained sketch-photo datasets demonstrated the effectiveness of the proposed method. For future work, we will investigate how the design of visual attributes affects quality of the learned coupled subspace, with the immediate hope to further improve retrieval performance on the chair dataset.

Acknowledgment. This work was partly supported by National Natural Science Foundation of China (NSFC) grant No. 61402047, Beijing Natural Science Foundation (BNSF) grant No. 4162044, NSFC-RS joint funding grant Nos. 61511130081 and IE141387, the Open Projects Program of National Laboratory of Pattern Recognition grant No. 201600018, NSFC grant No. 61273217, and the Fundamental Research Funds for the Central Universities under Grant No. 2016RC11.

References

1. Cao, Y., Wang, C., Zhang, L., Zhang, L.: Edgel index for large-scale sketch-based image search. In: CVPR (2011)
2. Cao, Y., Wang, H., Wang, C., Li, Z., Zhang, L., Zhang, L.: Mindfinder: interactive sketch-based image search on millions of images. In: ACM MM (2010)
3. Costa Pereira, J., Coviello, E., Doyle, G., Rasiwasia, N., Lanckriet, G.R., Levy, R., Vasconcelos, N.: On the role of correlation and abstraction in cross-modal multimedia retrieval. TPAMI **36**(3), 521–535 (2014)

4. Eitz, M., Hildebrand, K., Boubekeur, T., Alexa, M.: Sketch-based image retrieval: Benchmark and bag-of-features descriptors. IEEE Trans. Visual Comput. Graphics **17**(11), 1624–1636 (2011)
5. Gorodnitsky, I.F., Rao, B.D.: Sparse signal reconstruction from limited data using focuss: a re-weighted minimum norm algorithm. IEEE Trans. Signal Process. **45**(3), 600–616 (1997)
6. Hardoon, D.R., Szedmak, S., Shawe-Taylor, J.: Canonical correlation analysis: an overview with application to learning methods. Neural Comput. **16**(12), 2639–2664 (2004)
7. He, R., Zhang, M., Wang, L., Ji, Y., Yin, Q.: Cross-modal subspace learning via pairwise constraints. TIP **24**(12), 5543–5556 (2015)
8. Hu, R., Collomosse, J.: A performance evaluation of gradient field hog descriptor for sketch based image retrieval. CVIU **117**(7), 790–806 (2013)
9. Jia, Y., Salzmann, M., Darrell, T.: Learning cross-modality similarity for multinomial data. In: ICCV (2011)
10. Kim, T.K., Kittler, J., Cipolla, R.: Discriminative learning and recognition of image set classes using canonical correlations. TPAMI **29**(6), 1005–1018 (2007)
11. Li, K., Pang, K., Song, Y., Hospedales, T., Zhang, H., Hu, Y.: Fine-grained sketch-based image retrieval: the role of part-aware attributes. In: WACV (2016)
12. Li, Y., Hospedales, T.M., Song, Y.Z., Gong, S.: Fine-grained sketch-based image retrieval by matching deformable part models. In: BMVC (2014)
13. Li, Y., Hospedales, T.M., Song, Y.Z., Gong, S.: Free-hand sketch recognition by multi-kernel feature learning. CVIU **137**, 1–11 (2015)
14. Lin, Y.L., Huang, C.Y., Wang, H.J., Hsu, W.C.: 3d sub-query expansion for improving sketch-based multi-view image retrieval. In: ICCV (2013)
15. Mignon, A., Jurie, F.: CMML: a new metric learning approach for cross modal matching. In: ACCV (2012)
16. Ouyang, S., Hospedales, T., Song, Y.-Z., Li, X.: Cross-modal face matching: beyond viewed sketches. In: Cremers, D., Reid, I., Saito, H., Yang, M.-H. (eds.) ACCV 2014. LNCS, vol. 9004, pp. 210–225. Springer, Heidelberg (2015). doi:10.1007/978-3-319-16808-1_15
17. Parui, S., Mittal, A.: Similarity-invariant sketch-based image retrieval in large databases. In: Fleet, D., Pajdla, T., Schiele, B., Tuytelaars, T. (eds.) ECCV 2014. LNCS, vol. 8694, pp. 398–414. Springer, Heidelberg (2014). doi:10.1007/978-3-319-10599-4_26
18. Putthividhy, D., Attias, H.T., Nagarajan, S.S.: Topic regression multi-modal latent dirichlet allocation for image annotation. In: CVPR (2010)
19. Qi, Y., Guo, J., Song, Y.Z., Xiang, T., Zhang, H., Tan, Z.H.: Im2sketch: sketch generation by unconflicted perceptual grouping. Neurocomputing **165**, 338–349 (2015)
20. Rasiwasia, N., Costa Pereira, J., Coviello, E., Doyle, G., Lanckriet, G.R., Levy, R., Vasconcelos, N.: A new approach to cross-modal multimedia retrieval. In: ACM MM (2010)
21. Rasiwasia, N., Moreno, P.J., Vasconcelos, N.: Bridging the gap: query by semantic example. TMM **9**(5), 923–938 (2007)
22. Sharma, A., Jacobs, D.W.: Bypassing synthesis: Pls for face recognition with pose, low-resolution and sketch. In: CVPR (2011)
23. Sharma, A., Kumar, A., Daume III., H., Jacobs, D.W.: Generalized multiview analysis: a discriminative latent space. In: CVPR (2012)
24. Wang, F., Kang, L., Li, Y.: Sketch-based 3d shape retrieval using convolutional neural networks. In: CVPR (2015)

25. Wang, H., Nie, F., Huang, H.: Multi-view clustering and feature learning via structured sparsity. In: ICML (2013)
26. Wang, K., He, R., Wang, W., Wang, L., Tan, T.: Learning coupled feature spaces for cross-modal matching. In: ICCV (2013)
27. Wu, W., Xu, J., Li, H.: Learning similarity function between objects in heterogeneous spaces. Microsoft Research Technique report (2010)
28. Yu, Q., Liu, F., Song, Y., Xiang, T., Hospedales, T., Loy, C.C.: Sketch me that shoe. In: CVPR (2016)
29. Yu, Q., Yang, Y., Song, Y.Z., Xiang, T., Hospedales, T.M.: Sketch-a-net that beats humans. In: BMVC (2015)
30. Zhuang, Y., Wang, Y., Wu, F., Zhang, Y., Lu, W.: Supervised coupled dictionary learning with group structures for multi-modal retrieval. In: AAAI (2013)

IIIT-CFW: A Benchmark Database of Cartoon Faces in the Wild

Ashutosh Mishra[1], Shyam Nandan Rai[1],
Anand Mishra[2(✉)], and C.V. Jawahar[1,2]

[1] IIIT Chittoor, Sri City, India
[2] CVIT, KCIS, IIIT Hyderabad, Hyderabad, India
anand.mishra@research.iiit.ac.in

Abstract. In this paper, we introduce the cartoon faces in the wild (IIIT-CFW) database and associated problems. This database contains 8,928 annotated images of cartoon faces of 100 public figures. It will be useful in conducting research on spectrum of problems associated with cartoon understanding. Note that to our knowledge, such realistic and large databases of cartoon faces are not available in the literature.

Keywords: Cartoon faces · Cartoon face synthesis · Sketches · Fine art

1 Introduction

We introduce a database of 8,928 annotated cartoon faces designed as an aid in studying the problem of unconstrained cartoon understanding. The database can be downloaded from our project website[1].

Our database which we refer as IIIT cartoon faces in the wild (or IIIT-CFW in abbreviation) is designed to study spectrum of problems associated with cartoon understanding. Some of these problems are listed in Sect. 5. Oxford dictionary defines cartoon as follows: *a simple drawing showing the features of its subjects in a humorously exaggerated way, especially a satirical one in a newspaper or magazine.* However, the modern usage of cartoon has extended to any non-realistic, semi-realistic drawing or painting intended for satire, caricature, or humor, or to the artistic style of such works. Following the modern definition, our database of cartoon faces contains caricatures, paintings, cartoons and sketches of internationally well-known public figures.

Research in face recognition has been significantly advanced in last few years [10,14,17,21,24,28]. Thanks to multiple databases introduced (we have discussed few of them in Sect. 2). These databases have triggered the research and study in face recognition domain. On the other hand, there have been only very few attempts to address the problem of recognizing cartoon faces [3,22], that too with experiments on small test sets. Cartoon understanding has many

---

[1] http://cvit.iiit.ac.in/projects/cartoonFaces/.

G. Hua and H. Jégou (Eds.): ECCV 2016 Workshops, Part I, LNCS 9913, pp. 35–47, 2016.
DOI: 10.1007/978-3-319-46604-0_3

(a)   (b)

Fig. 1. Who are these and what are they doing? There has been lots of advancement in face recognition. However, the problem of recognizing cartoon characters has not been looked rigorously. Our database: the IIIT-CFW will be useful for comprehensive studies of understanding cartoon images.

application areas. One of the fundamental application is: given an image containing cartoons of people, answering questions, such as who are in the image and what are they doing? (See Fig. 1). Such understanding, (i) can help visually impaired people to understand cartoon images or movies, and (ii) can be used to automatically censor communal or politically incorrect cartoons in the social media. Other applications of understanding cartoons are generating realistic cartoon faces, generating various realistic facial expression in cartoons, etc. These applications have enormous importance in fine art.

Cartoon face recognition is the first step towards larger understanding of cartoon images. The problem of cartoon face recognition is closely related to real face recognition, however poses many additional challenges. For example, (i) artistic variations, (ii) limited examples, (iii) magnitude less data than real faces, (iv) highly caricatured. The other challenges such as pose, expression, age, illumination variations, race (e.g., cartoon faces of Asian characters are very different in look from that of European characters) and gender variations remain similar as face databases. We show some examples of our database illustrating the above mentioned challenges in Fig. 2. Another closely related area to cartoon face recognition is *sketch recognition* [2,7]. However, in sketch recognition, most of the attempts were made to recognize handwritten geometric objects. Our database of cartoon faces is much broader and challenging than simple geometric sketches or drawing, and sketch recognition techniques may not be directly applicable to these images. We believe that the IIIT-CFW will prove a first important step towards conducting research in broad area of cartoon understanding.

Before proceeding with the details, we briefly summarize the IIIT-CFW database here:

- This database contain cartoon images of 100 international celebrities (politician, actor, singer, sports person, etc.) and 8,928 images in all.
- The images in this database are harvested from the web. These images contain cartoons drawn in totally unconstrained setting.
- The IIIT-CFW contains detailed annotations and it can be used for wide spectrum of problems including cartoon face recognition, cartoon face verification,

(a) Age

(b) Appearance

(c) Artistic variation

(d) Expression

(e) Gender

(f) Amount of caricaturing

(g) Pose

(h) Race

Fig. 2. Sample faces of the IIIT-CFW. It has a lot of variations, such as (a) age (young and old), (b) appearance (with beard, with glass), (c) artistic (pure cartoon, sketch and caricature) (d) expression (happy, sad, seducing, angry, etc.), (e) gender (male and female), (f) amount of caricaturing, (g) pose (frontal and non-frontal), and (h) race (Asian, American, African, etc.).

cartoon image retrieval, relative attributes in cartoons, gender or age group estimation from the cartoon faces, and cartoon faces synthesis.

- We provide face bounding box along with some additional attributes such as age group, view, expression, pose etc.
- Most of the images of this database are in color with very few in gray scale.
- We provide standard train and test splits according to the problem.

More details are provided in the remainder of this paper which is organized as follows. In Sect. 2, we discuss some of the related databases. Since cartoon understanding is novel problem, however, closely related to face recognition, we provide brief discussion on popular face recognition databases, and compare them with ours. Section 3 describes image collection and annotation scheme. We give detail database statistics and analyze the complexity of the database in Sect. 4. We then discuss intended usage of this database where we discuss about spectrum of problems which can be studied on this database. We finally provide concluding remarks for this database paper in the Sect. 6.

2   Related Databases

The problem of cartoon face understanding lacks standard benchmark databases. On the other hand, the real face recognition community has a clear advantage of having plethora of standard benchmarks. Starting from popular ORL database [16] in the year 1994 and Yale database [1] in the year 1997, numerous standard benchmarks have been released to address face recognition problem. Each of these databases are more challenging and realistic as compared to their past counterparts. In this section we present a brief survey of some of the popular face databases and compare them with our cartoon face database. We summarize this comparison in Table 1.

- **ORL face database** [16]. This database consists of 400 face images of 40 distinct characters. The images for some characters were taken at different time, with varying lighting and facial conditions. The images are face centered and taken against a dark background.
- **Yale face database** [1]. This database contains 165 face images of 15 characters. The faces in this database are frontal and have very small variations.
- **Labeled Wikipedia faces (LWF)** [8]. The LWF database contains 8.5 K faces of approximately 1.5 K individuals. These images were collected from the Wikipedia living people category. The database, in addition to images, contains some meta data, e.g., the source images, image captions (if available) and person name detection results.
- **FaceScrub** [13]. It contains 1,06,863 images of 530 celebrities, with about 200 faces per person. The images in the database were harvested from the web and are taken under real-world situations (i.e., uncontrolled settings). Images apart from the queried person were discarded in order to build the database.
- **FEI face database** [23]. Is a Brazilian face database that contains a set of 2800 face images, 14 images for each of 200 individuals. Equal number of male and female subjects are present in the database. Colored images taken against a white homogeneous background in an upright frontal position with profile rotation of up to about 180 degrees are present in the database.
- **Indian face database** [11]. Is a database consisting eleven different images, each of 40 distinct subjects. The images were acquired in an upright frontal position against a bright homogeneous background. The database also provide

Table 1. Variations, size and target applications of various face databases vs our cartoon database. Our database provides suitable annotations and train-test splits to study wide range of problems (R: race, G: gender, P: pose, E: expression, A: appearance, P_1: face recognition, P_2: face verification, P_3: face detection, P_4: photo2cartoon P_5: cartoon2photo P_6: attributes based search P_7:relative attributes in faces, *: Not available publicly).

Databases	Variation					Size (# people, # images)	Target applications
	R	G	P	E	A		
ORL [16]	✓	✓	✓	✓	✓	(40, 400)	P_1
Yale [1]	✓	✓	×	✓	✓	(15, 165)	P_1
Indian Face [11]	×	✓	✓	✓	✓	(40, 440)	P_1
LFW [9]	✓	✓	✓	×	✓	(5749, 13233)	P_1, P_2
Texas 3D [5,6]	✓	✓	×	✓	✓	(105, 1149)	P_1
FEI [23]	×	✓	✓	✓	✓	(200, 2800)	P_1
PubFig83 [15]	✓	✓	✓	✓	✓	(100, 8300)	P_2
Celeb Faces [19]	✓	✓	✓	✓	✓	(5346, 87628)	P_1,P_2
IMFDB [18]	×	✓	✓	✓	✓	(100, 34512)	P_1, P_2
LWF [8]	✓	✓	✓	✓	✓	(1500, 8500)	P_1, P_2
FaceScrub [13]	✓	✓	✓	✓	✓	(530, 106863)	P_1,P_3
Facebook [21]	-	-	-	-	-	(200 M, 8 M)	*
Google [17]	-	-	-	-	-	(4.4 M, 4030 M)	*
VGG [14]	✓	✓	✓	✓	✓	(2363, 2.6 M)	P_1,P_2
The IIIT-CFW	✓	✓	✓	✓	✓	(100, 8927)	$P_1,P_2,P_3,P_4,P_5,P_6,P_7$

detail annotations for face orientation. Some emotions such as neutral, smile, laughter, sad or disgust are also included in annotation of this database.

- **Labeled faces in the wild** [9]. The LFW database of face images is designed for studying the problem of unconstrained face recognition. The database contains more than 13,000 images of 1680 characters. These images were collected from the web. The faces in the database are result of Viola-Jones face detector [25] and hence, are roughly frontal.
- **CelebFaces** [19]. This database contains 5436 characters and 87628 face images in all. It contains faces of those celebrity who do not exist in LFW. Images in this database were collected from web.
- **Youtube face** [27]. The database contains 3,425 videos of 1,595 different people. All the videos were downloaded from YouTube.
- **PubFig83** [15]. The PubFig83 database contains 8300 cropped facial images of 83 unique public figures. This database aims to provide the solution for the problem of recognizing identities from near-frontal faces.
- **Indian Movie Face Database (IMFDB)** [18]. Is a large unconstrained face database consisting of 34512 images of 100 Indian actors from more than 100 videos. The images have been obtained manually by cropping them from video frames in turn leading to high degree of variability in terms of scale, pose, expression, illumination, age, resolution, occlusion, and makeup. The

IMFDB provides a detailed annotation of every face in terms of age, pose, gender, expression and type of occlusion. Standard train-val-test division is missing in this database.

- **Industrial benchmarks** [17,21]. These face databases introduced by Google and Facebook are the largest in size. However, they are not publicly available. The Google and Facebook database contains 200 Million and 4.4 Million faces of 4030 and 8 Million characters respectively.
- **VGG face database** [14]. This database is introduced by Visual geometry group of Oxford university. It contains 2.6 Million faces of 2363 characters harvested from the web.

Contrary to the real face databases, ours is a first attempt to create a realistic and large database of cartoon faces. In many ways our database is similar to pubFig and celebFace, e.g., both these databases and ours contain faces of public figures harvested from the web. However, our database has additional challenges due to the fact that it contains cartoon faces. Moreover, unlike pubFig which can only be used for face verification, our database can be used to address many different problems (see Sect. 5). In short, the major highlights of our database are as follows: (i) it is a first large database of cartoon faces, (ii) it contains detail annotations, and hence, it can be used to study spectrum of problems associated with cartoon understanding.

3   Data Collection and Annotations

The CFW is harvested from Google image search. We have used queries like 'Obama + cartoon', 'Emma Watson + cartoon', and so on, to collect cartoon images of 100 public figures. These public figures are chosen from different categories such as sports, politics, art, science, etc. and different countries such as USA, UK, Australia, India, etc. Once images are collected, we use manual filtering to remove irrelevant images. We then gave these images to our annotation team of three people who were asked to draw face bounding boxes and provide following attributes to each face:

- Type of cartoon: cartoon, cartoon sketch, caricature
- Pose: frontal, non frontal
- Expression: happy, sad, thoughtful, seductive, sorrow, angry, serious, frightened, crying, shocked
- Age group: young, old
- Gender: male, female
- Beard: yes, no
- Glass: yes, no

For the subjective attributes like age group and expression, we used voting scheme among the annotators. In addition to face annotation, attributes for each face, some metadata details such as the name of the personality and the identity number (id number) is also assigned.

Fig. 3. Example of annotations provided in the IIIT-CFW.

Annotation is stored and described in the form of XML. The XML contains the information about the unique id number assigned to each personality in addition to the name of the personality and the above seven attributes. Moreover, the coordinates $(x_1, y_1, width, height)$ of the face bounding box are also included in the XML description. Figure 3 shows an example of annotations we provide in the CFW. For annotation, image markup tool which was released by Mozilla under public license version–1.1 was used[2].

4   Statistical Details and Complexity Analysis of Database

We now provide statistical details of the IIIT-CFW which is collected in totally unconstrained manner. The IIIT-CFW has large variations in attributes. These variations make the database realistic and challenging. This database contains 8928 cartoon images of 100 public figures. The variations in this database across the attributes are shown through pie-charts in Fig. 4. In this figure, we illustrate variations in data across seven attributes (discussed in Sect. 3) and variations in race. We observe that the introduced database posses large diversity.

We also analyze the complexity of the database by analyzing the mean face and eigenfaces of the database and compare it with some of the popular face database, namely, Yale [1], LFW [9] and pubFig [15]. These comparisons are shown in Figs. 6 and 7 respectively. Here, we show mean and eigenfaces of Yale

[2] http://tapor.uvic.ca/~mholmes/image_markup/.

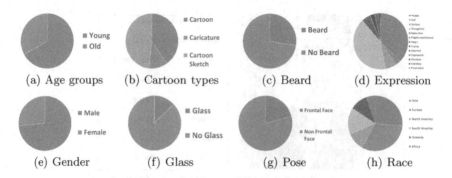

(a) Age groups   (b) Cartoon types   (c) Beard   (d) Expression

(e) Gender   (f) Glass   (g) Pose   (h) Race

Fig. 4. Wide variations in attributes in our database. We show distribution of face images across eight attributes and observe that our database has lots of diversity across various attributes.

(a) pubFig   (b) Ours

Fig. 5. Mean faces of Angelina Jolie (1st and 3rd column) and Barack Obama (2nd and 4th column) in pubFig [15] and ours. We observe that in pubFig [15] celebrities are clearly recognizable but not in ours.

database [1] and relatively harder databases such as LFW [9] and pubFig [15]. We observe that as compared to ours, the mean and the top eigenfaces of these databases clearly look like faces. This implies that these popular database have lesser variations in pose and appearance of faces as compared to ours. We also compare celebrity wise mean faces of our database with that of pubFig [15] which also contain faces of public figures. This comparison is shown in Fig. 5. We choose faces of Angelina Jolie and Barack Obama for this study. As can be seen, one can easily recognize the mean faces of these two celebrities in case of pubFig [15]. However, the mean face of these celebrities in our cartoon database is hard to recognize. These observation justify our claim that our database contains cartoon images collected in a totally unconstrained setting and it has a large variations.

5   Spectrum of Problems

The IIIT-CFW has been introduced to study a spectrum of problems. These problems are summarized in Fig. 8. Although many of these problems are fundamental in real face domain, but due to the unavailability of detail annotations and problem specific train-test splits existing face databases facilitate research

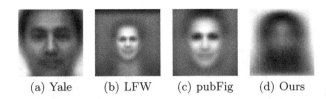

(a) Yale   (b) LFW   (c) pubFig   (d) Ours

Fig. 6. Mean faces of our cartoon database in (d) as compared to (a) Yale [1] (b) LFW [9] and (c) pubFig [15]. We observe that mean face of Yale database clearly looks like a face as compared to the relatively harder databases such as LFW and pub-Fig. On the other hand, our database: the IIIT-CFW contains large variations, and hence the mean face does not clearly look like a face.

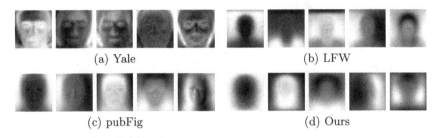

(a) Yale   (b) LFW

(c) pubFig   (d) Ours

Fig. 7. Top-5 eigenfaces of (a) Yale [1] (ii) LFW [9], (c) pubFig [15] and (d) Ours

only on selected problems. On the other hand, we not only provide problem specific train-val-test splits, but also detail annotations to study wide range of problems associated with cartoon faces. In this section, we briefly describe the problems which can be studied on our database, and explain the train-val-test split strategy. Table 2 summarizes the training, validation and test sets in our database.

1. **Cartoon face recognition.** The problem of cartoon face recognition is to recognize the given cartoon face as one of the C classes.
2. **Cartoon face verification.** Given two cartoon faces the problem of face verification is to answer weather the pair is of same person or not. For this problem we have labeled face pairs as same or different based on if they are of same public figure or not. The train-test division is done such that if a pair of cartoon characters c belong to train set, then it does not belong to validation and test set.
3. **Cartoon gender identification.** It is binary classification problem where given a cartoon face the system has to answer weather it is a male or a female. We provide a standard train and test split by making sure that if a cartoon character is present in train set, examples of this cartoon character will not be present in test set.
4. **Photo2cartoon and cartoon2photo.** The problem here is: given real face of a public figure, can we retrieve all the cartoon faces of that public figure from a large database of cartoons, and vice-versa. This database provide

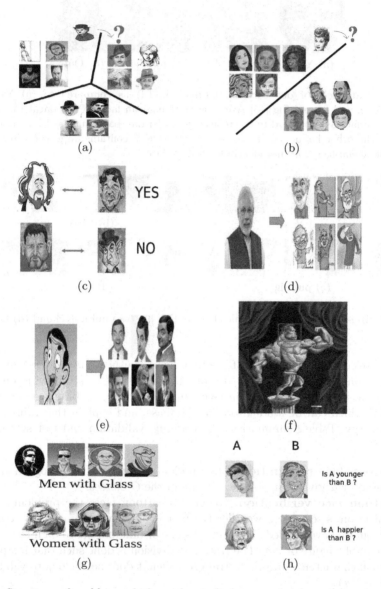

Fig. 8. Spectrum of problems which can be studied on our database: (a) cartoon face recognition, (b) cartoon gender classification (c) cartoon face verification, (d) photo to cartoon search (e) cartoon to photo search, (f) cartoon face detection (e) attribute based search in cartoons, and (f) relative attributes in cartoons. We provide **suitable annotations** and **problem specific train-val-test split** to conduct study on various problems associated with cartoon faces.

Table 2. Training, testing and validation splits in our database (the CFG) for various problems (CF: cartoon faces, RF: real faces, CFP: cartoon face pairs).

Problem	Train set	Validation set	Test set	Query set
Face recognition	4464 CF	2232 CF	2232 CF	NA
	100 classes	100 classes	100 classes	
Gender identification	6007 CF	1857 CF	1064	NA
	2 classes	2 classes	2 classes	
Face verification	1,80,39,021 CFP	17,23,296 CFP	5,65,516 CFP	NA
	2 classes	2 classes	2 classes	
Attribute based search	NA	NA	NA	Query: 10 strings
				Databse: 8928 CF
Photo2cartoon	NA	NA	NA	Query: 1000 RF
				Databse: 8928 CF
cartoon2photo	NA	NA	NA	Query: 8928 CF
				Databse: 1000 RF

support for studying such problems. Along with cartoon faces we provide 1000 real faces (ten real face of each character). These real faces are harvested from Google image search and can be used as query for photo2cartoon retrieval and database for cartoon2photo retrieval. Further for cartoon2photo retrieval all the cartoon in the database should be used as query.

5. **Face detection, pose estimation and landmark detection.** This has been a well studied problem of real face images [29]. On other side, cartoon faces have lots of artistic variations and detecting face, landmark points such as eyes, nose, mouth etc. can prove challenging for the state of the art methods. For example: results of face detection using the famous Viola-Jones method [25] is shown in Fig. 9. We see that face detection in cartoon is not a trivial task and needs special attention. Our database can also facilitate research for this problem.

6. **Relative attributes in Cartoon.** Relative attributes in faces has been a well studied problem. Given a pair of cartoon faces (A, B) the problem is to answer some questions such as: Is A older than B? Is A happier than B? Are A and B of similar age group? We also provide annotation for this problem and a standard train-val-test split similar to face verification problem.

7. **Attribute based cartoon search.** The IIIT-CFW database also provides annotation for attribute based cartoon search, such as search all cartoon faces with glass, search all female cartoon faces who are happy, and so on. We provide 10 such string queries along with associated relevant images.

Other exciting problems. Generating photo-realistic images of human faces has been a fascinating yet a hard problem in computer vision and computer graphics. This problem has gained attention of researchers in the last decade, and some interesting works have been published in this space, such as, face hallucination [12], facial expression generation [20]. There have also been some works on face sketches, which are the subset of our database, e.g., face sketch synthesis and recognition [26], sketch inversion [4].

Fig. 9. Results of Viola-Jones [25] face detection on our database: first four images show some successful face detection. The last four images are few examples where Viola-Jones fails to detect faces. In general, we observe that seminal method Viola-Jones is not very successful in detecting cartoon faces.

These problems in real faces or sketch faces domain can be also studied for cartoons, and our database can be used for conducting such study. Generating realistic cartoon faces with various facial expressions can be an exciting application in the fine art perspective.

6 Conclusions

We have introduced a large database of cartoon faces and discussed the spectrum of problems which can be studied on this database. We believe the database will trigger research in cartoon face understanding and can prove a turning point in the way of how computers see the cartoons.

References

1. Belhumeur, P.N., Hespanha, J.P., Kriegman, D.J.: Eigenfaces vs. fisherfaces: recognition using class specific linear projection. IEEE Trans. Pattern Anal. Mach. Intell. **19**(7), 711–720 (1997)
2. Field, M., Valentine, S., Linsey, J., Hammond, T.: Sketch recognition algorithms for comparing complex and unpredictable shapes. In: IJCAI (2011)
3. Glasberg, R., Samour, A., Elazouzi, K., Sikora, T.: Cartoon-recognition using video & audio descriptors. In: European Signal Processing Conference (2005)
4. Güçlütürk, Y., Güçlü, U., van Lier, R., van Gerven, M.A.: Convolutional sketch inversion. arXiv preprint arXiv:1606.03073 (2016)
5. Gupta, S., Castleman, K.R., Markey, M.K., Bovik, A.C.: Texas 3d face recognition database. In: Image Analysis & Interpretation (SSIAI), pp. 97–100. IEEE (2010)
6. Gupta, S., Markey, M.K., Bovik, A.C.: Anthropometric 3d face recognition. Int. J. Comput. Vis. **90**(3), 331–349 (2010)
7. Hammond, T.A., Logsdon, D., Paulson, B., Johnston, J., Peschel, J.M., Wolin, A., Taele, P.: A sketch recognition system for recognizing free-hand course of action diagrams. In: IAAI (2010)
8. Hasan, M.K., Pal, C.J.: Experiments on visual information extraction with the faces of wikipedia. In: AAAI (2014)
9. Huang, G.B., Ramesh, M., Berg, T., Learned-Miller, E.: Labeled faces in the wild: A database for studying face recognition in unconstrained environments. Technical report 07–49, University of Massachusetts, Amherst, October 2007
10. Jafri, R., Arabnia, H.R.: A survey of face recognition techniques. JIPS **5**(2), 41–68 (2009)

11. Jain, V., Mukherjee, A.: The Indian face database (2002). http://vis-www.cs.umass.edu/vidit/IndianFaceDatabase

12. Liu, C., Shum, H., Freeman, W.T.: Face hallucination: theory and practice. Int. J. Comput. Vis. **75**(1), 115–134 (2007)

13. Ng, H.W., Winkler, S.: A data-driven approach to cleaning large face datasets. In: ICIP (2014)

14. Parkhi, O.M., Vedaldi, A., Zisserman, A.: Deep face recognition. In: BMVC (2015)

15. Pinto, N., Stone, Z., Zickler, T., Cox, D.: Scaling up biologically-inspired computer vision: a case study in unconstrained face recognition on facebook. In: CVPRW (2011)

16. Samaria, F.S., Harter, A.C.: Parameterisation of a stochastic model for human face identification. In: WACV (1994)

17. Schroff, F., Kalenichenko, D., Philbin, J.: Facenet: A unified embedding for face recognition and clustering. In: CVPR (2015)

18. Setty, S., et al.: Indian movie face database: a benchmark for face recognition under wide variations. In: NCVPRIPG (2013)

19. Sun, Y., Wang, X., Tang, X.: Hybrid deep learning for face verification. In: ICCV (2013)

20. Susskind, J.M., Anderson, A.K., Hinton, G.E., Movellan, J.R.: Generating facial expressions with deep belief nets. INTECH Open Access Publisher (2008)

21. Taigman, Y., Yang, M., Ranzato, M., Wolf, L.: Deepface: closing the gap to human-level performance in face verification. In: CVPR (2014)

22. Takayama, K., Johan, H., Nishita, T.: Face detection and face recognition of cartoon characters using feature extraction. In: Image, Electronics and Visual Computing Workshop, p. 48 (2012)

23. Thomaz, C.E., Giraldi, G.A.: A new ranking method for principal components analysis and its application to face image analysis. Image Vis. Comput. **28**(6), 902–913 (2010)

24. Tolba, A., El-Baz, A., El-Harby, A.: Face recognition: a literature review. Int. J. Sig. Process. **2**(2), 88–103 (2006)

25. Viola, P.A., Jones, M.J.: Robust real-time face detection. Int. J. Comput. Vis. **57**(2), 137–154 (2004)

26. Wang, X., Tang, X.: Face photo-sketch synthesis and recognition. IEEE Trans. Pattern Anal. Mach. Intell. **31**(11), 1955–1967 (2009)

27. Wolf, L., Hassner, T., Maoz, I.: Face recognition in unconstrained videos with matched background similarity. In: CVPR (2011)

28. Zhao, W., Chellappa, R., Phillips, P.J., Rosenfeld, A.: Face recognition: a literature survey. ACM Comput. Surv. (CSUR) **35**(4), 399–458 (2003)

29. Zhu, X., Ramanan, D.: Face detection, pose estimation, and landmark localization in the wild. In: CVPR (2012)

Identifying Emotions Aroused from Paintings

Xin Lu[1]([✉]), Neela Sawant[2], Michelle G. Newman[3],
Reginald B. Adams Jr.[3], James Z. Wang[3], and Jia Li[3]([✉])

[1] Adobe Systems Inc., Mountain View, USA
xinl@adobe.com
[2] Amazon.com, Inc., Seattle, USA
neela.sawant@gmail.com
[3] The Pennsylvania State University, State College, USA
{mgn1,radams,jwang,jiali}@psu.edu

Abstract. Understanding the emotional appeal of paintings is a significant research problem related to affective image classification. The problem is challenging in part due to the scarceness of manually-classified paintings. Our work proposes to apply statistical models trained over photographs to infer the emotional appeal of paintings. Directly applying the learned models on photographs to paintings cannot provide accurate classification results, because visual features extracted from paintings and natural photographs have different characteristics. This work presents an adaptive learning algorithm that leverages labeled photographs and unlabeled paintings to infer the visual appeal of paintings. In particular, we iteratively adapt the feature distribution in photographs to fit paintings and maximize the joint likelihood of labeled and unlabeled data. We evaluate our approach through two emotional classification tasks: distinguishing positive from negative emotions, and differentiating reactive emotions from non-reactive ones. Experimental results show the potential of our approach.

Keywords: Classification · Evoked emotion · Adaptive learning · Photograph · Visual art

1   Introduction

Visual artworks such as paintings can evoke a variety of emotional responses from human observers, such as calmness, dynamism, turmoil, and happiness. Automatic inference of the emotions aroused from a given painting is an important research question due to its potential application in large-scale image management and human perception understanding. For instance, the affective capability of paintings might be leveraged to determine which artwork might be used to decorate workplaces, hospitals, gymnasia, and schools. The problem is highly

This material is based upon work supported by the National Science Foundation under Grant No. 1110970. The work was done when X. Lu and N. Sawant were with Penn State University.

G. Hua and H. Jégou (Eds.): ECCV 2016 Workshops, Part I, LNCS 9913, pp. 48–63, 2016.
DOI: 10.1007/978-3-319-46604-0_4

challenging because many paintings are abstract in nature. The exact association between visual features and evoked emotions is often not obvious.

An applicable framework that has been used to quantify general emotion recognition problem from color photographs [3,8,13,14] is to learn a statistical model that connects handcrafted visual features extracted from the training images with their associated emotional labels. However, unlike emotion recognition in photographs which can leverage existing annotated datasets such as the International Affective Picture System (IAPS) [10], we do not have a validated dataset with sufficient manually-labeled paintings. Previous methods [7,11,12] conducted training on a small collection (around a hundred pieces) of labeled paintings, which is insufficient and not publicly accessible. As the features of images from the same emotional category form a perplexing distribution in the feature space, a large labeled training dataset is needed to provide good coverage of possible variations. Establishing a large collection of paintings associated with emotional labels is time-consuming in that the subjectivity of visual appeal judgment to paintings requires the validation of the emotional labels to a collection of images.

One intuitive alternative is to apply those model learned from labeled photographs onto paintings straightforwardly. However, due to the difference in feature distributions between paintings and color photographs, as we will illustrate in Sect. 3, the statistics captured by the model is quite different from those in paintings. Experimental results (Sect. 5) also confirm that the model trained on photographs is inaccurate in recognizing emotions in paintings.

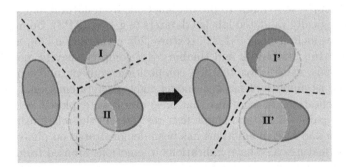

Fig. 1. Simplified illustration of distribution adaptation between photographs and paintings. **Left:** solid ellipses represent initially-estimated feature spaces of photographs from different emotional categories (indicated by different colors); orange dashed ellipses represent feature spaces of paintings whose emotional categories are unknown. The decision boundaries derived from photographs (black dashed lines) are unfit for paintings as they cut through feature spaces of paintings. **Right:** the estimation of photograph feature spaces adjusted according to the overlaps of photographs and paintings (region I and II). The new decision boundaries are more reasonable for paintings. (Color figure online)

This paper proposes an adaptive learning approach to recognize emotions in paintings, which leverages both labeled photographs and unlabeled paintings. The idea is to transfer the learned knowledge of photographs to paintings through distribution adaptation, a process wherein the distribution of the source domain is gradually adapted to the distribution of the target domain. Specifically, each photograph is associated with a weight; we account for the difference between the two distributions by re-weighting the weights. Figure 1 illustrates the basic intuition of this approach.

The rest of this paper is organized as follows: Sect. 2 provides a summary of related work. We present extensive statistical analysis to identify the dramatic distributions in paintings and color photographs in Sect. 3. The proposed algorithm is detailed in Sect. 4. Experimental results are presented in Sect. 5. Discussions and conclusions are provided in Sect. 6.

2   Related Work

2.1   Affective Image Classification

The analysis of emotions evoked through paintings has been under-explored by the research community, likely due to the scarcity of manually labeled paintings. Few studies have estimated aesthetics or emotions with a relatively small number of painting images [7,11,12]. Sartori *et al.* have studied abstract paintings using statistical analysis [16]. Our work is different in that we train statistical models on labeled photographs and adapt the learned models to paintings.

Some attempts were made to predict emotions from natural images [3,14,24] with psychologically validated labeled datasets (e.g., the IAPS). Commonly used visual features included color [2,22], texture [26], composition [25], and content of the image [15]. Machajdik and Hanbury [14] comprehensively modeled categorical emotions, using color, texture, composition, content, and semantic level features such as number of faces to model eight discrete emotional categories. Other representations of emotions that have also been explored by researchers include word pairs [18,23] and shape features [13]. As the relationship between these features and human emotions has been demonstrated on photographs, we believe these features also have indications to emotions aroused from paintings. In particular, our work adopted four groups of features: color, texture, composition, and content.

2.2   Domain Adaptation/Adaptive Learning

Many domain adaptation techniques have been developed in the past decades for building robust classifiers with data drawn from mismatched distributions. The two major directions are adapting feature distributions [6,17,20,21] and adapting classifier training [1,4,5].

To adapt feature distributions, Sugiyama *et al.* directly provided an estimate of the importance function by matching the two distributions in terms of the Kullback-Leibler divergence [20]. Shi and Sha proposed an approach to learn domain-invariant features and use them to minimize a proxy misclassification error on the target domain [17]. Kang *et al.* [21] proposed an unsupervised domain adaptation approach where the classifier was trained iteratively, such that each iteration used an increased number of automatically discovered target domain examples, and a decreased number of source domain examples. Jhuo *et al.* [6] transformed the visual samples in the source domain into an intermediate representation such that each transformed source sample could be linearly reconstructed by the samples of the target domain. The intrinsic relatedness of the source samples was then captured by using a low-rank structure.

To build robust classifiers for data drawn from mismatched distributions, Bickel *et al.* [1] proposed a logistic regression classifier to explicitly model classification problems without having to estimate the marginal distributions for shift correction. Gopalan *et al.* [5] computed the domain shift by learning shared subspaces between the source and target domains for classifier training. In [9], joint bias and weight vectors were estimated as a max-margin optimization problem for domain adaptation. The authors of [4] enforced the target classifier to share similar decision values on the unlabeled consumer videos with the selected source classifiers.

Our work proposes an adaptive learning approach that integrates the feature adaptation and classifier training. We then leverages labeled photographs and unlabeled paintings to infer the visual appeal of paintings.

3   Feature Distributions in Paintings and Photographs

To better illustrate the problem and introduce the proposed adaptive learning algorithm, we first conduct statistical analyses to identify the differences of feature distributions between color photographs and paintings.

3.1   Settings

We analyzed the feature differences by taking the color photographs within the IAPS [10] and randomly crawling 10,000 paintings from Flickr.com. Photograph and painting examples are shown in Figs. 2 and 3.

We represent an image (photograph or painting) with five types of visual features: 21-dimensional global color features including statistics of saturation, brightness, hue, and colorfulness; 39-dimension region-based color features describing region-based color statistics; 27-dimensional texture features composed of wavelet textures and features that depict the contrast, correlation, and homogeneity for each of the HSV channels of the images; 14-dimensional feature encoding the depth of field, dynamics, and the rule of thirds to represent the composition of an image; and 4-dimensional content feature referring to the number and size of frontal faces and the number of skin-colored pixels. All dimensions of the feature vectors are normalized to $[0, 1]$. Detailed descriptions of those features are presented in [14].

Fig. 2. Examples of photographs in the IAPS dataset [10]. (Color figure online)

Fig. 3. Examples of the painting images that we have collected for this study. (Color figure online)

3.2   Differences of Feature Distributions

This section unveils the underlying difference of feature distributions of paintings and photographs. We calculate the differences for each type of features using Euclidean distance as follows.

For each painting t from the set of paintings $T = \{t_i\}_{i=1}^{N_t}$ and its feature vector $f_c(t)$ ($c \in \{\text{color(global), color(region), texture, content, composition}\}$), we pair it with its nearest neighbor $S^*(t)$ from the photograph set $S = \{s_i\}_{i=1}^{N_s}$, where $S^*(t) = \arg\min_s D(f_c(t), f_c(s))$. N_s and N_t are the sizes of the photograph set and the painting set respectively. Distance $D(f_c(t), f_c(S^*(t)))$, denoted by $D_c(t)$, is defined as the distance between a single painting t and the collection of photographs $\{s_i\}$ in terms of feature type c. We normalize $D_c(t)$ by

$$\tilde{D}_c(t) = \frac{D_c(t)}{D(f_c(s'), f_c(S^*(t)))}, \qquad (1)$$

where s' is the photo whose feature vector $f_c(s')$ is the nearest one to $f_c(S^*(t))$. $\tilde{D}_c(t) < 1$ means that the visual feature extracted from painting t is close to at least one feature vector in the photograph collection S, while $\tilde{D}_c(t) \geq 1$ indicates the existence of a larger difference between t's feature and one of the features from S. The greater $\tilde{D}_c(t)$ is, the larger the difference is between $f_c(t)$ and the photograph set S.

In Fig. 4, we show the distributions of the normalized distance $\tilde{D}_c$ between a feature vector (global color features, region-based color features, texture, composition, and content) in a painting and its nearest vector from the photograph set. As shown in the fourth plot, paintings differ from photographs most in terms

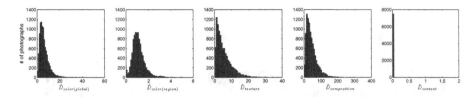

Fig. 4. Distributions of the normalized distance ($\tilde{D}$) from a painting to its nearest photograph, in terms of color (global), color (region), texture, composition and content feature, respectively. (Color figure online)

$$\tilde{D} = 20 \qquad \tilde{D} = 40 \qquad \tilde{D} = 60 \qquad \tilde{D} = 80 \qquad \tilde{D} = 100$$

Fig. 5. Examples of painting-photograph pairs with different value of $\tilde{D}_{composition}$. The first row are paintings. Their associated photographs are in the second row.

of the composition; the value of $\tilde{D}_{composition}$ at the peak of the distribution is about 17. This indicates that there is dramatic differences in composition features between most paintings and photographs. Paintings and photographs also differ a lot in terms of the global color feature (first plot) and the texture feature (third plot), as their curves peak at $\tilde{D}_{color(global)}$ around 4 and $\tilde{D}_{texture}$ around 2, respectively. Finally, in the last plot, $\tilde{D}_{content}$ are close to 0 for almost all paintings, which indicates that photographs and paintings have similar content features. The reason may be that the content features we extracted only describe the existence and the number of human faces, as well as the size of human skin areas. The dramatic differences between feature distributions and paintings indicate the necessity to perform the proposed adaptive learning in order to leverage the labeled photographs for recognizing emotions in paintings.

In Figs. 5, 6 and 7, we provide some examples of painting-photograph pairs with different distances. Pairs with small $\tilde{D}_c$ are similar in terms of feature c.

4   Adaptive Learning Approach

We now introduce the detailed formulation of the proposed adaptive learning approach. We first explain the notations and provide a formal description of the common covariant shift approach mentioned in Sect. 2. We then present our

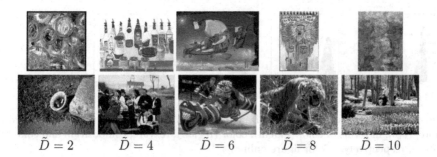

$\tilde{D} = 2$ $\tilde{D} = 4$ $\tilde{D} = 6$ $\tilde{D} = 8$ $\tilde{D} = 10$

Fig. 6. Examples of painting-photograph pairs with different value of $\tilde{D}_{texture}$. The first row are paintings. Their associated photographs are in the second row.

$\tilde{D} = 3$ $\tilde{D} = 6$ $\tilde{D} = 9$ $\tilde{D} = 12$ $\tilde{D} = 15$

Fig. 7. Examples of painting-photograph pairs with different value of $\tilde{D}_{color}$. The first row are paintings. Their associated photographs are in the second row.

approach that integrates the adaptive feature adaptation and classifier training. Finally, we describe how we jointly solve the maximization problem.

4.1 Notation

Let x be the p-dimensional data and the class labels of x be $y \in \{1, 2, \ldots, K\}$. For binary classification, K is set to two. Let S and T be the sets of photographs (source domain) and paintings (target domain), respectively, and the marginal probabilities $P_{X \in S}(X)$ and $P_{X \in T}(X)$ are denoted by $\Psi(x)$ and $\Phi(x)$, respectively. Let $\hat{\Phi}(x)$ and $\hat{\Psi}(x)$ denote the estimated distributions using the observed data samples.

4.2 Covariant Shift

Given the same feature observation $X = x$, the photograph set S and the painting set T, the conditional distributions of emotion labels Y are expected to be the same in both datasets, i.e., $P_{x \in S}(Y|X = x) = P_{x \in T}(Y|X = x)$. However, the marginal distributions of X may be different, i.e. $\Psi(X) \neq \Phi(X)$. This difference between the two domains is called covariate shift [19]. This is a problem if a mis-specified statistical model from a parametric model family is trained by minimizing the expected classification error over S. A common covariate shift correction approach assigns fixed weights to each labeled instance in S proportional to the ratio $\frac{\Psi(X)}{\Phi(X)}$. Then a classifier $P(Y|X)$ is trained to minimize the weighted classification error. We call it static covariate shift correction, as the estimation of instance weights is fixed before the subsequent classifier training task.

4.3   Adaptive Learning Approach

We devise a semi-supervised adaptive learning algorithm using both labeled and unlabeled data. As in standard covariate shift correction approaches, we compute a weight $w(x) = \frac{\hat{\Phi}(x)}{\hat{\Psi}(x)}$ for each $x \in S$. Essentially $w(x)$ is a form of importance sampling where data from the photographs is selected with a weight that corrects the covariate shift in both photographs and paintings. Then, all labeled and unlabeled data can be treated in a common semi-supervised framework to maximize the following objective:

$$O = \sum_{(x,y)\in S\times Y} w(x)(\log P(x,y)) + \alpha \sum_{x'\in T} \log P(x') , \qquad (2)$$

where α is a pre-determined scaling factor associated with incomplete (unlabeled) data. In Eq. 2, $P(x') = \hat{\Phi}(x')$ and $P(x,y) = \hat{\Phi}(x)P(y|x)$. In the static way, $w(x)$ is estimated once as $\frac{\hat{\Phi}(x)}{\hat{\Psi}(x)}$ and then maintained constant throughout the optimization of Eq. 2. Such strategy does not incorporate any information from the consequent classification task. On the contrary, we update the weights in each iteration.

4.4   Mixture Discriminant Analysis

The iterative estimation of $P(x,y), x \in T$ and $\Phi(x)$ can be readily embodied in a semi-supervised framework using a mixture discriminant analysis (MDA). A K-class Gaussian mixture discriminant is computed as $P(X = x, Y = k) = a_k \sum_{r=1}^{R_k} \pi_{kr}\phi(x|\mu_{kr}, \Sigma_{kr})$, where a_k is the prior probability of class $k (0 \leq a_k \leq 1)$, $\sum_{k=1}^{K} a_k = 1$. R_k is the number of mixture components used to model class k and the total number of mixture components for all the classes is $M = \sum_{k=1}^{K} R_k$. π_{kr} is the mixing proportion for the rth component in class k, $0 \leq \pi_{kr} \leq 1$, and $\sum_{k=1}^{K} \pi_{kr} = 1$. $\phi(.)$ denotes the pdf of a Gaussian distribution with μ_{kr} the centroids of component r in class k and σ_{kr} as the corresponding covariance matrix. To simplify the notation, the mixture model can be written as

$$P(X = x, Y = k) = \sum_{m=1}^{M} \pi_m p_m(k)\phi(x|\mu_m, \sigma_m) , \qquad (3)$$

where $1 \leq m \leq M$ is the new component label assigned in a consecutive manner to all the components in the classes. The prior probability for the mth component $\pi_m = a_k \pi_{kr}$ if m is the new label for the rth component in the kth class. The quantity $p_m(k) = 1$ if the component m belongs to class k and 0 otherwise. This ensures that the density of X within class k is a weighted sum over only the components inside class k.

Formulation of Joint Optimization. With weights initialized, we optimize Eq. 2 using expectation maximization algorithm with an intermediate classification step for the unlabeled examples in the paintings. Iterations are denoted by τ.

– *E-step*: Compute the posterior probability of each sample $(x, y) \in S \times Y$ belonging to component m.

$$q_m(x) \propto \pi_m^{(\tau)} p_m(y) \phi(x | \mu_m^{(\tau)}, \sigma_m^{(\tau)}), \quad \text{subject to} \sum_{m=1}^{M} q_m(x) = 1 . \quad (4)$$

For the unlabeled data $x' \in T$, the labels y' are to be treated as missing parameters. We first compute the posterior probability over each component m.

$$f_m(x') \propto \pi_m^{(\tau)} \phi(x | \mu_m^{(\tau)}, \sigma_m^{(\tau)}) . \quad (5)$$

Next, classification is conducted to estimate $y'^{(\tau)} = \arg\max_k \sum_{m \in \mathbb{R}_k} f_m(x')$. The quantity $p_m(y'^{(\tau)}) = 1$ and all other $p_{m' \neq m}(y'^{(\tau)}) = 0$. The posterior for unlabeled data is updated as:

$$q_m(x') \propto \pi_m^{(\tau)} p_m(y'^{(\tau)}) \phi(x' | \mu_m^{(\tau)}, \sigma_m^{(\tau)}), \quad \text{subject to} \sum_{m=1}^{M} q_m x' = 1 . \quad (6)$$

– *Maximization*: In this step, the parameters for paintings are updated using all data.

$$\pi_m^{(\tau+1)} \propto \sum_{x \in S} w^{(\tau)}(x) q_m(x) + \alpha \sum_{x' \in T} q_m(x'), \quad \text{subject to} \sum_m \pi_m^{(\tau+1)} = 1 . \quad (7)$$

$$\mu_{m,p}^{(\tau+1)} = \frac{\sum_{x \in S} w^{(\tau)}(x) q_m(x) x_p + \alpha \sum_{x' \in T} q_m(x') x_p'}{\sum_{x \in S} w^{(\tau)}(x) q_m(x) + \alpha \sum_{x' \in T} q_m(x')} . \quad (8)$$

Let

$$A = \sum_{x \in S} w^{(\tau)}(x) q_m(x) (x_p - \mu_{m,p}^{(\tau+1)})^2 , \quad (9)$$

$$B = \alpha \sum_{x' \in T} q_m(x')(x'_p - \mu_{m,p}^{(\tau+1)})^2 \,, \tag{10}$$

$$C = \sum_{x \in S} w^{(\tau)}(x)q_m(x) \,, D = \alpha \sum_{x' \in T} q_m(x') \,. \tag{11}$$

Then

$$\sigma_{m,p}^{2(\tau+1)} = \frac{A + B}{C + D} \,. \tag{12}$$

– *Weight Update*: Compute $P(X = x|Y = y), \forall(x,y) \in S$, using the updated parameters of class Y and update their weights as follows:

$$w(x)^{(\tau+1)} = \frac{\sum_m \pi_m p_m(y)\phi(x|y; \mu_m^{(\tau+1)}, \sigma_m^{2(\tau+1)})}{\hat{\Psi}(x)} \,. \tag{13}$$

In the above formulation, the parameters for unlabeled paintings (i.e., $\hat{\Psi}(x)$) always remain constant. Thus the adaptation is sensitive to the classification for paintings (the numerator), and weights are refined iteratively to consider both classification and clustering error.

5   Experiments

5.1   Settings

Datasets: We use three datasets: photograph dataset with emotional labels, unlabeled painting dataset, and a collection of 200 labeled paintings.

– *Labeled photographs:* We used the IAPS [10] as labeled photographs (Fig. 2). The IAPS dataset is a popular and validated dataset for the study of emotions evoked by natural photographs. The IAPS dataset contains $1,149$ images, each of which is associated with an empirically derived mean of valance and arousal. Valence describes the positive or negative aspect of human emotions, where common emotions, such as joy and happiness, are positive, whereas anger and fear are negative. Arousal represents the human physiological state of being

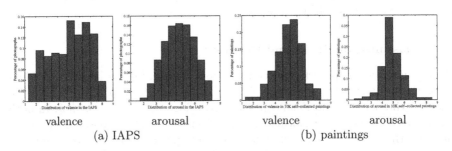

valence	arousal	valence	arousal
(a) IAPS		(b) paintings	

Fig. 8. Distributions of valence and arousal in the IAPS dataset and the 10,000-painting dataset.

reactive to stimuli. A higher value of arousal indicates higher excitation. We generate the ground truth emotional ratings of the four classification tasks based on the value of valence and arousal of photographs. The range of valence in the IAPS is [1.3, 8.3], and the range of arousal is [1.7, 7.4]. The distribution of valence and arousal in the IAPS is presented in Fig. 8(a).

- *Unlabeled paintings:* We randomly crawled 10, 000 paintings from Flickr as the unlabeled painting set. Examples have been presented in Sect. 3. A subset or a whole set of these paintings were used in our approach.
- *Labeled paintings:* We randomly crawled an alternative collection of paintings (200) from Flickr for the purpose of evaluation. We recruited participants to rate those paintings in terms of valence and arousal. The participants included college students with major in psychology and community individuals recruited from Amazon Mechanical Turk. Each painting was rated by at least five participants, and ratings were collected with the same guidelines as in the IAPS. The range of valence in rated paintings was [1.3, 8.1], and the range of arousal was [1.5, 8.5]. The distribution of valence and arousal of labeled paintings is presented in Fig. 8(b).

Model selection and parameter tuning: To make it more convenient to introduce the tasks, we first briefly discuss the settings for the model selection and initialization.

- *Model selection:* We randomly selected 100 images from the labeled painting set as a validation set and used the remaining 100 paintings for test. We used a grid search to tune α and the number of unlabeled images to be used for semi-supervised learning using a validation dataset. Within each task, the number of mixture components (clusters) was determined using Bayesian Information Criterion (BIC). Several random initializations were evaluated to select a good model using the validation dataset.
- *Weight initialization:* We first approximated $\hat{\Phi}(x)$ and $\hat{\Psi}(x)$ by independently estimating Gaussian mixture models (ϕ) for the photograph domain and the painting domain. The initial weights of photograph domain data were computed by taking the ratio of $\hat{\Phi}(x)/\hat{\Psi}(x)$.

In the following three subsections, we present the settings and experimental results of the two classification tasks.

5.2   Classification Tasks and Results

We evaluated our approach with two emotion classification tasks. We first identified the positivity or negativity of emotion aroused from paintings. Then we analyze whether the emotional content in paintings was reactive or not. In both tasks, we compared the performance of our approach with the baseline approach in which the model was trained on labeled photographs and tested on paintings.

Task 1 - Identifying positivity and negativity of emotional content: As valence describes the positive or negative aspect of human emotions, we divided paintings into two groups based on valence value. We calculated the mean value of valence in the IAPS, which was 5. Images with valence larger than 5 were labeled as positive (Class 1), and others were labeled as negative (Class 0). This results in 631 positive images and 514 negative images. In the validation set, there were 64 positive paintings and 36 negative ones. In the test set, 62 images were positive, and 38 were negative.

Task 2 - Identifying reactivity of emotional content: According to the psychology literature, the dimension of arousal refers to the human physiological state of being reactive to stimuli. We let images with arousal values larger than 4.8 as images with stronger reactive emotional content (Class 1) and lower than 4.8 has weaker reactive emotional content (Class 0). This results in 597 positive images and 551 negative images in training. In the validation set, there were 41 positive paintings and 59 negative ones. In the test set, 61 images were positive, and 39 were negative.

For both tasks, we compared our results with the baseline approach (MDA) in which the model was trained on labeled photographs and tested on paintings. Our approach outperformed the MDA approach in both the validation dataset and the test dataset for both tasks. For Task 1, the classification accuracy by MDA for the test dataset is 59 % (61 % for the validation dataset), while that

Fig. 9. Correctly classified and misclassified test paintings in the test set of the task 1. Paintings were annotated with TP, TN, FP, and FN, referring to correctly classified strongly reactive paintings, correctly classified weakly reactive paintings, misclassified strongly reactive paintings, and misclassified weakly reactive paintings, respectively. (Color figure online)

by our approach is 61 % (63 % for validation). For Task 2, the accuracy by MDA for the test dataset is 54 % (52 % for the validation dataset), while that by our approach is 61 % (62 % for validation).

Fig. 10. Correctly classified and misclassified paintings in the test set of the task 2. Paintings were annotated with TP, TN, FP, and FN, referring to correctly classified positive paintings, correctly classified negative paintings, misclassified positive paintings, and misclassified negative paintings, respectively. (Color figure online)

We show classification results on example images for the two tasks in Figs. 9 and 10. Abstract paintings with a strong visual difference from natural photographs tend to be misclassified by the learned model. This indicates that emotional responses evoked by similar stimuli (such as color and texture) might be different in natural photographs and abstract paintings. To better predict emotions aroused from abstract paintings, it is necessary to include labeled abstract paintings in the training set in addition to natural photographs. We also observe that some stimuli have different emotional indications in photographs and paintings. For instance, the color of blue is associated with negative emotions aroused from natural photographs, whereas the color of red and yellow are associated with positive emotions. However, this is not necessarily true in paintings as shown in Fig. 10. To improve the prediction accuracy on paintings in the wild, we may need to generalize the proposed algorithm in cases that we have some labeled paintings besides a large collection of labeled photographs and unlabeled paintings. We would like to take this direction as future work.

6   Discussions and Conclusions

We investigated the problem of emotion classification on paintings. Due to the scarcity of paintings with emotional labels, we proposed an adaptive learning approach that leveraged color photographs with emotion labels and unlabeled paintings to infer the emotional appeal of paintings. Our approach takes into account differences in feature distributions in paintings and color photographs as we use photographs with emotional ratings. We performed two emotion classification tasks. The experimental results showed that our approach achieved a higher accuracy in recognizing emotions in paintings.

Although we have shown that the adaptive learning approach improves clearly upon a baseline approach without adaption, the classification accuracies we achieved for classification of emotional responses are nevertheless low, indicating ample room for enhancement. We believe that the main reason for the limited performance is the intrinsic complexity of the problem. The visual features we have experimented with seem to have weak association with the evoked emotions of paintings, and it is quite possible that a fundamental breakthrough is needed to push further the technology. In addition, our adaptive learning approach relies on the assumption that the non-zero density support of the feature distribution of the source is the same as that of the target, under which reweighting is viable to approximate the distribution of the target. The validity of this assumption calls for thorough examination in the future.

References

1. Bickel, S., Brückner, M., Scheffer, T.: Discriminative learning for differing training and test distributions. In: International Conference on Machine Learning (ICML), pp. 81–88 (2007)
2. Changizi, M.A., Zhang, Q., Shimojo, S.: Bare skin, blood and the evolution of primate colour vision. Biol. Lett. **2**(2), 217–221 (2006)
3. Datta, R., Li, J., Wang, J.Z.: Algorithmic inferencing of aesthetics and emotion in natural image: an exposition. In: International Conference on Image Processing (ICIP), pp. 105–108 (2008)
4. Duan, L., Xu, D., Chang, S.F.: Exploiting web images for event recognition in consumer videos: a multiple source domain adaptation approach. In: IEEE Conference on Computer Vision and Pattern Recognition (CVPR), pp. 1338–1345 (2012)
5. Gopalan, R., Ruonan, L., Chellappa, R.: Domain adaptation for object recognition: an unsupervised approach. In: International Conference on Computer Vision (ICCV), pp. 999–1006 (2011)
6. Jhuo, I.H., Liu, D., Lee, D., Chang, S.F.: Robust visual domain adaptation with low-rank reconstruction. In: IEEE Conference on Computer Vision and Pattern Recognition (CVPR), pp. 2168–2175 (2012)
7. Jia, J., Wu, S., Wang, X., Hu, P., Cai, L., Tang, J.: Can we understand van Gogh's mood? Learning to infer affects from images in social networks. In: ACM International Conference on Multimedia, pp. 857–860 (2012)
8. Joshi, D., Datta, R., Fedorovskaya, E., Luong, Q.T., Wang, J.Z., Li, J., Luo, J.: Aesthetics and emotions in images. IEEE Sig. Process. Mag. **28**(5), 94–115 (2011)

9. Khosla, A., Zhou, T., Malisiewicz, T., Efros, A.A., Torralba, A.: Undoing the damage of dataset bias. In: Fitzgibbon, A., Lazebnik, S., Perona, P., Sato, Y., Schmid, C. (eds.) ECCV 2012. LNCS, vol. 7572, pp. 158–171. Springer, Heidelberg (2012). doi:10.1007/978-3-642-33718-5_12

10. Lang, P.J., Bradley, M.M., Cuthbert, B.N.: International affective picture system: affective ratings of pictures and instruction manual. In: Technical report A-8, University of Florida, Gainesville, FL (2008)

11. Li, C., Chen, T.: Aesthetic visual quality assessment of paintings. IEEE J. Sel. Top. Sig. Process. **3**(2), 236–252 (2009)

12. Li, C.T., Shan, M.K.: Emotion-based impressionism slideshow with automatic music accompaniment. In: ACM International Conference on Multimedia, pp. 839–842 (2007)

13. Lu, X., Suryanarayan, P., Adams Jr., R.B., Li, J., Newman, M.G., Wang, J.Z.: On shape and the computability of emotions. In: ACM International Conference on Multimedia, pp. 229–238 (2012)

14. Machajdik, J., Hanbury, A.: Affective image classification using features inspired by psychology and art theory. In: ACM International Conference on Multimedia, pp. 83–92 (2010)

15. Rodgers, S., Kenix, L.J., Thorson, E.: Stereotypical portrayals of emotionality in news photos. Mass Commun. Soc. **10**(1), 119–138 (2007)

16. Sartori, A., Yanulevskaya, V., Salah, A.A., Uijlings, J., Bruni, E., Sebe, N.: Affective analysis of professional and amateur abstract paintings using statistical analysis and art theory. ACM Trans. Interact. Intell. Syst. **5**(2), 8 (2015)

17. Shi, Y., Sha, F.: Information-theoretical learning of discriminative clusters for unsupervised domain adaptation. In: International Conference on Machine Learning (ICML), pp. 1079–1086 (2012)

18. Shibata, T., Kato, T.: Kansei image retrieval system for street landscape-discrimination and graphical parameters based on correlation of two image systems. In: International Conference on Systems, Man, and Cybernetics, pp. 274–252 (2006)

19. Shimodaira, H.: Improving predictive inference under covariate shift by weighting the log-likelihood function. J. Stat. Plan. Infer. **90**(2), 227–244 (2000)

20. Sugiyama, M., Nakajima, S., Kashima, H., Buenau, P.V., Kawanabe, M.: Direct importance estimation with model selection and its application to covariate shift adaptation. In: Neural Information Processing Systems (NIPS), pp. 1433–1440 (2008)

21. Tang, K., Ramanathan, V., Li, F.F., Koller, D.: Shifting weights: adapting object detectors from image to video. In: Neural Information Processing Systems (NIPS), pp. 647–655 (2012)

22. Valdez, P., Mehrabian, A.: Effects of color on emotions. J. Exp. Psychol. Gen. **123**(4), 394–409 (1994)

23. Wang, H.L., Cheong, L.F.: Affective understanding in film. IEEE Trans. Circ. Syst. Video Technol. **16**(6), 689–704 (2006)

24. Yanulevskaya, V., van Gemert, J., Roth, K., Herbold, A., Sebe, N., Geusebroek, J.: Emotional valence categorization using holistic image features. In: International Conference on Image Processing (ICIP), pp. 101–104 (2008)

25. Yao, L., Suryanarayan, P., Qiao, M., Wang, J.Z., Li, J.: Oscar: on-site composition and aesthetics feedback through exemplars for photographers. Int. J. Comput. Vis. **96**(3), 353–383 (2012)
26. Zhang, H., Augilius, E., Honkela, T., Laaksonen, J., Gamper, H., Alene, H.: Analyzing emotional semantics of abstract art using low-level image features. In: Advances in Intelligent Data Analysis, pp. 413–423 (2011)

Fast Face Sketch Synthesis via KD-Tree Search

Yuqian Zhang, Nannan Wang$^{(\boxtimes)}$, Shengchuan Zhang, Jie Li, and Xinbo Gao

State Key Laboratory of Integrated Services Networks,
Xidian University, Xi'an, China
yuqianz@yeah.net, nnwang@xidian.edu.cn, zsc_2007@163.com,
{leejie,xbgao}@mail.xidian.edu.cn

Abstract. Automatic face sketch synthesis has been widely applied in digital entertainment and law enforcement. Currently, most sketch synthesis algorithms focus on generating face portrait of good quality, but ignoring the time consumption. Existing methods have large time complexity due to dense computation of patch matching in the neighbor selection process. In this paper, we propose a simple yet effective fast face sketch synthesis method based on K dimensional-Tree (KD-Tree). The proposed method employs the idea of divide-and-conquer (*i.e.* piece-wise linear) to learn the complex nonlinear mapping between facial photos and sketches. In the training phase, all the training images are divided into regions and every region is divided into some small patches, then KD-Tree is built up among training photo patches in each region. In the test phase, the test photo is first divided into some patches as the same way in the training phase. KD-Tree search is conducted for K nearest neighbor selection by matching the test photo patches in each region against the constructed KD-Tree of training photo patches in the same region. The KD-Tree process builds index structure which greatly reduces the time consumption for neighbor selection. Compared with synthesis methods using classical greedy search strategy (*i.e.* KNN), the proposed method is much less time consuming but with comparable synthesis performance. Experiments on the public CUHK face sketch (CUFS) database illustrate the effectiveness of the proposed method. In addition, the proposed neighbor selection strategy can be further extended to other synthesis algorithms.

Keywords: Neighbor selection · KD-Tree · Local search · Face sketch synthesis

1 Introduction

Face sketch synthesis has attracted growing attentions due to its applications in both digital entertainment and law enforcement. For example, in mobile Internet application, scene portrait effect generation in video chat makes people enjoy the conversation. In social network, people are more willing to use face sketches generated from their own photos as avatars in Twitter or Facebook. In the cartoon industry, in order to save time, artists use an automatic sketch synthesis system

© Springer International Publishing Switzerland 2016
G. Hua and H. Jégou (Eds.): ECCV 2016 Workshops, Part I, LNCS 9913, pp. 64–77, 2016.
DOI: 10.1007/978-3-319-46604-0_5

to product animations. And in the law enforcement, because a suspect's face photo is not available in most cases, police officers need to match a simulated sketch of a suspect drawn by an artist with the recollection of an eyewitness against a mug-shot database to help identify the suspect. Face sketch synthesis can assist to narrow down the modality gap between face photos and face sketches, and then achieve effective matching. As a result, face sketch synthesis becomes a key technique and research hotspot of sketch-photo recognition.

1.1   Related Work

Currently face sketch synthesis can be mainly categorized as image-based method [7,9] and exemplar-based methods [18,22]. The image-based sketch synthesis methods commonly utilize edges in the input image to produce shadings and strokes. Although image-based methods can produce meaningful stylistic effects in some sense, their results are usually missing important facial details and consequently more like the input photos and rather than the artistic work. On the other hand, exemplar-based methods generate new sketches with rich textures from a set of training face photo-sketch pairs, and can synthesize face sketch of different styles from different training sample sets. Compared with image-based methods, exemplar-based approaches can capture important facial structures more effectively and handle the artistic styles which are difficult to describe in a parametric manner. Thus, exemplar-based methods outperform traditional image-based methods.

There mainly exist two types of exemplar-based face sketch synthesis algorithms: profile sketch synthesis [4,24,27] and shading sketch synthesis [18,23,28]. Compared with profile sketches, shading sketches with both contours and textures are more expressive in representing facial structures and more popular in research. Tang and Wang [18] used a global eigen-transformation to synthesize face sketches from photos. It is not difficult to notice that approximating the sketch drawing process of an artist as a linear process is not accurate. This process is more like a nonlinear process for the complex hair style among different people. To overcome this problem, Liu *et al.* [8] proposed a local geometry preserving based nonlinear method to approximate the mapping function and patch-based reconstruction. Gao *et al.* [6,20] employed sparse representation to adaptively determine the number of nearest neighbors instead of fixed number of neighbors as in [8]. Aforementioned approaches generate local patches independently and cannot learn the face structures well. In order to overcome the drawbacks, a state-of-the-art approach using a multiscale Markov random field (MRF) model [23] has been proposed. This approach can well synthesize complicated face structures and significantly reduce artifacts by learning the face structure across different scales. Nevertheless, the MRF model cannot synthesize new sketches and the optimization problem in solving the MRF is NP-hard. For this problem, Zhou *et al.* proposed a Markov weight fields (MWF) model [28] for face sketch synthesis. The method is capable of synthesizing new sketch patches as a linear combination of candidate sketch patches. There are also some improvements on the MRF model and MWF model, *e.g.* [12–14,21].

In spite of the great achievement that exemplar-based methods can usually produce higher-quality sketches, there exist a common drawback among exemplar-based approaches, that is the matching process to a large amount of training data is too computationally intensive. Patch matching is the most time-consuming part in exemplar-based face sketch synthesis. To solve this problem, Song et al. [16] proposed a real-time spatial sketch denoising (SSD) based sketch synthesis algorithm. This method formulates face sketch synthesis as an image denoising problem. The box filter [19] is applied to the KNN search for achieving real-time performance.

1.2 Our Approach

In this paper, we propose a novel and fast exemplar-based face sketch synthesis method based on KD-Tree. The method adopts the idea of divide-and-conquer (i.e. piece-wise linear) to learn the nonlinear mapping relationship between the facial photos and sketches. Firstly we divides all the training images into overlapping regions and each region is divided into patches, and then KD-Tree is conducted among training photo patches of the same region in the training phase. In the test phase, KD-Tree search are conducted to accelerate the neighbor selection process by matching the test photo patches against the training photo patches. Generally most data shows clustering modality, the efficiency of nearest neighbor selection can be greatly improved by building efficient KD-Tree index structure. In order to enforce local compatibility and smoothness between adjacent synthetic sketch patches, we adopt an average operation for overlapping regions in the final reconstructed results. The effectiveness of the proposed approach is evaluated on the CUHK face sketch (CUFS) database. The experimental results validate that the proposed approach significantly improves the performance of face sketch synthesis in time consumption, and the proposed method is more effective to synthesize sketch compared with the face sketch synthesis method using classical greedy search strategy (i.e. KNN).

2 Face Sketch Synthesis

Due to the large differences between photos and sketches caused by different generation mechanisms and information expression manners, it is difficult to identify the suspect by directly matching the photo-sketch pair. In this condition, by firstly transforming a photo into its corresponding sketch, we can reduce the difference between photos and sketches significantly, then allowing effective matching between the two. In this paper, we assume that the mapping function between photos and sketches is complicated nonlinear. We construct KD-Tree in the training phase and then to search the K nearest neighbor patches of a test photo patch from the KD-Tree in the test phase. The idea of piece-wise linear is applied to learn the nonlinear mapping relationship between photo-sketch pairs. Then we can generate the synthesized sketch patch from the linear combination of K nearest sketches corresponding to the K candidate photo patches. Figure 1 is the whole framework of the proposed method.

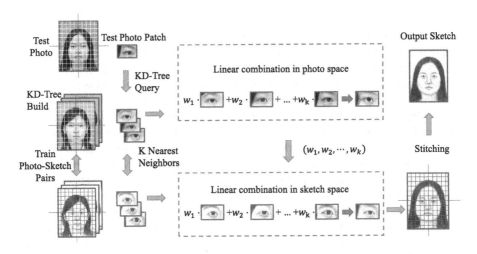

Fig. 1. The framework of our proposed method

KD-Tree is a high-dimensional index tree data structure [26]. KD-Tree has a wide application of approximate nearest neighbor search [1] and nearest neighbor search [3] in large high-dimensional data space, such as K nearest neighbor searching and matching of high-dimensional feature vectors in image retrieval and identification. In practice, most data show a clustering pattern. By constructing effective index structure of KD-Tree, the speed of data retrieval can be greatly improved.

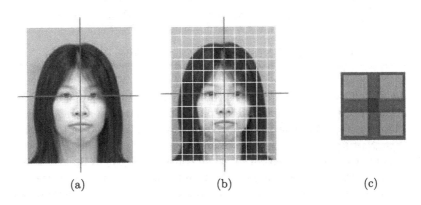

Fig. 2. (a) region division; (b) patch division; (c) overlapping pattern

We assume that all the face images to be studied are plain style and geometrically normalized by fixing the locations of eyes. We adopt the region division strategy to local search. We divide the test photo and all the training photo-sketch pairs into M overlapping regions as shown in Fig. 2(a) for local search.

Compared with global search, local search strategy can not only improve the matching accuracy under the intuition that patches in the same region are more similar to each other, but also reduce the computation in patch matching to save synthesis time. Due to the complexity of face structure, instead of directly learning the global face structure, which might be too complicated to estimate, we target at local patches with simpler structure. Every face region is divided into N overlapping patches in the same way as shown in Fig. 2(b), the overlapping local neighbors can provide global information, sketch patches overlap in the way shown in Fig. 2(c). Let $\mathbf{I}_p^{mn}$ and $\mathbf{I}_s^{mn}$ denote the test photo patch and the sketch patch to be synthesized respectively, $m = 1, 2, \ldots, M$, $n = 1, 2, \ldots, N$. During sketch synthesis, we build KD-Tree for all the photo patches of each region in training photo set as shown in Fig. 3. For a photo patch $\mathbf{I}_p^{mn}$ from test face photo, we find its K most similar photo patches $\mathbf{I}_{pk}^{mn}$ from the training photo set $\mathbf{T}_p^m$ by KD-Tree query, and use its corresponding sketch patches $\mathbf{I}_{sk}^{mn}$ in the training portrait set $\mathbf{T}_s^m$ and reconstruction weights $\mathbf{w}_k^{mn}$ to estimate the sketch patch to be synthesized $\mathbf{I}_s^{mn}$. The underlying assumption is that, if two photo patches are similar, then their sketch patches should also be similar. The proposed face sketch synthesis algorithm is summarized as in Algorithm 1:

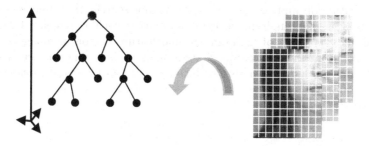

Fig. 3. Constructing a KD-Tree for all photo patches in one region

Stitching sketch patches: In order to strengthen local smoothness and compatibility between adjacent synthetic sketch patches, we adopt an average operation for overlapping areas to make the final synthetic sketch result own the same size as the test photo image.

In step (1) (line 3 in Algorithm 1), when constructing the KD-Tree, we select mean value as threshold of maximum variance dimension to divide the image patch data. We integrate the KD-tree search and best bin first method (BBF) to find the nearest neighbors, and the Euclidean distance is utilized as similarity measure.

In step (2) (line 4 in Algorithm 1), we obtain the weight coefficients by minimize the reconstruction error

$$\varepsilon^{mn}(w) = \|\mathbf{I}_p^{mn} - \sum_{k=1}^{K} \mathbf{w}_k^{mn} \mathbf{I}_{pk}^{mn}\|^2, s.t. \sum_{k=1}^{K} \mathbf{w}_k^{mn} = 1 \qquad (1)$$

Algorithm 1. KD-Tree search based face sketch synthesis

1: **For** $m = 1$ to M

2: **For** $n = 1$ to N

3:     Neighbor selection: We build KD-Tree for all the photo patches of each region in training photo set. For a test photo patch $\mathbf{I}_p^{mn}$, we search the K nearest neighbor patches $\mathbf{I}_{pk}^{mn} \in \mathbf{T}_p^m$ at the same region in training photo set by KD-Tree query, $k = 1, 2, \ldots, K$;

4:     Computing reconstruction weights: We calculate the reconstruction weights $\mathbf{w}_k^{mn}$ of K photo candidates $\mathbf{I}_{pk}^{mn}$ by minimizing the error of reconstructing $\mathbf{I}_p^{mn}$;

5:     Sketch patch estimation: We combine the weight coefficients $\mathbf{w}_k^{mn}$ and the K nearest neighbor sketch patches $\mathbf{I}_{sk}^{mn} \in \mathbf{T}_s^m$ corresponding to the K candidate photo patches $\mathbf{I}_{pk}^{mn}$ linearly to estimate the pseudo-sketch patch $\mathbf{I}_s^{mn}$.

6: **End For**

7: **End For**

This constrained least squares problem can be solved by defining a $K \times K$ matrix Q,

$$Q(i,j) = (\mathbf{I}_p^{mn} - \mathbf{I}_{pi}^{mn})^T (\mathbf{I}_p^{mn} - \mathbf{I}_{pj}^{mn}) \tag{2}$$

and $R = Q^{-1}$, the constrained least squares problem has a close-form solution,

$$\mathbf{w}_k^{mn} = \frac{\sum_{t=1}^{K} R(k,t)}{\sum_{i=1}^{K} \sum_{i=1}^{K} R(i,j)} \tag{3}$$

where $k = 1, 2, \ldots, K$. The close-form solution can be directly applied to compute the reconstruction weights.

In step (3) (line 5 in Algorithm 1), the sketch patch to be synthesized can be estimated from the linear combination of the K candidate sketch patches $\mathbf{I}_{sk}^{mn} \in \mathbf{T}_s^m$,

$$\mathbf{I}_s^{mn} = \sum_{k=1}^{K} \mathbf{w}_k^{mn} \mathbf{I}_{sk}^{mn} \tag{4}$$

3   Experiments

In order to verify the effectiveness of the proposed face sketch synthesis algorithm based on KD-Tree, we conduct experiments in the CUFS database, which contains 606 face photo-sketch pairs with photos from three sub databases (*i.e.* the CUHK student database [9], the AR database [10] and the XM2VTS database [11]). The CUHK student consists of 188 photo-sketch pairs where 88 pairs used for training and the rest are for testing. In the AR database which consists of 123 photo-sketch pairs, we randomly choose 80 pairs for training and the rest for test. And for the XM2VTS database, 100 pairs are randomly selected for training and the rest 195 pairs are used for test. Figure 4 shows examples of photo-sketch pairs in the CUFS database. All the face images in the database are in a fontal pose,

Fig. 4. The examples of photo-sketch pairs in CUFS database

with neutral expression, plain style, normal lighting, and without occlusions. In our experiments, the size of face images are aligned to 250×200, and the locations of eyes are geometrically normalized by fixing to $(75, 125)$ and $(125, 125)$, respectively. We implement the proposed method using MATLAB and experimented on a computer with i7-4790 Intel core 3.6 GHZ CPU. In following first two experiments, we test the influence of different parameter values to synthesis performance and running time performance. In the third experiment, we evaluate the proposed algorithm against the face sketch synthesis method based on locally linear embedding (LLE) using KNN search [8] (instead of KD-Tree used in our proposed method) and the MRF based approach to validate the efficiency and effectiveness of the proposed method.

In our proposed method, there are following parameters which could affect the final performance: the divided region size, the patch size, the number of neighbors K, the degree of overlapping between adjacent regions and patches. For the patch size, some face details disappear when the size is too large, and noises appear when it is too small. In all the experiments, the patch size is set as 20×20, which can generate good sketch synthesis result. To ensure smooth transition between two adjacent regions or patches, we keep $2/3$ region overlapping.

3.1 Synthetic Results of Different Divided Region Size

In the first experiment, we fix the values of all other parameters, and only change the divided region size to see how it impacts on the sketch synthesis result. Figure 5 shows the comparison of region size as 150×150, 100×100, 50×50, and 30×30 with $K = 1$. The sketch synthesis results illustrate that we can obtain a better pseudo-sketch when region size is 50×50. The synthesized sketch is

Table 1. The running time of different divided region size (unit: second)

	Training time	Test time
150×150	5.0	32.2
100×100	11.6	27.9
50×50	13.2	4.8
30×30	7.0	3.0

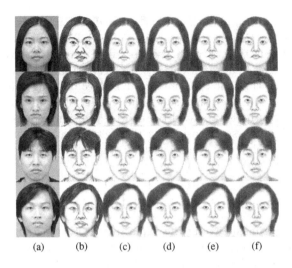

Fig. 5. The face sketch synthesis results of different divided region size: (a) test photo; (b) sketch drawn by the artist; (c) 150×150; (d) 100×100; (e) 50×50; (f) 30×30.

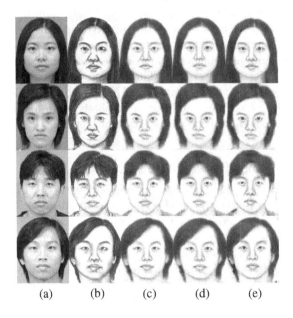

Fig. 6. The face sketch synthesis results of different neighbor number: (a) test photo; (b) sketch drawn by the artist; (c) $K = 1$; (d) $K = 5$; (e) $K = 25$.

noisier when the divided region size is too large (such as 150×150, 100×100), but generated dominant facial structures have no much difference with 50×50. When the region size is too small, there appears mosaic effects as shown in Fig. 5(f).

Table 1 shows the running time when divided region size is set as different values. The training time is the total time of KD-Tree building, and the test time is the synthesis time of each pseudo-sketch generating averaged by the number of test images in a statistical sense. As Table 1 implied, with the divided region size changes, the time consuming of KD-Tree building is irregular, so we can not consider it. On the other hand, the smaller of divided region size, the faster the sketch synthesis rate, and the shorter the time required for KD-Tree query and sketch synthesis. Considering the sketch synthetic quality and time simultaneously, we think that the proposed method achieves better results when region size is 50×50.

3.2   Synthetic Results of Different Neighbor Number

In the second experiment, we fix the values of all other parameters, and only change the number of neighbors K to see how it impacts on the sketch synthesis result. Figure 6 shows the comparison of $K = 1, 5, 25$ with region size 50×50. The sketch synthesis results illustrate that we can obtain a better pseudo-sketch when $K = 5$. We find that when the neighbor number is too small (such as $K = 1$), there are too much noise in synthesized hair, mouth, and chin areas. When K is too large (such as $K = 25$), blurring effect appears in synthesized face contour and the dominant facial details for the linear combination of neighbors. Table 2 shows the running time of pseudo-sketch generating when the number of neighbors K is set as different values. The data in Table 2 show that, with the increase of neighbors, the time consuming of KD-Tree building is still irregular, but the speed of KD-Tree query and sketch synthesis is gradually slowing down, and the method needs more time to synthesize a sketch.

3.3   Results of Different Synthesis Methods

In the third experiment, we compare our method with the LLE method and the MRF method to illustrate the effectiveness and efficiency of the proposed method. For the LLE approach, we set the patch size as 20×20, the number of neighbors $K = 5$, the search region is 5 (that is, search region size $|\triangle| = 30 \times 30$), and keep 2/3 region overlapping. For our method, we set the patch size 20×20, the number of neighbors K=5, the divided region size 50×50, and keep 2/3 region overlapping. Qualitative evaluation results of the proposed method and the LLE method are shown in Fig. 7. The holistic results illustrates that the two method

Table 2. The running time of different neighbor number K (unit: second)

	Training time	Test time
$K = 1$	13.2	4.8
$K = 5$	20.8	9.2
$K = 25$	17.8	157.6

Table 3. Running time of different synthesis methods

	MRF	LLE	Our method
Time (second)	180	670.3	9.2
Program. Language	MATLAB	MATLAB	MATLAB

can both synthesize dominant facial structures and clear contour with less noise. Table 3 shows the running time of different synthesis methods for generating one sketch. The LLE method needs more than 11 min to synthesize a sketch, while our method only cost 9.2 s. The MRF method could achieve the performance of 180 s as reported [23]. All these algorithms could be further speeded up through efficient programming language such as C or C++. We have tested the available MRF codes and it consumes about 8.6 s to synthesize a sketch by using C++ in comparison to 180 s using MATLAB. It is expected that the proposed method could reach the performance of less than 1 s for synthesizing one sketch.

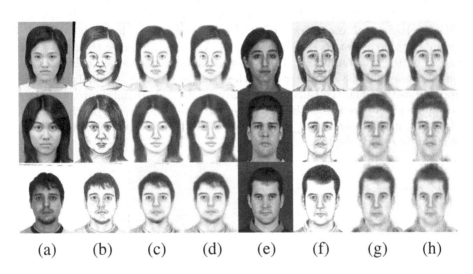

(a)   (b)   (c)   (d)   (e)   (f)   (g)   (h)

Fig. 7. The face sketch synthesis results of the baseline method and our method: (a) and (e) test photo; (b) and (f) sketch drawn by the artist; (c) and (g) the LLE method; (d) and (h) our method.

In addition, we perform face sketch recognition evaluation on the whole 338 synthesized sketches from the CUFS database. The proposed KD-Tree method is also compared with the LLE method [8] and the state-of-the-art MRF method [23] (synthetic results of the MRF method are generated based on the codes download from [17]) about face sketch recognition accuracy at Rank-1 using two metrics: Fisherface [2] and Null-space linear discriminant analysis (NLDA) [5]. Table 4 shows the face sketch recognition accuracies. We randomly partition 338

Table 4. Rank-1 recognition accuracy using different face sketch synthesis methods and face recognition methods

	Fisherface	NLDA
MRF (%)	78.76	87.72
LLE (%)	84.92	91.04
Our method (%)	84.56	90.12

synthesized sketches into two groups: 150 for training classifiers and the rest 188 for test. We repeat this partition 50 times and the averaged accuracy is reported as shown in Table 4. From the results, we can see that the proposed method and the LLE method achieves higher recognition rates than the MRF approach [23]. The proposed method and the LLE can obtain basically comparable recognition accuracy. The image quality evaluation also conducted on the whole 338 synthesized sketches. Figure 8 shows the quality evaluation results of the proposed method, the LLE method and MRF method using structural similarity index metric (SSIM) [25] and visual information fidelity (VIF) metric [15]. The horizontal axis marks the IQA score and the vertical axis labels the percentage of synthesized sketches whose IQA scores are larger than the score marked on the horizontal axis. Table 5 gives the averaged image quality assessment scores on all 338 synthesized sketches. As shown in Fig. 8 and Table 5, the proposed method and the LLE method have comparable performance, and they are superior compared with the MRF method. In summary, our method could achieve comparable synthesis performance with conventional LLE method but significantly reduce the time consuming.

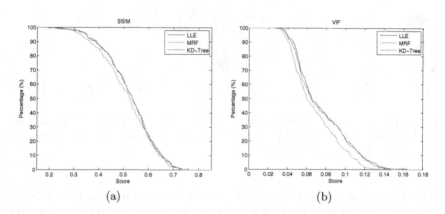

(a)   (b)

Fig. 8. Quality evaluation results of different sketch synthesis methods: (a) SSIM; (b) VIF

Table 5. The quality evaluation scores of different synthesis methods

	SSIM	VIF
The MRF method (%)	51.32	6.78
The LLE method (%)	52.58	7.52
The proposed method (%)	52.83	7.39

4 Conclusions

In this paper, we proposed a fast face sketch synthesis algorithm based on KD-Tree. The algorithm learns the nonlinear mapping function between photos and sketches based on the idea of piece-wise linear. And KD-Tree construction and KD-Tree search are conducted in neighbor selection process to accelerate sketch patch synthesis. The proposed approach is tested in CUFS database including 606 faces. Judging from the results, the proposed method can synthesize face sketch well with smooth and clear facial detail. Compared with the synthesis approaches using KNN, the method can greatly improve the synthetic effectiveness and significantly reduce the synthesis time consumption. In addition, the proposed neighbor selection strategy can be further extended to other synthesis algorithms to speed up the sketch synthesis process.

Acknowledgement. This work was supported in part by the National Natural Science Foundation of China (under Grant 61432014, 61501339, and 61671339), in part by the Fundamental Research Funds for the Central Universities (under Grant XJS15049,and JB160104), in part by the China Post-Doctoral Science Foundation under Grant 2015M580818 and Grant 2016T90893 and in part by the Shaanxi Province Post-Doctoral Science Foundation.

References

1. Beis, J., Lowe, D.: Shape indexing using approximate nearest-neighbour search in high-dimensional spaces. In: Conference on Computer Vision and Pattern Recognition, pp. 1000–1006 (1997)
2. Belhumeur, P., Hespanha, J., Kriegman, D.: Eigenfaces vs. fisherfaces: recognition using class specific linear projection. IEEE Trans. Pattern Anal. Mach. Intell. **19**(7), 711–720 (1997)
3. Bentley, J.: Multidimensional binary search trees used for associative searching. Commun. ACM **18**(9), 509–517 (1975)
4. Chen, H., Xu, Y., Shum, H., Zheng, N.: Example based facial sketch generation with non-parametric sampling. In: Proceedings of IEEE Conference on Computer Vision, pp. 433–438 (2010)
5. Chen, L., Liao, H., Ko, M.: A new lda-based face recognition system which can solve the small sample size problem. Pattern Recogn. **33**(10), 1713–1726 (2000)
6. Gao, X., Wang, N., Tao, D., Li, X.: Face sketch-photo synthesis and retrieval using sparse representation. IEEE TCSVT **22**, 1213–1226 (2012)

7. Gastal, E., Oliveira, M.: Domain transform for edge-aware image and video processing. ACM Trans. Graph. **30**(4), 1244–1259 (2011)
8. Liu, Q., Tang, X., Jin, H., Lu, H., Ma, S.: A nonlinear approach for face sketch synthesis and recognition. In: Proceedings of IEEE Conference on Computer Vision and Pattern Recognition, pp. 1005–1010 (2005)
9. Lu, C., Xu, L., Jia, J.: Combining sketch and tone for pencil drawing production. In: Eurographics Association, pp. 65–73 (2012)
10. Martinez, A., Benavente, R.: The AR face database. Technical report 24, CVC, Barcelona, Spain, June 1998
11. Messer, K., Matas, J., Kittler, J., Luettin, J., Maitre, G.: XM2VTSDB: the extended M2VTS database. In: Proceedings of the International Conference on Audio- and Video-Based Biometric Person Authentication, pp. 72–77, April 1999
12. Peng, C., Gao, X., Wang, N., Li, J.: Superpixel-based face sketch-photo synthesis. IEEE TCSVT **PP**, 1 (2015)
13. Peng, C., Gao, X., Wang, N., Li, J.: Graphical representation for heterogeneous face recognition. IEEE TPAMI (2016)
14. Peng, C., Gao, X., Wang, N., Tao, D., Li, X., Li, J.: Multiple representations-based face sketch-photo synthesis. IEEE TNNLS (2015)
15. Sheikh, H., Bovik, A.: Image information and visual quality. IEEE Trans. Image Process. **15**(2), 430–444 (2006)
16. Song, Y., Bao, L., Yang, Q., Yang, M.: Real-time exemplar-based face sketch synthesis. In: Proceedings of Eureopean Conference on Computer Vision, pp. 800–813 (2014)
17. Song, Y., Bao, L., Yang, Q., Yang, M.: Real-time exemplar-based face sketch synthesis (2014). http://www.cs.cityu.edu.hk/yibisong/eccv14/index.html. Accessed 19 June 2016
18. Tang, X., Wang, X.: Face sketch synthesis and recognition. In: IEEE International Conference on Computer Vision, p. 687 (2003)
19. Viola, P., Jones, M.: Rapid object detection using a boosted cascade of simple features. In: Proceedings of Computer Vision and Pattern Recognition, p. 511 (2001)
20. Wang, N., Li, J., Tao, D., Li, X., Gao, X.: Heterogeneous image transformation. Pattern Recogn. Lett. **34**(1), 77–84 (2013)
21. Wang, N., Tao, D., Gao, X., Li, X., Li, J.: Transductive face sketch-photo synthesis. IEEE TNNLS **24**(9), 1364–1376 (2013)
22. Wang, N., Tao, D., Gao, X., Li, X., Li, J.: A comprehensive survey to face hallucination. IJCV **31**(1), 9–30 (2014)
23. Wang, X., Tang, X.: Face photo-sketch synthesis and recognition. IEEE Trans. Pattern Anal. Mach. Intell. **31**(11), 1955–1967 (2009)
24. Wang, X., Tang, X.: Style and abstraction in portrait sketching. ACM Trans. Graph. **32**(4), 96–96 (2013)
25. Wang, Z., Bovik, A., Sheikh, H., Simoncelli, E.: Image quality assessment: from error visibility to structural similarity. IEEE Trans. Image Process. **13**(4), 600–612 (2004)
26. Wikipedia: k-d tree (2016). https://en.wikipedia.org/wiki/K-d_tree. Accessed 19 June 2016

27. Xu, Z., Chen, H., Zhu, S., Luo, J.: A hierarchical compositional model for face representation and sketching. IEEE Trans. Pattern Anal. Mach. Intell. **30**(6), 955–969 (2008)
28. Zhou, H., Kuang, Z., Wong, K.: Markov weight fields for face sketch synthesis. In: Proceedings of IEEE Conference on Computer Vision and Pattern Recognition, pp. 1091–1097 (2012)

W08 – Computer Vision for Road Scene Understanding and Autonomous Driving

Preface

Analyzing road scenes using cameras could have a crucial impact in many domains, such as autonomous driving, advanced driver assistance systems (ADAS), personal navigation, mapping of large scale environments, and road maintenance. For instance, vehicle infrastructure, signage, and rules of the road have been designed to be interpreted fully by visual inspection. As the field of computer vision becomes increasingly mature, practical solutions to many of these tasks are now within reach. Nonetheless, there still seems to exist a wide gap between what is needed by the automotive industry and what is currently possible using computer vision techniques. The goal of this workshop was to allow researchers in the fields of road scene understanding and autonomous driving to present their progress and discuss novel ideas that will shape the future of this area. In particular, this workshop aimed to bridge the large gap between the community that develops novel theoretical approaches for road scene understanding and the community that builds working real-life systems performing in real-world conditions.

October 2016

Mathieu Salzmann
Jose Alvarez
Lars Petersson
Fredrik Kahl
Bart Nabbe

W08 – Computer Vision for Road Scene Understanding and Autonomous Driving

Preface

Monocular Visual-IMU Odometry:
A Comparative Evaluation
of the Detector-Descriptor Based Methods

Xingshuai Dong[1], Xinghui Dong[2(✉)], and Junyu Dong[1]

[1] Ocean University of China, Qingdao 266071, China
[2] Centre for Imaging Sciences, University of Manchester,
Manchester M13 9PT, UK
xinghui.dong@manchester.ac.uk

Abstract. Visual odometry has been used in many fields, especially in robotics and intelligent vehicles. Since local descriptors are robust to background clutter, occlusion and other content variations, they have been receiving more and more attention in the application of the detector-descriptor based visual odometry. To our knowledge, however, there is no extensive, comparative evaluation investigating the performance of the detector-descriptor based methods in the scenario of monocular visual-IMU (Inertial Measurement Unit) odometry. In this paper, we therefore perform such an evaluation under a unified framework. We select five typical routes from the challenging KITTI dataset by taking into account the length and shape of routes, the impact of independent motions due to other vehicles and pedestrians. In terms of the five routes, we conduct five different experiments in order to assess the performance of different combinations of salient point detector and local descriptor in various road scenes, respectively. The results obtained in this study potentially provide a series of guidelines for the selection of salient point detectors and local descriptors.

Keywords: Monocular visual-IMU odometry · Odometry · Navigation · Salient point detectors · Local descriptors · Evaluation

1 Introduction

Ego-motion estimation in real-world environments has been studied over the past decades. As one of the commonly-used methods for this problem, Visual Odometry (VO) estimates the pose of a vehicle by matching the consecutive images captured using the onboard camera [28]. According to the camera involved, visual odometry can be divided into two categories: monocular and stereo [28]. However, the architecture of stereo visual odometry systems is normally complex, which limits their practical applications. Stereo visual odometry also tends to degenerate to a monocular system when the distance between objects and the camera is large. On the other hand,

Electronic supplementary material The online version of this chapter (doi:10.1007/978-3-319-46604-0_6) contains supplementary material, which is available to authorized users.

© Springer International Publishing Switzerland 2016
G. Hua and H. Jégou (Eds.): ECCV 2016 Workshops, Part I, LNCS 9913, pp. 81–95, 2016.
DOI: 10.1007/978-3-319-46604-0_6

monocular visual odometry systems are simple and can be easily used in practical applications. In addition, the joint use of the Inertial Measure Unit (IMU) and the camera (referred to as Visual-IMU Odometry) normally improves both the reliability and accuracy of motion estimation [19] because they are complementary [3]. Hence, the scope of this research is limited to the study of monocular visual-IMU odometry.

Considering local descriptors are insensitive to occlusion, background clutter and other changes [23], they have been extensively applied to visual odometry [26], visual-SLAM (Simultaneous Localization and Mapping) [5] and visual tracking [9]. Local descriptors are normally extracted at the salient points detected from images in order to accelerate the speed of feature matching. In this context, salient point detection and feature extraction are key to the detector-descriptor based visual odometry systems. As a result, an extensive evaluation of detectors and descriptors in a unified visual odometry framework is required in order to obtain guidelines for the choice of these.

To the authors' knowledge, however, there is no research which extensively assesses the performance of salient point detectors and local descriptors for the applications of monocular visual-IMU odometry. In this paper, we therefore conduct an extensive, comparative evaluation of different combinations of detector and descriptor in the scenario of monocular visual-IMU odometry. The contributions of this paper are: (1) we design a unified evaluation framework based on five typical routes containing different road scenes and a well-established monocular visual-IMU odometry system [15]; and (2) we survey five salient point detectors and eight local descriptors (in which HOG [4], LIOP [34], LM [18] and LSSD [32] have not been applied to visual odometry) and perform a comparative evaluation on different combinations of detector and descriptor, which produces a set of useful benchmarks and insights.

The remainder of this paper is organized as follows. Related work is reviewed in Sect. 2. In Sect. 3, the detail and implementation notes of the salient point detectors and local descriptors are described. The experiments are introduced in Sect. 4 and the results are reported in Sect. 5. Finally, conclusions are drawn in Sect. 6.

2 Related Work

In this section, we briefly review the existing work related to salient point detectors and local descriptors, the application and the evaluation studies of these methods.

2.1 Salient Point Detectors

Salient points are normally used to avoid the heavy computational cost of matching all the pixels in two images. Harris and Stephens [13] proposed a corner detector using the image gradient matrix. Based on this detector, Mikolajczky and Schmid [21] proposed the Harris-Laplace corner detector. The FAST (Features from Accelerated Segment Test) corner detector [27] was introduced based on a discretized circle of pixels surrounding the corner candidate point. Although corner points can be fast computed, they are less distinctive. In contrast, the points detected using blob detectors are more distinctive and redetected [28]. These detectors include the Difference of Gaussian

(DoG) detector [20] and the Fast Hessian detector [1]. In addition, Geiger et al. [11] proposed a blob and corner detector in order to capture both types of points.

2.2 Local Descriptors

Local descriptors have been widely applied in computer vision due to their powerful representation abilities. Local descriptors, for example, Scale-Invariant Feature Transform (SIFT) [20] and Histogram of Orientation Gradient (HOG) [4], can be computed from local gradient histograms. As a faster alternative to SIFT, Bay et al. [1] introduced the Speeded-Up Robust Features (SURF) descriptor. Local descriptors can also be extracted in the form of filter responses [18] or image patches [33]. Besides, Shechtman and Irani [32] introduced a Local Self-Similarity Descriptor (LSSD) while Wang et al. [34] proposed a Local Intensity Order Pattern (LIOP) descriptor.

2.3 Detector-Descriptor Based Monocualr Visual (-IMU) Odometry

The application of local descriptors can be found in many visual odometry tasks. Nister et al. [26] applied the image patches extracted at the Harris corner points to monocular visual odometry, while Bloesch et al. [2] used the FAST detector and multi-level patches for monocular visual-inertial odometry. As one of the most famous local descriptors, SIFT [20] has been used in monocular visual-IMU odometry systems [15, 24]. Nilsson et al. [25] also proposed a monocular visual-aided inertial navigation system using SURF [1]. However, these descriptors are normally extracted from gray level images. In order to exploit richer image characteristics, Dong et al. [7] applied three sets of multi-channel image patch features to monocular visual-IMU odometry.

2.4 Comparative Evaluations of Salient Point Detectors and Local Descriptors

Many evaluation studies have been conducted for computer vision tasks. Schmid et al. [31] compared salient point detectors under different scale, viewpoint, lighting and noise conditions. Mikolajczyk and Schmid further assessed different affine-invariant detectors [22] and descriptors [23]. Recently, Gauglitz et al. [9] compared different salient point detectors and local descriptors for visual tracking. An evaluation study of local descriptors was also performed in the field of geographic image retrieval [35].

On the other hand, the similar comparative studies have also been performed for the visual odometry tasks in the indoor [30] and outdoor scenes [12, 16, 29]. However, only a small number of combinations of detector and descriptor were tested in these studies. In addition, the datasets used are not representative to road scenes. Therefore, we conduct a series of extensive (more detectors and descriptors) evaluation experiments based on a unified monocular visual-IMU odometry framework containing five particularly typical real-world routes. To our knowledge, this is the first extensive evaluation study in the scenario of monocular visual-IMU odometry.

3 Salient Point Detectors and Local Descriptors

We briefly review the salient point detectors and local descriptors tested in this study. The parameters used for these methods can be found in the supplementary material.

3.1 Salient Point Detectors

The five salient point detectors examined in this study are described as follows.

Blob and Corner (Blob&Corner). Geiger et al. [11] first convolved the blob and corner masks with an image. Then, non-maximum and non-minimum suppressions were applied to response images. Four types of points: "corner max", "corner min", "blob max", and "blob min" were derived.

Difference of Gaussian (DoG). Lowe [20] introduced a salient point detector by finding local extrema in an image. The convolution of the image and the DoG functions is performed at different scales. Thus, the salient points can be derived by convolving the extrema of the scale space in the DoG functions with the input image.

Fast Hessian. As a scale-invariant salient point detector, Fast Hessian [1] was developed on the basis of the Hessian matrix. In order to reduce the computational cost, Bay et al. [1] used a set of box filters to approximate the Laplace of Gaussian functions. The salient points in an image can be obtained by detecting the local maximum of the determinate of the Hessian matrix over spatial locations and scales.

Features from Accelerated Segment Test (FAST). Rosten et al. [27] proposed the FAST detector. This detector operates on a circle of 16 pixels around the candidate corner point p. The point p is treated as a corner if there is a continuous arc of at least nine pixels that are darker than the pixel $I_p - s$ (s is a threshold) or brighter than the candidate pixel $I_p + s$. The FAST detector can be further accelerated by learning a decision tree in order to examine fewer pixels.

Harris-Laplace. The Harris-Laplace detector [21] locates potential salient points in the scale space based on a multi-scale Harris corner detector. The key idea of the Harris-Laplace detector is to obtain the representative scale of a local pattern, which is the extremum of the Laplacian function across different scales. This scale is representative in the quantitative viewpoint because it measures the scale at which the maximal similarity between the detector and the local image pattern is reached.

3.2 Local Descriptors

In total, we tested eight different local descriptors in this study. We briefly introduce these below. For more details, please refer to the original publications.

Histogram of Oriented Gradients (HOG). The HOG descriptor computes the occurrence of the gradient orientation in the sub-regions of an image [4]. It first partitions the image into blocks which are further divided into cells. Then, a gradient orientation histogram is derived over each cell. The histograms obtained over each block are concatenated into a vector. We computed a 9-bin histogram from each 5×5 cell in the 15×15 block around a salient point in this study.

Image Patches (IMGP). The simplest description of a salient point is the image patch around this point. Extraction of image patches only requires cropping the image at a given point. The non-warped image patches retain the original image characteristics [33]. In our experiments, the size of image patches was set as 11×11 pixels.

Integral Channel Image Patches (ICIMGP). Dollár et al. [6] proposed a set of integral channels, including the gray level (or color) channel(s), the gradient magnitude channel and six gradient histogram channels. Dong et al. [7] first extracted the image patch around a point in each channel. Then, each patch was L_2 normalized separately. All patches were combined into a single ICIMGP feature vector. In this study, the size of patches was set as 11×11 pixels.

Leung-Malik (LM) Filter Bank. The LM filter bank [18] contains 36 first- and second-order derivatives of Gaussian filters built at six orientations and three scales, eight Laplace of Gaussian filters, and four Gaussian filters. We applied the LM filter bank at each salient point in this study.

Local Intensity Order Pattern (LIOP). Given the image patch around a point, the LIOP descriptor [34] first partitions it into sub-regions using the overall ordinal data. Then, a LIOP is computed over the neighborhood of each pixel. The LIOPs contained in each sub-region are accumulated into an ordinal bin. The LIOP descriptor is obtained by combining different ordinal bins.

Local Self-Similarity Descriptor (LSSD). Given an image, LSSD [32] first computes a correlation surface for each pixel by comparing its local neighborhood with the neighbourhood of each pixel within a larger surrounding region. Then, the surface is partitioned into log-polar bins, which contains n_r radial bins and n_θ angular bins. Finally, the descriptor is obtained as the normalized bins by linearly stretching these bins into the range of [0, 1].

Scale-Invariant Feature Transform (SIFT). The SIFT descriptor [20] is extracted by computing a 128-bin histogram of local oriented gradient magnitudes and orientations in the neighborhood of a salient point.

Speeded-Up Robust Features (SURF). The SURF descriptor [1] first obtains an orientation from the disk around a salient point. Then, a square neighborhood that is parallel to this orientation is derived. The neighborhood is further divided into four 4×4 patches. The features computed from these patches are concatenated into a 64-D feature vector. Compared to SIFT features [20], the lower dimensionality boosts the computational and matching speed.

4   Evaluation Experiments

In this study, a monocular visual-IMU odometry system [15] was used and five experiments were conducted using different routes. In each experiment, we tested different combinations of salient point detector and local descriptor. The GPS/IMU navigation unit data [10] was used as ground-truth, while the pure inertial method (referred to as IMU, whose navigation data was obtained by integrating acceleration and angular velocity) was used as a baseline. The Euclidean distance and the rotation angle were used to compute the position and orientation errors respectively.

4.1   The Monocular Visual-IMU Odometry System

Hu and Chen [15] proposed a monocular visual-IMU odometry system (see Fig. 1 for pipeline) based on the multi-state constraint Kalman filter (MSCKF) [24]. In this system, the trifocal geometry relationship [14] between three consecutive frames is used as camera measurement. Hence, the estimation of the 3D position of feature points is avoided. Also, the trifocal tensor model [14] is used to map the matched feature points between the first two frames into the third frame. A "bucketing" method [17] is further used to choose a subset of the matched points. Finally, the Random Sample Consensus (RANSAC) [8] method is applied in order to reject outlier points.

We used the modified version [7] of the system [15]. The feature matching and outlier rejection module was replaced with a self-adaptive scheme in order to prevent the system from exceptionally crashing when insufficient inliers were returned. The feature matching algorithm introduced by Lowe [20] was utilized in this study.

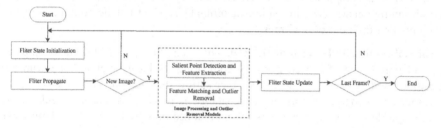

Fig. 1. The pipeline of the monocular visual-IMU odometry system [15] used in this study.

4.2   Dataset and Ground-Truth

In order to assess the detectors and descriptors fairly and explicitly, we selected five typical routes (see Figs. 2 and 3) from the KITTI dataset [10] according to the length and shape, the impact of the independent motion of other vehicles and pedestrians. (The configurations of the routes can be found in the supplementary material). The three factors are challenging for the existing visual odometry systems. Specifically, (1) Route 1 (Straight Line) and Route 2 (Quarter Turn) are on the urban road, in which other vehicles can be found; (2) Route 3 (Multiple Quarter Turns) and Route 4 (Multiple Curved Turns) are in the residential area, and are longer and more complicated; and (3) Route 5 (Loop Line) is also in the residential area and is a closed path. All images included in these routes are real-world driving sequences with the GPS/IMU ground-truth data. These images were captured at 10 fps using a recording platform equipped with multiple sensors [10]. We used the synchronized grayscale images in this study.

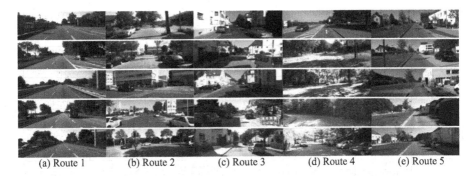

(a) Route 1   (b) Route 2   (c) Route 3   (d) Route 4   (e) Route 5

Fig. 2. Example images (corresponding images of the left color camera) of the five routes selected from the KITTI dataset [10]. (Color figure online)

4.3 Performance Measures

Since the measures based on the error of trajectory endpoints are usually misleading, we used the Root Mean Square Error (RMSE) measure computed from the position or orientation data. This measure has been extensively used for the navigation and autonomous driving systems. The RMSE measure is defined as:

$$RMSE = \sqrt{\frac{\sum_{i=1}^{n} \left[(x_i - \hat{x}_i)^2 + (y_i - \hat{y}_i)^2 \right]}{n}}, \tag{1}$$

where (x_i, y_i) means the ground-truth data while $(\hat{x}_i, \hat{y}_i)$ stands for the estimated data.

5 Experimental Results

In this section, we report the position and orientation RMSE measures derived in the five experiments. (More figures are provided in the supplementary material).

5.1 Route 1: Straight Line

Since Route 1 was gathered on the express way, the average speed involved was high. Table 1 lists the overall position and orientation RMSE values computed between the estimated trajectories obtained using different methods and the ground-truth trajectory. Figure 3(a) further shows the ground-truth trajectory and the estimated trajectories obtained using IMU and the best descriptor for each detector in this experiment.

It can be seen from Table 1 that: (1) the joint use of Fast Hessian [1] and ICIMGP [7] yields the best performance; (2) ICIMGP [7] can also achieve proper performance when used with other detectors, except the DoG detector [20]; (3) the HOG [4] and LSSD [32] descriptors perform properly when combined with FAST [27] while SIFT [20], SURF [1] and LM [18] generates promising results when used with DoG [20];

Table 1. The overall position and orientation RMSE values computed between the ground-truth trajectory and the trajectories obtained using different methods on Route 1.

		BLOB& CORNER [11]	DOG [20]	FAST [27]	FAST HESSIAN [1]	HARRIS LAPLACE [21]
Position RMSE (m)	IMU	19.7514 (Salient point detector is not applicable)				
	HOG [4]	11.8107	136.1566	**11.0005**	52.1558	16.7228
	ICIMGP [7]	**8.8652**	57.4174	17.9052	**5.2729**	**10.5965**
	IMGP [33]	152.6954	33.1861	36.6821	45.0751	42.7403
	LIOP [34]	110.3710	96.4385	254.7819	355.2067	162.6288
	LM [18]	30.4017	11.1896	18.7077	50.2143	40.8369
	LSSD [32]	48.7660	221.8634	13.6568	238.2317	198.0097
	SIFT [20]	78.9520	**5.4794**	17.7088	16.7066	44.4767
	SURF [1]	60.8664	8.8896	15.9851	15.3137	26.1256
Orientation RMSE (deg)	IMU	2.4215 (Salient point detector is not applicable)				
	HOG [4]	2.3897	9.9110	**2.2235**	2.9339	2.4759
	ICIMGP [7]	**1.9690**	3.9674	2.3187	**1.7411**	**2.1637**
	IMGP [33]	2.3714	2.5128	2.5516	2.5728	2.7986
	LIOP [34]	3.0980	2.7016	4.2099	4.1999	2.2773
	LM [18]	2.3281	2.6195	2.5136	2.3939	2.8105
	LSSD [32]	2.1357	7.1138	2.4031	9.1309	6.5336
	SIFT [20]	2.7823	**2.3661**	2.5850	2.6820	2.8603
	SURF [1]	2.5319	2.4400	2.4226	2.3399	2.8067

(4) IMGP [33] and LIOP [34] do not provide good performance. Especially, LIOP performs worse than all its counterparts; and (5) the IMU method performs properly.

5.2   Route 2: Quarter Turn

The route used in this experiment is a simple quarter turn. Table 2 reports the overall position and orientation RMSE values derived using IMU and different combinations of salient point detector and local descriptor. As can be seen, (1) the ICIMGP de-scriptor [7] performs the best, especially, when combined with the FAST detector [27]; (2) the combination of HOG [4] and FAST [27] is comparable to this result; (3) SIFT [20] and SURF [1] yield proper performances; (4) the performance of LIOP [34] is better than that it obtained in Sect. 5.1 but is still worse than those of the other descriptors in most cases; (5) LM [18] and LSSD [32] perform well when combined with the Blob&Corner detector [11]; (6) IMGP [33] performs properly when used with the FAST [27] or DoG [20] detectors; and (7) the performance of the IMU method is proper. In addition, the ground-truth trajectory and the trajectories obtained using IMU and the best descriptor for each salient point detector are shown in Fig. 3(b).

5.3   Route 3: Multiple Quarter Turns

The route used in this experiment was captured in the residential area. Compared to Routes 1 and 2, this route is longer and more complicated. Table 3 lists the overall position and orientation RMSE values obtained using different methods. It can be observed that: (1) the best result is produced by the combination of Fast Hessian [1] and ICIMGP [7]; (2) HOG [4] also performs well, especially, when used with the Harris Laplace detector [21]; (3) the performance of IMGP [33] is even comparable to

Table 2. The overall position and orientation RMSE values computed between the ground-truth trajectory and the trajectories obtained using different methods on Route 2.

<table>
<tr><th colspan="2"></th><th>BLOB&
CORNER [11]</th><th>DOG [20]</th><th>FAST [27]</th><th>FAST
HESSIAN [1]</th><th>HARRIS
LAPLACE [21]</th></tr>
<tr><td rowspan="10">Position
RMSE
(m)</td><td>IMU</td><td colspan="5">19.2885 (Salient point detector is not applicable)</td></tr>
<tr><td>HOG [4]</td><td>5.1639</td><td>8.0799</td><td>4.1790</td><td>13.9958</td><td>8.9684</td></tr>
<tr><td>ICIMGP [7]</td><td>4.2406</td><td>5.8100</td><td>3.5711</td><td>4.9501</td><td>8.4941</td></tr>
<tr><td>IMGP [33]</td><td>25.5154</td><td>14.4854</td><td>10.8527</td><td>22.5591</td><td>21.9990</td></tr>
<tr><td>LIOP [34]</td><td>22.6505</td><td>45.1004</td><td>35.8729</td><td>35.1246</td><td>18.4742</td></tr>
<tr><td>LM [18]</td><td>8.6962</td><td>13.6695</td><td>14.1090</td><td>14.9695</td><td>24.6382</td></tr>
<tr><td>LSSD [32]</td><td>7.4026</td><td>7.7328</td><td>7.4474</td><td>62.5453</td><td>15.2898</td></tr>
<tr><td>SIFT [20]</td><td>13.1014</td><td>13.9049</td><td>13.5340</td><td>19.0370</td><td>14.2213</td></tr>
<tr><td>SURF [1]</td><td>22.5823</td><td>9.0183</td><td>14.5184</td><td>16.0266</td><td>18.1139</td></tr>
<tr><td>IMU</td><td colspan="5">3.9190 (Salient point detector is not applicable)</td></tr>
<tr><td rowspan="9">Orientation
RMSE
(deg)</td><td>HOG [4]</td><td>1.6664</td><td>1.8306</td><td>1.6076</td><td>1.7836</td><td>1.6327</td></tr>
<tr><td>ICIMGP [7]</td><td>1.4627</td><td>1.5223</td><td>1.4032</td><td>1.4785</td><td>1.5449</td></tr>
<tr><td>IMGP [33]</td><td>4.1985</td><td>2.0223</td><td>1.8827</td><td>3.9470</td><td>4.2121</td></tr>
<tr><td>LIOP [34]</td><td>4.3496</td><td>4.2128</td><td>4.5956</td><td>4.1954</td><td>4.2518</td></tr>
<tr><td>LM [18]</td><td>1.4296</td><td>1.6533</td><td>1.6976</td><td>1.7509</td><td>4.1327</td></tr>
<tr><td>LSSD [32]</td><td>1.5367</td><td>1.4339</td><td>1.5818</td><td>9.8677</td><td>2.2354</td></tr>
<tr><td>SIFT [20]</td><td>1.6483</td><td>1.5586</td><td>1.5179</td><td>2.9828</td><td>2.6253</td></tr>
<tr><td>SURF [1]</td><td>3.9259</td><td>1.5555</td><td>1.6213</td><td>2.3997</td><td>2.5474</td></tr>
</table>

the best result when combined with DoG [20] and is proper when used with the other detectors; (4) LM [18] performs properly and yields its best performance when combined with the Harris Laplace detector [21] while SIFT [20] and SURF [1] perform properly in most cases; (5) LIOP [34] produces better results than it did on Routes 1 and 2, and yields its best performance when used with Harris Laplace [21]; (6) LSSD [32] provides proper performance when combined with Blob&Corner [11], DoG [20] or FAST [27]; and (7) the performance of the IMU method is worse than those of all the descriptors. Besides, the ground-truth trajectory and the trajectories obtained using IMU and the best descriptor for each salient point detector are shown in Fig. 3(c).

5.4   Route 4: Multiple Curved Turns

The route used in this experiment contains several curved turns. Table 4(a) lists the overall position and orientation RMSE values derived using different methods. It can be seen that: (1) the joint use of Fast Hessian [1] and ICIMGP [7] achieves the best result; (2) SIFT [20] yields the comparable performance to this result when used with FAST [27] and performs better than it did on Routes 1, 2 and 3; (3) HOG [4], SURF [1] and LM [18] perform properly while LSSD [32] only produces proper performance when used with Blob&Corner [11], DoG [20] or FAST [27]; (4) IMGP [33] yields its best performance when combined with DoG [20] and also performs properly when used with the other detectors; (5) the trajectories obtained using LIOP [34] suffer from the drift issue except when used with Harris Laplace [21] and are even worse than that obtained using IMU. Figure 3(d) also shows the ground-truth trajectory and the trajectories derived using IMU and the best descriptor for each detector.

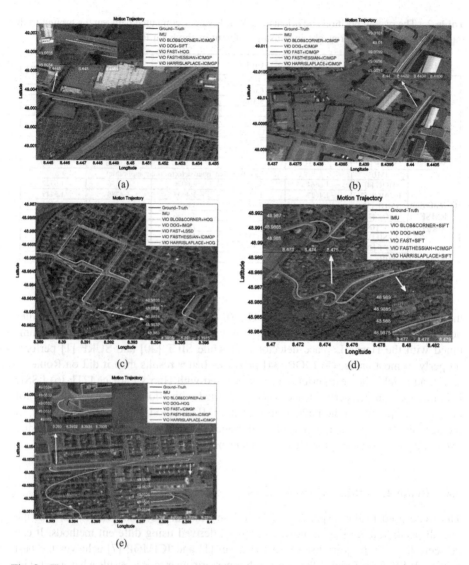

Fig. 3. The ground-truth trajectory and the trajectories (best viewed in color) obtained using IMU and the best descriptor for each detector in five experiments: (a) Straight Line (express way, ≈ 780 m, ≈ 60 km/h); (b) Quarter Turn (urban road, ≈ 330 m, ≈ 28 km/h); (c) Multiple Quarter Turns (residential area, ≈ 960 m, ≈ 26 km/h); (d) Multiple Curved Turns (residential area, ≈ 1050 m, ≈ 40 km/h); and (e) Loop Line (residential area, ≈ 930 m, ≈ 38 km/h). (Color figure online) (Map source: GoogleEarth).

5.5   Route 5: Loop Line

A closed route is used in this experiment. Table 4(b) reports the overall position and orientation RMSE values computed between the trajectories obtained using different methods and the ground-truth data. As can be seen, (1) the combination of FAST [27]

Table 3. The overall position and orientation RMSE values computed between the ground-truth trajectory and the trajectories obtained using different methods on Route 3.

		BLOB& CORNER [11]	DOG [20]	FAST [27]	FAST HESSIAN [1]	HARRIS LAPLACE [21]
	IMU	1540 (Salient point detector is not applicable)				
	HOG [4]	9.0217	17.1248	15.1831	9.2064	4.9899
	ICIMGP [7]	12.1206	7.7111	16.9728	4.4340	6.2895
Position	IMGP [33]	18.3862	4.8790	19.2680	20.4940	10.0586
RMSE	LIOP [34]	15.1372	39.5007	14.8697	15.4606	9.7781
(m)	LM [18]	12.9940	14.2923	22.6583	14.3077	9.6142
	LSSD [32]	16.0244	11.8442	12.4355	37.3118	34.9911
	SIFT [20]	13.4720	9.2277	24.5953	10.8567	6.8956
	SURF [1]	32.1153	7.0529	25.2071	8.5964	6.3545
	IMU	11.2301 (Salient point detector is not applicable)				
	HOG [4]	2.6607	4.3870	2.5740	1.8785	1.4192
	ICIMGP [7]	2.7049	2.9338	2.6542	1.3711	1.7284
Orientation	IMGP [33]	2.8369	2.7518	2.8495	2.8208	1.7913
RMSE	LIOP [34]	2.7034	2.7309	2.6419	3.2402	1.7431
(deg)	LM [18]	2.7518	2.9264	2.6755	2.9101	1.7195
	LSSD [32]	2.7423	2.9747	2.3698	4.4367	3.2621
	SIFT [20]	2.6880	2.7993	2.7558	1.8593	1.7595
	SURF [1]	2.5756	2.8834	2.8303	1.8531	1.7349

and ICIMGP [7] performs the best; (2) HOG [4] yields promising results except when it is used with Blob&Corner [11]; (3) LM [18], IMGP [33], SIFT [20] and SURF [1] generate proper performance while LSSD [32] only yields proper performance when used with DoG [20] or FAST [27]; (4) LIOP [34] performs properly when combined with the Blob&Corner [11], DoG [20] or Harris Laplace [21] detectors; and (5) the performance of IMU is the worst while it can be improved by being jointly used with local descriptors. In addition, Fig. 3(e) shows the ground-truth trajectory and the trajectories obtained using IMU and the best descriptor for each salient point detector.

5.6 Summary

The performance of the descriptors varies when they are used with different detectors or on different routes. To summarize, a set of insights can be obtained as follows:

(1) In the five experiments, the best result is always produced by ICIMGP [7], especially, when it is used with the FAST [27] or Fast Hessian [1] detectors. It suggests that ICIMGP [7] is suitable for monocular visual-IMU odometry. Those promising results should be attributed to the fact that ICIMGP [7] encodes richer image characteristics than its counterparts that are normally extracted from gray level images;

(2) The HOG [4] and LSSD [32] descriptors perform properly when they are used with FAST [27]. However, their performance varies when used with other detectors;

(3) The DoG detector [20] is the best choice for IMGP [33]. In this case, IMGP [33] performs better than ICIMGP [7] on Routes 3 and 4. However, it does not yield promising results on the straight express way (Route 1). The similar finding can be obtained for LIOP [34] when it is used with Harris Laplace [21]. These results show that gray level image patches are not sufficient for the use on the straight express way and probably need to be combined with other image characteristics (see ICIMGP);

Table 4. The overall position and orientation RMSE values computed between the ground-truth trajectory and the trajectories obtained using different methods on (a) Route 4 and (b) Route 5.

		BLOB& CORNER [11]	DOG [20]	FAST [27]	FAST HESSIAN [1]	HARRIS LAPLACE [21]
Position RMSE (m)	IMU	86.6306 (Salient point detector is not applicable)				
	HOG [4]	28.1719	10.8526	8.0639	16.6777	18.0063
	ICIMGP [7]	14.5597	9.1290	15.3423	6.5293	14.3628
	IMGP [33]	18.0994	8.1375	15.3857	24.7288	28.3987
	LIOP [34]	133.3808	250.2128	164.4068	190.7820	33.4962
	LM [18]	12.1501	16.7098	8.3151	18.9811	18.6905
	LSSD [32]	13.3530	22.0602	11.6544	42.8612	50.3251
	SIFT [20]	10.1651	11.4728	6.9466	7.4098	10.8258
	SURF [1]	12.2692	8.2212	10.2553	12.2840	19.8987
Orientation RMSE (deg)	IMU	3.6691 (Salient point detector is not applicable)				
	HOG [4]	3.9045	2.6484	2.6698	2.7958	2.8306
	ICIMGP [7]	2.9066	2.6197	2.8062	2.5820	2.8042
	IMGP [33]	3.0646	2.5938	2.8138	3.4242	2.8374
	LIOP [34]	6.7869	8.6987	8.7326	7.9277	5.5268
	LM [18]	3.0063	2.7083	2.7701	2.7169	2.8940
	LSSD [32]	3.0072	2.8973	3.4745	6.7956	4.9426
	SIFT [20]	2.7768	2.6617	1.5408	2.6173	2.7813
	SURF [1]	2.8159	2.6166	2.8096	2.5472	2.8429

(a)

		BLOB& CORNER [11]	DOG [20]	FAST [27]	FAST HESSIAN [1]	HARRIS LAPLACE [21]
Position RMSE (m)	IMU	314.4739 (Salient point detector is not applicable)				
	HOG [4]	61.4032	6.4047	12.5497	29.8080	18.2804
	ICIMGP [7]	18.0249	8.9149	4.5590	9.1430	6.9035
	IMGP [33]	14.4585	15.2747	13.3215	35.9567	19.8309
	LIOP [34]	16.2077	14.4689	35.1219	51.8146	9.0775
	LM [18]	12.2945	8.6872	18.3456	13.8273	21.9467
	LSSD [32]	64.8867	17.0492	20.7358	64.2704	57.0051
	SIFT [20]	22.6322	6.7678	14.7502	14.0927	8.0781
	SURF [1]	27.8902	11.8585	11.1392	11.5467	35.0271
Orientation RMSE (deg)	IMU	9.7546 (Salient point detector is not applicable)				
	HOG [4]	3.8551	2.4639	3.5458	3.9671	3.5270
	ICIMGP [7]	3.5059	3.5002	2.3885	2.6783	2.6362
	IMGP [33]	3.2276	3.6311	3.3802	3.5993	3.4252
	LIOP [34]	3.2975	3.3220	3.4657	6.1507	2.7783
	LM [18]	3.1867	3.3307	3.2962	3.2579	3.3887
	LSSD [32]	3.7195	3.7232	3.4236	7.0683	3.6475
	SIFT [20]	3.3112	3.3340	3.3997	3.4244	2.7540
	SURF [1]	3.5203	3.4688	3.2930	3.5448	3.6012

(b)

(4) The LM [18], SIFT [20] and SURF [1] descriptors produce promising results when used with DoG [20] while their performances are not stable when used with the other detectors. Surprisingly, SURF [1] normally performs better when combined with DoG [20] than Fast Hessian [1] even if the latter was proposed for it; and

(5) According to the average position RMSE, Route 3 is the easiest (15.0 ± 8.8) but Route 1 is the most difficult (65.2 ± 79.2) for the detectors and descriptors tested here.

The above insights provide the meaningful guidelines for choosing the salient point detector and local descriptor in the monocular visual-IMU odometry applications.

We did not compare the computational speed of different detectors and descriptors because they were implemented in different programming languages. However, the time cost of feature matching depends on the dimensionality of the local descriptors

Table 5. The dimensionality of the local descriptors examined in this paper.

Descriptor	HOG [4]	ICIMGP [7]	IMGP [33]	LIOP [34]	LM [18]	LSSD [32]	SIFT [20]	SURF [1]
Dim.	279	968	121	144	48	36	128	64

extracted at the same salient points. Table 5 lists the dimensionality of the eight local descriptors. It can be seen that the dimensionality of the ICIMGP [7] descriptor is the highest while it did produce the best results in this study.

6 Conclusions and Future Work

In this paper, we first reviewed five salient point detectors and eight local descriptors. Then, we conducted a comparative evaluation study on different combinations of detector and descriptor using a unified monocular visual-IMU odometry framework and five typical routes [10]. To our knowledge, this is the first extensive comparative evaluation on salient point detectors and local descriptors for monocular visual-IMU odometry by using these explicit types of routes. The experimental results can be used as a set of baselines in the further research. The analysis of these results also provides a set of useful insights to the community, which could be used as guidelines for the selection of the detector-descriptor combinations.

However, the experiments presented in this paper are not exhaustive and only investigate different combinations of detector and descriptor using a monocular visual-IMU odometry system. In the next stage of this study, we will tune the parameters of the detectors and descriptors and also test a different monocular visual odometry system in order to augment the results reported in this paper.

Acknowledgement. This work is partially supported by the National Natural Science Foundation of China (NSFC) (No. 61271405).

References

1. Bay, H., Ess, A., Tuytelaars, T., Van Gool, L.: Speeded-up robust features (SURF). Comput. Vis. Image Underst. 110(3), 346–359 (2008)
2. Bloesch, M., Omari, S., Hutter, M., Siegwart, R.: Robust visual inertial odometry using a direct EKF-based approach. In: IEEE/RSJ International Conference on Intelligent Robots and Systems, pp. 298–304 (2015)
3. Corke, P., Lobo, J., Dias, J.: An introduction to inertial and visual sensing. Int. J. Robot. Res. 26(6), 519–535 (2007)
4. Dalal, N., Triggs, B.: Histograms of oriented gradients for human detection. In: IEEE Conference on Computer Vision and Pattern Recognition, pp. 886–893 (2005)
5. Davison, A., Reid, I., Molton, N., Stasse, O.: MonoSLAM: real-time single camera SLAM. IEEE Trans. Pattern Anal. Mach. Intell. 29(6), 1052–1067 (2007)

6. Dollár, P., Tu, Z., Perona, P., Belongie, S.: Integral channel features. In: British Machine Vision Conference (2009)
7. Dong, X., He, B., Dong, X., Dong, J.: Monocular visual-IMU odometry using multi-channel image patch exemplars. Multimedia Tools and Applications (in press)
8. Fischler, M., Bolles, R.: Random sample consensus: a paradigm for model fitting with applications to image analysis and automated cartography. Commun. ACM **24**(6), 381–395 (1981)
9. Gauglitz, S., Höllerer, T., Turk, M.: Evaluation of interest point detectors and feature descriptors for visual tracking. Int. J. Comput. Vis. **94**(3), 335–360 (2011)
10. Geiger, A., Lenz, P., Stiller, C., Urtasun, R.: Vision meets robotics: the KITTI dataset. Int. J. Robot. Res. **32**, 1229–1235 (2013)
11. Geiger, A., Ziegler, J., Stiller, C.: StereoScan: dense 3D reconstruction in real-time. In: IEEE Intelligent Vehicles Symposium, pp. 963–968 (2011)
12. Govender, N.: Evaluation of feature detection algorithms for structure from motion. Council for Scientific and Industrial Research, Technical report (2009)
13. Harris, C., Stephens, M.: A combined corner and edge detector. In: Alvey Vision Conference (1988)
14. Hartley, R., Zisserman, A.: Multiple View Geometry in Computer Vision, 2nd edn. Cambridge University Press, Cambridge (2008)
15. Hu, J., Chen, M.: A sliding-window visual-IMU odometer based on tri-focal tensor geometry. In: IEEE International Conference on Robotics and Automation, pp. 3963–3968 (2014)
16. Jiang, Y., Xu, Y., Liu, Y.: Performance evaluation of feature detection and matching in stereo visual odometry. Neurocomputing **120**, 380–390 (2013)
17. Kitt, B., Geiger, A., Lategahn, H.: Visual odometry based on stereo image sequences with RANSAC-based outlier rejection scheme. In: IEEE Intelligent Vehicles Symposium, pp. 486–492 (2010)
18. Leung, T., Malik, J.: Representing and recognizing the visual appearance of materials using three-dimensional textons. Int. J. Comput. Vis. **43**(1), 29–44 (2001)
19. Li, M., Mourikis A I.: Improving the accuracy of EKF-based visual-inertial odometry. In: IEEE International Conference on Robotics and Automation, pp. 828–835 (2012)
20. Lowe, D.G.: Distinctive image features from scale-invariant keypoints. Int. J. Comput. Vis. **60**(2), 91–110 (2004)
21. Mikolajcyk, K., Schmid, C.: An affine invariant interest point detector. In: International Conference on Computer Vision, pp. 128–142 (2002)
22. Mikolajczyk, K., Schmid, C.: Scale & affine invariant interest point detectors. Int. J. Comput. Vis. **60**(1), 63–86 (2004)
23. Mikolajczyk, K., Schmid, C.: A performance evaluation of local descriptors. IEEE Trans. Pattern Anal. Mach. Intell. **27**(10), 1615–1630 (2005)
24. Mourikis, A., Roumeliotis, S.: A multi-state constraint Kalman filter for vision-aided inertial navigation. In: IEEE International Conference on Robotics and Automation, pp. 3565–3572 (2007)
25. Nilsson, J.O., Zachariah, D., Jansson, M., Handel, P.: Realtime implementation of visual-aided inertial navigation using epipolar constraints. In: IEEE Position Location and Navigation Symposium (PLANS), pp. 711–718 (2012)
26. Nistér, D., Naroditsky, O., Bergen, J.: Visual odometry. In: IEEE Conference on Computer Vision and Pattern Recognition, pp. 652–659 (2004)
27. Rosten, E., Porter, R., Drummond, T.: Faster and better: a machine learning approach to corner detection. IEEE Trans. Pattern Anal. Mach. Intell. **32**(1), 105–119 (2010)

28. Scaramuzza, D., Fraundorfer, F.: Visual odometry [tutorial]. IEEE Robot. Autom. Mag. **18** (4), 80–92 (2011)
29. Scaramuzza, D., Fraundorfer, F., Siegwart, R.: Real-time monocular visual odometry for on-road vehicles with 1-point RANSAC. In: IEEE International Conference on Robotics and Automation, pp. 4293–4299 (2009)
30. Schmidt, A., Kraft, M., Kasiński, A.: An evaluation of image feature detectors and descriptors for robot navigation. In: Bolc, L., Tadeusiewicz, R., Chmielewski, L.J., Wojciechowski, K. (eds.) ICCVG 2010, Part II. LNCS, vol. 6375, pp. 251–259. Springer, Heidelberg (2010)
31. Schmid, C., Mohr, R., Bauckhage, C.: Evaluation of interest point detectors. Int. J. Comput. Vis. **37**(2), 151–172 (2000)
32. Shechtman, E., Irani, M.: Matching local self-similarities across images and videos. In: IEEE Conference on Computer Vision and Pattern Recognition, pp. 1–8 (2007)
33. Varma, M., Zisserman, A.: A statistical approach to material classification using image patch exemplars. IEEE Trans. Pattern Anal. Mach. Intell. **31**, 2032–2047 (2009)
34. Wang, Z., Fan, B., Wu, F.: Local intensity order pattern for feature description. In: International Conference on Computer Vision, pp. 603–610 (2011)
35. Yang, Y., Newsam, S.: Geographic image retrieval using local invariant features. IEEE Trans. Geosci. Remote Sens. **51**(2), 818–832 (2013)

Road Segmentation for Classification of Road Weather Conditions

Emilio J. Almazan, Yiming Qian$^{(\boxtimes)}$, and James H. Elder

Centre for Vision Research, York University, Toronto, Canada
ealmazanm@gmail.com, {yimingq,jelder}@yorku.ca

Abstract. Using vehicle cameras to automatically assess road weather conditions requires that the road surface first be identified and segmented from the imagery. This is a challenging problem for uncalibrated cameras such as removable dash cams or cell phone cameras, where the location of the road in the image may vary considerably from image to image. Here we show that combining a spatial prior with vanishing point and horizon estimators can generate improved road surface segmentation and consequently better road weather classification performance. The resulting system attains an accuracy of 86 % for binary classification (bare vs. snow/ice-covered) and 80 % for 3 classes (dry vs. wet vs. snow/ice-covered) on a challenging dataset.

Keywords: Linear perspective · Vanishing point · Horizon · Road segmentation · Weather conditions

1 Introduction

Automatic assessment of road weather conditions using vehicle camera data can be used to inform the human driver, driver-assist controls and autonomous control systems. Moreover, the information can be shared across connected vehicles, alerting following vehicles to conditions ahead. Another application is automatic dispatch and verification of snow ploughs and service vehicles. Given their typically wide geographic distribution, these service vehicles can provide real-time data on road conditions to central management, which can then use the data to verify maintenance and optimize dispatch.

While future generations of service vehicles may be manufactured with appropriate built-in cameras, in the meantime there is interest in retrofitting existing vehicles with removable dash cams that can be used for multiple purposes. This poses a challenge for video analytics, as the pose of the camera relative to the road surface may vary considerably. Since the cameras are mounted inside the vehicle, imagery may be partially occluded by the hood of the vehicle, For snow ploughs, the road surface may also be occluded further by the plough, depending on its position (Fig. 1).

To address these challenges a reliable algorithm for segmenting the road surface from the imagery is required. This method must be able to handle variations

© Springer International Publishing Switzerland 2016
G. Hua and H. Jégou (Eds.): ECCV 2016 Workshops, Part I, LNCS 9913, pp. 96–108, 2016.
DOI: 10.1007/978-3-319-46604-0_7

Bare		Covered		
Bare dry $n = 32$	Bare wet $n = 14$	Iced covered $n = 8$	Snow covered $n = 16$	Snow packed $n = 30$

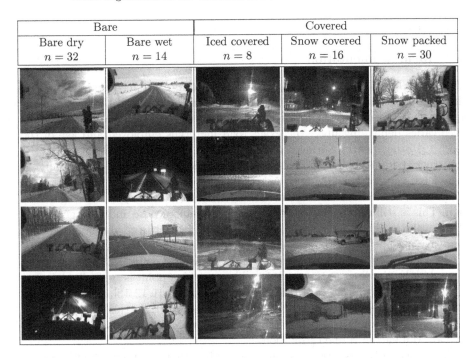

Fig. 1. Example images from training dataset, and the number n in each class.

in the position and pose of the camera as well as geometry of the road surface. Using appearance features of the road surface (e.g., texture) for segmentation is unlikely to be reliable across diverse weather conditions, since the road appearance will vary considerably and sometimes may strongly resemble other surfaces in the scene. For these reasons, we focus here on geometric methods for identifying the road surface and show that by fusing a combination of these methods we can significantly improve road weather classification performance.

In particular we develop a novel method for estimating the road vanishing point, which yields a triangular road segmentation hypothesis. This vanishing point method also delivers a measure of reliability, which can be used to identify when the vanishing point is ill-defined (in a parking lot, for example). Under these conditions we revert to a weaker segmentation based upon detection of the horizon line. Combining these with a spatial prior then delivers an estimated road segmentation tailored to each image.

This paper is organized as follows: Sect. 2 reviews prior work, Sect. 3 details our road segmentation algorithm, Sect. 4 describes our classification process, Sect. 5 reports results and finally Sect. 6 presents our conclusions and plans for future work.

2 Prior Work

2.1 Road Segmentation

One might initially imagine using surface appearance properties to distinguish the road pavement surface from other surfaces in the scene [2,3]. However, this approach is problematic here for at least three reasons: (1) pavement appearance varies depending upon the exact road materials employed and age of the road; (2) other nearby surfaces (e.g., sidewalks, driveways, buildings) may be constructed from similar materials; (3) the road surface may be partially or completed covered by snow and/or ice.

For these reasons, we use geometric methods to estimate the road segmentation. This is still non-trivial due to diversity in camera pose and road geometry. Roads vary in shape, are sometimes relatively unstructured, non-homogeneous and vary in appearance under varying weather and illumination conditions.

Previous approaches have estimated the vanishing point [12,18,19], horizon [1] and/or border lines of the road [13]. The vanishing point is typically detected using texture information from Gabor wavelet filters [1,12,18], using a Hough transform [24] or with a line segment voting scheme [20]. In this work we adapt recent work on Hough-based vanishing point detection [21] that has proven effective for Manhattan frame estimation.

The horizon line is often estimated as the line that partitions the image into two regions that differs maximally in appearance [6,7], however more elaborate approaches based on gist descriptors [1,15] have also been employed. Here we identify the horizon as the vertical location that maximizes the RMS first derivative in the vertical direction across all horizontal locations and colour channels.

2.2 Road Weather Classification

Since the focus of this paper is on road segmentation, we will review the literature on road weather classification only briefly.

Much of the prior work on road condition classification has focused on the use of polarization and infrared cameras [5,8–10,14,25], which can be expensive and installation can be complex. However, there are also a number of efforts employing standard RGB cameras. Omer and Fu [16] used an SVM with RGB and gradient histogram features to classify conditions as bare, covered or covered with bare tire tracks. However their approach required manual cropping of each image to extract the image region projecting from the ground surface, which is impractical for a real system. Kauai et al. [11] used colour cues to add some degree of illumination invariance, however their approach depends on detecting white line markings to identify the road area, which will fail under snowy conditions or for roads that are poorly marked. In a very recent paper, Amthor et al. [4] proposed a spatiotemporal approach that integrates over many frames to detect specular reflections indicative of wet conditions. While their method improves over prior approaches, it requires integration over many frames, increasing computational load and delay.

For the present paper we employ the classifier reported recently by Qian et al. [17], which uses a naive Bayes classifier over texton and luminance features. Please see Sect. 4 for more details.

2.3 Dataset

To train and evaluate our algorithm, we employ the challenging dataset of 100 2048×1536 pixel images (Fig. 1) introduced by Qian et al. [17], obtained directly from the authors. The dataset contains roads under different weather conditions, from bare dry to snow packed. Each of the five classes was randomly and evenly split between training and test datasets, each consisting of 50 images.

The pictures were taken at different times of the day, thus covering a wide range of illumination conditions and the camera pose varied considerably. The road condition class was identified manually by our industrial partner. For training and evaluation purposes, we manually segmented the road surface from the background. Running our classifier on the manually segmented imagery allows us to estimate the potential for increasing classification performance through further improvements in segmentation.

3   Road Segmentation

The main challenge for segmenting the road surface is the variability of the road appearance under different weather conditions, which limits the utility of appearance features such as luminance, colour, texture and detailed road markings. We therefore propose a method that relies on contextual information to define the vanishing point of the road and horizon line. The process consists of four stages: (1) estimation of the vanishing point of the road; (2) assessment of the reliability of this vanishing point estimate; (3) direct estimation of the horizon line, for vanishing points assessed to be unreliable; (4) fusion with a spatial prior to identify the region of the image corresponding to the road surface.

3.1   Vanishing Point Estimation

A vanishing point is defined as a point in the image plane where parallel lines converge. We use the line detector algorithm of Tal and Elder, 2012 [21] (code obtained directly from authors). The detector returns betwen 122 and 746 lines for each of the images in the training dataset. It also returns the estimated total length l of the line segments along each detected line. As revealed in Fig. 2, the geometry (position ρ, orientation θ, length l) of each line provides some information about the likelihood that it is generated by the vanishing point (ON) versus a background process (OFF). We therefore rerank the lines using a naive Bayes model to approximate the likelihood ratio L_i for each line i:

$$L_i = \frac{p(\rho_i, \theta_i, l_i | \text{ON})}{p(\rho_i, \theta_i, l_i | \text{OFF})} \approx \frac{p(\rho_i | \text{ON}) p(\theta_i | \text{ON}) p(l_i | \text{ON})}{p(\rho_i | \text{OFF}) p(\theta_i | \text{OFF}) p(l_i | \text{OFF})}. \tag{1}$$

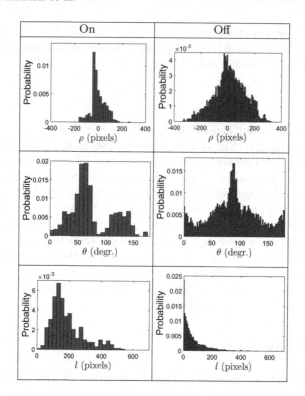

Fig. 2. Likelihood distributions for the three line features (ρ, θ and l).

We estimate the vanishing point as the point in the image that minimizes the distance to the top-ranked n lines. Specifically, we adopt a naive Bayes approach and choose the point v that maximizes

$$p(v|\mathrm{L}) \propto \prod_{i}^{n} p(d_i|v)p(v) \tag{2}$$

where $\mathrm{D} = (d_1, d_2, ..., d_n)$ are the distances to the detected lines. The spatial prior $p(v)$ is modelled as a Gaussian distribution, and the likelihoods $p(d_i|v)$ are determined from the training data as shown in Fig. 3.

Equation 2 is not convex in general; to maximize we select the optimal solution from 50 gradient descent solutions (MATLAB fminsearch), initialized by randomly sampling from the prior $p(v)$.

Figure 4 compares performance of the vanishing point algorithm on the training dataset with and without the re-ranking step. We find that generally the re-ranking improves results and that error is minimizec by using the top-ranked 20 lines. Note also that using the lines to estimate the vanishing point yields much lower error than using the centroid of vanishing points from the training set (Prior model). Figure 5 shows examples of automatically estimated vanishing points.

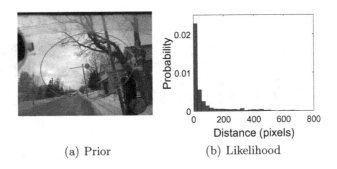

(a) Prior   (b) Likelihood

Fig. 3. (a) Vanishing point prior distribution plotted on a sample image from the dataset. The red ellipse indicates the 95 % confidence interval for the vanishing point. (b) Likelihood distribution for the distance of the top-ranked 20 detected lines from the vanishing point. (Color figure online)

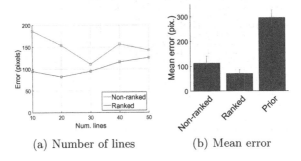

(a) Number of lines   (b) Mean error

Fig. 4. (a) Average Euclidean error of the estimated vanishing point as a function of the number n of lines employed. (b) Mean error and standard error of the mean, collapsing over n.

There are some situations where the vanishing point of the road is not readily apparent, such as in parking lots or intersections (Fig. 10(c–f)). Our vanishing point algorithm will tend to produce large errors for these cases, which could in turn lead to large errors in the road segmentation. To prevent this, we assess the reliability of vanishing point estimates as the average distance $\bar{D}_k$ of the top k lines closest to the estimated vanishing point; If $\bar{D}_k$ exceeds a threshold t, we reject the vanishing point estimate and use an alternate method to determine the horizon line (see below). There are two free parameters for this reliability measure: the number k of lines and the threshold t. We optimize using the training data based on the ultimate error in estimating the horizon line, assessed as the average absolute error at left and right image boundaries (Fig. 6): values of $k = 12$ and $t = 21$ were found to be optimal.

(a)   (b)   (c)

Fig. 5. Examples of automatically estimated vanishing points.

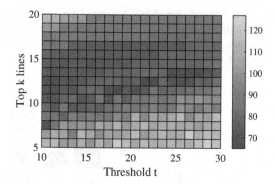

Fig. 6. The error graph of different combinations of threshold t and top k lines.

3.2 Horizon Estimation

When vanishing point estimation fails it may still be possible to constrain the road location using the horizon line. The horizon line can be defined by two parameters, for example, its vertical location and orientation. For our dataset, however, we found that orientation estimation could be quite unreliable. We therefore fixed the orientation to horizontal.

To estimate the vertical location of the horizon, we used the training images for which our vanishing point estimates were judged (automatically) to be unreliable as a horizon training dataset ($k = 23$ images in all). We then (1) normalized each image to have zero mean and unit variance, (2) registered them vertically so that their horizons aligned, (3) extracted the luminance channel from each image, (4) averaged over horizontal position (see Fig. 7(a)) and (5) cropped to extract a luminance vector l_i of length n centred at the horizon. Finally, we computed the first m principal components u_i (see Fig. 7(b)) of length n over these k vectors.

To estimate the vertical position y_h of the horizon for a target image, we (1) normalize the image to have zero mean and unit variance, (2) extract the luminance channel, (3) average over horizontal position and (4) convolve the resulting vector l with each of the m principal component vectors to generate m

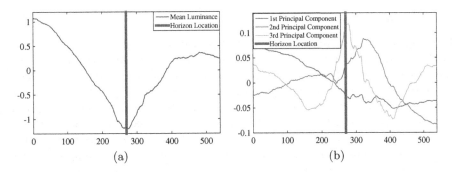

(a)   (b)

Fig. 7. (a) Mean normalized luminance of horizon training images as a function of vertical displacement from horizon. (b) First three principal components of vertical luminance distribution around horizon location.

projection vectors $\tilde{l}_i$. Approximating the training data as multivariate normal, the log probability that the horizon lies at vertical location y can be estimated as:

$$\log p\left(y_h = y\right) \propto - \sum_{i=1}^{m} \left(\tilde{l}_i(y) - \bar{\mathbf{l}}^T \mathbf{u}_i\right)^2 / \lambda_i, \qquad (3)$$

where $\bar{\mathbf{l}}$ is the mean over the training vectors $\mathbf{l}_i$ and λ_i is the ith eigenvalue. The horizon is then estimated by maximizing this log probability over y.

The two free parameters of this method are the length n of the principal component filters and the number m of these filters to employ. We optimized these parameters by grid search over the training data (Fig. 8), finding $n = 300$ pixels and $m = 6$ to be optimal. Examples of horizon lines estimated on the test dataset are shown in Fig. 10(c–f).

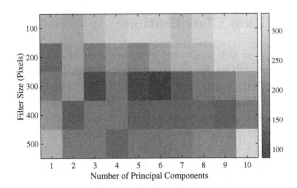

Fig. 8. Mean vertical location error in horizon estimate over training data, as a function of the length n and number m of principal components filters.

3.3   Region of Interest

The road vanishing point and horizon line provide crucial geometric constraints on the location of the road surface. To turn these constraints into an approximate segmentation of the road, we fuse them with a spatial prior that has been conditioned on the estimated vanishing point or horizon. Figure 9(a) shows the spatial prior, learned over the training dataset, without conditioning. The prior is quite diffuse, due not only to the variability in road geometry but also to the variation in camera placement. Figures 9(b–c) show the same prior, computed relative to the vanishing point location for images where a vanishing point can be identified (a) and relative to the horizon line for images where it cannot (c). Note that conditioning on the geometry leads to a more focused and accurate indicator of the road surface location.

In order to segment the road for a novel image, we first estimate the vanishing point. If the estimate is judged reliable, we register the associated prior (Fig. 9(b)) with the estimated vanishing point and label all pixels above a threshold probability p_0 to be road pixels. If the vanishing point is judged to be unreliable we follow the same procedure for the estimated horizon line and prior. If our vanishing point and horizon line estimates were perfectly accurate, a threshold of $p_0 = 0.5$ would maximize proportion correct pixel labelling (road/non-road). Figure 9(d) shows that our road segmentation algorithm performs substantially better than the method of Qian et al. [17], which involved simply thresholding the spatial prior, with no estimation of road geometry. This figure also confirms that a threshold of 0.5 works well in practice and is the value we adopt for road weather classification.

Figure 10 shows representative road segmentation results on the test dataset. There remain some failure modes for both road vanishing point and horizon detection, but generally speaking the results are good, as indicated by the median examples (b).

4   Road Condition Classification

To assess the utility of the improved road segmentation, we use it to define the region of interest (ROI) for road weather classification. In particular, we use an adaptation of the method of Qian et al. [17], which employs scale- and orientation-invariant MR8 filters [23]. These filters produce an 8-dimensional feature vector at each pixel in the ROI. Each ground truth ROI in the training set is divided into 8×8 pixel non-overlapping patches, each of which is then represented by an $8 \times 8 \times 8 = 512$-dimensional feature vector. K-means is then used to cluster the feature vectors from the training data into $k = 74$ textons.

While MR8 is roughly luminance-invariant, luminance can carry information about weather (snow is bright, wet roads tend to be darker). Qian et al. therefore augmented this texton descriptor with a 20-bin histogram of grey level deviations from the mean image luminance.

Qian et al. based their classifier on a naive Bayes model of exponential-χ^2 distances of input vectors from their class-conditional means. Here we take a

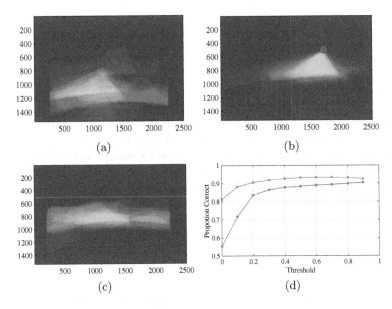

Fig. 9. (a) Prior spatial distribution of road pixels, in absolute image coordinates. (b) Prior horizontally and vertically registered to vanishing point. (c) Prior vertically registered to horizon. (d) Proportion of correctly labelled image pixels for the test set, as a function of the probability threshold p_0.

Fig. 10. Example road segmentations on the test dataset. Results are evaluated based on proportion of correctly labelled pixels (road/non-road). (a)–(c) show best, median and worst-case (failure mode) examples for cases where a vanishing point could be estimated. (d)–(f) show best, median and worst-case examples for cases where the vanishing point was deemed unreliable and a horizon estimator was used.

simpler approach, using an SVM with RBF kernel in a one-versus all design (the SVM implementation provided in the MATLAB Statistics and Machine Learning Toolbox). We found this to yield very similar results.

5   Performance Evaluation

Classification results on the test set for two classes (bare vs snow/ice covered), three classes (dry, wet, snow/ice covered) and five classes (dry, wet, snow, ice, packed) are shown in Fig. 11. We evaluate results using three different methods to define the ROI: (1) manual segmentation; (2) the automatic segmentation method proposed here; (3) automatic segmentation using the fixed prior of Fig. 9(a) [17]. As a baseline we also show performance for a classifier that simply selects the highest *a priori* probability. Note that the manual segmentation provides an upper bound on the possible payoff from further improvements to segmentation.

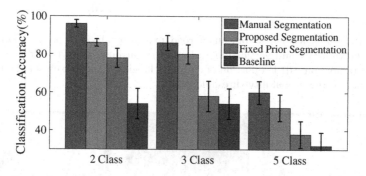

Fig. 11. Results comparison for 2, 3 and 5 classification using manual, Proposed Segmentation, Fixed prior segmentation against random guesses

Our proposed segmentation method achieved an accuracy of 86 % for two-classes, 80 % for three-classes, and 52 % for 5 classes. Given the challenging nature of the dataset, these are promising results.

The proposed segmentation method improves classification accuracy over the fixed segmentation method used by Qian et al. [17] in all cases. Statistical significance of this improvement can be assessed by computing the posterior probability that the underlying probability of correct classification is greater for our proposed method, assuming a flat prior over the performance for the two methods. This yields a posterior probability of 0.81 for the 2-class case, 0.99 for the 3-class case and 0.90 for the 5-class case, corresponding to p-values of .19, .01 and .10 in the language of null-hypothesis testing.

6   Summary

In this paper we have proposed a novel algorithm for road segmentation from uncalibrated dash cameras, to support road weather analysis. The algorithm was designed to operate robustly over a a diverse range of camera poses on both structured (highway/local road) and unstructured roads (parking lots). The approach consist of finding the vanish point, or horizon and fusing with a registered spatial prior. Classification performance on a challenging dataset was 86 % and 80 % for two- and three-class problems, respectively, representing a significant improvement over prior work [17]. Our analysis reveals that further improvements in performance will likely depend on improvements in both the segmentation and classification stages.

In recent years concern has been raised regarding the lack of generalization of traditional supervised road segmentation techniques, which tend to fail when facing situations not covered in the training set. To overcome this issue, attempts have been made to use online learning methods to adapt the parameters of the algorithm to the image data [1,22]. These methods typically assume that the bottom of the image projects from the road surface [1,2,7,22], which unfortunately is not the case for our dataset (Fig. 1). Nevertheless, this is an important issue, and we hope to increase the adaptiveness of our method in the near future.

References

1. Alvarez, J.M., Gevers, T., Lopez, A.M.: 3D scene priors for road detection. In: 2010 IEEE Conference on Computer Vision and Pattern Recognition (CVPR), pp. 57–64. IEEE (2010)
2. Álvarez, J.M., López, A.M.: Road detection based on illuminant invariance. IEEE Trans. Intell. Transp. Syst. **12**(1), 184–193 (2011)
3. Álvarez, J.M., López, A.M., Baldrich, R.: Shadow resistant road segmentation from a mobile monocular system. In: Martí, J., Benedí, J.M., Mendonça, A.M., Serrat, J. (eds.) IbPRIA 2007. LNCS, vol. 4478, pp. 9–16. Springer, Heidelberg (2007). doi:10.1007/978-3-540-72849-8_2
4. Amthor, M., Hartmann, B., Denzler, J.: Road condition estimation based on spatio-temporal reflection models. In: Gall, J., Gehler, P., Leibe, B. (eds.) GCPR 2015. LNCS, vol. 9358, pp. 3–15. Springer, Heidelberg (2015). doi:10.1007/978-3-319-24947-6_1
5. Casselgren, J.: Road surface classification using near infrared spectroscopy. Ph.D. thesis
6. Dahlkamp, H., Kaehler, A., Stavens, D., Thrun, S., Bradski, G.R.: Self-supervised monocular road detection in desert terrain. In: Proceedings of Robotics: Science and Systems, Philadelphia (2006)
7. De Cristóforis, P., Nitsche, M.A., Krajník, T., Mejail, M.: Real-time monocular image-based path detection. J. Real Time Image Process. **11**, 1–14 (2013)
8. Jokela, M., Kutila, M., Le, L.: Road condition monitoring system based on a stereo camera. In: IEEE 5th International Conference on Intelligent Computer Communication and Processing, ICCP 2009, pp. 423–428. IEEE (2009)
9. Jonsson, P.: Remote sensor for winter road surface status detection. In: Proceedings of 2011 IEEE Sensors, pp. 1285–1288. IEEE (2011)

10. Jonsson, P., Casselgren, J., Thornberg, B.: Road surface status classification using spectral analysis of NIR camera images. IEEE Sens. J. **15**(3), 1641–1656 (2015)
11. Kawai, S., Takeuchi, K., Shibata, K., Horita, Y.: A method to distinguish road surface conditions for car-mounted camera images at night-time. In: 2012 12th International Conference on ITS Telecommunications (ITST), pp. 668–672. IEEE (2012)
12. Kong, H., Audibert, J.Y., Ponce, J.: Vanishing point detection for road detection. In: IEEE Conference on Computer Vision and Pattern Recognition, CVPR 2009, pp. 96–103. IEEE (2009)
13. Kong, H., Audibert, J.Y., Ponce, J.: General road detection from a single image. IEEE Trans. Image Process. **19**(8), 2211–2220 (2010)
14. Lim, S.H., Ryu, S.K., Yoon, Y.H.: Image recognition of road surface conditions using polarization and wavelet transform. J. Korean Soc. Civil Eng. **27**(4D), 471–477 (2007)
15. Oliva, A., Torralba, A.: Modeling the shape of the scene: a holistic representation of the spatial envelope. Int. J. Comput. Vis. **42**(3), 145–175 (2001)
16. Omer, R., Fu, L.: An automatic image recognition system for winter road surface condition classification. In: 2010 13th International IEEE Conference on Intelligent Transportation Systems (ITSC), pp. 1375–1379. IEEE (2010)
17. Qian, Y., Almazan, E.J., Elder, J.H.: Evaluating features and classifiers for road weather condition analysis. In: 2016 IEEE International Conference on Image Processing (ICIP). IEEE (2016)
18. Rasmussen, C.: Grouping dominant orientations for ill-structured road following. In: Proceedings of the 2004 IEEE Computer Society Conference on Computer Vision and Pattern Recognition, CVPR 2004, vol. 1, pp. I-470. IEEE (2004)
19. Rasmussen, C.: Texture-based vanishing point voting for road shape estimation. In: BMVC, pp. 1–10. Citeseer (2004)
20. Suttorp, T., Bucher, T.: Robust vanishing point estimation for driver assistance. In: IEEE Intelligent Transportation Systems Conference, ITSC 2006, pp. 1550–1555. IEEE (2006)
21. Tal, R., Elder, J.H.: An accurate method for line detection and Manhattan frame estimation. In: Park, J.-I., Kim, J. (eds.) ACCV 2012. LNCS, vol. 7729, pp. 580–593. Springer, Heidelberg (2013). doi:10.1007/978-3-642-37484-5_47
22. Tan, C., Hong, T., Chang, T., Shneier, M.: Color model-based real-time learning for road following. In: IEEE Intelligent Transportation Systems Conference, ITSC 2006, pp. 939–944. IEEE (2006)
23. Varma, M., Zisserman, A.: Classifying images of materials: achieving viewpoint and illumination independence. In: Heyden, A., Sparr, G., Nielsen, M., Johansen, P. (eds.) ECCV 2002. LNCS, vol. 2352, pp. 255–271. Springer, Heidelberg (2002). doi:10.1007/3-540-47977-5_17. http://www.robots.ox.ac.uk/ vgg
24. Wang, Y., Teoh, E.K., Shen, D.: Lane detection and tracking using B-snake. Image Vis. Comput. **22**(4), 269–280 (2004)
25. Yang, H.J., Jang, H., Kang, J.W., Jeong, D.S.: Classification algorithm for road surface condition. IJCSNS **14**(1), 1 (2014)

Recognizing Text-Based Traffic Guide Panels with Cascaded Localization Network

Xuejian Rong[1], Chucai Yi[2], and Yingli Tian[1(✉)]

[1] The City College, City University of New York, New York, NY 10031, USA
{xrong,ytian}@ccny.cuny.edu
[2] HERE North America LLC, Chicago, IL 60606, USA
gschucai@gmail.com

Abstract. In this paper, we introduce a new top-down framework for automatic localization and recognition of text-based traffic guide panels (http://tinyurl.com/wiki-guide-signs) captured by car-mounted cameras from natural scene images. The proposed framework involves two contributions. First, a novel Cascaded Localization Network (CLN) joining two customized convolutional nets is proposed to detect the guide panels and the scene text on them in a coarse-to-fine manner. In this network, the popular character-wise text saliency detection is replaced with string-wise text region detection, which avoids numerous bottom-up processing steps such as character clustering and segmentation. Text information contained within detected text regions is then interpreted by a deep recurrent model without character segmentation required. Second, a temporal fusion of text region proposals across consecutive frames is introduced to significantly reduce the redundant computation in neighboring frames. A new challenging Traffic Guide Panel dataset is collected to train and evaluate the proposed framework, instead of the unsuited symbol-based traffic sign datasets. Experimental results demonstrate that our proposed framework outperforms multiple recently published text spotting frameworks in real highway scenarios.

Keywords: Road scene understanding · Traffic Guide Panel · Text spotting · Video OCR

1 Introduction

With the recent advances in vehicle intelligence, advanced driver assistance, and road surveying, the vehicle mounted systems are expected to have a deep understanding of the surrounding environment and provide reliable information for the drivers or autonomous navigation. As one of the most important context indicators in driving status, traffic signs (symbol-based or text-based) have attracted considerable attention in the fields of detection and recognition. Symbol-based traffic signs such as *Stop* or *Exit* signs usually have relatively smaller size and unique shape, while text-based traffic signs/panels often have a standard rectangular shape containing numerous text information.

© Springer International Publishing Switzerland 2016
G. Hua and H. Jégou (Eds.): ECCV 2016 Workshops, Part I, LNCS 9913, pp. 109–121, 2016.
DOI: 10.1007/978-3-319-46604-0_8

Most existing algorithms for traffic sign recognition were developed specifically for symbol-based traffic signs under limited conditions. Some systems demanded sophisticated hardware setup to capture high-resolution images, and others worked well on individual static frames but could not meet the efficiency requirement of the real-time video processing. Moreover, these methods usually ignored a large amount of valuable semantic information resided in the text-based traffic signs such as guide signs or panels, as shown in Fig. 1. The semantic information from guide panel could notify drivers or autonomous control systems of interchange, toll plaza, and exit direction. In most cases, this information is not completely available or up-to-date on car-mounted navigation systems.

Fig. 1. Samples of traffic guide panels and the corresponding text information in the highway environments.

In this paper, a framework is proposed to detect and recognize text-based traffic guide panels captured in highway environments (see examples in Fig. 1). This framework could help deliver the text information from guide panels to human drivers as head-up display information, and also to autonomous driving vehicles in case of un-updated digital mapping. On a set of continuous image frames, we first detect candidate traffic guide panels in each frame by using a set of learned convolutional neural network (CNN) features, and then eliminate false positive candidates by using temporal information from the continuous frames. The preliminary guide panel candidates are then further enhanced. Afterward, a fine CNN-based text detector is trained to localize all the detected text regions within the guide panel candidates. These text regions are finally recognized by a deep recurrent model in a sequence-to-sequence encoder-decoder fashion. Although several general scene text detection and recognition methods [1–3] have been developed to localize and recognize the text information in the natural scenes, most of these methods used exhaustive manner such as sliding window to search for all possible regions containing text information across an entire image. This process is time-consuming and error-prone, leading to more false alarms. The shape, color, and geometric cues of the traffic signs are not completely modeled in these approaches. In contrast, our proposed framework could largely reduce the searching space in each frame and improve the efficiency.

The remainder of the paper is organized as follows: Sect. 2 reviews related work on traffic sign reading and text spotting in the wild. Section 3 describes our methodology for localizing the traffic guide panels and corresponding scene texts, and the enhancement of the guide panels. The temporal information fusion of consecutive video frames, and the recognition of the detected text regions are described in details in Sect. 4. The collected highway traffic guide panels benchmark dataset and the experimental results are presented and discussed in Sect. 5. The proposed framework and future work are concluded in Sect. 6. It is worth noting that the single-word based guide signs (e.g., $STOP$ sign) are out of the scope of this paper since their inside text information is always fixed and they could be directly detected and recognized as specific types of traffic signs.

2   Related Work

In recent years, many researchers worked on the research topics associated with text extraction from natural scene images and its associated applications. Most state-of-the-art methods of scene text extraction [1, 2, 4–10] comprise two stages, detection to obtain image regions containing text information, and recognition to transform image-based text information into text codes. The detection methods could be further divided into three groups: region-based methods, e.g., [10], connected component based methods, e.g., [11–13], and convolutional neural network (CNN) based methods, e.g., [8]. Region-based text detection approaches rely on local features like the texture to locate text regions, while connected component-based methods focus on segmenting individual text characters using specific text patterns such as the intensity, colors, and edges. And CNN-based approaches usually attempt to generate the character saliency maps based on the extracted CNN features on multiple scales, and apply clustering afterward.

For the text recognition, a number of techniques [9, 14, 15] have been reported which follow a bottom-up fashion to train their own scene character classifiers. The recognized characters are then grouped into a word based on the context information, while some errors including spelling and ambiguities are recovered by incorporating the Lexicon and n-gram language model. Most of these methods require robust and accurate character-level segmentation and recognition. To avoid the above numerous local computation, several methods based on recurrent neural network (RNN) with long short-term memory (LSTM) are recently proposed [16,17], which model a word image as an unsegmented sequence and does not require character-level segmentation and recognition.

Although scene text extraction has been a fairly popular research field, there are a limited number of publications that specifically concentrated on the extraction of text information from traffic guide signs and panels captured in the form of continuous frames by car-mounted cameras. The main challenges which prevent the exploration might be the wide diversity of the information contained within traffic panels which are difficult to analyze, and the computation complexity of the popular text extraction approaches which cannot meet the efficiency requirement in realistic environments.

Specifically, Gonzlez et al. [18] attempted to use maximally stable extremal regions (MSERs) to detect both traffic signs and text characters. The traffic panels were detected in each frame based on color segmentation and bag of visual words, and the detected regions were further classified using both support vector machines and Naive Bayes classifiers. However, this method was only applied to the single frame and ignored the temporal information. Greenhalgh et al. [19] introduced more scene cues like the scene structure to define search regions within each frame, and exhaustedly located a large number of guide sign candidates using MSERs, hue, saturation and value color thresholding. The text characters contained within detected candidate regions are further detected as MSERs and grouped into lines, before being interpreted with optical character recognition (OCR) engines. This approach outperforms previous methods, but is still sophisticated and computationally expensive. Notice, these methods mainly only focus on locating the general traffic signs and rely on the OCR engines for the following text detection and recognition inside the guide signs. However, our proposed method attempts to provide more accurate and useful text region proposals and their interpretation besides the basic guide panel locations which are relatively meaningless to the drivers or autonomous driving systems.

For the system validation, several datasets have also been proposed, including the German traffic sign detection benchmark [20], the German traffic sign recognition benchmark [21], and the Belgian traffic sign dataset [22]. However, these datasets focus on the detection of the symbol-based traffic sign, and therefore not applicable to the validation for extracting text information from the guide panel.

3   Cascaded Localization of Text-Based Guide Panels

In this section, the localization process of the traffic guide panels and the text regions within are presented. The enhancement of the preliminarily localized guide panels is also described. Specifically, to accurately and efficiently localize the guide panels and text regions of interest, we establish a two-stage cascaded framework, and model each stage as a unified detection process, inspired by the You Only Look Once (YOLO) detector [23]. The first stage of the proposed Cascaded Localization Network (CLN) aims to find all the guide panels candidates with a high recall rate, and the second stage focuses on the accurate localization

Fig. 2. Demonstration of localizing guide panel candidates. The highlighted grids in orange represent where the center of the guide panel falls into, and predict the exact shape of the corresponding bounding box. The green bounding box represents the final regressed shape of the panel prediction. The input resolution of the first layer of the guide panel localization net is 448 × 448. And the total number of grids is 7 × 7 = 49. (Color figure online)

of the text regions and eliminates the false alarms, including the non-panel and redundant detections, with the text localization results.

3.1 Unified Localization of Traffic Guide Panels

For an image frame captured at the highway, we first search for all the possible locations of traffic guide panels by integrating the separate components of object detection into a single neural network. Therefore the network reasons globally about the full image and all the candidates, and predicts all the bounding boxes simultaneously. In practice, the detector first evenly divides the input highway scene image (rescaled to 448 × 448) into a $S \times S$ grid, in which each grid cell is responsible for detecting and localizing the guide panel whose center falls into this grid cell, by predicting B bounding boxes and confidence scores for those boxes. The confidence scores represent the probability of the box containing a guide panel and also the accuracy of the box prediction. The confidence is formally defined as $Pr(Panel) * IoU_{Pre}^{GT}$, which would be forced to zero if there is no object existing in the cell, and otherwise equal the intersection over union (IoU) between the predicted box and the ground truth.

Different from the original YOLO detector, here each bounding box is composed of 7 predictions: $\{x, y, w, h, \cos\theta, \sin\theta\}$ and the presence confidence. The (x, y) coordinates and the width/height (w, h) denote respectively the location (center of the box w.r.t. the bounds of the grid cell) and size of a bounding box tightly enclosing the guide panel. θ represents the bounding box rotation. And the presence confidence denotes the IoU between the predicted guide panel bounding box and any ground truth bounding box. The implementation details of this localization network are as follows. We set $S = 7, B = 2$ in the experiments on the newly collected Traffic Guide Panel dataset. The final prediction is a $S \times S \times (B*7+1) = 7 \times 7 \times 15$ tensor. To boost the efficiency of the localization process, this network has 9 convolutional layers followed by 2 fully connected layers w.r.t. the 24 convolutional layers used in regular YOLO detector. We pretrain our convolutional layers on the ImageNet 1000-class competition dataset [24], and fine-tune the model on the training set of the Traffic Guide Panel dataset including the ground truth annotations for all the text-based traffic guide panels. The localization results are illustrated in Fig. 2.

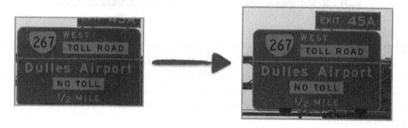

Fig. 3. Illustration of the enhancement of initial localized guide panels by extending each edge of the bounding box with 20 %.

Compared with previously CNN-based object detection approaches which attempt to generate the saliency map and verify the clustered bounding box for specific object category, here the regression-based guide panel detector directly outputs the localization results without extra panel/non-panel classification. The generated bounding boxes of guide panels are then enlarged by 20 % to each side, as illustrated in Fig. 3, since the predicted panel bounding boxes, are sometimes too tight which will affect the following text region localization. In addition, this enlargement is able to make up missing parts of guide panels from small bounding boxes. This process also involves context information of the guide panels to benefit the following recognition stage.

3.2   Fine Text Region Localization

In this section, we introduce the second stage CNN architecture of the cascaded localization network for text region localization in the enhanced guide panel image patches. This stage also follows the strategy of the YOLO detector and

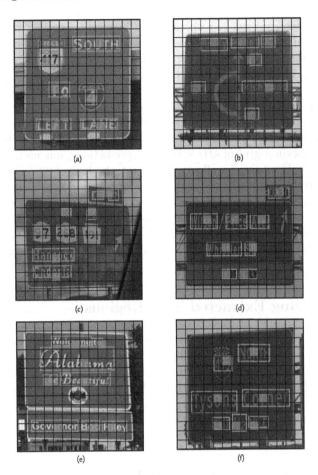

Fig. 4. Localization results of the text region candidates within detected traffic guide panels. The highlighted grids in orange predict the exact shape of the bounding box, and represent where the center of the text region candidates fall into. The green bounding boxes represent the finally regressed shape of the text region prediction. The red dashed bounding boxes represent the missed ground truth text region. (Color figure online)

its variant [25] by constructing a fixed field of predictors, each of which specializes in predicting the presence of a word string around a specific image location. To better localize the text regions instead of the general objects, additional Hough Voting predictor is implemented to pool evidence from the whole image. Since the text occurrences are usually smaller and more variable compared to general objects, the grid number is also increased from $G_I = 7$ to $G_I = 14$ to solve the problems. In details, the architecture comprised 9 convolutional layers, each of which is followed by the Rectified Linear Unit non-linearity (ReLU), four of which by a max-pooling layer (2×2, with a stride of 2). The stride of all linear filters is 1, and the resolution of feature maps is kept through zero padding.

In testing each grid cell is responsible to localize a word string if the word center falls within this cell, by regressing five numbers: the text region presence confidence c, and the other four parameters $p = (x, y, w, h)$, where the (x, y) coordinates represent the text location (center of the box w.r.t. the bounds of the grid cell), and the width and height (w, h) represent the size of the text region. Here we do not need to predict the bounding box rotations of multiple text regions as in [25], since all the text lines are parallel to the edge of the guide panels based on observation. Therefore, for an input guide panel patch of size $H_I \times W_I$, we obtain a grid of $(H_I \times W_I)/\Sigma^2$ predictions, one each for an image cell of size $\Sigma \times \Sigma$ pixels. To effectively detect the large text instances in the guide panel, we further apply the text region localization net on multiple scales. The input image is first downsampled by factors $\{1, 1/2, 1/4\}$, and the localization results at multiple down-scaled levels of the input image are finally merged via non-maximal suppression. In two overlapping detections, the one with the lower probability is suppressed. The final localization results are demonstrated in Fig. 4.

4   Recognizing Extracted Text Regions

On the localized guide panels and their text regions from a sequence of continuous frames, text recognition is performed to extract readable text codes. The temporal information across continuous frames is modeled to reduce the computation cost and eliminate the false alarms. This fusion step is unnecessary if the proposed localization pipeline is applied on a static image or individual frame. A deep recurrent model is then introduced to directly recognize all the localized text regions.

4.1   Temporal Fusion in Consecutive Frames

In the practical driving process, the proposed cascaded localization networks should run on each of the continuous frames captured from the car-mounted camera/recorder, and the occurrence of the guide panels would be relatively rare in a long frame sequence. Moreover, the resolution and quality of the guide panel would gradually increase as car proceeded close and then suddenly vanish. Therefore, it would be computationally time-consuming and unnecessary to apply all the cascaded localization stages for every video frame as many previous traffic sign detection methods [13, 18, 19].

In our experiments, only the guide panel localizer is applied on each frame, and the enhancement and text region localizer are only applied in the last t frames, where the actual value of t is determined by the trade-off between the effective text recognition time and average text recognition accuracy. The last available frame is determined by the distance between the guide panel image patch and the three image boundaries (top, left, and right). Some specific localization results are regarded as false alarms if they are not successfully localized by the guide panels at the last t frames. In our test, $t = 10$ works well for the fusion process, which usually takes $1/6 \sim 1/3$ of the whole time of successful panel detection in the highway environments.

4.2 Recognizing Text Regions with Deep Recurrent Model

After the finally refined text regions are generated, the text recognition process is modeled as a sequence labeling problem by using a deep recurrent model. In the traditional framework of text recognition in traffic signs or license plates, character segmentation has a great influence on the success of recognition. The text information would be recognized incorrectly if the segmentation is improper, even if a high-performance character recognizer is adopted. Here we model the text region recognition problem as a single-pass sequence labeling process. In details, each input text region x ideally contain a piece of text with horizontal orientation from left to right. The overall procedure of the sequence labeling based text region recognition starts with converting the text region bounding box into a sequence of feature vectors which are extracted by using the pre-trained 9-layer CNN model sliding across the bounding box. Afterward, a bi-directional recurrent neural network (RNN) model with long short-term memory (LSTM) is trained to label the sequence features, with stochastic gradient descent (SGD) algorithm. Connectionist temporal classification is applied at last to the output layer of RNN to analyze the labeling results of RNN and generate the final recognition result. The recognition process is demonstrated in Fig. 5.

5 Experimental Results

In this section, experiments are performed to verify the effectiveness of the proposed Cascaded Localization Network on new Traffic Guide Panel dataset which

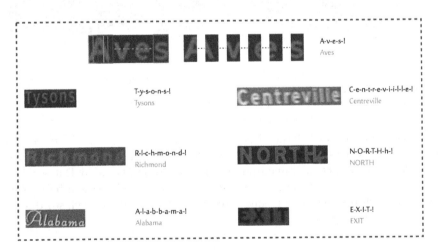

Fig. 5. The sequence-to-sequence encoder-decoder recognition demonstration of the extracted text region candidates.

contains a variety of individual highway guide panels, compared with multiple recent text spotting approaches in the realistic highway scenes.

Benchmark Dataset. Since there is no publicly available dataset specifically on traffic guide panels, we collect a new challenging dataset of traffic guide panels at the highway. This dataset contains a variety of highway guide panels {3841 high-resolution individual images in total, 2315 containing traffic guide panel level annotations (1911 for training and 404 for testing, and all the testing images are manually labeled with ground truth tight text region bounding boxes), 1526 containing no traffic signs}. All the images are collected from *AAroads* website[1], and captured from the view of car-mounted dash camera, including numerous kinds of traffic guide panel such as direction, toll plaza, destination distance, and exit indication.

Fig. 6. Comparison of the Top-5 text region localization proposals from the proposed approach and the best competing baseline method [8].

In the experiments, all the traffic guide panel annotations in 1911 of the 2315 images are used to fine-tune the guide panel localization net. The text region localization net is trained on the SynthText in the Wild Dataset [25], which consisted of 800 k images with approximately 8 million synthetic word instances. Each text instance is annotated with its text-string-level, word-level, and character-level bounding boxes.

---

[1] http://www.aaroads.com.

Table 1. Text localization results and average processing times on the Traffic Guide Panel dataset. Precision P and recall R at the maximum f-measure F, and the localization time t_l (in seconds).

Method	P	R	F	t_l
Proposed	**0.73**	0.64	**0.68**	0.16
Jaderberg et al. [8]	0.59	**0.71**	0.64	4.53
Gomez et al. [26]	0.46	0.53	0.49	1.32
Epshtein et al. [11]	0.35	0.41	0.38	2.51

(a)   (b)

Fig. 7. Failure cases of the proposed Cascaded Localization Networks due to kinds of image degradations, e.g., reflection and occlusion.

Comparison to Existing Methods. First our proposed approach is compared with three recent methods for lexicon-free text detection.

- Stroke Width Transform, Epshtein et al. [11]: a well-known method[2] that leverages the consistency of characters' stroke width to detect arbitrary fonts.
- MSER Text Detection, Gomez et al. [26]: uses maximally stable extremal regions (MSERs), a popular tool in text detection[3], which is combined with a perceptual organization framework.
- Deep Text Spotting, Jaderberg et al. [8]: a state-of-the-art method[4] that uses multiple stages of convolutional neural networks to predict text saliency score at each pixel, and cluster to form the region predictions afterward.

For the first two methods, the outputs are ranked by the bounding box size, which is a sensible way to favor the more prominent detected texts since the codes do not produce confidence values. For [8], the summed text saliency

---

[2] https://github.com/lluisgomez/DetectText.
[3] https://github.com/lluisgomez/text_extraction.
[4] https://bitbucket.org/jaderberg/eccv2014_textspotting.

scores are used for candidates ranking. Table 1 shows the text localization performance and computation efficiency (i.e., average processing time) on a standard PC with dual 3.2 GHz CPU and a NVIDIA Geforce Titan X GPU. We follow the standard PASCAL VOC detect criterion: a detection is correct if the IoU between its bounding box and the ground truth exceeds 50 %. Overall, our method outperforms the existing text localization methods in the highway environments, and the gains over the two non-learning methods [11, 26] are large in terms of f-measure. Moreover, the proposed method outperforms the conventional R-CNN based text detection approach [8] on the precision and f-measure, and is comparable in terms of recall rate. As to the computation efficiency, due to the straightforward and precise regression architect, the proposed cascaded localization network performs significantly faster than the previous learning and non-learning methods.

Qualitative Examples. Finally, we present text detection examples in Fig. 6 to qualitatively demonstrate the performance of the proposed approach and the best competing baseline [8]. These images illustrate the advantages of our proposed method for narrowing down the search space and improving the computation efficiency. Failure cases in certain frames caused by image degradations, such as uneven illumination, reflection, and occlusion, are demonstrated in Fig. 7. However, these localization results could be effectively eliminated through temporal fusion in practice.

6   Conclusion and Future Work

In this paper, we have presented a new top-down CNN-based cascaded framework for automatic detection and recognition of text-based traffic guide panels in the wild. The proposed framework performed in an efficient coarse-to-fine manner, and effectively reduced the redundant computation in continuous frames. The future work will focus on further improving the accuracy and efficiency of the cascaded localization network on traffic guide panels, and extending the newly collected text-based guide panel dataset to a larger scale for future validation and comparison.

Acknowledgement. This work was supported in part by NSF grants EFRI-1137172, IIP-1343402, and FHWA grant DTFH61-12-H-00002.

References

1. Ye, Q., Doermann, D.: Text detection and recognition in imagery: a survey. IEEE Trans. Pattern Anal. Mach. Intell. **37**(7), 1480–1500 (2015)
2. Yin, X., Zuo, Z., Tian, S., Liu, C.: Text detection, tracking and recognition in video: a comprehensive survey. IEEE Trans. Image Process. **25**(6), 2752–2773 (2016)
3. Zhu, Y., Yao, C., Bai, X.: Scene text detection and recognition: recent advances and future trends. Front. Comput. Sci. **10**(1), 19–36 (2016)

4. Zhang, Z., Zhang, C., Shen, W., Yao, C., Liu, W., Bai, X.: Multi-oriented text detection with fully convolutional networks. arXiv.org, April 2016

5. Qin, S., Manduchi, R.: A fast and robust text spotter. In: WACV (2016)

6. Zini, L., Odone, F.: Portable and fast text detection. Mach. Vis. Appl. **27**, 1–15 (2016)

7. Jaderberg, M., Simonyan, K., Vedaldi, A., Zisserman, A.: Reading text in the wild with convolutional neural networks. Int. J. Comput. Vis. **116**(1), 1–20 (2015)

8. Jaderberg, M., Vedaldi, A., Zisserman, A.: Deep features for text spotting. In: Fleet, D., Pajdla, T., Schiele, B., Tuytelaars, T. (eds.) ECCV 2014. LNCS, vol. 8692, pp. 512–528. Springer, Heidelberg (2014). doi:10.1007/978-3-319-10593-2_34

9. Neumann, L., Matas, J.: Efficient scene text localization and recognition with local character refinement. arXiv.org (2015)

10. Yin, X., Yin, X., Huang, K., Hao, H.: Robust text detection in natural scene images. IEEE Trans. Pattern Anal. Mach. Intell. **36**(5), 970–983 (2014)

11. Epshtein, B., Eyal, O., Yonatan, W.: Detecting text in natural scenes with stroke width transform. In: CVPR (2010)

12. Yi, C., Tian, Y., Arditi, A.: Portable camera-based assistive text and product label reading from hand-held objects for blind persons. IEEE/ASME Trans. Mechatron. **19**(3), 808–817 (2014)

13. Wu, W., Chen, X., Yang, J.: Detection of text on road signs from video. IEEE Trans. Intell. Transp. Syst. **6**, 378 (2005)

14. Wang, T., Wu, J., Coates, A., Ng, A.: End-to-end text recognition with convolutional neural networks. In: ICPR (2012)

15. Rong, X., Yi, C., Yang, X., Tian, Y.: Scene text recognition in multiple frames based on text tracking (2014)

16. Su, B., Lu, S.: Accurate scene text recognition based on recurrent neural network. In: Cremers, D., Reid, I., Saito, H., Yang, M.-H. (eds.) ACCV 2014. LNCS, vol. 9003, pp. 35–48. Springer, Heidelberg (2015). doi:10.1007/978-3-319-16865-4_3

17. Shi, B., Wang, X., Lv, P., Yao, C., Bai, X.: Robust scene text recognition with automatic rectification. arXiv.org, March 2016

18. Gonzalez, A., Bergasa, L., Yebes, J.: Text detection and reocnition on traffic panels from street-level imagery using visual apperance. IEEE Trans. Intell. Transp. Syst. **15**(1), 228–238 (2014)

19. Greenhalgh, J., Mirmehdi, M.: Real-time detection and recognition of road traffic signs. IEEE Trans. Intell. Transp. Syst. **16**(3), 1360–1369 (2012)

20. Houben, S., Stallkamp, J., Salmen, J., Schlipsing, M., Igel, C.: Detection of traffic signs in real-world images: the German traffic sign detection benchmark. In: Proceedings IJCNN, 1–8 August 2013

21. Stallkamp, J., Schlipsing, M., Salmen, J., Igel, C.: The German traffic sign recognition benchmark: a multi-class classification competition. In: Proceedings of IJCNN, pp. 1453–1460, July 2013

22. Timofte, R., Zimmermann, K., Gool, L.V.: Multi-view traffic sign detection, recognition, 3D localisation. In: WACV (2009)

23. Redmon, J., Divvala, S., Girshick, R., Farhadi, A.: You only look once: unified real-time object detection. In: CVPR (2016)

24. Krizhevsky, A., Sutskever, I., Hinton, G.E.: Imagenet classification with deep convolutional neural networks. In: NIPS, pp. 1097–1105 (2012)

25. Gupta, A., Vedaldi, A., Zisserman, A.: Synthetic data for text localisation in natural images. arXiv.org, April 2016

26. Gomez, L., Karatzas, D.: Multi-script text extraction from natural scenes. In: ICDAR(2013)

The Automatic Blind Spot Camera:
A Vision-Based Active Alarm System

Kristof Van Beeck[✉] and Toon Goedemé

EAVISE, KU Leuven, Technology Campus De Nayer, Sint-Katelijne-Waver, Belgium
{kristof.vanbeeck,toon.goedeme}@kuleuven.be

Abstract. In this paper we present a vision-based active safety system targeting the blind spot zone of trucks. Each year, these blind spot accidents are responsible for numerous fatalities and heavily injured. Existing commercial systems seem not to be able to cope with this problem completely. Therefore, we propose a vision-based safety system relying solely on the blind spot camera images. Our system is able to detect all vulnerable road users (VRUs) in the blind spot zone, and automatically generates an alarm towards the truck driver. This inherently is a challenging task. Indeed, such active safety system implicitly requires extremely high accuracy demands at very low latency. These two demands are contradictory, and thus very difficult to unite. However, our real-life experiments show that our proposed active alarm system achieves excellent accuracy results while meeting these stringent requirements.

Keywords: Computer vision · Real-time · Active safety systems

1 Introduction and Related Work

Each year the blind spot zone of trucks is responsible for an estimate of about 1300 casualties in Europe alone [9]. These accidents almost always occur in a similar fashion: the truck driver takes a right hand turn at an intersection and overlooks vulnerable road users (VRUs – e.g. pedestrians or bicyclists) which continue their way straight ahead. They have one of two distinctive causes: inattentiveness of the truck driver or the fact that these victims were located in a blind spot zone around the truck. Several such zones around the truck exist where the driver has only limited or no view. Evidently, the zone starting from the front right corner of the truck's cabin which extends further to the right hand side of truck is the most crucial one. To cope with these blind spot zones, several commercial systems were developed. However, each of them has specific disadvantages, and as such none of them seem to handle this blind spot problem completely. These commercial systems can be subdivided into two main groups: *passive* and *active* systems. Passive safety systems still rely on the attentiveness of the truck driver himself. The most widely used passive systems are the – since 2003 obliged by law – blind spot mirrors. However, their introduction did not resulted in a decrease in the number of casualties [14]. A second passive safety

© Springer International Publishing Switzerland 2016
G. Hua and H. Jégou (Eds.): ECCV 2016 Workshops, Part I, LNCS 9913, pp. 122–135, 2016.
DOI: 10.1007/978-3-319-46604-0_9

system is found in passive blind spot cameras. These systems are mounted in a robust manner and – using wide-angle lenses – display the blind spot zone on a monitor in the truck's cabin when a right hand turn is signalled. However, these systems again rely on the attentiveness of the truck driver. Active safety systems automatically generate an auditive, visual or haptic alarm signal towards the truck driver (e.g. ultrasonic distance sensors) and as such avoid this disadvantage. However, existing active safety systems are unable to *interpret* the environment. No distinguishment between static objects (e.g. traffic signs) and VRUs is made, and often false positive alarms are generated. As such, the truck driver experiences this as annoying, and tends to disable the system. To overcome the aforementioned challenges, we present an active safety system relying solely on the input images from the blind spot camera. Using computer vision object detection methodologies, our system is able to efficiently detect VRUs in these challenging blind spot images, and automatically warns the truck driver of their presence. Such a system eliminates all disadvantages mentioned above: it is always adjusted correctly, is easily integratable in existing passive blind spot camera setups, does not rely on the attentiveness of the truck driver and implicitly provides some scene understanding. However, this is not an easy task. Indeed, these VRUs are multiclass (they consist of pedestrians, bicyclists, children and so on) and appear in very different viewpoints and poses. Furthermore excellent accuracy results need to be achieved for such a system to be usable in real-life scenarios. However, achieving high accuracy often comes at the cost of high computational complexity. This is unfeasible for our application: we aim to develop an active safety system which runs in real-time on low-cost embedded hardware. Additionally, we need to cope with the large viewpoint and lens distortion induced by traditional blind spot cameras. As a starting point, we employ the vanilla implementation of a VRU detection and tracking framework that we proposed in previous work [16], able to efficiently detect and track both pedestrians and bicyclists in these challenging blind spot camera images. However, currently this framework focuses on the aspect of VRU detection and tracking only. As such, the framework remains far away from a total active safety system. Therefore, in this paper we extend, polish and elevate this tracking-by-detection VRU framework into such an active alarm system. We present extensive real-life experiments and indicate that our final active alarm system meets the stringent requirements that such a system should achieve to be usable in practice.

To efficiently generate an alarm, we employ object detection algorithms that enable the detection of vulnerable road users in the blind spot images. A vast amount or literature concerning pedestrian detection exists. Since a detailed discussion is out of the scope of this work, we refer the reader to [1,6–8,18] for an extensive overview on the evolution of different pedestrian detectors. Several works exist which perform pedestrian and bicycle detection specifically for traffic safety applications, and are thus related to our work. However, to the best of our knowledge, no publications exist which explicitly discuss accuracy and usability results at safety system level. Furthermore only forward-looking cameras [3,13] or stationary cameras [15] are used. Indeed, traditionally only forward-looking

Fig. 1. Our final active alarm system. See http://youtu.be/0S-uEPA_R5w.

datasets are employed. The images in Fig. 1 display example frames of the blind spot safety application we target here. As seen, the specific viewpoint and lens distortion significantly increases the difficulty. The remainder of this paper is structured as follows. In Sect. 2 we briefly discuss the vanilla implementation of [16] which we use as our baseline. In Sect. 3 we then discuss our extension, and elevate this baseline framework into a complete active safety system. We present accuracy results at system level. Based on these results, we discuss the usability of our safety system for real-life scenarios in Sect. 4. We conclude this paper and discuss future work in Sect. 5.

2   Baseline Algorithm

As baseline framework we start from the VRU detection and tracking framework for blind spot camera images presented in [16]. An overview of this VRU detection and tracking framework is visualised in Fig. 2. In a nutshell, the framework works as follows. As seen in the images of Fig. 1, the vulnerable road users appear distorted, rotated and scaled based on the position in the image. This scene knowledge is exploited as follows. We assume that the blind spot camera is mounted at a fixed position w.r.t. the ground plane. In this case, the exact transformation only depends on the position in the image. During an offline calibration, this distortion is modelled as a perspective transformation. Thus, for each region of interest (ROI) in the input image the transformation due to the viewpoint distortion is locally modelled. Based on this information each ROI is rewarped to an upright, undistorted fixed-height image patch. Since the scale is fixed, only a single search scale needs to be evaluated for the detection models. Next, image features are extracted on this rewarped patch. Three different detection models are evaluated. As object detection methodology, the deformable part based models (DPM) are employed [10,11]. Apart from the standard pedestrian model, an upper body model and one of three bicycle components (i.e. different viewpoint) – selected depending on the position in the image – are evaluated. This upper body model, combined with a bicycle model enables the efficient detection of bicyclists. For each of these three models a probability map is generated. These hypothesis maps are then combined into a single detection probability map for that image patch. Finally, to cope with missing detections these detection maps are integrated in a tracking-by-detection methodology. For this,

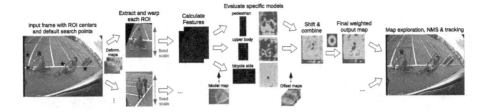

Fig. 2. An overview of the baseline blind spot VRU detection algorithm [16].

at strategic positions in the image initial search locations are defined (indicated with the black asterisks in Fig. 2). Each of these initial search locations is evaluated in each frame. If a VRU is found, a Kalman filter is instantiated based on a constant velocity motion model. In future frames, the next location is predicted and evaluated using the detection pipeline discussed above.

3   An Active Vision-Based Blind Spot Safety System

Our VRU detection and tracking framework from [16] is able to detect and track both pedestrians and bicyclists with high accuracy at reasonable processing speeds. Here we now elevate the tracking-by-detection methodology into an active safety system, and present extensive experiments as such. In its current form the existing framework has several caveats which need to be tackled first. Currently, the calculation time is non-deterministic. The tracking-by-detection framework relies on initial search coordinates which are defined at strategic positions in the image. When VRUs are detected at these positions, a new track is instantiated and evaluated in the consecutive frames. This approach thus implies that the processing speed depends on the number of tracks that are evaluated. Such non-deterministic behaviour is not suited for hard real-time applications where predictable *latency* and *processing speed* are of crucial importance. We must be able to guarantee that the system reacts within a constant time. Therefore, in Subsect. 3.1 we propose a methodology which tackles the non-deterministic behaviour of this framework. In Subsect. 3.2 we then elevate the tracking approach, convert it into a final active alarm system and present accuracy experiments as such.

3.1   Deterministic Calculation Time

We first define a blind spot zone in the image in which all pedestrians and bicyclists ought to be detected. Determining this zone correctly is of crucial importance for the effectiveness of our final alarm system. A strong correlation exists between the size of this detection zone and the latency of our final detection system. Most accidents occur when the truck makes a right turn without noticing pedestrians or bicyclists that continue their way straight ahead. Research indicates that it takes a worst-case reaction time of about 1.5 s for a

Fig. 3. Blind spot zone.   **Fig. 4.** 4 × 3 search grid.   **Fig. 5.** 5 × 4 search grid.
(Color figure online)

truck driver to react when confronted with an event and undertake the effective break action [4]. Thus, an early detection of the VRUs is crucial. For this, a large detection zone is needed, which ideally starts far behind the truck itself. In such scenarios, e.g. fast moving bicyclists are detected early and enough time remains for the truck driver to interpret the alarm signals and undertake a corresponding action. However, such a large detection zone requires significant calculation power. Indeed, the size of this blind spot detection zone essentially determines a trade-off between the latency of our alarm system and the required computation power. To perform our consecutive validation experiments, we constructed a detection zone denoted in red in Fig. 3 (on the ground plane). All VRUs which enter this zone (approximately 6.60 m by 2.60 m) ought to be detected as soon as possible. The vanilla implementation performs the transformation based on the centroids of the VRUs. Therefore, we define the slightly larger and higher positioned detection zone displayed in green.

We now determine fixed search points within this previously defined (green) blind spot zone. At each point we perform the exact same approach as in [16]. Note that we still employ the tracking-by-detecting approach to cope with missing detections and to increase the robustness. However, we do not utilise the predicted Kalman future locations as input to our warping framework. These future locations are now only used to match detections from the previous frames in future frames. This is needed to cope with missing detections (e.g. in between two search points). Evidently, since the number of search points now is fixed, the calculation time becomes deterministic. We positioned these search points on a linear grid distributed in the above mentioned green detection zone. Evidently, the number of grid points determines a trade-off between the computational complexity and the accuracy. To determine this trade-off we evaluated the performance of five different grids, ranging from dense to fine: a 3 × 3 grid, a 4 × 3 grid, a 4 × 4 grid, a 5 × 4 grid and finally a 5 × 5 grid. As an example, two of these grids are visualised in Figs. 4 and 5. However, due to the non-linear distortion and specific viewpoint a linear grid does not represent the most optimal distribution. Therefore we developed an algorithm which splits up the blind spot zone in segments of optimal sizes, taking into account the rotation and scale robustness of our detector. For this we first we evaluated the invariance of our deformable part detectors with respect to both rotation and scale variation. These results are visualised in Figs. 6 and 7. As seen, slight variations on both

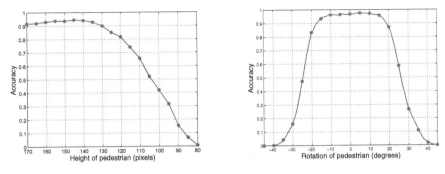

Fig. 6. Acc. of DPM vs. height.   **Fig. 7.** Acc. of DPM vs. rotation.

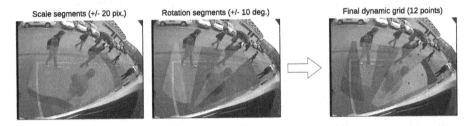

Fig. 8. The construction of the dynamic search grid.

the exact height and rotation cause negligible loss in accuracy. Based on these results, the delineated blind spot zone is segmented and search points are determined automatically as visualised in Fig. 8. This results in a grid of 12 points, which we coined the *dynamic grid*. We executed thorough experiments concerning both accuracy and speed when using these detection grids. To validate our algorithms we recorded real-life experiments using a commercially available blind spot camera (Orlaco 115°) and a genuine truck (Volvo FM12). For this, several dangerous blind spot scenarios were simulated, including both pedestrians and bicyclists. Our final test set consists of about 5500 blind spot image frames, in which about 8000 VRUs were labelled. Since we now only detect VRUs in this delineated blind spot zone, we evidently discard all annotations outside this zone. About 42 % of all annotations are maintained. Figure 9 displays these accuracy results for all grids, and the original tracking-by-detection accuracy. The dashed black line indicates the accuracy of the VRU tracking-by-detection implementation from [16] which relies on initial search coordinates without the use of our blind spot zone. The full black line displays the accuracy for this original implementation when only taking into account detections and annotations in the blind spot zone as discussed above. As seen, a significant gain in accuracy is achieved. When only detecting the VRUs in the delineated blind spot zone, the framework achieves an average precision of 91.92 %. This is due to multiple reasons. Annotations far outside the blind spot zone are difficult to detect, since they are very small. Furthermore, several different annotators were involved.

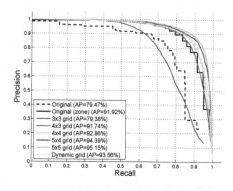 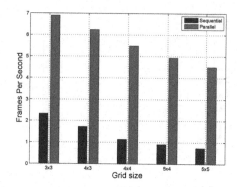

Fig. 9. Acc. when using fixed grids.   **Fig. 10.** Speed when using fixed grids.

This induced that often the exact location behind the truck, where the annotations start, significantly diverges between different sets. Due to the position of the initial search points in the tracking-by-detection framework, sometimes it was unfeasible to detect specific pedestrian or VRUs early enough. As seen, the 3×3 grid evidently is not dense enough. Similar accuracy performance as to the original tracking-by-detection framework is achieved with a grid of 4×3 points. Apart from the deterministic calculation time, these grids have another significant advantage over the standard tracking-by-detection framework. There, a VRU that is being tracked might be lost if for multiple frames in a row no detection is found (e.g. due to occlusions). No new search point is predicted in such cases. When using this default grid, tracks are much more easily recovered. Furthermore, we also performed experiments with additional datasets which include children. Our experiments indicated that, apart from adults, our approach is able to efficiently detect children without the need for additional search scales. This is due to the perspective transformation: when enough search points are utilised the probability that a child incidentally is retransformed to the fixed adult scale increases. Note that the accuracy results of Fig. 9 are still on single VRU detection capacity, the accuracy of the overarching blind spot alarming system is to be discussed in the next subsection.

Figure 10 displays the processing speed when using the fixed detection grids in the delineated blind spot zone. The evaluation is performed on an Intel Xeon E5 CPU at 3.1 GHz. The framework is mainly implemented in Matlab with time-consuming parts in both C and OpenCV. We tested both a sequential and a parallel implementation of our framework. Parallelisation was simply obtained by evaluating each grid point on a parallel CPU core. When using for example a 4×3 grid (an identical size to the dynamic grid), we achieve a parallel processing speed of 6.2 frames per second (FPS). However, even when evaluated in parallel, increasing the size of the detection grid lowers the detection speed. Note that we still employ Matlab which implies that multi-threaded processing and the data transfer between different threads is far from optimal.

3.2   Final Safety System

We now elevate the tracking-by-detection framework towards an autonomous active safety system. We step away from individual bounding boxes for each VRU, and generate an alarm if one or more VRUs are detected in the blind spot zone delineated as discussed above. Figure 1 shows how our final alarm system currently displays the detection of VRUs in the blind spot zone. For each frame we determine if an alarm needs to be generated. For validation we thus classify each frame as a *true positive* (TP), *false positive* (FP), *false negative* (FN) and *true negative* (TN). Thus, for each frame, we validate the effectiveness of our system. This is far from ideal, since no temporal information is taken into account. Furthermore, such evaluation metric is pessimistic when evaluating an alarm system such as in our application. Take for example the scenario where multiple true positive frames in a row occur when one of more VRU(s) enter the blind spot zone at the end of the truck. In such cases the truck driver is warned. Now suppose – due to e.g. missed detections – a few consecutive frames are classified as *false negatives*. While not optimal, in real-world scenarios this is less of a concern since the truck driver was already warned. In such cases only a short interruption of the (auditory) alarm signal would be noticed. However, the evaluation results presented here fail to take these considerations into account. To further improve the accuracy of our system, we evaluated the integration of temporal smoothing as follows. We aim to reject single (or short periods of) false positives. For this, we perform *majority voting* on a window sliding over the temporal frame per frame detection results. The exact size of this window (number of frames, N) is used as a parameter in our accuracy experiments. Figure 11 displays the accuracy results of our final active alarm system (black line), as compared to the accuracy of the original tracking-by-detection framework when only VRUs are accounted in the delineated blind spot zone (as discussed above, indicated with the dashed black line). Our active alarm system achieves an average precision of 97.26 %. We observe a significant accuracy improvement over the vanilla tracking-by-detection framework where the accuracy is defined by taking into account each individual VRU track. This improvement is explained by the fact that the exact accuracy conditions are now shifted towards the system level. Take for example two pedestrians walking side by side in the blind spot zone, where one pedestrian is (partially) occluded by the other. If in such case our tracking framework only detects the non-occluded pedestrian, and fails to detect the occluded pedestrian a false negative is counted resulting in a lower recall. Regarding our alarm system, finding only the non-occluded pedestrian in the blind spot zone is sufficient, since this already generates an alarm (and thus the frame is regarded as being a *true positive*). A similar observation for false positives exist. As mentioned, to further increase the detection accuracy we employ a sliding majority voting over a window of N frames. For this, we simply take the most occurring classification in the window of the N previous frames as a final decision for that frame. Figure 12 displays the precision recall curves of our alarm system for increasing sizes of this majority window (zoomed in on the top right corner). The black curve indicates our original algorithm ($N = 1$).

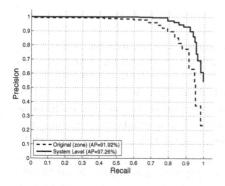 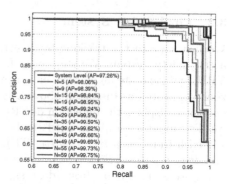

Fig. 11. Acc. of our final alarm system.   **Fig. 12.** Acc. for different sizes of N.

An increase in size of this window evidently increases the accuracy. The latency introduced by our majority voting scheme equals $\frac{N+1}{2}$ frames on average, 1 frame best-case and N frames worst-case. Take for example $N = 29$ frames. In such cases, our final alarm system achieves an average precision of about 99.5 %. At a frame rate of 15 FPS (and taken into account real-time detection performance), an alarm is generated after worst-case two seconds.

4   Discussion

The acceptability and usability of an active alarm system as presented in the previous sections depends on many considerations. These range from reliability, predictiveness, false error rate and so on. An active blind spot detection system consists of at least two main components: the detection of the VRUs in the blind spot zone, and communicating this information to the truck driver. Although this latter component is of extreme importance towards the development of a commercial system, in this paper we focused on the first component: detecting the VRUs in an efficient manner. According to [12], two main technical criteria exist: the system should be able to perform *good* VRU detection and the system should be able to give an alarm system *in time* such that enough time remains for the truck driver to take action. We translated both criteria in three distinctive requirements: the *throughput, latency* and *accuracy* of the system. Here, we now discuss the required specifications and discuss the usability of our final alarm system in real-life situations.

Throughput. The throughput, defined in the number of FPS, is easily quantifiable. Evidently, to be used in hard real-time scenarios our alarm system should be able to classify each detection frame at least as fast as the rate at which new frames need to be analysed. Typical commercial blind spot cameras achieve a frame rate of 15 FPS. The detection speed of our final active alarm system depends on the number of grid points. At e.g. a 3×3 detection grid, a processing speed of about 7 FPS is achieved. Our final alarm system fails to meet this requirement. However, the final multiclass detection framework (used as a baseline in our final active alarm system) served as a proof-of-concept Matlab implementation. Plenty of room for speed optimisation exists. Indeed, in [5] we proposed a highly optimised hybrid CPU/GPU implementation of the VRU detection system presented in [17], and proofed that real-time performance is achieved. Increasing the throughput of our final alarm system is only a matter of a more efficient implementation, e.g. no algorithmic redevelopment is needed.

Latency. The latency is defined as the time delay between the moment that VRUs enter the blind spot zone, and the moment that the system was able to raise an alarm. In the most extreme case, the truck driver should be warned before at least his reaction time (worst case 1.5 s) added with the time needed to perform a stopping maneuver in advance. Quantifying the time needed to perform this stopping maneuver is difficult, since it depends on several factors such as weather conditions, the combined mass of the HGV and its truckload. Due to the methodology of our active alarm system presented above, the maximally allowed latency depends on several factors. In our current final alarm system we defined that the zone in which VRU detection needs to be performed starts about 6.60 m behind the front of the truck's cabin. However, this is only a design parameter and as such can be increased – at the cost of higher computational complexity. Indeed, an increase of this detection zone allows for a larger latency. Furthermore, the allowed latency of our detection system is correlated with the relative speed difference between the VRUs and the truck. For pedestrians, this is of limited concern. However, for bicyclists this needs to be taken into account. Additionally, when the *majority voting* scheme presented above is used, the latency is correlated with the accuracy. When increasing the number of frames (N) of the sliding majority window, the latency increases. The optimal value of this parameter depends on how the system is employed. Evidently, when no majority voting is used (i.e. $N = 1$) an immediate decision is taken for each individual frame. The latency thus equals the detection time for a single frame. If e.g. a detection speed of 15 FPS is achieved, a latency of only 67 ms exist. However, this ideal scenario is based on offline processing of the image frames, and ignores the latency introduced by e.g. the frame grabber when capturing the image frames from the camera. For the remainder of this section we assume that this latter time is negligible. When majority voting is used to increase the accuracy, an increase in latency occurs. As an example, suppose $N = 5$. The (worst case) latency between a bicyclist who enters the frame at the rear of the truck, and the generation of an alarm now takes 333 ms (at 15 FPS and real-time detection performance). The relative speed difference between the bicyclist and the size of the detection zone needs to be taken into account to determine if this latency is small enough. Suppose a bicyclist with a velocity of 20 km/h approaches a truck taking a right hand turn at 10 km/h. In such scenario, the time between entering the delineated detection zone and reaching the front right corner of the truck's cabin equals about 2.4 s. Thus, slightly more than 2 s remain for the truck driver to react in this particular situation. As noticed, determining the minimal latency that such an alarm system requires is a difficult task. At

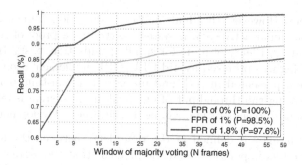

Fig. 13. The recall of our alarm system for three fixed values of the FPR.

best, when achieving real-time performance, our alarm system achieves a detection latency of 67 ms. In such cases, we achieve an average precision of 97.26 % on our test set. If needed, the detection accuracy could further be increased at the cost of an increase in latency. If such an increase in latency is not allowed, the VRU detection zone could be extended at the cost of extra computational complexity.

Accuracy. The system should be able to perform *good* VRU detection. As such, the false alarm rate and miss rate should be minimal. Exact quantitative figures of these false positive rates (FPR) are difficult to find and not consistent in the literature. For example, research on vehicle-based pedestrian collision warning systems state a maximum false alarm rate of 2 % and a miss rate of 1 % [2] need to be achieved, whereas [12] indicates a false alarm rate of up to 5 % is allowed. In Fig. 13 we plot the recall of our final alarm system in function of N for three fixed values of the false positive rate (and thus precision): 0 % (perfect precision), 1 % (P=98.5 %) and 1.8 % (P=97.6 %). This last FPR rate approximately equals the allowed rate in the literature. If we allow for a false positive alarm rate of 1.8 %, our final alarm system achieves for e.g. $N = 5$ a recall of 89.3 % (at a precision of 97.6 %). Thus, when allowing for a false positive rate of 2 %, about 90 % of the time VRUs are in the blind spot zone, an alarm is generated. For increasing N this raises quickly to about 98 % at 1.8 % missed detections ($N = 29$). A perfect recall is achieved for $N = 55$. However, defining the usability of a detection system solely on a specific value of the false positive rate is not optimal. For example, research indicates that a correlation exists between the acceptance of false alarms and the predictiveness of an alarm system [12]. The false alarms are easier accepted if the circumstances in which they occur are predictable. A safety system of which is known that false alarms occur during e.g. rainy conditions is easier accepted as compared to a safety system which produces a similar amount of false alarms at random moments. Furthermore, a fixed value for the false positive rate implies a specific operating point (i.e. detection threshold) of our system. At low detection thresholds most VRUs are detected, at the cost of relatively many false alarms (i.e. high recall at low precision). At high detection thresholds only instances that have a high probability of being a VRU are detected (i.e. low recall at high precision. Defining the exact operating point of our active alarm system (and thus the trade-off between precision and recall) remains open for discussion. This highly depends on *how* the system is used. If utilised as autonomous safety system (e.g. as an autonomous emergency braking system), a perfect accuracy is needed. Currently, our active alarm system fails to achieve perfect performance. However, if used as a decision support safety system for the driver, it offers a significant advantage if a high recall is achieved at (almost) perfect precision, which is the case. For such scenarios the accuracy and usability of our alarm system is excellent. Take for example the precision recall curve in Fig. 12, for $N = 9$. If set for a perfect precision (i.e. no false alarms), a recall of 80.3 % is achieved. Thus, in 80 % of the time VRUs are present in the blind spot zone, our system generates an alarm. If a low false positive rate is allowed, the recall further increases. For example, at a recall of 85.4 %, a false positive rate of only 1 % is achieved. At these settings, about 34 frames of our entire dataset were classified as false positives, on a total of about 5500 frames (i.e. 0.62 %). When measured in time units, about 27 s for each driven hour a false alarm is generated. Keep in mind that these false positive frames are not distributed randomly over the entire dataset, since such single frame false positives are easily filtered out. The remaining false positives occur where an object in our dataset is misclassified as being a VRU for multiple frames in a row. After further examination, for these specific settings the main cause of the false positive frames was due to the false detections where, due to shadows – with some imagination – an upper body-like appearance is seen. Such false positives are easily eliminated when validated with e.g. an additional ultrasonic distance sensor. Furthermore, currently we assume that our alarm system continuously performs detection. However, commercial alarm systems are only activated at low speeds (using GPS) or when the driver signals a right hand turn.

5   Conclusions and Future Work

In this paper we presented a vision-based active alarm safety system guarding the blind spot zone of trucks. Our alarm system manages to efficiently detect vulnerable road users that are present in the blind spot zone, and actively generates an alarm. We showed that our system is able to meet the stringent requirements that such an active safety system requires, when used as a decision support active alarm system. At perfect precision, a recall rate of more than 80 % is achieved. At low false positive rates and slightly higher latency, our alarm system reaches recall values of up to three nines five. These results are promising when keeping a commercial system in mind. However, we note that further large-scale tests are needed to draw final conclusions with respect to the usability of our active alarm system. Furthermore, the inclusion of additional sensors (such as long wave infrared and ultrasonic distance sensors) allow to further boost the accuracy.

References

1. Benenson, R., Omran, M., Hosang, J., Schiele, B.: Ten years of pedestrian detection, What have we learned? In: Agapito, L., Bronstein, M.M., Rother, C. (eds.) ECCV 2014. LNCS, vol. 8926, pp. 613–627. Springer, Heidelberg (2015). doi:10. 1007/978-3-319-16181-5_47
2. Chan, C.Y., Bu, F., Shladover, S.: Experimental vehicle platform for pedestrian detection. California PATH Program, Institute of Transportation Studies, University of California at Berkeley (2006)
3. Cho, H., Rybski, P.E., Zhang, W.: Vision-based bicycle detection and tracking using a deformable part model and an EKF algorithm. In: Proceedings of the 13th IEEE International Conference on Intelligent Transportation Systems (2010)
4. Coley, G., Wesley, A., Reed, N., Parry, I.: Driver reaction times to familiar but unexpected events (2008)
5. De Smedt*, F., Van Beeck*, K., Tuytelaars, T., Goedemé, T.: Pedestrian detection at warp speed: exceeding 500 detections per second (* indicates equal contribution). In: Proceedings of the Conference on Computer Vision and Pattern Recognition Workshops, Portland, Oregon (2013)
6. Dollár, P., Wojek, C., Schiele, B., Perona, P.: Pedestrian detection: a benchmark. In: Proceedings of the IEEE Conference on Computer Vision and Pattern Recognition (2009)
7. Dollar, P., Wojek, C., Schiele, B., Perona, P.: Pedestrian detection: an evaluation of the state of the art. IEEE Trans. PAMI **34**(4), 743–761 (2012)
8. Enzweiler, M., Gavrila, D.M.: Monocular pedestrian detection: survey and experiments. IEEE Trans. PAMI **31**(12), 2179–2195 (2009)
9. EU: Commission of the European Communities, European Road Safety Action Programme: mid-term review, 22 february 2006
10. Felzenszwalb, P., McAllester, D., Ramanan, D.: A discriminatively trained, multiscale, deformable part model. In: Proceedings of the IEEE Conference on Computer Vision and Pattern Recognition (2008)
11. Felzenszwalb, P.F., Girshick, R.B., McAllester, D., Ramanan, D.: Object detection with discriminatively trained part based models. IEEE Trans. PAMI **32**(9), 1627–1645 (2010)
12. Hoedemaeker, D., Doumen, M., De Goede, M., Hogema, J., Brouwer, R., Wennemers, A.: Modelopzet voor dodehoek detectie en signalerings systemen (2010)
13. Jung, H., Ehara, Y., Tan, J.K., Kim, H., Ishikawa, S.: Applying MSC-HOG feature to the detection of a human on a bicycle. In: Proceedings of the 12th International Conference on Control, Automation and Systems (2012)
14. Knight, I.: A study of the implementation of dir. 2007/38/EC on the retrofitting of blind spot mirrors to HGVs (2011)
15. Takahashi, K., Kuriya, Y., Morie, T.: Bicycle detection using pedaling movement by spatiotemporal gabor filtering. In: Proceedings of the IEEE Region 10 Conference (2010)
16. Van Beeck, K., Goedemé, T.: Efficient multiclass object detection: detecting pedestrians and bicyclists in a truck's blind spot camera. In: Proceedings of the 3rd IAPR Asian Conference on Pattern Recognition, Kuala Lumpur, Malaysia (2015)

17. Van Beeck, K., Goedemé, T., Tuytelaars, T.: Real-time vision-based pedestrian detection in a trucks blind spot zone using a warping window approach. In: Ferrier, J.-L., Bernard, A., Gusikhin, O., Madani, K. (eds.) Informatics in Control, Automation and Robotics. LNEE, vol. 283, pp. 251–264. Springer, Heidelberg (2014). doi:10.1007/978-3-319-03500-0_16
18. Zhang, S., Benenson, R., Omran, M., Hosang, J., Schiele, B.: How far are we from solving pedestrian detection?. In: Proceedings of the IEEE Conference on Computer Vision and Pattern Recognition (2016)

Extracting Driving Behavior: Global Metric Localization from Dashcam Videos in the Wild

Shao-Pin Chang[1], Jui-Ting Chien[2], Fu-En Wang[1], Shang-Da Yang[2], Hwann-Tzong Chen[2], and Min Sun[1(✉)]

[1] Departmant of Electrical Engineering, National Tsing Hua University, Hsinchu, Taiwan
s104061554@m104.nthu.edu.tw, s102061149@m102.nthu.edu.tw, sunmin@ee.nthu.edu.tw
[2] Departmant of Computer Science, National Tsing Hua University, Hsinchu, Taiwan
s104062535@m104.nthu.edu.tw, s102062322@m102.nthu.edu.tw, htchen@cs.nthu.edu.tw

Abstract. Given the advance of portable cameras, many vehicles are equipped with always-on cameras on their dashboards (referred to as dashcam). We aim to utilize these dashcam videos harvested in the wild to extract the driving behavior—global metric localization of 3D vehicle trajectories (Fig. 1). We propose a robust approach to (1) extract a relative vehicle 3D trajectory from a dashcam video, (2) create a global metric 3D map using geo-localized Google StreetView RGBD panoramic images, and (3) align the relative vehicle 3D trajectory to the 3D map to achieve global metric localization. We conduct an experiment on 50 dashcam videos captured in 11 cities under various traffic conditions. For each video, we uniformly sample at least 15 control frames per road segment to manually annotate the ground truth 3D locations of the vehicle. On control frames, the extracted 3D locations are compared with these manually labeled ground truths to calculate the distance in meters. Our proposed method achieves an average error of 2.05 m and 85.5 % of them have error no more than 5 m. Our method significantly outperforms other vision-based baseline methods and is a more accurate alternative method than the most widely used consumer-level Global Positioning System (GPS).

Keywords: Camera localization · Structure from motion

1 Introduction

Recently, self-driving car is one of the hottest topic in computer vision and it has received a huge amount of industrial investment to solve this holy-grail problem. One very important topic for advancing self-driving car is to build a realistic simulation environment, in particular, realistic driving behavior of other AI agents in the environment. Collecting in-house driving behavior data from humans is time-consuming and not scalable to cover many corner cases. Hence,

© Springer International Publishing Switzerland 2016
G. Hua and H. Jégou (Eds.): ECCV 2016 Workshops, Part I, LNCS 9913, pp. 136–148, 2016.
DOI: 10.1007/978-3-319-46604-0_10

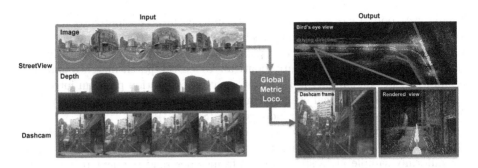

Fig. 1. Global Metric Localization of 3D vehicle trajectory. Left-Panel: inputs including StreetView RGBD panorama images (Top) and dashcam frames (Bottom). Right-Panel: output—3D trajectory (yellow dots) in bird's eye view (Top). A rendered view compared to a dashcam frame is shown at the Bottom. (Color figure online)

we propose to crowd-source driving behavior from many individual drivers using cheap portable cameras.

Thanks to the advance of portable camera, many vehicles are equipped with always-on cameras on their dashboards (referred to as dashcam). For instance, dashcams are equipped on almost all new cars in Taiwan, South Korea, and Russia. Its most common use case is to report special events such as traffic violations. Due to the popularity of these videos on video sharing website such as YouTube, many dashcam videos can be harvested on the web. In this work, we aim for extracting the driving behavior—"global metric localization" of 3D vehicle trajectories—in these dashcam videos. This is a challenging task, since dashcams typically are uncalibrated wide field-of-view cameras. Nevertheless, these driving behaviors can potentially be very valuable due to its diversity—it is captured by different drivers at different times and locations under different traffic conditions.

We define the task of "global metric localization" as localizing the 3D vehicle trajectory in the global metric 3D map. The 3D map is referred to as global and metric, since the whole world shares the same map and the unit in the 3D map can be converted into meters, respectively. The idea is that, with 3D vehicle trajectories in global metric 3D map, the extracted driving behavior can be analyzed to create realistic AI driving agents in the future. We propose a three-step approach to extract the driving behavior. First, we apply state-of-the-art structure from motion technique [1] to jointly estimate the camera intrinsic, the camera motion, and the 3D structure of the scene (referred to as Dashcam 3D). At this point, the 3D information of each video is in each coordinate system (Sect. 3.1). Hence, we cannot accumulate driving behavior in a single reference coordinate. Second, we use Google StreetView to create a 3D map in a single reference coordinate (Sect. 3.2). We modify the approach of Cavallo [2] and combine many geo-localized scans of Google StreetView RGBD panoramic images to create a simplified 3D map (referred to as StreetView 3D).

Finally, we apply a cascade of image-level and feature-level matching methods to efficiently find image patch matches between the StreeView 3D and Dashcam 3D. We further extract the ground plans in both StreeView and Dashcam 3D and assume two ground plans are identical. Given the patch matches and this assumption, we can simplify a 3D transformation estimation problem into a 2D transformation and vertical scale estimation problem. This significantly makes the RANSAC model estimation more robust (Sect. 3.3).

As a first step toward this direction, we conduct an experiment on 50 dashcam videos captured in 11 cities under various traffic conditions. For each video, we uniformly sample at least 15 control frames per road segment to manually annotate the ground truth 3D coordinates of the vehicle. Each extracted 3D trajectory is compared with these manually labeled ground-truth 3D control frames to calculate the distance in meters. Our proposed method achieves an average distance of 2.04 m and 85.5 % of them have distance no more than 5 m. Our method significantly outperforms other vision-based baseline methods and is a more accurate alternative method for vehicle localization than the most widely used consumer-level Global Positioning System (GPS).

2   Related Work

Extracting vehicle trajectory is related to three types of visual localization tasks: image-based landmark localization, landmark localization using 3D point clouds in a map, and vehicle localization.

Image-Based Landmark Localization. [3,4] are early work showing the ability to match query images to a set of reference images. Schindler et al. [5] improve the performance to handle city-scale localization. Hays and Efros [6] further demonstrate that query images can be matched to a collection of 6 million GPS-tagged images dataset (within 200 km) at a global scale. Zamir and Shah [7] propose to use Street View images as reference images with GPS-tags, and match SIFT keypoints in a query image efficiently to SIFT keypoints in reference images by using a tree structure. A voting scheme is also introduced to jointly localize a set of nearby query images (within 300 m). As a result of voting, it is able to outperform [5]. Vaca-Castano et al. [8] propose to estimate the trajectory of a moving camera in the longitude and latitude coordinate using Bayesian filtering to incorporate the map topology information. Similar to [7,8], we also use Street View images as reference images. However, unlike [7], we assume a video sequence is captured across an arbitrary distance (not restricted to within 300 m). Unlike [8], we use not only the topology of the map, but also the relative 3D position of the dashcam frames to improve the localization accuracy. Cao and Snavely [9] propose to match a query image to reference images with a graph-based structure to reliably retrieve a sub-group of images corresponding to a representative landmark. This method can be used to improve single image matching accuracy at the first stage of our method. Bettadapura et al. [10] also use Street View images as reference images to match the point-of-view images captured by a cellphone camera. Moreover, the method utilizes accelerometers, gyroscopes and compasses on the cellphone to improve the matching accuracy. The final estimated point-of-view is used as an approximation of the users' attention in applications such as egocentric video tours at museums.

Landmark Localization Using 3D Point Clouds in a Map. Accurate image-based camera 6 Degrees of Freedom (DoF) pose estimation can also be achieved by utilizing 3D point clouds in a map [11–14]. In our approach, we use many geo-localized Google StreetView RGBD panoramic images to create a 3D map using a modified method of [2]. Yu et al. [15] treat each frame in a dashcam video as a separate image query to estimate the 6DoF camera pose in the StreetView 3D map by solving the Perspective-n-Point (PnP) problem [16]. Our method is similar to [15]. Except that we treat frames in the same video as a whole sequence. Hence, our method additionally integrates all frames in the relative 3D trajectory. This makes our proposed method more robust.

Vehicle Localization. For egocentric vehicle localization, many methods combining image-based sensors with other sensors or map information have been proposed. Given the vehicle speed at all time and the rough initial vehicle location, Badino et al. [17] use Bayesian filter and a per-frame-based visual feature to align a current frame to pre-recorded frames in the database while considering the candidate location of previous frames. Taneja et al. [18] propose a similar but lightweight method requiring images sparsely sampled in space (in average every 7 m). Lategahn et al. [19] combine frame-based visual matching and Inertial Measurement Unit (IMU) for localization. However, it also assumes the GPS information of the first frame is also given. Both [20,21] utilize relative position information from visual odometry with map information from OpenStreetMaps to globally localize a vehicle. However, these methods require the vehicle trajectory to be complex enough to be uniquely identified on the map (i.e., many turns, etc.). Dashcam videos on YouTube do not come with additional speed or initial location information. Moreover, a video is typically less than 5 min with simple trajectories. In contrast, our method does not require an initial location of the first frame or any extra sensor, and it can even localize vehicles with simple trajectories using a global metric 3D map created from StreetView RGBD panoramic images. However, we do assume some weakly location information of the whole video sequence such as city, road name, etc. are known.

3   Our Method

In order to extract the driving behavior, we propose a three-step approach for "global metric localization" of 3D vehicle trajectories. The pipeline of the approach includes (1) extracting a relative 3D vehicle trajectory (Fig. 2(a)), (2) creating a global metric 3D map (Fig. 2(b)), and (3) aligning the 3D trajectory to the 3D map (Fig. 2(c)). In these steps, we utilize state-of-the-art Structure-from-Motion (SfM), Geographical Information Systems (GIS), and dense matching.

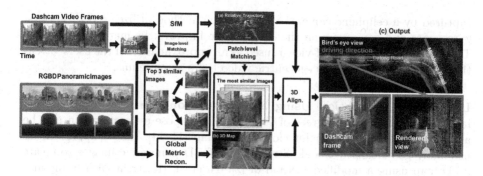

Fig. 2. System Pipeline. Panel (a): the obtained relative 3D trajectory given the dash-cam video. Panel (b): the obtained global metric 3D map given StreetView RGBD panorama images. Panel (c): the output – global metric vehicle 3D trajectory.

Moreover, we propose a novel 3D alignment method utilizing a ground-plane prior information in StreetView scenes to achieve the best result.

3.1 Extracting 3D Vehicle Trajectory

A dashcam video can be interpreted as sequential images captured along with the movement of the vehicle. Hence, we treat the dashcam 3D camera trajectory as the proxy of the 3D vehicle trajectory. In order to obtain the 3D vehicle trajectory, we apply sequential Structure-from-Motion (SfM) techniques to the estimation of relative camera positions with respect to the first frame. Note that our problem is not a classical Visual Odometry (VO) problem, since we do not have the camera intrinsic information of the harvested dashcam video. Moreover, most of the dashcam videos are captured by a wide-angle or even a fisheye camera, which introduces an unknown camera distortion in raw video frames. Therefore, it is critical to estimate the camera intrinsic including camera distortion. We use a state-of-the-art sequential Structure-from-Motion (SfM) method [1] to jointly estimate the camera intrinsic and extrinsic, and the sparse 3D point cloud representation of the scene. We refer to the coordinate system of the reconstruction as "Dashcam 3D". Note that the 3D vehicle trajectory in Dashcam 3D has two drawbacks. Firstly, the trajectory is only known up-to-scale (not metric). For instance, we can know the car is driving with constant speed, but we do not know the exact speed in meters. Secondly, Dashcam 3D is isolated from other meta information in GIS. For instance, we can know the car is making a turn, but we do not know the car is turning at a specific intersection (e.g., between market street and main street). Hence, we need a coordinate system which is metric and is globally consistent with meta information such as road intersections, traffic signs, etc.

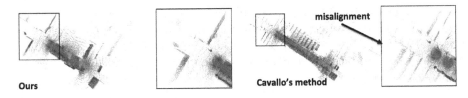

Fig. 3. Our Global Metric 3D Map (Left Panel) vs. Cavallo's method [2] (Right Panel). It shows that our method generates a much better aligned 3D Map.

3.2 Creating Global Metric 3D Map

Google StreetView is one of the largest and most information-rich street-level GIS with millions of RGBD panoramic images captured all over the world. Every panoramic image is geotagged with an accurate GPS position and covers a 360° horizontal and 180° vertical field-of-view (FoV). The spherical projection of the RGB and Depth images are shown in the bottom-left corner of Fig. 2. Note that the depth image is calculated from normal directions and distances of dominant surfaces in the scene. This allows to map building facades and roads while ignoring smaller entities such as vehicles or pedestrians. This also implies the depth image is an approximation of the true depth image of the scene. Generally, there is a panorama every 6 to 15 m with a nearly uniform street coverage. Hence, it is very likely that a dashcam observes many similar StreetView panoramas along the path of the vehicle. Our goal is to use Google StreetView to create a metric 3D Map which is consistent with other meta information such as roads, intersections, etc. at a global scale. We modify Cavallo's method [2] to create a global metric 3D Map. In particular, Cavallo's method places the 3D Map of each panorama onto a 2D plane according to the associated GPS position. This introduces noticeable approximation error when the 3D Map becomes large. Alternatively, we place the 3D Map of each panorama onto a 3D sphere as below,

$$r = E_r \cdot \cos(lat), \tag{1}$$
$$y = E_r \cdot \sin(lat), \tag{2}$$
$$x = r \cdot \sin(lon), \tag{3}$$
$$z = r \cdot \cos(lon), \tag{4}$$

where lat stands for latitude, lon stands for longitude, E_r denotes the radius of the Earth, and $[x, y, z]$ denotes a location in the global metric 3D map coordinate. This mitigates the approximation error even when the 3D Map is large (Fig. 3).

3.3 Aligning 3D Trajectory to 3D Map

In order to obtain the global metric vehicle 3D trajectory, we propose to align the trajectory in Dashcam 3D to the global metric 3D Map obtained from Google StreetView. We introduce the following coarse-to-find steps for alignment.

Weak Location Information. Since most dashcams are equipped with a consumer-level GPS, we roughly know that the video is captured close to a few geo-locations. For instance, a set of road intersections. Then, we use Google StreetView API to retrieve all StreetView panoramic images within M meters of the known geo-locations.

Image-Level Matching. Given a set of retrieved panoramic images and a dashcam video, we want to find a set of matched image pairs—one panorama matched with one dashcam frame. Since dashcam video typically captures the viewing direction parallel to the road direction, we crop each panoramic image into two "reference images" (i.e., two directions per road), each with 36° vertical FoV and 72° horizontal FoV (i.e., one fifth of the FoV of a panoramic image). We use the following techniques to measure the similarity of a pair of images.

- Holistic feature similarity. For both the reference images and frames, we detect sparse SIFT keypoints and represent each keypoint using SIFT descriptor [22]. Then, we use Fisher vector encoding [23] to generate our holistic feature representation for all images. The cosine similarity between a pair of Fisher vectors is used to efficiently measure the similarity of a pair of reference image and frame.
- Geometric verification. The similarity between a pair of reference image and frame can be more reliably confirmed by applying geometric verification method consisting of (1) raw SIFT keypoint matches with ratio test, and (2) RANSAC matching with epipolar geometric verification. However, geometric verification is more computationally expensive than calculating similarity using holistic feature.

In our application, we assume the reference images densely cover a region on the map containing the path of the dashcam. This implies that we only need a small set of reference images for the path. Therefore, we start from each frame and use holistic feature to retrieve its top K similar reference images. Then, we apply geometric verification only on the retrieved images to re-order them according to the number of inlier matches which is referred to as the "confidence score". At this point, we obtain a ranked list of pairs of frames and their corresponding reference images. Since some frames have very generic appearance such that they are similar to many reference images, we use the standard ratio test to keep only discriminative frames. In particular, the ratio of the confidence score between the top-1 and the second similar reference image needs to be larger than γ.

Patch-Level Matching. Given a matched image pair, we further want to obtain the matched image patch pairs between the frame and matched reference images. Note that every image patch in a dashcam frame is associated with a 3D location in Dashcam 3D coordinate. Similarly, every image patch in a reference image is associated with a 3D location in StreetView 3D coordinate. Hence, we can establish 3D correspondences between Dashcam and StreetView 3D coordinates given matched image patch pairs. Although we already obtain

SIFT keypoint matches while obtaining image-level matching, we find it is not very reliable and the keypoints are very sparse. In order to improve both the precision and recall of 3D correspondence between Dashcam and StreetView 3D coordinates, we apply a state-of-the-art dense matching method [24] to all matched image pairs and obtain a much more reliable set of 3D correspondences than other keypoint-based matches. To further increase the precision, we remove all pairs of images with less than Q matched image patches.

3D Alignment. Given the 3D correspondence between Dashcam and StreetView 3D coordinates, we aim to estimate the best 3D transformation to align these two coordinates. This task can be solved using a classical Random Sample Consensus (RANSAC) with 3D transformation method. However, we have found this classical approach often generates alignment results where the ground planes from both coordinates are not the same after alignment. Therefore, we propose to first make sure that the ground planes in both Dashcam and StreetView 3D coordinates occupy the (x, y) plane. Next, to ensure the aligned ground plane still occupies the (x, y) plane, we propose the following "ground-prior" 3D transformation to be estimated as described below,

$$\begin{bmatrix} x \\ y \\ z \end{bmatrix} = \begin{bmatrix} a & b & 0 \\ c & d & 0 \\ 0 & 0 & e \end{bmatrix} \begin{bmatrix} \hat{x} \\ \hat{y} \\ \hat{z} \end{bmatrix} + \begin{bmatrix} f \\ g \\ 0 \end{bmatrix} , \tag{5}$$

where $[x, y, z]$ is a location in StreetView 3D, $[\hat{x}, \hat{y}, \hat{z}]$ is a coordinate in Dashcam 3D, parameters $[a, b, c, d, f, g]$ encode 2D affine transformation in the x, y plane, and parameter e encodes scaling in z axis. Given many 3D correspondences (i.e., $[x, y, z]$ and $[\hat{x}, \hat{y}, \hat{z}]$), we can estimate parameters $[a, b, c, d, e, f, g]$ by solving least squares problem, and a reliable set of parameters can be estimated by using RANSAC with "ground-prior" 3D transformation. Note that our proposed transformation only have 7 degrees of freedom compared to 12 and 9 for 3D affine and rigid transformations, respectively. Moreover, we do not assume that the output point cloud of the sfm is isotropic (i.e., scalings in x,y,z direction are equal). Our proposed "ground-prior" 3D transformation allows different scaling factor for each axis. As a result, we found our proposed "ground-prior" 3D transformation achieves much smaller alignment error.

3.4 Implementation Details

The value of M, which controls the number of Google StreetView panoramas to be considered, depends on the uncertainty of the known geo-locations. In our case, we found $M = 500\,\text{m}$ is a good value considering noise in consumer-level GPS. For image-level matching, We found that $K = 3$ and $\gamma = 1.3$ retrieves sufficient number of good matched image pairs. For patch-level matching, we found $Q = 10$ gives us good results.

Fig. 4. Annotation interface. Left panel: StreetView 3D map, where yellow circle denotes the 3D location of a specific frame. Top-Right panel: Dashcam video. Bottom-Right panel: StreetView cropped image. All three panels are synchronized according to the 3D trajectory. By marking a yellow circle into a red circle, a user can drag it to modify the 3D location of a specific frame in 3D map. (Color figure online)

4   Experiments

We evaluate our proposed method on real-world dashcam videos downloaded from the Internet, and show that our method achieves state-of-the-art global metric 3D trajectory results compared to other baseline methods.

4.1   Data and Annotation

We harvest 50 dashcam videos on YouTube with good video quality and resolution higher than or equal to 720p. We also retrieve one GPS location for each video as mentioned in the description of the video or provided by the video owner. From the GPS locations, we know these videos are captured in a diverse set of 11 cities in Taiwan. In order to have the ground-truth global metric 3D trajectories, we build a web-based user annotation interface to compare the rendered view of StreetView 3D Map and a dashcam frame (Fig. 4). For each road segment, the users uniformly select at least 15 control frames and use the interface to drag the camera pose of each frame to the correct location in 3D Map. The dashcam videos and annotations will be released once the paper is accepted.

4.2   Evaluation Metric

To measure the quality of the predicted 3D trajectory, we calculate the distance between the ground truth and the predicted locations in Google StreetView 3D coordinate for the control frames. The smaller the distance the better the quality of the prediction. We refer to this distance as error.

Table 1. List of methods for comparison with their detailed steps, where steps differing from our proposed method are highlighted using bold fonts. Average error (Avg.) and standard deviation (SD) are reported at the last two columns, where the smallest values are highlighted using bold fonts. Geo-Verification stands for geometric verification. DHOG stands for dense HOG. DSIFT stands for dense SIFT. SfM stands for Structure-from-Motion. * indicates that the performance is evaluated on successfully estimated control frames which are only 10.2 % of all control frames.

	Feature-match	3D estimation	SfM	Avg	SD
Our	Deepmatch	ground prior + 3D alignment + RANSAC	Yes	**2.05**	**2.88**
Baseline 1	Deepmatch	**3D Rigid alignment** + RANSAC	Yes	7.44	12.04
Baseline 2	Deepmatch	**3D Affine alignment** + RANSAC	Yes	10.52	28.23
Baseline 3	**DHOG match**	ground prior + 3D alignment + RANSAC	Yes	67.96	75.26
Baseline 4	**DSIFT match**	ground prior + 3D alignment + RANSAC	Yes	85.01	80.39
Baseline 5	Deepmatch	**PnP RANSAC**	No	17.12*	22.8*

4.3 Baseline Methods

We compare our method with several variants (Table 1):

- Baseline 1. Estimating 3D rigid transformation with no ground-prior.
- Baseline 2. Estimating 3D affine transformation with no ground-prior.
- Baseline 3. Using dense HOG-based matching rather than [24].
- Baseline 4. Using dense SIFT-based matching [25] rather than [24].
- Baseline 5 [2]. Each frame is matched to one panoramic image. If there are enough patch correspondences, we use PnP [16] to estimate the 3D camera pose in StreetView 3D coordinate.

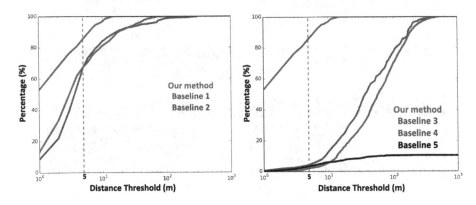

Fig. 5. Percentage of control frames vs. error threshold. We highlight the percentage with 5 m as threshold using a dash purple line. (Color figure online)

Fig. 6. Typical examples. Top-panel: the bird's eye view. Bottom-panel: rendered view compared with dashcam frame. Yellow dot denotes the location of each frame. Two consecutive dots are connected by a dark yellow edge. Green arrow indicates the driving direction. Light blue edges denote the road information. (Color figure online)

4.4 Results

For each method, we calculate the average error and standard deviation over all control frames (Table 1). Our method achieves the smallest average error of 2.05 m and standard deviation of 2.88 m. We confirm that our proposed ground-prior 3D alignment outperforms 3D rigid (Baseline 1) and affine (Baseline 2) transformations. Moreover, deepmatch [24] significantly outperforms other dense matching methods (Baseline 3 and 4). Finally, We also report the percentage of control frames with error lower than a threshold. By changing the threshold, we can plot a curve with percentage at the vertical axis (Fig. 5). Our method predicts 85.5 % locations with error no more than 5 m. We show many typical examples in Fig. 6. In each example, we show the bird's eye view of the global metric 3D trajectory in StreetView 3D coordinate, where a yellow dot denotes the location of each frame, two consecutive dots are connected by a dark yellow edge, the green arrow indicates the driving direction, and the light blue edges denote the road information. Two comparisons between rendered view and dashcam frame are also shown for each example. From these examples, we can see that our estimated trajectories are accurate at lane-level. For instance, the car is driving on the outside lane in the first example of Fig. 6.

5 Conclusion

We propose a robust method to obtain global metric 3D vehicle trajectories from dashcam videos in the wild. Our method potentially can be used to crowd-source driving behaviors for developing self-driving car simulator. On 50 dashcam videos, our proposed method achieves an average error of 2.05 m and 85.5 % of them have error no more than 5 m. Our method significantly outperforms other vision-based baseline methods and is a more accurate alternative method than the most widely used consumer-level Global Positioning System (GPS).

Acknowledgements. We thank MOST 104-3115-E-007-005 in Taiwan for its support.

References

1. Gargallo, P., Kuang, Y.: Opensfm. https://github.com/mapillary/OpenSfM/
2. Cavallo, M.: 3d city reconstruction from google street view. Comput. Graph. J. (2015)
3. Robertson, D., Cipolla, R.: An image-based system for urban navigation. In: BMVC (2004)
4. Zhang, W., Kosecka, J.: Image based localization in urban environments. In: 3DPVT (2006)
5. Schindler, G., Brown, M., Szeliski, R.: City-scale location recognition. In: CVPR (2007)
6. Hays, J., Efros, A.A.: Im2gps: estimating geographic information from a single image. In: CVPR (2008)

7. Zamir, A.R., Shah, M.: Accurate image localization based on google maps street view. In: Daniilidis, K., Maragos, P., Paragios, N. (eds.) ECCV 2010. LNCS, vol. 6314, pp. 255–268. Springer, Heidelberg (2010). doi:10.1007/978-3-642-15561-1_19
8. Vaca-Castano, G., Zamir, A., Shah, M.: City scale geo-spatial trajectory estimation of a moving camera. In: CVPR (2012)
9. Cao, S., Snavely, N.: Graph-based discriminative learning for location recognition. In: CVPR (2013)
10. Bettadapura, V., Essa, I., Pantofaru, C.: Egocentric field-of-view localization using first-person point-of-view devices. In: WACV (2015)
11. Irschara, A., Zach, C., Frahm, J., Bischof, H.: From structure-from-motion point clouds to fast location recognition. In: CVPR (2009)
12. Li, Y., Snavely, N., Huttenlocher, D.P.: Location recognition using prioritized feature matching. In: Daniilidis, K., Maragos, P., Paragios, N. (eds.) ECCV 2010. LNCS, vol. 6312, pp. 791–804. Springer, Heidelberg (2010). doi:10.1007/978-3-642-15552-9_57
13. Sattler, T., Leibe, B., Kobbelt, L.: Fast image-based localization using direct 2d-to-3d matching. In: ICCV (2011)
14. Li, Y., Snavely, N., Huttenlocher, D., Fua, P.: Worldwide pose estimation using 3d point clouds. In: Fitzgibbon, A., Lazebnik, S., Perona, P., Sato, Y., Schmid, C. (eds.) ECCV 2012. LNCS, vol. 7572, pp. 15–29. Springer, Heidelberg (2012). doi:10.1007/978-3-642-33718-5_2
15. Yu, L., nad Guillaume Bresson, C.J., Moutarde, F.: Monocular urban localization using street view. Arxiv (2016)
16. Lepetit, V., Moreno-Noguer, F., Fua, P.: Epnp: an accurate o(n) solution to the pnp problem. Int. J. Comput. Vis. **81**(2), 155 (2009)
17. Badino, H., Huber, D., Kanade, T.: Real-time topometric localization. In: ICRA (2012)
18. Taneja, A., Ballan, L., Pollefeys, M.: Never get lost again: vision based navigation using StreetView images. In: Cremers, D., Reid, I., Saito, H., Yang, M.-H. (eds.) ACCV 2014. LNCS, vol. 9007, pp. 99–114. Springer, Heidelberg (2015). doi:10.1007/978-3-319-16814-2_7
19. Lategahn, H., Schreiber, M., Ziegler, J., Stiller, C.: Urban localization with camera and inertial measurement unit. In: Intelligent Vehicles Symposium (IV) (2013)
20. Floros, G., van der Zander, B., Leibe, B.: OpenStreetSLAM: global vehicle localization using openstreetmaps. In: ICRA (2013)
21. Brubaker, M., Geiger, A., Urtasun, R.: Lost! leveraging the crowd for probabilistic visual self-localization. In: CVPR (2013)
22. Lowe, D.G.: Distinctive image features from scale-invariant keypoints. Int. J. Comput. Vision **60**(2), 91–110 (2004)
23. Jegou, H., Perronnin, F., Douze, M., Snchez, J., Perez, P., Schmid, C.: Aggregating local image descriptors into compact codes. TPAMI **34**, 1704–1716 (2011)
24. Weinzaepfel, P., Revaud, J., Harchaoui, Z., Schmid, C.: DeepFlow: Large displacement optical flow with deep matching. In: ICCV (2013)
25. Kim, J., Liu, C., Sha, F., Grauman, K.: Deformable spatial pyramid matching for fast dense correspondences. In: CVPR (2013)

From On-Road to Off: Transfer Learning Within a Deep Convolutional Neural Network for Segmentation and Classification of Off-Road Scenes

Christopher J. Holder[1,2(✉)], Toby P. Breckon[2], and Xiong Wei[1]

[1] Institute for Infocomm Research, Singapore, Singapore
[2] School of Engineering and Computer Sciences,
Durham University, Durham, UK
c.j.holder@durham.ac.uk

Abstract. Real-time road-scene understanding is a challenging computer vision task with recent advances in convolutional neural networks (CNN) achieving results that notably surpass prior traditional feature driven approaches. Here, we take an existing CNN architecture, pre-trained for urban road-scene understanding, and retrain it towards the task of classifying off-road scenes, assessing the network performance within the training cycle. Within the paradigm of transfer learning we analyse the effects on CNN classification, by training and assessing varying levels of prior training on varying sub-sets of our off-road training data. For each of these configurations, we evaluate the network at multiple points during its training cycle, allowing us to analyse in depth exactly how the training process is affected by these variations. Finally, we compare this CNN to a more traditional approach using a feature-driven Support Vector Machine (SVM) classifier and demonstrate state-of-the-art results in this particularly challenging problem of off-road scene understanding.

1 Introduction

Scene understanding is a vital step in an autonomous vehicle processing pipeline, but this can be especially challenging in an off-road, unstructured environment. Knowledge about upcoming terrain and obstacles is necessary for deciding on the optimum path through such an environment, and can also be used to inform vehicle driving parameters to improve traction, efficiency and maximise passenger comfort and safety.

Whole scene understanding is a well-discussed problem with applications in many domains [1, 2]. Recent contributions have used convolutional neural network (CNN) based approaches to achieve state-of-the-art results [3], while approaches combining hand-crafted features with linear classifiers have been somewhat side-lined [4].

Work in the domain of scene understanding for autonomous vehicles has followed this trend [5, 6], however there is very little work applying deep-learning techniques to the more challenging off-road environment. This paper aims to assess the applicability to such an environment of a state-of-the-art CNN architecture that was originally designed and trained to perform per-pixel classification on urban road scene images [6].

© Springer International Publishing Switzerland 2016
G. Hua and H. Jégou (Eds.): ECCV 2016 Workshops, Part I, LNCS 9913, pp. 149–162, 2016.
DOI: 10.1007/978-3-319-46604-0_11

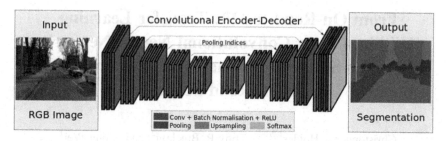

Fig. 1. Architecture of the Segnet convolutional neural network [6]. The encoder network, consisting of convolution and pooling layers, is followed by a mirror-image decoder network, consisting of convolution and up-sampling layers

Within this work we perform transfer learning, taking a CNN architecture that has already been originally trained to classify a large, often more generic data set and re-training it from this initialization to a more specific or alternative task (for which data is often more limited). In this case, a CNN trained for urban street scene classification is subsequently re-trained with a smaller, more specialised data set of off-road scenes. The idea is that the weights learned on the larger data set act to build a set of generic image filters that can be easily adapted for the task of classifying the more specialised imagery used later [7]. Transfer learning is generally thought to be beneficial when training with a small specialised data set or when the time to train a new network from scratch is not available, so we investigate the effects of data set size and training time on the classification performance of networks that have performed different amounts of pre-training or no pre-training at all.

Most existing work in the area of off-road classification does not make use of deep-learning techniques: the approach described in [8] aims to classify different parts of a colour image of an off-road scene using Gaussian Mixture Models, while the approach outlined in [9] uses a combination of features from colour imagery and 3D geometry from a laser rangefinder to classify the different parts of an off-road scene.

For comparison with our CNN based approach, we use a method based on the state-of-the-art object category retrieval work in [10]: dense gradient features are clustered to build a histogram encoding that is fed into a support vector machine (SVM) [11] for classification.

2 Methodology

We primarily propose a convolutional neural network approach and compare this to a secondary support vector machine approach for relative performance evaluation.

2.1 CNN Architecture

The convolutional neural network architecture we use is nearly identical to the 'Segnet' architecture described in [6], with only minor changes made to the final layer of the network in order to output eight classes and to adjust the class weightings for our off-road data set. Similar network architectures exist [3], however we down-selected Segnet due to the focus of its creators on autonomous vehicle applications and its ability to perform real-time classification.

Fig. 2. An example image from the Camvid dataset along with its annotations

The Segnet architecture is visualised in Fig. 1. It is comprised of a symmetrical network of thirteen 'encoder' layers followed by thirteen 'decoder' layers. The encoder layers correspond to the convolution and pooling layers of the VGG16 [12] object classification network, while the decoder layers up-sample their input so that the final output from the network has the same dimensions as the input image. During the encoding phase, each pooling layer down-samples its input by a factor of two and stores the location of the maximum value from each 2×2 pooling window. During the decoding phase, these locations are used by the corresponding up-sampling layer to populate a sparse feature map, with the convolution layers on the decoder side trained to fill the gaps. This technique facilitates full pixel-wise classification to be achieved in real-time, making Segnet an ideal architecture for use in further autonomous vehicle applications.

2.2 CNN Training

We begin by training the network on the Camvid dataset [13] that was used by the original authors to assess Segnet. By training on a large, well labelled dataset that has already been shown to work well with this network architecture we can ensure that our network learns a set of weights that are relevant to a vehicular scene understanding task. We then perform transfer learning, retraining the network on our own off-road data so that it can adjust its weights to better suit an off-road environment and discriminate between the classes present in these scenes.

The benefits of transfer learning are in the ease with which an existing trained network can be adapted to a new specialised task. The time taken to train the network and learn optimum weights should be greatly reduced when compared to a network being trained from scratch with randomly initialised weights. In cases where the specialised data set is small or only partially labelled, a network trained from a random starting point may never achieve satisfactory results, however by performing the bulk of training with a larger set of data and only utilising the specialised data set for the last few iterations, a better outcome can be achieved [7].

In our case, the initial training data consists of 367 labelled images of urban street scenes from the Camvid data set, resized to a resolution of 480 × 360. An example image from the dataset, along with its annotations, can be seen in Fig. 2. The original authors chose eleven pixel classes for the Segnet classification task, *{sky, building, pole, road marking, road, pavement, tree, sign, fence, car, pedestrian, and bicycle}*. As the network architecture performs classification of every pixel, this gives us up to 172,800 samples per image, or 63,417,600 samples in total. In practice, the total is slightly less than this as some images have pixels that do not fit into any of the eleven original classes and are labelled 'void'.

 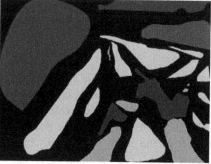

Fig. 3. An example image from our off-road dataset next to its partially labelled training image

Our off-road data consists of 332 images captured by a vehicle mounted camera driven at two different off-road driving facilities encompassing a variety of environments, which we split into roughly 90 % training data and 10 % test data, giving us 295 training images. For the CNN, our images have been resized to the same resolution of 480 × 360 as the Camvid images. We identified 8 pixel class labels for our off-road data set, *{sky, water, dirt, paved road, grass, foliage, tree, and man-made obstacle}*, 3 of which also existed in the Camvid data.

Fully labelling every pixel in even a small set of images can be very time consuming, so we only partially label our training images to assess whether good classification results can still be achieved without full labelling. Our labelling strategy consists of hand drawing a shape that is entirely contained by, but not touching the edges of, each image segment. Every pixel within that shape is then considered a member of the chosen class. Another reason this approach was chosen is the lack of clear boundaries to delineate classes in off-road scenes, for example when a muddy surface gradually gives way to gravel, or where long grass becomes foliage. This provided us with a total of 35,016,288 labelled pixels for training, with the rest of the pixels (roughly 31 % of the total) labelled as void so that the network would ignore them. An example image from our dataset, along with its annotations, can be seen in Fig. 3. For testing our classification results, we use one set of 37 images labelled in the same manner, as well as another set of 4 fully labelled images. Figure 4 shows the partial and fully labelled versions of one of our test images.

To test the effects of transfer learning when the specialised training is carried out with a small data set, we train several versions of the network using different sized subsets of this data, one each containing 140, 70, 35, 17, and 8 of the original images.

Snapshots are taken at several points during the Camvid training, so that we can observe the effects of different amounts of pre-training. Seven versions of the network will be trained and assessed on our off-road dataset: one which has been randomly initialised with no prior training, along with networks trained for 1000, 2000, 5000, 10,000, 20,000 and 30,000 iterations on the Camvid data.

Our training is performed on an NVidia Tesla K40 GPU, taking roughly one hour per thousand training iterations.

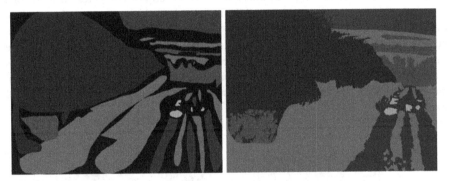

Fig. 4. Partial and fully labelled versions of the same image from our off-road data set. Fully manually annotating an image like this can take a person several hours, while a partially annotated image can be created in a few minutes. In our partially labelled training set, 69 % of pixels are labelled

2.3 Support Vector Machine

For comparison, we will be training a SVM to classify the same data using dense gradient features, based on the approach used in [10] for object classification. For our approach we will be classifying image segments, as this will allow us to cluster feature points to build up a bag-of-words vocabulary. The segments in this case are those created manually while labelling the data, as in this case we are only interested in the performance of the classifier itself and so a perfect segmentation is assumed. In practice, an imperfect segmentation algorithm would be used, potentially leading to errors in the segmentation that could impact classifier performance.

To ensure enough local gradient information is available at each feature point, we use images with a resolution of 1280 × 720, higher than those used to train the CNN. The memory and time that would be required to train the CNN using images at this resolution would be infeasibly high, however by clustering our features before passing them to the SVM, the size of data it uses to train and classify is constant per data sample regardless of image resolution.

Our labelled data set gives us 5664 labelled segments, which we split into 90 % for training data and 10 % for testing data. We ignore any samples too small to provide at least 50 feature points, leaving us with between 3000 and 4000 viable segments, depending on the feature grid density used.

We train a Support Vector Machine for a maximum of 20,000 iterations using a radial basis function to perform a grid search over the kernel parameter space.

Dense Feature Descriptors. A dense grid of feature points is computed for each segment. The grid density, g pixels between grid nodes in both x and y direction, is chosen empirically by testing values between 2 and 10 pixels. Generally, a denser grid should contain a greater amount of information at the expense of computation time, so a lower number should give better results in most cases.

The Speeded Up Robust Features (SURF) algorithm [14] is used to create a descriptor for each remaining grid node. A SURF descriptor computes Haar wavelet responses within a square region around the initial point, which are summed to produce a vector describing the intensity distribution of pixels within the region. This results in either a 128 or 64 dimension vector that describes the local texture. Empirically we found a 64 dimension vector to give better results at this task. Every SURF descriptor is computed at the same orientation of 0 radians with a radius of r pixels. r is chosen empirically after assessing classification results using a range of values from 2 to 20 pixels.

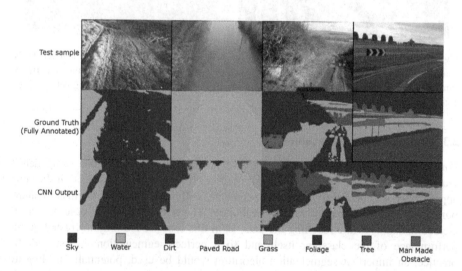

Fig. 5. Results from the CNN after 30,000 iterations of pre-training and 10,000 iterations of training with the full off-road dataset. The middle row shows the fully annotated test images for comparison, and class colour labels are shown below

Feature Encoding. Descriptors resulting from grid-wise feature extraction over a given segment are encoded into a fixed length vector for subsequent classification.

We use a histogram encoding (traditional bag-of-words [15]) approach: for histogram encoding, we first use K-means clustering to create a visual vocabulary, or bag of words, of K clusters within the 64 dimensional space of our SURF descriptors. For each segment, a histogram is computed accumulating the number of its SURF descriptors assigned to each cluster within the vocabulary. This histogram is normalised to provide a K-dimensional descriptor for the segment as the input feature vector to the SVM. The optimum value for K is chosen empirically, after testing values from 200 to 1600.

3 Results

We evaluate our classifiers using two sets of test data: a set of images partially labelled in the same manner as our training data, and a smaller set that are fully labelled (i.e. every single pixel in the image is labelled). The output layer of the CNN assigns a label to every pixel, while the SVM outputs a label for each segment. Figure 5 shows some example images with their respective CNN outputs and ground truth annotations.

Due to the lack of clearly defined boundaries in some areas of off-road scenes, there exist some pixels could have more than one correct label in terms of true ground truth. This should not have much effect on the partially labelled data, as boundary regions remain largely unlabelled, however this is likely to have a negative effect on classification results when testing against fully labelled data. To limit this effect, when deciding whether a pixel is correctly labelled we search for a match within a 5 pixel radius in the ground truth image. When testing with partially labelled data, a pixel is only labelled correctly if a match is found at its exact location in the ground truth image.

When discussing the CNN, unless stated otherwise, accuracy is defined as the number of correctly labelled pixels divided by the total number of labelled pixels in the

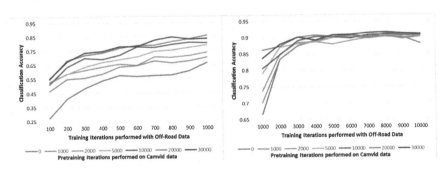

Fig. 6. Comparison of training progress for networks that have undergone different amounts of pre-training on the Camvid urban data set. We plot classification accuracy at every 100th iteration during training with our off-road data set for the first 1000 iterations, then at every further 1000th iteration until 10,000 iterations have been trained

test data. When discussing the SVM, accuracy is defined as the number of correctly labelled segments divided by the total number of labelled segments in the test data.

3.1 CNN with Partially Labelled Test Data

First we compare classification accuracy from training the network on our full off-road data set as well as smaller subsets thereof after different amounts of pre-training, and testing on our partially labelled test data set.

Table 1. Accuracy of the CNN on the Camvid test data at the points when snapshots are taken to perform transfer learning

Iterations trained	1000	2000	5000	10000	20000	30000
Classification accuracy	0.31	0.36	0.48	0.68	0.75	0.79

Pre-training Iterations. Table 1 shows the performance of the network on Camvid test data before any training with off-road data, with accuracy recorded at the six points from which transfer learning was to be performed. As the Camvid data is mostly fully labelled, we use the same measure of accuracy as we use with our fully labelled off-road test data set, wherein a label is deemed to be correct if it is within a 5 pixel radius of a similarly labelled pixel in the ground truth image.

These results demonstrate the network has rapid performance improvement over its first 10,000 training iterations, followed by a slower but consistent improvement in performance during later training iterations.

Figure 6 shows the results achieved by each pre-trained version of the network on our full data set. Each version of the network was trained for 10,000 iterations, with a snapshot taken and accuracy recorded first at every 100 iterations, then at every 1000 iterations.

The results show that the first few thousand iterations clearly benefit from transfer learning, with the networks that have performed a greater amount of pre-training generally performing better. However, by 5000 iterations of training, even the network

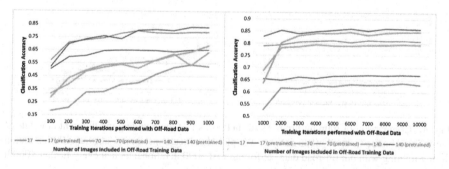

Fig. 7. Comparing pre-trained and non-pre-trained networks using different sized subsets of our off-road data set

initialised with random weights has achieved an accuracy of close to 0.9, beyond which there is very little improvement from any of the networks.

As the training continues, the networks pre-trained for longer give marginally better results. The highest accuracy achieved is 0.917, which comes after 8000 iterations of the network that was pre-trained for 30,000 iterations. The networks pre-trained for 20,000 and 30,000 iterations show very similar results throughout the training, suggesting a limit to the performance gains that can be achieved by pre-training.

Training was continued up to 20,000 iterations with each network, however this gave no further increase in accuracy and so only the first 10,000 iterations are shown.

It is interesting to note that our results surpass those achieved by their respective networks on the Camvid test data within a few hundred iterations, and then go on to perform significantly better. This could partly result from our data-set containing fewer classes (8 vs 11). Another factor could be our partially labelled test data, which features very few class boundary regions, however further testing with fully labelled data shows similar performance. It is possible that partially labelled training data could lead to a better performing classifier due to the lack of potentially confusing boundary pixels, although to fully test this we would need to compare these results to those obtained by training an identical network with a fully labelled version of the same data set, which is beyond the scope of this paper.

Data Set Size. To consider the effect the amount of training data used has on classification, we train networks using five different sized subsets of our training data, containing 140, 70, 35, 17 and 8 images, both with and without pre-training. Figure 7 compares results for three of these subsets, each trained for 10,000 iterations.

The effects of transfer learning are similar: for the first 1000 iterations, the benefits of pre-training are clear, however after just a few thousand more, both pre-trained and un-pre-trained networks have achieved close to their optimum performance. As training progresses, the pre-trained network consistently outperforms the non-pre-trained network by a small margin, which generally increases as the dataset size decreases: After

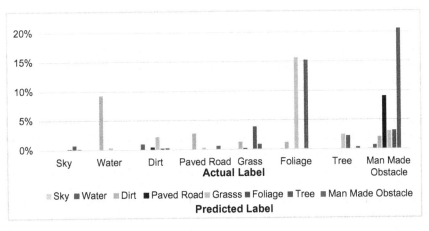

Fig. 8. Misclassified pixels, per class, as a percentage of the total number of pixels belonging to that class (correctly labelled pixels are not shown)

10,000 iterations with a dataset of 140 images, the accuracy of the pre-trained network is just 0.01 better than the un-pre-trained network, while with the dataset of 8 images, this margin increases to 0.09.

Per Class Results. We now discuss in more detail the results from the CNN trained for 10,000 iterations on the full data set after 30,000 iterations of pre-training. This is the network configuration that we would expect to typically perform best, with the highest amount of pre-training and largest data set, and it consistently achieves an accuracy of 0.91 against our partially labelled test data once it has passed 5000 iterations. Figure 8 shows the proportion of pixels belonging to each class that were given each possible incorrect label.

The most common misclassifications are between grass, foliage and trees, which is understandable given their visual similarities. Proportionally to class size, the largest is the 20.5 % of pixels containing Man Made Obstacles that are misclassified as Tree. This is likely because many of the man-made obstacles in the off-road environment, such as fences, posts and gates, are made of wood and so have a similar appearance to trees.

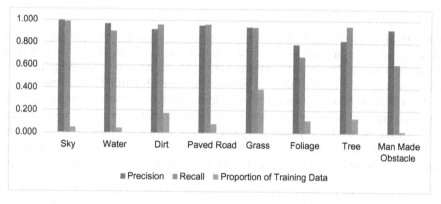

Fig. 9. Per class statistics for the CNN classifier. CNN was trained for 10,000 iterations on the full off-road data set after 30,000 iterations of pre-training. Testing was performed on the partially labelled testing set. As well as class precision and recall, we plot the number of pixels comprising each class within the training data as a proportion of the total number of labelled pixels in the set

Figure 9 plots the precision and recall of each class along with the proportion of the training data set that each class makes up. The foliage class performed worst, likely due to its visual similarity to both grass and trees, while sky gave the best results. Camera exposure was set to capture maximum detail at ground level, so in most instances the sky is much brighter than the rest of the scene, which combined with its lack of high frequency detail and consistent placement at the top of an image makes it easily distinguishable from other classes.

For the most part, classes that achieve high precision also achieve high recall, however man-made obstacle is an exception, with a very high precision (0.92) but

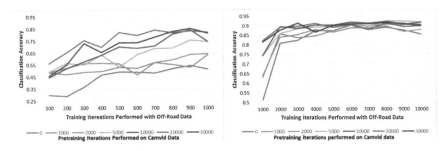

Fig. 10. Classification results using the fully labelled test set, comparing networks that have undergone different amounts of pre-training on the Camvid urban data set

lowest overall recall (0.613), meaning very few pixels are misclassified as man-made obstacle, while many pixels which should be labelled man-made obstacle are not. The fact that it is the class with fewest training samples (594,125 pixels) is likely to have played a part in this, as well as its visual similarity to trees, as discussed above.

There would appear to be some correlation between the frequency of a class within the data set and its recall, possibly because of the way the output is weighted towards classes that appear more often.

3.2   Fully Labelled Test Images

Currently we have only discussed the results obtained through testing the CNN classifier against partially labelled data, thus we also test it against a set of fully annotated images to demonstrate that it can achieve similar results.

Figure 10 show the results obtained, and demonstrates that testing with fully labelled images yields results very similar to those of the partially labelled set. The highest accuracy seen was with the network pre-trained for 5,000 iterations, with an accuracy of 0.924 after 8000 iterations of training with the full off-road data set.

Interestingly, the network snapshots that perform poorly on the partially labelled set (i.e. those that have not yet been through enough training iterations or have only been trained on a small data set) tend to perform worse on the fully labelled images. By contrast, those that perform well on the partially labelled data exhibit less deterioration, and in some cases even demonstrate an improvement in accuracy, when the fully labelled set is used. This would appear to suggest that a more comprehensively trained network performs much better in class boundary regions.

Another point of note is that with the partially labelled data set, a network that had undergone greater pre-training would almost always perform better, however, when testing with the fully labelled data set, the networks that have undergone 5000 and 10,000 pre-training iterations consistently outperform those with 20,000 and 30,000 iterations, although only by a very small margin, at the later stages of training. This could be because the networks that have undergone more pre-training begin to overfit to the data they were originally trained on. The fact that this only occurs when the fully

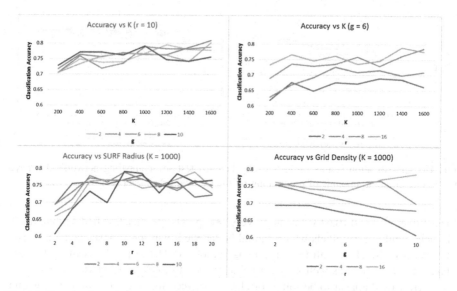

Fig. 11. Results from SVM classifier using various feature configurations. K represents the number of clusters used for bag-of-words encoding, g is the density of feature grid, i.e. number of pixels in both the x and y direction between feature points, and r is the radius, in pixels, of the area that each feature point takes account of when building its SURF descriptor

labelled data is used might suggest that this overfitting only has a noticeable effect when classifying class boundary regions, which are not present in the partially labelled data.

3.3   SVM

For Comparison, we test the SVM approach on its ability to classify segments from our off-road data set. The SVM parameters are automatically optimised through cross-validation, however we test several different configurations for the features that we pass into the classifier. The parameters that we alter are g, the number of pixels between feature points in our grid, r, the radius in pixels around each feature point that our descriptors take account of, and K, the number of clusters used to build our bag-of-words. Figure 11 shows several comparisons to demonstrate how performance is affected.

We would expect a decrease in g to improve results, as a greater amount of detail is being considered. This partly holds true in our results, although not consistently so. As r changes, we initially see a consistent improvement in results, which begins to tail off after a while. This is likely because with r set too restrictively, each feature point only has access to a limited region of local gradient information. By contrast, with r set too large, high frequency detail is lost as the descriptor is built from a greater number of pixels. The optimum value appears to be around $r = 10$. The general trend for K is that larger is better, but memory and time constraints make too large a value impractical.

The best result attained by the SVM was an accuracy of 0.813, using the parameters $g = 6$, $r = 12$, $K = 1400$.

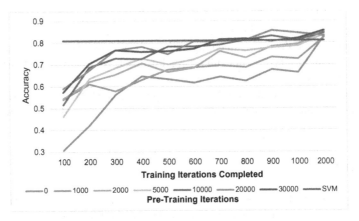

Fig. 12. Training progress of the CNN after different amounts of pre-training, measured as accuracy on the segment classification task for comparison to the SVM classifier

To properly compare SVM and CNN performance, we adapted our CNN classifier to label whole segments. This was done by winner-takes-all vote of pixel labels within the segment. Figure 12 shows the segment classification results as the CNN is trained after different amounts of pre-training. The CNNs pre-trained for 10,000 or more iterations all achieve results better than those of the SVM before 1000 iterations, and by 2000 iterations all, including the CNN that has undergone no pre-training, have surpassed the SVM. After further training, segment classification results are very similar to those for pixel classification, peaking at around 0.91, confirming that the CNN is significantly more effective at this classification task than the SVM.

4   Conclusions

This work demonstrates how an existing deep convolutional neural network classification and segmentation architecture can be adapted to a new task with minimal intervention. We have shown how quickly the network can learn to classify new kinds of images, and visualised CNN training performance by testing classification accuracy throughout the cycle, allowing us to compare networks as training progresses to show the effects that transfer learning and data-set size can have on performance.

Notably, we have demonstrated that pre-training is of limited utility when a large data set is used for a long training period. While pre-training was shown to improve performance when smaller data sets were used, results were still well below those observed with larger training data, even without pre-training, suggesting that pre-training is no substitute for an adequately sized data set. Pre-training was also shown to improve results early in the training cycle, although as training continues these effects diminish until a network with no pre-training will almost match the performance of a pre-trained one. In our testing, this happened as early as 5000 iterations, which represents just 5 h of training. However, our results have shown that networks that have undergone more pre-training tend to perform marginally better, even after many iterations of training, however the results obtained from our fully labelled test set appear to show the opposite effect above 5000 iterations of pre-training, suggesting that there is a limit. With that in mind, it would appear the optimum configuration of CNN for this task, using the Segnet architecture [6] and trained on our full off-road data set, is around 10,000 iterations of pre-training followed by 10,000 iterations of training.

Our results show that such a CNN can outperform a SVM based classifier using dense gradient features by a significant margin, even after a limited amount of training.

References

1. Li, L.-J., Socher, R., Fei-Fei, L.: Towards total scene understanding: classification, annotation and segmentation in an automatic framework. In: IEEE Conference on Computer Vision and Pattern Recognition, CVPR 2009. IEEE (2009)
2. Gupta, S., et al.: Indoor scene understanding with RGB-D images: bottom-up segmentation, object detection and semantic segmentation. Int. J. Comput. Vis. **112**(2), 133–149 (2015)
3. Long, J., Shelhamer, E., Darrell, T.: Fully convolutional networks for semantic segmentation. In: Proceedings of the IEEE Conference on Computer Vision and Pattern Recognition (2015)
4. Tang, I., Breckon, T.P.: Automatic road environment classification. IEEE Trans. Intell. Transp. Syst. **12**(2), 476–484 (2011)
5. Alvarez, J.M., Gevers, T., LeCun, Y., Lopez, A.M.: Road scene segmentation from a single image. In: Fitzgibbon, A., Lazebnik, S., Perona, P., Sato, Y., Schmid, C. (eds.) ECCV 2012, Part VII. LNCS, vol. 7578, pp. 376–389. Springer, Heidelberg (2012)
6. Badrinarayanan, V., Kendall, A., Cipolla, R.: Segnet: a deep convolutional encoder-decoder architecture for image segmentation. arXiv preprint arXiv:1511.00561 (2015)
7. Shin, H.-C., et al.: Deep convolutional neural networks for computer-aided detection: CNN architectures, dataset characteristics and transfer learning. IEEE Trans. Med. Imaging **35**(5), 1285–1298 (2016)
8. Jansen, P., et al.: Colour based off-road environment and terrain type classification, Piscataway, NJ. IEEE (2005)
9. Manduchi, R., et al.: Obstacle detection and terrain classification for autonomous off-road navigation. Auton. Robots **18**(1), 81–102 (2005)
10. Chatfield, K., Zisserman, A.: VISOR: towards on-the-fly large-scale object category retrieval. In: Lee, K.M., Matsushita, Y., Rehg, J.M., Hu, Z. (eds.) ACCV 2012, Part II. LNCS, vol. 7725, pp. 432–446. Springer, Heidelberg (2013)
11. Cortes, C., Vapnik, V.: Support-vector networks. Mach. Learn. **20**(3), 273–297 (1995)
12. Simonyan, K., Zisserman, A.: Very deep convolutional networks for large-scale image recognition. arXiv preprint arXiv:1409.1556 (2014)
13. Brostow, G.J., Fauqueur, J., Cipolla, R.: Semantic object classes in video: a high-definition ground truth database. Pattern Recogn. Lett. **30**(2), 88–97 (2009)
14. Bay, H., Tuytelaars, T., Van Gool, L.: SURF: speeded up robust features. In: Leonardis, A., Bischof, H., Pinz, A. (eds.) ECCV 2006, Part I. LNCS, vol. 3951, pp. 404–417. Springer, Heidelberg (2006)
15. Sivic, J., Zisserman, A.: Video Google: a text retrieval approach to object matching in videos. In: Proceedings of the Ninth IEEE International Conference on Computer Vision. IEEE (2003)

Joint Optical Flow and Temporally Consistent Semantic Segmentation

Junhwa Hur[✉] and Stefan Roth

Department of Computer Science, TU Darmstadt, Darmstadt, Germany
junhwa.hur@visinf.tu-darmstadt.de

Abstract. The importance and demands of visual scene understanding have been steadily increasing along with the active development of autonomous systems. Consequently, there has been a large amount of research dedicated to semantic segmentation and dense motion estimation. In this paper, we propose a method for jointly estimating optical flow and temporally consistent semantic segmentation, which closely connects these two problem domains and leverages each other. Semantic segmentation provides information on plausible physical motion to its associated pixels, and accurate pixel-level temporal correspondences enhance the accuracy of semantic segmentation in the temporal domain. We demonstrate the benefits of our approach on the KITTI benchmark, where we observe performance gains for flow and segmentation. We achieve state-of-the-art optical flow results, and outperform all published algorithms by a large margin on challenging, but crucial dynamic objects.

1 Introduction

Visual scene understanding from movable platforms has been gaining increased attention due to the active development of autonomous systems and vehicles. Semantic segmentation and dense motion estimation are two core components for recognizing the surrounding environment and analyzing the motion of entities in the scene. The performance of techniques in both areas has been steadily increasing, reported and fueled by public benchmarks (e.g., KITTI [9], MPI Sintel [4], or Cityscapes [6]). Along with the increasing popularity and importance of the two areas, there has been a recent trend in the literature considering how to bridge the two themes and analyzing which benefits these tasks can additionally derive from one another.

There have been a few basic attempts to utilize optical flow to enforce temporal consistency of semantic segmentation in a video sequence [5,10,22]. Also, segmenting the scene into superpixels (without clear semantics) has been shown to help estimating more accurate optical flow, assuming that object boundaries may give rise to motion boundaries [30,36,37]. Strictly speaking, however, previous work so far simply uses the results from one task as supplementary information for the other, and there have not been many attempts to relate the two tasks

© Springer International Publishing Switzerland 2016
G. Hua and H. Jégou (Eds.): ECCV 2016 Workshops, Part I, LNCS 9913, pp. 163–177, 2016.
DOI: 10.1007/978-3-319-46604-0_12

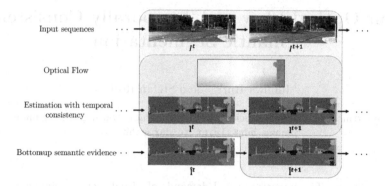

Fig. 1. Overview of our approach. The red region contributes to estimating optical flow, and the blue region ensures temporal consistency of the semantic segmentation, both given two frames. The overlapping region defines the output of our method. (Color figure online)

more closely or to solve them jointly. Yet, off-the-shelf motion estimation algorithms are not accurate enough to fully rely on [5, 22]. The only exception is very recent work that uses both semantic information and segmentation to increase the accuracy of optical flow [27], however without considering the benefits of temporal correspondence for semantic labeling.

In this paper, we address this gap and present an approach for joint optical flow estimation and temporally consistent semantic segmentation from monocular video, in which both tasks leverage each other. Figure 1 shows the overview of our method. We begin by assuming that a bottom-up semantic segmentation for each frame is given. Then we estimate accurate optical flow fields by exploiting the semantic information from the given semantic segmentation. The benefit of semantic labels is that they can give us information on the likely physical motion of the associated pixels. At the same time, accurate pixel-level correspondence between consecutive frames can establish temporally consistent semantic segmentations and help refining the initial results.

We make two major contributions. First, we introduce an accurate piecewise parametric optical flow formulation, which itself already outperforms the state of the art, particularly on dynamic objects. Our formulation explicitly handles occlusions to prevent the data term from unduly influencing the results in occlusion areas. As a result, our method additionally provides occlusion information such as occlusion masks and occlusion types. Our second contribution is to jointly estimate optical flow and temporally consistent semantic segmentation in a monocular video setting. For the flow estimation, we additionally apply the epipolar constraint for pixels that should be consistent with the camera ego-motion, as inferred by the semantic information. At the same time, accurately estimated flow helps to enforce temporal consistency on the semantic segmentation. We effectively realize these ideas in our joint formulation and make them feasible using inference based on patch-match belief propagation (PMBP) [2].

Our experiments on the popular KITTI dataset show that our method yields state-of-the-art results for optical flow. For estimating flows on dynamic foreground objects, which are particularly crucial from an autonomous navigation standpoint, our method outperforms all published optical flow algorithms in the benchmark by a significant margin.

2   Related Work

Piecewise Parametric Flow Estimation. Piecewise parametric approaches using a homography model have recently shown promising results on standard benchmarks [4, 9] for motion estimation. Representing the scene as a set of planar surfaces significantly reduces the number of unknowns; at the same time, parametrizing the motion of surfaces by 9-DoF or 8-DoF transforms ensures sufficient diversity and generality of their motion [12, 20, 31–33, 38]. In the stereo setting, Vogel *et al.* [31–33] proposed a scene representation consisting of piecewise 3D planes undergoing 3D rigid motion and demonstrate the most accurate results to date for estimating the 3D scene flow on the KITTI benchmark.

On the other hand, the monocular case with its limited amount of data (i.e., two consecutive images) makes the problem more challenging, hence the type of regularization becomes much more important [12, 38]. Hornacek *et al.* [12] introduced a 9-DoF plane-induced model for optical flow via continuous optimization. Their method shows its strength on rigid motions, but is weaker on poorly textured regions because of the lack of global support. Yang and Li [38] instead use a 8-DoF homography motion in 2D space with adaptive size and shape of the pieces via discrete optimization.

Our approach also relies on an 8-DoF parameterization, which we found to yield accurate optical flow estimates in practice.

Epipolar Constraint-Based Flow Estimation. Several approaches have relied on the epipolar constraint for estimating motion [1]. Strictly enforcing the constraint gives the benefit of reducing the search space significantly, but causes an inherent limitation for handling independently moving objects whose motion usually violates the constraint [13, 23, 36, 37]. Adding the constraint as a soft prior can resolve this issue, but there is still the challenge of determining where to relinquish the constraint by only depending on the data term [34, 35].

Our approach explicitly resolves this ambiguity with the aid of semantic information, which provides information on the physical properties of objects (e.g., static or movable).

Temporally Consistent Semantic Segmentation. Among a broad literature on enabling temporal consistency of video segmentation, we specifically consider the case of semantic segmentation here. One common way to inject temporal consistency is to utilize motion and structure features from 3D point clouds obtained by Structure from Motion (SfM) [3, 7, 29]. Another way is to jointly reconstruct a scene in 3D with semantic labels through a batch process, naturally enabling temporally consistent segmentation [14, 26, 40]. In causal approaches that rely on temporal correspondence, previous approaches achieve accurate temporal correspondence using sparse feature tracking [25] or dense flow maps with a similarity function in feature space [22]. A recent work [15] introduces feature space optimization for spatio-temporal regularization in partitioned batches with overlaps.

We achieve temporal consistency for semantic segmentation using a jointly estimated, accurate dense flow map, which leverages the semantic information.

Optical Flow with Semantics. The question of exploiting semantics for optical flow has only received very limited attention so far. The most related approach is the very recent work by Sevilla-Lara *et al.* [27], which treats the problem sequentially. First, the scene is segmented into 3 semantic categories, things, planes and stuff. Second, motion is estimated individually for these semantic parts and later composited. In contrast, we treat the entire problem as the minimization of a single unified energy. Moreover, motion estimation and semantic segmentation are inferred jointly instead of sequentially, hence may mutually leverage each other. Experimentally, we report significantly more accurate motion estimates for dynamic objects and demonstrate improved segmentation performance.

3   Approach

The core idea put forward in this paper is that optical flow and semantic segmentation are mutually beneficial and are best estimated jointly to simultaneously improve each other. Figure 1 shows the flow of our proposed method in the temporal domain and explains which elements contribute to achieving which task. Here, we assume that some initial bottom-up semantic evidence is already given by an off-the-shelf algorithm, such as a CNN (e.g., [16]), which is subsequently refined by having temporal consistency. In the red-shaded region, a pair of consecutive images and their refined semantic segmentation contribute to estimating optical flow more accurately. At the same time, the temporally consistent semantic labeling at time $t + 1$ is inferred from its bottom-up evidence, the previously estimated semantic labeling at time t, and the estimated flow map. For longer sequences, our approach proceeds in an online manner on two frames at a time.

Similar to [38], our formulation is based on an 8-DoF piecewise-parametric model with a superpixelization of the scene. Superpixels play an important role in our formulation for connecting the two different domains: optical flow and semantic segmentation. One superpixel represents a global motion as well as a semantic label for its pixels inside, and the motion is constrained by the physical properties that the semantic label implies. For example, the motion of pixels corresponding to some physically-static objects (e.g., building or road) can only be caused by camera motion. Thus, enforcing the epipolar constraint on those pixels can effectively regularize their motion.

Another important feature of our formulation is that we explicitly formulate the occlusion relationship between superpixels [36,37] and infer the occlusion mask as well. This directly affects the data term such that it prevents occluded pixels from dominating the data term during the optimization.

3.1 Preprocessing

Superpixels. As superpixels generally tend to separate objects in images, they can be a good medium for carrying semantic labels and representative motions for their pixels. Our approach uses the recent state-of-the-art work of Yao *et al.* [39], which has shown to be well suited for estimating optical flow.

Semantic Segmentation. For the bottom-up semantic evidence, we use an off-the-shelf fully convolutional network (FCN) [16] trained on the Cityscapes dataset [6], which contains typical objects frequent in street scenes.

Fundamental Matrix Estimation. In order to apply the epipolar constraint on superpixels for which their semantic label tells us that they are surely static objects (e.g. roads, buildings, etc.), our approach requires the fundamental matrix resulting from the camera motion. We use a standard approach, i.e. matching SIFT keypoints [18] and using the 8-point algorithm [11] with RANSAC [17].

3.2 Model

Our model jointly estimates *(i)* the optical flow between reference frame I^t and the next frame I^{t+1}, and *(ii)* a temporally consistent semantic segmentation l^{t+1} given bottom-up semantic evidence $\hat{l}^{t+1}$ and the previously estimated semantic labeling l^t. l is a semantic label probability map, which has the same size as the input image and L channels, where L is the number of semantic classes. Instead of using a single label, we adopt label probabilities so that we can more naturally and continuously infer the semantic labels in the time domain. Note that we assume an online setting (i.e., no access to future information) and hence infer the segmentation at time $t+1$ rather than t. Optical flow is represented by a set of piecewise motions of superpixels in the reference frame. We define the motion of a superpixel through a homography and formulate the objective for estimating the 8-DoF homography $\mathbf{H}_s$ of each superpixel s and the temporally consistent semantic segmentation l^{t+1} as:

$$E(\mathbf{H}, l^{t+1}, o, b) = E_\mathrm{D}(\mathbf{H}, o) + \lambda_\mathrm{L} E_\mathrm{L}(\mathbf{H}, l^{t+1}, o) \\ + \lambda_\mathrm{P} E_\mathrm{P}(\mathbf{H}) + \lambda_\mathrm{C} E_\mathrm{C}(\mathbf{H}, o, b) + \lambda_\mathrm{B} E_\mathrm{B}(b). \tag{1}$$

Here, E_D, E_L, E_P, E_C, and E_B denote color data term, label data term, physical constraint term, connectivity term, and boundary occlusion prior, respectively.

We adopt two kinds of occlusion variables: the boundary occlusion label b between two superpixels, and the occlusion mask o defined at the pixel level. The boundary occlusion label b regularizes the spatial relationship between two neighboring superpixels (i.e., co-planar, hinge, left occlusion, or right occlusion) [36,37]. The occlusion mask o explicitly models whether a pixel is occluded or not. One important difference to previous superpixel-based work [37] is that we additionally infer a pixelwise occlusion mask, which prevents occluded pixels from adversely affecting the data cost.

Data Terms. The data terms aggregate photometric differences

$$E_D(\mathbf{H}, o) = \sum_{s \in S} \frac{1}{|s|} \underbrace{\sum_{\mathbf{p} \in s} (1 - o_{\mathbf{p}}) \rho_D \left(I^t(\mathbf{p}), I^{t+1}(\mathbf{p}') \right) + o_{\mathbf{p}} \lambda_o}_{\text{image data}} \tag{2}$$

and semantic label differences

$$E_L(\mathbf{H}, \mathbf{l}^{t+1}, o) = \sum_{s \in S} \frac{1}{|s|} \sum_{\mathbf{p} \in s} \phi_l(\mathbf{H}, \mathbf{l}_{\mathbf{p}'}^{t+1}, o) \qquad \text{with} \tag{3}$$

$$\phi_l(\mathbf{H}, \mathbf{l}_{\mathbf{p}'}^{t+1}, o) = \frac{1}{2} \sum_i^L (1 - o_{\mathbf{p}}) \left\| \mathbf{l}_{\mathbf{p}',i}^{t+1} - (\alpha \hat{\mathbf{l}}_{\mathbf{p}',i}^{t+1} + (1 - \alpha) \mathbf{l}_{\mathbf{p},i}^t) \right\|^2 \tag{4}$$

over each pixel of each superpixel. Here, $\mathbf{p}'$ is the corresponding pixel in I^{t+1} of pixel $\mathbf{p}$ in I^t, which is determined according to the homography $\mathbf{H}_{\mathcal{S}(\mathbf{p})} \in \mathbb{R}^{3 \times 3}$ of its superpixel

$$\mathbf{p}' = \mathbf{H}_{\mathcal{S}(\mathbf{p})} \mathbf{p}, \tag{5}$$

where $\mathcal{S} : I^t \to S$ is a mapping that assigns a pixel $\mathbf{p}$ to its superpixel $s \in S$.

In the image data term in Eq. (2), the function $\rho_D(\cdot, \cdot)$ measures the photometric differences between two pixels using the ternary transform [28] and a truncated linear penalty. If a pixel $\mathbf{p}$ is occluded (i.e., $o_{\mathbf{p}} = 1$), a constant penalty λ_o is applied.

The label data term in Eq. (3) measures the distance between two semantic label probability distributions over each pixel: *(i)* our estimation $\mathbf{l}_{\mathbf{p}'}^{t+1}$ and *(ii)* a weighted sum of the previous estimation $\mathbf{l}_{\mathbf{p}}^t$, which is propagated by the optical flow, and the bottom-up evidence $\hat{\mathbf{l}}_{\mathbf{p}'}^{t+1}$, while considering its occlusion status. The motivation of the term is to penalize label differences to the bottom-up evidence and at the same time propagate label evidence over time, except when an occlusion takes place.

Physical Constraint Term. Semantic labels can provide useful cues for estimating optical flow. If pixels are labeled as physically static objects, such as building, road, or infrastructure, then they normally do not undergo any 3D motion, hence their observed 2D motion is caused by camera motion and should thus satisfy the epipolar constraint. We define the corresponding term as

$$E_P(\mathbf{H}) = \sum_{s \in S} \min(\phi_P(s, \mathbf{H}_s), \lambda_{\text{non\_st}} + \beta[l_s^t \in L_{\text{st}}]), \tag{6}$$

$$\text{where} \quad \phi_{\text{st}}(s, \mathbf{H}_s) = \frac{1}{|s|} \sum_{\mathbf{p} \in s} \left\| (\mathbf{p}'^{\top} \mathbf{F} \mathbf{p}) \right\|_1 = \frac{1}{|s|} \sum_{\mathbf{p} \in s} \left\| ((\mathbf{H}_{\mathcal{S}(\mathbf{p})} \mathbf{p})^{\top} \mathbf{F} \mathbf{p}) \right\|_1 \tag{7}$$

measures how well the homography matrix $\mathbf{H}_s$ of a superpixel s meets the epipolar constraint from the fundamental matrix $\mathbf{F}$. For non-static objects, such as pedestrians or vehicles, we still apply the epipolar penalty, however a weak one

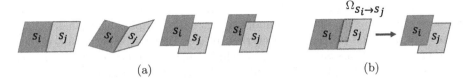

Fig. 2. *(a)* Four cases of boundary relations between two superpixels: co-planar, hinge, left occlusion, and right occlusion. *(b)* The visualization of the set of occluded pixels $\Omega_{s_i \to s_j}$ in the case of a left occlusion (black-colored region).

using a low truncation threshold $\lambda_{\mathrm{non\_st}}$. This is motivated by the fact that possibly dynamic objects may in fact stand still and thus obey epipolar geometry, but we do not want to penalize them too much if they do not. For static objects, on the other hand, we augment the truncation threshold by β in order to give a stricter penalty. L_{st} is the set of semantic labels that corresponds to the physically static objects. l_s is a representative semantic label of superpixel s, which has the highest probability over the pixels in the superpixel: $l_s = \mathrm{argmax}_i \sum_{\mathbf{p} \in s} l^t_{\mathbf{p},i}$.

Connectivity Term. The connectivity term encourages the smoothness of motion between two neighboring superpixels based on their occlusion relationship:

$$E_C(\mathbf{H}, o, b) = \sum_{s_i \sim s_j} \phi_C(\mathbf{H}_{s_i}, \mathbf{H}_{s_j}, o, b_{ij}) \qquad (8)$$

$$\text{with} \quad \phi_C(\mathbf{H}_{s_i}, \mathbf{H}_{s_j}, o, b_{ij}) = \begin{cases} \phi_{\mathrm{co}}(\mathbf{H}_{s_i}, \mathbf{H}_{s_j}, o) & \text{if } b_{ij} = \text{co-planar,} \\ \phi_{\mathrm{h}}(\mathbf{H}_{s_i}, \mathbf{H}_{s_j}, o) & \text{if } b_{ij} = \text{hinge,} \\ \phi_{\mathrm{occ}}(s_i, s_j, o) & \text{if } b_{ij} = \text{left occlusion,} \\ \phi_{\mathrm{occ}}(s_j, s_i, o) & \text{if } b_{ij} = \text{right occlusion.} \end{cases} \qquad (9)$$

As shown in Fig. 2(a), the boundary occlusion flag b_{ij} expresses the relationship between two neighboring superpixels s_i and s_j as co-planar, hinge, left-occlusion, or right-occlusion [36,37]. This categorization helps to regularize the motion of two superpixels defined by their homography matrices. We distinguish between three different potentials:

$$\phi_{\mathrm{co}}(\mathbf{H}_{s_i}, \mathbf{H}_{s_j}, o) = \frac{1}{|s_i \cup s_j|} \sum_{\mathbf{p} \in s_i \cup s_j} \|\mathbf{H}_{s_i}\mathbf{p} - \mathbf{H}_{s_j}\mathbf{p}\|_1 + \sum_{\mathbf{p} \in s_i \cup s_j} \lambda_{\mathrm{imp}}[o_p = 1] \qquad (10)$$

$$\phi_{\mathrm{h}}(\mathbf{H}_{s_i}, \mathbf{H}_{s_j}, o) = \frac{1}{|\mathcal{B}_{s_i, s_j}|} \sum_{\mathbf{p} \in \mathcal{B}_{s_i, s_j}} \|\mathbf{H}_{s_i}\mathbf{p} - \mathbf{H}_{s_j}\mathbf{p}\|_1 + \sum_{\mathbf{p} \in s_i \cup s_j} \lambda_{\mathrm{imp}}[o_p = 1] \qquad (11)$$

$$\phi_{\mathrm{occ}}(s_{\mathrm{f}}, s_{\mathrm{b}}, o) = \sum_{\mathbf{p} \in s_{\mathrm{f}}} \lambda_{\mathrm{imp}}[o_p = 1]$$
$$+ \sum_{\mathbf{p} \in s_{\mathrm{b}}} \Big(\lambda_{\mathrm{imp}}[\mathbf{p} \in \Omega_{s_{\mathrm{f}} \to s_{\mathrm{b}}}][o_p = 0] + \lambda_{\mathrm{imp}}[\mathbf{p} \notin \Omega_{s_{\mathrm{f}} \to s_{\mathrm{b}}}][o_p = 1] \Big) (12)$$

These are motivated as follows: When two superpixels are co-planar, all pixels within should follow the identical homography matrix as they are on the same plane. For a hinge relationship, only the pixels on the boundary set $\mathcal{B}_{s_i, s_j}$ can satisfy the motion from two superpixels s_i and s_j. In both cases, there should be no occluded pixels, hence we adopt a very large 'impossible' penalty λ_{imp} to prevent occluded pixels from occurring. In case that one superpixel occludes another, their motions only affect the occlusion masks. Equation (12) expresses the case that pixels of the front superpixel s_f occlude some pixels of the back superpixel s_b. As shown in Fig. 2(b), $\Omega_{s_f \to s_b}$ is a set of pixels in s_b that is occluded by some pixels in s_f from the motion. All pixels in the front superpixel s_f should not be occluded, and only pixels in the set of $\Omega_{s_f \to s_b}$ in s_b should be occluded.

Boundary Occlusion Prior. Without an additional prior term, the boundary occlusion flag in the connectivity term would prefer to take the occlusion cases. We thus define a prior term to yield proper biases for each case:

$$E_{\text{B}}(b) = \begin{cases} \lambda_{\text{co}}[l_{s_i} \neq l_{s_j}] & \text{if } b_{ij} = \text{co-planar,} \\ \lambda_{\text{h}} & \text{if } b_{ij} = \text{hinge,} \\ \lambda_{\text{occ}} & \text{if } b_{ij} = \text{occlusion,} \end{cases} \tag{13}$$

where $\lambda_{\text{occ}} > \lambda_{\text{h}} > \lambda_{\text{co}} > 0$. Because it is less likely that two different objects are co-planar in the real world, we only apply the prior penalty for the co-planar case λ_{co} when the respective semantic labels of the superpixels differ.

3.3   Optimization

The minimization of our objective is challenging, as it combines discrete (i.e., $\{l^{t+1}, b, o\}$) and continuous (i.e., $\mathbf{H}$) variables. We use a block coordinate descent algorithm. As shown in Algorithm 1, we iteratively update each variable in the order: *(i)* homography matrices $\mathbf{H}$ for superpixels, *(ii)* occlusion variables b, o, and *(iii)* semantic label probability maps l^{t+1}. Optimizing the homography matrices $\mathbf{H}$ is especially challenging because the matrices have 8 DoF in 2D space and their parameterization incurs a high-dimensional search space. We address this using PatchMatch Belief Propagation (PMBP) [2]; see below for details.

Once the motion $\mathbf{H}$ is updated, occlusion variables can be easily updated independently for each pair of neighboring superpixels, while other variables are held fixed. Given their motions, we first calculate the overlapping region, which can potentially be the occluded region for one of the two superpixels. Then, we calculate the energy in Eq. (1) for all four boundary occlusion cases with the candidate occlusion pixels given. The boundary occlusion case that has the minimum energy is taken, including the corresponding occlusion mask state. Finally, the semantic label probability map l^{t+1} can also be easily updated independently for all superpixels by minimizing label data term in Eq. (3).

Optimizing Homography Matrices Using PMBP. Our method optimizes the homography matrices in the continuous domain using PatchMatch Belief Propagation (PMBP) [12]. PMBP is a simple but powerful optimizer based on Belief Propagation. Instead of using a discrete label set, PMBP uses a set of particles that is randomly sampled and propagated in the continuous domain.

Algorithm 1. Optimization

---

initialization();
for $m = 1$ *to n-outer-iters* **do**
    for $n = 1$ *to n-inner-iters* **do**
        | Optimizing $E(\mathbf{H}, l^{t+1}, o, b)$ for $\mathbf{H}$ using PMBP
    end
    $\{b, o\} = \text{argmin}_{b,o}\, E(\mathbf{H}, l^{t+1}, o, b)$
    $l^{t+1} = \text{argmin}_{l^{t+1}}\, E(\mathbf{H}, l^{t+1}, o, b)$
end

PMBP requires an effective way of proposing the random particles; typically they are obtained from a normal distribution defined over some parameters. In our approach, however, we devise several strategies for proposing particles of the homography matrices without over-parameterization. Between two image patches, a superpixel and its corresponding region in the other frame, we estimate the homography matrix by using *(i)* LK warping, *(ii)* 3 correspondences and the fundamental matrix, *(iii)* 4 randomly perturbed correspondences, and *(iv)* sampled correspondences from neighboring superpixels. Empirically, we find that these strategies generate reasonable particles without requiring an over-parameterization, and only 5 outer-iterations are enough to be converged.

4 Experiments

We verify the effectiveness of our approach with a series of experiments on the well-established KITTI benchmark [9]. To the best of our knowledge, there is no dataset that simultaneously provides ground truth for optical flow and semantic segmentation in the same scenes; while ground truth for both is available in the KITTI benchmark, the evaluation is carried out on disjoint sequences.

We first evaluate our optical flow results on the KITTI Optical Flow 2015 benchmark and compare to the top-performing algorithms in the benchmark. In addition, we analyze the effectiveness of the semantics-related terms to understand how effectively the semantic information contributes to the estimation of optical flow. Finally, we demonstrate qualitative and quantitative results for temporally consistent semantic segmentation. We use DiscreteFlow [21] to initialize the flow estimation and utilize the FCN model [16] trained on the Cityscapes dataset [6] for bottom-up semantic segmentation evidence. We set our parameters automatically using Bayesian optimization [19] on the training portion.

4.1 KITTI 2015 Optical Flow

We compare to the top-scoring optical flow methods on the KITTI Optical Flow 2015 benchmark, which have been published at the time of submission. Note that we do not consider scene flow methods here, as they have access to multiple views. Table 1 shows the results. *Fl-bg*, *Fl-fg*, and *Fl-all* denote the flow error

Table 1. KITTI optical flow 2015: comparison to the published top-performing optical flow methods in the benchmark. Our method leads to state-of-the-art results and significantly increases the performance on challenging dynamic regions (*fg*).

Method	Non-occluded pixels			All pixels		
	Fl-bg	Fl-fg	Fl-all	Fl-bg	Fl-fg	Fl-all
MotionSLIC [36]	**6.19 %**	64.82 %	16.83 %	14.86 %	66.21 %	23.40 %
PatchBatch [8]	10.06 %	26.21 %	12.99 %	19.98 %	30.24 %	21.69 %
DiscreteFlow [21]	9.96 %	22.17 %	12.18 %	21.53 %	26.68 %	22.38 %
SOF [27]	8.11 %	23.28 %	10.86 %	**14.63 %**	27.73 %	**16.81 %**
Ours (JFS)	7.85 %	**18.66 %**	**9.81 %**	15.90 %	**22.92 %**	17.07 %

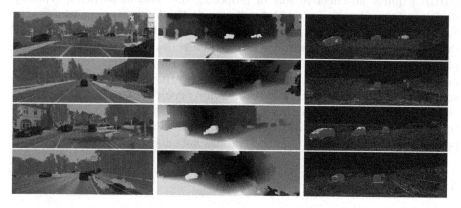

Fig. 3. Results on KITTI Optical Flow 2015. Left: Source images overlaid with semantic segmentation results. **Middle**: Our flow estimation results. **Right**: Qualitative comparison with DiscreteFlow: gray pixels – both methods correct, skyblue pixels – our method is correct but DiscreteFlow is not, red pixels – DiscreteFlow is correct but ours is not, and yellow pixels – both failed. (Color figure online)

evaluated for background pixels only, foreground pixels only, or for all pixels, respectively. Our method outperforms all top-scoring methods when considering all non-occluded pixels and performs very close to the leading method when considering all pixels. Especially for the flow of dynamic foreground objects, our method outperforms all published results by a large margin. This is of particular importance in the domain of autonomous navigation where understanding the motion of other traffic participants is crucial. This substantial performance gain stems from several design decisions. First, our piecewise motion representation effectively abstracts the planar surfaces of foreground vehicles, and the 8-DoF homography successfully describes the rigid motion of each surface.

The soft epipolar constraint of our model, derived from the jointly estimated semantics, contributes to the flow estimation particularly on background pixels and clear performance gains are observed for non-occluded pixels. When including occluded pixels, however, SOF [27] slightly outperforms ours.

The main reason is that their localized layer approach and planar approximation with large pieces can regularize the occluded regions better than our piecewise model based on superpixels. In future work, this gap may be addressed through an additional global support model or coarse-to-fine estimation. MotionSLIC [36] still performs better than ours on background pixels by strictly enforcing the epipolar constraint. As a trade-off, however, their strict epipolar constraint yields significant flow errors for foreground pixels and eventually increases the overall error.

Figure 3 shows visual results on the KITTI dataset (visualized as in [27]) and provides a direct comparison to DiscreteFlow, which highlights where the performance gain over the initialization originates. Our method provides more accurate flow estimates on foreground objects, but also on static objects.

4.2 Effectiveness of Semantic-Related Terms

Next we analyze the effectiveness of the semantic-related terms, the epipolar constraint term and the label data term, in order to understand how much the semantic information contributes to optical flow estimation over our basic piecewise optical flow model. We turned off each term and evaluated how each setting affects the flow estimation results on the KITTI Flow 2015 training dataset. The analysis is shown in Table 2.

We find that the label term clearly contributes to more accurate flow estimation overall, but it has a side-effect on background areas where the initial semantic segmentation may have some outliers. Using the epipolar constraint term results in more accurate flow estimates on background areas, which majorly satisfy the epipolar assumption. On foreground objects, however, the flow error slightly increases. This performance loss is coming from the trade-off of our assumption that non-static objects (e.g., vehicles) sometimes do not move, which made us apply the epipolar cost but with a small truncation threshold.

One interesting observation is that our basic piecewise flow model, without the semantic-related terms, still demonstrates competitive performance for estimating optical flow on non-occluded pixels.

Table 2. Effectiveness of semantic-related terms: the performance of our basic piecewise optical flow model is boosted further (KITTI 2015 training set).

Usage of terms		Non-occluded pixels			All pixels		
Label	Epi	Fl-bg	Fl-fg	Fl-all	Fl-bg	Fl-fg	Fl-all
✓	✓	8.27 %	17.40 %	**9.83 %**	16.44 %	20.02 %	**16.98 %**
✓	✗	8.45 %	**16.97 %**	9.90 %	16.73 %	**19.61 %**	17.17 %
✗	✓	**8.20 %**	17.82 %	9.84 %	**16.35 %**	20.41 ,%	16.99 %
✗	✗	8.51 %	17.21 %	10.00 %	16.84 %	19.86 %	17.31 %

Table 3. Performance of temporally consistent semantic segmentation.

IoU (%)	Sky	Building	Road	Sidewalk	Fence	Vegetation	Pole	Car	Sign	Pedestrian	Cyclist	Mean
FCN [16]	69.35	78.53	73.75	38.19	33.33	68.37	23.68	77.60	31.27	20.11	21.42	48.69
Ours	71.80	79.97	77.99	41.01	36.27	69.21	16.44	78.58	39.05	23.50	25.44	50.84

FCN [16]

Ours

time t-1   time t   time t+1
(a) Results on three consecutive frames.

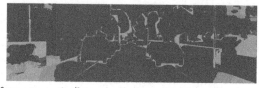

(b) Performance gain/loss over bottom-up semantic segmentation.

Fig. 4. Temporally consistent semantic segmentation results.

4.3 Temporally Consistent Semantic Segmentation

We finally evaluate the performance of our temporally consistent semantic segmentation on a sequence from the KITTI dataset, which has a 3rd-party ground truth semantic annotation [24]. This, however, is a preliminary result, since the semantic segmentation model we used here is trained on the higher-resolution Cityscapes dataset [6], which possesses somewhat different statistics. Better results are expected from a custom-trained model. Table 3 shows that our joint approach increases the segmentation accuracy over the bottom-up segmentation results [16] by 2 % points in the intersection-over-union (IoU) metric. The accuracy is increased on all object classes except for the pole class, which is not well captured by our superpixels. Figure 4(a) shows our results on three consecutive frames, and Fig. 4(b) demonstrates our performance gain/loss over the bottom-up segmentation using the visualization of Fig. 3. With the aid of accurate temporal correspondences, our method revises inconsistent results and effectively reduces false positives in the time domain.

5   Conclusion

We have proposed a method for jointly estimating optical flow and temporally consistent semantic segmentation from monocular video. Our results on the challenging KITTI benchmark demonstrated that both tasks can successfully leverage each other. A piecewise optical flow model with PMBP inference builds the basis and itself already achieves competitive results. Embedding semantic information through label consistency and epipolar constraints further boosts the performance. For dynamic objects, which are particularly important from the viewpoint of autonomous navigation, our method outperforms all published results in the benchmark by a large margin. Preliminary results on temporally consistent semantic segmentation further demonstrate the benefit of our approach by reducing false positives and flickering. We believe that a refinement of the superpixels may lead to further performance gains in the future.

Acknowledgement. We thank Marius Cordts for providing a pre-trained semantic segmentation model. The research leading to these results has received funding from the European Research Council under the European Union's Seventh Framework Programme (FP7/2007–2013)/ERC Grant Agreement No. 307942.

References

1. Baker, S., Scharstein, D., Lewis, J.P., Roth, S., Black, M.J., Szeliski, R.: A database and evaluation methodology for optical flow. Int. J. Comput. Vis. **92**(1), 1–31 (2011)
2. Besse, F., Rother, C., Fitzgibbon, A., Kautz, J.: PMBP: PatchMatch belief propagation for correspondence field estimation. Int. J. Comput. Vis. **110**(1), 2–13 (2013)
3. Brostow, G.J., Shotton, J., Fauqueur, J., Cipolla, R.: Segmentation and recognition using structure from motion point clouds. In: Forsyth, D., Torr, P., Zisserman, A. (eds.) ECCV 2008. LNCS, vol. 5302, pp. 44–57. Springer, Heidelberg (2008). doi:10.1007/978-3-540-88682-2_5
4. Butler, D.J., Wulff, J., Stanley, G.B., Black, M.J.: A naturalistic open source movie for optical flow evaluation. In: Fitzgibbon, A., Lazebnik, S., Perona, P., Sato, Y., Schmid, C. (eds.) ECCV 2012. LNCS, vol. 7577, pp. 611–625. Springer, Heidelberg (2012). doi:10.1007/978-3-642-33783-3_44
5. Chen, A.Y.C., Corso, J.J.: Temporally consistent multi-class video-object segmentation with the video graph-shifts algorithm. In: WACV (2011)
6. Cordts, M., Omran, M., Ramos, S., Scharwächter, T., Enzweiler, M., Benenson, R., Franke, U., Roth, S., Schiele, B.: The cityscapes dataset for semantic urban scene understanding. In: CVPR (2016)
7. Floros, G., Leibe, B.: Joint 2D–3D temporally consistent semantic segmentation of street scenes. In: CVPR (2012)
8. Gadot, D., Wolf, L.: PatchBatch: a batch augmented loss for optical flow. In: CVPR (2016)
9. Geiger, A., Lenz, P., Urtasun, R.: Are we ready for autonomous driving? The KITTI vision benchmark suite. In: CVPR (2012)
10. Grundmann, M., Kwatra, V., Han, M., Essa, I.: Efficient hierarchical graph-based video segmentation. In: CVPR (2010)
11. Hartley, R.I.: In defense of the eight-point algorithm. IEEE Trans. Pattern Anal. Mach. Intell. **19**(6), 580–593 (1997)
12. Hornáček, M., Besse, F., Kautz, J., Fitzgibbon, A., Rother, C.: Highly overparameterized optical flow using PatchMatch belief propagation. In: Fleet, D., Pajdla, T., Schiele, B., Tuytelaars, T. (eds.) ECCV 2014. LNCS, vol. 8691, pp. 220–234. Springer, Heidelberg (2014). doi:10.1007/978-3-319-10578-9_15

13. Kitt, B., Lategahn, H.: Trinocular optical flow estimation for intelligent vehicle applications. In: ITSC (2012)
14. Kundu, A., Li, Y., Dellaert, F., Li, F., Rehg, J.M.: Joint semantic segmentation and 3D reconstruction from monocular video. In: Fleet, D., Pajdla, T., Schiele, B., Tuytelaars, T. (eds.) ECCV 2014. LNCS, vol. 8694, pp. 703–718. Springer, Heidelberg (2014). doi:10.1007/978-3-319-10599-4_45
15. Kundu, A., Vineet, V., Koltun, V.: Feature space optimization for semantic video segmentation. In: CVPR (2016)
16. Long, J., Shelhamer, E., Darrell, T.: Fully convolutional networks for semantic segmentation. In: CVPR (2015)
17. Lourakis, M.: Fundest: a C/C++ library for robust, non-linear fundamental matrix estimation (2011). http://www.ics.forth.gr/~lourakis/fundest/
18. Lowe, D.G.: Distinctive image features from scale-invariant keypoints. Int. J. Comput. Vis. **60**(2), 91–110 (2004)
19. Martinez-Cantin, R.: BayesOpt: a Bayesian optimization library for nonlinear optimization, experimental design and bandits. J. Mach. Learn. Res. **15**, 3735–3739 (2014)
20. Menze, M., Geiger, A.: Object scene flow for autonomous vehicles. In: CVPR (2015)
21. Menze, M., Heipke, C., Geiger, A.: Discrete optimization for optical flow. In: Gall, J., Gehler, P., Leibe, B. (eds.) GCPR 2015. LNCS, vol. 9358, pp. 16–28. Springer, Heidelberg (2015). doi:10.1007/978-3-319-24947-6_2
22. Miksik, O., Munoz, D., Bagnell, J.A., Hebert, M.: Efficient temporal consistency for streaming video scene analysis. In: ICRA (2013)
23. Mohamed, M.A., Mirabdollah, M.H., Mertsching, B.: Differential optical flow estimation under monocular epipolar line constraint. In: Nalpantidis, L., Krüger, V., Eklundh, J.-O., Gasteratos, A. (eds.) ICVS 2015. LNCS, vol. 9163, pp. 354–363. Springer, Heidelberg (2015). doi:10.1007/978-3-319-20904-3_32
24. Ros, G., Ramos, S., Granados, M., Bakhtiary, A., Vazquez, D., Lopez, A.M.: Vision-based offline-online perception paradigm for autonomous driving. In: WACV (2015)
25. Scharwächter, T., Enzweiler, M., Franke, U., Roth, S.: Stixmantics: a medium-level model for real-time semantic scene understanding. In: Fleet, D., Pajdla, T., Schiele, B., Tuytelaars, T. (eds.) ECCV 2014. LNCS, vol. 8693, pp. 533–548. Springer, Heidelberg (2014). doi:10.1007/978-3-319-10602-1_35
26. Sengupta, S., Greveson, E., Shahrokni, A., Torr, P.H.S.: Urban 3D semantic modelling using stereo vision. In: ICRA (2013)
27. Sevilla-Lara, L., Sun, D., Jampani, V., Black, M.J.: Optical flow with semantic segmentation and localized layers. In: CVPR (2016)
28. Stein, F.: Efficient computation of optical flow using the census transform. In: Rasmussen, C.E., Bülthoff, H.H., Schölkopf, B., Giese, M.A. (eds.) DAGM 2004. LNCS, vol. 3175, pp. 79–86. Springer, Heidelberg (2004). doi:10.1007/978-3-540-28649-3_10
29. Sturgess, P., Alahari, K., Ladicky, L., Torr, P.H.S.: Combining appearance and structure from motion features for road scene understanding. In: BMVC (2012)
30. Sun, D., Liu, C., Pfister, H.: Local layering for joint motion estimation and occlusion detection. In: CVPR (2014)
31. Vogel, C., Roth, S., Schindler, K.: View-consistent 3D scene flow estimation over multiple frames. In: Fleet, D., Pajdla, T., Schiele, B., Tuytelaars, T. (eds.) ECCV 2014. LNCS, vol. 8692, pp. 263–278. Springer, Heidelberg (2014). doi:10.1007/978-3-319-10593-2_18
32. Vogel, C., Schindler, K., Roth, S.: Piecewise rigid scene flow. In: ICCV, pp. 1377–1384 (2013)

33. Vogel, C., Schindler, K., Roth, S.: 3D scene flow estimation with a piecewise rigid scene model. Int. J. Comput. Vis. **115**(1), 1–28 (2015)
34. Wedel, A., Pock, T., Braun, J., Franke, U., Cremers, D.: Duality TV-L1 flow with fundamental matrix prior. In: IVCNZ (2008)
35. Wedel, A., Cremers, D., Pock, T., Bischof, H.: Structure- and motion-adaptive regularization for high accuracy optic flow. In: ICCV, pp. 1663–1668 (2009)
36. Yamaguchi, K., McAllester, D., Urtasun, R.: Robust monocular epipolar flow estimation. In: CVPR (2013)
37. Yamaguchi, K., McAllester, D., Urtasun, R.: Efficient joint segmentation, occlusion labeling, stereo and flow estimation. In: Fleet, D., Pajdla, T., Schiele, B., Tuytelaars, T. (eds.) ECCV 2014. LNCS, vol. 8693, pp. 756–771. Springer, Heidelberg (2014). doi:10.1007/978-3-319-10602-1_49
38. Yang, J., Li, H.: Dense, accurate optical flow estimation with piecewise parametric model. In: CVPR (2015)
39. Yao, J., Boben, M., Fidler, S., Urtasun, R.: Real-time coarse-to-fine topologically preserving segmentation. In: CVPR (2015)
40. Zhang, C., Wang, L., Yang, R.: Semantic segmentation of urban scenes using dense depth maps. In: Daniilidis, K., Maragos, P., Paragios, N. (eds.) ECCV 2010. LNCS, vol. 6314, pp. 708–721. Springer, Heidelberg (2010). doi:10.1007/978-3-642-15561-1_51

Fusing Convolutional Neural Networks with a Restoration Network for Increasing Accuracy and Stability

Hamed H. Aghdam$^{(\boxtimes)}$, Elnaz J. Heravi, and Domenec Puig

Department of Computer Engineering and Mathematics,
University Rovira i Virgili, Tarragona, Spain
{hamed.habibi,elnaz.jahani,domenec.puig}@urv.cat

Abstract. In this paper, we propose a ConvNet for restoring images. Our ConvNet is different from state-of-art denoising networks in the sense that it is deeper and instead of restoring the image directly, it generates a pattern which is added with the noisy image for restoring the clean image. Our experiments shows that the Lipschitz constant of the proposed network is less than 1 and it is able to remove very strong as well as very slight noises. This ability is mainly because of the shortcut connection in our network. We compare the proposed network with another denoisnig ConvNet and illustrate that the network without a shortcut connection acts poorly on low magnitude noises. Moreover, we show that attaching the restoration ConvNet to a classification network increases the classification accuracy. Finally, our empirical analysis reveals that attaching a classification ConvNet with a restoration network can significantly increase its stability against noise.

Keywords: Image restoration · Image denoising · Traffic sign classification · Deep learning

1 Introduction

Convolutional Neural Networks (ConvNets) have considerably advanced compared with AlextNet [1] which won the ImageNet competition in 2012. In particular, depth of ConvNets have greatly increased last years. Szegedy et al. [2] created a network consisting of multiple Inception modules. Besides, Simonyan and Zisserman [3] proposed a network with 19 layers. The idea behind this ConvNet is to increase the depth rather than its width. Srivastava et al. [4] showed how to train very deep networks by directly flowing information from previous layers to next layers through a gate function. Recently, He et al. [5] trained a 152-layer ConvNet and won the ImageNet competition. Their ConvNet is similar to [4] in the sense that information flows directly to the following layers. However, the gate function in [4] has been replaced with an identity mapping function.

© Springer International Publishing Switzerland 2016
G. Hua and H. Jégou (Eds.): ECCV 2016 Workshops, Part I, LNCS 9913, pp. 178–191, 2016.
DOI: 10.1007/978-3-319-46604-0_13

Despite the impressive results obtained by ConvNets, Szegedy *et al.* [6] showed that small perturbation of input images can alter their classification result. The perturbed samples are called *adversarial examples*. The difference between the original image and its adversarial sample is not sometimes even recognizable to human eye. They study the reason by computing the *upper bound* of the Lipschitz constant for each layer. The results suggest that instability of ConvNets might be due to the fact that they are highly non-linear functions. As the result, a small change in the input may considerably change the output. We also carried out an empirical study on various ConvNet architectures trained on different datasets [7]. In this work, we generated 1200 noisy images for each sample in the test sets using a Gaussian noise with $\sigma \in [1 \dots 40]$. The results showed that all the ConvNets in our experiments were unstable to image degradation even when the samples were degraded using the Gaussian noise with $\sigma = 1$. Moreover, the ConvNets were unstable regardless of the class of the object.

Contribution: In this paper, we deal with adversarial examples from another perspective. Denoting the *softmax* layer of a ConvNet (*i.e.* the last layer in a classification ConvNet) by $\mathcal{L}_\theta(x)$, the general idea is to find a parameter vector θ such that:

$$\forall_{\|\nu\| \le \epsilon} \; \mathcal{L}_\theta(x + \nu) = \mathcal{L}_\theta(x) \tag{1}$$

where ν is an additive noise vector whose magnitude is less than ϵ. As we mentioned earlier, solving instability problem using the above formulation may require to add new terms to the loss function or devise new sets of layers to our ConvNet. Instead, we utilize currently available layers, optimization technique and loss function to increase the stability of the ConvNets. Mathematically, we are looking for two sets of parameters θ_1 and θ_2 such that:

$$\forall_{\|\nu\| \le \epsilon} \; \mathcal{L}_{\theta_1}(\mathcal{F}_{\theta_2}(x + \nu)) = \mathcal{L}_{\theta_1}(\mathcal{F}_{\theta_2}(x)). \tag{2}$$

In other words, our aim is to find a function $\mathcal{F} : \mathbb{R}^n \to \mathbb{R}^n$ that is able to map all points around $x \in \mathbb{R}^n$ to the same point. If we can find such a function, the sample x and all its adversarial examples will be mapped to the same point. Then, the classification ConvNet will be able to produce the same output for all adversarial examples. In Sect. 3, we explain how to model the function $\mathcal{F}$ using a ConvNet and train a classification ConvNet using $\mathcal{F}$. Our experiments in Sect. 4 show that the proposed formulation is able to increase the stability of ConvNets against additive noise. Also, it increases the classification accuracy. Last but not the least, we show that our formulation is able to deal with high magnitude as well as low magnitude noises.

2   Related Work

Szegedy *et al.* [6] discovered that ConvNets are sensitive to small variations of the input. They found the additive noise ν which was able to reduce the score of the true class close to zero. They also studied the non-linearity of ConvNets using the Lipschitz theorem. Similarly, Papernot *et al.* [8] produced adversarial samples which were incorrectly classified by the ConvNet. They produced these samples by modifying 4.02 % of the input features. We also proposed an objective function to find the minimal additive noise ν in the closest distance to the decision boundary in which $x+\nu$ falls into the wrong class [7]. Goodfellow *et al.* [9] argued that the instability of ConvNet to adversarial examples is due to linear nature of ConvNets. Based on this idea, they proposed a method for quickly generating adversarial examples. They used these examples to reduce the test error.

Gu and Rigazio [10] stacked a denoising autoencoder (DAE) to their ConvNet and preprocessed the adversarial examples using the DAE before feeding them to the ConvNet. They mentioned that the resulting network can be still attacked by new adversarial examples. Inspired by contractive autoencoders, they added a smoothness penalty to the objective function and trained a more stable network.

Instead of trying to minimize the classification score, Sabour *et al.* [11] tried to find a degraded image closest to the original image that its representation mimics those produced by natural images. Fawzi *et al.* [12] provided a theoretical framework for explaining the adversarial examples. Their framework suggests that the instability to noise is due to low flexibility of classifiers.

3   Proposed Method

As we mentioned in (2), our aim is to learn the function $\mathcal{F}(.)$ that is able to map the clean sample x and adversarial sample $x + \nu$ to vector y. In this paper, we set $y = x$ for simplicity. In other words, $\mathcal{F}(x + \nu) = \mathcal{F}(x) = x$. With this formulation, $\mathcal{F}$ can be seen as a function for denoising the additive noise from x. In contrast to [13], we do not restrict $\mathcal{F}$ to Gaussian noise. Furthermore, contrary to [14] that models $\mathcal{F}$ using 16 M parameters, we are interested in models with much fewer parameters and higher capacity.

Our model, $\mathcal{F}$, must be able to model wide range of random noises. From one perspective, $\mathcal{F}$ can be seen as an associative memory that is able to memorize all patterns $X = \{x_1 \ldots x_i \ldots_M\}, x_i \in \mathbb{R}^N$ in our dataset and map every sample $\{x_i + \nu | \|\nu\| \leq \epsilon\}$ to x_i. Here, x_i is an image patch and X is the set of all possible image patches collected from all classes of objects in our dataset.

The required memorizing capacity of $\mathcal{F}$ directly depends on the diversity and complexity of the patterns in X. Neural networks are non-linear functions with high capacity to memorize complex patterns. On the one hand, conventional neural networks (consisting only of fully connected layers) cannot be deep if we want to increase the width of the network since it can dramatically increase the number of the parameters. Another disadvantage of fully connected networks for modeling $\mathcal{F}$ is their computational complexity. On the other hand, complex patterns can be modeled and memorized better using deep models. Convolutional neural networks address both these problems using the weight sharing strategy. This makes it possible to increase both width and depth of the network. For this reason, we model $\mathcal{F}$ using a deep ConvNet. Compared with [14] and [15], our ConvNet is deeper and has more representation power. Also, in contrast to [17]

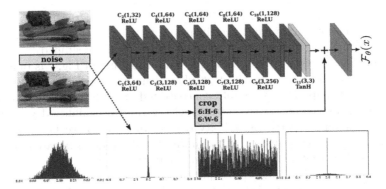

Fig. 1. The proposed ConvNet for modeling $\mathcal{F}$ in (2). Different noises including the Gaussian noise are generated as ν in (2). The histograms indicate a fews examples of probability density functions utilized for generating noise.

that uses a network with 4.5 M parameters, our ConvNet requires only 0.4 M (400 K) parameters. Finally, our network is different from all these networks in the sense that it facilitates learning $\mathcal{F}(x) = x$ using a shortcut connection. Figure 1 illustrates the architecture of our ConvNet.

The network consists of 11 convolution layers in which it only utilizes 3×3 or 1×1 kernels. Except the last convolution layer, there is a 1×1 convolution layer after every 3×3 convolution layer. The 1×1 kernels have been mainly used for two purposes. First, they apply a non-linear transformation on the input similar to the idea in [16]. Second, they reduce the number of the parameters in the next layer by decreasing the number of the feature maps. In fact, the number of the feature maps in each 1×1 layer is half of the number of the feature maps in the previous 3×3 layer.

Since the depth of the network is high, it is not practical (*e.g.* vanishing gradient problem) to use saturating non-linearities such as the hyperbolic or sigmoid functions. For this reason, we use *leaky rectified liner units* [17] with $\alpha = 0.01$ as the activation function in our network. However, the activation function of the last convolution layer is the *hyperbolic* function. Using this activation function, the last convolution layer is able to generate negative values which is crucial to remove noise from the image. In addition, the noise level must be in $[-1, 1]$.

In contrast to the previous methods that we mentioned in Sect. 2, the last convolution layer does not produce the restored image. Instead, it predicts a pattern that in which the clean image is restored by adding this pattern with the degraded image. In the case of additive noise, the output of the last convolution layer is $-\nu$ (see (2)). Adding $-\nu$ with the noisy input $x + \nu$ produces the clean input x. It should be noted that our network is able to denoise any kind of noise and it is not restricted to additive noise. In the case of non-additive noise, the last convolution layer generates a pattern that restores the clean image when it is added to the degraded image. The shortcut connection in our network plays a similar role as in [4,5] and it facilitates the training of the deep network. However, its major advantage is that it makes it easier for the network to learn the identity mapping function (*e.g.* when the image is not degraded).

It should be noted that the noise generation module in Fig. 1 is only used during the training phase. In the test phase, the noise generation module is omitted. In this paper, we have only concentrated on additive noise. The noise generation module creates noisy patterns with various probability density functions. Five examples of the probability density functions have been shown in the figure. Besides the Gaussian and uniform distributions, there are also other density functions that generate sparse noise patterns.

The proposed network accepts inputs bigger than 12×12 pixels. Given a $H \times W$ image, the output of the last convolution layer is a $H - 12 \times W - 12$ image. Hence, the input image cannot be directly added with the output of the last convolution layer. To this end, the image is cropped (central cropping) in the shortcut connection before adding with the last convolution layer. Although the need for cropping could be solved by padding the input image in the first convolution layer, notwithstanding, our experiments showed that 0-padding the image in the first layer decreases the training performance due to the border effect. However, after the network has been trained, we zero-pad the image in the first convolution layer and omit the cropping module in the test phase.

Finally, although the receptive field of each convolution kernel is small, the whole network works with 13×13 receptive fields. In other words, any element in the last convolution layer is computed using a 13×13 patch in the input image. In terms of associative memory network, our ConvNet tries to associate 13×13 image patches to a single number. It is possible to increase the receptive field by adding more 3×3 layers to the network and keep the number of the parameters low by adding 1×1 layers. However, we did not find a significant improvement by adding more layers to the network and the performances were comparable to the 11-layer network when they are trained on the datasets that we have used in this paper.

As we show in the next section, the trained network can be stacked to any classification network to restore the input images. The classification network (all layers) must be fine-tuned after freezing the layers of the restoration network.

4   Experiments

The restoration network is trained by minimizing the L_2 regularized *mean square error*:

$$E = \frac{1}{NM} \sum_{i=1}^{N} \sum_{j=1}^{M} \|x_i - \mathcal{F}_\theta(x_i + \nu_j)\|^2 + \lambda \|\theta\|^2 \tag{3}$$

where N is the total number of the images and M is the number of times that a noise pattern is generated for each sample. Also, θ is the set of network weights and biases and λ is the regularization coefficient. It is worth mentioning that the noisy patterns are generated on the fly. That said, we have implemented a degradation module which accepts a mini-batch of clean images and outputs their degraded version. Each sample in the mini-batch is degraded M times.

4.1 Implementation Details

We implemented the proposed network using Caffe framework [18]. However, the original Caffe framework is only able to generate Gaussian and uniform noises with known standard deviation and ranges. For this reason, we modified the noise generation class in the library[1] in order to generate Gaussian noises with random standard deviations and uniform noises with random ranges. Also, the generated noises are probabilistically processed by sparsifying the results or manipulating noise intensities heuristically.

All the weights in the network are initialized using the method in [19]. Although the input of the network could be images bigger than 12×12 pixels, we use 48×48 image patches as the input of the network. It is also possible to use bigger image patches, but, it will reduce the mini-batch size because of limitations of the memory on the GPU device. The network is trained using the momentum stochastic gradient descend, mini-batch size 50 and exponential learning rate annealing. We set momentum to 0.9, learning rate to 0.001, learning rate annealing to 0.99996, λ to $1e-6$ and maximum number of iterations to 10^5. Also, following the idea in [15] we set the learning rate of the last convolution layer to 0.0001. Note that we *do not* apply zero-padding in the training phase. Besides, the network input is normalized to $[0, 1]$. This is important since if we do not normalize the input of the network to this range, the output of the last convolution layer must be scaled accordingly to be in the same range as the input image.

After training the network, zero-padding is applied only in the first convolution layer (the size of padding is 6 for each side). Also, it is possible to feed images with arbitrary size to the network. We only need to always crop the network input 6 pixels from each side before adding with the output of the last convolution layer. Last but not the least, it is possible to use other color spaces instead of RGB space. The only modification that the network needs is to set the number of the feature map in the last convolution layer equal to the number of the channels in the input layer.

4.2 Dataset

In this section, we first assess the restoration capability of our ConvNet. Then, we evaluate how preprocessing of the inputs of a classification network using our ConvNet can affect the accuracy. To this end, we carry out our experiments on the German Traffic Sign Recognition Benchmark (GTSRB) dataset [20] which contains 43 classes of vertical traffic signs. Each color image in this dataset contains one traffic sign and they vary from 15×15 to 250×250 pixels. The training set consists of $39,209$ images and the test set contains $12,630$ images.

---

[1] We added a new function to filler.hpp file.

We use 10 % of the training set for validation. We first crop the image within the annotated bounding box and resize all the images to 48 × 48 pixels.

The GTSRB dataset has some important characteristics. First, it has been collected considering real scenarios and it contains many degraded images. Second, the imaging device is noisy and it has degraded edges of the objects in some cases. Third, the resolution of images are low. Therefore, a slight change in the image may affect the classification score.

Qualitative analysis: We randomly degraded some of the samples in the test set and restored them using our ConvNet. Figure 2 shows the results. Four different images have been shown for each sample starting from the noisy image in the left. Next, the output of the last convolution layer (*i.e.* ν) and the restored image are illustrated in the second column and third columns. Finally, the fourth column shows ν after normalizing the values between $[0, 1]$.

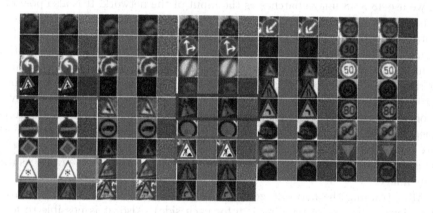

Fig. 2. Samples of restored images for each classes of traffic signs (best viewed in color and electronically). (Color figure online)

First we observe that samples indicated by the red rectangles are not strongly degraded. In other words, the restored image must be very close to the degraded image. We see that the ConvNet is able to accurately restore the image without manipulating the edges of the traffic sign. However, it slightly changes the background of the object. In addition, the background of the sample inside the green rectangle is completely bright. Also, the white color inside the traffic sign is not noisy. However, due to excessive amount of illumination, the edges of the traffic sign are slightly degraded. As it is clear from the normalized ν inside this rectangle, the ConvNet only manipulates the edges and ignores the clean pixels of the image. Finally, the strongly degraded image in the blue rectangle has been properly recovered using our ConvNet. In particular, the edges of the traffic sign are more clean and its background it more smoother. As we will discuss shortly, these three properties improves the classification accuracy of the classification ConvNet trained on this dataset.

Exploratory analysis: In order to analyze the performance of the proposed ConvNet, we created several versions of our ConvNets with various depth. In addition, we also implemented the ConvNet in [15] for the task of restoration. The architecture of the ConvNets are illustrated in Table 1. In the case of our ConvNets, the activation function of the last layer is the hyperbolic function. Also, the architecture and training procedure of last row in the table is exactly the same as in [15] except it is adapted on RGB images. It is worth mentioning that there is no shortcut connection in [15].

Table 1. Different ConvNet architectures trained for image restoration. The activation function of the last layer in all the ConvNets is hyperbolic function. Refer to the text for explanation.

ConvNet	#3x3	#1x1	#3x3	#1x1	#3x3	#1x1	#3x3	#1x1	#3x3	#1x1	#3x3
L11 (our)	64	32	128	64	128	64	128	64	256	128	3
L9	64	32	128	64	128	64	128	64	3	-	-
L7	64	32	128	64	128	64	3	-	-	-	-
L5	64	32	128	64	3	-	-	-	-	-	-
L3	64	32	3	-	-	-	-	-	-	-	-
	#9x9	#1x1	#5x5								
Dong [15]	64	32	3								

We analyzed the restoration capability of these ConvNets as follows: We picked 1263 samples from the test set and for each sample, 150 noisy samples were generated using the same generation module as in Fig. 1. Then, the noisy samples were fed to every ConvNet and the *peak signal to noise ratio* (PSNR) of the restored images were computed using the following equation:

$$psnr = 10 \log_{10} \left(\frac{255^2}{\frac{1}{HW} \sum_{m=i}^{H} \sum_{n=j}^{W} (x - x')^2} \right). \tag{4}$$

In the above equation, x is the clean image and x' is the noisy or restored image. Figure 3 shows different properties of the above ConvNets. The top plots show the PSNR of the noisy images versus the PSNR of the restored images along with the best polynomial line fitted on the result of each ConvNet, separately. We have fitted a line on the top-left plot and a second order polynomial on the top-right plot. In terms of restoration, the model in [15] has the lowest PSNR if the PSNR of the noisy image is more than 20 dB. In addition, L7, L9 and L11 ConvNets show similar performances. However, L5 ConvNet starts to act poorly compared with these three network when the PSNR of the input is more than 37 dB. Finally, L3 shows a more accurate behavior in higher PSNRs but its performance decreases quickly when the PSNR of the input is less than 35 dB.

Note that we are not only looking for a network that is able to accurately restore images. In (2) we mentioned that our aim is to increase the performance

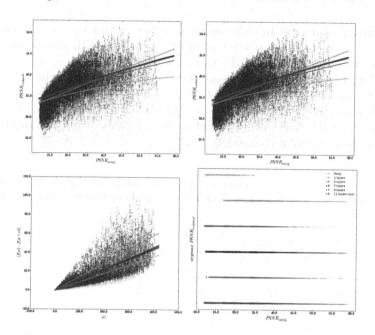

Fig. 3. PSNR of the ConvNet in Table 1 computed on the test samples. Refer to text for explanation (best viewed in color and electronically). (Color figure online)

and the stability a ConvNet by mapping all nearby samples around x to the same point. In other words, the output of the ConvNet must change slightly when the input changes dramatically. We have investigated this in the bottom-left plot in Fig. 3. The horizontal axis shows the magnitude of noise and the vertical axis shows the difference between the output of the networks supplied with the clean and noisy images. First, we observe that all the network are contraction. This means that the Lipschitz constant is in range $[0, 1)$ which is a desirable property for our task. Second, the network in [15] has the smallest value of K since for any magnitude of noise, the difference between the output of the clean image and the output of the noisy image is smallest compared with the other networks. Third, L5, L7, L9 and L11 act similarly but the level of contraction in L11 is more than L7 and L9. Also, L3 acts poorly compared with the other networks.

Quantitative results: We have tested the above networks by generating $1263 \times 150 = 189,450$ images. For each network in our experiment, we counted the number of the samples that each network has produced the highest PSNR. Table 2 shows the results. We observe that L11 has the highest number of hits by producing the best result in 52 % of the noisy samples. In addition, its output is within the top-2 PSNRs in the case of 76 % of the samples. The bottom-right plot in Fig. 3 shows the distribution of hits of each network, separately. We observe that L11 is able to produce the highest PSNR in noisy images with any magnitude of noise. This is consistent with the results shown in Fig. 2 in which we illustrated that the network is able to produce accurate results for slightly degraded (the red and green rectangles) as well as the strongly degraded (blue rectangle) images. Moreover, we observe that the network proposed in [15] is only able to produce accurate results for strongly degraded images. In other words, if the image is not noisy, this network might discard some of the important details of the object in the restored image.

Table 2. Number of times that each network has produced the output with highest PSNR.

Network	Top-1	Top-2
L11	95739	146854
L9	5184	32874
L7	36395	117268
L5	6759	24903
L3	39548	47250
Dong [15]	5825	9751

Based on these results, L11 is the better choice for restoring images compared with L3, L5, L7 and L9 since it produces images with higher PSNR and also its value of K is small. Although [15] posses smallest K among other network, it has also the worst restoration power compared with other networks. Consequently, we pick L11 as the restoration model for the task of classification in following experiments.

Classification of traffic signs: We have previously proposed a ConvNet for classifying traffic signs which is able to classify 99.51 % of the test samples in the GTSRB dataset correctly using an ensemble of 5 ConvNets [21]. Also the best accuracy of a single ConvNet is 99.05 % in this work. After training the restoration network, we attach the input of the classification ConvNet to the output of the restoration ConvNet. Then, the layers of the restoration ConvNet are frozen and the classification network is fine-tuned using noisy samples generated by the same module as in Fig. 2. Note that, we do not train the classification ConvNet from scratch. Instead, we use the pre-trained model from our previous work to initialize the weights of the classification network.

We finetuned the classification ConvNet using the mini-batch size 50 and 15000 iterations. After fusing the classification ConvNet with the restoration network, classification accuracy of the single ConvNet was increased to 99.37 % after 6500 iterations. We also noticed that the accuracy was converged after 15000 iterations. Table 3 shows the results.

We observe that the classification accuracy increases 0.47 % which is equal to 59 samples in the test set. Note that the winner of the GTSRB competition [22] classified 99.46 % of the test samples using an ensemble of 25 ConvNets where a

Table 3. Classification of the traffic signs before and after attaching the restoration network.

Network	Top-1(%)	Top-2(%)	Top-5(%)
Single network	99.05	99.69	99.81
Restoration+single network	99.52	99.80	99.85
Single network in [22]	98.80	NA	NA

single network consisted of 1.5 M parameters. However, harnessing our classification ConvNet with the proposed restoration network, we could correctly classify 99.52 % of the test samples. Our fused network consists of 1.5 M parameters. Taking into account the fact that [22] have achieved a comparable result to our network using an ensemble of 25 network, our fused ConvNet is approximately 25 faster than the ensemble in [22]. Yet, it is also more accurate. We analyzed the samples that are incorrectly classified using our single network and they are correctly classified after fusing the classification ConvNet with the restoration network. Figure 4 shows some of these samples.

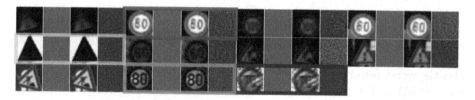

Fig. 4. Some of the samples that are incorrectly classified using the single network but they are correctly classified in the fused network (best viewed in color and electronically). (Color figure online)

Looking at the noisy sample inside the red and green rectangles, we observe that the restoration network has removed some artifacts from the pictograph area while it has improved the quality of the pictographs. Similarly, the edges of the sample inside the yellow rectangle is noisy due to excessive background illumination. The restoration network reduces this effect and produces an image that is correctly classified by the network. Last but not the least, the background noise has been reduced in the sample indicated by the blue rectangle.

Analyzing Stability: In order to analyze the stability of the fused network, we considered four different ConvNets including the original network before and after attaching the restoration network, the original network finetuned using a training set that is augmented with many noisy samples and the original network that applies a Gaussian smoothing in the first layer.

Next, to empirically study the stability of the ConvNets against noise, the following procedure is conducted. First, we pick the test images from the original

Table 4. Accuracy of the ConvNets obtained by degrading the *correctly classified test images* in the original datasets using a Gaussian noise with various values of σ.

Network	Accuracy (%) for different values of σ											
	1	2	4	8	10	15	20	25	30	35	40	Overall
Original	99.0	98.9	98.9	98.3	97.8	96.5	93.4	90.3	87.0	83.7	80.6	93.2
Noisy augmented	100.0	99.9	99.8	99.3	99.0	98.3	96.8	95.0	92.9	90.7	88.4	96.4
Smoothing	99.9	99.9	99.8	99.3	98.9	97.7	95.2	92.6	89.6	86.5	83.6	94.9
Restore+original	100.0	100.0	99.9	99.8	99.7	99.4	98.8	98.1	97.1	95.9	94.4	98.5

datasets which are *correctly classified* by each ConvNets. Then, 150 noisy images are generated for each $\sigma \in \{1, 2, 4, 8, 10, 15, 20, 25, 30, 35, 40\}$. In other words, 1650 noisy images are generated for each of correctly classified test images from the original datasets. We only consider the correctly classified samples since we are interested in finding how noise can change the class of the correctly classified samples. In other words, it might not be logical to add noise to a misclassified sample to see whether or not it is misclassified by the ConvNet. Table 4 shows the accuracy of the ConvNets per each value of σ.

It is clear that the network equipped with the restoration network produces better results with a significant margin to other methods. This is mainly due to the same reasons that we mentioned on Fig. 4. The restoration network is able to recover important parts of the degraded image but simple noise removal techniques such as smoothing is not able to do a complex restoration. In addition, we observe that augmenting the dataset with noisy images is advantageous. But, it is still prone to samples that are strongly degraded.

5   Conclusion

In this paper, we proposed a ConvNet to accurately restore degraded images. Our ConvNet is different from rest of the networks proposed for image denoising in the sense that it is deeper and it utilizes a shortcut connection to find a pattern which is added with the noisy image in order to restore the clean image. This is different from other networks in the sense that they try to directly restore the clean image. Our experiments showed that the proposed ConvNet is able to accurately restore strong and slightly degraded images. Restoring slightly degraded images is not trivial since ConvNets are highly non-linear functions and a slight change in the input can cause a significant change in the output. We showed this problem using a previously proposed ConvNet. However, because of the shortcut connection, our ConvNet is able to deal with small magnitude noises. Furthermore, we attached our network to the classification ConvNet proposed for the GTSRB dataset and showed that the accuracy of the same ConvNet increase from 99.05 % to 99.52 %. Finally, we empirically analyzed stability of the fused classification ConvNet and showed that it produces more accurate results compared with other methods.

Acknowledgements. Hamed H. Aghdam and Elnaz J. Heravi are grateful for the supports granted by Generalitat de Catalunya's Agècia de Gestió d'Ajuts Universitaris i de Recerca (AGAUR) and University Rovira i Virgili through the FI-DGR 2015 fellowship and the Marti Franques fellowship, respectively.

References

1. Krizhevsky, A., Sutskever, I., Hinton, G.: Imagenet classification with deep convolutional neural networks. In: NIPS, pp. 1097–1105. Curran Associates, Inc. (2012)
2. Szegedy, C., Reed, S., Sermanet, P., Vanhoucke, V., Rabinovich, A.: Going deeper with convolutions. In: arXiv preprint, pp. 1–12 (2014). arXiv:1409.4842
3. Simonyan, K., Zisserman, A.: Very deep convolutional networks for large-scale image recognition. In: International Conference on Learning Representation (ICLR), pp. 1–13 (2015)
4. Srivastava, R.K., Greff, K., Schmidhuber, J.: Highway networks (2015). arXiv:1505.00387
5. He, K., Zhang, X., Ren, S., Sun, J.: Deep residual learning for image recognition. In: arXiv prepring (2015). arXiv:1506.01497
6. Szegedy, C., Zaremba, W., Sutskever, I.: Intriguing properties of neural networks. In: International Conference on Learning Representations (ICLR), pp. 1–10 (2014)
7. Aghdam, H.H., Heravi, E.J., Puig, D.: Analyzing the stability of convolutional neural networks against image degradation. In: Proceedings of the 11th International Conference on Computer Vision Theory and Applications (2016)
8. Papernot, N., McDaniel, P., Jha, S., Fredrikson, M., Celik, Z.B., Swami, A.: The limitations of deep learning in adversarial settings. In: 1st IEEE European Symposium on Security and Privacy, Saarbrucken. IEEE (2016)
9. Goodfellow, I.J., Shlens, J., Szegedy, C.: Explaining and harnessing adversarial examples. In: International Conference on Learning Representation (ICLR), pp. 1–11 (2015)
10. Gu, S., Rigazio, L.: Towards deep neural network architectures robust to adversarial examples (2013), pp. 1–9 (2014). arXiv:1412.5068
11. Sabour, S., Cao, Y., Faghri, F., Fleet, D.J.: Adversarial manipulation of deep representations. arXiv preprint, pp. 1–10 (2015). arXiv:1511.05122
12. Fawzi, A., Fawzi, O., Frossard, P.: Analysis of classifiers' robustness to adversarial perturbations. In: Number 2014, pp. 1–14 (2015). arXiv:1502.02590
13. Jain, V., Seung, S.: Natural image denoising with convolutional networks. In: NIPS 21, pp. 769–776. Curran Associates, Inc. (2009)
14. Eigen, D., Krishnan, D., Fergus, R.: Restoring an image taken through a window covered with dirt or rain. In: Proceedings of the IEEE International Conference on Computer Vision, pp. 633–640 (2013)
15. Dong, C., Loy, C.C., He, K.: Image super-resolution using deep convolutional networks. arXiv preprint 8828(c), pp. 1–14 (2014)
16. Lin, M., Chen, Q., Yan, S.: Network in network. arXiv preprint, p. 10 (2013)
17. Maas, A.L., Hannun, A.Y., Ng, A.Y.: Rectifier nonlinearities improve neural network acoustic models. In: ICML Workshop on Deep Learning, vol. 30 (2013)
18. Jia, Y., Shelhamer, E., Donahue, J., Karayev, S., Long, J., Girshick, R., Guadarrama, S., Darrell, T., Eecs, U.C.B.: Caffe: convolutional architecture for fast feature embedding. In: ACM Conference on Multimedia (2014)

19. Glorot, X., Bengio, Y.: Understanding the difficulty of training deep feedforward neural networks. In: Proceedings of the 13th International Conference on Artificial Intelligence and Statistics (AISTATS), vol. 9, pp. 249–256 (2010)
20. Stallkamp, J., Schlipsing, M., Salmen, J., Igel, C.: Man vs. computer: benchmarking machine learning algorithms for traffic sign recognition. Neural Netw. **32**, 323–332 (2012)
21. Aghdam, H.H., Heravi, E.J., Puig, D.: Recognizing traffic signs using a practical deep neural network. In: Reis, L.P., Moreira, A.P., Lima, P.U., Montano, L., Muñoz-Martinez, V. (eds.) AISC 2006. AISC, vol. 417, pp. 399–410. Springer, Heidelberg (2016). doi:10.1007/978-3-319-27146-0_31
22. Cirean, D., Meier, U., Masci, J., Schmidhuber, J.: Multi-column deep neural network for traffic sign classification. Neural Netw. **32**, 333–338 (2012)

Global Scale Integral Volumes

Sounak Bhattacharya[1][✉], Lixin Fan[1], Pouria Babahajiani[1],
and Moncef Gabbouj[2]

[1] Nokia Technologies, Tampere, Finland
{sounak.bhattacharya.ext,lixin.fan,pouria.babahajiani.ext}@nokia.com
[2] Tampere University of Technology, Tampere, Finland
moncef.gabbouj@tut.fi

Abstract. Integral volume is an important image representation technique, which is useful in many computer vision applications. Processing integral volumes for large scale 3D datasets is challenging due to high memory requirements. The difficulties lie in efficiently computing, storing, querying and updating the integral volume values. In this work, we address the above problems and present a novel solution for processing integral volumes for large scale 3D datasets efficiently. We propose an octree-based method where the worst-case complexity for querying the integral volume of arbitrary regions is $\mathcal{O}(\log n)$, here n is the number of nodes in the octree. We evaluate our proposed method on multi-resolution LiDAR point cloud data. Our work can serve as a tool to fast extract features from large scale 3D datasets, which can be beneficial for computer vision applications.

Keywords: Integral volume · Octree · Point cloud · LiDAR

1 Introduction

Integral images are probably best known for their use in real-time face detection [1]. Since its first introduction in the '80s [2], integral images have found many important applications in computer vision research [3–6].

In general, the sum of pixels inside any rectangular shaped region in an 2D image can be calculated in constant time using its integral image representation. Integral images can be easily extended for 3D data. 3D version of integral images or integral volumes can be used to calculate sum of pixels of different cube shaped regions in constant time. However, the additional dimension poses some new challenges as huge amount of memory is required for storing the integral volumes and it also becomes computationally expensive to query and modify the integral volumes.

Computation of integral volumes of 3D datasets are difficult as all existing approaches require the data to be loaded into memory to get the integral representations. This approach becomes impossible if we consider large scale datasets: Multi resolution world map data, 3D model of a city, country or the whole world.

© Springer International Publishing Switzerland 2016
G. Hua and H. Jégou (Eds.): ECCV 2016 Workshops, Part I, LNCS 9913, pp. 192–204, 2016.
DOI: 10.1007/978-3-319-46604-0_14

These datasets are just too huge to load into memory. Various compression techniques [7,8] can be used to mitigate the primary memory requirement to an extent but they will not work in case of the global scale datasets mentioned before. Another challenge is updating the integral volume values. For example, if the original data changes by a single pixel, all the values of its integral representation can change. Needless to say we need efficient methods to store, query and update integral volumes for global scale datasets in order to apply many computer vision algorithms.

Hierarchical octree data structures are often used to represent these kind of large scale multi-resolution data [9]. However, there is no existing method for efficient integral volume processing for them. The problem still lies in efficiently querying and updating the integral values.

A simple approach towards this problem would be to compute and store the integral volumes locally in the leaf nodes of the tree. The integral volume value of any query region can be simply found by adding the values of all the nodes inside that region. With this design we achieve efficient storage and also deal with the updating issue. If some data changes, we only need to update the integral volume values of that specific leaf node, which saves significant computational overheads. However, this approach is very in-efficient in case of querying the integral volume value of a point or a region, as the values from the number of nodes to be accumulated to get the result may be very high. This design can be improved to work really well if the query region is aligned with the tree node-structure (see baseline method) but can be extremely slow in case of misalignment, as we show in our experiment. Thus, we need a more robust design for integral volume query while keeping the querying computation complexity low.

In this paper we present a novel approach which queries integral volumes for global scale data, and which has querying time complexity $\mathcal{O}(\log n)$, where n is the number of nodes in the octree representation of the data. We achieve significant speed gain by storing extra values in non-leaf nodes. Thus, we settle for higher offline memory usage for fast integral volume query. We experiment and demonstrate our method on large point-cloud data (Fig. 1.) and show that it is possible to fast query integral volumes from 3D global scale datasets.

2   Related Works

Integral Images and Volumes. Integral images was first introduced in 1984 by F. Crow as summed area tables which was used for texture mapping [2]. The 3D extension i.e., the idea of three-dimensional sum-tables was later given by A. Glassner [10]. In 2004, Integral Images became greatly popular by their use in Robust Real-Time Face Detection [1]. In this work a very large number of rectangular features were evaluated for each detection window and integral image representation made it possible to perform these evaluations very quickly, consequently making the system real-time in a conventional computation environment.

Fig. 1. Plot of a section of point cloud data at zoom 22 (maximum zoom is 23). It represents a volume of around $(612\,\mathrm{m})^3$ in about 15.2 million data points.

Despite significant speed gain while computing certain features, a common issue with using Integral Images and Volumes is that they require great amount of storage and large word length. Methods to reduce the storage size and word length has been introduced by H. Belt [8]. In that work, a lossless and a lossy method of word length reduction is introduced. The lossless method takes advantage of numerical properties of complement-coded arithmetic and the lossy method is based on rounding the original image prior to the integral image calculation. In the 3D extension, memory efficient data structure introduced by Urschler et al. [7] is very useful to reduce the memory usage when dealing with integral volumes. It works by dividing the integral volume data into equal-sized blocks and estimating the integral volume value for the points of each block using a one-parameter model and then storing the differences between the estimated values and the actual values using different word length per block. They tested their method in a weak learner ensemble based machine learning framework and the memory usage was 3 times less. However, these methods still rely on loading the input data into memory for integral volume processing. Thus, they cannot be scaled to work with global scale datasets. Also, updating the integral volume values as the dataset gets larger remains an issue with these methods.

Octrees, Point Clouds. First introduced in 1982 by D. Meagher [11] for geometric modelling, octrees have found wide range of applications. Octrees are used in efficient rendering techniques [12]. In the field of robotics, octree based 3D mapping frameworks are used [13]. Web mapping services such as Bing Maps uses 2D version of octree (quadtree) based tiling system for efficient indexing and retrieval of map data [14].

LiDAR (Light Detection and Ranging) is a great remote sensing tool to scan and record urban environments. It works by emitting beams of laser in the surrounding and recording the reflection time to create a highly detailed map. LiDAR scans usually generate large point cloud data. The octree data structure is often a common choice for efficiently storing and processing of the point clouds generated by these kind of remote sensing technologies [9,15,16]. Also, octree based region growing algorithms have been used for segmentation of point cloud data [17].

3   Method

3.1   Octrees, Octkeys and General Offline Computation

Octrees are hierarchical data structures, where any internal node can have at most eight children. The most important property of octrees, is that they are based on the principle of recursive decomposition. For example, when representing region data, the root node of the tree represents the entire region. Each child node represents one of the eight equal cube-shaped part of the region represented by its parent node. This division of space is recursively continued until we reach a maximum depth of the tree.

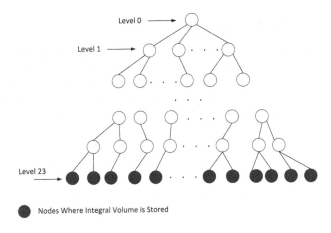

Fig. 2. Integral volumes stored at the leaf nodes of the octree

To efficiently access and visualise the data we use an octkey based tile system which is a 3D extension of the quadkey based tile system used in Bing Maps [14]. Each node in the tree is analogous to a tile at a certain zoom level and is identified by an octkey. All the tiles at a certain depth have octkeys of the same length. Also, the number of digits in the octkey is always equal to the depth of the node in the octree. In this work, we use the word tile and node interchangeably.

To achieve the task of querying the integral volume value of any point or region, we first need to compute and store the integral volume values for all the data points. As the maximum resolution data is stored at the leaf nodes, we visit all the leaf nodes of the tree and calculate the integral volume, and store it in a file in the respective nodes. This can be visualized in Fig. 2. These computations are strictly local and are restricted to each leaf node.

We worked with 3D LiDAR scans of the city of Tampere, Finland. This data was collected by driving cars through the streets while simultaneously scanning the environment through LiDAR sensors. The range of values for the global coordinates at full resolution was $(0, 2^{31} - 1)$, as 31 bits were used to represent the coordinate values. For efficiency, the points were grouped at level 23. That means, 8 bit local displacement offset was stored in the nodes at depth 23 [15]. That's why we have an octree of height 23. The integral volumes at each leaf node are of the dimension $2^8 \times 2^8 \times 2^8$.

Now, to query the integral volume for any arbitrary region, we can add up all the tiles inside the queried region. As mentioned earlier, this is a challenge as the region gets bigger, the number of tiles to be added also gets bigger. In the worst case, if the queried region represents the root, we have to add 8^{23} tiles; Which is prohibitively inefficient. Thus, we need smarter ways to accumulate values to produce the desired result. In the next subsections we analyse different approaches to tackle this problem.

3.2   The Base-Line System

The integral volume value of a queried region can be calculated in a faster way if we can decrease the number of tiles to be added. To achieve this, we need to store values at the non-leaf nodes of the tree, otherwise we will not be able to access the integral volume values of bigger tiles without breaking it into children. Thus, we do a bottom up traversal of the tree and sum up all the children's value and store it in a file in their parents node.

Now, given a query region, if a tile partially intersects the query region, it is recursively divided into its children and tested whether the children tiles intersect the query region. A recursive branch stops if a leaf node is reached or there is no intersection of the query region with the tile. If a tile completely falls inside the queried region, its value is returned. The base line system starts with tile 0 and continues this process for tiles 1, 2 and 3.

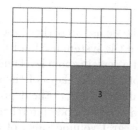 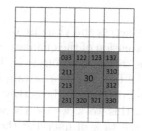

Fig. 3. Queried Region aligned with tiles (left). Queried Region not aligned with the tiles (right)

To visualise this, let's consider a simplified two-dimensional case consisting of only three zoom levels. The tiling convention is exactly same with bing map tile systems [14]. In Fig. 3, we can see the two queried regions are marked in orange. Let's consider the left image; The queried region is totally aligned with tile number 3. The tiles which actually return value are numbered in the Figure. The total number of nodes visited for querying is 4 (Tiles 0, 1, 2 and 3).

On the right image, the queried region is not very well aligned with the bigger tiles. Consequently, there are more recursive calls to break down tiles. The number of nodes visited for this query is 52 (Tiles 0, 00, 01, 02, 03, 030, 031, 032, 033, 1, 10, 11, 12, 120, 121, 122, 123, 13, ... , 333).

Evidently, there are some significant advantages as well as disadvantages of this approach. As we see from the given example, if the query region is aligned with the tile distribution, then the querying is very fast. However, if the query region is not aligned with the tiles then the system has to recurse down the tree to find smaller tiles to add. Thus there is a possibility of the number of nodes visited increasing exponentially as the query region gets larger.

3.3   Integral Volume by Storing Surfaces

We propose an alternative way, which bypasses the shortcoming of the base-line system. For each non-leaf node, we compute the integral volume locally at full resolution but only store 3 different surfaces. These are specifically the surfaces which do not touch $(0, 0, 0)$th coordinate of the tile. Figure 4 shows the surfaces coloured in orange.

The surface arrays are of length $2^{8+(23-d)}$ in both dimensions, where d is the depth of the non-leaf node. For example, at depth 22 the surface arrays are of the dimension 512×512. The reason behind the careful choice of these three particular surfaces for each tile is the design of how we intend to query the integral volume of a point or a region.

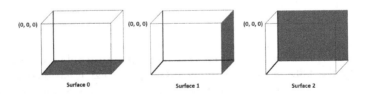

Fig. 4. Stored surfaces of a tile (Color figure online)

We calculate the integral volume value of a given query point, by starting at the root node of the tree and traversing the path towards the leaf node representing the query point. We call it the main recursion branch. For each node on this path, we calculate the projection of the query point on the relevant neighbouring sibling nodes at that particular depth. As the projected point is always on the surface of a node, we easily get the integral volume value of the projected point from the stored surface arrays at the neighbouring nodes. We keep accumulating all the neighbour values as we repeat this process for every node on the main recursion branch. We stop the recursion at the leaf node. As there is integral volume present in the leaf node, we instantly get the integral volume value of the query point local to the leaf node. We then add this value to the accumulated neighbour values to get the desired result.

From Fig. 5 we can visualise a simple case of how the methods works. We start with a tile, which is the root node and a query point at which we intend to evaluate the integral volume value. In the figure, the root node is the cube on the top of the main recursion branch and the query point can be seen as the orange dot (a). We break down the root into children and then select the one in which the query point belongs (b). We then calculate the projection of the query point on the relevant sibling neighbours. In this case we only need to find the projection on the neighbour immediately left to the node as the starting point of the region is on the top left corner. The projected point can be seen as a black dot (c). We get the value of the projected point from the stored surfaces in the neighbour node. The surface is shown in orange colour. We then repeat this process for the selected children node. This time also, we only need to calculate the projection on the neighbour which is on the immediate left (e). We don't need to recurse down further as we have reached the maximum depth in this example (d). As the integral volume is stored here, we retrieve the integral volume value of the query point local to this tile. We then add this integral volume value with all the retrieved neighbour values to get the final result.

Now, given a cube shaped query region, we find out the integral volume value of all its corner points. Then by simple arithmetic addition and subtraction operation we can get the integral volume value of the queried region. For example, In Fig. 6. we see an cube whose corners are numbered by letters A−H. To get the integral volume for this cube, we calculate the integral volume value for each corner point using surface method. These values indicate the sum of all the point from the beginning of the global region represented by the octree to that specific point. Once we have the values for all corners A−H, we get the integral volume value by Eq. 1 shown above the figure.

$$iv_{cube} = (H - G - F + E) - (D - C - B + A) \qquad (1)$$

The advantage of this approach is, for each query point we only have to go down on one particular path of the tree. Thus, if the query region has 8 corner points and the depth of the tree is d, when need to visit at most $8 \times d$ nodes in the main recursion branches. Considering the visits to the neighbours the maximum number of total nodes visited will be $k \times d$. Thus, the time complexity of this method is $\mathcal{O}(\log n)$, where n is the number of nodes in the tree. This approach is also totally independent of the alignment of the query region with the tiles. While the best case of the base-line system might be better than this method, the surface method is much better for the average case and the worst case.

This method can be further optimized if we choose the starting node to be the common ancestor node of all the 8 query points, which has the highest depth in the tree. This way we don't always have to start at the root node for small

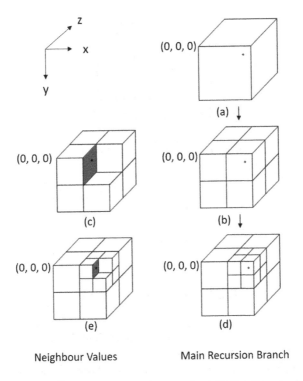

Neighbour Values   Main Recursion Branch

Fig. 5. Visualisation of the surface method (Color figure online)

query regions, we can start at a node much lower in the tree. We only have to start at the root node when the query region is big enough.

3.4   Integral Volume by Storing Surface Borders

The method described in the previous section works by storing surfaces at different non-leaf nodes. This approach is fast but relies on the offline storage of the surfaces at full resolution. This may be challenging as the surface size becomes significantly big, especially near the root node. For example, in our dataset we use an octree of height 23. Each surface at depth 14 is of the dimension $2^{17} \times 2^{17}$. With gzip compression this array takes around 100 Gbs of storage space. For each node we need to store 3 of them, i.e., 300 Gbs of storage per node. If we want to store them at the root, each surface would require approximately 36000 Petabytes of storage. Thus, to tackle this offline storage problem, we present another approach which works by only storing the boundary vectors of the surfaces. Previously, we were storing 3 surface arrays per node. In this approach we only store two boundary vectors for each of the surface arrays. Thus, we store 6 different vectors per non-leaf node.

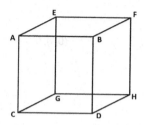

Fig. 6. Integral volume of a cube

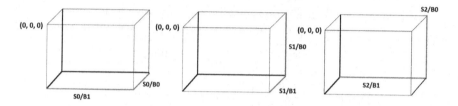

Fig. 7. Stored borders of a tile

This approach hugely reduces the off-line memory storage requirement. Instead of storing $3 \times m^2$ elements per node, where m is the width of the surface array, we now store $3 \times 2 \times m$ elements per node. Thus, the storage requirement decreases by $\frac{m}{2}$ times. This factor increases exponentially as we move up the tree. At depth 14, now we need to store $3 \times 2 \times 2^{17}$ elements per node instead of $3 \times 2^{17} \times 2^{17}$, i.e., 2^{16} times less elements. Thus, the off-line storage decreases from 300 Gbs to around 5 Megabytes per node.

However, as a consequence of not storing surfaces, now we cannot readily access neighbour values if the projection is not exactly on the border. In that case, we need to start at the root and recursively accumulate values similar to the surface method, until we reach the depth where integral volume is stored. We need to do this every time a neighbour value needs to be accessed. Thus, in this method there are two separate sets of recursion. The first set is the main branch of recursion, which starts from the root node and ends at the leaf node containing the query point; The number of recursive calls is equal to the depth of the tree. The other set of recursive calls are related to the task of accumulating each neighbour values. Obviously, this approach is computationally more expensive than the previous one, as it has to recurse down the tree every time a neighbouring value needs to be accessed. This method can be used if there is a not enough memory available to store surface arrays.

4   Experiments and Results

In this section we will discuss about the experiment and analyse the results. All the implementations were done using python 2.7 in a Linux environment (4 GB Ram, 8-cores).

4.1 Construction

On an average it took 0.4 s per leaf node to compute and store integral volumes. In the LiDAR scan of the city of Tampere, there were 509,652 leaf nodes. The total time taken was approximately 53 h. For the surface method the construction of surfaces were done by traversing the tree in bottom up direction, each depth at a time. When the surface sizes became too big, they were constructed chunk wise. The surface borders were also constructed in a similar manner. All the data were stored in hdf5 files.

4.2 Experiment Setup

We chose different sizes of query region and compared the performances of all the three methods (base-line, storing surfaces, storing surface-border). As a performance measure we chose the average nodes visited per query. The average nodes visited is a good metric of performance as it is implementation and hardware independent. For a fixed sized query region, we randomly shifted it thousands of time and recorded the average number of nodes visited for all the methods.

We use the term blocksize as a measure of the queried region size. The unit blocksize has the same dimension as the smallest tile, i.e., tiles at level 23. Block size 2 means the queried region is two unit blocks long in each dimension, and so on. The ground resolution at zoom level 23 is 0.0187 m per pixel. Each tile at zoom level 23 is of the dimension $256 \times 256 \times 256$ pixels. Thus, the unit block size physically represents a region of approximately $5\,\text{m} \times 5\,\text{m} \times 5\,\text{m}$. We repeat the experiment for increasing block sizes and observe how the methods behave.

4.3 Comparison: Average Nodes Visited

From Fig. 8 we can see that the average number of nodes visited for the base-line system increases almost exponentially as the query block size increases. This is expected as high number of nodes visited when the query regions are not aligned. The base line system has to recurse down to the leaf nodes many times. As the query region gets bigger the cost of the mis-alignment also increases.

The number of nodes visited by our proposed method (storing surfaces) stays almost constant as at most $k \times d$ number of recursive calls are required for each of the 8 query point corners. This is the key advantage as the number of nodes visited remains totally independent of the query region size.

The nodes visited in the surface-border method is much higher than the surface method as it needs to recurse down the tree to the maximum depth each time there is a neighbour call. Interestingly, there is no significant growth of average nodes visited with increasing block size, as its complexity is directly proportional to the depth of the tree. As the tree depth remains constant in this experiment there is no observable growth in the average nodes visited measure.

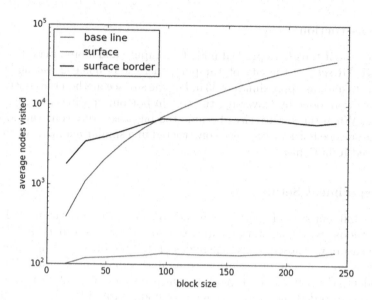

Fig. 8. Average nodes visited vs block size

4.4 Comparison: Querying Time

In Table 1 we see the average query time per block size in seconds for different methods. The naive approach refers to the conventional integral volume query. It is not possible to query the integral volume for a region greater than blocksize 4 with our setup as the memory required exceeds the memory available. We observe that base line system is faster for small sized query region. From block size 8 onwards the surface method performs better. Block size 8 corresponds to a physical region of approximately 40 m × 40 m × 40 m. The surface-border method has the poorest performance in terms of querying time for all block sizes due to high amount of overhead.

Table 1. Average Querying Time for different methods

Block sizes	1	2	4	8	16	32	64
Naive	0.005	0.008	-	-	-	-	-
Base line	0.05	0.06	0.08	0.17	0.33	2.91	3.26
Surface	0.13	0.12	0.15	**0.16**	**0.17**	**0.38**	**0.46**
Surface border	0.46	0.60	0.78	1.50	2.28	4.24	5.25

5 Discussion and Conclusion

Discussion. There are some limitations with our proposed systems. One of them is offline storage. To fast compute the integral volume values we need to store the surfaces at each non-leaf node in full resolution. This is not so difficult for nodes at higher depth of the tree but as we get nearer to the root of the octree, the size of the stored surfaces can be huge. We can consider various compression techniques to achieve this task, but as we get closer and closer to the root level it will become increasingly difficult to store the surfaces. This problem is mitigated by using the surface-border method and the base line system, but both of them are significantly slower than the surface method. All the methods can be viewed from a compromise between storage and computation perspective. The base line system is most memory efficient but it's poorest performing due to exponential growth. The surface method is the best in terms of performance but it is difficult to implement due to high storage requirement near the root. The surface-border method is very slow but relatively much more memory efficient than surface method. The user can choose between these methods according to memory and computation constraints.

Secondly, we cannot query the integral volumes in constant time. However, unlike traditional methods, our methods make it possible to query integral volumes for global scale data in a reasonably fast way.

Conclusion. In this paper, we presented novel methods for querying integral volume for global scale data. Our methods are based on octree hierarchical data structures. We can query the integral volume of any region with time complexity $\mathcal{O}(\log n)$ by storing surfaces at non-leaf nodes, where n is the number of nodes in the octree. The query time is independent of the size of the query region. Thus, our method preserves this beneficial and crucial property of integral representations.

In the future, we may think of a system which is a mixture of Surface and Surface-Border methods. As storing the surfaces are difficult near root, we can store surface-borders there, and we can store surfaces at the nodes with less height. We can choose the mixture according the memory and computation constraints.

References

1. Viola, P., Jones, M.J.: Robust real-time face detection. International J. Comput. Vis. **57**(2), 137–154 (2004)
2. Crow, F.C.: Summed-area tables for texture mapping. ACM SIGGRAPH Comput. Graph. **18**(3), 207–212 (1984)
3. Bay, H., Ess, A., Tuytelaars, T., Van Gool, L.: Speeded-up robust features (surf). Comput. Vis. Image Understand. **110**(3), 346–359 (2008)
4. Holzer, S., Rusu, R.B., Dixon, M., Gedikli, S., Navab, N.: Adaptive neighborhood selection for real-time surface normal estimation from organized point cloud data using integral images. In: 2012 IEEE/RSJ International Conference on Intelligent Robots and Systems, pp. 2684–2689. IEEE (2012)

5. Shafait, F., Keysers, D., Breuel, T.M.: Efficient implementation of local adaptive thresholding techniques using integral images. In: Electronic Imaging 2008, International Society for Optics and Photonics, pp. 681510–681510 (2008)
6. Wang, X., Doretto, G., Sebastian, T., Rittscher, J., Tu, P.: Shape and appearance context modeling. In: IEEE 11th International Conference on Computer Vision, 2007, ICCV 2007, pp. 1–8. IEEE (2007)
7. Urschler, M., Bornik, A., Donoser, M.: Memory efficient 3d integral volumes. In: Proceedings of the IEEE International Conference on Computer Vision Workshops, pp. 722–729 (2013)
8. Belt, H.: Storage size reduction for the integral image. Technical report, Philips Research (2007)
9. Elseberg, J., Borrmann, D., Nüchter, A.: One billion points in the cloud-an octree for efficient processing of 3d laser scans. ISPRS J. Photogrammetry Remote Sens. **76**, 76–88 (2013)
10. Glassner, A.S.: Multidimensional sum tables. In: Graphics Gems, pp. 376–381. Academic Press Professional, Inc. (1990)
11. Meagher, D.: Geometric modeling using octree encoding. Comput. Graph. Image Process. **19**(2), 129–147 (1982)
12. Laine, S., Karras, T.: Efficient sparse voxel octrees-analysis, extensions, and implementation. NVIDIA Corporation 2 (2010)
13. Wurm, K.M., Hornung, A., Bennewitz, M., Stachniss, C., Burgard, W.: Octomap: a probabilistic, flexible, and compact 3d map representation for robotic systems. In: Proceedings of the ICRA 2010 Workshop on Best Practice in 3D Perception and Modeling for Mobile Manipulation, vol. 2 (2010)
14. Schwartz, J.: Bing maps tile system. https://msdn.microsoft.com/en-us/library/bb259689.aspx
15. You, Y., Fan, L., Roimela, K., Mattila, V.V.: Simple octree solution for multi-resolution lidar processing and visualisation. In: 2014 IEEE International Conference on Computer and Information Technology (CIT), pp. 220–225. IEEE (2014)
16. Babahajiani, P., Fan, L., Gabbouj, M.: Object recognition in 3d point cloud of urban street scene. In: Jawahar, C.V., Shan, S. (eds.) ACCV 2014, Part I. LNCS, vol. 9008, pp. 177–190. Springer, Heidelberg (2015). doi:10.1007/978-3-319-16628-5_13
17. Vo, A.V., Truong-Hong, L., Laefer, D.F., Bertolotto, M.: Octree-based region growing for point cloud segmentation. ISPRS J. Photogrammetry Remote Sens. **104**, 88–100 (2015)

Aerial Scene Understanding Using Deep Wavelet Scattering Network and Conditional Random Field

Sandeep Nadella[1], Amarjot Singh[2(✉)], and S.N. Omkar[3]

[1] Department of ECE, National Institute of Technology, Warangal, India
[2] Department of Engineering, University of Cambridge, Cambridge, UK
as2436@cam.ac.uk
[3] Department of Aerospace Engineering, Indian Institute of Science, Bangalore, India

Abstract. This paper presents a fast and robust architecture for scene understanding for aerial images recorded from an Unmanned Aerial Vehicle. The architecture uses Deep Wavelet Scattering Network to extract Translation and Rotation Invariant features that are then used by a Conditional Random Field to perform scene segmentation. Experiments are conducted using the proposed framework on two annotated datasets of 1277 images and 300 aerial images, introduced in the paper. An overall pixel accuracy of 81 % and 78 % is achieved for the datasets. A comparison with another similar framework is also presented.

Keywords: Aerial scene understanding · Unmanned aerial vehicle · Deep wavelet scattering · Conditional random field

1 Introduction

Unmanned air vehicles (UAVs) have recently become a useful information gathering medium for numerous applications such as surveillance [15], vegetation management [23], disaster management (flood) [18], atmosphere pollution monitoring [22] and coastline management [2]. UAVs have particularly gained popularity for data collection in the aftermath of natural catastrophes such as floods [18] and earthquakes [18] due to their ease of deployment, ability to fly at low altitudes and capture images at higher resolution. These systems have been used in the past to segment the aerial image into regions to develop emergency route plans that can help to rescue trapped victims and estimate the incurred damage.

Numerous attempts have been made in the past to segment regions from aerial imagery. Initial methods in this area focused only on segmenting roads from aerial images. Some of them achieved this task by using traditional methods such as active contours and snakes [9] while others used features such as higher order movements [17] and intensity [3]. These methods were further extended to segment the aerial image into other natural and man-made landmarks (in addition to roads) that can help to construct detailed maps of the terrain of interest and further benefit route planning. Ghiasi et al. [7], Dubuisson-Jolly et al. [6]

© Springer International Publishing Switzerland 2016
G. Hua and H. Jégou (Eds.): ECCV 2016 Workshops, Part I, LNCS 9913, pp. 205–214, 2016.
DOI: 10.1007/978-3-319-46604-0_15

and Rezaeian et al. [16] used a fusion of color and texture features to achieve semantic segmentation of aerial images. Lathuiliere et al. [10] combined a Markov model with SVM to achieve the task of aerial scene segmentation while Montoya-Zegarra et al. [13] used class specific priors with Conditional Random Field (CRF) to achieve the pixel-wise labeling. Marmanis et al. [12] used an ensemble of Convolutional Neural Networks (CNNs) to segment out vegetation regions from aerial images.

Hand-engineered color and texture features achieve only a nominal scene segmentation accuracy while despite the success of CNNs, design and optimal configuration of these networks is not well understood making it difficult to develop these networks. In addition, it is difficult to train CNNs for aerial scene segmentation due to the availability of limited training dataset. Bruna et al. [1] and Sifre et al. [21] have shown that wavelet-based ScatterNets can give a performance that is competitive to that of trained networks, based on our accumulated knowledge of geometrical image properties. Hence, we use the Deep Wavelet scattering architecture proposed by Mallat [21] as the front-end of our proposed pipeline to extract translation and rotation invariant scattering features. Condition Random field (CRF) is the obvious choice from the back-end as they give superior performance over Markov Random Field (MRF) [5]. Hence, CRF is used as the back-end of the proposed network that uses the translation and rotation invariant features extracted by the scattering network to perform the desired scene segmentation.

This paper presents a framework for Scene Understanding for aerial images recorded from an unmanned air vehicle. The main contributions of the paper are stated below:

- Scene Understanding Architecture: The proposed architecture extracts Translation and Rotation Invariant features using a handcrafted computationally efficient Deep Wavelet Scattering network (front-end) that are further used by a Condition Random Field (CRF) (back-end) to achieve the necessary scene segmentation.
- Datasets: Since, CRF is a supervised learning algorithm, a dataset of 1277 annotated images carefully collected from Stanford Background dataset [8] and CMU Urban Image dataset [14], that contains the selected natural and man-made landmarks that appear in aerial images is introduced (Please note that these features are not recorded from the UAV). This dataset is used to pre-train the CRF. Next, an UAV aerial image dataset of 300 annotated images recorded from an UAV with the same man-made landmarks is used to fine tune the pre-trained CRF.

The proposed framework is used to perform scene understanding on the introduced datasets. The average segmentation accuracy for each class for both datasets is presented. In addition, an extensive comparison of the proposed pipeline with other scene segmentation methods is presented.

The paper is divided into the following sections. Section 2 presented the Datasets introduced in the paper while Sect. 3 presents the proposed Scene

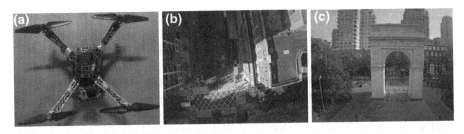

Fig. 1. Illustration presents (a) Unmanned Air Vehicle (UAV) used to record the aerial images (b-c) Sample of aerial images recorded by the UAV.

Segmentation Framework. Section 4 presents the experimental results and Sect. 5 draws conclusions.

2   Introduced Annotated Datasets

The paper presents two annotated datasets which contain natural and man-made landmarks which appear in aerial images. The landmarks quite commonly seen in aerial images are included in the datasets. The landmarks are namely: 'Sky', 'Tree', 'Road', 'Grass', 'Water', 'Building', 'Mountain.', 'Foreground objects'. The first dataset (D1) is a collection of 1277 annotated images carefully chooses from Stanford Background dataset [8] and CMU Urban Image Dataset [14]. All images are forced to a fixed resolution of 200×300. The second UAV aerial image dataset (D2) introduced in the paper includes 300 annotated images takes from the UAV. The images contain the landmarks mentioned above. The UAV and example of two images from the UAV aerial image dataset are shown in Fig. 1.

3   Scene Understanding Framework

This section introduces the proposed scene understanding framework that is used to segment the image regions which can be then utilized to interpret the scene. The framework is composed of a front-end that extracts discriminatory features while a back-end that uses these features to segment the image into different regions. We use the Deep Wavelet scattering architecture proposed by Mallat [21] as the front-end of our proposed pipeline to extract translation and rotation invariant scattering features while Conditional Random field (CRF) is used as the back-end of the proposed network that utilizes the extracted features to perform the desired scene segmentation. The pipeline is shown in Fig. 2.

3.1   Deep Wavelet Scattering Network

Deep wavelet scattering networks are multilayer networks that incorporate geometric knowledge to produce high-dimensional image representations that are discriminative and approximately invariant to translation and rotation [1,21]. The invariants at the first layer of the network are obtained by filtering the image with multi-scale and multi-directional complex Morlet wavelet decompositions followed by a point-wise nonlinearity and local averaging. The high frequencies lost due to averaging are recovered at the later layers using cascaded wavelet transformations with non-linearities, justifying the need for a multilayer network. Bruna et al. [1] and Sifre et al. [19–21] have proposed numerous convolutional scattering architectures that produce invariant and discriminative feature descriptors. We present the generic idea behind all the models below.

ScatterNets decompose an input image x using multi-scale and multi-directional complex Morlet wavelets that are obtained by dilating and rotating a single band-pass filter ψ for any scale j and direction θ. A wavelet filters a signal x using a complex wavelet ψ_{θ,j_1} using the following formulation:

$$x \star \psi_{\theta,j_1} = x \star \psi^a_{\theta,j_1} + \iota x \star \psi^b_{\theta,j_1} \tag{1}$$

where ψ^a is the real and ψ^b is the imaginary part of the wavelet. A wavelet transform response commutes with translations, and is therefore not translation invariant. To build a translation invariant representation, a L_2 point-wise is first applied to the wavelet coefficient as shown below:

$$|x \star \psi_{\theta,j_1}| = \sqrt{|x \star \psi^a_{\theta,j_1}|^2 + |x \star \psi^b_{\theta,j_1}|^2} \tag{2}$$

L_2 is a good non-linearity as it is stable to deformations and non-expansive that makes it stable to additive noise [1]. This results in the regular envelope of the filtered signal which still commutes with translations.

The resulting wavelet-modulus operator applied on the signal x is given by:

$$\widetilde{W_1}x = (x \star \phi_J, |x \star \psi_{\theta,j}|_{\theta,j}) = (S_0 x, U_1 x) \tag{3}$$

where $x \star \phi_J$ is the low-pass coefficient and $|x \star \psi_{\theta,j}|_{\theta,j}$ is the high pass coefficient. The invariant part of U_1 is computed with an averaging over the spatial and angle variables. It is implemented for each scale j, fixed with a roto-translation convolution of $Y(h) = U_1 x(h, j_1)$ along the $h = (u', \theta')$ variable, with an averaging kernel $\Phi_J(h)$. For $p_1 = (g_1, j_1)$ and $g_1 = (u, \theta_1)$, this is written

$$S_1 x(p_1) = U_1 x(., j_1) \star \Phi_J(g_1) \tag{4}$$

We choose $\Phi_J(u', \theta') = (2\pi)^{-1} \Phi_J(u')$ to perform an averaging over all angles θ and over a spatial domain proportional to 2^J.

The high frequencies lost by this averaging are recovered through roto-translation convolutions with separable wavelets. Roto-translation wavelets are computed with three separable products. Complex quadrature phase spatial wavelets $\psi_{\theta_2,j_2}(u)$ or averaging filters $\Phi_J(u)$ are multiplied by complex 2π periodic wavelet $\psi_k(\theta)$ or by $\bar{\phi}(\theta) = (2\pi)^{-1}$

$$\Psi_{\theta_2,j_2,k_2}(u, \theta) = \psi_{\theta_2,j_2}(u)\bar{\psi}_{k_2}(\theta) \tag{5}$$

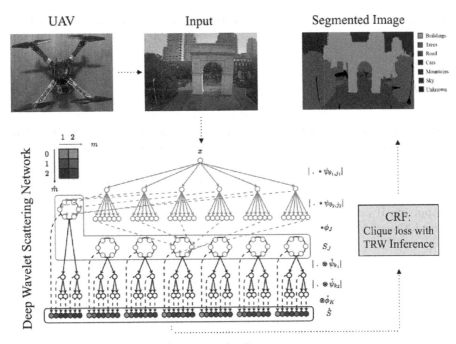

Fig. 2. Separable scattering architecture. First spatial scattering layers in grey, second scattering layers in black. Spatial wavelet-modulus operators (grey arrows) are averaged (doted grey arrows), as in [1]. Outputs of the first scattering are reorganized in different orbits (large black circles) of the action of the rotation on the representation. A second cascade of wavelet-modulus operators along the orbits (black arrows) splits the angular information in several paths that are averaged (doted black arrows) along the rotation to achieve rotation invariance. Output nodes are colored with respect to the order m, $\overset{\circ}{m}$ of their corresponding paths. Modified from [19].

$$\Psi_{0,J,k_2}(u,\theta) = \Phi_J(u)\bar{\psi}_{k_2}(\theta) \tag{6}$$

$$\Psi_{\theta_2,j_2,0}(u,\theta) = \psi_{\theta_2,j_2}(u)\bar{\phi}(\theta) \tag{7}$$

Finally, roto-translation wavelets for second layer are computed as $\widetilde{W_2}U_1x = (S_1x, U_2x)$ where S_1x is defined in (4) and

$$U_2x(p_2) = |U_1x(.,j_1) \star \Psi_{\theta_2,j_2,k_2}(g_1)| \tag{8}$$

with $g_1 = (u, \theta_1)$, $p_2 = (g_1, \bar{p}_2)$, and $\bar{p}_2 = (j_1, \theta_2 - \theta_1, j_2, k_2)$. Since $U_2x(p_2)$ is computed with a roto-translation convolution, it remains covariant to the action of the roto-translation group. Fast computations of roto-translation convolutions with separable wavelet filters $\Psi_{\theta_2, j_2, k_2}(u, \theta) = \psi_{\theta_2, j_2}(u) \bar{\psi}_{k_2}(\theta)$ are performed by factorizing

$$Y \star \Psi_{\theta_2, j_2, k_2}(u, \theta) = \sum_{\theta'} \left(\sum_{u'} Y(u', \theta') \psi_{\theta_2, j_2}(r_{-\theta'}(u - u')) \right) \bar{\psi}_{k_2}(\theta - \theta') \quad (9)$$

It is thus computed with a two-dimensional convolution of $Y(u, \theta')$ with $\psi_{\theta_2, j_2}(r_\theta u)$ along $u = (u_1, u_2)$, followed by a convolution of the output and a one-dimensional circular convolution of the result with k_2 along θ. This convolution which rotates the spatial support of $\psi_{\theta_2, j_2}(u)$ by θ while multiplying its amplitude by $\bar{\psi}_{k_2}(u)$.

Applying $\widetilde{W}_3 = \widetilde{W}_2$ to $U_2 x$ computes second order scattering coefficients as a convolution of $Y(g) = U_2 x(g, \bar{p}_2)$ with $\Phi_J(g)$, for $\bar{p}_2$ fixed is given as:

$$S_2 x(p_2) = U_1 x(., \bar{p}_2) \star \Phi_J(g) \quad (10)$$

The output roto-translation of a second order scattering representation is a vector of coefficients given by:

$$Sx = (S_0 x(u), S_1 x(p_1), S_2 x(p_2)) \quad (11)$$

with $p_1 = (u, \theta_1, j_1)$ and $p_2 = (u, \theta_1, j_1, \theta_2, j_2, k_2)$.

3.2 Conditional Random Field

Conditional Random Field (CRF) is a probabilistic framework that allows us to describe the relationship between related output variables such as labels for pixels in an image as a function of observed features: pixel colors or features [5]. This framework is thus ideal for combining multiple visual cues for scene understanding.

The CRF undirected graphical model used in this paper uses pairwise 4-connected grid consisting of finite number of vertices or nodes and edges connecting these nodes. Each node corresponds to a random variable denoted by X. Edges define the neighbourhood relation between these unobserved random variables.

A loss equation, required to be minimized to achieve the optimal labelling is defined by fitting two matrices F and G to the unary and edge features. γ_i represent the set of parameter values $\gamma(x_i)$ for all values of x_i. Let $k(\mathbf{y}, i)$ represent the unary features for variable i for a given input image y. Therefore:

$$\gamma_i = Fk(\mathbf{y}, i) \quad (12)$$

In the similar fashion, the parameter values for all x_i, x_j is denoted by γ_{ij}. Given that $v(\mathbf{y}, i, j)$ represents the edge feature for pair (i, j), then:

$$\gamma_{ij} = Gv(\mathbf{y}, i, j) \quad (13)$$

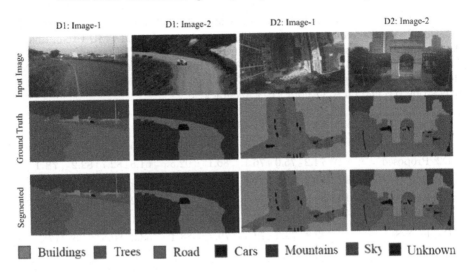

Fig. 3. The figure shows the two images from the D1: 1277 image dataset collected from Stanford Background dataset [8] and CMU Urban Image Dataset [14]. D2 is selected from the 300 image dataset collected from an UAV. Their ground truth and segmentation obtained by the proposed pipeline is also presented.

The gradients needed for optimization can be obtained using the following equation:

$$\frac{\partial L}{\partial F} = \sum_i \frac{\partial L}{\partial \gamma_i} k(\mathbf{y}, i)^T, \frac{\partial L}{\partial G} = \sum_{ij} \frac{\partial L}{\partial \gamma_{ij}} v(\mathbf{y}, i, j)^T \qquad (14)$$

This is under the assumption that $\frac{\partial L}{\partial \gamma}$ has been calculated.

A clique loss function is used in the paper to achieve the scene segmentation with Tree-Reweighted [5] inference which uses LBFGS optimization algorithm. In this process, the number of images used for trained is repeatedly doubled, with the number of learning iterations halved. Marginal based clique loss function is used to calculate the loss at each iteration. After every iteration, the loss value is checked and if bad search direction is encountered, L-BFGS is reinitialized [5].

4   Results

The proposed scene segmentation pipeline was evaluated and compared with another similar framework on both datasets introduced in the Sect. 2.

The front-end of the pipeline uses the deep wavelet scattering network to extract features using Morlet filters at 4 scales (j) and 8 pre-defined orientations (θ), as explained in Sect. 3.1. The features are extricated from each image from the 1277 annotated image dataset (D1) constructed by combining images from the Stanford Background dataset [8] and CMU Urban Image Dataset [14]. Each image of the dataset has a fixed resolution of 200×300. The condition random

Table 1. Table presents overall pixel accuracy for each label on both datasets. D1: 1277 image dataset collected from Stanford Background dataset [8] and CMU Urban Image Dataset [14]. D2: 300 image datset collected from an UAV. HOG: Histogram of oriented gradients [4], RGB-I [5]: RGB Intensities, PL [5]: Pixel Locations, BL: Building, MN: Mountain, FGO: Foreground Object, FCN-8s: Fully Convolutional Network with 8 pixel stride [11] and OPA: Overall Pixel Accuracy

Features	Sky	Tree	Road	Grass	Water	BL	MN	FGO	OPA
D1: Proposed	77.5	76.3	71.8	91.9	96.5	63.5	98.5	80.5	**81.3**
D2: Proposed	74.2	75.0	76.1	80.1	92.5	61.5	82.7	82.2	**78.1**
D1: RGB-I+HOG+PL	91.4	69.6	87.7	83.3	65.3	79.4	64.2	66.2	76.7
D2: RGB-I+HOG+PL	89.0	69.1	78.5	80.9	60.3	80.2	34.0	69.3	69.8
D1: FCN-8s	74.8	77.1	72.2	90.6	97.4	60.1	96.1	77.1	80.2
D2: FCN-8s	72.8	78.2	79.3	79.7	88.4	58.2	80.5	84.6	77.3

field is trained on the image features obtained using a 5-fold cross-validation split on the dataset. The average accuracies for 'Sky', 'Tree', 'Road', 'Grass', 'Water', 'Building', 'Mountain', 'Foreground object' is presented in Table 1. Two images selected from the D1 dataset along with the ground truth and segmentation using the trained CRF is shown in Fig. 3. The trained CRF is able to recognize the above-mentioned landmarks from images contained in D1 dataset.

Next, the trained CRF is fine tuned to detect the same landmarks for aerial images recorded from the UAV. The trained CRF model is fine-tuned on the features extracted from the UAV annotated aerial image dataset (D2) presented in Sect. 2. The features are extracted with the deep wavelet scattering network using Morlet filters with the above-mentioned parameters, from images of resolution 200×300 obtained using a 5-fold cross-validation split on the UAV image dataset. The average accuracies for the above-mentioned labels for the UAV image dataset is presented in Table 1. Two images selected from the D2 dataset along with the ground truth and segmentation using the Fine-tuned CRF is shown in Fig. 3.

The proposed scene segmentation pipeline is compared with segmentation pipelines that use: (i) hand-crafted or (ii) learned features to achieve this task. The scene segmentation results of the proposed method are compared with the segmentation performed by a handcrafted feature obtained by combining RGB intensities, HOG [4] and pixel locations that are then used in a CRF framework to achieve segmentation for both datasets. The proposed method is then compared with the scene segmentation results obtained by training a Fully Convolutional Network (FCN) with 8-pixel stride [11] on D1 dataset and then fine tuning the learned network on D2 dataset. The results are presented in Table 1. It is evident from Table 1 that the proposed method outperforms the segmentation pipeline that makes use of the hand-crafted features for scene segmentation on both datasets. The proposed method is also able to outperform the Fully Convolutional Network [11] on both datasets. The reason for this seems to be the small size of the D1 and D2 datasets resulting into the inefficient learning of the FCN network.

5   Conclusions

The paper introduces a novel application area of scene understanding to aerial images, which can be vital in surveillance and disaster management applications. The proposed architecture has also shown the importance of Scatternet that can extract invariant features which can replace popular hand-crafted features due to its superior performance. The proposed framework can also be used in an application with less availability of training data as only the back-end of our framework requires learning. The proposed framework achieves decent overall pixel accuracy for scene segmentation on both annotated datasets introduced in the paper. We hope to extend our framework to make use of large corpora of partially labeled data, or perhaps by using motion cues in videos to obtain segmentation labels. An important and natural extension of our method can be provided by incorporating object-based reasoning directly into our model which can lead to better understanding of images.

References

1. Bruna, J., Mallat, S.: Invariant scattering convolution networks. IEEE Trans. Pattern Anal. Mach. Intell. **35**(8), 1872–1886 (2013)
2. Casella, E., Rovere, A., Pedroncini, A., Mucerino, L., Casella, M., Cusati, L.A., Vacchi, M., Ferrari, M., Firpo, M.: Study of wave runup using numerical models and low-altitude aerial photogrammetry: A tool for coastal management. Estuar. Coast. Shelf Sci. **149**, 160–167 (2014)
3. Christophe, E., Inglada, J.: Robust road extraction for high resolution satellite images. In: 2007 IEEE International Conference on Image Processing, pp. 437–440. IEEE (2007)
4. Dalal, N., Triggs, B.: Histograms of oriented gradients for human detection. In: IEEE Conference on Computer Vision and Pattern Recognition (CVPR) (2005)
5. Domke, J.: Learning graphical model parameters with approximate marginal inference. IEEE Trans. Pattern Anal. Mach. Intell. **35**, 2454–2467 (2013)
6. Dubuisson-Jolly, M., Gupta, A.: Color and texture fusion: application to aerial image segmentation and gis updating. Image Vis. Comput. **18**, 823–832 (2010)
7. Ghiasi, M., Amirfattahi, R.: Fast semantic segmentation of aerial images based on color and texture. In: 8th Iranian Conference on Machine Vision and Image Processing (MVIP) (2013)
8. Gould, S., Fulton, R., Koller, D.: Decomposing a scene into geometric and semantically consistent regions. In: International Conference on Computer Vision (ICCV) (2009)
9. Laptev, I., Mayer, H., Lindeberg, T., Eckstein, W., Steger, C., Baumgartner, A.: Automatic extraction of roads from aerial images based on scale space and snakes. Mach. Vis. Appl. **12**(1), 23–31 (2000)
10. Lathuiliere, S., Vu, H., Le, T., Tran, T., Hung, D.: Semantic regions recognition in UAV images sequence. Knowl. Syst. Eng. **326**, 313–324 (2015)

11. Long, J., Shelhamer, E., Darrell, T.: Fully convolutional network for semantic segmentation. In: IEEE Computer Vision and Pattern Recognition (CVPR) (2015)
12. Marmanis, D., Wegner, J.D., Galliani, S., Schindler, K., Datcu, M., Stilla, U.: Semantic segmentation of aerial images with an ensemble of CNNs. ISPRS Ann. Photogrammetry Remote Sens. Spatial Inf. Sci. **3**, 473–480 (2016)
13. Montoya-Zegarra, J., Wegner, J., Ladicky, L., Schindler, K.: Semantic segmentation of aerial images in urban areas with class-specific higher-order cliques. ISPRS Ann. Photogrammetry Remote Sens. Spatial Inf. Sci. **2**, 127–133 (2015)
14. Munoz, D., Bagnell, J.A., Hebert, M.: co-inference for multi-modal scene analysis. In: Fitzgibbon, A., Lazebnik, S., Perona, P., Sato, Y., Schmid, C. (eds.) ECCV 2012. LNCS, vol. 7577, pp. 668–681. Springer, Heidelberg (2012). doi:10.1007/978-3-642-33783-3_48
15. Penmetsa, S., Minhuj, F., Singh, A., Omkar, S.: Autonomous UAV for suspicious action detection using pictorial human pose estimation and classification. Electron. Lett. Comput. Vis. Image Anal. **3**(1), 18–32 (2014)
16. Rezaeian, M., Amirfattahi, R., Sadri, S.: Semantic segmentation of aerial images using fusion of color and texture features. J. Comput. Secur. **1**, 225–238 (2013)
17. Rochery, M., Jermyn, I.H., Zerubia, J.: Higher order active contours. Int. J. Comput. Vis. **69**(1), 27–42 (2006)
18. Şerban, G., Rus, I., Vele, D., Breţcan, P., Alexe, M., Petrea, D.: Flood-prone area delimitation using UAV technology, in the areas hard-to-reach for classic aircrafts: case study in the north-east of apuseni mountains, transylvania. Nat. Hazards, **82**, 1–16 (2016)
19. Sifre, L.: Rigid-motion scattering for image classification. Ph.D. thesis (2014)
20. Sifre, L., Mallat, S.: Combined scattering for rotation invariant texture analysis. In: European Symposium on Artificial Neural Networks (ESANN) (2012)
21. Sifre, L., Mallat, S.: Rotation, scaling and deformation invariant scattering for texture discrimination. In: IEEE conference on Computer Vision and Pattern Recognition (CVPR), pp. 1233–1240 (2013)
22. Šmídl, V., Hofman, R.: Tracking of atmospheric release of pollution using unmanned aerial vehicles. Atmos. Environ. **67**, 425–436 (2013)
23. Su, Y., Guo, Q., Fry, D.L., Collins, B.M., Kelly, M., Flanagan, J.P., Battles, J.J.: A vegetation mapping strategy for conifer forests by combining airborne lidar data and aerial imagery. Can. J. Remote Sens. **42**(1), 1–15 (2016)

W10 – BioImage Computing

Preface

Bioimage computing has known tremendous developments in recent years. State-of-the-art light microscopy (LM) can visualize living cells with unprecedented image quality and resolution in space and time. Novel LM modalities provide biologists with formidable means to explore cell mechanisms, embryogenesis, or neural development, to mention just a few biological applications. Electron microscopy (EM) supplies complementary information about the cell structure down to nanometer resolution. In view of the massive bioimage data sets produced in the field, amounting to multiple terabytes per volume or video, with exceedingly complex information content to be analyzed, state-of-the-art computational methods are very much needed.

With the aim to address at least part of this need, the second Workshop on Bioimage Computing (BIC) was held in conjunction with the 14th European Conference on Computer Vision (ECCV 2016), following the success of the first edition at the 28th IEEE Conference on Computer Vision and Pattern Recognition (CVPR 2015). The workshop brought together a diverse crowd of researchers active in computer vision and bioimage analysis to discuss the latest challenges and promising solutions in image modeling, restoration, segmentation, registration, object detection, counting, clustering, tracking, and many other topics at the crossroads of computer vision and biology.

We are very grateful to the invited speakers, Charless Fowlkes, Pascal Fua, Jeroen van der Laak, Gonzalo de Polavieja, Jens Rittscher, Michael Unser, Thomas Walter, for sharing their expert vision at the workshop. In addition to invited talks, 10 contributed presentations (two talks and eight posters) were carefully selected from in total 14 submissions. We thank the authors for choosing to present their work at the workshop and for contributing to its success. Each submitted paper received at least three independent reviews. We gratefully acknowledge the effort of the 22 anonymous expert reviewers in assessing the technical and scientific quality of the papers. Special thanks to Florian Jug for maintaining the BIC website (bioimagecomputing.com).

The final accepted papers presented at the workshop are found in the following pages. We hope they are valuable to your research and we look forward to welcoming you at future editions of the workshop.

October 2016

Patrick Bouthemy
Fred Hamprecht
Erik Meijering
Thierry Pécot
Pietro Perona
Carsten Rother

Single-Image Insect Pose Estimation by Graph Based Geometric Models and Random Forests

Minmin Shen[✉], Le Duan, and Oliver Deussen

INCIDE Center, University of Konstanz, Konstanz, Germany
minmin.shen@uni-konstanz.de

Abstract. We propose a new method for detailed insect pose estimation, which aims to detect landmarks as the tips of an insect's antennae and mouthparts from a single image. In this paper, we formulate this problem as inferring a mapping from the appearance of an insect to its corresponding pose. We present a unified framework that jointly learns a mapping from the local appearance (image patch) and the global anatomical structure (silhouette) of an insect to its corresponding pose. Our main contribution is that we propose a data driven approach to learn the geometric prior for modeling various insect appearance. Combined with the discriminative power of Random Forests (RF) model, our method achieves high precision of landmark localization. This approach is evaluated using three challenging datasets of insects which we make publicly available. Experiments show that it achieves improvement over the traditional RF regression method, and comparably precision to human annotators.

Keywords: Insect pose estimation · Landmark detection · Random forest

1 Introduction

Automated image based tracking and pose estimation receives increasing interests of both biology and computer science community, as its developments enable remotely quantify and understand individual behavior previously impossible [1]. Therefore, automatic insect tracking techniques have been an research topic in biological image analysis [2–4]. The movements of harnessed insects' bodyparts, such as antennae or mouthparts, provide information for behavioral study. Motivated by latest behavioral studies in biology [5], we aim to localize the landmark as the tips of bodyparts (e.g. a bee's antennae or tongue shown in Fig. 1) to provide detailed pose information.

In contrast to most existing works that aim at estimating the center of mass (position), detecting the detailed body posture and position of appendages (pose) is more challenging. Most existing tracking/pose estimation algorithms are not applicable for our task, due to a number of specific challenges and constraints:

© Springer International Publishing Switzerland 2016
G. Hua and H. Jégou (Eds.): ECCV 2016 Workshops, Part I, LNCS 9913, pp. 217–230, 2016.
DOI: 10.1007/978-3-319-46604-0_16

- **Occlusion.** Insect body parts are highly clustered due to their small sizes, thus self occlusions are prevalent in insect body parts (Fig. 1b). As a result, it is difficult to estimate the pose.
- **Unstructured appearance.** Insect body parts have dark appearance, similar shape and no texture. Moreover, our image data is a set of 2D videos, and does not contain depth information. Their unstructured appearance makes them difficult to differentiate.
- **Complex motion.** A varying number of body parts are observed in consecutive video frames (e.g. the bee tongue does not appear in Fig. 1c), thus we have incoherent motion paths and the trajectories have long tracking gaps. Motion cues furthermore provide only little information to predict the current pose.

In the videos to be analyzed, the insect will be fed with sugar water by a stick and it may respond by extending its tongue. It is required to infer the presence of the tongue before localizing it. Similarly, an antenna may be absent when it moves above the head (Fig. 1d) or suffers from heavy motion blur (Fig. 1e). As pointed out in [6], the state-of-the-art tracking algorithms do not perform well when applied to our task. In [6], a track linking approach was used for estimating landmarks in merge conditions, i.e. the tips of two body parts are bounded within the same bounding box (BB). In contrast to our fully automated method, the approach in [6] is a multi-frame pose estimation framework, and it requires additional human intervention to rectify probable erroneous hypotheses at some frames. In this paper, we formulate this problem as inferring a mapping from the appearance of an insect to its corresponding pose. We focus on single-image pose estimation, because this strategy could further improve the performance of a multi-frame framework as per-frame initialization and recovery.

Some related pose estimation techniques have been proposed, such as model based methods [4,7] and Random Forest (RF) regression methods [8]. There are some recently emerged studies on pose estimation of humans [9], heads [10], and hands [11], as well as medical image analysis for localization of landmarks [12,13]. The success of these RF regression methods comes from two factors. One is the discriminative power of RF model. The other factor is the strategy of localizing landmarks by estimating its relative displacements with regards to other image patches, making it suitable for highly structured objects but not for our case. For example, these relative displacements do not change dramatically in medical images in 2D grids. Similarly, relative positions between joints of body parts are relatively stable for humans, heads or hands in 3D coordinates, so that these methods work well with depth images [9–11]. Our task is more challenging, due to the large variance of relative position between landmarks in 2D grids. Besides, it is difficult to infer the configuration (pose) with varying number of landmarks based on local appearance.

To address these aforementioned issues, we present a unified framework that incorporates the geometric model as the prior, and utilizes the RF model to estimate the possible positions of body part in pixel precision. Under this framework, the maximum a posteriori (MAP) estimation is found as the landmarks positions.

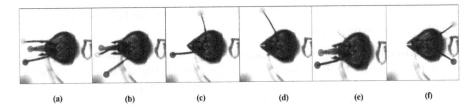

Fig. 1. Example frames of various poses and the outputs by our method. The tips of three body parts are marked in different colors: a blue circle represents for the left antenna, red for the tongue and green for the right antenna. (a) all body parts are present; (b) the tongue is partially occluded by the right antenna; (c)–(e) some body parts are absent; (f) in some rare cases, the antennae move backwards. (Color figure online)

The main contributions of our work are:

- To the best of our knowledge, the proposed framework is the first method for detailed insect pose estimation from a single frame.
- This is an exemplar of random forest based pose estimator with data-driven regularization. Given the landmark candidate positions predicted by Random Forests, we propose a data-driven approach to adaptively weight and select precise landmark positions, incorporating probable global structure of the anatomy to be estimated.
- We benchmark our approach on a set of large challenging datasets and make it publicly available for future studies.

2   Related Work

Animal tracking. Recently, a number of tracking techniques emerged in biology for tracking various types of animals [1]. Particle filtering is used in some insect tracking algorithms to maintain the identity of objects throughout a whole video sequence [2,14,15]. However, as pointed out in [16], particle filtering is often only effective for short tracking gaps and the search space becomes significantly larger for long gaps. Similarly, data association techniques that have been applied in [17] are also not able to tackle the tracking gaps. To develop a more efficient algorithm, some studies incorporate higher level attributes that characterize specific insect motion into a learning diagram. In [18], overlapping larvae are separated by assigning object labels to each pixel, given user-annotated examples of encounters of two larvae as boundary conditions. For modeling occluded spatiotemporal regions, dozens of examples of encounters of two larvae need to be selected. A behavior model is proposed in [14] by firstly abstracting local motions and by modeling the behavior as a dynamical model on such local motions. However, the Markov model used in [14] for behavior limits its applications to some latest behavioral studies which require multi-target tracking, because the number of parameters to specify the transition and observation models is exponential in the number of moving objects.

Pose estimation. While some animal tracking algorithms also provide some information about pose (e.g. orientation of the animal) based on contour models [4], few works have been done for directly addressing the pose estimation problem. Given a rough initial guess of the pose parameters, a cascaded pose regression is proposed to progressively refine the pose estimation until it converges [7]. Our task is more challenging in that we have to address the self-occlusion problem. Moreover, instead of an iterative solution, we present a one-pass algorithm. Different from [6] and [7], our algorithm does not require an initial guess of the target position.

Random Forest based pose estimator/landmark detector. Random Forests (RF) [19] describe an ensemble of decision trees trained independently on a randomized selection of features. Recent works on Hough Forests [8] have shown that objects can be effectively located by training RF regressors to predict the position of a point relative to the sampled region, then running the regressors over a region and accumulating votes for a likely position. In these studies, the final estimation is found as the center of the densest vote mass by mean shift [20]. If the objects are occluded or missing on the test image, the candidates of the target point returned by the trained RF regressor will contain outliers. Therefore, it is crucial to remove such outliers to guarantee a reasonable estimation under the condition of occlusion. In [10], the authors assume the pose parameters stored in a single leaf will follow a Gaussian distribution, and discard the leaves with high variances by simple thresholding when performing mean shift. Similarly, the hand pose estimator in [11] is refined by a mean shift based method to recover the poorly detected joints when they are occluded or missing. Besides the occlusion problems our input images have also less informative visual features for disambiguating objects with similar appearance. As pointed out in [12], landmark detectors based on classification may produce highly interchangeable responses due to very similar local appearance patterns of different anatomical body (sub)parts. Further disambiguation is required that incorporates the global structure of objects. Existing works on medical image analysis for localization of landmarks exploit global landmark relation represented by either repetitive anatomical patterns [12] or shape models [13] for regularization. In our task, however, such stable global landmark relation is not applicable. In this paper, we propose a method to learn the global landmark relation from training data based on a graph based geometric model.

3   Problem Statement

In this paper, we aim to estimate the pose $\mathbf{X} = \{\mathbf{x}^n | 1 \leq n \leq N, \forall \mathbf{x}^n \in \Re^5\}$ from a single image I, where the state of part n is defined as $\mathbf{x}^n = \{\mathbf{y}^n, \theta^n, s^n, t^n\}$. $\mathbf{y}^n$ is the position of the landmark in our defined coordinate system as shown in Fig. 2, θ^n is the angle, and s^n is the scale. Specifically, $t^n = \{0, 1\}$ is the

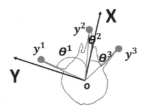

Fig. 2. The coordinate is defined by setting the centroid of head as the origin **o**, the line from the origin towards the mouth center as the x-axis. The head centroid and the mouth center are assumed to be known.

state indicating the presence of part n. The images are acquired from the top view of observed individual insects. Six example frames of an insect images with the outputs of our method are shown in Fig. 1 to visualize various insect poses. Taking a bee for example, we aim to estimate the tips of its three body parts: left antenna (blue circle), tongue (red circle) and right antenna (green circle). Figure 1b illustrates that these body parts are highly clustered, and self-occlusion usually occurs. Body parts may be present or absent. The antennae usually move forwards while occasionally backwards.

4   Combined Landmark Position Proposals

To map the image I to the corresponding pose $\mathbf{X}$ is difficult because the mapping from visual input to poses is highly complicated, our framework imposes constraints to the solution space based on two cues: local appearance and global structure. On one hand, we use RF model for predicting the class label c ($c = \{1$: right antenna, 2: left antenna, 3: tongue$\}$ and 0 as background.) at pixel precision based on patch appearance. On the other hand, we propose a method based on Pictorial Structure (PS) model [21,22] to learn the global structure. We do *not* make any specific assumption about the anatomical model of an insect's head (which was done in [6]), instead we use a common assumption that holds for generic objects: for the same type of insects, they have similar appearances when they are in similar poses. The global structure of an insect is represented by its silhouette, which is a d-dimensional datapoint $\mathbf{f} \in \Re^d$. Based on this assumption, it is expected that these datapoints will lie on or near a low dimensional manifold, in which the neighborhood of each datapoint is preserved. The likelihood of global structure of the unknown pose is learned by the nearest neighbor (NN) method, and used as a constraint to regularize the mapping estimated by the RF model.

Given the image I, the posterior probability $p(\mathbf{X}|I)$ is computed as

$$p(\mathbf{X}|I) \propto p(I|\mathbf{X})p(\mathbf{X}) \tag{1}$$

where $p(I|\mathbf{X})$ is the likelihood of the image evidence given a particular pose, and the $p(\mathbf{X})$ corresponds to a tree prior according to the PS model. Both terms are learned from training data. Specifically we propose a method to adaptively construct the graph for the insect geometric model.

4.1 Geometric Model

Typical PS models assume that, an object can be decomposed into parts connected with pairwise constraints that define the prior probability of part configurations. As we aim to estimate the tips of body parts appended to the insect's head, we build a complete graph based on the pairwise relations between tips as well as each tip $\mathbf{x}^n$ and the centroid of the head $\mathbf{x}^0$. Then the PS model $G = (V, E)$ is learned from the training data by computing the minimum spanning tree of a graph. The resultant E is the set of pairs of each tip and the centroid, and the centroid is the root. Based on the assumption that part likelihoods are conditionally independent [21], Eq. (1) is factorized as

$$p(\mathbf{X}|I) \propto p(\mathbf{x}^0) \prod_{n=0}^{N} p(\mathbf{r}^n|\mathbf{x}^n) \prod_{(i,j)\in E} p(\mathbf{x}^i, \mathbf{x}^j|\Phi_{ij}) \qquad (2)$$

where $p(\mathbf{r}^n|\mathbf{x}^n)$ is the likelihood of position based on local appearance $\mathbf{r}^n$. The joint probability $p(\mathbf{x}^i, \mathbf{x}^j|\Phi_{ij})$ indicates the spatial relations between $\mathbf{x}^i$ and $\mathbf{x}^j$ with parameters Φ_{ij}.

Although we model the global structure as the form of Eq. (2), it is different from typical PS models that assume all parts are present. As we focus on pose estimation rather than detecting the insect head, $\mathbf{x}^0$ is assumed to be known. To represent the global structure of a pose, we extract a feature vector $\mathbf{f} \in \Re^d$ for each image combining five types of silhouette features: Edge Histogram Descriptor [23], the Geometrical Feature [24], the Shape Signature Histogram [25], the Fourier Descriptor [26] and the Hu moments [27]. The dimensionality of $\mathbf{f}$ is $d = 88$, thus no dimensionality reduction is required. For a new visual input represented by silhouette features $\mathbf{f}$ of image I, we find its K neighbors in the visual feature space and construct the neighborhood $\mathbf{K}$ in the pose space.

As the nodes of landmarks of G are all leafs, and the likelihood of individual landmarks are conditionally independent, the node representing $\mathbf{x}^n$ will be removed if the frequency of the presence of $\mathbf{x}^n \in \mathbf{K}$ is lower than a threshold value τ. The new graph $G^* = (V^*, E^*)$ remains a tree structure. Based on G^*, Eq. (2) is changed to

$$p(\mathbf{X}|I) \propto \prod_{n\in E^*} p(\mathbf{r}^n|\mathbf{x}^n)p(\mathbf{x}^n, \mathbf{x}^0|\Phi_{n0}) \qquad (3)$$

We assume that Φ_{n0} takes the form of unimodal Gaussian distribution over $\mathbf{y}^n, s^n$, and the von Mises distribution over θ^n. Thus, the model parameters $(\boldsymbol{\mu}_{\mathbf{y}}^n, \Sigma_{\mathbf{y}}^n)$, (μ_s^n, σ_s^n) and $(\mu_\theta^n, \sigma_\theta^n)$ are learned from the training samples in $\mathbf{K}$. The joint probability is computed as

$$p(\mathbf{x}^n, \mathbf{x}^0|\Phi_{n0}) = \mathcal{N}(\mathbf{y}^n|\boldsymbol{\mu}_{\mathbf{y}}^n, \Sigma_{\mathbf{y}}^n)\mathcal{N}(s^n|\mu_s^n, \sigma_s^n)\mathcal{M}(\theta^n|\mu_\theta^n, \sigma_\theta^n) \qquad (4)$$

4.2   Random Forest Based Classifier

We use RF model to compute the likelihood of landmark position based on local appearance evidence $p(\mathbf{r}^n|\mathbf{x}^n)$. Taking bee images for example, each datapoint in the training dataset D is an image patch $(I(\mathbf{y}_i)$, where $\mathbf{y}_i$ is the image coordinate) sampled in the following way: We randomly sample the patches with centroids located along the contour (see the light blue contours in Fig. 3) as examples of corresponding class c and the patches with centers inside or outside the contour as examples of background. A class labels c is assigned to every datapoint. As shown in Fig. 3a, a class label $c \in [0, N]$ of each patch (colored square) is the index of its closest tip (colored circle) along the contour: {1: right antenna, 2: left antenna, 3: tongue} and 0 as background. A similar sampling strategy is applied for ant images, as shown in Fig. 3c. $N = 3$ for a bee and $N = 2$ for an ant. We classify left or right antenna to balance the distribution of classes, since the samples of class $c = 3$ are much fewer than the class $c = 1$ or $c = 2$.

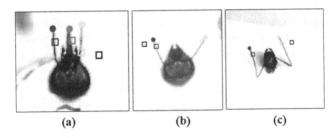

(a)   (b)   (c)

Fig. 3. The image sizes of Dataset A, B and C are (a) 275×235, (b) 350×320 and (c) 415×420 in pixels, respectively. The patch size (denoted by a square) is 16×16 pixels. The images have been scaled for better visualization.

To train the forest R, we randomly extract patches from D and use the information gain criterion to select the split function. The split function of a node is represented by a simple two-pixel test as in [9]. The forest R is constructed, with each leaf L_j created when the maximum depth is reached or a minimum number of patches are left. Each leaf stores the patches from D that end here. Each patch of a given test image I passes down a tree and ends in a leaf $L_j(\mathbf{y}_i)$, which gives the class probabilities $p(c|I(\mathbf{y}_i))$. A class label c is assigned to each pixel with the highest $p(c|I(\mathbf{y}_i))$, and $p(\mathbf{r}^c|\mathbf{x}^c)$ is set to be 1. Specifically, we set $p(\mathbf{r}^c|\mathbf{x}^c) = 1, \forall c = 1, 2$, since the RF model may not correctly differentiate the left or the right antenna. We will address this problem by solving Eq. (3).

4.3   Final Landmark Localization

According to Eq. (3), the posterior probability of configuration $p(\mathbf{X}|I)$ is computed as the product of the posterior probability of the landmarks $n \in E^*$. We construct a response image by computing the posterior probability for each of these landmarks at an image coordinate. To localize a landmark, a simple strategy by selecting the pixel with highest probability may fail due to the outlying pixels. Instead, we use mean shift [28] with a flat kernel to find the modes of probability mass for each part, and assume that it lies in the connected component that contains the landmark. Finally, the landmark is simply estimated as the furthest pixel within the connected component.

5   Experiments

As pointed out in [6], the state-of-the-art tracking algorithms do not perform well when applied to our task. In this experiment, as our method combines the strength of the traditional regression forest [8] and Pictorial Structure model, it is compared with the methods directly applying these two concepts.

5.1   Datasets and Evaluation Metric

In this experiment, our method was evaluated on three challenging datasets of individual insects (i.e. bees and ants) during a behavioral experiment, among which two datasets of individual bees are recorded in different light conditions or other experimental settings. For example, Dataset A contains images from a video recording a bee in different trials of experiments, while Dataset B is of various bees in different trials. The image data comes from our biological partner:

- Dataset A (bee): 5633 training images, 2788 testing images
- Dataset B (bee): 3625 training images, 9003 testing images
- Dataset C (ant): 215 training images, 238 testing images

The spatial resolution is 39 pixels per μm for bee images and 22 pixels per μm for ant images. More details about the three datasets are shown in Fig. 3.

As our method directly estimates the position of landmarks, it does not produce bounding box (BB) hypotheses. Some popular pose estimation metrics, such as average precision of keypoints (AFK) [29], require ground truth BBs for evaluation, thus not suitable for our method. Results of our method are compared with the two aforementioned methods as well as ground truth landmark positions, which are manually annotated by a human. We compute the rate of false positives (FP) and false negatives (FN) of inferring the presence of each landmark to validate the adequacy of our geometric model, e.g. a FP of the tongue indicates that the tongue is inferred to be present while it is absent actually. The accuracy of localization is measured by the average Euclidean distance in pixels between the results and the groundtruth.

5.2   Implementation Details

For learning the geometric model, we found $K = 100$ nearest neighbors to construct $\mathbf{K}$ in Sect. 4.1. We construct 10 trees for the RF and each tree has the depth of 5. Each tree converges until the maximum tree depth is reached or the amount of remaining patches is less than 50. The bandwidth of meanshift kernel is set as 0.05 for all images.

The complexity of the algorithm is measured by the processing time. For constructing a random forest, we use the code of Hough Forest [8]. Using a Matlab implementation of our method, testing takes around 4 seconds per frame on an Intel i7 machine with 8 GB RAM. It takes about 1 s for RF classification, and 3 s for computing Eq. (3) and final landmark localization.

5.3   Results and Discussion

For quantitative evaluation, Table 1 shows the average position error (pixels) in three datasets. The average position errors of each part are merely 10.2, 5.3 and 18.0 pixels, respectively. They are rather small compared to the size of an insect head (shown as Fig. 3). The position error on Dataset C is larger than the others because ant images have more severe motion blur (e.g. the right antenna in Fig. 5f), and the exact positions of landmarks are ambiguous.

Table 1. Quantitative evaluation on three datasets.

Datasets	Position error (pixels)	FN (%)	FP (%)
A	10.2	5	0
B	5.3	3	0.2
C	18.0	0	0

To validate the advantage of our method over RF and the typical PS model, we compare the three methods on Dataset A, which is the most challenging one due to the complex background. The typical PS model in Eq. (2) assumes that all landmarks are present, and the spatial relations between parts are learned from all the training samples. As shown in Table 2, this method produces a high FP rate when inferring the presence of the tongue. With the learned geometric model in Eq. (3), our method achieves a significant improvement over both the PS model and the RF regressor in terms of both the localization precision and the ability to disambiguate different objects.

Table 2. Comparison of three methods on dataset A.

Methods	L. antenna			Tongue			R. antenna		
	pos. error	FN(%)	FP(%)	pos. error	FN(%)	FP(%)	pos. error	FN(%)	FP(%)
Ours	10.2	4	0	14.9	11	0	8.4	3	0
PS	17.6	2	0	18.4	4	13	16.7	4	0
RF	24.5	2	0	26.3	26	44	25.3	8	0

Figure 4 shows the localization errors of each landmark from Dataset A for a more detailed discussion. We show nine image sequences where either the RF or the PS method produces large localization errors, while our method achieves very low position errors in most of the frames.

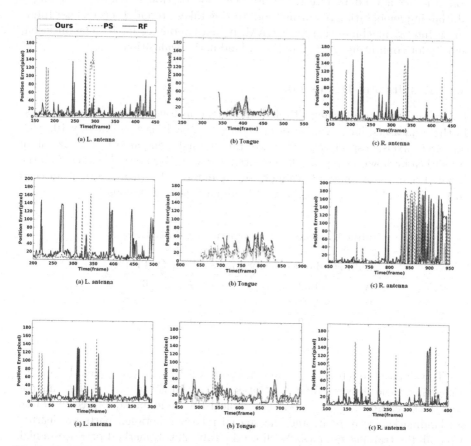

Fig. 4. Quantitative results by our method (green), RF regressor (blue) and PS model (red). (Colour figure online)

We visualize more results in Figs. 5 and 6 to discuss the advantage of our method in more details. As shown in Fig. 5a and e, our method successfully localizes the two antennae even in complex background, while the RF regressor fails to distinguish the left antenna from the noise of background and thus produces high position errors. Besides, the RF regressor may incorrectly recognize an antenna as the tongue (as shown in Fig. 5c–d), indicating a high FP rate of the tongue in Table 2. In contrast, our method is able to disambiguate the tongue and the right antenna even when they are very close to each other (see Fig. 5a).

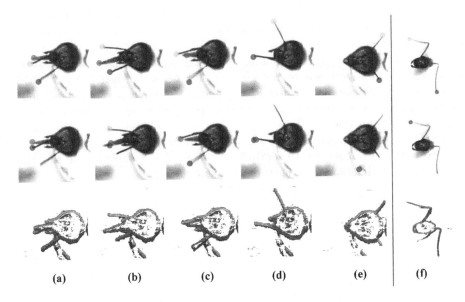

Fig. 5. Qualitative results by our method (the first row), RF regressor (the second row) and RF classification (the bottom row).

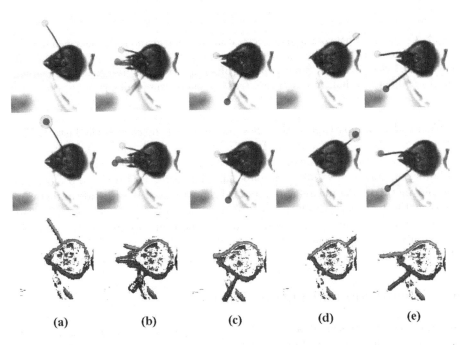

Fig. 6. Qualitative results by our method (the first row), PS model (the second row) and RF classification (the bottom row).

Figure 6 shows the advantage over typical PS models in inferring the number of landmarks present. Without inferring the presence of a landmark, it will be localized at some position. A naïve approach for rejecting the potentially incorrect position is that a landmark falling inside the region of insect head will be rejected, e.g. the tongue has been rejected in Fig. 6a and d. But it cannot deal with more general cases as shown in Fig. 6b and e. Moreover, the spatial relations between parts learned from all training data provides little information in our case, since the possible positions of antennae in all training images are nearly uniformly distributed. As shown in Fig. 6a and d, the left antenna is incorrectly located in the right antenna. In contrast, our method is capable of inferring the absence of a landmark by the learned geometric model.

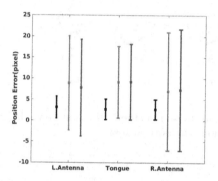

Fig. 7. Comparison between human annotators and our method: the means and standard deviations of the Euclidean distance between the landmark positions of human annotator A vs. the results of our method (blue), human annotator B vs. our method (green) and between human raters only (red). (Colour figure online)

As for the running time of the three methods, our method is the fastest. The PS model takes 8 s for computing Eq. (2), while ours only takes 3 s for Eq. (3).

To validate that the localization precision of our method are comparable to human annotators, we also compare the pixel error between two annotators and our method. The means and standard deviations of the Euclidean distance between the landmark positions of human annotator A vs. the results of our method (blue), human annotator B vs. our method (green) and between human raters only (red), are illustrated in Fig. 7. The results show that the estimation of our method is comparably accurate as human annotators in most cases.

6   Conclussion and Future Work

In summary, we presented a new algorithm exploiting local appearance and global geometric structure of an insect to infer its pose from a single image. Our method is a data-driven approach to incorporate geometric constraints. The model parameters are learned from the training data. Our method addresses the issue of interchangeable estimations by solely using RF model for landmark detection, and presents nice interplay between RF and PS model. The performance of our method has been validated on three large challenging datasets of different types of insects, which achieves comparable position accuracy to that of human annotators.

Future work includes incorporating our method into a multi-frame pose estimation framework. Given the high accuracy of pose estimated based on single frames by our method, merging it into an interactive tracking framework such as [6] could result in a new approach for insect behavioral analysis.

References

1. Dell, A.I., Bender, J.A., Branson, K., Couzin, I.D., de Polavieja, G.G., Noldus, L.P., Pérez-Escudero, A., Perona, P., Straw, A.D., Wikelski, M., et al.: Automated image-based tracking and its application in ecology. Trends Ecol. Evol. **29**(7), 417–428 (2014)
2. Branson, K., Belongie, S.: Tracking multiple mouse contours (without too many samples). In: IEEE Computer Society Conference on Computer Vision and Pattern Recognition (CVPR), vol. 1, pp. 1039–1046. IEEE (2005)
3. Khan, Z., Balch, T., Dellaert, F.: MCMC data association and sparse factorization updating for real time multitarget tracking with merged and multiple measurements. IEEE Trans. Pattern Anal. Mach. Intell. **28**(12), 1960–1972 (2006)
4. Branson, K., Robie, A.A., Bender, J., Perona, P., Dickinson, M.H.: High-throughput ethomics in large groups of drosophila. Nat. Method **6**(6), 451–457 (2009)
5. Huston, S.J., Stopfer, M., Cassenaer, S., Aldworth, Z.N., Laurent, G.: Neural encoding of odors during active sampling and in turbulent plumes. Neuron **88**(2), 403–418 (2015)
6. Shen, M., Li, C., Huang, W., Szyszka, P., Shirahama, K., Grzegorzek, M., Merhof, D., Duessen, O.: Interactive tracking of insect posture. Pattern Recogn. **48**(11), 3560–3571 (2015)
7. Dollár, P., Welinder, P., Perona, P.: Cascaded pose regression. In: IEEE Conference on Computer Vision and Pattern Recognition (CVPR), pp. 1078–1085. IEEE (2010)
8. Gall, J., Yao, A., Razavi, N., Van Gool, L., Lempitsky, V.: Hough forests for object detection, tracking, and action recognition. IEEE Trans. Pattern Anal. Mach. Intell. **33**(11), 2188–2202 (2011)
9. Shotton, J., Sharp, T., Kipman, A., Fitzgibbon, A., Finocchio, M., Blake, A., Cook, M., Moore, R.: Real-time human pose recognition in parts from single depth images. Commun. ACM **56**(1), 116–124 (2013)
10. Fanelli, G., Gall, J., Van Gool, L.: Real time head pose estimation with random regression forests. In: IEEE Conference on Computer Vision and Pattern Recognition (CVPR), pp. 617–624. IEEE (2011)
11. Tang, D., Yu, T.H., Kim, T.K.: Real-time articulated hand pose estimation using semi-supervised transductive regression forests. In: IEEE International Conference on Computer Vision (ICCV), pp. 3224–3231. IEEE (2013)
12. Donner, R., Menze, B.H., Bischof, H., Langs, G.: Global localization of 3d anatomical structures by pre-filtered hough forests and discrete optimization. Med. Image Anal. **17**(8), 1304–1314 (2013)

13. Chen, C., Xie, W., Franke, J., Grutzner, P., Nolte, L.P., Zheng, G.: Automatic x-ray landmark detection and shape segmentation via data-driven joint estimation of image displacements. Med. Image Anal. **18**(3), 487–499 (2014)
14. Veeraraghavan, A., Chellappa, R., Srinivasan, M.: Shape and behavior encoded tracking of bee dances. IEEE Trans. Pattern Anal. Mach. Intell. **3**, 463–476 (2008)
15. Landgraf, T., Rojas, R.: Tracking honey bee dances from sparse optical flow fields. FB Mathematik und Informatik FU, pp. 1–37 (2007)
16. Perera, A., Srinivas, C., Hoogs, A., Brooksby, G., Hu, W.: Multi-object tracking through simultaneous long occlusions and split-merge conditions. In: IEEE Conference on Computer Vision and Pattern Recognition (CVPR), vol. 1, pp. 666–673 (2006)
17. Balch, T., Khan, Z., Veloso, M.: Automatically tracking and analyzing the behavior of live insect colonies. In: Proceedings of the Fifth International Conference on Autonomous Agents, pp. 521–528. ACM (2001)
18. Fiaschi, L., Diego, F., Gregor, K., Schiegg, M., Koethe, U., Zlatic, M., Hamprecht, F., et al.: Tracking indistinguishable translucent objects over time using weakly supervised structured learning. In: IEEE Conference on Computer Vision and Pattern Recognition (CVPR), pp. 2736–2743. IEEE (2014)
19. Breiman, L.: Random forests. Mach. Learn. **45**(1), 5–32 (2001)
20. Cheng, Y.: Mean shift, mode seeking, and clustering. IEEE Trans. Pattern Anal. Mach. Intell. **17**(8), 790–799 (1995)
21. Andriluka, M., Roth, S., Schiele, B.: Pictorial structures revisited: people detection and articulated pose estimation. In: IEEE Conference on Computer Vision and Pattern Recognition (CVPR), pp. 1014–1021. IEEE (2009)
22. Felzenszwalb, P.F., Girshick, R.B., McAllester, D., Ramanan, D.: Object detection with discriminatively trained part-based models. IEEE Trans. Pattern Anal. Mach. Intell. **32**(9), 1627–1645 (2010)
23. Frigui, H., Gader, P.: Detection and discrimination of land mines in ground-penetrating radar based on edge histogram descriptors and a possibilistic K-Nearest neighbor classifier. Fuzzy Syst. **17**(1), 185–199 (2011)
24. Li, S.Z.: Shape matching based on invariants. In: Omidvar, O. (ed.) Shape Analysis, Progress in Neural Networks, pp. 203–228. Ablex, Norwood (1999)
25. Zhang, D., Liu, G.: Review of shape representation and description techniques. Pattern Recogn. **37**(1), 1–19 (2004)
26. Zhang, D., Lu, G.: A comparative study of curvature scale space and fourier descriptors for shape-based image retrieval. J. Visual Commun. Image Represent. **14**(1), 39–57 (2003)
27. Hu, M.K.: Visual pattern recognition by moment invariants. IRE Trans. Inf. Theor. **8**(2), 179–187 (1962)
28. Comaniciu, D., Meer, P.: Mean shift: a robust approach toward feature space analysis. IEEE Trans. Pattern Anal. Mach. Intell. **24**(5), 603–619 (2002)
29. Yang, Y., Ramanan, D.: Articulated human detection with flexible mixtures of parts. IEEE Trans. Pattern Anal. Mach. Intell. **35**(12), 2878–2890 (2013)

Feature Augmented Deep Neural Networks for Segmentation of Cells

Sajith Kecheril Sadanandan[1,2]([✉]), Petter Ranefall[1,2], and Carolina Wählby[1,2]

[1] Department of Information Technology, Uppsala University, Uppsala, Sweden
sajith.ks@it.uu.se
[2] SciLifeLab, Uppsala, Sweden

Abstract. In this work, we use a fully convolutional neural network for microscopy cell image segmentation. Rather than designing the network from scratch, we modify an existing network to suit our dataset. We show that improved cell segmentation can be obtained by augmenting the raw images with specialized feature maps such as eigen value of Hessian and wavelet filtered images, for training our network. We also show modality transfer learning, by training a network on phase contrast images and testing on fluorescent images. Finally we show that our network is able to segment irregularly shaped cells. We evaluate the performance of our methods on three datasets consisting of phase contrast, fluorescent and bright-field images.

Keywords: Deep neural network · Feature augmentation · Cell segmentation · Convolutional neural network · Unstained cells

1 Introduction

Observation of biological samples over prolonged periods of time is commonly used to study phenotypical changes due to variations in environmental conditions or genetic modifications. High-throughput high-content screening is used to analyse many biological processes simultaneously [1]. It is tedious for human observers to monitor changes at the cellular level over long time. Automated image analysis algorithms are widely used to simplify and quantify the analysis process [2].

For automated image analysis at the cellular level, a commonly used approach is to segment the cellular regions and track the cell segments over time [3]. The cell segmentation is a crucial step in this process, which affects the quality of the cell tracking results. In this work, we aim to segment cells in time-lapse microscopy image sequences. Cell segmentation is a challenging process, especially when the cells are unstained. Deep Neural Networks (DNN) using Fully Convolutional Neural Networks (FCNN) have shown excellent results in semantic segmentation [4]. FCNNs were also used in segmenting unstained cells in microscopy images [5,6]. The network structures of these high performing FCNNs, as opposed to traditional DNNs [7,8], suggest that designing the proper

© Springer International Publishing Switzerland 2016
G. Hua and H. Jégou (Eds.): ECCV 2016 Workshops, Part I, LNCS 9913, pp. 231–243, 2016.
DOI: 10.1007/978-3-319-46604-0_17

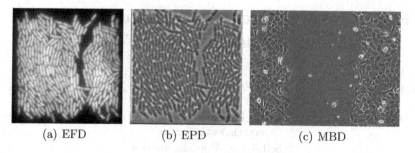

      (a) EFD   (b) EPD   (c) MBD

Fig. 1. (a) Input *E. coli* fluorescent dataset (EFD) (b) *E. coli* phase contrast dataset (EPD) and (c) mouse mammary cells bright-field dataset (MBD).

deep network is non-trivial. Often, a network that gives good results on a particular dataset may not give good results on another dataset. Fusing features from different layers of deep networks [9] or combining deep features with hand-crafted features [10] were used in video action recognition tasks, where the authors used 'late fusion', i.e., they combined features at later layers of the deep network for classification. A combination of Gabor filters and Convolutional Neural Networks was used for face detection [11], where the author performed an 'early fusion', by combining hand-crafted features in the first layer of the neural network. Recently, DNNs with a reduced number of parameters [12,13] were also successfully used for classification. In this work, we augment features at the first layer by combining hand-crafted features with raw images, and train an FCNN with a reduced number of parameters. We use wavelet filtering and eigen value based enhancement for feature augmentation. For one of our datasets we create ground-truth semi-automatically, using an existing method [14]. In Sect. 2, we describe how to modify a deep network with augmented features for two different datasets of *E. coli* cells and mouse cells. In Sect. 3, we perform a quantitative evaluation of our results with an existing method for the *E. coli* dataset and a qualitative evaluation of our results on the mouse cells dataset. We also show how the feature augmentation improves segmentation of the cells.

2   Materials and Methods

2.1   Input Images

The input images comprise two time-lapse datasets- (1) a prokaryotic cell dataset, consisting of *E. coli* and (2) a eukaryotic cell dataset, consisting of mouse mammary gland cells. The *E. coli* cell images were acquired using a phase contrast microscope and we call this dataset *E. coli* phase dataset (EPD) and the mouse cells were acquired using a bright-field microscope and we call it mouse bright-field dataset (MBD), hereafter. The EPD consists of 500 images of size 1024×1360 pixels in vertical and horizontal directions respectively, while the bright-field dataset consists of 411 images of size 1040×1392 pixels. These two datasets are used for both training and testing of our FCNNs. In addition, we use a single image of the *E. coli* sample, imaged under a fluorescence microscope and we name this dataset *E. coli* fluorescent dataset (EFD), for additional testing of a modality that is different from the one used for training the FCNN. Sample images from the image datasets are shown in Fig. 1.

2.2   Image Preprocessing

The EPD contains regions outside the cell colony area. We therefore crop the images to a size of 860×860 pixels to set the field of view to cell regions alone. The images in the MBD, are not cropped as the raw images contain cells in the full field of view. We create three different types of feature maps depending on the dataset, such as eigen value based contrast enhancement [15], wavelet coefficient filtering [16] and truncated Singular Value Decomposition (SVD) [17]. The idea behind the feature augmentation is to highlight certain regions in the input images and make the network learn features from those regions resulting in improved segmentation of cellular regions. The choice of these features depends on the imaging modality and the type of cells imaged.

For the EPD, we use the eigen value based contrast enhancement and truncated SVD. The eigen value based contrast enhancement was successfully used in [3] to segment *E.coli* cells. This method improves the contrast between the regions of touching cells. The contrast enhancement using this approach helps the network to learn features for better cell segmentation than the network that does not use additional contrast enhancements, by accurately segmenting the touching cells. We use truncated SVD as denoising method and wanted to see if denoising has any impact on the segmentation results, especially for the EFD, which is more noisy than either the EPD or the MBD. The eigen value based contrast enhancement is done by extracting the minimum curvature of the intensity landscape in the input image. For this, first we find the Hessian matrix, H, which is created by finding the second derivative at each pixel position in the x and y directions of the image. The maximum and minimum curvatures (principal curvatures) at a position are the eigen values of the Hessian matrix. The eigen values are found by the following equation [15].

$$k_{1,2} = \frac{trace(H) \pm \sqrt{trace(H)^2 - 4 \times det(H)}}{2} \tag{1}$$

Here, k_1 and k_2 are the principal curvatures with $k_1 < k_2$. To perform contrast enhancement, we create an image with k_1, the lowest eigen value, from all spatial locations of the input image. To find the truncated SVD, we find singular values sorted in decreasing order, for the full raw image, and add the values till they sum upto 99 % of the sum of all singular values. All the singular values after 99 % are set to zero and an image is reconstructed from the new set of singular values. For the EPD, we use four different input combinations for the FCNN such as- (1) raw images, (2) eigen images, (3) combined raw and eigen images, and (4) truncated SVD images as summarized in Table 1.

Table 1. The inputs used for training. The EFD is not used for training

Dataset	Raw	Eigen	Raw + Eigen	SVD	Raw + Wavelet
EPD	yes	yes	yes	yes	-
MBD	yes	-	-	-	yes
EFD	-	-	-	-	-

For the MBD, we first find the wavelet transform using Daubechies 4 wavelet [16] (db4) to four decomposition levels and set the approximation coefficients to zero and then reconstruct the image using these modified coefficients. Two deep networks with raw images and a stack of combined raw images with wavelet filtered images as input are created for the MBD. We use open-source code available at [18] to find wavelet features. Table 1 shows the inputs used for training both the EPD and the MBD. All these input images were preprocessed by normalizing to the range [0, 1] and subtracting the median value.

2.3   Semi-automatic Ground Truth Generation

Training data generation is one of the crucial steps for any FCNN application. We observed that the quality of the training set was equally important as the quantity. In this work, we employed two different strategies for training set generation. For the EPD, we generated the training set semi-automatically. We used the open-source code available at [14] to segment *E. coli* cells. Once the segmentation was finished, we manually removed the false positives to improve the quality of our training set. We observed that even a single false postive could adversely affect the results when testing the FCNN. This could be due to two reasons- (1) when false positives are present, the network learns parameters to detect foreground regions that actually have the features of the background, resulting in poor performance during testing. (2) since we perform data augmentation there is a high chance that the false positives are present in multiple training samples. We selected 30 images, equally spaced at regular intervals in the EPD consisting of 500 images, for training our FCNN. After selecting representative images, we set the input image size of the FCNN to 540×540 pixels through cropping. From every representative raw input image, we cropped 5 patches to cover the entire image region. The regions we cropped were such that the patches cover the top-left corner, bottom-left corner, top-right corner, bottom-right corner and the centre of the images. We created data augmentation using these representative images. The data augmentation step consisted of spatial transformations such as flipping, rotation and elastic deformations [5]. We did two experiments- (1) with the original U-Net and (2) with a modified U-Net. For the experiment with the original U-Net, we created a training set of 20000 images, while for the experiment with the modified U-Net, we created a training set of 600 images, followed by feature augmentation. Finally, we created weight maps to give additional weights to the foreground regions for weighted

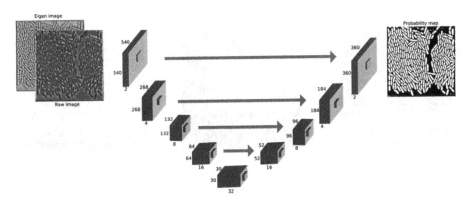

Fig. 2. Architecture of the network. Each block represents two convolutions with a kernel of size 3 × 3 without padding. An input image with its augmented feature map and the corresponding output probability map is also shown. The feature map is contrast enhanced for better visualization.

softmax [5]. Additional weights force the network to learn parameters in such a way that it can separate touching cells. We set the border weight value to 10 for the feature augmented networks and 3 for the single input image networks and standard deviation to 3 for all the networks to create the weighted labels.

For the MBD, there is no previously existing method that gives a satisfactory cell segmentation, to the best of our knowledge. Therefore semi-automated ground truth generation cannot be used in this case. We manually marked the boundary of each cell in two images. There were approximately 300 cells per image. Then, by data augmentation, 600 training samples were generated from these images, followed by feature augmentation. The rest of the processing pipeline is similar to the one used for the EPD.

2.4 Deep Neural Network Architecture and Training

The FCNN we use in this work, is inspired by the recent FCNN known as U-Net [5]. Initially we trained the original U-Net [5] architecture using 20000 training images, created through data augmentation, for 200000 training iterations. During testing, we found that the network was under-performing and the final segmentation result was poor for our dataset. This may be because of the large number of parameters in the network model and also that our dataset may be lying in a lower dimensional feature space. The details regarding these results are given in Sect. 3.1. Next, we modified the original network structure and combined it with traditional image processing techniques to improve performance on our dataset. We modified the original architecture by reducing the feature map size, i.e. number of featuremaps, to 1/32 of the original size. For example, the original U-Net has a feature map size of 64 in the first layer while our modified network has two feature maps in the first layer. The architecture of the network, a raw image, a feature map, and an output probability map is shown in Fig. 2.

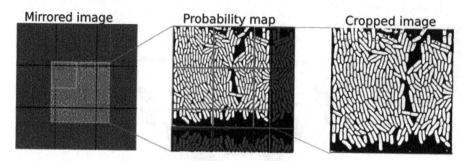

Fig. 3. Overlap-tiling to find the probability map of the entire image. The raw image or the stack of raw images with augmented feature maps is mirrored on all sides to take care of the boundary problem. Then patch-wise probability maps are created to cover the entire image and finally the probability map is cropped to the size of the raw input image.

Here, we reduced the training set size to 600 images. We used the following hyperparameters for training: the number of training iterations was set to 20000 with base learning rate to 0.01 and momentum to 0.9 and reduced the learning rate to 1/10 of the current value after every 5000 iterations. We used the open-source framework Caffe [19], with an additional weighted softmax loss layer and a crop layer, to implement the FCNN. We trained all different networks on a workstation with Intel(R) Core(TM) i7-5930K CPU running at 3.50 GHz and a Nvidia Titan X GPU.

2.5   Segmentation and Postprocessing

For the EPD, testing was done on the whole time-lapse sequence comprising of 500 images, to quantify its usability for cell tracking applications. The final network had an input size of 540 × 540 or 540 × 540 × 2, depending on network architecture, and the output probability map size was 356 × 356. So to create a probability map for the entire image, we first created an image that was 9 times the size of the original image by mirroring on all eight neighborhood positions of the image followed by feature map generation. After the mirroring step, we traversed through the whole image, in an overlap-tile strategy of input, in such a way that the output probability maps did not overlap, similarly as in [5]. The overlap-tiling along with cropping of the probability map is shown in Fig. 3. For the EPD, we empirically found a threshold of 0.2 for binarization and removed objects that were smaller than 200 pixels to eliminate false positive pixels. Finally, we filled holes in the output mask to get a final segmentation mask. For the MBD, a similar procedure was followed to create a probability map. The probability map for the MBD was not as sharp as the one for the EPD. We therefore applied watershed segmentation to the probability map to find the final segmentation mask. We used the openly available CellProfiler software [20] for watershed segmentation. In CellProfiler, we set the parameters minimum and

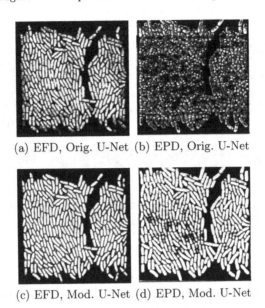

(a) EFD, Orig. U-Net (b) EPD, Orig. U-Net

(c) EFD, Mod. U-Net (d) EPD, Mod. U-Net

Fig. 4. Probability maps from the original U-Net and the modified U-Net when raw images were used as input. (a) and (b) show the probability maps for the EFD and the EPD, respectively, for the original U-Net. (c) and (d) show the corresponding probability maps for the modified U-Net with architecture shown in Fig. 2.

maximum diameter of objects to 30 and 100 respectively, for the segmentation, and kept other parameters at their default values.

2.6 Modality Transfer Learning

Finally, we investigated if a trained network can be transfered to a new imaging modality, in this case moving from phase contrast to fluorescence microscopy. For the EFD, we re-used the network trained on the EPD. We inverted the input image, so that the cells appeared as dark objects and the background was bright. After inverting the image, we created feature augmentation and fed to the corresponding network trained on the EPD. This way we were able to re-use the same network for testing on a different modality, that was not used for training.

3   Results and Discussions

In this section, we show the results obtained from the modified network for our image datasets.

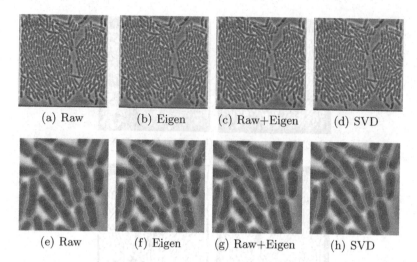

Fig. 5. (a–d) Segmentation result overlayed on the EPD (e–h) zoomed-in regions of corresponding segmentation results on highlighted (red) regions from (a–d). (Color figure online)

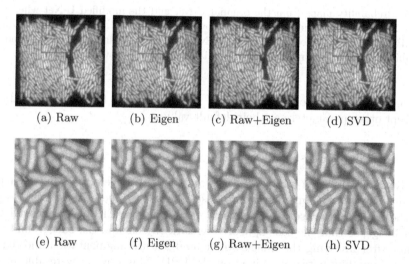

Fig. 6. (a–d) Segmentation result overlayed on the EFD (e–h) zoomed-in regions of corresponding segmentation results on highlighted (red) regions. (Color figure online)

3.1 Deep Neural Network

A comparison of results from the original U-Net and our modified network for raw input images is shown in Fig. 4. Visual inspection of these results shows that the modified network performs better than the original one for our dataset. This might be attributed to the small number of parameters for the network and low feature dimensionality of our dataset.

Table 2. The average F-score ± standard deviation for the previously published CBA method and the here proposed methods using raw images, eigen images, raw images with eigen images and truncated SVD images for the EPD and the EFD

Dataset	CBA	Raw	Eigen	Raw + Eigen	SVD
EPD	0.81 ± 0.27	0.37 ± 0.24	0.60 ± 0.21	$\mathbf{0.82 \pm 0.29}$	0.78 ± 0.28
EFD	0.83 ± 0.25	0.78 ± 0.29	0.84 ± 0.26	0.84 ± 0.25	$\mathbf{0.85 \pm 0.25}$

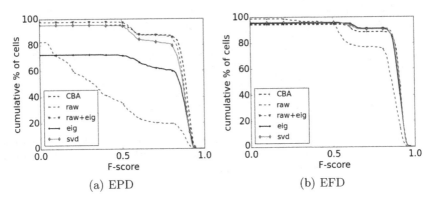

(a) EPD   (b) EFD

Fig. 7. Percentage of cells above particular F-score value v/s F-score for the EPD and the EFD.

3.2 Segmentation Evaluation

The segmentation results for the EPD and the EFD for different networks are shown in Figs. 5 and 6 respectively. Zoomed-in regions of highlighted areas (in red) are also shown in these figures. For the EPD, a performance improvement for the proposed method can be seen from the results of our feature augmented networks, giving comparatively better results than single input networks as shown in Fig. 5. For the EFD, qualitative evaluation of the results shows that similar performance is obtained for all networks as shown in Fig. 6. Next we did a quantitative evaluation of the segmentation result on the EPD and the EFD. We compared all the segmentation results with the corresponding ground truth images. The results of the comparison are shown in Fig. 7(a) for the EPD and Fig. 7(b) for EFD. The average F-score value per cell, together with standard deviations for the EPD (288 cells) and the EFD (308 cells) with respect to the different methods are shown in Table 2. The evaluation on the EFD shows that our proposed method, using feature augmentation, is comparable to the state-of-the-art method, refered to as CBA [3]. The evaluation on the EPD shows that the feature augmentation based deep network using the raw image + the eigen image is better than the deep networks using either the raw image or the eigen image alone. Furthermore we found that our proposed method is better than the previous method for detecting irregularly shaped cells. The segmentation results for two images with irregularly shaped cells are shown in Fig. 8. The results show

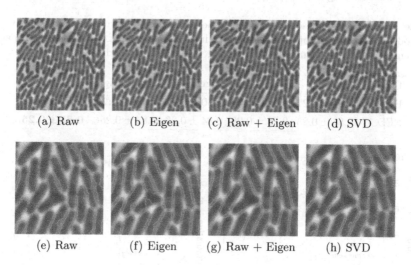

(a) Raw   (b) Eigen   (c) Raw + Eigen   (d) SVD

(e) Raw   (f) Eigen   (g) Raw + Eigen   (h) SVD

Fig. 8. (a–d) show segmentation results, on a selected region, using our networks when an unusually long cell is present in the input image. Similarly (e–h) show results when an irregular shaped cell is present in the input image.

that our method can detect *E. coli* cells of any length or other abnormalities. We observed that the networks with raw image and truncated SVD image as input had a low perfomance because the regions between the cells had a high value in the output probability map and were detected as foreground regions after thresholding. It is worth noting that the truncated SVD gave better results than the raw image. This might be due to the reduction in noise while doing SVD truncation. We observed that 99 % of the sum of all singular values gave the best performance, when the sum was varied from 80 % to 99 % of the total sum of all singular values. Since the truncated SVD acts as a denoising filter, it might be possible to use other denoising filters to achieve similar performance. Qualitative analysis on the MBD showed that the feature augmented network, using wavelet filtering, gave visibly improved results as compared to the network using only the raw images. The probability maps are shown in Fig. 9(a) and (b). Comparing the two results we can see that the regions inside the cells are brighter, indicating high probability of being cells, while the boundaries are dark. We did watershed segmentation on the probability maps to get a final segmentation mask. The final segmentation mask overlayed on raw input image is shown in Fig. 9(c) and (d). The results from the MBD also showed that improved performance can be obtained using feature augmentation.

We compared the execution speed of the CBA method with our deep neural network approach. A direct comparison of the CBA method with the proposed method is not possible since CBA is a CPU based algorithm while the proposed method is GPU based. For the comparison, we used the faster version of CBA [14]. We found that the CBA method took 1.86 s to segment the EPD of size 860×860 on a laptop with quad core Intel(R) Core(TM) i7 CPU running at

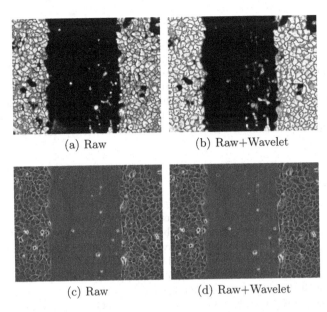

(a) Raw   (b) Raw+Wavelet

(c) Raw   (d) Raw+Wavelet

Fig. 9. Segmentation result of the MBD. Probability maps of results using the raw image alone and using the raw image along with feature augmentation using wavelet filtering is shown in (a) and (b) and corresponding segmentation results using the watershed algorithm on the probability maps are shown in (c) and (d). Training and testing was done on separate images.

2.7 GHz with 8 Gb RAM on Ubuntu 14.04. The proposed approach took 0.91 s to segment the same image on a workstation with six core Intel(R) Core(TM) i7 CPU running at 3.50 GHz with 32 Gb RAM and a Nvidia Titan X GPU on Ubuntu 14.04.

4   Conclusion and Future Work

In this work, we have modified an existing FCNN and augment the input layer with hand-crafted features to improve the performance. We used an existing method to generate the ground truth semi-automatically, for training our FCNNs. We showed that modality transfer learning is possible by training the FCNN on one imaging modality, such as phase contrast microscopy images and test on a different modality, such as fluorescence microscopy images. We also showed that our proposed feature augmentation technique improved the segmentation of cells on three different datasets. The previous state-of-the-art method (CBA) fails in finding cells that do not have an elliptical shape, while the proposed FCNN does not have such restrictions. It should be noted that these irregularly shaped cells were not part of the training set, and we believe that the success is due to the ability of the FCNN to identify the local structures that enables better segmentation of individual cells. In the future, we plan to use other features for improved segmentation accuracy for unstained cultured cells and use the segmentation results for cell tracking applications.

Acknowledgements. This work was supported by the Swedish research council under Grant 2012-4968 (to CW) and the Swedish strategic research program eSSENCE. Image data was kindly provided by Johan Elf at the Department of Cell and Molecular Biology, Computational and Systems Biology, Uppsala University, Sweden and Theresa Vincent at the Department of Physiology and Pharmacology, Karolinska Institutet, Sweden.

References

1. Ishii, N., Nakahigashi, K., Baba, T., et al.: Multiple high-throughput analyses monitor the response of E. coli to perturbations. Science **316**(5824), 593–597 (2007)
2. Lin, S.C., Yip, H., Phandthong, R., Davis, B., Talbot, P.: Evaluation of dynamic cell processes and behavior using video bioinformatics tools. In: Bhanu, B., Talbot, P. (eds.) Video Bioinformatics. CB, vol. 22, pp. 167–186. Springer, Heidelberg (2015). doi:10.1007/978-3-319-23724-4_9
3. Sadanandan, S.K., Baltekin, Ö., Magnusson, K.E.G., et al.: Segmentation and track-analysis in time-lapse imaging of bacteria. IEEE J. Sel. Topics Signal Process. **10**(1), 174–184 (2016)
4. Long, J., Shelhamer, E., Darrell, T.: Fully convolutional networks for semantic segmentation. In: IEEE Conference on Computer Vision and Pattern Recognition (CVPR), pp. 3431–3440 (2015)
5. Ronneberger, O., Fischer, P., Brox, T.: U-Net: convolutional networks for biomedical image segmentation. In: Navab, N., Hornegger, J., Wells, W.M., Frangi, A.F. (eds.) MICCAI 2015. LNCS, vol. 9351, pp. 234–241. Springer, Heidelberg (2015). doi:10.1007/978-3-319-24574-4_28
6. Chen, H., Qi, X.J., Cheng, J.Z., et al.: Deep contextual networks for neuronal structure segmentation. In: Proceedings of the Thirtieth AAAI Conference on Artificial Intelligence, pp. 1167–1173 (2016)
7. Lecun, Y., Bottou, L., Bengio, Y., et al.: Gradient-based learning applied to document recognition. Proc. IEEE **86**(11), 2278–2324 (1998)
8. Krizhevsky, A., Sutskever, I., Hinton, G.E.: Imagenet classification with deep convolutional neural networks. In: Advances in Neural Information Processing Systems, vol. 25, pp. 1097–1105. Curran Associates, Inc. (2012)
9. Feichtenhofer, C., Pinz, A., Zisserman, A.: Convolutional two-stream network fusion for video action recognition. arXiv:1604.06573v1 (2016)
10. Wang, P., Li, Z., Hou, Y., et al.: Combining convnets with hand-crafted features for action recognition based on an HMM-SVM classifier. arXiv:1602.00749v1 (2016)
11. Kwolek, B.: Face detection using convolutional neural networks and gabor filters. In: Duch, W., Kacprzyk, J., Oja, E., Zadrożny, S. (eds.) ICANN 2005. LNCS, vol. 3696, pp. 551–556. Springer, Heidelberg (2005). doi:10.1007/11550822_86
12. Liu, B., Wang, M., Foroosh, H., et al.: Sparse convolutional neural networks. In: 2015 IEEE Conference on Computer Vision and Pattern Recognition (CVPR), pp. 806–814, June 2015
13. Iandola, F.N., Moskewicz, M.W., Ashraf, K., et al.: Squeezenet: alexnet-level accuracy with 50x fewer parameters and <1mb model size. arXiv:1602.07360v3 (2016)

14. Sadanandan, S.K.: CBA segmentation. https://bitbucket.org/sajithks/fastcba/. Accessed 21 May 2016
15. Woodford, C., Philips, C.: Numerical Methods with Worked Examples, Matlab edn. Springer, New York (2012)
16. Daubechies, I.: Ten Lectures on Wavelets. SIAM, vol. 61. Springer, New York (1992)
17. Golub, G., Kahan, W.: Calculating the singular values and pseudo-inverse of a matrix. J. Soc. Ind. Appl. Math. Ser. B: Numer. Anal. **2**(2), 205–224 (1965)
18. Wasilewski, F.: Pywavelets. http://www.pybytes.com/pywavelets/. Accessed 21 May 2016
19. Jia, Y., Shelhamer, E., Donahue, J., et al.: Caffe: Convolutional architecture for fast feature embedding. arXiv preprint arXiv:1408.5093 (2014)
20. Carpenter, A.E., Jones, T.R., Lamprecht, M.R., et al.: Cellprofiler: image analysis software for identifying and quantifying cell phenotypes. Genome Biol. **7**, R100 (2006)

3-D Density Kernel Estimation for Counting in Microscopy Image Volumes Using 3-D Image Filters and Random Decision Trees

Dominic Waithe[3(✉)], Martin Hailstone[4], Mukesh Kumar Lalwani[2],
Richard Parton[4], Lu Yang[3], Roger Patient[2], Christian Eggeling[1,3],
and Ilan Davis[4]

[1] MRC Human Immunology Unit, University of Oxford, Oxford, UK
[2] MRC Molecular Haematology Unit, University of Oxford, Oxford, UK
[3] Wolfson Imaging Centre, Weatherall Insitute of Molecular Medicine,
University of Oxford, Oxford, UK
dominic.waithe@imm.ox.ac.uk
[4] Department of Biochemistry, University of Oxford, Oxford, UK

Abstract. We describe a means through which cells can be accurately counted in 3-D microscopy image data, using only weakly annotated images as input training material. We update an existing 2-D density kernel estimation approach into 3-D and we introduce novel 3-D features which encapsulate the 3-D neighbourhood surrounding each voxel. The proposed 3-D density kernel estimation (DKE-3-D) method, which utilises an ensemble of random decision trees, is computationally efficient and achieves state-of-the-art performance. DKE-3-D avoids the problem of discrete object identification and segmentation, common to many existing 3-D counting techniques, and we show that it outperforms other methods when quantification of densely packed and heterogeneous objects is desired. In this article we successfully apply the technique to two simulated and to two experimentally derived datasets and show that DKE-3-D has great potential in the biomedical sciences and any field where volumetric datasets are used.

Keywords: Density kernel estimation · 3-D · Random decision trees · Microscopy · Counting

1 Introduction

For over 30 years 3-D fluorescence light-microscopy has been used to visualise and investigate many aspects of cell biology and physiology. In recent years however, microscopy has seen unprecedented advances in resolution and speed allowing unobtrusive visualisation of live specimens at very high speeds. These microscopes which include highly sensitive confocal microscope, structured illumination, 3D-STED and light-sheet microscopes are capable of generating gigabytes of information from individual experiments [1–6]. These systems create

© Springer International Publishing Switzerland 2016
G. Hua and H. Jégou (Eds.): ECCV 2016 Workshops, Part I, LNCS 9913, pp. 244–255, 2016.
DOI: 10.1007/978-3-319-46604-0_18

significant challenges in terms of image processing and analysis which remains a bottleneck for the effective use of data generated by these systems [7]. As a consequence there is a real demand for combining intelligent analysis solutions which are powerful and computationally efficient. For this study images were acquired using a confocal microscope, but the technique could be equally applied to images taken on other microscopes.

Within the field of 3-D microscopy the most common approach to quantification of structures or objects within a specimen rely on segmentation of the global intensity histogram and often require a number of processing and filtering steps to isolate the cell-type or structure of interest [8,9]. These solutions require a skilled image analyst who is familiar with image processing techniques to process each image. From the medical imaging community discriminative and generative machine learning approaches have also been applied to segment organs in 3-D medical imaging of the body [10–12]. These approaches are advanced, yet do not tend to tackle the broad needs of the light microscopy imaging community which require algorithms that can be tuned to a number of similar yet discrete applications by relatively unskilled users.

The method proposed here is a discriminative approach utilising regression random decision trees to learn the association between features generated using basic image filters and a structured representation of each object within the training dataset. This approach follows on from the 2-D density approaches which were first applied to density estimation in biological images and also for estimating the number of individuals in a crowd [13–19]. The core strength of the density estimation approach is that it does not try to identify objects in their entirety but instead learns to associate pixel features with a particular density value. This approach means that if objects differ in morphology or appearance or are densely packed, the technique can still provide an accurate prediction of the number of objects present. The density estimation approach is perfect for application in microscopy due to the dense and heterogeneous nature of the objects being counted. The current state of the art for density estimation in 2-D is achieved through using Fully Convolutional Regression Networks (FCRNs) which out-perform regression decision trees with sufficient training [19]. In this study we decided to use regression random decision trees however, due to there high speed and their top performance, especially with relatively small amounts of training. Processing time when analysing 3-D data is a key consideration and also, in biomedical applications, dataset sizes can be small and so optimum performance with a small amount of training is key advantage.

In previous density kernel estimation approaches, images features have been calculated from pixels using dense SIFT or an array of basic image filters which describe the pixel and its local environment in 2-D data [13,14]. We found that these filters could be applied to 3-D data by processing each slice of the image volume independently and through ensuring that the input density kernel used for the training was 3-D and not 2-D. We denote this adapted 2-D density kernel estimation algorithm as DKE-2-D. A more powerful approach however, that we developed during this study, was to use image filters that function in

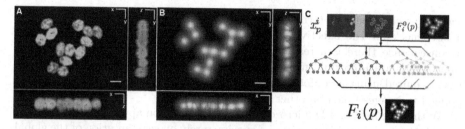

Fig. 1. Training scheme in 3-D. (A) Input image volume with dot annotation (red, exaggerated) in xy dimension and also orthogonal max projections (zy, right) (xz, bottom). (B) Ground-truth density function in xy dimension and also orthogonal max projections (zy, right) (xz, bottom). Scale bar is 40 pixels. (C) Schematic for data input and output with the ensemble of decision trees. Input features are calculated from input image volumes and associated with ground-truth density volume. Sampled voxel features and associated ground-truth voxels are then concatenated into a long vector (number of voxels, number of features) and used to train the ensemble of decision trees. Each decision tree receives a boot-strap sample of input voxels. At inference time, for a given voxel, the output density is calculated using the average output of each tree for that voxel to produce the predicted density image. (Color Figure online)

3-D and aggregate information from the local 3-D environment into the feature description of each voxel, a technique we call DKE-3-D. For this method we have developed an array of image filters which can process and aggregate the local 3-D voxel environment to provide a very rich description of each voxel within the 3-D image volume. Through applying these filters with our density kernel estimation method we have achieved a high level of accuracy. Our main contributions in this study are therefore, that we outline the theoretical basis of density kernel estimation in 3-D, we develop specialised 3-D filters for feature description, which out-perform comparable 2-D filters, and we validate our technique against competitive methods on four distinct 3-D volumetric datasets.

2   Method

The training data is provided by the user in the form of N image volumes $(I_{i=1}, I_2, I_3, ..., I_N)$ with N corresponding annotations $(A_{i=1}, A_2, A_3, ..., A_N)$. A_i is a sparse matrix $(\mathbf{R}^3)$ where the location of each cell in the corresponding image is marked with a single point (dot), by the user (Fig. 1). Each point in the annotation is stored in a vector of 3-D centroid positions $Pi = \{P_1, P_2, ..., P_{C(i)}\}$ and C_i is the total cell count for a particular image. From each annotation volume in the training set we produce a ground-truth density representation which for each pixel (p) is defined as the sum of all the Gaussian kernels centred on the dot annotations:

$$\forall p \in I_i, \ F_i^0(p) = \sum_{\mu \in \mathbf{P_i}} \mathcal{N}(p; \mu, \sigma^2) \tag{1}$$

and $\sigma^2 = diag(\sigma_x^2, \sigma_y^2, \sigma_z^2)$. The kernel is anisotropic as the acquisition sampling resolution is often different in the axial z-dimension compared to the x-y lateral dimension. Figure 1 shows an example input image with dot annotations superimposed (Fig. 1A) and also the ground-truth density image calculated from these annotations (Fig. 1B). For this application we chose the sigma to represent approximately 1/3 the dimensions of the cells being counted which allows the whole kernel to be contained within an average cell, due to the so-called three-sigma rule of thumb [20]. For example if on average the cells being counted have dimension which is $30 \times 30 \times 10$ pixels it would have a kernel of sigma $10 \times 10 \times 3$ applied to it. Typically, the ground-truth density map is produced by convolving A_i with a 3-D Gaussian kernel of size σ. The integral of the ground-truth density map and the sum of the annotation volume can differ for a particular image when one or more of the cells are overlapping the periphery of the scene. It is a desirable consequence that the integral density be slightly reduced with respect to the annotations in this case, as we only want to consider the parts of cells within the scene. For each pixel in the input image, during training and testing, a corresponding feature vector is calculated, $x_i^p \in \mathbf{R}^{21}$ for DKE-2-D and $x_i^p \in \mathbf{R}^{25}$ for DKE-3-D. Each descriptor of the feature vector is created through processing of the input image or volume with one of a bank of filters which included: Gaussian, magnitude of Gaussian, Laplacian of Gaussian, eigenvalues of curvature, as in [14]. These filters are applied at multiple scales (sigma = 0.8, 1.6, 3.2 and 6.4) to aggregate data from the surrounding voxels into the feature descriptor at that pixel or voxel. This scale range was sufficient for the cases used in this study and were not changed. If the objects being counted are large with respect to the pixel resolution and smooth in appearance one should consider downsampling the images to improve the computational efficiency of the system. For the DKE-2-D algorithm, 2-D features were calculated. For the DKE-3-D algorithm, 3-D features were calculated, whereby the filters were calculated in 3-D across each volume and responses encoded as a feature vector for each pixel. The same filters were used as in the 2-D case but using 3-D implementations of each. The sigma range used was also the same as in the 2-D case using isotropic kernels throughout.

2.1 Decision Tree Framework

To solve the 3-D counting problem a machine learning density kernel estimation (DKE) approach was employed using an ensemble of decision trees [14]. The role of the DKE approach is to learn the non-linear mapping $\mathcal{F} : x_p^i \rightarrow F_i(p)$ which maps the input pixel features to the annotation derived ground-truth densities. Once optimised, this model would then allow us to predict the density values associated with a given pixel and allow estimation of the cell count for an entire image volume through summation of the individual densities. We chose an ensemble of regression decision trees as our non-linear model [21]. Regression trees are simple binary trees which are built according to a classical top-down procedure [22]. In general, regression trees are fast to train, as split parameters are chosen randomly, and also they can handle large amounts of data as their complexity increases linearly with the number of data samples. Both of these factors are important for 3-D datasets where a typical image volume can contain more than 7 million pixels. From the top of the tree to the bottom, the data is split recursively into more and more specialised subsets based on the features and labels of the training data. Before generation of the first decision tree the training data from each image volume is concatenated into a single 2-D array (S) with dimension (num. of pixels × num. of features). The total volume of data is then reduced through random sampling by (1/200), as this was found to improve the speed of the fitting without deleterious affects on the accuracy of the algorithm due to pixel redundancy in each image. The recursive function which splits the data at each node, does so through selecting K candidate descriptors at random and with replacement from the available feature list. For each candidate, a threshold value is generated at random within the permissible min/max range for that feature $[a_{min}^s, a_{max}^s]$ producing a list of candidate splits $s_1, ..., s_K$. Some decision tree types will enforce that multiple thresholds be considered for each feature selected, but in this case we kept the value as one, to keep the fitting efficient. A cost function (Score(s_i, S)) is calculated for each candidate split based on the subset of data at the node. The score used in this application was based on reducing the output variance in the labels associated with the left and right side of the proposed split:

$$- \sum_{p \in S_R} (F(p) - \bar{F}_R) - \sum_{p \in S_L} (F(p) - \bar{F}_L) \tag{2}$$

where S_L represents all the pixels which had values less than the proposed split point and S_R represents the complementary set within the superset S. $\bar{F}^L$ and $\bar{F}^R$ represent the mean value for all the pixel labels in the left and right side of the split respectively. From the K candidates the highest scoring feature and threshold which splits the accompanying density labels is chosen. The recursive splitting is repeated on the left and right node subsets until one of the stop conditions is fulfilled. Termination in this case was fulfilled when a decision tree reached a depth of 20, or there were only 20 samples left in a split. Each terminal node is then assigned the average density of the labels which descended into it. During inference, unlabelled image pixel features descend the trees based on the now fixed test functions at each split. The pixels will inherit the density value associated with the node in which their descent terminates. The generation of just one decision tree will tend to result in overfitting of data and so typically with random decision tree methods an ensemble of trees is generated from bootstrap samples of the input data. In this case 30 trees were generated during training. The average density value for a pixel, from all the generated trees, is then used to generate the output density label for that location.

2.2   Alternative Methods

As a means of comparison for our adapted approach (DKE-2-D) proposed approach (DKE-3-D) we compare our techniques to two current methodologies for

3-D counting of cells in 3-D volumetric data as well as to a competitive state-of-the-art technique known as FARSIGHT. The first comparative method is a generic segmentation strategy based on analysis of the image volume intensity histogram. For this, a Matlab script was developed which first thresholds the images automatically using the Otsu algorithm and then applies a 3-D water-shedding algorithm to the image to split any clumped cells. The number of cells was then counted through Matlab's in-built region-props functions [23,24]. A second approach, which is a simple regression analysis was also developed using Matlab's in-built poly function. Using 10 randomly selected training images, the relationship between the independent variable (the cell number in each image) and the dependent variable (the integral intensity) was learnt through linear regression and then inference was performed by querying unseen image intensities using this learnt distribution. Our third method of comparison represents the current state-of-the-art for counting cells in 3-D microscopy data which is a technique employing a morphological multi-model approach to segmentation and cell classification and has been shown to be highly accurate (FARSIGHT) [25,26]. The FARSIGHT algorithm required no additional parameters to perform segmentation and required no training.

3 Results

3.1 The Datasets

To establish the efficacy of the proposed technique we created/acquired four datasets and assessed the performance of the algorithm on each. The datasets and source code for this project are available through the website: http://github.com/dwaithe/Density_Kernel_Estimation_3D.

The first dataset (dataset 1) comprised of simulated 3-D image volumes which contain relatively few cells, with between 1 and 33 cells in each image. The simulation closely resembles cultures of HL60 cells with their nuclei stained with DAPI, which is a fluorescent DNA binding agent commonly applied in the life sciences for cell counting [27]. The assumption is that each cell only contains one nucleus, which is usually the case, and so can be used to directly estimate the number of cells present. The dataset contains 30 image volumes in total with dimension $404 \times 283 \times 65$ and also included corresponding dot annotations. The texture and shape of the nuclei staining varies across each example and varies from cell-to-cell. The dimension of the input kernel applied at each dot in the image was set to $\sigma_x = \sigma_y = 12, \sigma_z = 13$.

The second dataset (dataset 2) has been designed to closely simulate colon tissue sampled from human patients suffering from adenocarcinoma, a type of cancer [27]. This dataset comprises 30 images volumes of dimension $325 \times 258 \times 65$ and includes ground-truth data which exactly represents cell numbers present in each scene. This dataset is challenging due to the density of cells within the scene and their close packing. Images were reduced in scale before processing as this was found to improve the computational speed without reducing the quality of the prediction. No other preprocessing was performed. The input kernel dimension applied at each dot in the image was set to $\sigma_x = \sigma_y = 6, \sigma_z = 10$.

The third test dataset (dataset 3) is experimentally derived and consists of 3-D confocal micrographs acquired from *Drosophila melanogaster* fly brains cultured for several days, fixed and then stained with DAPI nuclear dye, which stained the nuclei of the cells within the brain. 26 images were acquired on a Olympus Fluoview FV1000 microscope for this application with dimension varying between $512 \times 512 \times 15$ and $512 \times 512 \times 33$. The ground-truth for this data was created through manual identification of cell centres using commercially available Imaris software, due to its excellent 3-D visualisation capabilities, although any other software could have been used. The dimension of the kernel used to generate the ground-truth density image from the annotation image was set to $\sigma_x = \sigma_y = 15, \sigma_z = 4$.

The fourth dataset (dataset 4) represents deep 3-D volume imaging of the heart organ from intact Zebrafish embryos. In this study, a transgenic zebrafish line Tg(*myl7*:EGFP; *myl7*:dsRednuc) was used which expresses red fluorescent protein (dsRed) in nuclei and enhanced green fluorescent protein (EGFP) in the cytoplasm of cardiomyocytes. The zebrafish embryos were stained for immunofluorescence so that the ventricular cardiomyocytes could be specifically counted. The red (dataset 4a) and green (dataset 4b) channels were imaged using a Zeiss confocal microscope and reconstructed independently to form two discrete image volumes varying in z-depth between specimen from $256 \times 256 \times 73$ to $256 \times 256 \times 212$. The red fluorescence staining is relatively punctate, representing the nuclei of the cells, whereas the cytoplasmic signal is much more diffuse and is continuous across the entire organ. For counting cells in the red nuclear fluorescence channel a sigma kernel of dimension $\sigma_x = \sigma_y = \sigma_z = 1.8$ was used. The ground-truth for this data was created through manual identification of cell centres using commercially available Imaris software. Cells could not be recognised from the green channel alone, due to the diffuse nature of the cytoplasmic staining, so for the basis of training on this dataset, the same cell positions and kernel sigma values from the red channel annotation were used.

To judge the performance of each of the algorithms, for datasets 1–3, a thorough cross-validation strategy was employed. For each comparison the algorithm was trained on 10 image volumes and then used to estimate the counts in 15 hold-out images, with the exception of the segmentation and FARSIGHT approaches which required no training. For the fourth dataset, which is a smaller dataset, training was performed on 8 image volumes and then the evaluation was performed on 2 hold-out images. Results for each assessment are described in terms of a percentage accuracy metric: $Acc.(\%) = (1 - ((GT - PC)/GT)) * 100$, GT is the integral of the ground-truth density image and PC is the integral of the predicted density image. For each algorithm and dataset comparison, the training and test images were shuffled and the procedure repeated ten times with the average accuracy and its standard deviation being recorded for all the comparisons.

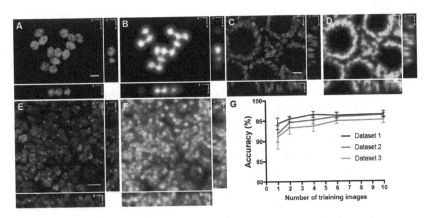

Fig. 2. DKE-3-D evaluation data. Example images (A) from dataset 1 with (B) density estimation, (C and D) dataset 2 and (E and F) dataset 3. Scale bar is 40 pixels in A and B and 6 μm in C. The depth of each stack is 65 pixels in A and B and 13.75 μm (25 pixels) in C. Orthogonal views show middle point of xy image in zy and xz plane. (D) The line plot shows the accuracy of the DKE-3-D algorithm when between 1 and 10 images are used in training. Error bars represent standard deviation of data.

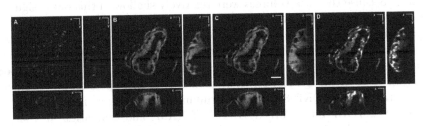

Fig. 3. Indirect density estimation. Example image from dataset 4 (A) in green channel (cytoplasmic stain) (B) in red channel (nuclear stain) (C) merged image of red and green channel. (D) Indirect predicted density output from model when using cytoplasmic stain for input features and ground-truth cell positions from red nuclear stain. Scale bar is 30 μm, image volume is 117 μm (77 pixels) deep. Orthogonal views show middle point of xy image in zy and xz plane. (Color figure online)

Table 1. Performance of algorithms. Performance is shown as percentage accuracy ± standard deviation.

Method	Dataset 1	Dataset 2	Dataset 3	Dataset 4a	Dataset 4b
DKE-2-D	93.9 ± 1.3 %	93.1 ± 1.3 %	**95.4 ± 0.8%**	73.3 ± 24.9 %	**88.5 ± 8.1%**
DKE-3-D	**96.5 ± 0.8%**	**96.4 ± 0.5%**	95.2 ± 0.9%	**85.6 ± 10.8%**	84.0 ± 16.1%
FARSIGHT	96.1 ± 2.0 %	81.2 ± 3.0 %	< 0 %	82.8 ± 3.5 %	NA
Otsu water	92.5 ± 1.1 %	46.2 ± 0.7	< 0 %	65.0 ± 3.4 %	NA
Lin. Reg.	94.3 ± 1.1 %	92.3 ± 1.2	88.3 ± 2.4 %	38.5 ± 72.5 %	76.7 ± 15.8 %

The DKE-3-D approach proved to be a highly effective means of predicting the number of cells in each sample and out-performed the adapted DKE-2-D approach, the standard approaches (linear regression, Otsu watershed) and the FARSIGHT algorithm especially in dense scenes (dataset 2 and 3). Table 1 shows that the accuracy of the proposed algorithm (DKE-3-D) was better than the other approaches for dataset 1, although all the techniques performed well on this data. Dataset 1 represents a relatively sparse dataset with relatively few cells in each image and represents typical data for which a basic segmentation approach would normally be sufficient. Each technique achieved accuracy of over 92.5 % with the DKE-3-D approach being slightly more accurate with an average accuracy of 96.5 %. This shows that in relatively simple datasets, with few cells, it is probably sufficient to use a conventional approach like segmentation or linear regression, as top accuracy can be achieved. In datasets 2 the proposed DKE-3-D algorithm proved to be the most effective, out-performing all the other approaches including the DKE-2-D approach and achieved accuracy of 96.4 % compared to 93.1 % and 92.3 % for the DKE-2-D and linear regression approaches respectively. The performance of the proposed algorithm is also evident in Dataset 3 where it out-performed the linear regression approach by over 7 % and the segmentation approaches failed almost completely. Interestingly the DKE-2-D and DKE-3-D approaches performed equally well on this dataset probably because the data volumes were relatively shallow in this data (sigma z = 4) and so aggregation of 3-D data was less impactful. The FARSIGHT algorithm performed well on the relatively sparse dataset 1 (96.1 %) and respectably well on the denser dataset 2 (81.2 %) but failed completely on dataset 3, showing that even cutting-edge segmentation strategies fail on data where cells are densely packed. Although slower, than both the linear regression and segmentation strategies the DKE-3-D is fast, training with 10 input images takes 5 s (dataset 1, 2.3 GHz Intel Core i7, 16 GB of RAM) and evaluation of a single image volume takes 10 s. The largest bottleneck for DKE-3-D is calculating the pixel features as this took around 40 s per image volume twice as long as it took for DKE-2-D (20 s), this could however be sped up considerably through parallelization. For the accuracy comparisons ten training images were used to train the DKE-3-D algorithm, but it is possible to train the algorithm with far fewer images and still achieve highly accurate results at test time. Figure 2D shows the average performance of the DKE-3-D algorithm when trained with between 1 and 10 images and evaluated on 15 holdout images as before. The DKE-3-D algorithm will after being trained with 2 images achieve an average 94.4 % accuracy (Datasets 1–3) which is less than 2 % less than the accuracy achieved with 10 training images 96.0 %.

Dataset 4 represents challenging data for any of the tested counting systems (Fig. 3). DKE-3-D performed best on this dataset however it is clear that the heterogeneity in the intensity of cells proved challenging for all the tested algorithms. Although DKE-3-D is able to handle a large diversity of object appearances, the accuracy will drop when their is too much diversity. This data was useful for showing the limits of the present approaches but also offered a unique opportunity, due to its two colour channels, to showcase a unique advantage of the DKE algorithm. Dataset 4a represents the red nuclear stain (Fig. 3A) which can be accurately annotated by a human, to label every cell in the heart tissue. When trained on this data the DKE-3-D algorithm achieved an accuracy of 85.6 % which was better than any of the other tested techniques. Dataset 4b represents the cytoplasmic channel from the same image volumes as the red channel(Fig. 3B), a ground-truth cannot be made directly using the green channel due to the diffuse and overlapping nature of the stain. If however we use the ground-truth positions from Dataset 4a with the features calculated in Dataset 4b we can achieve a respectable 88.5 and 84.0 % accuracy for DKE-2-D and DKE-3-D respectively (example output Fig. 2D). It is likely that the reason the DKE-2-D algorithm outperformed the DKE-3-D algorithm on this data because the diffuse nature of the cytoplasmic data means the 3-D features present in the DKE-3-D algorithm did not contribute much information. This indirect learning has great potential, whereby we can indirectly approximate cell counts based on stains which are not easily quantifiable by a human annotator. This means acquisition times and sample preparation times could be reduced as it would only be necessary to fully label and image samples for the training and then the technique could be applied to different potentially cheaper or more coarsely imaged representation. The only other technique, which can do this, is the simple linear regression approach but this technique achieved only 76.7 % accuracy, due to most likely insufficient feature description, when compared to the DKE-3-D technique.

4   Conclusion and Limitations

The DKE method is a highly accurate and computationally efficient means through which 3-D objects with complex intensity distributions can be easily counted using only a dot annotation as training. This work shows that density kernel estimation is a invaluable approach for solving complex counting tasks in 3-D microscopy data. We make a significant step towards perfecting the technique through incorporating novel 3-D filters into the work-flow. The conventional DKE-2-D approach, adapted to 3-D, works relatively well on all data, but the proposed DKE-3-D algorithm with 3-D filters outperforms all other techniques, especially in dense environments where the boundaries of cells are not easily identified. This technique is suitable for counting any object which is roughly spheroidal or spherical in shape, but is limited, like other techniques, if the integral intensity between cells is wildly different. In summary, the DKE-3-D algorithm is a vital approach for tackling counting in 3-D volumes and due to its unique density approach can out-perform conventional methodologies on a range of data.

Acknowledgements and Funding. We acknowledge the WIMM, The Dunn School of Pathology and the Biochemistry Department for infrastructure support. Authors are grateful to the staff of the Biomedical Services Unit at the John Racliffe Hospital site for aquatic support. We thank the Wolfson Imaging Centre Oxford and to MICRON

Oxford (http://micronoxford.com, supported by the Wellcome Trust Strategic Award 091911) for access to equipment and assistance with data acquisition and analysis. MKL and RP acknowledge funding from the BHF-Centre for Regenerative Medicine, Oxford-UK (grant ref RM/13/3/30159). The work was supported by the Wolfson Foundation, the Medical Research Council (MRC, grant number MC_UU_12010/unit programmes G0902418 and MC_UU_12025), MRC/BBSRC/ EPSRC (grant number MR/K01577X/1), and Wellcome Trust (grant ref 104924/ 14/Z/14). MH was supported through the ONBI DPhil programme in biomedical imaging technology development funded by the MRC and Engineering and Physical Sciences Research Council (EPSRC) (grant number EP/L016052/1). I.D. and R.M.P. were supported by a Wellcome Trust Senior Research Fellowship (081858) to I.D. LY was supported by a Clarendon Fund Scholarship in Humanities and by a Goodger fund Scholarship. DW was supported by funding from the MRC and EPSRC (grant number EP/L016052/1). None of the funding organisations have had any role in study design, data collection and analysis, decision to publish, or preparation of the manuscript.

References

1. Streibl, N.: Three-dimensional imaging by a microscope. JOSA A **2**(2), 121–127 (1985)
2. Chen, B.-C., Legant, W.R., Wang, K., Shao, L., Milkie, D.E., Davidson, M.W., Jane-topoulos, C., Wu, X.S., Hammer, J.A., Liu, Z., et al.: Lattice light-sheet microscopy: Imaging molecules to embryos at high spatiotemporal resolution. Science **346**(6208), 1257998 (2014)
3. Reynaud, E.G., Krzic, U., Greger, K., Stelzer, E.H.: Light sheet-based fluorescence microscopy: more dimensions, more photons, and less photodamage. HFSP J. **2**(5), 266–275 (2008)
4. Huang, B., Wang, W., Bates, M., Zhuang, X.: Three-dimensional super-resolution imaging by stochastic optical reconstruction microscopy. Science **319**(5864), 810–813 (2008)
5. Harke, B., Ullal, C.K., Keller, J., Hell, S.W.: Three-dimensional nanoscopy of colloidal crystals. Nano Lett. **8**(5), 1309–1313 (2008)
6. Shao, L., Kner, P., Rego, E.H., Gustafsson, M.G.: Super-resolution 3d microscopy of live whole cells using structured illumination. Nat. Method **8**(12), 1044–1046 (2011)
7. Reynaud, E.G., Peychl, J., Huisken, J., Tomancak, P.: Guide to light-sheet microscopy for adventurous biologists. Nat. Method **12**(1), 30–34 (2015)
8. Long, F., Zhou, J., Peng, H.: Visualization and analysis of 3d microscopic images. PLoS Comput. Biol. **8**(6), e1002519–e1002519 (2012)
9. Peng, H., Bria, A., Zhou, Z., Iannello, G., Long, F.: Extensible visualization and analysis for multidimensional images using Vaa3D. Nat. Protoc. **9**(1), 193–208 (2014)
10. Cuingnet, R., Prevost, R., Lesage, D., Cohen, L.D., Mory, B., Ardon, R.: Automatic detection and segmentation of kidneys in 3D CT images using random forests. In: Ayache, N., Delingette, H., Golland, P., Mori, K. (eds.) MICCAI 2012. LNCS, vol. 7512, pp. 66–74. Springer, Heidelberg (2012). doi:10.1007/978-3-642-33454-2_9
11. Lempitsky, V., Verhoek, M., Noble, J.A., Blake, A.: Random forest classification for automatic delineation of myocardium in real-time 3D echocardiography. In: Ayache, N., Delingette, H., Sermesant, M. (eds.) FIMH 2009. LNCS, vol. 5528, pp. 447–456. Springer, Heidelberg (2009). doi:10.1007/978-3-642-01932-6_48

12. Hu, S., Hoffman, E., Reinhardt, J.M., et al.: Automatic lung segmentation for accurate quantitation of volumetric x-ray CT images. IEEE Trans. Med. Imag. **20**(6), 490–498 (2001)
13. Lempitsky, V., Zisserman, A.: Learning to count objects in images. In: Advances in Neural Information Processing Systems, pp. 1324–1332 (2010)
14. Fiaschi, L., Nair, R., Koethe, U., Hamprecht, F., et al.: Learning to count with regression forest and structured labels. In: 2012 21st International Conference on Pattern Recognition (ICPR), pp. 2685–2688. IEEE (2012)
15. Arteta, C., Lempitsky, V., Noble, J.A., Zisserman, A.: Interactive object counting. In: Fleet, D., Pajdla, T., Schiele, B., Tuytelaars, T. (eds.) ECCV 2014. LNCS, vol. 8691, pp. 504–518. Springer, Heidelberg (2014). doi:10.1007/978-3-319-10578-9_33
16. Waithe, D., Rennert, P., Brostow, G., Piper, M.D.: Quantifly: robust trainable software for automated drosophila EGG counting. PloS one **10**(5), e0127659 (2015)
17. Pham, V.-Q., Kozakaya, T., Yamaguchi, O., Okada, R.: COUNT forest: Co-voting uncertain number of targets using random forest for crowd density estimation. In: Proceedings of the IEEE International Conference on Computer Vision, pp. 3253–3261 (2015)
18. Kainz, P., Urschler, M., Schulter, S., Wohlhart, P., Lepetit, V.: You should use regression to detect cells. In: Navab, N., Hornegger, J., Wells, W.M., Frangi, A.F. (eds.) MICCAI 2015. LNCS, vol. 9351, pp. 276–283. Springer, Heidelberg (2015). doi:10.1007/978-3-319-24574-4_33
19. Xie, W., Noble, J.A., Zisserman, A.: Microscopy cell counting with fully convolutional regression networks. In: Computer Methods in Biomechanics, Biomedical Engineering: Imaging and Visualization MICCAI 1st Workshop on Deep Learning in Medical Image Analysis (2015)
20. Pukelsheim, F.: The three sigma rule. Am. Stat. **48**(2), 88–91 (1994)
21. Breiman, L.: Random forests. Mach. Learn. **45**(1), 5–32 (2001)
22. Geurts, P., Ernst, D., Wehenkel, L.: Extremely randomized trees. Mach. Learn. **63**(1), 3–42 (2006)
23. Otsu, N.: A threshold selection method from gray-level histograms. Automatica **11**(285–296), 23–27 (1975)
24. Meyer, F.: Topographic distance and watershed lines. Signal Process. **38**(1), 113–125 (1994)
25. Schmitz, C., Eastwood, B.S., Tappan, S.J., Glaser, J.R., Peterson, D.A., Hof, P.R.: Current automated 3D cell detection methods are not a suitable replacement for manual stereologic cell counting. Front. Neuroanat. **8**, 1–34 (2014)
26. Lin, G., Chawla, M.K., Olson, K., Barnes, C.A., Guzowski, J.F., Bjornsson, C., Shain, W., Roysam, B.: A multi-model approach to simultaneous segmentation and classification of heterogeneous populations of cell nuclei in 3D confocal microscope images. Cytom. Part A **71**(9), 724–736 (2007)
27. Svoboda, D., Homola, O., Stejskal, S.: Generation of 3D digital phantoms of colon tissue. In: Kamel, M., Campilho, A. (eds.) ICIAR 2011. LNCS, vol. 6754, pp. 31–39. Springer, Heidelberg (2011). doi:10.1007/978-3-642-21596-4_4

Dendritic Spine Shape Analysis:
A Clustering Perspective

Muhammad Usman Ghani[1(✉)], Ertunç Erdil[1], Sümeyra Demir Kanık[1],
Ali Özgür Argunşah[2], Anna Felicity Hobbiss[2], Inbal Israely[2], Devrim Ünay[3],
Tolga Taşdizen[4], and Müjdat Çetin[1]

[1] Faculty of Engineering and Natural Sciences, Sabanci University, Istanbul, Turkey
{ghani,sumeyrakanik,mcetin}@sabanciuniv.edu
[2] Champalimaud Neuroscience Programme,
Champalimaud Centre for the Unknown, Lisbon, Portugal
{ali.argunsah,anna.hobbiss,inbal.israely}@neuro.fchampalimaud.org
[3] Faculty of Engineering and Computer Sciences,
Izmir University of Economics, Izmir, Turkey
devrim.unay@ieu.edu.tr
[4] Electrical and Computer Engineering Department,
University of Utah, Salt Lake City, USA
tolga@sci.utah.edu

Abstract. Functional properties of neurons are strongly coupled with
their morphology. Changes in neuronal activity alter morphological characteristics of dendritic spines. First step towards understanding the
structure-function relationship is to group spines into main spine classes
reported in the literature. Shape analysis of dendritic spines can help
neuroscientists understand the underlying relationships. Due to unavailability of reliable automated tools, this analysis is currently performed
manually which is a time-intensive and subjective task. Several studies on
spine shape classification have been reported in the literature, however,
there is an on-going debate on whether distinct spine shape classes exist
or whether spines should be modeled through a continuum of shape variations. Another challenge is the subjectivity and bias that is introduced
due to the supervised nature of classification approaches. In this paper,
we aim to address these issues by presenting a clustering perspective. In
this context, clustering may serve both confirmation of known patterns
and discovery of new ones. We perform cluster analysis on two-photon
microscopic images of spines using morphological, shape, and appearance
based features and gain insights into the spine shape analysis problem.
We use histogram of oriented gradients (HOG), disjunctive normal shape
models (DNSM), morphological features, and intensity profile based features for cluster analysis. We use x-means to perform cluster analysis that
selects the number of clusters automatically using the Bayesian information criterion (BIC). For all features, this analysis produces 4 clusters
and we observe the formation of at least one cluster consisting of spines
which are difficult to be assigned to a known class. This observation
supports the argument of intermediate shape types.

Keywords: Dendritic spines · Shape analysis · Clustering · x-means ·
Microscopy · Neuroimaging

© Springer International Publishing Switzerland 2016
G. Hua and H. Jégou (Eds.): ECCV 2016 Workshops, Part I, LNCS 9913, pp. 256–273, 2016.
DOI: 10.1007/978-3-319-46604-0_19

Fig. 1. A dendritic branch with several spines imaged using a two-photon laser scanning microscope (2PLSM).

1   Introduction

Dendritic spines, small protrusions of the dendritic shaft, are one of the most important structures of neurons. Ramón y Cajal first identified spines in the 19th century and suggested that neuronal activity variations change the spine morphology [1,2]. This claim has been supported by several studies reporting changes in the morphology and density with changes in neuronal activity [3–6]. Spines are the post-synaptic partners of a synapse [7] and are main receivers for synaptic input [2]. Dendritic spines in the hippocampal neurons are related with learning and short-term memory [8,9]. Studies also reported that spine density is decreased due to some neuro-degenerative diseases such as Alzheimer's [9].

A dendritic branch with several spines is shown in Fig. 1. Each spine has two segments, head and neck. Spine head is connected to the parent dendrite through the neck [10]. Dendritic spines exhibit extraordinary diversity [11]; they have different sizes and densities across different cell types, brain areas, and animal species [2]. A great variety in spine head and neck dimensions is usually demonstrated even within the same cell [2]. These facts emphasize the challenging nature of the spine analysis task. Dendritic spines have different shape types; researchers suggest that different morphological variations could possibly be related to various developmental stages or functional roles [12]. In the literature, dendritic spines have mostly been grouped into four shape classes: filopodia, mushroom, thin, and stubby [2,8,13–15]. Filopodia spines have long necks and no heads, mushroom spines have long necks and large bulbous heads, thin spines have long necks and small heads, and stubby spines are known to have either no necks or short necks [2]. An example of each of these classes is given in Fig. 2. Distribution of different shape types varies in different areas of the brain; it is also dependent upon the age of the animal being imaged, for instance stubby spines are dominant during early postnatal development [2].

This classification of spine shapes has been widely used in the literature, however, there is an open research question concerning whether distinct classes of spines shapes exist or whether spines should be modeled through a continuum of shape variations. Parnass et al. [12] proposed that morphological groups of spine shapes do not represent inherent shape types, instead they depict shape variations a spine can go through during its life time. Bourne and Harris [16] noticed spine enlargement as a result of synaptic enhancement, causing transition of thin spines to mushroom type. Peters and Kaiserman-Abramof [15] reported the existence of spines with intermediate shape types and they found it difficult

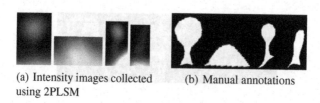

(a) Intensity images collected using 2PLSM   (b) Manual annotations

Fig. 2. Spine Classes: Mushroom, Stubby, Thin, Filopodia (Left to Right). Intensity and corresponding manually annotated images are shown for each shape class.

to assign them to one of the standard shape types. Basu et al. [17] reported a human expert being unsure while assigning labels to some of the spines. Arellano et al. [18] who used morphological features for spine analysis, also found several spines with intermediate morphological characteristics in their dataset. Spacek and Hartman [19] could not classify some spines into standard shape types and introduced a new class between mushroom and stubby, and thin and mushroom spines. Ruszczycki et al. [11] hinted towards a different classification standard: classifying spines into large and small, they reported better sensitivity with this classification approach. Wallace and Bear [20] used spine length and head diameter to perform spine analysis and found a continuous distribution. Mancuso et al. [21] suggested using morphological features to perform clustering and count spines in different clusters. In summary, different groups work with single or multiple neuroscience experts and each group uses their defined rules for classification, which results in subjectivity.

Quantitative analysis of dendritic spines is important for neurobiological research as it can help neuroscientists understand the underlying structure-function relationship. Currently this analysis is performed manually due to unavailability of reliable automated spine shape analysis tools. Manual analysis is a laborious, time-intensive, and most importantly subjective task. Rodriguez et al. [13] reported inter-operator and intra-operator variations in the spine type labeling task. Availability of reliable automated analysis tools can expedite research in this domain and assist neuroscientists decode the underlying relationship between neuron function and structure.

One might question why perform clustering rather than treating this as a classification problem. First of all, classification methods use manually provided labels as ground truth and extracting those labels is a time-intensive task. It also introduces subjectivity, which could be reduced by employing several experts and using a majority vote approach but this would make the labeling effort even more time-intensive. Inter-operator and intra-operator variability reported by Rodriguez et al. [13] emphasizes that subjectivity is a major issue in performing classification. Another issue with supervised classification is that it inherently starts from a pre-defined set of classes and does not allow exploration of potential intermediate shapes or possible continuous variation of shapes. Although clustering does not explicitly enable the latter either, it can be viewed as a step in that direction. Furthermore, some existing techniques require manual annotation of spines either to directly use them for feature extraction or for training segmentation algorithms. The objective of clustering in this context is two-fold: confirm the hypothesis of some distinct shape classes and discover new natural groups. We discover natural groups in the data using different features and analyze whether they support the existing hypotheses or add new information to our understanding of spine shapes.

As suggested by Mancuso et al. [21], we present a clustering-based approach for spine shape analysis. We perform cluster analysis using several feature representations and gain insights by performing analysis of discovered natural groups. We use Disjunctive Normal Shape Models (DNSM) [22], Histogram of Oriented Gradients (HOG) [23], intensity profiles [24], and morphological features [25]. We use an extension of k-means, x-means [26], to perform cluster analysis that uses the Bayesian Information Criterion (BIC) to select the number of clusters automatically. This study is based on two-photon laser scanning microscopy (2PLSM) images. Analyzing 2PLSM images is more challenging in comparison to confocal laser scanning microscopy (CLSM) images due to low signal to noise characteristics. Additionally, following the Abbe's law [27], resolution of 2PLSM images is half of the CLSM images. The reason behind using 2PLSM is that it allows imaging of living cells, which would capture shape transitions during synaptic process [10, 28].

The major contribution of this paper is application of HOG-based features for spine analysis and cluster analysis of dendritic spines with different representations. To the best of the authors' knowledge, this is the first paper that performs such an analysis of dendritic spine shapes with a wide range of feature sets. The rest of this paper is structured as follows. A brief summary of some of the related work is presented in Sect. 2. Section 3 discusses the methodology of our approach in detail. Experimental analysis and results are presented and discussed in Sect. 4. Section 5 summarizes the findings and conclusions of this paper.

2 Related Work

There exist several studies on supervised spine classification but none of these studies have reported performing unsupervised cluster analysis of dendritic spine shapes. Rodriguez et al. [13] performed spine classification on 3D images using morphological features. They developed a decision tree based classifier and evaluated its performance using labels provided by human experts. Son et al. [8] also developed a classification approach using morphological features and evaluated their approach with labels assigned by a human expert. Shi et al. [7] developed a semi-supervised learning approach for spine classification based on morphological features, and used human experts for validation of their results. A recent study on spine analysis applied ISOMAP [29] to study the importance of different morphological parameters and found neck length and head diameter to be the most prominent features for mushroom and stubby spines [30]. Ghani et al. [31] exploited the parametric nature of the DNSM approach and used its parameters for spine classification; they also used labels assigned by a human expert for performance evaluation. Erdil et al. [24] developed a joint classification and segmentation approach, within which they used intensity profiles for classification of spines. Labels assigned by a human expert were used to evaluate the performance of their algorithm.

As it can be noticed from a small subset of studies on classification summarized here, most of the groups use one or more human experts to assign class labels which are later used to evaluate the performance of their supervised classification approaches. Even though using the manually extracted labels as ground truth is a viable approach for this problem, it introduces subjectivity. We attempt to address this issue by presenting a clustering approach aiming to discover natural groups of spine shapes in an unsupervised fashion using various feature representations.

3 Methodology

We provide the details of our methodology in this section. Post natal 7 to 10 days old mice are imaged using 2PLSM.[1] We have acquired 15 stacks of 3D images using 2PLSM. After applying median filtering, we project 3D images to 2D using maximum intensity projection (MIP) [32]. We used 2D projections for this analysis, because resolution along the z-axis in our data is $0.3\,\mu\text{m}$ which is much worse than lateral resolution, which is $0.019\,\mu\text{m}$ or $0.024\,\mu\text{m}$ for different stacks. The slices along z-axis provide limited information [33]. The spines consist of a small head ($\sim 1\,\mu\text{m}$ diameter) and a thin neck ($\sim 0.2\,\mu\text{m}$ diameter), and are generally $0.5\,\mu\text{m}$ to several μm long [2]. Due to low 2PLSM resolution, complete spine covers only a few slices along the z-axis. The low axial resolution makes the spine analysis in 3D very challenging even for human experts [34]. While there are other projection methods available, MIP is a standard projection procedure used in most of the neuroscience studies [10,17,33–35]. In total, 242 dendritic spines have been selected from 15 dendritic branches for this study.

3.1 HOG Features

HOG [23] computes histogram of gradient orientations and applies contrast normalization to improve performance. It is observed that spine heads have uniform intensities whereas intensity in the neck region is not uniform. A decreasing intensity pattern can be noticed in the neck part of the spines. Using this appearance information would help us discover clusters with different appearance patterns. In order to compute HOG features, we select a region of interest (ROI) in intensity images such that the spine is completely inside the ROI. This does not require the ROI for all spines to have the same dimensions. Further, we rotate the ROI such that spine necks are vertically aligned. Examples resulting from this process are shown in Fig. 3.

---

[1] All animal experiments are carried out in accordance with European Union regulations on animal care and use, and with the approval of the Portuguese Veterinary Authority (DGV).

Fig. 3. Sample images from the dataset prepared for HOG.

In order to capture fair amount of small-scale details, we selected the cell size as a function of width and height: $CellSize = \left[height/5, width/5\right]$; cells are small spatial regions. A large block size value allows to suppress local intensity changes; blocks are relatively large spatial regions. To keep moderate level of information about local illumination variations, we selected a block size value equal to twice the $CellSize$. Contrast normalization is controlled through block overlap, and we selected a block overlap of 1 cell. We used 9 signed histogram orientation bins, because using signed orientation allows to track light to dark and dark to light intensity changes. We computed 576-dimensional HOG feature vectors with these settings and later used these features for cluster analysis.

3.2 DNSM Features

DNSM is a parametric shape model, proposed recently by Ramesh et al. [36]. DNSM represents a shape as a union of convex polytopes, which are constructed by intersections of half spaces. DNSM attempts to approximate the characteristic function of a shape. For further details of the DNSM, readers are referred to [22,36]. DNSM-based features provide a shape representation; it would be an interesting experiment to perform clustering using DNSM-based shape features. We apply DNSM to segment dendritic spine images following the approach in [31] and use 384-dimensional DNSM parameters as feature vectors to perform cluster analysis. A few images from the dataset used for DNSM features are presented in Fig. 4.

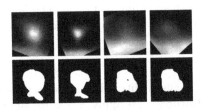

Fig. 4. A few images from dataset prepared for DNSM features: before segmentation (above) and segmented images (below).

Table 1. List of Morphological features used.

Neck Length, Head Diameter, Circularity, Shape Factor
Width and Height of bounding box, Perimeter, Area
Neck Length to Head Diameter Ratio (NHR)
Foreground to background pixels ratio in bounding box

3.3 Morphological Features

Morphology of dendritic spines has been extensively studied in the literature. Most of the studies on spine analysis compute morphological parameters to perform classification of spines. In this paper, we use 12 morphological features suggested in a recent study on spine classification [25]. The morphological features we use are listed in Table 1. In order to compute these morphological features, we perform segmentation using DNSM and apply methods suggested in [25].

3.4 Intensity Profiles Based Features

Erdil et al. [24] suggests that intensity information in the regions in which a potential neck is likely to be contained can be used to differentiate spine classes. Regions where the neck might appear is found using the assumption that the spine neck lies below the spine head. Once the spine head is found by minimizing an intensity-based energy function using active contours [37], the approach in [24] creates two rectangular regions below the spine head as shown in Fig. 5. The first region shown in Fig. 5(a) is constructed such that the bottom point of the spine head (shown by a red cross) lies at the center of the rectangle. The second rectangular region shown in Fig. 5(b) is a narrower one and is drawn such that it is located just below the spine head. Erdil et al. [24] extract three sets of feature vectors by exploiting intensities in these rectangular regions which are combined to form 378-dimensional feature vectors. The first set of feature vectors is obtained by summing up the intensities in the first rectangle horizontally. Similarly, the second set of feature vectors are obtained by vertical summation of the intensities in the corresponding rectangle. The final set of feature vectors are the histograms of intensities in the second rectangular region.

3.5 Feature Selection

Considering the high-dimensionality of feature representations being used (except morphological features), we apply a feature similarity based unsupervised feature selection algorithm [38]. Mitra et al. [38] introduced the maximum information compression index, which attempts to minimize the information loss while selecting a certain number of features. Here, the aim of feature selection is to aid the clustering algorithm, we select 100 features for each feature representation (except morphological features) and use these selected features to perform clustering.

(a) First region   (b) Second region

Fig. 5. Regions in which a potential neck is likely to be contained. (Color figure online)

3.6   Clustering

Jain [39] suggests there are two objectives for clustering: (i) exploratory: when there is no existing hypothesis or model, the aim is to discover patterns, and (ii) confirmatory: when a pre-specified model or hypothesis exists, the objective of cluster analysis is to confirm the model on the dataset being used. For dendritic spine analysis, the literature provides a pre-specified model as described in the introduction section. The nature of our analysis is: (i) an attempt to analyze how well a pre-specified model fits our data, (ii) if such a model does not fit our data, discover and explore natural groups within the data.

Jain [39] argues that there is no best clustering algorithm, because every clustering technique implicitly or explicitly imposes a structure on the data, and it gives good results if there is a good match. Jain further emphasizes that it is rather crucial to select the appropriate representation that implicitly or explicitly makes the pattern discovery an easy process. Considering the clustering analysis problem as a selection of appropriate representation rather than selection of a clustering method, we have compared different feature representations in terms of clustering results. We applied x-means [26], an extended version of k-means, which does not require the number of clusters to be provided. It uses BIC to automatically select the number of clusters in the available data from a given range of number of clusters, which we set as 2 to 10. It begins with lower bound of given range for number of clusters and continues computing clusters until upper bound for number of clusters have been reached; during this process it also computes BIC score for each cluster assignment. Finally, it selects the number of clusters based on best BIC score.

4   Results and Discussion

Our dataset consists of 242 dendritic spines selected from 15 dendritic branches for this analysis. These are spines that have been labeled as mushroom or stubby by a human expert. Analysis of clusters formed using different feature representations is presented in this section.

4.1   HOG Features Based Analysis

Using HOG based appearance feature representation for x-means clustering resulted in 4 clusters. The average image for each cluster is computed by averaging manually segmented binary images in that cluster. The resulting images are shown in Fig. 6. There are 49 spines in cluster 1, 93 spines in cluster 2, 72 spines in cluster 3, and 28 spines in cluster 4. As it is evident from the average images, cluster 2 and cluster 3 represent mushroom spines (long neck and big head). However, clusters 1 and 4 appear to consist either of spines from both classes or of spines that may possibly lie in between these two classes in the shape space. When we examine individual samples from these clusters, illustrated in Fig. 7, we observe that they exhibit similar characteristics, i.e., have small heads and no necks. However, closer analysis of intensity images shows existence of short necks, i.e., low intensity regions just below the head part. These observations support the produced clusters in the sense that although there are some spines which are easy to be classified (grouped in clusters 2 and 3), even a human expert would have difficult time providing labels for most of the spines in cluster 1 and cluster 4. This analysis also points to what one might call two subclasses (cluster 2 and cluster 3) within the mushroom class.

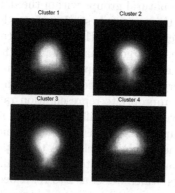

Fig. 6. Average image for each cluster generated using the HOG features.

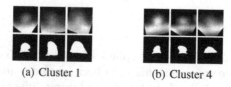

(a) Cluster 1   (b) Cluster 4

Fig. 7. Intensity (top) and corresponding manually annotated images (bottom) for some of the spines grouped in cluster 1 and cluster 4 using the HOG features.

4.2   DNSM Features Based Analysis

We computed shape features using DNSM and performed clustering on this representation. The algorithm produced 4 clusters consisting of 32, 48, 50, and 112 spines. Average images of these clusters are given in Fig. 8. Most of the spines in cluster 1 have short or no necks; their head diameter to neck diameter ratio is approximately 1. A few spines from cluster 1 are presented in Fig. 9. This cluster appears to contain spines that clearly exhibit the characteristics of stubby spines as well as spines with distinct heads and thick necks. Cluster 2, cluster 3, and cluster 4 are mostly mushroom clusters.

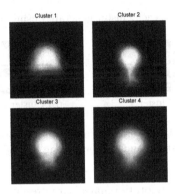

Fig. 8. Average image for each cluster generated using the DNSM features.

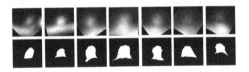

Fig. 9. Intensity (top) and corresponding manually annotated images (bottom) for some of the spines grouped in cluster 1 using the DNSM representation.

4.3   Morphological Features Based Analysis

Clustering analysis with morphological features resulted in 4 clusters with sizes: 102, 64, 64, and 12 spines. Average image for each of the produced clusters is given in Fig. 10. It is clear from Fig. 10 that cluster 1, and 2 are mushroom majority clusters. However, cluster 3 and cluster 4 show a mixed pattern, most of the spines have short thick neck, small head, and most importantly their neck diameters and head diameters are similar. A few spines from cluster 3 and cluster 4

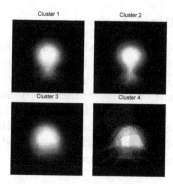

Fig. 10. Average image for each cluster generated using morphological features.

(a) Cluster 3   (b) Cluster 4

Fig. 11. Intensity (top) and corresponding manually annotated images (bottom) for some of the spines from cluster 3 and cluster 4 using the morphology based features.

along with their manually annotated images are presented in Fig. 11. These cluster appear to contain many stubby spines as well as spines with distinct heads and thick necks. It would be interesting to analyze which features are dominant in the clustering process, which might provide important information to neuroscientists. In this context, we perform an initial analysis using information gain [40] and conclude that neck length is the most dominant feature for data used in this study, which confirms analysis performed in some of our previous studies [25,30].

4.4   Intensity Profile Features Based Analysis

Using the intensity profile based features resulted in 4 clusters consisting of 45, 81, 48, and 68 spines. The average image for each of these clusters is presented in Fig. 12. It is clear that cluster 1, cluster 2, and cluster 3 are similar and appear to consist mostly of mushroom-like spines, i.e., they have big heads and long necks. Spines in cluster 3 have relatively shorter necks as compared to cluster 2, spines in cluster 4 have big heads and very short or no necks. Some of the spines clustered in cluster 4 are shown in Fig. 13. This cluster appears to contain many stubby spines as well as spines with distinct heads and thick necks.

4.5   Combined Features Based Analysis

Since, shape and appearance are complementary features, it is intuitive to combine both types of features and perform cluster analysis. We have already selected

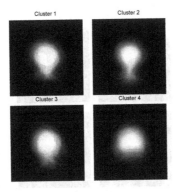

Fig. 12. Average image for each cluster generated using the intensity profile based features.

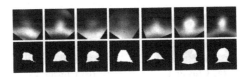

Fig. 13. Intensity (top) and corresponding manually annotated images (bottom) for some of the spines from cluster 4 generated using the intensity profile based features.

100 features from each group using a feature similarity based approach. We combine these selected features to perform clustering in this section. Using a combination of HOG and DNSM based features results in 4 clusters consisting of 30, 78, 22, and 112 spines. The average image for each of these clusters is presented in Fig. 14. It is clear that cluster 2 and cluster 4 are similar and consist most of the mushroom-like spines, i.e., they have big heads and long necks. Spines in cluster 1 and cluster 3 are similar to one another in the sense that they have big heads and very short or no necks, as illustrated in Fig. 15.

Using a combination of DNSM and intensity profile based features results in 4 clusters consisting of 32, 62, 36, and 112 spines. Average image for each cluster is presented in Fig. 16. Cluster 2, cluster 3, and cluster 4 consist of mostly mushroom-like spines, having big heads and long necks. However, cluster 1 consists of spines with intermediate properties: short, thick necks and big heads, as illustrated in Fig. 17. These spines have some morphological properties similar to mushroom spines and some similar to stubby spines, therefore, we may call cluster 1 a mixed or intermediate cluster.

4.6   Clustering vs. Human Expert

In this section, we compare the clustering results achieved using different representations to the labels assigned by a neuroscience expert. The idea is that similar data samples (belonging to same class) should be clustered in the same

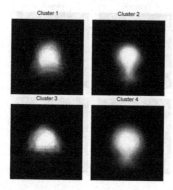

Fig. 14. Average image for each cluster generated using HOG+DNSM features.

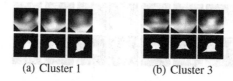

(a) Cluster 1   (b) Cluster 3

Fig. 15. Intensity (top) and corresponding manually annotated images (bottom) for some of the spines from cluster 1 and cluster 3 using HOG+DNSM based features.

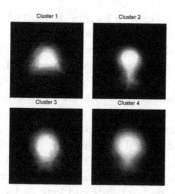

Fig. 16. Average image for each cluster generated using DNSM+IntensityProfile features.

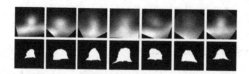

Fig. 17. Intensity (top) and corresponding manually annotated images (bottom) for some of the spines from cluster 1 generated using DNSM+IntensityProfile features.

group. There are two challenges in spine shape analysis: (i) separating mushroom spines from stubby spines, and (ii) separating thin spines from filopodia type spines. Because of the developmental age of the animals we use, we see few filopodia in our data, this is why we focused on mushroom vs. stubby problem for this study. Stubby vs. mushroom analysis is a challenging task due to 2PLSM resolution limits. In fact, in stimulated emission depletion (STED) microscopy images, many reported stubby spines look like mushroom spines [41].

Table 2. Comparison of clustering results and labels from human expert

Features	Acc.	Class	Clusters			
			1	2	3	4
DNSM	79.34 %	m	11	48	38	85
		s	21	0	12	27
Morphology	81.82 %	m	88	64	26	4
		s	14	0	38	8
HOG	**88.02 %**	m	15	91	68	8
		s	34	2	4	20
IntensityProfile	80.17 %	m	39	81	34	28
		s	6	0	14	40
HOG+DNSM	79.34 %	m	15	76	6	85
		s	15	2	16	27
DNSM+IntensityProfile	80.17 %	m	10	62	25	85
		s	22	0	11	27

A human expert manually labeled 242 spine images, 182 spines as mushroom and 60 as stubby. Table 2 shows the class membership of the spines in each of the clusters formed using each feature type. We observe that some clusters are dominated by shapes from one class whereas other are mixed. We have already analyzed the similarity within each of these clusters in the previous subsections, and observed the exploratory nature of our approach pointing to possibly intermediate shapes. Given the availability of manual labels, let us now carry out an analysis on the confirmatory aspects of our approach. In particular, to evaluate how strongly each clustering approach based on a different feature set confirms the manual shape labels, let us evaluate our clustering results using the manual labels as ground truth. To this end, let us pretend our clustering methods assign each cluster to the shape class with the majority of samples in that cluster. Then we can count the number of "correct and incorrect classifications". Using this approach, we evaluate these feature representations and find out that HOG features perform best on the available data taking the human expert's labels as the ground truth, viewing this it as a classification problem we can achieve 88.02 % classification accuracy.

According to expert's labels, clusters 2, 3, and 4 formed with the DNSM representation correspond to the mushroom class, whereas cluster 1 is the stubby majority cluster. Sample images shown in Fig. 9 suggests that spines in cluster 1 have similar characteristics, however, the expert has labeled some of these spines as mushroom and others as stubby. This itself depicts the challenging nature of spine analysis and subjective nature of the manual labeling task. We have similar observations on clusters formed through the use of the other features. In particular, we observe both the confirmatory role of the clustering methods through the formation of clusters dominated by one of the classes as labeled by the human expert (e.g., HOG clusters 2 and 3), as well as the exploratory nature of clustering through the generation of clusters with mixed membership (e.g., HOG clusters 1 and 4). Our experimental analysis suggests that the possibility of intermediate shape types in addition to the conventional shape classes should be considered in spine shape analysis. One further step along this direction could involve efforts to characterize the distribution of spines in a continuous shape space.

5   Conclusion

In this paper, we have proposed a clustering approach to perform spine shape analysis. The advantages of adopting a clustering approach for spine shape analysis are: such an approach would not suffer from subjectivity, and analysis time would be reduced by avoiding manual labeling tasks. To the best of our knowledge an extensive clustering analysis of spine shapes has not been published. We use appearance, shape, and morphological feature based representations to perform clustering and shed some light on this problem. We perform clustering using x-means that uses BIC to select the number of clusters automatically; interestingly it produces 4 clusters for all of the features considered here, this implies there are 4 sub-groups in our data. Additionally, we have observed that, for the data used in our analysis, although there are many spines which easily fit into the definition of standard shape types (confirming the hypothesis), there are also a significant number of others which do not comply with standard shape types and demonstrate intermediate properties. Existence of intermediate shape types has been observed using all representations. It would be interesting to perform a neuroscientific analysis of produced clusters and understand biological meaning of each cluster produced. This is an initial analysis that provides clustering perspective on spine analysis and compare it with expert labels, it would also be interesting to use proposed approach to perform an analysis tying clusters to different experimental conditions.

The emergence of this phenomenon can be explained in several ways. It is a known fact that dendritic spines exhibit shape type transitions over time, this phenomenon happens over the period of hours. If the spines are captured at these transition periods, for instance a mushroom spine changing to a stubby spine, it might happen to have a short and thick neck and a head diameter to neck diameter ratio close to 1. As some spines in our data demonstrate such properties, it would be difficult to label them as mushroom or stubby. An alternative solution could be to define an intermediate class/group/cluster. A temporal analysis of several spine shapes would provide more insight into this phenomenon. It should also be noted that based on the expert labels, our data consists of two shape classes: mushroom and stubby. Including other shapes of spines such as thin and filopodia in the type of analysis we have proposed here might facilitate an even better understanding of the nature of shape classes and distribution. It might also be interesting to pose this as unsupervised regression problem, which would allow to study continuum of shape variations in a principled manner. It is important to mention that the distribution of spine shapes are dependent on various aspects of the data used, including which anatomical region of the brain the imaged neurons belong to as well as the age of the imaged neurons. This might also contribute towards different conclusions from different studies on spine shapes. Another potential issue might be performing the analysis on 2D projections versus 3D data. Therefore, it would be interesting to perform similar analysis with different 2D projection methods as well as 3D data. To conclude, the clustering perspective we propose in this paper can both be used to perform automated spine shape analysis to identify known shape classes as well as to help neuroscientists discover and explore unknown patterns in the shape space which have been previously ignored.

Acknowledgement. This work has been supported by the Scientific and Technological Research Council of Turkey (TUBITAK) under Grant 113E603, and by TUBITAK-2218 Fellowship for Postdoctoral Researchers.

References

1. Lippman, J., Dunaevsky, A.: Dendritic spine morphogenesis and plasticity. J. Neurobiol. **64**(1), 47–57 (2005)
2. Yuste, R.: Dendritic Spines. MIT Press, Cambridge (2010)
3. Yuste, R., Bonhoeffer, T.: Morphological changes in dendritic spines associated with long-term synaptic plasticity. Annu. Rev. Neurosci. **24**, 1071–1089 (2001)
4. Matsuzaki, M., Honkura, N., Ellis-Davies, G.C., Kasai, H.: Structural basis of long-term potentiation in single dendritic spines. Nature **429**(6993), 761–766 (2004)
5. Harvey, C.D., Svoboda, K.: Locally dynamic synaptic learning rules in pyramidal neuron dendrites. Nature **450**(7173), 1195–1200 (2007)
6. Govindarajan, A., Israely, I., Huang, S.Y., Tonegawa, S.: The dendritic branch is the preferred integrative unit for protein synthesis-dependent ltp. Neuron **69**(1), 132–146 (2011)
7. Shi, P., Zhou, X., Li, Q., Baron, M., Teylan, M.A., Kim, Y., Wong, S.T.: Online three-dimensional dendritic spines mophological classification based on semi-supervised learning. In: ISBI 2009 IEEE International Symposium on Biomedical Imaging: From Nano to Macro, pp. 1019–1022 (2009)
8. Son, J., Song, S., Lee, S., Chang, S., Kim, M.: Morphological change tracking of dendritic spines based on structural features. J. Microsc. **241**(3), 261–272 (2011)
9. Xu, X., Wong, S.: Optical microscopic image processing of dendritic spines morphology. IEEE Signal Process. Mag. **23**(4), 132–135 (2006)

10. Koh, I.Y., Lindquist, W.B., Zito, K., Nimchinsky, E.A., Svoboda, K.: An image analysis algorithm for dendritic spines. Neural Comput. **14**(6), 1283–1310 (2002)
11. Ruszczycki, B., Szepesi, Z., Wilczynski, G.M., Bijata, M., Kalita, K., Kaczmarek, L., Wlodarczyk, J.: Sampling issues in quantitative analysis of dendritic spines morphology. BMC Bioinformatics **13**, 213 (2012)
12. Parnass, Z., Tashiro, A., Yuste, R.: Analysis of spine morphological plasticity in developing hippocampal pyramidal neurons. Hippocampus **10**(5), 561–568 (2000)
13. Rodriguez, A., Ehlenberger, D.B., Dickstein, D.L., Hof, P.R., Wearne, S.L.: Automated three-dimensional detection and shape classification of dendritic spines from fluorescence microscopy images. PloS one **3**(4), 1–12 (2008)
14. Chang, F., Greenough, W.T.: Transient and enduring morphological correlates of synaptic activity and efficacy change in the rat hippocampal slice. Brain Res. **309**, 35–46 (1984)
15. Peters, A., Kaiserman-Abramof, I.R.: The small pyramidal neuron of the rat cerebral cortex. The perikaryon, dendrites and spines. Am. J. Anat. **127**, 321–356 (1970)
16. Bourne, J., Harris, K.M.: Do thin spines learn to be mushroom spines that remember? Curr. Opin. Neurobiol. **17**(3), 381–386 (2007)
17. Basu, S., Plewczynski, D., Saha, S., Roszkowska, M., Magnowska, M., Baczynska, E., Wlodarczyk, J.: 2dSpAn: semiautomated 2-D segmentation, classification and analysis of hippocampal dendritic spine plasticity. Bioinformatics (2016)
18. Arellano, J.I., Benavides-Piccione, R., DeFelipe, J., Yuste, R.: Ultrastructure of dendritic spines: correlation between synaptic and spine morphologies. Frontiers Neurosci. **1**(1), 131–143 (2007)
19. Spacek, J., Hartmann, M.: Three-dimensional analysis of dendritic spines. i. quantitative observations related to dendritic spine and synaptic morphology in cerebral and cerebellar cortices. Anat. Embryol. **167**, 289–310 (1983)
20. Wallace, W., Bear, M.F.: A morphological correlate of synaptic scaling in visual cortex. J. Neurosci. **24**(31), 6928–6938 (2004)
21. Mancuso, J.J., Chen, Y., Li, X., Xue, Z., Wong, S.T.: Methods of dendritic spine detection: from Golgi to high-resolution optical imaging. Neuroscience **251**, 129–140 (2013)
22. Mesadi, F., Cetin, M., Tasdizen, T.: Disjunctive normal shape and appearance priors with applications to image segmentation. In: Navab, N., Hornegger, J., Wells, W.M., Frangi, A.F. (eds.) MICCAI 2015. LNCS, vol. 9351, pp. 703–710. Springer, Heidelberg (2015). doi:10.1007/978-3-319-24574-4_84
23. Dalal, N., Triggs, B.: Histograms of oriented gradients for human detection. In: IEEE Computer Society Conference on Computer Vision and Pattern Recognition, CVPR 2005, vol. 1, pp. 886–893. IEEE (2005)
24. Erdil, E., Argunşah, A.O., Tasdizen, T., Unay, D., Cetin, M.: A joint classification and segmentation approach for dendritic spine segmentation in 2-photon microscopy images. In: IEEE 12th International Symposium on Biomedical Imaging (ISBI), pp. 797–800. IEEE (2015)
25. Ghani, M.U., Kanik, S.D., Argunşah, A.O., Tasdizen, T., Unay, D., Cetin, M.: Dendritic spine shape classification from two-photon microscopy images. In: IEEE Signal Processing and Communications Applications (SIU) (2015)
26. Pelleg, D., Moore, A.W., et al.: X-means: extending k-means with efficient estimation of the number of clusters. In: ICML, vol. 1 (2000)
27. Lipson, A., Lipson, S.G., Lipson, H.: Optical Physics. Cambridge University Press, Cambridge (2010)

28. So, P.T., Dong, C.Y., Masters, B.R., Berland, K.M.: Two-photon excitation fluorescence microscopy. Annu. Rev. Biomed. Eng. **2**(1), 399–429 (2000)
29. Tenenbaum, J.B., de Silva, V., Langford, J.C.: A global geometric framework for nonlinear dimensionality reduction. Science **290**(5500), 2319 (2000)
30. Ghani, M.U., Argunşah, A.O., Israely, I., Unay, D., Tasdizen, T., Cetin, M.: On comparison of manifold learning techniques for dendritic spine classification. In: IEEE 13th International Symposium on Biomedical Imaging (ISBI). IEEE (2016)
31. Ghani, M.U., Mesadi, F., Kanik, S.D., Argunşah, A.O., Israely, I., Unay, D., Tasdizen, T., Cetin, M.: Dendritic spine shape analysis using disjunctive normal shape models. In: IEEE 13th International Symposium on Biomedical Imaging (ISBI). IEEE (2016)
32. Wallis, J.W., Miller, T.R., Lerner, C.A., Kleerup, E.C.: Three-dimensional display in nuclear medicine. IEEE Trans. Med. Imaging **8**(4), 297–303 (1989)
33. Zhang, Y., Zhou, X., Witt, R.M., Sabatini, B.L., Adjeroh, D., Wong, S.T.: Dendritic spine detection using curvilinear structure detector and lda classifier. Neuroimage **36**(2), 346–360 (2007)
34. Bai, W., Zhou, X., Ji, L., Cheng, J., Wong, S.T.: Automatic dendritic spine analysis in two-photon laser scanning microscopy images. Cytometry Part A **71**(10), 818–826 (2007)
35. Xu, X., Cheng, J., Witt, R.M., Sabatini, B.L., Wong, S.T.: A shape analysis method to detect dendritic spine in 3D optical microscopy image. In: 3rd IEEE International Symposium on Biomedical Imaging: Nano to Macro, pp. 554–557. IEEE (2006)
36. Ramesh, N., Mesadi, F., Cetin, M., Tasdizen, T.: Disjunctive normal shape models. In: IEEE 12th International Symposium on Biomedical Imaging (ISBI), pp. 1535–1539, April 2015
37. Chan, T.F., Vese, L.A.: Active contours without edges. IEEE Trans. Image Process. **10**(2), 266–277 (2001)
38. Mitra, P., Murthy, C., Pal, S.K.: Unsupervised feature selection using feature similarity. IEEE Trans. Pattern Anal. Mach. Intell. **24**(3), 301–312 (2002)
39. Jain, A.K.: Data clustering: 50 years beyond k-means. Pattern Recogn. Lett. **31**(8), 651–666 (2010)
40. Cover, T.M., Thomas, J.A.: Elements of Information Theory. Wiley, New York (1991)
41. Tonnesen, J., Katona, G., Rózsa, J., Nagerl, U., et al.: Spine neck plasticity regulates compartmentalization of synapses. Nature Neuroscience **17**(5), 678–685 (2014)

Cell Counting by Regression Using Convolutional Neural Network

Yao Xue[1], Nilanjan Ray[1(✉)], Judith Hugh[2], and Gilbert Bigras[2]

[1] Department of Computing Science, University of Alberta, Edmonton, Canada
nray1@ualberta.ca
[2] Department of Laboratory Medicine, University of Alberta, Edmonton, Canada

Abstract. The ability to accurately quantitate specific populations of cells is important for precision diagnostics in laboratory medicine. For example, the quantization of positive tumor cells can be used clinically to determine the need for chemotherapy in a cancer patient. In this paper, we describe a supervised learning framework with Convolutional Neural Network (CNN) and cast the cell counting task as a regression problem, where the global cell count is taken as the annotation to supervise training, instead of following the classification or detection framework. To further decrease the prediction error of counting, we tune several cutting-edge CNN architectures (e.g. Deep Residual Network) into the regression model. As the final output, not only the cell count is estimated for an image, but also its spatial density map is provided. The proposed method is evaluated with three state-of-the-art approaches on three cell image datasets and obtain superior performance.

Keywords: Cell counting · Convolution neural network · Deep residual net · Detection · Classification

1 Introduction

1.1 Problem Definition

Automatic cell counting is to obtain the number of certain types of cells in a medical image like microscopic images. It is of great interest to a wide range of medical scenarios [2,4,23]. An example is the diagnosis and treatment of breast cancer, which is one of the most common female diseases leading to death worldwide. The number of proliferating (e.g. Ki67 positive) tumor cells is an important index associated with the severity of disease clinically. One available method of quantization involves counting the nuclei of proliferating cells using traditional image analysis techniques on a microscopic image. However, it has been proven to be challenging because of inability to distinguish tumor cells from surrounding normal tissue like vessels, fat and fibrous tissue [11], especially in reality the resolution of input medical image could be very high, at the same time the target cells could easily be extremely dense. Consequently, it is quite difficult to manually count target cells one by one. This is the principal motivation of automatic cell counting.

© Springer International Publishing Switzerland 2016
G. Hua and H. Jégou (Eds.): ECCV 2016 Workshops, Part I, LNCS 9913, pp. 274–290, 2016.
DOI: 10.1007/978-3-319-46604-0_20

1.2 Background

From the perspective of computer vision community, automatic cell counting is a branch task of the object counting problem. Many methods have chosen to fulfill object counting task following the detection pipeline [17,20,21,27,30,32]. In this case, an object detection framework is designed to localize each object (e.g. cell, head or vehicle) one by one, after that a counter naturally takes all the detected objects and produces the final count. Following the success of deep learning applied in computer vision like detection, segmentation and localization [13,14,33], most recent counting-by-detection works choose learning based approach, where each training object has annotation information, sometimes dot annotation indicating the centroid of the object [8,18,31], sometimes bounding-box annotation around the object [30]. However, it is well known that the problem of detecting and localizing individual object instance is far from being solved, especially in real world application of cell counting, where the cell density can be extremely high [7,15,29]. For example, the number of cells can easily reach or exceed thousands per image, and the cells also show huge variations in terms of type, size, shape and appearance etc. Another related work is Fully Convolutional Neural Network (FCNN) [26], which has remarkable result in semantic segmentation and spatial density prediction (in some way, object counting can be seen as an integration over spatial density prediction). To build the end-to-end and pixel-to-pixel FCNN, its training phase requires the pixel-wise annotation, which is strongly supervised information and gives much benefit to FCNN, consequently work like [9] is proposed to compensate.

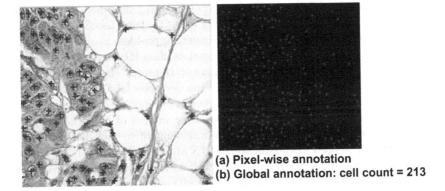

(a) Pixel-wise annotation
(b) Global annotation: cell count = 213

Fig. 1. Counting-by-detection framework, most of which requires the pixel-wise annotation, is not a good choice in cell counting task, where cells could be extremely dense.

Figure 1 shows a cell image example with its two level of annotations: (a) pixel-wise annotation, where the nuclei of each cell is dot-annotated; (b) global count, where the total number of cell in the image is provided. Most counting-by-detection framework takes the strongly supervised pixel-wise annotation as input during training, and then generate global count (i.e. the total number of target cells) for test image. However, the automatic cell counting task is to predict a global count only, thus it is a limitation and also unnecessary to design an object counting framework relying on the more expensive annotation data, which will make system unpractical in the real-world application of cell counting.

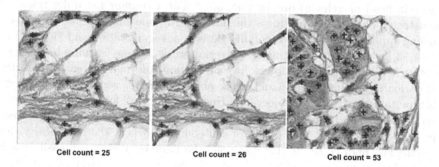

Fig. 2. Cell counting is better to be modeled as a regression problem rather than a classification problem.

Here we expand the scope of our related work study from purely cell counting to all the object counting problem. Object (including cell, people, vehicle, etc.) counting task [3,7,8,15,18,19,24,29,35] benefits a lot from the superior performance of Convolutional Neural Network (CNN) in recent years. Several work [3,7,15] exploit CNN to enable their counting system work in dense and crowded environment. While [24,29] focus on extracting deep features from pre-trained or fine-tuned CNN models. However a multi-class classification CNN is usually trained and used. That means the counting problem is cast as a classification problem, where the cell count is treated as class ID, and images with the same number of objects are seen as belonging to the same class. During its test phase, each test image is predicted with an integer class label (for example: 25, 26 or 53 in Fig. 2), which indicates the number of objects in the image. However as we know in object classification task, training images of different categories (for example: cat, bicycle and airplane) are independent to each other, and softmax loss function is used in classification CNN architectures [13,14]. Actually, a classification-orientated CNN model treats cell counts 25 and 53 as far apart as counts 25 and 26. However from the nature of cell counting, the distance between different cell counts is very important. It is beneficial to treat the object counting task as a regression task [29], where counts 25 and 26 should be closer and that could be correctly reflected in the regression setting.

Taking all the discussion above into consideration, the advantages of cell counting approach proposed in this paper can be summarized into the following aspects:

1. To capture the relationship between RGB cell image and its overall cell count, we cast the cell counting task as developing an end-to-end regression

framework, which is more suitable for counting task compared to counting by detection. Additionally, instead of being applied for classification purpose, a convolutional neural network architecture with Euclidean loss function is used for regression.

2. As the final output, the proposed approach not only estimate the global number of certain cells in an image but also produce the spatial density prediction, which is able to describe the local cell density of an image sub-region. In many clinical imaging systems [10, 28, 34], researchers have confirmed that the topographic map that illustrate the cell density distribution is a valuable tool correlated with the disease diagnose and treatment.

3. We utilize several mainstream CNN architectures (including the Deep Residual Network [13], AlexNet [14]) into our regression model. To the best of our knowledge, this is the first piece of work to expand the deep residual network from classification, detection, segmentation to object counting.

2   The Proposed Framework

2.1   System Overview

In this section, we give a general overview on the proposed approach, details of every part are provided in the following sections. In this paper, we propose a supervised learning framework for cell counting task shown in Fig. 3.

In the training phase, a Convolutional Neural Network (CNN) is utilized to build a regression model between image patch and its cell count number. We employ several kinds of CNN architectures and use Euclidean loss function during training, to enable the regression model fit for the cell counting task. To prepare the training data, we generate a large number of square patches from every training image. Along with each training patch, there is a patch count number, which indicates the number of target cells present in the patch. After that, patch rotation is performed on the collected training patches for the purpose of making the system more robust to rotational variance and data augmentation.

In the test phase, one test image is cropped into a number of overlapping test patches with the same size as the training patches in the sliding-window manner. Each of these test patches is passed into the CNN-based regression model, and then the estimated cell count of the input test patch is output from the last layer of the CNN model. After predicting cell counts for all the patches, we perform a 2-D Linear Interpolation over the estimated cell count and its corresponding x-y coordinates to build a heatmap, which provides a spatial density prediction as shown in Fig. 3. Lastly, integrating these interpolated counts on pixel locations provides us the final count on the test image. The whole procedure is illustrated in Fig. 3.

2.2   Data Preparation and Processing

In the real application of automatic cell counting, the resolution of input medical image could be very high, at the same time the target cells could be very dense.

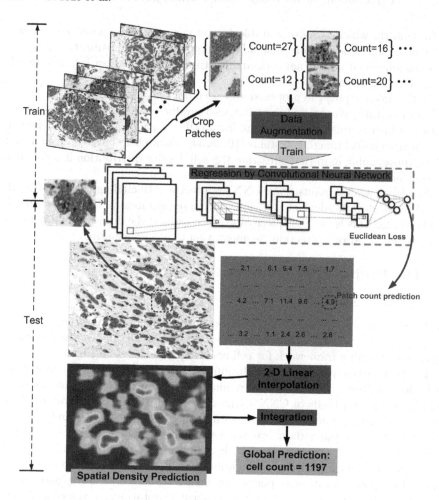

Fig. 3. System overview

Consequently, it is quite difficult to manually count target cells one by one. This is the original motivation of automatic cell counting. Considering the nature of these medical images, which need automatic cell counting, data preparation and processing is naturally necessary. In this work, we crop image into consistent patches and then perform training and prediction over these patches, in order to (1) make the approach more robust to scale variance, (2) avoid resizing original microscope image, which could cause information loss, (3) prepare more training data to prevent the CNN based regression model from overfitting during training.

The proposed method operates by first partitioning image to smaller patches. Patches are generated in a sliding window manner: from the top-left corner of a large W-by-H image with a certain patch size and stride size. Usually, stride size is set smaller than half of path size to ensure that adjacent patches have overlapping region. To construct training data, every training patch is accompanied by a patch count, which is an integer indicating how many cells exist in the patch. Then for data augmentation, a training patch is rotated from 0 degree to 360 degree with a certain rotation step, for example 30 degrees.

2.3   Convolutional Neural Network Regression Model

2.3.1   Classification vs. Regression for Counting

As we know, in a CNN-based classification model, the network outputs a vector whose size is the same size as the number of classes. The i-element in the vector describes the confidence score that the input image belongs to the i-th class. During test phase, the index with the highest confidence score is selected as the final classification result. Softmax loss is widely used for classification problem.

However for counting problems, it is not proper to take cell count number as class index. The reason why regression is a better choice than classification for counting task has been explained in detail in introduction part. In our counting-by-regression model, the difference between ground-truth value and the estimated value can be better preserved during calculating the error. This information is quite helpful for optimizing the CNN weights more accurately in the back-propagation phase. The layer of our regression model outputs a single number, indicating the number of cells that our model predicts. In our model, we employ two kinds of CNN architectures, the first one is AlexNet [14] which consists of 5 convolution layers + 3 fully connected layers; the other is the deep residual network (ResNet) [13] which we will explain in the next section. In both of these architectures, the loss function is defined as the Euclidean loss, which measures the sum of squares of differences between the ground truth and prediction. We train the AlexNet model from scratch with Softmax and Euclidean loss layer respectively, the performance improvement of regression over classification is experimentally explained in detail at Sect. 3.4.

2.3.2   Deep Residual Network for Regression

Since the 2012 ImageNet competition, convolutional neural networks have become popular in large scale image recognition tasks, several milestone networks (including AlexNet [14] VGGNet [22] and GoogLeNet [6], etc.) have been proposed. Recently, the introduction of residual connections into deep convolutional networks has yielded state-of-the-art performance in the 2015 ILSVRC challenge. This raises the question of whether there is any benefit in introducing deep residual network (ResNet) [13] in to the cell counting task. In the following section, we are going to explain the network architecture and its components used in this paper.

Convolutional layer. It consists of a set of learnable filters. During the forward pass, we slide each filter along the width and height of the input volume and compute dot products between its weights and the activation map from previous layer. Intuitively, the filters will be trained to be active to some type of visual feature such as an edge of some orientation or a blotch of some color on the first layer.

Pooling layer. It works by down-sampling the convolutional features using the max operation (*max-pooling*) or average operation (*average-pooling*). Pooling layer is usually inserted between successive convolutional layers, in order to reduce the amount of network parameters and also to control overfitting.

Batch Normalization layer. In the ResNet architecture, authors [13] deploy Batch Normalization (BN) layer [25] right after each convolution and before activation. As we know, normalization is often used as a pre-processing step to make the data consistent. When the input flows through a deep network, the weights and parameters adjust the values of the input, sometimes making the data too big or too small again. Batch Normalization layer allows us to normalize the data in each mini-batch across the network rather than just performing normalization once in the beginning, thus this problem is largely avoided. [25] has demonstrated that batch normalization helps to boost the learning speed and also increase the overall accuracy.

Fully-Connected layer. As the name implies, each neuron in a Fully-Connected (FC) layer has full connections to all neurons in the previous layer. After gathering all the responses from previous layers into each of its neuron, fully connected layer is responsible for computing a class-specific confidence vectors, where its each neuron outputs a score for a certain class. For example, the ResNet ends with a 1000-way fully-connected layer, on which the class with maximum score is selected as its final predicted label.

Overall Architecture. Different from other CNN architectures, ResNet consists of a number of Residual Blocks. Each residual block is a made up of Convolutional layer, Batch Normalization layer and a shortcut that connects the original input with the output as shown in Fig. 4 (a) and (b), where a Residual Block with Identity Shortcut (RB-IS) and a Residual Block with Projection Shortcut (RB-PS) is illustrated, respectively. The mathematical model of residual block can be summarized as:

$$y_l = F(X_l, \{W_l\}) + h(X_l) \qquad X_{l+1} = f(y_l) \tag{1}$$

$$h(X_l) = \begin{cases} X_l & identity\,mapping \\ W_p X_l & projection\,mapping \end{cases} \tag{2}$$

X_l and X_{l+1} are the input and output of the l-th residual block, $F(X_l, \{W_l\})$ stands for the residual function, and f is a activation function (e.g. ReLU). $h(X_l)$ represents the shortcut connection: identity mapping or projection mapping. If the dimension of X_l and X_{l+1} is the same, the identity shortcuts is used; otherwise a linear projection W_p is performed on the shortcut connections to match the dimension, that is projection mapping. The central idea [13] of ResNet is to learn the additive residual function F with respect to $h(X_l)$, with a key choice of using an identity mapping and/or projection mapping.

Figure 4 (a) and (b) show two types of Residual Blocks, which are used in different layers of ResNet model (c) according to whether the dimensions of

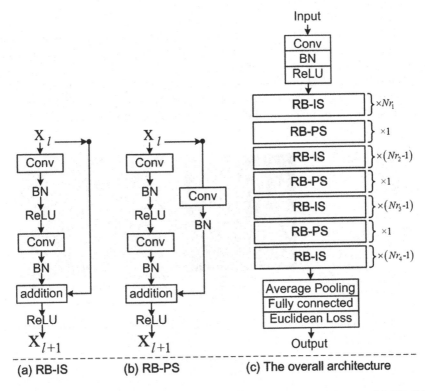

Fig. 4. (a) RB-IS stands for the Residual Block with Identity Shortcut; (b) RB-PS is the Residual Block with Projection Shortcut; (c) An illustration of the architecture that we used in this paper.

input and output are the same. Nr_1, Nr_2, Nr_3 and Nr_4 represent the number of residual blocks used in four sections of ResNet model. For example, $Nr_1 = 3$, $Nr_2 = 4$, $Nr_3 = 6$ and $Nr_4 = 3$ in ResNet-50. Additionally, it has been demonstrated that pre-trained network can be adjusted to be effective for other computer vision tasks. We modify the last fully-connected layer of ResNet from outputting a 1000-D vector to outputting 1 item indicating the predicted number of cells. Additionally, we replace the softmax loss with Euclidean loss. After that, we perform fine-tuning on the weights in fully-connected layer of the ResNet using cell datasets, the parameters of previous layers are preserved. Finally, we obtain three ResNet based regression models for cell counting.

3   Experiment and Performance

3.1   Datasets

First, we describe the three cell datasets, on which the proposed method and other comparison methods are evaluated. The first dataset [12] involves 100 H&E

stained histology images of colorectal adenocarcinomas. A total of 29,756 nuclei were marked at/around the center with over 22,000 labeled with the cell type. The second dataset [1] consists of 200 highly-realistic synthetic emulations of fluorescence microscopic images of bacterial cells. The third dataset comprise of 55 high-resolution RGB images, each of them is a microscopic image of proliferative tumor cells area with a resolution of 1920-by-2560 pixels. The tumor cell size is about 10 to 20 pixels in diameter or 10 μm in physical length.

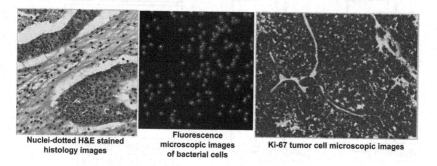

Nuclei-dotted H&E stained histology images   Fluorescence microscopic images of bacterial cells   Ki-67 tumor cell microscopic images

Fig. 5. Example images from the three evaluation datasets and their dotted annotation. (Color figure online)

Table 1. Details of three datasets: *Size* is the image size; *Ntr/Nte* is the number of images selected for training and testing; *AC* indicates the average number of cells; *MinC-MaxC* is the minimum and maximum numbers of cells in a dataset.

Cell dataset	Size	Ntr/Nte	AC	MinC-MaxC
Nuclei [12]	500×500	50/50	310.22	1–1189
Bacterial [1]	256×256	100/100	171.47	74–317
Ki67 cell	1920×2560	45/10	2045.85	70–4808

To build this Ki-67 cell image dataset, a 10X microscopic field representing the highest proliferative area was acquired using a Nikon Eclipse E600 microscope with 0.25 aperture and a QImaging Micropublisher 5.0 RTV camera equipped with a Sony ICX282 CCD, finally it gives us 24-bit color pictures with a resolution of 1920×2560 pixels. All of the three evaluation cell datasets have their dotted annotation available, which represents the location of cells as shown in Fig. 5. For the three datasets, we randomly select images for training and testing. Details of the three evaluation datasets are summarized in Table 1.

3.2   Implementation Details

The proposed method is implemented in Matlab, and we utilize Caffe [33], a fully open source implementation of Convolutional Neural Network, which affords clear access to Matlab/Python with support for GPU computation. As discussed in image partion part, each original RGB images is partitioned under certain rotation, stride size, and patch size. After taking experiments under different settings, we use stride size = 30 (pixels), patch size = 60×60 (pixels) and rotation step = 30 for the nuclei data; stride size = 20 (pixels), patch size = 40×40 (pixels) and rotation step = 30 for the bacterial data; stride size = 50 (pixels), patch size = 200×200 (pixels) and rotation step = 30 for the Ki-67 cell data. All the experiments are run on a machine with Intel Core i7-4790K CPU@4.00 GHz $\times$ 8 and GPU GeForce GTX TITAN Black/PCIe/SSE2.

3.3   Evaluation Metric and Counting Examples

In all the experiments, we use the Mean Relative Error (MRE) and Mean Absolute Error (MAE) as the metric for quantitative evaluation: where N is the total number of test images, t_i and p_i are the true and predicted numbers of cells in the i-th test image. MRE and MAE are defined as follows:

$$MRE = \frac{1}{N} \sum_{i=1}^{N} \frac{|t_i - p_i|}{t_i} \tag{3}$$

$$MAE = \frac{1}{N} \sum_{i=1}^{N} |t_i - p_i| \tag{4}$$

3.4   Counting Performance Using Different Models

First, we are going to investigate the performance difference between Classification (C) model and Regression (R) model for the cell counting task. The whole framework follows the pipeline shown in Fig. 3. As for the CNN architecture, we employ AlexNet (5conv + 3fc) and ResNet (50 layers) separately. And softmax loss function and Euclidean loss function are used respectively in the classification and regression model. We conduct this comparison experiment on all the three cell datasets and evaluate the performance in terms of Mean Relative Error and Mean Absolute Error (std also provided). Table 2 shows that on all the three datasets regression model shows lower prediction error by considerable margins than the classification model, which experimentally support the discussion in Sect. 2.3.1. It is also necessary to note that the AlexNet based regerssion model outperforms the ResNet based classification model. Table 3 shows the counting performances using ResNets with different number of layers. The 50/101/152-layer ResNet based regression models are used in this experiment. We can observe that ResNet-152 model shows the lowest prediction error, followed by ResNet-101 and ResNet-50 respectively.

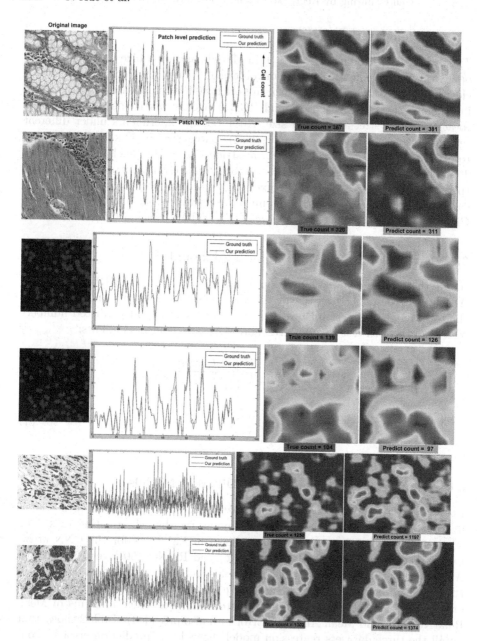

Fig. 6. Spatial density prediction and counting results on the cell datasets. Figure 6 provides several cell counting results on the three evaluation datasets. Original cell image is shown in on left side; the middle panel shows the patch level prediction, which is a middle result of our cell counting result; The right panel shows the spatial density prediction map (measured in number/square pixel) as well as the global counts of ground-truth and our prediction. From the patch level prediction curve, we can see that our estimated counts for each patch approximate the pattern of ground truth counts well.

Table 2. Counting performance in terms of MRE and MAE±std comparison between Classification (C) and Regression (R) model

MRE	Nuclei-dataset	Bacterial-dataset	Ki67-dataset
AlexNet(C)	0.2175	0.0918	0.1226
AlexNet(R)	0.2019	0.0651	0.0959
ResNet(C)	0.2104	0.0772	0.1170
ResNet(R)	0.1925	0.0539	0.0775
MAE±std	Nuclei-dataset	Bacterial-dataset	Ki67-dataset
AlexNet(C)	20.7636±13.9416	12.9667±4.5361	213.5302±65.7220
AlexNet(R)	18.5720±12.6055	9.2591±3.3142	151.2059±44.6032
ResNet(C)	19.8742±13.5217	11.8711±3.8247	169.5076±50.2124
ResNet(R)	17.1437±11.5073	8.2064±2.8515	128.7426±40.5621

Table 3. Counting performance in terms of MRE and MAE±std using different models.

MRE	Nuclei-dataset	Bacterial-dataset	Ki67-dataset
ResNet-50(R)	0.1925	0.0539	0.0775
ResNet-101(R)	0.1845	0.0507	0.0697
ResNet-152(R)	0.1666	0.0450	0.0641
MAE±std	Nuclei-dataset	Bacterial-dataset	Ki67-dataset
ResNet-50(R)	17.1437±11.5073	8.2064±2.8515	128.7426±40.5621
ResNet-101(R)	16.3164±10.8762	7.7542±2.4580	116.3076±39.0215
ResNet-152(R)	14.9275±10.4368	7.4741±2.2248	108.3014±40.4698

3.5 Comparison with State of the Art

We carry out experimental performance comparison between our method and three other state-of-the-art approaches (presented in [5,16,24]) on three evaluation datasets. The counting result from ResNet-152 regression model is used as our approach result during this comparison. Figure 7 provides the cell counts of ground-truth and four predictions of "Le.count" [16], "Le.detect" [5], "Deep-Feat" [24] and "The proposed" on every test image. To quantify Fig. 7, Table 4 reports the performance in terms of Mean Relative Error (MRE) and Mean Absolute Error (MAE) over the three evaluation datasets.

The proposed method has achieved very competitive result on Nuclei dataset and Ki67 dataset, MRE = 16.66 % and 6.41 % respectively. The images from Nuclei and Ki67 datasets contain 310.22 and 2045.85 cells on average, our proposed method is able to predict with only 14.93 and 108.30 cells in terms of mean absolute error; while other three methods gives 33.89–71.80 and 189.35–259.67 error cells on average.

Table 4. Counting performance (MRE) and (MAE±std) comparison on the three evaluation datasets.

MRE	Nuclei-dataset	Bacterial-dataset	Ki67-dataset
DeepFeat [24]	0.3581	0.1751	0.1249
Le.count [16]	0.2674	**0.0208**	0.1151
Le.detect [5]	0.3206	0.1083	0.1540
The proposed	**0.1666**	0.0450	**0.0641**
MAE±std	Nuclei-dataset	Bacterial-dataset	Ki67-dataset
DeepFeat [24]	71.8046 ± 51.4109	25.4792 ± 19.1504	189.3559 ± 53.6329
Le.count [16]	51.4479 ± 39.8087	**6.4061 ± 3.5657**	185.9391 ± 60.5042
Le.detect [5]	33.8995 ± 23.9252	18.1937 ± 13.4393	259.6736 ± 85.0594
The proposed	**14.9275 ± 10.4368**	7.4741 ± 2.2248	**108.3014 ± 40.4698**

On Bacterial dataset, the proposed method gives MRE = 4.50 %, but [16] makes 2.4 % further improvement over our result. The central idea of [16] is to estimate a density function whose integral over any image region gives the count of objects within that region. In its learning phase, each cell is dot-annotated and is assigned a real-valued Sift feature vector describing the local appearance. It means that for each cell, [16] needs its x-y coordinate on an image and then compute the Sift feature on the image sub-region around this cell. In comparison, the proposed method only takes the number of cells as annotation to an image patch during training. As one can imagine, for an image containing hundreds to thousands of cells, the complexity and time consuming of [16] will increase greatly. Furthermore, when it comes to the much more dense datasets (Nuclei and Ki67), the Sift descriptor based learning of [16] becomes less reliable.

It is also necessary to mention that the MRE values of all the four methods on Nuclei dataset are higher than those on other two datasets, because Nuclei dataset has several test images, which only contains a few cells e.g. 1, 4 or 8. For example, predicting the cell count from 1 (ground truth) to 2 or from 4 (ground truth) to 6 will greatly affect the final MRE value.

4   Conclusions

In this paper, we propose a novel regression based framwork for cell counting. As the output, spatial density map and global cell count are provided. The proposed method is able to handle dense cell microscopy image, where the cells also present huge variation in appearance. We have experimentally demonstrated that the proposed approach achieved superior performance compared with several recent related methods.

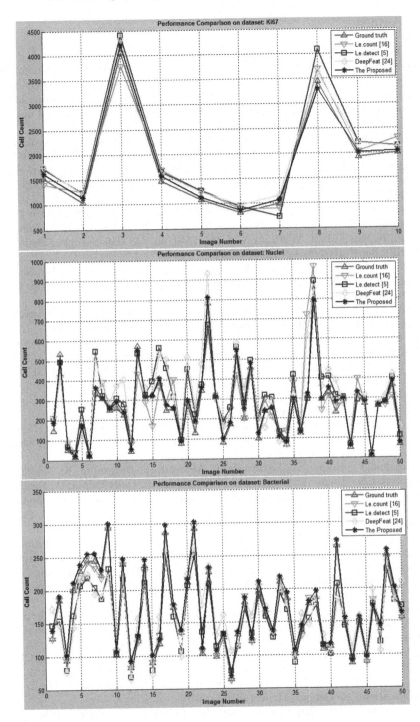

Fig. 7. The estimated count versus ground-truth of different approaches on the three evaluation datasets.

References

1. http://www.robots.ox.ac.uk/vgg/research/counting/
2. Goldhirsch, A., Gelber, R.D., Gnant, M., Piccart-Gebhart, M., Thrlimann, B., Coates, A.S., Winer, E.P., Senn, H.-J.: Tailoring therapies - improving the management of early breast cancer: St. gallen international expert consensus on the primary therapy of early breast cancer 2015. Ann Oncol first published online 4 May 2015. doi:10.1093/annonc/mdv221
3. Li, H., Zhang, C., Wang, X: Cross-scene crowd counting via deep convolutional neural network. In: Computer Vision and Pattern Recognition (CVPR) (2015)
4. Rimm, D.L., Camp, R.L., Chung, G.G.: Automated subcellular localization and quantification of protein expression in tissue microarrays. Nat. Med. **8**, 1323–1327 (2002)
5. Arteta, C., Lempitsky, V., Noble, J.A., Zisserman, A.: Learning to detect cells using non-overlapping extremal regions. In: Ayache, N., Delingette, H., Golland, P., Mori, K. (eds.) MICCAI 2012. LNCS, vol. 7510, pp. 348–356. Springer, Heidelberg (2012). doi:10.1007/978-3-642-33415-3_43
6. Jia, Y., Sermanet, P., Reed, S., Anguelov, D., Erhan, D., Vanhoucke, V., Rabinovich, A., Szegedy, C., Liu, W.: Going deeper with convolutions. In: Computer Vision and Pattern Recognition (2014)
7. Yang, L., Liu, S., Cao, X., Wang, C., Zhang, H.: Deep people counting in extremely dense crowds. In: ACM International Conference on Multimedia (2015)
8. Cireşan, D.C., Giusti, A., Gambardella, L.M., Schmidhuber, J.: Mitosis detection in breast cancer histology images with deep neural networks. In: Mori, K., Sakuma, I., Sato, Y., Barillot, C., Navab, N. (eds.) MICCAI 2013. LNCS, vol. 8150, pp. 411–418. Springer, Heidelberg (2013). doi:10.1007/978-3-642-40763-5_51
9. Pathak, D., Krahenbuhl, P., Darrell, T.: Constrained convolutional neural networks for weakly supervised segmentation. In: ICCV (2015)
10. Hart, N.S., Collin, S.P., Garza-Gisholt, E., Hemmi, J.M.: A comparison of spatial analysis methods for the construction of topographic maps of retinal cell density. PLoS One **9**(4), e93485 (2014)
11. Cantaloni, C., Eccher, C., Bazzanella, I., Aldovini, D., Bragantini, E., Morelli, L., Cuorvo, L.V., Ferro, A., Gasperetti, F., Berlanda, G., Dalla Palma, P., Fasanella, S., Leonardi, E.: Proliferative activity in human breast cancer: Ki-67 automated evaluation and the influence of different ki-67 equivalent antibodies. Diagn. Pathol. (2011)
12. Tsang, Y.W., Cree, I.A., Snead, D.R.J., Rajpoot, N.M., Sirinukunwattana, K., Raza, S.E.A.: Locality sensitive deep learning for detection and classification of nuclei in routine colon cancer histology images. IEEE Trans. Med. Imaging (2016)
13. Ren, S., Sun, J., He, K., Zhang, X.: Deep residual learning for image recognition. In: CVPR (2015)
14. Sutskever, I., Krizhevsky, A., Hinton, G.E., Imagenet classification with deep convolutional neural networks. In: Neural Information Processing Systems, pp. 1097–1105 (2012)
15. Lebanoff, L., Idrees, H.: Counting in dense crowds using deep learning. In: CRCV (2015)
16. Lempitsky, V., Zisserman, A.: Learning to count objects in images. In: Neural Information Processing Systems (NIPS) (2010)
17. Lin, Z., Davis, L.S.: Shape-based human detection and segmentation via hierarchical part-template matching. IEEE Trans. Pattern Anal. Mach. Intell. (T-PAMI) **32**, 604–618 (2010)

18. Liu, F., Yang, L.: A novel cell detection method using deep convolutional neural network and maximum-weight independent set. In: Navab, N., Hornegger, J., Wells, W.M., Frangi, A.F. (eds.) MICCAI 2015. LNCS, vol. 9351, pp. 349–357. Springer, Heidelberg (2015). doi:10.1007/978-3-319-24574-4_42

19. Habibzadeh, M., Krzyżak, A., Fevens, T.: White blood cell differential counts using convolutional neural networks for low resolution images. In: Rutkowski, L., Korytkowski, M., Scherer, R., Tadeusiewicz, R., Zadeh, L.A., Zurada, J.M. (eds.) ICAISC 2013. LNCS (LNAI), vol. 7895, pp. 263–274. Springer, Heidelberg (2013). doi:10.1007/978-3-642-38610-7_25

20. Sivic, J., Rodriguez, M., Laptev, I., Audibert, J.-Y.: Density-aware person detection and tracking in crowds. In: IEEE International Conference on Computer Vision (ICCV) (2011)

21. Kholi, P., Barinova, O., Lempitsky, V.: On detection of multiple object instances using hough transforms. IEEE Trans. Pattern Anal. Mach. Intell. (T-PAMI) 34, 1773–1784 (2012)

22. Zisserman, A., Parkhi, O.M., Vedaldi, A.: Deep face recognition. In: BMVC (2015)

23. McShane, L.M., Gao, D., Hugh, J.C., Mastropasqua, M.G., Viale, G., Zabaglo, L.A., Penault-Llorca, F., Bartlett, J.M., Gown, A.M., Symmans, W.F., Piper, T., Mehl, E., Enos, R.A., Hayes, D.F., Dowsett, M., Nielsen, T.O., Polley, M.Y., Leung, S.C.: An international ki67 reproducibility study. J. Natl. Cancer Inst. 105(24), 1897–1906 (2013)

24. Pujol, O., Seguí, S., Vitrià, J.: Learning to count with deep object features. In: Computer Vision and Pattern Recognition (CVPR) (2015)

25. Szegedy, C., Ioffe, S.: Batch normalization: accelerating deep network training by reducing internal covariate shift. In: ICML (2015)

26. Long, J., Shelhamer, E., Darrell, T.: Fully convolutional networks for semantic segmentation. In: CVPR (2015)

27. Subburaman, V.B., Descamps, A., Carincotte, C.: Counting people in the crowd using a generic head detector. In: IEEE Ninth International Conference on Advanced Video and Signal-Based Surveillance (AVSS), pp. 470–475 (2012)

28. Messinger, J.D., Zhang, T., Bentley, M.J., Gutierrez, D.B., Ablonczy, Z., Smith, R.T., Sloan, K.R., Curcio, C.A., Ach, T., Huisingh, C., McGwin Jr., G.: Quantitative autofluorescence and cell density maps of the human retinal pigment epithelium. Invest. Ophthalmol. Vis. Sci. 55(8), 4832–4841 (2014)

29. Tota, K., Idrees, H.: Counting in dense crowds using deep features. In: CRCV (2015)

30. Wang, M., Wang, X.: Automatic adaptation of a generic pedestrian detector to a specific traffic scene. In: IEEE Conference on Computer Vision and Pattern Recognition (CVPR) (2011)

31. Zisserman, A., Xie, W., Noble, J.A.: Microscopy cell counting with fully convolutional regression networks (2015)

32. Wu, B., Nevatia, R.: Detection of multiple, partially occluded humans in a single image by bayesian combination of edgelet part detectors. In: IEEE Computer Society Conference on IEEE International Conference on Computer Vision (ICCV) Vision and Pattern Recognition (CVPR) (2005)

33. Donahue, J., Karayev, S., Long, J., Girshick, R., Guadarrama, S., Darrell, T., Jia, Y., Shelhamer, E.: Caffe: convolutional architecture for fast feature embedding. In: IEEE Conference on Computer Vision and Pattern Recognition (CVPR) (2014)

34. Zhang, X., Chen, Y.: Study of cell behaviors on anodized tio 2 nanotube arrays with coexisting multi-size diameters. Nano-Micro Lett. **8**, 61–69 (2015)
35. Xie, Y., Xing, F., Kong, X., Su, H., Yang, L.: Beyond classification: structured regression for robust cell detection using convolutional neural network. In: Navab, N., Hornegger, J., Wells, W.M., Frangi, A.F. (eds.) MICCAI 2015. LNCS, vol. 9351, pp. 358–365. Springer, Heidelberg (2015). doi:10.1007/978-3-319-24574-4_43

Measuring Process Dynamics and Nuclear Migration for Clones of Neural Progenitor Cells

Edgar Cardenas De La Hoz[1], Mark R. Winter[1], Maria Apostolopoulou[2],
Sally Temple[2], and Andrew R. Cohen[1(✉)]

[1] Department of Electrical and Computer Engineering,
Drexel University, Philadelphia, PA, USA
`acohen@coe.drexel.edu`
[2] Neural Stem Cell Institute, Rensselaer, NY, USA

Abstract. Neural stem and progenitor cells (NPCs) generate processes
that extend from the cell body in a dynamic manner. The NPC nucleus
migrates along these processes with patterns believed to be tightly coupled to mechanisms of cell cycle regulation and cell fate determination.
Here, we describe a new segmentation and tracking approach that allows
NPC processes and nuclei to be reliably tracked across multiple rounds
of cell division in phase-contrast microscopy images. Results are presented for mouse adult and embryonic NPCs from hundreds of clones, or
lineage trees, containing tens of thousands of cells and millions of segmentations. New visualization approaches allow the NPC nuclear and
process features to be effectively visualized for an entire clone. Significant differences in process and nuclear dynamics were found among type
A and type C adult NPCs, and also between embryonic NPCs cultured
from the anterior and posterior cerebral cortex.

Keywords: Neural stem cells · Neural progenitor cells · Stem cell
processes · Segmentation · Tracking · Lineaging · Stem cell process
dynamics · Interkinetic nuclear migration

1 Introduction

Neural progenitor cells (NPCs) play a key role in the generation and maintenance
of the nervous system. NPCs are proliferative, undergoing mitosis to generate
daughter cells that are genetic copies of the parent. As this process repeats, a
family tree, or clone of related cells develops. NPCs are also migratory, with
cells moving as needed to form and maintain the functionally, spatially and
morphologically distinct components of the nervous system.

Individual NPCs exhibit a complex cellular morphology, with rapidly forming
and changing cellular processes or protrusions [1]. These NPC processes may
be used to attach to different regional structures such as the apical or basal
surface of the neuroepithelium during development [2], and may also be used
to explore the environment. During the non-mitotic, or interkinetic portion of

© Springer International Publishing Switzerland 2016
G. Hua and H. Jégou (Eds.): ECCV 2016 Workshops, Part I, LNCS 9913, pp. 291–305, 2016.
DOI: 10.1007/978-3-319-46604-0_21

the cell cycle, NPC nuclei undergo distinct motion along the processes. This interkinetic nuclear migration (INM) has been observed in a wide variety of vertebrate cell types [3], and has been associated with the cell fate, or type of daughter cells that will be produced post-mitosis [4]. The relationship between INM and mechanisms controlling cell cycle and mitosis is an important open question [5,6].

Fluorescence microscopy is most commonly used to visualize INM. Because INM generally involves the spatial patterning or organization of a 3-D structure such as the cortex or retina, 3-D fluorescence microscopy, either confocal or multi-photon, is a way to observe not only the INM, but also the resulting divisions and tissue formation. Fluorescence microscopy allows for images to be captured with distinct nuclear and cytoplasmic markers, making the analysis of INM easier for both manual and computational approaches. However, fluorescence imaging of NPCs places a limit on the duration of the imaging experiment because of the increased photo-toxicity. Long-term observation of proliferating NPCs at a temporal frequency sufficient to establish accurate tracking of cells requires the use of transmitted light microscopy [7,8].

Using phase-contrast microscopy to image live NPCs can capture multiple rounds of cell division over a period of 5–7 days or even longer without the photo-toxic effects of fluorescence. This time duration allows mouse cells to complete as many as 8 or even 10 rounds of cell divisions. *In vitro* phase contrast imaging is able to capture both the NPC nucleus, or cell body, as well as the processes. The quantification of INM from phase microscopy is more challenging compared to fluorescence imaging. The processes appear and disappear at a high temporal frequency, sometimes over a period of minutes making it difficult to integrate temporal information into the process segmentation. The process intensities vary only slightly from the background, and generally do not exhibit the phase contrast halo artifact that makes it possible to more reliably segment the cell nuclear region. Any clutter in the image sequence can be hard to differentiate from cell processes, with dead cells or other detritus appearing virtually identical to actual processes. Another challenge is the quantity of image data involved in a typical experiment. Stem cell populations often exhibit heterogeneous behaviors, so experiments examining behaviors for clones of cells can require the analysis of hundreds of clones, tens of thousands of cells and millions of individual cell segmentations. Adding process dynamics to such an experiment makes analysis by hand impossible - automated techniques are required.

Analyzing NPC process dynamics from time-lapse microscopy image sequences requires the cell body and processes to be segmented in each frame. The segmentation results are associated temporally by a tracking algorithm. Lineaging identifies mitotic events and establishes parent-daughter relationships. Together, the tracking and lineaging results establish the lineage tree showing the temporal and mitotic relationships among all cells in the clone. Here we present a new technique for segmenting and tracking NPC processes in time-lapse phase contrast microscopy. Our approach first uses an existing open-source software tool known as LEVER (for Lineage Editing and Validation) to segment, track and lineage the cells [7–11]. The LEVER analysis segments and tracks cells throughout the image sequence and is the basis for the subsequent segmentation and tracking of the NPC processes. The phase contrast LEVER segmentation [12] captures the cell soma, and the centroid of this is used as the nuclear location. LEVER can optionally integrate fluorescence markers for identifying the nucleus or process boundaries, but these are not required.

Once the LEVER analysis is complete, each image is thresholded to identify the foreground pixels that may belong to processes. Morphological processing on this threshold image is used to remove any background clutter in the images such as dead cells or detritus. Each of the process foreground pixels is then assigned to the LEVER segmentation result that is closest in the sense of minimizing the geodesic distance, or the distance in traversing only foreground process pixels to the LEVER nuclear segmentation results. Once the process pixels have been assigned to LEVER cell tracks, the process bounding box is computed, and the projection of the nuclear location onto the principal axis of the bounding box is taken. This provides the location of the cell in every image frame, and also the location of the nucleus relative to the processes, the key features for characterizing both cellular and nuclear motion.

Figure 1 illustrates the process segmentation and analysis steps. Starting with the LEVER segmentation and tracking results (panel A), the image is next adaptively thresholded to identify possible process pixels, shown in red (B). Process pixels are assigned to the nearest segmentation using a geodesic distance (C). Finally, the process bounding box is established, and the nuclear location is projected onto the process principal axis, shown as a white dot (D).

2   Related Literature

Examining Fig. 1, it can be observed that NPC process segmentation appears similar to the problem of neuron tracing, or neurite segmentation. Neuron tracing is an extremely well studied problem, including in phase contrast images [13]. A broad overview of the neuron tracing problem is given by Meijering [14]. Despite the superficial similarity between neurite segmentation and NPC process segmentation, the two applications are actually very different. Unlike neurons, NPCs are highly motile. The morphology of the cell body and of the processes changes dramatically over short periods of time. Also unlike neurons, NPCs are also proliferative, dividing to produce new cells. Finally, NPCs are more adherant compared to neurons, with cells frequently in close contact. For 2-D *in vitro* imaging, cells may also crawl on top of each other, causing significant overlap. Separating these touching cells is one of the principle challenges in working with NPC image sequence data.

The first automated computer algorithm for NPC segmentation, tracking and lineaging in phase contrast images was described by Al Kofahi, *et al.* [15]. More advanced tracking approaches for phase contrast images were descibed by Li *et al.* [16,17]. For fluorescency microscopy images, Amat *et al.* describe an approach used with light-sheet microscopy images [18]. The CellProfiler program also has support for lineage analysis with track editing [19]. Winter *et al.* developed a tracking approach called Multitemporal Associate Tracking (MAT) that

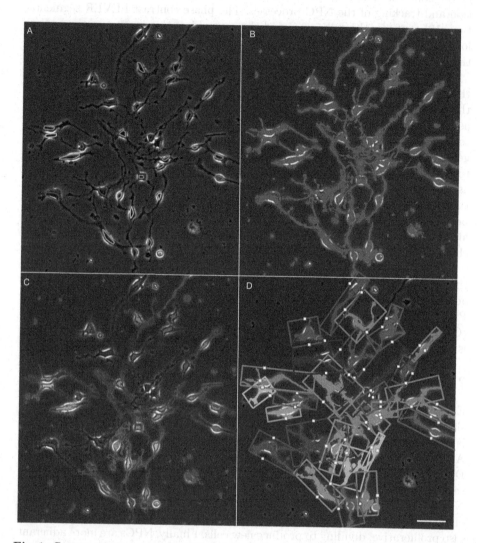

Fig. 1. Segmentation and tracking of adult neural progenitor cell (NPC) processes. Results are shown for a single image from an 1100 frame time-lapse sequence, with convex hulls showing cell segmentation, colored by tracking assignment (A). A thresholding step identifies pixels that may belong to processes (B). A geodesic distance transform on the thresholded image is used to assign each process pixel to the nearest connected cell segmentation, with unassigned pixels in gray (C). Nuclear location and migration are established by projecting the nuclear centroid onto the principal axis of the bounding box of each cells processes, shown as the white dot (D). Scale bar indicates 50 μm. (Color figure online)

was designed specifically for objects that split and merge [20,21]. The open-source LEVER program combines the MAT tracking algorithm with an online user-based validation [8]. LEVER works with 2-D+time phase contrast images, 5-D (3-D+multichannel+time) [11] and also with mixed phase and fluoresence microscopy images [9,10]. LEVER uses an inference approach to incorporating human-provided corrections into the segmentation and tracking results. LEVER also uses contextual information about the cell populations obtained from the lineage tree to reduce the error rates of the automated analysis algorithms by more than 80 % [7]. The LEVER program is used here to generate the cell segmentation, tracking and lineaging results.

3   Results

Two different experimental questions involving adult and embryonic mouse NPCs are addressed in this paper. First, differences in process dynamics are compared between type C and type A adult NPCs, two distinct sub-populations of adult NPCs. The second dataset that was analyzed consisted of embryonic NPCs cultured at E12.5 (12.5 days post-fertilization) from either the anterior or the posterior regions of the cerebral cortex. This dataset was previously used to study differences between anterior and posterior NPCs [7], and has been further analyzed here with process segmentation and tracking. The results of the automated segmentation, tracking and lineaging algorithms have been fully validated by human observers using the LEVER program [8]. This validation corrects any errors in the tracking or lineaging results. Validation of the segmentation by the human observer establishes that every cell has a segmentation result in every image frame. Validation of individual pixels assigned to each cell segmentation is detailed in Sect. 4. All of the automated image analysis results, including lineaging, tracking, nuclear and process segmentation, can be viewed interactively together with the image data using the CloneView program [7] as described in Sect. 5.

3.1   Type A and Type C Adult NPCs

The adult NPC dataset contains movies from four different imaging experiments. The data consists of 142 NPC clones, with a total of 1,350 cells or tracks and 361,867 individual cell segmentations. A total of 48 movies were processed. At the end of each experiment, cells were stained using immunohistochemistry to identify the cell types including type C and type A NPCs.

Figure 2 shows NPC process segmentation for a clone of cells that produces both type A and type C NPCs. The LEVER segmentation results are shown with different colors to indicate track IDs (A). Process pixels (half-tone) are assigned to the closest cell segmentation (solid-tone pixels) using a geodesic distance (B). Process pixels colored in gray could not be assigned to any cell track. Bounding boxes for the process pixels are colored according to cell fate commitment, with type A committed NPCs in red and type C committed NPCs in blue (C). Cell fate is established for each cell at the end of the experiment by fixing and staining the cells. Fate commitment is then applied to the tree retrospectively. A cell is considered committed to a fate iff all cells in the subtree rooted at the given cell are of the same fate. The lineage tree is colored by the generation of fate commitment, with subsequent generations having a darker hue. The lineage tree also shows process area (green line) and soma area (yellow line), each normalized per-clone, plotted next to each cell. Showing features on the lineage tree in this manner is a new and effective way to visualize nuclear and process dynamics for an entire clone.

Figure 3 shows summary statistics for fate-committed type A and C NPCs. Type C cells have significantly larger soma area ($p = 10^{-46}$) and larger process area ($p = 10^{-62}$) compared to type A cells. Type C cells exhibit lower nuclear velocity measured along the normalized process principal axis ($p = 10^{-20}$). Type C cells can also be seen to exhibit different patterns of motion compared to type A cells, with a higher entropy of nuclear migration ($p = 10^{-5}$). This means that the type C cells are more uniformly distributed along the process principal axis as compared to the type A cells.

3.2 Anterior and Posterior Cerebral Cortex Embryonic NPCs

The embryonic NPC dataset consists of 129 movies imaged in 3 different experiments. A total of 160 clones were analyzed, with 10,644 cells and 1,585,104 segmentations. The same analysis approach as used for adult NPCs was applied to the embyronic NPC data. Embryonic NPC clones are generally larger compared to adult clones. Figure 4 shows an example of the process segmentation and tracking results for an embryonic NPC clone. This clone contains 331 cells or tracks, and 30,229 individual cell segmentations. Starting with an unprocessed image frame (A), the LEVER segmentation and tracking results (B) are shown as the convex hulls of the cell pixels colored by track ID. The process pixels are shown segmented and tracked, colored by track assignment and with process pixels blended and cell pixels colored at full saturation (C). The process bounding box is shown in (D), with the projection of the nuclear centroid onto the process principal axis shown as a white dot. The feature used for analyzing nuclear location and velocity is the position of the nuclear centroid along this principal process axis, with the extents of the process axis normalized per frame to $[-1,1]$.

The lineage tree from Fig. 4 also renders the time sequence of normalized nuclear location for each cell. For cell tracks that occur later in the movie, that lineage tree becomes very difficult to read as the spacing between cells on the lineage becomes quite tight. Figure 5 shows an alternative rendering for the lineage tree based on a radial tranform of cell relationships. The radius in this case corresponds to time, and angular orientation is used to position daughter cells below their parent. This alternative rendering for the lineage tree makes better use of the available space, making it easier to visualize the process features throughout the cell cycle.

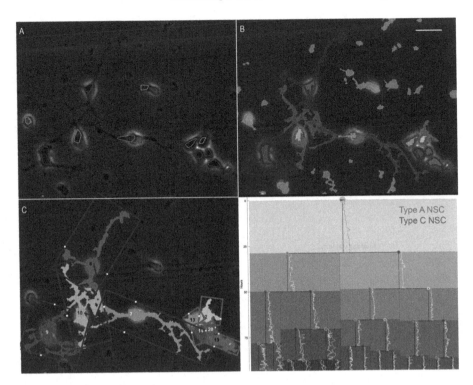

Fig. 2. Segmentation, tracking and lineage results with cell fate commitment and soma and process areas for type A and type C NPCs. Single image from 1100 frame sequence with cell segmentation and tracking results obtained from the LEVER program (A). Process segmentation and tracking result, with cell pixels shown in solid-tone and process pixels in half-tone (B). Bounding boxes are colored by cell fate commitment, with NPCs producing only type A NPCs in red and NPCs that produce only type C NPCs in blue (C). Lineage tree colored by fate commitment, with color hue darkening for each mitotic generation and soma and process areas ploted next to each cell cycle line. Process area for each cell is plotted in green normalized to the maximum process area per clone. Soma area for each cell is shown in yellow. Area values are normalized to the largest value on the clone. Scale bar indicates 25 μm. (Color figure online)

A statistical summary of cell and process size, as well as nuclear migration features is shown in Fig. 6. Posterior cells have larger soma ($p = 10^{-43}$) and process ($p = 10^{-10}$) areas as compared to anterior cells. Posterior cells also exhibit signficantly different patterns of motion, with lower nuclear velocity ($p = 10^{-10}$) and nuclear migration entropy ($p = 10^{-19}$).

One of the advantages of an analysis that follows the cells across multiple rounds of cell division is the ability to analyze cells based on what mitotic generation they were produced in. Figure 7 shows the nuclear and process area, as well as the nuclear velocity and the entropy of nuclear location all separated

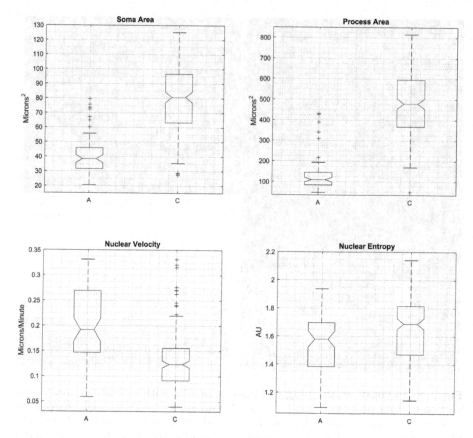

Fig. 3. Summary statistics for type A and type C adult neural progenitor cells. Box plots show median value as red line, blue box extents indicate the 25th−75th percentile of the data, data beyond whiskers are outliers. Notches indicate 95 % confidence interval for the median. Type C cells have larger soma and processes, lower nuclear migration velocity and have increased entropy of nuclear location compared to type A cells. (Color figure online)

by generation. Generation 0 refers to the initially plated NPC, generation 1 are the cells created in the first division, *etc.* Note that anterior and posterior cells exhibit similar patterns of soma and process size, and nuclear migration dynamics (entropy and velocity) across generations. Interestingly, anterior NPCs show a later peak in process and soma area compared to posterior cells. This increase is driven by a small number of anterior clones that are larger, both in the cell and process size, compared even to the generally larger posterior cells.

4   Methods

The cell culture and image acquisition uses the same approaches as described previously [7,8,22]. Following image acquistion, the images are segmented, tracked

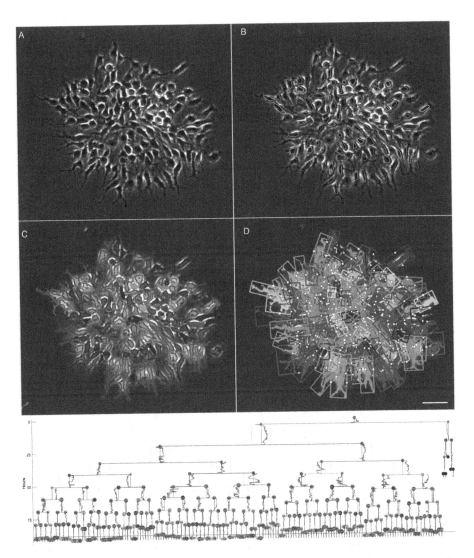

Fig. 4. Cell and process segmentation and tracking with lineage tree for embryonic neural progenitor cell clone. One image from an 1100 frame sequence (A), with LEVER segmentation and tracking results shown as convex hulls colored by track ID (B). After thresholding, processes are assigned to a cell track as indicated by the color (C), with solid tone for the cell segmentation, half tone for the process pixels and unassigned process pixels shown in gray. The centroid of the cell nucleus is projected onto the principal axis of the bounding box enclosing each cell and its processes, shown as a white dot (D). A new rendering combines conventional lineage information with the nuclear location feature (bottom), with the location of the nucleus for each cell along the normalized principal axis of the process bounding box plotted alongside the cell cycle indicator on the tree. Scale bar indicates 50 μm. (Color figure online)

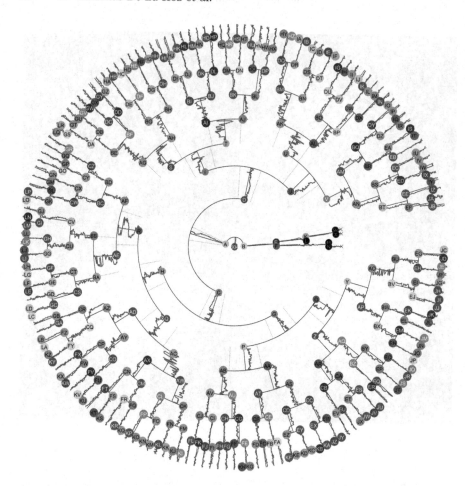

Fig. 5. Radial rendering of the lineage tree with process dynamics. A new visualization for the lineage from Fig. 4 is shown, with time represented by the radius and cells distributed rotationally. Nuclear location along the process principal axis, normalized to [−1,1] is plotted alongside the radial line representing each cell lifespan. This visualization allows features associated with the lineage tree to be more clearly rendered at the distal cells in larger trees.

and lineaged using the LEVER program. LEVER uses separate segmentation algorithms for the adult and embryonic cells. LEVER requires two parameters for each – maximum cell size and maximum velocity. The same parameters were applied to all of the embryonic data and all the adult data.

Validation identifies and corrects errors in the automated algorithms [23]. The LEVER program is designed to make any errors in the segmentation, tracking and lineaging easy to identify and quick to correct [8]. Validation using the LEVER program verifies that tracking assignments and parent-daughter relationships are correct and that every cell has a segmentation in every image frame.

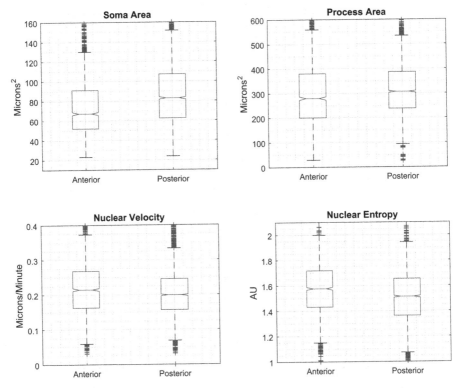

Fig. 6. Summary statistics for anterior and posterior cerebral cortex neural progenitor cells. Box plots show median value as red line, blue box extents indicate the 25th–75th percentile of the data, data beyond whiskers are outliers. Notches indicate 95 % confidence interval for the median. Anterior cells have smaller soma and process areas compared to posterior cells. Anterior cells also exhibit significantly different patterns in the motion of the nucleus along the processes, with increases to both nuclear velocity and to the entropy of the nuclear location.

Validation of the segmentation algorithms at the individual pixels was presented previously using the tracking algorithm and also using externally measured size differences between different cell populations based on flow cytometry [7].

Process segmentation and tracking consists of denoising, followed by thresholding and then assignment. Starting with a two dimensional image I, we invert the image and compute the morphological opening $I_{\mathrm{open}} = \max(\min(I))$ and then construct the denoised image from the white top-hat transform of I,

$$I_{\mathrm{wth}} = I - I_{\mathrm{open}}. \tag{1}$$

A disk shaped kernel with a radius of seven pixels is used for the opening. This removes variations in the phase contrast background across I. This I_{wth} has negative values at the phase contrast halo pixels – the bright artifacts surrounding

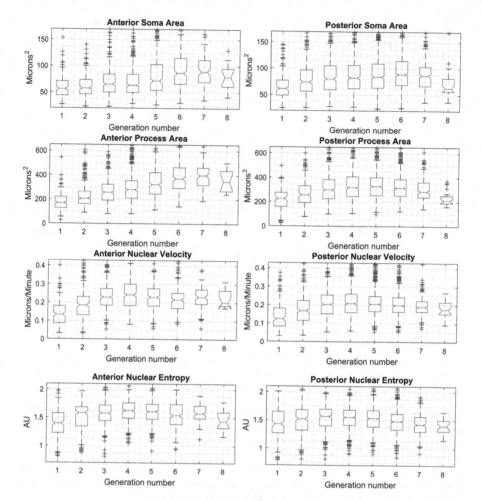

Fig. 7. Summary statistics for anterior and posterior cerebral cortex neural progenitor cells by generation. Cells are initially plated at generation zero, with each mitotic event producing a subsequent generation. Box plots show median value as red line, blue box extents indicate the 25th–75th percentile of the data, data beyond whiskers are outliers. Notches indicate 95 % confidence interval for the median. Anterior cells and clones are generally smaller compared to posterior cells and clones. A small subset of anterior clones contributes to a late and significant increase in cell and process size. (Color figure online)

thick regions associated with the cell body, and postive values interior to the cells and processes. Negative values are removed,

$$I_{\text{denoise}} = \max(I_{\text{wth}}, 0), \tag{2}$$

and the intensities are normalized to [0,1] forming the denoised image.

A dual-thresholding approach reduces the amount of background debris detected as process pixels (false positives). This uses the Otsu transform, T_{Otsu}, weighted by $[\alpha_L, \alpha_H] = [0.3, 0.6]$,

$$BW_1 = I_{\text{wth}} > \alpha_H * T_{\text{Otsu}}. \tag{3}$$

Any connected components with area smaller than ten pixels are removed from this image, and then a morphological reconstruction uses this first thresholded image to identify high-intensity regions in I_{denoise},

$$I_{\text{final}} = \text{reconstruct}(BW_1, I_{\text{denoise}}). \tag{4}$$

Finally, the second threshold is applied to form the final thresholded image,

$$BW_{\text{final}} = I_{\text{final}} > \alpha_L * T_{\text{Otsu}}. \tag{5}$$

Following thresholding, each pixel is assigned the tracking ID as the nearest nuclear segmentation using a geodesic distance across BW_{final}.

Once all foreground pixels from BW_{final} have been assigned a tracking ID from the nearest segmentation result, the process bounding box is computed from the process pixel locations for track ID i, $(x, y)_i$. The process pixels are centered, subtracting the mean value of the process pixel location,

$$(x, y) = (x, y)_i - \text{mean}(x, y)_i. \tag{6}$$

The bounding box is computed using the singular value decomposition (SVD) of the spatial locations of the process pixels,

$$\text{SVD}(x, y) = USV, \tag{7}$$

where the vectors V form an orthonormal basis that gives the principal axis directions for the process pixels [24]. The process pixels are projected into the V coordinate system, $(x', y') = (x, y) * V$. The bounding box in the orthogonal space is computed $[x'_{\text{min}}, x'_{\text{max}}, y'_{\text{min}}, y'_{\text{max}}]$ and projected to the original space,

$$[x_{\text{min}}, y_{\text{min}}; x_{\text{max}}, y_{\text{max}}] = [x'_{\text{min}}, y'_{\text{min}}; x'_{\text{max}}, y'_{\text{max}}] * V^{-1} + \text{mean}(x, y)_i. \tag{8}$$

The projection of the nuclear centroid on the first coordinate in the V space, or the principal axis, is used as the nuclear location feature for velocity and entropy calculations. For entropy calculations, the principal axis is divided into ten bins.

Finally, all statistical tests were done with the non-parametric Wilcoxon Rank-Sum test for difference of medians [25].

5   Open Source Software and Data Availability

The LEVER program is available under the GNU Public License (GPL v2 or later). Details on obtaining source code or compiled executables are available from http://n2t.net/ark:/87918/d9rp4t. All of the image analysis results described here, together with the image data, are available interactively on the CloneView website: http://n2t.net/ark:/87918/d9wc73.

6   Conclusions

This paper describes new a new segmentation and tracking approach for NPC processes. One key challenge is to reject debris including dead cells while still capturing fine processes in cluttered images. New visualization techniques for the lineage tree enhance the ability to show nuclear and process dynamics for entire clones. Analyzing hundreds of clones found previously unknown significant differences in nuclear and process dynamics among functionally different populations of NPCs.

Acknowledgments. Portions of this research were supported by the NIH NINDS (R01NS076709), and by the NIH NIA (R01AG041861).

References

1. Ayala, R., Shu, T., Tsai, L.: Trekking across the brain: the journey of neuronal migration. Cell **128**(1), 29–43 (2007)
2. Strzyz, P.J., Lee, H.O., Sidhaye, J., Weber, I.P., Leung, L.C., Norden, C.: Interkinetic nuclear migration is centrosome independent and ensures apical cell division to maintain tissue integrity. Dev. Cell **32**(2), 203–219 (2015)
3. Kosodo, Y.: Interkinetic nuclear migration: beyond a hallmark of neurogenesis. Cell. Mol. Life Sci. **69**(16), 2727–2738 (2012)
4. Baye, L.M., Link, B.A.: Interkinetic nuclear migration and the selection of neurogenic cell divisions during vertebrate retinogenesis. J. Neurosci. **27**(38), 10143–10152 (2007)
5. Meyer, E.J., Ikmi, A., Gibson, C.M.: Interkinetic nuclear migration is a broadly conserved feature of cell division in pseudostratified epithelia. Curr. Biol. **21**(6), 485–491 (2011)
6. Spear, C.P., Erickson, C.A.: Interkinetic nuclear migration: a mysterious process in search of a function. Dev. Growth Differ. **54**(3), 306–316 (2012)
7. Winter, M., Liu, M., Monteleone, D., Melunis, J., Hershberg, U., Goderie, S., Temple, S., Cohen, X.R.: Computational image analysis reveals intrinsic multigenerational differences between anterior and posterior cerebral cortex neural progenitor cells. Stem Cell Rep. **5**(4), 609–620 (2015)
8. Winter, M., Wait, E., Roysam, B., Goderie, S., Kokovay, E., Temple, S., Cohen, A.R.: Vertebrate neural stem cell segmentation, tracking and lineaging with validation and editing. Nat. Protoc. **6**(12), 1942–1952 (2011)
9. Mankowski, W.C., Winter, M.R., Wait, E., Lodder, M., Schumacher, T., Naik, S.H., Cohen, A.R.: Segmentation of occluded hematopoietic stem cells from tracking. In: Conference Proceedings of IEEE Engineering in Medicine and Biology Society, pp. 5510–5513 (2014)
10. Mankowski, W.C., Konica, G., Winter, M.R., Chen, F., Maus, C., Merkle, R., Klingmüller, U., Höfer, T., Kan, A., Heinzel, S., Oostindie, S., Hodgkin, P., Cohen, A.R.: Multi-modal segmentation for quantifying fluorescent cell cycle indicators throughout clonal development. In: Bioimage Informatics Conference (2015)
11. Wait, E., Winter, M., Bjornsson, C., Kokovay, E., Wang, Y., Goderie, S., Temple, S., Cohen, A.R.: Visualization and correction of automated segmentation, tracking and lineaging from 5-d stem cell image sequences. BMC Bioinf. **15**(1), 328 (2014)

12. Cohen, A.R., Gomes, F., Roysam, B., Cayouette, M.: Computational prediction of neural progenitor cell fates. Nat. Meth. **7**(3), 213–218 (2010)
13. Al-Kofahi, O., Radke, R.J., Roysam, B., Banker, G.: Automated semantic analysis of changes in image sequences of neurons in culture. IEEE Trans. Biomed. Eng. **53**(6), 1109–1123 (2006)
14. Meijering, E.: Neuron tracing in perspective. Cytometry Part A **77A**(7), 693–704 (2010)
15. Al-Kofahi, O., Radke, R.J., Goderie, S.K., Shen, Q., Temple, S., Roysam, B.: Automated cell lineage tracing: a high-throughput method to analyze cell proliferative behavior developed using mouse neural stem cells. Cell Cycle **5**(3), 327–335 (2006)
16. Li, K., Miller, E.D., Weiss, L.E., Campbell, P.G., Kanade, T.: Online tracking of migrating and proliferating cells imaged with phase-contrast microscopy. In: 2006 Conference on Computer Vision and Pattern Recognition Workshop, p. 65 (2006)
17. Li, K., Miller, E.D., Chen, M., Kanade, T., Weiss, L.E., Campbell, P.G.: Cell population tracking and lineage construction with spatiotemporal context. Med. Image Anal. **12**(008), 546–566 (2008)
18. Amat, F., Lemon, W., Mossing, D.P., McDole, K., Wan, Y., Branson, K., Myers, E.W., Keller, P.J.: Fast, accurate reconstruction of cell lineages from large-scale fluorescence microscopy data. Nat. Meth. **11**(9), 951–958 (2014)
19. Bray, M., Carpenter, A.E.: Cellprofiler tracer: exploring and validating high-throughput, time-lapse microscopy image data. BMC Bioinf. **16**(1), 1–7 (2015)
20. Winter, M.R., Fang, C., Banker, G., Roysam, B., Cohen, A.R.: Axonal transport analysis using multitemporal association tracking. Int. J. Comput. Biol. Drug Des. **5**(1), 35–48 (2012)
21. Chenouard, N., Smal, I., de Chaumont, F., Maska, M., Sbalzarini, I.F., Gong, Y., Cardinale, J., Carthel, C., Coraluppi, S., Winter, M., Cohen, A.R., Godinez, W.J., Rohr, K., Kalaidzidis, Y., Liang, L., Duncan, J., Shen, H., Xu, Y., Magnusson, K.E., Jalden, J., Blau, H.M., Paul-Gilloteaux, P., Roudot, P., Kervrann, C., Waharte, F., Tinevez, J.Y., Shorte, S.L., Willemse, J., Celler, K., van Wezel, G.P., Dan, H.W., Tsai, Y.S., de Solorzano, C.O., Olivo-Marin, J.C., Meijering, E.: Objective comparison of particle tracking methods. Nat. Meth. **11**(3), 281–289 (2014)
22. Kokovay, E., Wang, Y., Kusek, G., Wurster, R., Lederman, P., Lowry, N., Shen, Q., Temple, S.: Vcam1 is essential to maintain the structure of the svz niche and acts as an environmental sensor to regulate svz lineage progression. Cell Stem Cell **11**(2), 220–230 (2012)
23. Cohen, A.R., Bjornsson, C., Temple, S., Banker, G., Roysam, B.: Automatic summarization of changes in biological image sequences using algorithmic information theory. IEEE Trans. Pattern Anal. Mach. Intell. **31**(8), 1386–1403 (2009)
24. Theodoridis, S., Koutroumbas, K.: Pattern Recognition, 4th edn. Academic Press, San Diego (2009)
25. Bain, L.J., Engelhardt, M.: Introduction to Probability and Mathematical Statistics. Duxbury, Boston (1992)

Histopathology Image Categorization with Discriminative Dimension Reduction of Fisher Vectors

Yang Song[1](✉), Qing Li[1], Heng Huang[2], Dagan Feng[1], Mei Chen[3,4], and Weidong Cai[1]

[1] BMIT Research Group, School of IT, University of Sydney, Sydney, Australia
yang.song@sydney.edu.au
[2] Department of Computer Science and Engineering,
University of Texas, Arlington, USA
[3] Computer Engineering Department,
State University of New York at Albany, Albany, USA
[4] Robotics Institute, Carnegie Mellon University, Pittsburgh, USA

Abstract. In this paper, we present a histopathology image categorization method based on Fisher vector descriptors. While Fisher vector has been broadly successful for general computer vision and recently applied to microscopy image analysis, its feature dimension is very high and this could affect the classification performance especially when there is small amount of training images available. To address this issue, we design a dimension reduction algorithm in a discriminative learning model with similarity and representation constraints. In addition, to obtain the image-level Fisher vectors, we incorporate two types of local descriptors based on the standard texture feature and unsupervised feature learning. We use three publicly available datasets for experiments. Our evaluation shows that our overall approach achieves consistent performance improvement over existing approaches, our proposed discriminative dimension reduction algorithm outperforms the common dimension reduction techniques, and different local descriptors have varying effects on different datasets.

1 Introduction

Tissue examination using histopathology images is regularly performed in the clinical routine for cancer diagnosis and treatment. Computerized histopathology image classification supports automated categorization of cancer status (benign or malignant) or subtypes, where manual analysis can be subjective and error-prone due to the complex visual characteristics of histopathology images. The majority of existing studies in this area have focused on image feature representation. For example, custom feature descriptors have been designed based on structures of cells or regions [3,11,14]. Other approaches propose to use automated feature learning techniques such as convolutional sparse coding [16], dictionary learning [12], and deconvolution network [2].

© Springer International Publishing Switzerland 2016
G. Hua and H. Jégou (Eds.): ECCV 2016 Workshops, Part I, LNCS 9913, pp. 306–317, 2016.
DOI: 10.1007/978-3-319-46604-0_22

As a less studied feature representation for biomedical imaging, Fisher vector (FV) [7] has recently been applied to microscopy image analysis [2,14]. FV is a feature encoding algorithm that aggregates a dense set of locally extracted features, such as dense scale-invariant feature transform (DSIFT) descriptors, based on the Gaussian mixture model (GMM) to form a high-dimensional image-level descriptor. Classification of FV descriptors is then performed using the linear-kernel support vector machine (SVM). This approach has shown excellent performance in many general imaging applications such as face recognition, texture classification, and object detection.

On the other hand, due to the high dimensionality, the classification performance using FV descriptors could be affected if there are insufficient training data to represent the complex visual characteristics of the problem domain. This issue would be especially important for histopathology image studies, due to the cost of preparing training data. While it could be intuitive to apply standard dimension reduction techniques such as principal component analysis (PCA), it has been shown that with FV descriptors, discriminative dimension reduction is more effective for face recognition [10]. However, we are not aware of existing studies on the design of suitable dimension reduction algorithms for FV descriptors of histopathology images.

In this work, we propose an automated method to categorize histopathology images. Our algorithm contributions are two-fold. First, we design two FV descriptors to represent the histopathology images, based on the local DSIFT features and patch-level features that are learned using a deep belief network (DBN) [4] model, respectively. Second, to address the issue of small training data, we design a discriminative dimension reduction method to reduce the feature dimension and enhance the discriminative power of FV descriptors. Our design is inspired by [10], but we find direct application of this method reduces the classification performance on some datasets. We thus further improve the model [10] by devising a classification score-based training set selection technique and introducing an additional representation constraint into the optimization objective. For evaluation, three public histopathology image datasets (Fig. 1) are used. We demonstrate better categorization performance compared to other feature representation and dimension reduction techniques.

2   Methods

2.1   Fisher Vector Descriptors

FV is analogous to the bag-of-words (BOW) encoding that it encodes a dense set of local descriptors into an image-level descriptor. The encoding works by first generating a GMM from all local descriptors. Based on the soft assignments of local descriptors to the Gaussian modes, the first and second-order difference vectors between the local descriptors and each of the Gaussian centers are computed. The FV descriptor is then the concatenation of all difference vectors. Assume that the local descriptor is d dimensional and k Gaussian modes are used. The resultant FV descriptor is $2dk$ dimensional.

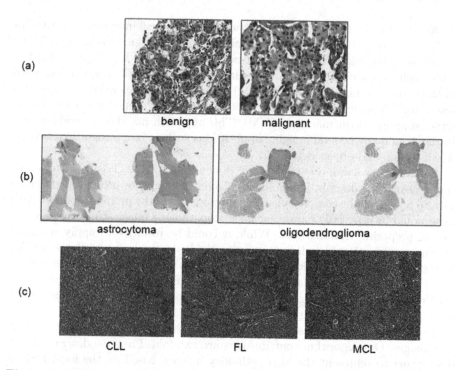

(a)

benign   malignant

(b)

astrocytoma   oligodendroglioma

(c)

CLL   FL   MCL

Fig. 1. Example images of three datasets: (a) UCSB breast cancer dataset, (b) MICCAI 2015 CBTC challenge training set, and (c) IICBU 2008 malignant lymphoma dataset. Each image represents one image category.

The local descriptors can be any patch-level features. In this study, we use two types of local descriptors. (1) Following the standard FV computation, DSIFT descriptors are extracted at multiple scales with spatial bins of 4, 6, 8, 10 and 12 pixels and sampled every two pixels. (2) Unsupervised feature learning using DBN is performed on half-overlapping patches of 8×8 pixels. The network comprises two layers with each layer producing 64 features. The patch-level local descriptor is the concatenation of features from the two layers. The use of unsupervised feature learning is inspired by existing work [2,6], which shows that unsupervised feature learning is highly effective and can be more representative than supervised feature learning for microscopy images. We have also evaluated DBN with other numbers of layers and nodes, using only the features from the last layer, or generating local descriptors at multiple scales. The proposed structure is found to provide the best results.

For each type of local descriptor, we set a common feature dimension of 128 to make the different local descriptors directly comparable. PCA is then used to reduce the local descriptor dimension to 64, and based on which, GMM of 64 modes is generated. The image-level FV descriptor is consistently $d = 2 \times 64 \times 64$ dimensional for each of the two types of local descriptors.

2.2   Discriminative Dimension Reduction

We design a discriminative learning-based dimension reduction algorithm, which helps to enhance the discriminative power of the FV descriptor. Formally, given a training set of n images $\{I_i : i = 1, \ldots, n\}$, the FV descriptor (regardless of the local descriptor type) of image I_i is denoted as f_i with category label y_i. The objective is to learn a linear projection matrix $W \in \mathbb{R}^{h \times d}$ with $h \ll d$ indicating the reduced dimension. The descriptor f_i is then transformed to $W f_i$, which is expected to meet the similarity and representation constraints. The dimension-reduced descriptors are finally used to train a linear-kernel SVM to categorize the histopathology images. The overall method flow is illustrated in Fig. 2.

Similarity constraint. This constraint specifies that after dimension reduction, descriptors of the same class should be similar and descriptors of different classes should be dissimilar. As a result, such descriptors would be more easily classified

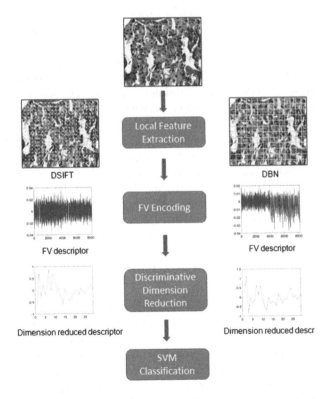

Fig. 2. Illustration of our method design. To categorize an image, the local DSIFT or patch-wise DBN features are first extracted then encoded as FV descriptors. These descriptors are then dimension reduced using our discriminative dimension reduction method, and finally classified using linear-kernel SVM. Unsupervised learning is involved in DBN feature extraction and FV encoding, and supervised learning is used in discriminative dimension reduction and SVM classification.

compared to the original FV descriptors. We formulate this constraint based on the Euclidean distance between pairs of descriptors:

$$\|Wf_i - Wf_j\|_2^2 < b, \ \forall y_i = y_j; \quad \|Wf_i - Wf_j\|_2^2 > b, \ \forall y_i \neq y_j; \qquad (1)$$

where i and j index the n training data, and b is a learned threshold. By imposing a margin of at least one, the constraint is rewritten as:

$$\theta_{ij}(b - \|Wf_i - Wf_j\|_2^2) > 1 \qquad (2)$$

where θ_{ij} is 1 if $y_i = y_j$, and -1 otherwise. This is equivalent to the following learning objective:

$$\operatorname*{argmin}_{W,b} \sum_{i,j} \max[1 - \theta_{ij}(b - (f_i - f_j)^T W^T W(f_i - f_j)), 0] \qquad (3)$$

An iterative optimization process can be used to update W and b by incorporating one pair of descriptors at each iteration [10].

An important issue of this learning process is the selection of descriptor pairs f_i and f_j. If all possible pairs of training data are enumerated, there would be a large number of descriptor pairs imposing contradicting optimization goals hence affecting the effectiveness of the learned matrix. To overcome this issue, we design a classification score-based training data selection approach. Specifically, our idea is that for each f_i, we select positive f_j (i.e. $\theta_{ij} = 1$) that has high classification score of class y_j, and negative f_j (i.e. $\theta_{ij} = -1$) that has low classification score of class y_j. The positive f_j represents the good data that f_i should move towards, and the negative f_j represents the hard examples that f_i should move further from. The classification score is the probability estimate from a linear-kernel SVM trained using all the training data. The scores of all training data from one class are then sorted and the score at the pth percentile is chosen as the threshold. The positive (or negative) f_j having a score above (or below) this threshold is selected to form a training pair with f_i. In addition, we further reduce the number of descriptor pairs by restricting that only images with classification scores lower than the threshold are used as f_i, so that training will focus on hard examples.

Representation constraint. While the similarity constraint measures the pairwise similarity between descriptors, the representation constraint evaluates the representativeness of the descriptor by the overall class space. In the lower dimensional space, we expect the descriptor f_i to be well represented by the correct class only. Specifically, assume that there are n_j descriptors from class j, and the descriptor set is denoted as $R_j \in \mathbb{R}^{d \times n_j}$ (note for simplicity j is now used to index the classes). The representation of f_i by class j, defined as $\mu_{i,j}$, is computed as the sparse reconstruction from R_j, $\mu_{i,j} = R_j c_{i,j}$. Here $c_{i,j} \in \mathbb{R}^{n_j}$ is a weight vector with q nonzero elements and is derived analytically using locality-constrained linear coding (LLC) [13]:

$$\min_{c_{i,j}} \|f_i - R_j c_{i,j}\|^2 + \lambda \|v_{i,j} \odot c_{i,j}\|^2 \quad s.t. \mathbf{1}^T c_{i,j} = 1, \ \|c_{i,j}\|_0 = q \qquad (4)$$

where $v_{i,j} \in \mathbb{R}^{n_j}$ contains the Euclidean distances between f_i and each descriptor in R_j, and the constant $\lambda = 0.01$. Note that f_i is excluded from R_j if $y_i = j$.

The representation constraint is then defined in a similar construct to the similarity constraint, but replacing the distance between pairs of descriptors by distance between the descriptor and its reconstructions. Formally, this constraint is formulated as:

$$\theta_{ij}(b - \|Wf_i - W\mu_{i,j}\|_2^2) > 1 \tag{5}$$

where $\theta_{ij} = 1$ if $y_i = j$, and otherwise $\theta_{ij} = -1$. The learning objective is thus:

$$\operatorname*{argmin}_{W,b} \sum_{i,j} \max[1 - \theta_{ij}(b - (f_i - \mu_{i,j})^T W^T W(f_i - \mu_{i,j})), 0] \tag{6}$$

Note that we can set multiple q values $q = \{q_1, q_2, \ldots\}$, so that for f_i and each class j, we obtain multiple representations $\{\mu_{i,j} : q = q_1, q_2, \ldots\}$ and expect each of the representation to satisfy Eq. (5). In this way, we increase the number of training pairs for the representation constraint.

Algorithm 1. Discriminative Dimension Reduction

Data: Training data $\{f_1, y_1\}, \ldots, \{f_n, y_n\}$.

Result: Linear projection matrix W.

Train a linear kernel SVM on the training data;

Based on the classification scores of the training data, create a set of training pairs $\{(f_i, f_j), i \in \{1, \ldots, n\}, j \in \{1, \ldots, n\}\}$;

Initialize W using PCA on the training data;

Initialize b as the threshold that can satisfy $\theta_{ij}(b - \|Wf_i - Wf_j\|_2^2) > 1$ for most training pairs;

repeat

    for *each training pair* (f_i, f_j) **do**

        if $\theta_{ij}(b - \|Wf_i - Wf_j\|_2^2) \leq 1$ **then**

            $\Delta_{ij} = (f_i - f_j)(f_i - f_j)^T$;

            $W_{t+1} = W_t - \gamma\theta_{ij}W_t\Delta_{ij}, \quad b = b + \alpha\theta_{ij}$;

        end

    end

    for *each training data* f_i, *class* j, *and parameter* q **do**

        $\min_{c_{i,j}} \|f_i - R_j c_{i,j}\|^2 + \lambda\|v_{i,j} \odot c_{i,j}\|^2 \quad s.t. \mathbf{1}^T c_{i,j} = 1, \|c_{i,j}\|_0 = q$;

        $\mu_{i,j} = R_j c_{i,j}$;

        if $\theta_{ij}(b - \|Wf_i - W\mu_{i,j}\|_2^2) \leq 1$ **then**

            $\Delta_{ij} = (f_i - \mu_{i,j})(f_i - \mu_{i,j})^T$;

            $W_{t+1} = W_t - \gamma\theta_{ij}W_t\Delta_{ij}, \quad b = b + \alpha\theta_{ij}$;

        end

    end

until *convergence or maximum number of iterations is reached*;

Combined optimization. W is first initialized using PCA on the training data. Then, W and b are learned using a stochastic sub-gradient method combining

Table 1. Classification accuracy (%) comparing feature representations.

	UCSB	CBTC	IICBU
DSIFT-BOW	47.9	53.1	73.8
DBN-BOW	44.5	43.8	70.9
DSIFT-FV	87.8	50.0	90.9
DBN-FV	86.2	65.6	90.1
DSIFT-FV-DDR (proposed)	**89.7**	56.3	**93.3**
DBN-FV-DDR (proposed)	**89.7**	**75.0**	91.2

Eqs. (3) and (6). First, at each iteration t, the algorithm takes a descriptor pair f_i and f_j. If Eq. (2) is not met, W and b are updated by:

$$W_{t+1} = W_t - \gamma\theta_{ij}W_t\Delta_{ij}, \quad b = b + \alpha\theta_{ij} \tag{7}$$

where $\Delta_{ij} = (f_i - f_j)(f_i - f_j)^T$, γ and α are constant learning rates and default to 0.25 and 1. After the selected descriptor pairs are enumerated, the training pair f_i and $\mu_{i,j}$ is used at each iteration to update W and b using Eq. (7) with $\Delta_{ij} = (f_i - \mu_{i,j})(f_i - \mu_{i,j})^T$. The iteration continues until convergence or maximum number of iterations is reached. The overall discriminative dimension reduction method is summarized in Algorithm 1.

With the derived linear projection matrix W, a descriptor f_i is dimension reduced to Wf_i. SVM training and classification are then performed on these lower dimensional descriptors to obtain the image category. Our empirical analysis shows that a linear-kernel SVM is more effective than the polynomial and radial basis function (RBF) kernels.

2.3   Datasets and Implementation

We use three public histopathology image datasets: (1) UCSB breast cancer dataset of 58 hematoxylin and eosin (H&E) stained tissue microarray (TMA) images, including 32 benign (B) and 26 malignant (M) cases; (2) MICCAI 2015 CBTC challenge training set, containing 32 whole-slide images of brain tumors with $40\times$ apparent magnification, out of which 16 are astrocytoma (A) and 16 are oligodendroglioma (O); and (3) IICBU 2008 malignant lymphoma dataset of 374 H&E stained image sections from brightfield microscopy, including 113 chronic lymphocytic leukemia (CLL), 139 follicular lymphoma (FL), and 122 mantle cell lymphoma (MCL) cases. The first two datasets represent problems with small numbers of training data, and the third dataset demonstrates multiclass categorization. Example images are shown in Fig. 1.

For all datasets, we employ four-fold cross validation with three parts of the data for training and one part for testing, following the same protocol used in existing studies for the UCSB breast cancer dataset [3,5]. For the first two datasets, we set h (the reduced feature dimension) to half of the number of

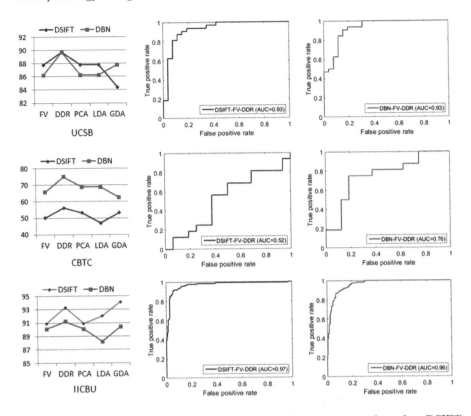

Fig. 3. Classification results comparing dimension reduction approaches when DSIFT or DBN is used as the local descriptor. The left column shows the classification accuracies (%). The middle and right columns show the ROC curves and AUCs using our approaches DSIFT-FV-DDR and DBN-FV-DDR.

images and p (the pth percentile of classification score) to 80. For the third dataset, due to the relatively large number of images, h is set to a quarter of the number of images, and p is set to 60. For the representation constraint, we set q to 3 and 5 for all datasets. These parameter settings are determined using 10-fold cross validation within the training set.

3   Experimental Results

We first evaluate the effect of different local descriptors (DSIFT, DBN) and feature encoding algorithms (BOW, FV), and our proposed method. Table 1 shows that in general FV encoding outperformed the BOW encoding by a large extent. DBN-FV is particularly effective for the CBTC dataset while DSIFT-FV is more descriptive for the other two datasets. With our proposed discriminative dimension reduction (DDR), we achieve the best performance for all three datasets. DBN-FV-DDR is more effective for the CBTC dataset while DSIFT-FV-DDR

Table 2. AUCs on the UCSB breast cancer dataset compared to existing studies.

DSIFT-FV-DDR	DBN-FV-DDR	[3]	[5]	[9]
0.93	0.93	0.92	0.93	0.95

Table 3. Classification accuracies (%) on the IICBU 2008 lymphoma dataset compared to existing studies.

DSIFT-FV-DDR	DBN-FV-DDR	[8]	[15]
93.3	91.2	85	70.9

is more effective for the IICBU dataset. Overall, the results suggest that FV can provide more discriminative power than BOW, but the choice of local descriptors (DSIFT or DBN) needs to be evaluated for different datasets.

Figure 3 shows the results using the original FV descriptor (no dimension reduction), our proposed discriminative dimension reduction (DDR) algorithm, and the other popular dimension reduction techniques: PCA (unsupervised), linear discriminative analysis (LDA) and generalized discriminative analysis (GDA) [1] (supervised). It can be seen that PCA is useful for the CBTC dataset only. While GDA with DSIFT local descriptors performs the best for the IICBU dataset, the performance using GDA fluctuates largely for different datasets and local descriptors. Our DDR method provides more consistent advantage.

The receiver operating characteristic (ROC) curves using our methods are shown in Fig. 3 as well. For the UCSB dataset, although the DSIFT-FV-DDR and DBN-FV-DDR methods produced the same classification accuracy (89.7 %) and AUC (0.93), differences exist in the ROC curves. It can be seen that to obtain 100 % true positive rate, DBN-FV-DDR outputs a lower false positive rate; and with 0 % false positive rate, DBN-FV-DDR gives a higher true positive rate, when compared to SIFT-FV-DDR. Similar performance differences are observed for the other two datasets as well. This indicates the overall advantage of using DBN as the local descriptors over DSIFT.

Table 2 lists the AUCs of our methods and those reported in the existing studies [3,5,9] for the UCSB dataset. The existing methods are based on multiple instance learning (MIL) models and a combination of texture and morphological features. Our method can be considered as related to MIL that only image-level label is available; however, in our method, local descriptors are combined using FV encoding and classification is performed at the image-level only. The results show that while the advanced MIL method with joint clustering and classification [9] is more effective, our method performs better than or comparably to the other approaches [3,5]. We suggest that our method can be a viable and conceptually simpler alternative to the MIL models.

Table 3 lists the classification accuracies of methods and those reported in the literature [8,15] for the IICBU dataset. The approach [8] is standard benchmark for the IICBU dataset, and performs image classification by extracting texture and shape features and then using a variation of kNN classification. The more recent approach [15] provides another open platform for the microscopy image classification task with a different set of features and SVM classification. Our results show large improvement over these approaches. We note that for the CBTC dataset, to the best of our knowledge, there is no available benchmark for performance comparison.

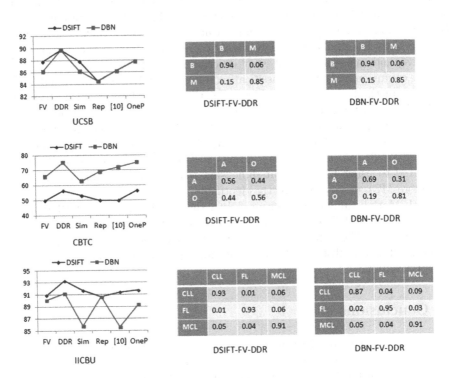

Fig. 4. Classification accuracy (%) comparing our DDR method with several variations (Sim, Rep, and OneP) when DSIFT or DBN is used as the local descriptor. Results using FV (without dimension reduction) or [10] are also included. Confusion matrices of classification using our methods are shown as well.

The effects of individual components in our DDR method are evaluated by comparing the following approaches: (1) Sim: only the similarity constraint is used for discriminative dimension reduction; (2) Rep: only the representation constraint is used; and (3) OneP: a single p value ($p = 3$) is used when constructing the representation constraint. We also compare with the original discriminative dimension reduction algorithm [10], which is equivalent to using only the similarity constraint but without the classification score-based training data selection, i.e. all possible positive and negative pairs are used in training. As shown in Fig. 4, when DSIFT is used as the local descriptor, Sim provides some performance improvement over FV; but when DBN is used as the local descriptor, Rep is more effective than Sim. Combining Sim and Rep (i.e. DDR) gives the best classification. The performance difference between Sim and [10] illustrates the usefulness of having training data selection. It can be seen that Sim outperforms [10] in most cases except when DBN is used as the local descriptor on the CBTC dataset. We suggest that this is because the CBTC dataset contains a small number of images, and including all possible training data is helpful to better exploit the feature space characteristics. The overall advantage of our DDR method over the compared approaches demonstrates that it is essential to have both the similarity and representation constraints in the optimization objective, and to use only a subset of descriptor pairs for training.

The confusion matrices of classification using our DSIFT-FV-DDR and DBN-FV-DDR methods are shown in Fig. 4. For the CBTC dataset, with DBN-FV-DDR, there is a tendency that more images are classified as oligodendroglioma than astrocytoma, hence resulting in a high recall (81 %) but low precision rate (72 %) of oligodendroglioma. For the IICBU dataset, DSIFT-FV-DDR generates more balanced results among the various classes compared to DBN-FV-DDR. Compared to using FV (without dimension reduction), the main difference is that more MCL cases are correctly identified.

With Matlab implementation on a PC, the training process of DDR needs about 3.8 s on the UCSB dataset, 1.8 s on the CBTC dataset, and 36.4 s on the IICBU dataset. The different sizes of datasets affect the size and complexity of training data, and subsequently affect the number of iterations and time required for optimization.

4   Conclusions

We present a histopathology image categorization method in this paper. Our method comprises two major components: FV encoding of local descriptors that are computed using DSIFT or based on unsupervised learning with DBN; and discriminative dimension reduction of FV descriptors with similarity and representation constraints. Our method is evaluated on three public datasets of breast cancer, brain tumor and malignant lymphoma images, and we show better performance in comparison with some existing approaches and other feature representation and dimension reduction techniques.

References

1. Baudat, G., Anouar, F.: Generalized discriminant analysis using a kernel approach. Neural Comput. 12(10), 2385–2404 (2000)
2. BenTaieb, A., Li-Chang, H., Huntsman, D., Hamarneh, G.: Automatic diagnosis of ovarian carcinomas via sparse multiresolution tissue representation. In: Navab, N., Hornegger, J., Wells, W.M., Frangi, A.F. (eds.) MICCAI 2015. LNCS, vol. 9349, pp. 629–636. Springer, Heidelberg (2015). doi:10.1007/978-3-319-24553-9_77

3. Kandemir, M., Zhang, C., Hamprecht, F.A.: Empowering multiple instance histopathology cancer diagnosis by cell graphs. In: Golland, P., Hata, N., Barillot, C., Hornegger, J., Howe, R. (eds.) MICCAI 2014, Part II. LNCS, vol. 8674, pp. 228–235. Springer, Heidelberg (2014). doi:10.1007/978-3-319-10470-6_29

4. Keyvanrad, M.A., Homayounpour, M.M.: A brief survey on deep belief networks and introducing a new object oriented toolbox (DeeBNet) arXiv:1408.3264 (2014)

5. Li, W., Zhang, J., McKenna, S.J.: Multiple instance cancer detection by boosting regularised trees. In: Navab, N., Hornegger, J., Wells, W.M., Frangi, A.F. (eds.) MICCAI 2015. LNCS, vol. 9349, pp. 645–652. Springer, Heidelberg (2015). doi:10.1007/978-3-319-24553-9_79

6. Otálora, S., et al.: Combining unsupervised feature learning and riesz wavelets for histopathology image representation: application to identifying anaplastic medulloblastoma. In: Navab, N., Hornegger, J., Wells, W.M., Frangi, A.F. (eds.) MICCAI 2015. LNCS, vol. 9349, pp. 581–588. Springer, Heidelberg (2015). doi:10.1007/978-3-319-24553-9_71

7. Perronnin, F., Sánchez, J., Mensink, T.: Improving the Fisher kernel for large-scale image classification. In: Daniilidis, K., Maragos, P., Paragios, N. (eds.) ECCV 2010, Part IV. LNCS, vol. 6314, pp. 143–156. Springer, Heidelberg (2010). doi:10.1007/978-3-642-15561-1_11

8. Shamir, L., Orlov, N., Eckley, D.M., Macura, T.J., Johnston, J., Goldberg, I.G.: Wndchrm - an open source utility for biological image analysis. Source Code Biol. Med. 3(1), 13 (2008)

9. Sikka, K., Giri, R., Bartlett, M.: Joint clustering and classification for multiple instance learning. In: BMVC, pp. 1–12 (2015)

10. Simonyan, K., Parkhi, O.M., Vedaldi, A., Zisserman, A.: Fisher vector faces in the wild. In: BMVC, pp. 1–12 (2013)

11. Sparks, R., Madabhushi, A.: Explicit shape descriptors: novel morphologic features for histopathology classification. Med. Image Anal. 17(1), 997–1009 (2013)

12. Vu, T.H., Mousavi, H.S., Monga, V., Rao, G., Rao, A.: Histopathological image classification using discriminative feature-oriented dictionary learning. IEEE Trans. Med. Imag. 35(3), 738–751 (2016)

13. Wang, J., Yang, J., Yu, K., Lv, F., Huang, T., Gong, Y.: Locality-constrained linear coding for image classification. In: CVPR, pp. 3360–3367 (2010)

14. Xu, X., Lin, F., Ng, C., Leong, K.P.: Adaptive co-occurrence differential texton space for HEp-2 cells classification. In: Navab, N., Hornegger, J., Wells, W.M., Frangi, A.F. (eds.) MICCAI 2015. LNCS, vol. 9351, pp. 260–267. Springer, Heidelberg (2015). doi:10.1007/978-3-319-24574-4_31

15. Zhou, J., Lamichhane, S., Sterne, G., Ye, B., Peng, H.: BIOCAT: a pattern recognition platform for customizable biological image classification and annotation. BMC Bioinformatics 14, 291 (2013)

16. Zhou, Y., Chang, H., Barner, K., Spellman, P., Parvin, B.: Classification of histology sections via multispectral convolutional sparse coding. In: CVPR, pp. 3081–3088 (2014)

Automatic Detection and Segmentation of Exosomes in Transmission Electron Microscopy

Karel Štěpka[1], Martin Maška[1], Jakub Jozef Pálenik[1], Vendula Pospíchalová[2],
Anna Kotrbová[2], Ladislav Ilkovics[3], Dobromila Klemová[3], Aleš Hampl[3],
Vítězslav Bryja[2], and Pavel Matula[1(✉)]

[1] Faculty of Informatics, Centre for Biomedical Image Analysis,
Masaryk University, 602 00 Brno, Czech Republic
pam@fi.muni.cz
[2] Department of Experimental Biology, Masaryk University,
602 00 Brno, Czech Republic
[3] Department of Histology and Embryology, Masaryk University,
602 00 Brno, Czech Republic

Abstract. Exosomes are nanosized, cell-derived vesicles that appear
in different biological fluids. They attract a growing interest of the
researcher community due to their important role in intercellular communication. An easy to use and reliable method for their quantification
and characterization at the single-vesicle level is tremendously needed
to help evaluating exosomal preparations in research as well as clinical studies. In this paper, we present a morphological method for automatic detection and segmentation of exosomes in transmission electron
microscopy images. The exosome segmentation is carried out using morphological seeded watershed on gradient magnitude image, with the seeds
established by applying a series of hysteresis thresholdings, followed by
morphological filtering and cluster splitting. We tested the method on
a diverse image data set, yielding the detection performance of slightly
over 80 %.

Keywords: Exosome · Detection · Segmentation · Transmission electron microscopy · Image processing

1 Introduction

Exosomes are small (30–200 nm) vesicles appearing in biological fluids, such as
blood and urine. They play important roles in intercellular signaling and have
garnered interest due to their therapeutic and diagnostic potential, e.g. in relation to oncological diseases [1,2]. However, to utilize this potential, novel automated approaches for isolation and characterization of these vesicles are required.

Due to their nanosize, exosomes are usually observed using transmission electron microscopy (TEM). Not limited by the diffraction limit for visible light,

© Springer International Publishing Switzerland 2016
G. Hua and H. Jégou (Eds.): ECCV 2016 Workshops, Part I, LNCS 9913, pp. 318–325, 2016.
DOI: 10.1007/978-3-319-46604-0_23

TEM enables us to visualize structures several orders of magnitude smaller than those viewable with optical microscopes. Nevertheless, TEM alone is not very suitable as a method for quantification and characterization of exosomes, and therefore, image analysis tools for automated quantitative characterization of TEM exosomal images are heavily sought after.

A number of algorithms have been proposed for the analysis of various structures in electron microscopy images over the past decade. These primarily include segmentation of neurons [3], their synapses [4], and mitochondria [5,6] from scanning electron microscopy stacks using machine learning, reconstruction of nuclear envelopes [7] from TEM stacks using region growing, and detection of virus particles [8,9] in TEM images using size priors and texture descriptors. Nevertheless, to the best of our knowledge, there are no image analysis tools for the quantification of exosomes in TEM images currently available. As all of the above, exosome analysis requires a special treatment to properly discriminate between desired exosomes of nearly oval shapes of highly variable sizes and typical contaminants, such precipitated stain, proteins, and other impurities, found in the preparations.

In this paper, we introduce a novel method for automatic quantification of exosomes in TEM images. The method employs traditional morphological seeded watershed, the performance of which depends significantly on the proper choice of seeds. We establish them by applying a gradual edge growing procedure followed by size and shape filtering, and by a cluster splitting step. The proposed method is validated over a diverse data set of TEM exosomal images, achieving a promising detection performance in terms of F_1 score.

2 Input Data

The data set used to validate the proposed algorithm consisted of 20 heterogeneous 16-bit images, containing 63 exosomes of roughly oval shapes in total, together with a coarse, grainy background and non-exosome structures. The exosomes were isolated by ultracentrifugation from the ascites of ovarian cancer patients, negatively contrasted with ammonium molybdate [10], and imaged with a Morgagni 268D microscope (FEI) equipped with Megaview III (Soft Imaging System), at 70 kV. The dimensions of the individual images were 500×500 pixels, with scales ranging from 1.0 to 2.5 nanometers per pixel. Three examples of the analyzed images can be seen in Fig. 1.

3 Proposed Approach

The high variability of the input images calls for a segmentation approach that would be successful across a wide range of scenarios. Since some of the exosomes were lighter than their surrounding, while other were darker, or of similar intensity as the background, the intensity could not be reliably used as a discriminating feature. The identifying feature that showed to be most consistent across various images was the exosome border, and its roughly oval shape. The

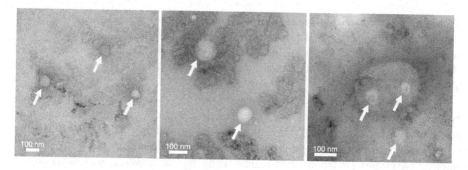

Fig. 1. Three examples of the analyzed images at different scales, with exosomes indicated by the arrows. Note the precipitated stain and other impurities in the background, and the varying exosome intensity relative to their surrounding.

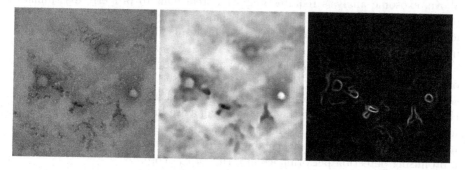

Fig. 2. Left: The input grayscale image. Center: The result of edge-enhancing filtering ($\lambda = 0.0050$). Right: The edge map of the filtered image displayed in the central panel.

backbone of our segmentation method is based on morphological watershed, with the identification of the exosome seeds being the crucial step.

To reduce the amount of noise and enhance the exosome borders, we start by preprocessing the input image with edge-enhancing diffusion (EED) filtering (100 iterations with the time step of 0.1, and a contrast parameter λ) [11]. The initial edge map, G, is then obtained as the gradient magnitude of the preprocessed image, normalized to the $[0, 1]$ interval (Fig. 2). As the gradient magnitude often varies along the exosome borders considerably (which would lead to disconnected edge segments if a simple thresholding of G were used), we apply a gradual edge growing routine to identify the exosome borders in the edge map G as follows.

The strongest segments of the exosome borders are found by thresholding G with the threshold T, fixed as the top 2 % of the cumulative histogram of G. To find the seeds for exosome interiors, we then let the edge segments grow along the ridges until they fully enclose the exosomes. We do this by performing a sequence of hysteresis thresholdings for $n = 1, 2, \ldots$. The upper threshold stays at T, whereas the lower threshold $T - n\Delta t$ gets progressively lower. The lowest possible threshold was chosen as 0.05 to account for all important edges.

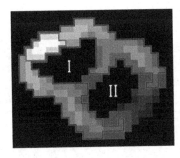 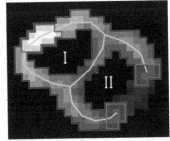

Fig. 3. Finding the exosome borders and interiors in the gradient magnitude image in two successive iterations of the gradual edge growing procedure. The red area shows the edge segmented with the highest threshold, T. The blue area shows the edge segmented with the lower threshold, $T - (n-1)\Delta t$ and $T - n\Delta t$, right before and at the moment the component I becomes fully enclosed, respectively. At the latter moment, the blue area gets frozen, except for the tips of the branches (marked in green) of the blue area skeleton (marked in yellow), allowing the edge to grow further to fully enclose also the component II, without potentially corrupting the edge around the component I. (Color figure online)

Each time the growing edge segments create a new interior component, that component is stored as a new candidate seed, and the edge component surrounding it is frozen, preventing it from growing any further, and thus distorting or removing the candidate seed. However, this may potentially prevent some of the edge segments from completely enclosing the corresponding exosomes, if multiple exosomes are touching. In such cases, the first exosome interior to be fully enclosed causes the common edge component of all the touching exosomes to get frozen before it can grow enough to fully enclose the others. To prevent this, we analyze the skeleton of the edge component at the time of freezing, and if it contains any long branches (exceeding approximately 5 % of the expected exosome circumference), their tips are kept unfrozen, allowing them to grow further along the respective gradient magnitude ridges. An illustrative example of such a situation is depicted in Fig. 3.

Once the hysteresis thresholdings are computed, the candidate seeds are processed based on their size and shape. The size criterion discards those candidate seeds not falling within the expected exosome dimensions. To filter out the candidate seeds by shape, they are subjected to morphological opening, with a disc structuring element of the size corresponding to a user-defined fraction α of the expected exosome size. If the area of a candidate seed decreases by more than 10 % after the opening, it indicates its boundary is not smooth enough, and the candidate seed is discarded.

If the image contains any touching exosomes that have not been separated during the gradual edge growing due to weak edges between them, they usually form non-convex clusters. Such clusters are split by computing the Euclidean distance transform (EDT) over them, and taking its HCONVEX transform [12], with $h = 3$, yielding a single seed for each of the EDT distinct local maxima.

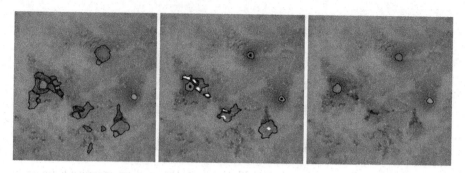

Fig. 4. Left: The candidate seed contours after the gradual edge growing procedure, overlaid over the input image. Center: The seeds established after the basic filtering, and the corresponding auxiliary watershed segmentation. The white seeds are those that will be removed by the additional filtering, since the corresponding components in the auxiliary segmentation are not round enough. Right: Three exosomes segmented from the black seeds depicted in the central panel.

When the seeds have been established, they can either be directly used for the final segmentation, or an additional, optional filtering step can be taken to improve the detection performance. This step involves an auxiliary watershed segmentation based on the seeds. For each resulting component c, we calculate its roundness R_c as

$$R_c = \frac{4\pi A_c}{P_c^2},$$

where A_c and P_c denotes the component area and perimeter, respectively. If $R_c < 0.75$, the component c of the auxiliary segmentation is not considered round, and its corresponding seed is discarded. This helps especially in images with strong and complex background, where false seeds may be detected among the EED-processed background structures (such random structures generally tend to have low roundness).

For the final segmentation, the gradient magnitude of the input image is used as the segmentation function in morphological seeded watershed, but the exact choice of the segmentation function is less critical than finding the seeds properly, and can be adapted for particular needs. As an alternative, the final segmentation can also be based on an energy minimization approach. The results of the basic and additional filtering, and the final segmentation, are depicted in Fig. 4, showing the segmentation of three exosomes.

4   Results and Discussion

We applied the proposed algorithm to the image data set described in Sect. 2, and expressed the detection success rate in terms of Precision, Recall, and the combined F_1 score:

$$Precision = \frac{TP}{TP + FP}, \quad Recall = \frac{TP}{TP + FN},$$

$$F_1 = 2 \cdot \frac{Precision \cdot Recall}{Precision + Recall},$$

where TP is the number of True Positives, FP is the number of False Positives, and FN is the number of False Negatives.

The detected seeds were compared with expert-annotated reference images. A detected seed was labeled as a True Positive, if it intersected with exactly one reference seed, and no other detected seed intersected with the same reference seed. In other cases, the detected seeds were labeled as False Positives. The reference seeds with no corresponding True Positive (i.e., missed exosomes) were counted as False Negatives.

In order to find the optimal values of λ and α, for which the proposed method achieves the highest F_1 score measured over all the analyzed 20 images, 306 different configurations were examined in total, with $\lambda = 0.0010, 0.0015, \dots, 0.0095$ and $\alpha = 0.10, 0.15, \dots, 0.90$. We also evaluated the influence of the additional filtering step that involved the auxiliary watershed segmentation, as mentioned in Sect. 3. The obtained results are summarized in Table 1, showing the best F_1 scores, together with the corresponding Precision and Recall values, and the optimal parameter values. Furthermore, we performed a leave-one-out cross-validation for the both versions of the proposed method to estimate their expected performance for new images from the same source. The measured F_1 score was approximately 2.2 % and 0.7 % lower than that obtained for the optimal parameter setting (Table 1) in case of the basic and additional filtering, respectively.

In some cases, the additional filtering may lower the Recall value by mistakenly removing True Positive seeds. However, the best F_1 score for the basic processing was achieved with a different parameter setting than that for the complete alternative, resulting in the clear improvement of both Precision and Recall when the additional filtering was used.

Apart from this, low Recall can be caused by a very low contrast of the edges of some exosomes. Due to the nature of the hysteresis thresholding, each exosome or cluster of touching exosomes needs to have at least one edge segment

Table 1. Performance of the proposed method with the optimal λ and α setting for the basic and additional seed filtering, and of a machine-learning method that combines fourth-order algebraic curve fitting [6] with ilastik's random-forest object classifier [13].

Method	Precision	Recall	F_1	λ_{opt}	α_{opt}
Proposed (basic filtering)	0.7963	0.6825	0.7350	0.0045	0.40
Proposed (extended filtering)	0.9184	0.7143	0.8036	0.0050	0.15
Algebraic curve fitting+ilastik	0.8511	0.6349	0.7273	NA	NA

where the gradient magnitude exceeds the upper threshold T; otherwise, that exosome or cluster is completely missed.

We also compared the performance of our method with a machine-learning approach that combines algebraic curve fitting [6] with object classification provided by ilastik [13]. To account for variable exosome sizes, the input images were first divided into five independent series of patches of different sizes (50×50, 90×90, 150×150, 200×200, and 250×250 pixels) with a 50 % overlap between neighboring patches. A fourth-order algebraic curve was then fitted to the patch intensities, and the patch was binarized using the zero level set of the fitted curve. Finally, all 4-connected components not touching the patch border were established as exosome candidates and classified using a random-forest classifier provided by ilastik, using 32 shape and textural features calculated over the gradient magnitude of the corresponding input image data. To utilize all data for both training and classification, we performed a 10-fold cross-validation. As shown in Table 1, the machine-learning approach achieved approximately 0.8 % and 7.6 % less accurate results in terms of the combined F_1 score than our proposed algorithm with the basic and additional filtering, respectively.

Altogether, our proposed algorithm reliably detects most of the exosomes, and a preliminary analysis of the quantitative results showed that the size distribution of the exosomes obtained using our approach corresponds well with the size distribution patterns obtained using an alternative measurement method, tunable resistive pulse sensing [14].

5   Conclusion

To the best of our knowledge, we present for the first time an image analysis method specifically developed for a quantitative analysis of TEM exosomal images. The method exploits morphological seeded watershed, with the seed detection being the important step. We identify the seeds by performing a series of hysteresis thresholdings, followed by size and shape filtering, and optionally by the additional filtering step based on an auxiliary watershed segmentation.

The method is capable of detecting exosomes both lighter and darker than their surrounding, and of distinguishing them from common artifacts in TEM images, such as precipitated stain and other impurities in sample preparations. Moreover, it provides their basic characteristics: number, size, area, and roundness, offering a fully automated way to study and evaluate exosomal preparations both for research and clinical purposes. We believe the ever-growing exosomal research would benefit from the presented tool significantly. The implementation of this tool and all relevant data used for generating the results described in this paper are made publicly available at http://cbia.fi.muni.cz/exosome-analyzer, free of charge for noncommercial and research purposes.

Acknowledgements. This work was supported by the Grant Agency of Masaryk University (MUNI/M/1050/2013).

References

1. Yang, C., Robbins, P.D.: The roles of tumor-derived exosomes in cancer pathogenesis. Clin. Dev. Immunol. **2011**, 842–849 (2011)
2. Nikitina, I.G., Sabirova, E.Y., Karpov, V.L., Lisitsyn, N.A., Beresten, S.F.: Role of exosomes and microvesicles in carcinogenesis. Mol. Biol. **47**(5), 668–673 (2013)
3. Andres, B., Köthe, U., Helmstaedter, M., Denk, W., Hamprecht, F.A.: Segmentation of SBFSEM volume data of neural tissue by hierarchical classification. In: Rigoll, G. (ed.) DAGM 2008. LNCS, vol. 5096, pp. 142–152. Springer, Heidelberg (2008). doi:10.1007/978-3-540-69321-5_15
4. Kreshuk, A., Straehle, C.N., Sommer, C., Köthe, U., Knott, G., Hamprecht, F.A.: Automated segmentation of synapses in 3D EM data. In: IEEE International Symposium on Biomedical Imaging, pp. 220–223 (2011)
5. Lucchi, A., Smith, K., Achanta, R., Knott, G., Fua, P.: Supervoxel-based segmentation of mitochondria in EM image stacks with learned shape features. IEEE Trans. Med. Imaging **31**(2), 474–486 (2012)
6. Seyedhosseini, M., Ellisman, M.H., Tasdizen, T.: Segmentation of mitochondria in electron microscopy images using algebraic curves. In: IEEE International Symposium on Biomedical Imaging, pp. 860–863 (2013)
7. Wood, S.: A semi-automated segmentation of electron microscopy images for 3D reconstruction of the nuclear envelope. Master's thesis, Imperial College London (2012)
8. Kylberg, G., Uppström, M., Hedlund, K.O., Borgefors, G., Sintorn, I.M.: Segmentation of virus particle candidates in transmission electron microscopy images. J. Microsc. **245**(2), 140–147 (2012)
9. Proença, M.C., Nunes, J.F.M., De Matos, A.P.A.: Automatic virus particle selection-the entropy approach. IEEE Trans. Image Process. **22**(5), 1996–2003 (2013)
10. Pospíchalová, V., Svoboda, J., Dave, Z., Kotrbová, A., Kaiser, K., Klemová, D., Ilkovics, L., Hampl, A., Crha, I., Jandáková, E., Minář, L., Weinberger, V., Bryja, V.: Simplified protocol for flow cytometry analysis of fluorescently labeled exosomes and microvesicles using dedicated flow cytometer. J. Extracellular Vesicles **4** (2015)
11. Weickert, J.: Anisotropic Diffusion In Image Processing. Teubner, Stuttgart, Germany (1998)
12. Soille, P.: Morphological Image Analysis. Springer-Verlag, Heidelberg (2003)
13. Sommer, C., Straehle, C., Köthe, U., Hamprecht, F.A.: Ilastik: interactive learning and segmentation toolkit. In: IEEE International Symposium on Biomedical Imaging, pp. 230–233 (2011)
14. Coumans, F., van der Pol, E., Böing, A., Hajji, N., Sturk, G., van Leeuwen, T., Nieuwland, R.: Reproducible extracellular vesicle size and concentration determination with tunable resistive pulse sensing. J. Extracellular Vesicles **3** (2014)

Poisson Point Processes for Solving Stochastic Inverse Problems in Fluorescence Microscopy

Ihor Smal[✉] and Erik Meijering

Biomedical Imaging Group Rotterdam,
Departments of Medical Informatics and Radiology,
Erasmus University Medical Center,
P.O. Box 2040, 3000 CA Rotterdam, The Netherlands
ihor@smal.ws

Abstract. Despite revolutionary developments in fluorescence based optical microscopy imaging, the quality of the images remains fundamentally limited by diffraction and noise. Hence, deconvolution methods are often applied to obtain better estimates of the biological structures than the measured images are providing prima facie, by reducing blur and noise as much as possible through image postprocessing. However, conventional deconvolution methods typically focus on accurately modeling the point-spread function of the microscope, and put less emphasis on properly modeling the noise sources. Here we propose a new approach to enhancing fluorescence microscopy images by formulating deconvolution as a stochastic inverse problem. We solve the problem using Poisson point processes and establish a connection between the classical Shepp-Vardi algorithm and probability hypothesis density filtering. Results of preliminary experiments on image data from various biological applications indicate that the proposed method compares favorably with existing approaches in jointly performing deblurring and denoising.

Keywords: Stochastic reconstruction · Poisson point process · Probability hypothesis density filter · Fluorescence microscopy · Deconvolution

1 Introduction

Fluorescence microscopy imaging is an indispensable tool in numerous biological studies for visualizing (intra)cellular structures and dynamic processes. However, the quality of the acquired images is often rather poor, mainly due to low photon counts and the usage of diffraction-limited optics. This is especially true in single-molecule imaging experiments, where the objects of interest (generally termed "particles") are smaller than the optical resolution of the microscope and the fluorescence signal is weak. As a result, fluorescently labeled vesicles, peroxisomes, or other particles are typically rendered as blurred spots with Gaussian-like intensity profiles, severely corrupted by Poisson noise [1,2]. But also in the case of imaging larger objects, such as microtubules and actin filaments within cells,

© Springer International Publishing Switzerland 2016
G. Hua and H. Jégou (Eds.): ECCV 2016 Workshops, Part I, LNCS 9913, pp. 326–338, 2016.
DOI: 10.1007/978-3-319-46604-0_24

or the dendritic and axonal arbors of neurons, the effects of noise and blurring may adversely affect subsequent analyses.

The main sources of noise in fluorescence microscopy are the signal itself (photon shot noise) and the digital imaging electronics. The mechanics of both noise sources is well understood and the statistical distributions of noise are known [3,4]. The signal-dependent noise is described by a Poisson distribution, while the noise arising from the imaging system often follows a Gaussian distribution. In practice, especially with low-excitation or single-molecule fluorescence imaging, the signal-dependent noise dominates, and the Gaussian noise caused by the imaging device can be ignored. The latter source of noise, for example, can also be substantially reduced by cooling the detector/camera.

To reduce both noise and blurring, deconvolution methods are frequently used [5,6]. Most existing deconvolution methods, however, are primarily designed for deblurring, involving careful modeling of the point-spread-function (PSF) of the microscope optics. Although noise is often also reduced in the process, the underlying algorithms typically do not focus on this aspect and do not properly model the noise distributions, but assume that noise can be easily removed as a preprocessing step by applying specific image filters.

Here we approach the deconvolution problem in a novel and more fundamental way, by considering the blurring due to the PSF and the statistics of the noise as equally important aspects of one and the same "stochastic" inverse/reconstruction problem. Because of the Poissonian nature of photon emission, so-called Poisson point processes (PPPs) [7] are especially suitable for solving such problems. Similar reconstruction problems appeared in the field of positron emission tomography (PET), where they were tackled using the well-known Shepp-Vardi algorithm [8]. There, PPPs also played a major role in developing reconstruction algorithms that are still used in clinical PET imaging devices. We demonstrate how the Shepp-Vardi solution to the stochastic reconstruction problem can be adapted for microscopy imaging, and we show its performance for several biological applications.

Surprisingly, the final iterative update equations of the solution coincide with the update equation of the so-called probability hypothesis density (PHD) filter [9]. In computer vision and robotics, the PHD filter (which is derived in a very complex and rigorous way using the theory of random finite sets [10]) is a state-of-the-art method for multi-object tracking in image sequences. However, contrary to tracking applications, our solution (as an extension of the Shepp-Vardi algorithm) is equal to employing the PHD filter unconventionally: not to an image sequence but a static image, and not for tracking but for iterative denoising/deconvolution. The power of our problem formulation and the proposed solution is in the ability to fully model the acquisition process, to incorporate the noise statistics, and even to model such events as scattering of emitted photons and failure of a detector to produce photoelectrons.

This paper is organized as follows. In Sect. 2 we provide the problem statement, including necessary definitions. Next, in Sect. 3, we describe the classical Shepp-Vardi algorithm, which forms the basis for solving our reconstruction problem, and its relation to the PHD filter. Section 4 describes how the algorithm can be further improved by introducing prior knowledge about the smoothness of the reconstructed image. In Sect. 5 we present first examples of the proposed method in comparison with alternative solutions for several biological applications. Concluding remarks are made in Sect. 6.

2   Problem Statement

A point process is a random variable whose realizations are sets containing only points of some state space $\mathcal{X}$ (usually the Euclidean space $\mathbb{R}^m, m \geq 1$). For a Poisson point process (PPP), the distribution of the points is fully characterized by a density (also called "intensity") function $\lambda(x) \geq 0$ over $\mathcal{X}$ (Fig. 1). The number of points (realizations of PPP) on any subset $\mathcal{R}$ of $\mathcal{X}$ is Poisson distributed with mean $N_{\mathcal{R}} = \int_{\mathcal{R}} \lambda(x) dx$. In our case, the space $\mathcal{X}$ is defined as the physical space, where the light-emitting fluorophores are located.

The points on the input space $\mathcal{X}$ (emissions of photons) occur as a PPP with the intensity function $\{\lambda(x) : x \in \mathcal{X}\}$. By means of a microscope, the points of this process are observed with a detector/camera after a random translation (due to the PSF of the optical system) to the output space $\mathcal{Y}$ (also Euclidean space $\mathbb{R}^m, m \geq 1$). According to the theory [11], points on the output space occur as a Poisson process with intensity function $\{\mu(y) : y \in \mathcal{Y}\}$ given by

$$\mu(y) = \int_{\mathcal{X}} P_d(x) p(y|x) \lambda(x) dx + \mu_0(y), \qquad (1)$$

where $P_d(x)$ is the probability that a point (e.g. an emitted photon) will be translated according to the PSF $p(y|x)$ from the input location x to the output space $\mathcal{Y}$. The intensity $\mu_0(y)$ models the observed clutter (background noise). The spurious emissions (e.g. caused by autofluorescence) are assumed to be uniformly distributed over $\mathcal{X}$, with a constant intensity λ^c. In principle, λ^c can be made spatially dependent in order to model more complex clutter (e.g. false light emissions originating within an inhomogeneous cell background). In any case, the clutter intensity is defined as $\mu_0(y) = \int_{\mathcal{X}} P_d(x) p(y|x) \lambda^c dx$.

The observed microscopy image $\mathcal{I}$ is the result of binning the points of the PPP on $\mathcal{Y}$ into $N_{\tilde{y}}$ bins, which constitute the pixels of the image. The pixels in $\mathcal{I}$ are defined as disjoint bounded sets $R_1, \ldots, R_{N_{\tilde{y}}}, \tilde{\mathcal{Y}} = \cup_{i=1}^{N_{\tilde{y}}} R_i \in \mathbb{R}^2$. The number of points of the process that lie in R_i (the pixel value) is denoted as Y_i. No record is kept of the location of the points within any set R_i.

The inverse problem is defined as the inference about the points in the input space on the basis of points observed in the output space. In general, there are two problems that complicate the estimation of $\lambda(x)$ using the observed pixel values or observed points on $\mathcal{Y}$. The first one is present even if so much data are available that the function $\mu(y)$ can be regarded as known perfectly. In this case, the integral in (1) must be solved for $\lambda(x)$ for a given kernel $p(y|x)$. This is generally termed a deterministic inverse problem, and a deconvolution problem if the kernel $p(y|x)$ depends only on the difference $y - x$. The second problem

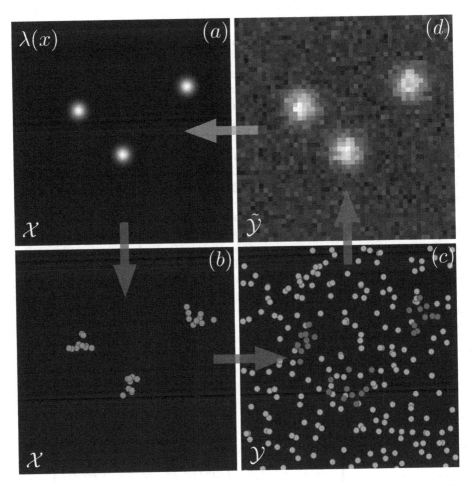

Fig. 1. Example of (a) the density function $\lambda(x)$, (b) the realization (*yellow*) of the PPP on $\mathcal{X}$, obtained by sampling from $\lambda(x)$, (c) the translated PPP (*green*) with superimposed clutter (*cyan*) on $\mathcal{Y}$, and (d) the resulting binned measurements (an image), with the number of bins (pixels) $N_{\tilde{y}}$. (Color figure online)

is that the point-process data available are random, so estimating $\lambda(x)$ from measurements on the output space $\mathcal{Y}$ is a stochastic inverse problem.

Considering our problem statement, the log-likelihood of the probability density function $p(Y_1, \ldots, Y_{N_{\tilde{y}}}, N_{\tilde{y}} | \lambda(x))$ of the binned data, which describes how likely it is to observe image $\mathcal{I}$ given intensity $\lambda(x)$, is given by [11,12]

$$\mathcal{L}(\lambda) = -\int_{\mathcal{Y}} \mu(y)dy + \sum_{i=1}^{N_{\tilde{y}}} Y_i \ln\left(\int_{R_i} \mu(y)\right)dy + \sum_{i=1}^{N_{\tilde{y}}} \ln\left(Y_i!\right). \qquad (2)$$

To solve the stochastic inverse problem, we seek a solution in terms of $\lambda(x)$ that maximizes the log-likelihood $\mathcal{L}(\lambda)$. In trying to solve the problem straightforwardly, using the calculus of variations, one can employ functional derivatives (to find a local maximum) and form a system of nonlinear equations, which can be solved only in some special (but not practically useful) cases. Fortunately, this difficulty can be avoided by employing the expectation-maximization (EM) algorithm, which results in a recursion for the maximum-likelihood (ML) estimate of $\lambda(x)$, avoiding directly solving any nonlinear equations [11,12]. For PET, the EM approach yields the well-known Shepp-Vardi algorithm [8].

3   Shepp-Vardi Algorithm and the PHD Filter

The Shepp-Vardi algorithm was originally proposed for PET and solves the problem of estimating the intensity function of the emission of short-lived radioisotopes. The algorithm was derived via the EM method, which at that time was not widely known [8]. In PET, radioisotope emissions are modeled as a nonhomogeneous Poisson point process. The Shepp-Vardi algorithm produces the ML estimate of the intensity function of this process, which provides an image of the radioisotope spatial density. This density is directly proportional to the intensity $\lambda(x)$ of radioisotope decay at the point x. In PET reconstruction the assumptions with respect to (1) are $P_d(x) = 1$ and $\mu_0(y) = 0$. The EM recursion for iteratively estimating $\lambda(x)$ is then given by [12]

$$\lambda^{(k+1)}(x) = \lambda^{(k)}(x) \sum_{i=1}^{N_{\tilde{y}}} Y_i \frac{p(Y_i|x)}{\int_{\mathcal{X}} p(Y_i|x')\lambda^{(k)}(x')dx'}. \tag{3}$$

Following the derivation of the Shepp-Vardi algorithm, but taking P_d and $\mu_0(y)$ into account, we similarly find

$$\lambda^{(k+1)}(x) = \lambda^{(k)}(x) \left\{ 1 - P_d(x) + \sum_{i=1}^{N_{\tilde{y}}} Y_i \frac{P_d(x)p(Y_i|x)}{\int_{\mathcal{X}} p(Y_i|x')\lambda^{(k)}(x')dx' + \mu_0(Y_i)} \right\}. \tag{4}$$

This recursion turns out to be identical to the estimate update in the well-known PHD filter [9,13], which has been developed for multi-target tracking (a completely different application). This surprising connection is established by proving that the first step of the Shepp-Vardi algorithm is essentially identical to the information update step of the PHD intensity filter. Thus, the recursion (4) actually describes a PHD filter, which is applied iteratively (and is therefore referred to as iPHD in the sequel) to a single image in order to solve the stochastic inverse problem and produce the estimate of $\lambda(x)$. It extends the Shepp-Vardi algorithm to a more general solution, capable of dealing with clutter and imperfect detection and scattering of photons.

4   Improving Stability by Regularization

The described stochastic reconstruction procedure has a fundamental noise instability which results in artifacts that are visually similar to the Gibbs phenomenon [11]. These artifacts are not caused by the EM method, but arise in any algorithm that estimates an infinite dimensional quantity (in our case $\lambda(x)$) from a finite number of measurements. In practice, several regularization procedures can be used, e.g. Grenander's method of sieves, penalty functions, Markov random fields (extending penalty functions to multiple dimensions), or resolution kernels [11,12]. Sophisticated combinations of these can be very effective in reducing not only noise but also edge artifacts. Since microscopic images from biological experiments typically do not contain structures with sharp edges, we concentrate here only on two basic noise suppression techniques.

Grenander's method of sieves, which preserves the EM form of the intensity estimator, is one of the simplest techniques to suppress noise. The idea is to constrain the estimate $\lambda(x)$ to be in a smooth subset, called a sieve, of the set of nonnegative functions. By allowing the size of the sieve to grow in an appropriate manner with the number of measurement points, it is hoped that the constrained estimate is consistent in the sense that it converges to the true intensity. The sieve restricts $\lambda(x)$ to the collection of all functions of the form

$$S \equiv \left\{ \lambda(x) = \int_{\mathcal{Z}} \kappa(x|z)\zeta(z)dz, \quad \text{for some} \quad \zeta(z) \right\}, \tag{5}$$

where the kernel of the sieve, $\kappa(x|z)$, is a specified pdf (e.g. an appropriately dimensioned Gaussian pdf) for each $z \in \mathcal{Z}$, so that $\int_{\mathcal{X}} \kappa(x|\cdot)dx = 1$, and $\zeta(z) \geq 0$, and $\int_{\mathcal{Z}} \zeta(z)dz < \infty$. For our applications, without loss of generality, we can assume that $\mathcal{Z} = \mathcal{X}$. In effect, the integral (5) is a low pass filter applied to the intensity $\zeta(z)$. The basic idea is to compute the ML estimate $\hat{\zeta}(z)$ from the data and subsequently compute the ML intensity $\hat{\lambda}(x)$ from $\hat{\lambda}(x) = \int_{\mathcal{Z}} \kappa(x|z)\hat{\zeta}(z)dz$. The estimate $\hat{\zeta}(z)$ is computed by the EM method, which is directly applicable to estimating $\zeta(z)$ using a modified PSF $g(y|z) = \int_{\mathcal{X}} p(y|x)\kappa(x|z)dx$. Iterating until convergence by means of

$$\zeta^{(k+1)}(z) = \zeta^{(k)}(z) \sum_{i=1}^{N_{\tilde{y}}} Y_i \frac{g(Y_i|z)}{\int_{\mathcal{X}} g(Y_i|z')\zeta^{(k)}(z')dz'} \tag{6}$$

gives the ML estimate $\hat{\zeta}(z)$ from which $\hat{\lambda}(x)$ can be computed [11,12]. This method is also compatible with the PHD intensity filter.

Alternatively, the difficulty of maximizing $\mathcal{L}(\lambda)$ without introducing artifacts can be also partially solved by introducing a regularization (penalty) term $\mathcal{E}(\lambda)$, which describes the prior knowledge about the smoothness of the intensity $\lambda(x)$ using Markov random fields (MRFs). The ML estimation problem is then transformed into a maximum a posteriori (MAP) estimation problem. Specifically, the approach is to maximize the functional $\mathcal{G}(\lambda)$ defined by

$$\mathcal{G}(\lambda) = \mathcal{L}(\lambda) - \mathcal{E}(\lambda), \tag{7}$$

where $\mathcal{L}(\lambda)$ is the log-likelihood functional given by (2), and $\mathcal{E}(\lambda)$ is the penalty that describes the prior knowledge about $\lambda(x)$. For 2D images, the prior density of the MRF is defined on a discrete lattice (i,j) which discretizes the space $\mathcal{X}$,

Table 1. SNR values for the synthetic images and the reconstructed intensity $\lambda(x)$ obtained using the described methods

Initial SNR	10	1
SVA	4.7	0.5
SVA (Sieves)	9.5	1.0
SVA (MRF)	10.4	1.1
HPS	2.1	1.0

and is based on penalizing large gradients in $\lambda(x)$. The EM algorithm can be combined with the prior for deriving the MAP estimator by simply adding the prior to the maximization at each stage of the algorithm. In practice, this leads to a set of nonlinear equations that can be solved by performing several steps of Jacobi-like gradient iterations at each stage of the EM algorithm to solve the nonlinear difference equations [11,14].

5   Experimental Results

5.1   Evaluation of Regularization

Before presenting examples of the described techniques for biological applications we first study the effects of regularization. We simulated 2D images size of 128×128 pixels using (1) and applying binning (Fig. 2(a), (g)). The intensity $\lambda(x)$ had a constant value of, respectively, 100 (Fig. 2(a)) and 1 (Fig. 2(g)) within a square region of size of 50×50 pixels in the center of the image, and was equal to 0 outside the square. This corresponds to a signal-to-noise ratio (SNR) of, respectively, 10 and 1. The transition density $p(y|x)$ was selected as a normal density with the standard deviation of 1 pixel, and we used $P_d(y|x) = 1$.

The results of estimating the underlying intensity $\lambda(x)$ using the Shepp-Vardi algorithm (SVA), SVA with sieves, SVA with MRF, and with state-of-the-art commercial deconvolution tool Huygens Professional Software (HPS, Scientific Volume Imaging B.V., Hilversum, the Netherlands, https://svi.nl/) are shown in Fig. 2. We observe that using regularization clearly produces smoother results than using no regularization, but there appears to be no striking difference between the sieves and MRF methods (see also Table 1). In practice, regularization with sieves is preferable because it avoids solving nonlinear equations (as in the case with MRF) and allows easy integration into the EM optimization. The HPS tool, which tries to solve the deterministic inverse problem, produces inferior results. It should be noted that in the case of stochastic reconstruction one should not expect to get an ideal constant-valued square as $\lambda(x)$ and that some "artifacts" are unavoidable. The purpose of these experiments was merely to show how noisy typical estimates of the intensity function can be and how regularization techniques deal with it.

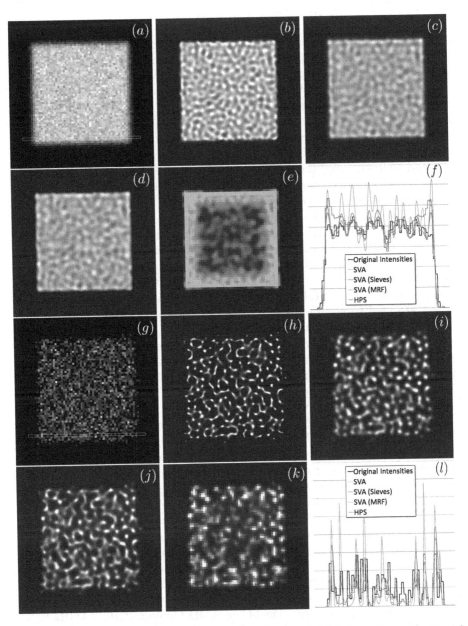

Fig. 2. Results of reconstructing a square-shaped density $\lambda(x)$ from the realization of a PPP with $\text{SNR} = 10$ (top two rows) and $\text{SNR} = 1$ (bottom two rows). The panels correspond to original noisy image (a, g), the density $\lambda(x)$ obtained by SVA (b, h), SVA regularized with sieves (c, i), SVA regularized with MRF (d, j), the result of HPS (e, k), and the intensity profiles along the indicated yellow regions (lines) of interest (f, l). For this example (with no clutter) the iPHD filter simplifies to SVA (Color figure online)

5.2 Evaluation for Biological Applications

We explored the potential of the proposed iPHD filter for deconvolution in various biological applications in comparison with SVA and HPS. As a first example we used images from the particle tracking challenge (http://bioimageanalysis. org/track/). The images show subresolution objects modeled as PSF-shaped bright spots on top of a noisy background [15]. The noise in the background was modeled using the Poisson distribution with mean equal to 10. The amplitudes of the spot intensity were chosen to obtain SNRs in the range from 2 to 7 [15]. The results of applying iPHD, SVA, and HPS, are shown in Fig. 3. The iPHD filter clearly outperformed the other methods, producing more localized estimates of object positions in comparison with HPS, and fewer spurious local maxima in the background regions compared to the SVA.

As a second example we used data from the single-molecule localization microscopy challenge (http://bigwww.epfl.ch/smlm/). The data contain sequences of images from single-molecule imaging experiments [16]. A typical image contains hundreds of PSF-shaped blurred spots, representing a subset of emitting fluorophores (at a specific time point), located on an underlying subcellular structure (e.g. a tubulin filament). In super-resolution microscopy, such images are used to accurately detect the positions of the fluorophores, which, taken all together yield a super-resolved image of the structure. For our experiments we combined the individual images of a sequence using maximum intensity projection to form a single image corresponding to the case when all fluorophores would be emitting simultaneously. Having this single blurred image we studied the power of iPHD, SVA, and HPS to obtain a better, deconvolved image of the biological structures. The results are shown in Fig. 4. In this case, with negligible noise in the background areas, iPHD and SVA performed comparably. The deconvolution results of HPS were found to be slightly worse.

As a final example we applied the described techniques to fluorescence microscopy images of neurons. The images were acquired with a confocal microscope and in this case the background areas contained low levels of noise. The results of deconvolving such images using iPHD, SVA, and HPS, are shown in Fig. 5. The iPHD filter performed slightly better in the sense that it produced sharper image structures than HPS and with less noise than SVA.

The iPHD filter was implemented in the Java programming language (Oracle Corporation, Redwood Shores, CA, USA) as a plugin for ImageJ (National Institutes of Health, Bethesda, MD, USA) [17,18]. Executing 100 iterations of the described approach for an image of size 128×128 pixels on a single thread on a standard personal computer (Dual-Core AMD Opteron 2216, 2.4 GHz CPU, 8 GB RAM) takes approximately 30 s. The method is highly parallelizable and can be implemented for GPU (Graphics Processing Unit) hardware.

6 Discussion and Conclusion

In contrast with existing solutions for image deconvolution we have proposed to formulate the problem more fundamentally as a stochastic reconstruction

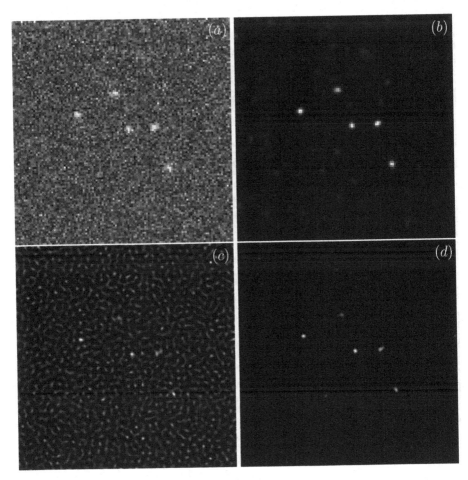

Fig. 3. Example of deconvolving an image from the particle tracking challenge. The image contains PSF-shaped objects embedded in noise (a). Results are shown of reconstructing $\lambda(x)$ using HSP (b), SVA (c), and the proposed iPHD filter (d). The ability of the iPHD filter to better account for noise is clearly visible.

problem. Using the theory of Poisson point processes, which perfectly suits our needs, we have shown how the solution to the stochastic inverse problem can be obtained as an iterative recursion. In doing so we have established a connection between the classical Shepp-Vardi algorithm and the more recently proposed PHD filter. The advantage of our proposed deconvolution method is that it provides a better theoretical framework for modeling the entire image acquisition process including the noise sources. We have presented first examples of deconvolution using our method for various biological applications, demonstrating that it performs comparable or better than even state-of-the-art commercial deconvolution software. The image data used in these examples contained realistic amounts of noise and/or blur, for which our method is especially useful.

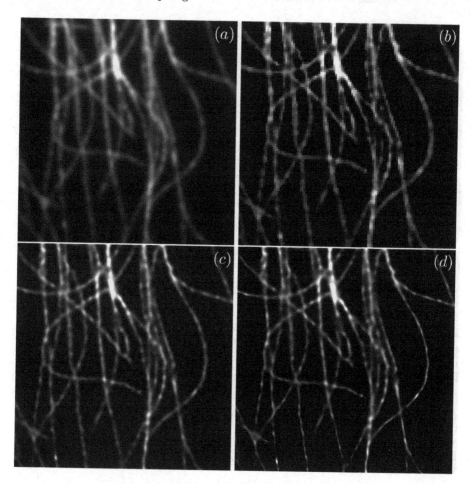

Fig. 4. Example of deconvolving an image from the single-molecule localization microscopy challenge. The image contains filamentous cellular structures (a). Results are shown of reconstructing $\lambda(x)$ using HSP (b), SVA (c), and the proposed iPHD filter (d). The absence of background noise in the original image makes the iPHD filter perform comparably to SVA.

We note that in high-quality (low-noise) images the advantage of our method over other methods may be less pronounced. In future work we aim to extend the proposed solution to deal with more general classes of point processes and to incorporate other sources of noise (different distributions). We also aim to explore further improvements by incorporating prior information about the relevant object structures to be reconstructed (e.g. by modeling the appearance of microtubules as elongated structures). In terms of further application and experimental validation we plan to quantify the improvements potentially offered by our method in fluorophore localization for super-resolution microscopy.

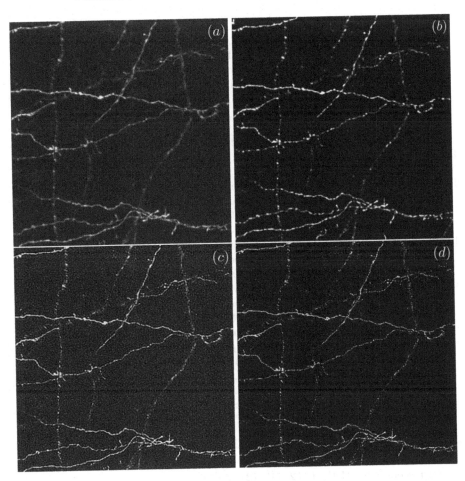

Fig. 5. Example of deconvolving a confocal fluorescence microscopy image showing dendritic structures. The panels show the original image (a) and the results of reconstructing $\lambda(x)$ using HSP (b), SVA (c), and the proposed iPHD filter (d). It can be appreciated that the iPHD filter is better able to deal with background noise and produces more consistent and sharper results than SVA and HPS.

References

1. Vonesch, C., Aguet, F., Vonesch, J.L., Unser, M.: The colored revolution of bioimaging. IEEE Sig. Process. Mag. **23**(3), 20–31 (2006)
2. Zhang, B., Zerubia, J., Olivo-Marin, J.C.: Gaussian approximations of fluorescence microscope point-spread function models. Appl. Opt. **46**(10), 1819–1829 (2007)
3. van Vliet, L.J., Sudar, D., Young, I.T.: Digital fluorescence imaging using cooled CCD array cameras. In: Celis, J.E. (ed.) Cell Biology: A Laboratory Handbook, vol. 3, 2nd edn, pp. 109–120. Academic Press, New York (1998)
4. Pawley, J.B.: Handbook of Biological Confocal Microscopy, 3rd edn. Springer, New York (2006)

5. Sarder, P., Nehorai, A.: Deconvolution methods for 3-D fluorescence microscopy images. IEEE Sig. Process. Mag. **23**(3), 32–45 (2006)
6. Topor, P., Zimanyi, M., Mateasik, A.: Increasing axial resolution of 3D data sets using deconvolution algorithms. J. Microsc. **243**(3), 293–302 (2011)
7. Kingman, J.F.C.: Poisson Processes. Clarendon Press, Oxford (1998)
8. Shepp, L.A., Vardi, Y.: Maximum likelihood reconstructions for emission tomography. IEEE Trans. Med. Imaging **1**(2), 113–122 (1982)
9. Mahler, R.: Multi-target Bayes filtering via first-order multi-target moments. IEEE Trans. Aerosp. Electron. Syst. **39**, 1152–1178 (2003)
10. Goutsias, J., Mahler, R., Nguyen, H.: Random Sets Theory and Applications. Springer, New York (1997)
11. Snyder, D.L., Miller, M.I.: Random Point Processes in Time and Space. Springer Texts in Electrical Engineering. Springer, New York (1991)
12. Streit, R.L.: Poisson Point Processes: Imaging, Tracking, and Sensing. Springer, New York (2010)
13. Streit, R.L.: PHD intensity filtering is one step of a MAP estimation algorithm for positron emission tomography. In: Proceedings of 12th International Conference on Information Fusion, pp. 308–305 (2009)
14. Roysam, B., Shrauner, J.A., Miller, M.I.: Bayesian imaging using Good's roughness measure. In: Proceedings of IEEE International Conference of Acoustics, Speech and Signal Processing, pp. 932–935 (1988)
15. Chenouard, N., Smal, I., de Chaumont, F., Maska, M., Sbalzarini, I.F., Gong, Y., Cardinale, J., Carthel, C., Coraluppi, S., Winter, M., Cohen, A.R., Godinez, W.J., Rohr, K., Kalaidzidis, Y., Liang, L., Duncan, J., Shen, H., Xu, Y., Magnusson, K.E.G., Jalden, J., Blau, H.M., Paul-Gilloteaux, P., Roudot, P., Kervrann, C., Waharte, F., Tinevez, J.Y., Shorte, S.L., Willemse, J., Celler, K., van Wezel, G.P., Dan, H.W., Tsai, Y.S., de Solorzano, C.O., Olivo-Marin, J.C., Meijering, E.: Objective comparison of particle tracking methods. Nat. Methods **11**, 281–289 (2014)
16. Sage, D., Kirshner, H., Pengo, T., Stuurman, N., Min, J., Manley, S., Unser, M.: Quantitative evaluation of software packages for single-molecule localization microscopy. Nat. Methods **12**, 717–724 (2015)
17. Abràmoff, M.D., Magalhães, P.J., Ram, S.J.: Image processing with ImageJ. Biophotonics Int. **11**(7), 36–42 (2004)
18. Schneider, C.A., Rasband, W.S., Eliceiri, K.W.: NIH Image to ImageJ: 25 years of image analysis. Nat. Methods **9**(7), 671–675 (2012)

Deep Convolutional Neural Networks for Human Embryonic Cell Counting

Aisha Khan[1(✉)], Stephen Gould[1], and Mathieu Salzmann[1,2]

[1] College of Engineering and Computer Science,
The Australian National University, Canberra, Australia
aisha.sj.khan@gmail.com
[2] CVLab, EPFL, Lausanne, Switzerland

Abstract. We address the problem of counting cells in time-lapse microscopy images of developing human embryos. Cell counting is considered as an important step in analyzing biological phenomenon such as embryo viability. Traditional approaches to counting cells rely on hand crafted features and cannot fully take advantage of the growth in data set sizes. In this paper, we propose a framework to automatically count the number of cells in developing human embryos. The framework employs a deep convolutional neural network model trained to count cells from raw microscopy images. We demonstrate the effectiveness of our approach on a data set of 265 human embryos. The results show that the proposed framework provides robust estimates of the number of cells in a developing embryo up to the 5-cell stage (i.e., 48 h post fertilization).

1 Introduction

Counting the number of objects in an image is an important and challenging computer vision problem that arises in many real-world applications ranging from crowd monitoring to biological research. In biological research counting cells is a fundamental first step for further analysis (e.g., cell mitosis detection and cell lineage analysis). In this paper we focus on the problem of determining the number of cells in time-lapse microscopy images of developing human embryos. We are primarily interested in images of embryos up to the 5-cell stage, which have been used in other works for computing biomarkers (e.g., cell timing parameters) to assess embryo viability in the context of *in vitro* fertilization (IVF) treatments [14,19].

Manual cell counting, is an extremely tedious process that is prone to error and subject to intra- and inter-individual variability. Automating the process has the benefit of reducing time and cost, minimizing errors, and improving consistency of results between individuals and clinics. To simplify the task and improve robustness, many researchers stain the cells prior to automatic counting [1,4,5,20]. However, cell staining is not feasible for many applications (such as IVF embryo assessment).

Counting non-stained cells in dark-field microscopy images is difficult because of constraints in the imaging process. For example, the exposure time, the light

© Springer International Publishing Switzerland 2016
G. Hua and H. Jégou (Eds.): ECCV 2016 Workshops, Part I, LNCS 9913, pp. 339–348, 2016.
DOI: 10.1007/978-3-319-46604-0_25

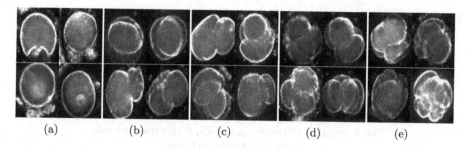

Fig. 1. Examples of developing embryos: (a) one-cell stage, (b) two-cell stage, (c) three-cell stage, (d) four-cell stage and (e) 5-or-more cell stage

intensity and the transparency of the specimen all cause variations in the image quality and result in faint cell boundaries. Analysis of human embryonic cells is further challenged by the fact that the cells exhibit variability in appearance and shape. Also, each embryo grows (cells undergo divisions) in a compact manner where cells severely overlap with each other. Moreover, cells are surrounded by distracting noise such as extra cellular material (fragments) attached to the growing embryo and surrounding gel material (see Fig. 1 and Fig. 2 (e)–(f) for examples). All these difficulties make hand crafted algorithms for automated cell counting brittle.

In this paper, we utilize non-stained dark-field microscopy images of developing human embryos. Our goal is to automatically count the number of cells in the developing embryos up to the 5-cell stage (with higher cardinality being grouped into a "5-or-more" category). We do so using a convolutional neural network (CNN) that can learn from vast amount of training data to overcome the difficulties presented above. Our network significantly outperform the previous state-of-the-art is this task.

2   Related Work

Counting objects in images is typically achieved by training either an object detector or directly a counter. Detection-based methods first localize the individual objects in the input image and then simply count them. In the context of cell biology, this strategy was employed in [5,7,15]. One of the main drawbacks of this approach, however, is that it requires training data labeled with the locations of the objects of interest, which is time-consuming and expensive to acquire, if possible at all. A different, yet related approach, consists of predicting object density instead of precise object locations. This was proposed by Lempitsky and Zisserman [13] in the general context of computer vision and by Xie et al. [20] for microscopy images. While effective, this again suffers from the fact that it requires detailed annotations, if not of the objects themselves, then of their local density.

By contrast, directly learning a counter bypasses the hard detection problem and reduces labelling cost by only requiring the true number of objects in each training image. When the number of such objects can be arbitrarily large, and thus not all possible numbers can be observed during training, such as for people counting in crowds [21], regression approaches are typically best-suited. By contrast, when the number of object instances that can appear in an image is small, classification becomes the method of choice. This approach has recently become popular in the context of human embryonic cell counting. For example, Wang et al. [18] proposed a 3-level classification method to predict the embryo cell stage without performing detection. In Khan et al. [8], a conditional random field (CRF) framework was developed to count the cells in sequences of microscopy images. Thanks to their accuracy, these methods have become a key ingredient in cell detection and early-stage embryo development analysis algorithms [7,9,15]. Following their success, in this paper, we introduce a method to directly count the number of cells in an early-stage embryo without requiring any detection phase.

Traditional counting methods rely on hand crafted feature descriptors [7–9,15,18]. Recently, however, learning features via deep convolutional neural network (CNN) models [12] has proven highly effective for a variety of tasks, such as recognizing handwritten digits [3], handwritten characters [2], faces [17] and natural images [11], and, in the biomedical domain, detecting cell mitosis [1,4]. CNNs were also recently applied to the problem of cell counting [16,20]. In both cases, however, the networks were trained to perform in well-controlled environments, with clean background and little cell overlap on synthetic images. In practice, however, and in particular in the case of human embryos, the images background contains a lot of noise, such as fragments, and the cells of the growing embryo greatly overlap each other.

In this paper, we therefore address the cell counting problem in this challenging scenario. To this end, we introduce a CNN-based counting approach that requires minimal annotations, i.e., only the number of cell in each image. Furthermore, we incorporate temporal information via a CRF, which smoothes the individual CNN predictions across the entire sequence. Our experiments demonstrate that our approach outperforms, by a large margin, the state-of-the-art method on the challenging task of counting cells in early stage human embryo development.

3 Deep Learning Based Cell Counter

Our goal is to count cells directly from the microscopy images of developing human embryos. We formulate cell counting as a classification problem and employ an end-to-end deep CNN framework. The main objective for our cell counting model is to learn a mapping $F : \mathbb{R}^{m \times n} \to \mathcal{L}$, where $m \times n$ is the size of the microscopy image and $\mathcal{L} = \{1, \ldots, N^{max}\}$ is the cell cardinality of the image, with the last label corresponding to N^{max}-or-more cells in the embryo. In practice, we use $N^{max} = 5$.

Our framework uses raw pixel intensity as input and, in contrast to previous cell counting approaches [5,13,20], only uses the cell count in each training image as annotation, without requiring any information about the objects shape, size and location. In this setting, our goal is to learn a mapping from an input image to the number of cells in this image, which we propose to do with a CNN, as discussed below.

3.1 CNN-Based Embryonic Cell Counting

In this work, we make use of images of developing embryos that were acquired using the $Eeva~System^{TM}$, for capturing microscopy images developed by Auxogyn, Inc. Embryos are placed in a petri dish inside an incubator and image acquisition software acquires a single-plane image every five minutes over a five day period. Below, we first present our approach to obtaining the training data and then discuss our CNN framework.

Computing Embryo Bounding Boxes. The microscopy images that we used as input contain a well boundary, which we remove by applying a pre-calculated boundary mask (see Fig. 2(b) for boundary-removed image). These images also contain extracellular material and noise that could easily confuse a classifier. To reduce the impact of this noise, we introduce a fully automatic approach to select a region of interest by computing a bounding box that encloses the embryo. To this end, we first determine the largest connected component in the thresholded boundary-removed intensity image and compute the centroid of this component. Each image contains one embryo only (in our application only one embryo is grown per well as shown in Fig. 2), so the centroid can be computed as the point within the component with maximum shortest distance to the region boundary [10]. We then crop the image around this centroid to obtain an image of size 151×151 pixels. The result is shown in Fig. 2(c). The dimension of the bounding box reflects the size of a fully developed embryo and is determined by the known optical setup of the image acquisition system. After processing all the training images in this manner, we normalize the results by subtracting the mean intensity taken over the whole dataset. The same mean is subtracted from test images.

Cell counting is invariant to rotation. Therefore, we generate additional training instances by applying arbitrary rotations and mirroring to the original data. This reduces overfitting and, as shown in our experiments, improves accuracy.

Our CNN Framework. We follow the architecture of Krizhevsky et al. [11]. Our CNN model contains eight layers (five convolutional ones and three fully connected ones). The first convolutional layer (Conv1) filters the 151×151 input image with 96 kernels of size 11×11. Conv2 has 256 filters of size 5×5, Conv3 and Conv4 have 384 filters of size 3×3, and the last Conv5 layer has 256 filters of size 3×3. The fully connected layers have 4096 neurons each with 50 % dropout ratio used during training. Max pooling layers with a 3×3 kernel size are used after Conv1, Conv2 and Conv5. We employ a Rectified Linear Unit (ReLU) activation function after every convolutional and fully connected layer.

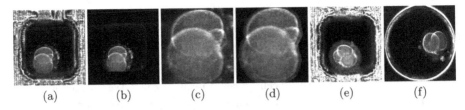

(a)   (b)   (c)   (d)   (e)   (f)

Fig. 2. Example of (a) raw intensity image; (b) boundary-removed image; (c) cropped image; and (d) masked cropped image [10]. Notice that the noise at the right of the image (c) is removed in (d) but that some boundary pixels are also affected. Also shown is (e) surrounding gel material; and (f) fragments attached to the embryo

Furthermore, we apply local response normalization to Conv1 and Conv2. The output layer encodes an ($N^{\mathrm{max}} = 5$)-way classification problem for which we use a softmax function to produce a distribution over the five class labels. The network maximizes the multinomial logistic log loss of the softmax output.

We use the Caffe [6] package to implement our model. All the configuration settings are standard other than those specified here. In particular, we initialize the learning rate to 0.005 and decrease it by a factor of 10 after half of the iterations. The momentum term is set to 0.9, and the weight decay to 0.0005. The network is trained for 5,000 iterations, taking three hours on an Nvidia K40 GPU. These parameters are obtained by cross-validation.

3.2   Enforcing Temporal Constraints

The CNN framework described above provides a cell count for each frame individually. However, in sequential data, as ours, adjacent frames are more likely to have the same number of cells. Considering neighboring frames can thus further improve the cell count over a complete time-lapse sequence. Following the work of Khan et al. [10], we capture this by making use of a conditional random field (CRF) with a unary and pairwise terms.

Formally, we represent the number of cells at time t with a discrete random variable N_t. Each variable N_t for $t \in \{1, \ldots, T\}$ can take a label from the set $\mathcal{L} = \{1, \ldots, N^{\mathrm{max}}\}$. Let $N_t \in \mathcal{L}$ denote the label assigned to frame t. Then we can define the energy of a complete labeling over all frames as

$$E(N_1, \ldots, N_T) = \sum_{t=1}^{T} \psi_t^{\mathrm{U}}(N_t) + \sum_{t=1}^{T-1} \psi_{t,t+1}^{\mathrm{P}}(N_t, N_{t+1}), \qquad (1)$$

where the unary term (ψ_t^{U}) represents a score for each cell count in each frame and is obtained from the log of the softmax output of our CNN-based cell counter. The pairwise term (ψ_t^{P}) enforces consistency between neighboring frames by imposing a biological constraint encoding the fact that the cell count should be monotonically non-decreasing over time and is expressed as

$$\psi_{t,t+1}^{\mathrm{P}}(N_t, N_{t+1}) = \begin{cases} 0, & \text{if } N_t \le N_{t+1} \\ \infty, & \text{if } N_t > N_{t+1} . \end{cases} \qquad (2)$$

Table 1. Cell stage prediction performance. Here, the average is computed as the arithmetic mean of the one to five cell predictions, and the overall represents the fraction of correct instances

Experiments	Cell stage prediction (%)						
	1-cell	2-cell	3-cell	4-cell	5-cell	Avg	Overall
RawImg	98.48	89.36	60.44	77.33	89.08	82.94	87.36
RawImgCRF	98.87	94.18	63.07	81.67	91.11	85.78	90.25
CroppedImg	99.19	94.51	70.41	82.90	92.89	87.98	91.45
CroppedImgCRF	**99.48**	**97.60**	**73.91**	**87.30**	**95.23**	**90.70**	**94.05**
Khan et al. [8]	95.66	87.93	23.91	65.91	73.12	69.31	77.93

We search for the most likely number of cells in each frame, and ultimately the most likely sequence. This corresponds to the assignment that minimizes $E(N_1, \ldots, N_T)$, which can be obtained efficiently by dynamic programming.

4   Experiments

We evaluated our approach on 265 time-lapse image sequences consisting of a total of 148,993 frames (with 21%, 24%, 4%, 23%, 28% of samples for 1 to 5-or-more cell cardinality, respectively). The sequences capture the embryos from 53 different patients and show a high degree of variation, such as extra cellular material artifacts and cell reabsorption. We used a 10-fold cross validation strategy and report the cell stage prediction accuracy, computed as the percentage of frames where the correct number of cells was predicted. We compare the results of our approach against the cell counting results of Khan et al. [8]. To obtain ground-truth, we manually annotated the sequences with the number of cells in each frame.

Table 1 compares the results of our approach with different types of input, with and without using the CRF, and against those of the state-of-the-art method of Khan et al. [8]. Note that, independently of the kind of input and of the use of a CRF, our approach always significantly outperforms Khan et al. [8]. In particular, our basic CNN cell counter, with raw intensity images as input, yields on average 13.63% and overall 9.43% improvement over Khan et al. [8]. The performance further improves by 5.04% on average and 4.09% overall by training our CNN with images cropped around the bounding box. The use of a CRF yields additional boost of roughly 3% both in average and overall accuracy. We note that the computational cost of the CRF is minimal and that our running time is well within the 5-minute interval between frames. Analyzing the performance for each cardinality reveals that our approach can reliably predict the correct number of cells up to the 5-cell stage. The improvement over the state-of-the-art method of Khan et al. [8] is highest in the 3-cell case (from 23.91% to 73.91%), which is the most challenging one due to the small amount of data available for this stage. Note that this lack of data also explains why

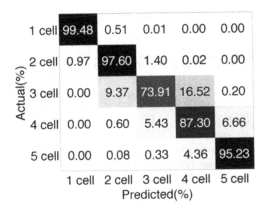

Fig. 3. Confusion matrix (CroppedImgCRF) %

Table 2. Ablation analysis. Here, the average is computed as the arithmetic mean of the one to five cell predictions, and the overall represents the fraction of correct instances

Experiments	(%)	
	Avg	Overall
CroppedImg w/o aug	80.32	85.82
CroppedImg w/o augCRF	83.65	89.08
CroppedImg w Mirror	83.32	87.79
CroppedImg w MirrorCRF	86.31	91.15
BRmImg	84.54	88.20
BRmCRF	88.09	92.12
MaskedImg	85.98	90.71
MaskedImgCRF	88.98	93.26

the 3-cell stage remains comparatively lower than the other stages even with our approach. The confusion matrix in Fig. 3 shows that our errors typically occur with adjacent classes. We show some error cases in Fig. 4.

In Table 2, we analyze the influence of several components of our method via an ablation study. To this end, we first evaluate the impact of data augmentation. Our results show that augmenting the data by mirroring and rotation (Cropped-Img vs CroppedImg w/o aug) increases the overall performance by 5.63 %. In particular, we observed a substantial improvement in the 3-cell case (17.62 %), which, as mentioned above suffers from data scarcity. Note that only using mir-roring augmentation (CroppedImg w Mirror and CroppedImg w MirrorCRF) improves over no augmentation at all, but still does not reach the accuracy when using rotation and mirroring. In addition to data augmentation, we also study the influence of our image pre-processing steps, described in the method section,

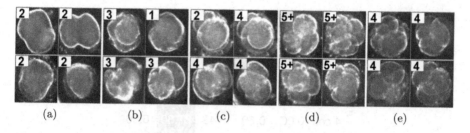

(a)   (b)   (c)   (d)   (e)

Fig. 4. Examples of cell counting error with CroppedImgCRF variant for 1-cell stage (a), 2-cell stage (b), 3-cell stage (c), 4-cell stage (d) and 5-or-more cell stage (e). Here, predicted cell count is mentioned on top left of each image

Table 3. Cell detection analysis. Here, the average is computed as the arithmetic mean of the one to four cell predictions, and the overall represents the fraction of correct instances

Experiments	Cell stage prediction (%)						
	1-cell	2-cell	3-cell	4-cell	5-cell	Avg	Overall
Khan et al. [9]	96.89	89.77	16.48	49.37	65.32	63.57	72.05
Detection w CroppedImgCRF	100.00	99.47	89.20	76.06	90.54	91.05	92.18

on our results. In particular, we observed an improvement of 0.84 % by training the CNN with the boundary-removed images (RawImg vs. BRmImg). As a pre-processing step, the method of Khan et al. [8] subtracts the background from the images by performing embryo segmentation [10] (see Fig. 2 (d)). To compare the impact of this background subtraction to our simpler bounding boxes, we trained a CNN with such background subtracted images. This resulted in performance drop of 0.74 % (MaskedImg vs. CroppedImg). The drop can be explained by the errors in the embryo masks, which occasionally include background and exclude foreground. These results suggest that our simpler bounding box based approach is more robust to these phenomena.

To summarize, all of the variants of our method yield significantly higher accuracy than the state-of-the-art (Khan et al. [8]) on this dataset. While the alternative method of Wang et al. [18] also performs cell counting directly from the masked microscopy images, they only evaluate on a subset of our data, and, more importantly, only up to the 4-cell case. A direct comparison is therefore not truly possible. However, we believe that the fact that their accuracy on the 4-cell stage was substantially lower than ours (-16.44 %) illustrates the superiority of our approach. Also, comparisons done by Khan et al. [8] showed that their method performed better than Wang et al. [18].

Finally, we also study the impact of our improved cell counts on the task of cell detection. To this end, we employed the method of Khan et al. [9] and replaced their cell counter with ours. For cell detection, we used the 35 sequences, consisting of 19,147 frames, in which the ground-truth cell locations were manually annotated. In Table 3, we can observe a substantial improvement (20.13 %) in cell detection accuracy, thanks to our better counting strategy.

5 Conclusion

Previous approaches to cell counting in microscopy images of early-stage embryo development [7–9,15,18] have put a lot of effort in designing features that are well-suited for the task. These approaches, however, do not scale up to the large variability observed in ever growing datasets. In this paper, we have therefore proposed to directly learn the relevant features from images. To this end, we have introduced a deep CNN approach to cell counting in microscopy images. Our experiments have demonstrated that our basic CNN counter outperforms previous cell counting methods by a margin of 16.12 % in overall accuracy. Furthermore, we have shown that this performance could be significantly improved by automatically computing a bounding box enclosing the embryo and by incorporating temporal information via a CRF. Altogether, our approach yields state-of-the-art results on the task of counting human embryonic cells in microscopy images. In the future, we plan to apply deep learning to analyze complete embryo sequences and find correlations with embryo viability. This will help embryologists to identify new biomarkers and, eventually, improve IVF success rates.

References

1. Chen, T., Chefd'hotel, C.: Deep learning based automatic immune cell detection for immunohistochemistry images. In: Wu, G., Zhang, D., Zhou, L. (eds.) MLMI 2014. LNCS, vol. 8679, pp. 17–24. Springer, Heidelberg (2014)
2. Cireşan, D.C., Meier, U., Gambardella, L.M., Schmidhuber, J.: Convolutional neural network committees for handwritten character classification. In ICDAR (2011)
3. Ciresan, D.C., Meier, U., Masci, J., Gambardella, L.M., Schmidhuber, J.: Flexible, high performance convolutional neural networks for image classification. In IJCAI (2011)
4. Cireşan, D.C., Giusti, A., Gambardella, L.M., Schmidhuber, J.: Mitosis detection in breast cancer histology images with deep neural networks. In: Mori, K., Sakuma, I., Sato, Y., Barillot, C., Navab, N. (eds.) MICCAI 2013, Part II. LNCS, vol. 8150, pp. 411–418. Springer, Heidelberg (2013)
5. Flaccavento, G., Lempitsky, V., Pope, I., Barber, P., Zisserman, A., Noble, J., Vojnovic, B., Learning to count cells: applications to lens-free imaging of large fields. Microscopic Image Analysis with Applications in Biology (2011)
6. Jia, Y., Shelhamer, E., Donahue, J., Karayev, S., Long, J., Girshick, R., Guadarrama, S., Darrell, T. Caffe: convolutional architecture for fast feature embedding. In: Proceedings of the 22nd ACM international conference on Multimedia (2014)
7. Khan, A., Gould, S., Salzmann, M.: A linear chain markov model for detection and localization of cells in early stage embryo development. In: WACV (2015)
8. Khan, A., Gould, S., Salzmann, M.: Automated monitoring of human embryonic cells up to the 5-cell stage in time-lapse microscopy images. In: ISBI (2015)

9. Khan, A., Gould, S., Salzmann, M.: Detecting abnormal cell division patterns in early stage human embryo development. In: Zhou, L., Wang, L., Wang, Q., Shi, Y. (eds.) MLMI 2015. LNCS, vol. 9352, pp. 161–169. Springer, Heidelberg (2015). doi:10.1007/978-3-319-24888-2_20
10. Khan, A., Gould, S., Salzmann, M.: Segmentation of developing human embryo in time-lapse microscopy. In: ISBI (2016)
11. Krizhevsky, A., Sutskever, I., Hinton, G.E.: Imagenet classification with deep convolutional neural networks. In: NIPS (2012)
12. LeCun, Y., Boser, B., Denker, J.S., Henderson, D., Howard, R.E., Hubbard, W., Jackel, L.D.: Backpropagation applied to handwritten zip code recognition. Neural Comput. 1(4), 541–551 (1989)
13. Lempitsky, V., Zisserman, A.: Learning to count objects in images. In: Advances in Neural Information Processing Systems (2010)
14. Meseguer, M., Herrero, J., Tejera, A., Hilligse, K.M., Ramsing, N.B., Jose, R.: The use of morphokinetics as a predictor of embryo implantation. Hum. Reprod. 26(10), 2658–2671 (2011)
15. Moussavi, F., Yu, W., Lorenzen, P., Oakley, J., Russakoff, D., Gould, S.: A unified graphical model framework for automated human embryo tracking. In: ISBI (2014)
16. Seguí, S., Pujol, O., Vitria, J.: Learning to count with deep object features. In: CVPR Workshops (2015)
17. Strigl, D., Kofler, K., Podlipnig, S.: Performance and scalability of GPU-based convolutional neural networks. In: PDP (2010)
18. Wang, Y., Moussavi, F., Lorenzen, P.: Automated embryo stage classification in time-lapse microscopy video of early human embryo development. In: Mori, K., Sakuma, I., Sato, Y., Barillot, C., Navab, N. (eds.) MICCAI 2013. LNCS, vol. 8150, pp. 460–467. Springer, Heidelberg (2013). doi:10.1007/978-3-642-40763-5_57
19. Wong, C., Loewke, K., Bossert, N., Behr, B., Jonge, C.D., Baer, T., Pera, R.R.: Non-invasive imaging of human embryos before embryonic genome activation predicts development to the blastocyst stage. Nature Biotechnol. 28(10), 1115–1121 (2010)
20. Xie, W., Noble, J.A., Zisserman, A.: Microscopy cell counting with fully convolutional regression networks. In: DLMIA (2015)
21. Zhang, C., Li, H., Wang, X., Yang, X.: Cross-scene crowd counting via deep convolutional neural networks. In: CVPR (2015)

W15 – Robust Reading

Preface

The Second International Workshop on Robust Reading (IWRR 2016) was organised in the context of ECCV 2016 in Amsterdam. The IWRR series, initiated at ACCV 2014 (Singapore), aims at bringing together computer vision researchers and practitioners in reading systems that operate on images acquired in unconstrained conditions, such as scene images, video sequences, born-digital images, wearable camera, lifelog feeds, social media images, etc. The automatic extraction and interpretation of textual content in images is a hot topic in the computer vision community with new datasets being released and the application areas being diversified. As an indicator of interest of the community, the Robust Reading Competition has received more than 4300 submissions to date.

Text content is not always present in images, but when it is, it tends to be important for scene understanding. Recent statistics from the large-scale Coco-Text dataset indicate that about 50% of the images contain some textual information. Text offers high-level semantic information, not easily obtainable from analysing the rest of the scene. As such, it requires an explicit and accurate recognition. It is interesting to see how visual question answering systems, which perform extremely well when interpreting visual content, seem to encounter difficulties when the answer sought lies in the textual content present in the scene. The time of celebrating this workshop marks a milestone in robust reading research, as the availability of large scale datasets, combined with latest developments in Deep Learning, enable for a holistic contextual reasoning between scene text and the rest of the scene contents.

IWRR 2016 received 12 original paper submissions, out of which 7 (59%) were accepted for oral presentation. The selection process was based on a double-blind reviewing process. At least 3 reviews were solicited for each paper. We cordially thank the program committee members for their excellent and time conscious responses. The programme featured 3 keynotes by distinguished invited speakers: M. Jaderberg (Google Deep Mind, UK), S. Belongie (Cornell Tech, USA) and R. Manmatha (A9.com, USA), who delivered outstanding talks covering both the industry and academia viewpoints. We want to thank Google Deep Mind and A9.com for sponsoring the corresponding invited talks. A panel discussion concluded the workshop, which allowed the participants to debate on a number of open challenges in the field.

We hope you will enjoy the proceedings of IWRR 2016!

October 2016

Dimosthenis Karatzas
Pramod Sankar Kompalli
Faisal Shafait
Jiri Matas
Masakazu Iwamura

Robust Text Detection
with Vertically-Regressed Proposal Network

Donglai Xiang[1(✉)], Qiang Guo[2], and Yan Xia[3]

[1] Tsinghua University, Beijing, China
xdl13@mails.tsinghua.edu.cn
[2] National University of Defense Technology, Changsha, China
[3] SenseTime Group Limited, Beijing, China

Abstract. Methods for general object detection, such as R-CNN [4] and Fast R-CNN [3], have been successfully applied to text detection, as in [7]. However, there exists difficulty when directly using RPN [10], which is a leading object detection method, for text detection. This is due to the difference between text and general objects. On one hand, text regions have variable lengths, and thus networks must be designed to have large receptive field sizes. On the other hand, positive text regions cannot be measured in the same way as that for general objects at training. In this paper, we introduce a novel vertically-regressed proposal network (VRPN), which allows text regions to be matched by multiple neighboring small anchors. Meanwhile, training regions are selected according to how much they overlap with ground-truth boxes vertically and the location of positive regions is regressed only in the vertical direction. Experiments on dataset provided by ICDAR 2015 Challenge 1 demonstrate the effectiveness of our methods.

Keywords: Text detection · Vertical regression · Regional Proposal Network

1 Introduction

Text detection, or text localization, plays a key role in robust text reading. Due to the special pattern of text regions, most traditional efforts utilize some specially designed features for text detection, such as the Maximally Stable Extremal Region (MSER) method [9] or the Stroke Width Transform (SWT) method [2]. Recently, the success of convolutional neural network in general object detection motivates researchers to bring the experience from general objects to text regions. For example, the method in [7] first generates some text proposals, and then performs classification and regression on them, which is similar to R-CNN [4] and Fast R-CNN [3] in a nutshell.

Text regions, as a special type of object regions, can be effectively detected by utilizing the detection framework of general objects, as revealed by [7]. Then we

---

D.Xiang and Q.Guo—Contributed equally to this work.

© Springer International Publishing Switzerland 2016
G. Hua and H. Jégou (Eds.): ECCV 2016 Workshops, Part I, LNCS 9913, pp. 351–363, 2016.
DOI: 10.1007/978-3-319-46604-0_26

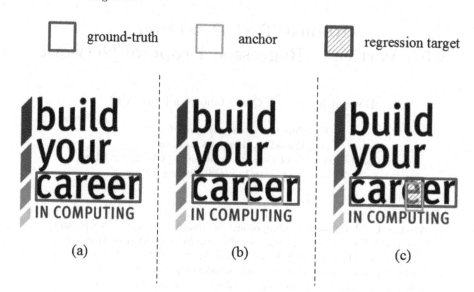

Fig. 1. (a) An example of text region that occupies almost the whole width of the image is shown in red box. (b) The anchor is shown in green, and it is excluded from positive training samples according to the measurement of RPN, but is included in our method. (c) Our method uses "thin" anchors (in green color) and only regresses the locations of ground-truth in vertical direction (in blue color). (Color figure online)

wonder how the most recent Faster R-CNN method [10] can be adopted for text detection. The core of Faster R-CNN [10] lies in a Region Proposal Network (RPN), in which object proposals are selected based on convolutional feature maps. Although RPN is originally used as a proposal generator, it can serve as a powerful detector itself. This paper will investigate the usage of RPN in the task of text detection.

However, directly applying RPN to text detection may suffer from a number of limitations. First, RPN selects positive training regions based on the intersection-over-union between an anchor and a ground-truth. In this way, anchors which fully overlap with a ground-truth in vertical direction but partly overlap in the horizontal direction are likely to be excluded from positive training samples, although they are text regions indeed (Fig. 1(b)). Second, the length of text regions varies substantially, and there always exist text regions that almost occupy the whole width of image (Fig. 1(a)). In this situation, the networks must be designed to have extremely large receptive field in horizontal direction in order to "see" large text regions thoroughly. As a result, the network is difficult to design: it must either have very deep convolutional layers, or skip many details in early steps by pooling.

To tackle the above problems, in this work we propose a vertically-regressed proposal network (VRPN) for the task of text detection. We select training samples in the view of what are text regions and what are not. In VRPN, positive training samples are not measured by the intersection-over-union between anchor regions and ground-truth boxes any more. Instead, anchor regions which largely overlap with a ground-truth box in vertical direction while lying inside the ground-truth box in horizontal direction are treated as positives (Fig. 1(b)). Considering that a text region is not a single object but a union of text patterns, we use very "thin" anchors and only regress the vertical coordinates of positive samples (Fig. 1(c)). In this way, training samples are selected based on the nature of text regions and it is not rigid to have a network with an extremely large receptive field size.

The contribution of this work is summarized as follows:

1. We show that the RPN method can be borrowed from general object detection to the task of text detection.
2. We demonstrate that the size of receptive field in a network is critical to the detection of text regions of variable sizes.
3. We propose a novel VRPN method that fully utilizes information in the images and effectively solves the challenge of detecting text regions with variable length.

In experiments, our VRPN method shows substantial improvement compared with the RPN method on the ICDAR 2015 Robust Reading Competition Challenge 1 [8], which demonstrates the effectiveness of the proposed method.

2   Related Works

A lot of efforts have been devoted to the task of text detection in literature. The proposed methods can be categorized in two lines: the connected-component methods and the sliding-window methods.

2.1   Connected-component Methods

Traditionally, connected-component methods [5,6,12,14,15] have been more prevalent for the text detection task, because text regions which have special patterns are favorable as detection targets by connected-component methods. Text in images, no matter in what language, consists of a number of disconnected characters with sharp boundaries and obvious patterns against the background. Therefore, connected-component methods rely on some manually designed features, usually pixel-level information, to build fast detectors for charter components, including MSER [9], SWT [2] and EdgeBox [16]. False alarms are then filtered out by text/non-text classifiers, such as SVM and CNN, and then character components are connected to get text lines with complex post-processing procedures.

The connected-component approaches have a great advantage in terms of speed, but their drawbacks are obvious as well. First, detectors based on low-level features generate a number of false alarms, leading to difficulties in filtering them out. Second, the process of combining all character components into text lines is usually quite complicated and inelegant. In addition, using CNNs as merely filters doesn't fully tap their potential, which we can see in the sliding-window methods where CNNs are used as powerful detectors.

2.2 Sliding-window Methods

Compared with connected-component methods, sliding-window approaches share more common techniques with general object detections. In sliding-window methods, a window (or windows) scans over the image in different locations and sizes, and features are extracted for the areas inside the window. Then the areas are classified as text or non-text by classfiers [1,11,13]. The windows can be boxes with pre-defined sizes, or just be region proposals. Similar to R-CNN [4] and Fast R-CNN [3], the recent text detection method in [7] first generates some text proposals, and then classifies and regresses them.

Notably, Ren *et al.* [10] propose a Faster R-CNN framework, which exploits convolutional features for proposing candidate windows. The core of Faster R-CNN is the Regional Proposal Network (RPN). In RPN, anchors are distributed all over the images in a sliding-window fashion, and then regions associated with the anchors are classified and regressed based on convolutional features. Although RPN is originally used as a proposal generator, it can be adopted as a powerful detector itself with great accuracy and high efficiency. However, there are still no works that show how RPN performs when used for text detection.

3   Vertically-Regressed Proposal Network for Text Detection

In this section, we introduce our vertically-regressed proposal network (VRPN). We first briefly review the Regional Proposal Network (RPN) proposed by Ren *et al.* [10]. Then we explain its limitation when used for text detection, and introduce our motivation. The proposed VPRN method is presented at last.

3.1 Regional Proposal Network

In RPN [10], classification and regression share the same convolutional layers. A number of anchors (k) with various sizes and aspect ratios are pre-defined, in order to explore the shape of objects. At training stage, images are fed into a convolutional network to obtain convolutional feature maps. Then a small network (usually a convolutional layer with 3×3 kernels followed by ReLU) slides on the feature map. Each point on the feature map corresponds to k anchors that are centered at the sliding window. Output of the sliding window is then fed into two sibling 1×1 convolutional layers: one with $2k$ outputs for classification (cls), and another with $4k$ outputs for bounding box regression (reg). For each anchor region, its intersection-over-union (IoU) with all ground-truth boxes is computed. If its IoU with any ground-truth box is higher than a threshold, the region is labeled as positive. The regression target for a positive

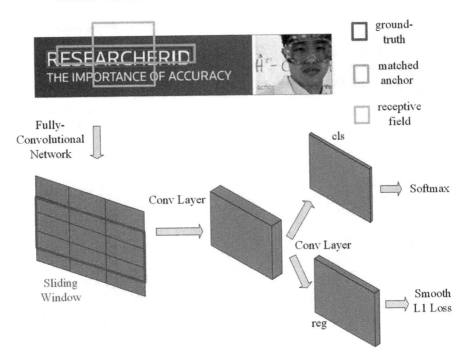

Fig. 2. Architecture of regional proposal network for the problem of text detection.

sample is its best-matched ground-truth box. At test stage, the network predicts a number of boxes regressed from the anchors, together with their objectiveness scores. Then non-maximal supression (NMS) is applied on these boxes to remove redundancy. The architecture of RPN is illustrated in Fig. 2.

3.2   Vertically-Regressed Proposal Network

Motivation. We find that there are a number of limitations when trying to apply RPN to text detection due to the following reasons.

First, the substantially varying sizes of text regions make the network designing challenging. In the original RPN method, networks usually don't have a receptive field that is large enough to cover all long text regions, so the detected location might deviate severely from the ground-truth. This problem might possibly be solved by enlarging the receptive field of the network. This can be achieved by either increasing the stride in early layers, or making the network deeper by adding more convolutional layers. However, on one hand, larger stride in early stage leads to inaccurate representation, which means a lot of details will be missing. This might hinder the accuracy of the prediction. On the other hand, adding more convolutional layers in order to deepen the network usually costs more computation. Neither solution is favorable for a text detection

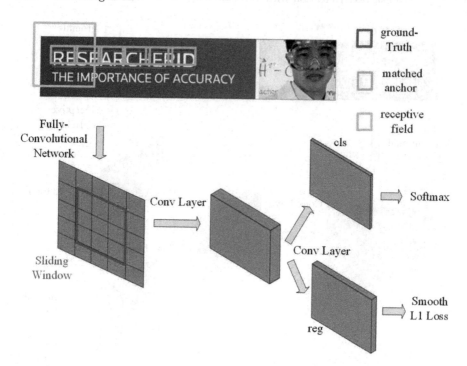

Fig. 3. Architecture of our proposed vertically-regressed proposal network.

system. Therefore, we hope to have a network that is able to deal with large text regions with moderate receptive field size and network size.

Second, as the aspect ratio of text regions are quite different, a large number of anchors with different height and width would be required in order to match the ground-truth boxes. This also increases the computation cost. We expect to have a network that can solve the problem with fewer anchors and less computation effort.

Third, in the training stage of RPN, positive and negative labels are assigned to anchors according to their IoU values with ground-truth. Therefore, some regions that are indeed textual would be excluded from positives. To illustrate, we show an example in Fig. 3. We can see that each of the green anchors region only covers a small part of the whole text region in red, so they will not be selected as positive samples. And even worse, the green regions may be selected as negatives. However, these regions are indeed textual, and the information within these regions might be contributive to training a powerful detector.

Network Description. Vertically-regressed proposal network shares a similar network structure to regional proposal network. However, VRPN adopts different approaches in selecting training samples and defining loss.

Our approach defines a new measurement of how well an anchor matches a ground-truth box for text regions. We denote the ground-truth bounding boxes inside an image by $\{G_j\} = \{(G_{jx1}, G_{jy1}, G_{jx2}, G_{jy2})\}$, where G_{jx1}, G_{jy1}, G_{jx2} and G_{jy2} are the x and y coordinates of the top-left and bottom-right vertices of G_j, respectively. Given an anchor $A_i = (A_{ix1}, A_{iy1}, A_{ix2}, A_{iy2})$, we define a candidate target bounding box for A_i and G_j as

$$t_{ij} = (\max\{G_{jx1}, A_{ix1}\}, G_{jy1}, \min\{G_{jx2}, A_{ix2}\}, G_{jy2}) \, . \tag{1}$$

The candidate target box is empty if $\max\{G_{jx1}, A_{ix1}\} > \min\{G_{jx2}, A_{ix2}\}$.

Then, the matching score between A_i and G_j is defined as

$$S_{ij} = \text{IoU}(A_i, t_{ij}) \, . \tag{2}$$

The class label assigned to A_i is

$$c_i^* = \begin{cases} 1 & \text{if } \max_j\{S_{ij}\} > \text{threshold}, \\ 0 & \text{otherwise.} \end{cases} \tag{3}$$

If A_i is assigned as positive, we also define the regression target associated with A_i as $T_i = t_{ij}$ where $j = \text{argmax}_k\{S_{ik}\}$.

To explain the rule in plain words, we select A_i as a positive training sample if the matching score between A_i and any ground-truth box is greater than a threshold. If the anchor is assigned a positive label, it is also trained for regression, and the regression target is just the candidate target bounding box t_{ij} that has the best matching score with A_i. This rule to match anchors with ground-truth boxes is illustrated in Fig. 4.

Loss Definition. The training loss for VRPN is given as

$$L(\{c_i\}, \{r_i\}) = \frac{1}{N_{\text{cls}}} \sum_i L_{\text{cls}}(c_i, c_i^*) + \frac{\lambda}{N_{\text{reg}}} \sum_i \sum_{j \in \{x, y, w, h\}} c_i^* L_{\text{reg}}(r_i^j, r_i^{j*}). \tag{4}$$

Here i is the index of anchor regions. c_i is the class prediction of A_i and c_i^* is its label for classification. r_i^x is a parameterized coordinate of the anchor's x-center, and r_i^{x*} is the parameterized coordinate of regression target associated with the anchor. $r_i^y, r_i^{y*}, r_i^w, r_i^{w*}, r_i^h$, and r_i^{h*}, are defined likewise. The parameterized coordinates are:

$$r^x = (x - x_a)/w_a, r^y = (y - y_a)/h_a,$$
$$r^w = \log(w/w_a), r^h = \log(h/h_a), \tag{5}$$

and

$$r^{x*} = (x^* - x_a)/w_a, r^{y*} = (y^* - y_a)/h_a,$$
$$r^{w*} = \log(w^*/w_a), r^{h*} = \log(h^*/h_a), \tag{6}$$

where $[x_a, y_a, w_a, h_a]$ are the x-center coordinate, y-center coordinate, width and height of the anchor A_i, respectively, while $[x, y, w, h]$ and $[x^*, y^*, w^*, h^*]$ are similarly defined for the prediction and the regression target T_i associated with A_i. L_{cls} is the classification loss, computed by softmax and cross-entropy loss over the text/non-text classes. L_{reg} is the regression loss, for which we adopt smooth L_1 loss as defined in [3]. The parameter λ is a weight to balance them.

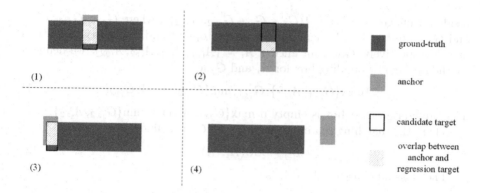

Fig. 4. Four cases for matching an anchor with a ground-truth box. In case (1), the anchor has an IoU above a threshold 0.7 with its candidate target box; in case (2), the anchor deviates too much from the ground-truth in the vertical direction to be matched with it; in case (3), the left end of the anchor is outside the ground-truth so the candidate target has a different left boundary with the anchor; in case (4), the anchor is completely outside the ground-truth and they don't match each other. Whether an anchor region is assigned as positive or not is based on its IoU with its target.

3.3 Implementation Details

Our VRPN method measures how well an anchor matches a ground-truth box mainly according to how much they overlap vertically (if the anchor lies inside the ground-truth box in the horizontal direction). A ground-truth can be matched by several neighbouring anchors, whose x-coordinates differ by a total stride of the network one by one. Therefore, the width of the anchors can be set to be slightly larger than the total stride to ensure that they leave no space in between, and only their height varies to fit different text areas.

At test stage, just like RPN, the output of the network is a bunch of filtered boxes regressed from the anchors. Then non-maximal suppresion (NMS) is performed on these boxes at some threshold. Then some of them are merged together if they overlap horizontally in order to match long words.

4   Experiments

4.1   Dataset and Evaluation Metric

We conduct experiments on the dataset provided for Challenge 1: "Born-Digital Images (Web and Email)" of ICDAR 2015 Robust Reading Competition [8]. The dataset contains 410 images for training and 141 images for testing. We train all networks with the 410 training images in this dataset and conduct testing using the 141 test images.

Considering the fact that NMS and other post-processing steps actually have quite a large impact on the detection results, while what we really want to compare is the ability of the networks to cover ground-truth boxes with few false alarms, we first evaluate methods by their raw outputs without post-processing. So we use a pixel-level evaluation. We compare the performance of methods by f-measure, which is defined as

$$F_\beta = (1 + \beta^2) \frac{\text{precision} \cdot \text{recall}}{\beta^2 \text{precision} + \text{recall}} \ . \tag{7}$$

The f-measure is a combination of recall and precision. Recall is defined as the number of pixels in ground-truth boxes that are covered by at least one output box divided by the total number of ground-truth pixels in the dataset. And precision is defined as the number of detected ground-truth pixels divided by all pixels in the output boxes, with repeatedly detected pixels counted only once. We use $\beta = 1$ in evaluation, *i.e.* the F_1 score, which is the harmonic mean of precision and recall values.

Although post-processing steps are not our focus in this paper, we still provide the performance of all methods after non-maximal suppresion (NMS) and basic merging, which will be explained more detailedly in the next paragraph, in order to demonstrate that our conclusion on methods won't be challenged when post-processing steps are added to the pipeline. We still use F_1 score to evaluate performance and the threshold of NMS is set at 0.3 for this experiment setting.

Merging of Bounding Boxes. After NMS is performed on the raw output boxes, some of them are merged together in order to match long words and extract text lines. All the boxes in a connected component are merged to one box. The connected components are built by adding two boxes which overlap with each other. Here the "overlap" means one box is completely enclosed by the other or the height of their intersection box divided by the maximum of their heights is above a certain threshold. The four boundaries of the final output box are computed as the leftmost one and the rightmost one, as well as the averaged upper and lower boundaries of boxes inside a connected component.

4.2   Experiments on Vertically-Regressed Proposal Network

In this subsection, we verify the motivation of our VRPN method and demonstrate its superiority to RPN for the task of text detection by a number of experiments.

How Receptive Field Size Affects the Performance of RPN? In Sect. 3.2 we argue that, in order for the RPN network to regress the box locations accurately, the receptive field of the network has to be large enough, especially in horizontal direction. In order to validate it, we conduct the following experiments in regard to RPN.

We compare two networks with different receptive field sizes, using the RPN method. The structures of the two networks are shown in Table 1. The same 10

Table 1. Structure of RPN networks

Layer	Parameters			
Network index	RPN I		RPN II	
Conv	kernel=5, pad=2, stride_w=2, stride_h=1, output=16			
ReLU	-			
Conv	kernel=5, pad=2, stride=1, output=16			
ReLU	-			
Max pooling	kernel=2, stride=2			
Conv	kernel=3, pad=1, stride=1, output=32		kernel=5, pad=2, stride=1, output=32	
ReLU	-		-	
Conv	kernel=3, pad=1, stride=1, output=32		kernel=5, pad=2, stride=1, output=32	
ReLU	-		-	
Max pooling	kernel=2, stride=2		kernel=2, stride=2	
Conv	kernel=3, pad=1, stride=1, output=64		kernel=5, pad=2, stride=1, output=64	
ReLU	-		-	
Conv	kernel=3, pad=1, stride=1, output=64		kernel=5, pad=2, stride=1, output=64	
ReLU	-		-	
Conv (sliding window)	kernel=3, pad=1, stride=1, output=256			
relu	-			
Conv	kernel=1, pad=0, stride=1, output=20	kernel=1, pad=0, stride=1, output=40	kernel=1, pad=0, stride=1, output=20	kernel=1, pad=0, stride=1, output=40
Loss	softmax loss	smooth L_1 loss	softmax lost	smooth L_1 loss
Receptive field size	horizontal: 67, vertical: 36		horizontal: 115, vertical: 60	

anchors with different sizes are used, which are obtained by clustering ground-truth boxes in training set. The two networks only differ in the kernel sizes in four convolutional layers, and RPN II has a larger receptive field.

As can be seen from Table 2, the network with a larger receptive field performs better, no matter with or without post-processing. However, having a receptive field size large enough to cover all text regions results in a number of problems, as has been discussed in Sect. 3.2. This motivates us to develop the VRPN method.

Comparison Between RPN and VRPN. In this section we conduct experiments to compare the performance of RPN and VRPN. In VRPN, we use the same network structure and anchors as RPN II. So in this experiment, the

Table 2. Comparisons between RPN I and RPN II with different receptive field size.

	w/o post-processing			with post-processing		
	Precision	Recall	F_1	Precision	Recall	F_1
RPN I	0.666	0.513	0.579	0.678	0.654	0.666
RPN II	0.666	0.630	0.648	0.744	0.660	0.699

difference between RPN and VRPN lies in the selection of positive/negative training samples. Results are shown in Table 3. We can see that VPRN achieves a much higher recall and overall F_1 score than RPN. The improvement is because, VRPN selects positive training samples mainly according to how well anchors overlap with ground-truth vertically, which allows much more anchors assigned as positive. At test stage, more anchors are located in text areas where they will be scored higher according to our method of training, and therefore cover more text pixels to achieve a better recall. Also, our precision is close to RPN. This experiment verifies the superiority of VRPN.

How to Choose Anchors for VRPN? The VRPN method makes the selection of anchors easy. Because in VRPN, the anchors only need to explore the heights of ground-truth boxes and their width can be fixed to a value slightly larger than the horizontal stride of the network. This makes detection more accurate than using wider anchors as in RPN. We use the following experiments to validate this idea. We compare two VRPN settings with different anchors. For VRPN I, we use the same 10 anchors as before; and for VRPN II, we use 5 anchors whose widths are fixed at 10 (the horizontal stride of the network is 8) and heights range from 8 to 40. The network structure and other hyperparameters remain the same. Experimental results are shown in Table 4.

From the results we can see that VRPN with anchors selected in our designed method achieves better performance than the original manner even with fewer anchors and less computation cost. The improvement is presumably due to finer regression of target bounding boxes, which is a benefit of the smaller anchors. Some examples of detection outputs by VRPN II are shown in Fig. 5.

Table 3. Comparisons between RPN and VRPN with the same network structure and anchors.

	w/o post-processing			with post-processing		
	Precision	Recall	F_1	Precision	Recall	F_1
RPN II	0.666	0.630	0.648	0.744	0.660	0.699
VRPN I	0.645	0.858	0.736	0.730	0.777	0.753

Table 4. Comparison between two ways of selecting anchors

	w/o post-processing			with post-processing		
	Precision	Recall	F_1	Precision	Recall	F_1
VRPN I	0.645	0.858	0.736	0.730	0.777	0.753
VRPN II	0.709	0.822	0.761	0.707	0.826	0.762

Fig. 5. Example detections by the VRPN II network. For each column in this figure, the first row shows the original image; the second row shows the raw outputs of the method; and the third row shows the final detection result after merging.

5   Conclusion

In this paper, we present a vertically-regressed proposal network. This method originates from RPN and is developed for text detection. In the proposed method, text regions are matched by several consecutive anchor regions, and each anchor region is regressed to predict the upper and lower boundaries of text regions. This allows the network to perform accurate and robust text detection with moderate network structure, fewer anchors and lower computation cost.

Using "thin" anchors in VRPN can be treated as making anchor-level inference on dense feature maps. For future work, we can investigate pixel-level detection which makes inference on a feature map of the same size as the original image.

References

1. Chen, X., Yuille, A.L.: Detecting and reading text in natural scenes. In: Proceedings of the 2004 IEEE Computer Society Conference on Computer Vision and Pattern Recognition, CVPR 2004, vol. 2, pp. II-366. IEEE (2004)
2. Epshtein, B., Ofek, E., Wexler, Y.: Detecting text in natural scenes with stroke width transform. In: 2010 IEEE Conference on Computer Vision and Pattern Recognition (CVPR), pp. 2963–2970. IEEE (2010)
3. Girshick, R.: Fast R-CNN. In: Proceedings of the IEEE International Conference on Computer Vision, pp. 1440–1448 (2015)
4. Girshick, R., Donahue, J., Darrell, T., Malik, J.: Rich feature hierarchies for accurate object detection and semantic segmentation. In: Proceedings of the IEEE Conference on Computer Vision and Pattern Recognition, pp. 580–587 (2014)
5. Huang, W., Lin, Z., Yang, J., Wang, J.: Text localization in natural images using stroke feature transform and text covariance descriptors. In: Proceedings of the IEEE International Conference on Computer Vision, pp. 1241–1248 (2013)
6. Huang, W., Qiao, Y., Tang, X.: Robust Scene text detection with convolution neural network induced MSER trees. In: Fleet, D., Pajdla, T., Schiele, B., Tuytelaars, T. (eds.) ECCV 2014, Part IV. LNCS, vol. 8692, pp. 497–511. Springer, Heidelberg (2014)
7. Jaderberg, M., Simonyan, K., Vedaldi, A., Zisserman, A.: Reading text in the wild with convolutional neural networks. Int. J. Comput. Vis. **116**(1), 1–20 (2016)
8. Karatzas, D., Gomez-Bigorda, L., Nicolaou, A., Ghosh, S., Bagdanov, A., Iwamura, M., Matas, J., Neumann, L., Chandrasekhar, V.R., Lu, S., et al.: ICDAR 2015 competition on robust reading. In: 2015 13th International Conference on Document Analysis and Recognition (ICDAR), pp. 1156–1160. IEEE (2015)
9. Matas, J., Chum, O., Urban, M., Pajdla, T.: Robust wide-baseline stereo from maximally stable extremal regions. Image and Vis. Comput. **22**(10), 761–767 (2004)
10. Ren, S., He, K., Girshick, R., Sun, J.: Faster R-CNN: towards real-time object detection with region proposal networks. In: Advances in Neural Information Processing Systems, pp. 91–99 (2015)
11. Tian, S., Lu, S., Su, B., Tan, C.L.: Scene text recognition using co-occurrence of histogram of oriented gradients. In: 2013 12th International Conference on Document Analysis and Recognition (ICDAR), pp. 912–916. IEEE (2013)
12. Tian, S., Pan, Y., Huang, C., Lu, S., Yu, K., Lim Tan, C.: Text flow: a unified text detection system in natural scene images. In: Proceedings of the IEEE International Conference on Computer Vision, pp. 4651–4659 (2015)
13. Wang, K., Babenko, B., Belongie, S.: End-to-end scene text recognition. In: 2011 IEEE International Conference on Computer Vision (ICCV), pp. 1457–1464. IEEE (2011)
14. Ye, Q., Huang, Q., Gao, W., Zhao, D.: Fast and robust text detection in images and video frames. Image Vis. Comput. **23**(6), 565–576 (2005)
15. Yin, X.C., Yin, X., Huang, K., Hao, H.W.: Robust text detection in natural scene images. IEEE Trans. Pattern Anal. Mach. Intell. **36**(5), 970–983 (2014)
16. Zitnick, C.L., Dollár, P.: Edge boxes: locating object proposals from edges. In: Fleet, D., Pajdla, T., Schiele, B., Tuytelaars, T. (eds.) ECCV 2014, Part V. LNCS, vol. 8693, pp. 391–405. Springer, Heidelberg (2014)

Scene Text Detection with Adaptive Line Clustering

Xinxu Qiao[✉], He Zhu, and Weiping Li

Department of Electronic Engineering and Information Science,
University of Science and Technology of China, Hefei, China
{qxx,ghost}@mail.ustc.edu.cn, wpli@ustc.edu.cn

Abstract. We propose a scene text detection system which can maintain a high recall while achieving a fair precision. In our method, no character candidate is eliminated based on character-level features. A weighted directed graph is constructed and the minimum average cost path algorithm is adopted to extract line candidates. After assigning three line-level probability values to each line, the final decisions are made according to the line candidate clustering of the current image. The proposed system has been evaluated on the ICDAR 2013 dataset. Compared with other published methods, it has achieved better performances.

Keywords: Line-level features · Weighted directed graph model · Minimum average cost path algorithm · Line candidate clustering

1 Introduction

Text detection and recognition in natural scenes is a key technology to potential applications such as autonomous navigation, multilingual translation, and assistance to the visually impaired people. While there have been significant advances in recent years, text detection still remains challenging due to the diversity of scene text and the complexity of background. For comprehensive surveys, refer to [8, 20, 24].

A typical text detection system usually consists of four components, namely, character candidate extraction, false candidate elimination, text line generation, and text line verification. Existing methods for scene text detection can be largely categorized into three groups: methods using the sliding window [7, 18, 23], methods using the connected components [2, 5, 15, 21], and hybrid methods [6].

Zhang et al. [23] adopted the sliding window which is based on the symmetry property of character groups. In the work [7] text saliency maps were computed by evaluating the character/background convolutional neural network classifier in a sliding window. Tian et al. [18] detected character candidates by combining the sliding window scheme with a fast cascade boosting algorithm that exhibited a high performance.

Compared with the methods using the sliding window, methods based on connected components have become popular during the last ten years, since

© Springer International Publishing Switzerland 2016
G. Hua and H. Jégou (Eds.): ECCV 2016 Workshops, Part I, LNCS 9913, pp. 364–377, 2016.
DOI: 10.1007/978-3-319-46604-0_27

these methods are usually more efficient and relatively insensitive to variations in scale, orientation, font, and language type. SWT [4] and MSER [11] are two representative component-based methods for scene text detection, which constitute the basis of a lot of subsequent works [2,5,15,21]. The method of Neumann and Matas [12] exploited the MSER detector and then classified the detected regions as either a character, a multi-character or the background. In [3] a fast stroke detector was proposed based on an efficient pixel intensity comparison to surrounding pixels.

However, the character candidate extraction brings in too many non-text components especially in component-based methods, making it difficult to attain a high precision. Meanwhile, the traditional text detection process often suffers from an error accumulation problem. In particular, the errors occurring in each of the four sequential steps will propagate to the subsequent steps and eventually lead to a low detection recall.

To address these issues, our scene text detection system is proposed from a new aspect. All the regions extracted in the first step are reserved to generate line candidates and the final text lines for each image are decided based on the clustering of line candidates which are represented by three line-level probability values.

Since we do not eliminate the character candidates based on character-level features, the system is able to obtain a high recall. But in the meantime, more false line candidates are generated which requires a high-performance classifier to pick out true text lines. In our system, thanks to the line-level probability values, the clustering strategy can successfully handle this problem and make the system adaptive to various scenes. Every component of the proposed framework is linked to each other and plays an essential role. Our system has been evaluated on the ICDAR 2013 dataset. Compared with other published methods, we have achieved better results.

The rest of the paper is organized as follows: In Sect. 2, we describe all the details of the proposed system. The experimental results and discussions are presented in Sect. 3, followed by the conclusions in Sect. 4.

2   The Proposed System

The proposed scene text detection system consists of character candidate extraction, character probability assignment, line candidate generation and line candidate clustering. The flow chart of the system is shown in Fig. 1.

To be specific, we extract character candidates on three image channels and assign a probability value to each region through a random forest classifier. A weighted directed graph is then constructed on each channel and a minimum average cost path algorithm is proposed to generate all the possible lines. Each line candidate has a potential line probability calculated on the components' probabilities. After that, line candidates from different channels are merged and sent through symmetry classifier and appearance classifier to get another two probabilities. Finally, all lines are split into text and non-text based on the clustering of the three probabilities.

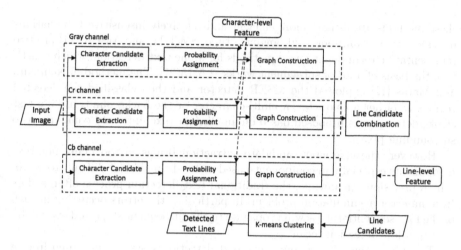

Fig. 1. The flow chart of the proposed scene text detection system

2.1 Character Candidate Extraction

The goal of this step is to detect as many text regions as possible to ensure the recall of the whole system. Sung et al. [15] introduced a high recall method to extract character candidates based on the extremal region (ER) tree. We improve this method by adding some post-processing steps to make it suitable for the following construction of graph.

The image is converted to YC_bC_r color space and the gray, C_r, C_b channels are used in the extraction method. An ER tree is first constructed on each channel and divided into multiple sub-trees according to the size and position similarities of adjacent regions. The similarity between two regions is computed as:

$$S(R_t, R_{t+1}) = \frac{A(R_t) \cap A(R_{t+1})}{A(R_t) \cup A(R_{t+1})} \tag{1}$$

where $A(\bullet)$ denotes the bounding box of an extremal region and t denotes the threshold level.

When the similarity between R_t and R_{t+1} is smaller than a threshold value, the tree is separated into two sub-trees. Then the sub-trees with small depth are pruned and only one region with the smallest regularized stability value is chosen as the character candidate from each sub-tree. The regularized stability value [21] is defined as:

$$\Psi(R_t) = \begin{cases} (|R_{t-1}| - |R_t|)/|R_t| + \theta_1(a - a_{max}) & if \quad a > a_{max} \\ (|R_{t-1}| - |R_t|)/|R_t| + \theta_2(a_{min} - a) & if \quad a < a_{min} \\ (|R_{t-1}| - |R_t|)/|R_t| & otherwise \end{cases} \tag{2}$$

where $|R_t|$ denotes the cardinality of R_t.

The candidates obtained so far are not suitable for graph construction because one region may cover some other regions. To tackle this issue, we apply Ostu method [13] on the candidate and its neighbor regions to get local binary images. These local images are added to a black image which has the same size as the input image. Finally, the connected components on the whole binary images are taken as the character candidates.

2.2 Character Probability Assignment

In this stage, we assign a probability value to each character candidate instead of removing the ones that are classified as non-character. This avoids wrongly removing character candidates. More specifically, the random forest is adopted as the classifier with the feature of Co-occurrence of Histogram of Oriented Gradients (Co-HOG). We take the output value of the random forest classifier as the candidate's probability.

Co-HOG as an extension of HOG is first proposed to deal with human detection task [19] and later used in text recognition [17]. It captures spatial information by counting frequency of co-occurrence of oriented gradients between pixel pairs. Thus it represents more shape information and is capable to identify text candidate.

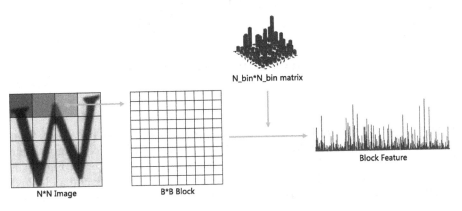

N_bin*N_bin matrix

Block Feature

N*N Image   B*B Block

Fig. 2. The extraction process of the Co-HOG feature

For each candidate as shown in Fig. 2, we take the bounding rectangle region of the binary image and divide it into several blocks without overlapping. The block feature is obtained by a co-occurrence matrix computed on each block and the Co-HOG feature descriptor of the whole region can then be constructed by concatenating all the normalized block features. The co-occurrence matrixs computation method in [17] is used.

We train our classifier on the training set of ICDAR 2013 dataset. The above character candidate extraction method is used on each training image to obtain candidate regions. The regions that satisfy the following condition are labeled as positive samples:

$$\frac{(Area(D) \cap Area(G))}{(Area(D) \cup Area(G))} > 0.8 \tag{3}$$

where D is a detected candidate and G is the ground truth character bounding box. Those regions that do not overlap with any ground truth character are labeled as negative samples.

2.3   Line Candidate Generation

The process of the proposed line candidate generation method consists of four steps: graph construction, minimum average cost path generation, potential line probability computation, and multiple channels combination.

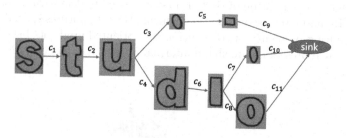

Fig. 3. Illustration of the weighted directed graph

Graph Construction. Based on the assumption that all text lines start from the left to the right, all character candidates are first sorted according to their horizontal coordinates. The weighted directed graph as illustrated in Fig. 3 can thus be constructed. Each character candidate stands for a vertex and a directed edge from vertex A to vertex B is created if they satisfy the following conditions:

$$D_x(N_A, N_B)/min(W_A, W_B) < T_x \tag{4}$$
$$D_y(N_A, N_B)/min(H_A, H_B) < T_y \tag{5}$$
$$min(H_A, H_B)/max(H_A, H_B) < T_s \tag{6}$$
$$min(P_A^c, P_B^c) > T_p \quad || \quad (P_A^c - 0.5) * (P_B^c - 0.5) > 0 \tag{7}$$

where $D_x(N_A, N_B)$ and $D_y(N_A, N_B)$ are the horizontal and vertical distances between the centers of vertex A and vertex B, W_A (W_B) and H_A (H_B) are the width and height of vertex A (B), P_A^c (P_B^c) is the character probability of vertex A (B).

The cost of an edge should be affected by two elements: the probabilities of the two vertices and the distance between them. When two linked vertices belong to a true text line, the cost of the edge should be small. So the cost is defined as below:

$$C(N_A, N_B) = \theta_1 * D(N_A, N_B) + \theta_2/(P_A^c + P_B^c) \qquad (8)$$

where $D(N_A, N_B)$ denotes the Euclidean distance between two vertex centers.

In addition, we increase a sink in the graph. If the out-degree of a vertex is zero, there will be an edge from the vertex to the sink and the cost is zero. The sink represents no physical existence, but it benefits the following minimum average cost path algorithm and reduces the number of generated line candidates.

Minimum Average Cost Path Generation. In every channel graph, there are vertices that have on one on the left and vertices that can reach no one on the right. These two kinds represent the beginning and the ending of a text line respectively. The algorithm aims to find a path from a starting vertex to the sink with the minimum average cost which should represent the most likely text line among all the paths from the same starting vertex. Then the minimum average cost paths from all starting vertices compose the line candidates.

The proposed minimum average cost path algorithm is a modified version of the Dijkstra algorithm. The Dijkstra algorithm measures the sum of the path cost in order to find the shortest path between two vertices. However, in our case a longer path may be more likely to represent a text line. So we change the criterion by computing the average cost of every path. The path with the minimum average cost is selected as a line candidate.

Potential Line Probability Computation. Once the minimum average cost path is found, the character candidates that compose this line are settled. Thus a potential line probability for this line can be computed based on the character probabilities.

Instead of simply averaging the values, we propose a context-based method. Such calculation should give the line candidate a higher value if most of the components are actually characters. On the contrary, the false lines are assigned with lower values than the averages. The specific formula is defined as follows:

$$P_i^l = \frac{P_{i-1}^l * (i-1) + (P_{i-1}^l + \theta_p) * P_i^c}{i} \quad i = 1, 2, \cdots, N \qquad (9)$$

where $P_0^l = 1 - \theta_p$ and N is the number of components in the line candidate. The potential line probability $P_L = P_N^l$.

The parameter θ_p should be corresponding to the threshold that is used to classify samples by the classifier. Generally speaking, a sample is classified as true if the probability of the random forest classifier is larger than 0.5. But it can also be set as another proper value according to the distribution of the classifier outputs.

Multiple Channels Combination. This step is designed to combine the line candidates from different image channels. For every line candidate, we first find a minimum rotated rectangle that can contain all the character level components. Then we divide all the line candidates into several subsets based on the overlapping between rotated rectangles from different channels. The candidates in a subset are supposed to correspond to the same line and the one with highest potential line probability is chosen to form the final line candidate set.

2.4 Line Candidate Clustering

The mechanism of how human identify and recognize text in natural scenes is still not clear at present, but it has been shown that people with normal vision can effortlessly discover text regions without looking into each individual character, even at a glance [23]. Taking advantage of this property, we introduce two line-level classifiers based on symmetry feature and appearance feature which give each line candidate two more probabilities. Together with the potential line probability, the line candidates separate into text and non-text according to the clustering algorithm.

Symmetry Feature. A text line usually exhibits high self-similarity to itself and strong contrast to its local background. Based on this property, we design our line-level symmetry feature. We improve Zhang et al.'s template [23] to fit the line boundary better and reduce the influences of close lines.

Fig. 4. Illustration of our template for line features extraction

As illustrated in Fig. 4, The template consists of four rectangles denoted by R_T, R_{MT}, R_{MB}, and R_B, respectively. The details of the template construction process are described as follows. For every line, a rough axle is obtained through the fitting of character component centers. Then the components whose center is obviously far away from the axle are eliminated. A new axle is calculated through the remaining components. Such operations repeat until the axle is stable. R_M is the minimum rotated rectangle of the final components. R_{MT}, R_{MB}, R_T, R_B are then obtained based on R_M. The height factor r of R_T and R_B ranges from 0.2 to 1 and is chosen with all line candidates taking into account. The criterion is to set the value of r as large as possible while making sure that the background region does not overlap with any other line candidate.

Let $h^c_{x,y}(R_P)$ denotes the histogram of the transformation image c in the rectangle R_P, where $(P \in T, M, B, MT, MB)$. The symmetry are defined as follows:

$$S^c_{x,y} = \chi^2(h^c_{x,y}(R_MT), h^c_{x,y}(R_MB)) \tag{10}$$

$$Ct^c_{x,y} = \chi^2(h^c_{x,y}(R_T), h^c_{x,y}(R_MT)) \tag{11}$$

$$Cb^c_{x,y} = \chi^2(h^c_{x,y}(R_B), h^c_{x,y}(R_MB)) \tag{12}$$

where $\chi^2(\bullet)$ is the χ^2-distance function [14]. We adopt four kinds of transformation image: gradient image, texture image [10], Laplacian image, and the corresponding channel image where the candidate is extracted. All these features are concatenated to form the 12-dimensional feature vector.

Appearance Feature. Besides the symmetry feature, appearance feature that contains enormous information also plays a significant role. We adopt affine transformation to get a horizontal rectangle based on the aforesaid R_T and the rectangle is resized to a new one whose aspect ratio is 2.5 but height remains unchanged. Then the Convolutional Co-HOG (ConvCo-HOG) feature [16] is calculated on the channel image that the line candidate is extracted on.

Compared with the Co-HOG feature, ConvCo-HOG feature is extracted based on a sliding block instead of dividing the image into non-overlapping blocks. But the calculation of the co-occurrence matrix is the same as Co-HOG.

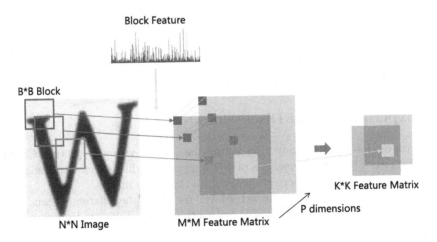

Fig. 5. The extraction process of the ConvCo-HOG feature

As illustrated in Fig. 5, the $N * N$ input image constructs P different feature matrixes with the size of $M * M$ where P is the dimension of co-occurrence matrix and $M = N - B + 1$. Then the average pooling strategy [1] is applied on each of the above feature matrix by averaging the feature vectors within a small non-overlapping window defined as follows:

$$F_{avg}(i,j) = (\sum F(i - T/2 : i + T/2, j - T/2 : j + T/2))/T^2 \qquad (13)$$

where F is a $M*M$ feature matrix and $T*T$ is the size of the average window. The final dimension of the ConvCo-HOG feature vector is $K^2 P$, where $K = M/T$. For more details, refer to [16].

Congeneric Line Candidates Clustering. Traditional text detection systems often adopt a line classifier in the final step to make hard decisions. However, text lines in natural scenes vary widely due to the various fonts, contents and so on. It is difficult to design a high-performance classifier to pick out the text lines while making the false alarms as few as possible.

In our system, we have obtained three line-level probabilities which inspire us to solve the problem with the clustering algorithm. Each line candidate corresponds to a point in a three-dimensional space and K-means algorithm is used to divide the candidates of an image into two classes. Compared to the fixed threshold of a classifier, this operation tactfully selects true text lines and it's robust to different scenes.

Notice that the initial state is crucial to K-means algorithm, an improper initial state can lead to very bad performance. Meanwhile, since we don't remove candidates based on character information, quite a few line probabilities are close to zero. If the clustering is based on all the line candidates, many false alarms will be introduced which will result in a low precision. To address these issues, we sort the line candidates based on the sum of the three probabilities and take the top fifteen candidates into clustering. The initial positive set only contains the candidate with the highest probability sum and the initial negative set only contains the candidate with the lowest probability sum. The other candidates are labeled according to their distance from the first-pass centers.

3 Experiments and Discussions

The proposed scene text detection system has been evaluated on the ICDAR 2013 dataset. The dataset consists of 462 images including 229 for training and 233 for testing. Our classifiers are trained on these 229 images.

First, we evaluated the character-level recall of the character candidate extraction method and compared it with others (see Table 1). Equation 14 is the criterion used in this experiment,

$$\frac{Area(D) \cap Area(G)}{Area(D) \cup Area(G)} > 0.5 \qquad (14)$$

where D is the detected candidate and G is the ground truth character bounding box.

Table 1. Character-level results on ICDAR 2013 dataset with Eq. 14 as criterion

Method	Precision(%)	Recall(%)
Proposed method	13.95	83.49
Sung et al. [15]	11.21	84.55
Tian et al. [18]	23.10	89.20

Our extraction method takes connected components on the whole processed image as candidates, a character candidate sometimes consists of two or more connected characters. This case makes the proposed method disadvantaged when comparing with others based on Eq. 14. However, in our system we don't eliminate character candidates, connected characters are still retained to generate line candidates. Thus we propose a new reasonable criterion as follows:

$$\frac{Area(D) \cap Area(G)}{Area(G)} > 0.7 \quad \&\& \quad \frac{min(Height(D), Height(G))}{max(Height(D), Height(G))} > 0.7 \quad (15)$$

We did not implement the extraction method of Tian et al., so our method is only compared with the one of Sung et al. based on this criterion. The new results are shown in Table 2.

Table 2. Character-level results on ICDAR 2013 dataset with Eq. 15 as criterion

Method	Precision(%)	Recall(%)
Proposed method	13.91	86.99
Sung et al. [15]	11.24	86.69

Then we assessed the line symmetry classifier and line appearance classifier. Both of them are random forest classifiers which are trained on the ICDAR 2013 training set. Notice that our classifiers do not aim to make hard decisions, they assign a high probability value to the candidate if it is true text. So Fig. 6 shows the performance of the classifiers in the form of probability distribution. The horizontal axis in the graph is the output value of the classifiers and the vertical axis is the frequency number of each output. The negative samples are marked with green while the positive ones are marked with red.

Finally, the performances of the proposed algorithm as well as other published methods on the ICDAR 2013 dataset are shown in Table 3. Since the character candidates are not eliminated in the first three steps, the proposed system successfully avoids the error accumulation problem and obtains a high recall as expected. In the meantime, the clustering strategy dynamically distinguishes candidates of the current image based on different line-level information rather than classifying all image candidates in a fixed way. This ensures a fair precision and makes the system adaptive to various scenes.

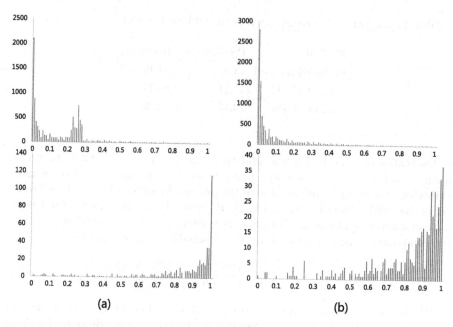

Fig. 6. The probability distribution of the line-level classifiers. (a) the performance of the symmetry feature; (b) the performance of the ConvCo-HOG feature. (Color figure online)

Table 3. Experimental results on the ICDAR 2013 dataset

Method	Precision(%)	Recall(%)	F-measure(%)
Proposed method	85.21	77.84	81.45
Sung et al. [15]	88.65	74.23	80.80
Tian et al. [18]	85.15	75.89	80.25
Zhang et al. [23]	88	74	80
Lu et al. [9]	89.22	69.58	78.19
Neumann and Matas [12]	81.8	72.4	77.1
Zamberletti et al. [22]	85.6	70.0	77.0
USTB TexStar [21]	86.3	68.3	76.2

A final text line of the proposed system often consists of several words which are several detection results in other methods. Thus a false alarm causes a larger decline to the result. But the proposed system still achieves a good precision thanks to the line clustering strategy. Compared with Tian et al.' method which solves the error accumulation problem by integrating the last three sequential steps into a single process, the proposed system obtained a higher recall and precision though the character extraction part behaved a little worse.

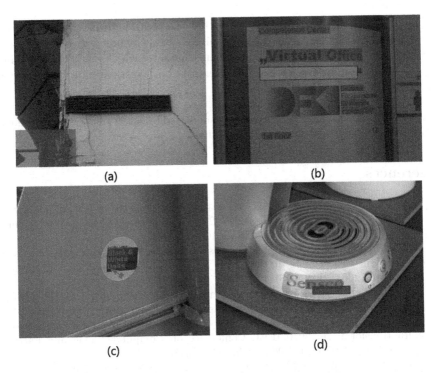

Fig. 7. Failure cases of the proposed method

Some failure cases of the proposed system are depicted in Fig. 7. In Fig. 7(a), the character candidate extraction algorithm is unable to deal with the text with extremely low contrast. The small text line in Fig. 7(c) which is even incognizable to human eyes is also not detected. The proposed method only detected part of the text lines in Fig. 7(b)(d) and they were regarded as false alarms. To be fair, such lines should not be counted when calculating the recall. But they can be considered as positive when it comes to the precision. We manually calculated the precision of the proposed method in this way and it achieved 91.25 %.

4   Conclusions

In this paper, we propose a scene text detection system that does not remove candidates based on character information. Instead, we assign a probability value to each one and adopt a minimum average cost path algorithm to extract line candidates. True text lines are picked out by clustering congeneric candidates of the current image. Compared to the traditional methods, our system can effectively deal with the error accumulation problem and it is adaptive to different scenes due to the clustering strategy. In addition, our system is very flexible. Every step can be easily replaced by a better method to obtain a higher recall or precision.

The main drawback of our system is that the recall is utterly dependent on the character extraction method. In the failure cases, the first step of our system extracted only part of the word or even none character which made the following steps helpless. Our future work will concentrate on investigating a higher-recall character extraction algorithm.

Acknowledgments. This work is partially supported by Intel Collaborative Research Institute on Mobile Networking and Computing.

References

1. Boureau, Y.L., Ponce, J., LeCun, Y.: A theoretical analysis of feature pooling in visual recognition. In: Proceedings of the 27th International Conference on Machine Learning (ICML-2010), pp. 111–118 (2010)
2. Busta, M., Neumann, L., Matas, J.: Fastext: efficient unconstrained scene text detector. In: Proceedings of the IEEE International Conference on Computer Vision. pp, 1206–1214 (2015)
3. Buta, M., et al.: Fastext: efficient unconstrained scene text detector. In: 2015 IEEE International Conference on Computer Vision (ICCV), pp. 1206–1214. IEEE (2015)
4. Epshtein, B., Ofek, E., Wexler, Y.: Detecting text in natural scenes with stroke width transform. In: 2010 IEEE Conference on Computer Vision and Pattern Recognition (CVPR), pp. 2963–2970. IEEE (2010)
5. Huang, W., Lin, Z., Yang, J., Wang, J.: Text localization in natural images using stroke feature transform and text covariance descriptors. In: Proceedings of the IEEE International Conference on Computer Vision, pp. 1241–1248 (2013)
6. Huang, W., Qiao, Y., Tang, X.: Robust scene text detection with convolution neural network induced MSER trees. In: Fleet, D., Pajdla, T., Schiele, B., Tuytelaars, T. (eds.) ECCV 2014, Part IV. LNCS, vol. 8692, pp. 497–511. Springer, Heidelberg (2014)
7. Jaderberg, M., Vedaldi, A., Zisserman, A.: Deep features for text spotting. In: Fleet, D., Pajdla, T., Schiele, B., Tuytelaars, T. (eds.) ECCV 2014, Part IV. LNCS, vol. 8692, pp. 512–528. Springer, Heidelberg (2014)
8. Liang, J., Doermann, D., Li, H.: Camera-based analysis of text and documents: a survey. Int. J. Doc. Anal. Recognit. (IJDAR) 7(2–3), 84–104 (2005)
9. Lu, S., Chen, T., Tian, S., Lim, J.H., Tan, C.L.: Scene text extraction based on edges and support vector regression. Int. J. Doc. Anal. Recognit. (IJDAR) 18(2), 125–135 (2015)
10. Martin, D.R., Fowlkes, C.C., Malik, J.: Learning to detect natural image boundaries using local brightness, color, and texture cues. IEEE Trans. Pattern Anal. Mach. Intell. 26(5), 530–549 (2004)
11. Neumann, L., Matas, J.: A method for text localization and recognition in real-world images. In: Kimmel, R., Klette, R., Sugimoto, A. (eds.) ACCV 2010, Part III. LNCS, vol. 6494, pp. 770–783. Springer, Heidelberg (2011)
12. Neumann, L., Matas, J.: Efficient scene text localization and recognition with local character refinement. In: 2015 13th International Conference on Document Analysis and Recognition (ICDAR), pp. 746–750. IEEE (2015)
13. Otsu, N.: A threshold selection method from gray-level histograms. Automatica 11(285–296), 23–27 (1975)

14. Rubner, Y., Puzicha, J., Tomasi, C., Buhmann, J.M.: Empirical evaluation of dissimilarity measures for color and texture. Comput. Vis. Image Underst. **84**(1), 25–43 (2001)
15. Sung, M.C., Jun, B., Cho, H., Kim, D.: Scene text detection with robust character candidate extraction method. In: 2015 13th International Conference on Document Analysis and Recognition (ICDAR), pp. 426–430. IEEE (2015)
16. Tian, S., Bhattacharya, U., Lu, S., Su, B., Wang, Q., Wei, X., Lu, Y., Tan, C.L.: Multilingual scene character recognition with co-occurrence of histogram of oriented gradients. Pattern Recogn. **51**, 125–134 (2016)
17. Tian, S., Lu, S., Su, B., Tan, C.L.: Scene text recognition using co-occurrence of histogram of oriented gradients. In: 2013 12th International Conference on Document Analysis and Recognition (ICDAR), pp. 912–916. IEEE (2013)
18. Tian, S., Pan, Y., Huang, C., Lu, S., Yu, K., Lim Tan, C.: Text flow: a unified text detection system in natural scene images. In: Proceedings of the IEEE International Conference on Computer Vision, pp. 4651–4659 (2015)
19. Watanabe, T., Ito, S., Yokoi, K.: Co-occurrence histograms of oriented gradients for pedestrian detection. In: Wada, T., Huang, F., Lin, S. (eds.) PSIVT 2009. LNCS, vol. 5414, pp. 37–47. Springer, Heidelberg (2009). doi:10.1007/978-3-540-92957-4_4
20. Ye, Q., Doermann, D.: Text detection and recognition in imagery: a survey. IEEE Trans. Pattern Anal. Mach. Intell. **37**(7), 1480–1500 (2015)
21. Yin, X.C., Yin, X., Huang, K., Hao, H.W.: Robust text detection in natural scene images. IEEE Trans. Pattern Anal. Mach. Intell. **36**(5), 970–983 (2014)
22. Zamberletti, A., Noce, L., Gallo, I.: Text localization based on fast feature pyramids and multi-resolution maximally stable extremal regions. In: Jawahar, C.V., Shan, S. (eds.) ACCV 2014 Workshops. LNCS, vol. 9009, pp. 91–105. Springer, Heidelberg (2015)
23. Zhang, Z., Shen, W., Yao, C., Bai, X.: Symmetry-based text line detection in natural scenes. In: 2015 IEEE Conference on Computer Vision and Pattern Recognition (CVPR), pp. 2558–2567. IEEE (2015)
24. Zhu, Y., Yao, C., Bai, X.: Scene text detection and recognition: recent advances and future trends. Front. Comput. Sci. **10**(1), 19–36 (2016)

From Text Detection to Text Segmentation: A Unified Evaluation Scheme

Stefania Calarasanu[1]([✉]), Jonathan Fabrizio[1], and Séverine Dubuisson[2]

[1] EPITA-LRDE, 14-16, rue Voltaire, 94276 Le Kremlin Bicêtre, France
{calarasanu,jonathan.fabrizio}@lrde.epita.fr
[2] Sorbonne Universités, UPMC Univ Paris 06, CNRS, UMR 7222, ISIR,
75005 Paris, France
severine.dubuisson@isir.upmc.fr

Abstract. Current text segmentation evaluation protocols are often incapable of properly handling different scenarios (broken/merged/partial characters). This leads to scores that incorrectly reflect the segmentation accuracy. In this article we propose a new evaluation scheme that overcomes most of the existent drawbacks by extending the EVAL-TEX protocol (initially designed to evaluate text detection at region level). This new unified platform has numerous advantages: it is able to evaluate a text understanding system at every detection stage and granularity level (paragraph/line/word and now character) by using the same metrics and matching rules; it is robust to all segmentation scenarios; it provides a qualitative and quantitative evaluation and a visual score representation that captures the whole behavior of a segmentation algorithm. Experimental results on nine segmentation algorithms using different evaluation frameworks are also provided to emphasize the interest of our method.

Keywords: Evaluation protocol · Evaluation metrics · Text segmentation

1 Introduction

During the last decade, text understanding systems have received a lot of attentions from both the research and the industry communities. In particular, end-to-end systems became popular due to their complex processing chain. Such systems rely on different processing stages, such as text segmentation, text grouping, text classification, text localization, text rectification or text recognition. Among these stages, text segmentation is a phase of crucial importance not only for many end-to-end systems but also for other applications that rely on it, such as the image inpaiting (*e.g.* subtitle removal [21]). The interest in this stage is also reflected by the organization of numerous competitions around this topic, such as ICDAR 2013 [15] and 2015 [13] *Robust Reading Competition* (Task 2) with Challenge 1 on born-digital images and Challenge 2 on natural scenes.

© Springer International Publishing Switzerland 2016
G. Hua and H. Jégou (Eds.): ECCV 2016 Workshops, Part I, LNCS 9913, pp. 378–394, 2016.
DOI: 10.1007/978-3-319-46604-0_28

The different stages of an end-to-end system are evaluated in different ways, with respect to the type of text representation at each level. For example, text segmentation implies evaluating a binary representation, while text localization is usually done by comparing bounding box positions in an image. Finally, the text recognition is evaluated based on the transcription obtained by using an OCR. Frequently, the evaluation of the transcription is also used as a final result for many end-to-end systems. This result provides a combined evaluation based on the recognition accuracy of the used OCR and the localization precision. Since text segmentation can be a vital pre-processing or post-processing stage in a document analysis application, it is important to quantify its contribution and quality independently.

Most of the times the output of the text segmentation is a binary image in which the foreground (white pixels) represents potential text objects (*i.e.* characters) and the background (black pixels) corresponds to the remainder.

As pointed in [20], among the existing evaluation choices (user-interaction, output OCR, pixel-based...) the most valuable evaluation procedure seems to be the pixel comparison between the ground truth (GT) and detection images. Nevertheless, evaluating text segmentation remains a difficult task due to a set of problems that can alter the evaluation scores such as: variation of characters' thickness, merged characters, partially detected characters or fragmented characters. For example, the variation of characters' thickness can often impact the evaluation scores when dealing with natural scene images, in which illumination properties and cluttered backgrounds can severely influence the accuracy of the character segmentation. We note that, due to these difficulties, some protocols have common drawbacks, the three most penalizing ones being:

- In pixel-based evaluation protocols, the penalty due to a character's segmentation failure varies usually with respect to the character's surface size, although the surface is not related to the size of the character.
- Conversely, many character-based evaluation protocols imply a binary approach to decide whether a character is well segmented or not; this leads to inaccurate evaluations of degraded character segmentations.
- Lastly, dealing with binary decisions implies a threshold dependency of critical parameters which are most of the times difficult to set up.

In this article we propose to overcome these issues by firstly adapting the EvaLTex protocol exposed in [2] initially designed for text localization and secondly using the visualization tool in [1], to evaluate text segmentation results. The advantages of the adaptation of this framework are numerous:

- It provides a more representative set of scores than classical evaluation methods.
- It comes with a visualization system which gives at a glance an overview of the accuracy of the evaluated methods and helps to compare different sets of results.
- It handles all types of atom detections: partial, broken, merged, broken and merged, missed.

– It produces an equal evaluation of all characters regardless of their size.
– It proposes a non-binary local evaluation which allows a proper evaluation of partial, broken and merged character detections.
– It is robust to character thickness variation.

Furthermore, the EVALTEX protocol, by design, is able to evaluate text detection systems at paragraph/line/word level. The adaptation of EVALTEX protocol for text segmentation unifies the evaluation at all detection levels: paragraph/line/word and now character. It is hence possible to evaluate an end-to-end system, at each step, by using a single tool.

This article is organized as follows. Section 2 presents a survey of the state-of-the-art evaluation methods used for text segmentation. This section also presents the EVALTEX protocol that is next adapted for the segmentation evaluation. Section 3 presents the evaluation framework details and its applicability to text segmentation evaluation tasks. Section 4 is dedicated to experiments and discussions on the scores obtained with different evaluation methods. Finally, concluding remarks and perspectives are given in Sect. 5.

2   Related Work

Text segmentation can be evaluated in different manners. For example, by user-interaction [4,6,12,25,26], in which humans are supposed to count manually the number of correct and incorrect matches between the GT and the detections. This approach is not sufficiently reliable as it inevitably implies a high level of subjectivity: different users can produce different evaluation scores.

Another approach for text segmentation evaluation consists in using the OCR recognition rate [3,10,27]. In such cases, the scores do not only depend on the segmentation correctness but also on the OCR recognition accuracy. For example, a good segmentation output can produce a low score if the used OCR does not recognize correctly all the characters.

The pixel-based evaluation methods [8,16,20,22,23,30] compute the difference between a binary GT image and a detection image and count the number of pixels that correctly match. In [22] five performance measurements were used to evaluate the binarization outputs: misclassification error (ME), edge mismatch (EMM), relative foreground area error (RAE), modified Hausdorff distance (MHD), and region non-uniformity (NU). Authors in [8] opted for recall, precision, accuracy and specificity rates to interpret historical documents binarization results. A normalized cross-correlation value between binarized and GT images has been employed in [16] to evaluate the degraded character level in color images. The main drawback of these approaches is the fact that the evaluation is done exclusively at pixel level and hence it depends on the character area size making it less robust to thickness variations. In [23], the authors presented an evaluation protocol for binarization methods, based on four metrics: pixel error ($PERR$), square error (MSE), signal to noise ratio (SNR) and peak signal to noise ratio ($PSNR$). The advantage of this method is that it comes together with a GT annotation technique consisting of adding noise to a clean document and hence assuring an objective pixel-based evaluation. In [30], authors also opted for the PSNR metric, together with a negative rate metric (NRM) and a misclassification penalty metric (MPM). In [20] the evaluation is also done at pixel level by producing a set of eight evaluation metrics computed directly on binarized images: F-measure, recall, precision, broken text, missing text, merge-deformation, deformation and false alarm. The advantage of this work is that it provides a method to produce a reliable GT by using skeletons. Hence, the method is not sensitive to character thickness variations and does not alter the scores. This protocol was used during the ICDAR 2015 *Robust Reading* competition (Challenge 1 and 2, Task 2). The advantage of this work is that it provides a method to produce a reliable GT by using skeletons. Hence, the method is not sensitive to character thickness variations and does not alter the scores. This protocol was used during the ICDAR 2015 *Robust Reading* competition (Challenge 1 and 2, Task 2).

Finally, the atom-based evaluation [2,5,9] consists in comparing atom-level objects (*i.e.* characters). Compared to pixel-based evaluations, this kind of approaches treats all characters in the same way, independently of their sizes. This is a major advantage with respect to pixel-based evaluations, because it can differentiate between various segmentation scenarios. Clavelli *et al.* [5] proposed a multi-level annotation scheme that represents text objects at pixel (text part), atom (e.g character), word and line levels. This framework, also used for the ICDAR 2015 *Robust Reading* competition (Challenge 1 and 2, Task 2) can evaluate text segmentation tasks, when text objects are represented at pixel and part levels. The matching protocol is based on two thresholds: T_{min} and T_{max}, used to validate the matchings between a GT and a detection represented by a set of connected components (CCs). The default values are set to: $T_{min} = 0.9$, $T_{max} = \min(5, 0.5 \cdot T)$, where T corresponds to the thickness of the text part. Based on this, the detection CCs are classified into several categories: background, fraction, whole, multiple, fraction & multiple and mixed. The main disadvantages of this method are the binary local evaluation approach and the fact that it does not handle broken character segmentations, which leads to low recall values when such cases occur. The ZoneMap metric proposed in [9] is a generalization of the metric proposed in [18] and of the DETEVAL framework [28] used for evaluating page segmentation and area classification in documents. It is computed based on the matching scenarios and different error rates. EVALTEX [2] is a framework introduced to evaluate text localization results. The main core of this protocol consists of a two-level ground truth annotation for each image: first, each word is bounded by a rectangular box; then, several words are grouped and bounded into text regions. This two-level annotation is then used to compare the GT text objects with the detection results. Based on the overlap between the GT and the detection objects, four types of matchings are identified: *one-to-one, one-to-many, many-to-one* or *many-to-many*. Depending on the matching type, a dedicated set of local performance metrics for each GT object is computed. Finally, seven global scores (global, quantity and quality recall and precision and *F*-Score) are computed for a dataset, by providing both a quality

Fig. 1. Example of a text segmentation image with labeled CCs.

and a quantity evaluation of the detection results. This protocol represents the starting point for the evaluation scheme presented in this paper.

3   Revision of EvaLTex and adaptation to text segmentation

In this section we show how, by respecting and adapting some of the metrics and rules of EvaLTex, we can evaluate not only text localization, but also text segmentation.

GT annotation. In order to evaluate a result, a GT is needed. For the character segmentation evaluation, we will consider the annotation representation to be a mask for a connected component (CC) or a set of CCs having the same label in the segmented image. In practice, in the Latin alphabet, a character is usually defined by one CC but it can also be defined by two or three CCs (*i.e.* characters with accents or tittles). An example of the used ground truth annotation is given in Fig. 1. In the following section we will discuss the matching rules and the metrics used to evaluate the text segmentation.

Matching strategies. Initially, the EvaLTex framework was designed to evaluate the localization of text regions such as words and lines represented through bounding boxes or blobs. It relies on the computation of two measurements: the coverage and the accuracy. The coverage measures the ratio between the matching surface of two objects with respect to the GT object, while the accuracy measures the ratio of the matching surface and the detection one. In order to provide a representative evaluation, these two measurements take into account many different detection situations. Simple cases involve an object from the GT being matched with a single object in the detection (*one-to-one* match). More challenging cases include GT objects being matched with multiple detections (*one-to-many*) or multiple detections matching the same object in the GT (*many-to-one*). Finally, it is possible that many objects in the GT match many objects in the detection (*many-to-many*). As the EvaLTex framework is able to handle all these cases and as it does not perform a binary evaluation but always provides a ratio of quality of the matching, the evaluation is more representative than many other frameworks that do not handle all different cases or simply perform a binary evaluation (match or failure). Furthermore, EvaLTex framework always considers slight variations of detected text elements by enlarging and reducing their surrounding regions during the comparison.

In order to apply the principles of EVALTEX to evaluate text segmentation one needs to move from the word/line/region representation to a character level using a connected component (CC) annotation. Similarly to text detection, text segmentation requires managing different matching scenarios. When a GT CC corresponds to a CC in the detection set, even if the coverage between the two is not complete, we deal with a whole or partial atom detection. When a CC in the GT is covered by multiple CCs in the detection set, we deal with a fragmented atom detection. The third case, which consists in multiple characters in the detection being linked together, is referred to a merged atom detection where a CC in the detection set corresponds to multiple CCs in the GT. Lastly, a fragmented and merged detection occurs when detections are fragmented and linked to other characters at the same time. One can observe that the matching cases that occur in text detection can be retrieved in the segmentation scenarios, making EVALTEX a good starting point to evaluate text segmentation algorithms. To do so, let us consider $\mathcal{G} = \{G_i\}_{i=1,...,N_G}$ a set of N_G GT text boxes and $\mathcal{D} = \{D_j\}_{j=1,...,N_D}$ a set of N_D detections.

Whole and Partial Atom Detection. To locally evaluate the quality of the matching between a GT atom G_i and a detection D_j we can use the *coverage* and the *accuracy* metrics defined in [2] (this corresponds to a *one-to-one* case). The coverage value is computed using the reduced GT object, while the accuracy using the enlarged GT object in order to remain robust to small detection size variations. When moving from the evaluation of words to characters, we want to keep this property by remaining robust to slight character thickness variations. However, applying the erosion could make small characters disappear. Hence, we will consider the computation of the coverage value, not by eroding the GT object but by dilating the detection atom. This change will further be reflected in the evaluation of all four types of atom detections. For a *partial* or *whole* segmented CC, the coverage and accuracy between G_i and D_j is computed in the following manner:

$$\text{Cov}_i = \frac{\text{Area}(G_i \cap Dd_j)}{\text{Area}(G_i)}, \quad \text{Acc}_i = \frac{\text{Area}(Gd_i \cap D_j)}{\text{Area}(D_j)}, \tag{1}$$

where Gd_i and Dd_j represent the dilated GT and detection CCs. In our experiments we use a square structuring element of size equal to 1.

Fragmented Atom Detection. In the case of a *fragmented* CC (corresponding to a *one-to-many* detection scenario), the same GT CC is detected multiple times. Here again, the coverage [2] is computed by taking into account all the intersections between the GT CC and the dilated detection CCs in the following manner:

$$\text{Cov}_i = \frac{\bigcup_{j=j_1}^{j_{s_i}} \text{Area}(G_i \cap Dd_j) - \bigcap_{j=j_1}^{j_{s_i}} Dd_j}{\text{Area}(G_i)} \cdot F_i, \tag{2}$$

$$\text{Acc}_i = \frac{\bigcup_{j=j_1}^{j_{s_i}} \text{Area}(Gd_i \cap D_j) - \bigcap_{j=j_1}^{j_{s_i}} Dd_j}{\bigcup_{j=1}^{s_i} \text{Area}(D_j)} \tag{3}$$

where s_i represents the number of fragmentations associated to G_i and F_i a fragmentation penalization applied to each GT CC. Contrary to the penalization proposed in [2], we propose here a smoother one, defined as:

$$F_i = \frac{1}{1 + \ln(s_i) \cdot \ln(s_i)} \cdot 0.6 + 0.4 \tag{4}$$

Merged Atom Detection. A merged atom case (equivalent to a *many-to-one* scenario) considers the coverage rate used during partial and whole atom detection (see Eq. 1), while the accuracy is computed as in [2]:

$$Acc_i = \frac{Area(Gd_i \cap D_j)}{Area(D_{j,i})}, \tag{5}$$

where $Area(D_{j,i})$ represents the corresponding detection area for each G_i and is defined as:

$$Area(D_{j,i}) = \frac{Area(Gd_i)}{TextArea_{D_j}} \cdot nonTextArea_{D_j}, \tag{6}$$

where $TextArea_{D_j}$ and $nonTextArea_{D_j}$ correspond to, respectively the total text area and the non text area, defined as:

$$TextArea_{D_j} = Area(\bigcup_{i=1}^{m_j}(Gd_i \cap D_j)) \tag{7}$$

$$nonTextArea_{D_j} = Area(D_j) - TextArea_{D_j}, \tag{8}$$

where m_j represents the number of merged GT CCs.

Fragmented and Merged. The coverage for the fragmented and merged scenarios (corresponding to *many-to-many* cases) is derived from the fragmented case (see Eq. 2). In [2], the accuracy is computed exclusively using Eq. 5. However, since this case involves a merged and fragmented atom detection, we redefine the accuracy and compute it by combining Eqs. 3 and 5. The accuracy then becomes the ratio between the union of all intersection areas between the GT CC G_i and the union of all detections k_i CC that are generated from the *merged* mappings as well as all s_i CC detections generated from the *whole* or *partial* mappings:

$$Acc_i = \frac{\bigcup_{j=j_1}^{j_{s_i}+k_i} Area(Gd_i \cap D_j) - \bigcap_{j=j_1}^{j_{s_i}} D_j}{(\bigcup_{j=j_1}^{j_{s_i}} Area(D_j) - \bigcap_{j=j_1}^{j_{s_i}} D_j) \cup (\bigcup_{j=j_1}^{j_{k_i}} Area(D_{k,i}))} \tag{9}$$

4   Experiments and Interpretation of Results

In this section we evaluate our evaluation scheme and compare our results with other evaluation protocols. This evaluation is performed on the segmentation results[1] of nine detection methods that participated to the *ICDAR 2013 and*

---

[1] Publicly available at http://rrc.cvc.uab.es/ [13].

2015 Robust Reading Competition [13,15]. The EvaLTeX tool and the corresponding GT format for the ICDAR datasets are available at https://www.lrde.epita.fr/wiki/Evaltex.

Evaluating an evaluation method is neither an easy, nor an obvious task. First of all, there are no precise rules that can decide the precision or correctness of such a protocol. Moreover, there is undoubtedly, always a level of subjectivity involved in the proposition of such a new protocol, either due to its metrics or its matching strategies. This raises a straightforward question of whether we can state that one evaluation protocol is better than other. While this statement seems too strong, we can however debate on the reliability of some metrics and computed scores in a given context. To validate at best our protocol, we first propose a qualitative evaluation (Sect. 4.1) using three evaluation methods: ours, one pixel-based [20] and one atom-based [5]. Next (Sect. 4.2), global scores on the entire dataset are computed using the different evaluation methods and compared. Lastly, in Sect. 4.3 we show the suitability of the histogram visualization tool to provide, at a glance, a more detailed overview of the behavior of segmentation methods.

4.1 Qualitative Evaluation

The purpose of having a qualitative comparison is to stimulate the analysis of concrete examples and interpret the representativity of certain scores with respect to others in order to illustrate possible inconsistencies and their impact on the scores produced by current used protocols. Figure 2 illustrates multiple common segmentation situations that will be used as a basis for further discussions. In this figure, from top to bottom, the first picture is the original image, the second picture is the expected segmentation (the GT) while the third represents the segmentation result. The next images correspond to the analysis of a pixel based evaluation, followed by an atom based evaluation analysis[2]. The sixth image corresponds to the histogram visualization of coverage and accuracy distributions for each segmentation example. Table 1 provides the scores computed using the atom-based, pixel-based and our evaluation method.

In Fig. 2.a one can observe that all text characters have been segmented. However, due to hole filled characters ("o", "d", "D" and "O") the atom-based evaluation does not consider the characters as segmented (in red) and underestimates the recall (78 %). As the evaluation is a binary one, the computed recall for this image is the same as if these letters would have been completely missed. The first conclusion is that such an evaluation does not allow precise comparisons. Moreover, the detected letters are considered as false positive which produces similar precision scores (70 %) which is clearly underestimated. The atom-based protocol considers better to miss the "o" than to detect it with its hole filled. The second conclusion is that the obtained scores with this framework are not a faithful representation of what we would intuitively expect.

---

[2] All pictures publicly available at http://rrc.cvc.uab.es/ [13].

Table 1. Recall, Precision and *F*-Score obtained using different evaluation methods on the segmentation examples depicted in Fig. 2.

Figure	PIXEL [20]			ATOM[5]			OUR EVALUATION		
	R	P	F	R	P	F	R	P	F
2.a	94.04	46.22	61.98	77.78	70	73.68	99.96	83.72	91.12
2.b	92.18	57.25	70.63	60		42.86	50	99.08	53.19	69.22
2.c	82.96	93.75	88.02	66.67	69.23	67.92	72.12	79.79	75.76
2.d	92.9	68.05	78.56	66.67	75	70.59	88.88	79.24	83.79

Figure 2.b illustrates an example of merged characters ("U" and "T"), which are correctly identified by the atom-based evaluator, but not taken into account when computing the recall value. This leads to a recall of 60 %, which is clearly not consistent with the segmentation efficiency.

In the example depicted in Fig. 2.c, we can observe the outline (*i.e.* border) segmentation of characters "c","o" and "m". Such cases of partial segmentation are not handled by the atom-based evaluator and counted as false positives, although the boundaries of these characters perfectly approximate their shapes and hence could successfully be recognized by an OCR. This example also illustrates a frequent problem involving characters with tittles (character "j"), which are missing from the segmentation result. The consequence is that the atom-based method considers the entire character "j" as not being segmented (false positive), decreasing both the recall (66.67 %) and precision (75 %).

In Fig. 2.d, one can see that the thickness of the segmentation of characters are slightly thicker than the GT. Here again the binary matching approach decision does not provide relevant comparisons between different segmentation cases. Due to the thickness variation, correct detections are counted as false positives and consequently both the recall and precision are under estimated (66.67 % and 75 %). This example also shows the difficulty of setting up correctly the decision thresholds and the huge impact of these parameters on the final scores.

Contrary to atom-based protocols, the pixel-based ones count all pixels that match the GT and reject all others. In the cases of Fig. 2.a, b and d, the recall seems to be more representative than that of the atom-based one. In Fig. 2.a, the four letters are well counted and the "filling" areas within the characters are considered as false positive pixels decreasing only the precision rate. The merged characters in Fig. 2.b are evaluate more fair than with the atom-based evaluation leading to a recall value of 92 %. In Fig. 2.d, the thickness variation does not penalize the pixel-based recall (92.9 %) as much as the atom-based one does (66.67). The large character area contributes however to an overestimation of recall (82.96 %) and precision (93.75 %) in Fig. 2.c. Here, the pixel evaluation method does not differentiate between the false positive pixels from character out-of-border pixels. Moreover, not all letters have the same weight, but highly depending on their area. For example, the characters in the word "life" contribute less to the overall recall than the characters of the word "jungle" because they have a bigger size. Similarly, because of the surface of the false positives in Fig. 2.a, the precision is severely underestimated (less then 50 %).

With our proposed method the filling of characters in Fig. 2.a does not affect the recall, which correctly states that all characters were segmented (99.96 %). The filling, however is penalized by the precision value. Similarly, the merged characters are correctly evaluated, producing an almost perfect recall score of 99.08 %. The thickness variation that exceeds the allowed dilation of the character together with the three false positives lead to a precision score of 53 %, which is rather logic if we assume that we have five out eight nearly correct segmentations. For the examples in Fig. 2.c the recall values are in between the ones produced by the atom-based and pixel evaluation protocols. This is consistent with the reasoning that the recall is over-estimated by the pixel evaluation due to the large text area and under-estimated by the atom-based one due to the minimal segmented area thresholds. The same is valid for the recall score obtained in Fig. 2.d. In this picture, 8 characters are detected among the 9 characters. This leads to 88 % of recall, which is the expected value correctly computed in spite of the thickness variation. The precision however seems over-estimated (79.24 %) if compared to the rates obtained with pixel and atom based methods. This is due to two reasons: firstly, we count only one false positive ("A") instead of three as in the case of the atom-base evaluation, and secondly, by allowing the thickness variation we are more permissive than the pixel method.

4.2 Quantitative Evaluation

Table 2 summarizes the rankings produced by the overall evaluation of nine text segmentation methods using four different protocols presented in Tables 3 and 4. As characterized by the standard deviation σ in Table 2 there is a significant discrepancy between some of the rankings produced by the pixel and atom-based evaluations (for example in the case of the *NSTextractor*). The difficulty now is to select the method that is the most reliable. To answer to this question, we have computed the mean of the ranking for each segmentation. First, one can observe that our method gives the nearest results to this mean. In a second time, we have ordered the segmentation results according to this mean. This gives us an average ranking. One can expect that, by collecting the rankings from various methods, the ranking would be smoothed and the impact of artifacts reduced in the evaluation protocols. Again our method is the nearest to this new ranking. This comparison to the mean ranking and to the new ranking is not an absolute prove but it provides however a reasonable clue for selecting the most appropriate evaluation method.

4.3 Results Visualization

Figure 3 illustrates the histogram representation [1] of the evaluation results of three segmentation methods (*NSTsegmentator* [19], *OCTYMIST* [17] and *Strad-Vision* [24]) on the ICDAR 2015 natural scene dataset. This visualization tool

Fig. 2. Four examples (a, b, c and d). For each example, from top to bottom: the original image, the GT, the segmentation, the pixel-based classification (false positive in red, correct in green, non-segmented in white), the atom-based classification (non-detected in red, correct in green, merged in blue) and the histogram visualization. (Color figure online)

is very useful as it provides at a glance important characteristics of the global segmentation efficiency, namely the distribution of coverage and accuracy values over an entire dataset. The first bin of the accuracy histogram represents the false positives, the last bin (*i.e.*] 0.9,1]) represents the rate of perfect detections, while all other bins represent the detection rates with accuracy values between 0.1 and 0.9. Similarly, the first bin of the coverage histogram represents the

Table 2. Ranking based on the F-Score and PERR scores in Tables 3 and 4. Mean and standard deviation of ranking. New ranking based on means of ranking.

Ranking Participants	Pixel [20]	Atom [5]	Stathis [23]	Our's	Mean of ranking	σ	Ranking based on the means
BUCT_YST [11]	3	2	4	2	2.75	0.96	3
I2R_NUS [14]	4	6	3	4	4.25	1.26	4
I2R_NUS_FAR [14]	2	3	2	3	2.5	0.58	2
NSTextractor [19]	7	4	6	6	5.75	1,26	6
NSTsegmentator [19]	8	7	9	8	8	0.82	8
OTCYMIST [17]	9	9	8	9	8.75	0.5	9
StradVision [24]	1	1	1	1	1	0	1
TextDetection [7]	6	8	5	7	6,5	1.29	7
USTB_FuStar [29]	5	5	7	5	5.5	1	5

rate of GT objects not detected, while the last bin symbolizes the number of GT atoms that have been perfectly segmented. All other bins represent the GT atoms with coverage ratio between 0.1 and 0.9.

By analyzing the three histograms we can observe that the *StradVision* method achieves the highest accuracy peek, while keeping its false positive rate close to zero. On the contrary, one can observe an approximately 40 % rate of false positives in the case of *NSTsegmentator* method, and a significantly larger rate for the *OCTYMIST* method, around 60 %. Concerning the coverage values, one can observe a narrower difference between the segmentation misses of *NSTsegmentator* and that of *StradVision*, both around 70 %. Another interesting aspect of this analysis consists in the fair distribution of missed and perfect atom segmentations produced by the *OCTYMIST* method (the value in the first and last bin are very close). By looking at the three histograms we can identify the same pattern, where most of the values fall in the first and last bins, meaning that all GT atoms where either well segmented or not at all, or that all produced segmentations perfectly match the GT atoms or they completely missed them. However, distributions of the accuracy and coverage values also appear within the bins between 0.1 and 0.9 as illustrated in the bottom of Fig. 3, although in a less important number.

One of the advantage of unifying the localization evaluation of EVALTEX with the segmentation evaluation is to benefit from this visualization scheme. To our knowledge, such a visualization tool for analyzing the precision of segmentation results does not yet exist. This visualization scheme can also be apply independently on segmentation examples as seen in Fig. 2.

Table 3. Quality, quantity and global scores obtained with alternative evaluation methods (Pixel, atom and Stiathos's method) on the detection results of all participants (in ascending order) during ICDAR'13 and ICDAR'15 Robust Reading Competition (Challenge 2, Task 2).

Participants	PIXEL EVALUATION [20]			ATOM EVALUATION [5]			STATHIS [23] EVALUATION			
	Recall	Precision	F-Score	Recall	Precision	F-Score	PERR	MSE	SNR	PSNR
BUCT_YST [11]	75.56	81.75	77.99	71.13	83.51	76.83	0.0235312	1530.12	39.8059	79.2717
I2R_NUS [14]	73.57	79.04	76.21	60.33	76.62	67.51	0.0233201	1516.39	39.3688	78.8345
I2R_NUS_FAR [14]	74.73	81.70	78.06	68.64	80.59	74.14	0.0228714	1487.22	39.73	79.1958
NSTextractor [19]	60.71	76.28	67.61	63.38	83.57	72.09	0.0306271	1991.53	38.2217	77.6875
NSTsegmentator [19]	68.41	63.95	66.10	68.00	54.35	60.41	0.0433068	2816.02	36.2739	75.7397
OTCYMIST [17]	46.11	58.53	51.58	41.79	31.60	35.99	0.0415516	2701.9	36.1228	75.5886
StradVision [24]	78.80	89.24	83.70	73.02	84.42	78.31	0.0187627	1220.04	40.512	79.9777
TextDetection [7]	64.74	76.20	70.01	62.03	57.43	59.64	0.0297574	1934.98	38.621	78.0868
USTB_FuStar [29]	69.58	74.45	71.93	68.03	72.46	70.18	0.0310387	2018.29	38.6495	798.1152

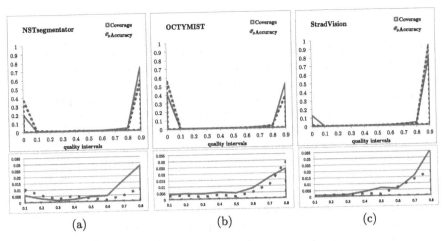

Fig. 3. Histogram representation of the coverage and accuracy rates on the ICDAR 2015 natural scene dataset of three segmentation methods: (a) *NSTsegmentator* [19]; (b) *OCTYMIST* [17]; (c) *StradVision* [24]. The bottom histograms represent the detailed distribution of rates over the intervals between 0.1 and 0.8. One can observe that the histograms provide a good inside on the behavior of a text segmentation algorithm. For example, the most powerful method is *StradVision* as it has the highest accuracy and coverage values in the last bin of the histogram. On the other hand, *OCTYMIST* has a higher rate of false positives (green values in the first bin) than correct character detections (green value in the last bin). Also, the number of true positives (magenta value in the last bin) is equal to the number of missed detection (magenta value in the first bin). The *NSTsegmentator* lies somewhere in between the two previous methods as it has a lower number of missed detections and false positives than *OCTYMIST* but higher than *StradVision*. (Color figure online)

Table 4. Quality, quantity and global scores obtained with our evaluation method on the detection results of all participants (in ascending order) during ICDAR'13 and ICDAR'15 Robust Reading Competition (Challenge 2, Task 2)

Participants	QUALITY		QUANTITY		GLOBAL		
	Recall	Precision	Recall	Precision	Recall	Precision	F-Score
BUCT_ YST [11]	97.73	97.81	84.25	95.92	82.34	93.83	87.71
I2R_ NUS [14]	96.94	96.91	81.17	93.06	78.68	90.18	84.04
I2R_ NUS_ FAR [14]	96.92	97.09	82.22	93.14	79.69	90.43	84.72
NSTsegmentator [19]	96.59	98.46	70.66	92.31	68.26	90.89	77.96
NSTsegmentator [19]	95.91	95.45	80.96	63.04	77.66	60.17	67.81
OCTYMIST [17]	93.23	94.73	59.76	43.63	55.72	41.33	47.46
StradVision [24]	97.36	98.32	87.52	98.34	85.21	96.69	90.59
TextDetection [7]	95.83	97.24	79.27	71.22	75.97	69.25	72.46
USTB_ FuStar [29]	98.01	97.31	80.59	83.10	78.99	80.87	79.92

5   Conclusion

In this article, we have presented a framework to evaluate text segmentation results. This framework was inspired from EVALTEX, a protocol initially designed to evaluate text detection systems.

The proposed evaluation scheme is able to deal efficiently with different possible segmentation scenarios such as broken, merged characters, partially detected characters or both broken and merged characters. Its robustness to slight variations in character thickness makes the protocol independent of the character's size. Moreover, the evaluation does not rely on a binary decision, which allows a better discrimination between different segmentation scenarios. For all these reasons, scores computed using this framework are not only representative for the segmentation quality but they also allow to characterize and compare segmentation methods. To sum up, as this work handles the segmentation evaluation (at character level) and is an adaptation of a framework capable of evaluating text detection at paragraph/line or word levels, we can state that the presented work is a unified tool to evaluate a text understanding chain at every stage of the detection process. Furthermore, we have shown that we can successfully apply the histogram visualization tool to segmentation evaluation results in order to provide a more detailed overview of the segmentation method's behavior.

In the future, a possible improvement would be to add an OCR evaluation step in the EVALTEX framework. This platform is already able to provide the correspondence between objects in the detection and objects in the GT. This would indicate which character in the GT would be associated to which character in the detection set. The release of this tool is equally planned.

References

1. Calarasanu, S., Fabrizio, J., Dubuisson, S.: Using histogram representation and earth mover's distance as an evaluation tool for text detection. In: Proceedings of International Conference on Document Analysis and Recognition (2015)
2. Calarasanu, S., Fabrizio, J., Dubuisson, S.: What is a good evaluation protocol for text localization systems? Concerns, arguments, comparisons and solutions. Image Vis. Comput. **46**, 1–17 (2016). http://www.sciencedirect.com/science/article/pii/S0262885615001377
3. Cao, H., Govindaraju, V.: Handwritten carbon form preprocessing based on Markov random field. In: Proceedings of Computer Vision and Pattern Recognition, pp. 1–7, June 2007
4. Chang, F., Liang, K.H., Tan, T.M., Hwan, W.L.: Binarization of document images using Hadamard multiresolution analysis. In: Proceedings of International Conference on Document Analysis and Recognition, pp. 157–160 (1999)
5. Clavelli, A., Karatzas, D., Llados, J.: A framework for the assessment of text extraction algorithms on complex color images. In: Proceedings of Document Analysis Systems, pp. 19–26 (2010)
6. Fabrizio, J., Marcotegui, B., Cord, M.: Text segmentation in natural scenes using toggle-mapping. In: Proceedings of the 16th IEEE International Conference on Image Processing, pp. 2349–2352 (2009)

7. Fabrizio, J., Robert-Seidowsky, M., Dubuisson, S., Calarasanu, S., Boissel, R.: Textcatcher: a method to detect curved and challenging text in natural scenes. Int. J. Doc. Anal. Recogn. **19**(2), 99–117 (2016)

8. Filho, C., Mello, C.A.B., Andrade, J.D., Falcao, D.M.A., Lima, M.P., Santos, W.P., Oliveira, A.L.I.: Based on color quantization by genetic algorithms. In: 19th IEEE International Conference on Tools with Artificial Intelligence (ICTAI 2007), vol. 1, pp. 488–491, October 2007

9. Galibert, O., Kahn, J., Oparin, I.: The zonemap metric for page segmentation and area classification in scanned documents. In: Proceedings International Conference on Image Processing, pp. 2594–2598 (2014)

10. He, J., Do, Q.D.M., Downton, A.C., Kim, J.H.: A comparison of binarization methods for historical archive documents. In: Proceedings of International Conference on Document Analysis and Recognition, pp. 538–542, August 2005

11. Huang, W.: Buctyst segmentation method. http://rrc.cvc.uab.es/?com=evaluation&ch=2&view=task2_method&id_submit=2608

12. Kang, B.H., Han, G.S., Kim, H.G., Kim, J.S., Yoon, C.R., Cho, M.S.: Fuzzy inference and logical level methods for binary graphic/character image extraction. In: 1998 IEEE International Conference on Systems, Man, and Cybernetics, vol. 5, pp. 4626–4629, October 1998

13. Karatzas, D., Gomez-Bigorda, L., Nicolaou, A., Ghosh, S., Bagdanov, A., Iwamura, M., Matas, J., Neumann, L., Chandrasekhar, V.R., Lu, S., et al.: ICDAR 2015 competition on robust reading. In: Proceedings of International Conference on Document Analysis and Recognition (2015)

14. Karatzas, D., Shafait, F., Uchida, S., Iwamura, M., Bigorda, L.G., Mestre, S.R., Mas, J., Mota, D.F., Almazan, J.A., de las Heras, L.P.: ICDAR 2013 robust reading competition. In: Proceedings of International Conference on Document Analysis and Recognition, pp. 1484–1493 (2013)

15. Karatzas, D., Shafait, F., Uchida, S., Iwamura, M., Bigorda, L.G.i., Mestre, S.R., Mas, J., Mota, D.F., Almazan, J.A., de las Heras, L.P.: ICDAR 2013 robust reading competition. In: International Journal on Document Analysis and Recognition, pp. 1484–1493 (2013)

16. Kohmura, H., Wakahara, T.: Determining optimal filters for binarization of degraded characters in color using genetic algorithms. In: Proceedings of International Conference on Pattern Recognition, vol. 3, pp. 661–664 (2006)

17. Kumar, D., Ramakrishnan, A.G.: OTCYMIST: Otsu-canny minimal spanning tree for born-digital images. In: Proceedings of Document Analysis Systems, pp. 389–393, March 2012

18. Mao, S., Kanungo, T.: Software architecture of PSET: a page segmentation evaluation toolkit. Int. J. Doc. Anal. Recognit. **4**(3), 205–217 (2002)

19. Milyaev, S., Barinova, O., Novikova, T., Kohli, P., Lempitsky, V.: Image binarization for end-to-end text understanding in natural images. In: Proceedings of International Conference on Document Analysis and Recognition, pp. 128–132 (2013)

20. Ntirogiannis, K., Gatos, B., Pratikakis, I.: An objective evaluation methodology for document image binarization techniques. In: Proceedings of Document Analysis Systems, pp. 217–224, September 2008

21. Robert-Seidowsky, M., Fabrizio, J., Dubuisson, S.: TextTrail: a robust text tracking algorithm in wild environments. In: Proceedings of the 10th International Conference on Computer Vision Theory and Applications, pp. 268–276, March 2015

22. Sezgin, M., Sankur, B.: Survey over image thresholding techniques and quantitative performance evaluation. J. Electron. Imaging **13**(1), 146–168 (2004). http://dblp.uni-trier.de/db/journals/jei/jei13.htmlSezinS04

23. Stathis, P., Kavallieratou, E., Papamarkos, N.: An evaluation technique for binarization algorithms. J. Univ. Comput. Sci. **14**(18), 3011–3030 (2008)
24. Sung, M.C., Jun, B., Cho, H., Kim, D.: Scene text detection with robust character candidate extraction method. In: Proceedings of International Conference on Document Analysis and Recognition, pp. 426–430, August 2015
25. Trier, O.D., Taxt, T.: Evaluation of binarization methods for document images. Pattern Anal. Mach. Intell. **17**(3), 312–315 (1995)
26. Wang, Q., Tan, C.L.: Matching of double-sided document images to remove interference. In: Proceedings of Computer Vision and Pattern Recognition, vol. 1, pp. I-1084–I-1089 (2001)
27. Wolf, C., Jolion, J.M., Chassaing, F.: Text localization, enhancement and binarization in multimedia documents. In: Proceedings of International Conference on Pattern Recognition, vol. 2,pp. 1037–1040 (2002)
28. Wolf, C., Jolion, J.M.: Object count/area graphs for the evaluation of object detection and segmentation algorithms. Int. J. Doc. Anal. Recogn. **8**(4), 280–296 (2006)
29. Yin, X.C., Yin, X., Huang, K., Hao, H.W.: Robust text detection in natural scene images. Pattern Anal. Mach. Intell. **36**(5), 970–983 (2014)
30. Zhu, Y., Wang, C., Dai, R.: Document image binarization based on stroke enhancement. In: Proceedings of International Conference on Pattern Recognition, vol. 1, pp. 955–958 (2006)

Dynamic Lexicon Generation
for Natural Scene Images

Yash Patel[1,2(✉)], Lluis Gomez[2], Marçal Rusiñol[2], and Dimosthenis Karatzas[2]

[1] CVIT IIIT, Hyderabad, India
yash.patel@students.iiit.ac.in
[2] Computer Vision Center, Universitat Autònoma de Barcelona, Barcelona, Spain
{lgomez,marcal,dimos}@cvc.uab.es

Abstract. Many scene text understanding methods approach the end-to-end recognition problem from a word-spotting perspective and take huge benefit from using small per-image lexicons. Such customized lexicons are normally assumed as given and their source is rarely discussed. In this paper we propose a method that generates contextualized lexicons for scene images using only visual information. For this, we exploit the correlation between visual and textual information in a dataset consisting of images and textual content associated with them. Using the topic modeling framework to discover a set of latent topics in such a dataset allows us to re-rank a fixed dictionary in a way that prioritizes the words that are more likely to appear in a given image. Moreover, we train a CNN that is able to reproduce those word rankings but using only the image raw pixels as input. We demonstrate that the quality of the automatically obtained custom lexicons is superior to a generic frequency-based baseline.

Keywords: Scene text · Photo OCR · Scene understanding · Lexicon generation · Topic modeling · CNN

1 Introduction

Reading systems for text understanding in the wild have shown a remarkable increase in performance over the past five years [1,2]. However, the problem is still far from being considered solved with the best reported methods achieving end-to-end recognition performances of 87 % in focused text scenarios [3,4] and 53% in the more difficult problem of incidental text [5].

The best performing end-to-end scene text understanding methodologies address the problem from a word spotting perspective and take a huge benefit from using customized lexicons. The size and quality of these custom lexicons has been shown to have a strong effect in the recognition performance [6].

The source of such per-image customized lexicons is rarely discussed. In most academic settings such custom lexicons are artificially created and provided to the algorithm as a form of predefined word queries. But, in real life scenarios lexicons need to be dynamically constructed.

© Springer International Publishing Switzerland 2016
G. Hua and H. Jégou (Eds.): ECCV 2016 Workshops, Part I, LNCS 9913, pp. 395–410, 2016.
DOI: 10.1007/978-3-319-46604-0_29

In one of the few examples in literature, Wang et al. [7] used Google's "search nearby" functionality to built custom lexicons of businesses that might appear in Google Street View images. In the document analysis domain, different techniques for adapting the language models to take into account the context of the document have been used, such as language model adaptation [8] and full-book recognition techniques [9]. Such approaches are nevertheless only feasible on relatively large corpuses were word statistics can be effectively calculated and are not applicable to scene images where text is scarce.

On the other hand, scene images contain rich visual information that could provide the missing context to improve text detection and recognition results. In the view of the authors, reading text in the wild calls for holistic scene understanding in a way where visual and textual cues are treated together providing mutual feedback for each others interpretation.

In this paper, we take a first step in this direction, and we propose a method that generates contextualized lexicons based on visual information. For this we make the following contributions: first, we learn a topic model using Latent Dirichlet Allocation (LDA) [10] using as a corpus textual information associated with scene images combined with scene text. This topic model is suitable for generating contextualized lexicons of scene text given image descriptions. Subsequently, we train a deep CNN model, based on the topic model, that is capable to produce on its output a probability distribution over the topics discovered by the LDA analysis directly from the image input. This way our method is able to generate contextualized lexicons for new (unseen) images directly from their raw pixels, without the need of any associated textual content. Moreover, we demonstrate that the quality of such automatically obtained custom lexicons is superior to generic frequency-based lexicons in predicting the words that are more likely to appear as scene text instances in a given image.

2   Related Work

End-to-end scene text recognition pipelines are usually based in a multi-stage approach, first applying a text detection algorithm to the input image and then recognizing the text present in the cropped bounding boxes provided by the detector [11].

Scene text recognition from pre-segmented text has been approached in two different conditions: using a small provided lexicon per image (also known as the word spotting task), or performing unconstrained text recognition, i.e. allowing the recognition of out-of-dictionary words.

Many of the existing text recognition methods [6,7,12–14] rely on individual character segmentation and recognition. After that, character candidates are grouped into larger sequences (words and text lines) using spatial and lexicon-based constraints. Such methods differ, apart from the features and classifiers used for individual character classification, in their language models, and the inference methods used to find the best character sequence, e.g. pictorial structures [7], Conditional Random Fields (CRF) [15], Viterbi decoding [6,12,13], or Beam Search [14]. Language models are usually based on a dictionary of the most frequent words in a given language and a character n-gram (usually a bi-gram). A much stronger language model, relying on large-scale data center infrastructure, is used in [14] combining a compact character-level 8-gram model and a word-level 4-gram model.

State of the art language models for document-based OCR have demonstrated good performance in scene text recognition when text instances can be properly binarized [16, 17].

In the case of the word spotting and retrieval tasks it is also possible to make use of holistic word recognizers that perform recognition without any explicit character segmentation (Goel 2013, Almazan 2013, jaderberg2016reading).

Obviously, either language-model based approaches and holistic word recognizers may benefit from using per-image customized lexicons: by reducing their search space or (in the case of holistic recognizers) the number of possible class-labels. As an example, Table 1 shows end-to-end recognition performance in [6] for different sizes of the per-image lexicon.

Table 1. Recognition performance drops when adding distraction words in the lexicon [6].

	5 distractors	20 distractors	50 distractors	860 distractors	Open vocabulary
F-score	76 %	74 %	72 %	67 %	38 %

However, having a small lexicon containing all the words that may appear in a given image is not realistic in many cases. Even for methods using large (frequency based) lexicons (e.g. the 90 k word dictionary used in [4]), it is not possible to recognize out-of-dictionary words such as telephone numbers, prices, url's, email addresses, or to some extent product brands. Notice that in the last edition of the ICDAR Robust Reading Competition [2] out-of-dictionary words are not included in the customized dictionaries provided for end-to-end recognition, as it is not realistic that such queries would be available in a real-life scenario.

An interesting method for reducing an initial large lexicon to a small image-specific lexicon is proposed in [18]. Since having a large lexicon poses a problem for CRF based methods because pairwise potentials become too generic, they propose a lexicon reduction process that alternates between recomputing priors and refining the lexicon.

Wang et al. [7] propose the use of geo-localization information to built custom lexicons of businesses that might appear in Google Street View images. This multimodal approach to generate contextualized lexicons from GPS data clearly helps in recognition of out-of-dictionary words that are strongly correlated with the location from which an image is taken, e.g. street names, touristic attractions, business front stores, etc.

In this paper we propose a method that generates contextualized lexicons based only on visual information. The main intuition of our method is that visual information may provide in some cases a valuable cue for text recognition algorithms: there are some words for which occurrence in a natural scene image correlates directly with objects appearing in the image or with the scene category itself. For example, if there is a telephone booth in the image the word "telephone" has a large probability of appearance, while if the image is a mountain landscape the "telephone" word is less likely to appear.

Evidence of this correlation between visual and textual information in natural scene images has been recently reported by Movshovitz et al. in [19]. A Deep Convolutional Neural Network trained for fine-grained classification of storefront street view images implicitly learns to read, i.e. to use textual information, when needed, despite it has been trained without any annotated text or language models. The network, by learning the correct representation for the task at hand, learned that some words are correlated with specific types of businesses, up to a point in which if the text in correctly classified images is removed the net loses classification confidence about their correct class. Moreover, the network is able to produce relevant responses when presented with a synthetic image containing only textual information (a word) that relates with a specific business.

On a totally different application but also in relation with exploiting the correlation between visual and textual information, Feng et al. [20] proposes a method that uses the topic modeling framework for generating automatic image annotations and text illustration. They presented a probabilistic model based on the assumption that images and their co-occurring textual data are generated by mixtures of latent topics.

A topic model [10,21] is a type of statistical model for discovering the abstract "topics" that occur in a collection of text documents. Topic modeling has been applied successfully in many text-analysis tasks such as document modeling, document classification, semantic visualization/organization, and collaborative filtering. But they also have applications in Computer Vision research. They have been used for unsupervised image classification by Li et al. [22] when Bag-of-Visual-Words was a dominant method for image classification. Nowadays they are a common tool for automatic image annotation methods.

In this paper we present a method that generates contextualized lexicons based on visual information. We use a similar approach to [20] in topic models to exploit correlation between visual and textual information. But distinctly to [20] we do not aim at generating annotations of the image, but instead the words that are more likely to appear in the image as scene text instances.

Our method is also related with the work of Zhang et al. [23] in which we use Latent Dirichlet Allocation (LDA) [10] within the topic modeling framework to supervise the training of a deep neural network (DNN), so that DNN can approximate the LDA inference. An idea that is motivated by the transfer learning approach of [24]. However, in our method we train a deep CNN that takes images as input instead of a text Bag-of-Words as in [23].

3   Method

The underlying idea of our lexicon generation method is that the topic modeling statistical framework can be used to predict a ranking of the most probable words that may appear in a given image. For this we propose a three-fold method: First, we learn a LDA topic model on a text corpus associated with the image dataset. Second, we train a deep CNN model to generate LDA's topic-probabilities directly from the image pixels. Third, we use the generated topic-probabilities, either from the LDA model (using textual information) or from the CNN (using image pixels), along with the word-probabilities from the learned LDA model to re-rank the words of a given dictionary. Figure 1 shows a diagram representation of the overall framework.

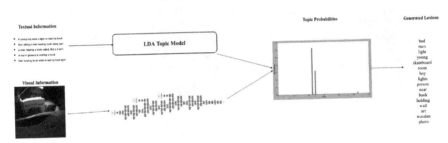

Fig. 1. We learn a LDA topic model on a text corpus associated with scene images. Then we train a deep CNN model to generate the probabilities over latent topics directly from image pixel information.

The training samples in our framework are composed by a couple of visual information (an image) and some associated textual information (e.g. a set of image captions and/or the annotations of words that appear in the image), see Fig. 2(a). Our model assumes that the textual information describe the content of the image either directly or indirectly and hence can be used to generate contextualized lexicons for natural images.

In the next section we explain how we learn the LDA topic model to discover latent topics from training data by using only the textual information. Then in Sect. 3.2 we show how it is possible to train a deep CNN model to predict the same probability distributions over topics as the LDA model but using only the image pixels (visual information) as input. Finally, in Sect. 3.3 we explain how using the topic probabilities we can generate word rankings, i.e. a per-image ranked lexicon, for new (unseen) images.

3.1   Learning the LDA Topic Model Using Textual Information

Our method assumes that the textual information associated with the images in our dataset is generated by a mixture of latent topics. Similar to [20], we propose the use of Latent Dirichlet Allocation [10] for discovering the latent topics in the

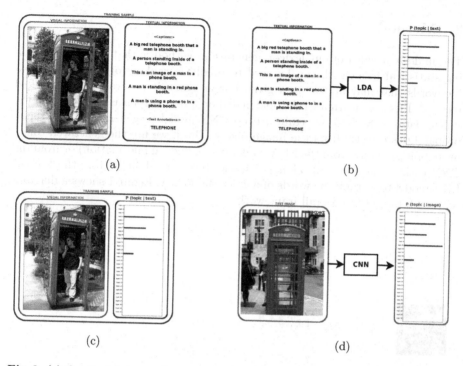

Fig. 2. (a) Our training samples consist in a couple of an image and some associated textual content. (b) Using a topic model we can represent the textual information as a probability distribution over topics $P(topic \mid text)$. (c) Training samples for our CNN use those probability values as labels. (d) The CNN takes an image as input and produces on its output a probability distribution over topics $P(topic \mid image)$.

dataset's text corpus, and thus to represent the textual information associated with a given image as a probability distribution over the set of discovered topics.

As presented in [10], LDA is a generative statistical model of a corpus (a set of text documents) where each document can be viewed as a mixture of various topics, and each topic is characterized by a probability distribution over words. LDA can be represented as a three level hierarchical Bayesian model. Given a text corpus consisting of M documents and a dictionary with N words, Blei et al. define the generative process [10] for a document d as follows:

– Choose $\theta \sim Dir(\alpha)$.
– For each of the N words w_n:
  • Choose a topic $z_n \sim Multinomial(\theta)$.
  • Choose a word w_n from $p(w_n \mid z_n, \beta)$, a multinomial probability conditioned on the topic z_n.

where θ is the mixing proportion and is drawn from a Dirichlet prior with parameter α. As [10] suggests, α and β are assumed to be sampled once in the process of generating a corpus. This way the documents are represented as topic probabilities $z_{1:K}$ (being K the number of topics) and word probabilities over topics. The learned LDA model has two sets of parameters, the topic probabilities given documents $P(z_{1:K} \mid d)$ and the word probabilities given topics $P(w \mid z_{1:K})$. This way any new (unseen) document can be represented in terms of a probability distribution over topics of the learned LDA model by projecting it in the topic space.

Notice that in our framework a document corresponds to the textual information associated to an image (e.g. image captions and scene text annotations). Thus, the text corpus is the set of all textual information (documents) in the whole dataset. By learning the LDA topic model using this corpus we discover a set of latent topics in our dataset, and we can represent the textual information associated to a given image as a probability distribution over those topics $p(topic|text)$ as shown in Fig. 2(b).

3.2 Training a CNN to Predict Probability Distributions Over LDA's Topics

Once we have the LDA topic model, we want to train a deep CNN model to predict the same probability distributions over topics as the LDA model does for textual information, but using only the raw pixels of new unseen images.

For this we can generate a set of training (and validation) samples as follows: given an image from the training set we represent its corresponding textual information (captions) as probability values over the LDA's topics. These probability values are used as labels for the given image as shown in Fig. 2(c).

This way we obtain a set of M training (and validation) examples of the form $\{(x_1, y_1), ..., (x_M, y_M)\}$ such that x_i is an image and y_i is the probability distribution over topics obtained by projecting its associated textual information into the LDA topic space.

Using this training set we train a deep CNN to predict the probability distribution y_i for unseen images, see Fig. 2(d), directly from the image pixels. In fact, we use a transfer learning approach here in order to shortcut the training process by fine-tuning the well known Inception [25] deep CNN model. Details on the training procedure are given in Sect. 4.2.

3.3 Using Topic Models for Generating Word Ranks

Once the LDA topic model is learned as explained in Sect. 3.1, we can represent the textual information corresponding to an unobserved image as probability distribution over the topics of LDA model $P(topic \mid text)$, which is done by projecting the textual information to the topic-space. Since the contribution of each word to each topic, $P(word \mid topic)$ was pre-computed when we learned the LDA model, we can calculate the probability of occurrence for each word in the dictionary $P(word \mid text)$ as follows:

$$P(word \mid text) = \sum_{i=1:K} (P(word \mid topic_i)P(topic_i \mid text)) \qquad (1)$$

Similarly, once the deep CNN is trained as explained in Sect. 3.2, we can obtain the probability distribution over topics for an unseen image $P(topic \mid image)$ as the output of the CNN when feeding the image pixels on its input. Again, since the word-probability for each topic which $P(word \mid topic)$ is known from the corresponding LDA model, which we used to supervise the training of deep CNN's training, we can calculate the probability of occurrence of each word in the dictionary $P(word \mid image)$ as follows:

$$P(word \mid image) = \sum_{i=1:K} (P(word \mid topic_i)P(topic_i \mid image)) \qquad (2)$$

Using the obtained probability distributions over words (i.e. $P(word \mid text)$), or $P(word \mid image)$) we are able to rank a given dictionary in order to prioritize the words that have more chances to appear in a given image.

In the following section we show how the word rankings obtained from both approaches are very similar, which demonstrates the capability of the deep CNN to generate topic probabilities directly from the image pixels. Moreover, the rankings generated this way prove to be better that a frequency-based word ranking in predicting which are the expected scene text instances (words) to be found in a given image.

4   Experiments and Results

In this section we present the experimental evaluation of the proposed method on its ability to generate lexicons that can be used to improve the performance of systems for reading text in natural scene images. First, we present the datasets used for training and evaluation in Sect. 4.1. Then, in Sect. 4.2, we provide the implementation details of our experiments. In Sect. 4.3, we analyze the performance of the word rankings obtained by representing image captions as a mixture of LDA topics as detailed in Sect. 3.3. Finally in Sect. 4.4, we show the performance of the word ranking obtained with our CNN network trained for predicting topic probabilities.

4.1   Datasets

In our experiments we make use of two standard datasets, namely the MS-COCO [26] and the COCO-Text [27] datasets.

The MS-COCO is a large scale dataset providing task-specific annotations for object detection, segmentation, and image captioning. The dataset consists of 2.5 million labeled object instances among 80 categories in 328 K images of complex everyday scenes. Images are annotated with multiple object instances and with 5 captions per image.

COCO-Text is a dataset for text detection and recognition in natural scene images that is based on the MS-COCO dataset. The images in this dataset were not taken with text in mind and thus it contains a broad variety of text instances. The dataset consists of 63,686 images, 173,589 text instances (words) and 3-fine grained text attributes. The dataset is divided in 43,686 training images and 20,000 validation images.

COCO-Text images are a subset of MS-COCO images, thus for our experiments we use the ground truth information of both datasets: image captions from MS-COCO and text instances (word transcriptions) from COCO-Text.

Since both the training and validation images of COCO-Text are a subset of the MS-COCO training set, we have done the following partition of the data: for training purposes we use the training and validation sets of MS-COCO but removing the images that are part of the validation set in COCO-Text. For validation purpose we use the validation set of COCO-Text. This way our training set consists of 103287 images and our validation set of 20000 images.

Apart of the MS-COCO and COCO-Text datasets we have used the entire english-wikipedia text, consisting of around 4 million text documents, for computing the word-frequency based lexicon used as a Baseline for word-rankings evaluation.

4.2 Implementation Details

In our experiments involving topic modeling we have used the gensim [28] Python library for learning and inferring the LDA model. We have learned multiple LDA models with a varying number of topics and have compared word ranking results as shown in Sect. 4.3.

On the other hand, we have used the TensorFlow [29] framework for finetuning of the Inception_v3 model [25]. We have trained the final layer of the net from scratch, accommodating it to the size of our topic modeling task, and leaving the rest of the net untouched. We used the cross entropy loss function and Gradient Descent optimizer with a fixed learning rate of 0.01 and a batch size of 100 for 100k iterations.

4.3 LDA Word Rankings from Image Captions

In this section we evaluate the performance of the different word rankings obtained with our method on predicting text instances (words) for COCO-Text validation images. The setup of the experiment is as follows:

Corpus: We learned the LDA topic model using two different corpuses: (1) we use 63686 documents made using the word annotations from both the train and validation images of COCO-Text and their corresponding captions (from MS-COCO); (2) we do the same but using only the 43686 images in the train set of COCO-Text and their corresponding captions (from MS-COCO).

Dictionary: We do experiments with two different dictionaries: (1) The list of 33563 unique annotated text instances (words) in the COCO-Text dataset; and (2) a generic dictionary of approximately 88172 words used in [4], but removing stop words thus giving rise to a dictionary of 88036 words.

Word-rankings using LDA: For each image, the words of the dictionary are ranked by obtaining the word probabilities as mentioned in Sect. 3.3.

Baseline ranking: Dictionary words are ranked according to their frequency of occurrences. Frequency of occurrence of dictionary words is computed on wikipedia-english corpus.

Given a fixed dictionary we are interested in word rankings that are able to prioritize the words that are more likely to appear in a given image as scene text instances. Thus, we propose the following procedure to evaluate and compare different word rankings: for every word ranking we count the percentage of COCO-Text ground truth (validation) instances that are found among the top-N words of the re-ranked dictionary. This way we can plot curves illustrating the number of COCO-Text instances found in different word lists (lexicons) that correspond to certain top percentages of the ranked dictionary. The larger the area under those curves the better is a given ranking.

Figure 3 evaluate our method for a varying number of topics of the LDA model, and compare their performance with the baseline frequency-based ranking using the above mentioned text corpuses and dictionaries. The x-axis in the plots represents percentage of words of the re-ranked dictionary. The y-axis represents percentage of instances of the validation set of COCO-Text dataset in the top-N percent of the re-ranked dictionary.

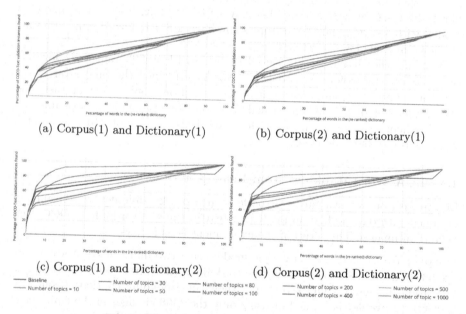

(a) Corpus(1) and Dictionary(1)   (b) Corpus(2) and Dictionary(1)

(c) Corpus(1) and Dictionary(2)   (d) Corpus(2) and Dictionary(2)

Fig. 3. Word ranking performance comparison.

Notice that we analyze our method only for the COCO-Text word instances that are present in the dictionary, this is why using 100 % of dictionary words we always reach 100 % of COCO-Text instances.

As can be appreciated the number of topics in the LDA topic model is an important parameter of the method. The best performance for our

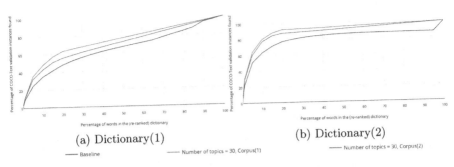

(a) Dictionary(1)   (b) Dictionary(2)

—— Baseline   —— Number of topics = 30, Corpus(1)   —— Number of topics = 30, Corpus(2)

Fig. 4. Word ranking performance comparison by using Corpus(1) and Corpus(2) with each dictionaries.

automatically generated rankings are found for the 30 topics model. In such a case the performance of the LDA based rankings is superior to the baseline in all the experiments. This demonstrates that the topic modeling analysis we propose is able to predict the occurrence of words as scene text instances much better than a frequency-based dictionary.

Figure 4 shows the performance comparison of the rankings generated with the 30 topics LDA model in both dictionaries. Obviously using the textual content associated with validation images, in Corpus(1), for learning the LDA topic model provides an extra boost to the method's performance. Still the word rankings provided by the LDA model learned only from training data, Corpus(2), clearly outperform the baseline ranking.

4.4 CNN Word Rankings

In this experiment we evaluate the performance of the deep CNN network trained with the procedure detailed in Sects. 3.2 and 4.2. Figure 5 shows the performance comparison of the word rankings obtained by the LDA model using 30 topics as in the previous section, and the word rankings obtained with the CNN as explained in Sect. 3.3. It is important to notice here that for training the CNN the train images' labels are generated from the LDA model learned only with Corpus(2). This is, our CNN model has never seen validation data (neither images or textual content) in a direct or indirect way.

As can be seen the CNN is able to produce word rankings with almost the same performance as projecting the images' captions in the LDA space, but using only the image raw pixels as input. Using the CNN for predicting the probability distribution over 30 topics for a given image takes takes 54 ms.

Figure 6 shows the cross entropy loss of the CNN during the training process, up to 100 k iterations. We also show the top-1 topic classification accuracy (i.e. as when we evaluate a classification task) because it's efficient and gives us a rough estimation on how the network is performing at every iteration. Thus, for visualization we calculate accuracy by looking only at the most important topic in ground-truth labels and in the CNN predictions.

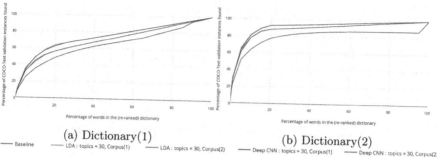

(a) Dictionary(1)   (b) Dictionary(2)

— Baseline   —— LDA : topics = 30, Corpus(1)   — LDA : topics = 30, Corpus(2)   —— Deep CNN : topics = 30, Corpus(1)   — Deep CNN : topics = 30, Corpus(2)

Fig. 5. Word ranking performance comparison of LDA model and deep CNN with 30 topics for Dictionaries (1) and (2).

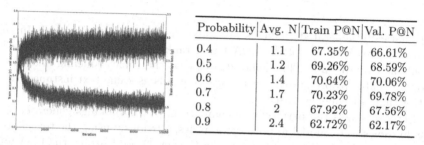

Probability	Avg. N	Train P@N	Val. P@N
0.4	1.1	67.35%	66.61%
0.5	1.2	69.26%	68.59%
0.6	1.4	70.64%	70.06%
0.7	1.7	70.23%	69.78%
0.8	2	67.92%	67.56%
0.9	2.4	62.72%	62.17%

Fig. 6. Cross entropy loss and top-1 classification accuracy during the CNN training process up to 100k iterations (left). CNN model train and validation precision at N for different probabilities.

Once the CNN model is trained we analyze its performance more precisely by looking at the top-N most important topics, defined as the set of top-N topics for which the sum of their probabilities reaches a certain threshold. Figure 6 shows the CNN precision at N (P@N) calculated this way for the train and validation sets. Notice that N might change for each image.

As can be appreciated in the table the CNN model is able to approximate the learned topic model consistently in both training and validation sets. While the obtained precision at N are far from a perfect model, we can see that in average the CNN is able to predict the top-2 topics pretty well in nearly 70 % of the images. Moreover, since as shown in Fig. 5 the performance of the word rankings obtained directly from the topic model and the CNN are almost identical, we can conclude that these values are only an estimator of the CNN real performance. In other words, the word rankings produces by the CNN can be as good as the ones using the LDA topic models even if the CNN prediction is not 100 % accurate.

Figure 7 shows qualitative results in which it can be appreciated the effectiveness of the proposed method to produce word rankings that prioritize the text instances annotated in different sample images. Figure 8 shows some unsuccessful cases.

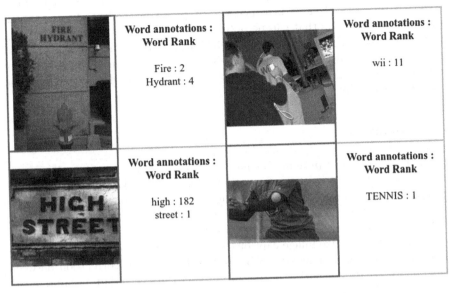

Fig. 7. Qualitative successful results of generated word rankings.

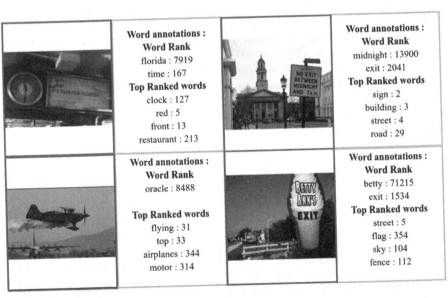

Fig. 8. Qualitative unsuccessful results of generated word rankings. Word instances without any semantic correlation with the visual information in the scene tend to be low ranked.

Images in Figs. 7 and 8 have been selected from the validation set in order to show a diversity of cases in which the proposed method produces particularly interesting results that can be potentially leveraged by end-to-end reading systems. For example, for the bottom-right image in Fig. 7 the top ranked word in the 33 K words dictionary(1) is "TENNIS", a word instance that is partially occluded in the image and whose recognition would be very difficult without the context provided by the scene.

5   Conclusion

In this paper we have presented a method that generates contextualized per-image lexicons based on visual information. This way we take a first step towards the use of the rich visual information contained in scene images that could provide the missing context to improve text detection and recognition results.

We have shown how in large scale datasets consisting in images and associated textual information, like image captions and scene text transcriptions, the topic modeling statistical framework can be used to leverage the correlation between visual and textual information in order to predict the words that are more likely to appear in the image as scene text instances. Moreover, we have shown that is possible to train a deep CNN model to reproduce those topic model based word rankings but using only an image as input.

Our experiments demonstrate that the quality of the automatically obtained custom lexicons is superior to a generic frequency based baseline, and thus can be used to improve scene text recognition methods. Future work will be devoted to integrate the proposed method in an end-to-end scene text reading system.

As a result of the work presented in this paper we have developed a cross API, which is made publicly available[1], to get captions from MS-COCO and corresponding word annotations from COCO-Text.

Acknowledgments. This project was supported by the Spanish projects TIN2014-52072-P and RYC-2009-05031.

References

1. Karatzas, D., Shafait, F., Uchida, S., Iwamura, M., i Bigorda, L.G., Mestre, S.R., Mas, J., Mota, D.F., Almazan, J.A., de las Heras, L.P.: ICDAR 2013 robust reading competition. In: 2013 12th International Conference on Document Analysis and Recognition, pp. 1484–1493. IEEE (2013)
2. Karatzas, D., Gomez-Bigorda, L., Nicolaou, A., Ghosh, S., Bagdanov, A., Iwamura, M., Matas, J., Neumann, L., Chandrasekhar, V.R., Lu, S., et al.: ICDAR 2015 competition on robust reading. In: 2015 13th International Conference on Document Analysis and Recognition (ICDAR), pp. 1156–1160. IEEE (2015)
3. Li, H., Shen, C.: Reading car license plates using deep convolutional neural networks and lstms. arXiv preprint arXiv:1601.05610 (2016)

---

[1] https://github.com/yash0307/MS-COCO_COCO-Text_CrossAPI.

4. Jaderberg, M., Simonyan, K., Vedaldi, A., Zisserman, A.: Reading text in the wild with convolutional neural networks. Int. J. Comput. Vision **116**(1), 1–20 (2016)
5. Gomez-Bigorda, L., Karatzas, D.: Textproposals: a text-specific selective search algorithm for word spotting in the wild. arXiv preprint arXiv:1604.02619 (2016)
6. Wang, T., Wu, D.J., Coates, A., Ng, A.Y.: End-to-end text recognition with convolutional neural networks. In: 2012 21st International Conference on Pattern Recognition (ICPR), pp. 3304–3308. IEEE (2012)
7. Wang, K., Belongie, S.: Word spotting in the wild. In: Daniilidis, K., Maragos, P., Paragios, N. (eds.) ECCV 2010. LNCS, vol. 6311, pp. 591–604. Springer, Heidelberg (2010). doi:10.1007/978-3-642-15549-9_43
8. Frinken, V., Karatzas, D., Fischer, A.: A cache language model for whole document handwriting recognition. In: 2014 11th IAPR International Workshop on Document Analysis Systems (DAS), pp. 166–170. IEEE (2014)
9. Xiu, P., Baird, H.S.: Towards whole-book recognition. In: The Eighth IAPR International Workshop on Document Analysis Systems, DAS 2008, pp. 629–636. IEEE (2008)
10. Blei, D.M., Ng, A.Y., Jordan, M.I.: Latent dirichlet allocation. J. Mach. Learn. Res. **3**, 993–1022 (2003)
11. Ye, Q., Doermann, D.: Text detection and recognition in imagery: a survey. IEEE Trans. Pattern Anal. Mach. Intell. **37**(7), 1480–1500 (2015)
12. Neumann, L., Matas, J.: On combining multiple segmentations in scene text recognition. In: 2013 12th International Conference on Document Analysis and Recognition, pp. 523–527. IEEE (2013)
13. Jaderberg, M., Vedaldi, A., Zisserman, A.: Deep features for text spotting. In: Fleet, D., Pajdla, T., Schiele, B., Tuytelaars, T. (eds.) ECCV 2014. LNCS, vol. 8692, pp. 512–528. Springer, Heidelberg (2014). doi:10.1007/978-3-319-10593-2_34
14. Bissacco, A., Cummins, M., Netzer, Y., Neven, H.: Photoocr: reading text in uncontrolled conditions. In: Proceedings of the IEEE International Conference on Computer Vision, pp. 785–792 (2013)
15. Mishra, A., Alahari, K., Jawahar, C.: Top-down and bottom-up cues for scene text recognition. In: 2012 IEEE Conference on Computer Vision and Pattern Recognition (CVPR), pp. 2687–2694. IEEE (2012)
16. Milyaev, S., Barinova, O., Novikova, T., Kohli, P., Lempitsky, V.: Image binarization for end-to-end text understanding in natural images. In: 2013 12th International Conference on Document Analysis and Recognition, pp. 128–132. IEEE (2013)
17. Gómez, L., Karatzas, D.: Scene text recognition: no country for old men? In: Jawahar, C.V., Shan, S. (eds.) ACCV 2014. LNCS, vol. 9009, pp. 157–168. Springer, Heidelberg (2015). doi:10.1007/978-3-319-16631-5_12
18. Roy, U., Mishra, A., Alahari, K., Jawahar, C.V.: Scene text recognition and retrieval for large lexicons. In: Cremers, D., Reid, I., Saito, H., Yang, M.-H. (eds.) ACCV 2014. LNCS, vol. 9003, pp. 494–508. Springer, Heidelberg (2015). doi:10.1007/978-3-319-16865-4_32
19. Movshovitz-Attias, Y., Yu, Q., Stumpe, M.C., Shet, V., Arnoud, S., Yatziv, L.: Ontological supervision for fine grained classification of street view storefronts. In: 2015 IEEE Conference on Computer Vision and Pattern Recognition (CVPR), pp. 1693–1702. IEEE (2015)
20. Feng, Y., Lapata, M.: Topic models for image annotation and text illustration. In: Human Language Technologies: The 2010 Annual Conference of the North American Chapter of the Association for Computational Linguistics, Association for Computational Linguistics, pp. 831–839 (2010)

21. Papadimitriou, C.H., Tamaki, H., Raghavan, P., Vempala, S.: Latent semantic indexing: a probabilistic analysis. In: Proceedings of the Seventeenth ACM SIGACT-SIGMOD-SIGART Symposium on Principles of Database Systems, pp. 159–168. ACM (1998)

22. Fei-Fei, L., Perona, P.: A bayesian hierarchical model for learning natural scene categories. In: 2005 IEEE Computer Society Conference on Computer Vision and Pattern Recognition (CVPR 2005). vol. 2, pp. 524–531. IEEE (2005)

23. Zhang, D., Luo, T., Wang, D., Liu, R.: Learning from lda using deep neural networks. arXiv preprint arXiv:1508.01011 (2015)

24. Hinton, G., Vinyals, O., Dean, J.: Distilling the knowledge in a neural network. arXiv preprint arXiv:1503.02531 (2015)

25. Szegedy, C., Vanhoucke, V., Ioffe, S., Shlens, J., Wojna, Z.: Rethinking the inception architecture for computer vision. arXiv preprint arXiv:1512.00567 (2015)

26. Lin, T.-Y., Maire, M., Belongie, S., Hays, J., Perona, P., Ramanan, D., Dollár, P., Zitnick, C.L.: Microsoft COCO: common objects in context. In: Fleet, D., Pajdla, T., Schiele, B., Tuytelaars, T. (eds.) ECCV 2014. LNCS, vol. 8693, pp. 740–755. Springer, Heidelberg (2014). doi:10.1007/978-3-319-10602-1_48

27. Veit, A., Matera, T., Neumann, L., Matas, J., Belongie, S.: Coco-text: Dataset and benchmark for text detection and recognition in natural images. arXiv preprint. arXiv:1601.07140 (2016)

28. Rehurek, R., Sojka, P.: Software framework for topic modelling with large corpora. In: Proceedings of the LREC 2010 Workshop on New Challenges for NLP Frameworks (2010)

29. Abadi, M., Agarwal, A., Barham, P., Brevdo, E., Chen, Z., Citro, C., Corrado, G.S., Davis, A., Dean, J., Devin, M., et al.: Tensorflow: Large-scale machine learning on heterogeneous distributed systems. arXiv preprint arXiv:1603.04467 (2016)

End-to-End Interpretation of the French Street Name Signs Dataset

Raymond Smith[✉], Chunhui Gu, Dar-Shyang Lee, Huiyi Hu,
Ranjith Unnikrishnan, Julian Ibarz, Sacha Arnoud, and Sophia Lin

Google Inc., 1600 Ampthitheatre Pkwy, Mountain View, CA 94043, USA
{rays,chunhui,dsl,clarahu,ranjith,julianibarz,sacha,sophi}@google.com

Abstract. We introduce the French Street Name Signs (FSNS) Dataset consisting of more than a million images of street name signs cropped from Google Street View images of France. Each image contains several views of the same street name sign. Every image has normalized, title case folded ground-truth text as it would appear on a map. We believe that the FSNS dataset is large and complex enough to train a deep network of significant complexity to solve the street name extraction problem "end-to-end" or to explore the design trade-offs between a single complex engineered network and multiple sub-networks designed and trained to solve sub-problems. We present such an "end-to-end" network/graph for Tensor Flow and its results on the FSNS dataset.

Keywords: Deep networks · End-to-end networks · Image dataset · Multiview dataset

1 Introduction

The detection and recognition of text from outdoor images is of increasing research interest to the fields of computer vision, machine learning and optical character recognition. The combination of perspective distortion, uncontrolled source text quality, and lack of significant structure to the text layout adds extra challenge to the still incompletely solved problem of accurately recognizing text from all the world's languages. Demonstrating the interest, several datasets related to the problem have become available: including ICDAR 2003 Robust Reading [11], SVHN [13], and, more recently, COCO-Text [16], with details of these and others shown in Table 1.

While these datasets each make a useful contribution to the field, the majority are very small compared to the size of a typical deep neural network. As the dataset size increases, it becomes increasingly difficult to maintain the accuracy of the ground-truth, as the task of annotating must be delegated to an increasingly large pool of workers less involved with the project. In the COCO-text [16] dataset for instance, the authors performed an audit themselves of the accuracy of the ground truth, and found that the annotators had found legible text regions with a recall of 84 %, and transcribed the text content with an accuracy

© Springer International Publishing Switzerland 2016
G. Hua and H. Jégou (Eds.): ECCV 2016 Workshops, Part I, LNCS 9913, pp. 411–426, 2016.
DOI: 10.1007/978-3-319-46604-0_30

of 87.5 %. Even at an edit distance of 1, the text content accuracy was still only 92.5 %, with missing punctuation being the largest remaining category of error.

Synthetic data has been shown [8] to be a good solution to this problem and can work well provided the synthetic data generator includes the formatting/distortions that will be present in the target problem. Some real-world data however, by its very nature, can be hard to predict, so real data remains the first choice in many cases where available.

The difficulty remains therefore, in generating a sufficiently accurately annotated, large enough dataset of real images, to satisfy the needs of modern data-hungry deep network-based systems, which can learn as large a dataset as we can provide, without necessarily giving back the generalization that we would like. To this end, and to make OCR more like image captioning, we present the French Street Name Signs (FSNS) dataset, which we believe to be the first to offer multiple views of the same physical object, and thus the chance for a learning system to compensate for degradation in any individual view.

Table 1. Datasets of outdoor images containing text, including larger than single character ground truth. Information obtained mostly from the iapr-tc11.org website

Name	Content	Size
ICDAR2003 [11]	Images with word and character bounding boxes	Train: 258 Images, 1,157 words Test: 251 Images, 1,111 words
SVHN [13]	Images of numbers and single digits from Google Street View with boxes	Train: 73,257 digits Test: 26,032 Additional: 531,131
COCO-text [16]	Images from the MS COCO dataset that contain text	63,686 images with 173,589 text regions
KAIST [9] scene text	Images with word and character boxes of Korean and English	3,000 images
NEOCR [12]	Images with text field boxes and perspective quadrangles.	659 images with 5,238 text fields
SVT [18]	Images from Google Street View, with names of businesses in them	Train: 100 images, 211 words Test: 250 images, 514 words
Synthetic word [8]	Synthetic images of real-world-like words	9 million images, 90k distinct words
FSNS	Images of French street name signs	>1,000,000 images

2   Basics of the FSNS Dataset

As its name suggests, the FSNS dataset is a set of signs, from the streets of France, that bear street names. Some example images are shown in Fig. 1. Each image carries four tiles of 150 × 150 pixels laid out horizontally, each of which contains a pre-detected street name sign, or random noise in the case that less than four independent views are available of the same physical sign. The text detection problem is thus largely eliminated, although the signs are still of variable size and orientation within each tile image. Also each sign carries multiple text lines, with a maximum of 3 lines of significant text, with the possibility of other additional lines of irrelevant text. Each of the tiles within an image is intended to be a different view *of the same physical sign*, taken from a different position and/or at a different time. Different physical signs of the same street name, from elsewhere on the same street, are included as separate images. There are over 1 million different physical signs.

Fig. 1. Some examples of FSNS images

The different views are of different quality, possibly taken from an acute angle, or blurred by motion, distance from the camera, or by unintentional privacy filtering. Occasionally some of the tiles may be views of a different sign altogether, which can happen when two signs are attached to the same post. Some examples of these problems are shown in Fig. 2. The multiple views can reduce some of the usual problems of outdoor images, such as occlusion by foreground objects, image truncation caused by the target object being at the edge

Fig. 2. Examples of blurring, obstruction, and incorrect spatial clustering

of the frame, and varied lighting. Other problems cannot be solved by multiple views, such as bent, corroded or faded signs.

The task of the system then is to obtain the best possible canonical text result by combining information from the multiple views, either by processing each tile independently and combining the results, or by combining information deep within the recognition system (most likely deep network).

3   How the FSNS Dataset Was Created

The following process was used to create the FSNS dataset:

1. A street-name-sign detector was applied to all Google Street View images from France. The detector returns an image rectangle around each street name sign, together with its geographic location (latitude and longitude).
2. Multiple images of the same geographic location were gathered together (spatially clustered).
3. Text from the signs was transcribed using a combination of reCAPTCHA [3], OCR and human operators.
4. Transcribed text was presented to human operators to verify the accuracy of the transcription. Incorrect samples were re-routed for human transcription (back to step 3) or discarded if already the result of a human transcription.
5. Images were bucketized geographically (by latitude/longitude) so that the train, validation, test, and private test sets come from disjoint geographic locations, with 100 m wide strips of "wall" in between that are not used, to ensure that the same physical sign can't be viewed from different sets.

6. Since roads are long entities that may pass between the disjoint geographic sections, there may be multiple signs of the same street name at multiple locations in different subsets. Therefore as each subset is generated, any images with truth strings that match a truth string in any previously generated subset are discarded. Each subset thereby has a disjoint set of truth strings.

7. All images for which the truth string included a character outside of the chosen encoding set, or for which the encoded label length exceeded the maximum of 37, were discarded. The character set to be handled is thus carefully controlled.

Note that the transcription was systematically Title Case folded from the original transcription, in order to make it represent the way that the street name would appear on a map. This process includes removal of text that is not relevant, including data such as the district or building numbers.

4   Normalized Truth Text

The FSNS dataset is made more interesting by the fact that the truth text is a normalized representation of the name of the street, as it should be written on the map, instead of a simple direct transcription of the text on the sign. The main normalization is Title Case transformation of the text, which is often written on the sign in all upper case. Title Case is specified as follows:

The words: au, aux, de, des, du, et, la, le, les, sous, sur always appear in lower-case. The prefixes: d', l' always appear in lower-case. All other words, including suffixes after d' and l', always appear with the initial letter capitalized and the rest in lower-case.

The other main normalization is that some text on the sign, which is not part of the name of the street, is discarded. Although this seems a rather vague instruction, for a human, even without knowledge of French, it becomes easy after reading a few signs, as the actual street names fit into a reasonably obvious pattern, and the extraneous text is usually in a smaller size.

Some examples of some of these normalizations of the text between the sign and the truth text are shown in Fig. 3. The task of transcribing the signs is thus not a basic OCR problem, but perhaps somewhat more like image captioning [17], by requiring an interpretation of what the sign *means*, not just its literal content. A researcher working with the FSNS dataset is hereby provided with a variety of design options between adding text post-processing to the output of an OCR engine and training a single network to learn the entire problem "end-to-end".

Truth: Impasse Jacques Guignard

Truth: Impasse René Lemonnier

Truth: Rue de Villers

Truth: Place Charles de Gaulle

Fig. 3. Examples of images with their normalized truth text

5   Details of the FSNS Dataset

The location of the FSNS dataset is documented in the **README.md** file.[1] There are 3 disjoint subsets, Train, Validation and Test[2]. Each contains images of fixed size, 600 × 150 pixels, containing 4 tiles of 150 × 150 laid out horizontally, and padded with random noise where less than 4 views are available.

The size and location of each subset are shown in Table 2, and some basic analysis of the word content of each subset is shown in Table 3. The analysis in Table 3 excludes frequent words with frequency in the Train set >100, and the words listed in Sect. 4 as lower-case. As might be expected, given the process by which the subsets have been made disjoint, the fraction of words in each subset that are out of vocabulary with respect to the Train subset is reasonably high at around 30 %. Such a rate of out-of-vocabulary words will also make it difficult for a system to learn the full vocabulary from the Train set.

---

[1] https://github.com/tensorflow/models/tree/master/street/README.md.
[2] An additional private test set will be kept back for the purposes of organizing competitions.

Table 2. Location and size of each subset of the FSNS dataset

Subset	Location	Number of images	Number of words
Train	train/train@512	1044868	3189576
Validation	validation/validation@64	16150	50218
Test	test/test@64	20404	62650
Private test	n/a	21054	65366

Table 3. Word counts excluding 'stop' words, (being the prefixes with a frequency >100, and the lower-cased words) in each subset and number out of vocabulary (OOV) with respect to (wrt) words in the Train subset

Subset	Non-stop words	Unique words	Unique words OOV wrt Train	Total OOV words	Percent OOV words
Train	1336341	93482	0	0	0
Validation	22250	7425	3482	7272	32.7
Test	28587	8675	4081	8526	29.8
Private Test	28752	8870	4265	9375	32.6

Each subset is stored as multiple TFRecords files of `tf.train.Example` protocol buffers, which makes them ready-made for input to TensorFlow [1,4]. The Example protocol buffer is very flexible, so the full details of the content of each example are laid out in Table 4.

Note that the ultimate goal of a machine learning system is to produce the UTF-8 string in "image/text." That may be achieved either by learning the byte sequences in the text field, or there is also a pre-encoded mapping to integer class-ids provided in "image/class" and "image/unpadded_class". The mapping between these class-ids and the UTF-8 text is provided in a separate file at `charset_size=134.txt`. Each line in that file lists a class-id, a tab character, and the UTF-8 string that is represented by the class-id. Class-id 0 represents a space, and the last class-id, 133, represents the "null" character, as used by the Connectionist Temporal Classification (CTC) alignment algorithm [5] typically used with an LSTM network. Note that some class-ids map to multiple UTF-8 strings, as some normalization has been applied, such as folding all the different shapes of double quote to the same class.

The ground truth text in the FSNS dataset uses a subset of these characters. In addition to all digits, upper and lower-case A-Z, there are the following accented characters: à À â Â ä ç Ç é É è È ê Ê ë Ë î Î ï ô Ô œ ù Ù û Û ü ÿ and these punctuation symbols: <= _ - , ; ! ? / . ' " ( )] & + a total of 109, including space.

For systems that process the multiple views separately, it is possible to avoid processing the noise padding. The number of real, non-noise views of a sign is given by the value of the field "image/orig_width" divided by 150.

Table 4. The content of each example proto in the TFRecords files

Key name	Type	Length	Content
Image/format	Bytes (string)	1	"PNG"
Image/encoded	Bytes (string)	1	Image encoded as PNG
Image/class	Int64	37	Truth class-ids padded with nulls
Image/unpadded_class	Int64	Variable	Truth class-ids unpadded
Image/width	Int64	1	Width of the image in pixels
Image/orig_width	Int64	1	Pre-padding width in pixels
Image/height	Int64	1	Height of the image in pixels
Image/text	Bytes (string)	1	Truth string in UTF-8

No sample in any of the subsets has a text field that encodes to more than 37 class-ids. 37 is not a completely arbitrary choice. When padded with nulls in between each label for CTC, $(2 \times 37 + 1 = 75)$ the classic sequences are no longer than half the width $(150/2 = 75)$ of a single input view, which allows for some shrinkage of the data width in the network.

6   The Challenge

The FSNS dataset provides a rich and interesting challenge in machine learning, due to the variety of tasks that are required. Here is a summary of the different processes that a model needs to learn to discover the right solution:

- Locating the lines of text within the sign within each image.
- Recognizing the text content within each line.
- Discarding irrelevant text.
- Title Case normalization.
- Combining data from multiple signs, ignoring data from blurred or inconsistent signs.

None of the above is an explicit goal of the challenge. The current trend in machine learning is to build and train a single large/deep network to solve all of a problem without additional algorithmic pieces on one end or another, or to glue trained components together [6,17]. We believe that the FSNS data set is large enough to train a single deep network to learn all of the above tasks, and we provide an example in Sect. 7. We therefore propose that a competition based on the FSNS dataset should measure:

- Word recall: Fraction of space-delimited words in the truth that are present in the OCR output.
- Word precision: Fraction of space-delimited words in the OCR output that are present in the truth.
- Sequence error: the fraction of truth text strings that are not produced exactly by the network, after folding multiple spaces to single space.

Word recall and precision are almost universally used, and need no introduction. We add sequence error here because the strings are short enough that we can expect a significant number of them to be completely correct. Using only these metrics allows for end-to-end systems to compete directly against systems built from smaller components that are designed for specific sub-problems.

7   An End-to-End Solution

We now describe a Tensor Flow graph that has been designed specifically to address the Challenge, end-to-end, using just the graph, with no algorithmic components. This means that the text line finding and handling of multiple views, including where there are less than four, is entirely learned and dealt with inside the network. Instead of using the orig_width field in the dataset, the images are input as fixed size and the random padding informs the network of the lack of useful content. The network is based on the design that has been shown to work well for many languages in Tesseract [14], with some extensions to handle the multi-line, multi-tile FSNS dataset. The design is named Street-name Tensor-flow Recurrent End-to-End Transcriber (STREET). To perform the tasks listed above, the graph design has a high-level structure with purpose, as shown in Fig. 4.

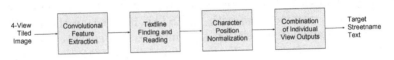

Fig. 4. High-level structure of the network graph

Conventional convolutional layers process the images to extract features. Since each view may contain up to three lines of text, the next step is intended to allow the network to find upto three text lines and recognize the text in each separately. The text may appear in different positions within each image, so some character position normalization is also required. Only then can the individual outputs be combined to produce a single target string. These components of the end-to-end system are described in detail below. Tensor Flow code for the STREET model described in this paper is available at the Tensor Flow Github repository[3].

7.1   Convolutional Feature Extraction

The input image, being 600 × 150, is de-tiled to make the input a batch of 4 images of size 150 × 150. This is achieved by a generic reshape, which is a combination of TensorFlow reshape and transpose operations that split one

---

[3] https://github.com/tensorflow/models/tree/master/street.

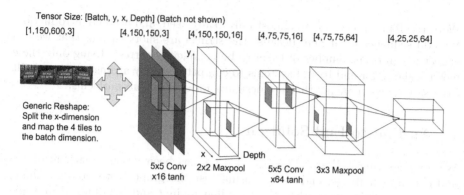

Fig. 5. Convolutional feature extraction and size reduction

dimension of the input tensor and map the split parts to other dimensions. Two convolutional layers are then used with max pooling, with the expectation that they will find edges, and combine them into features, as well as reduce the size of the image down to 25 × 25. Figure 5 shows the detail of the convolutions.

7.2 Textline Finding and Reading

Vertically summarizing Long Short-Term Memory (LSTM)[7] cells are used to find text lines. *Summarizing* with an LSTM, inspired by the LSTM used for sequence to sequence translation [15], involves *ignoring the outputs of all timesteps except the last*. A *vertically* summarizing LSTM is a summarizing LSTM that *scans the input vertically*. It is thus expected to compute a vertical summary of its input, which will be taken from the last vertical timestep. *Each x-position is treated independently.* Three different vertical summarizations are used:

1. Upward to find the top textline.
2. Separate upward and downward LSTMs, with depth-concatenated outputs, to find the middle textline.
3. Downward to find the bottom textline.

Although each vertically summarizing LSTM sees the same input, and could theoretically summarize the entirety of what it sees, they are organized this way so that they only have to produce a summary of the most recently seen information. Since the middle line is harder to find, that gets two LSTMs working in opposite directions. Each receives a copy of the output from the convolutional layers and passes its output to a separate bi-directional horizontal LSTM to recognize the text. Bidirectional LSTMs have been shown to be able to read text with high accuracy [2]. The outputs of the bi-directional LSTMs are concatenated in the x-dimension, to string the text lines out in reading order. Figure 6 shows the details.

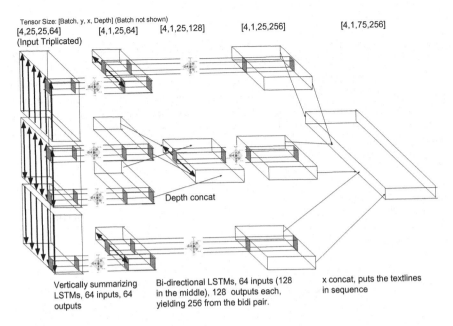

Tensor Size: [Batch, y, x, Depth] (Batch not shown)
[4,25,25,64]   [4,1,25,64]   [4,1,25,128]   [4,1,25,256]   [4,1,75,256]
(Input Triplicated)

Depth concat

Vertically summarizing LSTMs, 64 inputs, 64 outputs

Bi-directional LSTMs, 64 inputs (128 in the middle), 128 outputs each, yielding 256 from the bidi pair.

x concat, puts the textlines in sequence

Fig. 6. Text line finding and reading

7.3   Character Position Normalization

Assuming that each network component so far has achieved what it was designed to do, we now have a batch of four sets of one to three lines of text, spread spatially across the x-dimension. Each of the four sign images in a batch may have the text positioned differently, due to different perspective within each sign image. It is therefore useful to give the network some ability to reshuffle the data along the x-dimension. To that end we provide two more LSTM layers, one scanning left-to-right across the x-dimension, and the other right-to-left, as shown in Fig. 7. Instead of a bidirectional configuration, they operate in two distinct layers. This allows state information to be passed to the right or left in the x-dimension, allowing the characters in each of the four views to be aligned.

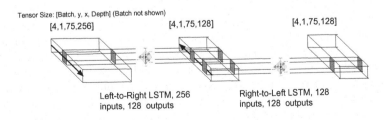

Tensor Size: [Batch, y, x, Depth] (Batch not shown)
[4,1,75,256]   [4,1,75,128]   [4,1,75,128]

Left-to-Right LSTM, 256 inputs, 128 outputs

Right-to-Left LSTM, 128 inputs, 128 outputs

Fig. 7. Character position normalization

7.4   Combination of Individual View Outputs

After giving the STREET network chance to normalize the position of the characters along the x-dimension, a generic reshape is used to move the batch of 4 views into the depth dimension, which then becomes the input to a single unidirectional LSTM and the final softmax layer, in Fig. 8. The main purpose of this last LSTM is to combine the four views for each sign to produce the most accurate result. If none of the layers that went before have done anything towards the Title Case normalization, this final LSTM layer is perfectly capable of learning to do that well.

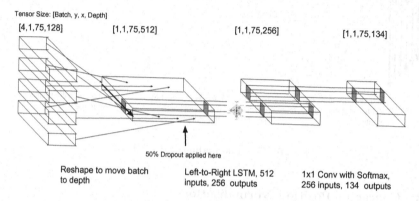

Fig. 8. Combination of individual view outputs

The only regularization used is a 50 % dropout layer between the reshape that combines the four signs and the last LSTM layer. Details of each component of the STREET graph can be found in Table 5.

8   Experiments and Results

As a baseline, Tesseract [14] was tested, but the FSNS dataset is extremely difficult for it. The best results were obtained from the LSTM-based engine in version 4.00, with the addition of pre-processing to locate the rectangle of the sign, and invert the projective transformation, plus post-processing to Title Case the output to match the truth text, as well as combination of the highest confidence results from the four views. Even with this help, Tesseract only achieves word recall of 20–25 %. See Table 6. The majority of failure cases revolve around the textline finder, which includes noise connected components, drops characters, or merges textlines. The main cause of these difficulties appears to be the tight line spacing, compressed characters, and tight border that appears on most signs.

The STREET model was trained using the CTC [5] loss function, with the Adam optimizer [10] in Tensor Flow, with a learning rate of 2×10^{-5}, and 40 parallel training workers. The error metrics outlined in Sect. 6 were used.

Table 5. Size and computational complexity of the layers in the graph

Name	Input	Output	Weights	Mult-add
Reshape0	$1 \times 150 \times 600 \times 3$	$4 \times 150 \times 150 \times 3$		
Conv0 ($5 \times 5 \times 16$)	$4 \times 150 \times 150 \times 3$	$4 \times 150 \times 150 \times 16$	1216	109 M
Maxpool0 2×2	$4 \times 150 \times 150 \times 16$	$4 \times 75 \times 75 \times 16$		
Conv1 ($5 \times 5 \times 64$)	$4 \times 75 \times 75 \times 16$	$4 \times 75 \times 75 \times 64$	25664	577 M
Maxpool1 3×3	$4 \times 75 \times 75 \times 64$	$4 \times 25 \times 25 \times 64$		
V-SumLSTMs ($4 \times$)	$4 \times 25 \times 25 \times 64$	$4 \times 1 \times 25 \times 128 \times 4$	33024×4	330 M
DepthConcat	$4 \times 1 \times 25 \times 128 \times 2$	$4 \times 1 \times 25 \times 256$		
BidiLSTMs ($3 \times$)	$4 \times 1 \times 25 \times 128 \times 2$ $+ 4 \times 1 \times 25 \times 256$	$4 \times 1 \times 25 \times 256 \times 3$	$263168 \times 2 +$ 394240	92 M
XConcat	$4 \times 1 \times 25 \times 256 \times 3$	$4 \times 1 \times 75 \times 256$		
LTRLSTM	$4 \times 1 \times 75 \times 256$	$4 \times 1 \times 75 \times 128$	197120	59 M
RTLLSTM	$4 \times 1 \times 75 \times 128$	$4 \times 1 \times 75 \times 128$	131584	39 M
Reshape1	$4 \times 1 \times 75 \times 128$	$1 \times 1 \times 75 \times 512$		
LTRLSTM	$1 \times 1 \times 75 \times 512$	$1 \times 1 \times 75 \times 256$	787456	59 M
Softmax	$1 \times 1 \times 75 \times 256$	$1 \times 1 \times 75 \times 134$	34438	2.6 M
Total			2.2M	1.3 B

Table 6. Error rate results

System	Test set	Word recall	Word precision	Sequence error
Tesseract	Validation	22.73	20.21	95.81
Tesseract	Test	23.58	20.49	98.91
Tesseract	Private test	23.93	21.05	95.93
STREET	Train	94.90	95.40	13.14
STREET	Validation	89.46	90.28	26.63
STREET	Test	88.81	89.71	27.54
STREET	Private test	89.48	90.32	26.64

The results are also shown in Table 6. The results show that the model is somewhat over-trained, yet the results for validation, test and private test are very close, which suggests that these subsets are large enough to be a good reflection of the model's true performance.

Some examples of error cases are shown in Fig. 9. In the first example, the model can be confused by obstructions. On the second line, the model drops a small word, perhaps as not relevant. On the third line, a less frequent prefix is replaced by a more frequent one. In the final example, an accent is dropped.

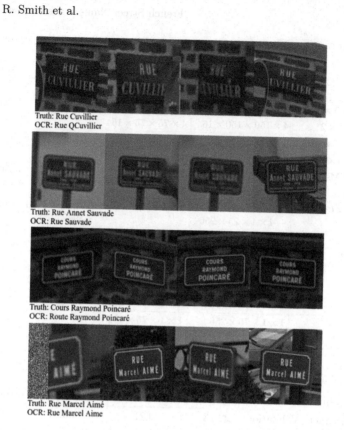

Truth: Rue Cuvillier
OCR: Rue QCuvillier

Truth: Rue Annet Sauvade
OCR: Rue Sauvade

Truth: Cours Raymond Poincaré
OCR: Route Raymond Poincaré

Truth: Rue Marcel Aimé
OCR: Rue Marcel Aime

Fig. 9. Some examples of error cases

9   Conclusion

The FSNS dataset provides an interesting machine learning challenge. We have shown that it is possible to obtain reasonable results for the entire task with a single end-to-end network, and the STREET network could easily be improved by application of common regularization approaches and/or changing the network structure. Alternatively there are many other possible approaches that involve applying algorithmic or learned solutions to parts of the problem. Here are a few:

- Detecting the position/orientation of the sign by image processing or even structure from motion methods, correcting the perspective, and applying a simple OCR engine.
- Text line finding followed by OCR on individual text lines.
- Detecting the worst sign(s) and discarding them, by blur detection, obstruction detection, contrast, or even determining that there is more than one physical sign in the image.

A comparison of these approaches against the end-to-end approach would be very interesting and provide useful information for the direction of future research.

References

1. Abadi, M., Agarwal, A., Barham, P., Brevdo, E., Chen, Z., Citro, C., Corrado, G.S., Davis, A., Dean, J., Devin, M., et al.: Tensorflow: large-scale machine learning on heterogeneous distributed systems. arXiv preprint arXiv:1603.04467 (2016)
2. Breuel, T.M., Ul-Hasan, A., Al-Azawi, M.A., Shafait, F.: High-performance OCR for printed English and Fraktur using LSTM networks. In: 2013 12th International Conference on Document Analysis and Recognition (ICDAR), pp. 683–687. IEEE (2013)
3. Google: reCAPTCHA. https://www.google.com/recaptcha/intro/index.html. Accessed 20 June 2016
4. Google: Tensorflow. https://www.tensorflow.org/. Accessed 20 June 2016
5. Graves, A., Fernández, S., Gomez, F., Schmidhuber, J.: Connectionist temporal classification: labelling unsegmented sequence data with recurrent neural networks. In: Proceedings of the 23rd International Conference on Machine Learning, pp. 369–376. ACM (2006)
6. Graves, A., Jaitly, N.: Towards end-to-end speech recognition with recurrent neural networks. In: Proceedings of the 31st International Conference on Machine Learning (ICML 2014), pp. 1764–1772 (2014)
7. Hochreiter, S., Schmidhuber, J.: Long short-term memory. Neural Comput. **9**(8), 1735–1780 (1997)
8. Jaderberg, M., Simonyan, K., Vedaldi, A., Zisserman, A.: Synthetic data and artificial neural networks for natural scene text recognition. arXiv preprint arXiv:1406.2227 (2014)
9. Jung, J., Lee, S., Cho, M.S., Kim, J.H.: Touch TT: scene text extractor using touchscreen interface. ETRI J. **33**(1), 78–88 (2011)
10. Kingma, D., Ba, J.: Adam: a method for stochastic optimization. arXiv preprint arXiv:1412.6980 (2014)
11. Lucas, S.M., Panaretos, A., Sosa, L., Tang, A., Wong, S., Young, R., Ashida, K., Nagai, H., Okamoto, M., Yamamoto, H., et al.: ICDAR 2003 robust reading competitions: entries, results, and future directions. Int. J. Doc. Anal. Recognit. (IJDAR) **7**(2–3), 105–122 (2005)
12. Nagy, R., Dicker, A., Meyer-Wegener, K.: NEOCR: a configurable dataset for natural image text recognition. In: Iwamura, M., Shafait, F. (eds.) CBDAR 2011. LNCS, vol. 7139, pp. 150–163. Springer, Heidelberg (2012)
13. Netzer, Y., Wang, T., Coates, A., Bissacco, A., Wu, B., Ng, A.Y.: Reading digits in natural images with unsupervised feature learning. In: NIPS Workshop on Deep Learning and Unsupervised Feature Learning, Granada, Spain, vol. 2011, p. 4. (2011)
14. Smith, R.: Tesseract blends old and new OCR technology. https://github.com/tesseract-ocr/docs/tree/master/das_tutorial2016. Accessed 20 June 2016
15. Sutskever, I., Vinyals, O., Le, Q.V.: Sequence to sequence learning with neural networks. In: Ghahramani, Z., Welling, M., Cortes, C., Lawrence, N.D., Weinberger, K.Q. (eds.) Advances in Neural Information Processing Systems vol. 27, pp. 3104–3112. Curran Associates Inc. (2014). http://papers.nips.cc/paper/5346-sequence-to-sequence-learning-with-neural-networks.pdf
16. Veit, A., Matera, T., Neumann, L., Matas, J., Belongie, S.: Coco-text: dataset and benchmark for text detection and recognition in natural images. arXiv preprint arXiv:1601.07140 (2016)

17. Vinyals, O., Toshev, A., Bengio, S., Erhan, D.: Show and tell: a neural image caption generator. In: Proceedings of the IEEE Conference on Computer Vision and Pattern Recognition, pp. 3156–3164 (2015)
18. Wang, K., Babenko, B., Belongie, S.: End-to-end scene text recognition. In: 2011 IEEE International Conference on Computer Vision (ICCV), pp. 1457–1464. IEEE (2011)

Efficient Exploration of Text Regions in Natural Scene Images Using Adaptive Image Sampling

Ismet Zeki Yalniz[✉], Douglas Gray, and R. Manmatha

A9.com, Palo Alto, USA
{izy,douggray,manmatha}@a9.com

Abstract. An adaptive image sampling framework is proposed for identifying text regions in natural scene images. A small fraction of the pixels actually correspond to text regions. It is desirable to eliminate non-text regions at the early stages of text detection. First, the image is sampled row-by-row at a specific rate and each row is tested for containing text using an 1D adaptation of the Maximally Stable Extremal Regions (MSER) algorithm. The surrounding rows of the image are recursively sampled at finer rates to fully contain the text. The adaptive sampling process is performed on the vertical dimension as well for the identified regions. The final output is a binary mask which can be used for text detection and/or recognition purposes. The experiments on the ICDAR'03 dataset show that the proposed approach is up to 7x faster than the MSER baseline on a single CPU core with comparable text localization scores. The approach is inherently parallelizable for further speed improvements.

Keywords: Adaptive image sampling · Scene text detection · 1D maximally stable extremal regions (1D MSER) · Mobile applications

1 Introduction

Recent advances in digital imaging technology enable users to take high quality digital pictures and videos in their natural environments. One can use these images and videos for automating various tasks such as product search, automatic navigation, license plate detection and recognition, surveillance and helping elderly or disabled people to recognize their environment. The existence of text in scene images provides valuable information about the content of the image. The research question is how to effectively detect and recognize text in scene images and perform it in real time using mobile devices.

Commercial Optical Character Recognition (OCR) systems are reasonably accurate (i.e., over 95 %) for recognizing text in document images [23]. However, text detection and recognition accuracies are generally much lower for natural scene images. In ICDAR'15, most methods performed below 40 % with the exception of "AJOU" [10] and "Stradvision-1". Both of these methods were based on variants of the MSER algorithm followed by different grouping approaches [8].

© Springer International Publishing Switzerland 2016
G. Hua and H. Jégou (Eds.): ECCV 2016 Workshops, Part I, LNCS 9913, pp. 427–439, 2016.
DOI: 10.1007/978-3-319-46604-0_31

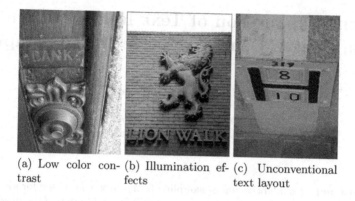

(a) Low color contrast

(b) Illumination effects

(c) Unconventional text layout

Fig. 1. Example scene images from the ICDAR'03 dataset ([12]).

Image blur, low resolution, low contrast, unconventional text layout, non-uniform background, lighting and perspective changes are among the factors which makes the problem challenging as seen in Fig. 1.

The most common approach for recognizing text in scene images is to localize each word and/or character in the input image and then classify each one of them independently [3, 22]. In these approaches, the performance of the overall text recognition framework heavily depends on the success of the text localization module. It is desirable to detect all the bounding boxes reliably with a high recall prior to recognition. There are also methods where the text detection and recognition modules are integrated [15, 21]. This is achieved by creating several hypotheses about the location and the content of the text and refining the results with the help of a character/word classifier. Integrated text localization and recognition schemes are typically much slower because of the character/word classification overhead and the overall success of the framework depends on the classifier's accuracy. More recently, deep neural networks have also been successfully used for end-to-end recognition of text in natural images [7]. Deep neural network approaches are not elaborated further, since the primary focus of this paper is to provide real-time performance for effective text-detection on mobile devices with minimal use of computational resources.

In the case of text localization task, the aim is not to recognize the text but reliably find the bounding boxes for each word and/or character in the input image. Sliding window based approaches have been widely used for this purpose [2, 3, 11]. The main problem with the sliding window approaches is the computational overload which is not desirable especially for mobile applications. The localization accuracy also depends on the sliding interval which defines the total number of windows to be tested. In total, there are $O(n^2)$ number of candidate windows for an input image of size n pixels. More recently pixel grouping/merging approaches have been shown to provide the best text localization results with lower computational load [5, 14, 15, 17, 25].

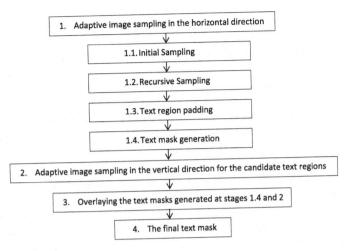

Fig. 2. The stages of the proposed image sampling framework for efficient text detection.

Text localization algorithms effectively use several features such as pixel intensity and local gradient information to group pixels and form candidate character glyphs for text detection purposes. Maximally Stable Extremal Regions (MSERs) [13] is currently the state-of-the-art approach to find text regions in scene images [14,15,24]. In a nut-shell, MSERs correspond to image blobs (i.e., connected components) in gray level images with the restriction that the size of the connected component is stable across several intensity thresholds. In the case of text localization, character glyphs are likely to be detected by the MSER approach, if there is sufficient contrast between the text and its background. The winning approaches in the ICDAR 2011, 2013 and 2015 competitions use MSERs to localize text in scene images [8,9,18]. The primary focus of our paper is, therefore, to improve upon the speed of the original MSER approach without losing its effectiveness. Text detection and recognition speed has prime importance especially for real-time mobile applications, where computational resources and battery power are always at premium [20].

In this paper, an adaptive image sampling framework is proposed for finding text regions efficiently in natural scene images. The observation is that most of the pixels in an input image do not belong to any text region and they can be eliminated at the early stages for efficient text detection. The proposed framework makes two assumptions for simplification purposes: (i) the text is composed of at least three characters, (ii) the text is aligned horizontally without significant skew. The requirement of at least three characters is a common assumption which is made by most text detection frameworks to eliminate false positives. The horizontal alignment of text is another general assumption which is also inherent in the ICDAR competition datasets.

The first stage of the proposed framework is to convert the input image to gray scale and sample a number of rows of pixels. The sampling frequency is determined according to the height of the smallest possible character in the input image. Each row is independently tested for containing any text or not. If the row is determined to contain any text, the rows nearby are also sampled in a recursive manner until the character glyphs are fully contained. The same image sampling process is applied to the vertical dimension as well for the candidate regions which are determined to contain text in the previous stage. The final output is a binary image where the candidate regions of texts are marked. The entire process is repeated for detecting text in the other image polarity as well. Figure 2 shows a flow chart of these stages.

The text region proposal results on the most widely used and cited ICDAR'03 dataset show that the effectiveness of the proposed approach is comparable to the most efficient linear time implementation of the original 2D MSER approach [16] while providing up to 7x speed improvement on a single CPU core. An unoptimized single threaded implementation of the proposed framework provides 20 frames per second even on a relatively old cell phone with an Apple A4 single core processor (released in 2010). Therefore the proposed framework can be used almost on any smart phone being used in the market as of today in 2016. Indeed, the proposed text region proposal algorithm is inherently parallelizable. Each row or columns of pixels can be independently evaluated for containing text without any need for a global priority queue or union-find data structure. These data structures are actually used by the most efficient implementations of the original MSER algorithm [13,16]. Parallelization of the original MSER algorithm is therefore not trivial and the speed gains might be bounded because of the global data structures being maintained. To our best knowledge, there is no publicly available GPU/parallel implementation of the original MSER algorithm. Our evaluations are constrained to the single threaded execution model in the rest of the paper.

The contributions of the paper may be summarized as follows:

(a) An adaptive image sampling methodology to filter out non-text regions without the need for evaluating each pixel in the input image.
(b) 1D adaptation of the original MSER algorithm for efficient image sampling and text detection.
(c) A text region detection framework which
  (i) is comparable to the original MSER algorithm in terms of effectiveness,
  (ii) provides up to 7x speed improvements on a single CPU core,
  (iii) is inherently parallelizable for further speed improvements.

The rest of the paper is organized as follows: the proposed adaptive image sampling framework is elaborated first in Sect. 2. The experiments are discussed in Sect. 3. Conclusions are drawn in Sect. 4.

2   The Adaptive Image Sampling Framework for Efficient Text Detection

The proposed adaptive image sampling framework operates on gray scale images to find text regions. The first stage is to determine the location of the character glyphs on the vertical axis by sampling rows of pixels in the input image.

Each sampled row is tested for containing any text by analyzing the position and length of connected components in the row image across different intensity thresholds. In this particular case, the connected components are extracted by generalizing the original MSER approach for 1D images. The surrounding rows of pixels which are determined to contain text are recursively sampled as well to fully recover the text. At this point, all the connected components of each sampled row are encoded one by one on a 2D image mask output. The same sampling process is applied in the vertical direction as well for the regions which are determined to contain text in the horizontal sampling stage. Those connected components are overlaid on the 2D image output using the AND logical operator. The resulting 2D image contains candidate character glyphs. The same process is applied to the other image polarity as well to detect text written in different polarities (i.e., dark text against lighter background or vice versa). Figure 3 illustrates the stages of the proposed approach. The details are given in the following subsections.

2.1   Initial Sampling

The aim of the initial sampling stage is to find the approximate location of the text and ensure that all the character glyphs satisfying certain size constraints can be fully reconstructed. This is achieved simply by sampling the input image uniformly at a certain rate. According to the "Nyquist-Shannon" sampling theorem [19], the sampling frequency must be at least twice the highest frequency object in the image in order to detect and/or reconstruct the original signal. In the case of text detection, the highest frequency objects are the smallest characters of interest in the input image. The sampling interval in the horizontal and vertical direction are, therefore, set to 10 and 2 pixels respectively for any input image of size 640×480. In this way, any character of height 20 and width 4 and above can be reliably detected.

2.2   Detecting Candidate Text Regions

The task is to classify the line represented by a row of image pixels whether it passes through any text region or not in the input image. The problem is not trivial because rows of pixels lack two dimensional contextual information. Our observation is that the change in the intensity values along the line gives clues about the existence of the text. More specifically, the intensity values increase rapidly and stay steady for a period and then fall back again to the intensity value of the text background. These "extremal regions" are detected by adapting the original MSER algorithm for 1D images. The original formal definition of 1D MSER regions [13] holds for the 1D images as well. The difference is that, 1D extremal regions are characterized by their length, start and end coordinates. The area of a given 1D extremal region is defined to be its length in the 1D image. Notice that MSER regions can be extracted from 1D images quite efficiently because of increased spatial locality and simplicity of 1D MSER regions. In this work, the 1D MSER regions are extracted separately for each image polarity (i.e.,

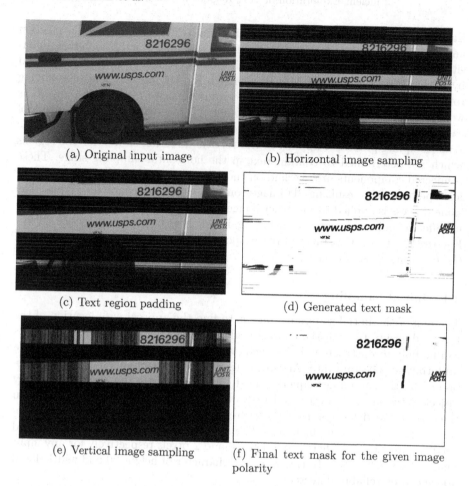

(a) Original input image   (b) Horizontal image sampling

(c) Text region padding   (d) Generated text mask

(e) Vertical image sampling   (f) Final text mask for the given image polarity

Fig. 3. The proposed adaptive image sampling scheme is illustrated for one image polarity of the input image (dark text against lighter background). Pixels which are not visited in stages (b), (c) and (e) are colored black.

negative and positive regions). For further speed improvements, it is possible to compute 1D MSER regions for both polarities at the same time with negligible computational overhead. Notice that the pixel gaps between extremal regions correspond to extremal regions in the other polarity for 1D images.

Having at least one MSER region is not a sufficient criterion for a row of image pixels to contain text. The rows are likely to have extremal regions even though the image does not contain any text. Therefore MSER regions with length less than two pixels and more than one sixth of the width of image are eliminated first. Next, a chaining mechanism is devised to further eliminate non-text regions. The key observation is that, if there exists any row which passes over a text region with at least three characters, then there must be at least three 1D MSER regions which are relatively close to each other. Two 1D MSER regions are assumed to be close by if the distance between them is smaller than the width of the preceding region multiplied by a constant (trained empirically to be 8). This analysis is done for every row sampled in the initial sampling stage and the rows which are determined to contain text are forwarded to the recursive sampling stage.

2.3   Recursive Sampling Stage

The output of the initial sampling stage is a number of rows which are likely to contain text. Here the aim is to efficiently sample rows of those regions at finer levels and reconstruct the character glyphs. It is achieved as follows: the two adjacent image regions bounded by the previous and next sampled rows are added to a stack for further sampling. This is done for all rows in the initial sampling stage if they are identified to contain text. The stack now contains a list of intervals which designate the start and end coordinates of the image regions on the vertical axis. Each interval in the stack is popped and the row in the center of the interval is tested for containing any text. If the result is positive, then the two sub regions divided by the center row are added to the stack as well. This is done recursively for all sampling intervals in the stack until the sampling interval contains a single row. At the end of the iterations, all the image regions which contain text are sampled horizontally and the regions which are very unlikely are not sampled. The output of this stage is a list of labels for each row indicating whether it is sampled or not. This is forwarded to the text region padding stage.

2.4   Text Region Padding

Additional sampling might be necessary to reconstruct the character glyphs. For example, "pad" is a word where there is only one connected component along the rows passing over the upper part of letter "d" and the lower part of letter "p". Since there are less than three regions along those rows, certain parts of the letters are classified as non-text during horizontal adaptive sampling stage. As a result, those characters are partially detected. This is not desirable because the aim is to fully reconstruct the character glyph. The solution is to pad around the regions where the rows are densely sampled. For the case of the word "pad", only the middle zone is classified as text in the recursive sampling stage because there are at least three 1D MSER regions in chain along each row in the respective region. Given the height h and start position s of each dense sampled region, all the rows positioned between $(s - h/2)$ and $(s + 3h/2)$ are also sampled and 1D MSER regions are calculated if they were not sampled before.

2.5   Text Mask Generation

1D MSER regions extracted from the sampled rows are used to generate a 2D binary mask which has the same size as the input image. This is simply done by printing all the 1D MSER regions of all the sampled rows on the respective row of the output image. If there are overlapping 1D MSER regions, they are printed on top of each other. This is actually equivalent to printing only the largest one among others. The output image contains extremal regions which are maximally stable along the horizontal direction.

2.6 Adaptive Image Sampling Along the Vertical Direction

The character glyphs exhibit similar characteristics when the pixels are sampled in the vertical dimension as well. In other words, the pixel intensity values increase and stay steady for a period if the column of pixels passes over a character glyph. In order to eliminate false positive text regions identified in the horizontal sampling stage, the adaptive image sampling is performed on the vertical direction as well for the candidate text regions. The sampling interval is determined to be half of the minimum width of a character which is set to 2 pixels. The column is classified to contain text if there exists at least one 1D MSER region without chaining the connected components. At the end, a mask image is generated using the extracted 1D MSER regions. Text masks obtained from the horizontal and vertical image sampling stages are combined simply using the logical AND operator over corresponding pixel values.

3 Experiments

The experiments are performed on the ICDAR'03 Robust Text Reading dataset. The dataset includes 251 scene images containing 1097 words and 5411 characters in total. The effectiveness of the proposed adaptive image sampling framework is compared to the fastest open source MSER implementation [1] which uses a linear time algorithm introduced by [16]. The evaluation metrics and the experimental results are discussed in the following subsections.

3.1 Evaluation Metrics

The aim is to evaluate the effectiveness of the proposed adaptive image sampling scheme for extracting the character glyphs from scene images. From the image sampling perspective, a high recall is desirable for recovering the character glyphs since the overall success of the text detection framework depends primarily on the success of the sampling stage. The evaluation measure therefore accounts for the overall amount of the character glyphs extracted from the test images and their localization accuracy. Given the ground truth bounding box t of a single character in the test image, the localization accuracy is determined by:

$$f(t, r) = \frac{|t \cap r|}{|t \cup r|} \tag{1}$$

where r is the estimated bounding box and the $|.|$ operator corresponds to the total number of pixels in the set respectively. If the two boxes fully overlap, the localization score is equal to 1.0. If there is no overlap between the two boxes, then the score is zero. Given a set of estimated bounding boxes R, the best matching box r_t is defined as

$$r_t = arg \max_{r \in R} f(t, r) \qquad (2)$$

for a ground truth character t in the test image. Precision and recall scores are computed for each character in the scene image as:

$$precision = \frac{|t \cap r_t|}{|r_t|}, recall = \frac{|t \cap r_t|}{|t|} \qquad (3)$$

where the average precision and recall scores over all the characters in the ground truth set are reported. It should be noted that this is a slightly modified version of the evaluation scheme used in ICDAR competitions focusing on the success of the glyph extraction task prior to any classification.

3.2   Evaluation

The experiments are performed for various settings of the proposed adaptive image sampling framework. In the first experiment, the vertical sampling is skipped and the character glyphs generated from the horizontal adaptive sampling stage are used for evaluation. The second experiment is designed to investigate the success of the adaptive sampling approach over dense sampling. Dense sampling is run in two modes. In the first case, all the rows in the input image are sampled and all the extracted 1D MSER regions are encoded in to the final mask output if they satisfy the length constraints discussed in Sect. 2.2. In the other case, the task masks are generated along the horizontal and vertical direction independently in the same way and the output masks are merged using the AND logical operator.

The baseline is the original 2D MSER approach [13]. The MSER parameters are independently trained for each system using the training set. The input images are not downsampled at any point. The sampling parameters are automatically adjusted for each image based on the image height. Notice that the maximum variation parameter for the 1D MSER is calculated over the length of 1D connected components whereas the original 2D MSER algorithm uses the area of the 2D connected components. In the experiments, the other MSER parameter delta is varied from 6 to 20 with an increment of 1 for both 1D and 2D MSER. It should be noted that most applications operate in this particular interval for delta. There is no post processing or glyph classification stage involved in the experiments. The aim is to understand to what extent the proposed approaches are able to extract character glyphs from the input images. The F-measure is defined as:

$$\frac{2 \times precision \times recall}{precision + recall} \qquad (4)$$

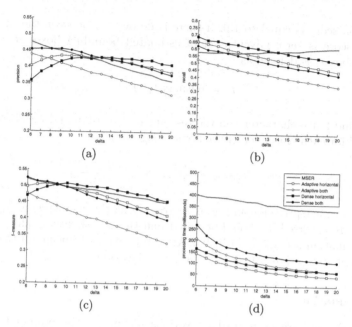

Fig. 4. Precision (a), recall (b), F-measure (c) and processing time plots (d) are given for different configurations of the adaptive image sampling framework in comparison with the original 2D MSER approach (baseline). Delta is the MSER parameter used for calculating the area stability of the region across different intensity levels. Depending on the application, it is typically set to be between 5 to 20 and it is set to 9 for the proposed application.

Figure 4 plots the localization scores, F-measure and processing time for all the configurations and the baseline for varying values of delta. It is clear that localization scores drop significantly if the vertical sampling stage is active for both adaptive and dense sampling tests. The dense sampling approach without vertical sampling provides the highest F-measure for values of delta above 8. The adaptive sampling approach with only horizontal sampling is the fastest method among others (up to 7x) providing F-measure scores comparable to the baseline. The speed gain becomes more drastic for increasing values of delta. The timing experiments are performed on a 32-bit operating system with an Intel i5 processor at 2.4 GHz. These approaches can be thought as different operating points in the space of precision, recall and processing time.

Figure 5 shows a number of examples for qualitative evaluation. The images are generated by coloring each connected component by averaging their pixel values in the original image. For the first two examples, all the character glyphs are extracted correctly in both images. The background of the text scene may look noisy due to sampling but this is not an issue for the task of text detection. In the last example, glyph extraction errors are shown with red circles for both the baseline 2D MSER output and the proposed approach. The errors are due

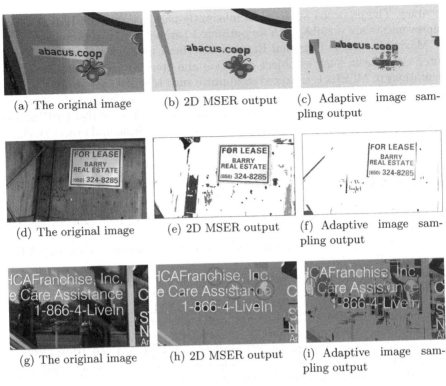

Fig. 5. The outputs of the 2D MSER and the proposed adaptive image sampling framework are visualized for three sample images. The glyph extraction errors are shown with red circles for the last example.

to connected glyphs and such errors are also expected under low contrast and image resolution for the MSER algorithm.

4   Conclusions

An efficient adaptive image sampling framework is presented for exploring text regions in natural scene images. The proposed approach exploits the fact that a small portion of pixels in the input images actually correspond to text regions and non-text regions should be avoided for efficient text detection. The sampling starts by sampling rows of pixels from the input image at a specific rate. Regions which may correspond to text regions are further sampled recursively until the text is fully contained. The same process is applied in the vertical dimension as well for the candidate text regions. The experiments on the ICDAR'03 dataset show that the effectiveness of the proposed approach is comparable to the MSER approach with a significant speed improvement. The proposed framework runs in real time on a mobile phone with an Apple A4 processor. It is expected to speed up the-state-of-the-art text detection and recognition systems with comparable accuracy. The proposed approach is inherently parallelizable and further speed improvements are possible with an optimized parallel implementation.

Maximally Stable Extremal Regions have been used for several other computer vision tasks such as object detection and tracking [4,6]. Efficient implementations of MSERs is expected to improve such MSER-based object tracking and recognition approaches. Future work includes (i) optimizing the adaptive image sampling framework for further speed gains with a parallel GPU implementation, and, (ii) adapting it for other image recognition and object tracking tasks.

References

1. Bradski, G.: The OpenCV library. Dr. Dobb's J. Softw. Tools. **25**(11), 120–129 (2000)
2. Chen, X., Yuille, A.L.: Detecting and reading text in natural scenes. In: CVPR, pp. 366–373 (2004)
3. Coates, A., Carpenter, B., Case, C., Satheesh, S., Suresh, B., Wang, T., Wu, D.J., Ng, A.Y.: Text detection and character recognition in scene images with unsupervised feature learning. In: ICDAR, pp. 440–445 (2011)
4. Donoser, M., Bischof, H.: Efficient maximally stable extremal region (MSER) tracking. In: Proceedings of the 2006 IEEE Computer Society Conference on Computer Vision and Pattern Recognition, CVPR 2006, vol. 1, pp. 553–560. IEEE (2006)
5. Epshtein, B., Ofek, E., Wexler, Y.: Detecting text in natural scenes with stroke width transform. In: CVPR, pp. 2963–2970 (2010)
6. Gómez, L., Karatzas, D.: Mser-based real-time text detection and tracking. In: 2014 22nd International Conference on Pattern Recognition (ICPR), pp. 3110–3115. IEEE (2014)
7. Jaderberg, M., Simonyan, K., Vedaldi, A., Zisserman, A.: Deep structured output learning for unconstrained text recognition. In: ICLR (2015)
8. Karatzas, D., Gomez-Bigorda, L., Nicolaou, A., Ghosh, S., Bagdanov, A., Iwamura, M., Matas, J., Neumann, L., Chandrasekhar, V.R., Lu, S., et al.: ICDAR 2015 competition on robust reading, pp. 1156–1160 (2015)
9. Karatzas, D., Shafait, F., Uchida, S., Iwamura, M., i Bigorda, L.G., Mestre, S.R., Mas, J., Mota, D.F., Almazn, J., de las Heras, L.P.: ICDAR 2013 robust reading competition. In: ICDAR, pp. 1484–1493. IEEE Computer Society (2013)
10. Koo, H.I., Kim, D.H.: Scene text detection via connected component clustering and nontext filtering. IEEE Trans. Image Process. **22**(6), 2296–2305 (2013)
11. Lee, J.J., Lee, P.H., Lee, S.W., Yuille, A.L., Koch, C.: Adaboost for text detection in natural scene. In: ICDAR, pp. 429–434 (2011)
12. Lucas, S., Panaretos, A., Sosa, L., Tang, A., Wong, S., Young, R.: ICDAR 2003 robust reading competitions. In: ICDAR, pp. 682–687 (2003)
13. Matas, J., Chum, O., Urban, M., Pajdla, T.: Robust wide-baseline stereo from maximally stable extremal regions. Image Vis. Comput. **22**(10), 761–767 (2004)
14. Neumann, L., Matas, J.: Text localization in real-world images using efficiently pruned exhaustive search. In: ICDAR, pp. 687–691 (2011)
15. Neumann, L., Matas, J.: Real-time scene text localization and recognition. In: CVPR, pp. 3538–3545 (2012)

16. Nistér, D., Stewénius, H.: Linear time maximally stable extremal regions. In: Forsyth, D., Torr, P., Zisserman, A. (eds.) ECCV 2008. LNCS, vol. 5303, pp. 183–196. Springer, Heidelberg (2008). doi:10.1007/978-3-540-88688-4_14

17. Pan, Y.F., Hou, X., Liu, C.L.: Text localization in natural scene images based on conditional random field. In: ICDAR, pp. 6–10 (2009)

18. Shahab, A., Shafait, F., Dengel, A.: ICDAR 2011 robust reading competition challenge 2: reading text in scene images. In: ICDAR, pp. 1491–1496 (2011)

19. Shannon, C.E.: Communication in the presence of noise. Proc. Inst. Radio Eng. **37**(1), 10–21 (1949)

20. Takeda, K., Kise, K., Iwamura, M.: Real-time document image retrieval on a smartphone. In: 2012 10th IAPR International Workshop on Document Analysis Systems (DAS), pp. 225–229. IEEE (2012)

21. Wang, K., Babenko, B., Belongie, S.: End-to-end scene text recognition. In: ICCV, pp. 1457–1464 (2011)

22. Wu, V., Manmatha, R., Riseman, E.M.: Textfinder: an automatic system to detect and recognize text in images. IEEE Trans. Pattern Anal. Mach. Intell. **21**(11), 1224–1229 (1999)

23. Yalniz, I.Z., Manmatha, R.: A fast alignment scheme for automatic ocr evaluation of books. In: ICDAR, pp. 754–758 (2011)

24. Yin, X.C., Yin, X., Huang, K., Hao, H.: Robust text detection in natural scene images. IEEE Trans. Pattern Anal. Mach. Intell. (TPAMI) **36**(5), 970–983 (2014)

25. Zhang, J., Kasturi, R.: Character energy and link energy-based text extraction in scene images. In: Kimmel, R., Klette, R., Sugimoto, A. (eds.) ACCV 2010. LNCS, vol. 6493, pp. 308–320. Springer, Heidelberg (2011). doi:10.1007/978-3-642-19309-5_24

Downtown Osaka Scene Text Dataset

Masakazu Iwamura[✉], Takahiro Matsuda, Naoyuki Morimoto, Hitomi Sato,
Yuki Ikeda, and Koichi Kise

Department of Computer Science and Intelligent Systems,
Graduate School of Engineering, Osaka Prefecture University, Sakai, Japan
{masa,kise}@cs.osakafu-u.ac.jp, morimoto@m.cs.osakafu-u.ac.jp

Abstract. This paper presents a new scene text dataset named Downtown Osaka Scene Text Dataset (in short, DOST dataset). The dataset consists of sequential images captured in shopping streets in downtown Osaka with an omnidirectional camera. Unlike most of existing datasets consisting of scene images intentionally captured, DOST dataset consists of uncontrolled scene images; use of an omnidirectional camera enabled us to capture videos (sequential images) of whole scenes surrounding the camera. Since the dataset preserved the real scenes containing texts as they were, in other words, they are *scene texts in the wild*. DOST dataset contained 32,147 manually ground truthed sequential images. They contained 935,601 text regions consisting of 797,919 legible and 137,682 illegible. The legible regions contained 2,808,340 characters. The dataset is evaluated using two existing scene text detection methods and one powerful commercial end-to-end scene text recognition method to know the difficulty and quality in comparison with existing datasets.

Keywords: Scene text in the wild · Uncontrolled scene text · Omnidirectional camera · Sequential image · Video · Japanese text

1 Introduction

Text plays important roles in our life. Imagining life in a world without text, in which, for example, neither book, newspaper, signboard, menu in a restaurant, texting on smartphone nor program source code exists or they exist in a completely different form, we can rediscovery not only the necessity of text but also importance of reading and interpreting text. Although only human being has been endowed with the ability of reading and interpreting text, researchers have struggled to enable computers to read text.

Focusing on camera-captured text and scene text, some pioneer works were presented in 1990s [21]. Since then, increasing attention was paid for recognizing scene text. Table 1 shows remarkable recent progress of scene text recognition techniques. In the table, most of reported accuracies of the latest methods exceeded 90 % on major benchmark datasets. However, does this mean these methods are powerful enough to read a variety of texts in the real environment? Many people would agree that the answer is no. Text images contained in these

© Springer International Publishing Switzerland 2016
G. Hua and H. Jégou (Eds.): ECCV 2016 Workshops, Part I, LNCS 9913, pp. 440–455, 2016.
DOI: 10.1007/978-3-319-46604-0_32

Table 1. Recent improvement of recognition performance in scene text recognition tasks. Based on Table 1 of [1], this table summarizes recognition accuracies of recent methods in percentage terms on representative benchmark datasets in the chronological order. "50," "1k" and "50k" represent lexicon sizes. "Full" and "None" represent with all per-image lexicon words and without lexicon, respectively.

Year	Method	IIIT5K [2]			SVT [3]		ICDAR03 [4]				ICDAR13 [5]
	Lexicon	50	1k	None	50	None	50	Full	50k	None	None
-	ABBYY [3]	24.3	-	-	35.0	-	56.0	55.0	-	-	-
2011	Wang et al. [3]	-	-	-	57.0	-	76.0	62.0	-	-	-
2012	Mishra et al. [2]	64.1	57.5	-	73.0	-	81.8	67.8	-	-	-
	Wang et al. [6]	-	-	-	70.0	-	90.0	84.0	-	-	-
	Novikova et al. [7]	-	-	-	72.9	-	-	82.8	-	-	-
2013	Goel et al. [8]	-	-	-	77.3	-	89.7	-	-	-	-
	Bissacco et al. [9]	-	-	-	90.4	78.0	-	-	-	-	87.6
2014	Alsharif and Pineau [10]	-	-	-	74.3	-	93.1	88.6	85.1	-	-
	Almazán et al. [11]	91.2	82.1	-	89.2	-	-	-	-	-	-
	Yao et al. [12]	80.2	69.3	-	75.9	-	88.5	80.3	-	-	-
	Jaderberg et al. [13]	-	-	-	86.1	-	96.2	91.5	-	-	-
	Su and Lu [14]	-	-	-	83.0	-	92.0	82.0	-	-	-
2015	Rodrguez-Serrano et al. [15]	76.1	57.4	-	70.0	-	-	-	-	-	-
	Gordo [16]	93.3	86.6	-	91.8	-	-	-	-	-	-
	Jaderberg et al. [17]	97.1	92.7	-	95.4	80.7	98.7	98.6	93.3	93.1	90.8
	Jaderberg et al. [18]	95.5	89.6	-	93.2	71.7	97.8	97.0	93.4	89.6	81.8
	Shi et al. [19]	97.6	94.4	78.2	96.4	80.8	98.7	97.6	95.5	89.4	86.7
2016	Shi et al. [1]	96.2	93.8	81.9	95.5	81.9	98.3	96.2	94.8	90.1	88.6
	Poznanski and Wolf [20]	97.9	94.2	-	96.6	83.6	-	-	-	-	-

datasets are far easier than the real. In the real environment, scene text is more diverse; for example, various designs/styles/shapes of texts under many different illuminations are taken from variety of angles/distances. In this regard, there is a big gap between scene texts contained in these existing datasets and observed in the real environment.

In this paper, to fill the gap, we present a new dataset named Downtown Osaka Scene Text Dataset (in short, DOST dataset) that preserved scene texts observed in the real environment as they were. The dataset contains videos (sequential images) captured in shopping streets in downtown Osaka with an omnidirectional camera equipped with five horizontal and one upward cameras shown in Fig. 1. In total, 30 image sequences (consisting of five shopping streets times six cameras) consisting of 783,150 images were captured. Among them, 27 image sequences consisting of 32,147 images were manually ground truthed. As a result, 935,601 text regions consisting of 797,919 legible and 137,682 illegible text regions were obtained. The legible regions contained 2,808,340 characters. Since the images were captured in Japan, they contained many Japanese texts. However, out of the whole (797,919) legible text regions, 283,940 consisted of only alphabets and digits. These legible text regions contained 1,138,091 non-Japanese characters. Because of the above mentioned features of the dataset, we can say that DOST dataset preserved *scene texts in the wild*. Figures 3, 4, 5 and 6 show examples of captured images ground truthed and segmented words

Fig. 1. Point Grey Ladybug3, an omnidirectional camera, captures six images consisting of five horizontal and one upward cameras at once. A panoramic view can be created from the six images.

Fig. 2. Equipment used for capturing.

contained in DOST dataset. Since the sequence images were captured with an omnidirectional camera and continuous in time, a single word was captured many times in multiple view angles. The DOST dataset was evaluated using two existing text detection and one powerful commercial end-to-end scene text recognition methods to measure the difficulty and quality in comparison with existing datasets.

2   Unique Features of DOST Dataset

Features of existing datasets are summarized in Table 2. Major differences of DOST dataset from existing datasets include following.

1. DOST dataset contains only real images. Unlike MJSynth [22] and Synth-Text [23] aiming at training a better classifier, DOST dataset aims at evaluation of scene text detection/recognition methods.
2. The images were completely not intentionally captured. In this regard, the most similar dataset is the one dedicated to ICDAR 2015 Robust Reading

Fig. 3. Samples of captured images ground truthed. The four images in this page are selected from ones ground truthed. Bounding boxes represent word regions and texts next to bounding boxes text annotations.

Fig. 4. Samples of captured images ground truthed (continued). The four images in this page are selected from ones ground truthed. Bounding boxes represent word regions and texts next to bounding boxes text annotations.

Fig. 5. Samples of captured images ground truthed (continued). The four images in this page are selected from ones ground truthed. Bounding boxes represent word regions and texts next to bounding boxes text annotations.

(a) Containing Japanese text

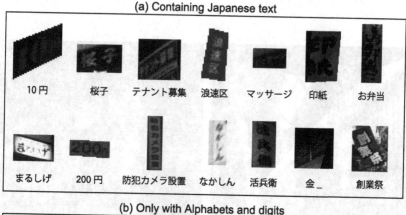

10 円   桜子   テナント募集   浪速区   マッサージ   印紙   お弁当

まるしげ   200 円   防犯カメラ設置   なかしん   活兵衛   金_   創業祭

(b) Only with Alphabets and digits

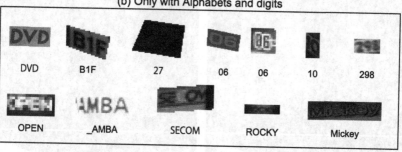

DVD   B1F   27   06   06   10   298

OPEN   _AMBA   SECOM   ROCKY   Mickey

Fig. 6. Samples of segmented words contained in DOST dataset. "_" means there is partially occluded character(s).

Competition Challenge 4 "incidental scene text." It is regarded not intentionally captured because images in the dataset were captured with Google Glass without having taken any prior action to cause its appearance in the field of view or improve its positioning or quality in the frame. DOST dataset is completely free from intention even from face direction of the user wearing Google glass.

3. The images are a video dataset (consecutive in time). There are already video datasets. The 2013 and 2015 editions of ICDAR Robust Reading Competition (RRC) Challenge 3 datasets [5,24] consists of sequential images. The biggest difference is that DOST dataset was captured with an omnidirectional camera. Another difference is that DOST dataset contains Japanese text while ICDAR RRC datasets consists of Latin text. Another video dataset YVT [25] contained YouTube videos. Some texts in the dataset are not scene texts but just captions.

4. DOST dataset contains multiple word images of a single word taken in different view angles.

5. The scale of DOST dataset is large. In the following discussion, let us exclude synthesized datasets and SVHN consisting of digit. Though the number of total images ground truthed in DOST dataset (32,147) is not very large

(almost half of the largest dataset, COCO-Text), the number of word regions (935,601 in total consisting of 797,919 legible and 137,682 illegible) is very large (a factor of 4.6 times larger than the second largest dataset, COCO-Text). This is because image sizes are relatively large ($1,200 \times 1,600$ pixels) and the images were captured in shopping streets where a lot of texts exist. DOST dataset is also the largest in terms of the number of unique word sequences, which is larger than the second largest, ICDAR2015 Challenge 3 dataset, by a factor of 6.3 times.

Another feature of DOST dataset is that it was manually ground truthed by students. The reason we did not use a crowdsourcing service such as Amazon Mechanical Turk[1] is most of workers cannot read Japanese text.

Yet another feature of DOST dataset is that it contains many Latin characters, though the images were captured in Japan. The number of characters per category and examples of Japanese characters and symbols are shown in Fig. 7. Kanji (aka. Chinese character) is a logogram. Katakana and Hiragana are syllabaries invented based on Kanji. Though symbols are originally not intended to be ground truthed, some were actually ground truthed. They include often used iteration marks such as ""々"" which represent a duplicated character. In the future, other than the iteration marks would be discarded by rigorously applying the ground truthing policy.

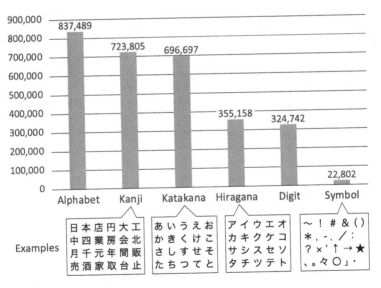

Fig. 7. Number of characters per category and examples of Japanese characters and symbols.

Table 2. Summary of publicly available datasets. "Video?" is whether the images are consecutive in time. "Real?" is whether the dataset consists of real images only (Yes) or not (No; note that captions are regarded as synthesized). #Image represents the total number of images (for a video dataset, the total number of frames). #Word represents the number of word regions ground truthed. In a video dataset, #WS represents the number of word sequences which do not consist of only "don't care" regions.

Name	Real?	Video?	#Image	#Word	#WS	Language
ICDAR2003 [4]	Yes	No	509	2,268	-	English
ICDAR2013 (Challenge 2)[5]	Yes	No	462	2,524	-	English
ICDAR2013 (Challenge 3) [5]	Yes	Yes	15,277	93,598	1,962	English, French, Spanish
ICDAR2015 (Challenge 3) [24]	Yes	Yes	27,824	125,141	3,562	English, French, Spanish
ICDAR2015 (Challenge 4) [24]	Yes	No	1,670	17,548	-	English
NEOCR [26]	Yes	No	659	5,238	-	English, German
KAIST [27]	Yes	No	3,000	3,000	-	English, Korean
SVT [3]	Yes	No	349	904	-	English
SVHN [28]	Yes	No	248,823	630,420[a]	-	Digit
IIIT5K [2]	Yes	No	5,000	5,000	-	English
YVT [25]	No	Yes	11791	16,620	245	English
MJSynth [22]	No	No	8,919,273	8,919,273	-	English
COCO-Text [29]	Yes	No	63,686	173,589	-	English, Germany, French, Spanish, etc.
SynthText [23]	No	No	800,000	800,000	-	English
DOST (this paper)	Yes	Yes	32,147	797,919	22,398	Japanese, etc

[a] The number of digits is shown

3   Construction of DOST Dataset

DOST dataset was constructed through the following procedure.

1. Image capture
   Scene images were captured with an omnidirectional camera, Point Grey Ladybug3, consisting of five horizontal and one upward cameras shown in Fig. 1. It was set up on a cart shown in Fig. 2 with a laptop computer and a battery for car. A pair of students walked in a shopping street putting the

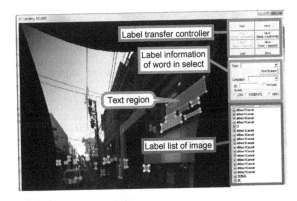

Fig. 8. Ground truthing software that can transfer text information (label) to neighboring frames.

cart. Images were captured in 6.5 fps in the uncompressed mode. The resolutions of each captured image were $1,200 \times 1,600$ pixels. Lens distortion of the captured images was rectified by a provided software by the vendor of the camera. This process completed in the year of 2012. Table 3 summarizes where, how long and how many images we captured.

2. Ground truthing
   Selected sequences were ground truthed by hand, unlike COCO-Text dataset [29] that used existing scene text detection/recognition methods. The reasons we did not use these methods were that scene texts contained in these images were very difficult for these methods. We developed a ground truthing tool shown in Fig. 8 to make it efficient. Similar to LabelMe Video [30], it had a functionality to transfer text information (text label) in a frame to neighboring frames using homography. However, things in the scene were not on a plane as homography assumes. Hence, following homography computation, more precise positions of words were determined by sliding window based template matching. Table 4 shows distribution of lengths of sequences. Each image is checked at least twice by different persons; one for ground truthing and the other for confirmation. When the ground truthing policy is updated, ground truths are updated by the confirmation opportunity. We spent more than 1,500 man hours for this process.

3. Privacy preservation
   Since the captured images preserved the real scene in shopping streets, we cannot avoid capturing passengers. To avoid privacy violation, we blurred face regions of passengers. At first, we used Amazon Mechanical Turk service. Later, however, we decided to ask this task also to our students so as to ensure the quality with less managing efforts.

Table 3. Place, time length (in hour), the number of images of capture.

Place	Length [h]	#Image
Sakai-Higashi	0.73	101,874
Namba	3.71	521,988
Shinsaibashi	0.25	35,100
Abiko	0.50	70,614
Tennoji	0.38	53,754
Total	5.57	783,150

Table 4. Distribution of lengths of image sequences.

Length of sequence	#sequence
5001	2
3181	1
2000 – 2009	4
1951	1
1500 – 1501	2
101 – 582	6
–100	9
Total	27

4 Ground Truthing Policy

The ground truthing policy of DOST dataset is almost shared with the 2013 and 2015 editions of ICDAR Robust Reading Competition Challenge 3 datasets [5, 24]. Since DOST dataset contained not only Latin but also Japanese text, in addition to the ground truthing policy for Latin scripts, we determined one for Japanese text. The ground truthing policy of DOST dataset is summarized below.

1. Basic unit
   A bounding box is created for each basic unit such as a word. In Latin text, word regions segmented by a space is a basic unit. On the other hand, a Japanese sentence is written without some space between words or grammatical units. Hence, as a basic unit of a Japanese sentence, we use *bunsetsu* which is the smallest unit of words that sounds natural in a spoken sentence. A proper noun is not divided.
   There is an exception. If the quality of text is "low," multiple texts of low quality are covered by a single bounding box (see "Transcription" below).
2. Partial occlusion and out of frame
   Even if the region of a basic unit is partially occluded or partially out of frame, it is regarded as a single basic unit without division.
3. Bounding box
   To cope with perspective distortion, a bounding box of a basic unit is represented by four isolated points.
4. Transcription
   The transcription of a basic unit region consists of visible characters. If a basic unit region is partially occluded or partially out of frame, visible characters are transcribed and invisible character(s) are represented by a space. For example, there is a segmented word region of "Barcelona" but "ce" is occluded. Then, the transcription should be "Bar lona." In Fig. 6, an underscore represents a space.

5. ID

The same ID is assigned to a sequence of a basic unit as long as it can be traced within the frame. An exception is the case a basic unit once completely disappears because it goes out of the frame; in such a case, even if it appears again, a different ID is assigned to the new one.

6. Quality

Either "high," "medium" or "low" is assigned to each basic unit based on subjective evaluation. Basic units with "high" and "medium" are regarded as legible. We allowed to enlarge the image to check if they are legible. Basic units with "low" are regarded as "don't care" regions where even if a text detection method detects such basic units, it is not considered as failure in detection.

7. Language

Either "Latin" or "Japanese" is assigned to each basic unit. A basic unit consisting of only alphabets and digits is labeled as "Latin." A basic unit containing at least one non-alphabet or non-digit character is labeled as "Japanese." This is useful for performing an experiment using only Latin text.

5   Comparison of Datasets

Difficulty of major datasets were compared using two detectors and one end-to-end recognition method. To reduce computational burden, in some datasets, a part of data were randomly sampled and used for the experiment. The datasets compared and how they were processed were described below.

1. ICDAR2003 [4]

All (258) images in the training set were used in the experiment.

2. ICDAR2013 (Challenge 2)[5]

All (229) images in the training set were used.

3. ICDAR2015 (Challenge 3) [24]

Images were sampled once in every 30 frames in 10 out of 24 training videos. As a result, 207 images were selected.

4. ICDAR2015 (Challenge 4) [24]

All (1,000) images in the training set of "End to End" task (Task 4.4) of ICDAR 2015 Robust Reading Competition Challenge 4 were used.

5. SVT [3]

All (350) images in both training and test sets were used.

6. YVT [25]

Images were sampled once in every 30 frames in all (30) videos. As a result, 420 images were selected.

7. COCO-Text [29]

300 images were randomly sampled from ones containing words annotated as English, legible and machine printed (say, target words). The 300 images contained 2,403 target words and words which do not satisfy the condition of the target words (say, non-target words). The non-target words were treated as "don't care" regions.

8. DOST (this paper)

   Images were sampled once in every 30 frames in all ground truthed sequences. As a result, 1,075 images were selected.

9. DOST Latin (this paper)

   This is to evaluate DOST dataset as a Latin scene text dataset containing only alphabets and digits. In text detection and recognition, the same images as "DOST" presented above were used. In evaluation, words containing characters other than alphabets and digits were treated as "don't care" regions. Thus, even if Japanese texts are detected, it does not affect the result.

Two detection methods were used for evaluation. One was the scene text detection method contained in the OpenCV API version 3.0. It was based on Neumann et al. [31]. The other was Matsuda et al. [32]. We were privately given the source code by courtesy of the authors of the paper. In addition, Google Vsion API[2] was used as a powerful commercial end-to-end recognition system. We could designate the language of texts. Only for "DOST," we designated Japanese. In this mode, English texts are also able to be detected and recognized while accuracies are expected to be lower. For other datasets including "DOST Latin," we designated English.

In performance evaluation, regardless of datasets, we shared the same evaluation criteria. For both text detection and end-to-end word recognition tasks, we followed the evaluation criteria used in the challenge of "incidental scene text" (Challenge 4) of ICDAR 2015 Robust Reading Competition. That is, for the scene text detection task, based on a single Intersection-over-Union (IoU) criterion with a threshold of 50 %, a detected bounding box was regarded as correct if it overlapped by more than 50 % with a ground truth bounding box. Recall

Table 5. Detection and Recognition results on selected datasets. Evaluation criteria are recall (R), precision (P) and F-measure (F) in percentage.

Dataset	Text detection						End-to-end		
	OpenCV API			Matsuda [32]			Google Vision API		
	R	P	F	R	P	F	R	P	F
ICDAR2003 [4]	17.6	20.0	21.1	35.0	74.2	47.5	77.3	86.1	81.8
ICDAR2013 (Challenge 2) [5]	11.4	4.2	6.1	4.8	5.2	4.8	70.9	71.8	71.3
ICDAR2015 (Challenge 3) [24]	9.7	7.5	8.5	2.4	10.4	3.9	38.2	52.0	44.1
ICDAR2015 (Challenge 4) [24]	11.4	15.1	13.0	3.8	18.1	6.3	40.5	61.6	48.5
SVT [3]	26.3	14.9	19.0	27.6	30.6	29.1	31.5	19.6	24.2
YVT [25]	36.4	23.4	28.5	1.1	5.3	1.9	33.1	43.8	37.7
COCO-Text [29]	9.3	16.5	11.9	0.8	11.3	1.5	11.9	30.5	17.1
DOST (this paper)	1.4	9.4	2.4	1.6	14.1	2.8	1.7	6.5	2.7
DOST latin (this paper)	0.8	2.2	1.2	1.3	5.2	2.1	6.6	39.6	11.2

---

[2] https://cloud.google.com/vision/.

and precision were simply calculated by the following equations.

$$\text{Recall} = \frac{\text{Number of correctly detected bounding boxes}}{\text{Number of bounding boxes in ground truth}} \tag{1}$$

$$\text{Precision} = \frac{\text{Number of correctly detected bounding boxes}}{\text{Number of detected bounding boxes}} \tag{2}$$

Then, F-measure was calculated as the harmonic mean of precision and recall. For the end-to-end word recognition task, a detected bounding box was regarded as correct if it satisfies the condition of the scene text detection task as well as the estimated transcription was completely correct. Recall, precision and F-measure were calculated in the same way as the detection task.

Results are summarized in Table 5. As can be seen, results of "DOST" and "DOST Latin" were far worse than others. This indicates that DOST dataset reflecting the real environment is more challenging than the major benchmark datasets.

6 Conclusion

Although many scene text datasets publicly available already exist, none of them are intentionally constructed to reflect the real environment. Hence, even though scene text detection/recognition methods achieve high accuracies on these existing major benchmark datasets, it was not possible to evaluate how they are good for practical use. To address the problem, we presented a new scene text dataset named Downtown Osaka Scene Text Dataset (in short, DOST dataset). Unlike most of existing datasets consisting of scene images intentionally captured, DOST dataset consists of uncontrolled scene images; use of an omnidirectional camera enabled us to capture videos (sequential images) of whole scenes surrounding the camera. Since the dataset preserved the real scenes containing texts as they were, in other words, they are *scene texts in the wild*. Through the evaluation conducted in the paper to know the difficulty and quality in comparison with existing datasets, we demonstrated that DOST dataset is more challenging than the major benchmark datasets.

Acknowledgments. The authors would like to thank the anonymous reviewers for their valuable comments and suggestions. This work is supported by JST CREST and JSPS KAKENHI #25240028.

References

1. Shi, B., Wang, X., Lyu, P., Yao, C., Bai, X.: Robust scene text recognition with automatic rectification. In: Proceedings of CVPR, pp. 4168–4176 (2016)
2. Mishra, A., Alahari, K., Jawahar, C.V.: Scene text recognition using higher order language priors. In: Proceedings of BMVC (2012)
3. Wang, K., Babenko, B., Belongie, S.: End-to-end scene text recognition. In: Proceedings of ICCV, pp. 1457–1464 (2011)

4. Lucas, S.M., Panaretos, A., Sosa, L., Tang, A., Wong, S., Young, R., Ashida, K., Nagai, H., Okamoto, M., Yamamoto, H., Miyao, H., Zhu, J., Ou, W., Wolf, C., Jolion, J.M., Todoran, L., Worring, M., Lin, X.: ICDAR 2003 robust reading competitions: Entries, results and future directions. IJDAR **7**(2–3), 105–122 (2005)
5. Karatzas, D., Shafait, F., Uchida, S., Iwamura, M., Gomez i Bigorda, L., Mestre, S.R., Mas, J., Mota, D.F., Almazan, J.A., de las Heras, L.P.: ICDAR 2013 robust reading competition. In: Proceedings of ICDAR, pp. 1115–1124 (2013)
6. Wang, T., Wu, D.J., Coates, A., Ng, A.Y.: End-to-end text recognition with convolutional neural networks. In: Proceedings of ICPR, pp. 3304–3308 (2012)
7. Novikova, T., Barinova, O., Kohli, P., Lempitsky, V.: Large-lexicon attribute-consistent text recognition in natural images. In: Fitzgibbon, A., Lazebnik, S., Perona, P., Sato, Y., Schmid, C. (eds.) ECCV 2012, Part VI. LNCS, vol. 7577, pp. 752–765. Springer, Heidelberg (2012)
8. Goel, V., Mishra, A., Alahari, K., Jawahar, C.V.: Whole is greater than sum of parts: recognizing scene text words. In: Proceedings of ICDAR, pp. 398–402 (2013)
9. Bissacco, A., Cummins, M., Netzer, Y., Neven, H.: Photoocr: reading text in uncontrolled conditions. In: Proceedings of ICCV, pp. 785–792 (2013)
10. Alsharif, O., Pineau, J.: End-to-end text recognition with hybrid HMM maxout models. In: International Conference on Learning Representations (ICLR) (2014)
11. Almazán, J., Gordo, A., Fornés, A., Valveny, E.: Word spotting and recognition with embedded attributes. IEEE TPAMI **36**(12), 2552–2566 (2014)
12. Yao, C., Bai, X., Shi, B., Liu, W.: Strokelets: a learned multi-scale representation for scene text recognition. In: Proceedings of CVPR (2014)
13. Jaderberg, M., Vedaldi, A., Zisserman, A.: Deep features for text spotting. In: Fleet, D., Pajdla, T., Schiele, B., Tuytelaars, T. (eds.) ECCV 2014, Part IV. LNCS, vol. 8692, pp. 512–528. Springer, Heidelberg (2014)
14. Su, B., Lu, S.: Accurate scene text recognition based on recurrent neural network. In: Cremers, D., Reid, I., Saito, H., Yang, M.-H. (eds.) ACCV 2014. LNCS, vol. 9003, pp. 35–48. Springer, Heidelberg (2015)
15. Rodriguez, J.A., Gordo, A., Perronnin, F.: Label embedding: a frugal baseline for text recognition. IJCV **113**(3), 193–207 (2015)
16. Gordo, A.: Supervised mid-level features for word image representation. In: Proceedings of CVPR (2015)
17. Jaderberg, M., Simonyan, K., Vedaldi, A., Zisserman, A.: Reading text in the wild with convolutional neural networks. IJCV **116**(1), 1–20 (2016)
18. Jaderberg, M., Simonyan, K., Vedaldi, A., Zisserman, A.: Deep structured output learning for unconstrained text recognition. In: Proceedings of ICLR (2015)
19. Shi, B., Bai, X., Yao, C.: An end-to-end trainable neural network for image-based sequence recognition and its application to scene text recognition. CoRR abs/1507.05717 (2015)
20. Poznanski, A., Wolf, L.: CNN-N-gram for handwritingword recognition. In: Proceedings of CVPR (2016)
21. Liang, J., Doermann, D., Li, H.: Camera-based analysis of text and documents: a survey. IJDAR **7**(2), 83–104 (2005)
22. Jaderberg, M., Simonyan, K., Vedaldi, A., Zisserman, A.: Synthetic data and artificial neural networks for natural scene text recognition. In: Proceedings of NIPS Deep Learning Workshop (2014)
23. Gupta, A., Vedaldi, A., Zisserman, A.: Synthetic data for text localisation in natural images. In: Proceedings of CVPR (2016)

24. Karatzas, D., Gomez-Bigorda, L., Nicolaou, A., Ghosh, S., Bagdanov, A., Iwamura, M., Matas, J., Neumann, L., Chandrasekhar, V.R., Lu, S., Shafait, F., Uchida, S., Valveny, E.: ICDAR 2015 robust reading competition. In: Proceedings of ICDAR, pp. 1156–1160 (2015)

25. Nguyen, P.X., Wang, K., Belongie, S.: Video text detection and recognition: dataset and benchmark. In: Proceedings of WACV (2014)

26. Nagy, R., Dicker, A., Meyer-Wegener, K.: NEOCR: a configurable dataset for natural image text recognition. In: Iwamura, M., Shafait, F. (eds.) CBDAR 2011. LNCS, vol. 7139, pp. 150–163. Springer, Heidelberg (2012)

27. Jung, J., Lee, S., Cho, M.S., Kim, J.H.: Touch TT: scene text extractor using touchscreen interface. ETRI J. **33**(1), 78–88 (2011)

28. Netzer, Y., Wang, T., Coates, A., Bissacco, A., Wu, B., Ng, A.Y.: Reading digits in natural images with unsupervised feature learning. In: Proceedings of NIPS Workshop on Deep Learning and Unsupervised Feature Learning (2011)

29. Veit, A., Matera, T., Neumann, L., Matas, J., Belongie, S.: COCO-Text: dataset and benchmark for text detection and recognition in natural images. CoRR abs/1207.0016 (2016)

30. Yuen, J., Russell, B., Liu, C., Torralba, A.: LabelMe video: building a video database with human annotations. In: Proceedings of ICCV, pp. 1451–1458 (2009)

31. Neumann, L., Matas, J.: Real-time scene text localization and recognition. In: Proceedings of CVPR, pp. 3538–3545 (2012)

32. Matsuda, Y., Omachi, S., Aso, H.: String detection from scene images by binarization and edge detection. Trans. IEICE **J93**(3), 336–344 (2010). In Japanese

W17 – Egocentric Perception, Interaction and Computing

Preface

This part constitutes the refereed proceedings of the First International Workshop on Egocentric Perception, Interaction and Computing (EPIC), held in Amsterdam (The Netherlands), in October 2016, in conjunction with the 14th European Conference on Computer Vision.

Egocentric perception introduces a series of challenging questions for Computer Vision and Multimedia as motion, real-time responsiveness and generally uncontrolled interactions in the wild are more frequently required or encountered. Questions such as what to interpret as well as what to ignore, how to efficiently represent egocentric actions and how captured information can be turned into useful data for guidance or log summaries become central.

Eyewear devices are becoming increasingly popular, both as research prototypes and off-the-shelf products. They can acquire images and videos, with different resolutions and frame rates, and can collect multimodal data such as gaze information, GPS position, IMU data, etc. Being connected with headmounted displays they can also provide new forms of visualization. Based on this rapid progress, we believe that we are only at the beginning and these technologies and their application can have a great impact on our life. In fact, these Eyewear devices will be able to automatically understand what the wearer is doing, acting, manipulating or where his attention is directed. They will also be able to recognize the surrounding scene and understand gestures and social relationships. This new EPIC@X series of workshops aims to bring together the various communities that are relevant to egocentric perception including Computer Vision, Multimedia, HCI and the Visual Sciences and is planned to be held alongside the major conferences in these fields.

This workshop received 19 submissions demonstrating the great interest of this timely topic from the scientific community. After a rigorous double-blind review process, 10 paper, which address very challenging issues of this field, have been accepted (acceptance rate 53 %).

October 2016

Giuseppe Serra
Rita Cucchiara
Walterio Mayol-Cuevas
Andreas Bulling
Dima Damen

DeepDiary: Automatically Captioning Lifelogging Image Streams

Chenyou Fan[✉] and David J. Crandall

School of Informatics and Computing, Indiana University, Bloomington, IN, USA
{fan6,djcran}@indiana.edu

Abstract. Lifelogging cameras capture everyday life from a first-person perspective, but generate so much data that it is hard for users to browse and organize their image collections effectively. In this paper, we propose to use automatic image captioning algorithms to generate textual representations of these collections. We develop and explore novel techniques based on deep learning to generate captions for both individual images and image streams, using temporal consistency constraints to create summaries that are both more compact and less noisy. We evaluate our techniques with quantitative and qualitative results, and apply captioning to an image retrieval application for finding potentially private images. Our results suggest that our automatic captioning algorithms, while imperfect, may work well enough to help users manage lifelogging photo collections.

Keywords: Lifelogging · First-person · Image captioning · Computer vision

1 Introduction

Wearable cameras that capture first-person views of people's daily lives have recently become affordable, lightweight, and practical, after many years of being explored only in the research community [1,12,22]. These new devices come in various types and styles, from the GoPro, which is marketed for recording high-quality video of sports and other adventures, to Google Glass, which is a heads-up display interface for smartphones but includes a camera, to Narrative Clip and Autographer, which capture "lifelogs" by automatically taking photos throughout one's day (e.g., every 30 s). No matter the purpose, however, all of these devices can record huge amounts of imagery, which makes it difficult for users to organize and browse their image data.

In this paper, we attempt to produce automatic textual *narrations* or captions of a visual lifelog. We believe that describing lifelogs with sentences is most natural for the average user, and allows for interesting applications like generating automatic textual diaries of the "story" of someone's day based on their lifelogging photos. We take advantage of recent breakthroughs in image captioning using deep learning that have shown impressive results for consumer-style images from social media [14,16], and evaluate their performance on the

© Springer International Publishing Switzerland 2016
G. Hua and H. Jégou (Eds.): ECCV 2016 Workshops, Part I, LNCS 9913, pp. 459–473, 2016.
DOI: 10.1007/978-3-319-46604-0_33

novel domain of first-person images (which are significantly more challenging due to substantial noise, blurring, poor composition, etc.). We also propose a new strategy to try to encourage diversity in the sentences, which we found to be particularly useful in describing lifelogging images from different perspectives.

Of course, lifelogging photo streams are highly redundant since wearable cameras indiscriminately capture thousands of photos per day. Instead of simply captioning individual images, we also consider the novel problem of jointly captioning lifelogging streams, i.e. generating captions for temporally-contiguous groups of photos corresponding to coherent activities or scene types. Not only does this produce a more compact and potentially useful organization of a user's photo collection, but it also could create an automatically-generated textual "diary" of a user's day based only on their photos. The sentences themselves are also useful to aid in image retrieval by keyword search, which we illustrate for the specific application of searching for potentially private images (e.g. containing keywords like "bathroom"). We formulate this joint captioning problem in a Markov Random Field model and show how to solve it efficiently.

To our knowledge, we are the first to propose image captioning as an important task for lifelogging photos, as well as the first to apply and evaluate automatic image captioning models in this domain. To summarize our contributions, we learn and apply deep image captioning models to lifelogging photos, including proposing a novel method for generating photo descriptions with diverse structures and perspectives; propose a novel technique for inferring captions for streams of photos taken over time in order to find and summarize coherent activities and other groups of photos; create an online framework for collecting and annotating lifelogging images, and use it to collect a realistic lifelogging dataset consisting of thousands of photos and thousands of reference sentences and evaluate these techniques on our data, both quantitatively and qualitatively, under different simulated use cases.

2   Related Work

While wearable cameras have been studied for over a decade in the research community [1,12,22], only recently have they become practical enough for consumers to use on a daily basis. In the computer vision field, recent work has begun to study this new style of imagery, which is significantly different from photos taken by traditional point-and-shoot cameras. Specific research topics have included recognizing objects [8,18], scenes [9], and activities [4,7,25,26]. Some computer vision work has specifically tried to address privacy concerns, by recognizing photos taken in potentially sensitive places like bathrooms [29], or containing sensitive objects like computer monitors [18]. However, these techniques typically require that classifiers be explicitly trained for each object, scene type, or activity of interest, which limits their scalability.

Instead of classifying lifelogging images into pre-defined and discrete categories, we propose to annotate them with automatically-generated, free-form image captions, inspired by recent progress in deep learning. Convolutional

Neural Networks (CNNs) have recently emerged as powerful models for object recognition in computer vision [6,10,19,28], while Recurrent Neural Networks (RNNs) and Long Short-Term Memory (LSTMs) have been developed for learning models of sequential data, like natural language sentences [5,11]. The combination of CNNs for recognizing image content and RNNs for modeling language have recently been shown to generate surprisingly rich image descriptions [14,23,32], essentially "translating" from image features to English sentences [15].

Some closely related work has been done to generate textual descriptions from videos. Venugopalan *et al.* [31] use image captioning model to generate video descriptions from a sequence of video frames. Like previous image captioning papers, their method estimates a single sentence for each sequence, while we explicitly generate multiple diverse sentences and evaluate the image-sentence matching quality to improve the captions from noisy, poorly-composed lifelogging images. Zhu *et al.* [33] use neural sentence embedding to model a sentence-sentence similarity function, and use LSTMs to model image-sentence similarity in order to align subtitles of movies with sentences from the original books. Their main purpose is to find corresponding movie clips and book paragraphs based on visual and semantic patterns, whereas ours is to infer novel sentences from new lifelogging image streams.

3   Lifelogging Data Collection

To train and test our techniques, two of the authors wore Narrative Clip lifelogging cameras over a period of about five months (June-Aug 2015 and Jan-Feb 2016), to create a repository of 7,716 lifelogging photos. To facilitate collecting lifelogging photos and annotations, we built a website which allowed users to upload and label photos in a unified framework, using the Narrative Clip API.[1]

We collected textual annotations for training and testing the system in two different ways. First, the two authors and three of their friends and family members used the online system to submit sentences for randomly-selected images, producing 2,683 sentences for 696 images. Annotators were asked to produce at least two sentences per image: one that described the photo from a first-person perspective (e.g., "I am eating cereal at the kitchen table.") and one from a third-person perspective (e.g. "A bowl of cereal sits on a kitchen table."). We requested sentences from each of these perspectives because we have observed that some scenes are more naturally described by one perspective or the other. Annotators were welcome to enter multiple sentences, and each image was viewed by an average of 1.45 labelers.

Second, to generate more diversity in annotators and annotations, we published 293 images[2] on Amazon's Mechanical Turk (AMT), showing each photo to at least three annotators and, as before, asking each annotator to give at

---

[1] https://open-staging.getnarrative.com/api-docs.
[2] We randomly chose 300, but removed 7 that we were not comfortable sharing with the public (e.g. photos of strangers whose permission we were not able to obtain).

least one first-person and one third-person sentence. This produced a set of 1,813 sentences, or an average of 6.2 sentences per image. A total of 121 distinct Mechanical Turk users contributed sentences.

Finally, we also downloaded COCO [21], a popular publicly-available dataset of 80,000 photos and 400,000 sentences. These images are from Internet and social media sources, and thus are significantly different than the lifelogging context we consider here, but we hypothesized that this may be useful additional training data to augment our smaller lifelogging dataset.

4   Automatic Lifelogging Image Captioning

We now present our technique for using deep learning to automatically annotate lifelogging images with captions. We first give a brief review of deep image captioning models, and then show how to take advantage of *streams* of lifelogging images by estimating captions jointly across time, which not only helps reduce noise in captions by enforcing temporal consistency, but also helps summarize large photo collections with smaller subsets of sentences.

4.1   Background: Deep Networks for Image Captioning

Automatic image captioning is a difficult task because it requires not only identifying important objects and actions, but also describing them in natural language. However, recent work in deep learning has demonstrated impressive results in generating image and video descriptions [14,31,33]. The basic high-level idea is to learn a common feature space that is shared by both images and words. Then, given a new image, we generate sentences that are "nearby" in the same feature space. The encoder (mapping from image to feature space) is typically a Convolutional Neural Network (CNN), which abstracts images into a vector of local and global appearance features. The decoder (mapping from feature space to words) produces a word vector using a Recurrent Neural Network (RNN), which abstracts out the semantic and syntactic meaning.

In the prediction stage, a forward pass of LSTM generates a full sentence terminated by a stop word for each input image. Similar image captioning models have been discussed in detail in recent papers [14,31,32]. In Sect. 4.2, we discuss in detail how to generate diverse captions for a single image.

4.2   Photo Grouping and Activity Summarization

The techniques in the last section automatically estimate captions for individual images. However, lifelogging users do not typically capture individual images in isolation, but instead collect long streams of photos taken at regular intervals over time (e.g., every 30 s for Narrative Clip). This means that evidence from multiple images can be combined together to produce better captions than is possible from observing any single image, in effect "smoothing out" noise in any particular image by examining the photos taken nearby in time. These sentences could provide more concise summarizations, helping people find, remember, and organize photos according to broad events instead of individual moments.

Suppose we wish to estimate captions for a stream of images $I = (I_1, I_2, ..., I_K)$, which are sorted in order of increasing timestamps. We first generate multiple diverse captions for each individual image, using a technique we describe in the next subsection. We combine all of these sentences together across images into a large set of candidates C (with $|C| = d|I|$, where d is the number of diverse sentences generated per image; we use $d = 15$). We wish to estimate a sequence of sentences such that each sentence describes its corresponding image well, but also such that the sentences are relatively consistent across time. In other words, we want to estimate a sequence of sentences $S^* = (S_1^*, S_2^*, ..., S_K^*)$ so as to minimize an energy function,

$$S^* = \operatorname*{argmin}_{S=(S_1,...,S_K)} \sum_{i=1}^{K} \text{Score}(S_i, I_i) + \beta \sum_{j=1}^{K-1} \mathbb{1}(S_j, S_{j+1}), \tag{1}$$

where each $S_i \in C$, $\text{Score}(S_i, I_i)$ is a unary cost function measuring the quality of a given sentence S_i in describing a single image I_i, $\mathbb{1}(S_a, S_b)$ is a pairwise cost function that is 0 if S_a and S_b are the same and 1 otherwise, and β is a constant. Intuitively, β controls the degree of temporal smoothing of the model: when $\beta = 0$, for example, the model simply chooses sentences for each image independently without considering neighboring images in the stream, whereas when β is very large, the model will try to find a single sentence to describe all of the images in the stream.

Equation (1) is a chain-structured Markov Random Field (MRF) model [17], which means that the optimal sequence of sentences S^* can be found efficiently using the Viterbi algorithm. All that remains is to define two key components of the model: (1) a technique for generating multiple, diverse candidate sentences for each image, in order to obtain the candidate sentence set C, and (2) the Score function, which requires a technique for measuring how well a given sentence describes a given image. We now describe these two ingredients in turn.

Generating Diverse Captions. Our joint captioning model above requires a large set of candidate sentences. Many possible sentences can correctly describe any given image, and thus it is desirable for the automatic image captioning algorithm to generate multiple sentences that describe the image in multiple ways. This is especially true for lifelogging images that are often noisy, poorly composed, and ambiguous, and can be interpreted in different ways. Vinyals et al. [32] use beam search to generate multiple sentences, by having the LSTM model keep b candidate sentences at each step of sentence generation (where b is called the beam size). However, we found that this existing technique did not work well for lifelogging sentences, because it produced very homogeneous sentences, even with a high beam size.

To encourage greater diversity, we apply the Diverse M-best solutions technique of Batra et al. [3], which was originally proposed to find multiple

MSCOCO + Lifelog

a man is sitting at a table
i am having a dinner with my friends
i am having a dinner with a friend
a man is sitting by side of a table
a man is sitting at a table
a man is looking at a man in a red shirt
there is a man with glasses on the table
there is a man sitting across the table
there is a man across the table with a
man

MSCOCO + Lifelog

I am typing on my computer
I am meeting with my friend
a person is typing on a laptop
there is a computer monitor on the table
there is a computer monitor in the room
two hands are typing on a computer
i am typing on my computer
i am working on my computer
i am sitting with my friend

MSCOCO + Lifelog

I am ordering food at a restaurant
I am ordering food in a restaurant
a man is preparing food in a restaurant
a woman and woman are preparing food
in a restaurant
a woman is preparing food in a restaurant
a woman is preparing food in a cafeteria
i am ordering my food at a restaurant
i am talking to my friend at a restaurant
there is a man and woman at the table

Fig. 1. Sample captions generated by models pre-trained with COCO and fine-tuned with lifelogging dataset. Three different colors show the top three predictions produced in three beam searches by applying the Diverse M-Solutions technique. Within each beam search, sentences tend to have similar structures and describe from similar perspective; between consecutive beam searches, structures and perspectives tend to be different. (Color figure online)

high-likelihood solutions in graphical model inference problems. We adapt this technique to LSTMs by performing multiple rounds of beam search. In the first round, we obtain a set of predicted words for each position in the sentence. In the second round, we add a bias term that reduces the network activation values of words found in the first beam search by a constant value. Intuitively, this decreases the probability that a word found during the previous beam search being selected again at the same word position in the sentence. Depending on the degree of diversity needed, additional rounds of beam search can be conducted, each time penalizing words that have occurred in any previous round.

Figure 1 presents sample automatically-generated results by using three rounds of beam search and a beam size of 3 for illustration purposes. We see that the technique successfully injects diversity into the set of estimated captions. Many of the captions are quite accurate, including "A man is sitting at a table" and "I am having dinner with my friends," while others are not correct (e.g. "A man is looking at a man in a red shirt"), and others are nonsensical ("There is a man sitting across the table with a man"). Nevertheless, the captioning results are overall remarkably accurate for an automatic image captioning system, reflecting the power of deep captioning techniques to successfully model both image content and sentence generation.

Image-Sentence Quality Alignment. The joint captioning model in Eq. (1) also requires a function $Score(S_i, I_i)$, which is a measure of how well an arbitrary sentence S_i describes a given image I_i. The difficulty here is that the

LSTM model described above tells us how to generate sentences for an image, but not how to measure their similarity to a given image. Doing this requires us to explicitly align certain words of the sentence to certain regions of an image – i.e. determining which "part" of an image generated each word. Karpathy et al. [16] propose matching each region with the word with maximum inner product (interpreted as a similarity measure) across all words in terms of learnable region vectors and word vectors, and to sum all similarity measures over all regions as the total score. We implement their method and train this image-sentence alignment model on our lifelogging dataset. To generate the matching score $\text{Score}(S_i, I_i)$ for Eq. (1), we extract region vectors from image I_i, retrieve trained word vectors for words in sentence S_i, and sum similarity measures of regions with best-aligned words.

Image Grouping Result. Finally, once captions have been jointly inferred for each image in a photostream, we can group together contiguous substreams of images that share the same sentence. Figure 2 shows examples of activity summarization. In general, the jointly-inferred captions are reasonable descriptions of the images, and much less noisy than those produced from individual images in Fig. 1, showing the advantage of incorporating temporal reasoning into the captioning process. For example, the first row of images shows that the model labeled several images as "I am talking with a friend while eating a meal in a restaurant," even though the friend is only visible in one of the frames, showing how the model has propagated context across time. Of course, there are still mistakes ranging from the minor error that there is no broccoli on the plate in the second row to the more major error that the last row shows a piano and not someone typing on a computer. The grammar of the sentences is generally good considering that the model has no explicit knowledge of English besides what it has learned from training data, although usage errors are common (e.g., "I am shopping kitchen devices in a store").

5   Experimental Evaluation

We first use automatic metrics that compare to ground truth reference sentences with quantitative scores. To give a better idea of the actual practical utility of technique, we also evaluate in two other ways: using a panel of human judges to rate the quality of captioning results, and testing the system in a specific application of keyword-based image retrieval using the generated captions.

5.1   Quantitative Captioning Evaluation

Automated metrics such as BLEU [24], CIDEr [30], Meteor [2] and Rouge-L [20] have been proposed to score sentence similarity compared to reference sentences provided by humans, and each has different advantages and disadvantages. We present results using all of these metrics (using the MS COCO Detection Challenge implementation[3]), and also summarize the seven scores with their mean.

---

[3] https://github.com/tylin/coco-caption.

Fig. 2. Randomly-chosen samples of activity summarization on our dataset.

Implementation. A significant challenge with deep learning-based methods is that they typically require huge amounts of training data, both in terms of images and sentences. Unfortunately, collecting this quantity of lifelogging images and annotations is very difficult. To try to overcome this problem, we augmented our lifelogging training set with COCO data using three different strategies: **Lifelog only** training used only our lifelogging dataset, consisting of 736 lifelogging photos with 4,300 human-labeled sentences; **COCO only** training used only COCO dataset; and **COCO then Lifelog** started with the **COCO only** model, and then used it as initialization when re-training the model on the lifelogging dataset (i.e., "fine-tuning" [19]).

For extracting image features, we use the VGGNet [27] CNN model. The word vectors are learned from scratch. Our image captioning model stacks two LSTM layers, and each layer structure closely follows the one described in [32]. To boost training speed, we re-implemented LSTM model in C++ using the Caffe [13] deep learning package. It takes about 2.5 h for COCO pre-training, and about 1 h for fine-tuning on Lifelog dataset with 10,000 iterations for both.

At test time, the number of beam searches conducted during caption inference controls the degree of diversity in the output; here we use three to match the three styles of captions we expect (COCO, first-person, and third-person perspectives).

Table 1. Bleu1-4, CIDEr, Meteor and Rouge Scores for Diverse 3-Best Beams of Captions on Test Set.

Datasets		Metric							
Training	Testing	Bleu-1	Bleu-2	Bleu-3	Bleu-4	CIDEr	METEOR	ROUGE	Mean
Lifelog	Lifelog 100	0.669	0.472	0.324	0.218	0.257	0.209	0.462	0.373
COCO		0.561	0.354	0.206	0.118	0.143	0.149	0.374	0.272
COCO+Lifelog		0.666	0.469	0.319	0.210	0.253	0.207	0.459	0.369
Lifelog@Usr1	Lifelog@Usr2	0.588	0.410	0.279	0.189	0.228	0.195	0.431	0.331
Lifelog@2015	Lifelog@2016	0.557	0.379	0.249	0.160	0.325	0.202	0.425	0.328

Samples of predicted sentences are shown in Fig. 1. This suggests that different genres of training sentences contribute to tune hidden states of LSTM and thus enable it to produce diverse structures of sentences in testing stage.

Results. Table 1 presents quantitative results of each of these training strategies, all tested on the same set of 100 randomly-selected photos having 1,000 ground truth reference sentences, using each of the seven automatic scoring metrics mentioned above. We find that the **Lifelog only** strategy achieves much higher overall accuracy than **COCO only**, with a mean score of 0.373 vs. 0.272. This suggests that even though COCO is a much larger dataset, images from social media are different enough from lifelogging images that the **COCO only** model does not generalize well to our application. Moreover, this may also reflect an artifact of the automated evaluation, because **Lifelog only** benefits from seeing sentences with similar vocabulary and in a similar style as in the reference sentences, since the same small group of humans labeled both the training and test datasets. More surprisingly, we find that **Lifelog only** also slightly outperforms **COCO then lifelog** (0.373 vs. 0.369). The model produced by the latter training dataset has a larger vocabulary and produces richer styles of sentences than Lifelog only, which hurts its quantitative score. Qualitatively, however, it often produces more diverse and descriptive sentences because of its larger vocabulary and ability to generate sentences in first-person, third-person, and COCO styles. Samples of generated diverse captions are shown in Fig. 1.

We conducted experiments with two additional strategies in order to simulate more realistic scenarios. The first scenario reflects when a consumer first starts using our automatic captioning system on their images without having supplied any training data of their own. We simulate this by training image captioning model on one user's photos and testing on another. Training set has 805 photos and 3,716 reference sentences; testing set has 40 photos and 565 reference sentences. The mean quantitative accuracy declines from our earlier experiments when training and testing on images sampled from the same set, as shown in Table 1, although the decline is not very dramatic (from 0.373 to 0.331), and still much better than training on COCO (0.272). This result suggests that the captioning model has learned general properties of lifelogging images, instead of overfitting to one particular user (e.g., simply "memorizing" the appearance of the places and activities they frequently visit and do).

The other situation is when an existing model trained on historical lifelogging data is used to caption new photos. We simulate this by taking all lifelogging photos in 2015 as training data and photos in 2016 as testing data. Training set has 673 photos and 3,610 sentences; testing set has 30 photos and 172 sentences. As shown in Table 1, this scenario very slightly decreased performance compared to training on data from a different user (0.328 vs. 0.331), although the difference is likely not statistically significant.

5.2 Image Captioning Evaluation with Human Judges

We conducted a small study using human judges to rate the quality of our automatically-generated captions. In particular, we randomly selected 21 images from the Lifelog 100 test dataset (used in Table 1) and generated captions using our model trained on the COCO then Lifelog scenario. For each image, we generated 15 captions (with 3 rounds of beam search, each with beam size 5), and then kept the top-scoring caption according to our model and four randomly-sampled from the remaining 14, to produce a diverse set of five automatically-generated captions per image. We also randomly sampled five of the human-generated reference sentences for each image.

For each of the ten captions (five automatic plus five human), we showed the image (after reviewing it for potentially private content and obtaining permission of the photo-taker) and caption to a user on Amazon Mechanical Turk, without telling them how the caption had been produced. We asked them to rate, on a five-point Likert scale, how strongly they agreed with two statements: (1) "The sentence or phrase makes sense and is grammatically correct (ignoring minor problems like capitalization and punctuation)," and (2) "The sentence or phrase accurately describes either what the camera wearer was doing or what he or she was looking at when the photo was taken." The task involved 630 individual HITs from 37 users.

Table 2 summarizes the results, comparing the average ratings over the 5 human reference sentences, the average over all 5 diverse automatically-generated captions (Auto-5 column), and the single highest-likelihood caption as estimated by our complete model (Auto-top). About 92 % of the human reference sentences were judged as grammatically correct (i.e., somewhat or strongly agreeing with statement (1)), compared to about 77 % for the automatically-generated diverse captions and 81 % for the single best sentence selected by our model. Humans also described images more accurately than the diverse captions (88 % vs. 54 %), although the fact that 64 % of our single best estimated captions were accurate indicates that our model is often able to identify which one is best among the diverse candidates. Overall, our top automatic caption was judged to be *both* grammatically correct and accurate 59.5 % of the time, compared to 84.8 % of the time for human reference sentences.

We view these results to be very promising, as they suggest that automatic captioning can generate reasonable sentences for over half of lifelogging images, at least in some applications. For example, for 19 (90 %) of the 21 images in the test set, at least one of five diverse captions was unanimously judged to be both

Table 2. Summary of grammatical correctness and accuracy of lifelogging image captions, on a rating scale from 1 (Strongly Disagree) to 5 (Strongly Agree), averaged over 3 judges. *Human* column is averaged over 5 human-generated reference sentences, *Auto-5* is averaged over 5 diverse computer-generated sentences, and *Auto-top* is single highest-likelihood computer-generated sentence predicted by our model.

Rating	*Grammar*			*Accuracy*		
	Human	Auto-5	Auto-top	Human	Auto-5	Auto-top
1	1.9%	7.6%	11.9%	2.9%	22.4%	21.4%
2	3.8%	10.0%	7.1%	3.8%	15.2%	7.1%
3	0.5%	5.7%	0.0%	4.8%	8.1%	7.1%
4	19.0%	17.6%	4.8%	22.4%	17.6%	19.0%
5	73.3%	59.0%	76.2%	65.2%	36.7%	45.2%
Mean	4.60	4.10	4.26	4.45	3.31	3.60

grammatically correct and accurate by all 3 judges. This may be useful in some retrieval applications where recall is important, for example, where having noise in some captions may be tolerable as long as at least one of them is correct. We consider one such application in the next section.

5.3   Keyword-Based Image Retrieval

Image captioning allows us to directly implement keyword-based image retrieval by searching on the generated captions. We consider a particular application of this image search feature here that permits a quantitative evaluation. As mentioned above, wearable cameras can collect a large number of images containing private information. Automatic image captioning could allow users to find potentially private images easily, and then take appropriate action (like deleting or encrypting the photos). We consider two specific types of potentially embarrassing content here: photos taken in potentially private locations like bathrooms and locker rooms, and photos containing personal computer or smartphone displays which may contain private information such as credit card numbers or e-mail contents.

We chose these two types of concerns specifically because they have been considered by others in prior work: Korayem *et al.* [18] present a system for detecting monitors in lifelogging images using deep learning with CNNs, while Templeman *et al.* [29] classify images according to the room in which they were taken. Both of these papers present strongly supervised based techniques, which were given thousands of training images manually labeled with ground truth for each particular task. In contrast, identifying private imagery based on keyword search on automatically-generated captions could avoid the need to create a training set and train a separate classifier for each type of sensitive image.

We evaluated captioning-based sensitive image retrieval against standard state-of-the-art strongly-supervised image classification using CNNs [19]

Table 3. Confusion matrices for two approaches on two tasks for detecting sensitive images. *Left:* Results on 3-way problem of classifying into not sensitive, sensitive place (bathroom), or digital display categories. *Right:* Results on 2-way problem of classifying into sensitive or not (regardless of sensitivity type). Actual classes are in rows and predicted classes are in columns.

3-way classification						2-way classification				
	CNN-based			Caption-based				CNN-based		Caption-based
	NotSen	Place	Display	NotSen	Place	Display		NotSen	Sen	NotSen	Sen
NotSen	0.730	0.130	0.140	0.686	0.117	0.197	NotSen	0.730	0.270	0.686	0.314
Place	0.189	0.811	0	0.151	0.792	0.057	Sen	0.317	0.683	0.161	0.839
Display	0.300	0.043	0.657	0.143	0.008	0.849					

(although we cannot compare directly to the results presented in [18] or [29] because we use different datasets). We trained the strongly-supervised model by first generating a training set consisting of photos having monitors and not having monitors, and photos taken in bathrooms and locker rooms or elsewhere, by using the ground truth categories given in the COCO and Flickr8k datasets. This yielded 34,736 non-sensitive images, 6,135 images taken in sensitive places, and 4,379 images with displays. We used pre-trained AlexNet model (1000-way classifier on ImageNet data) and fine-tuned on our dataset by replacing the final fully connected layer with a 3-way classifier to correspond with our three-class problem.

We also ran the technique proposed here, where we first generate automatic image captions, and then search through the top five captions for each image for a set of pre-defined keywords (specifically "toilet," "bathroom," "locker," "lavatory," and "washroom" for sensitive place detection, and "computer," "laptop," "iphone," "smartphone," and "screen" for display detection). If any of these keywords is detected in any of the five captions, the image is classified as sensitive, and otherwise it is estimated to be not sensitive.

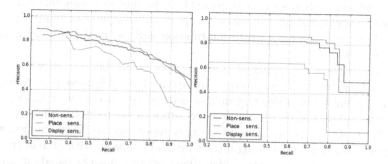

Fig. 3. Precision-recall curves for retrieving sensitive images using CNNs (left) and generated captions (right). (Color figure online)

Table 3 presents the confusion matrix for each method, using a set of 600 manually-annotated images from our lifelogging dataset as test data (with 300 non-sensitive images, 53 images in sensitive places, and 252 with digital displays). We see the supervised classifier has better prediction performance on finding sensitive places (0.811) than keyword based classifiers (0.792), while the caption-based technique classifier outperforms on predicting second type of sensitive images (0.849 vs. 0.657). In a real application, determining the type of private image is likely less important than simply deciding if it is private. The bottom table in Table 3 reflects this scenario, showing a confusion matrix which combines the two sensitive types and focuses on whether photos are sensitive or not.

From another point of view, sensitive photo detection is a retrieval problem. Figure 3 shows precision-recall curves for CNN and caption-based classifiers, respectively. They show the trade-off between selecting accurate sensitive photos (high precision) and obtaining a majority of all sensitive photos (high recall). For example, by using CNN classifier, we can obtain 80 % type 1 (sensitive place) photos with accuracy around 58 % (Fig. 3(left) green curve); by using the caption-based classifier, we can obtain 80 % of type 2 (digital display) sensitive photos with precision around 78 % (Fig. 3(right) blue curve).

The two approaches may also be complementary, since they use different forms of evidence in making classification decisions, and users in a real application could choose their own trade-off on how aggressively to filter lifelogging images.

6   Conclusion

In this paper, we have proposed the concept of using automatically-generated captions to help organize and annotate lifelogging image collections. We have proposed a deep learning-based captioning model that jointly labels photo streams in order to take advantage of temporal consistency between photos. Our evaluation suggests that modern automated captioning techniques could work well enough to be used in practical lifelogging photo applications. We hope our research will motivate further efforts of using lifelogging photos and descriptions together to help human memory recall the activities and scenarios.

Acknowledgments. This work was supported in part by the National Science Foundation (IIS-1253549 and CNS-1408730) and Google, and used compute facilities provided by NVidia, the Lilly Endowment through support of the IU PTI, and the Indiana METACyt Initiative. We thank Zhenhua Chen, Sally Crandall, and Xuan Dong for helping to label our lifelogging photos.

References

1. Azuma, R., Baillot, Y., Behringer, R., Feiner, S., Julier, S., MacIntyre, B.: Recent advances in augmented reality. IEEE Comput. Graph. Appl. **21**(6), 34–47 (2001)
2. Banerjee, S., Lavie, A.: METEOR: An automatic metric for MT evaluation with improved correlation with human judgments. In: ACL Workshop on Intrinsic and Extrinsic Evaluation Measures for Machine Translation and/or Summarization, pp. 65–72 (2005)
3. Batra, D., Yadollahpour, P., Guzman-Rivera, A., Shakhnarovich, G.: Diverse M-best solutions in markov random fields. In: Fitzgibbon, A., Lazebnik, S., Perona, P., Sato, Y., Schmid, C. (eds.) ECCV 2012. LNCS, vol. 7576, pp. 1–16. Springer, Heidelberg (2012). doi:10.1007/978-3-642-33715-4_1
4. Castro, D., Hickson, S., Bettadapura, V., Thomaz, E., Abowd, G., Christensen, H., Essa, I.: Predicting daily activities from egocentric images using deep learning. In: International Symposium on Wearable Computers (2015)
5. Elman, J.L.: Finding structure in time. Cogn. Sci. **14**(2), 179–211 (1990)
6. Erhan, D., Szegedy, C., Toshev, A., Anguelov, D.: Scalable object detection using deep neural networks. In: IEEE Conference on Computer Vision and Pattern Recognition. pp. 2155–2162 (2014)
7. Fathi, A., Li, Y., Rehg, J.M.: Learning to recognize daily actions using gaze. In: Fitzgibbon, A., Lazebnik, S., Perona, P., Sato, Y., Schmid, C. (eds.) ECCV 2012. LNCS, vol. 7572, pp. 314–327. Springer, Heidelberg (2012). doi:10.1007/978-3-642-33718-5_23
8. Fathi, A., Ren, X., Rehg, J.M.: Learning to recognize objects in egocentric activities. In: IEEE Conference on Computer Vision and Pattern Recognition, pp. 3281–3288 (2011)
9. Furnari, A., Farinella, G., Battiano, S.: Recognizing personal contexts from egocentric images. In: ICCV Workshops (2015)
10. Girshick, R., Donahue, J., Darrell, T., Malik, J.: Rich feature hierarchies for accurate object detection and semantic segmentation. In: IEEE Conference on Computer Vision and Pattern Recognition. pp. 580–587 (2014)
11. Graves, A.: Generating sequences with recurrent neural networks (2013). arXiv:1308.0850
12. Hodges, S., Williams, L., Berry, E., Izadi, S., Srinivasan, J., Butler, A., Smyth, G., Kapur, N., Wood, K.: Sensecam: a retrospective memory aid. In: ACM Conference on Ubiquitous Computing, pp. 177–193 (2006)
13. Jia, Y., Shelhamer, E., Donahue, J., Karayev, S., Long, J., Girshick, R., Guadarrama, S., Darrell, T.: Caffe: convolutional architecture for fast feature embedding (2014). arXiv:1408.5093
14. Karpathy, A., Fei-Fei, L.: Deep visual-semantic alignments for generating image descriptions (2014). arXiv:1412.2306
15. Karpathy, A., Johnson, J., Fei-Fei, L.: Visualizing and understanding recurrent networks (2015). arXiv:1506.02078
16. Karpathy, A., Joulin, A., Fei-Fei, L.: Deep fragment embeddings for bidirectional image sentence mapping. In: Advances in neural information processing systems, pp. 1889–1897 (2014)
17. Koller, D., Friedman, N.: Probabilistic Graphical Models Principles and Techniques. MIT Press, Cambridge (2009)
18. Korayem, M., Templeman, R., Chen, D., Crandall, D., Kapadia, A.: Enhancing lifelogging privacy by detecting screens. In: ACM CHI Conference on Human Factors in Computing Systems (2016)

19. Krizhevsky, A., Sutskever, I., Hinton, G.: Imagenet classification with deep convolutional neural networks. In: Advances in Neural Information Processing Systems, pp. 1097–1105 (2012)
20. Lin, C.Y.: Rouge: a package for automatic evaluation of summaries. In: Workshop On Text Summarization Branches Out (2004)
21. Lin, T.-Y., Maire, M., Belongie, S., Hays, J., Perona, P., Ramanan, D., Dollár, P., Zitnick, C.L.: Microsoft COCO: common objects in context. In: Fleet, D., Pajdla, T., Schiele, B., Tuytelaars, T. (eds.) ECCV 2014. LNCS, vol. 8693, pp. 740–755. Springer, Heidelberg (2014). doi:10.1007/978-3-319-10602-1_48
22. Mann, S., Nolan, J., Wellman, B.: Sousveillance: inventing and using wearable computing devices for data collection in surveillance environments. Surveill. Soc. 1(3), 331–355 (2002)
23. Mao, J., Xu, W., Yang, Y., Wang, J., Yuille, A.L.: Explain images with multimodal recurrent neural networks (2014). arXiv:1410.1090
24. Papineni, K., Roukos, S., Ward, T., Zhu, W.J.: BLEU: a method for automatic evaluation of machine translation. In: Annual Meeting of the Association for Computational Linguistics, pp. 311–318 (2002)
25. Ryoo, M., Matthies, L.: First-person activity recognition: what are they doing to me? In: IEEE Conference on Computer Vision and Pattern Recognition pp. 2730–2737 (2013)
26. Ryoo, M., Fuchs, T.J., Xia, L., Aggarwal, J.K., Matthies, L.: Robot-centric activity prediction from first-person videos: what will they do to me. In: ACM/IEEE International Conference on Human-Robot Interaction, pp. 295–302 (2015)
27. Simonyan, K., Zisserman, A.: Very deep convolutional networks for large-scale image recognition (2014). arXiv:1409.1556
28. Szegedy, C., Toshev, A., Erhan, D.: Deep neural networks for object detection. In: Advances in Neural Information Processing Systems, pp. 2553–2561 (2013)
29. Templeman, R., Korayem, M., Crandall, D.J., Kapadia, A.: Placeavoider: steering first-person cameras away from sensitive spaces. In: Network and Distributed Systems Security Symposium (2014)
30. Vedantam, R., Zitnick, C., Parikh, D.: Cider: Consensus-based image description evaluation. In: IEEE Conference on Computer Vision and Pattern Recognition, pp. 4566–4575 (2015)
31. Venugopalan, S., Rohrbach, M., Donahue, J., Mooney, R., Darrell, T., Saenko, K.: Sequence to sequence-video to text (2015). arXiv:1505.00487
32. Vinyals, O., Toshev, A., Bengio, S., Erhan, D.: Show and tell: a neural image caption generator (2014). arXiv:1411.4555
33. Zhu, Y., Kiros, R., Zemel, R., Salakhutdinov, R., Urtasun, R., Torralba, A., Fidler, S.: Aligning books and movies: Towards story-like visual explanations by watching movies and reading book (2015). arXiv:1506.06724

Temporal Segmentation of Egocentric Videos to Highlight Personal Locations of Interest

Antonino Furnari[✉], Giovanni Maria Farinella, and Sebastiano Battiato

Department of Mathematics and Computer Science,
University of Catania, Catania, Italy
{furnari,gfarinella,battiato}@dmi.unict.it

Abstract. With the increasing availability of wearable cameras, the acquisition of egocentric videos is becoming common in many scenarios. However, the absence of explicit structure in such videos (e.g., video chapters) makes their exploitation difficult. We propose to segment unstructured egocentric videos to highlight the presence of personal locations of interest specified by the end-user. Given the large variability of the visual content acquired by such devices, it is necessary to design explicit rejection mechanisms able to detect negatives (i.e., frames not related to any considered location) learning only from positive ones at training time. To challenge the problem, we collected a dataset of egocentric videos containing 10 personal locations of interest. We propose a method to segment egocentric videos performing discrimination among the personal locations of interest, rejection of negative frames, and enforcing temporal coherence between neighboring predictions.

Keywords: First person vision · Egocentric video · Context-based analysis · Aware computing · Video segmentation

1 Introduction and Motivation

Wearable cameras have recently become popular in many application scenarios including law enforcement [1], assistive technologies [2], life-logging [3] and social cameras [4]. Despite the large amount of information that such systems can potentially acquire, the exploitation of egocentric videos is quite difficult due to the lack of explicit structure, e.g., in the form of scene cuts or video chapters. Depending on the considered goal, long egocentric videos tend to contain much uninformative content like, for instance, transiting through a corridor, walking, or driving to the office. Therefore, as pointed out in [5], automated tools are needed to enable faster access to the information stored in such videos and index their visual content. Towards this direction, researches have investigated methods to produce short informative video summaries from long egocentric

Electronic supplementary material The online version of this chapter (doi:10.1007/978-3-319-46604-0_34) contains supplementary material, which is available to authorized users.

G. Hua and H. Jégou (Eds.): ECCV 2016 Workshops, Part I, LNCS 9913, pp. 474–489, 2016.
DOI: 10.1007/978-3-319-46604-0_34

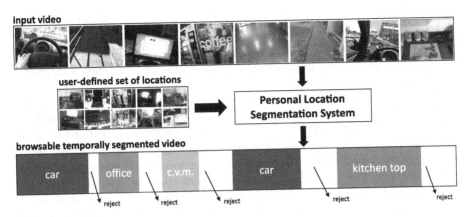

Fig. 1. Overall schema of the proposed temporal segmentation of an egocentric video.

videos [6–8], recognize the actions performed by the wearer [9–13], and segment the videos according to detected ego-motion patterns [5,14]. While current literature focuses on providing general-purpose methods which are usually optimized using data acquired by many users, we argue that, given the subjective nature of egocentric videos, more attention should be devoted to user-specific methods.

In this paper, we propose to segment unstructured egocentric videos into coherent shots related to user-specified personal locations of interest. Our notion of personal location builds on the one introduced in [15]: *a fixed, distinguishable spatial environment in which the user can perform one or more activities which may or may not be specific to the considered location.* According to this notion, a personal location is specified at the instance level (e.g., my kitchen, my office, my car), rather than at the category level (e.g., a kitchen, an office, a car). It should be noted that personal locations are very specific to the user defining them and should not be confused with the general concept of visual scene. Indeed, a given set of personal locations could include different instances corresponding to the same scene category (e.g., office vs lab office). Under such conditions, classical scene-tuned image descriptor such as GIST [16] would perform poorly as shown in [15]. Figure 1 shows a schema of the investigated problem. The user defines a number of locations of interest by providing minimal training data in the form of short videos (e.g., a 10 s video per location). The user is just asked to wear his camera and briefly look around while he is in the considered location. Therefore, each training video is deemed to contain the most common views of the considered location. Given the input egocentric video and the user-defined set of locations, the task is to establish for each frame in the video if it is related to either one of the considered personal locations or none of them (i.e., it is a negative sample). We want to emphasize that in a real-world scenario in which the system is set up by the end user himself, training must be simple and achievable with few training data. Moreover, given the large variability exhibited by egocentric videos, it is unfeasible to ask the user to acquire a significant quantity of negative samples [15]. Therefore, we assume that only positive samples of different locations are provided by the user and propose a method to detect negative samples automatically, without training on them. We would like to note that avoiding to learn from negative frames is not limiting from a performance stand point. In fact, as we show in the experiments, even when negative samples are available for learning purposes, training a multi-class classifier to correctly detect them is not trivial.

The proposed method uses a Convolutional Neural Network (CNN) to discriminate among different locations and a Hidden Markov Model (HMM) to enforce temporal coherence among neighbouring predictions. Differently from previous works, we treat the rejection of negative samples explicitly and introduces a non-parametric method to reject negative frames. Being non-parametric, our method does not need any negative samples at training time. We discuss the computational performances of the proposed method and also suggest a simplified system which is efficient enough to run in real-time. This allows possible uses in real-time, assistive-related applications. The main contributions of this paper are summarized in the following: (1) we study the problem of segmenting egocentric videos using minimal user-provided data and propose a dataset comprising more than 2 hours of labelled egocentric videos covering 10 different locations plus various negative environments, (2) we propose a method for egocentric video segmentation and negative sample rejection which trains only on the available positive samples, (3) we show how CNNs can be exploited in this domain (where training data is assumed to be scarce) experimenting a series of simple architectural tweaks to avoid over-fitting during fine-tuning and optimize computational performances. Experiments show that the proposed system outperforms baselines and existing approaches by a good margin and with an accuracy of over the 90 % on the challenging sequences included in the proposed benchmark dataset.

The remainder of the paper is organized as follows. Section 2 summarizes the related work. Section 3 describes the dataset. Section 4 presents the proposed system. Section 5 reports the experiments and discusses the results. Finally, Sect. 6 concludes the paper.

2   Related Work

Researchers have explored the issues and opportunities related to first person vision ever since the 90s. Relevant endeavors have focused on investigating contextual awareness and localization [17–19], improving human-machine interaction [20,21], understanding and recognizing human activities [10,22–24], indexing and summarizing egocentric videos [5,7,14]. In particular, our work is related to previous studies on contextual awareness in wearable and mobile computing. In [25], efficient computational methods for scene categorization are proposed for embedded devices. In [17], some basic tasks and locations related to the Patrol game are recognized from egocentric videos in order to assist the user during the game. In [18], personal locations are recognized from egocentric video based on the approaching trajectories observed from the camera point of view. In [19], a context-based vision system for place and scene recognition is proposed and deployed on a wearable system. In [26], still images of sensitive spaces are detected for privacy purposes combining GPS information and an image classifier. In [23], Convolutional Neural Networks and Random Decision Forests are exploited to recognize human activities from egocentric images. In [15], a benchmark of different wearable devices and image representation techniques for personal context recognition is proposed.

While current literature focuses primarily on providing general-purpose methods which can rely on data acquired by multiple user, we focus on a personalized scenario in which the user himself provides the training data and sets up the system. Under such conditions, it is not possible to rely on a big corpus of supervised data, since it is not feasible to ask the user to collect and label it. Moreover, differently from related works, we explicitly consider the problem of rejecting negative samples, i.e., recognizing locations the user is not interested in, so to discard irrelevant information.

3   Proposed Dataset

We collected a dataset of egocentric videos related to ten different personal locations, plus various negative ones. The considered locations arise from a possible daily routine: Car, Coffee Vending Machine (C.V.M.), Office, Lab Office (L.O.), Living Room (L.R.), Piano, Kitchen Top (K.T.), Sink, Studio, Garage. The dataset has been acquired using a hardware configuration similar to the best performing in the benchmark proposed in [15]: a Looxcie LX2 camera equipped with a wide angular converter. Such configuration allows to acquire videos at a resolution of 640 × 480 pixels and with a Field Of View of approximately 100°. The use of a wide-angular device is justified by the ability to acquire a large amount of information on the scene, albeit at the cost of radial distortion, which in some cases requires dedicated computation [27,28]. Figure 2 shows some example frames from the dataset. The dataset exhibits a high degree of intra-class variability (e.g., Car and Garage classes) and small inter-class variability in some cases (e.g., Office, Lab Office and Studio classes).

As discussed in the introduction, we assume that the user is required to provide only minimal data to define his personal locations of interest. Therefore, the training set consists in 10 short videos (one per each location) with an average length of 10 s per video. The test set consists in 10 video sequences covering the considered personal locations of interest, negative frames and transitions among locations. Each frame in the test sequences has been manually labeled as either one of the 10 locations of interest or as a negative. Table 1 summarizes the content of the test sequences with the related transitions. The dataset is also provided with an independent validation set which can be used to optimize the hyperparameters. The validation set contains 10 medium length (approximately 5 to 10 min) videos of activities performed in the considered locations (one video per location). Validation videos have been temporally subsampled in order to extract exactly 200 frames per location, while all frames are considered for training and test videos. We have also acquired 10 medium length videos containing negative samples from which we uniformly extract 300 frames for training and 200 frames

Car   C.V.M.   Office   L.O.   L.R.   Piano   K.T.   Sink   Studio   Garage

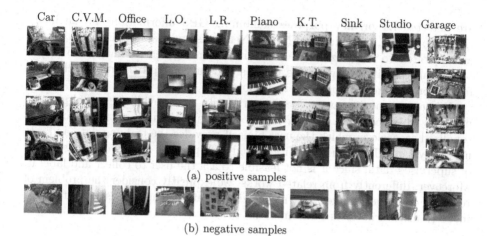

(a) positive samples

(b) negative samples

Fig. 2. Some sample frames from the proposed dataset (a) positive samples (b) negative samples.

Table 1. A summary of the location transitions contained in the test sequences. "N" represents a negative segment (to be rejected by the final system).

Sequence	Context transitions	Length
1	Car → N → Office → N → Lab Office	00:11:27
2	Office → N → Lab Office	00:05:55
3	Lab Office → N → Office → N → C.V.M.	00:07:24
4	TV → N → Piano → N → Sink	00:11:40
5	Kitchen → N → Sink → N → Piano	00:10:41
6	Kitchen → N → Sink → N → TV	00:11:18
7	Piano → N → Sink → N → TV	00:04:57
8	Studio → N → Car → N → Garage	00:06:51
9	Car → N → Garage → N → Studio	00:05:17
10	Car → N → Studio → N → Garage	00:06:05
Total length		01:21:35

for validation. Negative samples are provided in order to allow comparisons with methods which explicitly learn from negatives. Please note that the proposed method does not need to learn from negatives and hence it discards them at training time.

The proposed dataset contains 2142 positive, plus 300 negative frames for training, 2000 positive, plus 200 negative frames for validation and 132234 mixed (both positive and negative) frames for testing purposes. The dataset is available at the web page http://iplab.dmi.unict.it/PersonalContexts/.

4   Proposed Method

Given an egocentric video as an ordered collection of image frames $\mathcal{V} = \{I_1, \ldots, I_n\}$, our system must be able to (1) correctly classify each frame I_i as one of the considered locations, (2) reject negative frames, (3) segment temporally coherent sub-sequences related to the locations of interest. The system eventually returns the segmentation $\mathcal{S} = \{C_1, \ldots, C_n\}$, where $C_i \in \{0, \ldots, M-1\}$ is the class label associated to frame I_i ($C_i = 0$ representing the negative class label) and M is the total number of classes including negatives ($M = 11$ in our case - 10 locations, plus the negative class). Rejection of negative samples is usually tackled increasing the number of classes by one and explicitly learning to recognize negative samples. However, this procedure requires a number of training negative samples which may not be easily acquirable by the user in a real-world scenario. Indeed, given the large variability of visual content acquired by wearable devices, it would be infeasible to ask the user to acquire a sufficient number of representative negative samples. Therefore, we propose to treat negative rejection separately from classification and introduce a non-parametric rejection mechanism which does not need negative samples at training time.

We first consider a multi-class component which is trained solely on positive samples to discriminate among the considered positive $M-1$ classes. Since the multi-class model ignores the presence of negative frames, it only allows to estimate the posterior probability:

$$p(C_i | I_i, C_i \neq 0). \tag{1}$$

We propose to quantify the probability $p(C_i = 0 | I_i)$ of a given frame I_i to be negative as the uncertainty of the multi-class model in predicting the class labels related to last k frames (in our experiments we use $k = 30$, which is equivalent to one second at 30 fps). Specifically, considering that both the visual content and class label are deemed to change slowly in egocentric videos, we assume that the past k frames $\mathcal{I}_i^k = \{I_i, I_{i-1}, \ldots, I_{\max(i-k+1,1)}\}$ are related to the same class. Such assumption may be imprecise when $\mathcal{I}_i^k$ contains the boundary between two different locations. However, such cases are rather rare and if k spans over one second or less, the assumption only affects the boundary localization accuracy and is not expected to have a huge impact on the overall accuracy. Since the multi-class model has been tuned only on positive samples, we expect it to exhibit low uncertainty when the frames in $\mathcal{I}_i^k$ belong to one of the positive classes, while we expect a large uncertainty in the case of negative samples. Similarly to [29], we measure model uncertainty computing the variation ratio of the distribution of labels $\mathcal{Y}_i^k = \{y_i, \ldots, y_{\max(i-k+1,1)}\}$ predicted within $\mathcal{I}_i^k$ by maximizing the posterior probability in Eq. (1): $y_i = \arg\max_j p(C_i = j | I_i, C_i \neq 0), j = 1, \ldots, M-1$. We finally assign the probability of I_i being a negative sample as follows:

$$p(C_i = 0 | I_i) = 1 - \frac{\sum_j \mathbb{1}(y_j = \tilde{y}_i^k)}{\#\{\mathcal{Y}_i^k\}} \tag{2}$$

where $\mathbb{1}(\cdot)$ denotes the indicator function and $\tilde{y}_i^k$ represents the mode of y_i^k. It should be noted that the definition reported in Eq. (2) is totally arbitrary and encodes the belief that the model should agree on similar inputs if they are positive samples. In practice, given a number of predictions computed within a small temporal window, we quantify the probability of having a negative sample as the fraction of labels disagreeing with the mode.

Considering that $C_i = 0$ and $C_i \neq 0$ are disjoint events (and hence $p(C_i \neq 0|I_i) = 1 - p(C_i = 0|I_i)$), the probabilities reported in Eqs. (1) and (2) can be combined as follows:

$$p(C_i|I_i) = \begin{cases} p(C_i = 0|I_i) & \text{if } C_i = 0 \\ p(C_i \neq 0|I_i) \cdot p(C_i|I_i, C_i \neq 0) & \text{otherwise} \end{cases}. \qquad (3)$$

The final class prediction for frame I_i (including the rejection of negative samples) can be obtained maximizing Eq. (3) as follows:

$$C_i^* = \arg \max_j p(C_i = j|I_i) \qquad (4)$$

Given the nature of egocentric videos, subsequent frames will be likely related to the same location, while a sudden change of location is a rare event. Such a prior can be taken into account during the computation of the final segmentation using a Hidden Markov Model (HMM). We consider the probability $p(\mathcal{S}|\mathcal{V})$ which, according to the Bayes' rule, can be expressed as follows:

$$p(\mathcal{S}|\mathcal{V}) \propto p(\mathcal{V}|\mathcal{S})p(\mathcal{S}). \qquad (5)$$

Assuming conditional independence of the frames with respect to each other given their classes ($I_i \perp\!\!\!\perp I_j|C_i, \forall i,j \in \{1,2,\ldots,n\}, i \neq j$), and applying the Markovian assumption on the conditional probability distribution of the class labels ($p(C_i|C_{i-1}\ldots C_1) = p(C_i|C_{i-1})$), Eq. (5) can be written as:

$$p(\mathcal{S}|\mathcal{V}) \propto p(C_1) \prod_{i=2}^{n} p(C_i|C_{i-1}) \prod_{i=1}^{n} p(I_i|C_i). \qquad (6)$$

Probability $p(C_1)$ is assumed to be constant over the different classes and can be ignored when maximizing Eq. (6). Probability $p(I_i|C_i)$ can be inverted using the Bayes law $p(I_i|C_i) \propto p(C_i|I_i)p(I_i)$. Since I_i is observed, term $p(I_i)$ can be ignored, while $p(C_i|I_i)$ is estimated using Eq. (3). Equation (6) can be hence written as:

$$p(\mathcal{S}|\mathcal{V}) \propto \prod_{i=2}^{n} p(C_i|C_{i-1}) \prod_{i=1}^{n} p(C_i|I_i). \qquad (7)$$

The term $p(C_i|C_{i-1})$ is the HMM state transition probability. Transition probabilities in Hidden Markov Models can generally be learned from the data as done in [19], or defined ad hoc to express a prior belief as done in [26]. Since we assume that few training data should be provided by the user and no labeled sequences are available at training time, we define an ad-hoc transition probability as suggested by [26]:

$$p(C_i|C_{i-1}) = \begin{cases} \varepsilon, & \text{if } C_i \neq C_{i-1} \\ 1 - (M-1)\varepsilon, & \text{otherwise} \end{cases} \tag{8}$$

where ε is a small constant (we use the machine accuracy in double precision 2.22×10^{-16} in our experiments). The state transition probability defined in Eq. (8) enforces coherence between subsequent states and penalizes random state changes. The final segmentation of the input egocentric video is obtained choosing the one which maximizes the probability in Eq. (7) by using the Viterbi algorithm [30]:

$$\mathcal{S}^* = \arg \max_{\mathcal{S}} p(\mathcal{S}|\mathcal{V}). \tag{9}$$

5   Experimental Settings and Results

Experiments are performed on the dataset described in Sect. 3. All compared methods are trained on the whole training set and evaluated on the test sequences. The validation set is used to tune hyper-parameters and select the best performing iteration in the case of CNNs. In Sect. 5.1, we study the performances of the proposed method, paying particular attention to optimization. Specifically, we evaluate different architectural tweaks which help reducing over-fitting when fine-tuning Convolutional Neural Networks on our small realistic dataset (≈ 200 samples per class) and reduce computational requirements. Moreover, we discuss the influence of the different components included in our method (i.e., multiclass classifier, rejection mechanism, and HMM). In Sect. 5.2 we compare our method with respect to the state of the art.

5.1   Proposed Method: Optimization and Performances Evaluation

The multi-class classifier employed in the proposed method could be implemented using any algorithm able to output posterior probabilities in the form of Eq. (1). We consider Convolutional Neural Networks given their compactness and the superior performances shown on many tasks including personal location recognition [15]. In particular, following [15], we fine-tune the VGG-S network proposed in [31] on our training set. Since the VGG network has been trained on the ImageNet dataset, we expect the learned features to be related to objects and hence relevant to the task of location recognition, as highlighted in [32].

Optimization of the Multi-class Classifier. Fine-tuning a large CNN using a small training set (≈ 200 samples per class) is not trivial and some architectural details can be tuned in order to optimize performances. Specifically, we assess the impact of the following architectural settings: (1) locking the convolutional layers (i.e., setting their relative learning rate to zero), (2) disabling dropout in

Table 2. Optimization of the multi-class classifier. Architectural settings: ⟨L⟩ the convolutional layers are locked, ⟨ND⟩ dropout is disabled, ⟨128⟩ fully connected layers are reduced to 128 units and reinitialized, ⟨LR⟩ fully connected layers are replaced by a single logistic regression layer. Reported times are average per-image processing times. Maxima per column are reported in <u>**underlined bold digits**</u>, while second maxima are reported in **bold digits**.

Id	Settings			Accuracy			Computational performances	
				Discrim.	+Rejection	+HMM	Dimensions	Time
[a]				76.90	69.60	73.83	378 MB	13.23 ms
[b]	L			83.30	76.06	83.22	378 MB	13.13 ms
[c]	L	ND		**94.53**	**85.00**	**88.63**	378 MB	13.10 ms
[d]	L	128		83.07	77.49	82.84	34 MB	10.32 ms
[e]	L	ND	128	77.09	71.99	73.59	34 MB	10.28 ms
[f]	L	LR		**92.31**	**81.00**	**85.37**	26 MB	10.23 ms

Table 3. Per-class true positive rates for the considered configurations. See Table 2 for a legend.

Id	Settings			Per-Class True Positive Rate (TPR)										
				Car	C.V.M.	Gar.	K.T.	L.Off.	Off.	Piano	Sink	Stud.	L.R.	Neg.
[a]				91.28	**98.73**	**98.71**	**100.0**	95.87	**94.81**	98.52	**100.0**	99.40	**99.20**	36.91
[b]	L			90.71	98.53	98.41	99.60	93.83	**93.57**	98.48	99.00	98.50	98.91	47.77
[c]	L	ND		75.57	92.42	87.60	97.95	84.08	71.67	93.32	96.69	94.09	89.73	**82.34**
[d]	L	128		**99.09**	94.36	74.90	89.46	93.51	84.66	98.16	98.90	**99.72**	99.09	51.22
[e]	L	ND	128	**99.57**	95.43	98.31	**100.0**	**98.54**	90.25	**98.68**	**99.51**	**99.82**	99.14	36.51
[f]	L	LR		94.53	78.93	85.88	78.39	89.91	60.28	93.57	96.91	97.46	98.20	**61.66**

the fully connected layers, (3) reducing the number of units in the fully connected layers from 4096 to 128, (4) removing the fully connected layers and attaching a logistic regression (softmax) layer directly to the last convolutional layer. In the following, we discuss different combinations of the aforementioned architectural settings in order to assess the influence of each considered setting. Results for these experiments are reported in Tables 2 and 3.

Table 2 is organized as follows. Each row of the table is related to a different experiment. The first column (Id) reports unique identifiers for the considered methods. The second column (Settings) summarizes the architectural settings related to the specific method. The third column (Discrimination) reports the accuracy of the multi-class model alone (i.e., class labels are directly computed using Eq. (1)). Note that such accuracy values are computed removing all negative samples from the test set. The fourth column (+Rejection) reports the accuracy of the models after applying the proposed rejection method (i.e., labels are obtained using Eq. (4)). The fifth column (+HMM) reports the accuracy of the complete method including the Hidden Markov Model (i.e., final segmentation labels are obtained using Eq. (9)). Column 6 reports the size of the models in megabytes. Column 7 finally reports the average time needed to predict the class label of a single frame[1]. Table 3 reports per-class true positive rates for the considered configurations.

The reported results highlight the importance of tuning the considered architectural settings to improve both computational performances and accuracy. In particular, locking the convolutional layers allows to significantly improve the performances of the fine-tuned model (compare [b] to [a] in Table 2)[2]. Significant performance improvements are observable when the CNN is evaluated alone (Discrim. column) as well as when the model is integrated in the proposed system (columns +Rejection and +HMM). This result highlights how the unlocked network suffers from over-fitting, due to the high number of parameters to optimize with relatively few training data. It should be noted that, in our experiments, only convolutional layers are locked, while fully connected ones are still optimized. Locking convolutional layers, hence, allows to use part of the network as a bank of object-related feature extractors (the pre-trained convolutional layers), while optimizing the way such features are combined in the fully connected layers.

Disabling dropout has a positive impact when convolutional layers are locked and fully connected layers are fine-tuned ([c] vs [b]). This indicates that dropout is causing the model to underfit due to the scarcity of training data. Interestingly, when fully connected layers are reduced to 128 units and hence reinitialized with Gaussian noise, disabling dropout seems to favor overfitting as one would generally expect (compare [e] to [d]). This behavior is probably due to the inclination of randomly reinitialized layers to easily co-adapt [35]. Reducing the dimensionality of the fully connected layers to 128 units helps reducing the dimensions of the network and improving its speed, but results in a substantial loss in accuracy due to the needed reinitialization of the weights (compare [d] to [c]).

In order to devise a more compact model, we finally consider replacing the fully connected layers with a logistic regressor (i.e., a layer with 10 units followed by softmax). In this case, the locked convolutional layers of the VGG-S network are used as feature extractors, while predictions are performed combining them using a simple logistic regressor classifier. This configuration allows to greatly reduce memory and time requirements at the cost of a modest loss in terms of accuracy (compare [f] to [c], [d], [e]).

Among all compared method, the most accurate is [c], followed by the computationally efficient [f]. Both methods outperform the others by a good margin. Moreover, it is worth noting that [f] is more than 90 % smaller and 20 % faster than [c] while only about 3 % less accurate. Such result is particularly interesting in real-time scenarios involving low-resources and embedded devices (e.g., in smart glasses or in a drone). Finally, as can be noted from Table 3, only the two best configurations (methods [c] and [f]) succeed in correctly rejecting negative samples, while other methods yield lower true positive rates.

---

[1] Times have been estimated running the CNN models on a NVIDIA GeForce GTX 480 GPU using the Caffe framework [33]. They include the rejection of negative frames but do not take into account the application of the Hidden Markov Model.

[2] SVM models are tested on a Intel(R) Core(TM) i7-3930K CPU @ 3.20 GHz with LIBSVM [34].

Performances of the Proposed Method. As discussed above, columns 3 to 5 in Table 2 report performances related to the main components involved in the proposed method, i.e., multi-class classifier, rejection mechanism and Hidden Markov Model. As can be noted, high accuracies can be achieved when discriminating among a finite number of possible locations (column Discrim.). The need for a rejection mechanism in real-world scenarios makes the problem much harder, decreasing classification accuracy by 10 % in average (compare Discrim. with +Rejection columns). These results suggest that more efforts should be devoted to effective rejection mechanisms in order to make current classification systems useful in real world applications. Indeed, any real system devoted to distinguish among a number of classes must be able to deal with the negative ones. Enforcing temporal coherence using a Hidden Markov Model generally helps reducing the gap between simple discrimination and discrimination + rejection (consider for instance methods [c] and [f]). The effects of the rejection and HMM modules are qualitatively illustrated in Fig. 3. As can be noted, simple class discrimination (top row) yields noisy predictions when ground truth frames are negative. The rejection mechanism (second row) successfully detects negative segments. The use of a HMM (third row) finally helps reducing sudden changes in the predicted labels.

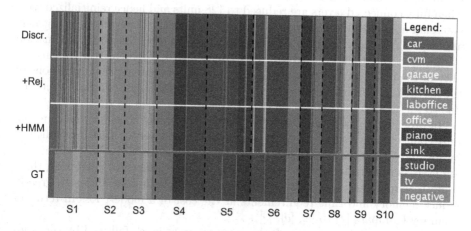

Fig. 3. Graphical representation of the labels produced by the proposed method (method [c] in Table 2). Each row reports the concatenation of labels produced for all test sequences. Boundaries between sequences are highlighted with black dashed lines and "S1" ... "S10" labels. The visualization is intended to qualitatively assess the influence of the rejection and HMM components on the performances of the overall system. Specifically, the first three rows report labels obtained using the multi-class classifier, the proposed rejection mechanism and the HMM, similarly to what discussed for Table 2. The last row reports the ground truth. Detailed visualizations for each sequence are available in the supplementary material available online. Best seen in color. (Color figure online)

5.2   Comparison with the State of the Art

To assess the effectiveness of the proposed method, we compare it with respect to two baselines and an existing method for personal location recognition [15]. The first baseline tackles the location recognition problem through feature matching. The system is initialized extracting SIFT feature points from each test image and storing them for later use. Given the current frame, SIFT features are extracted and matched with all images in the training set. To reduce the influence of outlier feature points, for each considered image pair, we perform a geometric verification using the MSAC algorithm [36] based on an affine model. Classification is hence performed considering the training set image presenting the highest number of inliers and selecting the class to which it belongs. In this case, the most straightforward way to perform rejection probably consists in setting a threshold on the number of inliers: if an image is a positive, it is expected to yield a good match with some example in the dataset, otherwise only weak matches should be obtained. Since it is not clear how such a threshold should be arbitrarily set, we learn it from data. To do so, we first normalize the number of inliers by the number of features extracted from the current frame. We then select the threshold which best separates the validation set from the training negatives. To speed up computation, input images are rescaled in order to have a standard height of 256 pixels (the same size to which images are resized when fed to CNN models), keeping the original aspect ratio.

The second considered baseline consists in a CNN trained to discriminate directly between locations of interest and negatives. In contrast with the proposed method, the baseline explicitly learns from negative samples. Hence, in our settings, the model is trained on 11 classes comprising 10 locations of interest, plus the negative class. This baseline is implemented adopting the same architecture as the one of method [c], which is the best performing configuration in our experiments. It should be noted that training negatives are independent

Table 4. Comparisons with the state of the art. Methods [c] and [f] are reported from Table 2 for convenience. Architectural settings: $\boxed{L}$ the convolutional layers are locked, $\boxed{ND}$ dropout is disabled, $\boxed{LR}$ fully connected layers are replaced by a single logistic regression layer, $\boxed{SIFT}$ the SIFT feature matching baseline, $\boxed{NE}$ the model is trained on both positive and negative samples, $\boxed{SVM}$ classification based on one-class and multiclass SVM classifiers.

Id	Settings	Accuracy			Computational performances	
		Discrim.	+Rejection	+HMM	Dimensions	Time
[c]	$\boxed{L}$ $\boxed{ND}$	**94.53**	**85.00**	**88.63**	378 MB	13.10 ms
[f]	$\boxed{L}$ $\boxed{LR}$	92.31	81.00	85.37	26 MB	10.23 ms
[g]	$\boxed{SIFT}$	34.64	33.16	–	71 MB	5170.1 ms
[h]	$\boxed{L}$ $\boxed{ND}$ $\boxed{NE}$	73.84	76.42	79.69	378 MB	12.82 ms
[i]	$\boxed{SVM}$ [15]	87.76	74.14	79.64	423 MB	97.83 ms

Table 5. Per-class true positive rates of the compared methods. See Table 4 for a legend.

Id	Settings			Per-Class True Positive Rate (TPR)										
				Car	C.V.M.	Gar.	K.T.	L.Off.	Off.	Piano	Sink	Stud.	L.R.	Neg.
[c]	L	ND		75.57	92.42	**87.60**	**97.95**	84.08	**71.67**	**93.32**	**96.69**	94.09	89.73	**82.34**
[f]	L	LR		**94.53**	78.93	85.88	78.39	**89.91**	60.28	**93.57**	**96.91**	**97.46**	98.20	61.66
[g]	SIFT			4.90	5.55	0.02	71.45	15.37	16.62	84.98	22.21	12.80	79.77	24.22
[h]	L	ND	NE	78.16	95.23	71.48	97.53	73.54	50.03	71.95	93.43	**95.70**	73.49	**95.72**
[i]	SVM	[15]		74.97	**98.16**	**97.63**	**98.45**	88.60	**92.27**	79.13	69.25	59.16	**99.13**	06.58

from validation and test negatives. We also compare our method with respect to the one proposed in [15]. Such method performs negative rejection and location recognition using a cascade of One-Class and multiclass SVM classifiers trained on features extracted employing the VGG network [31].

Tables 4 and 5 compare the performances of the considered methods. As can be noted, the proposed methods [c] and [f] retain the highest accuracies in Table 4. Requiring about 5 s to process each frame, the SIFT matching method ([g] in Table 4) is the slowest among the compared ones. Moreover, SIFT matching achieves poor results on the considered task, which indicates that it is not able to generalize to new views of the same scene and to cope with the many variabilities typical of egocentric videos. It should be noted that, since the SIFT baseline does not output any probability values, the HMM cannot be applied in this case.

Baseline [h] retains a high TPR on negative samples (see Neg. column in Table 5). However TPRs related to other classes and the accuracy of the overall

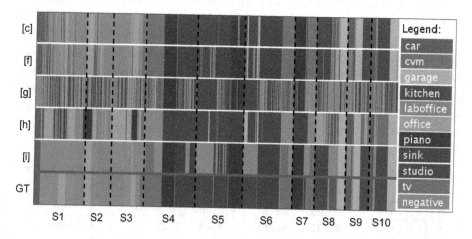

Fig. 4. Graphical representation of the segmentation results produced by the considered methods (see Table 4). Detailed visualizations for each sequence are available in the supplementary material. Best seen in color. (Color figure online)

system are lower when compared to the proposed approaches. This indicates how learning from negative samples is not trivial in the proposed problem. The method introduced in [15] is outperformed by the proposed methods (compare [i] to [c]-[f]) and gives inconsistent results in the rejection of negative frames (see column Neg. in Table 5). Moreover, the proposed approaches are significantly faster and have smaller size. Figure 4 finally reports segmentation results of all compared methods for qualitative assessment.

6   Conclusion

We have proposed a method to segment egocentric videos in order to highlight personal locations of interest. The system can be trained with few positive samples provided by the user. Convolutional Neural Networks are used to discriminate among positive locations, while a non-parametric rejection method is used to reject locations not specified by the user. A Hidden Markov Model is employed to enforce temporal coherence among neighboring predictions. We show how the architecture of the employed CNN can be tuned to optimize performances both in terms of accuracy and computational requirements. The effectiveness of the proposed method is assessed comparing it with respect to two baselines and a state of the art method. Future works will concentrate on studying the generalization ability of the method by considering multiple users in the personal location of interest recognition problem.

References

1. White, M.D.: Police Officer Body-worn Cameras: Assessing the Evidence. Office of Community Oriented Policing Services, Washington (2014)
2. Lee, M.L., Dey, A.K.: Lifelogging memory appliance for people with episodic memory impairment. In: Proceedings of the 10th International Conference on Ubiquitous Computing, pp. 44–53 (2008)
3. Gurrin, C., Smeaton, A.F., Doherty, A.R.: Lifelogging: personal big data. Found. Trends Inf. Retr. **8**(1), 1–125 (2014)
4. Ortis, A., Farinella, G.M., D'Amico, V., Addesso, L., Torrisi, G., Battiato, S.: RECfusion: automatic video curation driven by visual content popularity. In: ACM Multimedia (2015)
5. Poleg, Y., Arora, C., Peleg, S.: Temporal segmentation of egocentric videos. In: Computer Vision and Pattern Recognition, pp. 2537–2544 (2014)
6. Aizawa, K., Ishijima, K., Shiina, M.: Summarizing wearable video. In: International Conference on Image Processing. vol. 3, pp. 398–401 (2001)
7. Lu, Z., Grauman, K.: Story-driven summarization for egocentric video. In: Computer Vision and Pattern Recognition. pp. 2714–2721 (2013)
8. Xu, J., Mukherjee, L., Li, Y., Warner, J., Rehg, J.M., Singh, V.: Gaze-enabled egocentric video summarization via constrained submodular maximization. In: IEEE Conference on Computer Vision and Pattern Recognition pp. 2235–2244 (2015)
9. Kitani, K.M., Okabe, T., Sato, Y., Sugimoto, A.: Fast unsupervised ego-action learning for first-person sports videos. In: IEEE Conference on Computer Vision and Pattern Recognition, pp. 3241–3248 (2011)

10. Fathi, A., Farhadi, A., Rehg, J.M.: Understanding egocentric activities. In: IEEE International Conference on Computer Vision, pp. 407–414 (2011)
11. Ryoo, M.S., Rothrock, B., Matthies, L.: Pooled motion features for first-person videos (2014). arXiv preprint arXiv:1412.6505
12. Li, Y., Ye, Z., Rehg, J.M.: Delving into egocentric actions. In: IEEE Conference on Computer Vision and Pattern Recognition, pp. 287–295 (2015)
13. Spriggs, E.H., De La Torre, F., Hebert, M.: Temporal segmentation and activity classification from first-person sensing. In: Computer Vision and Pattern Recognition Workshops, pp. 17–24 (2009)
14. Poleg, Y., Ephrat, A., Peleg, S., Arora, C.: Compact CNN for indexing egocentric videos (2015). arXiv preprint arXiv:1504.07469
15. Furnari, A., Farinella, G.M., Battiato, S.: Recognizing personal contexts from egocentric images. In: Workshop on Assistive Computer Vision and Robotics (ACVR) in Conjunction with the IEEE International Conference on Computer Vision (2015)
16. Oliva, A., Torralba, A.: Modeling the shape of the scene: a holistic representation of the spatial envelope. Int. J. Comput. Vis. **42**(3), 145–175 (2001)
17. Starner, T., Schiele, B., Pentland, A.: Visual contextual awareness in wearable computing. In: International Symposium on Wearable Computing, pp. 50–57 (1998)
18. Aoki, H., Schiele, B., Pentland, A.: Recognizing personal location from video. In: Workshop on Perceptual User Interfaces, pp.79–82 (1998)
19. Torralba, A., Murphy, K.P., Freeman, W.T., Rubin, M.A.: Context-based vision system for place and object recognition. In: International Conference on Computer Vision (2003)
20. Starner, T., Weaver, J., Pentland, A.: Real-time american sign language recognition using desk and wearable computer based video. IEEE Trans. Pattern Anal. Mach. Intell. **20**(12), 1371–1375 (1998)
21. Antifakos, S., Kern, N., Schiele, B., Schwaninge, A.: Towards improving trust in context-aware systems by displaying system confidence. In: International Conference on Human Computer Interaction with Mobile Devices & Services (MobileHCI) (2005)
22. Fathi, A., Li, Y., Rehg, J.M.: Learning to recognize daily actions using gaze. In: Fitzgibbon, A., Lazebnik, S., Perona, P., Sato, Y., Schmid, C. (eds.) ECCV 2012, Part I. LNCS, vol. 7572, pp. 314–327. Springer, Heidelberg (2012)
23. Castro, D., Hickson, S., Bettadapura, V., Thomaz, E., Abowd, G., Christensen, H., Essa, I.: Predicting daily activities from egocentric images using deep learning. In: International Symposium on Wearable Computing (2015)
24. Damen, D., Leelasawassuk, T., Haines, O., Calway, A., Mayol-Cuevas, W.: You-do, i-learn: discovering task relevant objects and their modes of interaction from multi-user egocentric video. In: British Machine Vision Conference (2014)
25. Farinella, G.M., Ravì, D., Tomaselli, V., Guarnera, M., Battiato, S.: Representing scenes for real-time context classification on mobile devices. Pattern Recogn. **48**(4), 1086–1100 (2015)
26. Templeman, R., Korayem, M., Crandall, D., Apu, K.: PlaceAvoider: steering first-person cameras away from sensitive spaces. In: Annual Network and Distributed System Security Symposium, pp. 23–26 (2014)
27. Furnari, A., Farinella, G.M., Puglisi, G., Bruna, A.R., Battiato, S.: Affine region detectors on the fisheye domain. In: International Conference on Image Processing, pp. 5681–5685 (2014)
28. Furnari, A., Farinella, G.M., Bruna, A.R., Battiato, S.: Generalized sobel filters for gradient estimation of distorted images. In: International Conference on Image Processing (2015)

29. Gal, Y., Ghahramani, Z.: Dropout as a Bayesian Approximation: Representing Model Uncertainty in Deep Learning (2015). arXiv preprint arXiv:1506.02142
30. Bishop, C.M.: Pattern Recognition and Machine Learning. Springer, New York (2006)
31. Chatfield, K., Simonyan, K., Vedaldi, A., Zisserman, A.: Return of the devil in the details: delving deep into convolutional nets. In: British Machine Vision Conference (2014)
32. Zhou, B., Lapedriza, A., Xiao, J., Torralba, A., Oliva, A.: Learning deep features for scene recognition using places database. In: Advances in Neural Information Processing Systems, pp. 487–495 (2014)
33. Jia, Y., Shelhamer, E., Donahue, J., Karayev, S., Long, J., Girshick, R.B., Guadarrama, S., Darrell, T.: Caffe: convolutional architecture for fast feature embedding. In: ACM Multimedia, vol. 2, p. 4(2014)
34. Chang, C., Lin, C.: LIBSVM: a library for support vector machines. ACM Trans. Intell. Syst. Technol. **2**, 27:1–27:27 (2011)
35. Srivastava, N., Hinton, G., Krizhevsky, A., Sutskever, I., Salakhutdinov, R.: Dropout: a simple way to prevent neural networks from overfitting. J. Mach. Learn. Res. **15**(1), 1929–1958 (2014)
36. Torr, P., Zisserman, A.: MLESAC: a new robust estimator with application to estimating image geometry. Comput. Vis. Image Underst. **78**(1), 138–156 (2000)

Face-Off: A Face Reconstruction Technique for Virtual Reality (VR) Scenarios

M.S.L. Khan[1]([✉]), Shafiq Ur Réhman[1,3], Ulrik Söderström[1],
Alaa Halawani[1], and Haibo Li[2]

[1] Department of Applied Physics and Electronics, Umeå University,
90187 Umeå, Sweden
{muhammad.sikandar.lal.khan,shafiq.urrehman}@umu.se
[2] KTH Royal Institute of Technology, 100 44 Stockholm, Sweden
[3] University of East London, London, England

Abstract. Virtual Reality (VR) headsets occlude a significant portion of human face. The real human face is required in many VR applications, for example, video teleconferencing. This paper proposes a wearable camera setup-based solution to reconstruct the real face of a person wearing VR headset. Our solution lies in the core of asymmetrical principal component analysis (aPCA). A user-specific training model is built using aPCA with full face, lips and eye region information. During testing phase, lower face region and partial eye information is used to reconstruct the wearer face. Online testing session consists of two phases, (i) calibration phase and (ii) reconstruction phase. In former, a small calibration step is performed to align test information with training data, while the later uses half face information to reconstruct the full face using aPCA-based trained-data. The proposed approach is validated with qualitative and quantitative analysis.

Keywords: Virtual reality · VR headset · Face reconstruction · PCA · Wearable setup · Oculus

1 Introduction

Visualization is an important pillar for multimedia computing. The devices used for visualizing multimedia contents can be broadly categorized into (i) non-wearable computer devices and (ii) wearable computer devices. Non-wearable computer technologies employ two-dimensional (2-D) and/or three dimensional (3-D) displays/technologies for multimedia content rendering [13]. Three dimensional (3-D) technologies offer one more dimension for visualizing the data flow and the interplay of programs in complex multimedia applications. However, in past few years, this trend is shifting from non-wearable visualization to wearable visualization experience [12,15]. The wearable devices used for watching multimedia content are commonly known as virtual reality (VR) headsets and/or head mounted displays (HMD). These virtual reality (VR) headsets are becoming popular because of cheaper prices, more immersive experience, high quality,

© Springer International Publishing Switzerland 2016
G. Hua and H. Jégou (Eds.): ECCV 2016 Workshops, Part I, LNCS 9913, pp. 490–503, 2016.
DOI: 10.1007/978-3-319-46604-0_35

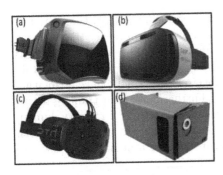

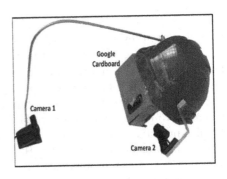

Fig. 1. Virtual reality headsets; (a) Oculus rift, (b) Gear VR, (c) HTC vive, (d) Google cardboard.

Fig. 2. Our wearable virtual reality setup: it consists of two RGB cameras along with a VR headset. Front camera is used for capturing lower face region and a side camera is used for capturing profile of an eye region.

better screen resolution, low latency and better control. According to statistics, around 6.7 million people have used VR headsets in year 2015 and it is expected to grow to 43 million users in year 2016 and 171 million users in year 2018 [31]. These headsets, for instance, Oculus rift, Play station VR, Gear VR, HTC vive, google cardboard, etc. [7] (see Fig. 1) are being used in many research and industrial applications, for example, medical simulation [21], gaming [8,24], 3D movie experience and scientific visualizations [23], etc. The integration of multimedia content inside VR headset is an interesting trend in the development of more immersive experience. The research community in wearable virtual reality field has been developing various hardware and software solutions to solve different issues related to virtual reality [18,27]. One of the major issues related to VR headsets is that they occlude half of the human face (upper face region) and to reconstruct the full human face is the main contribution of this research work.

We propose an optical sensor-based solution to address this issue. Our solution consists of a wearable camera setup where two cameras are used along with a VR headset as shown in Fig. 2. One camera is facing toward the lower face region (lips region) and the other camera is used to capture the side view of the eye-region. The full face is reconstructed using optical information of lower face region and partial eye region. We have used a google cardboard for our prototypic solution that can be extended to any VR headset.

Reconstructing a full face while wearing a VR headset is not an easy task [6]. The only efforts so far are done by Hao Li et al. [18] and Xavier et al. [3]. The former used an RGB-D camera and eight strain sensors to animate facial feature movements. They animate the facial movements through an avatar however they do not reconstruct the real face of a person wearing a VR headset. On the other hand, the later created a real-looking 3D human face model, where they trained a system to learn the facial expressions of the user from the lower part of the face only, and used it to change the model accordingly during testing. Compared to Hao Li et al., they came up with 3D face model of a person rather than using a 3D animated face. They have estimated the upper face information (eye region) based on lower face information (mouth region). But in literature, there is no direct correlation between upper and lower face regions [2,34], hence estimating one based on the other is not a good practice. Furthermore, their training model is limited to few (e.g. six) discrete facial expression. However, in theory, human facial expressions are continuous and a combination of different expressions with intermediary emotions [10,20,35]. Hence, reconstructing a human face based on few emotions can be problematic.

Considering the above-mentioned limitations, we have revisited the same question (face reconstruction while wearing a VR headset) with an innovative approach, where both upper and lower face information is considered during training and testing phases. We have used an asymmetrical principal component analysis algorithm (aPCA) [26] to reconstruct an original face using lips and eye information. The lips information is used to estimate lower facial expression and eye information is used for the upper facial expression. The proposed approach is validated with qualitative and quantitative evaluation. To the best of our knowledge, we are among the first to consider this problem.

The rest of the paper is disposed as following. Section 2 presents related work for face reconstruction under occlusion. Section 3 gives a description of asymmetrical principal component analysis (aPCA) model. This section further describes training and testing phases. In Sect. 4, a qualitative and quantitative analysis is done on our proposed approach. Section 5 presents the discussion and limitations. Conclusion is presented in Sect. 6.

2   Background and Related Work

Full face Reconstruction of a person wearing VR headset is required in many multimedia applications. The most prominent advantage is in video teleconferencing applications. Face reconstruction while using VR headset has been less studied because headset obstructs a significant portion of human face. The closest works to our research are from Hao et al. [18] and Xavier et al. [3]. Hao et al. have developed a real time facial animation system that augments a VR display with strain gauges and a head-mounted RGB-D camera for facial performance capture in virtual reality. Xavier et al. have recently proposed a solution to reconstruct a real human face by, (i) building a 3D texture model of a person, (ii) building an expression shape model, (iii) projecting a 3D face model on occluded face and (iv) finally combining 3D face model with occluded test image/video. In this section, we further present previously developed optical techniques for face reconstruction.

Optical systems confront occluded faces very often due to the use of accessories, such as scarf or sunglasses, hands on the face, the objects that persons carry, and external sources that partially occlude the camera view. Different computer vision techniques have been developed to counter face occlusion problems [16]. Texture based face reconstruction technique first detects the occluded region of the face and then run a recovery process to reconstruct the original face [11,19]. The recovery stage exploits the prior knowledge of the face and non-occluded part of the input image to restore the full face image. Furthermore, different model-based techniques have been proposed which exploit both shape and texture model of the face to reconstruct the original face [22,29]. These techniques extract the facial feature points of the input face, fit the face model, and detect occluded region according to these facial feature points.

Principal Component Analysis (PCA) has been a fundamental technique for face reconstruction, for example, simple-PCA [17], FR-PCA [28], Kernal-PCA [4] and FW-PCA [9]. It starts by training the non-occluded face images by creating an eigenspace based on full image pixel intensities and/or some selective samples of pixel intensities. During testing phase, the occluded image is mapped to eigenspace and the principle component coefficients are restored by iteratively optimizing the error between the original image and the reconstructed image from eigenspace. The above-mentioned PCA based methods are successful if the occluded regions are not larger than the face region. However, the main challenge in our work is that the VR headset occludes a significant portion of a user's face (nearly whole upper face), preventing effective face reconstruction from traditional PCA techniques. Hence, there is a need of an alternative method.

3   Extended Asymmetrical Principal Component Analysis (aPCA)

Asymmetrical principal component analysis (aPCA) has been previously used for video encoding and decoding [30]. In this work, we have extended aPCA for full face reconstruction for VR applications. Our algorithm consists of two phases, (i) training phase and (ii) testing phase. In training phase, we build an aPCA model by using the full frame and two half frames video sequences. Here, the full frame refers to full face of a person without VR headset and half frames refer to lips and eye regions. A person-specific aPCA based training model is built by synchronously recording full frame and half frames videos. The training model consists of mean faces and eigenspaces for full and half frames. The full frame eigenspace is created by using eigenvalues from half frames. The components spanning this space are called pseudo principal components and this space has the same size as a full frame. In this work, a user-specific training model is constructed for each individual, where each individual is asked to perform certain facial expressions during training session. During testing phase, a person wears a VR headset along with a wearable camera setup. A short calibration step is performed to align test half frames with trained half frames. When a new half frame is presented to a trained model, its own weights are found by projecting the new half frames onto the collection of trained half frame eigenspaces. These new weights with full-frame mean face and full-frame eigenspace are used to reconstruct the original face with all facial deformations (more prominently eyes and mouth deformation).

(a) Training   (b) Testing

Fig. 3. Our setup: on the left we have a training setup where two cameras are used to capture full face, eye-region and lips-region. On the right we have a testing setup where we have an attached VR-headset with wearable setup, two cameras are used to capture eye-region and lips-region.

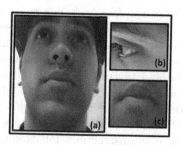

Fig. 4. A sample frame output of (a) full face, (b) eye region and (c) lips region.

3.1 Training Phase

A user-specific training model is build based on three synchronous video sequences. Our wearable training setup is shown in Fig. 3(a). Our training setup consists of two cameras denoted by Fc and Sc. Fc captures the full face and lips region of a person as show in Fig. 4a and c, respectively. Sc captures the side region of an eye as shown in Fig. 4b. Let ff, hf_l and hf_e denote the full face, lips region and eye region information, respectively. A Full frame (ff) training is performed by exploiting information from half frames (hf_l and hf_e).

Let, I_e and I_l be the intensity values of the eye and lips regions, respectively. The combined intensity matrix I_{hf} is denoted by,

$$I_{hf} = [I_e \quad I_l] \tag{1}$$

The mean I_{hfo} is calculated as,

$$I_{hfo} = \frac{1}{N} \sum_{n=1}^{N} I_{hf_{(n)}} \tag{2}$$

where, N is the total number of training frames. The mean is then subtracted from each basis in the training data, ensuring that the data is zero-centered.

$$\hat{I}_{hf} = I_{hf} - I_{hfo} \tag{3}$$

Mathematically, PCA is an optimal transformation of an input data in the form of least square error sense. Due to space constraint, we direct readers to [26,30] for more details. To this end, we need to find out the eigen vectors of the covariance matrix ($\hat{I}_{hf} \hat{I}_{hf}^T$). This can be done by singular value decomposition

(SVD) [33]. SVD is a factorization method which divides a square matrix into three matrices,

$$\hat{I}_{hf} = U\Sigma V^T \tag{4}$$

where, $V = [b_1, b_2 \dots b_N]$ is a matrix of an eigen vector and variable b_n corresponds to the eigen vector. The eigen space for the half frame $\phi_{hf} = [\phi_{hf}^1 \dots \phi_{hf}^N]$ is constructed by multiplying V with the $\hat{I}_{hf}$,

$$\phi_{hf} = \sum_i b_i \hat{I}_{hf(i)} \tag{5}$$

The half frame coefficients (α_{hf}) from training frames are calculated as,

$$\alpha_{hf} = \phi_{hf} (I_{hf} - I_{hfo})^T \tag{6}$$

Similarly, for full frame intensity values I_{ff}, we follow Eqs. 2 and 3 to get,

$$I_{ffo} = \frac{1}{N} \sum_{n=1}^{N} I_{ff(n)} \tag{7}$$

$$\hat{I}_{ff} = I_{ff} - I_{ffo} \tag{8}$$

The eigen space for the full frame $\phi_{ff} = [\phi_{ff}^1 \dots \phi_{ff}^N]$ is constructed by multiplying the eigen vector from half frame $V = [b_1, b_2 \dots b_N]$ with the $\hat{I}_{ff}$. This eigen space is spanned by half frame components. The component spanning this space are called pseudo principal components; information where not all the data is a principal component. This space has the same size as of full frame.

$$\phi_{ff} = \sum_i b_i \hat{I}_{ff(i)} \tag{9}$$

The full and half frame Eigen spaces and mean intensities values are saved and are used in the online testing session.

3.2   Testing Phase

A VR display is attached to a wearable camera setup as shown in Fig. 3(b). The full frame (ff) is no more active during the testing phase. The testing phase is sub-divided into calibration and reconstruction phase.

Calibration Phase: In the start of the testing phase a manual calibration step is performed. The camera position during the training phase can be inconsistent with the camera position during the testing phase. To align test half-frame with trained half-frame, we propose the following calibration step.

The mean half frames from the training phase and the first half-frames from the testing phase are used for the calibration. Figure 5 (top row) shows half frames from the training phase and Fig. 5 (bottom row) shows half frames from

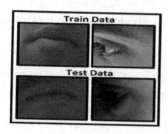

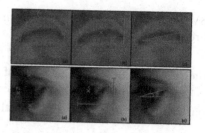

Fig. 5. The half frames: top row contains frames from training phase and bottom row contains frames from testing phase

Fig. 6. Top row - Lips geometry, Bottom row - Eye Geometry. (a) four feature points, (b) width, height and center, (c) geometry used for angle calculation.

the testing phase. We manually learn the feature parameters for both trained and test frames by using lips and eyes feature points. Let,

$$P_l = [P_l^1 \quad P_l^2 \quad P_l^3 \quad P_l^4] \tag{10}$$

$$w_l = \sqrt{(P_{l_x}^2 - P_{l_x}^1)^2 + (P_{l_y}^2 - P_{l_y}^1)^2}$$
$$h_l = \sqrt{(P_{l_x}^4 - P_{l_x}^3)^2 + (P_{l_y}^4 - P_{l_y}^3)^2}. \tag{11}$$

The center coordinates c_l are calculated as,

$$c_l = [w_l, \ h_l] \tag{12}$$

The w_l, h_l and c_l are graphically shown in Fig. 6b (top row). The in-plane rotational angle θ_l is calculated as,

$$\theta_l = arctan(\frac{P_{l_y}^2 - P_{l_y}^1}{P_{l_x}^2 - P_{l_x}^1}) \tag{13}$$

The angle calculation θ_l is graphically shown in Fig. 6c (top row). The scale s_l, rotation R_l and translation t_l between the trained and test lips frames are calculated as,

$$s_l = [w_l^{test}/w_l^{train}]$$
$$R_l = [\theta_l^{test} - \theta_l^{train}]$$
$$t_l = [c_l^{test} - c_l^{train}]. \tag{14}$$

A similar procedure is applied to calculate scale s_e, rotation R_e and translation t_e between the trained and test eyes frames as given below,

$$s_e = [w_e^{test}/w_e^{train}]$$
$$R_e = [\theta_e^{test} - \theta_e^{train}]$$
$$t_e = [c_e^{test} - c_e^{train}]. \tag{15}$$

Reconstruction Phase: During testing phase, half frame information is only available (see Fig. 5 (bottom row)). This half frame information along with trained model from training phase are used to reconstruct the original face of a person with respective facial deformation. The first step is to adjust the test half frames according to calibration step. Let, I_{hfe} and I_{hfl} are the test half frames, then $\bar{I}_{hfe}$ and $\bar{I}_{hfl}$ are calculated as,

$$\bar{I}_{hfe} = s_e\, R_e\, I_{hfe} + t_e$$
$$\bar{I}_{hfl} = s_l\, R_l\, I_{hfl} + t_l. \qquad (16)$$

The calibrated test half frames ($\bar{I}_{hf} = [\bar{I}_{hfe} \quad \bar{I}_{hfl}]$) are then subtracted from the mean half frames (Eq. 2),

$$I^t_{hf} = \bar{I}_{hf} - I_{hfo} \qquad (17)$$

where, superscript t denotes the test phase. The coefficients (α^t_{hf}) are calculated by using half frame Eigen space ϕ_{hf} (Eq. 5),

$$\alpha^t_{hf} = \phi_{hf}\,(\bar{I}_{hf} - I_{hfo})^T \qquad (18)$$

The entire frame containing full face information is constructed by using following equation,

$$I = I_{ffo} + \sum_{n=1}^{M} \alpha^t_{hf}\, \phi_{ff(n)} \qquad (19)$$

where, I_{ffo} is taken from Eq. 7, α^t_{hf} from Eq. 18 and ϕ_{ff} from Eq. 9. The M is a selected number of principal components used for reconstruction ($M < N$). The N is the total number of frames available for training and M is the number of most significant eigen images. In our experiment, N is around 1000 frames and M is 25 frames. The qualitative and quantitative results are presented in evaluation section.

4   Evaluation

We have performed an experiment with five subjects. For each subject, a training session of two minutes is done using our wearable setup as shown in Fig. 3(a). Each participant is requested to perform different (but natural) facial expressions, e.g. neutral, happy, sad, eye-blink, etc. Three synchronous video sequences of eye, mouth and full face regions are recorded as shown in Fig. 4. An offline training (Sect. 3.1) is performed for each individual using the recorded sequences. During testing session, a person wears a VR headset along with our wearable setup as shown in Fig. 3(b). A full face of a participant is reconstructed using two half frames according to the details in Sect. 3.2. Qualitative and Quantitative analyses are performed on our proposed approach. Qualitative analysis measures the reconstruction quality of a human face. Whereas, quantitative analysis measures the accuracy of our proposed approach.

4.1   Qualitative Analysis

The 75 % of data acquired during the training session is used for training and remaining 25 % of data is used for validation and testing purpose. Please note that we cannot do proper analysis with test data as upper face region is completely occluded by the VR display. The data is qualitatively analyzed with three different scenarios; (i) When just mouth information is used as a half frame during training (similar to [3]), (ii) when just eye information is used as a half frame during training and (iii) when both eye and mouth are used as a half frame during training. Figure 7 shows qualitative results on three users given the above-mentioned three scenarios. Left most face is the original face, second is the reconstructed face from mouth information (scenario i), third is the reconstructed face from the eye information (scenario ii) and the last is the reconstructed face from both mouth and eye information (scenario iii). The results clearly show that facial mimic is not just dependent on mouth area, facial mimic of a person can be modelled accurately by modeling the mouth and eye regions. The qualitative results on the test data is shown in Fig. 8.

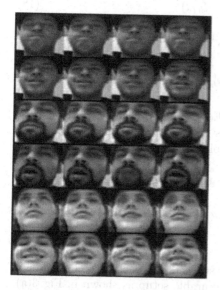

Fig. 7. From left to right: (i) Original frame. (ii) Reconstructed frame from mouth information. (iii) Reconstructed frame from eye information. (iv) Reconstructed frame from eye and mouth information.

Fig. 8. Reconstruction results from test data.

4.2   Quantitative Analysis

We have performed two types of quantitative analysis;

1. Shape based quantitative analysis.
2. Appearance based quantitative analysis.

In shape based quantitative analysis, we have compared the differences between the original facial feature points and the reconstructed facial feature points. We have used constrained local model (CLM) [5] to capture these facial feature points. Figure 9 shows the CLM on the human face. The left side of Fig. 9 shows the original face frame and the right side shows the reconstructed face frame. The shape based analysis is performed on 25 % of validation data for each individual and the results are presented in Table 1 according to the following equation.

$$mse_{shape} = \sum_{i=1}^{F} \frac{1}{F} [\sum_{j=1}^{N} \frac{|(s_j - \bar{s}_j)|}{N}] \tag{20}$$

where, s, $\bar{s}$, N and F refer to spatial locations of original facial feature points, spatial locations of reconstructed facial feature points, number of facial feature points and number of frames, respectively. For this work, $N = 66$ and $F = 250$–500. The shape analysis results show a small difference between the facial points of original and reconstructed face with an average difference of 1.5327 pixels.

In appearance based quantitative analysis, we have compared the intensity differences between the reconstructed face and the original test face. We have used the mouth region for comparison as upper face region is occluded during real testing. Appearance quality is measured through peak signal to noise ration (PSNR). This ratio depends on the mean square error (mse_{app}) between the original and reconstructed face. mse_{app} and PSNR is calculated according to:

$$mse_{app} = \sum_{j=1}^{h*v} \frac{(I_j - \bar{I}_j)^2}{h * v} \tag{21}$$

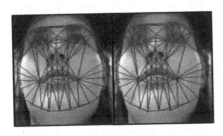

Fig. 9. Constrained local model (CLM) on human face; Left - original face, Right - reconstructed face.

Fig. 10. VR plus Embodied telepresence based video teleconferencing scenario.

Table 1. Shape based quantitative analysis.

Participants	mse_{shape}
Subj. 1	1.4530
Subj. 2	1.1207
Subj. 3	2.023
Subj. 4	0.7285
Subj. 5	2.3383

Table 2. Appearance based quantitative analysis.

Participants	PSNR [db]
Subj. 1	61.6
Subj. 2	74.95
Subj. 3	48.5
Subj. 4	62.7074
Subj. 5	56.08

where, h and v are the horizontal and vertical resolution of the frames, respectively. I_j is the original test face and $\bar{I}_j$ is the reconstructed face.

$$PSNR = 20 * \log(\frac{(255)^2}{mse_{app}})$$

(22)

where 255 is the maximum value for the pixel intensity. The results are presented in Table 2. A higher PSNR value means that there is a low difference in pixel intensity between the original and reconstructed faces.

5   Discussion

The qualitative and quantitative results show the validity of proposed aPCA-based approach. The qualitative results are presented in the form of reconstructed face frames, whereas quantitative results yield high PSNR and low difference in facial feature points. The PSNR values greater than 40 is considered good [25] and our experiment yields between 48–75 PSNR values. Similarly, shape-based analysis give good results with maximum difference of 2.34 (pixels).

We plan to use the reconstructed face of a wearer in virtual reality (VR) based video teleconferencing application. We will use our embodied telepresence agent (ETA) [14] along with a VR headset for teleconferencing purpose. The application scenario is shown in Fig. 10 and will be considered in future work. In this work, we have used two half frames for face reconstruction. However, this work could be simplified with just one half frame information with some compromise on results.

We have cut a portion of a cardboard for an eye camera. The eye camera is mounted smartly which does not affect significantly the virtual reality experience. The eye camera is mounted externally for this work but this work can be extended by integrating small camera inside VR displays, for example in other works, such as [1,27]. Furthermore, we have developed our own wearable setup for cameras. However, initially, we have mounted two cameras on google cardboard for testing purpose as shown in Fig. 11. There were two issue with this setup, (i) increase in weight and (ii) normalization issue between training and testing video sequences. These issues will be considered in future work.

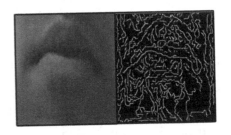

Fig. 11. Modified google cardboard setup.

Fig. 12. From left to right (a) the RGB half frame. (b) the edge image of the half frame.

This version of the work uses manual calibration step. In our future work, we plan to automate the calibration step by developing feature point localization technique. Furthermore, a problem with PCA is that it is very sensitive to light. To counter this problem, we are working to use edge feature information [32]. The half frame image will be converted to an edge map using a sobel filter (see Fig. 12) and the magnitude values of an edge image will be used to train the full face. During testing phase, the half frame edge map will be used to reconstruct the full face of a person. This work is in progress and will be considered in future publication.

6   Conclusion

We have proposed a novel technique for face reconstruction, when face is occluded by virtual reality (VR) headset. Full face reconstruction is based on asymmetrical principal component analysis (aPCA) framework. The aPCA framework exploits lips and eye appearance information for full face reconstruction. We have estimated the upper face expressions by partial eye information and lower face expression by lips information. This version uses appearance information for face modeling. In future, we plan to use shape based (or feature based) technique for full face reconstruction.

References

1. Fove eyetracker, January 2016. http://www.getfove.com/
2. Bentsianov, B., Blitzer, A.: Facial anatomy. Clin. Dermatol. **22**(1), 3–13 (2004)
3. Burgos-Artizzu, X.P., Fleureau, J., Dumas, O., Tapie, T., LeClerc, F., Mollet, N.: Real-time expression-sensitive hmd face reconstruction. In: SIGGRAPH Asia 2015 Technical Briefs, p. 9. ACM (2015)
4. Chakrabarti, A., Rajagopalan, A., Chellappa, R.: Super-resolution of face images using kernel pca-based prior. IEEE Trans. Multimedia **9**(4), 888–892 (2007)
5. Cristinacce, D., Cootes, T.F.: Feature detection and tracking with constrained local models. In: BMVC, vol. 2, p. 6 (2006)

6. Ekenel, H.K., Stiefelhagen, R.: Why is facial occlusion a challenging problem? In: Tistarelli, M., Nixon, M.S. (eds.) ICB 2009. LNCS, vol. 5558, pp. 299–308. Springer, Heidelberg (2009). doi:10.1007/978-3-642-01793-3_31

7. VR Headset, January 2016. http://www.wareable.com/headgear/the-best-ar-and-vr-headsets

8. Hoberman, P., Krum, D.M., Suma, E.A., Bolas, M.: Immersive training games for smartphone-based head mounted displays. In: 2012 IEEE Virtual Reality Short Papers and Posters (VRW), pp. 151–152. IEEE (2012)

9. Hosoi, T., Nagashima, S., Kobayashi, K., Ito, K., Aoki, T.: Restoring occluded regions using fw-pca for face recognition. In: 2012 IEEE Computer Society Conference on Computer Vision and Pattern Recognition Workshops (CVPRW), pp. 23–30. IEEE (2012)

10. Hupont, I., Baldassarri, S., Cerezo, E.: Facial emotional classification: from a discrete perspective to a continuous emotional space. Pattern Anal. Appl. 16(1), 41–54 (2013)

11. Hwang, B.W., Lee, S.W.: Reconstruction of partially damaged face images based on a morphable face model. IEEE Trans. Pattern Anal. Mach. Intell. 25(3), 365–372 (2003)

12. Jäckel, D.: Head-mounted displays. In: Proceedings of RTMI, pp. 1–8 (2013)

13. Javidi, B., Okano, F.: Three-Dimensional Television, Video, and Display Technologies. Springer, Heidelberg (2002)

14. Khan, M., Li, H., Rehman, S.: Telepresence mechatronic robot (tebot): toward the design and control of socially interactive bio-inspired system. J. Intell. Fuzzy Syst., Special Issue: Multimedia in Technology Enhanced Learning (2016)

15. Kimura, S., Fukuomoto, M., Horikoshi, T.: Eyeglass-based hands-free videophone. In: Proceedings of the 2013 International Symposium on Wearable Computers, pp. 117–124. ACM (2013)

16. Kuo, C.J., Lin, T.G., Huang, R.S., Odeh, S.F.: Facial model estimation from stereo/mono image sequence. IEEE Trans. Multimedia 5(1), 8–23 (2003)

17. Leonardis, A., Bischof, H.: Robust recognition using eigenimages. Comput. Vis. Image Underst. 78(1), 99–118 (2000)

18. Li, H., Trutoiu, L., Olszewski, K., Wei, L., Trutna, T., Hsieh, P.L., Nicholls, A., Ma, C.: Facial performance sensing head-mounted display. ACM Trans. Graph. (Proceedings SIGGRAPH 2015) 34(4), 47 (2015)

19. Lin, D., Tang, X.: Quality-driven face occlusion detection and recovery. In: IEEE Conference on Computer Vision and Pattern Recognition, CVPR 2007, pp. 1–7. IEEE (2007)

20. Liu, L., et al.: Vibrotactile rendering of human emotions on the manifold of facial expressions. J. Multimedia 3(3), 18–25 (2008)

21. McCloy, R., Stone, R.: Virtual reality in surgery. BMJ 323(7318), 912–915 (2001)

22. Mo, Z., Lewis, J.P., Neumann, U.: Face inpainting with local linear representations. In: BMVC, pp. 1–10 (2004)

23. Reinhard Friedl, M.: Virtual reality and 3d visualizations in heart surgery education. In: The Heart Surgery Forum, vol. 2001, p. 03054 (2002)

24. Schild, J., LaViola, J., Masuch, M.: Understanding user experience in stereoscopic 3d games. In: Proceedings of the SIGCHI Conference on Human Factors in Computing Systems, pp. 89–98. ACM (2012)

25. Sderstrm, U.: Very low bitrate video communication: a principal component analysis approach. Ph.D. thesis, Ume Unviersity (2008)

26. Söderström, U., Li, H.: Asymmetrical principal component analysis: theory and its applications to facial video coding. Effective Video Coding for Multimedia Applicationss, Dr. Sudhakar Radhakrishnan (ed.) (2011). InTech, ISBN: 978-953-307-177-0

27. Stengel, M., Grogorick, S., Eisemann, M., Eisemann, E., Magnor, M.A.: An affordable solution for binocular eye tracking and calibration in head-mounted displays. In: Proceedings of the 23rd Annual ACM Conference on Multimedia Conference, pp. 15–24. ACM (2015)

28. Storer, M., Roth, P.M., Urschler, M., Bischof, H.: Fast-robust PCA. In: Salberg, A.-B., Hardeberg, J.Y., Jenssen, R. (eds.) SCIA 2009. LNCS, vol. 5575, pp. 430–439. Springer, Heidelberg (2009)

29. Tu, C.-T., Lien, J.-J.J.: Facial occlusion reconstruction: recovering both the global structure and the local detailed texture components. In: Mery, D., Rueda, L. (eds.) PSIVT 2007. LNCS, vol. 4872, pp. 141–151. Springer, Heidelberg (2007)

30. Soderstrom, U., Li, H.: Asymmetrical principal component analysis for video coding. Electron. Lett. **44**, 276–277 (2008)

31. V.R. Users, January 2016. http://www.statista.com/statistics/426469/active-virtual-reality-users-worldwide/

32. Vincent, O., Folorunso, O.: A descriptive algorithm for sobel image edge detection. In: Proceedings of Informing Science & IT Education Conference (InSITE), vol. 40, pp. 97–107 (2009)

33. Wall, M.E., Rechtsteiner, A., Rocha, L.M.: Singular value decomposition and principal component analysis. In: Berrar, D.P., Dubitzky, W., Granzow, M. (eds.) A Practical Approach to Microarray Data Analysis, pp. 91–109. Springer, US (2003)

34. Waters, K.: A muscle model for animation three-dimensional facial expression. ACM SIGGRAPH Comput. Graph. **21**, 17–24 (1987). ACM

35. Whissell, C.: The dictionary of affect in language. Emot. Theor. Res. Exp. **4**(113–131), 94 (1989)

GPU Accelerated Left/Right Hand-Segmentation in First Person Vision

Alejandro Betancourt[1,2]([✉]), Lucio Marcenaro[1], Emilia Barakova[2],
Matthias Rauterberg[2], and Carlo Regazzoni[1]

[1] Department of Engineering (DITEN), University of Genova, Genova, Italy
abetan16@gmail.com
[2] Department of Industrial Design, Eindhoven University of Technology,
Eindhoven, Netherlands

Abstract. Wearable cameras allow users to record their daily activities from a user-centered (First Person Vision) perspective. Due to their favourable location, they frequently capture the hands of the user, and may thus represent a promising user-machine interaction tool for different applications. Existent First Person Vision, methods understand the hands as a background/foreground segmentation problem that ignores two important issues: (i) Each pixel is sequentially classified creating a long processing queue, (ii) Hands are not a single "skin-like" moving element but a pair of interacting entities (left-right hand). This paper proposes a GPU-accelerated implementation of a left right-hand segmentation algorithm. The GPU implementation exploits the nature of the pixel-by-pixel classification strategy. The left-right identification is carried out by following a competitive likelihood test based the position and the angle of the segmented pixels.

Keywords: Egovision · Hand-segmentation · GPU · Hand-detection · Wearable cameras

1 Introduction

Computer Vision and video analysis are nowadays two of the most explored topics in computer science. The increasing computational power, the data availability and the recent algorithmic developments are quickly attracting high-tech companies and computer scientist to develop systems to process and understand video streams. In particular, wearable cameras, by taking advantage of a privileged location, stand out as one of the most promising video perspectives nowadays. The videos recorded from this point of view are referred as First-Person Vision (FPV) or Egocentric videos [6].

The 90's idea of a device that can understand our surroundings and provide valuable assistance is nowadays technically possible. During the last couple of years, several successful applications of wearable cameras have been proposed in different fields such as Law Enforcement [10], Medical Applications [13], Lifelogging [14], among others. Due to the tight link with the user and its advantageous

© Springer International Publishing Switzerland 2016
G. Hua and H. Jégou (Eds.): ECCV 2016 Workshops, Part I, LNCS 9913, pp. 504–517, 2016.
DOI: 10.1007/978-3-319-46604-0_36

location, wearable cameras are commonly pointed out as a promising strategy to enhance user-machine interaction by exploiting the hands usage as interaction instrument.

In seek of such intuitive interaction, hand-based methods constitute the most explored field in EgoCentric videos. Hand signals have been used for several purposes, for example, to understand conscious interactions with the device [1], to infer the gaze of the user without using eye-trackers [9], to infer the active objects in the scene [20], among others.

The authors in [4] propose a unified structure to develop hand-based methods in egocentric videos. The proposed structure highlights the importance of decomposing the understanding of the hands in multiple levels, starting with simple questions like the presence of the hands [2,3,5] and finally obtaining more complex variables like the shape of each hand [8], to finally analyze its trajectories and interactions.

Within the Unified Framework proposed by Betancourt [4], the most explored level is the hand-segmentation. Its goal is to extract the shape of the hands by following a background/foreground segmentation at a pixel-by-pixel level. As shown in the literature this pixel-by-pixel approach achieves reliable results; However it has to deal with challenging aspects such as the illumination changes and the significant number of operations required. For instance, the camera of the Google glasses has a resolution of 720 p and records 30 fps, implying 928.800 pixel classifications per frame and a total of 27'864.000 per second of video.

Regarding the illumination changes, this is partially alleviated by using depth sensors or by combining multiple hand-segments, each of them trained to deal with particular light conditions. The former is usually restricted by the use of bigger devices with extra battery requirements; while the training data availability limits the latter [8]. About the computational complexity, a promising strategy is to simplify the frames by using SLIC superpixels [22]. On one side, the superpixel approach reduces the number of classifications tasks per frame and includes the concept of an edge in the segmentation; on the other side, it is necessary to run the SLIC algorithm frame by frame and the classification errors are considerably larger.

In addition to the technical challenges, the traditional background/foreground also carries the conceptual issues in the definition of hands understanding. On one side, the background/foreground approach assumes that both hands are equal and constitute the foreground of the scene, while on the other side, based on human studies, the hands are commonly defined as coupled system centrally coordinated by the brain to achieve a particular goal. Furthermore, there are considerable differences in the motion skills of both hands. In average, 9 out of 10 individuals are right-handed and as a consequence, their upper limb movement skills are asymmetric concerning speed, control, and strength. These differences are significantly larger in patients with upper limb motor problems such as cerebral palsy or upper limb stroke.

This paper proposes an accelerated strategy to segment and identifies the hands of the user when recorded by a wearable camera. The proposed approach follows the unified framework introduced by [4], but targets, in particular, the segmentation and identification level. The novelties of this paper are three folded:

(i) Formalises a multi-model hand-segmenter based on Random Forest and K-Nearest-Neighbors. The proposed hand-segmenter is inspired by the work of [18].

(ii) Proposes a GPU implementation of the multi-model hand-segmenter. The experimental results show that the accelerated version can process frames 6.2 times faster than a sequential CPU.

(iii) The accelerated hand segmenter is extended with the hand-identification level proposed in [8]. The experimental results show that using an acceptable compression rate it is possible to obtain reliable left/right hand-segmentations in real time.

The remaining of this paper is organized as follows: Sect. 2 introduces our approach. Subsection 2.1 formalizes the hand-segmentation and explains the single and multimodel hand-segmenters. Subsection 2.2 introduces the Random Forest classification algorithm and introduces two GPU kernels. Subsection 2.3 proposes the hand-identification mechanism. Finally, Sect. 3 evaluates the performance of the proposed kernels and the identification model. Section 4 concludes the paper.

2   Our Approach

The goal of this paper is to develop a strategy to delineate the left and right-hand silhouette by exploiting the GPU processing capabilities. Our approach extends the traditional pixel-by-pixel hand-segmentation approach by proposing an additional hand-identification step as suggested by [8]. Figure 1 summarizes the difference between the background/foreground approach and the Left/Right hand-segmentation. This section briefly introduces the pixel-by-pixel hand-segmentation problem, the algorithmic procedure behind random forests and the required improvements to segment each pixel as a separate thread in the GPU. Finally, the identification level is introduced. For more details about the identification step, please refer to [8].

2.1   Hand-Segmentation

It is probably the more explored problem in FPV. The main task is to delineate the silhouette of the hands at a pixel level. The more promising results are reported in [18] and [23] achieving F-scores around 90 % under slightly stable illumination conditions. The general idea behind these methods is to reduce the problem to a pixel binary classification problem, and then construct the frame result as the composition of the individual decisions.

In the most basic form, it is possible to train a single hand-segmenter by using a set of input frames and the ground truth masks (pixels belonging to the hands). This approach can be considered the evolution of the seminal work of

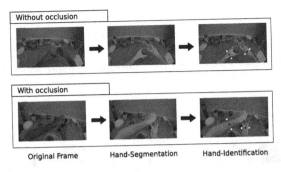

Fig. 1. The difference between hand-segmentation and hand-identification. The hand-to-hand occlusions are captured by following [8].

Jones and Rehg 1999 [16], with some differences in the used colour space and the classification algorithm. Recent works show that by using the *Lab* colour space (Lightness and a/b components) it is possible to alleviate the effect of small illumination changes. Figure 2 illustrates the general procedure to build a single hand-segmenter. In the first columns are the original frames, the training masks and their matrix representation. In the second column the training and testing stage. For illustrative purposes the training stage shows a decision tree; However, in practice, this can be a different type of classifier. Our experiments, as well as the state-of-the-art, are based on Random Forest classifiers.

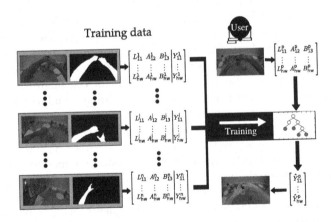

Fig. 2. Single-model hand-segmentation

In general a single hand-segmenter easily fails when applied to videos recorded with slightly changing light conditions. This problem can be partially alleviated by increasing the number of training frames, which in turns, could end up reducing the separability of the color space and producing excessive false-positives and false-negatives. Recent literature propose to train multiple hand-segmenters, one per frame and switch between them depending of the light conditions of the frame. The latter can be captured by built-in light sensors or estimated indirectly by global features like color histograms or GIST [7]. Figure 3 summarizes our implementation of the multi-model hand-segmenter.

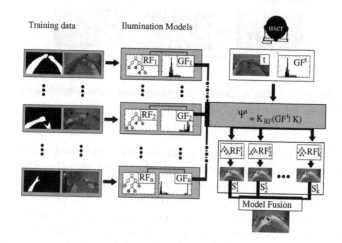

Fig. 3. Multi-model hand segmentation. Source [8]

The first column of the figure contains the manually labelled masks and their corresponding raw frames. Let us denote N as the number of manual labels available in the dataset, and n as the number of training pairs selected to build a multi-model binary hand-segmenter. For each training pair, $i = 1 \ldots n$ a trained binary random forest (RF_i) and its global feature (GF_i) are obtained and stored in a pool of illumination models (second column of the figure). Each RF_i is trained using the LAB values of each pixel in the frame i and as the class their corresponding values in the binary masks. As global feature (GF_i) we use the flatten HSV histogram. The choice of the colour spaces is based on the results reported by [17, 21]. Finally, we train a K-Nearest-Neighbor K_{RF} with the global features to switch between the more suitable illumination models.

In the testing phase, the K_{RF} is used as a recommender system which, given the global features of a new frame, provides the indexes of the closest K illumination models (RF^t). These models are subsequently used to obtain K possible segmentations (S^t), which are finally fused to get the final binary hand-segmentation (HS^t). The third column of the figure illustrates this part of the procedure. Formally, let's denote the testing frame as t and its HSV-histogram as GF^t, the indexes of the closest K illumination models ordered from closest to furthest based on the Euclidean distance as Eq. (1), their corresponding K random forest as Eq. (2), and their pixel-by-pixel segmentation applied to t as Eq. (3).

$$\Psi^t = K_{RF}(GF^t|K)$$

$$= \{\psi_1^t, \ldots, \psi_K^t\} \tag{1}$$

$$RF^t = \{RF_{\psi_1^t}, \ldots, RF_{\psi_K^t}\} \tag{2}$$

$$S^t = \{RF_{\psi_1^t}(t), \ldots, RF_{\psi_K^t}(t)\}$$

$$= \{S_1^t, \ldots, S_K^t\} \tag{3}$$

The binary hand-segmentation of the frame is the normalised weighted average of the individual segmentations in S^t, defined by Eq. (4). Where λ is a decaying weight factor, selected as 0.9.

$$HS^t = \frac{\sum_{j=1}^{K} \lambda^j \cdot S_j^t}{\sum_{j=1}^{K} \lambda^j} \tag{4}$$

2.2   Random Forest and Decision Trees

The egocentric literature points to Random Forest (RF) as the most suitable classifier for the hand-segmentation problem. They offer a fast classification, a reliable skin detection and are less prone to overfitting. As shown in [8,23], under a proper training, the use of multiple random forests could provide a robust hand segmentations even under changing light conditions.

On its general definition, a Random Forests is an ensemble method that fuses the result of multiple Decision Trees, each of which is in turn on a subset of the training data [15]. In this way, the main classification workload is carried out by its decision trees. A Decision Tree, respectively, is an algorithmic strategy to divide the feature space in such a way that the proposed division fit the output variable [19].

Without loosing generality lets assume a set of N observations, each of them containing containing p features and a response: that is (x_i, y_i) for $i = 1, 2, \ldots, N$, with $x_i = (x_{i1}, x_{i2}, \ldots x_{ip})$. Lets define an arbitrary partition of the input space X^p into M regions as $R_1, R_2, \ldots, R_M$, and the response of the model in each region as the constant c_m. In this way, the goal of the decision tree is to find, by using the input data, an appropriate partition and response constants to map the input space to the output space.

Given an space partition, the values of c_m can be obtained by defining an error function $J(c_m) = J(f(y_i, x_i, cm)|(x_i, y_i) \in R_m)$ and finding the constants that minimize it for each region (6). Finding the best partition of the space is computationally expensive for highly dimensional input spaces; However, it is possible to design recursive binary partitions in an efficient way.

$$\hat{c}_m = \operatorname*{argmin}_{cm} J(c_m) \qquad\qquad \forall m \in 1, \ldots, M \tag{5}$$

$$= \operatorname*{argmin}_{cm} J(f(y_i, x_i, cm)|(x_i, y_i) \in R_m) \qquad \forall m \in 1, \ldots, M \tag{6}$$

Starting with all the inputs consider a splitting feature j and value s to divide the feature space in two half-planes, namely R_1 and R_2 defined in (7). The best pair of (j, s) is the one that minimize the overall error of R_1 and R_2 as shown in (8). The same splitting procedure can be applied recursively on each half-plane until a stop criteria reached. Different stop criteria can be used to finish the procedure, such as the maximum tree depth or the minimum error required to consider valid a partition. Other options include the construction of large trees and then prune the unnecessary branches. The resulting regions and the model responses are defined by the leafs of the tree and their model responses respectively. The obtained tree can be applied to process new observations by following the rules captured by the sequences of (j, s) and returning the constant assigned to the final leaf.

$$R_1(j, s) = \{X | X_j \leq s\} \text{ and } R_2(j, s) = \{X | X_j > s\} \tag{7}$$

$$min_{j,s} \left[J(\hat{c}_1) + J(\hat{c}_2) \right] = min_{j,s} [J(f(y_i, x_i, \hat{c}_1) | (x_i, y_i) \in R_1(j, s))$$
$$+ J(f(y_i, x_i, \hat{c}_2) | (x_i, y_i) \in R_2(j, s))] \tag{8}$$

Once obtained the decision tree it can be represented by using 5 arrays: The decision variables J, the splitting values S, the position of the left and right nodes L and R respectively, and the response constants C. Each of these vectors has as many elements as nodes in the trained decision tree. For a Random Forest, the arrays of all its Decision Trees can be merged by keeping control of the position of the first node of each decision tree. These positions can be stored in a sixth array F. Algorithm 1 shows the Random Forest decision procedure. To obtain the Decision Tree pseudocode it is necessary to modify lines 3, 7 and 9, or define $F = [0]$ in the Random Forest procedure.

Algorithm 1. Random Forest Pseudocode.

```
 1: function SEGMENTPIXEL(pixel)
 2:     result = 0
 3:     for i ∈ F do
 4:         node = F[i]
 5:         while L[node]! = −1 do
 6:             if pixel[J[node]] ≤ S[node] then
 7:                 node = L[node] + F[i]
 8:             else
 9:                 node = R[node] + F[i]
10:             end if
11:         end while
12:         result+ = C[node]
13:     end for
14:     return result
15: end function
```

Existent hand-segmenters process each single pixel sequentially in the CPU of the device. This approach highly restricts the number of pixels being process at every time instance and creates long queues of pixels to be processed. Additionally, by analysing Algorithm 1, it is clear that the traversing algorithm is the result of a sequential access to the decision arrays (J, S, L, R) comparing the input features with (S) to return the average value (C) finally. This description

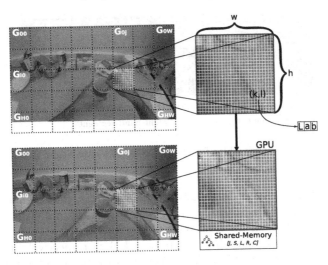

Fig. 4. Summary of the GPU hand-segmenter, including the block and grid dimensions and the information stored in the shared memory.

and easily fits the single instruction multiple data paradigm (SIMD) and point to promising speed improvements if processed by GPUs [11].

Figure 4 summarizes the intuition behind our GPU implementation. In practice we store the decision vectors in the shared memory of the GPU to guarantee that they can be accessed quickly by all the threads. This is done only once after the training phase is finished. In addition to the decision arrays the processing kernel must be uploaded to processing units. For comparative purposes we propose two kernels; The first kernel (GPU-DT) only parallelize the decisions of each Decision Tree, while the second kernel (GPU-RF) also includes the average of the decision trees. The pseudocode, as the final kernels, assume that J, S, C, L, R, and F are stored in the shared memory of the device. These arrays does not change and can be submitted to the shared memory immediately after the training phase.

2.3   Hand-Identification

Once obtained the hand-segmentation it is possible to fit an ellipse to the contours of the hands. A quick analysis of egocentric videos of daily activities easily points to the angle of the hands with respect to the lower frame border (θ), and the normalized horizontal distance to the left border (x) as two discriminative variables to build our L/R hand-identification model. Figure 5 illustrates these variables.

For the identification level, we use the Maxwell model proposed in [8]; where the identity of the hand is decided according to the result of a likelihood ratio test between two maxwell distributions. The reasons behind the choice of the Maxwell distribution are two: (i) It is positive defined (ii) It allows to include

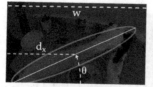 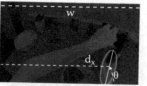

(a) Geometric problem of the (b) Geometric problem of the
left hand-segment   right hand-segment

Fig. 5. Input variables for the L/R hand-identification model.

an asymmetry factor in our formulation. The mathematical formulation for the
left hand (p_l) and the right hand (p_r) is given by Eqs. (9) and (10) respectively,
where p_x is the Maxwell distribution with parameters $\Theta = [d, a]$. The values
of x and θ are defined in the interval $[0, 1]$ and $[0, \pi]$ respectively. In general d
controls the displacement of the distribution (with respect to the origin) and a
controls its amplitude.

$$p_l(x, \theta|\Theta_l^x, \Theta_l^\theta) = p(x|\Theta_l^x)p(\theta|\Theta_l^\theta) \tag{9}$$

$$p_r(x, \theta|\Theta_r^x, \Theta_r^\theta) = p(1 - x|\Theta_r^x)p(\pi - \theta|\Theta_r^\theta) \tag{10}$$

$$p(x|\Theta) = p(x|d, a) = \sqrt{\frac{2}{\pi}} \frac{(x-d)^2}{a^3} e^{-\frac{(x-d)^2}{2a^2}} \tag{11}$$

In total this formulation contains 8 parameters summarized in Eq. (12). As
notation, the subindex of Θ refers to the left (l) or right (r) parameters, and
the super-index refer to the horizontal distance (x) or the anti-clockwise angle
(θ). The parameters of the model are selected by fitting the model to the angles
observed in the Kitchen dataset of subject 1. The final values are given by
Eq. (13). For more details about the fitting procedure and the motivation behind
the Maxwell formulation please refer to [8].

$$\begin{bmatrix} \Theta_l^x & \Theta_l^\theta \\ \Theta_r^x & \Theta_r^\theta \end{bmatrix} = \begin{bmatrix} d_l^x & a_l^x & d_l^\theta & a_l^\theta \\ d_r^x & a_r^x & d_r^\theta & a_r^\theta \end{bmatrix} \tag{12}$$

$$= \begin{bmatrix} -0.05 & 0.24 & -0.63 & 0.94 \\ -0.08 & 0.21 & -0.91 & 1.10 \end{bmatrix} \tag{13}$$

To compare the goodness of fit of the L/R hand-identification models given
by Eqs. (9) and (10) we perform a Likelihood ratio test on the post-processed
hand-like segments. The Likelihood ratio test is given by Eq. (14).

$$\Lambda(x, \theta) = \frac{L_l(\Theta_l^x, \Theta_l^\theta|x, \theta)}{L_r(\Theta_r^x, \Theta_r^\theta|x, \theta)} = \frac{p_l(x, \theta|\Theta_l^x, \Theta_l^\theta)}{p_r(x, \theta|\Theta_r^x, \Theta_r^\theta)}, \tag{14}$$

Relying only on the likelihood ratio, could lead to cases where two hand-like
segments are assigned the same label (left or right). To avoid this cases, and given
that a frame cannot have two left nor two right hands, we follow a competitive

rule in the following way. Lets assume two hands-like segments in the frame described by $z_1 = (x_1, \theta_1)$ and $z_2 = (x_2, \theta_2)$ as explained in Fig. 5, and their respective likelihood ratios given by $\Lambda(x_1, \theta_1)$ and $\Lambda(x_2, \theta_2)$. The competitive ids are assigned by Eq. (15).

$$
id_{z_1}, id_{z_2} = \begin{cases} \Lambda(x_1, \theta_1) > \Lambda(x_2, \theta_2) \rightarrow & id_{z_1} = l \\ & id_{z_2} = r \\ \\ \Lambda(x_1, \theta_1) \leq \Lambda(x_2, \theta_2) \rightarrow & id_{z_1} = r \\ & id_{z_2} = l \end{cases} \tag{15}
$$

3   Results

To measure the speed improvement of the accelerated hand-segmenter we use the subject 1 sequences of the kitchen dataset and two different GPU hand-segmentation kernels: The first kernel (DT_{GPU}) performs each Decision Tree as separate task in the GPU[1] and fuses the results in the CPU[2]. The second kernel (RF_{GPU}) evaluates the full Random Forest including the average directly in the GPU. Finally, the CPU sequential implementation of the algorithm is used as the baseline.[3] For comparative purposes the segmentation is performed at different compression levels. The results reported use 20 illumination models and fuses the closest 5 on each frame.

Figure 6 shows the time in seconds required by each hand-segmenter to process each frame at a particular compression width. It is noteworthy from the figure that the largest benefits, as expected, are obtained when the full image is segmented where the GPU_{RF} and GPU_{DT} kernels process in average 6.2 and 4.8 times faster than the CPU counterpart. The GPU_{RF} takes 0.052 s per frame while the CPU takes 0.32 s. In the worst case scenario, the CPU implementation takes 0.41 s, and the GPU_{RF} takes 0.058 s, which means that a throughput of 17.24 full resolution frames per second.

If a detailed segmentation is not required a common practice is to compress the frames before segmentation. If compressed to $180px$ width and assuming the worst scenario the GPU_{RF} and CPU could segment 141 and 44 fps respectively. It is noteworthy that this compression rate strongly compromises the detail of the segmentation but could lead to real-time analysis of the motion patterns of the user. The dashed and dotted lines in the figure shows the processing speed required to process video streams of 40 and 60 fps respectively.

To evaluate the segmentation quality we use the coffee sequence for training and the remaining ones for testing (i.e. CofHoney, HotDog, Tea, Pealette). Table 2 shows the performance of the Left/Right segmentation for each video sequence and the overall performance in the last columns. For this table the

---

[1] NVIDIA Corporation GF116 [GeForce GT 640 OEM].

[2] Intel(R) Core(TM) i7-3770 CPU @ 3.40 GHz.

[3] For the CPU baseline we use the Cython procedure available in sklearn.

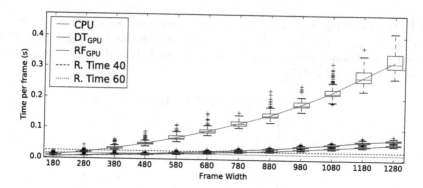

Fig. 6. GPU vs. CPU comparison.

Table 1. L/R hand-segmentation confusion matrix. This table uses the "Coffe" video sequence for training [8].

	CofHoney			Hotdog			Tea			Pealette			Total		
	No-hands	Left	Right	No-hands	Left	Right	No-hands	Left	Right	No-hands	Left	Right	No-hands	Left	Right
No-hands	0.990	0.003	0.007	0.989	0.005	0.006	0.996	0.002	0.002	0.991	0.006	0.003	**0.992**	**0.004**	**0.004**
Left	0.064	0.932	0.004	0.040	0.958	0.002	0.056	0.943	0.001	0.120	0.871	0.009	**0.073**	**0.923**	**0.004**
Right	0.092	0.002	0.906	0.136	0.001	0.864	0.082	0.000	0.918	0.112	0.002	0.886	**0.096**	**0.001**	**0.903**

hand-to-hand occlusions were disambiguated by using the algorithm proposed in [8] (Table 1).

Finally, Table 2 compares the multi-model hand-segmenter with previous works. Compared with a single pixel by pixel classifier of [18], our approach achieves improvements between 3 and 5 $F1$ score points. After the post-processing and identification process our method achieves a total $F1$ improvement of 9, 12 and 14 $F1$ points on the Coffee, Tea and Peanut video sequences respectively. In comparison to the shape aware hand-segmenter proposed by [23], our implementation performs better in all the video sequences. In particular, the "Tea" video sequence is improved by 10 $F1$ points.

Table 2. Hand-Segmenter state of the art comparison [8].

	Coffee	Tea	Peanut
1999 - Single pixel color [16]	0.83	0.80	0.73
2011 - stabilization + gPb + superpixel + CRF [12]	0.71	0.82	0.72
2013 - Li 1 × 1 window [18]	0.85	0.82	0.74
2013 - Li 9 × 9 window [18]	0.88	0.88	0.76
2014 - Shape Aware Forest (post-process) [23]	0.90	0.84	0.84
2016 - Ours (k = 20, m = 50)	0.88	0.87	0.77
2016 - Ours (k = 20, m = 50) + Hand-Id Post Process	**0.94**	**0.94**	**0.88**

4   Conclusions and Future Research

This paper contributes to 3 of the more challenging aspects of hand-segmentation methods in egocentric videos. The contributions of this paper are three folded:

(i) It proposes a hand-segmenter that fuse multiple hand-segmenter to alleviate illumination changes.

(ii) The proposed hand-segmenter is accelerated by using two different GPU kernels. The GPU hand-segmenter process 6.2 times faster that the sequential version.

(iii) A probabilistic hand-identification framework is introduced. This identification level seek to reduce the conceptual differences of traditional background/foreground hand segmenters and the human understanding of the hands as two cooperative entities. The proposed method properly identifies 99 % of the left and right hands.

As future research we highlight two possible extensions of this work: The first one is to migrate the implementation to embedded hardware. This would require additional work in the hardware side. (ii) Another interesting research line is to extend the identification level with tracker systems as proposed in the Unified Framework of Betancourt 2015 [4]. This is a promising research line for example to understand the motion patterns in patients of upper limb motor diseases.

Acknowledgement. This work was partially supported by the Erasmus Mundus joint Doctorate in Interactive and Cognitive Environments, which is funded by the EACEA, Agency of the European Commission under EMJD ICE.

References

1. Baraldi, L., Paci, F., Serra, G., Benini, L., Cucchiara, R.: Gesture Recognition using wearable vision sensors to enhance visitors' museum experiences. IEEE Sens. J. **15**(5), 1 (2015). http://ieeexplore.ieee.org/lpdocs/epic03/wrapper.htm?arnumber=7058423
2. Betancourt, A., Lopez, M., Regazzoni, C., Rauterberg, M.: A sequential classifier for hand detection in the framework of egocentric vision. In: Conference on Computer Vision and Pattern Recognition, vol. 1, pp. 600–605. IEEE, Columbus, June 2014. http://ieeexplore.ieee.org/lpdocs/epic03/wrapper.htm?arnumber=6910041
3. Betancourt, A., Morerio, P., Barakova, E.I., Marcenaro, L., Rauterberg, M., Regazzoni, C.S.: A dynamic approach and a new dataset for hand-detection in first person vision. In: Azzopardi, G., Petkov, N., Yamagiwa, S. (eds.) CAIP 2015. LNCS, vol. 9256, pp. 274–287. Springer, Heidelberg (2015). doi:10.1007/978-3-319-23192-1_23
4. Betancourt, A., Morerio, P., Marcenaro, L., Barakova, E., Rauterberg, M., Regazzoni, C.: Towards a unified framework for hand-based methods in first person vision. In: IEEE International Conference on Multimedia and Expo (Workshops). IEEE, Turin (2015)
5. Betancourt, A., Morerio, P., Marcenaro, L., Rauterberg, M., Regazzoni, C.: Filtering SVM frame-by-frame binary classification in a detection framework. In: International Conference on Image Processing. IEEE, Quebec (2015)

6. Betancourt, A., Morerio, P., Regazzoni, C., Rauterberg, M.: The evolution of first person vision methods: a survey. IEEE Trans. Circuits Syst. Video Technol. **25**(5), 744–760 (2015). http://ieeexplore.ieee.org/lpdocs/epic03/wrapper.htm?arnumber=7055926

7. Betancourt, A., Díaz-Rodríguez, N., Barakova, E., Marcenaro, L., Rauterberg, M., Regazzoni, C.: Unsupervised understanding of location and illumination changes in egocentric videos (2016). arXiv preprint: http://arxiv.org/abs/1603.09200

8. Betancourt, A., Morerio, P., Marcenaro, L., Barakova, E., Rauterberg, M., Regazzoni, C.: Left/Right Hand Segmentation in Egocentric Videos. ArXiv e-prints Under Revi (2016)

9. Buso, V., Benois-Pineau, J., Domenger, J.P.: Geometrical cues in visual saliency models for active object recognition in egocentric videos. In: Proceedings of the 1st International Workshop on Perception Inspired Video Processing - PIVP 2014, pp. 9–14. ACM Press, New York (2014). http://dl.acm.org/citation.cfm?id=2662996.2663007

10. Coudert, F., Butin, D., Le Métayer, D.: Body-worn cameras for police accountability: opportunities and risks. Comput. Law Secur. Rev. **31**(6), 749–762 (2015). http://dx.doi.org/10.1016/j.clsr.2015.09.002

11. Duncan, R.: A survey of parallel computer architectures. Computer **23**(2), 5–16 (1990)

12. Fathi, A., Ren, X., Rehg, J.M.: Learning to recognize objects in egocentric activities. In: Proceedings of the IEEE Computer Society Conference on Computer Vision and Pattern Recognition, pp. 3281–3288. IEEE, Providence, June 2011. http://ieeexplore.ieee.org/lpdocs/epic03/wrapper.htm?arnumber=5995444

13. Feng, S., Caire, R., Cortazar, B., Turan, M., Wong, A., Ozcan, A.: Immunochromatographic diagnostic test analysis using google glass. ACS Nano **8**(3), 3069–3079 (2014). http://pubs.acs.org/doi/abs/10.1021/nn500614k

14. Harvey, M., Langheinrich, M., Ward, G.: Remembering through lifelogging: a survey of human memory augmentation. Pervasive Mobile Comput. **27**, 14–26 (2016). http://www.sciencedirect.com/science/article/pii/S157411921500214X

15. Hastie, T., Tibshirani, R.J., Friedman, J.: The Elements of Statistical Learning, vol. 1, 10th edn. Springer, Heidelberg (2009). http://www.springerlink.com/index/D7X7KX6772HQ2135.pdf

16. Jones, M.J., Rehg, J.M.: Statistical color models with application to skin detection. Int. J. Comput. Vis. **46**, 81–96 (2002). IEEE Computer Society, Fort Collins, CO

17. Li, C., Kitani, K.: Model recommendation with virtual probes for egocentric hand detection. In: 2013 IEEE International Conference on Computer Vision, pp. 2624–2631. IEEE Computer Society, Sydney (2013). http://ieeexplore.ieee.org/lpdocs/epic03/wrapper.htm?arnumber=6751437

18. Li, C., Kitani, K.: Pixel-level hand detection in ego-centric videos. In: 2013 IEEE Conference on Computer Vision and Pattern Recognition, pp. 3570–3577. IEEE, June 2013. http://ieeexplore.ieee.org/lpdocs/epic03/wrapper.htm?arnumber=6619302

19. MathSoft: Classification and regression trees. Guide to Statistics 1, 369–401, February 1999

20. Matsuo, K., Yamada, K., Ueno, S., Naito, S.: An attention-based activity recognition for egocentric video. In: 2014 IEEE Conference on Computer Vision and Pattern Recognition Workshops, pp. 565–570. IEEE, June 2014. http://ieeexplore.ieee.org/lpdocs/epic03/wrapper.htm?arnumber=6910036

21. Morerio, P., Marcenaro, L., Regazzoni, C.: Hand detection in first person vision. In: Fusion, p. 6. University of Genoa, Istanbul (2013). http://www.isip40.it/resources/papers/2013/fpv_FUSION2013.pdf

22. Singhai, S., Satsangi, C.: Hand segmentation for hand gesture recognition. In: Workshop on Interactive Multimedia on Mobile & Portable Devices, vol. 1, pp. 48–52. ACM Press, New York (2014). http://dl.acm.org/citation.cfm?id=2505490

23. Zhu, X., Jia, X., Wong, K.-Y.K.: Pixel-level hand detection with shape-aware structured forests. In: Cremers, D., Reid, I., Saito, H., Yang, M.-H. (eds.) ACCV 2014, Part IV. LNCS, vol. 9006, pp. 64–78. Springer, Heidelberg (2015). doi:10.1007/978-3-319-16817-3_5

Egocentric Vision for Visual Market Basket Analysis

Vito Santarcangelo[1,2], Giovanni Maria Farinella[1(✉)], and Sebastiano Battiato[1]

[1] Department of Mathematics and Computer Science,
University of Catania, Catania, Italy
gfarinella@dmi.unict.it
[2] Centro Studi S.r.l., Buccino, SA, Italy

Abstract. This paper introduces a new application scenario for egocentric vision: Visual Market Basket Analysis (VMBA). The main goal in the proposed application domain is the understanding of customers behaviours in retails from videos acquired with cameras mounted on shopping carts (which we call narrative carts). To properly study the problem and to set the first VMBA challenge, we introduce the VMBA15 dataset. The dataset is composed by 15 different egocentric videos acquired with narrative carts during users shopping in a retail. The frames of each video have been labelled by considering 8 possible behaviours of the carts. The considered cart's behaviours reflect the behaviour of the customers from the beginning (cart picking) to the end (cart releasing) of their shopping in a retail. The inferred information related to the time of stops of the carts within the retail, or to the shops at cash desks could be coupled with classic Market Basket Analysis information (i.e., receipts) to help retailers in a better management of spaces and marketing strategies. To benchmark the proposed problem on the introduced dataset we have considered classic visual and audio descriptors in order to represent video frames at each instant. Classification has been performed exploiting the Directed Acyclic Graph SVM learning architecture. Experiments pointed out that an accuracy of more than 93 % can be obtained on the 8 considered classes.

1 Introduction and Motivations

Egocentric vision is a new emerging area in Computer Vision [1,2]. By exploiting wearable devices it is possible to collect hours of videos that can be processed to obtain a log of the monitored scenarios. Different papers on egocentric vision applications have been published in the recent literature. The main tasks addressed in this area are related to scene recognition [3], motion understanding [4], objects and actions recognition [5–8], 3D reconstruction [9,10] and summarization [11,12]. Among the others, context aware computing is an important research area for egocentric (first-person) vision domain [3,13,14]. Temporal segmentation of Egocentric Vision is also fundamental to understand the behavior of the users wearing a camera [4,15]. Recently, the retail scenario has

© Springer International Publishing Switzerland 2016
G. Hua and H. Jégou (Eds.): ECCV 2016 Workshops, Part I, LNCS 9913, pp. 518–531, 2016.
DOI: 10.1007/978-3-319-46604-0_37

Fig. 1. Information useful for VMBA.

become of particular interest for applications related to the geo-localization of the user's positions and the reconstruction of the spaces [16]. In the retail context, one of the possible developments of interest concerns the monitoring of the paths of customers, thereby enabling to carry out an analysis of their behaviors. Nowadays customers monitoring is partially employed by using loyalty cards, counting devices connected with Bluetooth and WiFi systems, employing RFID tags [17], as well as fixed cameras (e.g., video surveillance). Differently than classic approaches and considering the potentials and spread of egocentric cameras, in this paper we consider to turn an ordinary cart in a "narrative shopping cart" by equipping it with a camera. The acquired egocentric videos are processed with algorithms able to turn the visual paths in customers' behaviour. By doing so it is possible to acquire all over the route travelled by carts and (hence by the customers), from the cart picking to its release. Visual and audio data can be collected and processed to monitor pauses, to understand the areas of personal interest, to estimate the path speed, to estimate the most busy areas of the retail by clustering routes, to register the reactions opposite to the audio announcements in the store, as well as to infer the inefficiencies (e.g., slowness at cash desk). We call this kind of behavioral monitoring in a retail "Visual Market Basket Analysis" (VMBA) since it can be useful to enrich the classic "Market Basket Analysis" methods [18] used to infer the habits of customers.

In this paper we introduce the problem of VMBA considering three different high-level information related to the customers which is carrying the narrative cart (Fig. 1): location (i.e., indoor vs outdoor), action (i.e., stop vs moving), and scene context (i.e., cash desk, retail, parking, road). These high-level information can be organized in a hierarchy to produce 8 different behaviors useful in the retail domain to log the storyline of the shopping of the customers that can be eventually associated to others information (e.g., receipts) for retail management purposes. The 8 classes are shown as path, from the root to the leaves, of the tree in Fig. 2. Given a frame of the video acquired with the narrative cart camera, at

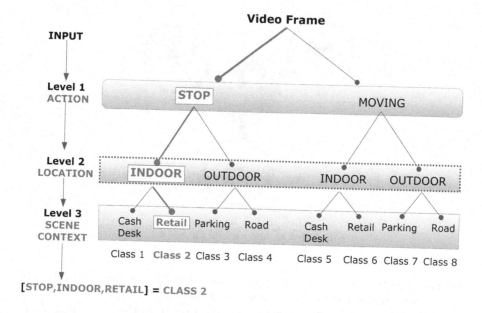

Fig. 2. Considered VMBA behavioral classes organized in a hierarchy.

Fig. 3. VMBA timeline temporally segmented considering the 8 classes. t denotes the time, whereas s denotes the stopping time.

each instant we wish to know a triplet corresponding to a path in the tree (e.g., [STOP, INDOOR, RETAIL] in Fig. 2). By classifying each frame of the acquired egocentric videos with the proposed 8 classes (i.e., the 8 possible triplet of the hierarchy in Fig. 2), it will be simple to perform an analysis of what are the custom behaviors, and also understand if there are problem to be managed in the store. An example of a narrative cart egocentric video together with a temporal segmentation with respect to the 8 defined classes is shown in Fig. 3. For example from the segmented narrative cart video it will be simple to understand how long are the stops to the cash desk by considering the frames classified with the triplets [STOP, INDOOR, CASH DESK] and [MOVING, INDOOR, CASH DESK]. This can be useful to eventually plan the opening of more cash desks to provide a better service to the customers. By analyzing the inferred triplets of a narrative cart video, it will be simple to understand if there are carts outside the cart parking spaces in order to take actions (e.g., if there is a long sequence of the triplet [STOP, OUTDOOR, ROAD] which does not change for long time). A lot of other considerations for a better management of the retail can be done by considering the narrative cart egocentric videos when those have been temporal segmented by classifying each frame with the 8 possible triples (i.e., behavioral classes). By combining the receipt with the temporal segmented video and with algorithms for visual re-localization [19] it will be simple to establish the order in which the products have been taken, hence increasing the information that are usually exploited by the classic "Market Basket Analysis" algorithms [18] and opening new research perspectives (Fig. 3). To set the first VMBA challenge we propose a new dataset of 15 sequences (VBMA) obtained by collecting and labeling real video sequences acquired in a retail. The proposed dataset is available for the research community upon request to the authors. We benchmark the dataset by considering a Direct Acyclic Graph SVM approach [20] coupled with classic descriptors for the representation of visual content (GIST [21]), motion (Optical Flow [22]), and audio (MFCC [23]). Experiments show that a classification accuracy of more than 93 % can be obtained on the proposed VMBA dataset when the 8 behavioral classes are considered.

The reminder of the paper is organized as follows: in Sect. 2, we describe the approach used to perform the benchmark study. Section 3 presents the dataset acquired with the narrative cart in a retail of Southern of Italy. Section 4 discuses the results. Finally, Sect. 5 concludes the paper and gives hints and open challenges.

2 Proposed Approach

The main goal of this paper is the segmentation of egocentric videos acquired with narrative carts in chapters automatically labeled with one of the 8 possible classes defined by the path of the tree presented in Fig. 2. A chapter is a set of consecutive frames of the video which present the same behavior (e.g., a sequence of frames with the same label [stop, indoor, cash desk]). The proposed behavioral tree has three layers (Fig. 2). The first layer is related to the action of moving or stopping the narrative carts (which reflect the user's basic actions in a retail). The second level of the tree identifies the high level location where the user is acting (indoor vs outdoor). The third level is related to the scene context during the shopping. Regarding the scene context we have considered four classes: parking, road, cash desk and retail. Looking at the VMBA hierarchy defined in Fig. 2, it is straightforward to understand that the different scene contexts are observed depending on the main location where the user is acting (indoor vs outdoor). Hence the scene contexts cash desk and retail can be observed only in indoor location, whereas the scene contexts parking and road can be observed only in outdoor locations. To perform the classification of a narrative cart video frame in order to automatically assign to it a triplet [action, location, scene context], two main "ingredients" are needed: the representation of the frame and

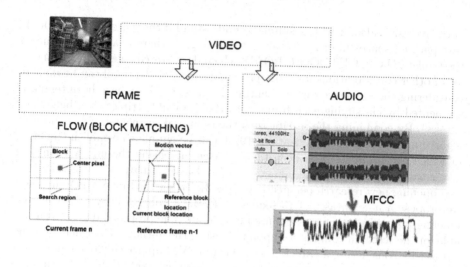

Fig. 4. Features used at the first level.

the classification modality. To benchmark the problem we have employed classic simple features for the representation and standard discriminative classifiers. In the following subsections we will detail the representations used for the three different layers of the tree in Fig. 2 and the classification method employed.

2.1 Representation at the First Level: Actions

The first level analyzes the customer behavior from the point of view of the motion of the narrative cart by considering two possible states: stop and moving. In order to understand such states from the egocentric video, in our benchmark we tested the MFCC audio features [24] and the optical flow features computed with the classic block matching approach [25] (Fig. 4). For the optical flow we have considered the frames divided in 9 blocks, so for each frame we have got a 9-dimensional features vector. The audio processing produced a feature vector of 62 components. We have decided to consider the audio because there is a visual correlation between the audio waveform with the narrative cart motion and locations (Fig. 5). The exploitation of the optical flow feature is straightforward since the problem under consideration. In our experiments we have tested the two considered features separately and jointly.

2.2 Representation at the Second Level: Location

The second level of the tree in Fig. 2 has the scope to identify the high level location where the user is acting: indoor vs outdoor. As for the first level we have considered MFCC features after visual inspection of waveform (Fig. 5). Indeed the waveform is more pronounced in the outdoor environment than in the indoor location. To benchmark the VMBA problem addressed in this paper for indoor

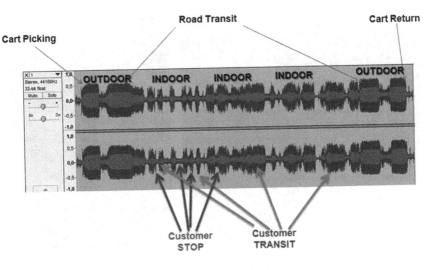

Fig. 5. Audio waveform and behaviors.

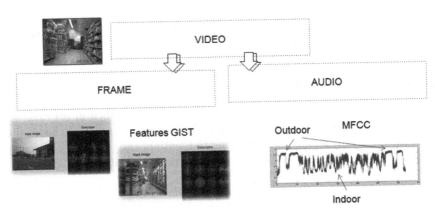

Fig. 6. Features used at the second level.

vs outdoor locations discrimination we have also tested the popular GIST visual descriptor [26], which is able to encode the scene context with a feature vector composed by 512 components (Fig. 6). In our experiments we tested indoor vs outdoor classification by considering audio and visual features independently and combined.

2.3   Representation at the Third Level: Scene Context

The third level of the hierarchy in Fig. 2 is related to the analysis of the scene context considering four different classes: cash desk, retail, parking and road. As described before, the first two contexts are related to the indoor environment, whereas the other two describe in more details the outdoor location. For this level

Fig. 7. Narrative carts.

of description we have used the GIST descriptor [26] again since its property in capturing the shape of the scene for context discrimination.

2.4 Classification Methods

After representing a frame of the egocentric video as described in previous sections, a classifier has to be employed to infer one of the 8 considered classes (i.e., one of the 8 possible triplet corresponding to a path of the tree in Fig. 2). In this paper we benchmarked three different classification modalities:

- combination of the results obtained by three different SVM classifiers in correspondence of the three different levels of the hierarchy;
- a single Multi-Class SVM trained on the 8 possible classes;
- a Direct Acyclic Graph SVM learning architecture (DAGSVM) [20] which reflects the hierarchy in Fig. 2 on each node.

Experiments reported in Sect. 4 demonstrate that good classification accuracy can be obtained considering the hierarchical classification performed by DAGSVM.

3   VMBA15 Dataset

To set the first VMBA challenge and perform the benchmark on the considered problem we acquired a dataset composed by 15 different egocentric videos with narrative carts in a retail of the Southern of Italy during real shopping. To this aim we have mounted a narrative cam veho muvi pro [27] into the front of a classic shopping cart as depicted in Fig. 7. Each narrative cart video has a

Fig. 8. Some visual examples of frames related to the egocentric videos of the VMBA15 dataset. The eight scenes represent the eight possible classes with order from top to bottom, left to right. Notice that some classes are characterized by similar visual content but different actions, such as in the case of the image at the first row of the second column (CLASS 2) and the third image in the second column (CLASS 6). The images at the first row are related to CLASS 1 (left) and CLASS 2 (right), and share the same location (INDOOR) but show different scene context (RETAIL vs CASH DESK).

Table 1. Number of samples per class for each egocentric video.

VIDEO	C_1	C_2	C_3	C_4	C_5	C_6	C_7	C_8	Total
1	0	13	2	0	8	193	17	89	322
2	0	17	4	0	9	266	10	84	390
3	0	19	4	0	12	226	10	96	367
4	0	20	3	0	10	277	13	106	429
5	0	20	4	0	10	213	9	107	363
6	69	10	28	2	59	134	35	91	428
7	0	3	13	0	7	102	16	119	260
8	6	36	7	0	8	233	8	75	373
9	142	186	8	0	18	550	9	85	998
10	0	5	3	0	7	106	13	75	209
11	42	90	31	0	10	406	16	89	684
12	0	36	22	0	26	436	23	104	647
13	56	80	57	4	7	130	28	133	495
14	50	396	7	0	3	485	11	46	998
15	81	528	0	27	3	310	3	46	998

duration between 3 to 20 min and resolution of 640×480 pixels. Audio has been also recorded since it can be useful to discriminate indoor vs outdoor environment. From each narrative cart video we have sampled and manually labeled frames and audio at 1 fps considering the 8 possible paths of the tree shown in Fig. 2. The total number of sample is 7961 (see Table 1 for more retails about the dataset). Some examples of frames extracted from the VMBA15 dataset are shown in Fig. 8. The labeled data is available upon request to the authors.

4   Experimental Settings and Results

We have performed experiments by randomly splitting that dataset in three parts composed by five egocentric video each. The experiments have been repeated three times considering 10 videos for the training and 5 video for the tests. The final results are obtained by averaging among the three runs. As first we have compared the different features employed at the different levels of the hierarchy independently by exploiting a SVM classifier with RBF kernel. This was useful to understand which are the best features (or combination of them) to be employed at each level for the final classification of each frame with respect to the 8 classes. In Table 2 are reported the results of the stop vs moving classification (i.e. First Level). Both audio and visual feature achieve good performance, however, visual feature (the flow) outperforms the audio features with a margin of about 5 %. Interestingly the combination by concatenation of audio and visual features improve the results and obtains an accuracy of 94.50 % in discriminating stop vs moving actions. The obtained results pointed out that the combination of MFCC and flow features has to be used at the first level.

Also in the case of the discrimination of the main location where the narrative cart is moving (or stopping), the visual features outperform audio features with a good margin by obtaining 95.79 % of accuracy (see Table 3). Differently than in the first level, the combination of audio and visual features do not improve the indoor vs outdoor classification. Hence for the second level we decided to employ the GIST descriptor alone.

For the third level of the hierarchy we have obtained an accuracy of 92.42 % with the GIST descriptor. Note that in this case a multi-class SVM with RBF kernel has been trained to discriminate this four possible scene contexts without considering the prior indoor vs outdoor. The results respect to the four scene contexts are reported in Table 4. The main confusion is related to the class parking and retail (first column in Table 4). This is probably due to the encoding of the scene information by the GIST descriptor. Indeed, when the narrative cart is in the parking space, the scene is mainly composed by vertical and horizontal edges that can be confused with the vertical and horizontal edges of some scenes in the retail (see Fig. 9). As demonstrated by the results reported later, this problem is mitigated when the classification is performed by the DAGSVM approach since it introduces a prior on the main location (indoor vs outdoor). One more problem in the classification is due to strong occlusions as the one in the examples reported in Fig. 10.

The aforementioned experiments pointed out that the best features to be employed in the hierarchy are the combination of MFCC and FLOW for the first level, whereas the GIST descriptor for the second and third level. Since the main goal is the classification with respect to the 8 possible triplets generated by the hierarchy in Fig. 2, after selecting the features for the three levels independently we have compared the three classification modalities described in Sect. 2.4. For the combination of three different classifiers (one for each level) we have considered the concatenation of the labels given by three different SVM (with RBF kernel) when trained independently on the best selected features of

Table 2. STOP vs MOVING classification

	FLOW	MFCC	COMBINED
Accuracy %	92.50	87.04	94.50
TP RATE %	73.03	61.54	84.76
TN RATE %	99.18	95.21	97.65
FP RATE %	0.82	4.79	2.35
FN RATE %	26.97	38.46	15.24

Table 3. INDOOR vs OUTDOOR classification

	GIST	MFCC	COMBINED
Accuracy %	95.79	88.00	91.77
TP RATE %	89.3	49.51	67.49
TN RATE %	97.8	97.66	97.1
FP RATE %	2.20	2.34	2.90
FN RATE %	10.7	50.49	32.51

Table 4. Scene Context classification

PREDICTED				
	PARKING	ROAD	RETAIL	CASH DESK
PARKING	54.25 %	17.01 %	25.09 %	3.64 %
ROAD	0.55 %	88.94 %	9.5 %	1.01 %
RETAIL	0.17 %	1.09 %	98.46 %	0.28 %
CASH DESK	0.13 %	7.47 %	17.21 %	75.19 %

Fig. 9. On the left a typical scene of the narrative cart when in the parking space. On the right an example of a frame acquired by the narrative cart in retail. The distribution of vertical and horizontal edges could generate confusion in the classification.

Fig. 10. Some examples of frames with occlusions (at the cash desk).

Fig. 11. Examples of frames correctly classified by the proposed DAGSVM approach. These frames are misclassified by the other two compared approaches. The frame on the left is related to the parking space of the carts, but is recognized as retail by both the combined approach and Multi-Class SVM. The frame on the right is related to outdoor, but is recognized as indoor by both the combined approach and Multi-Class SVM.

Table 5. Results of the classification considering the 8 classes

	Combination	Multi-Class SVM	DAGSVM
Accuracy %	87.36	69.54	93.47

the three levels. For the multi-class SVM with 8 classes we have trained a SVM with RBF kernel on the concatenation of MFCC, GIST and FLOW features. Finally, we have trained a DAGSVM [20] reflecting the hierarchy in Fig. 2. Each node of the DAG is composed by a SVM with RBF kernel in which the best features to solve the problem at each node are exploited. The results of the three different approaches are reported in Table 5.

The final results are in favor of the DAGSVM approach which obtain an accuracy of 93.47 %. It is worth to note that a concatenation of the MFCC features with the FLOW and GIST descriptors does not allow a multi-class SVM to reach good accuracy (69.54 %). Finally, the results of the combination of the three different classifiers stated at the second place in the classification a ranking (87.36 %). The visual examples for the assessment of the output given by the proposed DAGSVM-based approach are available in Fig. 11 and at the following URL: http://iplab.dmi.unict.it/epic2016.

5   Conclusion

This paper introduces the problem of "Visual Market Basket Analysis" (VMBA). To set the first VMBA challenge a new egocentric video dataset (VBMA15) has been acquired in a retail with cameras mounted on shopping carts. The VBMA15 dataset has been labeled considering 8 different classes corresponding to a hierarchical organization of actions, location and scene contexts. A first benchmark has been performed considering different classic representations and classification modalities. Experiments pointed out that audio, motion and global visual features are all useful in the VMBA application domain when coupled with a Direct Acyclic Graph based SVM leaning architecture. Our future works will be devoted to a complete formalization of the VMBA problem and to the augmentation of both dataset and labels to reflect the domain. We will also consider different retails to introduce a more realistic variability in the dataset. Moreover, recently appeared learning mechanisms to encode audio and flow features will be considered [3,22,28]. Also we will take into account egocentric camera with low capabilities for the recognition of the scene context [21]. The problem of re-localization [19] for the narrative carts will be explored to infer the order of the products acquired in a retail in order to combine visual location recognition and receipts. Finally, structure from motion based techniques [29] will be considered to automatically reconstruct the 3D shape of the store and to track the paths of the narrative carts to extract information useful for retails management.

Acknowledgment. The authors would like to thank Antonino Furnari, for his support in the development of this work.

References

1. Betancourt, A., Morerio, P., Regazzoni, C.S., Rauterberg, M.: The evolution of first person vision methods: a survey. IEEE Trans. Circuits Syst. Video Technol. **25**(5), 744–760 (2015)
2. Mann, S., Kitani, K.M., Lee, Y.J., Ryoo, M.S., Fathi, A.: An introduction to the 3rd workshop on egocentric (first-person) vision. In: 2014 IEEE Conference on Computer Vision and Pattern Recognition Workshops, pp. 827–832 (2014)
3. Furnari, A., Farinella, G.M., Battiato, S.: Recognizing personal contexts from egocentric images. In: 2015 IEEE International Conference on Computer Vision Workshop (ICCVW), pp. 393–401 (2015)
4. Poleg, Y., Arora, C., Peleg, S.: Temporal segmentation of egocentric videos. In: 2014 IEEE Conference on Computer Vision and Pattern Recognition, pp. 2537–2544 (2014)

5. Agrawal, P., Carreira, J., Malik, J.: Learning to see by moving. In: 2015 IEEE International Conference on Computer Vision (ICCV), pp. 37–45 (2015)
6. Damen, D., Leelasawassuk, T., Haines, O., Calway, A., Mayol-Cuevas, W.W.: You-do, i-learn: Discovering task relevant objects and their modes of interaction from multi-user egocentric video. In: British Machine Vision Conference (2014)
7. Fathi, A., Rehg, J.M.: Modeling actions through state changes. In: Computer Vision and Pattern Recognition, pp. 2579–2586 (2013)
8. Fathi, A., Ren, X., Rehg, J.M.: Learning to recognize objects in egocentric activities. In: Computer Vision and Pattern Recognition, pp. 3281–3288 (2011)
9. Poleg, Y., Halperin, T., Arora, C., Peleg, S.: Egosampling: Fast-forward and stereo for egocentric videos. In: Computer Vision and Pattern Recognition, pp. 4768–4776 (2015)
10. Lee, Y.J., Ghosh, J., Grauman, K.: Discovering important people and objects for egocentric video summarization. In: Computer Vision and Pattern Recognition, pp. 1346–1353 (2012)
11. Xiong, B., Kim, G., Sigal, L.: Storyline representation of egocentric videos with an applications to story-based search. In: International Conference on Computer Vision, pp. 4525–4533 (2015)
12. Lu, Z., Grauman, K.: Story-driven summarization for egocentric video. In: Computer Vision and Pattern Recognition, pp. 2714–2721 (2013)
13. Xu, Q., Li, L., Lim, J.H., Tan, C.Y.C., Mukawa, M., Wang, G.: A wearable virtual guide for context-aware cognitive indoor navigation. In: International Conference on Human-computer Interaction with Mobile Devices and Services, pp. 111–120 (2014)
14. Starner, T., Schiele, B., Pentland, A.: Visual contextual awareness in wearable computing. In: Second International Symposium on Wearable Computers, Digest of Papers, pp. 50–57, October 1998
15. Ortis, A., Farinella, G.M., D'Amico, V., Addesso, L., Torrisi, G., Battiato, S.: Organizing egocentric videos for daily living monitoring. Submitted to the ACM MM International Workshop on Lifelogging Tools and Applications (2016)
16. Wang, S., Fidler, S., Urtasun, R.: Lost shopping! monocular localization in large indoor spaces. In: International Conference on Computer Vision, pp. 2695–2703 (2015)
17. Ali, Z., Sonkusare, R.: Rfid based smart shopping: an overview. In: International Conference on Advances in Communication and Computing Technologies, pp. 1–3 (2014)
18. Tan, P.N., Steinbach, M., Kumar, V.: Introduction to Data Mining, 1st edn. Addison-Wesley Longman Publishing Co., Inc., Boston (2005)
19. Kendall, A., Grimes, M., Cipolla, R.: Posenet: a convolutional network for real-time 6-dof camera relocalization. In: International Conference on Computer Vision, pp. 2938–2946 (2015)
20. Platt, J.C., Cristianini, N., Shawe-taylor, J.: Large margin dags for multiclass classification. In: Advances in Neural Information Processing Systems, vol. 12, pp. 547–553 (2000)
21. Farinella, G., Raví, D., Tomaselli, V., Guarnera, M., Battiato, S.: Representing scenes for real-time context classification on mobile devices. Pattern Recogn. 48(4), 1086–1100 (2015)
22. Dosovitskiy, A., Fischery, P., Ilg, E., Häusser, P., Hazirbas, C., Golkov, V., Smagt, P.V.D., Cremers, D., Brox, T.: Flownet: learning optical flow with convolutional networks. In: International Conference on Computer Vision, pp. 2758–2766 (2015)

23. Muda, L., Begam, M., Elamvazuthi, I.: Voice recognition algorithms using mel frequency cepstral coefficient (MFCC) and dynamic time warping (DTW) techniques. CoRR abs/1003.4083 (2010)
24. Sahidullah, M., Saha, G.: Design, analysis and experimental evaluation of block based transformation in mfcc computation for speaker recognition. Speech Commun. **54**(4), 543–565 (2012)
25. Barron, J.L., Fleet, D.J., Beauchemin, S.S., Burkitt, T.A.: Performance of optical flow techniques. In: Computer Vision and Pattern Recognition, pp. 236–242 (1992)
26. Oliva, A., Torralba, A.: Modeling the shape of the scene: a holistic representation of the spatial envelope. Int. J. Comput. Vision **42**(3), 145–175 (2001)
27. Veho Muvi Cam: Narrative cam. www.vehomuvi.com. Accessed April 2016
28. Bengio, Y., Courville, A., Vincent, P.: Representation learning: a review and new perspectives. IEEE Trans. Pattern Anal. Mach. Intell. **35**(8), 1798–1828 (2013)
29. Wu, C.: Towards linear-time incremental structure from motion. In: International Conference on 3D Vision, pp. 127–134 (2013)

SEMBED: Semantic Embedding
of Egocentric Action Videos

Michael Wray[✉], Davide Moltisanti, Walterio Mayol-Cuevas,
and Dima Damen

Department of Computer Science, University of Bristol, Bristol, UK
{michael.wray,davide.moltisanti,walterio.mayol-cuevas,
dima.damen}@bristol.ac.uk

Abstract. We present SEMBED, an approach for embedding an egocentric object interaction video in a semantic-visual graph to estimate the
probability distribution over its potential semantic labels. When object
interactions are annotated using unbounded choice of verbs, we embrace
the wealth and ambiguity of these labels by capturing the semantic relationships as well as the visual similarities over motion and appearance
features. We show how SEMBED can interpret a challenging dataset of
1225 freely annotated egocentric videos, outperforming SVM classification by more than 5 %.

Keywords: Egocentric action recognition · Semantic ambiguity ·
Semantic embedding

1 Introduction

An egocentric camera captures rich and varied information of how the wearer
interacts with their environment. The challenge for the visual understanding
of this information is currently significant and not only incited by the enormous variety of such interactions but also by limitations in the available visual
descriptors, e.g. those rooted in motion or appearance. Supervised learning from
labelled examples is used to alleviate some of these ambiguities. Egocentric
datasets [6,10,12,34] and interaction recognition methods [9,10,23,28] differ in
the features used and classification techniques adopted, yet they all assume a
semantically distinct set of *pre-selected* verbs or verb-noun combinations for
supervision. When free annotations are available – unbounded choice of verbs or
verb-nouns – from audio scripts [1] or textual annotations [6], a single label is
selected to represent each interaction using a majority vote. Less frequent annotations are treated as outliers, though they typically represent a meaningful and

---

M. Wray and D. Moltisanti contributed equally to this work.

Electronic supplementary material The online version of this chapter (doi:10.
1007/978-3-319-46604-0_38) contains supplementary material, which is available to
authorized users.

G. Hua and H. Jégou (Eds.): ECCV 2016 Workshops, Part I, LNCS 9913, pp. 532–545, 2016.
DOI: 10.1007/978-3-319-46604-0_38

correct annotation. For example, lifting an object from a workspace could be described as *pick-up*, *lift*, *take* or *grab*; all valid labels. Note that assuming multiple *valid* labels is different from the problem of Ambiguous Label Learning, [3,14], where the aim is to find a single valid label from a mixed set of related and unrelated labels.

Egocentric video offers a unique insight into object interactions in particular. The camera is ideally positioned to capture objects being used and, equally interesting, the different ways in which the same object is used. One interaction (e.g. *open*) applies to a wide variety of objects, and each video can be labelled by multiple valid labels (e.g. *open door* vs. *push door*). In this context, recognition cannot be simplified as a one-vs.-all classification task. Capturing the semantic relationships between annotations and the visual ambiguities between accompanying video segments can better represent the space of possible interactions. Figure 1 shows a graphical abstract of our work.

Given a dataset of egocentric object interactions with free annotations, we contribute four diversions from previous attempts: (i) We treat all free annotations as valid, correct labellings, (ii) A graph that combines semantic relationships with visual similarities is built, inspired by previous work on object class categories in single images [8] (Sect. 3.1), (iii) A test video is embedded into the previously learnt semantic-visual graph and the probability distribution over its possible annotations is estimated (Sect. 3.2) and (iv) When verb meanings are available, we discover semantic relationships between annotations using WordNet (Sect. 3.3).

We test semantic embedding (SEMBED) on three public egocentric datasets [6,9,34]. We show that as the number of verb annotations and their semantic ambiguities increase, SEMBED outperforms classification approaches. We

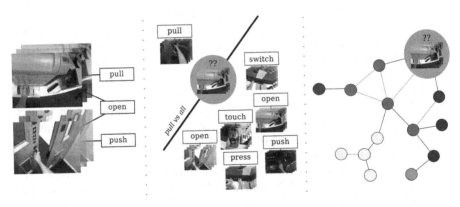

Fig. 1. Given a dataset of free annotations, with potentially ambiguous semantic labelling (left), we propose to deviate from the one-vs.-all classical approach (middle) and instead build a graph that encapsulates semantic relationships and visual similarities in the training set (right). Recognition then amounts to embedding an unlabelled video (denoted by '??') into the graph and estimating the probability distribution over potential labels.

also show that incorporating higher level semantic relationships, such as the hyponymy relationship, improves the results. Note that while we focus on *ego-centric object interaction recognition* as a rich domain of semantic and visual ambiguities, some of the arguments can apply to action recognition in general.

2   Embedding Object Interactions - Prior Work

To the best of our knowledge, embedding for egocentric action recognition has not been attempted previously. We first review works on recognising egocentric object interactions, then review works which incorporate semantic knowledge for recognition tasks.

Egocentric Object Interaction Recognition: Egocentric action recognition works range from self-motion [17] (e.g. walk, cycle) to high-level activities (e.g. [2,18,20,34,35]). On the task of object interaction recognition, approaches vary in whether they use hand-centred features [15,19], object-specific features [6,10,23,29] or a combination [12,21]. Ishihara *et al.* [15] use dense trajectories in addition to global hand shape features and apply a linear SVM to determine the action class. Kumar *et al.* [19] sample and describe superpixel regions around the hand. Their method allows for hand detectors to be trained spontaneously with the user performing the action.

Object-specific features are better suited for recognising verb-noun actions (e.g. *pick-cup vs. pick-plate*) rather than a general *picking* action. In Damen *et al.* [6], spatio-temporal interest points have been used to discover object interactions in an unsupervised manner. The works of Fathi *et al.* [9–11,21] have tested features including gaze, colour, texture and shape for verb-noun action classification. Of these, [10] specifically discusses the change in the object state as a useful feature to recognise object interactions. Though attempting video summarisation primarily, Ghosh *et al.* [12] introduces a collection of features that could be used to classify object-interactions such as distance from the hand, saliency, objectness represented using a spatio-temporal pyramid to detect change. These features were proven useful for segmenting object-interactions from a lengthy video, but have not been tested for action classification *per se.* On several publicly available datasets, Li *et al.* [21] compare motion, object, head motion and gaze information along with a linear SVM for object interaction classification. Their results prove that Improved Dense Trajectories (IDT) proposed by [37] outperform other motion features.

With the emergence of highly-discriminative appearance-based features, pre-trained Convolutional Neural Networks (CNN) on ImageNet have also been tested. In [25], CNN is evaluated for distinguishing manipulation from non-manipulation actions on an RGB-D egocentric dataset. Ryoo *et al.* [30] combine CNN with IDT along with novel time series pooling for dog-centric manipulation and non-manipulation actions. More recently, fine-tuned multi-stream CNN approaches have achieved state of the art results on egocentric datasets [22,33], though are tuned on each dataset independently.

Based on [21,30] conclusions, in this work we report results on IDT as a state-of-the-art motion feature and pre-trained CNN features a state-of-the-art appearance feature. Testing tuned CNNs is left for future work.

Semantic Embedding for Object and Action Recognition: Using linguistic semantic knowledge for Computer Vision tasks, including action recognition, has been fuelled by the accessibility of text or audio descriptions from online sources.

One such dataset which made this possible was gathered from YouTube videos [4] with free annotations. The dataset includes a variety of real-world scenarios, though not limited to egocentric or object-interactions. For each video, multiple annotators were asked to describe the video. Both [13,26] use this dataset for action recognition. In Motwani and Mooney [26], the most frequently annotated verb for each video is used, and verbs are grouped into classes using semantic similarity measures, extracted from the WordNet hierarchy as well as information corpuses. Videos are described by HoG and HoF features around spatio-temporal interest points. Guadarrama et al. [13] find subject, object and verb triplets in an attempt to automatically annotate the action. They create a separate semantic hierarchy for each, formulated by co-occurrences of words within the free annotations and use Spearman's rank to find the distances between clusters. Semantic links are used to generate specific, rather than general, annotations and a classifier is trained for each leaf node within the hierarchies. Their method allows zero-shot action annotation by trading-off specificity and semantic similarity. While combining semantics, both works use majority voting to limit the description per class to a single verb.

Another recent YouTube dataset was collected of users performing tasks while narrating their actions [1]. Labels are extracted from audio descriptions using automatic speech recognition. Verb labels are then used to align videos using a WordNet similarity measure as well as visual similarity (HoF and CNN) to find the sequence of actions in a task. Semantics have also been used for object recognition with images. Jin et al. [16] use WordNet to remove noisy labels from images which have multiple labels. Similarly, Ordonez et al. [27] use WordNet to find the most frequently-used object labels amongst multiple annotations. We build our work on Fang and Torresani [8], where images are embedded in a semantic-visual graph. In [8], images are clustered depending on the semantic relationships between the labels and edges of the graph are weighted with the visual similarity. They use ImageNet as the database for training, and benefit from the fact that images within ImageNet are organised according to the WordNet hierarchy. We differ from [8] in how we add visual links to the semantic graphs as will be explained next.

3 Semantic Embedding of Egocentric Action Videos

We next, in Sect. 3.1, explain how we build a semantic-visual graph (SVG) that encodes label and visual ambiguities in the training set. In Sect. 3.2, we detail how videos with an unknown class are embedded in SVG, and how the probability distribution over their annotations is estimated. Finally, in Sect. 3.3 we explore further semantic relationships when verb meanings are annotated.

3.1 Learning the Semantic-Visual Graph

The Semantic-Visual Graph (SVG) is a representation of the training videos, with three sources of information encoded. First, videos that are semantically linked, e.g. have the same label, are linked in SVG. Second, nodes that are visually similar, yet semantically distinct, should also be linked as these indicate visual ambiguities. Third, edge weights correspond to the normalised visual similarity, over neighbouring nodes, using a visual descriptor and a defined distance measure. In this section we explain how SVG_u, an undirected graph, is constructed, then normalised to achieve the directed graph SVG.

SVG_u is an undirected graph, where one node $x_i \in SVG_u$ corresponds to one training video. Assume $AX(x_i, x_j)$ is a binary function that checks whether two video labels are semantically related. Initially, $AX(x_i, x_j)$ is *true* when both videos are annotated by the exact same verb. This assumption is revisited in Sect. 3.3. Edges in SVG_u are created between nodes with a semantic relationship:

$$x_i \frown x_j \in SVG_u \iff AX(x_i, x_j) = true \qquad (1)$$

The undirected edge $x_i \frown x_j \in SVG_u$ is assigned a weight $w_{x_i \frown x_j} = D_v(x_i, x_j)$ where D_v is a distance measure defined over the visual descriptor chosen. Assume $rank(D_v(x_i, x_j))$ is a function that returns the relative position of the distance measure amongst all the remaining pairs of videos such that,

$$rank(D_v(x_i, x_j)) = n \iff D_v(x_i, x_j) = min_n(D_v(x_k, x_l)) \ \forall x_k, x_l \in SVG_u$$
$$and \ \ AX(x_k, x_l) \neq true \qquad (2)$$

and min_n is the nth minimum element in the list. In addition, assume $rank_i(D_v(x_i, x_j))$ is a function that returns the relative position of $D_v(x_i, x_j)$ amongst all nodes not connected to x_i such that,

$$rank_i(D_v(x_i, x_j)) = n \iff D_v(x_i, x_j) = min_n(D_v(x_i, x_l)) \ \forall x_l \in SVG_u$$
$$and \ \ AX(x_i, x_l) \neq true \qquad (3)$$

Further links are added to SVG_u to encode visual ambiguities such that,

$$x_i \frown x_j \in SVG_u \iff rank(D_v(x_i, x_j)) \leq m \ \ or \ \ rank_i(D_v(x_i, x_j)) = 1 \quad (4)$$

where m is the number of visual connections in SVG_u that correspond to the top m visually similar and semantically dissimilar nodes in SVG_u. We differ from [8] in that we ensure each node is connected to its top visually similar but semantically distinct node.

The undirected graph SVG_u is then converted to a directed graph by replacing each edge with two directed edges.

$$x_i \frown x_j \in SVG_u \Rightarrow \{x_i \rightarrow x_j, x_j \rightarrow x_i\} \in SVG \qquad (5)$$

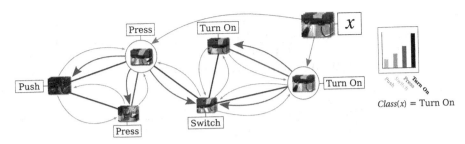

Fig. 2. The Semantic-Visual Graph (SVG) is built for training data, with semantic links (green) and visual links (blue) between videos. Given a test video x, two nearest neighbours are found (yellow) and a Markov Walk of 2 steps (step1-red and step2-orange) finds the probability distribution over potential labellings. Ref. supplementary material for animation. (Color figure online)

The weights of directed edges are initially the same as the weights for their undirected counterparts however they are normalised to define the probability of traversing from video x_i to x_j,

$$P(x_i \rightarrow x_j) = \frac{1/w_{x_i \rightarrow x_j}}{\sum_k 1/w_{x_i \rightarrow x_k}} \qquad \forall x_i \rightarrow x_k \in \text{SVG} \qquad (6)$$

The reciprocal of the weights is taken so that the most visually similar path will have the highest probability.

3.2 Embedding in Semantic-Visual Graph

Given a test video, x, we first embed the video into SVG then use the Markov Walk (MW) method from [8] to determine $Class(x)$. To embed x, we begin by finding the set $\mathcal{R}$ which contains the z closest neighbours to x based on visual distance, such that

$$\mathcal{R} = \{x_i \in \text{SVG} \mid rank(D_v(x, x_j)) \leq z\} \qquad (7)$$

We embed x into SVG by adding directed edges connecting x to nodes in $\mathcal{R}$: $x \rightarrow x_i \quad \forall x_i \in \mathcal{R}$ with normalised weights $P(x \rightarrow x_i)$. Following the embedding, MW attempts to traverse the nodes in the directed graph to estimate the probability of $Class(x)$. Given the Markovian assumption and a predefined number of steps t, we calculate the probability distribution of reaching a node x_i as follows

$$P(x_{i+t} \mid x) = \prod_{x_i \in R} \left(P(x \rightarrow x_i) \prod_{j=1}^{t} P(x_{i+j-1} \rightarrow x_{i+j}) \right) \qquad (8)$$

To perform MW efficiently, we construct the vector q such that

$$q(i) = \begin{cases} P(x \rightarrow x_i) & x_i \in \mathcal{R} \\ 0 & \text{otherwise} \end{cases} \qquad (9)$$

We also construct a matrix A such that $A(i,j) = P(x_i \rightarrow x_j)$ (Eq. 6), note that this matrix is asymmetrical as nodes have a different set of neighbours in SVG. Accordingly, $P(x_{i+t} \mid x) = q^T A^t$ where q^T is the transpose of q and t is the number of steps in MW. We can then accumulate $P(Class(x))$ for every unique annotation $ax \in AX$ as follows

$$P(Class(x) = ax) = \sum_{AX(x_{i+t},ax)=true} P(x_{i+t} \mid x) \qquad (10)$$

We then select $\arg\max_{Class(x)} P(Class(x))$ as the semantic label of x. Figure 2 shows an example of SVG and video embedding. In the figure, given two nearest neighbours $z = 2$ and two steps in MW $t = 2$, the probability distribution over possible labellings is calculated.

3.3 Semantic Relationships: Synsets and Hyponyms

In Sect. 3.1, videos are considered semantically linked only when the annotated verbs are the same. SVG then enables handling ambiguities via incorporating visual similarity links in the graph. However, further semantic relationships, such as synonymy and hyponymy relationships, can be exploited between annotations. In linguistics, two words are *synonyms* if they have the same meaning, and the set of all synonyms is a *synset*. Moreover, two words are described as a *hyponym* and a *hypernym* respectively if the first is a more specific instance of the second. The terms originate from the Greek word *hypó* and *hypér* - *under* and *over*.

Synonymy and hyponymy relationships are encoded in lexical databases. WordNet (v3.1, 2012) is a commonly-used lexical database that is based on six semantic relations [24]. In the WordNet verb hierarchy, verbs are first separated into their various meanings by the notation $\langle word \rangle.v.\langle s \rangle$ where $s \geq 1$ is the number of disjoint meanings. The meanings are then arranged in hierarchies that encapsulate semantic relationships. To benefit from such hierarchies, verbs should be annotated with their meanings. We annotate [6] using verb meanings, and Fig. 3 shows how such annotations of the same action can be synonyms and hyponyms, as annotators chose different or more specific action descriptions.

Given annotated meanings, we define the term action synsets (AS) to indicate that annotations are linked by a synonymy relationship solely, and the term action hyponym (AH) to indicate that annotations are linked by both the synonymy or the hyponymy relationships. For comparison, we define the term action meaning (AM) where annotations are linked only when the annotation matches exactly. We use the general term AX where $AX \in \{AM, AS, AH\}$ is one of the possible types of semantic relationships tested.

4   Datasets, Experiments and Results

We selected three publicly available datasets that primarily focus on object interactions from egocentric videos [6,7,9] (Fig. 4).

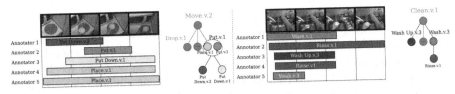

Fig. 3. Five free annotations for two sequences from the BEOID dataset [6], and the respective semantic relationships between the annotations from WordNet [24]. In the hierarchy, each parent-child relationship represents a hypernym-hyponym pair. The dotted circle encapsulates a synonymy relationship. The start and end times of the actions are also shown. For placing a cup on a mat (left), synonyms *put.v.*1 and *place.v.*1 were chosen by annotators. *put_down.v.*1, a hyponym of *put.v.*1 was also used. For washing a cup (right), the verbs *wash.v.*3, *wash up.v.*3 and *rinse.v.*1 were chosen. *rinse.v.*1 is a hyponym of *wash.v.*3.

Verb annotations: We exploited the annotations provided by the authors to split the CMU and GTEA+ sequences into object-interaction segments. For CMU, object-interaction annotations are only provided for the activity of *making brownies*. Annotators chose from 12 disjoint verbs to ground-truth segments. In GTEA+ annotators chose from verb-noun pairing to ground-truth, e.g. *cut_cucumber* versus *divide_bun* and similarly *squeeze_ketchup* versus *compress_bun*. When removing the nouns, verbs could be used interchangeably but free annotations were not available to annotators.

Name	Users	Seq.	OI Seg.s	Used OI Seg.s	Semantic Verbs
CMU [7]	5	35	516	406	12 (33.8, 30.5)
GTEA+ [9]	13	30	3371	1000*	25 (40.0, 75.5)
BEOID [6]	3-5	58	1488	1225	75 (16.3 34.2)

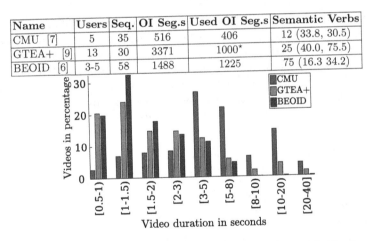

Fig. 4. Dataset details (top) and video length distributions (bottom). Number of users, segments, Object-Interaction (OI) segments and used segments in the results (length < 40 s) are detailed. We report the number of annotated verbs along with μ and σ for the number of segments per verb. *: Due to the size of GTEA+ we sampled 1000 videos randomly. Ref. supplementary material for frequencies of verb annotations per dataset.

While BEOID contains a variety of activities and locations, ranging from a desktop to operating a gym machine, it does not provide action-level annotations so we annotated BEOID using free annotations[1], allowing annotators to split video sequences into object-interaction segments in addition to choosing the verb. We recruited 20 native English speakers. These annotators were given a free textbox to label each segment with the verb that best described the seen interaction *in their opinion*. Once a verb has been chosen, the annotators were given the set of potential meanings extracted from WordNet for the chosen verb. Again, they were asked to select the meaning that, *in their opinion*, best suited the segment. Multiple annotators (8–10) were asked to label each task to intentionally introduce variability in the choice of verbs and start-end times of object interaction segments.

Motion and Appearance Features: We test two state-of-the-art feature descriptors to represent both the motion and the appearance of the videos. These are the Improved Dense Trajectories (IDT) [38] and Overfeat Convolutional Neural Networks pre-trained for ImageNet classes (CNN) [32]. For CNN features, we take every 5th frame from 30 fps video, starting always from the first frame, and rescale to 320×240 pixels.

Encodings: We test two encodings, using Bag of Words (BoW) [5] and Fisher Vectors (FV) [31] with Euclidean distance. For IDT, when creating the BoW and FV representations, we use a 25 % random sample from every video to model the Gaussians for efficiency. We vary the number of Gaussians (γ_{fv}) and the size of the codebook (γ_{bow}) in reported results.

Classification: In all results, leave-one-person-out cross validation has been used. Namely, when testing a video containing one person performing an action, all other videos captured from the same person are excluded from the training set. For SVM results, as the tested datasets contain an imbalance in the distribution of instances per class, we weight the classes by the term $w(c) = 1/prior(c)^{\lambda}$ where $\lambda \in [0,1]$ is the exponent that best fits the distribution of segments per verb for a given dataset (ref supplementary material).

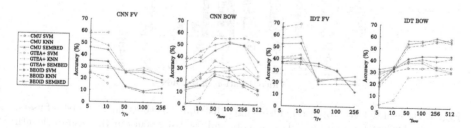

Fig. 5. Results as γ_{fv} and γbow vary for CMU, GTEA+, BEOID. Results were shown with $k = 5$, $m = 240$, $z = 10$, $t = 10$. Similar performance is seen for other parameters.

---

[1] Annotations can be found at: http://www.cs.bris.ac.uk/~damen/BEOID/.

Table 1. As the number of verbs increases from 12 to 75, the best performance changes from SVM to SEMBED. Results are obtained with $\gamma_{fv} = 10$ and $\gamma_{bow} = 256$, $k = \{3, 5, 5\}$, $m = 240$, $z = \{2, 6, 4\}$, $t = \{20, 20, 8\}$ for CNN and $z = \{4,5,14\}$, $t = \{4,20,10\}$ for IDT. For completion, state-of-the-art results on verb-noun classes are reported under 'Other Works' thus are not directly comparable to our verb only results.

FEATURES	CNN						IDT							
ENCODING	FV			BOW			FV			BOW			Verbs	Other Works
METHOD	SVM	K-NN	SEMBED	SVM	K-NN	SEMBED	SVM	K-NN	SEMBED	SVM	K-NN	SEMBED		
CMU [7]	58.6	46.6	46.3	55.9	43.3	52.0	69.4	58.1	57.4	55.9	57.6	61.6	12	48.6 [34], 73.4 [36]
GTEA+ [9]	15.6	30.0	31.0	25.1	33.5	33.6	43.6	43.4	42.1	27.8	34.5	40.3	25	60.5 [21], 65.1 [22]
BEOID [6]	20.9	34.4	37.5	15.2	19.1	19.6	38.7	36.0	37.4	34.8	39.6	45.0	75	-

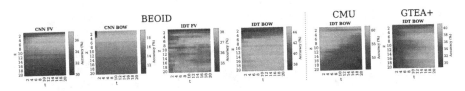

Fig. 6. Evaluation of SEMBED sensitivity to z and t parameters with $m = 240$.

Results on annotated verbs: Table 1 compares the three datasets for every ⟨features, encoding, classifier⟩ combination. The following conclusions can be made: (i) for all datasets, motion features (IDT) outperform appearance features (CNN) when classifying verbs without considering the object used. (ii) for CMU and GTEA+, we produce comparable results to published results using motion information on the same datasets. These are reported under 'Other Works' but are not directly comparable as published works tend to report on verb-noun classes. (iii) For the three datasets with varying number of verbs, as the number of verbs increases (12 → 75) with an increase in semantic ambiguity, SEMBED outperforms standard classifiers (SVM and K-NN). While the table shows the best results for encoding, Fig. 5 reports comparative results as γ is changed - $\gamma_{fv} = 10$ generally led to higher accuracies on all datasets, compared to $\gamma_{bow} = 256$.

We test the sensitivity of SEMBED to its key parameters z and t and report results in Fig. 6 showing the accuracy over various features for BEOID and across the three datasets for IDT-BOW (Ref. supplementary material for all combinations). As noted, z and t behave differently for the various appearance and motion descriptors as well as for different encodings. Generally, SEMBED is more sensitive to the choice of z than t. This is because the Markovian Walk (MW) is unable to represent the probability distribution over labels unless the starting positions are representative of the visual ambiguity. Figure 6 also shows that MW isn't too helpful for CMU (as t increases, accuracy decreases) because it has visually distinctive verb classes. On all datasets, SEMBED is resilient to changing m values; the results are comparable on $180 \leq m \leq 400$.

Table 2. As synonymy (AS) and then hyponymy (AH) semantic relationships are incorporated, accuracy increases for all features on the BEOID dataset. $\gamma_{fv} = 10$, $\gamma_{bow} = 256$, $m = 240$, {AM,AS,AH}: $z_{CNN} = \{3,3,2\}$, $t_{CNN} = \{20,20,14\}$, $z_{IDT} = \{6,10,13\}$, $t_{IDT} = \{20,20,2\}$

FEATURES	CNN						IDT						
ENCODING	FV			BOW			FV			BOW			
METHOD	SVM	K-NN	SEMBED	SVM	K-NN	SEMBED	SVM	K-NN	SEMBED	SVM	K-NN	SEMBED	Classes
AM	13.2	24.6	26.2	12.1	7.8	11.7	25.9	28.5	32.2	26.1	31.6	38.2	108
AS	17.9	25.6	27.1	12.7	8.1	12.7	29.8	30.4	33.5	29.6	33.6	**40.6**	102
AH	18.1	25.0	26.9	12.2	7.4	16.3	36.2	33.1	34.5	29.1	35.2	**41.9**	84

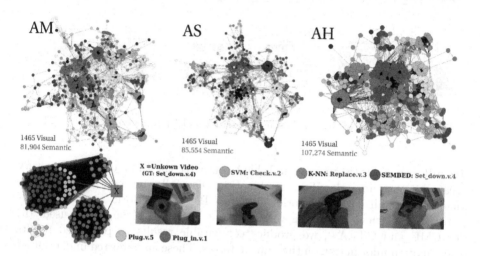

Fig. 7. SVG for three semantic levels on BEOID (top). Example using AH (bottom), SVM and K-NN produce incorrect results. The Markov walk of SEMBED allows the video to be correctly classified.

Results on annotated verbs and meanings: As mentioned earlier, we also annotate BEOID with verb-meaning ground-truth. This resulted in 108 $\langle word \rangle.v.\langle s \rangle$ annotations for the 1225 segments in the dataset. Note the increase in the number of classes from 75 when using verbs only to 108 when using verb-meaning ground-truth. This increase is due to two reasons - one *helpful*, another *problematic*. For example, it is *helpful* when annotators choose between *hold.v*.1: *"keep in a certain state, position"* and *hold.v*.2: *"hold in one's hand"*. Annotators would then use the first for when a button is pressed and the second for when an object is grasped. However, frequently, WordNet meanings can appear ambiguous resulting in *problematic* cases, especially in the context of egocentric actions. An example of this is the action of turning a tap on so water would flow. Annotators used *turn.v*.1: *"change orientation or direction"* and *turn.v*.4: *"cause to move around or rotate"* interchangeably. In WordNet though, *turn.v*.1 and *turn.v*.4 are not semantically related, introducing unwanted ambiguity affecting the ground-truth labels. While we accept that WordNet may not be the best method to incorporate meaning, we report results as semantic links are incorporated.

We test the three types of semantic relationships $AX = \{AM,AS,AH\}$. Histograms of all classes for the various semantic relationships are included in the supplementary material. Table 2 shows that embedding consistently improved performance as synsets and then hypernyms are grouped. Results also demonstrate the advantages of introducing semantic links between videos. Additionally, IDT continues to outperform CNN. Figure 7 shows one example of SEMBED in action when using meanings and AH semantic links[2]. It should be noted that the best performance of SEMBED on meanings is inferior to using verbs only. This is due to the difficulty in assigning meanings to verbs as previously noted. Approaches to address meaning ambiguities are left for future work.

5 Conclusion and Future Directions

The paper proposes embedding an egocentric action video in a semantic-visual graph to estimate the probability distribution over potentially ambiguous labels. SEMBED profits from semantic knowledge to capture interchangeable labels for the same action, along with similarities in visual descriptors.

While showing clear potential, outperforming classification approaches on a challenging dataset, results merely evaluate the $\arg\max$ label when compared to ground-truth. Further analysis of the probability distribution will be targeted next. Other approaches to identify semantically related object-interaction labels from, for example, other lexical sources, overlapping annotations or object labels will also be attempted. SEMBED's ability to scale to other object interactions and more discriminative visual descriptors will also be tested.

References

1. Alayrac, J., Bojanowski, P., Agrawal, N., Laptev, I., Sivic, J., Lacoste-Julien, S.: Unsupervised learning from narrated instruction videos. In: CVPR (2016)
2. Bleser, G., Damen, D., Behera, A., Hendeby, G., Mura, K., Miezal, M., Gee, A., Petersen, N., Macaes, G., Domingues, H., Gorecky, D., Almeida, L., Mayol-Cuevas, W., Calways, A., Cohen, A., Hogg, D., Stricker, D.: Cognitive learning, monitoring and assistance of industrial workflows using egocentric sensor networks. PLOS ONE (2015)
3. Chen, C.H., Patel, V.M., Chellappa, R.: Matrix completion for resolving label ambiguity. In: Proceedings of the IEEE Conference on Computer Vision and Pattern Recognition (2015)
4. Chen, D., Dolan, W.: Collecting highly parallel data for paraphrase evaluation. In: Annual Meeting of the Association for Computational Linguistics: Human Language Technologies (2011)
5. Csurka, G., Dance, C., Fan, L., Willamowski, J., Bray, C.: Visual categorization with bags of keypoints. In: Workshop on statistical learning in computer vision, ECCV (2004)

---

[2] Video with results available at: http://youtu.be/6bDDTIJUuic.

6. Damen, D., Leelasawassuk, T., Haines, O., Calway, A., Mayol-Cuevas, W.: You-do, I-learn: discovering task relevant objects and their modes of interaction from multi-user egocentric video. In: BMVC (2014)
7. De La Torre, F., Hodgins, J., Bargteil, A., Martin, X., Macey, J., Collado, A., Beltran, P.: Guide to the Carnegie Mellon University Multimodal Activity (CMU-MMAC) database. Robotics Institute (2008)
8. Fang, C., Torresani, L.: Measuring image distances via embedding in a semantic manifold. In: Fitzgibbon, A., Lazebnik, S., Perona, P., Sato, Y., Schmid, C. (eds.) ECCV 2012, Part IV. LNCS, vol. 7575, pp. 402–415. Springer, Heidelberg (2012)
9. Fathi, A., Li, Y., Rehg, J.M.: Learning to recognize daily actions using gaze. In: Fitzgibbon, A., Lazebnik, S., Perona, P., Sato, Y., Schmid, C. (eds.) ECCV 2012, Part I. LNCS, vol. 7572, pp. 314–327. Springer, Heidelberg (2012)
10. Fathi, A., Rehg, J.: Modeling actions through state changes. In: CVPR (2013)
11. Fathi, A., Ren, X., Rehg, J.: Learning to recognize objects in egocentric activities. In: CVPR (2011)
12. Ghosh, J., Lee, Y.J., Grauman, K.: Discovering important people and objects for egocentric video summarization. In: CVPR (2012)
13. Guadarrama, S., Krishnamoorthy, N., Malkarnenkar, G., Venugopalan, S., Mooney, R., Darrell, T., Saenko, K.: Youtube2text: Recognizing and describing arbitrary activities using semantic hierarchies and zero-shot recognition. In: ICCV (2013)
14. Hüllermeier, E., Beringer, J.: Learning from ambiguously labeled examples. In: Intelligent Data Analysis, pp. 419–439 (2006)
15. Ishihara, T., Kitani, K., Ma, W., Takagi, H., Asahawa, C.: Recognizing hand-object interactions in wearable camera videos. In: ICIP (2015)
16. Jin, Y., Khan, L., Wang, L., Awad, M.: Image annotations by combining multiple evidence & Wordnet. In: ACM international conference on Multimedia (2005)
17. Kitani, K., Okabe, T., Sato, Y., Sugimoto, A.: Fast unsupervised ego-action learning for first-person sports videos. In: CVPR (2011)
18. Kuehne, H., Serre, T.: Towards a generative approach to activity recognition and segmentation. AXiv preprint arXiv:1509.01947 (2015)
19. Kumar, J., Li, Q., Kyal, S., Bernal, E., Bala, R.: On-the-fly hand detection training with application in egocentric action recognition. In: CVPRW (2015)
20. Lade, P., Krishnan, N., Panchanathan, S.: Task prediction in cooking activities using hierarchical state space markov chain and object based task grouping. In: ISM (2010)
21. Li, Y., Ye, Z., Rehg, J.: Delving into egocentric actions. In: CVPR (2015)
22. Ma, M., Fan, H., Kitani, K.: Going deeper into first-person activity recognition. In: CVPR (2016)
23. McCandless, T., Grauman, K.: Object-centric spatio-temporal pyramids for egocentric activity recognition. In: BMVC (2013)
24. George, A.M.: Wordnet: a lexical database for english. Commun. ACM 38(11), 39–41 (1995)
25. Moghimi, M., Azagra, P., Montesano, L., Murillo, A., Belongie, S.: Experiments on an rgb-d wearable vision system for egocentric activity recognition. In: CVPRW (2014)
26. Motwani, T., Mooney, R.: Improving video activity recognition using object recognition and text mining. In: ECAI (2012)
27. Ordonez, V., Liu, W., Deng, J., Choi, Y., Berg, A., Berg, T.: Predicting entry-level categories. IJCV 115(1), 29–43 (2015)
28. Pirsiavash, H., Ramanan, D.: Detecting activities of daily living in first-person camera views. In: CVPR (2012)

29. Ren, X., Gu, C.: Figure-ground segmentation improves handled object recognition in egocentric video. In: CVPR (2010)
30. Ryoo, M., Rothrock, B., Matthies, L.: Pooled motion features for first-person videos. In: CVPR (2015)
31. Sánchez, J., Perronnin, F., Mensink, T., Verbeek, J.: Image classification with the fisher vector: theory and practice. IJCV **105**(3), 222–245 (2013)
32. Sermanet, P., Eigen, D., Zhang, X., Mathieu, M., Fergus, R., LeCun, Y.: Overfeat: Integrated recognition, localization and detection using convolutional networks. ICLR (2013)
33. Singh, S., Arora, C., Jawahar, C.: First person action recognition using deep learned descriptors. In: CVPR (2016)
34. Spriggs, E., De La Torre, F., Hebert, M.: Temporal segmentation and activity classification from first-person sensing. In: CVPRW (2009)
35. Sundaram, S., Mayol-Cuevas, W.W.: Egocentric visual event classification with location-based priors. In: Bebis, G., et al. (eds.) ISVC 2010, Part II. LNCS, vol. 6454, pp. 596–605. Springer, Heidelberg (2010)
36. Taralova, E., De La Torre, F., Hebert, M.: Source constrained clustering. In: ICCV (2011)
37. Wang, H., Kläser, A., Schmid, C., Liu, C.: Action recognition by dense trajectories. In: CVPR (2011)
38. Wang, H., Schmid, C.: Action recognition with improved trajectories. In: ICCV (2013)

Interactive Feature Growing for Accurate Object Detection in Megapixel Images

Julius Schöning[✉], Patrick Faion, and Gunther Heidemann

Institute of Cognitive Science, Osnabrück University, Osnabrück, Germany
juschoening@uos.de

Abstract. Automatic object detection in megapixel images is quite inaccurate and a time and memory expensive task, even with feature detectors and descriptors like *SIFT, SURF, ORB,* and *KAZE.* In this paper we propose an interactive feature growing process, which draws on the efficiency of the users' visual system. The performance of the visual system in search tasks is not affected by the pixel density, so the users' gazes are used to boost feature extraction for object detection.

Experimental tests of the interactive feature growing process show an increase of processing speed by 50 % for object detection in 20 megapixel scenes at an object detection rate of 95 %. Based on this method, we discuss the prospects of interactive features, possible use cases and further developments.

Keywords: Feature growing · Interactive object detection · Eye tracking · Multivariate detectors

1 Introduction

In available datasets [7,8,14,25] the resolution of images for e.g. feature and interest point detection are mostly way below common camera resolution between 5 and 20 megapixel (mp). Nevertheless, feature detection and description are usually key components in modern computer vision application like 3D reconstruction [18,19], object recognition, as well as scene awareness [16,17] and understanding [22]. One common way to start bottom-up analysis of still images is to apply feature detectors, such as *SIFT* [9], *SURF* [3], *ORB* [15], and *KAZE* [2]. For video data, these techniques have been extended with time as an additional dimension, cf. *3D SIFT* [20].

In this paper, we propose to extend available feature detectors and descriptors by integrating multimodal information generated by user interaction. We expect that interactive feature detectors and descriptors yield a minimum of feature points while maximizing information content and robustness. Further, down-sampling of images will be avoided and computation time reduced. To get an

Electronic supplementary material The online version of this chapter (doi:10. 1007/978-3-319-46604-0_39) contains supplementary material, which is available to authorized users.

© Springer International Publishing Switzerland 2016
G. Hua and H. Jégou (Eds.): ECCV 2016 Workshops, Part I, LNCS 9913, pp. 546–556, 2016.
DOI: 10.1007/978-3-319-46604-0_39

idea of the potential of interactive features, we perform object detection in scenes of 19.9 mp (5152 × 3864) resolution. For highlighting the need of high scene resolution, our data set consists of both very small and very large objects within various scenes. Starting with a brief overview of used features, we benchmark the detection rate and processing time of *SURF*, *SIFT*, *ORB*, and *KAZE* features in Sect. 3. Based on the detector with the best detection rate, the interactive feature growing process is introduced in Sect. 4. This guided process uses the effectiveness of the human vision system in search tasks. In experimental tests, we are able show that processing time is halved and detection rate even slightly increases. Finally, we discuss possible applications, improvements and further work.

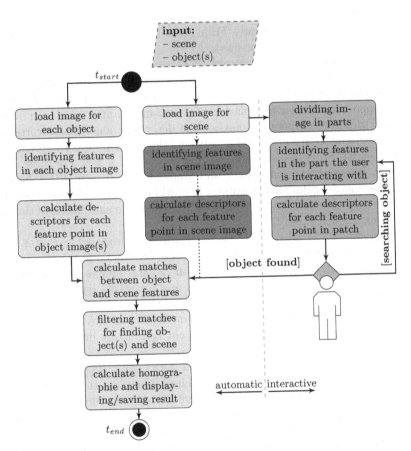

Fig. 1. Automatic and interactive object detection process—red blocks: processing time critical path of automatic feature detection and description process, especially, if high resolution scene images are used; green blocks: proposed interactive feature growing using, e.g., users' gaze information. By this additional information generated by user interaction, the number of feature points is reduced. (Color figure online)

2   State of the Art

In the following, we briefly summarize the feature processing stages and four common feature detection and description methods, that we used in our experiments.

Object recognition based on local features usually follows three processing stages [21, Chap. 4]:

- detection—identify the location of features,
- description—calculate a quantitative description of every feature,
- matching—find a best match between feature sets of different images, cf. yellow and red blocks of Fig. 1.

In order to integrate the user information into the whole process, one has to start at the detection level already. From there on, any classical combination of detection and description can be used.

Lowe [9] proposed the *Scale-invariant Feature Transform (SIFT)*. Its basic idea is to detect features as scale-space extrema in a pyramid of difference-of-Gaussian (DoG) filtered versions of the image. The DoG pyramid corresponds to a fast approximation for a Laplacian of Gaussian pyramid, which can be used effectively to detect corners in images. The descriptor algorithm incorporates local image gradients in a neighborhood around the keypoint into 4×4 orientation histograms with 8 orientation bins, leading to a $4 \times 4 \times 8 = 128$ dimensional descriptor. By using the scale space and gradient information, *SIFT* becomes invariant to image scaling and rotation. It is still one of the slowest algorithms for feature detection and description, mostly because the calculation of the DoG pyramid takes much time [13].

Speeded Up Robust Features (SURF) is another feature proposed by Bay et al. [3]. It also detects features as extrema in scale-space, but uses a fast approximation of the Hessian matrix, which is computed on integral images. For description, the responses of Haar-wavelets are recorded and quantized into 64 dimensions. The *SURF* algorithm needs roughly one third of the time of *SIFT* [3] with comparable detection performance. Still, both methods can only deal with linear illumination changes [13] and are therefore not completely invariant to photometric transformations.

Another robust feature is the *Oriented FAST and Rotated BRIEF* [15] (*ORB*), which combines two existing approaches. It employs the *FAST* detector, which detects points with an intensity difference between the center pixel and surrounding pixels greater than a predefined threshold. For *ORB*, this technique is applied on multiple levels of a scale pyramid. An orientation measure is added, which is lacking in *FAST*. The descriptor works with an orientation invariant extension of the *BRIEF* descriptor, which uses binary tests between pixels in an image patch. In principle, the *ORB* algorithm is not as robust as *SIFT* or *SURF*, but orders of magnitude faster, making it very useful for real-time applications [13].

The most recent method considered here is *KAZE* [2]. The fundamental difference to the previous ones is the computation of a nonlinear scale-space by diffusion filtering. Here, feature points are detected with Hessian matrices as well. The description is performed with the *M-SURF* descriptor, which is similar to *SURF*, but is adapted to the nonlinear scale space. *KAZE* does not offer much speedup and resides somewhere between *SIFT* and *SURF* in terms of computation time, but is more accurate even under non-linear transformations [2].

3   Feature Detectors and Descriptors

Due to the lack of available high-resolution image sets, that contain scenes with both small and large objects, we created our own data set for the evaluation of feature detectors and descriptors.

As shown in Fig. 2, it consists of four scenes—19.9 mp each— and nine objects with a large variation in resolution, scale and orientation. To provide an unbiased benchmark of the detection rate, the *OpenCV* implementation of *SIFT*, *SURF*, *ORB* and *KAZE* were used with their predefined parameters. Special boosted implementations have been deliberately left out. With all aforementioned features, an automatic object detection system corresponding to the yellow and red process blocks of Fig. 1 has been implemented. The feature matching between object and scene is done by a *Fast Library for Approximate Nearest Neighbors* (*FLANN*) [11] based matcher, followed by an outlier filter. Finally, the homography of the object in the scene is calculated and the resulting image is saved.

The random initialization of the algorithms has a minor effect on detecting the object. To reduce this effect, all twelve scene-object detection tasks[1] were repeated ten times.

As shown later in Fig. 3(a), the performance of *KAZE* is significantly better than *SIFT*, *SURF* and *ORB*. This result reflects the findings of Alcantarilla et al. [2]. Despite its nonlinear scale space, *KAZE* is computationally expensive, as shown later in Fig. 3(b). Nevertheless, because of its detection performance and its higher number of found corresponding features, *KAZE* is used for the implementation of our interactive feature growing process.

4   Interactive Feature Growing

The main idea of interactive feature growing is to detect and describe features, based on users gazes, during an object search task. Thus, a new time variant dimension—the users' gaze—is considered for the feature calculation, such that the information of the image is enriched by user interaction. Owing the fast response time of subjects in visual search tasks [6,24], our hypothesis is that users' gaze fixations on certain pixels contain information for boosting object detection. In consequence, an error-free object detection with a minimum of user keyboard and mouse interaction, as demonstrated in the supplemental video, can be realized.

---

[1] detect objects (e)-(h) in scene (a); detect objects (e),(g),(h) in scene (b); detect objects (i),(j) in scene (c); detect objects (k)-(m) in scene (d); cf. Fig. 2.

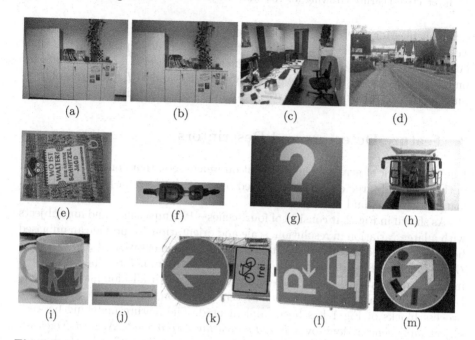

Fig. 2. Data set for scene-object detection tasks (See footnote 1) comprising four scene (a) to (d) each at a resolution of 5152 × 3864 pixel (19.9 mp) and nine object (e) to (m) in various resolution, scale and orientation

4.1 Process

To realize a first simple, temporal invariant implementation of interactive feature growing, we redesigned the normal automatic object detection process (Fig. 1, left hand side). Therefore, the path which is time critical for high resolution (red blocks) has been substituted by an interactive path (green blocks).

As a preprocessing step, the whole image is divided into a grid of small patches. In the current implementation, a simple rectangular grid is used, but meaningful image segmentation methods [4,5] could also be helpful. When the user interacts with a grid cell, the features in this cell are detected and described. The processing of image parts continues until the user finds the object in the scene. Then, the interactive process turns back to the automatic process and matches the features.

Additionally, after displaying the result, the user can directly decide whether the result is correct. Otherwise, the interactive process can be repeated.

4.2 User Interface

Considering user capacity for processing information [10], the user interface (UI) displays a maximum of five elements. Once the application is started, only a fixation element and a separator is displayed. All operating system elements are also hidden. As soon as the user presses the "start/found object" key, the scene is shown at the position of the fixation element. The object of interest for the detection task is displayed on the upper left. To provide the important instantaneous feedback in about a tenth of a second [12, Chap. 5], processed image parts are grayed out. The users' gaze point is visualized at all times during interactive key point growing. If the object of interest is found by the user, she/he presses the "start/found object" key again. After a brief processing time, the user can evaluate the result and is able to redo the current scene if the matching failed. A demonstration video of the UI is available within the supplemental material of this paper[2].

4.3 Implementation

The coding for the prototype and benchmark software was in $C++$ with $QT\ 5.3$, $OpenCV\ 3.0.0$ and $Tobii\ EyeX\ SDK\ 1.6$ as third-party components. To achieve a fast responding UI, the QT framework in conjunction with $OpenCV$ is used. On this basis, a low cost eye-tracking device, $Tobii\ EyeX$ [23], is implemented as singleton to capture the pixel at which the user is looking. To avoid blocking process elements within the UI and gaze capturing, the $KAZE$ feature detection and description is encapsulated as an independent thread. This design facilitates a continuous sampling of gaze data, such that the feature growing works even for very small eye movements.

5   Experimental Evaluation

In order to test our hypothesis and evaluating the interactive approach, the following tests were designed and performed.

5.1 Setup

As described in Sect. 3, the automatic tests are done with twelve randomized scene-object detection tasks, which were repeated ten times. Based on this procedure, the evaluation of the interactive feature growing was done with ten untrained subjects, using the randomized scene-object detection tasks. Taking a possible learning curve of the untrained subjects into account, the results in Fig. 3, and in the supplementary material contain the measurements with and without (marked with †) the first of twelve tasks.

To embed the human visual system in a natural manner, an eye-tracking device is used for machine interaction. This device requires calibration for every subject. After the calibration with the $Tobii$ tool, the subject performs the searching task using our implementation of interactive feature growing. The subjects were told to look at the object and find it in the scene as fast as possible. When they think they found it, they should press the "start/found object" key.

---

[2] see also https://ikw.uos.de/%7Ecv/publications/EPIC16.

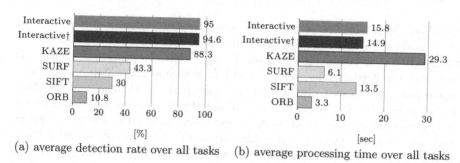

(a) average detection rate over all tasks   (b) average processing time over all tasks

Fig. 3. Average results over all twelve scene-object detection tasks (See footnote 1). †
first task of each subject is excluded with respect to the learning curve.

If the object was not detected correctly in a scene, the subject was able to repeat
this scene three times. In this case, the final reported processing time is the sum
over all retrials. A chinrest was used during the calibration and performing phase
to minimize errors due to head movements of the untrained subjects.

The processing time, in the automatic, as well as in the in interactive case,
is defined as difference between the stopping t_{end} and starting point t_{start}, cf.
Fig. 1. All tests were performed on the same *Intel i7-3770* computer with 24 GB
RAM.

5.2   Results

Interactive feature growing outperforms even the best automatic methods *KAZE*
with respect to the detection rate, see Fig. 3(a). On average, it has halved the
processing time of *KAZE* to a time comparable with *SIFT*, cf. Fig. 3(b). For
specific object-scene combinations, our interactive feature growing process is
29 %–69 % faster than *KAZE* with a slightly better detection rate. The detailed
results and statistics of each scene object combination are presented in a supplementary pdf document.

In two object-scene combinations users were not able to get the algorithm to
identify the right location, even after three retries. These object-scene combinations are illustrated in Fig. 4 – cf. detailed results Figs. 6 and 7 in supplementary
document.

6   Discussion

On average, interactive feature growing outperforms the automatic versions of
feature detection algorithms with respect to the detection rate. However, some
cases are problematic, cf. Fig. 4. By looking at these cases more closely, we
recognize that users only fixate their gazes on a small specific area of the object
within the scene and do not cover the complete object with their gazes. As
consequence, the number of features and descriptors were not sufficient to detect

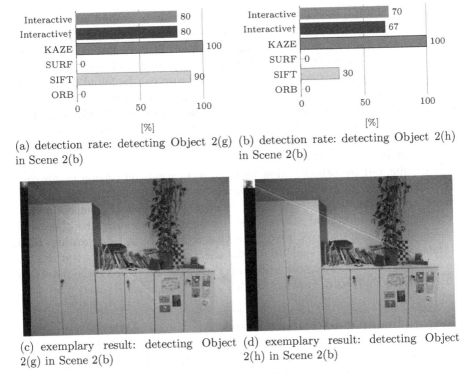

(a) detection rate: detecting Object 2(g) in Scene 2(b)

(b) detection rate: detecting Object 2(h) in Scene 2(b)

(c) exemplary result: detecting Object 2(g) in Scene 2(b)

(d) exemplary result: detecting Object 2(h) in Scene 2(b)

Fig. 4. Examples where the matching rate of interactive scene-object detection is below automatic approaches. This effect is caused by the rectangular processing grid.

the object in the scene. In addition, the fragmentation of the object through the grid resulted in even less features in the areas of the grid-lines. In further tests, we were able to reduce this effect by parameterization of the rectangular processing grid. Still, in order to avoid the problem even better, one should apply superpixels or segmentation based processing grids instead. Thus looking at one part of an object would lead to features being computed over the whole area of the object.

Another major point of discussion is why we omitted scaling down the scenes by some factor. Downscaling images until the task is just possible for humans, like it is common for image classification using deep convolutional neural networks, will reduce the processing time of the scene (Fig. 1, red blocks) drastically. But the varying size and resolution of the objects makes it almost impossible to define a scaling factor for the scenes, which works over the whole scene-object detection task. Scaling the images down too much would lead to drastically reduced detection rate for small objects. This behavior might also be an explanation on why *SIFT* does show such a low detection rate for objects with low resolution, like object 2(f), (h), (i), and (k).

Every interactive approach needs a user as operator over the complete processing time, which leads to the issue of use cases for such an expensive method. A potential use case is the creation of accurate ground truth annotations, which are essential in a large number e.g. for training of deep neuronal networks or of classifier ensembles. Currently, many of these ground truth data sets were created manually or operators review the results of automatic annotations to filter out incorrect data. Another use case can be found in situation where a user already exists, e.g. in research with driver assistance systems. Interactive feature growing could on the one hand boost detection of objects in front of the car, e.g. street signs. On the other hand it could support evaluation of driver behavior, e.g. in assessing if the driver missed some important signs or was distracted by other objects.

Regarding our hypothesis—that users' gaze fixations on certain pixels contains information for boosting object detection—we show in the results, that interactive identification of features can significantly improve the detection rate. By incorporating additional gaze features, like saccades, smooth pursuit, or total time spend on a certain pixel, we assume that interactive feature growing could be improved further. This leads to a more selective identification of features. In the end new feature descriptors using users' gazes could increase the detection rate of interactive feature growing to 100 %.

7   Conclusion and Future Work

In this paper, an interactive feature growing process has been presented. With a still naive and not yet optimized prototype of this novel method, the processing time for applying computationally expensive features on high quality images (20 mp) can be drastically reduced. In contrast to automatic methods, only the necessary areas of an image were processed. The decision, which parts of an image are necessary for e.g. a search task, is made by users' conscious and unconscious experiences in visual searching tasks. To support object detection, she/he uses her/his experiences of the real world, which include conceptual knowledge like "a pen is commonly placed on a table".

As further work, we plan to combine interactive feature growing with the FREAK [1] feature descriptor to get a fully bio-inspired system for scene understanding in high resolution images. Further, we want to investigate the impact of different image partition grids and temporal interaction of the user to describe completely new feature types. In addition to still images, the implementation of interactive feature growing for high definition video data is planned to improve our semi-automatic ground truth annotation *iSeg* [16,17].

Acknowledgments. This work was funded by German Research Foundation (DFG) as part of the Priority Program "Scalable Visual Analytics" (SPP 1335).

References

1. Alahi, A., Ortiz, R., Vandergheynst, P.: FREAK: fast retina keypoint. In: IEEE Conference on Computer Vision and Pattern Recognition (CVPR) (2012)

2. Alcantarilla, P.F., Bartoli, A., Davison, A.J.: KAZE features. In: Fitzgibbon, A., Lazebnik, S., Perona, P., Sato, Y., Schmid, C. (eds.) ECCV 2012. LNCS, vol. 7577, pp. 214–227. Springer, Heidelberg (2012). doi:10.1007/978-3-642-33783-3_16

3. Bay, H., Tuytelaars, T., Gool, L.: SURF: speeded up robust features. In: Leonardis, A., Bischof, H., Pinz, A. (eds.) ECCV 2006. LNCS, vol. 3951, pp. 404–417. Springer, Heidelberg (2006). doi:10.1007/11744023_32

4. Van den Bergh, M., Boix, X., Roig, G., de Capitani, B., Van Gool, L.: SEEDS: superpixels extracted via energy-driven sampling. In: Fitzgibbon, A., Lazebnik, S., Perona, P., Sato, Y., Schmid, C. (eds.) ECCV 2012. LNCS, vol. 7578, pp. 13–26. Springer, Heidelberg (2012). doi:10.1007/978-3-642-33786-4_2

5. Chen, H.-P., Shen, X.-J., Long, J.-W.: Histogram-based colour image fuzzy clustering algorithm. Multimedia Tools Appl. 75, 11417–11432 (2016). doi:10.1007/s11042-015-2860-6

6. Eriksen, C.W., Schultz, D.W.: Information processing in visual search: a continuous flow conception and experimental results. Percept. Psychophys. 25(4), 249–263 (1979)

7. Everingham, M., Van Gool, L., Williams, C.K.I., Winn, J., Zisserman, A.: The PASCAL Visual Object Classes Challenge 2012 (VOC2012) Results (2012). http://host.robots.ox.ac.uk:8080/pascal/VOC/voc2012/

8. Griffin, G., Holub, A., Perona, P.: Caltech-256 object category dataset. Technical report (2007)

9. Lowe, D.G.: Distinctive image features from scale-invariant keypoints. Int. J. Comput. Vis. 60, 91–110 (2004). doi:10.1023/B:VISI.0000029664.99615.94

10. Miller, G.A.: The magical number seven, plus or minus two: some limits on our capacity for processing information. Psychol. Rev. 63(2), 81 (1956)

11. Muja, M., Lowe, D.G.: Fast approximate nearest neighbors with automatic algorithm configuration. Proc. Int. Conf. Comput. Vis. Theor. Appl. (VISAPP) 2, 331–340 (2009)

12. Nielsen, J.: Usability Engineering. Morgan Kaufmann, San Francisco (1993)

13. Oliveira, I.O.d., Ono, K.V., Todt, E.: IGFTT: towards an efficient alternative to SIFT and SURF. In: International Conferences in Central Europe on Computer Graphics, Visualization and Computer Vision (WSCG), Full Papers Proceedings, pp. 73–80 (2015)

14. Romberg, S., Pueyo, L.G., Lienhart, R., van Zwol, R.: Scalable logo recognition in real-world images. In: Proceedings of the 1st ACM International Conference on Multimedia Retrieval, ICMR 2011, pp. 25: 1–25: 8. ACM, New York (2011)

15. Rublee, E., Rabaud, V., Konolige, K., Bradski, G.: ORB: an efficient alternative to SIFT or SURF. In: International Conference on Computer Vision (ICCV) (2011)

16. Schöning, J., Faion, P., Heidemann, G.: Semi-automatic ground truth annotation in videos: an interactive tool for polygon-based object annotation and segmentation. In: Proceedings of the 8th International Conference on Knowledge Capture (K-CAP), K-CAP 2015, pp. 17: 1–17: 4. ACM, New York (2015)

17. Schöning, J., Faion, P., Heidemann, G.: Pixel-wise ground truth annotation in videos - an semi-automatic approach for pixel-wise and semantic object annotation. In: Proceedings of the 5th International Conference on Pattern Recognition Applications and Methods (ICPRAM), pp. 690–697 (2016)

18. Schöning, J., Heidemann, G.: Evaluation of multi-view 3D reconstruction software. In: Azzopardi, G., Petkov, N. (eds.) CAIP 2015. LNCS, vol. 9257, pp. 450–461. Springer, Heidelberg (2015). doi:10.1007/978-3-319-23117-4_39

19. Schöning, J., Heidemann, G.: Interactive 3D modeling - a survey-based perspective on interactive 3D reconstruction. In: Proceedings of the 4th International Conference on Pattern Recognition Applications and Methods (ICPRAM) pp. 289–294 (2015)

20. Scovanner, P., Ali, S., Shah, M.: A 3-dimensional sift descriptor and its application to action recognition. In: Proceedings of the 15th ACM International Conference on Multimedia, MM 2007, pp. 357–360. ACM, New York (2007)

21. Szeliski, R.: Computer Vision: Algorithms and Applications. Springer, London (2011). doi:10.1007/978-1-84882-935-0

22. Tanisaro, P., Schöning, J., Kurzhals, K., Heidemann, G., Weiskopf, D.: Visual analytics for video applications. It-Inf. Technol. **57**, 30–36 (2015)

23. Tobii, A.B.: Tobii EyeX controller (2016). http://www.tobii.com/xperience/products/

24. Trick, L.M., Enns, J.T.: Lifespan changes in attention: the visual search task. Cogn. Dev. **13**(3), 369–386 (1998)

25. Xiao, J., Ehinger, K.A., Hays, J., Torralba, A., Oliva, A.: SUN database: exploring a large collection of scene categories. Int. J. Comput. Vis. **119**(1), 3–22 (2016). doi:10.1007/s11263-014-0748-y

Towards Semantic Fast-Forward and Stabilized Egocentric Videos

Michel Melo Silva[✉], Washington Luis Souza Ramos,
Joao Pedro Klock Ferreira, Mario Fernando Montenegro Campos,
and Erickson Rangel Nascimento

Departamento de Ciência da Computação,
Universidade Federal de Minas Gerais, Belo Horizonte, Brazil
{michelms,washington.ramos,mario,erickson}@dcc.ufmg.br, jpklock@ufmg.br

Abstract. The emergence of low-cost personal mobiles devices and wearable cameras and the increasing storage capacity of video-sharing websites have pushed forward a growing interest towards first-person videos. Since most of the recorded videos compose long-running streams with unedited content, they are tedious and unpleasant to watch. The fast-forward state-of-the-art methods are facing challenges of balancing the smoothness of the video and the emphasis in the relevant frames given a speed-up rate. In this work, we present a methodology capable of summarizing and stabilizing egocentric videos by extracting the semantic information from the frames. This paper also describes a dataset collection with several semantically labeled videos and introduces a new smoothness evaluation metric for egocentric videos that is used to test our method.

Keywords: Semantic information · First-person video · Fast-forward · Egocentric stabilization

1 Introduction

The popularity of first person videos, also known as egocentric videos, has considerably increased in social media. The large capacity of personal and video-sharing websites repositories and the ubiquity of easily operable devices such as smartphones, GoPro™ and Sony POV Action cameras are providing a compelling ecosystem for creating and storing different types of long-running egocentric videos. The wearer is free for recording long streams of regular activities such as working, cooking, driving, athletic activities like walking, running, bicycling,

---

M.M. Silva and W.L.S. Ramos contributed equally.

Electronic supplementary material The online version of this chapter (doi:10.1007/978-3-319-46604-0_40) contains supplementary material, which is available to authorized users.

G. Hua and H. Jégou (Eds.): ECCV 2016 Workshops, Part I, LNCS 9913, pp. 557–571, 2016.
DOI: 10.1007/978-3-319-46604-0_40

snowboarding, monitoring tasks (e.g. police patrol and life guarding) and home videos like family meetings and birthdays.

Despite the increasing popularity of recording egocentric videos, they are usually lengthy, monotonous and composed of an unedited content. The camera unsteadiness caused by the natural movements of the wearer makes them challenging to be analyzed [15]. Sampling at a fixed rate is the most simple manner to reduce their length. However, it amplifies the body movements producing disturbing and even nauseates videos.

Several works have been proposed to address the instability of egocentric videos aiming to create a pleasant experience when watching the reduced version. Such works borrowed the term *hyperlapse* from the exposure method in timelapse photography to name their methods. Similar to hyperlapse photography, where the camera moves through long distances and the images are aligned to create a final video with smooth transitions along the acquisition time, the hyperlapse algorithms also aim to downsize long and monotonous videos in short fast-forward watchable videos with no abrupt transitions between the frames. One challenge involving these approaches is that some portions of the video may be more significant to the users than others. For instance, one could be recording a celebratory event in its entirety, but in a posterior exhibition to the family the relevant parts are only those in which is possible to recognize the guests.

In this work, we propose a new frame segmentation approach and an egocentric video stabilizer based on the disparity between the semantic and non-semantic segments. Our method minimizes the shakiness in the final video avoiding the deletion of relevant frames for the user based as far as the semantic information is concerned. A new dataset composed of semantically labeled videos and an evaluation metric to measure the egocentric videos smoothness are presented and used in our experiments.

Similar to this work, our previous approach [18] slices the video into segments based on their relevance to the user to define their relative speed-ups. Although that approach is capable of creating a final video with the required speed-up avoiding the deletion of relevant segments, its optimization process increases the shakiness in the segments classified as no relevant. As stated by Poleg et al. [16] and Kopf et al. [10], egocentric videos do not present smooth transitions and continuous movement making hard to use traditional stabilization techniques which in the fast-forward videos is even more challenging due to the fact they are not composed of temporal consecutive frames. Additionally, like other works, the quantitative experiments is limited due to the use of a rough shakiness metric and an uncontrolled dataset, which generate misleading results.

Contributions: The contributions of this work can be summarized as:

i. A new frame segmentation approach combined with an egocentric video stabilizer. Our method uses the disparity between the semantic and non-semantic parts to segment the input video and stabilizes the segments by using homography transformations to smooth the output video and reconstruct the frames;

ii. A new dataset with several semantically labeled videos to fill the gap in the literature related to well-controlled datasets concerning the semantic information;

iii. A new evaluation metric able to measure the egocentric videos smoothness. We demonstrate through qualitative results that the most used metric for this kind of video which is the reduction of epipole/Focus of Expansion (FOE) jitter is not accurate.

2 Related Work

Video Summarization methods can capture the essential information of the video and create a shorter version, thus the amount of time necessary to interpret the video content can be reduced [19,20]. The summarization methods are basically divided into two approaches: static storyboard or still-image abstract, where the most representative keyframes are selected to represent the video as a whole [6,11] and; dynamic video skimming or moving-image abstract, where a series of video clips compose the output [3,14]. Despite the large number of video summarization techniques proposed over the past years, only few works address summarization on egocentric videos [4,11,13,17]. Besides video summarization techniques aim to keep semantic information, it cannot give a temporal perception of the video, because some parts of the input video are completely removed [16].

We can roughly divide smooth fast-forward techniques into two categories: 3D model approaches, which consists of methods that, in short, reconstruct the scene structure and create an optimal path where a virtual camera would navigate and; 2D approaches, where methods basically work on selecting frames adaptively to compose the final video. The main advantage of the former category is the freedom with respect to the camera pose, however, on the other hand, they require camera parallax and the reconstruction step can take a while to be performed. The latter avoids the 3D reconstruction by skipping a subset of the input frames in order to maximize the smoothness of the output video.

The work of Kopf et al. [10] is an example of the 3D model category. The authors present a method which reconstructs the 3D input camera path by using structure from motion and per-frame proxy geometries and, performs an optimization in path location and orientation to create a virtual path and render the final video. Although remarkable results are presented, their technique requires significant camera motion and parallax and, in addition, demands a high computational cost.

More recent methods have adopted the optimization of frame selection [5,8, 16]. Poleg et al. [16] focus on an adaptive frame selection based on minimizing an energy function. They modeled the video as a graph by mapping the frames as the nodes and the edges weight reflecting the cost of the transition between the frames in the final video. The shortest path in the graph produces the best frames transitions for the final video composition. In the work of Joshi et al. [8] they present a more sophisticated algorithm which optimally selects frames from the input video as result of a joint optimization of camera motion smoothing and speed-up. They also perform a 2D video stabilization to create the hyperlapse result. Halperin et al. [5] extended the work of Poleg et al. expanding the field of view of the output video by using a mosaicking approach on the input frames with single or multiple egocentric videos.

Although the output videos of the aforementioned methods are appreciable, they are limited by the lack of considering the existence of scenes with different relevance for the recorder. In our previous work [18] we addressed this issue by slicing the video into semantic and non-semantic segments and, based on the length of the segments we control the playback speed of each type of segment. In order to decrease the shakiness still present in the output videos of [18], which is caused by the increase of the playback speed in non-semantic segments, we propose in this work an egocentric video stabilizer which uses information from the original video. We also improve their slicing strategy to accurately define the semantic regions.

Despite the large number of proposed methods for video stabilization, they do not present good results for egocentric videos [9,16]. One example is the work of Hsu et al. [7]. In their work the input video is segmented in patches with α length and then a single homography matrix is applied to all frames belonging to a given patch. The α value utilized was 2 or 3-seconds, which represents, for example, around a half of a minute in a 10× fast-forward video. In this interval it is unlikely that all frames within a same patch are picturing the same scene, therefore it is impractical to find a homography consistency on them.

3   Methodology

In the following two sections we detail our proposed methodology to create semantic smooth fast-forward videos.

3.1   Semantic Egocentric Fast-Forwarding

The frame sampling process is composed of four steps. First, we build a graph for the egocentric video. In the graph frames are represented by nodes and the relation between two frames is modeled by an edge. Then, the semantic information, such as the Region of Interest (ROI) of detected faces or pedestrians, is extracted from each node in order to segment the video into relevant and non-relevant frames. Different speed-up rates are computed for relevant and non-relevant segments, such that the exhibition time of the semantic (the relevant segments) parts is enlarged to be contrasted over the non-semantic ones. At last, the final video is composed of the frames associated to the nodes in the shortest path in the graph. Figure 1 summarizes our approach.

Graph Building: Similar to the work of Poleg et al. [16], we build the graph with each node connected with τ_{max} subsequent frames. The weight $W_{i,j}$ of the edge that connects the i-th to j-th node is given by the linear combination of

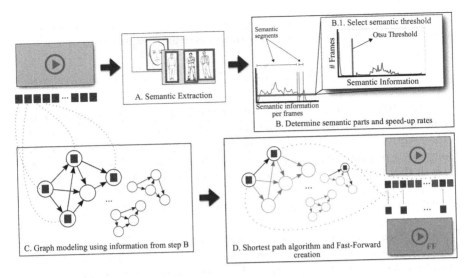

Fig. 1. Frame sampling process with an egocentric video as input. A. Perform a semantic extraction to compute the relevance of the frames; B. Calculate the semantic score along the frames and B.1 uses the Otsu method to find a meaningful semantic threshold, in order to identify semantic parts and speed-up rates; C. Graphs are created from the frames and their relations; D. Compute the shortest path and compose the final video with the selected nodes.

the terms related to the frames transition instability, appearance, velocity and semantic multiplied by a proportional factor, as shown in Eq. 1:

$$W_{i,j} = (\lambda_I \cdot I_{i,j} + \lambda_V \cdot V_{i,j} + \lambda_A \cdot A_{i,j} + \lambda_S \cdot S_{i,j}) \cdot \left\lceil \frac{(j-i)}{F} \right\rceil, \qquad (1)$$

where the proportional factor enhances transitions between frames with lower distance and F is the speed-up rate applied in the graph which the edge belongs.

The values of λ coefficients are the regularization factors for each of the costs terms and $I_{i,j}$ is the Instability Cost Term, which is calculated as the average distance of the FOE to the center of the image. $V_{i,j}$ is the Velocity Cost Term which is given by the difference between the desired optical flow magnitude in the whole video and the average of the optical flow magnitudes sum along the consecutive frames from i to j. $A_{i,j}$ is the Appearance Cost Term. We use a histogram comparison metric (Earth Mover's Distance) to measure the resemblance between the frame i and j.

Semantic Extraction: The Semantic Cost Term $S_{i,j}$ is used to penalize the transitions that are not composed by frames with relevant semantic information. Its values are given by Eq. 2:

$$S_{i,j} = \frac{1}{S_i + S_j + \epsilon}. \qquad (2)$$

The value of S_x presented in Eq. 2 is the semantic score of the frame x. For each frame of the input video, we extract the semantic information according to the semantic selected by the user (Fig. 1A). Let k be the k-th ROI returned by the extractor in the frame x, so the term S_x is defined as follows:

$$S_x = \sum_{k \in f_x} c_k \cdot a_k \cdot G_\sigma(k),\tag{3}$$

where c_k is the classifier confidence about the ROI k, assigning relevance proportional to the reliability of the semantic information in frames; a_k is the area of the k-th ROI, where ROIs with a bigger area represent a closer object, since it pictures a possible interaction and; $G_\sigma(k)$ is the value of the central point of the k-th ROI in the Gausian function with standard deviation σ centered at the frame f_x, which returns higher values to centralized information, once it is an egocentric video, so the wearer is focused on the relevant information.

Temporal Segmentation: Using the semantic information along the frames, the video is segmented into semantic and non-semantic parts. Differently from our previous work [18], that simply used the mean value (green line in Fig. 1B) to determine the segmentation threshold, we apply in this work the Otsu thresholding method to find the threshold, running it in a histogram of semantic information. The value returned by Otsu (green line in Fig. 1B.1) is used as the semantic threshold. Video segments composed of consecutive frames scored above this value are classified as semantic parts and the remaining ones as non-semantic.

Speed-up Rate Estimation: Estimating a lower speed-up rate for semantic segments and, consequently, a higher rate for non-semantic segments is not a trivial task, regarding their relation with the segment lengths. In order to manage the whole video in the desired speed-up F_d, the values of the semantic speed-up F_s and the non-semantic F_{ns} rates are computed by the minimization of the Eq. 4:

$$D(F_{ns}, F_s) = \left| \frac{L_s + L_{ns}}{F_d} - \left(\frac{L_s}{F_s} + \frac{L_{ns}}{F_{ns}} \right) \right|,\tag{4}$$

where L_s is the semantic segments length, in number of frames and, L_{ns} is the non-semantic segments length.

We solve the Eq. 4 by restricting the F_s and F_{ns} so that the F_s value is minimized as well as the difference between both, as presented in Eq. 5:

$$\underset{F_s, F_{ns}}{\arg\min} \left(D\left(F_{ns}, F_s \right) + \lambda_1 \cdot |F_{ns} - F_s| + \lambda_2 \cdot |F_s| \right),\tag{5}$$

where λ_1 and λ_2 are the regularization terms that give more importance either to keep the speed-up rates close or take the smaller F_s.

We reduce the search space of the Eq. 5 by considering the restrictions: (i) since we want more emphasis in the semantic parts, then $F_s \leqslant F_d$ and $F_s \leqslant F_{ns}$ and; (ii) because $F_s \leqslant F_d$, in order to manage the final video speed-up rate, $F_{ns} \geqslant F_d$. Since F_{ns}, F_s and $F_d \in \mathbb{N}$, then the search space is discrete and finite, due to the restrictions.

For each segment of the video we create a graph, with one source and one sink node, connecting with the τ_b border frames. For each graph we compute the shortest path through Bellman-Ford. All frames related with the nodes within the shortest path will compose the final video.

3.2 Egocentric Video Stabilization

In this section we present a novel stabilization method for fast-forward egocentric videos, thus its input is the output of a frame sampling method. Instead of using Homography Consistency with smooth transitions like Hsu et al. [7], we propose to segment the video into patches and look for the master frame of each patch. We then create a transition area with the intermediate frames of every pair of masters. The key idea of our method is to create a smooth transition by setting the target image planes on the masters and modifying the image planes of the frames that belong to the transition areas.

The first step of the stabilization methodology consists of segmenting the video into patches of size α and selecting one master frame M_k for each patch (Fig. 2a). We select as master of the k-th patch the frame f that belongs to it and maximizes the Eq. 6:

$$M_k = \arg\max_f \sum_{i \in p_k} R(f_i, f), \qquad (6)$$

where p_k is the k-th patch and the f_i is the i-th frame of the fast-forward video. The function $R(x, y)$ calculates the number of *inliers* in the RANSAC method [2] when computing the homography transformation from the image x to y.

The second step is to smooth the transitions, similar to the work of Hsu et al. For each frame, we calculate two homography transformation matrices, one from the current frame to the previous master frame and another to the posterior one. Both homography transformations are applied with weights set according to the

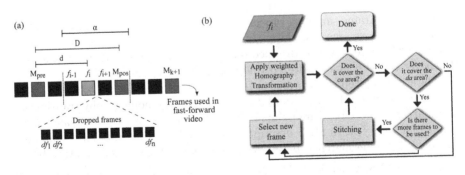

Fig. 2. Stabilization methodology for fast-forward egocentric videos. (a) Illustration of how the video is segmented in patches; dropped frames and the terms α, Δ and δ. (b) The diagram of the stabilization process.

distance to the masters. The i-th frame of the stabilized video $(\widehat{f_i})$ is given by:

$$\widehat{f_i} = H_{f_i,M_{pre}}^{1-w} \cdot H_{f_i,M_{pos}}^{w} \cdot f_i, \tag{7}$$

where f_i is the i-th frame of the fast-forward video, M_{pre} and M_{pos} are respectively the previous and posterior master frames to the frame f_i; the term $H_{x,y}^p$ is the p-th power of the homography transformation matrix from the image x to the image y; $w = (\delta \cdot (2 \cdot \alpha)/\Delta)$ is the weight that composes the p-th power, where δ is the distance (in number of frames) from the frame f_i to M_{pre}, and Δ is the distance between M_{pre} and M_{pos} (Fig. 2a). As stated by Hsu et al., choosing the α value to be a power of 2 makes the root calculation feasible by consecutive square roots.

As expected, after applying the homography transformations estimated in Eq. 7, black areas are generated due to the fact that the camera movements are abrupt and the elapsed time between consecutive frames in the fast-forward egocentric videos are large. Thus, the last step is to reconstruct these corrupted regions. To reconstruct these frames, we define two image areas centered in the frame: (i) the drop area (da) equals to $dp\%$ size of the frame and; (ii) the crop area (ca) equals to $cp\%$ size of the frame, where $cp > dp$.

The da area is the center of the image, where the viewer focuses on the majority of the time, then it is not allowed have any black or reconstructed areas in this region. On the other hand, the area between the ca and da is the peripheral vision, which is allowed to have artifacts but not black areas. The ca area is the cut region, thus regions outside this area are removed in the final video, therefore, having these black areas within them does not cause issues.

The reconstruction procedure is an iterative process depicted in Fig. 2(b). It starts with a new image f_i as input. Firstly, the algorithm applies the weighted homography transformation (Eq. 7) resulting the $\widehat{f_i}$. Then, it checks if the $\widehat{f_i}$ covers the ca area. If it does, no further actions are required and this frame is ready to compose the new stabilized video; otherwise the algorithm verifies if the $\widehat{f_i}$ covers the da area. If it does not, the frame $\widehat{f_i}$ is dropped and a new image is selected, if it covers, the algorithm checks weather still exist unused frames skipped by the frame sampling process to perform the reconstruction process. In an affirmative case, one new skipped frame is selected and used in the stitching process. Otherwise, the $\widehat{f_i}$ is dropped out and a new frame needs to be selected. Whenever a new frame is selected the process starts again.

The stitching step is performed as follows. We use the SURF detector to select feature points in the frames $\widehat{f_i}$ and d_j. To calculate the homography transformation matrix we match feature points between the images by describing all feature points of d_j and $\widehat{f_i}$ with SIFT descriptors and applying the brute force matching strategy. With the matched points we calculate the homography matrix $H_{d_j,\widehat{f_i}}$ using the RANSAC method. The $H_{d_j,\widehat{f_i}} \cdot d_j$ is now aligned with $\widehat{f_i}$ and copied to the back of it to compose the stitched image.

If it is necessary to select a new frame, it means that the $\widehat{f_i}$ does not yield a good transition in the final video. The algorithm selects a new frame d_j that belongs to interval $[f_{i-1}, f_{i+1}]$ in the original video and maximizes the Eq. 8:

$$\arg\max_{d_j} (G_\sigma(p) \cdot (R(d_j, \widehat{f}_{i-1}) + R(d_j, \widehat{f}_{i+1})) \cdot (\eta + S(d_j))), \qquad (8)$$

where, $G_\sigma(x)$ is the value of the Gaussian function with mean zero and standard deviation σ in the position x; p is the ar area percentage covered by d_j; η is a value used to prevent multiplication by zero, in case the function $S(d_j)$ that calculate the semantic information in the frame d_j returns zero. The final stabilized video is composed by all frames that achieved the Done step.

4   Experiments

In this section we present the experimental evaluation and results for our methodology using the new dataset and the evaluation metric. The next two sections contain details about our contributions: the dataset composition and the shakiness metric.

4.1   Semantic Egocentric Dataset

We propose a new labeled dataset to run the experiments and validate our methodology since there are no datasets in the literature that are semantically controlled. The dataset is composed of 11 videos divided in 3 categories of different activities: Biking; Driving and Walking. The videos under each one of these categories are classified according to their amount of semantic information. The classes are: 0p, which represents the videos with approximately no semantic information present (Biking 0p, Driving 0p and Walking 0p); 25p, for the videos containing relevant semantic information in ~25 % of its frames (Biking 25p, Driving 25p and Walking 25p); 50p, for the ones with around a half of their frames composed by semantics (Biking 50p, Biking 50p2, Driving 50p and Walking 50p) and; 75p, which represents videos with ~75 % of their frames containing relevant semantic information (Walking 75p).

We selected sections where the semantic was present to record the videos. We computed the semantic information in frames, according to Eq. 3, by either using the NPD (Normalized Pixel Difference) Face Detector [12] for the videos of the Walking category or, a pedestrian detector [1] for the videos of the other categories. We intended to use faces as the semantic information for all videos, but the usage of the pedestrian detector was necessary since the videos when biking or driving present a higher motion speed, what prevent the face detector from achieving a substantial accuracy.

We used a GoPro™Hero 3 camera mounted in a helmet for the Biking and Walking videos and attached to a head strap for the Driving videos. All videos were recorded in daylight so that the detectors could achieve a better accuracy. Figure 3 shows some frame examples of the sequences in the dataset. The complete dataset, including videos and the semantic labels, is publicly available to the research community[1].

---

[1] www.verlab.dcc.ufmg.br/fast-forward-video-based-on-semantic-extraction.

4.2   Shakiness Evaluation Metric

Most of hyperlapse methodologies focuses on producing smooth fast-forward ego-centric videos. In order to evaluate the smoothness of the output videos we need an evaluation metric that accurately express this value. The most popular quantitative measure present in the literature is the reduction of the epipole/FOE jitter [5,16,18]. However, this metric assigns a higher score for some videos that are visually more shaky than others. Based on that, we conducted an user study to verify the real smoothness of the video and to assess the quality of the metric.

Inspired by the qualitative comparison between videos made by Joshi et al. [8], where they made side-by-side comparisons using only the mean and standard deviation of consecutive output frames [8], we devised a quantitative metric to calculate the smoothness of the video. We use the fact that the presence of sharper images indicates a more stable video.

Thus, the smoothness estimation is computed as:

$$I = \frac{1}{N} \cdot \sum_{i=1}^{N} \frac{\sum_{j \in B_i} (f_j - \bar{f}_i)^2}{(N_B - 1)}, \tag{9}$$

where N is the number of frames of the video, B_i is the i-th buffer composed by N_B temporal neighborhood frames, f_j is the j-th frame of the video, $\bar{f}_i$ is the average frame of the buffer B_i and I indicates the instability index of the video. A smoother video yields a smaller I value.

For the qualitative evaluation, we generated output videos with average length of 35 s from 9 sequences using the smooth fast-forwarding techniques: EgoSampling (ES) [16]; Microsoft Hyperlapse (MH) [8] and Fast-Forward Based on Semantic Extraction (FFSE) [18], with a speed-up factor of 10. These sequences are publicly available and were previously used by those works. Then,

Fig. 3. Examples of the proposed semantic egocentric dataset. Frames in the first row represent the videos of the Biking category. Frames in the second row represent the videos of the Walking category. Frames in the third row represent the videos of the Driving category.

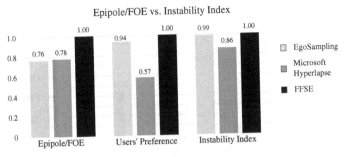

Fig. 4. Comparison among the epipole/FOE metric, the users' preference and the instability metric. The epipole/FOE metric present a low mean for the ES algorithm, which does not match the users' preference, differently from our proposed metric which seems to be a better match.

we asked for 33 subjects to watch the (unlabeled) videos and grade the video instability with respect to its smoothness in an assessment questionnaire. Unlike the quantitative measure of FOE locations differentiation, where the ES technique is superior to the other two techniques, the majority of the subjects preferred watching the MH output video, as shown in Fig. 4.

Figure 4 shows the normalized mean values of the 9 sequences for the metrics. The results reveal that the proposed metric really reflects the subjects' preferences, since it is more similar.

4.3 Results

The results of our methodology are presented in this section. We conducted our experiments using the whole semantic egocentric dataset proposed in Sect. 4.1.

In our work, we used as the semantic extractors a face detector [12] in videos where the wearer is walking and a pedestrian detector [1] in videos where the motion speed is higher. These detectors are responsible for giving us the c_k value of the Eq. 3. The Gaussian function is a Normal with parameters $\mu = 0$ and $\sigma = min(W/2, H/2)$, where W is the frame width and H is the frame height. The maximum allowed skip was set to $\tau_{max} = 100$ and $\epsilon = 1$ is the value which prevents division by zero in Eq. 2. The λ values in Eqs. 1 and 5 and the value of η in Eq. 8 were empirically defined, as well as the drop area, set as dp $= 50\%$ of the frame and the crop area, set as cp $= 5\%$ of the frame.

Our results were compared to three different approaches: (i) the EgoSampling (ES) technique proposed by [16]. We used their best reported parameters; (ii) the Microsoft Hyperlapse (MH) proposed by [8], which we used the desktop version of their algorithm to generate the videos and; (iii) the technique proposed in our previous work [18] (FFSE). All comparisons were made under quantitative metrics with respect to the visual instability, length and semantic information present in the output video. The metrics are:

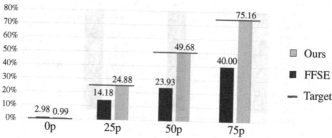

Fig. 5. The mean percentage of the semantic information present in videos per class. The values show how close the algorithms are from the ideal (target) value for the class. A peak in a frame with semantic information makes the FFSE segmentation strategy achieve poor results, differently from ours.

1. Output Speed-up: this metric indicates the speed-up achieved by the output video. It is better to have a speed-up close to the required speed-up. In this work, we set the speed-up to the factor of 10.
2. Semantic Content: it is the sum of the S_x value for all frames f_x of the video. We want to get a higher value over the other techniques.
3. Instability Index: this is the value of the Eq. 9. The lower is this value, the smoother is the video.

Figure 5 shows the mean percentage of semantic information present in videos per class for the FFSE algorithm and ours. We expect the methods to have the value as close as possible to the class. For instance, the methods should yield 25 % of semantics for the class 25p. The values obtained by our algorithm are closer to the expected values, which means that our segmentation strategy is more accurate. The reason of the poor accuracy of the FFSE algorithm is that a peak in semantic information interferes directly their approach, since they use the mean. In our case it does not happen, because we use a method that analyzes the semantic information globally to find the better threshold value.

We calculated the speed-up rates for the output videos. The ES algorithm reported a mean value of 23.904 and a standard deviation of 6.91, which is far from the ideal. The FFSE and our proposed technique achieved mean values of 12.764 and 12.188 and, standard deviation of 2.53 and 2.83 respectively, which means that they have a better accuracy with respect to the ES algorithm. The MH is the better one, because it achieves a mean of 9.44, which is the closest value to the required speed-up rate, and a standard deviation of 1.41.

Table 1 presents the results for the semantic content metric. Our algorithm is better than the others in the most of the cases. It is worth to note that for the videos with low semantic information present, our technique manages keep the same semantic information reported by the FFSE algorithm, which enforces our improvement with respect to the semantic.

Table 1. Semantic content

Name	ES	MH	FFSE	Ours
Biking 0p	**142.15**	54.47	114.76	114.76
Biking 25p	1,832.47	3,517.28	3,527.81	**3,758.44**
Biking 50p	4,640.36	3,374.42	6,247.30	**6,713.49**
Biking 50p2	2,650.41	4,760.14	**6,955.12**	5,744.19
Driving 0p	13.12	24.66	**39.70**	39.70
Driving 25p	121.76	216.17	220.69	**238.18**
Driving 50p	228.38	533.95	479.35	**569.66**
Walking 0p	161.87	239.28	**259.69**	259.69
Walking 25p	6,655.91	30,553.46	**78,752.01**	69,703.28
Walking 50p	5,817.10	3,497.56	51,603.23	**53,700.62**
Walking 75p	16,594.22	72,883.23	93,074.20	**125,766.91**

Table 2. Instability comparison

Name	ES	MH	FFSE	Ours	Ours + stabilization
Biking 0p	111.70	84.70	113.53	113.53	**81.76**
Biking 25p	187.25	166.77	185.57	185.03	**128.02**
Biking 50p	134.22	112.95	132.95	129.97	**90.68**
Biking 50p2	107.59	95.82	110.64	111.71	**76.75**
Driving 0p	164.51	153.33	177.60	177.60	**127.02**
Driving 25p	148.25	137.75	152.42	152.18	**124.07**
Driving 50p	154.38	131.06	154.82	153.85	**109.29**
Walking 0p	126.33	121.21	133.20	133.20	**94.26**
Walking 25p	134.96	126.06	129.73	132.49	**96.23**
Walking 50p	139.45	119.06	138.70	138.62	**92.53**
Walking 75p	150.18	127.55	145.75	137.15	**99.78**

We show in Table 2 results of the instability index metric for all approaches where lower values denote better results. We added a column to report the results for our stabilized videos in which we can see the improvement in the smoothness of the output videos.

5 Conclusions

In this work we proposed a novel method capable of producing smoother egocentric videos with more semantic content, by considering the shakiness, the required speed-up and the semantic information. We also introduced a new semantically controlled dataset and a smoothness evaluation metric to test fast-forward egocentric methods, once most of metrics in the literature do not reflect the watchers' preferences. We ran several experiments using the new dataset and the evaluation metric. The results showed the superiority of our new approach as far as smoothness and semantic information are concerned.

Acknowledgments. The authors would like to thank the agencies CAPES, CNPq, FAPEMIG, ITV (Vale Institute of Technology) and Petrobras for funding different parts of this work.

References

1. Dollár, P.: Piotr's Computer Vision Matlab Toolbox (PMT). https://github.com/pdollar/toolbox
2. Fischler, M.A., Bolles, R.C.: Random sample consensus: a paradigm for model fitting with applications to image analysis and automated cartography. Commun. ACM **24**(6), 381395 (1981)
3. Gong, Y., Liu, X.: Video summarization using singular value decomposition. In: Proceedings of the IEEE Conference on Computer Vision and Pattern Recognition, vol. 2, pp. 174–180, Hilton Head Island, SC, USA, June 2000
4. Gygli, M., Grabner, H., Riemenschneider, H., Van Gool, L.: Creating summaries from user videos. In: Fleet, D., Pajdla, T., Schiele, B., Tuytelaars, T. (eds.) ECCV 2014, Part VII. LNCS, vol. 8695, pp. 505–520. Springer, Heidelberg (2014)
5. Halperin, T., Poleg, Y., Arora, C., Peleg, S.: Egosampling: wide view hyperlapse from single and multiple egocentric videos. CoRR abs/1604.07741 (2016). http://arxiv.org/abs/1604.07741
6. Hari, R., Roopesh, C., Wilscy, M.: Human face based approach for video summarization. In: 2013 IEEE Recent Advances in Intelligent Computational Systems (RAICS), Trivandrum, India, pp. 245–250, December 2013
7. Hsu, Y.F., Chou, C.C., Shih, M.Y.: Moving camera video stabilization using homography consistency. In: 2012 19th IEEE International Conference on Image Processing, Orlando, FL, USA. IEEE, September 2012
8. Joshi, N., Kienzle, W., Toelle, M., Uyttendaele, M., Cohen, M.F.: Real-time hyperlapse creation via optimal frame selection. ACM Trans. Graph. **34**(4), 63:1–63:9 (2015)
9. Kopf, J., Cohen, M.F., Szeliski, R.: First-person hyper-lapse videos - supplemental material. http://research.microsoft.com/en-us/um/redmond/projects/hyperlapse/supplementary/index.html. Accessed 26 July 2016
10. Kopf, J., Cohen, M.F., Szeliski, R.: First-person hyper-lapse videos. ACM Trans. Graph. **33**(4), 78:1–78:10 (2014)
11. Lee, Y.J., Ghosh, J., Grauman, K.: Discovering important people and objects for egocentric video summarization. In: 2012 IEEE Conference on Computer Vision and Pattern Recognition (CVPR), Providence, RI, USA, pp. 1346–1353, June 2012
12. Liao, S., Jain, A., Li, S.: A fast and accurate unconstrained face detector. IEEE Trans. Pattern Anal. Mach. Intell. **38**(2), 211–223 (2016)
13. Lu, Z., Grauman, K.: Story-driven summarization for egocentric video. In: 2013 IEEE Conference on Computer Vision and Pattern Recognition (CVPR), Portland, OR, USA, pp. 2714–2721, June 2013

14. Ngo, C.W., Ma, Y.F., Zhang, H.: Automatic video summarization by graph modeling. In: Proceedings of the Ninth IEEE International Conference on Computer Vision, Nice, France, vol. 1, pp. 104–109, October 2003

15. Poleg, Y., Ephrat, A., Peleg, S., Arora, C.: Compact cnn for indexing egocentric videos. In: 2016 IEEE Winter Conference on Applications of Computer Vision (WACV), Lake Placid, NY, USA, pp. 1–9, March 2016

16. Poleg, Y., Halperin, T., Arora, C., Peleg, S.: Egosampling: fast-forward and stereo for egocentric videos. In: 2015 IEEE Conference on Computer Vision and Pattern Recognition (CVPR), Boston, MA, USA, pp. 4768–4776, June 2015

17. Potapov, D., Douze, M., Harchaoui, Z., Schmid, C.: Category-specific video summarization. In: Fleet, D., Pajdla, T., Schiele, B., Tuytelaars, T. (eds.) ECCV 2014, Part VI. LNCS, vol. 8694, pp. 540–555. Springer, Heidelberg (2014)

18. Ramos, W.L.S., Silva, M.M., Campos, M.F.M., Nascimento, E.R.: Fast-forward video based on semantic extraction. In: 2016 IEEE International Conference on Image Processing (ICIP), Phoenix, AR, USA. IEEE, September 2016

19. Yu, J., Kankanhalli, M., Mulhen, P.: Semantic video summarization in compressed domain MPEG video. In: Proceedings of the 2003 International Conference on Multimedia and Expo, ICME 2003, Baltimore, MD, USA, vol. 3, pp. III–329–332, July 2003

20. Zhuang, Y., Xiao, R., Wu, F.: Key issues in video summarization and its application. In: Proceedings of the 2003 Joint Conference of the Fourth International Conference on Information, Communications and Signal Processing and Fourth Pacific Rim Conference on Multimedia, Singapore, vol. 1, pp. 448–452, December 2003

A3D: A Device for Studying Gaze in 3D

Mahmoud Qodseya[✉], Marta Sanzari, Valsamis Ntouskos, and Fiora Pirri

ALCOR Lab, DIAG, Sapienza University of Rome, Rome, Italy
{qodseya,sanzari,ntouskos,pirri}@diag.uniroma1.it

Abstract. A wearable device for capturing 3D gaze information in indoor and outdoor environments is proposed. The hardware and software architecture of the device provides an estimate in quasi-real-time of 2.5D points of regard (POR) and then lift their estimations to 3D, by projecting them into the 3D reconstructed scene. The estimation procedure does not need any external device, and can be used both indoor and outdoor and with the subject wearing it moving, though some smooth constraint in the motion are required. To ensure a great flexibility with respect to depth a novel calibration method is proposed, which provides eye-scene calibration that explicitly takes into account depth information, in so ensuring a quite accurate estimation of the PORs. The experimental evaluation demonstrates that both 2.5D and 3D POR are accurately estimated.

Keywords: Wearable device · 3D gaze estimation · Point of regard in 3D scene

1 Introduction

Eye tracking has developed in the context of studying human visual selection mechanisms and attention (see [1–3] for a review on eye detection and gaze tracking in video-oculography). It is indeed well known that the points toward which humans direct the gaze are crucial for studying human perception and his ability to select the regions of interest out of a massive amount of visual information [4].

In the last few years the use of head-mounted eye tracking has spread in several research areas such as driving [5,6], learning [7], marketing [8], training [9], cultural heritage [10] and prevalently in human computer interfaces [11,12]; just to cite few of an increasing number of applications where gaze direction is studied. All these applications spotlight the need to move beyond prior models of computational attention and saliency [13–16] and move toward a deeper experimental analysis of gaze direction and eye-head motion, by collecting data to better understand the relation between *point of regard* (POR) and visual behavior [17], likewise strategies of search [18] and detection [19] in natural scenes.

However only quite recently models for head-mounted eye tracking have been extended first to include head motion tracking [20,21] and further to 3D, so as to be employed in real life experiments in unstructured settings [22–25]. In [26]

© Springer International Publishing Switzerland 2016
G. Hua and H. Jégou (Eds.): ECCV 2016 Workshops, Part I, LNCS 9913, pp. 572–588, 2016.
DOI: 10.1007/978-3-319-46604-0_41

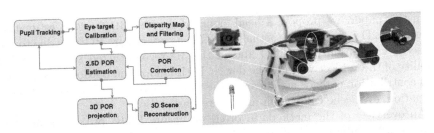

Fig. 1. On the left: a schema of the methods involved for projecting the PORs in the 3D reconstructed scene. On the right: the head-mounted eye-tracker with all its components.

Paletta and colleagues propose an interesting solution based on POR projection in an already reconstructed environment, exploiting an RGB-D sensor and the approach of [27]. To localize the PORs in the reconstructed scene they use key point detection and matching against those key points that are already in the reconstructed map. This said, 3D projection of the gaze in natural scenes is still an open research problem due to the difficulties of both designing lightweight wearable devices supporting complex computations for solving an ill-posed problem.

There is a considerable advantage in extending head-mounted eye-tracking to 3D. The advantages are formidable not only for the purpose of providing the depth of the field of view, not only for effectively understanding eye motion in natural scene, the shift and the inhibition of return [28], having the possibility of collecting PORs in the scene, but also to understand the relation between saliency and combined motion of eyes, head and body. All these factors can induce quite relevant advances in the comprehension of visual perception, and also would provide the possibility of collecting a huge amount of data in several contexts and for several useful applications.

Despite the remarkable advances in capturing head motion and real world scenes, in many of the above cited papers extension to 3D does not necessarily imply full 3D reconstruction of the scene nor the subject localization in the visually explored scene. For example in [24] the 3D gaze projection is obtained by remote recording, and localization and reconstruction is not considered. Similarly in [25] the head position and orientation are determined either by a remote camera or by fiducial markers, which have to be placed in the environment in such a way that at least one marker is visible in the scene camera image of the eye-tracker. It follows that no localization nor reconstruction is provided in so implying that the subject is not free to move in the environment.

However in order to be fully usable as a 3D device, both indoor and outdoor, and to provide a deep insight of visual perception, while the subject is performing simple activities, the point of regard needs to be localized in space likewise the head-mounted tracker. Therefore a 3D device requires not only eye and head tracking but also localization and depth perceptivity within the reconstructed scene, also to grant free motion to the subject.

In this paper, we propose a head-mounted device A3D for gaze estimation in both the 2D scene images (actually in 2.5D as images are RGB-D, due to the eye-scene calibration procedure) and in the 3D reconstructed scene, ensuring mobility of the subject wearing the device, both indoor and outdoor (see Fig. 1). This contribution extends significantly the work of [23,29] with respect to pupil estimation, eye-scene calibration and 3D reconstruction.

An overview of the methods involved, to ensure PORs projection in a 3D dense scene, is illustrated in Fig. 1. The proposed system works in quasi-real-time on a GPU, NVIDIA Corporation GK106GLM [Quadro K2100M]. However we are still far from a true gaze measurement device. In fact, the system has still severe limitations on freedom of movements. Indeed, approximatively correct localization and dense reconstruction is ensured under the proviso of smooth motion. In other words, erratic motion of the head, likewise sudden motions of the body must be avoided.

The remainder of this paper is organized as follow. In Sect. 2 and its subsections, we present the pipeline of the proposed system and the model for pupil detection, disparity map and filtering, localization and dense reconstruction, and finally the projection of PORs, or the visual axes in the reconstructed scene. In Sect. 3 and its subsections we present the details of the A3D device, the software, the performance and an analysis of errors computation for both the 2.5D and 3D PORs projections. We conclude the work with some considerations on present limits and future work.

2   Proposed Model

In this section we introduce the methods that are necessary to project PORs in the dense reconstructed scene. Note that we assume that the scene is static though the subject wearing the A3D device can move, however we shall show in Sect. 3 an example in slow motion. The A3D device is described in Sect. 3.

The methods we introduce take care of pupil detection, pupil and scene images calibration, disparity map construction together with filtering, the device localization, 3D scene reconstruction and, finally, the projection of the PORs in the scene. Though the solution proposed improves the Gaze machine of [23,29], we use mainly state of the art methods to solve each of the above mentioned problems. The whole pipeline extends the approaches where is needed, to make the whole system work properly.

Fig. 2. The calibration sequence: back, forward, head left, right, up and down

Fig. 3. Subjects performing the calibration procedure of the A3D device under different conditions.

2.1 Pupil Detection

A wealth of literature has faced the problem of pupil detection, as reported in [1–3]. Most approaches relies heavily on laboratory conditions, histogram thresholding and shape fitting, such as [30], which is also implemented in *Pupil* of [31]. Most 3D model-based approaches [21,32,33] rely on estimating the parameters of some model of the human eye. Due to the high complexity of the eye [34], shape based models are often hard to fit and usually require sophisticated settings like multiple light sources and cameras. On the other hand, those simpler models that are not complex enough to take into account eye shape and kinematics have to rely on simplifying assumptions, resulting in less accurate estimations. To overcome the limitations related to special assumptions on the eyeball or cornea shape and especially to cope with the eye dynamics, we introduce a model for estimating the POR on the basis of a set of learned parameters.

Dark pupil images are acquired with active IR illumination and a light filter is attached to the camera pointing the eye. The goal here is to predict whether a pixel $\mathbf{x} = (u, v, w)$, at location (u, v) with intensity w, in a test eye image belongs to the pupil or not, given a number of vectorized images and a vector of responses in $\{-1, +1\}$. The problem can be seen in terms of binary classification, by modelling a latent function g. Namely, given training data X, for a single pixel the probability of success $p(y = 1|X)$ is related to a latent function $g(X)$ which is mapped to the unit interval by a probit function φ, $p(y = 1|X) = \varphi(g(X))$, with $\varphi(g(X)) = 0.5(1 + \mathrm{erf}(g(X)/\sqrt{2})$. Due to the symmetry of φ, the likelihood of a single pixel, given the probit, is $p(y_i|g_i(X)) = \varphi(y_i g_i(X))$. Hence we rely on

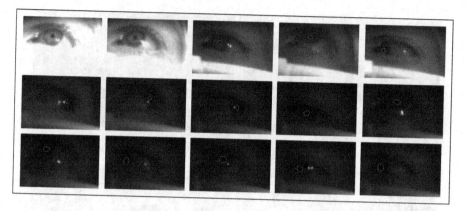

Fig. 4. Pupil detection with different eye orientations and sunlight intensities.

a Gaussian process as a prior on g, whose mean and variance gives a value for the prior $p(y = 1|X)$, somehow encoding the min and max variation of the pupil in the eye image. Using Gaussian process approximation $q(g|X, y)$ for binary classification [35,36], the posterior expectation and variance for $g_\star$, given a test pixel $\mathbf{x}_\star$ of a new test image can be computed analytically, namely, the predictive probability of $\mathbf{x}_\star$ to be of class 1 is given by

$$\int \varphi(g_\star)q(g_\star|X, \mathbf{y}, \mathbf{x}_\star)dg_\star \tag{1}$$

Both GP and visible light filter enable the method to work well for both indoor and outdoor environments, where the GP provides a dynamic threshold and the filter eliminates the effect of the visible light on the intensity of the eye image. An ellipse is finally fitted to bound the pupil. See Fig. 4.

2.2 Depth Map and Pupil-Target Calibration

Differently from other approaches (e.g. [37–39]) a real scene, as opposed to a screen, is here considered, hence we cannot exploit a calibration-free method based on a saliency map. Once the pupils are estimated, the optical axis is computed as the normal to the plane tangent to the cornea, approximated by a sphere, at the pupil center. The normal however does not correspond to the visual axis. This fact, together with noise, induces an error that increases with distance. To overcome this difficulty a calibration procedure is provided, minimizing this error. The important contribution here is that error minimization is parametric with respect to the distance measured along the optical axis.

In few words, the calibration requires the subject wearing the device to do the following motions in front of a calibration device as illustrated in Fig. 2: go forward toward the device, go backward, turn head up, down, left and right, keeping the eyes fixed to the target. Sequences of calibration performed by four subjects are illustrated in Fig. 3. By approximating the cornea with a sphere we obtain a function $f(\mathbf{x})$, with center $\mathbf{c}$. This last is computed exploiting anatomic ratios between the cornea center and the plica and between the plica and the camera centre. The camera centre is given in fact by visual odometry as detailed below. Given $f(\mathbf{x})$ then the normal $\mathbf{n} = \nabla f(\mathbf{p})$, with $\mathbf{p}$ the pupil center, where the z-coordinate of $\mathbf{p}$ is computed exploiting the above reasoning and recalling that $\mathbf{n}$ pass through $\mathbf{c}$. Hence, during the calibration the data

$$U = [(X_1, Y_1, x_1, y_1, d_1, \mathbf{n}_1^\top), \ldots, (X_N, Y_N, x_N, y_N, d_N, \mathbf{n}_N^\top)]^\top \in \mathbb{R}^{N \times 8} \quad (2)$$

are collected, with X_i, Y_i the target location in the scene image, x_i, y_i, the pupil center in the eye image, d_i the distance between the camera center and the target plane, $\mathbf{n}_i$ the normal, $i = 1, \ldots, N$, along the optical axis.

To obtain the distance d_i along the normal the target depth needs to be computed. Having the camera already calibrated, an early disparity map is computed by semiglobal matching [40]. Semiglobal matching considers pixelwise matching based on mutual information, and it approximates a global smoothness constraint. With semiglobal matching input images are not required to be rectified. We have used the approach of [41,42] for GPU implementation of semiglobal stereo matching. To obtain a dense disparity map we apply finally a global image smoothing based on weighted least square [43], following the real time implementation of [44].

Now we have to consider that at training time, each sample from U has size 1×8, while at test time we are given a measure 1×6, returning the pupil centre and the normal, and that the values X, Y of the real target in the image of the scene needs to be computed. To estimate these values in the image, corresponding to a specific eye orientation, we resort to multi task Gaussian process prediction, or to multi-output prediction (for a review see [45]), computing a Gaussian process for a vector valued function.

Given the depth map, we set the N distinct input vectors as $\mathbf{u_i} = (x_i, y_i, d_i, \mathbf{n}_i^\top)^\top$, $i = 1, \ldots, N$ and we set the $2N$ responses as $\mathbf{v} = (v_{x1}, \ldots, v_{xN}, v_{y1}, \ldots, v_{yN})^\top$ where v_{ij} is the response for task i to the input v_j, $i \in \{X, Y\}$. We note that the goal is to compute a latent function for predicting a good estimate for the X coordinate and a latent function for predicting a good estimate of the Y coordinate in the image, corresponding to the true reprojection of the observed target in the scene image. Placing a Gaussian process prior over the latent functions $\mathbf{f} = \{f_x, f_y\}$ a correlation is induced between the two tasks. Assuming zero means we have:

$$\langle f_X(\mathbf{u}) f_Y(\mathbf{u}') \rangle = K_{xy}^{\mathbf{f}} \kappa^{\mathbf{u}}(\mathbf{u}, \mathbf{u}') \text{ with } v_{ix} \sim \mathcal{N}(f_X(\mathbf{u}_i), \sigma_i^2) \quad (3)$$

where $K^{\mathbf{f}}$ is a positive semidefinite matrix that specifies the intertask correlation, $\kappa^{\mathbf{u}}$ is a covariance function on the input and σ_i^2 is the noise variance of the i-th task, $i \in \{X, Y\}$.

Inference is done using standard Gaussian process model. The mean prediction of a new point $\mathbf{u}_\star$ for task X is:

$$\hat{f}_X(\mathbf{u}_\star) = (\kappa_X^f \otimes \kappa_\star^u)^\top \Sigma^{-1} \mathbf{v} \quad (4)$$
$$\Sigma = K^f \otimes K^u + D \otimes I$$

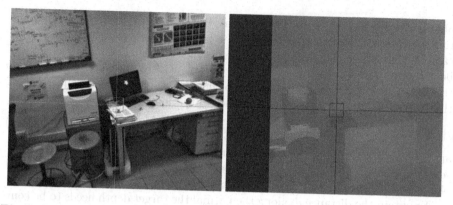

Fig. 5. On the left the 2.5POR in the RGB image of the scene, on the right the 2.5POR on the depth map.

Here $\otimes$ is the Kroneker product, κ_x^f selects the first column of K^f, $\kappa_\star^u$ is the vector of covariances between the point $u_\star$ and the training points, K^u is the matrix of covariances between the training data points, and D is a 2×2 matrix in which the element (i, i), $i \in \{X, Y\}$ is σ_i, and Σ is an $2N \times 2N$ matrix, we invite the reader to consult [46] for more details, also concerning hyperparameters estimation.

Once both hyperparameters and the matrix K^f are estimated, then the estimated values return the predicted position of the 2.5D POR (since being located in the image it is located in the depth map).

2.3   3D Reconstruction and POR Projection

Given the computed depth maps, the corresponding RGB image, and the location of the POR in the scene image, the 2.5D PORs are mapped from the left to the right image so that by epipolar geometry there is no more ambiguity between the visual axes. However to both localize the scene camera center and the 3D PORs in the images it is necessary to localize the scene camera with respect to the reference frame, hence we need to resort to visual SLAM. Recently [47] has proposed ElasticFusion as dense visual SLAM. We approach the problem of 3D reconstruction of the scene using the ElasticFusion of [47] that is based on GPU programming. The model uses an unordered list of surfels which are descriptors encoding position, normal, color, weight, time stamp update and initial time stamp. Surfels are divided into active and inactive, where the inactive parts are those no more observed. The concept is to verify loop closure when some active part of the model successfully registers with some inactive part. Successful loop closure induces non-rigid deformations of all the surfels, according to a deformation graph. Local loop closure are further incorporated in global loop closures.

The ElasticFusion model is defined over the space of RGB-D images, taking as input a depth and a color map. Therefore having them available we have been able to integrate the ElasticFusion model into our model, and obtain the dense visual slam, limited by the depth map estimation provided by the stereo pair. The advantage is that for outdoor experiments the stereo rig still provides interesting results for PORs projection, while most RGB-D sensors have some flaws. Furthermore RGB-D sensors at the current time are not enough lightweight for a wearable device designed to study perception.

Having the PORs in the depth maps he dense visual SLAM finally allows to locate the PORs in space, and then projected as spheres with radius inverse proportional to the depth.

3   Experiments

The hardware components of the A3D consist of a stereo camera rig, an Arduino unit, an eye camera, a mirror, and an IR LED. These components are supported on an ergonomically designed 3D printed frame (see Fig. 1). The stereo rig is composed by 2 XIMEA cameras (model: MQ013CG-E2) with a baseline equal to 14.4 cm, and it is configured to acquire synchronized image pairs at a frame rate of 25 fps with a resolution of 640×512 pixels. To guarantee this frame rate the upper limit for the exposure time is set to 30 ms. This has as a results less bright images at indoor scenes. The Arduino unit (model: Uno R3) is used to provide hardware synchronization to the stereo rig. The eye camera is a XIMEA camera (model: MU9PC-MH) and it is used to capture the motion of the eye. It captures images at a rate of 105 fps. The pupil detection software processes these images at the same frequency, as it needs 9.5 ms to detect the pupil in the eye images. The IR LED is required to facilitate pupil detection since it increases the overall contrast of the eye images, and in particular, the contrast between the pupil and the iris. The mirror is used in order to place the eye camera at the top of the A3D device, avoiding the scene occlusion caused by placing the camera in front of the eyes of the subject.

The main software modules of the A3D device consists of the data acquisition software, the pupil detection software, the depth computation software, and a

Fig. 6. Examples of the estimated 2.5D PORs for the first experiment

Table 1. Depth map average processing processing time for different image sizes

Image size	2828×1924	2262×1539	1696×1154	1131×769	565×384
Processing time (ms)	366	284	118	54	9

modified version of ElasticFusion [47]. The acquisition software, implemented in C++, manages the acquisition and rectification of the stereo images, the acquisition of the eye images, and the 2.5D POR estimation based on the calibration procedure. The depth estimation software consists of 2 parts: one based on the SGBM algorithm [40] and the other on the WLS filter [43]. Both are implemented in GPU in order to allow for real-time computation of the depth maps from the stereo image pairs. Finally, the modified version of ElasticFusion [47], also implemented in GPU, exploits here the computation of the depth map in place of the RGB-D sensor, which cannot be mounted on the device, and it is used to compute a 3D reconstruction of the scene and the projection of 3D PORs from the depth maps to the reconstructed scene.

3.1 Time Measurements

We report now the time performance for each software part of the A3D device. For each part we process 1000 frames and compute the average processing time. Pupil detection requires 9.5 ms on a region of interest with dimensions 180×120 pixels, while the depth estimation needs 25 ms for images of resolution 640×512 pixels. ElasticFusion and 3D POR estimation need 75 ms on the image resolution 640×512 pixels. Table 1 shows the average time for the depth map computation for different image resolutions. The computation time is computed using images taken from the Middlebury dataset [48], resized according to the different sizes required by the above measurements.

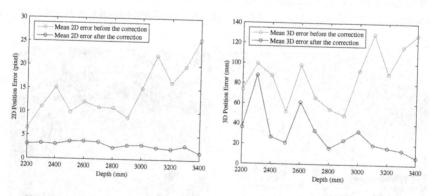

Fig. 7. 2.5D (left) and 3D (right) POR error before and after correction

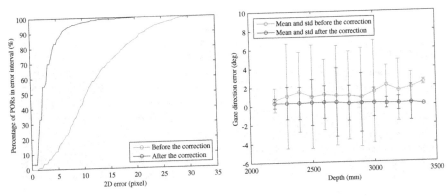

Fig. 8. On the left: cumulative error distribution for 2.5D PORs. On the right: angular error in gaze direction before and after correction.

3.2   Error Evaluation in Indoor Environments

In this section we describe a number of experiments that have been performed by 4 subjects. Note that PORs that are computed on the depth image are illustrated also on the 2D images.

The first experiment involves searching interest points in an indoor environment. Interest points taken in consideration are star-shaped stickers located within a workroom on walls, desks, devices or on the floor. The scene is considered static, so in the room there are no moving objects/persons.

The experiment is performed by a person wearing the A3D device and consists in performing first the calibration procedure described in Sect. 2, and then in a search task, which amounts to find all the stickers also moving inside the room. Some examples of scene images with overlaid POR visualizations are shown in Fig. 6.

In Fig. 7 the corresponding 2.5D and 3D errors are shown with respect to the depth of the interest points. The errors are considered to be the mean distances between estimated and ground truth PORs. In each plot the mean errors between and after the 2.5D and 3D corrections are shown, as described in Sect. 2. The error graphs point out the great improvement of the correction phase refining both 2.5D and 3D POR position estimation. The smaller improvement caused by the correction in the 3D case is due to occlusions and the great variance of 3D position estimation near edges.

In Fig. 8 the cumulative error distribution of the 2.5D PORs is shown. The area under the curve corresponding to the 2.5D PORs after the correction is much larger with respect to the curve obtained from the 2.5D PORs before the correction. This is representative of the large improvement achieved by the correction process.

Finally, for further evaluation we computed the error of the gaze direction corresponding to the estimated PORs before and after the correction. Denoting as K the camera calibration matrix and $\mathbf{p}$ the 2.5D POR position in homogeneous

Fig. 9. Examples of the estimated PORs for the second experiment.

Fig. 10. Examples of the reconstructed 3D scene during the second experiment showing reprojected PORs as red spheres. (Color figure online)

coordinates, the direction of the corresponding viewing ray is computed according to (see [49] for details):

$$\mathbf{d} = \mathrm{K}^{-1}\mathbf{p}. \tag{5}$$

Based on this, the angular error between the estimated and the ground truth PORs is given by

$$\theta = \arccos \frac{\mathbf{d}_{est}\mathbf{d}_{gt}}{\|\mathbf{d}_{est}\|\|\mathbf{d}_{gt}\|} \tag{6}$$

Here too the experiments show the improvements caused by the correction phase, which has as a result the decrease of both the mean and the standard deviation of the gaze direction error.

3.3 Qualitative Analysis in Indoor Environments

The second experiment is a qualitative study involving predefined objects search in the same indoor environment. The scene is considered to be static and the predefined objects are small plastic toys.

During the experiment subjects wearing the A3D have to look for several unknown toys inside the room. Some examples of the 2D images of the scene

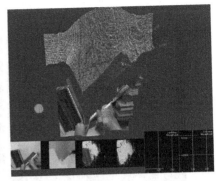

Fig. 11. Examples of the estimated PORs (left) and reconstructed 3D scene (right) during the third experiment.

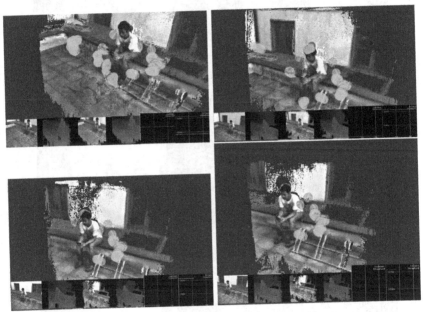

Fig. 12. 3D PORs in an outdoor sequence, with reconstruction and 3D PORs projection.

with PORs visualization are shown in Fig. 9. In Fig. 10 some examples of the 3D reconstructed scene are shown with the relative 3D PORs.

The third experiment is a qualitative study to visualize the gaze projection in slow motion in close range and dynamic indoor environments. During the experiment the subjects wearing the A3D have to pick up a book from the books on the shelf, which will cause changes in the environment and make it dynamic. Some examples of the 2D image of the scene with PORs visualization and the 3D reconstructed scene with relative reprojected PORs are shown in Fig. 11.

Fig. 13. 3D PORs in an outdoor sequence, observing two people talking.

3.4 Qualitative Analysis in Outdoor Environments

Finally a number of experiments have been performed for a qualitative study about focus on subjects in outdoor environments. The experiments consist first in a calibration procedure described in Sect. 2 and then the subjects wearing the A3D observe the people in the scene, moving around them. Some of the experiments are illustrated in Figs. 12 and 13. It is interesting to observe the projected PORs, in Fig. 13 as the subject is focusing on the person on the left, who is talking.

4 Conclusions

In this paper, we propose A3D, a head-mounted device for gaze estimation both in indoor and outdoor environments. By a suitable calibration procedure we can estimate the PORs on the depth images, hence in 2.5D, using the depth maps we exploited [47] ElasticFusion to both obtain the 3D reconstructed scene and 3D position of PORs in the scene.

Experiments on error analysis of the taken measures, together with cumulative error distribution and gaze direction errors studies, demonstrate the reliability of the introduced correction step.

The proposed system works in quasi-real-time, but limitations such as smooth head motion restrict its applications.

Future work include a much more reliable 3D reconstruction procedure to allow for fast head motions, and the possibility to extend the work to cover dynamic scenarios.

Acknowledgment. Supported by EU FP7 TRADR (609763) and EU H2020 SecondHands (643950) projects. The authors thank the anonymous reviewers for their comments.

References

1. Ji, Q., Wechsler, H., Duchowski, A.T., Flickner, M.: Special issue: eye detection and tracking. Comput. Vis. Image Underst. **98**(1), 1–3 (2005)
2. Hansen, D.W., Ji, Q.: In the eye of the beholder: a survey of models for eyes and gaze. IEEE Trans. Pattern Anal. Mach. Intell. **32**(3), 478–500 (2010)
3. Fuhl, W., Tonsen, M., Bulling, A., Kasneci, E.: Pupil detection for head-mounted eye tracking in the wild: an evaluation of the state of the art. Mach. Vis. Appl. 1–14 (2016). doi:10.1007/s00138-016-0776-4
4. Tsotsos, J., Culhane, S., Wai, W., Lai, Y., Davis, N., Nuflo, F.: Modeling visual attention via selective tuning. Artif. Intell. **78**, 507–547 (1995)
5. Ahlstrom, C., Victor, T., Wege, C., Steinmetz, E.: Processing of eye/head-tracking data in large-scale naturalistic driving data sets. IEEE Trans. Intell. Transp. Syst. **13**(2), 553–564 (2012)
6. Kasneci, E., Sippel, K., Aehling, K., Heister, M., Rosenstiel, W., Schiefer, U., Papageorgiou, E.: Driving with binocular visual field loss? A study on a supervised on-road parcours with simultaneous eye and head tracking. PloS One **9**(2), e87470 (2014)

7. Lai, M.L., Tsai, M.J., Yang, F.Y., Hsu, C.Y., Liu, T.C., Lee, S.W.Y., Lee, M.H., Chiou, G.L., Liang, J.C., Tsai, C.C.: A review of using eye-tracking technology in exploring learning from 2000 to 2012. Educ. Res. Rev. **10**, 90–115 (2013)
8. Wedel, M.: Attention research in marketing: a review of eye tracking studies. Robert H. Smith School Research Paper No. RHS 2460289 (2013)
9. Rosch, J.L., Vogel-Walcutt, J.J.: A review of eye-tracking applications as tools for training. Cogn. Technol. Work **15**(3), 313–327 (2013)
10. Alletto, S., Abati, D., Serra, G., Cucchiara, R.: Wearable vision for retrieving architectural details in augmented tourist experiences. In: 2015 7th International Conference on Intelligent Technologies for Interactive Entertainment (INTETAIN), pp. 134–139 (2015)
11. Jacob, R., Karn, K.S.: Eye tracking in human-computer interaction and usability research: ready to deliver the promises. Mind **2**(3), 4 (2003)
12. Jaimes, A., Sebe, N.: Multimodal human-computer interaction: a survey. Comput. Vis. Image Underst. **108**(1), 116–134 (2007)
13. Treisman, A., Gelade, G.: A feature-integration theory of attention. Cogn. Psychol. **12**, 97–136 (1980)
14. Koch, C., Ullman, S.: Shifts in selective visual-attention: towards the underlying neural circuitry. Hum. Neurobiol. **4**(4), 219–227 (1985)
15. Treisman, A.: Preattentive processing in vision. Comput. Vis. Graph. Image Process. **31**(2), 156–177 (1985)
16. Itti, L., Koch, C., Niebur, E.: A model of saliency-based visual attention for rapid scene analysis. IEEE PAMI **20**(11), 1254–1259 (1998)
17. Carmi, R., Itti, L.: Visual causes versus correlates of attentional selection in dynamic scenes. Vision. Res. **46**(26), 4333–4345 (2006)
18. Duncan, J., Humphreys, G.W.: Visual search and stimulus similarity. Psychol. Rev. **96**(3), 433–458 (1989)
19. Pessoa, L., Exel, S.: Attentional strategies for object recognition. In: Mira, J., Sánchez-Andrés, J.V. (eds.) IWANN 1999. LNCS, vol. 1606, pp. 850–859. Springer, Heidelberg (1999). doi:10.1007/BFb0098243
20. Beymer, D., Flickner, M.: Eye gaze tracking using an active stereo head. In: 2003 IEEE Computer Society Conference on Computer Vision and Pattern Recognition, 2003. Proceedings, vol. 2, pp. 451–458 (2003)
21. Zhu, Z., Ji, Q.: Novel eye gaze tracking techniques under natural head movement. IEEE Trans. Biomed. Eng. **54**(12), 2246–2260 (2007)
22. Munn, S.M., Pelz, J.B.: 3D point-of-regard, position and head orientation from a portable monocular video-based eye tracker. In: Proceedings of the 2008 Symposium on Eye Tracking Research and Applications, pp. 181–188. ACM (2008)
23. Pirri, F., Pizzoli, M., Rudi, A.: A general method for the point of regard estimation in 3D space. In: 2011 IEEE Conference on Computer Vision and Pattern Recognition (CVPR), pp. 921–928. IEEE (2011)
24. Bulling, A.: Pervasive attentive user interfaces. IEEE Computer **49**(1), 94–98 (2016)
25. Pfeiffer, T., Renner, P., Pfeiffer-Leßmann, N.: EyeSee3D 2.0: model-based real-time analysis of mobile eye-tracking in static and dynamic three-dimensional scenes. In: Proceedings of the Ninth Biennial ACM Symposium on Eye Tracking Research and Applications, pp. 189–196. ACM (2016)
26. Paletta, L., Santner, K., Fritz, G., Mayer, H., Schrammel, J.: 3D attention: measurement of visual saliency using eye tracking glasses. In: CHI 2013 Extended Abstracts on Human Factors in Computing Systems, pp. 199–204. ACM (2013)

27. Pirker, K., Rüther, M., Schweighofer, G., Bischof, H.: GPSlam: marrying sparse geometric and dense probabilistic visual mapping. In: BMVC, pp. 1–12 (2011)
28. Posner, M.I., Rafalb, R.D., Choatec, L.S., Vaughand, J.: Inhibition of return: neural basis and function preview. Cogn. Neuropsychol. **2**, 211–228 (1985)
29. Ntouskos, V., Pirri, F., Pizzoli, M., Sinha, A., Cafaro, B.: Saliency prediction in the coherence theory of attention. Biol. Inspir. Cogn. Archit. **5**, 10–28 (2013)
30. Świrski, L., Bulling, A., Dodgson, N.: Robust real-time pupil tracking in highly off-axis images. In: Proceedings of the Symposium on Eye Tracking Research and Applications, pp. 173–176. ACM (2012)
31. Kassner, M., Patera, W., Bulling, A.: Pupil: an open source platform for pervasive eye tracking and mobile, gaze-based interaction. CoRR abs/1405.0006 (2014)
32. Hennessey, C., Noureddin, B., Lawrence, P.: A single camera eye-gaze tracking system with free head motion. In: Proceedings of the 2006 Symposium on Eye Tracking Research and Applications, pp. 87–94. ACM (2006)
33. Ariz, M., Bengoechea, J.J., Villanueva, A., Cabeza, R.: A novel 2D/3D database with automatic face annotation for head tracking and pose estimation. Comput. Vis. Image Underst. **148**, 201–210 (2016)
34. Carpenter, R.H.: Movements of the Eyes, 2nd edn. Pion Limited, London (1988)
35. Williams, C.K., Rasmussen, C.E.: Gaussian processes for regression (1996)
36. Nickisch, H., Rasmussen, C.E.: Approximations for binary gaussian process classification. J. Mach. Learn. Res. **9**, 2035–2078 (2008)
37. Sugano, Y., Matsushita, Y., Sato, Y.: Appearance-based gaze estimation using visual saliency. IEEE Trans. Pattern Anal. Mach. Intell. **35**(2), 329–341 (2013)
38. Sugano, Y., Matsushita, Y., Sato, Y.: Calibration-free gaze sensing using saliency maps. In: 2010 IEEE Conference on Computer Vision and Pattern Recognition (CVPR), pp. 2667–2674. IEEE (2010)
39. Alnajar, F., Gevers, T., Valenti, R., Ghebreab, S.: Calibration-free gaze estimation using human gaze patterns. In: Proceedings of the IEEE International Conference on Computer Vision, pp. 137–144 (2013)
40. Hirschmuller, H.: Stereo processing by semiglobal matching and mutual information. IEEE Trans. Pattern Anal. Mach. Intell. **30**(2), 328–341 (2008)
41. Zhu, K., Butenuth, M., d'Angelo, P.: Comparison of dense stereo using CUDA. In: Kutulakos, K.N. (ed.) ECCV 2010. LNCS, vol. 6554, pp. 398–410. Springer, Heidelberg (2012). doi:10.1007/978-3-642-35740-4_31
42. Zhu, K., Butenuth, M., d'Angelo, P.: Efficient dense stereo matching using CUDA. Technical report, TUM (2013)
43. Farbman, Z., Fattal, R., Lischinski, D., Szeliski, R.: Edge-preserving decompositions for multi-scale tone and detail manipulation. ACM Trans. Graph. (TOG) **27**, 1–67 (2008). ACM
44. Li, Q., Zhao, H.: Real-time implementation for weighted-least-squares-based edge-preserving decomposition and its applications. In: Pan, Z., Cheok, A.D., Müller, W. (eds.) Transactions on Edutainment VI. LNCS, vol. 6758, pp. 256–263. Springer, Heidelberg (2011). doi:10.1007/978-3-642-22639-7_25
45. Alvarez, M.A., Rosasco, L., Lawrence, N.D.: Kernels for vector-valued functions: a review. Mach. Learn. **4**(3), 195–266 (2011)
46. Bonilla, E.V., Chai, K.M., Williams, C.: Multi-task Gaussian process prediction. In: Advances in Neural Information Processing Systems, NIPS, pp. 153–160 (2007)
47. Whelan, T., Leutenegger, S., Salas-Moreno, R.F., Glocker, B., Davison, A.J.: ElasticFusion: dense SLAM without a pose graph. In: Robotics: Science and Systems (RSS), Rome, Italy, July 2015

48. Scharstein, D., Hirschmüller, H., Kitajima, Y., Krathwohl, G., Nešić, N., Wang, X., Westling, P.: High-resolution stereo datasets with subpixel-accurate ground truth. In: Jiang, X., Hornegger, J., Koch, R. (eds.) GCPR 2014. LNCS, vol. 8753, pp. 31–42. Springer, Heidelberg (2014). doi:10.1007/978-3-319-11752-2_3

49. Hartley, R., Zisserman, A.: Multiple View Geometry in Computer Vision. Cambridge University Press, Cambridge (2003)

Context Change Detection for an Ultra-Low Power Low-Resolution Ego-Vision Imager

Francesco Paci[1]([✉]), Lorenzo Baraldi[2], Giuseppe Serra[2], Rita Cucchiara[2], and Luca Benini[1,3]

[1] Univeristà di Bologna, Bologna, Italy
{f.paci,l.benini}@unibo.it
[2] Università di Modena e Reggio Emilia, Modena, Italy
{lorenzo.baraldi,giuseppe.serra,rita.cucchiara}@unimore.it
[3] ETH Zürich, Zürich, Switzerland
lbenini@iis.ee.ethz.ch

Abstract. With the increasing popularity of wearable cameras, such as GoPro or Narrative Clip, research on continuous activity monitoring from egocentric cameras has received a lot of attention. Research in hardware and software is devoted to find new efficient, stable and long-time running solutions; however, devices are too power-hungry for truly always-on operation, and are aggressively duty-cycled to achieve acceptable lifetimes. In this paper we present a wearable system for context change detection based on an egocentric camera with ultra-low power consumption that can collect data 24/7. Although the resolution of the captured images is low, experimental results in real scenarios demonstrate how our approach, based on Siamese Neural Networks, can achieve visual context awareness. In particular, we compare our solution with hand-crafted features and with state of art technique and propose a novel and challenging dataset composed of roughly 30000 low-resolution images.

Keywords: Egocentric vision · ULP camera · Low-resolution · Deep learning

1 Introduction and Related Works

Understanding everyday life activities is gaining more and more attention in the research community. This has triggered a number of interesting applications, ranging from health monitoring, memory rehabilitation, lifestyle analysis to security and entertainment [13,14,31,32]. These are mainly based on two sources of data: sensor and visual data. Sensor data, such as GPS, light, temperature and acceleration have been extensively used for activity monitoring [15,22,25]: among others, Kwapisz *et al.* [17] describe how a smartphone can be used to perform activity recognition simply by keeping it in the pocket. Guan *et al.* [11] present a semi-supervised learning algorithm for action understanding based on 40 accelerometers strapped loosely to common trousers. Although sensor data

© Springer International Publishing Switzerland 2016
G. Hua and H. Jégou (Eds.): ECCV 2016 Workshops, Part I, LNCS 9913, pp. 589–602, 2016.
DOI: 10.1007/978-3-319-46604-0_42

can be easily collected for days, thanks to low energy consumption, its ability to recognize complex activities and the context around the user is low.

On the other hand, computer vision can indeed capture much richer contextual information which has been successfully used to recognize more complex activities [1,18,29]. Recently, several works that consider vision tasks from the egocentric perspective have been presented. Poleg *et al.* [26] propose a temporal segmentation that identifies 12 different activities (e.g. head motion, sitting, walking etc.). Castro *et al.* [5] present an approach based on the combination of a Convolutional Neural Network and a Random Decision Forest; this approach is able to recognize images automatically in 19 activity classes. Ryoo *et al.* [27] suggest a new feature representation for egocentric vision which captures both the entire scene dynamics and the salient local motion observed in video. However, these approaches are designed to recognize a limited set of activities and can be useful for specific applications only.

To address this limitation, some unsupervised temporal segmentation and context change detection techniques have been presented, which are capable of splitting an egocentric video into meaningful segments. Lu *et al.* [20] present an approach that discovers the essential moments of a long egocentric video. First, they segment the original video into a series of subshots. Then they represent a short sequence in term of visual objects, that appear within it, using a bank of object detectors. Dimiccoli *et al.* [9] present an approach for context change detection, which combines low-level features and detection of semantic visual concepts (high-level semantic labels are extracted using Imagga's auto-tagging system[1]). By relying on these features, a graph-cut technique is used to integrate agglomerative clustering and an adaptive windowing algorithm [4].

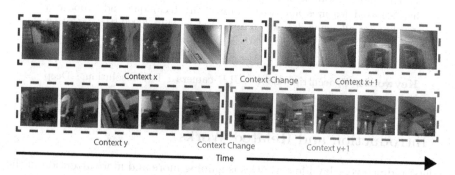

Fig. 1. We address the problem of recognizing context changes from low-Resolution images. Figure shows some images taken from the Stonyman Dataset

All of these approaches exploit high quality videos and images taken by egocentric cameras that can be worn, like GoPro, Narrative Clip, Looxcie, Google Glass and Microsoft SenseCam. Although these cameras have become smaller

---

[1] https://imagga.com/solutions/auto-tagging.html.

and cheaper, they are quite power-hungry. In fact, even if these devices take snapshots periodically, for example every 15 or 30 s, they have a short battery life ranging from one up to six hours. In addition, all presented solutions leverage imagers that, in the best case, consume several tens or hundreds of mW. These levels of power consumption are not affordable for continuous activity monitoring within a power envelope of a truly wearable system. Therefore, these solutions are not able to monitor human experience around the clock and their application in real contexts is limited in the analysis of short recording only.

We follow, therefore, another direction in contrast with the above mentioned. We explore how, even with very limited resolution, we can obtain context awareness and understand, at least, a change of context in our day-life. We present a context change detector for low-resolution images based on a wearable egocentric camera with ultra-low power consumption. An example of the task that we want to achieve is shown in Fig. 1. Low-resolution images can't "see" in the way we usually interpret, as good quality pictures, but can give visual context awareness, that can be exploited for context change detection. The system is able to collect data 24/7 laying the basis for the long-term analysis of egocentric vision activities. In this context, state of the art context change detection techniques, that are based on results of semantic classifiers, cannot be adopted. Therefore, we propose a novel approach that explores the use of Deep Convolutional Neural Networks on low level resolution images. Experimental results on a new challenging dataset demonstrate that the presented solution is able to detect context changes with good precision.

The paper is organized as follows. Section 2 gives an overview of the hardware system employed and presents the images and the pre-filtering stage, Sect. 3 describes in depth the Network architecture, Sect. 4 details the performance and accuracy of our solution, while Sect. 5 concludes the paper and gives some guidelines for future work.

2   Egocentric Vision Acquisition System

The egocentric vision acquisition system is based on a Texas Instrument Microntroller unit (MCU) and a low-power, low-resolution Stonyman Centeye imager. It is powered by a Li-Ion battery and embeds an energy harvester, that can supply the system while in operation or recharge the battery while the system is in standby. The main advantage of this platform is that it can continuously operate with a total power budget that is compatible with a small energy harvester or with 3, 5 days of lifetime with a small (1 Ah) battery. This platform is a development of Infinitime device [21], a wearable bracelet with human body harvesting. In Fig. 2 we show the core platform components and a picture of the real device.

The computational unit is an up-to 16 MHz Microcontroller by Texas Instruments, the MSP430FR5969 [23]. This MCU can run in several low power states, turning off unused memories and peripherals, or scaling down the operating frequency. The sensors that this board features are the above mentioned imager, plus an analog microphone, a temperature sensor and an accelerometer.

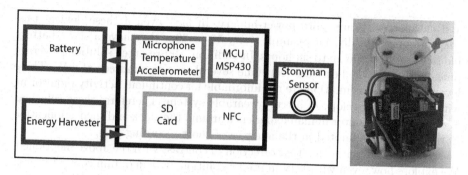

Fig. 2. Schema of the egocentric vision acquisition system

2.1 Stonyman Imager

The embedded camera sensor, as already mentioned, is a Stonyman sensor by Centeye [6]. The first step to acquire images from this analog sensor is to sample them by an Analog to Digital Converter (ADC) and then store them in the system FRAM. Then the platform can store images in an SD card or send them through the NFC to a seconds device (e.g. a smartphone or a tablet).

The analog sensor can capture 112×112 pixel wide grayscale images at up to 2.5 fps, while storing it into SD card. The power consumption of the imager itself is orders of magnitude less than a digital CMOS sensors in the marketplace. In fact, we observed that the power consumption while reading an image is 3.9 mW, while storing an image into SD card takes about 121 mW. In terms of performance, acquiring an image and storing to SD card takes 400 ms. The sending procedure via NFC is less expensive in terms of power budget, as it costs 0.35 mW. In sleep mode the MCU consmes only 0,005 mW. So engaging a battery of 1000 mAH, at 1 fps and storing images in the SD Card the device can run for 3,5 days with a full recharge. Further experiments conducted by Spadaro *et al.* [30] shows that with a kinetic harvester during running activity the harvester can supply enough energy to collect 36 images per minute, while walking activity permits to take 6 images per minute using the NFC to send the image to second device. This ultra-low power consumption enables this device to be used as a perpetual visual aware sensor.

Images captured by the imager and converted by the ADC are rather noisy. A pre-filtering step is thus required to enhance the image quality. Next section discusses the image quality issues and the noise removal technique that we propose.

2.2 Images Pre-processing

Images are sampled by a 12 bit ADC, so a normalization stage is needed to convert them in a 8-bit single channel format. In particular, images sampled from the Stonyman imager are mainly affected by static noise. Our noise removal system deals with it. Therefore, noise removal is carried out by subtracting a

Before Image Denoising

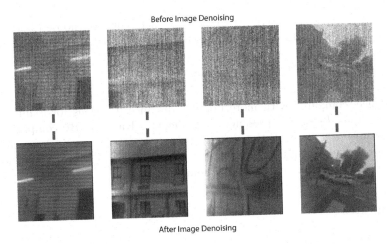

After Image Denoising

Fig. 3. Image Denoising results

mask to the images, which is created by averaging several pictures framing a white background in an average light condition. In Fig. 3 we show samples of images before and after denoising. After this stage, denoised images feed the temporal segmentation network described in next Section.

3 Temporal Segmentation Network

Learning to detect context changes can be addressed as a similarity learning task. In particular, we propose to learn a function $f(x, y)$ that compares an image x to another candidate image y of the same size and returns a high score if the two images capture the same context and a low score otherwise. The function f will be learned from a dataset of videos with labeled change points.

Given their widespread success in computer vision [10,16,19,28], we will use a deep ConvNet as the function f. The architecture of the network resembles that of a Siamese network [12], which is the most used model for addressing similarity learning with ConvNets. Siamese networks apply the same transformation ϕ to both inputs, and then combine their representations using a distance function. Therefore, function ϕ can be considered as an embedding, while the overall network can be seen as a learnable distance computation model.

To train the network, we employ a discriminative approach, by collecting positive and negative pairs. We define positive a pair of images which share the same temporal context, and negative a pair of images sampled from different contexts. At each iteration, we randomly sample a set of pairs $\mathcal{P}$, and minimize the following contrastive loss function:

$$L(\mathbf{w}) = \frac{1}{|\mathcal{P}|} \sum_{(x_i, y_i) \in \mathcal{P}} y_i f(x_i, y_i) + (1 - y_i) \max(0, 1 - f(x_i, y_i)) \tag{1}$$

where $y_i \in \{0, 1\}$ is the ground truth label of each pair. We choose to define the distance function f with respect to the embedding function ϕ through the cosine similarity:

$$f(x, y) = 1 - \frac{\phi(x) \cdot \phi(y)}{\|\phi(x)\| \cdot \|\phi(y)\|} \qquad (2)$$

This choice, compared with more popular distance functions for Siamese networks, such as L_1 or L_2, presents a significant advantage. By computing the angle between $\phi(x)$ and $\phi(y)$, and neglecting their magnitudes, it does not force the network to bring its activations into a given numerical range, thus saving training time and avoiding poor local minima.

4   Results

In this section we present the evaluation of our system in terms of accuracy in context change detection. The evaluation has been done by collecting a dataset of images that is described in the next section. In Sect. 4.2 we describe the evaluation measures, while in Sect. 4.3 we present accuracy in comparison with two baselines and a state-of-art work.

4.1   Stonyman Dataset

To evaluate our results we collected a dataset of 29261 images named "Stonyman Dataset", from the name of the imager. All the images are collected at 1 fps and from a single subject under several days. We define context change any point of the sequence which delimits two temporal segments representing different environments (i.e. we considered as context change going in a shop, enter in the workplace, going off for a pause, catch the bus, etc.).

In Table 1 we show the sets in which the dataset is divided and the number of images collected per day, while the third column shows the number of images

Table 1. Stonyman and Stonyman Quality Datasets: set names, number of images and number of context changes (CS)

Set name	Stonyman D.	Stonyman Quality D.	# of CS
2016-04-06	2734	2143	7
2016-07-05	12104	9257	13
2016-07-06	6256	5566	11
2016-07-07 - 9.00	2056	1544	5
2016-07-07 - 12.00	4367	4043	6
2016-07-08	868	424	3
2016-07-09	876	435	3
Total	29261	23412	48

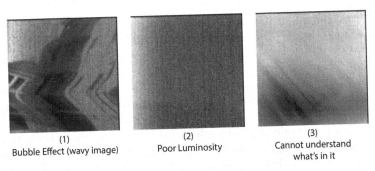

Fig. 4. Three examples, matching the three criteria used to remove images from Stonyman Dataset to create Stonyman Quality Dataset.

of a subset of the dataset that we called "Stonyman Quality dataset". This is an improved version of the dataset obtained by pruning images with poor quality or that cannot be understood by a human expert. In particular, three criteria were considered:

1. Images with bubble effect (wavy images).
2. Images with poor luminosity or completely black.
3. Images where the subject that took the dataset cannot understand what's in it.

In Fig. 4 an example of each of these defects is shown.

4.2 Evaluation Metrics

For the evaluation of context scene detection, the classical precision-recall scheme has been often used, with the important variation of adding a temporal tolerance factor to detections and ground truth cuts. Therefore, a detection is considered as positive if its distance to nearest ground truth cut is below a certain threshold, otherwise it is considered as a false positive. False negatives are computed by counting ground truth cuts which are further than the same threshold to the nearest detected cut. Formally, given a threshold θ, a set of detected change points $D = \{t_0, t_1, ..., t_n\}$ and the set of ground truth cuts $C = \{t_0^g, t_1^g, ..., t_m^g\}$, true positives, false positives and false negatives are computed as follows:

$$TP = \sum_{i=0}^{n} \max_{j=0}^{m} \mathbb{1}(|t_i - t_j^g| \leq \theta) \quad FP = \sum_{i=0}^{n} 1 - \max_{j=0}^{m} \mathbb{1}(|t_i - t_j^g| \leq \theta) \quad (3)$$

$$FN = \sum_{i=0}^{m} 1 - \max_{j=0}^{n} \mathbb{1}(|t_j - t_i^g| \leq \theta)$$

where $\mathbb{1}(\cdot)$ is an indication function that returns 1 when the given condition is true, and 0 otherwise. F-Score is then derived from Precision and Recall as usual.

Of course, the major drawback of this measure is the need to set an appropriate tolerance threshold. In our experiments, following previous works in the field [9], we set up a tolerance threshold of 5 frames, which given our frame rate correspond to 5 s.

The problem we address can be regarded as a temporal segmentation task, so appropriate measures can be taken from works that addressed temporal segmentation in other scenarios. One of them is surely scene detection, in which the objective is to temporally segment a broadcast video in semantically meaningful parts. In this setting, a measure based on intersection over union has been recently proposed [3]. Here, each temporal segment is represented as a closed interval, where the left bound of the interval is the starting frame, and the right bound is the ending frame of the sequence. The intersection over union of two segments a and b, $\text{IoU}(a, b)$, is written as

$$\text{IoU}(a, b) = \frac{a \cap b}{a \cup b} \tag{4}$$

A segmentation of a video can be seen as a set of non-overlapping sequences, whose union is the set of frames of the video. By exploiting this relation, [3] defines the intersection over union of two segmentations C and D as:

$$\overline{\text{IoU}}(C, D) = \frac{1}{2} \left(\frac{1}{\#C} \sum_{a \in C} \max_{b \in D} \text{IoU}(a, b) + \frac{1}{\#D} \sum_{b \in D} \max_{a \in C} \text{IoU}(a, b) \right) \tag{5}$$

It is easy to see that Eq. 5 computes, for each ground-truth segment, the maximum intersection over union with the detected segments. Then, the same is done for detected segments against ground-truth ones, and the two quantities are averaged.

4.3   Experimental Results

To quantitatively evaluate the difficulty of dealing with low resolution images, we first present two baseline experiments. They both use Histogram of Oriented Gradients [8] (HOG) as descriptors, and hierarchical agglomerative clustering with euclidean distance to group images in contexts.

In the former baseline test (named CT1, Clustering Test 1), we fix the number of clusters to eight, which is the number of unique contexts that we have in our dataset: biking, car, home, office, walking, stairs, supermarket/shop, outdoor. The idea behind this experiment is to test the ability of a popular handcrafted descriptor to distinguish between different contexts and places. HOG are extracted separately from each image and then descriptors are clustered in eight clusters.

In the latter test (named CT2, Clustering Test 2), instead, agglomerative clustering is applied with a different methodology, which resembles that of a Siamese network. Images are elaborated in subsequent couples from the beginning to end of the dataset. From each couple of images we extract HOG features, and compute the element-wise L_1 distance on feature vectors. We thus get a feature vector for each couple, having the same dimensionality of the HOG descriptor. The resulting features are then given as input to the agglomerative clustering, but instead of looking for eight clusters as the previous baseline test, we fix the number of clusters to two (similar and dissimilar pairs).

In Figs. 5 and 6 we present the accuracy measured respectively with F-Score and IoU on CT1 and CT2. We tested two different settings for HOG features extraction. For both we used a window size of 112×112, block size of 56×56 and block stride of 28×28, and tested two different cell sizes: 28×28 and 56×56. We selected these two settings after conducting a grid search on a subset of the dataset, and picked the top two feature sizes in accuracy.

As it can be seen from the two charts, F-Score and IoU values are very low, thus revealing that hand-crafted features are not well suitable for low-resolution noisy images. The best accuracy in terms of F-Score is achieved with CT1, since the solution of clustering into eight classes is a more easy task, and we see a slight improvement with Stonyman Quality with respect to the entire dataset. In Fig. 6 the same results are evaluated in terms of IoU. All settings results in similar values of IoU, and this is due to the completely different nature of the two performance measures.

Moving to the proposed approach, we employed the pre-trained 16 layers model from VGG [28] as the embedding function ϕ, since it is well known for its state-of-the-art performances on image classifications tasks, while still being a simple and lightweight model for modern GPUs. The overall network is then trained end-to-end using Stochastic Gradient Descent with learning rate 0.001 and batches of 20 couples.

In Table 2 we present the results of our system on the Stonyman and Stonyman Quality datasets. The performances are reported in terms of F-Score and IoU for each set. Notice that Stoneyman Quality compared to Stonyman produce 0.2 improvement in F-Score and 0.1 improvement in IoU, we attribute this behavior mostly to wavy images that are removed in Stonyman Quality. These distort images produce an altered feature that make the problem more challenging.

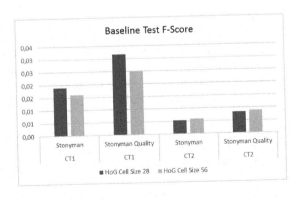

Fig. 5. CT1 and CT2 baselines in terms of F-Score

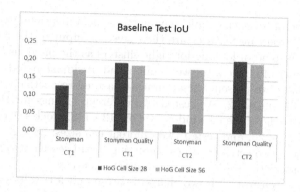

Fig. 6. CT1 and CT2 baselines in terms of IoU

Table 2. F-Score and IoU results of our system on Stonyman and Stonyman Quality datasets

	Stonyman D.		Stonyman Quality D.	
	F-Score	IoU	F-Score	IoU
2016-04-06	0.571	0.655	0.667	0.608
2016-07-05	0.216	0.411	0.357	0.539
2016-07-06	0.105	0.590	0.286	0.375
2016-07-07 - 9.00	0.133	0.397	0.625	0.791
2016-07-07 - 12.00	0.217	0.387	0.500	0.712
2016-07-08	0.143	0.618	0.400	0.552
2016-07-09	0.193	0.346	0.267	0.520
Average	0.226	0.486	0.443	0.585

Table 3 present a comparison of the two baselines (CT1 and CT2) and our system. We can observe that the techniques based on scene clustering achieve low performance. Whereas our system obtains promising results in both scenarios. We could not compare our solution with a state of the art Scene Clustering System called SR-Clustering [9], because, as mentioned before, a key element of their technique is the extensively usage of high-level semantic classifiers, which don't work with our low-resolution snapshots. This is clearly shown in Fig. 7, in which we present some examples of predictions obtained on our low-resolution images by the classifiers adopted in [9] and the corresponding Narrative Clip high quality image.

Therefore even if our system cannot exploit an high-level semantic classifier, we tested it on the reference dataset of SR-Clustering to show that results on color high quality images are in-line with the Stonyman Quality low-resolution images.

The SR-Clustering work proposes a dataset called EDUB-Seg which is composed of two sets: EDUB-Seg Set 1 and EDUB-Seg Set 2. The only publicly

Fig. 7. Imagga predicted tags on the same images shot with Stonyman (Grayscale) and Narrative (Color) (Color figure online)

Table 3. Comparison results between the proposed solution and the two baselines (CT1 and CT2) on Stonyman and Stonyman Quality datasets

	Stonyman D.		Stonyman Quality D.	
	F-Score	IoU	F-Score	IoU
CT1	0.019	0.170	0.032	0.192
CT2	0.006	0.179	0.009	0.204
Our system	**0.226**	**0.486**	**0.443**	**0.585**

Table 4. Performance results of our system on EDUB-Seg

	F-Score	IoU
Subject1_1	0.563	0.494
Subject1_2	0.545	0.536
Subject2_1	0.448	0.466
Subject2_2	0.500	0.473
Subject3_1	0.500	0.418
Subject3_2	0.400	0.574
Subject4_1	0.476	0.546
Subject4_2	0.774	0.560
Average	0.521	0.510

Table 5. Accuracy of our system and SR-Clustering in EDUB-Seg Set 1 Dataset

	F-Score
SR-Clustering	0.69
Our system	0.521

available one is EDUB-Seg Set 1. This dataset is composed 4912 color images (512 × 512 pixels) collected by 4 subjects with a Narrative Clip camera [24] at 2 fpm. In Table 4 is shown our results on this dataset. We trained the network with the technique leave-one-out: for each subset the network is trained on all the other subsets. The results shows an improvement in F-Score compared to Stoneyman Quality dataset, while on IoU there is a slight loss. This shows that in this dataset the low framerate is balanced by the quality of the images.

Lastly in Table 5 we report the results of SR-Clustering on EDUB-Seg set 1 and the average F-Score that we achieve with our system.

5   Conclusion and Further Work

In this paper we proposed a context change detection system. First, we presented an egocentric vision device with ultra-low power consumption that can capture images round the clock. Then, we suggested a similarity learning approach, based on Siamese ConvNets, that is able to deal with grayscale low-resolution snapshots. We finally run extensive experiments in real scenarios, showing the robustness and efficacy of the proposed method with respect to related approaches.

On future works we will explore an automatic technique for discarding images without a relevant semantic content. Moreover we will focus on embedding the network processing in an ultra-low power budget. The ultra-low power trend encourages deep-network based approaches [2,7]. Experts in computer vision and also VLSI and computer architecture communities are focusing on these approaches with promising results in terms of energy efficiency.

Acknowledgments. This work was partially supported by the Swiss National Foundation under grant 162524 (MicroLearn: Micropower Deep Learning), the ERC MultiTherman project (ERC-AdG-291125) and the Vision for Augmented Experiences through the Fondazione CRMO Project.

References

1. Alletto, S., Serra, G., Calderara, S., Cucchiara, R.: Understanding social relationships in egocentric vision. Pattern Recogn. **48**(12), 4082–4096 (2015)
2. Andri, R., Cavigelli, L., Rossi, D., Benini, L.: Yodann: an ultra-low power convolutional neural network accelerator based on binary weights. arXiv preprint arXiv:1606.05487 (2016)

3. Baraldi, L., Grana, C., Cucchiara, R.: A deep siamese network for scene detection in broadcast videos. In: Proceedings of the 23rd ACM International Conference on Multimedia, pp. 1199–1202. ACM (2015)
4. Bifet, A., Gavalda, R.: Learning from time-changing data with adaptive windowing. In: Proceedings of International Conference on Data Mining (2007)
5. Castro, D., Hickson, S., Bettadapura, V., Thomaz, E., Abowd, G., Christensen, H., Essa, I.: Predicting daily activities from egocentric images using deep learning. In: Proceedings of the ACM International symposium on Wearable Computers (2015)
6. Centeye: http://www.centeye.com/. Accessed 15 July 2016
7. Conti, F., Benini, L.: A ultra-low-energy convolution engine for fast brain-inspired vision in multicore clusters. In: DATE 2015 (2015)
8. Dalal, N., Triggs, B.: Histograms of oriented gradients for human detection. In: Proceedings of the IEEE Conference on Computer Vision and Pattern Recognition (2005)
9. Dimiccoli, M., Bolaños, M., Talavera, E., Aghaei, M., Nikolov, S.G., Radeva, P.: Sr-clustering: Semantic regularized clustering for egocentric photo streams segmentation. arXiv preprint arXiv:1512.07143 (2015)
10. Donahue, J., Jia, Y., Vinyals, O., Hoffman, J., Zhang, N., Tzeng, E., Darrell, T.: Decaf: A deep convolutional activation feature for generic visual recognition. In: Proceedings of the International Conference on Machine Learning (2014)
11. Guan, D., Yuan, W., Lee, Y.K., Gavrilov, A., Lee, S.: Activity recognition based on semi-supervised learning. In: Proceedings of the International Conference on Embedded and Real-Time Computing Systems and Applications (2007)
12. Hadsell, R., Chopra, S., LeCun, Y.: Dimensionality reduction by learning an invariant mapping. In: IEEE International Conference on Computer Vision and Pattern Recognition, vol. 2, pp. 1735–1742. IEEE (2006)
13. Hodges, S., Williams, L., Berry, E., Izadi, S., Srinivasan, J., Butler, A., Smyth, G., Kapur, N., Wood, K.: SenseCam: a retrospective memory aid. In: Dourish, P., Friday, A. (eds.) UbiComp 2006. LNCS, vol. 4206, pp. 177–193. Springer, Heidelberg (2006). doi:10.1007/11853565_11
14. Kelly, P., Doherty, A., Berry, E., Hodges, S., Batterham, A.M., Foster, C.: Can we use digital life-log images to investigate active and sedentary travel behaviour? Results from a pilot study. Int. J. Behav. Nutr. Phys. Act. 8(1), 1 (2011)
15. Khan, A.M., Tufail, A., Khattak, A.M., Laine, T.H.: Activity recognition on smartphones via sensor-fusion and kda-based svms. Int. J. Distrib. Sensor Netw. 2014, 14 (2014)
16. Krizhevsky, A., Sutskever, I., Hinton, G.E.: Imagenet classification with deep convolutional neural networks. In: Advances in Neural Information Processing Systems, pp. 1097–1105 (2012)
17. Kwapisz, J.R., Weiss, G.M., Moore, S.A.: Activity recognition using cell phone accelerometers. ACM SigKDD Explor. Newslett. 12(2), 74–82 (2011)
18. Li, Y., Fathi, A., Rehg, J.M.: Learning to predict gaze in egocentric video. In: Proceedings of the International Conference on Computer Vision (2013)
19. Long, J., Shelhamer, E., Darrell, T.: Fully convolutional networks for semantic segmentation. In: Proceedings of the IEEE Conference on Computer Vision and Pattern Recognition (2015)
20. Lu, Z., Grauman, K.: Story-driven summarization for egocentric video. In: Proceedings of the Conference on Computer Vision and Pattern Recognition (2013)

21. Magno, M., Brunelli, D., Sigrist, L., Andri, R., Cavigelli, L., Gomez, A., Benini, L.: Infinitime: multi-sensor wearable bracelet with human body harvesting. Sustainable Computing: Informatics and Systems (2016). http://www.sciencedirect.com/science/article/pii/S2210537916300816

22. Mannini, A., Sabatini, A.M.: Machine learning methods for classifying human physical activity from on-body accelerometers. Sensors 10(2), 1154–1175 (2010)

23. MSP430: Texas instruments. http://www.ti.com/ww/it/msp.430.html. Accessed 15 July 2016

24. Narrative: http://getnarrative.com/. Accessed 15 July 2016

25. Patel, S., Park, H., Bonato, P., Chan, L., Rodgers, M.: A review of wearable sensors and systems with application in rehabilitation. J. Neuroeng. Rehabil. 9(1), 1 (2012)

26. Poleg, Y., Arora, C., Peleg, S.: Temporal segmentation of egocentric videos. In: Proceedings of the Conference on Computer Vision and Pattern Recognition (2014)

27. Ryoo, M.S., Rothrock, B., Matthies, L.: Pooled motion features for first-person videos. In: Proceedings of the IEEE Conference on Computer Vision and Pattern Recognition, pp. 896–904 (2015)

28. Simonyan, K., Zisserman, A.: Very deep convolutional networks for large-scale image recognition. arXiv preprint arXiv:1409.1556 (2014)

29. Singh, K.K., Fatahalian, K., Efros, A.A.: Krishnacam: Using a longitudinal, single-person, egocentric dataset for scene understanding tasks. In: Proceedings of the IEEE Winter Conference on Applications of Computer Vision (2016)

30. Spadaro, L., Magno, M., Benini, L.: Kinetisee: A perpetual wearable camera acquisition system with a kinetic harvester: poster abstract. In: Proceedings of the 15th International Conference on Information Processing in Sensor Networks, IPSN 2016, pp. 68: 1–68: 2. IEEE Press, Piscataway (2016). http://dl.acm.org/citation.cfm?id=2959355.2959423

31. Su, Y.C., Grauman, K.: Detecting engagement in egocentric video. In: Proceedings of the European Conference on Computer Vision (2016)

32. Zhang, H., Li, L., Jia, W., Fernstrom, J.D., Sclabassi, R.J., Sun, M.: Recognizing physical activity from ego-motion of a camera. In: Proceedings of the IEEE Conference Engineering in Medicine and Biology (2010)

W22 – Web–scale Vision and Social Media

Preface

Welcome to the proceedings of the 4th Workshop on Web-scale Vision and Social Media (VSM), co-located with the 14th European Conference on Computer Vision, held on October 10, 2016 in Amsterdam, The Netherlands.

The Web has become a large ecosystem that reaches billions of users through information processing and sharing, and most of this information resides in pixels, either images or videos. Web-based services like YouTube and Flickr, and social networks such as Facebook have become increasingly popular, enabling us to easily upload, share and annotate massive numbers of images and videos. Therefore, the VSM workshop have aimed to bring together researchers from a diverse background to advocate and promote new research directions for problems involving web vision and social media such as large-scale visual content analysis, search and mining. The program contained novel, scalable methods that understand the visual data and exploit (noisy) user annotations in order to enable users to better navigate this content.

This year, we received 14 valid submissions of which 12 were fully reviewed. The others were either administratively rejected for technical reasons or withdrawn before review. A total of 7 papers were accepted (50 % of valid submissions); 3 of these were allocated long oral presentations (21 % of valid submissions) while the others were allocated short spotlight presentations. In addition, all oral and spotlight papers were presented at the poster session, together with extended abstracts describing relevant work that was recently published at major computer vision and multimedia conferences.

This workshop would not have been possible without the help of many. First of all we would like to thank the ECCV organisers for hosting the workshop in Amsterdam. Subsequently a big thank you to all the authors for their papers and the hard work of the reviewers. Finally we would like to thank the invited speakers for the exciting and inspiring talks and all the participants for making the workshop (again) a great success.

November 2016

Lamberto Ballan
Marco Bertini
Thomas Mensink

Label-Based Automatic Alignment of Video with Narrative Sentences

Pelin Dogan[1], Markus Gross[1], and Jean-Charles Bazin[2]([⊠])

[1] Department of Computer Science, ETHZ, Zurich, Switzerland
{pelin.dogan,grossm}@inf.ethz.ch
[2] Disney Research, Zurich, Switzerland
jean-charles.bazin@disneyresearch.com

Abstract. In this paper we consider videos (e.g. Hollywood movies) and their accompanying natural language descriptions in the form of narrative sentences (e.g. movie scripts without timestamps). We propose a method for temporally aligning the video frames with the sentences using both visual and textual information, which provides automatic timestamps for each narrative sentence. We compute the similarity between both types of information using vectorial descriptors and propose to cast this alignment task as a matching problem that we solve via dynamic programming. Our approach is simple to implement, highly efficient and does not require the presence of frequent dialogues, subtitles, and character face recognition. Experiments on various movies demonstrate that our method can successfully align the movie script sentences with the video frames of movies.

1 Introduction

Audio description consists of an audio narration track where the narrator describes what is happening in the video. It allows visually impaired people to follow movies or other types of videos. However the number of movies that provide it is considerably low, and its preparation is particularly time consuming. On the other hand, scripts of numerous movies are available online although they generally are plain text sentences. Our goal is to temporally align the script sentences to the corresponding shots in the video, i.e. obtain the timing information of each sentence. These sentences can then be converted to audio description by an automatic speech synthesizer or can be read by a human describer. This would provide a wider range of movies to visually impaired people.

Several additional applications could benefit from the alignment of video with text. For example, the resulting correspondences of video frames and sentences can be used to improve image/video understanding and automatic caption generation by forming a learning corpus. Video-text alignment also enables text-based video retrieval since searching for a part of the video could be achieved via a simple text search.

In this paper, we address temporal alignment of video frames with their descriptive sentences to obtain precise timestamps of the sentences with minimal manual intervention. A representative result is shown in Fig. 1. The videos

© Springer International Publishing Switzerland 2016
G. Hua and H. Jégou (Eds.): ECCV 2016 Workshops, Part I, LNCS 9913, pp. 605–620, 2016.
DOI: 10.1007/978-3-319-46604-0_43

are typically movies or some parts of movies with duration of 10 to 20 min. We do not assume any presegmentation or shot threading of the video. We start by obtaining the high-level labels of the video frames (e.g. "car", "walking", "street") with deep learning techniques [12] and use these labels to group the video frames into semantic shots. In this way, each shot contains relatively different semantics knowing that the information given by the different sentences is relatively different. Then we formulate the problem of text-video alignment as sentence-shot alignment by finding similarity between the high-level labels in the shots and the words of the sentences. This similarity is computed using the vectorial features of words and word-to-word distances. Our final alignment is formulated in a graph based approach computing the minimum distance path from the first to the last sentence-shot pair. The main contributions of our paper are:

- We align human-written sentences (such as scripts and audio description texts) with the complete set of shots that constitutes the video. Our approach does not require dialogues, subtitles, and face recognition. Our approach directly works on the raw video, i.e. no presegmentation or cut is needed.
- We automatically segment the input video into shots by using frame based high-level semantics so that a semantic change in a continuous camera shot can be detected. We refer this semantic change as *semantic cut* through the paper. We also introduce a refinement process to optimize the semantic cuts so that they tend to correspond to one sentence each.
- We introduce a novel dataset of script sentence alignments of various video sequences which are publicly available on the project page.

2   Related Work

Our goal is to temporally align a video with its script, which will provide a timestamp for each sentence in the script. In the following, we describe the related work on steps that will lead us towards this goal.

Image/video description. In the last years there has been an increasing interest in object/scene recognition, object labeling, and automatic caption generation, in part thanks to the availability of new datasets [4,29,30]. With the recent developments in deep convolutional architectures, large-scale visual recognition by convolutional neural networks [12] and recurrent neural networks [6] has achieved state-of-the-art results by surpassing the conventional methods. Moreover, impressive results have been obtained for describing images and videos with natural language [6,8,9,13,18,22,24]. These approaches rely on a corpus with strong annotations. The main reason why the current video description performance is falling behind the image description is the lack of large annotated video corpus that would provide better learning and understanding. Since the manual annotation of videos with text is very time consuming, automatic alignment methods of video-text pairs would increase the size of the corpus and the variety of the content.

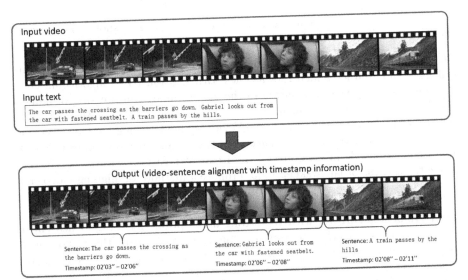

Fig. 1. Given an input movie and associated narrative sentences (e.g. from the movie script), our approach temporally aligns the video frames with the sentences and provides the timestamp information of the sentences. This figure illustrates a representative result for a 10-minutes long continuous video from the movie *Lucid Dreams of Gabriel*. For a better visibility of the figure, only a 8-seconds segment is shown here.

Text similarity. The recent developments of the deep neural networks improved the natural language processing tasks, with applications in information retrieval and artificial intelligence. The computation of the similarity and relation between words is an important step towards video-text alignment, for example to compute the similarity between the high-level labels of the video frames (e.g. "car", "walking") and the words of the script sentences(e.g. "She opens the car door"). Some approaches use either using a thesaurus or statistics from a large text corpus, or use both to compute word similarity [1,11,16,19,20]. In our work, we will use the approach of Pennington et al. [20]: they propose an unsupervised learning algorithm to obtain vector representations for words based on word-word co-occurrence statistics from a text corpus. Their vector representation demonstrates superior results in finding the semantic distance between words.

Shot segmentation. Aligning sentences with the corresponding video parts requires shot detection and shot segmentation. For this, many of the automated shot-change detection methods use color histograms [7,10,15,17] or visual descriptors [2,14,21]. These are mostly successful for shots that are bounded by camera cuts or abrupt visual transitions. In the context of video-text alignment, distinguishing a semantic change through a single camera shot is valuable because a semantic change in the video is usually associated to a new description sentence within the script. Therefore we are using semantic features, namely high-level labels, to segment the full video into "semantic shots" and in turn match the sentences with them.

Alignment. Tapaswi et al. [28] align book chapters with video scenes using dialogues and character identities as cues with a graph based algorithm. Their alignment requires face recognition in the video frames and presence of numerous dialogues which may fail in case the movie does not have these densely. Sankar et al. [26] align the scripts to TV videos/movies using location, face and speech recognition. However this success of the method is mostly limited to TV series, since it needs pre-training of the frequent locations within the video to divide the scenes. Bojanowski et al. [3] propose a method for aligning video clips to sentences given the vectorial features for both video and text. They require the segmentation of the video unlike us and solve the problem using a conditional gradient algorithm with the strong assumption that every video clip is corresponding to exactly one sentence. Instead, we segment the video jointly while performing alignment so that we do not require such strong assumption. Tapaswi et al. [27] present an approach to align plot synopses with the corresponding shots with the guidance of subtitles and character identities using dynamic programming. They require the extraction of character information both in textual and visual forms by using face detector and tracker. Rohrbach et al. [23] provide a dataset that contains transcribed descriptive video service, which is temporally aligned to full length movies. Their dataset provides video sentences with timestamps that match the video snippets. In contrast to our automatic method, they perform the fine alignment of the sentences manually which is significantly time consuming. Zhu et al. [31] aim to align books to their movie releases by using visual correspondences as well as the correspondences between the dialogues and the subtitles, which may fail for videos with very limited dialogues. Moreover their alignment is at a coarser level: they aim to match book chapters with TV episodes. In contrast, we aim for precise (frame-level) timestamps for sentences and shots.

3   Proposed Approach

In this section, we present our approach for aligning a video with its narrative sentences, which results in a timestamp for each sentence. To have an accurate alignment, the text input should provide at least one sentence for each shot in the movie. By the term *shot* we refer to a series of frames that runs for an uninterrupted period of time with the same semantics, not necessarily defined by camera cuts. An example of text input for our algorithm can be a movie script (dialogues not required). Another example would be a transcribed audio description of the movie containing rich descriptions for visually impaired people. We assume that the sentences are in the same temporal order as the movie, like movie scripts and audio descriptions. Our approach is designed for videos having a dynamic plot with different scenes and actions as in the typical Hollywood movies. A counter-example is a biographical documentary film, such as an interview, where a person speaks to the camera during the whole duration of the video, i.e. without any changes of scene or action.

3.1 Overview

We first obtain the high-level labels for all the video frames in the form of words, as well as their confidence scores, using deep learning techniques [12]. Then we smooth these through the time domain to obtain temporal coherency. The temporally coherent results are used to detect the semantic changes in the video, which corresponds to the beginnings and ends of the shots. Then the labels and their confidence scores of the frames of each detected shot are grouped together to represent the shots. We then calculate a similarity score for each shot-sentence pair using the labels from the shot and the sentence words. This provides a cost matrix and we then compute the minimum distance path assuming the matching of the first and last sentence-shot pairs are given. The nodes of the calculated path provides the matching of the sentence-shot pairs. This results in the annotation of each input sentence with the timestamp of the matched shot.

3.2 High-Level Features and Temporal Coherency

We start by obtaining the high-level features (labels) of each frame of the input video. Each video frame is processed independently and thus can be processed in parallel. These high-level labels are in the form of text words and typically refer to object (e.g. "car"), scene (e.g. "street") or action (e.g. "walking") visible in the video frame. We automatically obtain these labels, as well as their confidence score, by the deep learning based cloud service Clarifai[1] or Caffe framework [12] with pretrained models for its CNN architecture. As a result, for each video frame i we obtain a feature vector w_i whose number of entries is the total number of labels (around 1000) and the entry values are the confidence scores for the label corresponding to that entry index. A representative result vector for a frame from the movie *Lucid Dreams of Gabriel* is shown in Fig. 2.

By concatenating these column vectors w_i over time, we obtain a matrix $\mathbf{W}$ containing the confidence scores of the labels through time. A representative example is shown in Fig. 3-top. Each row of this matrix represents the scores of the label corresponding to that row index (e.g. "car") through time. If the entries of this row are all zero or very small, it means the corresponding label is not seen in the frames, e.g. no "car" object is visible in the entire video. The values in the matrix rows are noisy due to motion blur, occlusions, lighting change, and all the effects that decrease the performance of the automatic object/scene recognition tools. Therefore the obtained matrix requires smoothing in the temporal domain (x-axis) to provide temporal coherency between the neighboring frames. We aim to find the labels that have high confidence scores while eliminating the labels that are not temporally consistent. We find the labels by a graph based shortest

---

[1] https://www.clarifai.com/.

| tunnel | cave | crystal | quartz | hole | mineral | crypt | dungeon | leisure activities | walking |

$$\begin{bmatrix} 0.98 & 0.98 & 0.61 & 0.61 & 0.60 & 0.61 & 0.16 & 0.15 & 0.13 & 0.13 \end{bmatrix}$$

Fig. 2. Representative example of high-level labels and their confidence scores given an input video frame. Top: the input frame i from the movie *Lucid Dreams of Gabriel*. Bottom: the top 10 labels (in terms of confidence, out of 1000) and their confidence scores. The full confidence score vector (over all the labels) at frame i is written w_i.

path approach. We empirically set N to 10 and observed that higher values did not significantly change the final alignment results. We refer to the set of labels, one per frame through time, as a "path" q through the cost matrix, and our aim is to find the N shortest paths which will give us the N most dominant and temporally coherent labels for each frame. For this, we apply a shortest path algorithm N times in the following way. To find the first shortest path q_1, we consider the matrix $\mathbf{W}$ as a directed graph where the nodes are each $<frame, label>$ pair and the edges are defined using the entries of the matrix $\mathbf{W}$ (see Fig. 3). The weight of the edge from node (i, l) to node (i', l') is defined as

$$\phi\left((i, l), (i', l')\right) = \begin{cases} \lambda(1 - w_{i'}(l')) + \varphi(l, l') & \text{if } i' = i + 1 \\ \infty & \text{else} \end{cases} \tag{1}$$

where $\varphi(l, l')$ returns 1 when $l \neq l'$ and 0 otherwise, and where $w_i(l)$ is the score of the label indexed by l at frame i, i.e. node (i, l). The scaling factor λ sets the desired smoothness by penalizing the change of the label through the path and we set it to $\lambda = \frac{framerate}{10}$, where $framerate$ is the frame rate of the input video (usually 24 fps). We apply Dijkstra's algorithm [5] to obtain the minimum distance path solution. After finding the first path, we remove the edges pointing to the nodes of the calculated path so that those nodes cannot be selected for the future paths. We repeat this procedure to find the N shortest paths, that is to say the N most dominant labels. After the calculation of paths $q_1, ..., q_N$, the scores of the labels on the paths are smoothed with weighted moving average filter. A resulting temporally coherent matrix can be seen in Fig. 3-bottom. For writing simplicity, we still name this processed matrix as $\mathbf{W}$.

3.3   Shot Segmentation

So far, we explained how to obtain the temporally coherent labels and scores per frame stored in $\mathbf{W}$. We now aim to segment the whole input video into

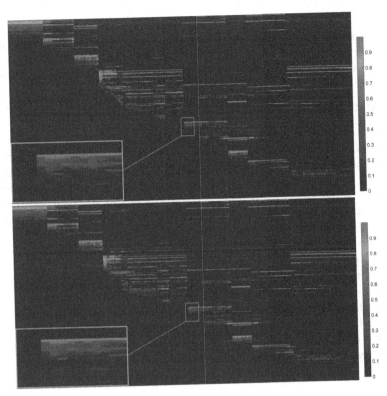

Fig. 3. Top: concatenated label vectors w_i. The height of this matrix depends on the number of unique labels detected through the whole video. Bottom: Temporally coherent result after path calculations where noisy labels are removed or smoothed.

shots by processing the matrix $\mathbf{W}$. For a frame to be the beginning of a new shot, it has to be different than the past neighboring frame and similar to the future neighboring frame. Since we already have applied temporal filtering, the scores in $\mathbf{W}$ carry temporal information from neighborhood, not just from the surrounding frames. We calculate a score S_i that represents the score of frame i to be the beginning of a new shot:

$$S_i = |D_C(w_i, w_{i-1})|(1 - |D_C(w_i, w_{i+1})|) \tag{2}$$

where w_i is the vector of label scores of the frame i and D_C computes the cosine distance of the input vectors.

Then we find the top K local maxima among all S_i, where K is the number of sentences in the input text. The frames corresponding to these maxima are our initial shot beginnings. It is important to note that we do not define *shots* by camera cuts. As discussed earlier, we refer to "shot" as a sequence of consecutive frames that have a similar semantic. Other than camera cuts, semantic cuts are considered as "shots" as well. For example, a continuous panning shot might have two different semantics with a soft border around the middle of the pan.

This panning shot needs to be segmented into two shots since there might be two different sentences describing it due to semantic change. Therefore our aim is not finding the camera cuts, but optimizing (and thus detecting) the semantic cuts -including camera cuts- that will match the sentences in the best way.

3.4   Alignment

Cost matrix. In the previous sections, we have automatically segmented the input video into shots according to their semantic contents and their smoothed features. As the basis of our method, we need a robust estimate of the alignment quality for all the shot-sentence pairs. We observe that a shot and a sentence are more likely to be alignable together if the words in this sentence and the labels of this shot are semantically similar. Using this concept, we compute a similarity value v_{ij} between each shot i and sentence j. Subsequently, we transform these values into a cost matrix $\mathbf{C} \in \mathbb{R}^{K \times K}$, in which each entry c_{ij} specifies a cost for aligning a pair of shot and sentence.

We represent the shot labels and the sentence words using GloVe word vector descriptors [20] of dimension $b = 300$. For each detected shot, we consider the set of all the N labels and scores found in all the frames of the shot. We denote the l-th label of the i-th shot by its confidence score $f_i(l)$ and its GloVe vector descriptor $d_i(l) \in \mathbb{R}^b$ where $l \in [1...N]$. Similarly, we denote the m-th word of the j-th sentence with its GloVe descriptor $d_j(m) \in \mathbb{R}^b$. The similarity between the label l and the word with index (j, m) is calculated as

$$z_{ij}(l, m) = |d_i(l) - d_j(m)| \tag{3}$$

which is modified by Lorentzian stopping function as

$$y_{ij}(l, m) = \left(1 + \left|\frac{z_{ij}(l, m)}{\sigma}\right|^{\alpha}\right)^{-1} \tag{4}$$

where $\alpha = 3$ and $\sigma = 0.5$ for all the experiments shown in this paper.

Finally the similarity values $y_{ij}(l, m)$ are used to compute the cost matrix $\mathbf{C}$ in which low values indicate shot-sentence pairs that are likely to be a good match. The entries of the cost matrix $\mathbf{C}'$ are computed as

$$c'_{ij} = 1 - \frac{1}{M} \sum_{m=1}^{M} f_i(l) \max_{l \in N} y_{ij}(l, m) \tag{5}$$

Lastly, we obtain the values of the cost matrix $\mathbf{C}$ by scaling the values of $\mathbf{C}'$ with an oriented 2D Gaussian factor which penalizes the elements in the upper right and lower left corner. In this way we incorporate the global likelihood of being at any node in the graph to our cost matrix considering passing through the nodes at the top-right or bottom-left corners are very unlikely.

$$c_{ij} = c'_{ij} \exp\left(-\frac{(i - j)^2}{2K^2}\right) \tag{6}$$

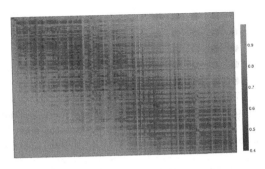

Fig. 4. Cost matrix whose elements c_{ij} are computed using similarity score between shot i (y-axis) and sentence j (x-axis).

An example of cost matrix for each pair of sentences and computed shots is available in Fig. 4.

Path calculation. So far we have described mappings between the shots and sentences. We now explain how to find a discrete mapping $p : \mathbb{R} \to \mathbb{R}^2$ in our cost matrix: for a time t, $p(t) = (i, j)$ means that the shot i corresponds to the sentence j. We refer to the discrete representation of a mapping p as a path through the cost matrix $\mathbf{C}$, and consider a graph based solution to find the minimum distance path. This path will provide the optimum shot-sentence pairings. We compute the cost of a path p as the average of all the entries in the cost matrix that the path goes through:

$$\psi(p) = \frac{1}{T} \sum_{t=1}^{T} \mathbf{C}(p(t)) \tag{7}$$

where T denotes the number of steps in the path.

To find the path with minimum cost, we consider the cost matrix as a directed graph where a path is defined as the set of connected nodes. We identify a node by its position (i, j) and edge as an ordered pair of nodes. Since we assume the input text sentences are in the same temporal order as the video, we only allow forward motion. In other words each node (i, j) is connected to its three neighbors $(i, j + 1)$, $(i + 1, j + 1)$, and $(i + 1, j)$. The weight of each edge is the value of the cost matrix at the node that the edge points to. An example graph of the possible connections is shown in Fig. 5.

We use dynamic programming to find the minimum distance path [25]. Computing the shortest path from the first node $(1, 1)$ to the last node (K, K) provides us the initial result for the shot-sentence pairings. An alignment result is shown in Fig. 6. The pink plot on the graph represents the ground truth alignment. The black plot shows the regions where our result is different than the ground truth. It is important to note that the y-axis represents the frames, not the shots. This is why paths have discrete vertical parts which corresponds to the set of frames corresponding to a shot.

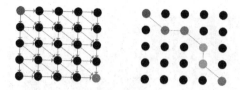

Fig. 5. Left: Possible oriented connections (in orange) between the nodes where the red node is considered the source and the green node is the sink. Right: An example path result from the source to the sink. (See text for details.) (Color figure online)

Refinement. As mentioned earlier, the sentences in the input text description do not have to correspond to the camera cuts. In addition, the result of the shot segmentation does not have to give the perfect shots for the sentences. This may cause the matching of a shot with more than one sentence (horizontal parts in the path) or matching of a sentence with more than one shot (vertical parts in the path). Therefore, the alignment that is obtained by the current cost matrix may not be the optimum.

We compute the optimum alignment by modifying the cost matrix in an iterative refinement procedure. Starting with the current optimum path, we combine the shots that are matched to the same sentence into a single shot. Conversely we segment the shot that is assigned to more than one sentence for another round. The segmentation of this shot is conducted in a way similar to Sect. 3.3. We find $r - 1$ local maxima among S_i in Eq. 2 in the corresponding region of frames during this shot, where r is the number of resulting sentences matched with it. In this way we obtain r shots that can be assigned to these r different sentences.

For example, the shots corresponding to the pink nodes (same column) on the path in Fig. 5 will be combined together, while the shot corresponding to the blue nodes (same row) will be split into two shots. After this refinement, we repeat all the steps starting from Sect. 3.4 to find the new optimal path. In our experiments, we observed that the result converges in less than 4 iterations. The effect of this refinement step is shown in the cost matrices of Fig. 6.

4   Applications

In this section we demonstrate different applications and the results obtained by our algorithm. Please refer to our project webpage for video results.

Video-sentence alignment. Aligning descriptive sentences to video in an automatic way can provide rich datasets for modeling video contents. The resulting video-sentence alignments can be used as training data to learn models for the task of automatic generation of video descriptions. An example of video-sentence alignment obtained by our algorithm is available in Fig. 7. It shows two consecutive shots separated by a sharp camera cut and the automatic alignment of the corresponding sentences. The sentences are marked automatically by the

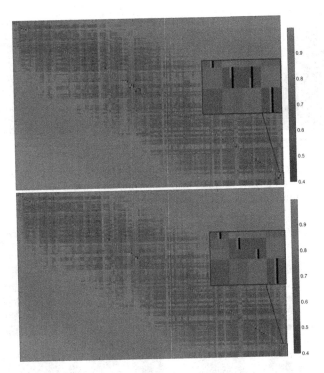

Fig. 6. The alignment result automatically obtained by our approach for the full movie (11 min) *Lucid Dreams of Gabriel* with its audio description sentences. Top: The initial alignment result using the initial shot segmentation results. The alignment of a shot to two consecutive sentences is seen in the close-up view (red box). Bottom: Our final alignment result after the refinement process. The close-up view shows that our result exactly matches with the ground truth alignment. (Color figure online)

timestamps that correspond to the very first frame of the shots by our algorithm since the beginning of these shots are captured perfectly.

Shot segmentation. Shot segmentation is used to split up a video into basic temporal units called shots. These units have consecutive frames taken contiguously by a single camera, representing a continuous action in time and space. Shot segmentation is an important step for various tasks such as automated indexing, content-based video retrieval and video summarization. While detecting sharp camera cuts is not a difficult task (as shown in Fig. 7 for a sharp camera cut), detecting only the camera cuts may not be sufficient for video-text alignment or other video retrieval tasks. The target material can have different types of separation. For example two sentences can take place in the same scene with a continuous camera shot while representing two different semantic information. A representative example of such a case is shown in Fig. 8 where the shot starts by a woman getting into the car and ends with a child having a chocolate bar. Although this scene is shot continuously by a panning camera

He leaves by the back door   *The mother is in the store and steals a chocolate from the cash desk.*

Fig. 7. Two consecutive shots (one frame of each shot is shown here) separated by a sharp camera cut and their aligned sentences, i.e. the nodes for these shot-sentence pairs are on the minimum distance path of the cost matrix.

Fig. 8. A continuous camera shot with two *semantic shots* aligned with the sentences from its audio description. Top row: *She opens the car door and gets in.* Bottom row: *She gives the chocolate to Gabriel that is in the car.* (From Lucid Dreams of Gabriel)

(i.e. not camera cut), it represents two different semantics which are expressed by two sentences in the audio description. Our joint segmentation approach is able to successfully detect the semantic cuts indicated by different sentences in the text input.

5   Evaluation and Discussion

We evaluated the proposed alignment method on a dataset of 12 videos with the sentences from their scripts or audio descriptions, including continuous long sections from the movies *Lucid Dreams of Gabriel, The Ninth Gate, The Wolf of Wall Street* and *Yes Man*. The duration of the videos in the dataset ranges from 10 to 20 min with 9.51 sentences per minute on average. The dataset is available on the project webpage and provides our results of shot segmentation, sentence alignment including timestamps, as well as ground truth data.

We now present the evaluation of our proposed alignment approach with respect to the manually obtained ground truth data. We measure the alignment accuracy by computing the temporal error between the ground truth timestamps of the sentences and the timestamps obtained by our approach. Figure 9 shows the distribution of the temporal error. It shows that 88.64% of the sentences have a temporal error of 0 s, i.e. our timestamps exactly correspond to the ground truth timestamps. This demonstrates the accuracy of our alignment approach.

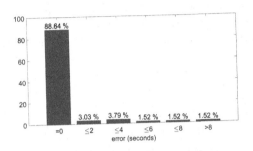

Fig. 9. Distribution of the absolute error in seconds on the timestamps obtained by our algorithm with respect to the ground truth timestamps. 88.64% of the sentences are matched perfectly to the first frame of the corresponding shot.

We now present the evaluation of our proposed shot segmentation approach with respect to the manually obtained ground truth shot segmentation. We consider two metrics again. Firstly we measure the number of shots detected by our approach over the total number of ground truth shots in the movie. Secondly, we measure the number of correctly detected shots by our approach over all detected shots, which includes false positives. The evaluation is shown in Fig. 10.

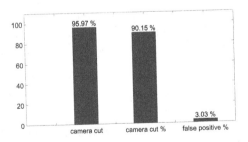

Fig. 10. Evaluation of our shot segmentation method. 95.97% of the ground truth camera shots are detected by our method. 90.15% of the shots detected by our algorithm correspond to the ground truth camera cuts. Meanwhile, only 3.03% of the shots detected by our approach are false positives.

Our method has some limitations. First, in order to correctly align the frames with the corresponding sentences, the image labeling tools (e.g. object/scene recognition) should provide sufficiently accurate labels and scores. The accuracy of our method can directly benefit from the next advances of the image labeling tools.

Another limitation is that our method is not designed for videos that mostly consist of close-up shots (e.g. interview videos) rather than scenes, actions and motion. Such video frames would not result in sufficient object/scene labels due to the lack of action and scene changes. We focused on more general movies because we believe they are more common. However, our method is suitable for a simple integration of dialogue-caption alignment approaches used in [28,31] that could be included as another variable in our global cost matrix. In future work, this integration could improve the results in videos that lack narrative sentences during dialogues.

A future application of our approach can be segmentation and structuring of videos that will allow important post-applications in content-based media analysis. Clustering of video units like shots and scenes allows unsupervised or semi-supervised content organization and has direct applications in browsing in massive data sources. Given the framewise high-level labels and timestamps of shot intervals of a video obtained by our algorithm, we can easily cluster these shots. Treating the rows of the cost matrix as the features of the segmented shots, one can simply apply a clustering method to obtain shot clusters.

In future work, it would be interesting to extend the proposed approach to cope with different types of media materials by bringing them into a common representation. For example a storyboard with drawing and sketches could be aligned with the corresponding shots in the movie using the high-level labels and their vector descriptors in an analogous way.

6   Conclusion

In this paper, we proposed an automatic method for temporally aligning the video frames of a movie with narrative sentences, for example issued from the movie script. Our approach segments the video into semantic shots and aligns them with the sentences in an iterative way by exploiting vector descriptors for text representation. Experiments on various movies successfully demonstrated the validity of our approach.

References

1. Agirre, E., Diab, M., Cer, D., Gonzalez-Agirre, A.: Semeval-2012 task 6: a pilot on semantic textual similarity. In: Joint Conference on Lexical and Computational Semantics, pp. 385–393 (2012)
2. Apostolidis, E., Mezaris, V.: Fast shot segmentation combining global and local visual descriptors. In: ICASSP (2014)
3. Bojanowski, P., Lajugie, R., Grave, E., Bach, F., Laptev, I., Ponce, J., Schmid, C.: Weakly-supervised alignment of video with text. In: ICCV (2015)

4. Deng, J., Dong, W., Socher, R., Li, L.J., Li, K., Fei-Fei, L.: ImageNet: a large-scale hierarchical image database. In: CVPR (2009)
5. Dijkstra, E.W.: A note on two problems in connexion with graphs. Numer. Math. **1**, 269 (1959)
6. Donahue, J., Anne Hendricks, L., Guadarrama, S., Rohrbach, M., Venugopalan, S., Saenko, K., Darrell, T.: Long-term recurrent convolutional networks for visual recognition and description. In: CVPR (2015)
7. Drew, M.S., Wei, J., Li, Z.N.: Illumination-invariant image retrieval and video segmentation. Pattern Recogn. **32**, 1369 (1999)
8. Farhadi, A., Hejrati, M., Sadeghi, M.A., Young, P., Rashtchian, C., Hockenmaier, J., Forsyth, D.: Every picture tells a story: generating sentences from images. In: Daniilidis, K., Maragos, P., Paragios, N. (eds.) ECCV 2010, Part IV. LNCS, vol. 6314, pp. 15–29. Springer, Heidelberg (2010)
9. Gupta, A., Srinivasan, P., Shi, J., Davis, L.S.: Understanding videos, constructing plots learning a visually grounded storyline model from annotated videos. In: CVPR (2009)
10. Hampapur, A., Jain, R., Weymouth, T.E.: Production model based digital video segmentation. Multimedia Tools Appl. **1**, 9 (1995)
11. Han, L., Kashyap, A., Finin, T., Mayfield, J., Weese, J.: UMBC ebiquity-core: semantic textual similarity systems. In: Proceedings of the Second Joint Conference on Lexical and Computational Semantics (2013)
12. Jia, Y., Shelhamer, E., Donahue, J., Karayev, S., Long, J., Girshick, R., Guadarrama, S., Darrell, T.: Caffe: convolutional architecture for fast feature embedding. In: ACM International Conference on Multimedia (2014)
13. Kulkarni, G., Premraj, V., Ordonez, V., Dhar, S., Li, S., Choi, Y., Berg, A.C., Berg, T.: BabyTalk: understanding and generating simple image descriptions. PAMI **35**, 2891 (2013)
14. Lankinen, J., Kämäräinen, J.K.: Video shot boundary detection using visual bag-of-words. In: VISAPP (2013)
15. Lee, J.C.M., Ip, D.M.C.: A robust approach for camera break detection in color video sequence. In: MVA (1995)
16. Mikolov, T., Chen, K., Corrado, G., Dean, J.: Efficient estimation of word representations in vector space (2013). arXiv preprint arXiv:1301.3781
17. Nagasaka, A., Tanaka, Y.: Automatic video indexing and full-video search for object appearances (1992)
18. Ordonez, V., Kulkarni, G., Berg, T.L.: Im2Text: describing images using 1 million captioned photographs. In: NIPS (2011)
19. Pedersen, T., Patwardhan, S., Michelizzi, J.: WordNet::Similarity - Measuring the Relatedness of Concepts. In: Proceedings of Demonstration Papers at HLT-NAACL (2004)
20. Pennington, J., Socher, R., Manning, C.D.: GloVe: global vectors for word representation. In: Proceedings of Empirical Methods in Natural Language Processing (EMNLP) (2014)
21. Qu, Z., Liu, Y., Ren, L., Chen, Y., Zheng, R.: A method of shot detection based on color and edge features. In: Proceedings of IEEE Symposium on Web Society (SWS) (2009)
22. Rohrbach, A., Rohrbach, M., Qiu, W., Friedrich, A., Pinkal, M., Schiele, B.: Coherent multi-sentence video description with variable level of detail. In: Jiang, X., Hornegger, J., Koch, R. (eds.) GCPR 2014. LNCS, vol. 8753, pp. 184–195. Springer, Heidelberg (2014). doi:10.1007/978-3-319-11752-2_15

23. Rohrbach, A., Rohrbach, M., Tandon, N., Schiele, B.: A dataset for movie description. In: CVPR (2015)
24. Rohrbach, M., Qiu, W., Titov, I., Thater, S., Pinkal, M., Schiele, B.: Translating video content to natural language descriptions. In: ICCV (2013)
25. Sakoe, H., Chiba, S.: Dynamic programming algorithm optimization for spoken word recognition. IEEE Trans. Acoust. Speech Sig. Process. **26**, 43 (1978)
26. Sankar, P., Jawahar, C., Zisserman, A.: Subtitle-free movie to script alignment. In: BMVC (2009)
27. Tapaswi, M., Bäuml, M., Stiefelhagen, R.: Story-based video retrieval in TV series using plot synopses. In: Proceedings of International Conference on Multimedia Retrieval (2014)
28. Tapaswi, M., Bauml, M., Stiefelhagen, R.: Book2Movie: aligning video scenes with book chapters. In: CVPR (2015)
29. Xiao, J., Ehinger, K.A., Hays, J., Torralba, A., Oliva, A.: SUN database: exploring a large collection of scene categories. IJCV **119**, 3 (2014)
30. Zhou, B., Lapedriza, A., Xiao, J., Torralba, A., Oliva, A.: Learning deep features for scene recognition using places database. In: NIPS (2014)
31. Zhu, Y., Kiros, R., Zemel, R., Salakhutdinov, R., Urtasun, R., Torralba, A., Fidler, S.: Aligning books and movies: towards story-like visual explanations by watching movies and reading books. In: CVPR (2015)

Towards Category Based Large-Scale Image Retrieval Using Transductive Support Vector Machines

Hakan Cevikalp[1]([✉]), Merve Elmas[1], and Savas Ozkan[2]

[1] Electrical and Electronics Engineering,
Eskisehir Osmangazi University, Eskişehir, Turkey
hakan.cevikalp@gmail.com, merveelmas1@gmail.com
[2] TUBITAK UZAY, Ankara, Turkey
savas.ozkan@tubitak.gov.tr

Abstract. In this study, we use transductive learning and binary hierarchical trees to create compact binary hashing codes for large-scale image retrieval applications. We create multiple hierarchical trees based on the separability of the visual object classes by random selection, and the transductive support vector machine (TSVM) classifier is used to separate both the labeled and unlabeled data samples at each node of the binary hierarchical trees (BHTs). Then the separating hyperplanes returned by TSVM are used to create binary codes. We propose a novel TSVM method that is more robust to the noisy labels by interchanging the classical Hinge loss with the robust Ramp loss. Stochastic gradient based solver is used to learn TSVM classifier to ensure that the method scales well with large-scale data sets. The proposed method improves the Euclidean distance metric and achieves comparable results to the state-of-art on CIFAR10 and MNIST data sets and significantly outperforms the state-of-art hashing methods on NUS-WIDE dataset.

Keywords: Image retrieval · Transductive support vector machines · Semi-supervised learning · Ramp loss

1 Introduction

Large-scale image retrieval has recently attracted great attention due to the rapid growth of visual data brought by Internet. Image retrieval can be defined as follows: Given a query image, finding and representing (in an ordered manner) the images depicting the same scene or objects in large unordered image collections. Despite the great research efforts, image retrieval is still a challenging problem since large-scale image search demands highly efficient and accurate retrieval methods.

For large scale image search, the most commonly used method is the hashing method that enables us to approximate the nearest neighbor search. Hashing methods convert each image feature vector in the database into a compact code

© Springer International Publishing Switzerland 2016
G. Hua and H. Jégou (Eds.): ECCV 2016 Workshops, Part I, LNCS 9913, pp. 621–637, 2016.
DOI: 10.1007/978-3-319-46604-0_44

(typically a binary code) and provide constant or sub-linear search time. Most of the current popular hashing methods [6,7,10,17,18,22,26,27,31] are unsupervised methods and they are built on the assumption that the similar images in the Euclidean space must have similar binary codes. Among these, Locality Sensitive Hashing (LSH) [6] chooses random projections so that two closest image samples in the feature space falls into the same bucket with a high probability. However, due to the semantic gap between the low-level features and semantics, Euclidean distances in the feature space do not reflect the semantic similarities between the images. Furthermore, the state-of-art image visual features are typically high-dimensional vectors ranging from several thousands to millions. As pointed out in [1], the performance of nearest-neighbor techniques using the Euclidean distances in high-dimensional spaces is poor since sparse and irregular distributions of data samples tend to have many holes (regions that have few or no nearby samples from the same classes), so it is necessary to learn more discriminative distance metrics. Therefore, relying Euclidean distances between image feature vectors for creating binary hash codes can be misleading. Our experimental results at the end also verify these claims.

To solve the challenging semantic gap problem, the most straightforward solution is to use label information. But, labeling all images in large image databases is too costly and difficult in practice. In contrast, relevant feedback given in terms of similar/dissimilar pairs is much easier to collect. Similarly, for most images on the web, some label tags can be collected at a more reasonable cost by using image file names or surrounding text. So, both semi-supervised and supervised hashing methods utilizing these types of information have been proposed [9,11,15,21,23,24,30,34]. Majority of these methods [9,21,24,30,34] use label information during creating similarity matrix and then projection directions that will preserve the similarities within the similarity matrix are found. Finally, these directions are used to produce binary codes. These methods cannot be applied directly to large-scale image datasets since they require computing and operating on a very large $n \times n$ sized similarity matrix, where n is the total number of image samples in the training (gallery) set. Generally, two procedures are followed to avoid this problem: In the first approach, only a small number of labeled data samples is used to learn binary codes and all unlabeled data samples are ignored. In the second procedure, some representative anchor points are created by random selection or clustering, and the similarity matrix of all data is approximated with much smaller sized similarity matrix of those anchor points. Both procedures are problematic in the sense that some potential information that may come from unlabeled data samples are ignored and propagation of supervised information from labeled samples to neighboring unlabeled samples has not been taken into consideration. The methods [11,15,23] that are more related to ours use SVM based large margin classifiers to learn compact binary codes. Both [11] and [23] use only labeled data since their methods require to operate on $n \times n$ sized kernel matrix. Thus, unlabeled data are ignored again and they do not contribute to label propagation. [15] does not need any supervision and the authors randomly select some samples and randomly assign them positive and negative labels. Then they run SVM algorithm to find the hyperplanes separating these samples and finally separating hyperplanes are used to produce binary codes. More recently, deep neural networks and CNN (Convolutional Neural Networks) features have been used for image retrieval [8,19,20,32,35–37]. These methods typically follow the similar structure of classifier networks that use a stack of convolutional layers to produce discriminative features, but the last layers use different loss functions that are more suitable for retrieval applications. For example, [19,35] use a triplet ranking loss designed to characterize one image is more similar to the second image than the third one whereas some methods use other loss functions such as surrogate loss [37], pair-wise ranking [8], or weighted approximate ranking [8]. Almost all these deep neural network methods are trained end-to-end fashion, which allows one to optimize the discriminative image features and hash functions simultaneously.

Similar to the hashing methods using large-margin based classifiers, we also use SVM classifiers to learn binary codes, but in contrast to other methods, we incorporate the unlabeled data during learning process in a transductive learning setting. Since the labeled data can be noisy in large-scale image retrieval applications, we introduce a more robust transductive SVM (TSVM) method to the noise present in labels. We use stochastic gradient based solver instead of sequential minimal optimization (SMO), thus our method scales well with large-scale data (to the best of our knowledge, it is the only transductive method that can be used with more than a million data). Finally, we introduce a novel method to learn class hierarchies based on graph cut and binary hierarchical trees to ensure the large margin between class samples.

2   Method

Here we consider the scenario where we have many unlabeled images with some limited amount of labeled image data. As we mentioned earlier, labels can be gathered from image file names or nearby text on the web. But, we have to keep in mind that the labels can be very noisy and there might be more than one labels attached to an image, e.g., if an image contains people, car, buildings etc., all these tags can be used to label the image. We use TSVMs to create binary hash codes. It should be noted that SVM like large-margin based classifiers are widely used for this goal and it was shown that larger margin between class samples yields to lower error rates in similarity search [15,23]. So, our goal is to find separating hyperplanes which will create balanced binary hash codes but at the same time they will yield to a large margin between the image samples of different classes.

In the proposed methodology, we first create image class hierarchies based on their visual content similarities and labels. To this end, we use binary hierarchical trees and Normalized Cuts clustering. This methodology is much better compared to the Wordnet based hierarchy used in [5] since it is created based on the separability of the visual classes. Then, we use TSVM to find the hyperlane that best separates the data samples (both labeled and unlabeled data) at each node of the binary hierarchical tree to make sure that the classes are split into two clusters with the largest margin possible. We first explain our novel TSVM algorithm and then describe how to create binary hierarchical trees and compact binary codes below.

2.1 Robust Transductive Support Vector Machines (RTSVMs)

Suppose that we are given a set of L labeled training samples $L = \{(\mathbf{x}_1, y_1), \ldots, (\mathbf{x}_L, y_L)\}$, $\mathbf{x} \in \mathbb{R}^d$, $y \in \{+1, -1\}$ and an unlabeled set of U vectors $U = \{\mathbf{x}_{L+1}, \ldots, \mathbf{x}_{L+U}\}$. Our goal is to find the best separating hyperplane characterized by $\theta = (\mathbf{w}, b)$, where $\mathbf{w}$ is the normal of the hyperplane and b is the bias term. We use separating hyperplanes to create binary codes and the sign of the following decision function defines the binary codes

$$f_\theta(\mathbf{x}) = \mathbf{w}^\top \mathbf{x} + b. \tag{1}$$

The main idea of TSVM learning is to find an hyperplane that separates the labeled samples with a large margin at the same time ensures that the unlabeled samples will be as far as possible from the margin. So, both the labeled and unlabeled data play a dominant role for finding the separating hyperplane. To this end, earlier methods [2,14] used the following optimization formulation

$$\operatorname*{arg\,min}_{\mathbf{w},b} \frac{1}{2}\|\mathbf{w}\|^2 + C\sum_{i=1}^{L} H_1(y_i(\mathbf{w}^\top\mathbf{x}_i + b)) + C^*\sum_{i=L+1}^{L+U} H_1(|\mathbf{w}^\top\mathbf{x}_i + b|), \tag{2}$$

where the function $H_1(t) = max(0, 1 - t)$ is the classical Hinge loss plotted in Fig. 1, and $C(C^*)$ is a user defined parameter that controls the weight of errors associated to the labeled (unlabeled) data samples. The loss function for unlabeled data is shown in Fig. 2(a). It turned out the TSVM formulation given in (2) has the potential to assign all unlabeled samples to only one of the classes with a very large margin, which yields a poor classification accuracy. In order to solve this problem, a balancing constraint that enforces the unlabeled data to be assigned to both classes based on the same fraction of labeled data samples is introduced in [14]. Chapelle and Zien [2] used the following relaxed balancing constraint, which we also use in this study to create balanced binary hash codes

$$\frac{1}{U}\sum_{i=L+1}^{L+U}(\mathbf{w}^\top\mathbf{x}_i + b) = \frac{1}{L}\sum_{i=1}^{L} y_i. \tag{3}$$

Collobert et al. [3] replaced the symmetric Hinge loss of unalabeled points with the symmetric Ramp loss defined as

$$SR_s(t) = R_s(t) + R_s(-t), \tag{4}$$

where $R_s(t) = min(1 - s, max(0, 1 - t))$ is the Ramp Loss function illustrated in Fig. 1. Here $-1 < s \leq 0$ is a parameter that must be set by the user.

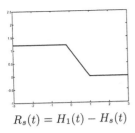 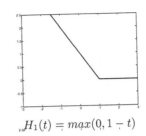 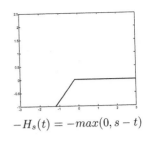

$$R_s(t) = H_1(t) - H_s(t) \qquad H_1(t) = max(0, 1 - t) \qquad -H_s(t) = -max(0, s - t)$$

Fig. 1. The illustration of the Ramp loss function, $R_s(t) = H_1(t) - H_s(t)$, where $H_a(t) = max(0, a - t)$ is the classical Hinge loss. Here, we set $s = -0.20$.

It should be noted that the loss functions for labeled and unlabeled data are not in the same range as shown in Figs. 1 and 2. For the symmetric Ramp loss used for unlabeled data, a sample can introduce at most a limited amount of cost value no matter of its position with respect to margin in the input space (the loss can be maximum 0.8 when s is set to -0.2). However, there is no bound for the Hinge loss used for labeled samples, e.g., a single outlying point farther from the margin can yield to a large loss. Therefore, the labeled outlying points – the samples that are misclassified outside the margin – start to play a dominant role in determining the separating hyperplane. As we mentioned earlier, labels can be very noisy in image retrieval applications, which aggravates the problem. To ameliorate this drawback, we interchange the convex Hinge loss with a more robust non-convex Ramp loss function. The Ramp loss also bounds the maximum amount of loss similar to the symmetric Ramp loss function and this helps to suppress the influence of misclassified examples. The superiority of the Ramp loss over the Hinge loss for supervised SVM training is well-proven and demonstrated in [4], so we adopt it to transductive learning here.

After these revisions, our robust TSVM method solves the following problem

$$\underset{\mathbf{w},b}{\arg\min} \; \frac{1}{2}\|\mathbf{w}\|^2 + C\sum_{i=1}^{L} R_s(y_i(\mathbf{w}^\top \mathbf{x}_i + b)) + C^* \sum_{i=L+1}^{L+U} SR_s(\mathbf{w}^\top \mathbf{x}_i + b)$$

$$\text{s.t.} \; \frac{1}{U}\sum_{i=L+1}^{L+U}(\mathbf{w}^\top \mathbf{x}_i + b) = \frac{1}{L}\sum_{i=1}^{L} y_i. \tag{5}$$

To use the symmetric Ramp loss function defined for unlabeled data samples, each unlabeled sample appears as two examples labeled with both negative and positive classes. More precisely, we create the new samples as follows

$$\begin{aligned}
y_i &= +1, \quad i \in [L+1, \ldots, L+U], \\
y_i &= -1, \quad i \in [L+U+1, \ldots, L+2U], \\
\mathbf{x}_i &= \mathbf{x}_{i-U}, \quad i \in [L+U+1, \ldots, L+2U].
\end{aligned} \tag{6}$$

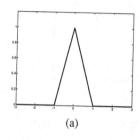 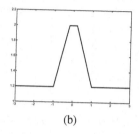

(a)   (b)

Fig. 2. Loss functions used for unlabeled data: (a) $H_1(|t|) = max(0, 1 - |t|)$, (b) The symmetric Ramp loss, $SR_s(t) = R_s(t) + R_s(-t)$. Here, we set $s = -0.20$.

Then, by using the equations $R_s(t) = H_1(t) - H_s(t)$ and $SR_s(t) = R_s(t) + R_s(-t)$, the above cost function without constraint can be written as

$$J(\theta) = J_{convex}(\theta) + J_{concave}(\theta), \tag{7}$$

where

$$J_{convex}(\theta) = \frac{1}{2}\|\mathbf{w}\|^2 + C\sum_{i=1}^{L} H_1(y_i(\mathbf{w}^\top\mathbf{x}_i + b)) + C^*\sum_{i=L+1}^{L+2U} H_1(y_i(\mathbf{w}^\top\mathbf{x}_i + b)), \tag{8}$$

and

$$J_{concave}(\theta) = -C\sum_{i=1}^{L} H_s(y_i(\mathbf{w}^\top\mathbf{x}_i + b)) - C^*\sum_{i=L+1}^{L+2U} H_s(y_i(\mathbf{w}^\top\mathbf{x}_i + b)). \tag{9}$$

The above cost function (7) is not convex but it can be decomposed into a convex (8) and concave (9) part, so we can apply concave-convex procedure (CCCP) [33] to solve the problem. By employing CCCP, the minimization of $J(\theta)$ with respect to $\theta = (\mathbf{w}, b)$ can be achieved by iteratively updating the parameter θ by the following rule

$$\theta^{t+1} = \arg\min_{\theta}(J_{convex}(\theta) + J'_{concave}(\theta^t)\theta), \tag{10}$$

under the constraint $\frac{1}{U}\sum_{i=L+1}^{L+U}(\mathbf{w}^\top\mathbf{x}_i + b) = \frac{1}{L}\sum_{i=1}^{L} y_i$.

After some standard derivations given in Appendix (available at http://mlcv. ogu.edu.tr/pdf/appendix.pdf), the resulting final robust TSVM method can be summarized as in Algorithm 1. It should be noted that the optimization problem that constitutes the core of the CCCP is convex. Instead of taking dual of this convex problem and solving it with a dual QP solver as in [3], we consider the primal problem and use SG algorithm given in Algorithm 2 to solve it. Thus, the proposed method scales well with large-scale data. To initialize the method, we use supervised linear SVM trained with labeled data samples only.

Algorithm 1. The Robust Transductive Support Vector Machines (RTSVM)

Initialize $\theta^0 = (\mathbf{w}^0, b^0)$, $t = 0$, $\epsilon_1 > 0$, $\epsilon_2 > 0$

Compute

$$\beta_i^0 \;=\; y_i \frac{\partial J_{concave}(\theta)}{\partial f_\theta(\mathbf{x}_i)} \;=\; \begin{cases} C, & \text{if } y_i((\mathbf{w}^0)^\top \mathbf{x}_i + b^0) < s \text{ and } 1 \le i \le L \\ C^*, & \text{if } y_i((\mathbf{w}^0)^\top \mathbf{x}_i + b^0) < s \text{ and } L+1 \le i \le L+2U \\ 0, & \text{otherwise.} \end{cases}$$

while $\|\mathbf{w}_{t+1} - \mathbf{w}_t\| \ge \epsilon_1$ or $\|\boldsymbol{\beta}_{t+1} - \boldsymbol{\beta}_t\| \ge \epsilon_2$ **do**

 – Solve the following convex minimization problem by using SG algorithm given in Algorithm 2

$$\underset{\mathbf{w}, b}{\arg\min} \; \frac{1}{2}\|\mathbf{w}\|^2 + C\sum_{i=1}^{L} H_1(y_i(\mathbf{w}^\top \mathbf{x}_i + b)) + C^* \sum_{i=L+1}^{L+2U} H_1(y_i(\mathbf{w}^\top \mathbf{x}_i + b)) +$$

$$\sum_{i=1}^{L+2U} \beta_i^t y_i(\mathbf{w}^\top \mathbf{x}_i + b)$$

such that $\frac{1}{U}\sum_{i=1}^{L+U}(\mathbf{w}^\top \mathbf{x}_i + b) = \frac{1}{L}\sum_{i=1}^{L} y_i$;

 – Set $\mathbf{w}^{t+1} = \mathbf{w}$, $b^{t+1} = b$;

 – Compute

$$\beta_i^{t+1} = \begin{cases} C, & \text{if } y_i((\mathbf{w}^{t+1})^\top \mathbf{x}_i + b^{t+1}) < s \text{ and } 1 \le i \le L \\ C^*, & \text{if } y_i((\mathbf{w}^{t+1})^\top \mathbf{x}_i + b^{t+1}) < s \text{ and } L+1 \le i \le L+2U \\ 0, & \text{otherwise.} \end{cases}$$

 – Set $t = t + 1$;

end while

2.2 Building Class Hierarchies

We use only labeled data to create class hierarchies. Assume that we are given some classes and corresponding labeled samples for each class (these are created by random selection of samples from each class or random selection of classes to create more independent hash functions). We use a binary hierarchical tree (BHT) that divides the image classes into two groups until each group consists of only one image class. In this setup, accuracy depends on the tree structure that creates well-balanced separable image class groups at each node of the tree. To this end, we use the Normalized Cuts (NCuts) algorithm of Shi and Malik [29] to split image classes into two groups (called positive and negative groups) since NCuts clustering algorithm maps the data samples into an infinite-dimensional feature space and cuts through the data by passing an hyperplane through the maximum gap in the mapped space [25]. In other words, it clusters the data into two balanced groups such that the margin between them is maximized. In our case, we must split image classes (not the individual image samples) into two groups. Therefore, we need to replace image data samples with image data classes. So, we approximate each class with a convex hull and use the convex

Algorithm 2. Stochastic Gradient Based Solver with Projection

---

Initialize
$\mathbf{w}_1, b_1, T > 0, \lambda_0 > 0, \epsilon > 0$
Description:
  for $t \in 1, ..., T$ **do**
    $\lambda_t \leftarrow \lambda_0/t;$
    for $i \in \text{randperm}(L + 2U)$ **do**
      – Compute sub-gradients
      $\mathbf{g}_t = \begin{cases} -y_i C(C^*)\mathbf{x}_i + \beta_i y_i \mathbf{x}_i, & \text{if } y_i(\mathbf{w}_t^T \mathbf{x}_i + b_t) \leq 1 \\ \beta_i y_i \mathbf{x}_i, & y_i(\mathbf{w}_t^T \mathbf{x}_i + b_t) > 1. \end{cases}$
      $h_t = \begin{cases} -y_i C(C^*) + \beta_i y_i, & \text{if } y_i(\mathbf{w}_t^T \mathbf{x}_i + b_t) \leq 1 \\ \beta_i y_i, & y_i(\mathbf{w}_t^T \mathbf{x}_i + b_t) > 1. \end{cases}$
      – Update hyperplane parameters
      $\tilde{\mathbf{w}}_t \leftarrow \mathbf{w}_t - \frac{\lambda_t}{L+2U}(\mathbf{w}_t + \mathbf{g}_t)$
      $\tilde{b}_t \leftarrow b_t - \frac{\lambda_t}{L+2U} h_t$
      – Project parameters onto the feasible set imposed by the constraint
      $(\mathbf{w}_t, b_t) = \mathcal{P}(\tilde{\mathbf{w}}_t, \tilde{b}_t)$
    end for
    if $(t > 2)$ & $(\|\mathbf{w}_t - \mathbf{w}_{t-1}\| < \epsilon)$, **break**
  end for

---

hulls distances between image classes to create similarity matrix. It should be noted that convex hulls are largely used to approximate classes, e.g., the linear SVM uses convex hull modeling. In this setting, the edges, w_{ij}, of the similarity matrix $\mathbf{W}$ is computed as

$$w_{ij} = \begin{cases} \exp(-d(H_i^{convex}, H_j^{convex})/t), & \text{if } i \neq j \\ 0, & \text{otherwise} \end{cases} \quad (11)$$

where t is the width of the Gaussian kernel function, and it must be set by the user. Note that the size of the similarity matrix is $C \times C$ where C is the number of classes. Thus, it is a much smaller sized matrix compared to other methods (mentioned at Introduction) using individual image samples. Then, we cluster the image classes into two groups by solving the generalized eigenvalue problem

$$\mathbf{L} = \lambda \mathbf{D} \mathbf{a}, \quad (12)$$

where $\mathbf{L} = \mathbf{D} - \mathbf{W}$ is the Laplacian matrix and $\mathbf{D}$ is a diagonal matrix whose entries are the column (or row) sums of $\mathbf{W}$. Finally, the components of the eigenvector $\mathbf{a}^*$ corresponding to the second smallest eigenvalue of (12) are thresholded to split image classes into two clusters, i.e.,

$$\begin{cases} y_i = -1, & \text{if } a_i^* \geq 0 \\ y_i = +1, & \text{if } a_i^* < 0 \end{cases} \quad (13)$$

Figure 3 illustrates the hierarchy obtained for 10-classes of CIFAR10 dataset. At the top node, it successfully separates man made vehicles (airplane, automobile,

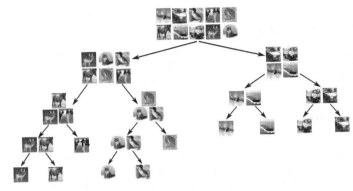

Fig. 3. Binary Hierarchical Tree obtained for CIFAR10 dataset using convex hull modeling of the classes. Each image represents an object class where it comes from.

ship, and truck) from the animals (bird, cat, deer, dog, frog, and horse). It also successfully groups visually similar groups such as automobile-truck, deer-horse, and airplane-ship together. So, our method produces both well-separated and well-balanced groups of classes, which is crucial for successful balanced binary hash codes. It should be noted this hierarchy is obtained automatically just by using the image feature samples and their labels. As mentioned earlier, more than one label can be assigned to image samples, e.g., assume that an image sample contains both *people* and *car*. In such cases, we treat groups with multiple labels as a new category and manually set the similarities between the related classes (*people* and *car* classes) to maximum. By doing so, we postpone to separate these related classes by grouping them as similar classes. So, they appear at the lower nodes of the class hierarchy where we can do a finer separation between them.

2.3   Creating Binary Hash Codes

Once we split image classes into two groups at each node of the BHT, we run TSVM algorithm by using both labeled and randomly chosen unlabeled data to find the separating hyperplanes. Then these hyperplanes can be used in two ways to produce hash codes. In the first place, we can use the following rule to create hash codes

$$h_i(\mathbf{x}) = \begin{cases} 1 & \text{when } \mathbf{w}_i^\top \mathbf{x} + b_i \geq 0 \\ 0 & \text{when } \mathbf{w}_i^\top \mathbf{x} + b_i < 0 \end{cases} \tag{14}$$

where $\mathbf{w}_i$s are the returned hyperplane normals and b_is are the corresponding bias parameters. Each BHT produces $C-1$ hash functions where C is the number of classes used to build BHT. So, the total number of hash bits will be $C-1$ times the number of BHTs. As a second choice, we can use hyperplane normals to embed the data samples onto a more discriminative space and then use an

Euclidean distance preserving hashing method (e.g., LSH) in the embedded space (this can be seen as metric learning followed by using a hashing method that approximates the learned distance metric). Lastly, we use Hamming distance to find the distances between hash codes, but weighted Hamming distances using hierarchy or margin can be also be used for this goal.

3 Experiments

Here, we conduct image retrieval experiments on three datasets. We compared the proposed hashing method, TSVMH-BHT (Transductive Support Vector Machine Hashing using Binary Hierarchical Tree), with both the supervised and unsupervised hashing methods: LSH [6], PCA-RR (Principal Component Analysis – Random Rotations) [7], PCA-ITQ (Principal Component Analysis – Iterative Quantization) [7], SKLSH (Shift-Invariant Kernel Locality Sensitive Hashing) [26], SH (Spectral Hashing) [31], SHD (Spherical Hamming Distance) [10], and SDH (Supervised Hashing) [21]. In addition to these hashing methods we also report the results obtained using PQ (Product Quantization) method of Jegou et al. [12] as a baseline. We also give the best reported accuracies of recent hashing methods using deep neural networks.

3.1   Experiments on CIFAR10 Dataset

Cifar10 dataset (available at http://www.cs.toronto.edu/~kriz/cifar.html) includes 60 K 32×32 small images of 10 objects: airplane, automobile, bird, cat, deer, dog, frog, horse, ship and truck. 50 K samples are used as training and they are split into 5 batches whereas the remaining 10 K samples are used for testing. We first used gray-scale GIST descriptors computed at three different scales (8,8,4), resulting in 320-dimensional image feature vectors as in [7]. But, the nearest-neighbor accuracy of this primitive feature representation was too small so we also used 16384 dimensional fisher vectors (FVs) and 4096 dimensional CNN features which significantly outperformed GIST descriptors in our experiments. We used a similar setup as in [28] to extract FVs. More precisely, we extracted many descriptors per image from 12×12 patches on a regular grid every two pixels at 3 scales. The dimensionality of the tested descriptors is reduced to 80 by using Principal Component Analysis (PCA), and 128-component Gaussian mixture model (GMM) components are used to obtain FVs. To extract CNN features, all images are first resized to 256×256 and then we used Caffe [13] implementation of the CNN described by Krizhevsky et al. [16] by using the identical setting used for ILSVRC 2012 classification with the exception that the base learning rate was set to 0.001. We used 80 % of the full training data for training and the remaining 20 % as validation to train the CNN classifier. The number of iterations is set to 120 K.

For all methods, we used the full training data to create hash functions, but we use only the samples in each batch to find the Hamming distances from the test samples. So, the results are averages over the results of 5 trials obtained

Table 1. mAP Scores (%) for CIFAR 10 dataset using GIST and FVs

GIST	32 bits	64 bits	128 bits	256 bits
TSVMH-BHT	**37.20**	**39.67**	**41.27**	**41.78**
SDH	34.51	36.64	37.88	38.59
LSH	23.10	24.57	26.25	26.38
SH	19.45	19.69	19.54	19.19
SHD	21.81	24.02	25.82	27.14
SKLSH	15.23	17.29	19.43	21.26
PCA-ITQ	24.51	26.08	27.10	28.05
PCA-RR	16.70	18.77	20.08	21.73
PQ	27.10	27.60	28.10	28.50
FVs	32 bits	64 bits	128 bits	256 bits
TSVMH-BHT	**46.74**	**51.37**	**53.94**	**55.10**
SDH	31.66	33.52	34.62	35.36
LSH	19.43	20.57	20.53	21.57
SH	19.60	20.43	21.44	21.86
SHD	19.47	21.91	24.09	25.77
SKLSH	11.10	11.38	11.93	12.68
PCA-ITQ	24.59	26.03	27.34	28.05
PCA-RR	23.07	24.53	25.83	36.76
PQ	24.30	23.80	22.90	22.00

Table 2. mAP Scores (%) for CIFAR 10 dataset using CNN features

CNN	32 bits	64 bits	128 bits	256 bits
TSVMH-BHT	79.97	81.89	82.45	82.79
SDH	**83.05**	**83.59**	**83.77**	**83.83**
LSH	73.98	74.87	75.56	76.40
SH	65.74	67.15	65.04	60.52
SHD	65.41	66.38	64.83	64.21
SKLSH	40.79	56.33	64.17	67.85
PCA-ITQ	80.78	81.27	81.86	82.05
PCA-RR	74.19	77.15	78.46	79.15
PQ	79.88	80.30	80.40	80.65
[19]	55.80	– –	– –	– –
[32]	52.10	– –	– –	– –
[35]	62.53	62.81	– –	– –
[36]	**≈86.0**	**≈86.0**	**≈86.0**	– –

for each training batch. We used randomly chosen 600 labeled samples and 900 unlabeled samples from each class to train our method. It should be noted the total training set size is 15 K and supervised hashing methods and unsupervised hashing methods that build dense similarity (or kernel) matrix cannot be used directly even for this moderate sized dataset. Therefore, randomly chosen anchor points are used in SDH [21]. The default value for the number of anchor points is 300 for SDH, but we increased it to 500 for better accuracies.

The mAP (mean Average Precision) scores using class labels as ground truth are given in Table 1 and Fig. 4 illustrates Precision curves obtained for different bit sizes. The mAP scores are obtained by using top 500 returned images as a function of code size as in [7]. [7] also reports mAP scores using the Euclidean distances as ground truth, but this is wrong in our opinion since the performance of the Euclidean distance is very poor: Euclidean Distance in the original input space yields to 27.15 % mAP for GIST, 28.22 % for FVs and 76.90 % for CNNs. As can be seen in Table 1, both supervised methods SDH and TSVMH-BHT dominate other unsupervised methods for GIST and FVs and our proposed method TSVMH-BHT achieves the best accuracies. The difference between the accuracies of these two methods is small for GIST but our proposed method significantly outperforms SDH for FVs. The mAP score for the proposed method is approximately 20 % better than the second best method SDH when 256 bits are used, which undoubtedly shows that the proposed method is better suited for high-dimensional visual image representations.

Table 2 shows the accuracies obtained using CNN features and some recently reported accuracies obtained using deep neural networks in the literature. It should be noted that the CNN features we extracted are different than the ones obtained by the methods given under PQ method in Table 2 since these methods are trained end-to-end fashion. Yet our proposed method outperforms all of them except the one given in [36]. SDH slightly beats our proposed method. The unsupervised PCA-ITQ also works well. [20] reports 89.4 % mAP accuracy for Cifar10 dataset. We verified this result by using their pre-trained models. But, their training files show that they used test data as validation data to train the CNN network, which is a violation of a fair testing procedure. Thus, we omitted this result in our table.

3.2 Experiments on NUS-WIDE Dataset

The NUS-Wide dataset has approximately 270 K images collected from Flickr. Each image is annotated with one or multi labels in 81 semantic classes. To comapre our results to the literature, we follow the settings in [19, 22, 32, 36] and we use the images associated with the 21 most frequent labels. The number of final training images is 96638 and the number of test images is 64704. Two images are considered as a true match if they share at least one common label as in [19, 22, 32, 36]. We used both FVs and CNN feature vectors for representing images. To obtain CNN feaures we first resized images to 256×256 as before and used the same setting we used in Cifar10. Note that this is a multi-label dataset, thus we selected images with non-overlapping unique labels to train the classifier network.

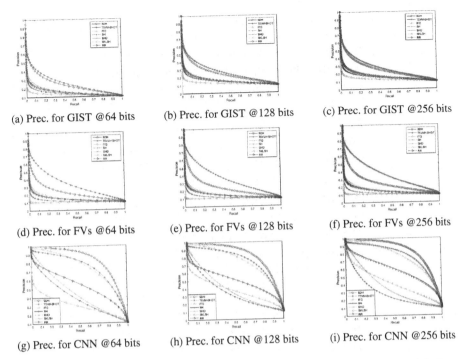

(a) Prec. for GIST @64 bits   (b) Prec. for GIST @128 bits   (c) Prec. for GIST @256 bits

(d) Prec. for FVs @64 bits   (e) Prec. for FVs @128 bits   (f) Prec. for FVs @256 bits

(g) Prec. for CNN @64 bits   (h) Prec. for CNN @128 bits   (i) Prec. for CNN @256 bits

Fig. 4. Comparisons of the hashing methods on CIFAR10 dataset using labels as ground truth.

But, results were very low compared to the ones obtained for FVs. We believe that the results were low mainly because the loss function is not designed for multi-label data. The noisy labels was another reason for the low accuracy. Thus, we used pre-trained Caffe model of ILSVRC 2012 to extract 4096-dimensional CNN features. Results are given in Table 3. Using Euclidean distance with full features yields to 52.20 % mAP for FVs and 69.65 % for CNN features. As in the previous case, hashing codes obtained CNN features yield to better accuracies. The proposed method achieves the best accuracies in all cases except for 32 bits and improves the Euclidean distance metric for 64 bits and above. The reported results for the best performing method [36] on Cifar10 are very low for NUS-WIDE. To the best our knowledge, our results are the best published mAP scores for NUS-WIDE dataset. As before, the performance difference is very significant for FVs. We believe that our better accuracies compared to the other state-of-art methods are due to the using robust Ramp loss for noisy labels.

3.3 Experiments on MNIST Dataset

The MNIST[1] digit dataset consists of 70 K hand-written digit samples, each of size 28×28 pixels. For this dataset, 60 K samples are allocated for training and

---

[1] Available at http://yann.lecun.com/exdb/mnist/.

Table 3. mAP Scores (%) for NUS-WIDE dataset using FVs and CNN features

FVs	32 bits	64 bits	128 bits	256 bits
TSVMH-BHT	53.97	**57.73**	**61.76**	**63.99**
SDH	**54.20**	56.41	58.14	58.93
LSH	30.25	36.27	39.50	43.20
SH	46.31	45.97	47.60	48.51
SHD	47.08	50.09	52.41	52.89
SKLSH	33.24	35.25	36.50	37.68
PCA-ITQ	50.41	51.95	52.63	53.17
PCA-RR	49.89	51.17	52.09	52.95
PQ	30.75	31.74	33.49	40.19
CNN	32 bits	64 bits	128 bits	256 bits
TSVMH-BHT	68.58	**72.90**	**74.64**	**76.21**
SDH	69.09	72.41	73.71	74.75
LSH	66.78	68.91	69.47	69.50
H	58.03	60.08	61.31	64.41
SHD	61.60	64.23	64.83	64.66
SKLSH	39.65	43.37	47.47	53.65
PCA-ITQ	68.62	70.91	72.48	73.55
PCA-RR	65.82	68.27	70.57	71.60
PQ	**71.07**	71.93	72.20	72.17
[19]	71.30	– –	– –	– –
[32]	62.90	– –	– –	– –
[35]	62.64	63.82	– –	– –
[36]	≈52.0	≈52.5	≈54.0	– –

Table 4. mAP Scores (%) for MNIST Digit dataset

Methods	32 bits	64 bits	128 bits	256 bits
TSVMH-BHT	**87.68**	**89.15**	**89.07**	**89.13**
SDH	81.29	85.37	86.10	86.26
LSH	72.15	74.40	79.30	82.43
SH	70.44	72.28	73.87	74.15
SHD	67.86	74.06	75.98	76.58
SKLSH	31.36	47.12	63.04	74.08
PCA-ITQ	79.55	83.37	85.50	86.23
PCA-RR	67.91	75.38	79.16	83.05
PQ	85.40	85.40	85.20	85.40

the remaining 10 K samples are reserved for test. We use gray-scale values as visual features, thus dimensionality of the sample space is 784. We use randomly chosen 5000 labeled samples and 800 unlabeled samples from each class to train the proposed method. It should be noted that test samples are not used as unlabeled samples during training. Results are given in Table 4. Euclidean Distance in the original input space yields to 85.95 % mAP score which is quite satisfactory. Yet, our proposed method gives better accuracies than NN for all bit sizes. SDH is the second best performing method and it can improve NN accuracy only for 128 bits and above.

4   Conclusion

In this study, we discussed the fact that the Euclidean distances in the high-dimensional feature spaces can be misleading, thus hashing methods approximating the Euclidean distances may perform poorly. To counter this, we proposed a hashing method that does both metric learning and fast image search. To this end, we used binary hierarchical trees and TSVM classifier. We proposed a more robust TSVM method designed for especially image retrieval applications. Using TSVM is extremely important here since it also exploits the unlabeled data that is neglected by many related hashing and distance metric learning methods.

We tested the proposed method on three image retrieval datasets. The results with high-dimensional FV features were particularly promising: Our method significantly outperformed all other tested hashing methods with FVs. We also obtained state-of-art results using CNN features on noisy labeled NUS-WIDE dataset which shows the importance of using our robust Ramp loss function. We also compared the proposed method to the recently published hashing methods using deep neural networks. These methods emphasize the importance of simultaneous learning of image features and binary codes, yet the results prove that this issue has not been resolved yet since majority of these deep neural networks methods yield very low accuracies compared to our method which learns hash codes independently from the pre-computed CNN features.

Acknowledgment. This work has been supported by the Scientific and Technological Research Council of Turkey (TUBİTAK) under Grant number TUBITAK-113E118.

References

1. Cevikalp, H., Triggs, B., Polikar, R.: Nearest hyperdisk methods for high-dimensional classification. In: ICML (2008)
2. Chapelle, O., Zien, A.: Semi-supervised classification by low density separation. In: Proceedings of 10th International Workshop on Artifical Intelligence and Statistics (2005)
3. Collobert, R., Sinz, F., Weston, J., Bottou, L.: Large scale transductive SVMs. J. Mach. Learn. Res. **7**, 1687–1712 (2006)
4. Ertekin, S., Bottou, L., Giles, C.L.: Nonconvex online support vector machines. IEEE Trans. Pattern Anal. Mach. Intell. **33**, 368–381 (2011)

5. Fergus, R., Bernal, H., Weiss, Y., Torralba, A.: Semantic label sharing for learning with many categories. In: Daniilidis, K., Maragos, P., Paragios, N. (eds.) ECCV 2010. LNCS, vol. 6311, pp. 762–775. Springer, Heidelberg (2010). doi:10.1007/978-3-642-15549-9_55

6. Gionis, A., Indyk, P., Motwani, R.: Similarity search in high dimensions via hashing. In: International Conference on Very Large Databases (1999)

7. Gong, Y., Lazebnik, S., Gordo, A., Perronnin, F.: Iterative quantization: a procrustean approach to learning binary codes for large-scale image retrieval. IEEE Trans. PAMI **35**, 2916–2929 (2013)

8. Gong, Y., Jia, Y., Leung, T., Toshev, A., Ioffe, S.: Deep convolutional ranking for multilabel image annotation. arXiv:1312.4894 (2013)

9. He, X., Cai, D., Han, J.: Learning a maximum margin subspace for image retrieval. IEEE Trans. Knowl. Data Eng. **20**, 189–201 (2008)

10. Heo, J.P., Lee, Y., He, J., Chang, S.F., Yoon, S.E.: Spherical hashing. In: CVPR (2012)

11. Hoi, S.C.H., Jin, R., Zhu, J., Lyu, M.R.: Semi-supervised svm batch mode active learning for image retrieval. In: CVPR (2008)

12. Jegou, H., Douze, M., Schmid, C.: Product quantization for nearest neighbor search. IEEE Trans. PAMI **33**, 117–128 (2010)

13. Jia, Y., Shelhamer, E., Donahue, J., Karayev, S., Long, J., Girshick, R., Guadarrama, S., Darrell, T.: Caffe: convolutional architecture for fast feature embedding. arXiv preprint arXiv:1408.5093 (2014)

14. Joachims, T.: Transductive inference for text classification using support vector machines. In: International Conference on Machine Learning (1999)

15. Joly, A., Buisson, O.: Random maximum margin hashing. In: CVPR (2011)

16. Krizhevsky, A., Sutskever, I., Hinton, G.E.: Imagenet classification with deep convolutional neural networks. In: NIPS (2012)

17. Kulis, B., Darrell, T.: Learning to hash with binary reconstructive embeddings. In: NIPS (2009)

18. Kulis, B., Grauman, K.: Kernelized locality-sensitive hashing for scalable image search. In: ICCV (2009)

19. Lai, H., Pan, Y., Yan, S.: Simultaneous feature learning and hash coding with deep neural networks. In: CVPR (2015)

20. Lin, K., Yang, H.F., Hsiao, J.H., Chen, C.S.: Deep learning of binary hash codes for fast image retrieval. In: IEEE Conference on Computer Vision and Pattern Recognition Workshops (CVPRW) (2015)

21. Liu, W., Wang, J., Ji, R., Jiang, Y.G., Chang, S.F.: Supervised hashing with kernels. In: CVPR (2012)

22. Liu, W., Wang, J., Kumar, S., Chang, S.F.: Hashing with graphs. In: ICML (2011)

23. Mu, Y., Shen, J., Yan, S.: Weakly-supervised hashing in kernel space. In: CVPR (2010)

24. Norouzi, M., Fleet, D.J.: Minimal loss hashing for compact binary codes. In: ICML (2011)

25. Rahimi, A., Recht, B.: Clustering with normalized cuts is clustering with a hyperplane. In: Statistical Learning in Computer Vision (2004)

26. Raginsky, M., Lazebnik, S.: Locality-sensitive binary codes from shift-invariant kernels. In: ICCV (2009)

27. Salakhutdinov, R., Hinton, G.: Semantic hashing. Int. J. Approximate Reason. **50**(12), 969–978 (2009)

28. Sanchez, J., Perronnin, F., Mensink, T., Verbeek, J.: Image classification with the fisher vector: theory and practice. Int. J. Comput. Vis. **34**, 1704–1716 (2013)
29. Shi, J., Malik, J.: Normalized cuts and image segmentation. IEEE Trans. PAMI **22**, 888–905 (2000)
30. Wang, J., Kumar, S., Chang, S.F.: Semi-supervised hashing for scalable image retrieval. In: CVPR (2010)
31. Weiss, Y., Torralba, A., Fergus, R.: Spectral hashing. In: NIPS (2008)
32. Xia, R., Pan, Y., Lai, H., Liu, C., Yan, S.: Supervised hashing for image retrieval via image representation learning. In: Proceedings of the 28 AAAI Conference on Artificial Intelligence (2014)
33. Yullie, A.L., Rangarajan, A.: The concave-convex procedure (cccp). In: Neural Information Processing Systems (2002)
34. Zhang, L., Wang, L., Lin, W.: Semi-supervised biased maximum margin analysis for interactive image retrieval. IEEE Trans. Image Process. **21**, 2294–2308 (2012)
35. Zhang, R., Lin, L., Zhang, R., Zuo, W., Zhang, L.: Bit-scalable deep hashing with regularized similarity learning for image retrieval and person re-identification. IEEE Trans. Image Process. **24**, 4766–4779 (2015)
36. Zhang, Z., Chen, Y., Saligrama, V.: Supervised hashing with deep neural networks. arXiv:1511.04524 (2015)
37. Zhao, F., Huang, Y., Wang, L., Tan, T.: Deep semantic ranking based hashing for multi-label image retrieval. In: CVPR (2015)

Solving Multi-codebook Quantization in the GPU

Julieta Martinez[✉], Holger H. Hoos, and James J. Little

University of British Columbia, Vancouver, Canada
{julm,hoos,little}@cs.ubc.ca

Abstract. We focus on the problem of vector compression using multi-codebook quantization (MCQ). MCQ is a generalization of k-means where the centroids arise from the combinatorial sums of entries in multiple codebooks, and has become a critical component of large-scale, state-of-the-art approximate nearest neighbour search systems. MCQ is often addressed in an iterative manner, where learning the codebooks can be solved exactly via least-squares, but finding the optimal codes results in a large number of combinatorial NP-Hard problems. Recently, we have demonstrated that an algorithm based on stochastic local search for this problem outperforms all previous approaches. In this paper we introduce a GPU implementation of our method, which achieves a 30× speedup over a single-threaded CPU implementation. Our code is publicly available (https://github.com/jltmtz/local-search-quantization).

1 Introduction

Approximate nearest neighbour search is often a computational bottleneck of computer vision and machine learning applications. For example, in structure from motion [1] (the task of reconstructing the 3d structure of a scene given multiple images), the bottleneck arises when computing the relative location of several image pairs, which amounts to nearest neighbour searches in datasets of millions of SIFT [2] descriptors. Another task where nearest-neighbour search is the computational bottleneck is image retrieval, also known as image-based image search; in this task we are given an image of an object, and the goal is to find similar objects in a large collection of images. In practice, this amounts to finding the nearest neighbours of the descriptor of the image query among the stored descriptors of the images in the database.

In the past, the nearest-neighbour problem has been addressed using data structures that, with high confidence, prune the number of vectors to which the distance has to be computed. Two prominent examples of this approach include randomized kd-trees and hierarchical k-means (both implemented in the very successful FLANN library [3]). These approaches, however, do not scale well for large datasets, as they need to store all the database vectors in memory, and incur additional memory costs for the data structures that they use.

In the light of memory limitations, hashing approaches have become increasingly popular [4,5]. Hashing aims to learn a compact embedding of the data

© Springer International Publishing Switzerland 2016
G. Hua and H. Jégou (Eds.): ECCV 2016 Workshops, Part I, LNCS 9913, pp. 638–650, 2016.
DOI: 10.1007/978-3-319-46604-0_45

whose Hamming distance (which can be computed very fast using the popcount operation of modern processors) approximates the Euclidean distance of two original vectors.

Recently, however, it has been demonstrated that hashing approaches are significantly less accurate than multi-codebook quantization (MCQ) methods. Multi-codebook quantization is a generalization of k-means where, instead of assigning each point to a single centroid, a vector is assigned to multiple codebooks. The indices of such assignments can be used as a compact representation for the original vector, and the codes can be used to compute approximate distances to previously-unseen vectors using a few table lookups.

In this work we focus on a variant of MCQ known as Additive Quantization (AQ) [6], which has a simple, constraint-free formulation, but has proven hard to optimize. We have recently demonstrated [7] that the AQ formulation can be lifted to achieve state-of-the-art performance on a series of standard retrieval benchmarks by leveraging an encoding algorithm based on stochastic local search (SLS) [8]. In this work, we explore a GPU implementation of such algorithm that has allowed us to run our method on very large-scale datasets, and has lead us to obtain state-of-the-art performance on SIFT1B – a dataset of 1 billion visual descriptors.

2   Related Work

The work that introduced the idea of using vector quantization for nearest neighbour search was [9], and is called product quantization (PQ). In PQ, the optimization is actually trivial because the codebooks are assumed to be orthogonal to each other. A recent improvement to PQ was introduced by Babenko and Lempitsky [6], and is called additive quantization (AQ). In AQ, the codebooks are full-dimensional, which makes the encoding problem NP-hard. Babenko and Lempitsky suggested using beam search to solve the encoding problem, but this was identified as the main computational bottleneck of the system. Moreover, the performance of AQ has been largely surpassed by composite quantization [10], a method that also uses full-dimensional codebooks, but enforces the products of centroids in different codebooks to be constant.

Our main contribution is a method that solves the encoding problem in AQ using Stochastic Local Search. As we will show, this encoding problem is equivalent to multiple fully-connected pairwise Markov random fields (MRFs). MRFs are widely used in computer vision, where they are often used to model visual context. For example, Tung and Little [11] use an MRF to perform scene parsing (i.e., labelling every pixel in an image) on city landscapes, and Krähenbühl and Kultun [12] use filtering to perform MAP inference on MRFs with binary terms which are restricted to be Gaussian kernels, and apply their optimization method to scene parsing on natural images.

2.1   MRF Optimization on the GPU

There has been some previous work on porting different MRF optimization algorithms to the GPU. For example, Vineet and Narayanan [13] introduce

CUDACuts, a CUDA-based implementation of graph cuts, an algorithm for exact MRF optimization that is applicable to submodular MRFs. The method exploits shared memory in the push-relabel step of graph cuts, and is demonstrated on a Nvidia GTX 280 GPU. Zach et al. [14] introduce a data-parallel approach to MRF optimization based on plane sweeping, which is applicable when the pairwise terms follow a Potts prior. The work dates back to 2008, when CUDA was a more difficult language to program in than it is today, so the authors used the OpenGL API to program their solution. The authors demonstrate an implementation on an Nvidia Geforce 8800 Ultra GPU.

Most previous work focuses on MRFs as they are applied to image-related tasks such as scene segmentation. In these applications, the MRFs typically have a large number of nodes (1 per pixel), have a low number of labels (e.g., 3 in [14]), are sparsely connected, and have special constraints on form of their pairwise terms (e.g. Potts in [14] and submodular in [13]). Thus, it is unlikely that those implementations will fit our problem, which has a low number of nodes $m = \{7, 15\}$, a large number of labels ($h = 256$), is densely connected, and whose pairwise terms do not follow any particular formulation. Moreover, in our application all the MRFs share the pairwise terms, which is a rare occurrence in other MRF applications. We believe that the implementation that we are introducing in this paper is the first one to address this particular MRF case using graphics processors.

3   Problem Formulation

First, we introduce some notation, following mostly Norouzi and Fleet [15]. Formally, we denote the set to quantize as $X \in \mathbb{R}^{d \times n}$, having n data points with d dimensions each; MCQ is the problem of finding m codebooks $C_i \in \mathbb{R}^{d \times h}$ and the corresponding codes B_i that minimize quantization error:

$$\min_{C_i, B_i} \left\| X - [C_1, C_2, \ldots, C_m] \begin{bmatrix} B_1 \\ B_2 \\ \vdots \\ B_m \end{bmatrix} \right\|_2^2, \tag{1}$$

where $B_i = [\mathbf{b}_{i1}, \mathbf{b}_{i2}, \ldots, \mathbf{b}_{in}] \in \{0, 1\}^{h \times n}$, and each subcode $\mathbf{b}_i$ is limited to having only one non-zero entry: $\|\mathbf{b}_i\|_0 = 1$, $\|\mathbf{b}_i\|_1 = 1$. Letting $C = [C_1, C_2, \ldots, C_m]$ and $B = [B_1, B_2, \ldots, B_m]^\top$, we can rewrite expression 1 more succinctly as

$$\min_{C, B} \|X - CB\|_2^2. \tag{2}$$

It can be seen that, if we have only $m = 1$ codebooks, then the problem is reduced to k-means. This suggests an EM-like optimization for Eq. 2 inspired by Lloyd's algorithm – a popular method used to solve k-means.

3.1   Iterative Optimization

MCQ, as stated in Eq. 2 is non-convex and, in general NP-hard. The standard approach to solve this problem is an iterative 2-step process known as coordinate descent, akin to Lloyd's algorithm widely used in k-means. We iteratively solve two sub-problems

1. $C^{t+1} = \min_C \|X - CB^t\|_2^2$ (codebook update)
2. $B^{t+1} = \min_B \|X - C^{t+1}B\|_2^2$ (encoding).

Subproblem 1 is a quadratic program over C, and amounts to solving large-scale least-squares problem. In this paper we focus on subproblem 2 which, on the other hand, amounts to solving n independent NP-hard problems that can be expressed as fully-connected Markov Random Fields (MRFs). We now explain how this formulation is derived.

3.2   MCQ Encoding as MAP Estimation in Multiple MRFs

To make the formulation of MCQ encoding as MRFs more evident, we focus on the problem of finding the codes $[\mathbf{b}_1, \mathbf{b}_2, \ldots, \mathbf{b}_m]$ that best approximate a single vector in $\mathbf{x}$. The goal in this case is to minimize the distance between $\mathbf{x}$ and its approximation $\hat{\mathbf{x}}$:

$$\min_{\hat{\mathbf{x}}} \|\mathbf{x} - \hat{\mathbf{x}}\|_2^2 = \min_{\hat{\mathbf{x}}} \|\mathbf{x}\|_2^2 - 2\langle \mathbf{x}, \hat{\mathbf{x}} \rangle + \|\hat{\mathbf{x}}\|_2^2 \tag{3}$$

In MCQ, the approximation $\hat{\mathbf{x}}$ is constrained to be the sum of single entries in m different subcodebooks C_i; that is, $\hat{\mathbf{x}} = \sum_{i=1}^m C_i \mathbf{b}_i$, therefore, we can rewrite the previous equation – during the encoding phase – as a minimization over the subcodebooks $\mathbf{b}_i$ that represent $\hat{\mathbf{x}}$

$$\min_{\{\mathbf{b}_1, \mathbf{b}_2, \ldots, \mathbf{b}_m\}} \|\mathbf{x} - \sum_{i=1}^m C_i \mathbf{b}_i\|_2^2 = \|\mathbf{x}\|_2^2 - 2\langle \mathbf{x}, \sum_{i=1}^m C_i \mathbf{b}_i \rangle + \|\sum_{i=1}^m C_i \mathbf{b}_i\|_2^2 \tag{4}$$

$$= \|\mathbf{x}\|_2^2 - 2\sum_{i=1}^m \langle \mathbf{x}, C_i \mathbf{b}_i \rangle + \|\sum_{i=1}^m C_i \mathbf{b}_i\|_2^2. \tag{5}$$

Finally, we expand the norm of the approximation as

$$\|\sum_{i=1}^m C_i \mathbf{b}_i\|_2^2 = \sum_{i=1}^m \|C_i \mathbf{b}_i\|_2^2 + \sum_i^m \sum_{j \neq i}^m \langle C_i \mathbf{b}_i, C_j \mathbf{b}_j \rangle \tag{6}$$

It now becomes apparent that we can express the objective function as a sum of unary (univariate) and pairwise (bi-variate) terms. First of all, we can drop the $\|\mathbf{x}\|_2^2$ term, because it is not a function of $\mathbf{b}_i$. Next, we can sum both $-2\sum_{i=1}^m \langle \mathbf{x}, C_i \mathbf{b}_i \rangle$ and $\sum_{i=1}^m \|C_i \mathbf{b}_i\|_2^2$, which are both functions of a single code $\mathbf{b}_i$, and make them the unary term of our MRF. Finally, the term $\sum_i^m \sum_{j \neq i}^m \langle C_i \mathbf{b}_i, C_j \mathbf{b}_j \rangle$, which is a function of two codes, becomes our pairwise term. Since there is a term for every pair of codes, the resulting MRF is fully connected.

For each vector that we are encoding, the codes may take any value from 1 to h; thus our search space consists of h^m possible solutions (typically, $m = \{7, 15\}$ and $h = 256$), which renders the problem inherently combinatorial and, in general, NP-Hard.

Not only is each problem hard, but the number of problems, n, usually scales with big data. For example, imagine that we want to build a visual search engine that searches for visual content on every image on the Internet – in that case, n can easily be in the order of several trillions. The scale of this problem calls for methods that are effective (i.e., achieve low-cost solutions), and efficient (do so without taking much time). We also need to make use of state-of-the-art computational resources to tackle the problem within reasonable timelines. In this paper, we present a GPU implementation of a promising algorithm that addresses this problem.

4 Solution Methodology

Our approach to MCQ encoding is based on stochastic local search (SLS), a prominent class of algorithms that have, at several points in time, achieved state-of-the-art performance on several NP-hard problems. The basic idea behind SLS is to iteratively alternate between a greedy (local) search procedure, and randomized perturbations to the current solution. SLS methods are typically anytime, trading off computation for solution quality, and are also often easy to implement.

Our algorithm is defined by

1. An initialization procedure
2. A perturbation procedure
3. A local search algorithm
4. An acceptance criterion

Our initialization procedure gives a starting solution by initializing each sub-code uniformly at random between 1 and h – this gives rise to an initial solution s. Similarly, our perturbation procedure takes the current solution, and changes $k \leq m$ subcodes to uniformly random values between 1 and h. Our local search algorithm is iterated conditional modes (ICM); an iterative algorithm itself that updates each subcode to its optimal value, while keeping the rest fixed. After perturbation and local search, we have a candidate solution s'. Our acceptance criterion simply keeps the solution with lower cost out of s and s'.

The pseucodode for our solution is given in the appendix as Algorithm 1.

4.1 Implementating SLS for Encoding

The initial implementation of our algorithm was done in Julia [16], a recent high-level language for scientific computing that runs on top of the LLVM compiler infrastructure[1], and as such is more suitable for low-level optimization. This implementation makes use of SIMD instructions where possible, and was heavily profiled and optimized.

A crucial observation that we obtained during the development of this single-threaded implementation was the importance of cached memory access when implementing ICM. In order to explain this subtlety, it is necessary that we talk about lookup tables in our implementation.

Shared Pairwise Tables. As we have mentioned, the objective function in encoding can be broken down in unary (single-parameter) and pairwise (two-parameter) terms – in fact, this is the easiest way to show that the problem is equivalent to an MRF. A first observation is that, although we have n different MRFs to solve, *they all actually share the same binary terms.* That is, the expression $\sum_i^m \sum_{j \neq i}^m \langle C_i \mathbf{b}_i, C_j \mathbf{b}_j \rangle$ is independent of $\mathbf{x}$, the vector that we are encoding. This means that we can precompute the values of the expression $\sum_i^m \sum_{j \neq i}^m \langle C_i \mathbf{b}_i, C_j \mathbf{b}_j \rangle$ for all the possible values of $C_i \mathbf{b}_i$ and $C_j \mathbf{b}_j$. For m codebooks, we have in total $m \cdot (m-1)/2$ tables of size $h \times h$. Handily, these tables are computed once and reused for all the MRFs that we are solving. For large n, the cost of computing these tables is negligible.

Unary Tables. The unary terms in our formulation correspond to the terms $-2 \sum_{i=1}^m \langle \mathbf{x}, C_i \mathbf{b}_i \rangle$ and $\sum_{i=1}^m \| C_i \mathbf{b}_i \|_2^2$. While the second unary term is independent of the encoded vector, $\mathbf{x}$, the first term actually has to be computed for each vector that we are encoding. To speed up SLS, we compute m tables of size $h \times 1$ that store the sum of both unary terms for each value of $\mathbf{b}_i \in \{1, 2, \ldots, h\}$ for each $i \in \{1, 2, \ldots, m\}$.

Batched Implementation. A straightforward implementation of Algorithm 1 encodes each point sequentially. The innermost statement of the algorithm, that is, the search for the best value of a single code given the rest (line 19), becomes the computational bottleneck of the system. Moreover, one can see that every time the expression

$$\mathbf{b}_k := \arg\min_{\mathbf{b}_k} -2 \langle \mathbf{x}, C_k \mathbf{b}_k \rangle + \| C_k \mathbf{b}_k \|_2^2 + \sum_{i \neq k}^m \langle C_k \mathbf{b}_k, C_i \mathbf{b}_i \rangle \qquad (7)$$

is evaluated for different k, a different pairwise $h \times h$ lookup table has to be loaded into cache. A straightforward optimization for cache performance of this bottleneck results from optimizing multiple codes at the same time. This is a common pattern in large-scale machine learning systems, which are typically throughput – not latency – oriented, and is commonly known as "batching". This results in about 4× speedup in our CPU implementation, and is also used in our GPU implementation.

---

[1] http://llvm.org/.

CUDA Kernel Breakdown. Our GPU implementation consists of three main kernels: (a) a setup kernel, which initializes the solutions, computes unary lookup tables and creates a series of random number generators; (b) a perturbation kernel, which alters random codes in the solution, and (c) a local search kernel, which implements ICM.

Initialization Kernel. Our initialization kernel creates a CUDA random (`curand`) state for each data point in the database and, during the first iteration, uses the samples to create a random initial solution. The implementation is fairly straightforward and takes less than 1/1000 of the total optimization time.

Perturbation Kernel. In this kernel, we have one thread per data point, with the goal of maximizing the work/thread ratio. The task of each kernel is to choose $k = 4$ (choosen via validation) entries in the current solution, and perturb them to random values between 1 and h.

The main challenge in this kernel is that the choice of $k = 4$ entries to perturb amounts to sampling *without replacement* from the uniform distribution between 1 and m. Since there are no off-the-shelf functions for sampling without replacement in the `curand` library, we implemented our own version of *reservoir sampling*[2]. The pseudocode for this kernel is shown in the appendix as Algorithm 2.

It is easy to show by induction that each code has an equal probability k/m of being perturbed, and the algorithm finishes when k samples have been perturbed – which is most likely achieved before visiting every code. Although elegant, reservoir sampling leads to large thread divergence, which is likely suboptimal for the GPU architecture. In any case, the time spent in this perturbation step is negligible compared to the ICM kernel that we discuss next.

ICM Kernel. The job of the ICM kernel is to perform local search after the solution has been perturbed; this corresponds to lines 16–21 in Algorithm 1. By far, this is the most expensive part of our pipeline, so we discuss the implementation in more detail.

In short, we have three main tasks: (a) copying the pre-computed unary terms to shared memory, (b) adding the corresponding pairwise terms to the unary terms for each possible value of each code, and (c) finding the minimum of all h possibilities in each code.

Task (a) is a only done once; its implementation is straightforward and makes bootstrapping the process faster when moving from one code to another. Task (b) is memory-limited – the pairwise tables are too big to fit in shared memory, so they have to be read from global memory. Task (c) amounts to a reduce operation, and is thus compute-limited.

The implementation of (b) is slightly complicated, as it requires us to use more global memory in order to achieve coalesced access in main memory. Now it is important that we remember the pairwise tables of size $h \times h$ that store

---

[2] https://en.wikipedia.org/wiki/Reservoir_sampling.

the pairwise terms $\sum_i^m \sum_{j \neq i}^m \langle C_i \mathbf{b}_i, C_j \mathbf{b}_j \rangle$. While in theory we only require $m \cdot (m-1)/2$ tables (and they need not be filled completely, as the dot products are symmetrical), in practice we create $m^2 - m$ tables, and fill all their h^2 entries. The purpose of this extra-memory use is to allow coalesced memory access to the pairwise terms. We keep a matrix of pointers to the tables, such that the table indexed by $[i, j]$ contains the dot-products between the ith and the jth code, such that the jth row contains all h possible values of the jth code for a constant value of the ith code. This means that, when adding the pairwise terms for all values of the jth code, we can access the precomputed values in a coalesced manner. However, since ICM optimizes each code sequentially, it is likely that we will at some point need the transpose of this table, so we store a copy of the $[i, j]$ table such that $[j, i] = [i, j]^\top$. Thanks to this transpose, we can preserve coalesced access when searching all the h possible values of the ith code w.r.t. a fixed value for the jth code.

Once all the pairwise terms have been added, we run task (c) as a reduce findmin operation on the unary + pairwise terms. This is a reduction over the h values that we computed in task (b). Note, however, that the output is not the minimum value itself, but its index (a number from 1 to h), so this requires an extra array of indices to keep track of during reduction. We implemented all the optimizations available in the CUDA reduce guide[3] for this step.

5   Experimental Setup

We are interested in MCQ as a means to fast and accurate approximate nearest neighbour search. The standard protocol in the literature uses three partitions of the data: (1) train, (2) query, and (3) base. Typically, the train partition is used to learn the codebooks C; then, one must encode (that is, derive B for) the base vectors using the previously learned codebooks C. Finally, one uses a smaller query set to search for approximate nearest neigbours in the base partition.

Performance is measured with recall@N curves. These curves are monotonically increasing, and reflect the empirical probability distribution, computed over the query set, that the first N computed approximate neighbours contain the actual nearest neighbour. In information retrieval, recall@1 is considered the most important point in this curve.

5.1   Datasets

We focus on two large-scale datasets: SIFT1B and SIFT10M. SIFT1B consists of 128-dimensional SIFT descriptors; the set has 100 million vectors for train, 10 thousand vectors for query, and 1 billion vectors for database. For expedience, we only used the first million vectors from the training set – this is a shorthand commonly used in previous work [10,15]. SIFT10M has the same data as SIFT1B, except that the first 10 million vectors of SIFT1B are used as base. The dataset is publicly available at http://corpus-texmex.irisa.fr/.

---

[3] https://docs.nvidia.com/cuda/samples/6_Advanced/reduction/doc/reduction.pdf.

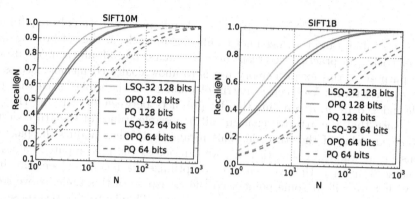

Fig. 1. Recall@N curves for very large-scale datasets: (left) the SIFT10M, and (right) SIFT1B.

5.2 Baselines

To compare nearest neighbour search performance, we use 3 baselines: product quantization (PQ) [9], which assumes that the codebooks are orthogonal, but initiated research in this area; optimized product quantization (OPQ) [15], which still assumes orthogonality, but also optimizes the subspace allocation via a rotation matrix $R \in SO(d)$, which can be solved for directly solving a Procrustes problem. Finally, we compare against composite quantization [10], a method that enforces the products between the codebooks (i.e., our pairwise terms), to be constant, and uses constrained optimization to find the codebooks. In CQ, codes are found using ICM, similar to our method. To reproduce PQ and OPQ we use the publicly available implementation of Norouzi and Fleet.[4] For CQ, we reproduce the values reported in [10]. We refer to our method as SLSQ-x, where x represents the number of ILS iterations used during database encoding. The number of ICM iterations (J in Algorithm 1, was set to 4).

6   Results

We report our results in recall@N, reproduced from our previous work [7] in Fig. 1, with detailed result on Table 1. Our method, when using 16 ILS iterations outperforms all the baselines, and when using 32 iterations further widens the performance advantage with respect to previous work. These results are shown here just for completeness, but are not the main focus of our work – when we set out to port our algoritm to the GPU, we already knew that it performed very well. Next, we report the speedups of our GPU implementation.

6.1   Speedups

For this particular report, the most important part for us to report is the speedup observed by our GPU implementation. We report those results on Table 2.

---

[4] https://github.com/norouzi/ckmeans.

Table 1. Detailed recall@N values for our method on large-scale datasets: SIFT10M and SIFT1B.

	SIFT10M – 64 bits			SIFT10M – 128 bits		
	R@1	R@10	R@100	R@1	R@2	R@5
PQ	15.79	50.86	86.57	39.31	54.74	74.89
OPQ	17.49	54.92	89.41	40.80	56.73	77.15
CQ [10]	21	63	93	47	64	84
LSQ-16	22.51	64.62	94.67	49.26	66.75	85.36
LSQ-32	22.94	65.20	94.85	49.50	67.31	86.33
	SIFT1B – 64 bits			SIFT1B – 128 bits		
	R@1	R@10	R@100	R@1	R@2	R@5
PQ	06.34	24.41	56.92	26.38	38.57	56.45
OPQ	07.02	27.34	61.89	28.43	40.80	59.53
CQ [10]	09	33	70	34	48	68
LSQ-16	09.73	35.82	73.84	35.32	50.84	70.66
LSQ-32	10.18	36.96	75.31	36.35	51.99	72.13

Table 2. Time spent per vector during encoding in our approach. "Sequential" refers to an LSQ implementation where ICM encodes each point sequentially (*i.e.*, does not take advantage of the shared pairwise terms). "Batched" is our LSQ implementation, which performs conditioning of shared pairwise terms among several data points.

Method	Sequential		Batched		Method	GPU (batched)		Method	Exhaustive NN	
codebooks (m)	7	15	7	15	codebooks (m)	7	15	codebooks (m)	8	16
LSQ-16 (ms.)	1.52	7.02	0.53	2.01	LSQ-16 (μs)	17.9	67.2	PQ (μs)	42.6	77.9
LSQ-32 (ms.)	3.01	13.93	1.05	4.03	LSQ-32 (μs)	35.7	134.3	OPQ (μs)	49.2	90.3

Focusing on the LSQ-32 results when using 15 codebooks, we see that our sequential implementation in Julia took almost 14 ms. per vector, our batched implementation reduced that time to roughly 4 ms. These times were measured on an Intel i7-3930K CPU, which runs at 3.2 GHz and has 12 MB of cache. The batched implementation was ported to a Titan X GTX GPU, and we observed a reduction in time to 134.3 µs, which results in a speedup of 30×. This means that encoding the SIFT1B base dataset can be done in slightly above 37 h, instead of the over 45 days that it would take with our single-threaded CPU implementation. Moreover, this GPU implementation has a running time comparable to that of PQ and OPQ in the CPU.

7   Conclusions and Future Work

We have demonstrated a GPU implementation of a recent SLS-based algorithm for encoding in multi-codebook quantization. The implementation takes advantage of the large-scale parallelism of modern GPUs by being throughput-oriented; it increases the load per thread during perturbation by making use of reservoir sampling, and ensures coalesced access to global memory by using multiple copies of the pairwise tables. We have shown that, in a typical scenario, our GPU implementation achieves a 30× speedup over a single-threaded CPU implementation. This has allowed us to tackle a dataset with 1 billion points in slightly over a day and a half of computation, instead of the month and half that it would take to do the same task with a single CPU.

A shortcoming of our comparison is that our CPU implementation is probably far from optimal. Ideally, we would like our CPU implementation to be based in C or C++, and even more ideally to be parallelized using `pthreads`. We dread the idea of doing the latter, and in any case we believe that the effort/speedup ratio will still highly favour the GPU implementation. On the other hand, we do not see any obvious ways of speeding up our current GPU implementation.

Future work may include further exploring the design space of stochastic local search algorithms for this problem, or improving the design of our CUDA program to obtain better performance from the GPU.

Appendix

```
1  // Initialize each code to a random value between 1 and h.
2  for i := 1, 2, ..., m do
3      b_i ~ U{1, h} ;
4  end
5  // Save the current solution
6  s := [b_i, b_2, ..., b_m]
7  // Loop over ILS iterations.
8  for i := 1, 2, ..., I do
9      // Perturb k codes.
10     for j := 1, 2, ..., k do
11         idx ~ U{1, m} // Sample a code to perturb (without replacement)
12         b_idx ~ U{1, h} // Perturb the code to a random value
13     end
14     // Run iterated conditional modes
15     // Loop over the number of ICM iterations
16     for j := 1, 2, ..., J do
17         // Update each code, keeping the rest fixed
18         for k := 1, 2, ..., m do
19             b_k := arg min_{b_k} -2⟨x, C_k b_k⟩ + ‖C_k b_k‖²₂ + Σ^m_{i≠k}⟨C_k b_k, C_i b_i⟩
20         end
21     end
22     // Compute the cost of the newly-found solution
23     s' := [b_i, b_2, ..., b_m]
24     // If the new solution is better, keep it
25     if cost(s') < cost(s) then
26         s := s'
27     end
28  end
29  return s
```

Algorithm 1. Our SLS algorithm for encoding in MCQ

```
1  needed := k // The number of codes that we still have to perturb
2  left := m // The number of codes that we can still visit
3  for i := 1, 2, ..., m do
4  |    // With probability needed/left, alter the ith code
5  |    r ~ U(0, 1);
6  |    if r < needed/left then
7  |    |    b_i ~ U{1, h}
8  |    |    needed := needed − 1
9  |    |    if needed ≤ 0 then
10 |    |    |    return
11 |    |    end
12 |    end
13 |    left := left − 1
14 end
```

Algorithm 2. Our perturbation method using reservoir sampling

References

1. Crandall, D.J., Owens, A., Snavely, N., Huttenlocher, D.P.: Sfm with mrfs: discrete-continuous optimization for large-scale structure from motion. IEEE Trans. Pattern Anal. Mach. Intell. **35**(12), 2841–2853 (2013)
2. Lowe, D.G.: Distinctive image features from scale-invariant keypoints. IJCV **60**(2), 91–110 (2004)
3. Muja, M., Lowe, D.G.: Fast approximate nearest neighbors with automatic algorithm configuration. In: VISApp, vol. 1 (2009)
4. Gong, Y., Lazebnik, S.: Iterative quantization: a procrustean approach to learning binary codes. In: CVPR (2011)
5. Norouzi, M., Fleet, D.J.: Minimal loss hashing for compact binary codes. In: ICML (2011)
6. Babenko, A., Lempitsky, V.: Additive quantization for extreme vector compression. In: CVPR (2014)
7. Martinez, J., Clement, J., Hoos, H., Little, J.: Revisiting additive quantization. In: ECCV (2016)
8. Hoos, H.H., Stützle, T.: Stochastic local search: Foundations & applications. Elsevier, Amsterdam (2004)
9. Jégou, H., Douze, M., Schmid, C.: Product quantization for nearest neighbor search. TPAMI **33**(1), 117–128 (2011)
10. Zhang, T., Du, C., Wang, J.: Composite quantization for approximate nearest neighbor search. In: ICML (2014)
11. Tung, F., Little, J.J.: CollageParsing: nonparametric scene parsing by adaptive overlapping windows. In: Fleet, D., Pajdla, T., Schiele, B., Tuytelaars, T. (eds.) ECCV 2014. LNCS, vol. 8694, pp. 511–525. Springer, Heidelberg (2014). doi:10.1007/978-3-319-10599-4_33
12. Krähenbühl, P., Koltun, V.: Efficient inference in fully connected crfs with gaussian edge potentials. arXiv preprint arXiv:1210.5644 (2012)
13. Vineet, V., Narayanan, P.: Cuda cuts: fast graph cuts on the gpu. In: IEEE Computer Society Conference on Computer Vision and Pattern Recognition Workshops, CVPRW 2008, pp. 1–8. IEEE (2008)

14. Zach, C., Gallup, D., Frahm, J.M., Niethammer, M.: Fast global labeling for real-time stereo using multiple plane sweeps. In: VMV, pp. 243–252 (2008)
15. Norouzi, M., Fleet, D.J.: Cartesian k-means. In: CVPR (2013)
16. Bezanson, J., Edelman, A., Karpinski, S., Shah, V.B.: Julia: a fresh approach to numerical computing. arXiv preprint arXiv:1411.1607 (2014)

Learning Joint Representations of Videos and Sentences with Web Image Search

Mayu Otani[1](✉), Yuta Nakashima[1], Esa Rahtu[2], Janne Heikkilä[2], and Naokazu Yokoya[1]

[1] Graduate School of Information Science,
Nara Institute of Science and Technology, Ikoma, Japan
{otani.mayu.ob9,n-yuta,yokoya}@is.naist.jp
[2] Center for Machine Vision and Signal Analysis,
University of Oulu, Oulu, Finland
{erahtu,jth}@ee.oulu.fi

Abstract. Our objective is video retrieval based on natural language queries. In addition, we consider the analogous problem of retrieving sentences or generating descriptions given an input video. Recent work has addressed the problem by embedding visual and textual inputs into a common space where semantic similarities correlate to distances. We also adopt the embedding approach, and make the following contributions: First, we utilize web image search in sentence embedding process to disambiguate fine-grained visual concepts. Second, we propose embedding models for sentence, image, and video inputs whose parameters are learned simultaneously. Finally, we show how the proposed model can be applied to description generation. Overall, we observe a clear improvement over the state-of-the-art methods in the video and sentence retrieval tasks. In description generation, the performance level is comparable to the current state-of-the-art, although our embeddings were trained for the retrieval tasks.

Keywords: Video retrieval · Sentence retrieval · Multimodal embedding · Neural network · Image search · Representation learning

1 Introduction

During the last decade, the Internet has become an increasingly important distribution channel for videos. Video hosting services like YouTube, Flickr, and Vimeo have millions of users uploading and watching content every day. At the same time, powerful search methods have become essential to make good use of such vast databases. By analogy, without textual search tools like Google or Bing, it would be nearly hopeless to find information from the websites.

Electronic supplementary material The online version of this chapter (doi:10.1007/978-3-319-46604-0_46) contains supplementary material, which is available to authorized users.

© Springer International Publishing Switzerland 2016
G. Hua and H. Jégou (Eds.): ECCV 2016 Workshops, Part I, LNCS 9913, pp. 651–667, 2016.
DOI: 10.1007/978-3-319-46604-0_46

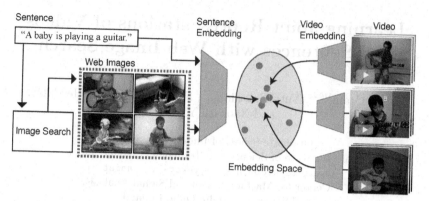

Fig. 1. An overview of our approach. Left side illustrates the image search results for a query "A baby is playing a guitar". Images highlight evidence of objects ("baby", "guitar") and actions ("playing"). Right side shows the most relevant videos in the YouTube dataset [1] obtained by ranking the clips according to Euclidean distance to the query sentence in an embedding space.

Our objective is to study the problem of retrieving video clips from a database using natural language queries. In addition, we consider the analogous problem of retrieving sentences or generating descriptions based on a given video clip. We are particularly interested in learning appropriate representations for both visual and textual inputs. Moreover, we intend to leverage the supporting information provided by the current image search approaches.

This topic has recently received plenty of attention in the community, and papers have presented various approaches to associate visual and textual data. One direction to address this problem is to utilize metadata that can be directly compared with queries. For instance, many web image search engines evaluate the relevance of an image based on the similarity of the query sentence with the user tags or the surrounding HTML text [4]. For sentence retrieval, Ordonez *et al.* [21] proposed to compare an image query and visual metadata with sentences.

While these methods using comparable metadata have demonstrated impressive results, they do not perform well in cases where appropriate metadata is limited or not available. Moreover, they rely strongly on the assumption that the associated visual and textual data in the database is relevant to each other. These problems are more apparent in the video retrieval task since video distribution portals like YouTube often provide less textual descriptions compared to other web pages. Furthermore, available descriptions (e.g. title) often cover only a small portion of the entire visual content in a video.

An alternative approach would be to compare textual and visual inputs directly. In many approaches, this is enabled by embedding the corresponding representations into a common vector space in such a way that the semantic similarity of the original inputs would be directly reflected in their distance in the embedding space (Fig. 1). Recent work [16, 27] has proposed deep neural network models for performing such embeddings. The results are promising, but developing powerful joint representations still remains a challenge.

In this paper, we propose a new embedding approach for sentence and video inputs that combines the advantages of the metadata-based web image search and deep neural network-based representation learning. More precisely, we use a standard search engine to obtain a set of supplementary images for each query sentence. Then, we pass the sentence and the retrieved images to a two-branch neural network that produces the sentence embedding. The video inputs are embedded into the same space using another neural network. The network parameters are trained jointly so that videos and sentences with similar semantic content are mapped to close points. Figure 1 illustrates the overall architecture of our approach. The experiments indicate a clear improvement over the current state-of-the-art baseline methods.

Our main contributions are as follows:

– We present an embedding approach for video retrieval that incorporates web image search results to disambiguate fine-grained visual concepts in query sentences.
– We introduce neural network-based embedding models for video, sentence, and image inputs whose parameters can be learned jointly. Unlike previous work that uses only videos and sentences, we utilize a sentence and corresponding web images to compute the sentence embedding.
– We demonstrate a clear improvement over the state-of-the-art in the video and sentence retrieval tasks with the YouTube dataset [1].
– We demonstrate description generation as an example of possible applications of our video embeddings. We observed that the performance is comparable with the state-of-the-art. This indicates that video contents are efficiently encoded into our video embeddings.

2   Related Work

Visual and Language Retrieval: Due to the explosive growth of images and videos on the web, visual retrieval has become a hot topic in computer vision and machine learning [4,20]. Several recent approaches for joint representation leaning enable direct comparison among different multimodalities. Farhadi *et al.* [7] introduced triplets of labels on object, action, and scene as joint representations for images and sentences. Socher *et al.* [27] proposed to embed representations of images and labels into a common embedding space. For videos, the approach proposed by Lin *et al.* [18] associates a parsed semantic graph of a query sentence and visual cues based on object detection and tracking.

The recent success of deep convolutional neural networks (CNNs) together with large-scale visual datasets [2,22,25] has resulted in several powerful representation models for images [5,33,35]. These CNN-based methods have been successfully applied to various types of computer vision tasks, such as object detection [10,23], video summarization [12], and image description generation [6,32].

Deep neural networks have also been used in the field of natural language processing [16,17]. For example, Kiros *et al.* [16] proposed sentence representation learning based on recurrent neural networks (RNNs). They also demonstrated image and sentence retrieval by matching sentence and image representations with jointly leaned linear transformations.

Representation learning using deep neural networks is explored in many tasks [3,9,14,19,34,37]. Frome et al. [9] proposed image classification by computing similarity between joint representations of images and labels, and Zhu et al. [37] addressed alignment of a movie and sentences in a book using joint representations for video clips and sentences. Their approach also computes similarity between sentences and subtitles of video clips to improve the alignment of video clips and sentences.

Our approach is the closest to work by Xu et al. [34]. They represent a sentence by a subject, verb, and object (SVO) triplet, and embed sentences as well as videos to a common vector space using deep neural networks. The main difference between ours and the work [34] is the use of an RNN to encode a sentence and supplementary web images. The use of an RNN enables our model to encode all words in a sentence and capture details of the sentence, such as an object's attributes and scenes, together with corresponding web images.

Exploiting Image Search: The idea of exploiting web image search is adopted in many tasks, including object classification [8] and video summarization [28]. These approaches collect a vast amount of images from the web and utilize them to extract canonical visual concepts. Recent label prediction for images by Johnson et al. [13] infers tags of target images by mining relevant Flickr images based on their metadata, such as user tags and photo groups curated by users. The relevant images serve as priors on tags for the target image. A similar motivation drives us to utilize web images for each sentence, which can disambiguate visual concepts of the sentence and highlight relevant target videos.

3 Proposed Approach

We propose neural network-based embedding models for the video and sentence retrieval tasks. In order to enhance the sentence embedding, we retrieve relevant web images that are assumed to disambiguate semantics of the sentence. For example, the word "keyboard" can be interpreted as a musical instrument or an input device for computers. If the word comes with "play," the meaning of "keyboard" narrows down to a musical instrument. This means that a specific combination of words can reduce the possible visual concepts relevant to the sentence, which may not be fully encoded even with the state-of-the-art RNN-based approach like [16].

We propose to take this into account by using web image search results. Since most image search engines use surrounding text to retrieve images, we can expect that they are responsive to such word combinations. Consequently, we retrieve web images using the input sentence as a query and download the results. The web images are fused with the input sentence by applying a two-branch neural network as shown in Fig. 2. Videos are also encoded by applying a neural network-based video embedding model. Relevance between sentence

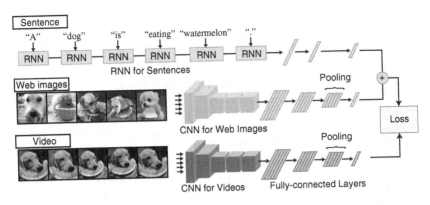

Fig. 2. Illustration of our video and sentence embedding. The orange component is the sentence embedding model that takes a sentence and corresponding web images as input. Video embedding model is denoted by the blue component. (Color figure online)

and video inputs is directly computed in the common embedding space using Euclidean distances. We jointly train our embedding models using video-sentence pairs by minimizing the contrastive loss [3].

3.1 Video Embedding

We extract frames from a video at 1 fps as in [34] and feed them to a CNN-based video embedding model. In our approach, we employ two CNN architectures: 19-layer VGG [26] and GoogLeNet [29], both of which are pre-trained on ImageNet [25]. We replace the classifier layer in each model with two fully-connected layers. Specifically, we compute activations of the VGG's fc7 layer or the GoogLeNet's inception 5b layer and feed them to additional embedding layers.

Let $X = \{x_i \mid i = 1, \ldots, M\}$ be a set of frames x_i, and $\mathrm{CNN}(x_i) \in \mathrm{R}^{d_v}$ be an activation of a CNN (d_v=4,096 for VGG, and d_v=1,024 for GoogLeNet). The video embedding $\phi_\mathrm{v}(X) \in \mathrm{R}^{d_e}$ is computed by:

$$\phi_\mathrm{v}(X) = \frac{1}{M} \sum_{x_i \in X} \tanh(W_{\mathrm{v}_2} \tanh(W_{\mathrm{v}_1} \mathrm{CNN}(x_i) + b_{\mathrm{v}_1}) + b_{\mathrm{v}_2}). \tag{1}$$

Here, $W_{\mathrm{v}_1} \in \mathrm{R}^{d_h \times d_v}$, $b_{\mathrm{v}_1} \in \mathrm{R}^{d_h}$, $W_{\mathrm{v}_2} \in \mathrm{R}^{d_e \times d_h}$, and $b_{\mathrm{v}_2} \in \mathrm{R}^{d_e}$ are the learnable parameters of the fully-connected layers.

3.2 Sentence and Web Image Embedding

The sentence embedding model consists of two branches that merge the outputs of a CNN-based network for web images and an RNN-based network for a sentence. Before computing the sentence embedding, we download top-K results of web image search with the input sentence as a query. Let $Z = \{z_j \mid j = 1, \ldots, K\}$

be a set of web images. We utilize the same architecture as the video embedding and compute an intermediate representation $e_z \in R^{d_e}$ that integrates the web images as:

$$e_z = \frac{1}{K} \sum_{z_j \in Z} \tanh(W_{z_2} \tanh(W_{z_1} \text{CNN}(z_j) + b_{z_1}) + b_{z_2}), \tag{2}$$

where $W_{z_1} \in R^{d_h \times d_v}$, $b_{z_1} \in R^{d_h}$, $W_{z_2} \in R^{d_e \times d_h}$, and $b_{z_2} \in R^{d_e}$ are the learnable parameters of the two fully-connected layers.

We encode sentences into vector representations using skip-thought that is an RNN pre-trained with a large-scale book corpus [16]. Let $Y = \{y_t \mid t = 1, \ldots, T_Y\}$ be the input sentence, where y_t is the t-th word in the sentence, and T_Y is the number of words in the sentence Y. Skip-thought takes a sequence of word vectors $w_t \in R^{d_w}$ computed from a word input y_t as in [16] and produces hidden state $h_t \in R^{d_s}$ at each time step t as:

$$r_t = \sigma(W_r w_t + U_r w_{t-1}), \tag{3}$$
$$i_t = \sigma(W_i w_t + U_i h_{t-1}), \tag{4}$$
$$a_t = \tanh(W_a w_t + U_a(r_t \odot h_{t-1})), \tag{5}$$
$$h_t = (1 - i_t) \odot h_{t-1} + i_t \odot a_t, \tag{6}$$

where σ is the sigmoid activation function, and $\odot$ is the component-wise product. The parameters W_r, W_i, W_a, U_r, U_i, and U_a are $d_s \times d_w$ matrices. Sentence Y is encoded into the hidden state after processing the last word w_{T_Y}, i.e., h_{T_Y}. We use combine-skip in [16], which is a concatenation of outputs from two separate RNNs trained with different datasets. We denote the output of combine-skip from sentence Y by $s_Y \in R^{d_c}$, where $d_c = 4,800$.

We also compute an intermediate representation e_s for sentence Y as:

$$e_s = \tanh(W_{s_2} \tanh(W_{s_1} s_Y + b_{s_1}) + b_{s_2}), \tag{7}$$

where $W_{s_1} \in R^{d_h \times d_c}$, $b_{s_1} \in R^{d_h}$, $W_{s_2} \in R^{d_e \times d_h}$, and $b_{s_2} \in R^{d_e}$ are the learnable parameters of sentence embedding.

Once the outputs e_s and e_z of each branch in our sentence embedding model are computed, they are merged into a sentence embedding $\phi_s(Y, Z)$ as:

$$\phi_s(Y, Z) = \frac{1}{2}(e_s + e_z). \tag{8}$$

By this simple mixture of e_s and e_z, the sentence and web images directly influence the sentence embedding.

3.3   Joint Learning of Embedding Models

We jointly train both embedding ϕ_v and ϕ_s using pairs of videos and associated sentences in a training set by minimizing the contrastive loss function [3]. In our approach, the contrastive loss decreases when embeddings of videos and sentences with similar semantics get closer to each other in the embedding space, and those with dissimilar semantics get farther apart.

The training process requires a set of positive and negative video-sentence pairs. A positive pair contains a video and a sentence that are semantically relevant, and a negative pair contains irrelevant ones. Let $\{(X_n, Y_n) \mid n = 1, \ldots, N\}$ be the set of positive pairs. Given a positive pair (X_n, Y_n), we sample irrelevant sentences $\mathcal{Y}'_n = \{Y'_f \mid f = 1, \ldots, N_c\}$ and videos $\mathcal{X}'_n = \{X'_g \mid g = 1, \ldots, N_c\}$ from the training set, which are used to build two sets of negative pairs $\{(X_n, Y'_f) \mid Y'_f \in \mathcal{Y}'_n\}$ and $\{(X'_g, Y_n) \mid X'_g \in \mathcal{X}'_n\}$. In our approach, we set the size of negative pairs N_c to 50. We train the parameters of embedding ϕ_v and ϕ_s by minimizing the contrastive loss defined as:

$$Loss(X_n, Y_n) = \tfrac{1}{1+2N_c} \left\{ d(X_n, Y_n) \right.$$

$$+ \sum_{Y'_f \in \mathcal{Y}'_n} \max(0, \alpha - d(X_n, Y'_f))$$

$$\left. + \sum_{X'_g \in \mathcal{X}'_n} \max(0, \alpha - d(X'_g, Y_n)) \right\}, \tag{9}$$

$$d(X_i, Y_j) = \|\phi_v(X_i) - \phi_s(Y_j, Z_j)\|_2^2, \tag{10}$$

where Z_n is the web images corresponding to sentence Y_n. The hyperparameter α is a margin. Negative pairs with smaller distances than α are penalized. Margin α is set to the largest distance of positive pairs before training so that most negative pairs influence the model parameters at the beginning of training.

Figure 3 shows the histograms of distances of positive and negative pairs before and after training. The initial distance distributions of positive and negative pairs overlap. After training, the distributions are pulled apart. This indicates that the

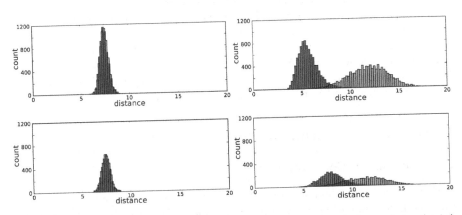

Fig. 3. Histograms of pairwise distances before training (left) and after training (right). Top row: Histograms of the training set. Bottom row: Histograms of the test set. Red represents positive pairs, and green represents negative pairs. (Color figure online)

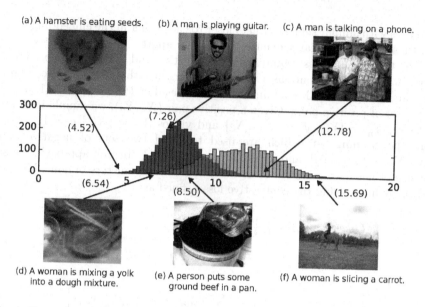

Fig. 4. Examples of positive (a)–(c) and negative (d)–(f) pairs in the test set with corresponding distances. The values (·) are distances of the pairs. The plot is the histograms of distances of positive (red) and negative (green) pairs. (Color figure online)

training process encourages videos and sentences in positive pairs to be mapped to closer points and those in negative ones to farther points.

The examples of positive and negative pairs in our test set with corresponding distances are shown in Fig. 4. The positive pair (a) and (b) are easy cases, in which sentences explicitly describe the video contents. The pair (c) is an example of hard cases. The sentence includes "a man" and "phone", but the video actually shows two men, and a phone is occluded by a hand.

The pairs (d) and (e) are hard negative cases. The pair (d) shows partial matches of contents, such as the action "mixing" and the object "yolk." Another negative pair (e) has a video and a sentence about cooking, although there is disagreement about details. As shown in these examples, the closer a video and a sentence are located in the embedding space, the more relevant they are. More examples can be found in the supplementary material.

4 Retrieval Experiments

4.1 Implementation Detail

With 19-layer VGG, the hidden layer size d_h of embedding ϕ_v and ϕ_s was set to 1,000 and the dimension of the embedding space d_e was set to 300. For model using GoogLeNet, we used $d_h = 600$ and $d_e = 300$.

We implemented our model using Chainer [30]. We used Adam [15] for optimization with a learning rate of 1×10^{-4}. The parameters of the CNNs and skip-thought were fixed. We applied dropout with a ratio of 0.5 to the input of the first and second layers of ϕ_v and ϕ_s. Our models were trained for 15 epochs, and their parameters were saved at every 100 updates. We took the model parameters whose performance was the best on the validation set.

4.2 Experimental Setup

Dataset: We used the YouTube dataset [1] consisting of 80K English descriptions for 1,970 videos. We first divided the dataset into 1,200, 100, and 670 videos for training, validation, and test, respectively, as in [11,34,35]. Then, we extracted five-second clips from each original video in a sliding-window manner. As a result, we obtained 8,001, 628, and 4,499 clips for the training, validation, and test sets, respectively. For each clip, we picked five ground truth descriptions out of those associated with its original video.

We collected top-5 image search results for each sentence using the Bing image search engine. We used a sentence modified by lowercasing and punctuation removal as a query. In order to eliminate cartoons and clip art, the image type was limited to photos using Bing API.

Video Retrieval: Given a video and a query sentence, we extracted five-second video clips from the video and computed Euclidean distances from the query to the clips. We used their median as the distance of the original video and the query. We ranked the videos based on the distance to each query and recorded the rank of the ground truth video. Since the test set has 670 videos, the probability of bringing the ground truth video at top-1 by random ranking is about 0.14 %.

Sentence Retrieval: For the sentence retrieval task, we ranked sentences for each query video. We computed the distances between a sentence and a query video in the same way as the video retrieval task. Note that each video has five ground truth sentences; thus, we recorded the highest rank among them. The test set has 3,500 sentences.

Evaluation Metrics: We report recall rates at top-1, -5, and -10, the average and median rank, which are standard metrics employed in the retrieval evaluation. We found that some videos in the dataset had sentences whose semantics were almost the same (*e.g.*, "A group of women is dancing" and "Women are dancing"). For the video that is annotated with one of such sentences, the other sentence is treated as incorrect with the recall rates, which does not agree with human judges. Therefore, we employed additional evaluation metrics widely used in the description generation task, *i.e.*, CIDEr, BLUE@4, and METEOR [2]. They compute agreement scores in different ways using a retrieved sentence and a set of ground truth ones associated with a query video. Thus, these metrics give high scores for semantically relevant sentences even if they are not annotated to a query video. We computed the scores of the top ranked sentence for each video using the evaluation script provided in the Microsoft COCO Evaluation Server [2]. In our experiments, all ground truth descriptions for each original video are used to compute these scores.

4.3 Effects of Each Component of Our Approach

In order to investigate the influence of each component of our approach, we tested some variations of our full model. The scores of the models on the video and sentence retrieval tasks are shown in Table 1. Our full model is denoted by ALL_2. ALL_1 is a variation of ALL_2 that computes embeddings with one fully-connected layer with the unit size of d_e. Comparison between ALL_1 and ALL_2 indicates that the number of fully-connected layers in embedding is not essential.

In order to evaluate the contributions of web images, we trained a model that does not use web images, $i.e.$, an embedding of a sentence Y is computed by $\phi_s(Y) = e_s$. We denote this model by VS. $VGG+ALL_2$ had better average rank than VGG+VS, and comparison between $GoogLeNet+ALL_2$ and GoogLeNet+VS also shows a clear advantage of incorporating web images.

We also tested a model without sentences, which is denoted by VI. It computes an embedding of web images by $\phi_s(Z) = e_z$. We investigated the effect of using both sentences and web images by comparing VI to our full model ALL_2. The results show that sentences are necessary. The comparison between VI and VS also indicates that sentences provide main cues for the retrieval task.

The scores of retrieved sentences computed by CIDEr, BLEU@4, and METEOR are shown in Table 2. In all metrics, our model using both sentences and web images (ALL_1 and ALL_2) outperformed to other models (VS and VI). In summary, contributions by sentences and web images were non-trivial, and the best performance was achieved by using both of them.

Table 1. Video and sentence retrieval results. R@K is recall at top K results (higher values are better). aR and mR are the average and median of rank (lower values are better). Bold values denotes best scores of each metric.

Models	Video retrieval					Sentence retrieval				
	R@1	R@5	R@10	aR	mR	R@1	R@5	R@10	aR	mR
Random Ranking	0.14	0.79	1.48	335.92	333	0.22	0.69	1.32	561.32	439
VGG+VS	6.12	21.88	33.22	58.98	24	7.01	18.66	27.16	131.33	35
VGG+VI	4.03	13.70	21.40	94.62	48	5.67	17.91	28.21	116.86	38
VGG+ALL₁	6.48	20.15	30.51	59.53	26	**10.60**	25.22	36.42	85.90	21
VGG+ALL₂	5.97	21.31	32.54	56.01	24	8.66	22.84	33.13	100.14	29
GoogLeNet+VS	7.49	22.84	33.10	54.14	22	8.51	21.34	30.45	114.66	33
GoogLeNet+VI	4.24	16.42	24.96	84.48	41	6.87	17.31	30.00	96.78	30
GoogLeNet+ALL₁	5.52	18.93	28.90	60.38	28	9.85	**27.01**	**38.36**	**75.23**	**19**
GoogLeNet+ALL₂	**7.67**	**23.40**	**34.99**	**49.08**	**21**	9.85	24.18	33.73	85.16	22
ST [16]	2.63	11.55	19.34	106.00	51	2.99	10.90	17.46	241.00	77
DVCT [34]	-	-	-	224.10	-	-	-	-	236.27	-

Table 2. Evaluated scores of retrieved sentences. All values are reported in percentage (%). Higher scores are better.

Models	CIDEr	BLEU	METEOR
VGG+VS	30.44	27.16	25.74
VGG+VI	29.00	22.42	22.99
VGG+ALL$_1$	42.52	**30.81**	**27.77**
VGG+ALL$_2$	32.56	27.39	26.58
GoogLeNet+VS	33.82	26.97	25.99
GoogLeNet+VI	35.08	24.56	24.16
GoogLeNet+ALL$_1$	**43.52**	29.99	27.48
GoogLeNet+ALL$_2$	38.08	29.28	26.50

Fig. 5. Examples of video retrieval results. Left: Query sentence and web images. Center: Top-3 retrieved videos by GoogLeNet+VS and VI. Right: Top-3 retrieved videos by GoogLeNet+ALL$_2$.

Query Video	GoogLeNet+All₂	GoogLeNet+VS
	1. A man is cutting a paper. 2. A man is cutting a paper by hands. 3. Someone is cutting the carrot into small pieces.	1. Someone is cutting the carrot into small pieces. 2. A person cuts a sock with scissors. 3. An oriental lady is cutting a carrot into thin pieces.
	1. A woman is talking while applying eyeshadow. 2. A woman applies Joker makeup to a man's face. 3. A woman is applying cosmetics to a man.	1. A woman is singing. 2. A woman is singing. 3. A woman wearing a headset is singing into a large microphone.
	1. A pair of zebras are playing with each other. 2. The zebras are playing. 3. A pair of zebras is nuzzling.	1. Leopards are congregating. 2. A group of deers are crossing road. 3. A pair of zebras is nuzzling.
	1. A man is playing keyboards. 2. A boy is playing a grand piano. 3. A boy is playing guitar.	1. A little boy is playing piano. 2. A little boy is playing a grand piano. 3. A boy is playing a piano.

Fig. 6. Examples of top-3 retrieved sentences. Left: Query videos. Center: Top-3 retrieved sentences by GoogLeNet+ALL₂. Right: Top-3 retrieved sentences by GoogLeNet+VS.

Some examples of retrieved videos by GoogLeNet+VS, GoogLeNet+VI, and GoogLeNet+ALL₂ are shown in Fig. 5. These results suggest that web images reduced the ambiguity of queries' semantics by providing hints on their visual concepts. For example, with sentence (1) "A man is playing a keyboard," retrieval results of GoogLeNet+VS includes two videos of a keyboard on a laptop as well as one on a musical instrument. On the other hand, all top-3 results by GoogLeNet+ALL₂ are about musical instruments. Compared to GoogLeNet+VI, our full model obtained more videos with relevant content. Moreover, the result of query (6) indicates that our model can recover from irrelevant image search results by combining a query sentence.

Some examples of sentence retrieval results are shown in Fig. 6. While our full model may retrieve sentences that disagree with query videos in details, most of the retrieved sentences are relevant to query videos.

4.4 Comparison to Prior Work

The approach for image and sentence retrieval by Kiros *et al.* [16] applies linear transformations to CNN-based image and RNN-based sentence representations to embed them into a common space. Note that their model was designed for the image and sentence retrieval tasks; thus, we extracted the middle frame as a keyframe and trained the model with pairs of a keyframe and a sentence. Xu *et al.* [34] introduced neural network-based embedding models for videos and sentences. Their approach embeds videos and SVO triplets extracted from sentences into an embedding space. Kiros *et al.*'s and Xu *et al.*'s approaches are denoted by ST and DVCT, respectively.

Scores in Table 1 indicates that our model clearly outperformed prior work in both video and sentence retrieval tasks. There is a significant difference in performance of DVCT and others. ST and ours encode all words in a sentence, while DVCT only encodes its SVO triplets. This suggests that using all words in a sentence together with an RNN is necessary to get good embeddings.

5   Video Description Generation

Automatic description generation for images [6,32] and videos [24,31,35] is another task to associate images or videos with sentences. As an application of our models, we performed the description generation task using our video embeddings. To analyze the information encoded by our video embedding, we trained a decoder that produces descriptions from our video embeddings.

A basic approach for description generation is to use long-short term memory (LSTM) that produces a sequence of probabilities over a vocabulary conditioned on visual representations [31,32]. We trained an LSTM as a decoder of video embeddings (Fig. 7). The decoder predicts the next word based on word vector w_t at each time step t as:

$$[a_t \; i_t \; f_t \; o_t]^T = W_u w_t + b_u + W_l h_{t-1}, \tag{11}$$

$$c_t = \tanh(a_t)\sigma(i_t) + c_{t-1}\sigma(f_t), \tag{12}$$

$$h_t = \tanh(c_t)\sigma(o_t), \tag{13}$$

$$p_t = \text{softmax}(W_p h_t + b_p) \tag{14}$$

where $W_u, W_l \in \mathbb{R}^{4d_w \times d_w}$ and $b_u \in \mathbb{R}^{4d_w}$ are parameters of the LSTM, and $[a_t \; i_t \; f_t \; o_t]^T$ is a column vector that is a concatenation of $a_t, i_t, f_t, o_t \in \mathbb{R}^{d_w}$. The matrix W_p and the vector b_p encode the hidden state into a vector with the vocabulary size. The output p_t is the probabilities over the vocabulary. We built a vocabulary consisting of all words in the YouTube dataset and special tags, *i.e.*, begin-of-sentence ("<bos >") and end-of-sentence ("<eos >"). The

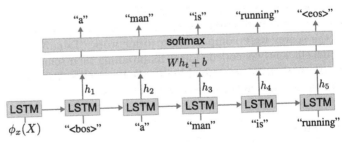

Fig. 7. Illustration of the decoder model. "<bos>" is a tag denoting the beginning of a sentence, and "<eos>" is the end of a sentence.

Women are dancing.　　A hamster eats seeds.　　A man is riding a motorcycle.

A woman is riding a horse.　　A man is playing a piano.　　A man is slicing a potato.

Fig. 8. Sentences generated from our video embeddings. The sentence in red is a failure. (Color figure online)

Table 3. Scores of generated sentences. TVNL + Extra Data is the TVNL model pretrained on the Flickr30k [36] and the COCO2014 [2] datasets.

Models	CIDEr	BLEU	METEOR
TVNL [31]	-	31.19	26.87
TVNL + Extra Data	-	33.29	29.07
DVETS [35]	51.67	41.92	29.60
Ours	41.62	33.69	28.47

generative process is terminated when "<eos >" is produced. We trained the decoder using the YouTube dataset. We computed the video embedding $\phi_v(X)$ using GoogLeNet+ALL$_2$ as an input to the LSTM at $t = 0$. We trained the decoder by minimizing the cross entropy loss. During training, we fixed the parameters of our embedding models.

Figure 8 shows generated sentences. Although video embeddings were trained for retrieval tasks and not finetuned for the decoder, we observed that most generated sentences were semantically relevant to their original videos.

We evaluated generated sentences with the COCO description evaluation. We found that the scores were comparable to prior work (Table 3). This indicates that our model efficiently encoded videos, maintaining their semantics. Moreover, this result suggests that our embeddings can be applied to other tasks that require joint representations of videos and sentences.

6   Conclusion

We presented a video and sentence retrieval framework that incorporates web images to bridge between sentences and videos. Specifically, we collected web image search results in order to disambiguate semantics of a sentence. We developed neural network-based embedding models for video, sentence, and image inputs which fuses sentence and image representations. We jointly trained video and sentence embeddings using the YouTube dataset. Our experiments demonstrated the advantage of incorporating additional web images, and our approach clearly outperformed prior work in the both video and sentence retrieval tasks. Furthermore, by decoding descriptions from video embeddings, we demonstrated that rich semantics of videos were efficiently encoded in our video embeddings. Our future work includes developing a video embedding that considers temporal structures of videos. It would be also interesting to investigate what kind of sentences benefit from image search results, and how to collect efficient images.

Acknowledgement. This work is partly supported by JSPS KAKENHI No. 16K16086.

References

1. Chen, D.L., Dolan, W.B.: Collecting highly parallel data for paraphrase evaluation. In: ACL, pp. 190–200 (2011)
2. Chen, X., Fang, H., Lin, T., Vedantam, R., Gupta, S., Dollr, P., Zitnick, C.L.: Microsoft COCO captions: data collection and evaluation server. arXiv preprint arXiv:1504.00325, 7 pages (2015)
3. Chopra, S., Hadsell, R., LeCun, Y.: Learning a similarity metric discriminatively, with application to face verification. In: CVPR, pp. 539–546 (2005)
4. Datta, R., Joshi, D., Li, J., Wang, J.Z.: Image retrieval: ideas, influences, and trends of the new age. ACM Comput. Surv. **40**(2), 5: 1–5: 60 (2008)
5. Donahue, J., Jia, Y., Vinyals, O., Hoffman, J., Zhang, N., Tzeng, E., Darrell, T.: DeCAF: a deep convolutional activation feature for generic visual recognition. In: ICML, pp. 647–655 (2014)
6. Fang, H., Gupta, S., Iandola, F., Srivastava, R.K., Deng, L., Dollar, P., Gao, J., He, X., Mitchell, M., Platt, J.C., Zitnick, C.L., Zweig, G.: From captions to visual concepts and back. In: CVPR, pp. 1473–1482 (2015)
7. Farhadi, A., Hejrati, M., Sadeghi, M.A., Young, P., Rashtchian, C., Hockenmaier, J., Forsyth, D.: Every picture tells a story: generating sentences from images. In: Daniilidis, K., Maragos, P., Paragios, N. (eds.) ECCV 2010. LNCS, vol. 6314, pp. 15–29. Springer, Heidelberg (2010). doi:10.1007/978-3-642-15561-1_2
8. Fergus, R., Fei-Fei, L., Perona, P., Zisserman, A.: Learning object categories from Google's image search. In: ICCV, pp. 1816–1823 (2005)
9. Frome, A., Corrado, G.S., Shlens, J., Bengio, S., Dean, J., Ranzato, M.A., Mikolov, T.: DeViSE: a deep visual-semantic embedding model. In: NIPS, pp. 2121–2129 (2013)
10. Girshick, R., Donahue, J., Darrell, T., Berkeley, U.C., Malik, J.: Rich feature hierarchies for accurate object detection and semantic segmentation. In: CVPR, pp. 580–587 (2014)
11. Guadarrama, S., Venugopalan, S., Austin, U.T., Krishnamoorthy, N., Mooney, R., Malkarnenkar, G., Darrell, T., Berkeley, U.C.: YouTube2Text: recognizing and describing arbitrary activities using semantic hierarchies and zero-shot recognition. In: ICCV, pp. 2712–2719 (2013)

12. Gygli, M., Grabner, H., Van Gool, L.: Video summarization by learning submodular mixtures of objectives. In: CVPR, pp. 3090–3098 (2015)
13. Johnson, J., Ballan, L., Fei-Fei, L.: Love thy neighbors: image annotation by exploiting image metadata. In: ICCV, pp. 4624–4632 (2015)
14. Karpathy, A., Joulin, A., Fei-Fei, L.: Deep fragment embeddings for bidirectional image sentence mapping. In: NIPS, pp. 1889–1897 (2014)
15. Kingma, D., Ba, J.: Adam: a method for stochastic optimization. In: ICLR, 11 pages (2015)
16. Kiros, R., Zhu, Y., Salakhutdinov, R.R., Zemel, R., Urtasun, R., Torralba, A., Fidler, S.: Skip-thought vectors. In: NIPS, pp. 3276–3284 (2015)
17. Le, Q.V., Mikolov, T.: Distributed representations of sentences and documents. In: ICML, pp. 1188–1196 (2014)
18. Lin, D., Fidler, S., Kong, C., Urtasun, R.: Visual semantic search: retrieving videos via complex textual queries. In: CVPR, pp. 2657–2664 (2014)
19. Lin, T.Y., Belongie, S., Hays, J.: Learning deep representations for ground-to-aerial geolocalization. In: CVPR, pp. 5007–5015 (2015)
20. Maybank, S.: A survey on visual content-based video indexing and retrieval. IEEE Trans. Syst. Man Cybern. Part C (Appl. Rev.) **41**(6), 797–819 (2011)
21. Ordonez, V., Kulkarni, G., Berg, T.: Im2Text: describing images using 1 million captioned photographs. In: NIPS, pp. 1143–1151 (2011)
22. Rashtchian, C., Young, P., Hodosh, M., Hockenmaier, J.: Collecting image annotations using Amazon's mechanical turk. In: NAACL-HLT, pp. 139–147 (2010)
23. Ren, S., He, K., Girshick, R., Sun, J.: Faster R-CNN: Towards real-time object detection with region proposal networks. In: NIPS, pp. 91–99 (2015)
24. Rohrbach, M., Qiu, W., Titov, I., Thater, S., Pinkal, M., Schiele, B.: Translating video content to natural language descriptions. In: ICCV, pp. 433–440 (2013)
25. Russakovsky, O., Deng, J., Su, H., Krause, J., Satheesh, S., Ma, S., Huang, Z., Karpathy, A., Khosla, A., Bernstein, M., Berg, A.C., Fei-Fei, L.: ImageNet large scale visual recognition challenge. Int. J. Comput. Vis. **115**(3), 211–252 (2015)
26. Simonyan, K., Zisserman, A.: Very deep convolutional networks for large-scale image recoginition. In: ICLR, p. 14 (2015)
27. Socher, R., Ganjoo, M., Manning, C.D., Ng, A.Y.: Zero-shot learning through cross-modal transfer. In: NIPS, pp. 935–943 (2013)
28. Song, Y., Vallmitjana, J., Stent, A., Jaimes, A.: TVSum: summarizing web videos using titles. In: CVPR, pp. 5179–5187 (2015)
29. Szegedy, C., Liu, W., Jia, Y., Sermanet, P., Reed, S., Anguelov, D., Erhan, D., Vanhoucke, V., Rabinovich, A.: Going deeper with convolutions. In: CVPR, pp. 1–9 (2015)
30. Tokui, S., Oono, K., Hido, S., Clayton, J.: Chainer: a next-generation open source framework for deep learning. In: NIPS, 6 pages (2015)
31. Venugopalan, S., Xu, H., Donahue, J., Rohrbach, M., Mooney, R., Saenko, K.: Translating videos to natural language using deep recurrent neural networks. In: NAACL-HLT, pp. 1494–1504 (2014)
32. Vinyals, O., Toshev, A., Bengio, S., Erhan, D.: Show and tell: a neural image caption generator. In: CVPR, pp. 3156–3164 (2015)
33. Wang, X., Gupta, A.: Unsupervised learning of visual representations using videos. In: ICCV, pp. 2794–2802 (2015)
34. Xu, R., Xiong, C., Chen, W., Corso, J.: Jointly modeling deep video and compositional text to bridge vision and language in a unified framework. In: AAAI, pp. 2346–2352 (2015)

35. Yao, L., Ballas, N., Larochelle, H., Courville, A.: Describing videos by exploiting temporal structure. In: ICCV, pp. 4507–4515 (2015)
36. Young, P., Lai, A., Hodosh, M., Hockenmaier, J.: From image descriptions to visual denotations: new similarity metrics for semantic inference over event descriptions. Trans. Assoc. Comput. Linguist. **2**, 67–78 (2014). https://tacl2013.cs.columbia.edu/ojs/index.php/tacl/article/view/229
37. Zhu, Y., Kiros, R., Zemel, R., Salakhutdinov, R., Urtasun, R., Torralba, A., Fidler, S.: Aligning books and movies: towards story-like visual explanations by watching movies and reading books. In: IEEE International Conference on Computer Vision (ICCV), pp. 19–27 (2015)

Depth2Action: Exploring Embedded Depth for Large-Scale Action Recognition

Yi Zhu[✉] and Shawn Newsam

University of California, Merced, USA
{yzhu25,snewsam}@ucmerced.edu

Abstract. This paper performs the first investigation into depth for large-scale human action recognition in video *where the depth cues are estimated from the videos themselves*. We develop a new framework called *depth2action* and experiment thoroughly into how best to incorporate the depth information. We introduce spatio-temporal depth normalization (STDN) to enforce temporal consistency in our estimated depth sequences. We also propose modified depth motion maps (MDMM) to capture the subtle temporal changes in depth. These two components significantly improve the action recognition performance. We evaluate our depth2action framework on three large-scale action recognition video benchmarks. Our model achieves state-of-the-art performance when combined with appearance and motion information thus demonstrating that depth2action is indeed complementary to existing approaches.

Keywords: Action recognition · Embedded depth

1 Introduction

Human action recognition in video is a fundamental problem in computer vision due to its increasing importance for a range of applications such as analyzing human activity, video search and recommendation, complex event understanding, etc. Much progress has been made over the past several years by employing hand-crafted local features such as improved dense trajectories (IDT) [39] or video representations that are learned directly from the data itself using deep convolutional neural networks (ConvNets). However, starting with the seminal two-stream ConvNets method [31], approaches have been limited to exploiting static visual information through frame-wise analysis and/or translational motion through optical flow or 3D ConvNets. Further increase in performance on benchmark datasets has been mostly due to the higher capacity of deeper networks [23,43,44,46] or to recurrent neural networks which model long-term temporal dynamics [2,24,47].

Electronic supplementary material The online version of this chapter (doi:10.
1007/978-3-319-46604-0_47) contains supplementary material, which is available to authorized users.

G. Hua and H. Jégou (Eds.): ECCV 2016 Workshops, Part I, LNCS 9913, pp. 668–684, 2016.
DOI: 10.1007/978-3-319-46604-0_47

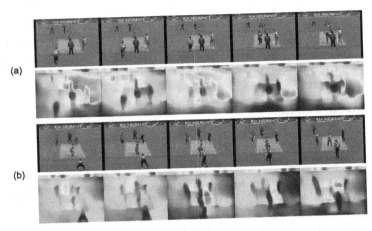

Fig. 1. (a) "CricketBowling" and (b) "CricketShot". Depth information about the bowler and the batters is key to telling these two classes apart. Our proposed depth2action approach exploits the depth information that is embedded in the videos to perform large-scale action recognition. This figure is best viewed in color (Color figure online)

Intuitively, *depth* can be an important cue for recognizing complex human actions. Depth information can help differentiate between action classes that are otherwise very similar especially with respect to appearance and translational motion in the red-green-blue (RGB) domain. For instance, the "CricketShot" and "CricketBowling" classes in the UCF101 dataset are often confused by the state-of-the-art models [44,46]. This makes sense because, as shown in Fig. 1, these classes can be very similar with respect to static appearance, human-object interaction, and in-plane human motion patterns. Depth information about the bowler and the batters is key to telling these two classes apart.

Previous work on depth for action recognition [3,40,45,50] uses depth information obtained from *depth sensors* such as Kinect-like devices and thus is not applicable to large-scale action recognition in RGB video. We instead estimate the depth information *directly from the video itself*. This is a difficult problem which results in noisy depth sequences and so a major contribution of our work is how to effectively extract the subtle but informative depth cues. To our knowledge, our work is the first to perform large-scale action recognition based on depth information embedded in the video data.

Our novel contributions are as follows: (i) We introduce *depth2action*, a novel approach for human action recognition using depth information embedded in videos. It is shown to be complementary to existing approaches which exploit spatial and translational motion information and, when combined with them, achieves state-of-the-art performance on three popular benchmarks. (ii) We propose STDN to enforce temporal consistency and MDMM to capture the subtle temporal depth cues in noisy depth sequences. (iii) We perform a thorough investigation on how best to extract and incorporate the depth cues including:

image- versus video-based depth estimation; multi-stream 2D ConvNets versus 3D ConvNets to jointly extract spatial and temporal depth information; ConvNets as feature extractors versus end-to-end classifiers; early versus late fusion of features for optimal prediction; and other design choices.

2   Related Work

There exists an extensive body of literature on human action recognition. We review only the most related work.

Deep ConvNets: Improved dense trajectories [39] dominated the field of video analysis for several years until the two-stream ConvNets architecture introduced by Simonyan and Zisserman [31] achieved competitive results for action recognition in video. In addition, motivated by the great success of applying deep ConvNets in image analysis, researchers have adapted deep architectures to the video domain either for feature representation [35,37,43,48,52] or end-to-end prediction [13,24,44,47].

While our framework shares some structural similarity with these works, it is distinct and complementary in that it exploits *depth* for action recognition. All the works above are based on appearance and translational motion in the RGB domain. We note there has been some work that exploits audio information [26]; however, not all videos come with audio and our approach is complementary to this work as well.

RGB-D Based Action Recognition: There is previous work on action recognition in RGB-D data. Chen et al. [3] use depth motion maps (DMM) for real-time human action recognition. Yang and Tian [50] cluster hypersurface normals in depth sequences to form a super normal vector (SNV) representation. Very recently, Wang et al. [45] apply weighted hierarchical DMM and deep ConvNets to achieve state-of-the-art performance on several benchmarks. Our work is different from approaches that use RGB-D data in several key ways:

(i) *Depth information source and quality*: These methods use depth information obtained from depth sensors. Besides limiting their applicability, this results in depth sequences that have much higher fidelity than those which can be estimated from RGB video. Our estimated depth sequences are too noisy for recognition techniques designed for depth-sensor data. Taking the difference between consecutive frames in our depth sequences only amplifies this noise making techniques such as STOP features [38], SNV representations [50], and DMM-based framework [3,45], for example, ineffective.

(ii) *Benchmark datasets*: RGB-D benchmarks such as MSRAction3D [19], MSRDailyActivity3D [42], MSRGesture3D [41], MSROnlineAction3D [51] and MSRActionPairs3D [27] are much more limited in terms of the diversity of action classes and the number of samples. Further, the videos often come with other meta data like skeleton joint positions. In contrast, our benchmarks such as UCF101 contain large numbers of action classes and the videos are less constrained. Recognition is made more difficult by the large intra-class variation.

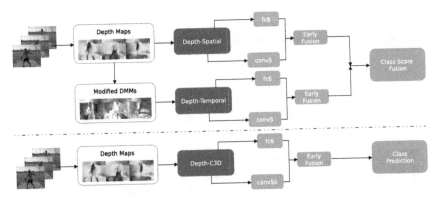

Fig. 2. Depth2Action framework. Top: Our *depth two-stream* model. Depth maps are estimated on a per-frame basis and input to a depth-spatial net. Modified depth motion maps (MDMMs) are derived from the depth maps and input to a depth-temporal net. Features are extracted, concatenated and input to two support vector machine (SVM) classifiers, to obtain the final prediction scores. Bottom: Our *depth-C3D* framework which is similar except the depth maps are input to a single depth-C3D net which jointly captures spatial and temporal depth information. This figure is best viewed in color (Color figure online)

We note that we take inspiration from [45,49] in designing our modified DMMs. The approaches in these works use RGB-D data and are not appropriate for our problem, though, since they construct multiple depth sequences using different geometric projections, and our videos are too long and our estimated depth sequences too noisy to be characterized by a single DMM.

In summary, our depth2action framework is novel compared to previous work on action recognition. An overview of our framework can be found in Fig. 2.

3   Methodology

Since our videos do not come with associated depth information, we need to extract it directly from the RGB video data. We consider two state-of-the-art approaches to *efficiently* extract depth maps from the individual video frames. We enforce temporal consistency in these sequences through inter-frame normalization. We explore different ConvNets architectures to extract spatial and temporal depth cues from the normalized depth sequences.

3.1   Depth Extraction

Extracting depth maps from video has been studied for some time now [29, 34,53]. Most approaches, however, are not applicable since they either require stereo video or additional information such as geometric priors. There are a few works [22] which extract depth maps from monocular video alone but they are computationally too expensive which does not scale to problems like ours.

Fig. 3. Depth maps estimated from the video v_ThrowDiscus_g05_c02.avi in the UCF101 dataset. (a): raw RGB frames; (b): depth maps extracted using [20]; (c): depth maps extracted using [4]; (d): the absolute difference between consecutive depth maps in (c). Blue indicates smaller values and yellow larger ones. This figure is best viewed in color (Color figure online)

We therefore turn to frame-by-frame depth extraction and enforce temporal consistency through a normalization step. Depth from images has made much progress recently [1,4,14,20] and is significantly more efficient for extracting depth from video. We consider two state-of-the-art approaches to extract depth from images, [4,20], based on their accuracy and efficiency.

Deep Convolutional Neural Fields (DCNF) [20]: This work jointly explores the capacity of deep ConvNets and continuous CRFs to estimate depth from an image. Depth is predicted through maximum a posterior (MAP) inference which has a closed-form solution. We apply the implementation kindly provided by the authors [20] but discard the time consuming "inpainting" procedure which is not important for our application. Our modified implementation takes only 0.09 s per frame to extract a depth map.

Multi-scale Deep Network [4]: Unlike DCNF above, this method does not utilize super-pixels and thus results in smoother depth maps. It uses a sequence of scales to progressively refine the predictions and to capture image details both globally and locally. Although the model can also be used to predict surface normals and semantic labels within a common ConvNets architecture, we only use it to extract depth maps. Our modified implementation takes only 0.01 s per frame to extract a depth map.

Figure 3 visually compares the per-frame depths maps generated by the two approaches. We observe that (1) [4] (Fig. 3c) results in smoother maps since it does not utilize super-pixels like [20] (Fig. 3b), and (2) [4] preserves structural details, such as the border between the sky and the trees, better than [20] due to its multi-scale refinement. An ablation study (see supplemental materials) shows [4] results in better action recognition performance so we use it to extract per-frame depth maps for the rest of the paper.

3.2 Spatio-Temporal Depth Normalization

We now have depth sequences. While this makes our problem similar to work on action recognition from depth-sensor data such as [45], these methods are not applicable for a number of reasons. First, their inputs are point clouds which allows them to derive depth sequences from multiple perspectives for a single video as well as augment their training data through virtual camera movement. We only have a single fixed viewpoint. Second, their depth information has much higher fidelity since it was acquired with a depth sensor. Ours is prohibitively noisy to use a single 2D depth motion map to represent an entire video as is done in [45]. We must develop new methods.

The first step is to reduce the noise by enforcing temporal consistency under the assumption that depth does not change significantly between frames. We introduce a temporal normalization scheme which constrains the furthest part of the scene to remain approximately the same throughout a clip. We find this works best when applied separately to three horizontal spatial windows and so we term the method spatio-temporal depth normalization (STDN). Specifically, let $\mathbf{x}$ be a frame. We then take n consecutive frames $[\mathbf{x}_{t1}, \mathbf{x}_{t2}, \ldots, \mathbf{x}_{tn}]$ to form a volume (clip) which is divided spatially into three equal-sized subvolumes that represent the top, middle, and bottom parts [25]. We take the 95th percentile of the depth distribution as the furthest scene element in each subvolume. The 95th percentile of the corresponding window in each frame is then linearly scaled to equal this furthest distance.

We also investigated other methods to enforce temporal consistency including intra-frame normalization, temporal averaging (uniform as well as Gaussian) with varying temporal window sizes, and warping. None performed as well as the proposed STDN (see supplemental materials).

3.3 ConvNets Architecture Selection

Recent progress in action recognition based on ConvNets can be attributed to two models: a two-stream approach based on 2D ConvNets [31,44] which separately models the spatial and temporal information, and 3D ConvNets which jointly learn spatio-temporal features [11,37]. These models are applied to RGB video sequences. We explore and adapt them for our depth sequences.

2D ConvNets: In [31], the authors compute a spatial stream by adapting 2D ConvNets from image classification [15] to action recognition. We do the same here except we use depth sequences instead of RGB video sequences. We term this our *depth-spatial stream* to distinguish it from the standard spatial stream which we will refer to as RGB-spatial stream for clarity. Our depth-spatial stream is pre-trained on the ILSVRC-2012 dataset [30] with the VGG-16 implementation [32] and fine-tuned on our depth sequences. [31] also computes a temporal stream by applying 2D ConvNets to optical flow derived from the RGB video. We could similarly compute optical flow from our depth sequences but this would be redundant (and very noisy) so we instead propose a different depth-temporal stream below in Sect. 3.4.

3D ConvNets: In [11,37], the authors show that 2D ConvNets "forget" the temporal information in the input signal after every convolution operation. They propose 3D ConvNets which analyze sets of contiguous video frames organized as clips. We apply this approach to clips of depth sequences. We term this *depth-C3D* to distinguish it from the standard 3D ConvNets which we will refer to as RGB-C3D for clarity. Our depth-C3D net is pre-trained using the Sports-1M dataset [13] and fine-tuned on our depth sequences.

3.4   Depth-Temporal Stream

Here, we look to augment our depth-spatial stream with a depth-temporal stream. We take inspiration from work on action recognition from depth-sensor data and adapt depth motion maps [49] to our problem. In [49], a single 2D DMM is computed for an entire sequence by thresholding the difference between consecutive depth maps to get per-frame (binary) motion energy and then summing this energy over the entire video. A 2D DMM summarizes where depth motion occurs.

We instead calculate the motion energy as the absolute difference between consecutive depth maps *without thresholding* in order to retain the subtle motion information embedded in our noisy depth sequences. We also accumulate the motion energy over clips instead of entire sequences since the videos in our dataset are longer and less-constrained compared to the depth-sensor sequences in [19,27,41,42,51] and so our depth sequences are too noisy to be summarized over long periods. In many cases, the background would simply dominate.

We compute one modified depth motion map (MDMM) for a clip of N depth maps as

$$\mathrm{MDMM}_{t_{start}} = \sum_{t_{start}}^{t_{start}+N} |\mathrm{map}^{t_{start}+1} - \mathrm{map}^{t_{start}}|, \tag{1}$$

where t_{start} is the first frame of the clip, N is the duration of the clip, and map^t is the depth map at frame t. Multiple MDMMs are computed for each video. Each MDMM is then input to a 2D ConvNet for classification. We term this our *depth-temporal stream*. We combine it with our depth-spatial stream to create our *depth two-stream* (see Fig. 2). Similar to the depth-spatial stream, the depth-temporal stream is pre-trained on the ILSVRC-2012 dataset [30] with the VGG-16 network [32] and fine-tuned on the MDMMs.

We also consider a simpler temporal stream by taking the absolute difference between adjacent depth maps and inputting this difference sequence to a 2D ConvNet. We term this our *baseline depth-temporal stream*. Figure 3d shows an example sequence of this difference. It does a good job at highlighting changes in the depth despite the noisiness of the image-based depth estimation.

3.5   ConvNets: Feature Extraction or End-to-End Classification

The ConvNets in our depth two-stream and depth-C3D models default to end-to-end classifiers. We investigate whether to use them instead as feature extractors followed by SVM classifiers. This also allows us to investigate early versus late fusion. We use our depth-spatial stream for illustration.

Features are extracted from two layers of our fine-tuned ConvNets. We extract the activations of the first fully-connected layer (fc6) on a per-frame basis. These are then averaged over the entire video and L2-normalized to form a 4096-dim video-level descriptor. We also extract activations from the convolutional layers as they contain spatial information. We choose the conv5 layer, whose feature dimension is $7 \times 7 \times 512$ (7 is the size of the filtered images of the convolutional layer and 512 is the number of convolutional filters). By considering each convolutional filter as a latent concept, the conv5 features can be converted into 7^2 latent concept descriptors (LCD) [48] of dimension 512. We also adopt a spatial pyramid pooling (SPP) strategy [7] similar to [48]. We apply principle component analysis (PCA) to de-correlate and reduce the dimension of the LCD features to 64 and then encode them using vectors of locally aggregated descriptors (VLAD) [10]. This is followed by intra- and L2-normalization to form a 16384-dim video-level descriptor.

Early fusion consists of concatenating the fc6 and conv5 features for input to a single multi-class linear SVM classifier [5] (see Fig. 2). Late fusion consists of feeding the features to two separate SVM classifiers and computing a weighted average of their probabilities. The optimal weights are selected by grid-search.

4   Experiments

The goal of our experiments is two-fold. First, to explore the various design options described in Sect. 3 Methodology. Second, to show that our depth2action framework is complementary to standard approaches to large-scale action recognition based on appearance and translational motion and achieves state-of-the-art results when combined with them.

4.1   Datasets

We perform experiments on three widely-used publicly-available action recognition benchmark datasets, UCF101 [33], HMDB51 [16], and ActivityNet [8].

UCF101 is composed of realistic action videos from YouTube. It contains 13320 videos in 101 action classes. It is one of the most popular benchmark datasets because of its diversity in terms of actions and the presence of large variations in camera motion, object appearance and pose, object scale, viewpoint, cluttered background, illumination conditions, etc. **HMDB51** is composed of 6766 videos in 51 action classes extracted from a wide range of sources. It contains both original videos as well as stabilized ones, but we only use the original videos. Both UCF101 and HMDB51 have a standard three split evaluation protocol and we report the average recognition accuracy over the three training and test splits. As suggested by the authors in [8], we use **ActivityNet** release 1.2 for our experiments due to the noisy crowdsourced labels in release 1.1. The second release consists of 4819 training, 2383 validation, and 2480 test videos in 100 activity classes. Though the number of videos and classes are similar to UCF101, ActivityNet is a much more challenging benchmark because it has greater intra-class variance and consists of longer, untrimmed videos. The evaluation metric we used in this paper is top-1 accuracy for all three datasets.

4.2   Implementation Details

We use the Caffe toolbox [12] to implement the ConvNets. The network weights are learned using mini-batch stochastic gradient descent (256 frames for two-stream ConvNets and 30 clips for 3D ConvNets) with momentum (set to 0.9).

Depth Two-Stream: We adapt the VGG-16 architecture [32] and use ImageNet models as the initialization for both the depth-spatial and depth-temporal net training. As in [44], we adopt data augmentation techniques such as corner cropping, multi-scale cropping, horizontal flipping, etc. to help prevent overfitting, as well as high dropout ratios (0.9 and 0.8 for the fully connected layers). The input to the depth-spatial net is the per-frame depth maps, while the input to the depth-temporal net is either the depth difference between adjacent frames (in the baseline case) or the MDMMs. For generating the MDMMs, we set N in Eq. 1 to 10 frames as a subvolume. For the depth-spatial net, the learning rate decreases from 0.001 to 1/10 of its value every 15K iterations, and the training stops after 66K iterations. For the depth-temporal net, the learning rate starts at 0.005, decreases to 1/10 of its value every 20K iterations, and the training stops after 100K iterations.

Depth-C3D: We adopt the same architecture as in [37]. The Depth-C3D net is pre-trained on the Sports-1M dataset [13] and fine-tuned on estimated depth sequences. During fine-tuning, the learning rate is initialized to 0.005, decreased to 1/10 of its value every 8K iterations, and the training stops after 34K iterations. Dropout is applied with a ratio of 0.5.

Note that since the number of training videos in the HMDB51 dataset is relatively small, we use ConvNets fine-tuned on UCF101, except for the last layer, as the initialization (for both 2D and 3D ConvNets). The fine-tuning stage starts with a learning rate of 10^{-5} and converges in one epoch.

4.3   Results

Effectiveness of STDN: Table 1(a) shows the performance gains due to our proposed normalization. STDN improves recognition performance for all approaches on all datasets. The gain is typically around 1–2 %. We set the normalization window (n in Sect. 3.2) to 16 frames for UCF101 and ActivityNet, and 8 frames for HMDB51. We further observe that (i) Depth-C3D benefits from STDN more than depth two-stream. This is possibly because the input to depth-C3D is a 3D volume of depth sequences while the input to depth two-stream is the individual depth maps. Temporal consistency is important for the 3D volume. (ii) Depth-temporal benefits from STDN more than depth-spatial. This is expected since the goal of the normalization is to improve the temporal

Table 1. Recognition performance of our proposed configurations on three benchmark datasets. (a): Our spatio-temporal depth normalization (STDN) indicated by (N) is shown to improve performance for all configurations on all datasets. (b): Using the ConvNets to extract features is better than using them as end-to-end classifiers. Also, early fusion of features is better than late fusion of SVM probabilities. See the text for discussion on depth two-stream versus depth-C3D

(a) Effectiveness of STDN

Model	UCF101	HMDB51	ActivityNet
Depth-Spatial	58.8%	37.9%	35.9%
Depth-Spatial (N)	59.1%	38.3%	36.4%
Depth-Temporal Baseline	61.8%	40.6%	38.2%
Depth-Temporal Baseline (N)	63.3%	42.0%	39.8%
Depth-Temporal	63.9%	42.6%	39.7%
Depth-Temporal (N)	65.1%	43.5%	40.9%
Depth Two-Stream	65.6%	44.2%	42.7%
Depth Two-Stream (N)	**67.0%**	**45.4%**	44.2%
Depth-C3D	61.7%	40.9%	45.9%
Depth-C3D (N)	63.8%	42.8%	**47.4%**

(b) Features or End-to-End Classifier

Model	UCF101	HMDB51	ActivityNet
Depth Two-Stream	67.0%	45.4%	44.2%
Depth Two-Stream fc6	68.2%	46.5%	45.3%
Depth Two-Stream conv5	70.1%	48.2%	47.0%
Depth Two-Stream Early	**72.5%**	**49.7%**	49.6%
Depth Two-Stream Late	70.9%	48.9%	48.7%
Depth-C3D	63.8%	42.8%	47.4%
Depth-C3D fc6	64.9%	43.9%	47.9%
Depth-C3D conv5b	66.7%	45.0%	49.1%
Depth-C3D Early	69.5%	46.6%	**52.1%**
Depth-C3D Late	67.8%	45.7%	51.0%

consistency of the depth sequences and only the depth-temporal stream "sees" multiple depth-maps at a time. From now on, all results are based on depth sequences that have been normalized.

Depth Two-Stream versus Depth-C3D: As shown in Table 1(a), depth two-stream performs better than depth-C3D for UCF101 and HMDB51, while the opposite is true for ActivityNet. This suggests that depth-C3D may be more suitable for large-scale video analysis. Though the second release of ActivityNet has a similar number of action clips as UCF101, in general, the video duration is much (30 times) longer than that of UCF101. Similar results for 3D ConvNets versus 2D ConvNets was observed in [21]. The computational efficiency of depth-C3D also makes it more suitable for large-scale analysis. Although our depth-temporal net is much faster than the RGB-temporal net (which requires costly optical flow computation), depth-two stream is still significantly slower than depth-C3D. We therefore recommend using depth-C3D for large-scale applications.

ConvNets for Feature Extraction versus End-to-End Classification: Table 1(b) shows that treating the ConvNets as feature extractors performs significantly better than using them for end-to-end classification. This agrees with the observations of others [2,37,54]. We further observe that the VLAD encoded conv5 features perform better than fc6. This improvement is likely due to the additional discriminative power provided by the spatial information embedded in the convolutional layers. Another attractive property of using feature representations is that we can manipulate them in various ways to further improve the performance. For instance, we can employ different (i) encoding methods: Fisher vector [25], VideoDarwin [6]; (ii) normalization techniques: rank normalization [18]; and (iii) pooling methods: line pooling [54], trajectory pooling [43,54], etc.

Early versus Late Fusion: Table 1(b) also shows that early fusion of features through concatenation performs better than late fusion of SVM probabilities. Late fusion not only results in a performance drop of around 1.0% but also requires a more complex processing pipeline since multiple SVM classifiers need to be trained. UCF101 benefits from early fusion more than the other two datasets. This might be due to the fact that UCF101 is a trimmed video dataset and so the content of individual videos varies less than in the other two datasets. Early fusion of multiple layers' activations is typically more robust to noisy data.

Depth2Action: We thus settle on our proposed depth2action framework. For medium-scale video datasets like UCF101 and HMDB51, we perform early fusion of conv5 and fc6 features extracted using a depth two-stream configuration. For large-scale video datasets like ActivityNet, we perform early fusion of conv5b and fc6 features extracted using a depth-C3D configuration. These two models are shown in Fig. 2.

4.4   Discussion

Class-Specific Results: We investigate the specific classes for which depth information is important. To do this, we compare the per-class performance of our depth2action framework with standard methods that use appearance and translational motion in the RGB domain. We first compute the performances of an RGB-spatial stream which takes the RGB video frames as input and an RGB-temporal stream which takes optical flow (computed in the RGB domain) as input. We then identify the classes for which our depth2action performs better than both the RGB-spatial and RGB-temporal streams. We compute these results for the first split of the UCF101 dataset. Figure 4a shows the 20 classes for which our depth2action framework performs best (in order of

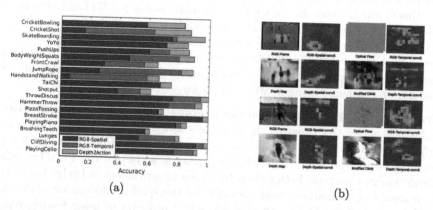

(a)   (b)

Fig. 4. (a) Recognition results on the first split of UCF101. Plot showing the classes for which our proposed depth2action framework (yellow) outperforms RGB-spatial (blue) and RGB-temporal (green) streams. (b) Visualizing the convolutional feature maps of four models: RGB-spatial, RGB-temporal, depth-spatial, and depth-temporal. Pairs of inputs and resulting feature maps are shown for each model for two actions, "CriketBowling" and "ThrowDiscus". This figure is best viewed in color (Color figure online)

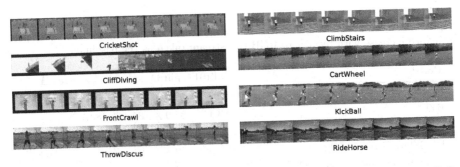

Fig. 5. Sample video frames of action classes that benefit from depth information. Left: UCF101. Right: HMDB51. This figure is best viewed in color (Color figure online)

decreasing improvement). For example, for the class CricketShot, RGB-spatial achieves an accuracy of around 0.18, RGB-temporal achieves around 0.62, while our depth2action achieves around 0.88. (For those classes where RGB-spatial performs better than RGB-temporal, we simply do not show the performance of RGB-temporal.) Depth2action clearly represents a complementary approach especially for classes where the RGB-spatial and RGB-temporal streams perform relatively poorly such as CriketBowling, CriketShot, FrontCrawl, HammerThrow, and HandStandWalking. Recall from Fig. 1 that CriketBowling and CriketShot are very similar with respect to appearance and translational motion. These are shown the be the two classes for which depth2action provides the most improvement, achieving respectable accuracies of above 0.8.

Sample video frames from classes in the UCF101 (left) and HMDB51 (right) datasets which benefit from depth information are show in Fig. 5 (see supplemental materials for more samples).

Visualizing Depth2Action: We visualize the convolutional feature maps (conv5) to better understand how depth2action encodes depth information and how this encoding is different from that of RGB two-stream models. Figure 4b shows pairs of inputs and resulting feature maps for four models: RGB-spatial, RGB-temporal, depth-spatial, and depth-temporal. (The feature maps are displayed using a standard heat map in which warmer colors indicate larger values.) The top four pairs are for "CriketBowling" and bottom four pairs are for "ThrowDiscus" (see supplemental materials for more action classes).

In general, the depth feature maps are sparser and more accurate than the RGB feature maps, especially for the temporal streams. The depth-spatial stream correctly encodes the bowler and the batter in "CriketBowling" and the discus thrower in "ThrowDiscus" as being salient while the RGB-stream gets distracted by other parts of the scene. The depth-temporal stream clearly identifies the progression of the bowler into the scene in "CriketBowling" and the movement of the discus thrower's leg into the scene in "ThrowDiscus" as being salient while the RGB-temporal stream is distracted by translational movement throughout the scene. These results demonstrate that our proposed depth2action

Table 2. Comparison of RGB two-stream, IDT computed from RGB video, and depth2action, and their combinations for the UCF101 dataset. Δ indicates the performance increase with respect to RGB two-stream taken as the baseline

Model	split01	split02	split03	Average	Δ
RGB Two-Stream baseline	90.8 %	92.0 %	91.3 %	91.4 %	0
IDT	83.1 %	85.9 %	85.1 %	84.7 %	-
Depth2Action	71.9 %	73.0 %	72.5 %	72.5 %	-
RGB Two-Stream+IDT	91.9 %	92.6 %	91.8 %	92.1 %	0.8 %
RGB Two-Stream+Depth2Action	91.7 %	92.5 %	91.8 %	92.0 %	0.7 %
Depth2Action+IDT	84.3 %	86.6 %	86.4 %	85.8 %	-
RGB Two-Stream+Depth2Action+IDT	92.5 %	93.8 %	92.8 %	93.0 %	1.8 %

approach does indeed focus on the correct regions in classes for which depth is important.

What About IDT? We compare our depth2action framework with improved dense trajectories (IDT) computed from RGB video. IDT has been shown to be the best hand-crafted features for action recognition [39]. It is known to perform well under various camera motions (e.g. pan, tilt and zoom) and zoom can be considered global depth change.

While the top part of Table 2 shows that IDT outperforms depth2action, which is not surprising due to how noisy our estimated depth maps are, we turn our attention to the performance obtained by combining these two approaches with an RGB two-stream model. Rows four and five show that the performance achieved by combining depth2action with RGB two-stream is on par with the combination of IDT with RGB two-stream (and both perform significantly better than IDT). The last column shows the improvement over RGB two-stream alone. This demonstrates that although depth2action is not as effective as IDT when taken alone, *it is as complementary to RGB two-stream as IDT.* This point is even more significant given the fact that IDT requires several orders of magnitude more computation time and storage space (mainly to extract and store the features) than depth2action. The combination of depth2action and RGB two-stream is much preferred over that of IDT and RGB two-stream for large-scale analysis. The last row of Table 2 shows the results of combining all three approaches. We again get an improvement. This result turns out to be state-of-the-art for this dataset and stresses the importance and complementarity of jointly exploiting appearance, translational motion, and depth for action recognition.

4.5   Comparison with State-of-the-Art

Table 3 compares our approach with a large number of recent state-of-the-art published results on the three benchmarks. For UCF101 and HMDB51, the reported performance is the mean recognition accuracy over the standard three splits. The last row shows the performance of combining depth2action with RGB

Table 3. Comparison with the state-of-the-art. * indicates the results are from our implementation of the method. Two-stream and C3D here is RGB based

Algorithm	UCF101	Algorithm	HMDB51	Algorithm	ActivityNet
Srivastava et al. [35]	84.3%	Srivastava et al. [35]	44.1%	Wang and Schmid [39]	61.3%*
Wang and Schmid [39]	85.9%	Oneata et al. [25]	54.8%	Simonyan and Zisserman [31]	67.1%*
Simonyan and Zisserman [31]	88.0%	Wang and Schmid [39]	57.2%	Tran et al. [37]	69.4%*
Jain et al. [9]	88.5%	Simonyan and Zisserman [31]	59.1%		
Ng et al. [24]	88.6%	Sun et al. [36]	59.1%		
Lan et al. [17]	89.1%	Jain et al. [9]	61.4%		
Zha et al. [52]	89.6%	Fernando et al. [6]	63.7%		
Tran et al. [37]	90.4%	Lan et al. [17]	65.1%		
Wu et al. [47]	91.3%	Wang et al. [43]	65.9%		
Wang et al. [43]	91.5%	Peng et al. [28]	66.8%		
Depth2Action	72.5%	Depth2Action	49.7%	Depth2Action	52.1%
+Two-Stream	92.0%	+Two-Stream	67.1%	+C3D	71.2%
+IDT+Two-Stream	**93.0%**	+IDT+Two-Stream	**68.2%**	+IDT+C3D	**73.4%**

two-stream for UCF101 and HMDB51, and RGB C3D for ActivityNet, and also IDT features. We achieve state-of-the-art results on all three datasets through this combination, again stressing the importance of appearance, motion, and depth for action recognition.

We note that since there are no published results[1] for release 1.2 of ActivityNet, we report the results from our implementations of IDT [39], RGB two-stream [31] and RGB C3D [37].

5   Conclusion

We introduced *depth2action*, the first investigation into depth for large-scale human action recognition where the depth cues are derived from the videos themselves rather than obtained using a depth sensor. This greatly expands the applicability of the method. Depth is estimated on a per-frame basis for efficiency and temporal consistency is enforced through a novel normalization step. Temporal depth information is captured using modified depth motion maps. A wide variety of design options are explored. Depth2action is shown to be complementary to standard approaches based on appearance and translational motion, and achieves state-of-the-art performance on three benchmark datasets when combined with them.

---

[1] The up-to-date leaderboard is at http://activity-net.org/evaluation.html.

In addition to advancing state-of-the-art performance, the depth2action framework is a rich research problem. It bridges the gap between the RGB- and RGB-D-based action recognition communities. It consists of numerous interesting sub-problems such as fine-grained action categorization, depth estimation from single images/video, learning from noisy data, etc. The estimated depth information could also be used for other applications such as object detection/segmentation, event recognition, and scene classification. We will make our trained models and estimated depth maps publicly available for future research.

Acknowledgements. This work was funded in part by a National Science Foundation CAREER grant, #IIS-1150115, and a seed grant from the Center for Information Technology in the Interest of Society (CITRIS). We gratefully acknowledge the support of NVIDIA Corporation through the donation of the Titan X GPU used in this work.

References

1. Baig, M.H., Torresani, L.: Coupled Depth Learning. In: WACV (2016)
2. Ballas, N., Yao, L., Pal, C., Courville, A.: Delving deeper into convolutional networks for learning video representations. In: ICLR (2016)
3. Chen, C., Liu, K., Kehtarnavaz, N.: Real-time human action recognition based on depth motion maps. J. Real-Time Image Process. **12**, 155–163 (2013)
4. Eigen, D., Fergus, R.: Predicting depth, surface normals and semantic labels with a common multi-scale convolutional architecture. In: ICCV (2015)
5. Fan, R.E., Chang, K.W., Hsieh, C.J., Wang, X.R., Lin, C.J.: LIBLINEAR: a library for large linear classification. J. Mach. Learn. Res. **9**, 1871–1874 (2008)
6. Fernando, B., Gavves, E., M., J.O., Ghodrati, A., Tuytelaars, T.: Modeling video evolution for action recognition. In: CVPR (2015)
7. He, K., Zhang, X., Ren, S., Sun, J.: Spatial pyramid pooling in deep convolutional networks for visual recognition. In: Fleet, D., Pajdla, T., Schiele, B., Tuytelaars, T. (eds.) ECCV 2014. LNCS, vol. 8691, pp. 346–361. Springer, Heidelberg (2014). doi:10.1007/978-3-319-10578-9_23
8. Heilbron, F.C., Escorcia, V., Ghanem, B., Niebles, J.C.: ActivityNet: a large-scale video benchmark for human activity understanding. In: CVPR (2015)
9. Jain, M., van Gemert, J.C., Snoek, C.G.M.: What do 15,000 object categories tell us about classifying and localizing actions? In: CVPR (2015)
10. Jegou, H., Perronnin, F., Douze, M., Sanchez, J., Perez, P., Schmid, C.: Aggregating local image descriptors into compact codes. TPAMI **34**, 1704–1716 (2012)
11. Ji, S., Xu, W., Yang, M., Yu, K.: 3D convolutional neural networks for human action recognition. TPAMI **35**, 221–231 (2012)
12. Jia, Y., Shelhamer, E., Donahue, J., Karayev, S., Long, J., Girshick, R., Guadarrama, S., Darrell, T.: Caffe: convolutional architecture for fast feature embedding. arXiv preprint arXiv:1408.5093 (2014)
13. Karpathy, A., Toderici, G., Shetty, S., Leung, T., Sukthankar, R., Fei-Fei, L.: Large-scale video classification with convolutional neural networks. In: CVPR (2014)
14. Kong, N., Black, M.J.: Intrinsic depth: improving depth transfer with intrinsic images. In: ICCV (2015)
15. Krizhevsky, A., Sutskever, I., Hinton, G.E.: Imagenet classification with deep convolutional neural networks. In: NIPS (2012)

16. Kuehne, H., Jhuang, H., Garrote, E., Poggio, T., Serre, T.: HMDB: a large video database for human motion recognition. In: ICCV (2011)
17. Lan, Z., Lin, M., Li, X., Hauptmann, A.G., Raj, B.: Beyond gaussian pyramid: multi-skip feature stacking for action recognition. In: CVPR (2015)
18. Lan, Z., Yu, S.I., Hauptmann, A.G.: Improving human activity recognition through ranking and re-ranking. arXiv preprint arXiv:1512.03740 (2015)
19. Li, W., Zhang, Z., Liu, Z.: Action recognition based on a bag of 3D points. In: CVPR (2010)
20. Liu, F., Shen, C., Lin, G.: Deep convolutional neural fields for depth estimation from a single image. In: CVPR (2015)
21. Liu, L., Zhou, Y., Shao, L.: DAP3D-Net: where, what and how actions occur in videos? arXiv preprint arXiv:1602.03346 (2016)
22. Liu, M., Salzmann, M., He, X.: Structured depth prediction in challenging monocular video sequences. arXiv preprint arXiv:1511.06070 (2015)
23. Ma, S., Bargal, S.A., Zhang, J., Sigal, L., Sclaroff, S.: Do less and achieve more: training CNNs for action recognition utilizing action images from the web. arXiv preprint arXiv:1512.07155 (2015)
24. Ng, J.Y.H., Hausknecht, M., Vijayanarasimhan, S., Vinyals, O., Monga, R., Toderici, G.: Beyond short snippets: deep networks for video classification. In: CVPR (2015)
25. Oneata, D., Verbeek, J., Schmid, C.: Action and event recognition with fisher vectors on a compact feature Set. In: ICCV (2013)
26. Oneata, D., Verbeek, J., Schmid, C.: The LEAR submission at THUMOS 2014 (2014)
27. Oreifej, O., Liu, Z.: HON4D: histogram of oriented 4D normals for activity recognition from depth sequences. In: CVPR (2013)
28. Peng, X., Zou, C., Qiao, Y., Peng, Q.: Action recognition with stacked fisher vectors. In: Fleet, D., Pajdla, T., Schiele, B., Tuytelaars, T. (eds.) ECCV 2014. LNCS, vol. 8693, pp. 581–595. Springer, Heidelberg (2014). doi:10.1007/978-3-319-10602-1_38
29. Raza, S.H., Javed, O., Das, A., Sawhney, H., Cheng, H., Essa, I.: Depth extraction from videos using geometric context and occlusion boundaries. In: BMVC (2014)
30. Russakovsky, O., Deng, J., Su, H., Krause, J., Satheesh, S., Ma, S., Huang, Z., Karpathy, A., Khosla, A., Bernstein, M., Berg, A.C., Fei-Fei, L.: Imagenet large scale visual recognition challenge. IJCV 115, 211–252 (2015)
31. Simonyan, K., Zisserman, A.: Two-stream convolutional networks for action recognition in videos. In: NIPS (2014)
32. Simonyan, K., Zisserman, A.: Very deep convolutional networks for large-scale image recognition. In: ICLR (2015)
33. Soomro, K., Zamir, A.R., Shah, M.: UCF101: a dataset of 101 human action classes from videos in the wild. In: CRCV-TR-12-01 (2012)
34. Sourimant, G.: A simple and efficient way to compute depth maps for multi-view videos. In: 3DTV-Conference (2010)
35. Srivastava, N., Mansimov, E., Salakhutdinov, R.: Unsupervised learning of video representations using LSTMs. In: ICML (2015)
36. Sun, L., Jia, K., Yeung, D.Y., Shi, B.E.: Human action recognition using factorized spatio-temporal convolutional networks. In: ICCV (2015)
37. Tran, D., Bourdev, L., Fergus, R., Torresani, L., Paluri, M.: Learning spatiotemporal features with 3D convolutional networks. In: ICCV (2015)

38. Vieiraa, A.W., Nascimentoa, E.R., Oliveiraa, G.L., Liuc, Z., Campos, M.F.: On the improvement of human action recognition from depth map sequences using space time occupancy patterns. Pattern Recogn. Lett. **36**, 221–227 (2014)
39. Wang, H., Schmid, C.: Action recognition with improved trajectories. In: ICCV (2013)
40. Wang, J., Liu, Z., Wu, Y.: Human Action Recognition with Depth Cameras. Springer, Heidelberg (2014)
41. Wang, J., Liu, Z., Chorowski, J., Chen, Z., Wu, Y.: Robust 3D action recognition with random occupancy patterns. In: Fitzgibbon, A., Lazebnik, S., Perona, P., Sato, Y., Schmid, C. (eds.) ECCV 2012. LNCS, vol. 7573, pp. 872–885. Springer, Heidelberg (2012)
42. Wang, J., Liu, Z., Wu, Y., Yuan, J.: Mining actionlet ensemble for action recognition with depth cameras. In: CVPR (2012)
43. Wang, L., Qiao, Y., Tang, X.: Action recognition with trajectory-pooled deep-convolutional descriptors. In: CVPR (2015)
44. Wang, L., Xiong, Y., Wang, Z., Qiao, Y.: Towards good practices for very deep two-stream convNets. arXiv preprint arXiv:1507.02159 (2015)
45. Wang, P., Li, W., Gao, Z., Tang, C., Zhang, J., Ogunbona, P.: Convnets-based action recognition from depth maps through virtual cameras and pseudocoloring. In: ACM MM (2015)
46. Wang, X., Farhadi, A., Gupta, A.: Actions transformations. In: CVPR (2016)
47. Wu, Z., Wang, X., Jiang, Y.G., Ye, H., Xue, X.: Modeling spatial-temporal clues in a hybrid deep learning framework for video classification. In: ACM MM (2015)
48. Xu, Z., Yang, Y., Hauptmann, A.G.: A discriminative CNN video representation for event detection. In: CVPR (2015)
49. Yang, X., Zhang, C., Tian, Y.: Recognizing actions using depth motion maps-based histograms of oriented gradients. In: ACM MM (2012)
50. Yang, X., Tian, Y.: Super normal vector for activity recognition using depth sequences. In: CVPR (2014)
51. Yu, G., Liu, Z., Yuan, J.: Discriminative orderlet mining for real-time recognition of human-object interaction. In: Cremers, D., Reid, I., Saito, H., Yang, M.-H. (eds.) ACCV 2014. LNCS, vol. 9007, pp. 50–65. Springer, Heidelberg (2015). doi:10.1007/978-3-319-16814-2_4
52. Zha, S., Luisier, F., Andrews, W., Srivastava, N., Salakhutdinov, R.: Exploiting image-trained CNN architectures for unconstrained video classification. In: BMVC (2015)
53. Zhang, G., Jia, J., Wong, T.T., Bao, H.: Consistent depth maps recovery from a video sequence. TPAMI **31**, 974–988 (2009)
54. Zhao, S., Liu, Y., Han, Y., Hong, R.: Pooling the convolutional layers in deep convnets for action recognition. arXiv preprint arXiv:1511.02126 (2015)

Cross-Dimensional Weighting for Aggregated Deep Convolutional Features

Yannis Kalantidis$^{(\boxtimes)}$, Clayton Mellina, and Simon Osindero

Computer Vision and Machine Learning Group Flickr, Yahoo, San Francisco, USA
ykal@yahoo-inc.com, clayton@yahoo-inc.com

Abstract. We propose a simple and straightforward way of creating powerful image representations via cross-dimensional weighting and aggregation of deep convolutional neural network layer outputs. We first present a generalized framework that encompasses a broad family of approaches and includes cross-dimensional pooling and weighting steps. We then propose specific non-parametric schemes for both spatial- and channel-wise weighting that boost the effect of highly active spatial responses and at the same time regulate burstiness effects. We experiment on different public datasets for image search and show that our approach outperforms the current state-of-the-art for approaches based on pre-trained networks. We also provide an easy-to-use, open source implementation that reproduces our results.

1 Introduction

Visual image search has been evolving rapidly in recent years with hand-crafted local features giving way to learning-based ones. Deep Convolutional Neural Networks (CNNs) were popularized by the seminal work of Krizhevsky *et al.* [19] and have been shown to "effortlessly" improve the state-of-the-art in multiple computer vision domains [29], beating many highly optimized, domain-specific approaches. It comes as no surprise that such features, based on deep networks, have recently also dominated the field of visual image search [3–5,29].

Many recent image search approaches are based on deep features, *e.g.*, Babenko *et al.* [4,5] and Razavian *et al.* [3,29] proposed different pooling strategies for such features and demonstrated state-of-the-art performance in popular benchmarks for *compact* image representations, *i.e.*, representations of up to a few hundred dimensions.

Motivated by these advances, in this paper we present a simple and straightforward way of creating powerful image representations via cross-dimensional weighting and aggregation. We place our approach in a general family of approaches for multidimensional aggregation and weighting and present a specific instantiation that we have thus far found to be most effective on benchmark tasks.

We base our cross-dimensional weighted features on a generic deep convolutional neural network. Since we aggregate outputs of convolutional layers before the fully connected ones, the data layer can be of arbitrary size [20]. We therefore avoid resizing and cropping the input image, allowing images of different

© Springer International Publishing Switzerland 2016
G. Hua and H. Jégou (Eds.): ECCV 2016 Workshops, Part I, LNCS 9913, pp. 685–701, 2016.
DOI: 10.1007/978-3-319-46604-0_48

aspect ratios to keep their spatial characteristics intact. After extracting deep convolutional features from the last spatial layer of a CNN, we apply weighting both spatially and per channel before sum-pooling to create a final aggregation. We denote features derived after such cross-dimensional weighting and pooling as *CroW* features.

Our contributions can be summarized as follows:

- We present a generalized framework that sketches a family of approaches for aggregation of convolutional features, including cross-dimensional weighting and pooling steps.
- We propose non-parametric weighting schemes for both spatial- and channel-wise weighting that boost the effect of highly active spatial responses and regulate the effect of channel burstiness respectively.
- We present state-of-the-art results on three public datasets for image search without any fine-tuning.

With a very small computational overhead, we are able to improve the state-of-the-art in visual image search. For the popular *Oxford* [26] and *Paris* [27] datasets, the mean average precision for our *CroW* feature is over 10 % higher than the previous state-of-the-art for compact visual representations. Additionally, our features are trivially combined for simple query expansion, enjoying even better performance. *We provide an easy-to-use, open source implementation that reproduces our results on GitHub[1].*

The paper is structured as follows: In Sect. 2 we present and discuss related work, while in Sect. 3 we present a general framework for weighted pooling to orient past work and our own explorations. In Sect. 4 we describe two complimentary feature weighting schemes, and we present experimental results for visual search in Sect. 5. The paper concludes with Sect. 6.

2   Related Work

Until recently, the vast majority of image search approaches were variants of the bag-of-words model [32] and were based on local features, typically SIFT [21]. Successful extensions include soft assignment [27], spatial matching [2,26], query expansion [1,6,7,35], better descriptor normalization [1], feature selection [36,38], feature burstiness [15] and very large vocabularies [22]. All the aforementioned strategies perform very well for object retrieval but are very hard to scale, as each image is represented by hundreds of patches, causing search time and memory to suffer.

The community therefore recently turned towards global image representations. Starting from local feature aggregation strategies like VLAD [16] or Fisher Vectors [24] multiple successful extensions have arisen [9,12,33,34], slowly increasing the performance of such aggregated features and closing the gap between global and bag-of-word representations for image search. Triangulation embedding with democratic aggregation [17] was shown to give state-of-the-art results for SIFT-based architectures, while handling problems related to

---

[1] https://github.com/yahoo/crow.

burstiness and interactions between unrelated descriptors prior to aggregation. Recently, Murray and Perronnin [23] generalized max-pooling from bag-of-words to Fisher Vector representations achieving high performance in search as well as classification tasks.

After the seminal work of Krizhevsky *et al.* [19], image search, along with the whole computer vision community, embraced the power of deep learning architectures. Out-of-the-box features from pre-trained Convolutional Neural Networks (CNNs) were shown to effortlessly give state-of-the-art results in many computer vision tasks, including image search [29].

Among the first to more extensively study CNN-based codes for image search were Babenko *et al.* [5] and Razavian *et al.* [3,29]. They experimented with aggregation of responses from different layers of the CNN, both fully connected and convolutional. They introduced a basic feature aggregation pipeline using max-pooling that, in combination with proper normalization and whitening was able to beat all aggregated local feature based approaches for low dimensional image codes. Gong *et al.* [10] used orderless VLAD pooling of CNN activations on multiple scales and achieved competitive results on classification and search tasks.

Very recently Tolias *et al.* [37] proposed max-pooling over multiple image regions sampled on the final convolutional layer. Their approach achieves state-of-the-art results and is complementary to our cross-dimensional weighting. Cimpoi *et al.* [8] also recently proposed using Fisher Vector aggregation of convolutional features for texture recognition. Their approach achieves great performace, it is however computationally demanding; PCA from 65 K dimensions alone requires multiplication with a very large matrix. Our approach is training- and parameter-free, with only a very small computational overhead.

In another very recent related work, Babenko and Lempitsky proposed the SPoC features [4] with slightly different design choices from the pipeline of [5] and sum- instead of max-pooling. As the latter approach is very related to ours, we discuss the differences of the two approaches in the following sections and explain SPoC in terms of the proposed aggregation framework.

The first approaches that *learn* features for landmark retrieval [11,28] are presented at the current ECCV conference. Both approaches use clean annotated data and fine-tune a deep CNN for feature extraction using a pairwise [28] or ranking [11] loss. These approaches are now state-of-the art in the most common benchmarks. Still, our proposed features are not far behind, without requiring training or clean annotated data.

3 Framework for Aggregation of Convolutional Features

3.1 Framework Overview

In this section we present a simple and straightforward way of creating powerful image representations. We start by considering a general family of approaches that can be summarized as proceeding through the following steps. Greater details and motivations for these steps will be given in subsequent sections, along with the specific instantiation that we have thus far found to be most effective on benchmark tasks.

1: Perform spatially-local pooling. Sum-pooling or max-pooling over a spatially local neighborhood within each channel of a convolutional layer, with neighborhood size $w \times h$ and stride s. Some limiting cases include: (1) a pooling neighborhood that occupies the full spatial extent of each channel (i.e. global pooling); and (2) a 1×1 pooling neighborhood (effectively not doing pooling at all). After pooling, we have a three-dimensional tensor of activities.

2: Compute spatial weighting factors. For each location (i, j) in the locally pooled feature maps we assign a weight, α_{ij}, that is applied to each channel at that location.

3: Compute channel weighting factors. For each channel k, we assign a weight, β_k that is applied to each location in that channel.

4: Perform weighted-sum aggregation. We apply the previously derived weights location-wise and channel-wise before using a channel-wise sum to aggregate the full tensor of activities into a single vector.

5: Perform vector normalization. The resulting vector is then normalized and power-transformed. A variety of norms can be used here.

6: Perform dimensionality reduction. We then reduce the dimensionality of the normed-vector. PCA is a typical choice here, and we may also choose to perform whitening or other per-dimension scalings on entries of the dimensionality reduced vector.

7: Perform final normalization. We then apply a second and final normalization step.

Algorithm 1 summarises these steps as pseudocode.

Algorithm 1. Framework for Aggregation of Convolutional Features

---

input : 3d feature tensor $\mathcal{X}$, pooling nhood size $w \times h$, stride s, and type p, spatial weight generation function, Ω_s, channel weight generation function, Ω_c, initial norm type, a, and power scaling, b, pre-trained whitening parameters W, final feature dimensionality K', final norm type, c

output: K'-dimensional aggregate feature vector $\mathcal{G} = \{g_1, \ldots, g_K\}$

1   $\tilde{\mathcal{X}} = \text{pool}(\mathcal{X}; w, h, s, p)$ // Initial local pooling

2   $\Omega_s(\tilde{\mathcal{X}}) \to \alpha_{ij} \; \forall \, i, j$ // Spatial weighting

3   $\Omega_c(\tilde{\mathcal{X}}) \to \beta_k \; \forall \, k$ // Channel weighting

4   $f_k = \sum_{i=1}^{W} \sum_{j=1}^{H} \alpha_{ij} \beta_k \mathcal{X}_{kij} \; \forall \, k$

5   $\widehat{\mathcal{F}} = \text{pnorm}(\mathcal{F}; a, b)$ // Normalize and powerscale

6   $\widetilde{\mathcal{F}} = \text{PCA}(\widehat{\mathcal{F}}; W, K')$ // dim. reduction and whitening

7   $\mathcal{G} = \text{norm}(\widetilde{\mathcal{F}}, c)$ // Normalize again

---

3.2 Cross-Dimensional Weighting

Let $\mathcal{X} \in \mathbb{R}^{(K \times W \times H)}$ be the 3-dimensional *feature* tensor from a selected layer l, where K is the total number of channels and W, H the spatial dimensions

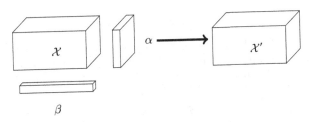

Fig. 1. Prior to aggregation, the convolutional features can be weighted channel-wise by a weight vector β and weighted location-wise by a weight matrix α such that $\mathcal{X}'_{kij} = \alpha_{ij}\beta_k\mathcal{X}_{kij}$. The weighted features $\mathcal{X}'$ are sum-pooled to derive an aggregate feature.

of that layer. As mentioned above, the spatial dimensions may vary per image depending on its original size, but we omit image-specific subscripts here for clarity.

We denote the entry in $\mathcal{X}$ corresponding to channel k, at spatial location (i, j) as $\mathcal{X}_{kij}$. For notational convenience, we also denote the channel-wise matrices of $\mathcal{X}$ as $\mathcal{C}^{(k)}$, where $\mathcal{C}^{(k)}_{ij} = \mathcal{X}_{kij}$. Similarly, we use $\boldsymbol{\lambda}^{(ij)}$ to denote the vector of channel responses at location (i, j), where $\lambda^{(ij)}_k = \mathcal{X}_{kij}$.

A weighted feature tensor $\mathcal{X}'$ is produced by applying per-location weights, α_{ij}, and per-channel weights, β_k, to feature tensor $\mathcal{X}$ as illustrated in Fig. 1:

$$\mathcal{X}'_{kij} = \alpha_{ij}\beta_k\mathcal{X}_{kij} \qquad (1)$$

The weighted feature tensor is aggregated by sum-pooling per channel. Let *aggregated feature* vector $\mathcal{F} = \{f_1, \ldots, f_k\}$ associated with the layer l be the vector of weight-summed activations per channel:

$$f_k = \sum_{i=1}^{W}\sum_{j=1}^{H} \mathcal{X}'_{kij} \qquad (2)$$

After aggregation, we follow what was shown to be the best practice [3,29] and L2-normalize $\mathcal{F}$, then whiten using parameters learnt from a separate dataset and L2-normalize again. We denote the features that are derived from the current framework as *Cross-dimensional Weighted* or *CroW* features.

4 Feature Weighting Schemes

In this section we present our non-parametric spatial and channel weighting for Steps 2 and 3 of the framework. We propose a spatial weighting derived from the spatial activations of the layer outputs themselves and a channel weighting derived from channel sparsity.

4.1   Response Aggregation for Spatial Weighting

We propose a method to derive a spatial weighting based on the normalized total response across all channels. Let $\boldsymbol{S}' \in \mathbb{R}^{(W \times H)}$ be the matrix of aggregated responses from all channels *per spatial location*, which we compute by *summing* feature maps $\boldsymbol{C}^{(k)}$:

$$\boldsymbol{S}' = \sum_k \boldsymbol{C}^{(k)}. \tag{3}$$

After normalization and power-scaling we get aggregated spatial response map $\boldsymbol{S}$, whose value at spatial location (i,j) is given by:

$$\mathcal{S}_{ij} = \left(\frac{S'_{ij}}{\left(\sum_{m,n} {S'_{mn}}^a \right)^{1/a}} \right)^{1/b}, \tag{4}$$

After computing the 2d spatial aggregation map $\boldsymbol{S}$ for feature $\boldsymbol{X}$, we can apply it independently on every channel, setting $\alpha_{ij} = \mathcal{S}_{ij}$ and using α_{ij} as in Eq. 1.

We experimented with different norms for normalizing the aggregate responses $\boldsymbol{S}'$, *i.e.*, L1, L2, *inf*, power normalization with $a = 0.5$ [25]. We found that image search performance remains very high in all cases and the differences are very small, usually less than 0.01 in mAP. We therefore choose to use the L2 norm and $b = 2$ for our spatial aggregation maps, before applying them to the features.

We visualize highly weighted spatial locations in Fig. 3 with images from the *Paris* [27] dataset. Our spatial weighting boosts features at locations with salient visual content and down weights non-salient locations. Notably, similar visual elements are boosted under our weighting despite large variation in lighting and perspective.

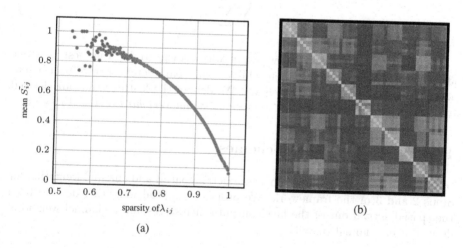

(a)

(b)

Fig. 2. Mean $\tilde{S}_{ij}$ plotted against channel sparsity at the corresponding location. The correlation of channel-wise sparsity for the 55 images in the query-set of the *Paris* dataset. Images are sorted by landmark class in both dimensions.

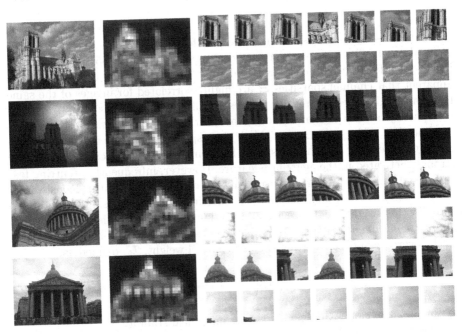

Fig. 3. Visualization of spatial weighting by aggregate response. On the left we show original images in the *Paris* dataset along with their spatial weights. On the right we visualize the receptive fields of the 7 highest weighted locations and the 7 lowest weighted locations for each image. The top two images are of Notre Dame and the bottom two are of the Panthéon.

In Fig. 2a we show the relationship between our spatial weights S_{ij} and the sparsity of the channel responses $\boldsymbol{\lambda}^{(ij)}$. We compute the spatial weight S_{ij} of every location in the *Paris* dataset and normalize each by the maximum spatial weight for the image in which it occurs, which we denote $\tilde{S}_{ij}$. The mean $\tilde{S}_{ij}$ for each level of channel sparsity at the corresponding location is plotted as cyan in Fig. 2a.

It can be seen that our spatial weighting tends to boost locations for which multiple channels are active relative to other spatial locations of the same image. This suggests that our spatial weighting is a non-parametric and computationally cheap way to favor spatial locations for which features co-occur while also accounting for the strength of feature responses. We speculate that these locations are more discriminative as there are combinatorially more configurations at mid-ranges of sparsity.

4.2 Sparsity Sensitive Channel Weighting

We now propose a method to derive a channel weighting based on the sparsity of feature maps. We expect that similar images will have similar occurrence rates for a given feature. For each channel k we find $\mathcal{Q}_k$, the proportion of non-zero responses, and compute the *per-channel sparsity*, Ξ_k, as:

$$\Xi_k = 1 - \mathcal{Q}_k, \tag{5}$$

where $\mathcal{Q} = \frac{1}{WH} \sum_{ij} \mathbb{1}[\boldsymbol{\lambda}^{(ij)} > 0]$. In Fig. 2b we visualize the pair-wise correlation of the vectors of channel sparsities $\boldsymbol{\Xi} \in \mathbb{R}^K$ for images in the query-set of the *Paris* dataset. The query-set for the *Paris* dataset contains 55 images total, 5 images each for 11 classes of Paris landmarks. We order the images by class. It is apparent that channel sparsities $\boldsymbol{\Xi}$ are highly correlated for images of the same landmark and less correlated for images of different landmarks. It appears that the sparsity pattern of channels contains discriminative information.

Since we sum-pool features $\boldsymbol{\lambda}^{(ij)}$ over spatial locations when we derive our aggregated feature, channels with frequent feature occurrences are already strongly activated in the aggregate feature. However, infrequently occurring features could provide important signal if, for example, the feature consistently occurs though only a small number of times in images of the same class. Motivated by this insight, we devise a channel weighting scheme similar to the concept of *inverse document frequency*. That is, we boost the contribution of rare features in the overall response by using the per-channel weight, $\mathcal{I}_k$, defined as:

$$\mathcal{I}_k = \log\left(\frac{K\epsilon + \sum_h \mathcal{Q}_h}{\epsilon + \mathcal{Q}_k}\right), \tag{6}$$

where ϵ is a small constant added for numerical stability.

Our sparsity sensitive channel weighting is also related to and motivated by the notion of intra-image visual burstiness [15]. Channels with low sparsity correspond to filters that give non-zero responses in many image regions. This implies some spatially recurring visual elements in the image, that were shown to negatively affect matching [15]. Although we don't go as far as [17] and try to learn a "democratic" matching kernel, our sparsity sensitive weights do down-weight channels of such bursty convolutional filters.

To provide further insight into the effect of our sparsity-sensitive channel weights (SSW), we visualize the receptive fields of active locations in channels that our weights boost.

Fig. 4. Regions corresponding to locations that contribute (are non-zero) to the 10 channels with the highest sparsity-sensitive weights for the four images of Fig. 3.

In Fig. 4 we show all receptive fields that are non-zero in (one or more) of the channels with the highest sparsity-sensitive channel weights. As values from these channels are increased before aggregation, our approach gives more weight to CNN outputs that correspond to the image regions shown on the right.

4.3 Discussion

Using the framework described in Sect. 3, we can explain different approaches in terms of their pooling, weighting and aggregation steps; we illustrate some interesting cases in Table 1. For example, approaches that aggregate the output of a max-pooling layer of the convolutional neural network are essentially performing max-pooling in Step 1.

In terms of novelty, it is noteworty to restate that the spatial weighting presented in Sect. 4.1 corresponds to a well known principle, and approaches like [8,17,23] have addressed similar ideas. Our spatial weighting is notable as a simple and strong baseline. Together with the channel weighting, the $CroW$ features are able to deliver state-of-the-art results at practically the same computational cost as off-the-self features.

Uniform Weighting. If we further uniformly set both spatial and channel weights and then perform sum-pooling per channel we end up with a simpler version of $CroW$ features, that we denote as *uniform CroW* or *uCroW*.

Relation to SPoC [4] Features. SPoC [4] can be described in terms of our framework as illustrated in Table 1. $CroW$ and SPoC features differ in their spatial pooling, spatial weighting, and channel weighting. For the first spatially-local pooling step, $CroW$ (and $uCroW$) max-pool (we are essentially using the outputs of the last pooling layer of the deep convolutional network rather than the last convolutional one as in SPoC). SPoC uses a centering prior for spatial weighting to boost features that occur near the center of the image, whereas we propose a spatial weighting derived from the spatial activations of the layer outputs themselves. Lastly, SPoC uses a uniform channel weighting, whereas we propose a channel weighting derived from channel sparsity. We demonstrate improvements for each of these design choices in Sect. 5.

Table 1. The pooling and weighting steps for three instantiations of our aggregation framework, *i.e.*, the proposed $CroW$, the simplified $uCroW$ and SPoC [4]. SW refers to the spatial weighting presented in 4.1, while SSW to the sparsity sensitive channel weighting presented in Sect. 4.2.

Step	SPoC [4]	$uCroW$	$CroW$
1: local pooling	None	Max	Max
2: spatial weighting	Centering prior	Uniform	SW
3: channel weighting	Uniform	Uniform	SSW
4: aggregation	Sum	Sum	Sum

5 Experiments

5.1 Evaluation Protocol

Datasets. We experiment on four publicly available datasets. For image search we report results on *Oxford* [26] and *Paris* [27], further combining them with the *Oxford100k* [26] dataset as distractors. We also present results on the *Holidays* [14] dataset. For Oxford we used the common protocol as in all other methods reported, *i.e.* the cropped queries. We regard the cropped region as input for the CNN and extract features. For Holidays we use the "upright" version of the images.

Evaluation Metrics. For image search experiments on *Oxford, Paris* and *Holidays* we measure mean average precision (mAP) over all queries. We use the evaluation code provided by the authors. For deep neural networks we use Caffe[2] [18] and the publicly available pre-trained VGG16 model [31]. As usual with Caffe, we zero-center the input image by *mean pixel subtraction*. In all cases, table rows including citations present results reported in the cited papers.

Query Expansion. One can trivially use simple query expansion techniques [7] with *CroW* features. Given the ranked list of database images by ascending distance to the query, we sum the aggregated feature vectors of the top M results, L2-normalize and re-query once again. Despite its simplicity, we show that this consistently improves performance, although it does come at the cost of one extra query.

5.2 Preliminary Experiments

Image Size and Layer Selection. In Fig. 5a we investigate the performance of *uCroW* features when aggregating responses from different layers of the network.

   Our *uCroW* features are in essence similar to the very recently proposed SPoC features of [4], but have some different design choices that make them more generic and powerful. Firstly, SPoC features are derived from the VGG19 model while our *uCroW* features are derived from the VGG16 model; in this section we show that our *uCroW* features performs much better even if we are using a smaller deep network. Secondly, we do not resize the input image to 586×586 as in [4] and instead keep it at its original size. SPoC is therefore comparable to the dotted cyan line in Fig. 5a.

   Choosing the last pooling and convolutional layers of the network significantly improves performance over the fourth, especially as the final dimension decreases. Moreover, the `pool5` layer consistently outperforms `conv5-3`, showing that max pooling in Step 1 is indeed beneficial.

   Regarding image size, we see that keeping the original size of the images is another factor that contributes to higher performance.

---

[2] http://caffe.berkeleyvision.org/.

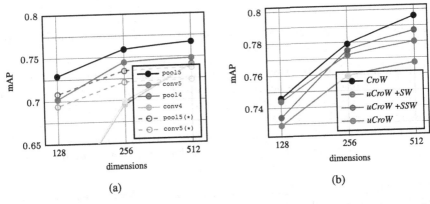

Fig. 5. Mean average precision on Paris. Different lines denote $uCroW$ features from the corresponding layers of VGG16; conv4 (conv5) corresponds to conv4_3 (conv5_3). Solid lines denote that the original image size is kept, while for dashed lines the images were resized to 586×586 as in [4]. Both conv4 and pool4 layers have very poor performance in low dimensions, with 0.58 mAP for $d = 128$. SPoC features [4] correspond to the dotted cyan line. Mean average precision on *Paris* when varying the dimensionality of the final features.

Effect of the Final Feature Dimensionality. In Fig. 5b we present mAP on *Paris* when varying the dimensionality of the final features. We present results for all weighting combinations of the proposed approach. $uCroW$ refers to uniform or no weighting. $uCroW +SW$ refers to using the only the spatial weighting of Sect. 4.1 on top of $uCroW$, $uCroW +SSW$ to using the sparsity sensitive channel weighting of Sect. 4.2 on top of $uCroW$, while $CroW$ refers to our complete approach with both weighting schemes. As we see, the $uCroW +SSW$ combination is affected more by dimensionality reduction than the rest. This can be interpreted as an effect of the subsequent dimensionality reduction. When calculating the sparsity sensitive weights all dimensions are taken into account, however, in the final reduced vector many of those were discarded.

Notes on Max-pooling. In preliminary experiments we also tested max-pooling instead of sum pooling for feature aggregation. Consistently with [4] we found it to be always inferior to sum-pooling when whitening was used.

Table 2. Mean average precision on Paris when learning the whitening parameters on Oxford, Holidays and Oxford100k for different values of d.

d		Oxford	Holidays	Oxford100k
512	$uCroW$	0.786	0.752	0.803
	$CroW$	0.797	0.792	**0.810**
256	$uCroW$	0.739	0.728	0.732
	$CroW$	**0.765**	0.784	0.762

Interestingly, max pooling performs better than sum-pooling in the non-whitened space, but mAP without whitening the features is much inferior (sometimes more than 10 % less) in all datasets tested.

Whitening. We learn the whitening parameters from a separate set of images. In Table 2 we present results on the *Paris* dataset when using 3 other datasets for whitening: the semantically related *Oxford* dataset, the *Holidays* dataset and the larger *Oxford100k* dataset. As we reduce the dimensionality, we see overfitting effects for the case where we learn on *Oxford* and this comes as no surprise: as dimensions are reduced, more dimensions that are selective for buildings are

Table 3. Mean average precision on *Paris*, *Oxford* and *Holidays* against the state-of-the-art for different values of d. QE denotes query expansion with the top $M = 10$ results. The fourth (sixth) column presents results when augmenting the *Paris* (*Oxford*) dataset with the 100 k distractors from *Oxford100k*. Results in the lowest set of rows correspond to methods with local features, followed by spatial verification.

Method	d	Paris	+Oxf100k	Oxford	+Oxf100k	Holidays
Tr. Embedding [17]	1024	—	—	0.560	0.502	0.720
Tr. Embedding [17]	512	—	—	—	—	0.700
Gong *et al.* [5]	512	—	—	—	—	0.783
Neural Codes [5]	512	—	—	0.435	0.392	—
R-MAC [37]	512	**0.830**	**0.757**	0.669	0.616	—
uCroW	512	0.786	0.710	0.697	0.641	0.839
CroW	512	0.797	0.722	**0.708**	**0.653**	**0.851**
Tr. Embedding [17]	256	—	—	—	—	0.657
Neural Codes [5]	256	—	—	0.435	0.392	0.749
Razavian *et al.* [30]	256	0.670	—	0.533	0.489	0.716
SPoC [4]	256	—	—	0.531	0.501	0.802
R-MAC [37]	256	0.729	0.601	0.561	0.470	—
uCroW	256	0.739	0.658	0.667	0.612	0.815
CroW	256	**0.765**	**0.691**	**0.684**	**0.637**	**0.851**
Tr. Embedding [17]	128	—	—	0.433	0.353	—
Neural Codes [5]	128	—	—	0.433	0.384	—
uCroW	128	0.699	0.610	0.625	0.559	—
CroW	128	**0.746**	**0.670**	**0.641**	**0.590**	**0.828**
CroW + QE	128	0.793	0.728	0.670	0.641	—
CroW + QE	256	0.815	0.753	0.718	0.676	—
CroW + QE	512	**0.848**	**0.794**	**0.749**	**0.706**	—
Tolias *et al.* [34]	—	0.770	—	0.804	0.750	—
Total Recall II [6]	—	0.805	0.710	0.827	0.767	—
Mikulik *et al.* [22]	—	0.824	0.773	0.849	0.795	—

kept when we learn the reduction parameters on a semantically similar dataset like *Oxford*.

To be directly comparable with related works, we learn the whitening parameters on *Oxford* when testing on *Paris* and vice versa, as accustomed. We use the *Oxford100k* dataset for whitening on the *Holidays*.

5.3   Image Search

In Table 3 we present comparisons of our approach with the state-of-the-art in image search on *Paris*, *Oxford* and *Holidays*. Both *uCroW* and *CroW* consistently outperform all other aggregation methods for different representation sizes, apart from R-MAC [37], which exhibits very high performance for Paris in 512 dimensions.

uCroW is a very strong baseline that gives state-of-the-art performance by itself. It therefore makes sense that improvement over *uCroW* is hard to get. *CroW* improves performance in all cases, with the gain increasing as the dimensionality of the final features decreases. For comparison, if we apply our weighting (instead of the centering prior) to SPoC features, the gain on *Paris* is around 3.9 % and 4.6 % for 256 and 512 dimensions respectively.

In Fig. 6 we present some interesting results *using just* $d = 32$ *dimensional features*. They demonstrate the invariance of *CroW* features to viewpoint and lighting variations even after heavy compression.

When further combining our approach with query expansion, we get even better results that compare to (or surpass on *Paris*) far more sophisticated approaches like [6,22,34] that are based on local features and include spatial verification steps.

In Fig. 7 we show the top-10 results for *all* 55 queries on the paris dataset using the uncompressed *CroW* features ($d = 512$). **We only have 3 false results in total** for precision@10. This illuminates why query expansion is so effective: the top ranked results are already of high quality.

Fig. 6. Sample search results using *CroW* features compressed to just $d = 32$ dimensions. The query image is shown at the leftmost side with the query bounding box marked in a red rectangle. (Color figure online)

Fig. 7. Top-10 results returned for all 55 queries of the Paris dataset, using the 512-dimensional *CroW* features (and no query expansion). The query image is shown on the leftmost place, with the query bounding box marked with a red rectangle. Our features produce just 3 false results in total, which are marked with an orange border. (Color figure online)

Although our approach is consistently better, the performance gap between *CroW* and the state-of-the-art is smaller in *Holidays*, where it outperforms the best competing method by about 4.9 % and 1.2 % for $d = 256, 512$, respectively.

6   Conclusions

In this paper we outline a generalized framework for aggregated deep convolutional features with cross-dimensional weighting which encompasses recent related works such as [4]. We propose simple, non-parametric weighting schemes for spatial- and channel-wise weighting and provide insights for their behavior by visualizing and studying the distributional properties of the layer output responses. Using this approach, we report results that outperform the state-of-the-art in popular image search benchmarks.

The *CroW* features are one instantiation of our generic aggregation framework. Still, it gives the current state-of-the-art results in image retrieval with minimal overhead and has intuitive qualities that offer insights on the nature of convolutional layer features.

Our aggregation framework is a valuable scaffold within which to discuss and explore new weighting schemes. The framework gave us a clear way to investigate channel and spatial weights independently. Learning weights for a particular task is a promising future direction. Likewise, with sufficient ground truth data, it is possible to fine-tune the entire end-to-end process within our proposed framework using, say, a rank-based loss as in [11,28], together with *attentional mechanisms* and spatial deformations [13].

References

1. Arandjelovic, R., Zisserman, A.: Three things everyone should know to improve object retrieval. In: CVPR (2012)
2. Avrithis, Y., Tolias, G.: Hough pyramid matching: speeded-up geometry re-ranking for large scale image retrieval. Int. J. Comput. Vision (IJCV), 1–19 (2013)
3. Azizpour, H., Razavian, A.S., Sullivan, J., Maki, A., Carlsson, S.: From generic to specific deep representations for visual recognition. In: DeepVision Workshop, CVPR (2015)
4. Babenko, A., Lempitsky, V.: Aggregating deep convolutional features for image retrieval. In: ICCV (2015)
5. Babenko, A., Slesarev, A., Chigorin, A., Lempitsky, V.: Neural codes for image retrieval. In: Fleet, D., Pajdla, T., Schiele, B., Tuytelaars, T. (eds.) ECCV 2014. LNCS, vol. 8689, pp. 584–599. Springer, Heidelberg (2014). doi:10.1007/978-3-319-10590-1_38
6. Chum, O., Mikulik, A., Perdoch, M., Matas, J.: Total recall II: query expansion revisited. In: CVPR (2011)
7. Chum, O., Philbin, J., Sivic, J., Isard, M., Zisserman, A.: Total recall: automatic query expansion with a generative feature model for object retrieval. In: ICCV (2007)
8. Cimpoi, M., Maji, S., Vedaldi, A.: Deep filter banks for texture recognition and segmentation. In: CVPR (2015)

9. Delhumeau, J., Gosselin, P., Jegou, H., Perez, P.: Revisiting the VLAD image representation. In: ACM Multimedia (2013)
10. Gong, Y., Wang, L., Guo, R., Lazebnik, S.: Multi-scale orderless pooling of deep convolutional activation features. In: Fleet, D., Pajdla, T., Schiele, B., Tuytelaars, T. (eds.) ECCV 2014. LNCS, vol. 8695, pp. 392–407. Springer, Heidelberg (2014). doi:10.1007/978-3-319-10584-0_26
11. Gordo, A., Almazán, J., Revaud, J., Larlus, D.: Deep image retrieval: learning global representations for image search. In: ECCV (2016)
12. Gosselin, P.H., Murray, N., Jégou, H., Perronnin, F.: Revisiting the fisher vector for fine-grained classification. Pattern Recogn. Lett. **49**, 92–98 (2014)
13. Jaderberg, M., Simonyan, K., Zisserman, A., Kavukcuoglu, K.: Spatial transformer networks. In: NIPS (2015)
14. Jegou, H., Douze, M., Schmid, C.: Hamming embedding and weak geometric consistency for large scale image search. In: Forsyth, D., Torr, P., Zisserman, A. (eds.) ECCV 2008. LNCS, vol. 5302, pp. 304–317. Springer, Heidelberg (2008). doi:10.1007/978-3-540-88682-2_24
15. Jégou, H., Douze, M., Schmid, C.: On the burstiness of visual elements. In: CVPR (2009)
16. Jégou, H., Douze, M., Schmid, C., Perez, P.: Aggregating local descriptors into a compact image representation. In: CVPR (2010)
17. Jégou, H., Zisserman, A.: Triangulation embedding and democratic aggregation for image search. In: CVPR (2014)
18. Jia, Y., Shelhamer, E., Donahue, J., Karayev, S., Long, J., Girshick, R., Guadarrama, S., Darrell, T.: Caffe: convolutional architecture for fast feature embedding. arXiv preprint arXiv:1408.5093 (2014)
19. Krizhevsky, A., Sutskever, I., Hinton, G.E.: Imagenet classification with deep convolutional neural networks. In: NIPS (2012)
20. Long, J., Shelhamer, E., Darrell, T.: Fully convolutional networks for semantic segmentation. arXiv preprint arXiv:1411.4038 (2014)
21. Lowe, D.: Local feature view clustering for 3D object recognition. In: CVPR (2001)
22. Mikulík, A., Perdoch, M., Chum, O., Matas, J.: Learning a fine vocabulary. In: Daniilidis, K., Maragos, P., Paragios, N. (eds.) ECCV 2010. LNCS, vol. 6313, pp. 1–14. Springer, Heidelberg (2010). doi:10.1007/978-3-642-15558-1_1
23. Murray, N., Perronnin, F.: Generalized max pooling. In: CVPR (2014)
24. Perronnin, F., Liu, Y., Sanchez, J., Poirier, H.: Large-scale image retrieval with compressed Fisher vectors. In: CVPR (2010)
25. Perronnin, F., Sánchez, J., Mensink, T.: Improving the fisher kernel for large-scale image classification. In: Daniilidis, K., Maragos, P., Paragios, N. (eds.) ECCV 2010. LNCS, vol. 6314, pp. 143–156. Springer, Heidelberg (2010). doi:10.1007/978-3-642-15561-1_11
26. Philbin, J., Chum, O., Isard, M., Sivic, J., Zisserman, A.: Object retrieval with large vocabularies and fast spatial matching. In: CVPR (2007)
27. Philbin, J., Chum, O., Sivic, J., Isard, M., Zisserman, A.: Lost in quantization: improving particular object retrieval in large scale image databases. In: CVPR (2008)
28. Radenović, F., Tolias, G., Chum, O.: CNN image retrieval learns from BoW: unsupervised fine-tuning with hard examples. In: ECCV (2016)
29. Razavian, A.S., Azizpour, H., Sullivan, J., Carlsson, S.: CNN features off-the-shelf: an astounding baseline for recognition. In: DeepVision Workshop, CVPR (2014)
30. Razavian, A.S., Sullivan, J., Maki, A., Carlsson, S.: Visual instance retrieval with deep convolutional networks. arXiv preprint arXiv:1412.6574 (2014)

31. Simonyan, K., Zisserman, A.: Very deep convolutional networks for large-scale image recognition (2014). CoRR abs/1409.1556
32. Sivic, J., Zisserman, A.: Video Google: a text retrieval approach to object matching in videos. In: ICCV, pp. 1470–1477 (2003)
33. Tolias, G., Avrithis, Y., Jégou, H.: To aggregate or not to aggregate: selective match kernels for image search. In: ICCV (2013)
34. Tolias, G., Avrithis, Y., Jégou, H.: Image search with selective match kernels: aggregation across single and multiple images. Int. J. Comput. Vision, 1–15 (2015)
35. Tolias, G., Jégou, H.: Visual query expansion with or without geometry: refining local descriptors by feature aggregation. Pattern Recogn. 47(10), 3466–3476 (2014)
36. Tolias, G., Kalantidis, Y., Avrithis, Y., Kollias, S.: Towards large-scale geometry indexing by feature selection. Comput. Vis. Image Underst. (CVIU) 120, 31–45 (2014)
37. Tolias, G., Sicre, R., Jégou, H.: Particular object retrieval with integral max-pooling of CNN activations. In: ICLR (2016)
38. Turcot, P., Lowe, D.: Better matching with fewer features: the selection of useful features in large database recognition problems. In: ICCV (2009)

LOH and Behold: Web-Scale Visual Search, Recommendation and Clustering Using Locally Optimized Hashing

Yannis Kalantidis[1]([⊠]), Lyndon Kennedy[2], Huy Nguyen[1], Clayton Mellina[1], and David A. Shamma[3]

[1] Computer Vision and Machine Learning Group, Flickr, Yahoo, San Francisco, USA
`ykal@yahoo-inc.com`, `huyng@yahoo-inc.com`, `clayton@yahoo-inc.com`
[2] Futurewei Technologies Inc., Santa Clara, USA
`lyndonk@acm.org`
[3] CWI: Centrum Wiskunde & Informatica, Amsterdam, The Netherlands
`aymans@acm.org`

Abstract. We propose a novel hashing-based matching scheme, called Locally Optimized Hashing (LOH), based on a state-of-the-art quantization algorithm that can be used for efficient, large-scale search, recommendation, clustering, and deduplication. We show that matching with LOH only requires set intersections and summations to compute and so is easily implemented in generic distributed computing systems. We further show application of LOH to: (a) large-scale search tasks where performance is on par with other state-of-the-art hashing approaches; (b) large-scale recommendation where queries consisting of thousands of images can be used to generate accurate recommendations from collections of hundreds of millions of images; and (c) efficient clustering with a graph-based algorithm that can be scaled to massive collections in a distributed environment or can be used for deduplication for small collections, like search results, performing better than traditional hashing approaches while only requiring a few milliseconds to run. In this paper we experiment on datasets of up to 100 million images, but in practice our system can scale to larger collections and can be used for other types of data that have a vector representation in a Euclidean space.

1 Introduction

The rapid rise in the amount of visual multimedia created, shared, and consumed requires the development of better large-scale methods for querying and mining large data collections. Similarly, with increased volume of data comes a greater variety of use cases, requiring simple and repurposeable pipelines that can flexibly adapt to growing data and changing requirements.

Recent advances in computer vision have shown a great deal of progress in analyzing the content of very large image collections, pushing the state-of-the-art for classification [27], detection [7,11] and visual similarity search

---

L. Kennedy and D.A. Shamma — Work done while author was at Yahoo Labs.

G. Hua and H. Jégou (Eds.): ECCV 2016 Workshops, Part I, LNCS 9913, pp. 702–718, 2016.
DOI: 10.1007/978-3-319-46604-0_49

[3, 20, 22, 31, 38]. Critically, deep Convolutional Neural Networks (CNNs) [23] have allowed processing pipelines to become much simpler by reducing complex engineered systems to simpler systems learned end-to-end and by providing powerful, generic visual representations that can be used for a variety of downstream visual tasks. Recently it has been shown that such deep features can be used to reduce visual search to nearest neighbor search in the deep feature space [5]. Complimentary work has recently produced efficient algorithms for approximate nearest neighbor search that can scale to billions of vectors [10, 17, 21].

In this paper, we present a novel matching signature, called *Locally Optimized Hashing (LOH)*. LOH extends LOPQ [21], a state-of-the-art nearest neighbor search algorithm, by treating the quantization codes of LOPQ as outputs of hashing functions. When applied to deep features, our algorithm provides a very flexible solution to a variety of related large-scale search and data mining tasks, including fast visual search, recommendation, clustering, and deduplication. Moreover, unlike [10, 17, 21], our system does not necessarily require specialized resources (*i.e.* dedicated cluster nodes and indexes for visual search) and is easily implemented in generic distributed computing environments.

Our approach sacrifices precision for speed and generality as compared to more exact quantization approaches, but it enables applications that wouldn't be computationally feasible with more exact approaches. LOH can trivially cope with large multi-image query sets. In practice, our approach allows datasets of *hundreds of millions* of images to be efficiently searched with query sets of *thousands of images*. We are in fact able to query with multiple large query sets, *e.g.* from Flickr groups, simultaneously and get visual recommendations for all the sets in parallel. We are also able to cluster web-scale datasets with MapReduce by simply thresholding LOH matches and running a connected components algorithm. The same approach can be used for deduplication of, *e.g.* search results.

Our contributions can be summarized as follows:

1. We propose Locally Optimized Hashing (LOH), a novel hashing-based matching method that competes favorably with the state-of-the-art hashing methods for search and allows approximate ordering of results.
2. We extend LOH to multiple image queries and provide a simple and scalable algorithm that can provide visual recommendations in batch for query sets of thousands of images.
3. We show that this same representation can be used to efficiently deduplicate image search results and cluster collections of hundreds of millions of images.

Although in this paper we experiment on datasets of up to 100 million images (*i.e.* using the YFCC100M dataset [29], the largest publicly available image dataset), in practice our system is suited to web-scale multimedia search applications with billions of images. In fact, on a Hadoop cluster with 1000 nodes, our approach can find and rank similar images *for millions of users from a search set of hundreds of millions of images in a runtime on the order of one hour*. The method can be adapted to other data types that have vector representations in Euclidean space.

2   Related Work

Large scale nearest neighbor search was traditionally based on hashing methods [6,26] because they offer low memory footprints for index codes and fast search in Hamming space [25]. However, even recent hashing approaches [19,28,34] suffer in terms of performance compared to quantization-based approaches [16,25] for the same amount of memory. On the other hand, quantization-based approaches traditionally performed worse in terms of search times, and it was only recently with the use of novel indexing methods [4] that quantization-based search was able to achieve search times of a few milliseconds in databases of billions of vectors [10,21,24].

A benefit of quantization approaches is that, unlike classic hashing methods, they provide a ranking for the retrieved points. Recently, approaches for binary code re-ranking have been proposed in [33,37]; both papers propose a secondary, computationally heavier re-ranking step that, although is performed on only the retrieved points, makes search slower than state-of-the-art quantization-based approaches. In the approach presented here, we try to keep the best of both worlds by producing an approximate ordering of retrieved points without re-ranking. We argue that for use cases involving multiple queries, this approximation can be tolerated since many ranked lists are aggregated in this case.

A similar approach to ours, *i.e.* an approach that aims to produce multipurpose, *polysemous* codes [8] is presented at the current ECCV conference. After training a product quantizer, the authors then propose to optimize the so-called index assignment of the centroids to binary codes, such that distances between similar centroids are small in the Hamming space.

For multi-image queries, there are two broad categories based on the semantic concepts that the query image set represents. The first is query sets that share the same semantic concept or even the same specific object (*i.e.* a particular building in Oxford) [1,9,31,39]. The second category is multi-image queries with *multiple* semantics. This category has been recently studied [15] and the authors propose a Pareto-depth approach on top Efficient Manifold Ranking [36] for such queries. Their approach is however not scalable to very large databases and they limit query sets to just be image pairs.

The current work uses visual features from a CNN trained for classification, thus similarities in our visual space capture broader category-level semantics. We focus on the first category of multi-image queries, *i.e.* multiple-image query sets with a single semantic concept, and provide a simple and scalable approach which we apply to Flickr group set expansion. However, it is straightforward to tackle the second category with our approach by introducing a first step of (visual or multi-modal) clustering on the query set with multiple semantics before proceeding with the LOH-based set expansion.

3   Locally Optimized Hashing

3.1   Background

Product Quantization. A *quantizer* q maps a d-dimensional vector $\mathbf{x} \in \mathbb{R}^d$ to vector $q(\mathbf{x}) \in \mathcal{C}$, where $\mathcal{C}$ is a finite subset of $\mathbb{R}^d$, of cardinality k. Each vector $\mathbf{c} \in \mathcal{C}$ is called a *centroid*, and $\mathcal{C}$ a *codebook*. Assuming that dimension d is a multiple of m, we may write any vector $\mathbf{x} \in \mathbb{R}^d$ as a concatenation $(\mathbf{x}^1, \ldots, \mathbf{x}^m)$ of m sub-vectors, each of dimension d/m. If $\mathcal{C}^1, \ldots, \mathcal{C}^m$ are m sub-codebooks of k sub-centroids in subspace $\mathbb{R}^{d/m}$, a *product quantizer* [16] constrains $\mathcal{C}$ to be a Cartesian product

$$\mathcal{C} = \mathcal{C}^1 \times \cdots \times \mathcal{C}^m, \tag{1}$$

making it a codebook of k^m centroids of the form $\mathbf{c} = (\mathbf{c}^1, \ldots, \mathbf{c}^m)$ with each sub-centroid $\mathbf{c}^j \in \mathcal{C}^j$ for $j \in \mathcal{M} = \{1, \ldots, m\}$. An optimal product quantizer q should minimize distortion $E = \sum_{\mathbf{x} \in \mathcal{X}} \|\mathbf{x} - q(\mathbf{x})\|^2$. as a function of $\mathcal{C}$, subject to $\mathcal{C}$ being of the form (1) [10]. This is typically done with a variant of k-means.

When codebook $\mathcal{C}$ is expressed as a Cartesian product, for each vector $\mathbf{x} \in \mathbb{R}^d$, the nearest centroid in $\mathcal{C}$ is

$$q(\mathbf{x}) = (q^1(\mathbf{x}^1), \ldots, q^m(\mathbf{x}^m)), \tag{2}$$

where $q^j(\mathbf{x}^j)$ is the nearest sub-centroid of sub-vector $\mathbf{x}^j$ in $\mathcal{C}^j$, for $j \in \mathcal{M}$ [10]. Hence finding an optimal product quantizer q in d dimensions amounts to solving m optimal sub-quantizer problems $q^j, j \in \mathcal{M}$, each in d/m dimensions.

Given a new *query* vector $\mathbf{y}$, the (squared) Euclidean distance to every point $\mathbf{x} \in \mathcal{X}$ may be approximated by

$$\delta^{SDC}(\mathbf{y}, \mathbf{x}) = \sum_{j=1}^{m} \|q^j(\mathbf{y}^j) - q^j(\mathbf{x}^j)\|^2, \tag{3}$$

or

$$\delta^{ADC}(\mathbf{y}, \mathbf{x}) = \sum_{j=1}^{m} \|\mathbf{y}^j - q^j(\mathbf{x}^j)\|^2, \tag{4}$$

where $q^j(\mathbf{x}^j) \in \mathcal{C}^j = \{\mathbf{c}_1^j, \ldots, \mathbf{c}_k^j\}$ for $j \in \mathcal{M}$. The superscripts SDC and ADC correspond to the symmetric and asymmetric distance computations of [16], respectively. In the latter case the query vector is not quantized using the product quantizer, distances $\|\mathbf{y}^j - \mathbf{c}_i^j\|^2$ are computed and stored for $i \in \mathcal{K}$ and $j \in \mathcal{M}$ prior to search, so (4) amounts to only $O(m)$ operations. Sacrificing distortion for speed, in this approach we are mostly exploring the symmetric approximation (3), where the query is also in quantized form. In this case, sub-quantizer distances $\|\mathbf{c}_l^j - \mathbf{c}_i^j\|^2$ can be pre-computed and stored for all $i, l \in \mathcal{K}$ and $j \in \mathcal{M}$ and again only $O(m)$ operations are needed for distance computations.

Locally Optimized Product Quantization. In their recent paper [21], the authors further extend product quantization by optimizing multiple product quantizers *locally*, after some initial, coarse quantization of the space. Similar to the IVFADC version of [16] or multi-index [4], they adopt a two-stage quantization scheme, where local optimization follows independently inside each cluster of a coarse quantizer Q, learnt on the residual vectors with respect to the cluster's centroid. They learn an *optimized* product quantizer [10] per cluster, jointly optimizing the subspace decomposition together with the sub-quantizers. Constraint (1) of the codebook is relaxed to

$$\mathcal{C} = \{R\hat{\mathbf{c}} : \hat{\mathbf{c}} \in \mathcal{C}^1 \times \cdots \times \mathcal{C}^m, R^T R = I\}, \tag{5}$$

where the $d \times d$ matrix R is orthogonal and allows for arbitrary rotation and permutation of vector components.

Given the coarse quantizer Q and the associated codebook $\mathcal{E} = \{\mathbf{e}_1, \ldots, \mathbf{e}_K\}$ of K *clusters*, for $i \in \mathcal{K} = \{1, \ldots, K\}$ we may define the set of residuals of all data points $\mathbf{x} \in \mathcal{X}_i$ quantized to cluster i as $\mathcal{Z}_i = \{\mathbf{x} - \mathbf{e}_i : \mathbf{x} \in \mathcal{X}_i, Q(\mathbf{x}) = \mathbf{e}_i\}$. Given a set $\mathcal{Z} \in \{\mathcal{Z}_1, \ldots, \mathcal{Z}_K\}$, the problem of locally optimizing both space decomposition and sub-quantizers can be expressed as minimizing distortion as a function of orthogonal matrix $R \in \mathbb{R}^{d \times d}$ and sub-codebooks $\mathcal{C}^1, \ldots, \mathcal{C}^m \subset \mathbb{R}^{d/m}$ per cell,

$$\begin{aligned} \text{minimize} \quad & \sum_{\mathbf{z} \in \mathcal{Z}} \min_{\hat{\mathbf{c}} \in \hat{\mathcal{C}}} \|\mathbf{z} - R\hat{\mathbf{c}}\|^2 \\ \text{subject to} \quad & \hat{\mathcal{C}} = \mathcal{C}^1 \times \cdots \times \mathcal{C}^m \\ & R^T R = I, \end{aligned} \tag{6}$$

where $|\mathcal{C}^j| = k$ for $j \in \mathcal{M} = \{1, \ldots, m\}$. Assuming a d-dimensional, zero-mean normal distribution $\mathcal{N}(\mathbf{0}, \Sigma)$ of residual data $\mathcal{Z}$, we can efficiently solve the problem by first aligning the data with PCA and then using the *eigenvalue allocation* [10] algorithm to assign dimensions to subspaces.

To achieve the state-of-the-art results on a billion-scale dataset, the inverted multi-index [4] is used with local optimization. In this setting, the original space is split into two subspaces first and then LOPQ follows within each one of the two subspaces separately, on the residual vectors.

Each data point now gets assigned in *two* clusters, one in each subspace. The intersection of two clusters gives a multi-index *cell* in the product space. However, as the space overhead to locally optimize per cell is prohibitive, in [21] the authors separately optimize *per cluster* in each of the two subspaces. They refer to this type of local optimization as *product optimization* and the complete algorithm as *Multi-LOPQ*, which is the approach we also adopt for training. As was shown in [21], using local rotations together with a single set of global subquantizers gave only a small drop in performance. We therefore choose to have a global set of sub-quantizers $q(\mathbf{x})$ defined as in (2) and trained on the projected residual vectors $\mathbf{x}$ from (10). We will refer to the two quantization stages as *coarse* and *fine* quantization, respectively.

3.2 Locally Optimized Hashing

The symmetric distance computation of (3) yields an approximation of the true distance in the quantized space. In pursuit of an even more scalable, fast and distributed-computing friendly approach, we propose to treat the sub-quantizer centroid indices as *hash codes*. This allows us to approximate the true distance via *collisions* without any explicit numeric computations apart from a final summation. As we demonstrate below, the proposed formulation further generalizes to querying with multiple vector queries, and, in fact, can perform many such queries in parallel very efficiently.

Lets begin by assuming a single coarse quantizer Q. The LOPQ model contains local rotations R_c and global sub-quantizers $q_c^j, j \in \mathcal{M}$ and $c \in \mathcal{K}$ that operate on the projected residuals. Let $\mathbf{x}, \mathbf{y} \in \mathcal{Z}_c$ be such residual vectors with respect to the same centroid of cluster c of the coarse quantizer. The symmetric distance computation of (3) is now given by

$$\delta_c^{SDC}(\mathbf{y}, \mathbf{x}) = \|q_c(\mathbf{y}) - q_c(\mathbf{x})\|^2 = \sum_{j=1}^{m} \|q_c^j(\mathbf{y}^j) - q_c^j(\mathbf{x}^j)\|^2, \qquad (7)$$

where q_c^j is the j-th sub-quantizer for cluster c, with $c \in \mathcal{K}, j \in \mathcal{M}$ and $\mathbf{x}, \mathbf{y} \in \mathcal{Z}_c$. A residual vector $\mathbf{x}$ is mapped via q_c to the corresponding sub-centroid indices $i_c(\mathbf{x}) = (i_c(\mathbf{x})^1, \ldots, i_c(\mathbf{x})^m)$. We may treat the indices as values of a set of hash functions $h_c = (h_c^1, \ldots, h_c^m)$, *i.e.* a mapping $h_c : \mathbb{R}^d \to \mathbb{Z}^m$ such that $h_c(\mathbf{x}) = i_c(\mathbf{x})$. We can then estimate the *similarity* between residual vectors $\mathbf{y}, \mathbf{x}$ using the function:

$$\sigma_h(\mathbf{y}, \mathbf{x}) = \sum_{j=1}^{m} \mathbb{1}[h_c(\mathbf{y})^j = h_c(\mathbf{x})^j], \qquad (8)$$

where $\mathbb{1}[a = b]$ equals to 1, iff $a = b$ and 0 otherwise. Our hash functions are defined locally, *i.e.* on residual vectors for a specific cluster, and therefore we call the proposed matching scheme *Locally Optimized Hashing* or *LOH*.

The LOH approach can be extended to work on top of a multi-LOPQ [21] model. Instead of having a single coarse quantizer, we learn two subspace quantizers Q^1, Q^2 of K centroids, with associated codebooks $\mathcal{E}^j = \{\mathbf{e}_1^j, \ldots, \mathbf{e}_K^j\}$ for $j = 1, 2$ in a product quantization fashion.

Each data point $\tilde{\mathbf{x}} = (\tilde{\mathbf{x}}^1, \tilde{\mathbf{x}}^2) \in \mathcal{X}$ is quantized using the two coarse quantizers into the tuple

$$(c_1, c_2) = (\arg\min_i \|\tilde{\mathbf{x}}^1 - \mathbf{e}_i^1\|, \arg\min_i \|\tilde{\mathbf{x}}^2 - \mathbf{e}_i^2\|), \qquad (9)$$

with $c_j \in [1, K]$ referring to the indices of the nearest clusters for the two subspaces $j = 1, 2$. We will refer to the tuple $c(\tilde{\mathbf{x}}) = (c_1, c_2)$ as the *coarse codes* of a data point. Following LOPQ, the residual vector $\mathbf{x} = (\mathbf{x}^1, \mathbf{x}^2)$ of point $\tilde{\mathbf{x}}$ is equal to:

$$\mathbf{x} = (R_{c_1}^1(\tilde{\mathbf{x}}^1 - \mathbf{e}_{c_1}^1), R_{c_2}^2(\tilde{\mathbf{x}}^2 - \mathbf{e}_{c_2}^2)), \qquad (10)$$

Algorithm 1. Data encoding for the multi-index case

---

    input : data point $\tilde{\mathbf{x}} \in \mathcal{X}$, number of subspaces m, coarse quantizer codebooks $\mathcal{E}^j$,
                 local rotations R_i^j where $i = 1, \ldots, K$ and $j = 1, 2$ and sub-quantizer
                 codebooks $\mathbf{c} = (\mathbf{c}^1, \ldots, \mathbf{c}^m)$.
    output: sets of coarse and fine codes

      // calculate coarse codes
  1   $(c_1, c_2) = (\arg\min_i \|\tilde{\mathbf{x}}^1 - \mathbf{e}_i^1\|, \arg\min_i \|\tilde{\mathbf{x}}^2 - \mathbf{e}_i^2\|)$

      // calculate locally projected residuals
  2   $\mathbf{x} = (R_{c_1}^1(\tilde{\mathbf{x}}^1 - \mathbf{e}_{c_1}^1), R_{c_2}^2(\tilde{\mathbf{x}}^2 - \mathbf{e}_{c_2}^2))$

      // split residual to m subvectors
  3   $\mathbf{x} = (\mathbf{x}^1, \ldots, \mathbf{x}^m)$

      // calculate fine codes
  4   $(f_1, \ldots, f_m) = (\arg\min_i \|\mathbf{x}^1 - \mathbf{c}_i^1\|, \ldots, \arg\min_i \|\mathbf{x}^m - \mathbf{c}_i^m\|)$

---

where R_i^j correspond to the local rotation of cluster i in subspace j and $\mathbf{x} \in \mathcal{X}$. We can split the concatenated vector $\mathbf{x}$ into m subvectors $\mathbf{x} = (\mathbf{x}^1, \ldots, \mathbf{x}^m)$ and use the global sub-quantizers for encoding into m codes. Therefore, given sub-quantizer $q(\mathbf{x})$ with codebooks $\mathbf{c} = (\mathbf{c}^1, \ldots, \mathbf{c}^m)$ and each sub-centroid $\mathbf{c}^j \in \mathcal{C}^j = \{\mathbf{c}_1^j, \ldots, \mathbf{c}_k^j\}$ for $j \in \mathcal{M} = \{1, \ldots, m\}$, we can compute

$$f_j = \arg\min_i \|\mathbf{x}^j - \mathbf{c}_i^j\|, \tag{11}$$

for all $j \in \mathcal{M}$ and get the sub-quantizer indices for the m subspaces in set $f(\mathbf{x}) = (f_1, \ldots, f_m)$. We will refer to this set as the *fine codes* of a data point. An overview of the encoding process is shown in Algorithm 1.

Now, given residual vectors $\mathbf{x}, \mathbf{y}$ with respect to the same set of coarse codes, and their sets of fine codes $f(\mathbf{x}), f(\mathbf{y})$, the similarity function of (8) can be expressed as

$$\sigma_h(\mathbf{y}, \mathbf{x}) = \sum_{i=1}^{m} \mathbb{1}[f_i(\mathbf{y}) = f_i(\mathbf{x})] \tag{12}$$

i.e. the sum of similarities for the m subspaces. We should note that since fine codes are calculated on residuals, *i.e.* given a coarse centroid, they are comparable only for points that share at least one of the coarse codes. If two points, for example share only the first coarse code of the two, only the first half of the fine codes are comparable.

3.3   Ranking with LOH

After we encode all database points using the approach summarized in Algorithm 1, each one will be assigned to the *cell* of the multi-index that corresponds to the pair of coarse codes of each data point. For indexing, an inverted list $\mathcal{L}_c$ is kept for each cell $c = c_{ij} = (c_i, c_j)$ of the multi-index, giving K^2 inverted lists in total.

For search one visits the inverted lists of multiple cells. The query vector is therefore not projected to just the closest coarse cluster for each of the coarse quantizers, but to multiple, and cells are visited in a sequence dictated by the multi-sequence algorithm [4]. As we are only counting collisions of fine codes within a coarse cluster, we need a way of incorporating the distance of the query to the centroid for each cell visited to further rank points *across* cells. The multi-sequence algorithm provides us with an (approximate) distance d_c for each cell which we use to extend the similarity function presented in the previous section. We introduce a weight w_c for each cell c visited that encodes the similarity of the query's residual to that cell's centroid, and modify the similarity function to be:

$$\sigma_w(\mathbf{y}, \mathbf{x}) = w_c + \sigma_h(\mathbf{y}, \mathbf{x}) = w_c + \sum_{i=1}^{m} \mathbb{1}[f_i(\mathbf{y}) = f_i(\mathbf{x})] \qquad (13)$$

We choose to set these weight to a simple exponential function of the approximate distances d_c used by the multi-sequence algorithm.

Similarities are evaluated for every vector in list $\mathcal{L}_c$, for every cell c returned by the multi-sequence algorithm. In [4], search is terminated if a quota of at least T vectors have been evaluated. For a query vector $\mathbf{y}$, we may assume that cells $\{c^1, \ldots, c^W\}$ were visited by the multi-index algorithm until termination. Let that sequence of lists visited be $\mathcal{L}^{\mathbf{y}} = \{\mathcal{L}_{c^1}, \ldots, \mathcal{L}_{c^W}\}$. Also let $\mathcal{X}^{\mathbf{y}} = \{\mathbf{x}_1, \ldots, \mathbf{x}_T\}$ be the sequence of the T database vectors evaluated during search, concatenated from W disjoint inverted lists. Let also set $\mathcal{S}^{\mathbf{y}} = \{\sigma_w(\mathbf{y}, \mathbf{x}_1), \ldots, \sigma_w(\mathbf{y}, \mathbf{x}_T)\}$, hold the similarity values of the query vector $\mathbf{y}$ with each of the top T database vectors returned by the multi-index. The ranked list of nearest neighbors returned for the query is the top elements of $\mathcal{S}^{\mathbf{y}}$ in descending order according to the approximate similarity values.

3.4 Searching with Large Query Sets

An application like recommendation requires the ability to jointly search with multiple query vectors and get aggregated results. Taking visual recommendation as an example, one can define query sets in multiple ways, *e.g.* the set of images in a given Flickr group, or the set of images that a given user has favorited. If each image is represented as a vector, *e.g.* using CNN-based global visual features, queries with *image sets* correspond to queries with *multiple vectors* and can produce results that are visually similar to the whole query image set.

Now let's suppose that the query is a set of Y vectors, $\mathcal{Y} = \{\mathbf{y}_1, \ldots, \mathbf{y}_Y\}$. If we query the index for each of the query vectors, we get sets $\mathcal{L}^{\mathbf{y}}$, $\mathcal{X}^{\mathbf{y}}$ and $\mathcal{S}^{\mathbf{y}}$ for each vector corresponding to cells, database vectors and similarities, respectively, with $\mathbf{y} = 1, \ldots, Y$. We can now define the set of similarity values

$$S_{\mathcal{Y}} = \{\sigma(\mathcal{Y}, \mathbf{x}_t)\} \text{ for } t \in \bigcup_{y \in Y} \mathcal{X}^{\mathbf{y}}, \qquad (14)$$

between the query set $\mathcal{Y}$ and all database vectors evaluated in any of the single-vector queries. The aggregation function $\sigma(\mathcal{Y}, \mathbf{x}) = g(\sigma_w(\mathbf{y}_1, \mathbf{x}), \ldots, \sigma_w(\mathbf{y}_Y, \mathbf{x}))$

Algorithm 2. Pseudo-code for batch search in PIG

---

input : queries, documents: flattened query and database files. Each row contains some id and a triplet of a fine code, its position in the ordered set and its corresponding coarse code.

output: scores: list of documents sorted by LOH similarity to the query set

// load flattened files for query set
1 Q = LOAD 'queries' AS (`user_id`, `image_id_q`, (`coarse_code,position,fine_code`) as `code_q`);

// load flattened files for the database set
2 D = LOAD 'documents' AS (`image_id_d`, (`coarse_code,position,fine_code`) as `code_d`);

// join by code
3 matches = JOIN Q by `code_q`, D BY `code_d`;

// group by document
4 grouped = GROUP matches BY (`user_id`, `image_id_d`);

// count the matches within each group
5 scores = FOREACH grouped GENERATE group.$0 as `user_id`, group.$1 as `image_id`, COUNT(matches) as `n_matches`;

// order by number of matches
6 scores = ORDER scores BY `user_id` ASC, `n_matches` DESC;

---

measures the similarity of the query set $\mathcal{Y}$ to database vector $\mathbf{x}$, where g can be any pooling function, for example

$$\sigma_{SUM}(\mathcal{Y}, \mathbf{x}) = \sum_{\mathbf{y} \in \mathcal{Y}} \sigma_w(\mathbf{y}, \mathbf{x}), \tag{15}$$

for sum-pooling or $\sigma_{MAX}(\mathcal{Y}, \mathbf{x}) = \arg\max_{\mathbf{y} \in \mathcal{Y}} \sigma_w(\mathbf{y}, \mathbf{x})$ for max-pooling. We experimentally found that sum-pooling performs better than max-pooling, which is understandable since the latter tends to under-weight results that appeared in the result sets of many query vectors. We also experimented with more complex functions, *e.g.* functions that combine max-pooling with the frequency that each database image appears in the result sets, but since the improvements were minimal we end up using the simpler sum-pooling function of (15) for the rest of the paper.

An advantage of representing images as multiple hash codes is that they can be naturally manipulated for a variety of tasks with MapReduce using tools such as PIG or HIVE for Hadoop. Returning to our example of image recommendations in Flickr, we might use a user's favorited images as a query set to produce a ranked set of recommended images that are visually similar to images the user has favorited. In this case we would like to produce recommendations for *all* users, and we would like an algorithm that can run many searches efficiently in batch to periodically recompute image recommendations for all users.

We show PIG pseudo-code for such a batch search in Algorithm 2. The algorithm assumes that the coarse and fine codes for each document have already been computed and are available in a *flattened* form. To get this form, we first

---

Algorithm 3. Pseudo-code for LOH clustering

---

input : documents $\mathcal{Y} = \{y_1, \dots, y_n\}$ with the set of flattened triplets, threshold t
output: clusters $\mathcal{R} = \{r_1, \dots, r_n\}$

1 Groups = HashMap<List>()
2 Matches = HashMap<Int>()
3 DocumentGraph = Graph()

   // group documents by matching LOH codes
4 **foreach** $d \in D$ **do**
5 | **foreach** $(c_i, j, f_j) \in d$ **do**
6 | | Groups$((c_i, j, f_j))$.append(d)

   // count num of matching codes for pairs of documents in each group
7 **foreach** $group \in Groups$ **do**
8 | **foreach** $(d_a, d_b) \in allPairs(group)$ **do**
9 | | Matches$((d_a, d_b))$++
10 | | **if** $Matches((d_a, d_b)) > t$ **then**
11 | | | DocumentGraph.addEdge(d_a, d_b)

   // find connected components in the document graph
12 $\mathcal{R} \longleftarrow$ DocumentGraph.findConnectedComponents()
13 **return** $\mathcal{R}$

---

split the m fine codes and create triplets by appending each fine code with its position in f and the corresponding coarse code. That is, for coarse and fine codes (c_1, c_2) and $(f_1, \dots, f_m)$, respectively, we would get the set of m triplets $((c_1, 1, f_1), (c_1, 2, f_2), \dots, (c_2, m, f_m))$ or *LOH codes*.

3.5 Clustering and Deduplication with LOH

LOH can also be used for efficient and scalable clustering. Unlike recent approaches that try to cluster data on a single machine [2,13], we are interested in the distributed case. Our clustering algorithm first constructs a graph of documents from an input set $\mathcal{Y}$ such that a pair of documents $\mathbf{x}, \mathbf{y} \in \mathcal{Y}$ is connected by an edge iff the LOH similarity of the pair is above some threshold t, i.e. $\sigma_h(\mathbf{y}, \mathbf{x}) > t$. Clustering then amounts to finding connected components in this graph.

We present pseudo-code for LOH clustering in Algorithm 3. The algorithm first groups documents by flattened code triplets. This grouping is used to efficiently count the number of matches for document pairs by greatly reducing the number of pairs we consider when constructing the graph. Like the batch search algorithm, LOH clustering is easily implemented in MapReduce frameworks. When running with a high threshold for a small set of images, e.g. for the top hundred or thousand results after image search, this algorithm can deduplicate the set in real-time, requiring only a few milliseconds.

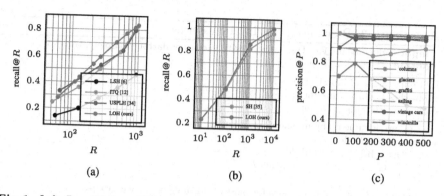

Fig. 1. *Left*: Recall@R on SIFT1M with 64bit codes. Recall is measured here as the percentage of times the true nearest neighbor is returned within the top R results returned by the index for all 10 K queries. $K = 1024$ for LOH. *Center*: Recall@R on SIFT1M for the proposed LOH and Spectral Hashing. LOH only takes into account the top $T = 10000$ results returned by the multi-index, while SH is exhaustive. *Right*: Precision@P for the 7 Flickr Group Photos dataset. Recommendations for the group "Portraits & Faces" are not depicted because they were flawless.

4   Experiments

We use the following four datasets:

SIFT1M Dataset [16]. This dataset contains of 1 million 128-dimensional SIFT vectors and 10 K query vectors and is a common benchmark dataset in related work [21,25,34].

Yahoo Flickr Creative Commons 100 M Dataset [30]. This dataset (YFCC100M) contains a subset of 100 million public images with a creative commons license from Flickr and is the largest such publicly available collection of social multimedia images.

Flickr Brad Pitt Search Dataset. This dataset contains the top 1048 photo results from a query for the search term "Brad Pitt" on the Flickr website. At the time that we collected this data, results from this query exhibited a large amount of "near-duplicate" results. We manually grouped each photo that looked visually similar into the same cluster. The dataset contains a total of 30 clusters with more than 1 image.

7 Flickr Groups Dataset. This dataset contains 70 K images in total and was constructed by collecting 10 K images from 7 popular Flickr groups: *Graffiti of the world, Sailboats and sailing, Glaciers, Icefields and Icebergs, Windmills, Columns and Columns, Vintage Cars and Trucks* and *Portraits and Faces*.

We use the $fc7$ features of the pretrained AlexNet model [23] from Caffe [18] and use PCA to reduce them to 128 dimensions. We learn a covariance matrix from 100 million images of the YFCC100M dataset and further permute the dimensions in order to balance variance between the two subspaces before multi-indexing [10]. As in all related work [10,16,21], we set the number of sub-quantizer centroids $k = 256$, $i.e.$ we require m bytes of memory in total per vector.

We adopt the Multi-LOPQ [21] approach to train[1] and index the database points. We use parameters $K = 1024$ ($K = 8192$), $m = 8$ ($m = 16$) and for $T=10\,K$ ($T=100\,K$) for SIFT1M (YFCC100M).

We use the recall metric to measure the performance of LOH against related methods and conduct experiments on the SIFT1M dataset. To compare with hashing methods that do not return any ordering of the retrieved points, we measure the percentage of times the true nearest neighbor is within the top R results returned by the index (therefore varying parameter T of the multi-index for LOH) for all $10\,K$ queries of the SIFT1M dataset. We use the precision-recall metric for evaluating deduplication.

4.1 Approximate Nearest Neighbor Search with LOH

We first investigate how the LOH approach compares with the hashing literature for the task of retrieving the true nearest neighbor within the first R samples seen. We compare against classic hashing methods like Locality Sensitive Hashing (LSH) [6], Iterative Quantization [12] and the recent Sequential Projection Learning Hashing (USPLH) [34] and report results in Fig. 1a. One can see that LOH, built on the inverted multi-index after balancing the variance of the two subspaces, compares well with the state-of-the-art in the field, even outperforming recently proposed approaches like [34] for large enough R. LOH provides a ranking for the items retrieved without requiring any further re-ranking process.

In Fig. 1b, we evaluate LOH ranking, $i.e.$ how well LOH orders the true nearest neighbor after looking at a fraction of the database. Here we compare against Spectral Hashing [35] (SH) that provides ranking of the binary signature and is shown to outperform a related approach using restricted Boltzmann machines [32].

4.2 Visual Recommendations for Flickr Groups

We conduct an experiment to evaluate the ability of the proposed approach to visually find images that might be topically relevant to a group of photos already curated by a group of users. On Flickr, such activity is common as users form groups around topical photographic interests and seek out high-quality photos relevant to the group. Group moderators may contact photo owners to ask them to submit to their group.

To evaluate this, we select 7 public Flickr groups that are representative of the types of topical interests common in Flickr groups, selected due to their clear thematic construction (*graffiti, sailing, glacier, windmill, columns, cars & trucks, portrait & face*), for ease of objective evaluation. For each group, we construct a

---

[1] https://github.com/yahoo/lopq.

large query of 10, 000 images randomly sampled from the group pool. We perform visual search using our proposed method on the YFCC100M dataset, aggregate results from all 10 thousand images and report precision after manual inspection of the top $k = 500$ results. We visually scanned the photo pools of the groups and consider true positives all images that look like images in the photo pool and follow the group rules as specified by the administrators of each group.

| (a) LOH-based results (proposed) | (b) Tag-based results (baseline) |

Fig. 2. Suggestions for Flickr group "vintage cars and trucks", false positives are marked by a red border. 2a: Our visual similarity-based suggestions; only 1 of the top results is false and the aesthetics fit the images in the group. 2b: Top images returned by tag-based search for "vintage cars and trucks"; we see more false positives in this case. (Color figure online)

Precision for each group is shown in Fig. 1c. For group "Portraits & Faces", for example *all* 500 top results were high-quality portraits. We see some confusion due to the nature of the visual representation chosen (*e.g.* our visual representation may confuse desert and cloud images with snow images), but overall, Precision@500 was over 0.96 for five out of the seven groups we tested.

Example results for the set expansion with our method and a baseline tag-based search are shown in Fig. 2 for Flickr group "vintage cars and trucks". For the proposed approach, precision is high, as is the aesthetic quality of the results. The tag-based Flickr search returns more false positives for such a specific group, as irrelevant images are likely improperly tagged.

4.3   Clustering and Deduplication Results

We evaluate the performance of LOH on the deduplication task using a dataset of Flickr searches for the query "Brad Pitt" with the LOH codes learned on the YFCC100M dataset. To measure precision and recall, we enumerate all pairs of images in the dataset and define a "positive" sample as a pair of images that belong to the same group in our dataset, and a "negative" sample as a pair of images that belong to different groups in our dataset.

In Fig. 3a we plot the precision-recall for LOH versus LSH [6] and PCA-E [14]. For LSH, we transform our PCA'd 128 dimensional image descriptor into a 128-bit binary code computed from random binary projection hash functions. For PCA-E we compute a 128-bit binary code by subtracting the mean of our PCA'd 128 dimensional image descriptor and taking the sign.

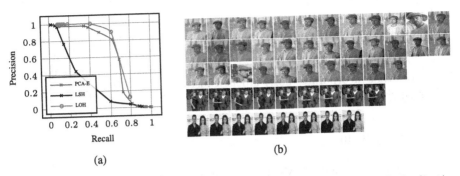

Fig. 3. *Left:* Precision-Recall curve on the Brad Pitt dataset. *Right:* Deduplication results on the Brad Pitt dataset; three clusters of duplicates are shown where each cluster shares at least 3 LOH codes.

We run LOH clustering for the 100 million images of the YFCC100M dataset on a small Hadoop cluster and sample clusters are shown in Fig. 4. We first did some cleaning and preprocessing, *i.e.* performed the edge extraction after performing deduplication and using a stoplist of codes (*i.e.* remove all triplets that appear more than 10 K or less than 10 times) for efficiency. For a threshold of $t = 3$, we get 74 million edges and approximately 7 million connected components. Of those, about 6.5 million are small components of size smaller than 5. Timewise, edge extraction for 100 M images took a couple of hours, while connected components run in a few minutes.

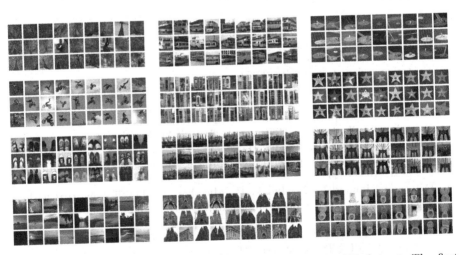

Fig. 4. Random images from sample clusters of the YFCC100M dataset. The first three rows show (mostly) coherent clusters that can be used for learning classifiers, while the bottom row shows failure cases. The sizes of the clusters depicted are (row-wise): 1194,976,920/272,320,873/139,151,164/6.8 M, 1363 and 94

By visual inspection, we notice that a large set of medium-sized clusters (*i.e.* clusters with $10^2 - 10^4$ images) contain visually consistent higher level concepts (*e.g.* from Fig. 4: "motorbikes in the air", "Hollywood St stars" or "British telephone booths"). Such clusters can be used to learn classifiers in a semi-supervised framework that incorporates noisy labels. Clustering YFCC100M gives us about 32 K such clusters.

5 Conclusions

In this paper we propose a system for web-scale search, recommendation, and cluster based on a novel matching scheme, Locally Optimized Hashing or LOH, that is computed on the very powerful and compact LOPQ codes. We show how LOH can be used to efficiently perform visual search, recommendation, clustering and deduplication for web-scale image databases in a distributed fashion.

While LOPQ distance computation gives high quality, fast distance estimation for nearest neighbor search, it is not as well suited for large-scale, batch search and clustering tasks. LOH, however, enables these use-cases by allowing implementations that use only highly parallelizable set operations and summations. LOH can therefore be used for massively parallel visual recommendation and clustering in generic distributed environments with only a few lines of code. Its speed also allows its use for deduplication of, *e.g.*, search result sets at query time, requiring only a few milliseconds to run for sets of thousands of results.

References

1. Arandjelovic, R., Zisserman, A.: Multiple queries for large scale specific object retrieval. In: BMVC (2012)
2. Avrithis, Y., Kalantidis, Y., Anagnostopoulos, E., Emiris, I.Z.: Web-scale image clustering revisited. In: ICCV (2015)
3. Avrithis, Y., Kalantidis, Y., Tolias, G., Spyrou, E.: Retrieving landmark and non-landmark images from community photo collections. In: ACM Multimedia (2010)
4. Babenko, A., Lempitsky, V.: The inverted multi-index. In: CVPR (2012)
5. Babenko, A., Slesarev, A., Chigorin, A., Lempitsky, V.: Neural codes for image retrieval. In: Fleet, D., Pajdla, T., Schiele, B., Tuytelaars, T. (eds.) ECCV 2014. LNCS, vol. 8689, pp. 584–599. Springer, Heidelberg (2014). doi:10.1007/978-3-319-10590-1_38
6. Datar, M., Immorlica, N., Indyk, P., Mirrokni, V.: Locality-sensitive hashing scheme based on p-stable distributions. In: Symposium on Computational Geometry (2004)
7. Dollár, P., Appel, R., Belongie, S., Perona, P.: Fast feature pyramids for object detection. PAMI **36**(8), 1532–1545 (2014)
8. Douze, M., Jégou, H., Perronnin, F.: Polysemous codes. In: ECCV (2016)
9. Fernando, B., Tuytelaars, T.: Mining multiple queries for image retrieval: on-the-fly learning of an object-specific mid-level representation. In: ICCV (2013)
10. Ge, T., He, K., Ke, Q., Sun, J.: Optimized product quantization. Technical report 4 (2014)

11. Girshick, R., Donahue, J., Darrell, T., Malik, J.: Rich feature hierarchies for accurate object detection and semantic segmentation. In: CVPR (2014)
12. Gong, Y., Lazebnik, S.: Iterative quantization: a procrustean approach to learning binary codes. In: CVPR (2011)
13. Gong, Y., Pawlowski, M., Yang, F., Brandy, L., Bourdev, L., Fergus, R.: Web scale photo hash clustering on a single machine. In: CVPR (2015)
14. Gordo, A., Perronnin, F., Gong, Y., Lazebnik, S.: Asymmetric distances for binary embeddings. PAMI **36**(1), 33–47 (2014)
15. Hsiao, K., Calder, J., Hero, A.O.: Pareto-depth for multiple-query image retrieval. arXiv preprint arXiv:1402.5176 (2014)
16. Jégou, H., Douze, M., Schmid, C.: Product quantization for nearest neighbor search. PAMI **33**(1) (2011)
17. Jégou, H., Tavenard, R., Douze, M., Amsaleg, L.: Searching in one billion vectors: re-rank with source coding. In: ICASSP (2011)
18. Jia, Y., Shelhamer, E., Donahue, J., Karayev, S., Long, J., Girshick, R., Guadarrama, S., Darrell, T.: Caffe: convolutional architecture for fast feature embedding. arXiv preprint arXiv:1408.5093 (2014)
19. Jin, Z., Hu, Y., Lin, Y., Zhang, D., Lin, S., Cai, D., Li, X.: Complementary projection hashing. In: ICCV (2013)
20. Kalantidis, Y., Tolias, G., Avrithis, Y., Phinikettos, M., Spyrou, E., Mylonas, P., Kollias, S.: Viral: visual image retrieval and localization. MTAP (2011)
21. Kalantidis, Y., Avrithis, Y.: Locally optimized product quantization for approximate nearest neighbor search. In: CVPR (2014)
22. Kennedy, L., Naaman, M., Ahern, S., Nair, R., Rattenbury, T.: How flickr helps us makesense of the world: context and content in community-contributed media collections. In: ACM Multimedia, vol. 3, pp. 631–640 (2007)
23. Krizhevsky, A., Sutskever, I., Hinton, G.E.: Imagenet classification with deep convolutional neural networks. In: NIPS (2012)
24. Norouzi, M., Fleet, D.: Cartesian k-means. In: CVPR (2013)
25. Norouzi, M., Punjani, A., Fleet, D.J.: Fast search in hamming space with multi-index hashing. In: CVPR (2012)
26. Paulevé, L., Jégou, H., Amsaleg, L.: Locality sensitive hashing: a comparison of hash function types and querying mechanisms. Pattern Recogn. Lett. **31**(11), 1348–1358 (2010)
27. Russakovsky, O., Deng, J., Su, H., Krause, J., Satheesh, S., Ma, S., Huang, Z., Karpathy, A., Khosla, A., Bernstein, M., et al.: Imagenet large scale visual recognition challenge. arXiv preprint arXiv:1409.0575 (2014)
28. Shen, F., Shen, C., Liu, W., Shen, H.T.: Supervised discrete hashing. In: CVPR (2015)
29. Thomee, B., Elizalde, B., Shamma, D.A., Ni, K., Friedland, G., Poland, D., Borth, D., Li, L.J.: Yfcc100m: the new data in multimedia research. Commun. ACM **59**(2), 64–73 (2016)
30. Thomee, B., Shamma, D.A., Friedland, G., Elizalde, B., Ni, K., Poland, D., Borth, D., Li, L.J.: The new data and new challenges in multimedia research (2015). arXiv preprint arXiv:1503.01817
31. Tolias, G., Avrithis, Y., Jégou, H.: Image search with selective match kernels: aggregation across single and multiple images. Int. J. Comput. Vision, 1–15 (2015)
32. Torralba, A., Fergus, R., Weiss, Y.: Small codes and large image databases for recognition. In: CVPR (2008)

33. Wang, J., Shen, H.T., Yan, S., Yu, N., Li, S., Wang, J.: Optimized distances for binary code ranking. In: Proceedings of the ACM International Conference on Multimedia, pp. 517–526. ACM (2014)
34. Wang, J., Kumar, S., Chang, S.F.: Sequential projection learning for hashing with compact codes. In: ICML (2010)
35. Weiss, Y., Torralba, A., Fergus, R.: Spectral hashing. In: NIPS (2008)
36. Xu, B., Bu, J., Chen, C., Cai, D., He, X., Liu, W., Luo, J.: Efficient manifold ranking for image retrieval. In: SIGIR (2011)
37. Zhang, L., Zhang, Y., Tang, J., Lu, K., Tian, Q.: Binary code ranking with weighted hamming distance. In: CVPR (2013)
38. Zheng, Y., Zhao, M., Song, Y., Adam, H., Buddemeier, U., Bissacco, A., Brucher, F., Chua, T.S., Neven, H.: Tour the world: building a web-scale landmark recognition engine. In: CVPR (2009)
39. Zhu, C.Z., Huang, Y.H., Satoh, S.: Multi-image aggregation for better visual object retrieval. In: ICASSP (2014)

W24 – Computer Vision for Art Analysis

Preface

Following the success of the 1st an 2nd Workshops on Computer VISion for ART Analysis held in 2012 (together with ECCV 2012) and in 2014 (together with ECCV 2014), we present the 3rd VISART (with ECCV 2016). The use of computer vision for the analysis of art has proven to be a fertile ground for research that continues to grow. For instance, the interdisciplinary nature of this research benefits the computer vision community with new tools that address new problems.

This workshop is relevant because it brings together leading researchers in the fields of computer vision, machine learning, art history, and multimedia information retrieval, with a special emphasis on art and cultural heritage applications. The scope of this workshop has been expanded from the first two editions not only to promote interdisciplinary collaborations and expose the audience to the problems and results in art analysis using the state-of-the-art techniques developed in the aforementioned fields, but also to understand the current challenges in art history that can be addressed by computer vision methodologies. In order to address the latter objective, the workshop chairs now include three art historians, and the invited keynote speakers are: Louisa Wood Ruby (Head of the Photoarchive Research at the Frick Art Reference Library New York, USA), Alexander Mordvintsev (Software Engineer at Google, who developed "Inceptionism: Going Deeper into Neural Networks"), and Maarten Wijntjes (Assistant Professor at Delft University of Technology, who is working on the problem of Visual Communication of Stuff and Things).

The first call for papers was distributed by mid-April, 2016 to several computer vision and art history mailing lists, and paper submission deadline was set to 30th June 2016. We have received 23 full paper submissions, out of which 13 papers have been accepted for presentation based on the three reviews each received from computer vision and art history experts. We would like to thank the excellent reviewers. We hope you enjoy the 3rd VISART!

October 2016

Joao Paulo Costeira
Gustavo Carneiro
Alessio Del Bue
Ahmed Elgammal
Peter Hall
Ann-Sophie Lehmann
Hans Brandhorst
Emily L. Spratt

The Art of Detection

Elliot J. Crowley$^{(\boxtimes)}$ and Andrew Zisserman

Visual Geometry Group, Department of Engineering Science,
University of Oxford, Oxford, UK
{elliot,az}@robots.ox.ac.uk

Abstract. The objective of this work is to recognize object categories in paintings, such as cars, cows and cathedrals. We achieve this by training classifiers from natural images of the objects. We make the following contributions: (i) we measure the extent of the *domain shift* problem for image-level classifiers trained on natural images vs paintings, for a variety of CNN architectures; (ii) we demonstrate that classification-by-detection (i.e. learning classifiers for regions rather than the entire image) recognizes (and locates) a wide range of small objects in paintings that are not picked up by image-level classifiers, and combining these two methods improves performance; and (iii) we develop a system that learns a region-level classifier *on-the-fly* for an object category of a user's choosing, which is then applied to over 60 million object regions across 210,000 paintings to retrieve localised instances of that category.

1 Introduction

"It is of the highest importance in the art of detection to be able to recognize out of a number of facts which are incidental and which vital. Otherwise your energy and attention must be dissipated instead of being concentrated."

– Sherlock Holmes, "The Reigate Puzzle"

The ability of visual classifiers to label the content of paintings is of great benefit to art historians, as it allows them to spend less time arduously searching through paintings looking for objects to study, and more time studying them. However, such visual classifiers are generally trained on natural images, for which there is a copious amount of annotation (and which is often lacking for paintings). Unfortunately, as Hall *et al.* observe [24], there is a drop in performance in training on natural images rather than paintings. So we ask, when it comes to classifying paintings using natural images as training data, *what are we missing?*

We investigate the answer to this question from two directions: first, by measuring quantitatively the *domain shift* problem for image-level classifiers, and second, by looking at what is missed by image-level classifiers, but not missed by *detectors*.

The task of interest here is image classification – classifying an image by the objects it contains. With increasingly powerful image representations provided by each generation of Convolutional Neural Networks (CNNs) there has been a

© Springer International Publishing Switzerland 2016
G. Hua and H. Jégou (Eds.): ECCV 2016 Workshops, Part I, LNCS 9913, pp. 721–737, 2016.
DOI: 10.1007/978-3-319-46604-0_50

steady increase in performance over a variety of challenging datasets of natural, photographic images [17,31,34] (and for a variety of tasks [15,22,29,32]). It has been shown that these representations transfer well between domains such as between DSLR and webcam images [39], natural images and sketches [43] and of particular interest to us, between images and paintings [11,12].

Our first contribution is to compare image-level-classifiers (i.e. representing an entire image by a single vector) trained on natural images to those trained on paintings at the task of painting classification. This allows us to observe how severe the drop in performance is for different architectures when they have to cope with domain shift.

It transpires that a major shortcoming of natural image-trained, image-level-classifiers is their inability to retrieve very small objects in paintings. Small objects are particularly prevalent in paintings, for example: animals dotted across the countryside in landscape scenes; boats that are often small regions in a seascape; and aeroplanes that are sometimes little more than a speck in the sky. Our second contribution is to demonstrate that classification-by-detection (i.e. finding regions in an image and classifying them) finds such objects for a variety of classes. We also show that combining the two methods, image-level classification and classification-by-detection, leads to improved performance.

Finally, we build upon the detector by contributing a system that detects an object of a user's choosing in paintings *on-the-fly*. The system downloads natural images from the web and learns a region-level classifier. This classifier is applied to over 60 million regions across 210,000 paintings to retrieve a large range of objects with high precision. The detected objects are given in their paintings with a bounding box, allowing for easy comparison of objects. We evaluate this system for many different queries.

The paper is organized as follows: Sect. 3 describes the datasets of natural images and paintings used in this work. An evaluation of painting classification for different network architectures with natural image-trained and painting-trained image-level classifiers is carried out in Sect. 4. In Sect. 5 object detectors are utilised for the retrieval of small objects in paintings. Lastly, we describe the on-the-fly learning system for detecting objects in paintings in Sect. 6.

2   Related Work

Domain Adaptation. There is a wealth of literature on adapting hand-crafted (i.e. shallow) features between domains (from a source domain to a target domain): Daumé [14] augments the feature space of source and target data. Others [27,30] have re-weighted source samples based on target sample similarity. Saenko *et al.* [35] map source and target data to a domain-invariant subspace; several later works build upon this idea [19,23,26,38]. For deep learning, Ganin and Lempitsky [20] incorporate a branch in their network architecture that classifies an input sample as being from one of two domains. The resulting loss is back-propagated, and then reversed before being passed to the original network to maximise domain confusion – the idea being that this should create a domain-invariant network. Tzeng *et al.* [39] learn domain invariant representations by adding two losses to their network architecture: (i) a loss based on a domain classifier similar to [20], and (ii) a 'domain confusion' loss that forces samples from different domains to appear similar to the network. Aljundi and Tuytelaars [3] propose a method that identifies those filters in the first convolutional layer of a network that are badly affected by domain shift. These filters are then reconstructed from filters less affected by the domain shift in order to achieve domain adaptation.

Natural Images to Paintings. In the vast majority of the domain adaptation literature, the source and target data both consist of natural images. Evaluation is mainly carried out on the 'Office Dataset' [35] where the domains in questions are images taken with a DSLR camera, a webcam, and images from the Amazon website. There is however, work on the specific problem of learning from natural images and retrieving paintings: Shrivastava *et al.* [36] use an Exemplar-SVM [28] to retrieve paintings of specific buildings. Aubry *et al.* [5] improve on this by utilising mid-level discriminative patches, the patches in question demonstrating remarkable invariance between natural images and paintings. Our previous work [13] demonstrates that this patch-based method can be extended to object categories in paintings beyond the instance matching of [5]. Others [41, 42] have considered the wider problem of generalising across many depictive styles (e.g. photo, cartoon, painting) by building a depiction-invariant graph model. Cai *et al.* [6] utilise query expansion to refine a DPM [18] model learnt on natural images with confident detections found on artwork.

3   Datasets

In this section we describe the datasets used in the paper: one of natural images, that will be used for training the *source* image classifiers and detectors; and the other of paintings that will be used to provide the *target* training images, and also a test set. The statistics for these datasets are given in Table 1.

3.1   Paintings

The Paintings Dataset introduced in [13], and available at the website [2], is a subset of the publicly available 'Art UK' dataset [1] – over 200,000 paintings from British galleries, of different styles and eras (formerly known as 'Your Paintings') – for which each painting is annotated for the occurrence of 10 classes – aeroplane, bird, boat, chair, cow, dining-table, dog, horse, sheep, train. The annotation is complete in the PASCAL VOC [16] sense – in that every occurrence is annotated at the image-level. These classes were chosen because they are all present in PASCAL VOC (used for the natural image dataset below), allowing us to assess the domain shift problem between the two datasets directly by class. Example images of the dataset are shown in Fig. 1.

Fig. 1. Example class images from the `Paintings Dataset`. From top to bottom row: aeroplane, cow, sheep. Notice that the dataset is particularly challenging: objects can be large or minuscule, may often be occluded, and are depicted in a large variety of styles such as photo-realistic, abstract and impressionist.

The entire 'Art UK' dataset [1] is used in the on-the-fly system (Sect. 6) to provide the variety required for general searches. This dataset consists of over 210,000 oil paintings.

3.2 Natural Images

The `VOC12` dataset is the subset of PASCAL VOC 2012 [16] TrainVal images that contain any of the 10 classes. Only 10 of the 20 VOC classes are used, because the 'Art UK' dataset does not have a sufficient number of annotated examples of the other 10 classes.

4 Domain Adaptation

In this section, we compare image-level classifiers trained on features from natural images (`VOC12`) to classifiers trained on features from paintings (the training set of the `Paintings Dataset`). In both cases these classifiers are evaluated on the test set of the `Paintings Dataset`. The classifiers trained on paintings are representative of the 'best-case scenario' since there is no domain shift to the target domain. Performance is assessed using Average Precision (AP) per class, and also precision at rank k (Pre@k) – the fraction of the top-k retrieved paintings that contain the object – as this places an emphasis on the accuracy of the highest classification scores. To evaluate the domain shift problem we examine the 'mAP gap' – the change in mean (over class) AP between natural image and painting-trained classifiers.

Table 1. The statistics for the datasets used in this paper: each number corresponds to how many images contain that particular class. Note, because each image can contain multiple classes, the total across the row does not equal the total number of images. Train/Validation/Test splits are also given.

Dataset	Split	Aero	Bird	Boat	Chair	Cow	Din	Dog	Horse	Sheep	Train	Total
VOC12	Train	327	395	260	566	151	269	632	237	171	273	3050
	Val	343	370	248	553	152	269	654	245	154	271	3028
	TrainVal	670	765	508	1119	303	538	1286	482	325	544	6078
Paintings Dataset	Train	74	319	862	493	255	485	483	656	270	130	3463
	Val	13	72	222	140	52	130	113	127	76	35	865
	TrainVal	87	391	1084	633	307	615	596	783	346	165	4328
	Test	113	414	1059	569	318	586	549	710	405	164	4301

The classifiers used are linear one-vs-rest SVMs, and the features are produced using a CNN. In Sect. 4.1 we determine how the mAP gap is affected by the CNN architecture used to produce the feature, and in Sect. 4.2 we discuss train and test augmentations, and the per class performance. Implementation details are given at the end of the section.

4.1 Networks

Three networks are compared, each trained on the ILSVRC-2012 image dataset with batch normalisation: first, the **VGG-M** architecture of Chatfield et al. [8] that consists of 8 convolutional layers. The filters used are quite large (7×7 in the first layer, 5×5 in the second). The features produced are 4096-D. Second, the popular 'very deep' model of Simonyan and Zisserman [37] **VD-16** that consists of 16 convolutional layers with very small 3×3 filters in each layer of stride 1. The features produced are again 4096-D. Third, the ResNets of He et al. [25] that treat groups of layers in a network as residual blocks relative to their input. This allows for extremely deep network architectures. The 152-layer ResNet model **RES-152** is selected for this work. The features extracted are 2048-D.

Network comparison. Table 2 gives the mAP performance for the three networks trained on VOC12 or the Paintings Dataset. Three things are clear: first, and unsurprisingly, for features from the same network, classifiers learnt on paintings are better at retrieving paintings than classifiers learnt on natural images; second, RES-152 features surpass VD-16 features, which in turn surpass VGG-M features; and finally, that the mAP gap decreases as the network gets better – from a 14.9 % difference for VGG-M to a 12.7 % for RES-152. Thus improved classification performance correlates with increased domain invariance.

From here on only ResNet features are used for image-level classifiers.

Table 2. mAP for retrieval using image-level classifiers trained on VOC12 vs the Paintings Dataset. Both the networks used to generate the features and the augmentation schemes are varied. 'Net' refers to the network used. 'none', 'f5', 'f25' and 'Stretch' are augmentation schemes and each column gives the corresponding mAP. Augmentation schemes are described further in Sect. 4.2. The last column shows the gap in mAP between natural image and painting-trained classifiers for 'Stretch' augmentation.

Net	Training set	None	f5	f25	Stretch	mAP gap
VGG-M	VOC12	50.8	51.9	52.9	52.9	14.9
VGG-M	Paintings Dataset	65.1	67.8	67.8	67.8	
VD-16	VOC12	54.8	56.2	56.7	56.8	14.0
VD-16	Paintings Dataset	68.7	71.2	71.2	70.8	
RES-152	VOC12	60.5	61.6	62.0	62.3	12.7
RES-152	Paintings Dataset	72.5	74.6	74.6	75.0	

4.2 Augmentation

Four augmentation schemes available in the MatConvNet toolbox [40] are compared, and are applied to each image to produce N crops. In all cases the image is first resized (with aspect ratio preserved) such that its smallest length is 256 pixels. Crops extracted are ultimately 224 × 224 pixels. The schemes are: **none**, a single crop ($N = 1$) is taken from the centre of the image; **f5**, crops are taken from the centre and the four corners. The same is done for the left-right flip of the image (N=10); **f25**, an extension of f5. Crops are taken at 25 % intervals in both width and height, this is also carried out for the left-right flip ($N = 50$); and finally, **Stretch**, a random rectangular region is taken from the image, linear interpolation across the pixels of the rectangle is performed to turn it into a 224 × 224 crop, there is then a 50 % chance that this square is left-right flipped. This is performed 50 times ($N = 50$). Note that the same augmentation scheme is applied to both training and test images.

Table 2 shows that the type of augmentation is important: 'stretch' generally produces the highest performance – a 2 % or more increase in mAP over 'none', and equal to or superior to 'f5' and 'f25'. This is probably because the stretch augmentation also mimics foreshortening caused by out-of-plane rotation for objects.

Results and discussion. Table 3 shows the per class AP and Pre@k for the best performing case (ResNet with stretch augmentation), with the corresponding PR curves given in Fig. 2. The datasets are not class balanced, and the ratio of number of TrainVal samples between natural images and paintings varies considerably over classes, but there does not seem to be an obvious correlation with performance – aeroplane classifiers learnt on paintings significantly outperform those learnt on natural images despite being trained with far fewer positive samples (87 vs. 670); and the 'chair', 'dining table' and 'dog' classes have similar numbers in the painting dataset, but with 'dining table' only having half the

Table 3. Retrieval performance comparison on the test set of the `Paintings Dataset` for classifiers trained using ResNet features. The images have been augmented using 'Stretch'. 'Set' refers to the training set used and the performance metric is given under 'Metric': Average Precision (AP) or Precision at rank k (Pre@k).

Set	Metric	Aero	Bird	Boat	Chair	Cow	Din	Dog	Horse	Sheep	Train	Avg
VOC	AP	69.4	42.0	88.7	57.3	62.4	48.4	50.5	73.5	48.7	81.9	62.3
	Pre@k=50	94.0	94.0	100.0	72.0	84.0	92.0	100.0	100.0	98.0	100.0	93.4
	Pre@k=100	61.0	82.0	99.0	72.0	89.0	84.0	98.0	100.0	86.0	98.0	86.9
Paint	AP	77.1	54.1	94.3	78.7	68.3	76.3	62.7	83.5	68.8	85.7	75.0
	Pre@k=50	96.0	100.0	100.0	98.0	92.0	94.0	100.0	100.0	100.0	100.0	98.0
	Pre@k=100	65.0	100.0	99.0	97.0	90.0	92.0	98.0	100.0	91.0	100.0	93.2

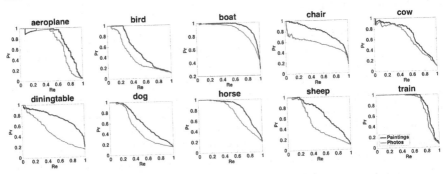

Fig. 2. Precision-Recall curves for different classes, comparing natural image-trained (red) and painting-trained (blue) classifiers learnt on ResNet features. Notice for 'sheep' that the gap in the curves is very significant even at low recall. (Color figure online)

TrainVal images of the other two in VOC12, yet (based on AP) their relative performance does not reflect these ratios at all.

One clear observation though is that the performance of natural image-trained classifiers is inferior to painting-trained classifiers, with an AP gap of around 0.1 for most classes. Pre@k sees a similar decrease. There are some particularly bad cases: 'sheep' has a colossal 20% decrease in AP, and the furniture classes ('chair' and 'dining table') endure a significant drop. There are several reasons for this inferior performance: first, a few of the paintings are depicted in a highly abstract manner, understandably hindering classification; second, some objects are depicted in a particular way in paintings that isn't present in natural images, e.g. aeroplanes in paintings can be WWII spitfires rather than commercial jets. A third reason is size in the painting; in spite of many paintings being depicted in quite a natural way small objects are missed. Some examples of paintings containing small objects that have been 'missed' (i.e. received a low classifier score) are given in Fig. 3. We investigate this problem in Sect. 5.

Fig. 3. Examples of paintings where a small object has been 'missed' (i.e. given a low score) by a classifier. In each case, the object under consideration is brought to attention with a red box. From left to right: aeroplane, dog, sheep, chair. These small objects are found with confidence by a detector. (Color figure online)

4.3   Implementation Details

Each image (both training and test) undergoes augmentation to produce N crops. The mean RGB values of ILSVRC-2012 are subtracted from each crop. These crops are then passed into a network, and the outputs of the layer before the prediction layer are recorded, giving N feature vectors. These are averaged and then normalised to produce a single feature. Linear-SVM Classifiers are learnt using the training features per class in a one-vs-the-rest manner for assorted regularisation parameters (C). The C that produces the highest AP for each class when the corresponding classifier is applied to the validation set is recorded. The training and validation data are then combined to train classifiers using these C parameters. These classifiers are then applied to the test features, which are ranked by classifier score. Finally, these ranked lists are used to compute APs.

5   Classification by Detection

In this section we classify images by using a detector which is capable of locating small objects. For this we use the VGG-16 Faster R-CNN network of Ren *et al.* [33]. Detection proceeds in two stages: first, a Region Proposal Network (RPN) with an architecture resembling VGG-VD-16 [37] takes in an image and produces up to 300 rectangular regions at a wide variety of scales and aspect ratios each with an "objectness" score. These regions are then used in a Fast R-CNN [21] network that identifies and regresses the bounding box of regions likely to contain PASCAL VOC classes. To obtain a ranked list for a given class, the entire VGG-16 Faster R-CNN network (both the RPN and the pre-trained Fast R-CNN) is applied to each painting in the test set, and the images are ranked according to the score of the highest confidence detection window.

Results and Discussion. Some example detections are given in Fig. 5. The AP and Pre@k per class is reported in Table 4. The pointwise average mAP and Pre@k curves are given in Fig. 4, and compared with those of the image-level classifiers.

Very interestingly, the mAP resulting from this detection network is higher than that of the image-level classifiers trained on natural images, marginally outperforming even the most powerful ResNet classifiers (62.7 % vs. 62.3 %).

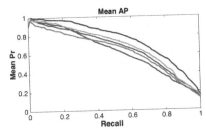
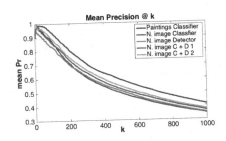

Fig. 4. Left: A point-wise average of mAP across Recall. Right: The average of class precision at rank k for $k < 1000$. Plots are given for image-level classifiers learnt on paintings (blue), and on natural images (red). The Faster-RCNN detector of Sect. 5 is given (yellow), as well as the combinations with image-level classifiers (green: ranked list combination, cyan: score combination). Notice the significant gap in the performance of natural image and painting-trained classifiers and how the classifier-detection combination ameliorates this. (Color figure online)

The most notable success is on the sheep class, $(70.6\,\% $ vs. $48.7\,\%)$. This is probably because sheep in natural images are typically quite large and near the foreground, whereas in paintings they are often tiny and dotted across an idyllic Welsh hillside. A similar, although smaller such discrepancy can be observed for dogs which are depicted in paintings not only as beloved pets, but also in hunting scenes where they are often small. However, Pre@k for small k is on average lower for the detector than the classifier. This is probably due to the detector fixating on shapes, and not seeing enough context. For example, the 'aeroplane' detector incorrectly fires with confidence on a dragonfly as its wingspan resembles that of a plane. The dragonfly is hovering above a table covered in fruit, clearly not a setting for an aeroplane. This mistake would not be made if images (with context) rather than regions were used for training.

In spite of this, we observe from the right-hand plot of Fig. 4 that when $k > 220$, the mean Pre@k of the detector overtakes that of the classifier. As we suspect, the detector is simply able to locate small objects the image-level classifier is not. This is confirmed by the plots of Fig. 6, which compares the image classifier score for each object label in a test image, to the size of the detection window given by the Faster R-CNN network. The tall bins/light colours in the lower-left corners confirms that typically, classifying the entire painting is poor when the regions found successfully by the detector are smaller.

Combining Detection and Image-Level Classification. We consider two methods of combining the ranked lists produced by the image-level classifiers (learnt on natural images), with those produced by the detector. Other methods are discussed in [4]. The first method is a simple rank merge that combines the two ordered lists (but does not require the scores). This obtains an mAP of $66.0\,\%$ (Table 4), closing the mAP gap to $9\,\%$. The second method uses a linear combination of the scores: $\alpha A + (1 - \alpha)B$, and orders on these, where A is the classifier score and B is the detector score. This gives an even higher mAP of

Table 4. Retrieval performance comparison for **image-level classifiers** trained using ResNet features where the images have been augmented using 'Stretch' vs. the Faster-RCNN detector used for **classification-by-detection** on the test set of the **Paintings Dataset**. Note that everything has been trained using natural images. C+D 1 refers to the combination of the classifier and detector ranked lists, and C+D 2 is the combination of their scores.

Method	Metric	Aero	Bird	Boat	Chair	Cow	Din	Dog	Horse	Sheep	Train	Avg
Classifier	AP	69.4	42.0	88.7	57.3	62.4	48.4	50.5	73.5	48.7	81.9	62.3
	Pre@k=50	94.0	94.0	100.0	72.0	84.0	92.0	100.0	100.0	98.0	100.0	93.4
	Pre@k=100	61.0	82.0	99.0	72.0	89.0	84.0	98.0	100.0	86.0	98.0	86.9
Detector	AP	67.4	36.2	88.8	32.8	65.1	48.7	57.6	79.6	70.6	80.0	62.7
	Pre@k=50	86.0	92.0	100.0	66.0	80.0	88.0	92.0	98.0	94.0	100.0	89.6
	Pre@k=100	58.0	71.0	99.0	58.0	84.0	80.0	91.0	98.0	92.0	100.0	83.1
C+D 1	AP	72.7	42.8	90.9	48.1	67.0	52.4	58.4	79.6	65.3	83.1	66.0
	Pre@k=50	90.0	92.0	100.0	74.0	86.0	96.0	96.0	98.0	94.0	100.0	92.6
	Pre@k=100	62.0	80.0	99.0	66.0	84.0	83.0	94.0	98.0	94.0	100.0	85.8
C+D 2	AP	75.2	45.0	92.3	54.8	69.1	53.3	60.4	80.8	70.5	83.7	68.5
	Pre@k=50	94.0	96.0	100.0	76.0	84.0	98.0	100.0	100.0	100.0	100.0	94.8
	Pre@k=100	64.0	77.0	99.0	76.0	90.0	89.0	99.0	100.0	94.0	100.0	88.8

Fig. 5. Example detection windows obtained using the Faster R-CNN network. From left to right: aeroplane, bird, chair, cow. Only, the highest ranked window is shown in each image, even though multiple successful detection windows may have been found. Notice that very small objects are captured, such objects are often missed by an image-level classifier.

68.5 % for $\alpha = 0.3$. The pointwise average mAP and Pre@k curves for these two combinations are given in Fig. 4. This high performance is probably because the image-level classifier and detector are able to complement each other: the classifier is able to utilise the context of a painting and the detector is able to reach small objects otherwise unnoticed.

6   Detecting Objects in Paintings On-the-Fly

It is evident from Sect. 5 that by using the network of [33] it is possible to retrieve objects in paintings through detection that are not retrieved using image-level classification. However, these objects are limited to those of PASCAL VOC, which isn't very useful if an art historian is interested in search for depictions of fruit or elephants. To accommodate for this, we provide a live system, inspired by [7,9,12] where a user may supply a query, and paintings are retrieved that contain the object with its bounding box provided. This improves on our image-level painting retrieval system [12] in two ways: Firstly, it retrieves small objects that cannot be located at image-level. Secondly, as the region containing the object is provided it is much easily to locate. The method is demonstrated over the entire 210,000 paintings of the 'Art UK' dataset [1].

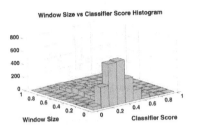
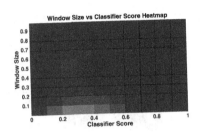

Fig. 6. Left: A 2-D histogram, showing the distribution of image classifier scores (computed from a single vector representing the entire image) against the window size of the highest scored detection window. Classifier scores are mapped between 0 and 1 and window sizes are relative to the size of the image (i.e. window area over image area). Note that the image classifier score is low when the window is small. Right: An overhead view of the histogram where tall peaks are represented by light colours, and short ones by dark colours. (Color figure online)

Overview. At run time, the user supplies an object query as text (e.g. "elephant"). Images are then downloaded for this query using Bing/Google Image Search, and object regions are extracted from them. The object regions are used to generate features, which are used with a pool of negative features to learn a classifier, which is then applied to the features of millions of object regions across the 'Art UK' dataset. The paintings containing the highest scoring object regions are retrieved with their object region annotated. A diagram of this system is provided in Fig. 7.

Feature Representation. Here, we describe how, given an image, features are produced for this system. The image is passed into the Region Proposal Network (RPN) of [33]. This produces up to 300 rectangular regions at a wide variety of scales and aspect ratios each with an "objectness" score. To allow for context, each region is expanded by 5 % in width and height. N of these regions are cropped from the image and resized to 224 by 224, then passed into the VGG-M-128 network of Chatfield et al. [8]. The 128-D output of fc7 (the fully connected layer before the prediction) is extracted and L2-normalised. This network is used primarily because the resulting small features minimise memory usage.

Off-line Processing. The features for object regions across the 'Art UK' dataset, and the features used as negative training examples for classification are computed offline. For each painting in 'Art UK', features are produced as above with $N = 300$ resulting in around 60 million features which are stored in memory. This amounts to ~32 GB. A fixed set of 16,000 negative features are computed for classification: Google and Bing image searches are performed for vague queries ('miscellanea', 'random stuff' and 'nothing in particular' to name a few) and the images are downloaded. For each image, the region from the RPN with the highest "objectness" score is used to produce a feature i.e. $N = 1$.

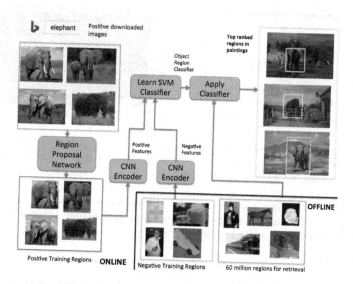

Fig. 7. A diagram of the on-the-fly system. The user types in a query, in this case elephant. Images of that object are downloaded from Bing/Google and passed into a region proposal network to localise the object. These localised regions are passed into a CNN to produce features, which are used in conjunction with pre-computed negative features to learn a region classifier. This region classifier is applied to 60 million object regions across 210,000 paintings and the highest scoring regions are retrieved.

On-line Processing. Computing positive training features and learning, then applying a classifier occur online. Positive features are obtained as follows: a Bing/Google Image Search is carried out using the query as a search term. The URLs for the first 100 images are recorded and downloaded in parallel across 12 CPU cores. Each of these images is passed into the RPN and the highest "objectness" region is used to produce a feature ($N = 1$), operating on the presumption that in these "Flickr style" images (the object is in focus, large and is often against a plain background) the region with the highest "objectness" score corresponds to the object in question. Instances of such windows can be seen in Fig. 8 where it is evident that this is often the case.

The positive and negative features are used in a Linear-SVM to produce a classifier. This can be done on a single core and takes a fraction of a second. The classifier is applied to 60 million painting features in a single matrix operation.

Fig. 8. Highest scoring "objectness" regions (in red) when images downloaded from Bing/Google are passed into an RPN. Top row: 'elephant', Bottom row: 'cottage'. Notice that the regions manage to contain the object, with quite a tight bound. (Color figure online)

6.1 Evaluation

The system is assessed for 250 different object queries over a variety of subjects. This include vehicles (boats, cars), animals (elephants, dogs), clothes (uniform, gown), structures (cottage, church), parts of structures (spires, roof) among others. Performance is evaluated quantitatively as a classification-by-detection problem as in Sect. 5: we rank each of the 210,000 paintings according to the score corresponding to its highest scoring object region and by eye, compute Pre@k – Precision at k, the fraction of the top-k retrieved paintings that contain the object – for the 50 top retrieved paintings. Some examples detections and Pre@k curves are provided in Fig. 9.

This system is crucially able to overcome one of the difficulties experienced by our image-level classification system [12]: a notable difference in performance occurs when an object is large in natural images and small in paintings. A good examples of this is 'wheel'. Bing/Google images of wheels mainly comprise of a single wheel, viewed head-on against a plain background. Conversely, wheels in paintings are often attached to carriages (or to a lesser extent, cars) and are a small part of the image. An image-level classifier succeeds if the natural images resemble the paintings in their entirety so cannot cope with this discrepancy, whereas a region-level classifier can cope with only a small part of a painting resembling the natural image. However, a drawback of the system relative to image-level classification occurs when the context of an object is lost. A similar observation was made in Sect. 5. A good example of this is for the query 'tie'. Some of the paintings retrieved are indeed of people wearing ties, but others are abstract **V** shapes. Several natural images for 'tie' are of a person's torso wearing a tie but by isolating the object, this context has been lost. The bounding boxes of the objects in paintings are often quite loose. Although not ideal, this isn't too important as the objects are sufficiently localised for human use.

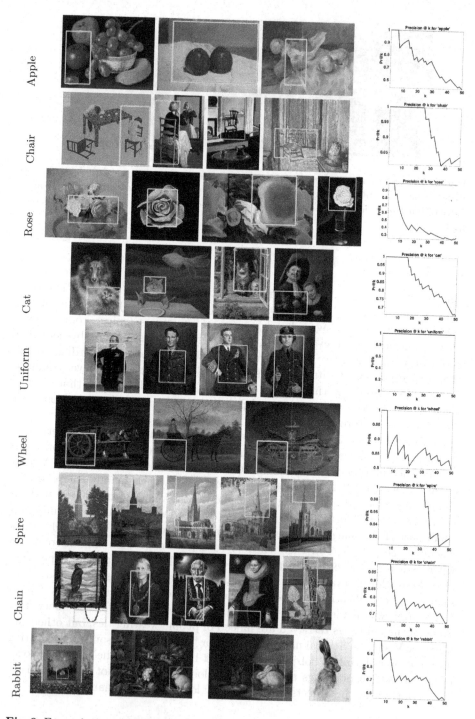

Fig. 9. Example detections for our on-the-fly system for assorted queries as well as the Pre@k curve for the top 50 results.

7   Conclusion and Future Work

In this paper, we have explored the domain shift problem of applying natural image-trained classifiers to paintings. We have further shown that detectors are able to find many objects in paintings that are otherwise missed, and based on this observation, have created an on-the-fly system that finds such objects across hundreds of different classes. Future work could consist of utilising the method of Cinbis *et al.* [10] to refine the locations of objects in natural images and paintings further. By doing this, the painting regions would be well suited for the query expansion method of [6].

Acknowledgements. Funding for this research is provided by EPSRC Programme Grant Seebibyte EP/M013774/1.

References

1. Art UK. http://artuk.org/
2. The Paintings Dataset. http://www.robots.ox.ac.uk/~vgg/data/paintings/
3. Aljundi, R., Tuytelaars, T.: Lightweight unsupervised domain adaptation by convolutional filter reconstruction. arXiv preprint arXiv:1603.07234 (2016)
4. Aslam, J., Montague, M.: Models for metasearch. In: Proceedings of the SIGIR, pp. 276–284. ACM, New York (2001)
5. Aubry, M., Russell, B., Sivic, J.: Painting-to-3D model alignment via discriminative visual elements. ACM Trans. Graph. **33**(2), 14 (2013)
6. Cai, H., Wu, Q., Hall, P.: Beyond photo-domain object recognition: benchmarks for the cross-depiction problem. In: Workshop on Transferring and Adapting Source Knowledge in Computer Vision, ICCV (2015)
7. Chatfield, K., Arandjelović, R., Parkhi, O.M., Zisserman, A.: On-the-fly learning for visual search of large-scale image and video datasets. Int. J. Multimedia Inf. Retr. **4**(2), 75–93 (2015)
8. Chatfield, K., Simonyan, K., Vedaldi, A., Zisserman, A.: Return of the devil in the details: delving deep into convolutional nets. In: Proceedings of the BMVC (2014)
9. Chatfield, K., Zisserman, A.: VISOR: towards on-the-fly large-scale object category retrieval. In: Lee, K.M., Matsushita, Y., Rehg, J.M., Hu, Z. (eds.) ACCV 2012. LNCS, vol. 7725, pp. 432–446. Springer, Heidelberg (2013). doi:10.1007/978-3-642-37444-9_34
10. Cinbis, R.G., Verbeek, J., Schmid, C.: Weakly supervised object localization with multi-fold multiple instance learning. IEEE Trans. Pattern Anal. Mach. Intell. (2016)
11. Crowley, E.J., Parkhi, O.M., Zisserman, A.: Face painting: querying art with photos. In: Proceedings of the BMVC (2015)
12. Crowley, E.J., Zisserman, A.: In search of art. In: Workshop on Computer Vision for Art Analysis, ECCV (2014)
13. Crowley, E.J., Zisserman, A.: The state of the art: object retrieval in paintings using discriminative regions. In: Proceedings of the BMVC (2014)
14. Daumé III., H.: Frustratingly easy domain adaptation arXiv preprint arXiv:0907.1815 (2009)

15. Donahue, J., Jia, Y., Vinyals, O., Hoffman, J., Zhang, N., Tzeng, E., Darrell, T.: DeCAF: a deep convolutional activation feature for generic visual recognition (2013). CoRR abs/1310.1531

16. Everingham, M., Eslami, S.M.A., Gool, L., Williams, C.K.I., Winn, J., Zisserman, A.: The pascal visual object classes challenge: a retrospective. IJCV **111**(1), 98–136 (2015). doi:10.1007/s11263-014-0733-5

17. Everingham, M., Van Gool, L., Williams, C.K.I., Winn, J., Zisserman, A.: The PASCAL Visual Object Classes Challenge 2012 (VOC 2011) (2012). http://host. robots.ox.ac.uk/pascal/VOC/voc2012/

18. Felzenszwalb, P.F., Grishick, R.B., McAllester, D., Ramanan, D.: Object detection with discriminatively trained part based models. IEEE PAMI **32**(9), 1627–1645 (2010)

19. Fernando, B., Tuytelaars, T.: Mining multiple queries for image retrieval: on-the-fly learning of an object-specific mid-level representation. In: Proceedings of the ICCV (2013)

20. Ganin, Y., Lempitsky, V.: Unsupervised domain adaptation by backpropagation. In: Proceedings of the ICLR (2015)

21. Girshick, R.B.: Fast R-CNN. In: Proceedings of the ICCV (2015)

22. Girshick, R.B., Donahue, J., Darrell, T., Malik, J.: Rich feature hierarchies for accurate object detection and semantic segmentation. In: Proceedings of the CVPR (2014)

23. Gopalan, R., Li, R., Chellappa, R.: Domain adaptation for object recognition: an unsupervised approach. In: Proceedings of the ICCV (2011)

24. Hall, P., Cai, H., Wu, Q., Corradi, T.: Cross-depiction problem: recognition and synthesis of photographs and artwork. Comput. Vis. Media **1**(2), 91–103 (2015)

25. He, K., Zhang, X., Ren, S., Sun, J.: Deep residual learning for image recognition. In: Proceedings of the ICCV (2015)

26. Hoffman, J., Darrell, T., Saenko, K.: Continuous manifold based adaptation for evolving visual domains. In: Proceedings of the CVPR (2014)

27. Huang, J., Gretton, A., Borgwardt, K.M., Schölkopf, B., Smola, A.J.: Correcting sample selection bias by unlabeled data. In: Advances in neural information processing systems, pp. 601–608 (2006)

28. Malisiewicz, T., Gupta, A., Efros, A.A.: Ensemble of exemplar-SVMs for object detection and beyond. In: Proceedings of the ICCV (2011)

29. Oquab, M., Bottou, L., Laptev, I., Sivic, J.: Learning and transferring mid-level image representations using convolutional neural networks. In: Proceedings of the CVPR (2014)

30. Pan, S.J., Tsang, I.W., Kwok, J.T., Yang, Q.: Domain adaptation via transfer component analysis. IEEE Trans. Neural Netw. **22**(2), 199–210 (2011)

31. Patterson, G., Hays, J.: Sun attribute database: discovering, annotating, and recognizing scene attributes. In: Proceedings of the CVPR, pp. 2751–2758 (2012)

32. Razavian, A., Azizpour, H., Sullivan, J., Carlsson, S.: CNN features off-the-shelf: an astounding baseline for recognition (2014). CoRR abs/1403.6382

33. Ren, S., He, K., Girshick, R., Sun, J.: Faster R-CNN: towards real-time object detection with region proposal networks. In: NIPS (2016)

34. Russakovsky, O., Deng, J., Su, H., Krause, J., Satheesh, S., Ma, S., Huang, S., Karpathy, A., Khosla, A., Bernstein, M., Berg, A., Li, F.: Imagenet large scale visual recognition challenge. IJCV **115**(3), 211–252 (2015)

35. Saenko, K., Kulis, B., Fritz, M., Darrell, T.: Adapting visual category models to new domains. In: Daniilidis, K., Maragos, P., Paragios, N. (eds.) ECCV 2010, Part IV. LNCS, vol. 6314, pp. 213–226. Springer, Heidelberg (2010)

36. Shrivastava, A., Malisiewicz, T., Gupta, A., Efros, A.: Data-driven visual similarity for cross-domain image matching. ACM Trans. Graph. **30**(6), 154 (2011)
37. Simonyan, K., Zisserman, A.: Very deep convolutional networks for large-scale image recognition. In: International Conference on Learning Representations (2015)
38. Sun, B., Saenko, K.: Subspace distribution alignment for unsupervised domain adaptation. In: Proceedings of the BMVC (2015)
39. Tzeng, E., Hoffman, J., Darrell, T., Saenko, K.: Simultaneous deep transfer across domains and tasks. In: Proceedings of the ICCV (2015)
40. Vedaldi, A., Lenc, K.: Matconvnet: convolutional neural networks for matlab. In: ACM International Conference on Multimedia (2015)
41. Wu, Q., Cai, H., Hall, P.: Learning graphs to model visual objects across different depictive styles. In: Fleet, D., Pajdla, T., Schiele, B., Tuytelaars, T. (eds.) ECCV 2014, Part VII. LNCS, vol. 8695, pp. 313–328. Springer, Heidelberg (2014)
42. Wu, Q., Hall, P.: Modelling visual objects invariant to depictive style. In: Proceedings of the BMVC (2013)
43. Yu, Q., Liu, F., Song, Y., Xiang, T., Hospedales, T.M., Loy, C.C.: Sketch me that shoe. In: Proceedings of the CVPR (2016)

A Streamlined Photometric Stereo Framework for Cultural Heritage

Chia-Kai Yeh[1]([✉]), Nathan Matsuda[1], Xiang Huang[3], Fengqiang Li[1], Marc Walton[2], and Oliver Cossairt[1]

[1] Department of EECS, Northwestern University, Evanston, USA
chiakaiyeh2017@u.northwestern.edu
[2] Northwestern University/Art Institute of Chicago Center for Scientific Studies in the Art (NU-ACCESS), Evanston, USA
[3] Argonne National Laboratory, Lemont, USA

Abstract. In this paper, we propose a streamlined framework of robust $3D$ acquisition for cultural heritage using both photometric stereo and photogrammetric information. An uncalibrated photometric stereo setup is augmented by a synchronized secondary witness camera co-located with a point light source. By recovering the witness camera's position for each exposure with photogrammetry techniques, we estimate the precise $3D$ location of the light source relative to the photometric stereo camera. We have shown a significant improvement in both light source position estimation and normal map recovery compared to previous uncalibrated photometric stereo techniques. In addition, with the new configuration we propose, we benefit from improved surface shape recovery by jointly incorporating corrected photometric stereo surface normals and a sparse $3D$ point cloud from photogrammetry.

Keywords: Photometric stereo · Reflectance transformation imaging · Near light position calibration · Photogrammetry · $3D$ surface shape reconstruction

1 Introduction

Computational Imaging techniques have been widely used for art history analysis and cultural heritage research in the last decade. Digital imaging technologies empower conservation scientists by revealing more information about works of art, helping to better preserve and protect their history for future generations. Accurate, automatic $3D$ surface recovery using only commodity cameras is particularly important for a number of applications in cultural heritage research. Since artifacts of historical significance are often located in public spaces or museums without the possibility of relocation to a laboratory environment, art conservators require $3D$ shape acquisition techniques that are portable, inexpensive, non-destructive, and fast, in order to uncover previously unknown information about artist techniques and materials. Two commonly used techniques that

© Springer International Publishing Switzerland 2016
G. Hua and H. Jégou (Eds.): ECCV 2016 Workshops, Part I, LNCS 9913, pp. 738–752, 2016.
DOI: 10.1007/978-3-319-46604-0_51

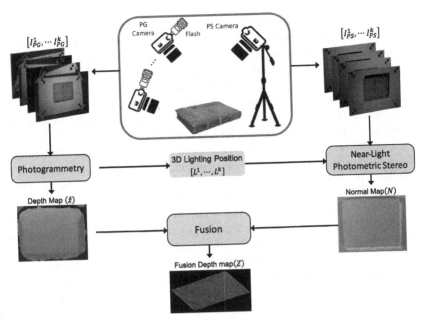

Fig. 1. Overview of the Streamlined photometric stereo framework for cultural heritage: We use photogrammetry to find the $3D$ light positions $[L^1, \cdots, L^k]$ relative to a stationary photometric stereo (PS) camera. The estimated $3D$ light positions then allow us to compute accurate surface normal N from the PS camera. We fuse the computed normal map with a depth map $\hat{z}$, computed using photogrammetry, to generate globally accurate $3D$ shapes Z with high-quality micro surface details.

fit these requirements are Reflectance Transformation Imaging (RTI) and Photogrammetry (PG).

RTI is a visualization technique that allows users to probe the appearance of an artwork under arbitrary illumination conditions computationally, in a post-processing step. RTIs are created from multiple photographs of the object captured by a camera with fixed position and varying illumination. Researchers use RTI to virtually re-light an object under arbitrary illumination conditions. Computational relighting can reveal fine details of the subject's $3D$ surface, for instance when strong raking light is used to visualize the surface appearance. However, because RTI is merely a visualization technique, it provides no direct access to depth information. Photometric stereo (PS) is a well established research topic in computer vision which estimates surface normal from a set of photographs taken with a fixed camera position and multiple known lighting directions. Intensity values in the captured images are modeled as a function of lighting angle, surface normal, and material reflectance. By inverting this model, PS techniques recover surface normal, which can then be integrated to produce $3D$ Surface shape.

Alternatively, Photogrammetry (PG) uses images taken at different camera positions, using triangulation to compute $3D$ surface shape. Using Structure from Motion (SfM) techniques, feature points common between/among multiple views can be used to jointly solve for both $3D$ location of the points and the corresponding camera positions. The resulting $3D$ result is globally accurate but not dense, since $3D$ information is computed only for each feature point, but not each pixel. These sparse $3D$ points can be interpolated to generate a low-resolution $3D$ mesh model of the object.

PS and PG techniques have been explored extensively in the literature, but still have fundamental drawbacks. For example, accurate PS normal output usually requires pre-calibrated lighting positions. In typical setups, this is achieved using either lighting with a fixed calibrated $3D$ geometry (e.g. a lighting dome), or by placing a reflective sphere in the scene to estimate incident lighting directions. $3D$ light position can be accurately pre-calibrated using a lighting dome, but this custom hardware solution is often inaccessible and sometimes impractical. A reflective sphere can accurately measure distant lighting, but produces significant errors when light sources violate the far light condition and are actually located near the object (e.g. within 4 times the size of the object), typical of many PS capture setups [13]. PG techniques do not require controllable lighting, but do require a high number of identifiable correspondence points in order to produce high resolution surface output, precluding the possibility of capturing low-texture or single-material objects frequently found in a wide variety of natural scenes. Furthermore, at large standoff distances, depth precision for PG methods is relatively coarse while PS solutions are capable of capturing highly detailed depth features.

In this paper, we present a robust $3D$ shape recovery capture framework for cultural heritage as shown in Fig. 1. Throughout the remainder of the paper we will refer to these two cameras as the PS camera, capturing reflectance information from a fixed position, and the PG camera, affixed to the light source and capturing scene structure for photogrammetry from multiple views of the object. The PG camera images are processed using existing SfM algorithms to recover the camera position for each frame, and thus the lighting positions for the PS camera as well. Using these computed $3D$ lighting positions we then produce an accurate PS normal map. Because we have generated a point cloud from the PG algorithm as well, we can fuse this sparse $3D$ information with the PS normal map to produce a $3D$ surface with both the fine surface detail typical of PS techniques and the absolute depth accuracy typical of PG techniques. The technique introduces minimal complexity beyond a conventional photometric stereo capture setup, yet can be used to significantly improve the accuracy of $3D$ surface reconstructions.

The specific contributions of this work are:

- **A simple, robust $3D$ capture system:** We present a simple system for the free-form photometric stereo capture system using just two camera with wireless synchronize triggers and a on-camera ring light. We show that our system simplifies reflectance capture and results in more accurate $3D$ surface reconstruction.

- **More accurate light position estimation:** Previous techniques estimate $3D$ light position directly from images from radiometric measurements [13], which are easily corrupted by shadows and specularities. In contrast, our light position estimation is based on geometric triangulation using SfM, and is therefore largely independent of scene reflectance and illumination.
- **Improved near-light PS surface recovery:** Traditional PS techniques assume infinitely distant light sources. Under this assumption, the lighting direction can be calibrated by placing a mirror ball in the scene. Our approach removes this far light assumption and eliminates the need for a lighting calibration object. Instead, $3D$ light position is estimated using a PG camera attached to the light source. We show that by accurately measuring the $3D$ location of the light sources, we can recover more accurate $3D$ surface shapes when using a PS setup that violates the far light assumption.
- **Large scale, high precision $3D$ reconstructions:** We show experimentally that our setup can be used to generate large field of view $3D$ shape reconstructions with high precision. This is done by fusing the fine details from dense normal estimation using PS, with the sparse $3D$ point clouds from our PG camera.

2   Previous Work

2.1   Reflectance Transformation Imaging

Reflectance transformation imaging is widely popular among art conservators through the use of the CHI RTI Builder and Viewer software suites [1]. RTI, originally known as Polynomial Texture Mapping (PTM), was first proposed by Malzbender [15] as a way to use a polynomial basis function for computational relighting. Later, the hemispherical harmonics (HSH) version [8] was introduced to reduce the directional bias in computational relighting results. Palma *et al.* [17] estimated normal from PTM RTIs by fitting the pixel intensity to a local bi-quadratic function of light angles and then setting the derivative to zero, which has the effect of finding the direction of the brightest pixel. Conservators use the CHI software to interactively explore image relighting and normal maps in the RTI Viewer, and also export those images offline for further research.

2.2   Photometric Stereo

In the original photometric stereo formulation introduced by Horn [12], light sources are assumed infinitely distant, the camera is orthographic, and the object surface is Lambertian and convex (*i.e.* no shadows or inter-reflections). Subsequent research has sought to generalize the technique for more practical camera, surface and lighting models. Belhumeur *et al.* [6] discovered that with an orthographic camera model and uncalibrated lighting, the object's surface can be uniquely determined to within a bas-relief ambiguity. Papadhimitri and Favaro et al. [18] recently pointed out that this ambiguity is resolved under the perspective camera model. Several researchers have also sought to relax the Lambertian reflectance assumption and incorporate effects such as specular highlights and shadows. New techniques have been introduced based on non-Lambertian reflectance models [5,10,11], or sophisticated statistical methods to automatically filter non-lambertian effects [14,26,27]. However, less attention has been paid to relaxing assumptions on the lighting model. Several researchers [13,19,24] recently investigated removing the far-light assumption to improve the accuracy of photometric stereo. Others consider non-isotropic illuminations [20]. Ackermann et al. [2] recently gave a more comprehensive surveys on earlier and recent photometric stereo techniques.

2.3   Photogrammetry

Developed in the 1990s, this technique has its origins in the computer vision community and the development of automatic feature-matching algorithms from the previous decade. To determine the 3D location of points within a scene, traditional photogrammetry methods require the 3D location and pose of the cameras, or the 3D location of a series of control points to be known. Later, Structure-from-Motion (SfM) relaxed this requirement, simultaneously reconstructing camera pose and scene geometry through the automatic identification of matching features in multiple images [22,23].

2.4   Combining Photometric Stereo and Photogrammetry

Although PS provides relatively accurate surface normal, it is still challenging to reconstruct a globally accurate surface shape. Some work has aimed to combine PG and PS techniques, such as the multi-view photometric stereo method by Hernandez et al. [9], which used RANSAC to estimate the light sources position and reconstruct 3D surfaces of Lambertian objects. For calibrated light sources, Birkbeck et al. [7] employed a variational method to estimate the surface and handle specular reflections using a Phong reflectance model. Ahmed et al. [4] used calibrated illumination and multi-view video to capture normal fields and improve the geometry templates. Wu et al. [25] performed a spherical harmonic lighting approximation to combine multi-view photometric stereo. Sabzevariuse et al. [21] used the 3D metric information computed with SfM from a set of 2D landmarks to solve for the bas-relief ambiguity for dense PS surface estimation. All of these algorithms require really critical environment constraint either accurate light-source calibration under far light model or careful illumination design. Nehab et al.'s [16] hybrid reconstruction algorithm focused on leveraging Poisson system to combine depths and normal information. Their fusion algorithm produces high quality reconstruction of 3D surfaces with a given parametric surface.

Our method relaxes the hardware setup constraints relative to these prior methods. To our knowledge ours is the first system to work on fusion between

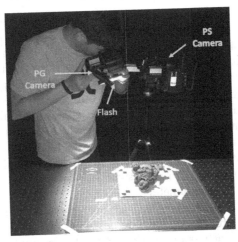

Fig. 2. Capture setup: We use two Canon 5D Mark III cameras with 50 mm prime lens. The PS camera is placed about 0.5 m away from the object.

near-light PS model and PG. Besides having more accurate light position and surface normal estimates, our method also can leverage the surface estimate obtained using photogrammetry. By fusing PS and PG results we can produce an improved 3D surface that retains the advantages of both PS and PG techniques.

3   Our Streamlined Photometric Stereo Framework

3.1   Hardware Setup

Our system setup consists of two Canon 5D Mark III DSLR cameras with 50 mm Canon Prime lenses. One of these, the PS camera was affixed to a tripod above the imaging area. A Polaroid 18 Super Bright Macro SMD LED Ring Light was mounted to the PG camera lens. Both cameras were attached to a PocketWizard FLex TT5 wireless trigger system to ensure synchronized exposures. Lastly a printed set of corner fiducial makers were affixed to the imaging area to provide a means to scale the PS and PG image sets to match the physical distances between the markers.

3.2   Framework Work Flow

We begin by capturing an image at each of k different PG camera positions (see Fig. 2). A ring light is placed around the lens of the PG camera so that the centroid location of the illumination coincides with the optical center of the lens. The PG camera captures a set of images $[I_{PG}^1, ..., I_{PG}^k]$ of the scene from a unique viewing location. The PS camera also captures k images $[I_{PS}^1, ..., I_{PS}^k]$, but from a fixed position. For the PG camera, illumination is always aligned with the camera axis. For the PG camera, a diversity of illumination directions is captures. The

PG images $[I^1_{PG}, ..., I^k_{PG}]$ are input into an off-the-shelf photogrammetry software Agisoft PhotoScan [3], which outputs the camera centers corresponding to the $3D$ light source positions $[L^1, ..., L^k]$. In addition, the software compute a sparse point cloud estimate of the objects $\hat{z}$. An image from the PS camera is input together with the PG camera images so that the extrinsic parameters from all cameras are determined in a unified global coordinate frame. Note that our PG images do not all have the same lighting and contain specularity and shadows under different lighting environment, none of which is ideal for typical passive multi-view stereo matching. However, we have sufficiently dense views under similar-enough lighting for the matching algorithm to find enough matching features between the images to reconstruct a photogrammetry model which is accurate to within a few millimeters.

Next, the $3D$ light positions $[L^1, ..., L^k]$ are used as input into a PS algorithm to accurately recover normal and albedo based on the spatially-varying incident lighting position at each point in the scene. To accomplish this, we solve a least squares problem to iteratively solve for the albedo a and normal N, given captured images $[I^1_{PS}, ..., I^k_{PS}]$ and corresponding 3D light positions $[L^1, ..., L^k]$, similar to the work by Papadhimitri et al. [19].

Finally, the PS algorithm generates a normal map $N = (n_x, n_y, n_z)$ for each pixel in the image. I, The relationship between the estimated normal and the depth map z is then $(\frac{\partial z}{\partial x}, \frac{\partial z}{\partial y}) = (p, q)$, where $(p, q) \triangleq (-\frac{n_x}{n_z}, -\frac{n_y}{n_z})$. The PG algorithm produces a depth map $\hat{z}$ of the scene only for a sparse subset of pixels. We assume $\hat{z}$ is transformed to the PS camera frame using the extrinsic parameters computed from the PG/SfM software. We then recover the PS-PG fused depth z_i for each pixel i by solving the following least squares problem:

$$\text{minimize} \sum_{i \in I} \left\| \begin{bmatrix} \partial z_i / \partial x_i \\ \partial z_i / \partial y_i \end{bmatrix} - \begin{bmatrix} p_i \\ q_i \end{bmatrix} \right\|^2_2 + \lambda \sum_{i \in \hat{I}} (z_i - \hat{z}_i)^2 \tag{1}$$
$$= \|\nabla Z - \Gamma\|^2_2 + \lambda \|MZ - \hat{Z}\|^2_2,$$

where Z, $\hat{Z}$, and Γ are the lexicographically vectorized versions of z_i, $\hat{z}_i$, and (p_i, q_i), ∇ is the gradient matrix, M is a binary selection matrix that only selects the pixels that have valid PG depths, and λ is the parameter depends on the confidence of PG depth.

Note that this formulation does not rely on any linear constraints or statistical priors; it is simply a weighted least-squares approach that attempts to satisfy, on average, the conditions observed by both the PS and PG recovery techniques. A wide variety of variations on this optimization could be employed depending on the type of object and intended usage of the recovered surface, but a detailed analysis of such possibilities is beyond the scope of this paper. We simply aim to demonstrate that the combination of both sets of simultaneously captured data, even with a rudimentary approach to optimization, characterizes the surface significantly better than either approach alone.

Table 1. Measure value *v.s.* ground truth for three light positions P1, P2, and P3: The first row shows the ground truth distance between the PG camera optical center and the 3D location of light sources P1, P2, and P3. The second and third rows show ΔL values for our technique and that of Huang *et al.* [13], respectively. The ΔL values reported are the distance between the estimated 3D position of the PG camera's optical center, and the ground truth 3D position, averaged over five measurements. The fourth and fifth rows report the standard deviation of the distance between the estimated and ground truth 3D location of the PG camera.

	P1	P2	P3
Ground truth distance (mm)	869.98	896.28	756.12
ΔL (Our method) (mm)	1.25	9.09	8.27
ΔL (Huang *et al.* [13]) (mm)	242.46	239.76	216.11
SD δ (Our method) (mm)	0.26	0.23	0.09
SD δ (Huang *et al.* [13]) (mm)	2.09	4.18	2.09

4   Experiments and Results

4.1   Light Position Estimation

First, we evaluated the accuracy and stability for our PG camera-based method for light position estimation. In order to compare to known physical lighting positions, we affixed the tripod mount of the PG camera onto an optical mounting post, which we then inserted sequentially into optical post holders at known locations on an optical table. Though we do not consider this manual procedure sufficient to provide ground truth data, the sub-millimeter tolerances of the machined optical table and mounting posts can demonstrate the extent to which the recovered lighting positions can be relied upon.

In Table 1, we repeated the three fixed lighting positions 5 times, which resulted in an average error relative to our measured positions of less than 10 mm, or well under 1 % error. The standard deviation of these values was less than 1 mm, indicating good repeatability of the technique. Compared to Huang *et al.* [13] using image intensity to estimate the lighting position, our approach using PG/SfM has more accurate lighting position estimation for a near-light photometric stereo model.

4.2   Normal Map Accuracy

To confirm that PG lighting position estimation produces a more accurate PS normal map, we compare normal map recovery for a sphere using our method, the near-light model in Huang *et al.* [13], a conventional distant-light PS model, and ground truth.

Figure 3 shows the X-component of the normal map sampled through the center of a sphere for the ground truth, conventional distant-light PS model, near-light model from Huang *et al.* [13], and our PG light estimation. Our method clearly demonstrates increased fidelity in normal map estimation.

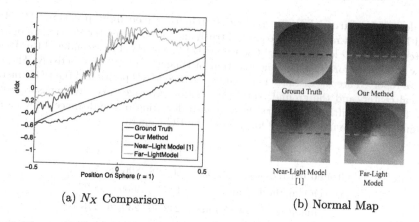

(a) N_X Comparison

(b) Normal Map

Fig. 3. Normal Map Accuracy for a sphere: Comparison between the x component of the estimated normal map for a sphere. The ground truth (shown in blue) normal for the sphere closely resembles a line (the gradient of a parabola is exactly a line). The normal estimate computed using the far light assumption (shown in cyan) and the uncalibrated photometric stereo method from Huang et al. [13] (shown in red) both produce significant errors. Our method (shown in green) accurately estimates 3D light position, and therefore produces the most accurate 3D normal. (Color figure online)

This method is a unique use case for PG techniques in surface reconstruction because it can be applied to texture less objects that would normally be a failure case for PG. So long as there is sufficient correspondence features to perform bundle adjustment somewhere in the PG camera field of view, our technique will produce accurate lighting positions, and thus more accurate normal maps, regardless of the amount of texture in the target object.

4.3 Fusion Surface Reconstruction

When objects have enough surface texture for the PG algorithm alone to produce a sparse point cloud, we can leverage this data for a more globally accurate surface reconstruction. Surface shape recovery remains a significant challenge for all PS techniques since small errors in normal recovery will produce incorrect geometry upon integration, and the absolute position of the surface can never be recovered. The formulation in Eq. 1 retains the fine surface detail recovered by PS and the gross geometric shape recovered by PG.

We chose to test the visual fidelity of surface fusion reconstructions using a cultural heritage object from our University's rare book collection, an object representative of the intended use case for this technique. Shown in Fig. 4, this 16th century reprinting of Hesiod's 'Works and Days', was covered with a reused parchment from an early manuscript that was scraped down to remove the letters from the top surface. Small ridges on the surface are aligned with the direction of the scraping motion. We hope to observe these abrasions in the context of the largely flat overall surface geometry. PS techniques alone will not retain the course flatness but will reveal the small ridges, while PG techniques alone will retain the flat surface but will not resolve the ridges at all. This object is thus an example of a surfaces our PS and PG fusion technique is well suited to recover.

Fig. 4. Test object: a 16*th* century book covered with reused parchment. Small surface abrasions on the surface are of interest to historians.

The λ parameter in Eq. 1 was set to 0.15, a value found experimentally that retained surface detail while preventing the large-scale PS errors to propagate into the final output.

In Fig. 5 we show side-by-side comparisons between the full surface and an inset revealing small details. The top row contains a reference image from the PS data set - the full book surface on the left, followed by the pink inset region expanded on the right. These regions are used in subsequent rows, where surface reconstructions are depicted in orthographic renders using a white Lambertian material and raking angle lights to highlight surface variation in blue along the y-axis and red along the x-axis. The 2*nd* row shows the surface output from the photometric stereo algorithm, which despite recovering small surface details exhibits extreme geometric errors which would significantly limit any object analysis based on the surface height. The 3*rd* row shows the PG surface mesh output from Agisoft Photoscan. The PG results correctly recover the general flatness of the object, but lose all fine surface detail. Finally in the bottom row we show our optimized PS+PG fusion results. We retain both the overall flat shape of the book surface while recovering the small wrinkles and abrasions present on the surface of the book.

In order to test our framework in more general settings, we have tested our method on several additional objects with complex geometry and fine surface detail. As shown in Fig. 6, our framework produces accurate 3*D* reconstructions that maintaining both global accuracy and high precision. The results are far superior to 3*D* reconstructions using either PS or PG alone.

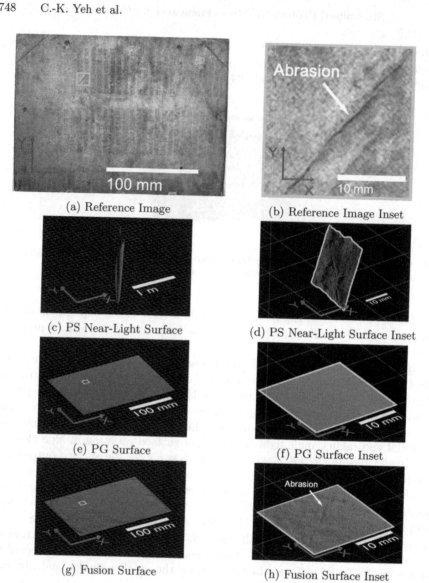

(a) Reference Image

(b) Reference Image Inset

(c) PS Near-Light Surface

(d) PS Near-Light Surface Inset

(e) PG Surface

(f) PG Surface Inset

(g) Fusion Surface

(h) Fusion Surface Inset

Fig. 5. Reconstruction Results: Comparison of reconstruction methods on a 16*th* century book shown in (a), and hi-resolution inset (b), corresponding to the outlined region to the left. After surface recovery, these results are depicted in orthographic perspective and illuminated by a red directional light along the x-axis and a blue directional light along the y-axis to reveal surface details without exaggerating the scale of the z-axis. The PS reconstructions using the method from [13], shown in (c) and (d), exhibit severe global geometry errors due to lack of absolute reference points (the scale in these images were reduced to accommodate the extreme range of z-axis values). PG output from Agisoft Photoscan is shown in (e) and (f). Our fusion results, produced by optimizing the surface for consistency with both PS and PG results are shown in (g), (h). Note that the fusion results exhibit a balance of course geometric accuracy (a flat book surface) while retaining small surface variations. (Color figure online)

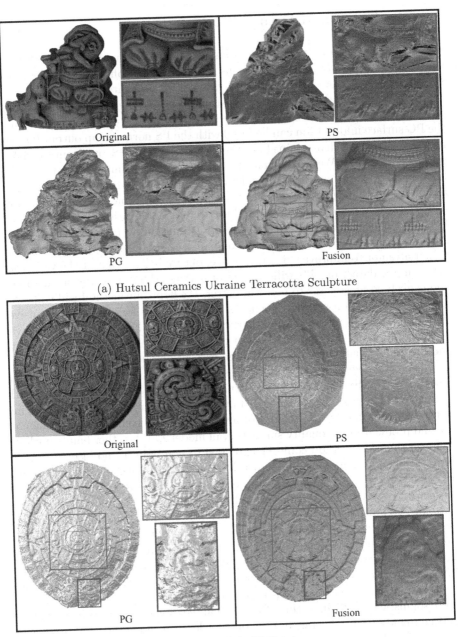

(a) Hutsul Ceramics Ukraine Terracotta Sculpture

(b) Chinese Jade BI Carvings

Fig. 6. Experimental Results using our Framework: We tested our framework on several objects with complex geometry and fine surface detail. These objects demonstrate that our system produces a good balance between global geometric accuracy and micro surface details. 3D reconstruction results using only photometric stereo (PS), and photogrammetry (PG) are shown for comparison. Our fusion results clearly demonstrate superior 3D reconstruction quality.

5 Conclusion and Future Work

We have presented a new technique using a PG camera attached to a flash light source to estimate 3D lighting positions for more robust photometric stereo 3D surface reconstructions. The resulting light position estimates are more accurate than conventional far-light directional estimates or near-light position estimates, and consequently produce more accurate normal maps. We also demonstrate that the PG surface information can be fused with the PS normal map output for surface reconstruction that retains both the fine details from PS and accurate global geometry from PG. We have demonstrated how to use a simple setup to acquire high quality 3D reconstruction results of several cultural heritage objects. Our initial results also give rise to another question: if fusion between poor normal recovery and good PG data produces a reasonable result, is the improved PS performance by accurate light position estimation even necessary? Further analysis is necessary to conclusively compare our results to fusion results that do not attempt to improve PS performance, but we believe that at the very least better input data from PS will not perform worse than other fusion methods, and is likely in most cases to perform better. We hope our method will empower conservators and conservation scientists with new tools for simple, inexpensive, 3D acquisition of cultural heritage artifacts. It is our belief that doing so will open the doors to new applications in monitoring the deterioration of objects and help inform new methods of damage prevention and preservation.

There are several possible directions for future work. Photometric stereo, technically, is a fix-view 2.5D reconstruction method that could not deal with the scene with lots of depth changes. In the future, we are interested in merging multi-view information to account for artifacts that photometric stereo can create and produce a high quality surface detail model. On the other hand, our light source estimation method could be extended to non-point or non-isotropic light sources, an extension applicable to nearly all real-world use cases. By performing PG camera pose estimation on both the PS camera and the PG camera, the full surface of a convex or more complicated surface shape may be recovered. From a systems perspective, the PG camera and flash component could be miniaturized (e.g. replaced with a point-and-shoot camera) to allow for greater freedom by the operator and quicker overall capture times. Two or more of these camera/flash units could be synchronized and processed to capture bidirectional reflectance information and ultimately used to recover more sophisticated material characterization jointly with surface shape. We are also interested in investigating more sophisticated PS algorithms that can handle difficult cases such as shadows and non-lambertian reflectance. Last but not least, although it is quite difficult to have a real ground truth to benchmark a 3D reconstruction system, still we would like to compare our framework with the state of art 3D acquisition method on cultural heritage application in the nearly future.

Acknowledgement. This project was undertaken at the Northwestern University/Art Institute of Chicago Center for Scientific Studies in the Arts (NU-ACCESS). NU-ACCESS is funded through a generous grant from the Andrew W.

Mellon Foundation. Supplemental support is provided by the Materials Research Center, the Office of the Vice President for Research, the McCormick School of Engineering and Applied Science and the Department of Materials Science and Engineering at Northwestern University. Additionally, this work was supported in part by NSF CAREER grant IIS-1453192.

References

1. Cultural heritage imaging: reflectance transformation imaging (rti) (2013). http://culturalheritageimaging.org/Technologies/RTI/index.html
2. Ackermann, J., Goesele, M.: A survey of photometric stereo techniques. Found. Trends Comput. Graph. Vis. **9**(3–4), 149–254 (2015). http://dx.doi.org/10.1561/0600000065
3. Agisoft LLC: Agisoft PhotoScan. http://www.agisoft.com
4. Ahmed, N., Theobalt, C., Dobrev, P., Peter Seidel, H., Thrun, S.: Robust fusion of dynamic shape and normal capture for high-quality reconstruction of time-varying geometry. In: Proceedings of IEEE Conference on Computer Vision and Pattern Recognition, pp. 1–8 (2008)
5. Alldrin, N., Zickler, T., Kriegman, D.: Photometric stereo with non-parametric and spatially-varying reflectance. In: 26th IEEE Conference on Computer Vision and Pattern Recognition, CVPR (2008)
6. Belhumeur, P.N., Kriegman, D.J., Yuille, A.L.: The bas-relief ambiguity. IJCV **35**(1), 33–44 (1999)
7. Birkbeck, N., Cobzas, D., Sturm, P., Jagersand, M.: Variational shape and reflectance estimation under changing light and viewpoints. In: Leonardis, A., Bischof, H., Pinz, A. (eds.) ECCV 2006, Part I. LNCS, vol. 3951, pp. 536–549. Springer, Heidelberg (2006)
8. Elhabian, S.Y., Rara, H., Farag, A.A.: Towards accurate and efficient representation of image irradiance of convex-Lambertian objects under unknown near lighting. In: Proceedings of the IEEE International Conference on Computer Vision, pp. 1732–1737 (2011)
9. Esteban, C.H., Vogiatzis, G., Cipolla, R.: Multiview photometric stereo. IEEE Trans. Pattern Anal. Mach. Intell. **30**(3), 548–554 (2008)
10. Goldman, D.B., Curless, B., Hertzmann, A., Seitz, S.M.: Shape and spatially-varying BRDFs from photometric stereo. IEEE Trans. Pattern Anal. Mach. Intell. **32**(6), 1060–1071 (2010)
11. Hertzmann, A., Seitz, S.: Shape and materials by example: a photometric stereo approach. In: 2003 IEEE Computer Society Conference on Computer Vision and Pattern Recognition, vol. 1, pp. 1–8 (2003)
12. Horn, B.K.P.: Obtaining shape from shading information. In: The Psychology of Computer Vision, pp. 115–155 (1975)
13. Huang, X., Walton, M., Bearman, G., Cossairt, O.: Near light correction for image relighting and 3D shape recovery. In: Guidi, G., Scopigno, R., Brunet, P. (eds.) International Congress on Digital Heritage - Theme 2 - Computer Graphics and Interaction. IEEE (2015)
14. Ikehata, S., Wipf, D., Matsushita, Y., Aizawa, K.: Robust photometric stereo using sparse regression. In: Proceedings of the IEEE Computer Society Conference on Computer Vision and Pattern Recognition, vol. 1, pp. 318–325 (2012)

15. Malzbender, T., Gelb, D., Wolters, H.: Polynomial texture maps. In: Proceedings of SIGGRAPH 2001. Annual Conference Series, pp. 519–528. ACM Press, New York (2001)
16. Nehab, D., Rusinkiewicz, S., Davis, J., Ramamoorthi, R.: Efficiently combining positions and normals for precise 3d geometry. ACM Trans. Graph. **24**(3), 536–543 (2005). http://doi.acm.org/10.1145/1073204.1073226
17. Palma, G., Corsini, M., Cignoni, P., Scopigno, R., Mudge, M.: Dynamic shading enhancement for reflectance transformation imaging. J. Comput. Cult. Heritage **3**(2), 1–20 (2010)
18. Papadhimitri, T., Favaro, P.: A new perspective on uncalibrated photometric stereo. In: Proceedings of the IEEE Computer Society Conference on Computer Vision and Pattern Recognition, pp. 1474–1481 (2013)
19. Papadhimitri, T., Favaro, P., Bern, U.: Uncalibrated near-light photometric stereo. In: Proceedings of the British Machine Vision Conference, pp. 1–12 (2014)
20. Quéau, Y., Durou, J.D.: Some illumination models for industrial applications of photometric stereo. In: QCAV (2015)
21. Sabzevari, R., Del Bue, A., Murino, V.: Structure from motion and photometric stereo for dense 3D shape recovery. In: Maino, G., Foresti, G.L. (eds.) ICIAP 2011, Part I. LNCS, vol. 6978, pp. 660–669. Springer, Heidelberg (2011)
22. Snavely, K.N.: Scene reconstruction and visualization from internet photo collections. Ph.D. thesis, Seattle, WA, USA (2009)
23. Snavely, N., Seitz, S.M., Szeliski, R.: Skeletal graphs for efficient structure from motion. In: Proceedings of Computer Vision and Pattern Recognition (2008)
24. Wetzler, A., Kimmel, R., Bruckstein, A.M., Mecca, R.: Close-range photometric stereo with point light sources. In: 2014 2nd International Conference on 3D Vision, pp. 115–122 (2014)
25. Wu, C., Liu, Y., Dai, Q., Member, S., Wilburn, B.: Fusing multiview and photometric stereo for 3d reconstruction under uncalibrated illumination. Trans. Vis. Comput. Graph. **17**(8), 1082–1095 (2011)
26. Wu, L., Ganesh, A., Shi, B., Matsushita, Y., Wang, Y., Ma, Y.: Robust photometric stereo via low-rank matrix completion and recovery. In: Kimmel, R., Klette, R., Sugimoto, A. (eds.) ACCV 2010. LNCS, vol. 6494, pp. 703–717. Springer, Heidelberg (2011). doi:10.1007/978-3-642-19318-7_55
27. Zhang, M.: Robust surface normal estimation via greedy sparse regression. Ph.D. thesis (2014)

Visual Link Retrieval in a Database of Paintings

Benoit Seguin[✉], Carlotta Striolo, Isabella diLenardo, and Frederic Kaplan

DHLAB, EPFL, Lausanne, Switzerland
{benoit.seguin,carlotta.striolo,isabella.dilenardo,
frederic.kaplan}@epfl.ch

Abstract. This paper examines how far state-of-the-art machine vision algorithms can be used to retrieve common visual patterns shared by series of paintings. The research of such visual patterns, central to Art History Research, is challenging because of the diversity of similarity criteria that could relevantly demonstrate genealogical links. We design a methodology and a tool to annotate efficiently clusters of similar paintings and test various algorithms in a retrieval task. We show that pre-trained convolutional neural network can perform better for this task than other machine vision methods aimed at photograph analysis. We also show that retrieval performance can be significantly improved by fine-tuning a network specifically for this task.

Keywords: Paintings · Visual search · Visual similarity

1 Introduction

In Art History, comparing paintings and finding relations between them is the basic block of many (if not most) analysis. The example of the painting of the *Virgin of the rocks*, by Leonardo da Vinci (Fig. 1), exemplifies how some painters were exposed in one way or another to the work of other's, and how the masterpiece represents the final culmination of several visual references and the starting point for other interpretations of a specific theme or *formula* that we can summarize with the name "pattern". These *visual links* are essential for studying the propagation of patterns and understanding the genesis of a single work of art, its reception and the history of a school of painting, and its influences, through centuries in Art History.

In order to study these visual links, art historians are often required to spend a lot of time in the few libraries which have acquired, across the years, the necessary amount of collections of photos to perform these analysis. Collecting and analyzing images is the starting point of the method for Art History. Starting by examining images of masterpieces was the approach that has characterized the largest schools of art criticism. It is clear that in order to define a set of homogeneous works attributed to a single author, or to the same painting school, historians made use of large photos datasets which helped them in cataloging and creating *corpora* [10]. In practice, however, scholars are still required to go

© Springer International Publishing Switzerland 2016
G. Hua and H. Jégou (Eds.): ECCV 2016 Workshops, Part I, LNCS 9913, pp. 753–767, 2016.
DOI: 10.1007/978-3-319-46604-0_52

manually over thousands of physical photos with limited metadata to navigate through them.

With the increasing efforts of digitization of artworks in various institutions, we have an unprecedented access to large iconographic databases of the past, with hundreds of thousands of images. However, art historians are in need of tools to navigate through such large collections of images other than just using text-queries.

In this work, we acquired a dataset encoding pairs of images which are considered as *visually linked* by art historians. We investigated the challenges of making a visual retrieval system, which from one painting could retrieve elements which share a visual link with the query. For this purpose, we compare various visual encoding methods. Finally, we propose a way to improve the retrieval accuracy by specializing our method to the task at hand.

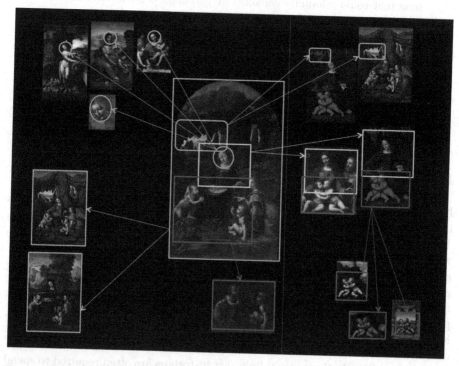

Fig. 1. Examples of visual links between artworks. The center image is the *Virgin of the rocks* by Leonardo da Vinci. It is easy to see how the global composition was reused by other painters (followers of Leonardo) on the bottom left. On the top left, other compositions by da Vinci himself reusing the same face. On the right, various sub-elements reused in other paintings. *(Best viewed in color)* (Color figure online)

2   Related Work

As far as analysis of paintings is concerned, most of the previous work actually comes from the Image Processing world with analysis such as brush-stroke extractions and image statistics to perform authorship ([20] for instance). But the goals and methods are not related to our project.

With the emergence of some online paintings datasets, some experiments trying to have automatic classification of style and/or artists have been done. Using CNN features [22] or combinations of them [9], the authors built classifiers to predict the painting style, genre or artist. In [31], they went slightly further by learning a metric to represent these classifications and used the learned metric to evaluate the "influence" of paintings [18].

In [12], the authors show that modern object classification frameworks based on convolutional neural network perform relatively well on paintings data. That way, they can have the user search for an object category in large collection of paintings from a simple text query.

Image retrieval is of course a well established field, with very powerful traditional methods based on local descriptors [21,26,32], and more recent methods using pre-trained CNN as global image descriptors with good performances [7,8,30]. However, the main benchmarks for image retrieval are *always* photographs, either of the same place (*Oxford5k, Paris6k, Holidays*) or of the same object (*UKB*). The closest dataset for our problem is probably the PRINTART database [11] but they only consider labels of scenes and not a fine grained visual similarity.

Since the signal of a painting image is different than a photograph. Applying methods that perform well on traditional datasets is not always straightforward. To our knowledge, there are only limited experiments for visual searches in paintings. Because of the extreme variety in style, working with them leads to tackling the issue of cross-domain matching. Previous work was mainly based on HoG [15] features used in a computationally expensive fashion to link paintings/sketches with photographs of the same scene [33] or with the 3D-model of the area [5]. The use of discriminant regions was also evaluated in [13].

3   Dataset Creation

Our first contribution is the creation of a dataset tackling the problem of visual links retrieval in paintings. Given a set of images of works of art P we consider two paintings $x, y \in P$ to be linked if an expert consider them to have a visual relation with each other. Each one of these links can actually be considered as an edge, building a graph linking elements of the dataset with each other.

Annotating such information is difficult in practice because it is a N-to-N problem. Unlike tasks like classification or prediction, an expert can not look at one image and give the complete ground-truth. In order to get the complete ground-truth, one would need to look at all pair-wise relationships ($O(N^2)$) which is impossible for a large N.

Hence, building the whole graph is intractable in practice, but our goal was to build a subset of it for evaluation purposes. Some of these visual links are actually known by the art history community, but often scattered in multiple books and separate analysis.

In fact, a fairly common approach is monographic. It is related to analyze a painter in particular, his artistic career, trying to track down all of his works, and that of his workshop. Rarely this analysis leaves the geographical boundaries and a specific time of diffusion [36,37].

Another main approach, however, seeks to analyze the dimensions and diffusion of the transmission of visual knowledge through several criteria. The images are used to understand the cultural contexts in which some elements, some patterns, have been taken, reformulated, and have been successful. This way takes into account different implications such as the "geography of art": the propagation of relationships trough countries and cultures [14]. The spread of a particular pattern in an author and his commercial success are related to the history of collecting and to the history of the taste, both aspects being relevant in order to explain the propagation [28,39].

In all these approaches finding the links between the images has a key role. For this our task was then to transfer this knowledge to a digitized format.

3.1 Choice of the Base Corpus

In order for experts to draw links between elements, we needed a base corpus of images. The fact that the migration of patterns in paintings is mainly important in the Modern Period (1400–1800) is an important factor in choosing our base *corpus*. As far as online catalogs of paintings are concerned, a few candidates are possible:

- **Google Art Project** [2]: large collection extracted unfortunately mainly from American museums, with poor coverage of the Renaissance.
- **BBC YourPaintings** [1]: British effort of categorization and labeling of the British museums collections. Mainly focused on British oil paintings of the 19th century. Used in [12,13] for object classification.
- **RKD Challenge** [25]: coming from the Rijksmuseum, this benchmark was created for scientists to test their algorithms on artists identification, labelling of materials and estimating the creation year. Boasting 112k elements, only 3'600 are actual paintings.
- **BnF Benchmark** [27]: created for the work in [27]. This benchmark coming from the Bibliotheque Nationale de France is made of 4'000 images with the goal of label propagation. Additionally, the diversity of mediums is high (paintings, drawings, illuminations, maps etc.).
- **Wikiart** [4]: large collection of images (126k) of paintings. Because it associates each painting with a style and a genre, it is the basis of various algorithms trying to predict these characteristics [9,18,22,31]. It was one our two main candidates.

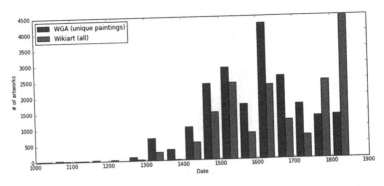

Fig. 2. Distribution of the artworks over time (until 1850) for two different datasets.

- **Web Gallery of Art** [3]: the Web Gallery of Art (WGA) is a smaller collection of almost 40k images. After taking out images which are not related to our analysis (sculpture, architecture...) and removing the images which are details of others, we get around 28k elements.

For the Wikiart and WGA datasets, we plotted the distribution of artworks over time on Fig. 2. It is obvious here that despite having less elements overall the WGA is a better choice for our analysis on the 1400–1800 period, making it our base corpus later in this work.

3.2 Gathering Method

We designed a web-based annotation tool that had three characteristics: the user can easily navigate through the database and compare images, the user can upload new images to the database and the user can make connections between entries of the database.

With this tool, an expert could find visual links by navigating the data through educated guesses and create a connection. Or if he knows about specific links (through the art-history literature and/or experience), he could transcribe the information to the system, either by finding the elements back in the database, or uploading the missing ones.

In practice, we realized it was impractical for the experts to annotate the links one by one. More precisely, in the examples we find, it is more common to find some "cluster-like" or group structure, where all the elements are linked with each other. Examples of such groups can be seen on Fig. 4. Most of these groups consist of a set of paintings (mostly between 2 and 7 elements) sharing a common pattern. In the end, we had users annotate these groups directly that we later translate to fully-connected clusters in the graph.

3.3 Data Gathered

Over the course of a month, an art historian was able to annotate 217 different groups of images. The numbers of images per group is variable and the distrib-

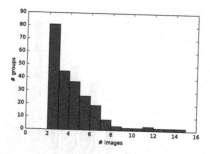

Fig. 3. Distribution of the number of images per annotated cluster.

ution can be seen on Fig. 3. This translates to 1'280 edges in the graph of visual links between 845 different images. 461 images were extracted from other sources and manually added when they were not found in the base corpus.

The extracted data provides us with a challenging benchmark as seen in Fig. 4. Variability in medium, style, and reuse of details is unique, and gives us a unique case of cross-domain visual matching.

4   Algorithms Evaluated

4.1   Bag-of-Words Methods

The main class of algorithms used very successfully in the problem of visual instance retrieval are based on local visual descriptors (mainly SIFT [24]). From the first Bag-of-Words representation for image retrieval [35], various improvements were proposed ranging from better clustering [21], spatial verification [21,26] or query expansion [32].

However, previous works on cross-domain matching [5,12,33] have shown that while these methods perform well on photographs, the performance of SIFT across domains drops drastically. Still, to support our claim, we implemented a version of the algorithm described in [26].

We computed the SIFT descriptors for every image of the dataset. We used 10M descriptors extracted from 5'000 randomly chosen images as our training data for our dictionary. Using K-means we clustered it in 100k visual words. Re-ranking is done by evaluating a simple scale + rotation transformation.

4.2   CNN Methods

In the recent years, deep Convolutional Neural Networks (CNN) [23] trained on very large corpus [16] have been shown to perform very well in almost every area of computer vision. For instance, reusing the first layers of a network have been shown to be an extremely good base representation of the visual information [17,29]. More specifically, applications of pre-trained CNN to the problem of visual instance retrieval have been studied in [6,8,30] on the classic *Oxford5k*, *Paris5k* and *Holidays* benchmarks.

Fig. 4. Examples of portions of annotated groups. **First row**: *Leda and the swan* different mediums (RUBENS, Peter Paul: painting; CORT, Cornelis: engraving; MICHELANGELO Buonarroti: drawing) **Second row**: similar composition (MASSYS, Quentin *The Moneylender and his Wife*; REYMERSWAELE, Marinus van *The Banker and His Wife*) **Third row**: *Adoration of the Child* different authors (DI CREDI Lorenzo, DEL SELLAIO Jacopo, DI CREDI Tommaso) **Fourth row**: similar element in the *Toilet of Venus* (ALBANI, Francesco first two; CARRACCI Annibale)

Building on these analysis, we use the VGG16 CNN architecture [34] as our base network (see Fig. 5). We extracted the activation of the *fc6* and *fc7* layers, almost mimicking [8], and the last convolutional layer activations *pool5*, inspired by [30].

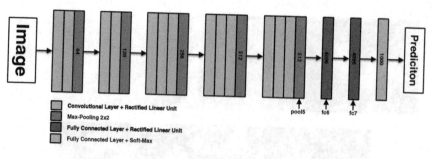

Fig. 5. The VGG16 architecture trained on the ImageNet competition. It is made by successively stacking two or three 3×3 convolutional layers, then using a max-pool layer to downsize the spatial resolution. Three fully connected layers are finally used, giving the class prediction scores. The number of feature maps at some layers is displayed. In order to use the fully-connected layers though, the result of pool5 is supposed to be 7×7 spatially, which forces the input image to be a 224×224 square.

In order to extract the fully-connected features (*fc6* and *fc7*), we need to give a square input of size 224×224 to the network. Because of the variable image ratio, we tried either extracting the center of the image or warping the image to a square. The feature vectors are then *l2*-normalized.

For the convolutional features (*pool5*), the image was isotropically resized for its smaller dimension to be equal to 256. Then we take a global sum-pool or max-pool operation (following [7] or [30] respectively) on the obtained feature-maps. We also experimented with *spatial-pooling* (SP) [30], which consists of performing the pooling operation separately on the four quadrants of the feature maps, hence multiplying the dimension of the feature vector by four. Finally *l2*-normalization is also applied. A schematic of this pipeline can be seen on Fig. 6.

Searches are then performed by using the *l2* distance between the image descriptors in a nearest neighbour fashion.

4.3 Fine-Tuning the Network

On the one hand, the visual variations across elements are high: the image can be grayscale or a sketch, the colors might be completely different, etc. On the other hand, the visual features we used were pre-trained on ImageNet which is only a collection of photographs of objects with their labels. It then makes sense to hope for improvements in the retrieval performance by fine-tuning the network.

A related approach was taken in [8] where they train a classification CNN on locations in cities, and then use the learned filters trained on this dataset instead of ImageNet, showing an improvment. Here, we want to learn the visual representation directly.

Our visual search is performed by doing nearest neighbour in our feature space from a query. To that regard, our feature extraction pipeline can be seen as a function embedding an image to a point in the feature space. Our goal

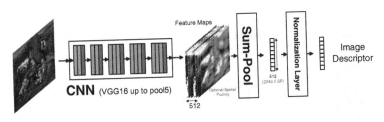

Fig. 6. Feature extraction pipeline.

would be to improve this embedding such that for two images to be close in this embedding would mean a high probability to share a visual connection.

In order to learn an embedding with a neural network, two approaches are possible. The first approach consists of submitting pairs of training images (X, Y) to the network, telling it if they are similar or not [19]. The second approach is to use triplets of images (A, B, C) telling the network that $d(f(A), f(B))$ should be smaller than $d(f(A), f(C))$ (where d is a distance function and f the embedding function) [38]. Since we are interested in making a ranking system, the order of proximity is what is important to us and the second approach then better suited.

In practice, we start with the feature extraction pipeline described above and represented on Fig. 6. Using some part of our dataset, we generate training queries. Each query $(Q_i, \{T_{i,j}\})$ consists of an image Q_i, and a set of images $\{T_{i,j}\}$ which all have a visual link with Q. Then we perform some hard-negative mining: we first run the query Q_i using the feature representations computed with our initial model, then we can easily generate interesting learning triplets by outputting $(Q_i, T_{i,j}, N_{i,j,k})$ where $N_{i,j,k}$ is an image not sharing a visual link with Q_i but is highly ranked if we search from Q_i in the original feature space.

From these triplets, we use a similar learning approach as [38]. If we consider the output of our network to be the function $f(.)$ then the loss we try to minimize is the Hinge loss:

$$\max(0, d(Q_i, N_{i,j,k}) - d(Q_i, T_{i,j}) - \delta)$$

In our case d is the $l2$ distance. Also, unlike [38] we did not use a regularization term, the $l2$ norm of the parameters was actually almost not varying during training.

Training was done with Stochastic Gradient Descent with momentum (learning rate: 10^{-5}, momentum term: 0.9) and took around 50 epochs to converge. Batches are slightly tricky to make as we need each part of the triplet to have similar sized images (i.e. all the Q_i of the batch to have size $s1$, all the $T_{i,j}$ to have size $s2$ etc.). Because of this, we had to discard a small portion of the data to make batches with a minimal size of 5 (and forced the maximum size to be 10). In the end, we used around 25k triplets for training and 5k for validation purposes.

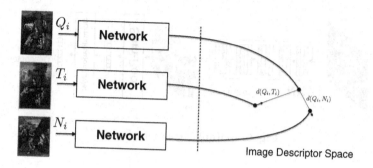

Fig. 7. Triplet learning framework.

5   Evaluation

Our goal is to make a search system to help art historians navigating through large collection of images. Hence, the main scenario is the user submitting an image as query, and we want to evaluate how well the system can give back the elements linked to it in our visual links graph. The metric we used is then the recall at certain ranks in the search results.

We divided our dataset into separate sub-graphs. 50 % of the data was kept for training, 25 % for validation purposes and 25 % for actual testing. The testing set was made of 199 images.

Given a ranking algorithm F that given an image input Q outputs an ordered list of images O_i, we want to evaluate its performance. Every image I of the testing set defines a query $(I, \{T_i^I\})$ where $\{T_i^I\}$ is the set of images sharing a visual connection with I. The recall at rank n for a single query is:

$$R^I[n] = \frac{|\{T_i^I\} \cap \{O_i\}_{i \leq n}|}{|\{T_i^I\}|}, \text{ where } \{O_i\} = F(I) \text{ and } |.| \text{ is the cardinal of a set.}$$

Computing the recall for the whole testing set is then just an aggregation of the recall for single queries:

$$R[n] = \sum_I w(I).R^I[n]$$

However, choosing the weights $w(.)$ to balance the influence of each query in the final result is a bit arbitrary. If we choose $w(I) = 1$, then all the queries would be considered equivalent, even if some have a higher number of visual connections than other. If we choose $w(I) = |\{T_i^I\}|$, then every visual connection is considered equally influent, which is not desirable either. Indeed, if we have a group of N elements which are close variations of each other, we have $\frac{N(N+1)}{2}$ separate links but which mainly encode the same visual relation. Taking this case as a basis, we want the weight of a fully connected group to be proportional to the square root of the number of visual links it represents. This gives us the weight function: $w(I) = \sqrt{\frac{|\{T_i'\}|}{|\{T_i'\}|+1}}$. In practice, the choice of $w(.)$ is not so important as it seems to have little impact on the ranking of the different methods.

6 Results

We evaluated the algorithms on the 199 queries of the testing set, using the whole WGA (38'500 images) as our search space. In Table 1, we are displaying various values of the *Recall* metric described in the previous section. We did not include results concerning the $fc7$ layer because they perform poorly compared to layer $fc6$ (this is in accordance with previous research of CNN features transferring for image retrieval).

The first observation from the results is the confirmation of our intuition that the Bag-of-Words method is not performing very well, even with a geometrical re-ranking step. The extreme variability in patterns, style and colors seems to be too strong for a dictionary of SIFT descriptor to handle.

As far as the output of the first fully-connected layer is concerned ($fc6$), it seems that extracting the squared-center of the image performs better than warping the image to a square. This seems to imply it is better to use only a sub-part of the image unmodified rather than using all of it, even if distorted.

Table 1. Recall metrics for the evaluated methods. D specifies the dimension of each representation.

Method	D	R[20]	R[50]	R[100]	R[200]
BoW	-	7.8	11.6	13.9	15.8
BoW + Geometrical Reranking	-	11.3	13.0	14.3	15.2
fc6 layer + Warp Extraction	4096	33.4	42.0	46.6	53.8
fc6 layer + Center Extraction	4096	37.2	43.1	50.1	57.7
fc6 layer + Center Extraction + PCA	2048	40.2	48.8	54.9	61.6
pool5 layer + max-pool	512	33.5	41.1	46.1	53.5
pool5 layer + sum-pool	512	36.4	43.0	51.7	58.1
pool5 layer + 2 × 2-sum-pool	2048	46.1	49.9	54.6	59.8
pool5 layer + 2 × 2-sum-pool + PCA	1024	46.5	51.4	56.4	62.5
pool5 layer + sum-pool + fine-tuning	512	45.3	53.4	60.3	68.3
pool5 layer + 2 × 2-sum-pool + fine-tuning	2048	47.5	55.5	60.8	68.3
pool5 layer + 2 × 2-sum-pool + fine-tuning + PCA	1024	48.2	57.5	63.6	70.8

When we use the output of the last convolutional layer (*pool5*), we do not need to crop or warp the image but we need to aggregate the activations of this layer. As already hinted by [7], using the *sum* operation instead of *max* during

Table 2. Example of queries of the testing set, and the retrieval rank of their respective linked images. Here *fc6*, *pool5* and *fine-tuned* represent respectively *fc6 layer + Center Extraction + PCA*, *pool5 layer + 2 × 2-sum-pool + PCA* and *pool5 layer + 2 × 2-sum-pool + fine-tuning + PCA* in the result table. For each table, the first image is the query and the others are the targets of the query.

fc6	>1000	>1000	1	>1000	3
pool5	504	716	1	764	3
fine-tuned	32	52	1	74	4

fc6	1	186	3	>1000	>1000	>1000
pool5	1	17	13	951	>1000	>1000
fine-tuned	2	3	1	91	813	968

fc6	>1000	238	53	>1000
pool5	>1000	4	76	92
fine-tuned	>1000	1	>1000	35

fc6	317	536	330	52	487
pool5	>1000	964	598	14	11
fine-tuned	>1000	>1000	126	1	27

fc6	449	>1000
pool5	633	>1000
fine-tuned	365	652

the pooling phase improves the results. Also, the spatial-pooling proposed by [30] (referred as *2x2-*-pool* in the table) allows a very efficient way to incorporate some structure in the image descriptor, improving the $R[20]$ score by 10 %. Although, it is probable this step greatly helps for similar global composition link (i.e. easy cases), but might hurt for links only defined by a detail.

After fine-tuning our convolutional filters through our triplet-learning procedure, we can observe a dramatic improvment in performance. The *pool5 + sum-pool* method improves by 8.9 % and 10.2 % for the $R[20]$ and $R[200]$ scores respectively. Comparatively speaking, the improvement in the case of spatial-pooling is smaller, especially for the first elements of the ranking (Table 2).

From a qualitative point of view, some examples of queries are displayed in Fig. 2. The first two queries are typical cases where fine-tuning the convolutional filters allow the retrieval system to better handle variations (color <-> grayscale, style,...). In the third row, we can see the improvment in rankings for the second and fourth target, but the actual loss of precision because of a mirroring composition for the third element. Finally, the last rows describes very difficult cases, either because the similarity is almost more semantic than local (fourth row), or because the medium is very different (fifth row).

7   Conclusion

In this paper, we interested ourselves in the retrieval of visual links in databases of paintings. Using a specific dataset created for this purpose, we showed that traditionally efficient methods based on Bags-of-Words fall short on this specific problem. However, recent methods based on pre-trained CNN perform favorably. Finally, we demonstrated how using some initial knowledge as training can dramatically improve the performance of the CNN descriptors at little cost.

References

1. BBC your paintings. www.artuk.org/discover/artworks
2. Google art project. www.google.com/culturalinstitute
3. Web gallery of art. www.wga.hu
4. WikiArt. www.wikiart.org
5. Aubry, M., Russell, B.C., Sivic, J.: Painting-to-3D model alignment via discriminative visual elements. ACM Trans. Graph. **33**(2), 1–14 (2014)
6. Azizpour, H., Razavian, A.S., Sullivan, J., Maki, A., Carlsson, S.: From generic to specific deep representations for visual recognition
7. Babenko, A., Lempitsky, V.: Aggregating local deep features for image retrieval (2015)
8. Babenko, A., Slesarev, A., Chigorin, A., Lempitsky, V.: Neural codes for image retrieval. In: Fleet, D., Pajdla, T., Schiele, B., Tuytelaars, T. (eds.) ECCV 2014. LNCS, vol. 8689, pp. 584–599. Springer, Heidelberg (2014). doi:10.1007/978-3-319-10590-1_38

9. Bar, Y., Levy, N., Wolf, L.: Classification of artistic styles using binarized features derived from a deep neural network. In: Agapito, L., Bronstein, M.M., Rother, C. (eds.) ECCV 2014. LNCS, vol. 8925, pp. 71–84. Springer, Heidelberg (2015). doi:10.1007/978-3-319-16178-5_5

10. Berenson, B.: Venetian Painters of the Renaissance (1894)

11. Carneiro, G., Silva, N.P., Bue, A., Costeira, J.P.: Artistic image classification: an analysis on the PRINTART database. In: Fitzgibbon, A., Lazebnik, S., Perona, P., Sato, Y., Schmid, C. (eds.) ECCV 2012. LNCS, vol. 7575, pp. 143–157. Springer, Heidelberg (2012). doi:10.1007/978-3-642-33765-9_11

12. Crowley, E.J., Zisserman, A.: In search of art. In: Agapito, L., Bronstein, M.M., Rother, C. (eds.) ECCV 2014. LNCS, vol. 8925, pp. 54–70. Springer, Heidelberg (2015). doi:10.1007/978-3-319-16178-5_4

13. Crowley, E.J., Zisserman, A.: The State of the Art: Object Retrieval in Paintings using Discriminative Regions (2014)

14. Da Costa Kaufmann, T.: Toward a Geography of Art. The University of Chicago Press Books, Chicago (2004)

15. Dalal, N., Triggs, B.: Histograms of oriented gradients for human detection. In: 2005 IEEE Computer Society Conference on Computer Vision and Pattern Recognition, vol. 1, pp. 886–893. IEEE (2005). http://ieeexplore.ieee.org/lpdocs/epic03/wrapper.htm?arnumber=1467360

16. Deng, J., Dong, W., Socher, R., Li, L.J., Li, K., Fei-Fei, L.: ImageNet: a large-scale hierarchical image database. In: 2009 Computer Society Conference on Computer Vision and Pattern Recognition, pp. 2–9 (2009)

17. Donahue, J., Jia, Y., Vinyals, O., Hoffman, J., Zhang, N., Tzeng, E., Darrell, T.: DeCAF: a deep convolutional activation feature for generic visual recognition. In: International Conference on Machine Learning, pp. 647–655 (2014). http://arxiv.org/abs/1310.1531

18. Elgammal, A., Saleh, B.: Quantifying creativity in art networks, June 2015. http://arxiv.org/abs/1506.00711

19. Hadsell, R., Chopra, S., LeCun, Y.: Dimensionality reduction by learning an invariant mapping. In: Proceedings of IEEE Computer Society Conference on Computer Vision and Pattern Recognition, vol. 2, pp. 1735–1742 (2006)

20. Hughes, J.M., Graham, D.J., Rockmore, D.N.: Quantification of artistic style through sparse coding analysis in the drawings of Pieter Bruegel the Elder. Proc. Natl. Acad. Sci. U.S.A. 107(4), 1279–1283 (2010)

21. Jegou, H., Douze, M., Schmid, C.: Hamming embedding and weak geometric consistency for large scale image search. In: Forsyth, D., Torr, P., Zisserman, A. (eds.) ECCV 2008. LNCS, vol. 5302, pp. 304–317. Springer, Heidelberg (2008). doi:10.1007/978-3-540-88682-2_24

22. Karayev, S., Trentacoste, M., Han, H., Agarwala, A., Darrell, T., Hertz-mann, A., Winnemoeller, H.: Recognizing image style. In: ECCV, pp. 1–20 (2014). http://arxiv.org/abs/1311.3715

23. Krizhevsky, A., Sutskever, I., Hinton, G.E.: Imagenet classification with deep convolutional neural networks. In: Advances in Neural Information Processing Systems, pp. 1097–1105 (2012)

24. Lowe, D.G.: Distinctive image features from scale-invariant keypoints. Int. J. Comput. Vis. 60(2), 91–110 (2004). http://link.springer.com/10.1023/B:VISI.0000029664.99615.94

25. Mensink, T., Gemert, J.V.: The Rijksmuseum Challenge: Museum-Centered Visual Recognition, pp. 2–5 (2014)

26. Philbin, J., Chum, O., Isard, M., Sivic, J., Zisserman, A.: Object retrieval with largevocabularies and fast spatial matching. In: Proceedings of IEEE Computer Society Conference on Computer Vision and Pattern Recognition (2007)

27. Picard, D., Gosselin, P.H., Gaspard, M.C.: Challenges in content-based imageindexing of cultural heritage collections. IEEE Signal Process. Mag. 95–102 (2015). https://hal.archives-ouvertes.fr/hal-01164409

28. Pomian, K.: Collectionneurs, amateurs, et curieux. XVIe - XVIIIe siècle. Paris, Venise (1987)

29. Razavian, A.S., Azizpour, H., Sullivan, J., Carlsson, S., Sharif, A., Hossein, R., Josephine, A., Stefan, S., Royal, K.T.H.: CNN features of-the-shelf: an astounding baseline for recognition. In: CVPR, pp. 512–519 (2014)

30. Razavian, A.S., Sullivan, J., Maki, A., Carlsson, S.: A baseline for visual instance retrieval with deep convolutional networks, December 2014. http://arxiv.org/abs/1412.6574

31. Saleh, B., Elgammal, A.: Large-scale classification of fine-art paintings: learning the right metric on the right feature, p. 21, May 2015. http://arxiv.org/abs/1505.00855

32. Shen, X., Lin, Z., Brandt, J., Avidan, S., Wu, Y.: Object retrieval and localization with spatially-constrained similarity measure and k-NN re-ranking. In: IEEE Conference on Computer Vision and Pattern Recognition, pp. 1–8 (2012)

33. Shrivastava, A., Malisiewicz, T., Gupta, A., Efros, A.A.: Data-driven visual similarity for cross-domain image matching. ACM Trans. Graph. 30(6), 1 (2011). http://dl.acm.org/citation.cfm?id=2070781.2024188

34. Simonyan, K., Zisserman, A.: Very deep convolutional networks for large-scaleimage recognition. arXiv Preprint, pp. 1–10 (2014). http://arxiv.org/abs/1409.1556

35. Sivic, J., Zisserman, A.: Video Google: a text retrieval approach to object matching in videos. In: Proceedings of CVPR (ICCV), pp. 2–9 (2003)

36. Giorgio, T., Bernard, A., Mancini Matteo, M.A.J.: Le botteghe di Tiziano. Alinari, Florence (2009)

37. van Hout, N., Merlu du Bourg, A., Gruber, G., Galansino, A., Howarth, D.: Rubens and His Legacy. Royal Academy of Arts, London (2014)

38. Wang, J., Song, Y., Leung, T., Rosenberg, C., Wang, J., Philbin, J., Chen, B., Wu, Y.: Learning fine-grained image similarity with deep ranking. In: CVPR, pp. 1386–1393 (2014)

39. Warnke, M.: Bilderatlas Mnemosyne. Akademie, Berlin (2000)

Hot Tiles: A Heat Diffusion Based Descriptor for Automatic Tile Panel Assembly

Susana Brandão[✉] and Manuel Marques

Instituto Superior Técnico, Universidade de Lisboa, Lisbon, Portugal
susana.brandao@tecnico.ulisboa.pt, manuel@isr.ist.utl.pt

Abstract. We revisit the problem of forming a coherent image by assembling independent pieces, also known as the jigsaw puzzle. Namely, we are interested in assembling tile panels, a relevant task for art historians, currently facing many disassembled panels. Existing jigsaw solving algorithms rely strongly on texture alignment to locally decide if two pieces belong together and build the complete jigsaw from local decisions. However, pieces in tile panels are handmade, independently painted, with poorly aligned patterns. In this scenario, existing algorithms suffer from severe degradation. We here introduce a new heat diffusion based affinity measure to mitigate the misalignment between two abutting pieces. We also introduce a global optimization approach to minimize the impact of wrong local decisions. We present experiments on Portuguese tile panels, where our affinity measure performs considerably better that state of the art and we can assemble large parts of a panel.

Keywords: Jigsaw puzzle · Heat diffusion descriptors

1 Introduction

We are interested in providing automatic tools to address a problem of great relevance for art historians: the assembly of tile panels (Fig. 1).

Tile panel assembly is an instance of jigsaw puzzle assembly. In jigsaw, an image, often photographs of natural scenery, is split into several pieces. The objective is then to, without knowing the position nor orientation of each individual piece, recover the initial image.

However, there are two main differences between tiles and jigsaw puzzles:

1. Tiles have poor texture: they often feature only two colors: white and blue.
2. Tiles have poor alignment between adjacent pieces: they are hand painted and individually baked

These two differences have a very strong impact on how we decide each piece position on the final panel. Namely, several algorithms [3,7,11] for jigsaw assembly rely strongly on texture alignment to **locally** decide if two pieces should be side by side and build the complete jigsaw from these local decisions. In this sense, the alignment between textures acts as an oracle that (almost) always

© Springer International Publishing Switzerland 2016
G. Hua and H. Jégou (Eds.): ECCV 2016 Workshops, Part I, LNCS 9913, pp. 768–782, 2016.
DOI: 10.1007/978-3-319-46604-0_53

Fig. 1. Unsorted tiles at the Portuguese Tile's Museum.

guesses if any two pieces belong together in a given orientation or not. With the local responses from an oracle, knowing the jigsaw shape and the position of an initial piece we can solve the puzzle using a simple algorithm:

input : Oracle; Jigsaw shape; Position of one piece; Unsorted pieces
output: Assembled jigsaw

for *Each position $\mathcal{P}_i$ occupied with a piece p_k* **do**
   for *each non occupied $\mathcal{P}_j$, abutting $\mathcal{P}_i$* **do**
      for *each piece p_l still in the unsorted pile* **do**
         isNeighbor← oracle(p_l,p_k)
         if *isNeighbor* **then**
            | movePieceFromUnsortedToPosition(p_l,P_j)
         end
      end
   end
end

Algorithm 1. Simple algorithm for solving jigsaw puzzles assuming the existence of an oracle.

The most recent algorithm, introduced by Paikin *et al.* [11], uses a very similar approach, identifying abutting pairs of pieces with a confidence of ~95 % using a dedicated affinity measure. These pairs are then used to ground the puzzle assembly. However, the affinity measure relies strongly on the existence of texture, and as we show in this paper, has only a 45 % accuracy when evaluated in tile panels. Thus, the problem of assembling tiles is considerably more difficult than the problem of assembling jigsaw puzzles from texture rich photographs.

In this work, we introduce a new affinity measure based on diffusion processes, that performs better than state of the art on our tile's dataset. The affinity leverages on existing diffusion based descriptors [2] that represent not only a pixel, but also its neighborhood, and thus is more robust to misalignments, achieving a performance of 0.55 % in tile panels (Fig. 2).

Notwithstanding the improvement we achieved, the affinity measure performance is still bellow the one obtained by the state of the art algorithms in

(a) Unsorted tiles   (b) Coherent panel, with misalignments

Fig. 2. Tile assembly: find the correct position and orientation of a set of pieces, or tiles, originally unsorted, so that they form a coherent image, or panel.

jigsaw puzzles from photographs. Thus it cannot be used to replace the local oracle and we have to move to **global** affinity criteria to assemble tile panels. I.e., we propose to maximize the sum of the affinity over all abutting sides on the final panel reconstruction. To avoid the exhaustive search associated with such global function, we formulate the tile selection as a graph edge selection, which we then solve using a linear relaxation. To recover a solution in the binary space, we use Monte Carlo projection and show that, while we do not guarantee that we achieve global optimal, we can recover large parts of the complete panel, even with a modest number of trials.

Thus, the current paper innovates by introducing:

- a tile panel dataset[1]
- a pairwise affinity measure that accounts for misalignments and poor texture;
- an algorithm for solving puzzles that uses a global affinity as criteria.

2   Dataset

In this work we introduce the seven 5×5 tile panels represented in Fig. 3. All panels are painted in white and blue. All free parameters in the affinity measure were estimated using as subset of Panel 1 tiles.

3   Related Work

Our objective is to reconstruct a tile panel, without knowing a-priori information besides the panel final shape. Namely, we have no information on the tiles' position nor orientation. This is an instance of a broader class of problems - the jigsaw puzzle assembly. Other instances have different constraints, e.g., there may be more a-priori information the pieces' orientation may be known a-priori, or we may not have all the pieces in the puzzles. The type of puzzles influences how the puzzles are assembled, i.e., they influence the implementation of

---

[1] Can be found at http://users.isr.ist.utl.pt/~sbrandao/tilePanels/.

Panel 1   Panel 2   Panel 3   Panel 4

Panel 5   Panel 6   Panel 7

Fig. 3. Dataset of tile panels

Algorithm 1 or other assembly approach. However, common to most approaches is the definition of the similarity between adjacent pieces, that acts as an oracle in those approaches but is very unreliable in tile panels. We here compare our affinity measure with previously propose ones, and discuss how the existing algorithms would fit the panel reconstruction problem.

3.1 Affinity Measure

As far as we are aware, all affinity measures between adjacent pieces compare color values, or similar functions, at a very shallow distance from the abutting boundary: no more that two rows/columns of pixels parallel to the boundary are used. Similar functions to the pixel color were based on the color gradient in the direction perpendicular to the abutting boundary.

Gallagher *et al.* [7] introduced a local affinity measure, linked to the difference in the gradient at the abutting edges of two adjacent pieces. Cho *et al.* [4] used directly the pixel color and Paikin *et al.* [11] compares not the color, but what the color should be based on the color gradient in the region perpendicular to the boundary.

The existing measures have showed very good results on current datasets created from photographs. In particular, Paikin showed very good results in finding best buddies (>95 %), as we show in Table 1. Best buddies correspond to pairs of pieces that are simultaneously the most affine to one another, and thus should have higher accuracy, but lower recall, than just nearest neighbors. Several assembly algorithms, e.g., [11,12], leverage on the identification of best buddies to assemble the whole puzzle.

The same table shows the results on the tile dataset, highlighting the need to define more relevant affinity measures to model the similarity between tiles. We note that, while we have obtained better results, we still have lower performances than those reported on photograph based datasets.

Table 1. Best buddies performance

Results on photographs (from [11])			Results on Tile Panels		
	Accuracy	Recall		Accuracy	Recall
Paikin [11]	0.96	0.86	Paikin[11]	0.45	0.16
Cho [3,4]	0.88	0.76	**This Paper**	0.55	0.15
Gallagher [7]	0.93	0.85			
Pomeranz [12]	0.94	0.84			

3.2   Assembly

The first attempts to automatically solve jigsaw puzzles have been proposed by Freeman and Garder in 1964 [6]. In the last 15 years it has received renew attention, leading to an increase in the size of puzzles solved. However, most algorithms correspond to elaborated versions of Algorithm 1.

For example, Gallagher *et al.* [7] represents the puzzle as a graph, where edges connect abutting sides and carry a weight associated with the affinity of the two sides. Initially the algorithm considers edges connecting all possible combinations between all pieces, and then trims edges by finding a Minimum Spanning Tree (MST) [9], so that the final edges correspond to the abutting edges in the assembled jigsaw. The main difficulty with this approach is that the jigsaw shape has to be verified and corrected during iterations of MST. We also use a graph representation, but we introduce the jigsaw shape on the graph construction, namely on the definition of neighboring positions. Thus can use a global criteria.

Sholomon *et al.* [13] proposed an automatic jigsaw puzzle solver using genetic algorithm. In each iteration they generated hundreds of possible solutions, merging two "parent" to an improved "child" solution. It is performed by detecting, extracting and combining assembled puzzle segments.

Pomeranz *et al.* [12] and Paikin *et al.* [11] introduced approaches that rely heavily in finding pairs of pieces that had a very high probability of being together. They obtain such pairs by searching for best buddies. Furthermore, Paikin *et al.* [11] takes a step forward by solving puzzles where pieces are in unknown orientations or are altogether missing. In their approach, Paikin *et al.* avoid the complexity introduced by focusing on local decision and improving affinity measures. In our work, we also account for unknown orientations, but still aim at a global criteria for deciding on tiles positions.

There are several approaches [1,4,10] that look into the optimization of affinity between adjacent pieces using global criteria. However, all these approaches assume that the pieces orientation is known and thus do not extent naturally to unknown orientations.

Andaló *et al.* [1] presented a global formulation for jigsaw problems, Puzzle Solving by Quadratic Programming (PSQP). Cho *et al.* [4] presented a graphical model based on the patch transform to solve the jigsaw puzzle assuming some sort of previous knowledge. The authors propose an algorithm that minimizes a probability function via loopy belief propagation. Both formulations assume a one to one correspondence between pieces and positions in the puzzle. This assumption does not hold when we need to consider different orientations for each piece.

In our work, we model the solution as a global optimization problem, as in [1], but we extend the set of available pieces so that each tile in each orientation is counted as a different tile, while not being necessarily in the final panel. As in [4], we can also easily incorporate previous knowledge by changing the affinity of some tiles depending on their position in the panel.

Recent work has also been introduced using neural networks, [10], which solve small puzzles, by unsupervised learning images structures in a manner similar to [5]. This approach radically differs from previous ones as it does not depend on the similarity between points in two adjacent tiles. Instead it depends on the overall structure of shapes in our environment. However, it again cannot handle problems where the pieces orientation is unknown.

4   Heat Based Affinity Measure

To address the problem of poor texture or limited descriptive patterns, we introduce a new diffusion based affinity measure that can represent not only compatibility between pixels across the abutting boundary, but also of their neighborhood, providing some level of resilience to misalignment. Furthermore, we also aim at enhancing the pattern information by looking the alignment between regions of color transition in the boundary direction.

Diffusion based descriptors are often used to represent 3D shapes, but it was also showed that they can represent color and textures. In this work, we follow [2] and consider a diffusion process where color influences the rate of diffusion, leading to a color dependent, but misalignment resilient, affinity measure. We illustrate what we mean by color dependent diffusion with the three examples in Fig. 4 where we simulate the diffusion of a heat source over a tile. In the first example, corresponding to the first row, we consider only the tile shape. In the second example, second row, we consider a source at a lighter part of the tile and, at the third example, we consider a source at a darker part. The source is showed in red in the first column of Fig. 4 and in the subsequent columns (b ∼ f) we show the temperature increasing around the source following more or less a concentric shape. While this general effect is the same over the three examples, the temperature at each point changes between examples as the different colors propagate heat at different rates. It is of especial interest to our problem the fact that the rate at which the heat propagates in the neighborhood affects the temperature evolution at the source itself. Also, the relation between color and diffusion rate can be defined by a map that minimizes the affinity between incorrect pairings.

In the following we describe how to simulate heat diffusion over surfaces, which the familiar reader may jump. Then we show how we estimate the affinity used to compute the results presented in Table 1, including how we define the map between color and diffusion rate, and how we introduce the alignment at the color transitions into the overall affinity

4.1   Heat Diffusion on Color Surfaces

Heat diffusion is an umbrella term for the dynamic process that affects some quantity, we here refer to as temperature, described by a function $f(\bar{x}, t) : \mathbb{R}^n \times \mathbb{R}^+ \to \mathbb{R}$ whose evolution in time is described by:

$$\nabla^2 f(\bar{x}, t) = c(\bar{x}) \partial_t f(\bar{x}, t), \tag{1}$$

where $\bar{x} = [x_1, ..., x_n]$ is a position vector, $\nabla^2 f(\bar{x}, t)$ is the Laplacian of function f and $c(\bar{x})$ is the heat conductivity at any given point.

The diffusion over tiles' surface is a discrete version of the above equation. In this case $f(\bar{x}, t)$ becomes a vector $\bar{f}(t) \in \mathbb{R}^N$ whose entry $[\bar{f}(t)]_i$ is the temperature at some pixel v_i in the surface and the conductivity is represented by a vector $\bar{c} \in \mathbb{R}^N$ with a vector corresponding to the color at each pixel. In this work, we discretize the Laplacian operator using a distance based representation of L, where L is a weighted graph Laplacian where the weight of each edge is the inverse of its length:

$$L\bar{f}(t) = (D - W)\,\bar{f}(t), \quad [W]_{v_i, v_j} = \begin{cases} 1/\|\bar{x}_{v_i} - \bar{x}_{v_j}\|^2, & \text{iff} \quad e_l = (v_j, v_i) \in E \\ 0, & \text{otherwise} \end{cases}, \tag{2}$$

and where D is a diagonal matrix with entries $D_{ii} = \sum_{j=1}^{N} [W]_{ij}$.

The equation allows to estimate a temperature at any time instant t given an initial temperature. In our work, and others previously [8], we consider a single source placed at some pixel s. In this case, the temperature can be written as

$$\bar{f}(t) = \sum_{i=1}^{N} \bar{\phi}_i^T \bar{f}(0) \exp(-\lambda_i t)[\bar{c}]_s \tag{3}$$

where λ_i and $\bar{\phi}_i$ are the solution to the generalized eigenvalue problem $L\bar{\phi}_i = C\bar{\phi}_i\lambda_i$. Here C is a diagonal matrix whose entry $C_{l,l}$ is a scalar c_l representing the color of pixel l. To move from RGB values to scalars, we use a map function $\gamma : \mathbb{R}^3 \to \mathbb{R}$, which we define shortly.

The temperature at each point will then depend both on the shape of the surface, in this case the rectangle formed by the two abutting tiles and in the color of both pieces. As the shape of the pieces is the same for all pairs, we remove this dependency. With that in mind, we first find the solution $\bar{f}_{\text{shape}}(t)$ corresponding to the upper row in Fig. 4, i.e., we solve Eq. 3 using the same L and the same initial condition but with $\bar{c} = \bar{1}$.

By dividing the solution with color $\bar{f}(t)$ by the solution at $\bar{f}_{\text{shape}}(t)$ we obtain a vector $\bar{g}(t) : [\bar{g}(t)]_i = [\bar{f}(t)]_i / [\bar{f}_{\text{shape}}(t)]_i$ that depends on the color and on the neighborhood, but is not affected by shape.

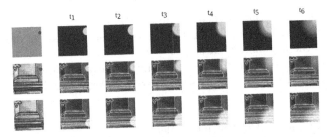

Fig. 4. Impact of color on diffusion. The first row corresponds to a diffusion process where all the points are equal. The second and third correspond to diffusion process where the rate depends on color. The red dot corresponds to the heat source on both cases. (Color figure online)

4.2 Affinity Measure

As heat diffusion depends on the neighborhood of each point, it should be similar across points in two abutting sides. We access the affinity between two tiles by first placing the two side by side, as showed in Fig. 5(a), and then consider multiple sources s_l, at each side of the boundary, as showed in Fig. 5(b). For each source individually, we estimate $[\bar{g}(t')]_{s_l}$ at a fixed time instant t'. Finally, Fig. 5(c), shows how much $\bar{g}$ changes across the boundary in the two cases. In this last graphic, we note that positive values correspond to higher temperatures in the left tile, associated with darker colors in this region.

We note that the vector $\bar{g}^i$, containing all the temperature of all the ordered sources at tile i, changes smoothly for neighboring sources, even under large changes in the tile's color. It is this smoothness that provides more resilient to misalignment than existing affinity measures. We thus compare the temperature for points in the same row/column, across boundaries: $\bar{\Delta}^{1,2} : \bar{g}^1(t) - \bar{g}^2(t)$. The affinity corresponds to the sum of the squares of $\bar{\Delta}$.

We note that, as with other affinity measures for jigsaw puzzles, $\bar{\Delta}^{1,2} \neq \bar{\Delta}^{2,1}$, as when we switch tiles positions, the connecting sides are no longer the same. In the remaining of the paper, we always assume that $\Delta^{1,2}$ corresponds to the

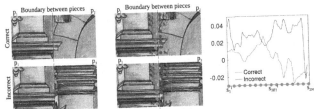

(a) Connecting two pieces   (b) Placing sources   (c) Temperature difference across the boundary

Fig. 5. Computing affinity between two abutting tiles. The top images corresponds to a correct pair, while the second correspond to an incorrect pair.

affinity between tile 1 and 2, when 1 is on the left side of 2 on a fixed orientation. By reasons that will be clear in Sect. 5, we consider all possible orientations of each physical tile as different tiles.

The overall process to compute the affinity measure between tiles p_i and p_j, when p_i is in the left side of p_j, is summarized in Algorithm 2.

---

input : Tiles p_i, p_j; Color map to scalar γ
output: Affinity: $\|\bar{\Delta}\|$
$\mathcal{I} \leftarrow$ connect(p_i, p_j)
$\bar{s}^{i,j} \leftarrow$ findSourcePosition$(p_{i,j})$
$L_{i,j} \leftarrow$ computeLaplacian$(\mathcal{I})$ (Eq. 2)
$C \leftarrow$ extractColor$(\gamma, \mathcal{I})$
$\bar{f}^{i,j}(t_s) \leftarrow$ computeTemperatureColor(L,C,$\bar{s}^{i,j}$) (Eq. 3)
$\bar{f}_{\text{shape}}(t_s) \leftarrow$ computeTemperatureColor(L,const,$\bar{s}^{i,j}$) (Eq. 3, C constant).
$\bar{\Delta} : [\bar{\Delta}]_l = \left([\bar{f}^i]_l - [\bar{f}^j]_l\right) / [\bar{f}_{\text{shape}}]_l$

Algorithm 2. Computing affinity between tiles p_i and p_j, when placed side by side, with p_i on the left of p_j.

4.3 Scalar Representation of Color

To use the above affinity definition, we need a map $\gamma : \mathbb{R}^3 \to \mathbb{R}$ between color and diffusion rate. We define such a map as the projection of each pixel color value $\mathcal{I}_{pixel}$ on an unit norm vector $\bar{\xi} \in \mathbb{R}^{+3}$. Such definition ensures that the map γ (i) has a lower positive bound, i.e., that all generalized eigenvalues are positive and that $\bar{f}(t)$ converges, and that (ii) has an bound making the problem feasible.

We parameterize such vector as: $\bar{\xi} = [\cos(\theta); \sin(\theta)\sin(\phi); \sin(\theta)\cos(\phi)]$, for all $\theta, \phi \in [0, \pi/2]$. Using several correct and incorrect pairs of puzzle 1 from the dataset, we searched for the parameters θ and ϕ that best minimized the distance between corrects and maximized the distance between incorrect.

Figure 6 shows that the distance function is convex on the chosen parameterization. Furthermore, it also shows that the minimum is close, but not equal, to

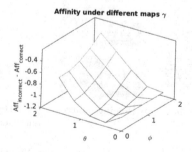

Fig. 6. Impact of different maps on the affinity measure.

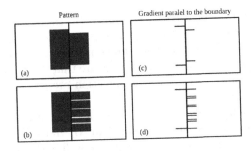

Fig. 7. Gradient alignment.

the vector $[0; 0; 1]$, which corresponds to a small deviation of the blue color. While we could have used convex optimization tools to further improve our estimation, we opted to use the minimum over this sparse sampling to avoid over-fitting to the small dataset of pairs we used to estimate the best distance.

4.4 Gradient Alignment

We want to align color transitions that occur in the boundary direction, so that Fig. 7(a) is less penalized than Fig. 7(b), as in the later there is match a between two distinctive patterns.

Thus we introduce a second affinity measure that matches the gradient parallel to the boundary in both tiles, as illustrated in Fig. 7(c and d). For each pair of pieces, the affinity depends on the norm of the vector with the difference between the two gradients.

We combine the two affinities by means of a coefficient α so that $\mathcal{A}_{affinity} = \mathcal{A}_{heat} + \alpha \mathcal{A}_{align}$. Using panel 1 we found that $\alpha = 0.11$ provided the best relation between precision and recall in best buddies.

5 Linear Programming for Tiling Reconstruction

As previously stated, we follow Gallagher [7] and represent the jigsaw problem as an edge selection problem in a graph. However, nodes in our graph representation correspond to all possible orientations of each tile at each position. Thus, for a panel with M tiles, the graph has $M^2 \times 4$ nodes. Edges in the graph connect the nodes at abutting positions in the panel leading to $(M \times 4)^2$ for each pair of positions in the panel. The complete set of edges in a panel with $M_x \times M_y = M$ tiles positions is $[(M_x - 1)M_y + (M_y - 1)M_x] \times 16M^2$. Figure 8 shows and example of all possible nodes and edges for a puzzle 2×2. In Fig. 8(a) we represent all possible orientations of the four pieces. Each position in the panel will have associated a set of nodes corresponding to these orientations. The nodes in two abutting positions will be connected by edges, as showed in Fig. 8(b). The complete set of edges and nodes is represented in Fig. 8(c).

Each edge has an associated weight given by the affinity of the two sides of the tiles that it connects. Our objective is to select a single edge between abutting positions so that the global affinity is high. However, the set of edges must respect some global constraints that ensure that the puzzle is feasible, e.g., that all the edges connecting to a given position are associated with the same node.

The edge selection problem associated with these global constraints can be written as binary linear program, but is still an NP-Hard problem. While we can solve it for small problems, it does not escalate well with the size of the puzzle. As an example, a 4×4 puzzle can take up to 2 h to solve. To allow scalability, we relax the problem to a linear program. To recover an integer solution from the relaxed problem, we introduce a Monte Carlo projection.

5.1   Binary Optimization Problem

To write the edge selection problem as an optimization problem, we represent any set of selected edges as vector $\bar{\tau} \in \{0, 1\}^{16 \times M^2}$, such that $[\bar{\tau}]_i = 1$ if we select edge i and $[\bar{\tau}]_i = 0$ otherwise. Thus we want to optimize the function $y(\bar{\tau}) = \bar{q}^T \bar{\tau}$, where $[\bar{q}]_i$ is the affinity between the two nodes connected by edge i.

We ensure a solution of the optimization problem corresponding to a feasible puzzle by introducing constraints in τ. We can divide such constraints in four families:

The first is that between two abutting positions, we select one, and only one edge:

$$\bar{\tau}^T \mathbb{1}_{\mathcal{E}}^{\text{edge}} = 1, \quad \forall \mathcal{E} = 1, ..., (2M - M_x - M_y) \tag{4}$$

where $\mathbb{1}_{\mathcal{E}}^{\text{tile}}$ is an indicator vector, where $[\mathbb{1}_{\mathcal{E}}^{\text{tile}}]_i = 1$ if and only if the edge i is associated with the abutting tiles at position $\mathcal{E}$ in the panel and zero otherwise.

The second is that each tile should be chosen once, and can be expressed as:

$$\sum_{\mathcal{P}=1}^{M} \bar{\tau}^T \mathbb{1}^{\text{tile}_{p,\mathcal{P}}} = w_{\mathcal{P}}, \quad \forall p = 1, ..., M \tag{5}$$

(a) Consider all possible pieces and orientations, Ω (b) For each edge position, $\mathcal{E}$, estimate affinity between all elements in Ω (c) Replicate for all positions.

Fig. 8. Modeling a jigsaw puzzle structure as a graph.

where $[\mathbb{1}_{p,\mathcal{P}}^{\text{tile}}]_i = 1$ if and only if the edge i connects with tile p at the panel position $\mathcal{P}$, and $w_{\mathcal{P}}$ is the number of abutting positions to $\mathcal{P}$, e.g., for a corner the weight is 2.

The third is that edges connecting to a given position have to connect to the same node:

$$\bar{\tau}^T \left(w_{\mathcal{P}} \mathbb{1}_{\omega,\mathcal{P}}^{\Omega} - [\mathbb{1}_{\omega,\mathcal{P}}^{\Omega}]_t \right) = 0 \quad \forall \omega \in \Omega \quad \mathcal{P} = 1, ..., M \quad t \in \mathcal{E}_{\omega,\mathcal{P}} \tag{6}$$

where $[\mathbb{1}_{\omega,\mathcal{P}}^{\Omega}]_i = 1$ if and only if the edge i connects with a node $\omega \in \Omega$, corresponding to some physical tile at a given orientation, at position $\mathcal{P}$ and zero otherwise. Furthermore, $\mathcal{E}_{\omega,\mathcal{P}}$ is the set of edges connecting to node ω in $\mathcal{P}$.

The forth removes symmetries resulting from the the puzzle structure, and is fundamental to avoid degenerate cases. The symmetries can be removed by considering that there is a tile with a single orientation. For example for $p = 1$, instead of considering the whole set Ω, we must consider only a single orientation regardless of its position in the panel:

$$\bar{\tau}^T \mathbb{1}_{\tilde{\omega}^1,\mathcal{P}}^{\Omega} = 0 \quad \forall \tilde{\omega}^1 = 1, ..., 3M \quad \mathcal{P} = 1, ..., M \quad t \in \mathcal{E}_{\omega,\mathcal{P}} \tag{7}$$

where $\tilde{\omega}^1$ corresponds to all possible orientations except 1.

Thus, we can formulate the jigsaw puzzle as the integer optimization problem:

$$\tau^* = \arg \max_x \quad \bar{q}^T \bar{\tau} \tag{8}$$

$$\text{s.t.} A\bar{\tau} = \bar{b} \quad [\bar{\tau}]_i \in \{0,1\} \tag{9}$$

where A is a matrix with entries $[A]_{i,j} \in \mathbb{N}$ sparse matrix with $(2M - M_x - M_y) + M + 4M^2$ rows and $16 \times M^2 \times (2M - M_x - M_y)$ columns. Each row of A corresponds to an indicator vectors $\mathbb{1}$ from the above constraints. Finally $\bar{b}$ also has integer entries $[\bar{b}]_i \in \mathbb{N}$.

Any prior information that we want to introduce in the solution, can be added directly by introducing more rows in A and $\bar{b}$.

5.2 Linear Relaxation

When we relax the above problem, we end up with a program whose solving time depends linearly on the total number of edges. The relaxed version of the above problem corresponds simply to replace Eq. 9 by $[\bar{\tau}]_i \in [0,1]$.

To recover an integer solution from the relaxed one, we use Monte Carlo projections. We first compute a relaxed version of the algorithm. Then, for each edge position $\mathcal{E}$, we associate the solution of the relaxed version to probability distributions on possible edges between tiles. We uniformly at random pick an edge position and, for that position, randomly select a connecting edge using the distribution. We then add the selected edge as a constraint to the linear optimization program and resolve it again. We iterate between sampling edges and solving the linear program until convergence, which often occurs after few iterations. After assigning an edge to each position, we have a binary solution, from which we can reconstruct a puzzle. However, we have no idea of how far we are from the minimum. We thus restart the projection several times, and look into the solutions with lower cost for the one that is able to better reconstruct tile panels.

Algorithm 3 summarizes the main steps of our algorithm for solving the relaxed version of our optimization formulation.

input : Affinity $\bar{c}$, Set of edge $\mathcal{E}$, Set of positions $\mathcal{P}$, Set of tiles in all possible orientations Ω
output: Selection vector $\bar{\tau} : [\bar{\tau}]_i \in \{0, 1\}$
$(A, \bar{b}) \leftarrow$ getConstraints$(\mathcal{E}, \mathcal{P}, \Omega)$, (Eqs. 4–7)
$(af_1, \bar{\tau}_1) \leftarrow$ solveLinearProgram$(\bar{c}, A, \bar{b})$, (Eq. 9)
for $i \leftarrow 1; i \leq N_s; i + +$ **do**
$\quad A_1 \leftarrow A; \bar{b}_1 \leftarrow \bar{b};$
$\quad$ **for** $j \leftarrow 1; j \leq M - 1; j + +$ **do**
$\quad\quad e \leftarrow$ randomWeightedEdgeSelection$(\mathcal{E}, \bar{\tau}_j)$
$\quad\quad (A_{j+1}, \bar{b}_{j+1}) \leftarrow addSelectedEdgeAsConstraint(e, A_j, \bar{b}_j)$
$\quad\quad (af_{j+1}, \bar{\tau}_{j+1}) \leftarrow$ solveLinearProgram$(\bar{c}, A_j, \bar{b})$
$\quad$ **end**
$\quad$ **if** $af_M < minAf$ **then**
$\quad\quad minAf \leftarrow af_M$
$\quad\quad \bar{\tau} \leftarrow \bar{\tau}_M$
$\quad$ **end**
end

Algorithm 3. Automatic tile panel assembly using linear programming

6   Results

Using the full binary solution, we were able to reconstruct a 4×4 subpanel of Panel 1 from Fig. 3, provided that we used as an a-priori information that the first and second piece were connected at the top left corner.

Panel 1   Panel 2   Panel 3   Panel 4

Panel 5   Panel 6   Panel 7

Fig. 9. Best reconstructions, where polygons highlight correctly assembled parts

For the full version of all the panels, without a-priori information and with the Monte Carlo projection, we cannot reconstruct the panels completely. However, we could recover large parts of each panel.

In Fig. 9 we present the best solutions, among the best 15 with highest affinity obtained from 100 independent Monte Carlo trials. And, to illustrate the difficulty of the dataset, we present in Table 2 the best buddies precision for each panel.

Table 2. Affinity precision on each panel

Affinity	Panel: 1	2	3	4	5	6	7
Paikin	0.50	0.47	0.56	0.10	0.20	0.50	0.57
This paper	0.64	0.61	0.5	0.57	0.29	0.8	0.38

7 Conclusions

In this paper we introduced a variation to the known jigsaw problem, where the affinity between pieces is not reliable. We have introduced a new dataset of tile panels, which correspond to jigsaws with very little texture and severe misalignment. We introduced a novel affinity measure, which showed considerably better results than previous state of the art on this particular dataset. Finally, we have introduced a global approach for assembling jigsaw puzzles.

While the affinity precision is still too small and we cannot correctly assemble whole panels without a small external help, when looking at the final assembled panels it is clear that many pairings resulting from our algorithm are still visually convincing, at least locally. We note that this is particularly true in panels 4 and 5, which also have small affinity precisions. This highlights the difficulty of automatically reconstruct puzzles with little texture. On the other hand, the proposed approach can be used interactively by an art historian in the reconstruction of the complete panel.

We note that the results here presented were obtained using only 100 Monte Carlo trials for the projections, which took one day of computing using an Intel Core i7-5500u, with no parallelization and the Gurobi optimization package. As each trial is independent from all previous ones, in future work we expect to be able to further explore and improve on these results.

Acknowledgements. This work was funded by FCT grant [UID/EEA/50009/2013] and FCT project: IF/00879/2012

References

1. Andalo, F.A., Taubin, G., Goldenstein, S.: Solving image puzzles with a simple quadratic programming formulation. In: 25th Conference on Graphics, Patterns and Images (SIBGRAPI), pp. 63–70 (2012)

2. Brandão, S., Costeira, J., Veloso, M.M.: The partial view heat kernel descriptor for 3D object representation. In: ICRA (2014)
3. Cho, T.S., Avidan, S., Freeman, W.T.: The patch transform. PAMI **32**(8), 1489–1501 (2010)
4. Cho, T.S., Avidan, S., Freeman, W.T.: A probabilistic image jigsaw puzzle solver. In: CVPR, pp. 183–190. IEEE (2010)
5. Doersch, C., Gupta, A., Efros, A.A.: Unsupervised visual representation learning by context prediction. In: ICCV (2015)
6. Freeman, H., Garder, L.: Apictorial jigsaw puzzles: The computer solution of a problem in pattern recognition. IEEE Trans. Electron. Comput. **EC–13**, 118–127 (1964)
7. Gallagher, A.C.: Jigsaw puzzles with pieces of unknown orientation. In: CVPR (2012)
8. Kovnatsky, A., Bronstein, M.M., Bronstein, A.M., Kimmel, R.: Photometric heat kernel signatures. In: Bruckstein, A.M., ter Haar Romeny, B.M., Bronstein, A.M., Bronstein, M.M. (eds.) SSVM 2011. LNCS, vol. 6667, pp. 616–627. Springer, Heidelberg (2012)
9. Kruskal, J.B.: On the shortest spanning subtree of a graph and the traveling salesman problem. Proc. Am. Math. Soc. **7**, 48–50 (1956)
10. Noroozi, M., Favaro, P.: Unsupervised learning of visual representations by solving jigsaw puzzles. arxiv abs/1603.09246 (2016), http://arxiv.org/abs/1603.09246
11. Paikin, G., Tal, A.: Solving multiple square jigsaw puzzles with missing pieces. In: CVPR, June 2015
12. Pomeranz, D., Shemesh, M., Ben-Shahar, O.: A fully automated greedy square jigsaw puzzle solver. In: CVPR, pp. 9–16 (2011)
13. Sholomon, D., David, O., Netanyahu, N.S.: A genetic algorithm-based solver for very large jigsaw puzzles. In: CVPR, pp. 1767–1774 (2013)

Novel Methods for Analysis and Visualization of Saccade Trajectories

Thomas Kübler[1], Wolfgang Fuhl[1], Raphael Rosenberg[3],
Wolfgang Rosenstiel[2], and Enkelejda Kasneci[1(✉)]

[1] Perception Engineering, University of Tübingen, Tübingen, Germany
{thomas.kuebler,wolfgang.fuhl,enkelejda.kasneci}@uni-tuebingen.de
[2] Computer Engineering, University of Tübingen, Tübingen, Germany
wolfgang.rosenstiel@uni-tuebingen.de
[3] Lab for Cognitive Research in Art History, University of Vienna, Vienna, Austria
raphael.rosenberg@univie.ac.at

Abstract. Visualization of eye-tracking data is mainly based on fixations. However, saccade trajectories and their characteristics might contain more information than sole fixation positions. Artists, for example, can influence the way our eyes traverse a picture by employing composition methods. Repetitive saccade trajectories and the sequence of eye movements seem to correlate with this composition. In this work, we propose two novel methods to visualize saccade patterns during static stimulus viewing. The first approach, so-called saccade heatmap, utilizes a modified Gaussian density distribution to highlight frequent gaze paths. The second approach is based on clustering and assigns identical labels to similar saccades to thus filter for the most relevant gaze paths. We demonstrate and discuss the strengths and weaknesses of both approaches by examples of free-viewing paintings and compare them to other state-of-the-art visualization techniques.

Keywords: Eye-tracking · Image viewing · Perception of art · Scanpath · Saccade clustering

1 Introduction

Studies on perception based on eye tracking are most often focused on the allocation and local density of fixations. Attention maps, fixation clustering [20], and aggregated values (e.g., dwell time on a region of interest (ROI)) are frequently used tools for such analysis. In fact, fixation-based analysis is motivated by the way our visual perception works; perception is only possible during fixations and suppressed during saccades, i.e., high velocity movements of the eyeball [11]. Therefore, saccadic patterns have mostly been studied indirectly, e.g., as transitions between ROIs [8]. Obviously, a large proportion of saccades will occur as

---

T. Kübler and W. Fuhl—Contributed equally to the paper.

© Springer International Publishing Switzerland 2016
G. Hua and H. Jégou (Eds.): ECCV 2016 Workshops, Part I, LNCS 9913, pp. 783–797, 2016.
DOI: 10.1007/978-3-319-46604-0_54

ROI transitions, e.g., between the faces of people in a painting. However, ROIs might be ambiguous in an art work. For example, when viewing abstract art, gaze is supposed to follow artistic composition principles [1] or in medieval art, by inserting reflective gold leafs in the painting [16]. Yarbus defined composition as *"[...] the means whereby the artist to some extent may compel the viewer to perceive what is portrayed in the picture"* [25]. Especially for abstract paintings, the definition of meaningful ROIs is questionable and an analysis of saccades and gaze transitions would be restrained to these ROIs. Benefits from art viewing analysis are deeper understanding of pictures and human perception, keypoint extraction from paintings [12], image compression [17] as well as saliency map creation [6].

This work focuses on the analysis of saccade trajectories. Thus, instead of asking the question *what* is looked at, we aim at proving techniques to tackle the questions *how* and *why* our gaze is driven and guided over an artwork in a particular way.

First, we show how saccade trajectories form patterns that are characteristic for the stimulus material and enable the artist to guide the viewer's gaze over the artwork. Then we introduce two methods to analyze saccade trajectories: (1) a novel visualization method, a saccadic heatmap, and (2) a clustering technique to cluster saccades for eye-tracking data of low temporal resolution. Both methods are compared to ROI transition diagrams and a trajectory clustering approach (attribute-driven edge bundling [18]). The proposed approaches allow to study saccadic patterns thoroughly and might contribute to a better understanding of the influence of image composition on visual scanning.

Both methods are implemented in the Eyetrace [15] software. Eyetrace is a visualization and analysis tool for static stimulus experiments, such as the viewing of fine art. It provides a variety of state-of-the-art algorithms for each processing step: Identification of fixations and saccades (e.g., [13,23]), clustering of fixation locations, automatic ROI annotation, and scanpath comparison (e.g., [14]). Eyetrace is available at http://www.ti.uni-tuebingen.de/Eyetrace.1751.0.html

2 Related Work

In eye-tracking recordings, data samples recorded during fixations outweigh by far the saccade samples. A first version of Eyetrace already tried to implement a feature for sampling saccades [9,22].

Dong et al. were among the first to work on simple heatmaps of saccades for the evaluation of enhanced imagery in cartography [7]. However, most studies work based on fixation heatmaps; sometimes even heatmaps containing both fixation and saccade data are employed, especially when no event filter is applied [3,4]. Popelka and Voženílek propose a space-time cube visualization, where saccades make up a large part of the visualization: as all samples are connected by a line, saccades result in the longest line segments [19].

Probably the best metaphor for a saccade heatmap is a grassland, where the grass is trampled down in paths that are frequently walked over. Trails emerge and enlarge as they are used more frequently. Similarly, the saccade heatmap visualizes frequently traversed gaze trails derived from the saccade point in eye-tracking data. Corresponding to the ROIs emerging from hot spots in the fixation heatmap, we will explore so-called saccade bundles, i.e., clusters of saccades.

Other methods, such as attribute-driven edge bundling techniques to cluster general trails, have successfully been applied to eye-tracking data [18]. A visually appealing and fast implementation can be found in the CUBu software [26] that can be accessed via Eyetrace [15], if a Nvidia GPU is available. In another approach, so-called saccade plots [5], saccades can be visualized in a more abstract way. Similar to a ROI transition diagram, saccades are split into x- and y- components and visualized, e.g., by arcs that connect different stimulus regions.

3 Eye Tracking Experiments

The proposed methods were applied to eye-tracking data collected during the viewing of paintings. Two paintings were chosen for this experiment that are at the center of a controversial methodological discussion in art history for several decades. In 1961 Kurt Badt argues that in order to interpret a painting one has to describe the path taken by the eye to go through it. His foremost examples are Jan Vermeer's Art of Painting at the Kunsthistorisches Museum, Vienna and Jacopo Tintoretto's Last Supper in S. Giorgio Maggiore, Venice [2]. Badt's argument was often discussed. But it could not yet be confirmed or falsified with empirical evidence.

(a) Vermeer, The art   (b) Tintoretto, The Last Supper

Fig. 1. Paintings employed in the eye-tracking experiments. (Color figure online)

Experiment 1: The Art of Painting: In the first experiment, nine subjects viewed Johannes Vermeer's *The art of painting* (Fig. 1(a)) on a screen for one minute. Eye movements were recorded by means of an EyeTribe eye tracker at 30 Hz sampling rate. Fixations and saccades were determined via a Gaussian mixture model [23, 24].

Experiment 2: The Last Supper (Tintoretto): This data set was recorded at the University of Vienna and contains eye-tracking data of 40 subjects viewing the painting shown in Fig. 1(b) for two minutes each. An IViewX RED 120 tracker was used and the painting shown on a 30" display (2560×1600 pixel) with a distance of 90 cm to the observer. The 20 art historians and 20 novices were instructed to judge whether they liked the picture to induce a sense for aesthetics.

4   Saccade Heatmap

Characterizing saccades requires at least two points, the origin and the target of the saccade. In addition, the representation of a saccade may contain its direction, amplitude, velocity and a whole trail of samples to show its ballistic nature. Clustering saccades is in contrast to clustering fixations a challenging task. Instead of comparing 2D fixation locations to each other, we need to assess the similarity of whole saccade trajectories. In this context, saccade direction, amplitude and the position of intra-saccadic measured points might also be relevant. The visualization of saccades without further post-processing might not be very informative. For example, Despite the relatively short viewing time of one minute and the small number of subjects, we extracted overall 959 saccades from the eye-tracking data collected during Experiment 1, Fig. 2. Each saccade is visualized by an arrow, resulting thus in a visual clutter and overlapping shapes. Given this visualization, it is pretty hard to derive any pattern; this is probably an additional reason why saccades are usually excluded from further analysis in many studies.

(a) Original artwork   (b) Raw saccades

Fig. 2. All saccades contained in a recording of nine subjects viewing *The Art of Painting* for one minute. Each saccade corresponds to one arrow in the visualization.

4.1   Construction of a Saccade Heatmap

To process saccadic data, we introduce a novel computational method for saccade heatmaps. The aim is to visualize the density of saccades, where frequently traversed areas gradually become *hot* while other areas stay *cold*. To achieve this, we have to (1) define a density function for a saccade, (2) integrate the density functions over all saccades, and (3) apply some post-processing, such as weighting. Each of these processing steps is described in detail in the following paragraph.

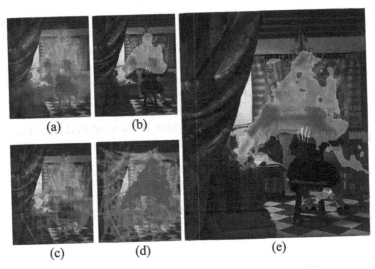

Fig. 3. (a) a raw saccade heatmap with Gaussian density functions stretched to cover the saccade trajectories. (b) thresholded at a minimum density to pronounce the most important paths. (c) raw heatmap with a small standard deviation for the saccade density function. As a result the heatmap is less smooth and more precise. (d) the heatmap was capped at a maximal density. The color resolution available for the remaining areas is therefore enlarged, but the resolution of the most frequently traveled paths is decreased. (e) Saccade heatmap with a low standard deviation, capped at a maximum density and with a minimum density threshold applied.

Density Functions: In the computation of fixation heatmaps, the density around a fixation location is usually modeled by a Gaussian. The mean of the Gaussian distribution is placed at the center of the fixation location and the standard deviation adjusted to represent 2–5° of the visual angle. Thus, it is supposed to represent the area of the fovea, the accuracy of the eye-tracker, or the area of *sharp, high-resolution* vision.

To compute saccade heatmaps, such a Gaussian with equal spread towards each direction obviously does not represent saccades very well. But the approach can be adapted by stretching the Gaussian along the saccade to cover its origin and target. More specifically, we apply the following Eqs. 1 and 2 to calculate the standard deviations of the Gaussian, where $dist$ is the length of the saccade.

In our implementation we used the pixel distance. To guarantee scale invariance, the pixel distance is calculated based on mm distances in the real world.

$$std_{dir}(dist) = \sqrt{dist} \cdot (1 + \ln(dist)) \tag{1}$$

$$std_{orto}(dist) = \sqrt{dist} \tag{2}$$

Note that in this case we have a covariance matrix that can be split into the contribution in the direction of the saccade std_{dir} and its orthogonal vector std_{orto}. The orthogonal contribution is chosen much smaller than the contribution along the saccade's major direction. This way a slim, ellipsoid shape is produced. We used the natural logarithm of the distance as stretching factor with e as base of the Gaussian and the idea that $e^{\ln dist} = dist$. For the Gaussian this is not completely correct (the standard deviation is the denominator), but the effect is as expected. The density function is then rotated and translated to align with the position and direction of the saccade vector.

$$g(x,y) = \frac{1}{2 * std_{dir} * std_{orto} * \pi} * e^{-\frac{1}{2}*(\frac{x^2}{std_{dir}^2} * \frac{y^2}{std_{orto}^2})} \tag{3}$$

Eq. 3 shows the complete Gaussian function, where x and y are the positions shifted from the saccade center.

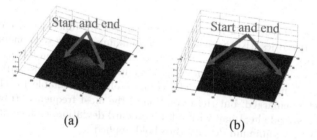

(a)   (b)

Fig. 4. Normal distribution density functions for two saccades. The height and color of the surface represents the density assigned to the respective position: (a) shows a short, (b) a long saccade.

Figure 4 visualizes the Gaussian distributions stretched along saccades. We can observe that the peak density is reached in the middle between the origin and target of the saccade and that positions along the saccade are not weighted equally. Furthermore, the start and end point are not contained within the high-density area. Figure 3(a) and (c) show the saccadic heatmap for two Gaussians with different standard deviations. In (a) the lines are smoothed and blurred by the high standard deviation. In (c) individual saccades are still visible and crisp. There is no obvious real-world equivalent to the spread of the Gaussian, like with the fovea for the fixation data. Instead, the parameter depends mainly on the eye-tracker's accuracy and the homogeneity of eye movements that the stimulus material invokes. If we want to study fine-grained details, a small standard deviation needs to be chosen. When general saccadic patterns are of interest, a larger standard deviation contributes to a faster convergence of the heatmap. Saccade trajectories are more likely to overlap when the spread is larger.

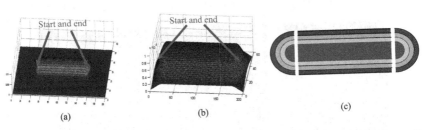

Fig. 5. Modified normal distribution density function that assigns the same gradient to each position along the saccade trajectory. (a) low standard deviation, leading to a crisp saccade representation. (b) larger standard deviation, resulting in a smooth but blurry heatmap. The width of the Gaussian is based on the user standard deviation. (c) Contour plot of the three components: two caps for the saccade start and end point, and a length-variable adapter piece between them.

To achieve an equal weight of the whole saccade trajectory, the central cross-section of the 2D Gaussian density function is *copied* along the trajectory (see Fig. 5). The start and end of the saccade are then modeled as a dissection of the Gaussian with one half applied to the start, the other to the end of the saccade (Fig. 5(c)).

Integrating Density Functions: Integration over all saccades in a recording is simple, as the density functions can be added. Using the modified density function without further modification would result in an increased number of saccade overlaps within the smaller ROIs (just as it happens in the example shown in Fig. 3(a) with the face of the woman): transitions to multiple other locations originate here, overlap each other, and cause the saccade heatmap to highlight the overlap region instead of the saccadic trajectory. A simple approach to avoid this effect is to reduce the length of the saccade (e.g., 10 % at each side). Endpoints will not accumulate anymore as the small shift assigns a lower weight to the periphery of the trajectory. Note that this effect is already built-in for the non-modified Gaussian density approach, since there exists only one maximum at the center of the saccade as described above.

Figure 6 shows the practical consequences of using either the modified density function (top row) or the non-modified density function (bottom row). When the modified density distribution is applied, frequent traversals between the painter,

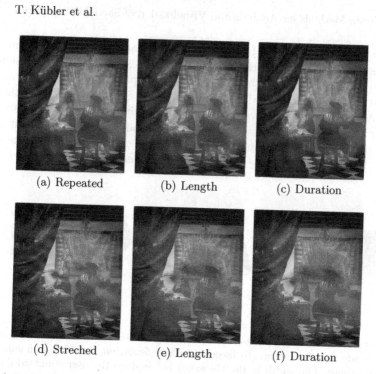

(a) Repeated   (b) Length   (c) Duration

(d) Streched   (e) Length   (f) Duration

Fig. 6. (a,b,c) In the top row, the modified density function is applied. (a) unweighted heatmap. (b) heatmap weighted by the length of the saccade highlights longer trajectories. (c) heatmap weighted by the duration of the enclosing fixations. (d,e,f) the bottom row employ the non-modified, stretched Gaussian density.

the woman and the mask are highlighted (first column). But there are also unwanted effects of saccadic overlay within the ROI regions of the faces (those are in fact the overall *hottest* areas). The stretched normal distribution compensates for this effect: hottest regions in this map are located in-between the face regions. However, the trail of gaze is not clearly visible. Especially the triangle between the two faces and the chandelier is not visible anymore.

A relevant drawback of the current implementation is that saccades sum up with each other independently of their direction. Theoretically, it would be possible to calculate separate heatmaps for saccades towards different directions. These heatmaps could then be merged by adding up only those heatmaps that stem from saccades with a similar direction. Heatmaps from different directions be then merged non-additively by taking the maximum of both maps. The implementation of these features is in scope of our future work.

Weighting and Post-processing: Just as the contribution of a fixation to a heatmap can be weighted by the fixation duration, the contribution of a saccade towards the saccade heatmap can be scaled. Figure 6(b) and (e) are weighted using the length of the saccade. Longer saccades contribute more towards the final heatmap, emphasizing the long-distance gaze transitions. For (e) and (f) saccades were weighted using the duration of both adjacent fixations. In these weighted heatmaps we can observe that the scaled normal distributions highlight the relevant gaze trails with only a minor overlap effect in the ROI regions when compared to the modified distribution.

Heatmaps of both, fixations and saccades, often suffer from the effect of one location that is so frequently looked at (or traversed), such that all other areas are covered by the large effect. This means that most of the color space is required to represent one spot and the remainder of the image has to be visualized with only a limited diversity of available colors. To cope with this effect, a parameter to cap the heatmap at some user defined maximum density is implemented. On the cost of resolution at the high density areas, low density effects can be studied in more detail. Figure 3 shows the saccadic heatmap with capped maximum and a minimum density threshold that cuts off non-relevant areas.

5   Saccade Clustering

This section introduces a new method for hierarchical clustering of saccades. In case of saccade clustering, we want to summarize most frequent gaze trails in the recording (similar to warm regions in the heatmap representing frequent gaze trails in the recording). Contrary to heatmaps we are working with the actual data that is not derived and generalized representation such as a probability distributions. This allows for a quantification and filtering of the results.

As for fixation clustering, we are then able to combine data from multiple recordings and subjects in order to reach a convergent gaze trail. Thereby, the most important, most repetitive elements are extracted from the recording. This process can be described as a denoising process that deletes individual variation from the data and highlights only the most common sequences.

When compared to visualization methods, clustering has several advantages: Each saccade can be uniquely assigned to one saccade bundle. These bundles can be quantified and compared to each other. Filtering and bundle selection can be applied (for example a visualization can select and display only the three most important gaze trails).

Clustering Algorithm: A hierarchical clustering [10] of a set of objects can be displayed as a binary tree. Each node represents one object of the set and the distance between two nodes represents the dissimilarity between the two objects. Constructing such a hierarchy tree consists of two steps. First calculating the dissimilarity between two nodes and second a linkage method for the dissimilarity between groups of nodes. Popular linkage criteria are maximum (or complete) linkage, minimum (or single) linkage and average linkage. Basically, maximum linkage will return the largest distance between any two elements contained in the two clusters, minimum linkage the smallest distance and average linkage the mean of all distances between any two nodes in the clusters.

For the definition of a distance metric between saccades we will consider both the orientation and the Euclidean distance between start and end points

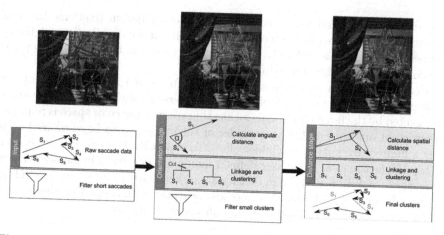

Fig. 7. Saccade clustering workflow. On the right side the raw data and clusters after the angular clustering as well as the subsequent distance clustering step are shown. Saccades of the same cluster are colored the same.

of the saccades. Data obtained from many or long recordings can easily contain some thousands saccades. As the dissimilarity calculation needs to be performed pairwise (resulting in a runtime of $\mathcal{O}(n^2)$), computational efficiency is an issue.

Saccade clustering is computed in a two-step approach as depicted in Fig. 7: in a first clustering step the orientation between saccades is used as similarity measure, afterwards a second clustering step based on the Euclidean distance between the saccades is performed, but only within the previously found clusters.

Runtime can be reduced by filtering short saccades that are unlikely to contribute much to driving gaze over the picture and by scanpath simplification, i.e., merging of temporally sequential saccades into the same direction.

Given a saccade with start point $A = (x_a, y_a)$ and end point $B = (x_b, y_b)$, the angle between $(-\pi; \pi]$ in relation to the positive x-axis plane is calculated as:

$$\angle(A, B) = atan2(y_b - y_a, x_b - x_a) \tag{4}$$

The angular difference between saccades S_1 and S_2 can then be computed as:

$$d(S_1, S_2) = \begin{cases} |\angle(S_1) - \angle(S_2)|, & \text{if } |angle(S_1) - angle(S_2)| \le \pi \\ 2\pi - |\angle(S_1) - \angle(S_2)|, & \text{otherwise} \end{cases} \tag{5}$$

The above equation can easily be adjusted for direction independence such that the saccades $S_1 = (A, B)$ and $S_2 = (B, A)$ are considered equal.

For the second clustering step, the spatial distance between two saccades $S_1 = (A, B)$ and $S_2 = (C, D)$ is calculated as the minimal distance of any of the start and end points to the line from start to end of the other saccade:

$$d(S_1, S_2) = min(d(A, (\overline{CD})), d(B, \overline{CD}), d(C, \overline{AB}), d(D, \overline{AB})) \tag{6}$$

The distance between a point A and a line segment $\overline{BC}$ is defined as the Euclidean distance between A and the closest point on the line segment $\overline{BC}$.

The construction of the clustering tree with the currently implemented method requires $\mathcal{O}(n^3)$, cutting the hierarchy tree can be done in $\mathcal{O}(n)$. The computational bottleneck is therefore the computation of the first clustering tree that includes many saccades. Due to the hierarchical clustering parameters can be adjusted easily and fast, allowing to choose between average cluster size and within-cluster similarity.

This ability to choose the detail-level after the computationally expensive part of the algorithm makes the method comfortable to use.

ROI Transitions: Figure 8 shows the transitions between ROIs. The depicted ROIs were calculated as cumulative clusters, i.e., clusters with the highest density of fixations shared by all participants. We distinguish between direct transitions, i.e., a saccade that connects two ROIs, and indirect transitions. Indirect transitions contain at least two saccades. The first saccade starts from a ROI but does not land in another ROI. We consider the following saccades until a ROI is hit. The indirect transition is then counted as a transition from the start ROI of the first saccade to the target ROI of the last saccade in this chain. This was already implemented in the first version of EyeTrace [9,22]. We added the capability to analyze indirect transitions.

6   Application of the Proposed Techniques to Art Viewing

The above approaches were applied to eye-tracking data of both free-viewing experiments introduced previously. For both eye-tracking datasets, the orientation clustering step was performed with maximum linkage criterion and direction

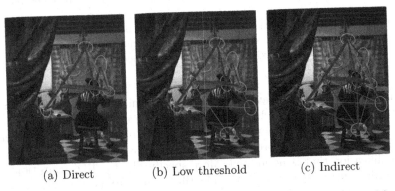

(a) Direct   (b) Low threshold   (c) Indirect

Fig. 8. Transitions between fixation clusters visualized by orange ellipses. (a) shows direct saccades that transition from one cluster to another. (b) shows the same clusters but includes also indirect transitions. In this visualization, the line width represents the transition frequency. Blue lines represent transitions that go from the left to the right, whereas green transitions stand for transitions in the opposite direction. (Color figure online)

dependency, whereas the distance-based clustering step with minimum linkage. Cutoff values were determined by successively easing the restrictiveness of the cutoff (i.e., increasing the cutoff threshold), until relatively many saccades were contained in the clusters. This parameter is necessarily subjective, as the homogeneity of saccades depends on the stimulus. While we are increasing the threshold, we are moving from very detailed saccade bundles towards a more general, coarser summary.

Results on Experiment 1: Figure 9(b) visualizes the clustering result for Experiment 1. Remarkably, saccade clustering reveals that the eye movements of the observers were driven by the social cue in the painting. The painter and the woman in this painting are displayed in a way that their gaze target can be estimated by the viewer. We can observe that the most frequent gaze trails computed by our clustering approach follow these social cues between the painter, the woman, and the plaster mask. We can further observe that the composition line of the painting that connects the mask, woman, and chandelier has a strong effect on gaze behavior.

(a) Sac. heatmap   (b) Sac. clusters   (c) ROI transitions   (d) Cubu bundling

Fig. 9. Comparison of the different approaches proposed in this paper (a,b,c) and one state-of-the-art visualization technique (d). In (b) the modified Gaussian (Fig. 5) with $std = 5.5$ and an absolute maxima of 25 overlapping saccades was applied.

In addition, Fig. 9 displays the spectrum of visualizations for saccades that is currently available in the Eyetrace software, where (a) visualizes the result of the saccade heatmap computation and (b) the result of the saccade clustering technique. Besides the different look, their main distinction lies in the amount of simplification that is performed. More specifically, the ROI transition graph as visualized in (c) builds upon the identification of ROIs (e.g., via mean-shift clustering of fixations). Its major advantage is that scanpath transitions instead of direct saccades between ROIs can be considered. Scanpath transitions may contain saccades to non-ROI areas in-between two ROIs and do not require a saccade directly from one ROI to another ROI.

The most recent and impressive example of clustering is attribute-driven edge bundling [18,26]. Edge bundling performs the mean-shift algorithm on both, saccadic start and end points as well as samples distributed equally along the saccadic trajectory. Therefore, clustered trajectories get an organic look, as if the exact ballistic eye movement was measured with an extremely high sampling rate and accuracy.

The edge bundling approach shown in (d) consists of various different steps (clustering of fixations, clustering of the trajectories, relaxation, color choice,...). Each step is associated with a set of parameters that require adjustment. The parameters were adjusted to emphasize the same effect that was also found by the other methods and we can clearly observe the primary gaze trajectories along the faces and towards the chandelier. When looking at the results it is important to keep in mind that the displayed data represents a considerable simplification and that the suggested level of detail is in fact not contained in the data. The samples along the saccade trajectory are interpolated. Contrary to the approach suggested here, the whole saccadic trail can be clustered - if a recording at a high enough frame rate is available. The proposed clustering approach uses only the start and end point of each saccade and can therefore also be run on the CPU while edge bundling requires the massive parallelization of a GPU.

Results on Experiment 2: Tintoretto was the first painter who represented the table of the Last Supper from the side, hence foreshortening it in the depth of the space. The main composition lines, as they have been described by Badt on the left (Apostes) and right (cat, servant, sideboard) lead into the depth of the space. Most saccade trajectories measured in Experiment 2 are along those composition lines with almost no transitions across the table. Also gaze escapes towards the light source in the top left corner mainly via the woman in-between the central image area and the light. The empirical experiment confirms the assumption of a correlation between composition lines (as generally analyzed by art historians) and eye movements of beholders. However, in this specific example the experiment falsifies Kurt Badt's analysis in one crucial point: His central assumption is that the viewer starting on the lower left corner will be refrained from following with his eyes the apostles along the table, and will instead follow the high-lighted leg of the left apostle, the dog and cat up to the servant and the right foreground. In the experiment, this connection was extremely rare (Fig. 10).

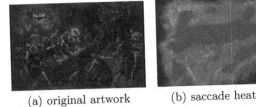

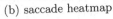

(a) original artwork   (b) saccade heatmap   (c) saccade bundles

Fig. 10. (a) *The last supper* by Tintoretto. (b) the saccade heatmap using the modified Gaussian (Fig. 5) with $std = 5.5$ and an absolute maxima of 100 overlapping saccades. (c) saccade clusters where the color represents the cluster membership.

This could be stated by using ROI transitions already before [21], but it becomes much more evident with our new visualization techniques. By employed our new visualization techniques, eye-tracking becomes an easier to use and very powerful tool to verify art historical theories about composition of pictures. This tools are useful for figurative paintings as those chosen in the present experiments. We expect them to be even more pertinent for abstract art and representational art without figures and or very salient objects (such as landscapes).

Conclusion: We introduced two novel computational techniques to process saccades: (1) the saccade heatmap and (2) a completely data-driven method for saccade clustering. Both methods were applied to two art viewing experiments alongside ROI transition diagrams and edge bundling. As they work without a definition of regions of interest, our methods are relatively easy to apply. In our future work, the method to compute saccade heatmaps will be adjusted for a sense of saccade direction in order to reduce the effect of overlapping saccades towards different directions.

References

1. Arnheim, R.: Art and Visual Perception: A Psychology of the Creative Eye. University of California Press, Berkeley (1954)
2. Badt, K., Dittmann, L., van Delft, J.V.: Modell und Maler von Jan Vermeer: Probleme der Interpretation: eine Streitschrift gegen Hans Sedlmayr. DuMont (1997)
3. Blascheck, T., Kurzhals, K., Raschke, M., Burch, M., Weiskopf, D., Ertl, T.: State-of-the-art of visualization for eye tracking data. In: EuroVis, vol. 2014 (2014)
4. Bojko, A.A.: Informative or misleading? heatmaps deconstructed. In: Jacko, J.A. (ed.) HCI International 2009, Part I. LNCS, vol. 5610, pp. 30–39. Springer, Heidelberg (2009)
5. Burch, M., Schmauder, H., Raschke, M., Weiskopf, D.: Saccade plots. In: ETRA, pp. 307–310. ACM (2014)
6. Condorovici, R.G., Vrânceanu, R., Vertan, C.: Saliency map retrieval for artistic paintings inspired from human understanding. In: SPAMEC (2011)
7. Dong, W., Liao, H., Roth, R.E., Wang, S.: Eye tracking to explore the potential of enhanced imagery basemaps in web mapping. Cartographic J. **51**(4), 313–329 (2014)
8. Ellis, S.R., Smith, J.D.: Patterns of Statistical Dependency in Visual Scanning, pp. 221–238. Elsevier Science Publishers BV, Amsterdam (1985)
9. Engelbrecht, M., Betz, J., Klein, C., Rosenberg, R.: Dem auge auf der spur: Eine historische und empirische studie zur blickbewegung beim betrachten von gemälden. IMAGE-Zeitschrift für interdisziplinäre Bildwissenschaft 11 (2010)
10. Härdle, W.K., Simar, L.: Applied Multivariate Statistical Analysis, vol. 22007. Springer, Heidelberg (2007)
11. Holmqvist, K., Nyström, M., Andersson, R., Dewhurst, R., Jarodzka, H., Van de Weijer, J.: Eye Tracking: A Comprehensive Guide to Methods and Measures. Oxford University Press, Oxford (2011)
12. Icoglu, O., Gunsel, B., Sariel, S.: Classification and indexing of paintings based on art movements. In: 2004 12th European Signal Processing Conference, pp. 749–752. IEEE (2004)

13. Kasneci, E., Kasneci, G., Kübler, T.C., Rosenstiel, W.: The applicability of probabilistic methods to the online recognition of fixations and saccades in dynamic scenes. In: ETRA, pp. 323–326. ACM (2014)
14. Kübler, T.C., Kasneci, E., Rosenstiel, W.: Subsmatch: scanpath similarity in dynamic scenes based on subsequence frequencies. In: ETRA, ACM (2014)
15. Kübler, T.C., Sippel, K., Fuhl, W., Schievelbein, G., Aufreiter, J., Rosenberg, R., Rosenstiel, W., Kasneci, E.: Analysis of eye movements with eyetrace. In: Fred, A., Gamboa, H., Elias, D. (eds.) BIOSTEC 2015. CCIS, vol. 574, pp. 458–471. Springer, Heidelberg (2015). doi:10.1007/978-3-319-27707-3_28
16. Leonards, U., Baddeley, R., Gilchrist, I.D., Troscianko, T., Ledda, P., Williamson, B.: Mediaeval artists: masters in directing the observers' gaze. Curr. Biol. **17**(1), R8–R9 (2007)
17. Ouerhani, N., Bracamonte, J., Hugli, H., Ansorge, M., Pellandini, F.: Adaptive color image compression based on visual attention. In: ICIAP, IEEE (2001)
18. Peysakhovich, V., Hurter, C., Telea, A.: Attribute-driven edge bundling for general graphs with applications in trail analysis. In: PacificVis, pp. 39–46. IEEE (2015)
19. Popelka, S., Voženílek, V.: Specifying of requirements for spatio-temporal data in map by eye-tracking and space-time-cube. In: ICGIP, p. 87684N. International Society for Optics and Photonics (2013)
20. Privitera, C.M., Stark, L.W.: Algorithms for defining visual regions-of-interest: comparison with eye fixations. PAMI **22**(9), 970–982 (2000)
21. Rosenberg, R.: Blicke messen: Vorschläge für eine empirische bildwissenschaft. Jahrbuch der Bayerischen Akademie der Schönen Künste **27**, 71–86 (2014)
22. Rosenberg, R., Klein, C.: The moving eye of the beholder: Eye tracking and the perception of paintings (2015)
23. Tafaj, E., Kasneci, G., Rosenstiel, W., Bogdan, M.: Bayesian online clustering of eye movement data. In: ETRA 2012, pp. 285–288. ACM (2012)
24. Tafaj, E., Kübler, T.C., Kasneci, G., Rosenstiel, W., Bogdan, M.: Online classification of eye tracking data for automated analysis of traffic hazard perception. In: Mladenov, V., Koprinkova-Hristova, P., Palm, G., Villa, A.E.P., Appollini, B., Kasabov, N. (eds.) ICANN 2013. LNCS, vol. 8131, pp. 442–450. Springer, Heidelberg (2013)
25. Tatler, B.W., Wade, N.J., Kwan, H., Findlay, J.M., Velichkovsky, B.M.: Yarbus, eye movements, and vision. i-Perception **1**(1), 7–27 (2010)
26. van der Zwan, M., Codreanu, V., Telea, A.: CUBu: universal real-time bundling for large graphs. IEEE Trans. Vis. Comput. Graph. **38**(1), 30–45 (2016)

Adversarial Training for Sketch Retrieval

Antonia Creswell[(⊠)] and Anil Anthony Bharath

BICV Group, Bioengineering, Imperial College London, London, UK
ac2211@ic.ac.uk

Abstract. Generative Adversarial Networks (GAN) are able to learn excellent representations for unlabelled data which can be applied to image generation and scene classification. Representations learned by GANs have not yet been applied to retrieval. In this paper, we show that the representations learned by GANs can indeed be used for retrieval. We consider heritage documents that contain unlabelled Merchant Marks, sketch-like symbols that are similar to hieroglyphs. We introduce a novel GAN architecture with design features that make it suitable for sketch retrieval. The performance of this sketch-GAN is compared to a modified version of the original GAN architecture with respect to simple invariance properties. Experiments suggest that sketch-GANs learn representations that are suitable for retrieval and which also have increased stability to rotation, scale and translation compared to the standard GAN architecture.

Keywords: Deep learning · CNN · GAN · Generative models · Sketches

1 Introduction

Recently, the UK's National Archives has collected over $70,000$ heritage documents that originate between the 16th and 19th centuries. These documents make up a small part of the "Prize Papers", which are of gross historical importance, as they were used to establish legitimacy of ship captures at sea.

This collection of documents contain *Merchant Marks* (see Fig. 4B), symbols used to uniquely identify the property of a merchant. For further historical research to be conducted, the organisation requires that the dataset be searchable by visual example (see Fig. 1). These marks are sparse line drawings, which makes it challenging to search for visually similar Merchant Marks between documents. This dataset poses the following challenges to learning representations that are suitable for visual search:

1. Merchant marks are line drawings, absent of both texture and colour, which means that marks cannot be distinguished based on these properties.
2. Many machine learning techniques, and most notably convolutional neural networks (CNNs), require large amounts of labelled training data, containing on the order of millions of labelled images [7]. None of the Merchant Marks are labelled, and in many cases it is not clear what labels would be assigned to them. This motivates an unsupervised approach to learning features.

G. Hua and H. Jégou (Eds.): ECCV 2016 Workshops, Part I, LNCS 9913, pp. 798–809, 2016.
DOI: 10.1007/978-3-319-46604-0_55

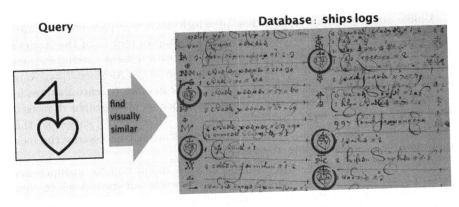

Fig. 1. An overview of the problem: the circled items contain examples of Merchant Marks; note that although some marks are distinct, they are still visually similar. We would like to retrieve visually similar examples, and find exact matches if they exist. Note that the two marks on the left are exact matches, while the others might be considered to be visually similar.

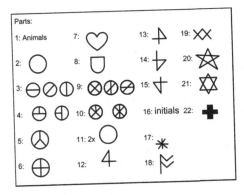

Fig. 2. Most marks in the Merchant Marks dataset are made of the above sub-structures which we refer to as *parts*.

3. The marks are not segmented from the dataset, limiting the number of examples available, and making it difficult to train CNNs.

To perform visual search on the Merchant Marks, a representation for the marks that captures their structure must be learned. Previous work has demonstrated that deep convolutional neural networks (CNNs) are able to learn excellent hierarchical representations for data [15]. CNNs have proven useful for tasks such as classification [7], segmentation [9] and have been applied to retrieval of art work [1,2]. However, these methods rely on large amounts of labelled data for learning the weights. In the absence of sufficient labelled training data, we propose the use of unsupervised techniques with CNN architectures to learn representations for the Merchant Marks.

Unlike some previous approaches in which feature representations were learned by using labelled datasets that differ in appearance from the retrieval set, we used the Merchant Marks dataset itself to learn dataset-specific features. For example, Crowley et al. [2] trained a network similar to AlexNet [7] on examples from the photographic scenes of ILSVRC-2012 in order to learn features for the retrieval of art work; they also trained a network on photographs of faces to learn features for retrieving paintings of faces [1]. Yu et al. [14] suggested that features suitable for understanding natural images are not necessarily the most appropriate for understanding sketches.

Convolutional Auto-encoders (CAE) can be a useful tool for unsupervised learning of features. They are made up of two networks, an encoder which compresses the input to produce an encoding and a decoder, which reconstructs the input from that encoding. It has been shown [8] that shallow CAEs often learn the delta function (a trivial solution) which is not a useful representation for the data. Instead, deep encoders are needed with strict regularisation on the activations. The Winner Take All CAE [8] imposes both spatial and life-time sparsity on the activations of the CAE in order to learn useful representations. Other regularisation techniques include the Variational Auto-encoder [6], which imposes a prior distribution on the encoding.

An alternative method, which learns representations from data without the need for regularisation, is the Generative Adversarial Network [3] (GAN). Deep convolutional generative adversarial networks [10] have been shown to learn good representations for data. In this paper, we propose the use of GANs for learning a representation of the Merchant Marks that can be used for visual search.

The key contribution is to show that GANs can be used to learn a representation suitable for visual search. We apply this novel idea to the Merchant Mark dataset, and compare two GAN architectures. The first GAN is designed to learn a representation for sketches, based on reported architectural considerations specific to sketches [14]. The second GAN is a modified version of the network proposed by Radford et al. [10] often used for learning representations for natural images. The representations are evaluated by comparing their invariance to shift, scale and rotation as well as the top 8 retrieval results for 15 examples.

2   Generative Adversarial Networks

Generative Adversarial Networks (see Fig. 3), (GANs) where first introduced by Goodfellow et al. [3], as a generative model that learned an excellent representation for the training dataset. GANs consist of two networks, a generative network, G and a discriminative network, D. The goal of the generative network is to learn the distribution of the training data, $p_{data}(x)$ where $x \in R^{dx}$ and dx is the dimensions of a data sample.

In a GAN, the generator takes as input a vector, $z \in R^{dz}$ of dz random values drawn from a prior distribution $p_z(z)$, and maps this to the data space, $G : R^{dz} \rightarrow R^{dx}$. The discriminator takes examples from both the generator and

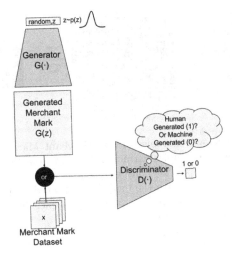

Fig. 3. Generative Adversarial Network: a random sample z is drawn from a prior distribution and fed into the generator, G to generate a sample. The discriminator will take a sample either from the generator, $G(z)$, or from the Merchant Mark dataset, $p_{data}(x)$, and predict whether the sample is machine or human generated. The discriminator's objective is to make the correct prediction, while the generator's objective is to generate examples that fool the discriminator.

real examples of training data and predicts whether the examples are human (or real) (1) or machine generated (0), $D : R^{d_x} \rightarrow [0, 1]$.

The objective of the discriminator is to correctly classify examples as human or machine generated, while the objective of the generator is to fool the discriminator into making incorrect predictions. This can be summarised by the following value function that the generator aims to minimise while the discriminator aims to maximise:

$$\min_G \max_D \mathbb{E}_{x \sim p_{data}(x)} \log D(x) + \mathbb{E}_{z \sim p_z(z)} \log(1 - D(G(z)))$$

Training an adversarial network, both the generator and the discriminator learn a representation for the real data. The approach considered here will use the representation learned by the discriminator.

3   Methods

Here, we show how the discriminator, taken from a trained GAN, can be modified to be used as an encoder for sketch retrieval. An overview of the methods used can be seen in Fig. 4.

3.1   Dataset Acquisition

The raw Merchant Mark dataset that we have been working with consists of 76 photographs of pages from the raw Merchant Mark dataset, similar to the one

Fig. 4. Overview: (A) Shows examples of raw Merchant Mark data, photographs of the documents. (B) Shows examples extracted by hand from the raw Merchant Mark dataset, a total of 2000 examples are collected. (C) An encoder is simply a discriminator, taken from a trained GAN with the final layer removed. Representations for both query and data samples are obtained by passing examples through the encoder, the representations are used for retrieval.

shown in Fig. 4A, which contain multiple Merchant Marks at different spatial locations on the page. The focus of this paper is on retrieval of visually similar examples rather than localisation, so the first step involved defining box regions from which Merchant Mark training examples could be extracted. The extracted examples are re-size to be 64×64 pixels to form a suitable dataset for training a GAN. In total there are 2000 training examples (see Fig. 4B).

3.2   Learning an Encoder

Training a GAN. To learn an encoding, the generator and the discriminator of a GAN are trained iteratively, as proposed by Goodfellow et al. [3]. See pseudo-code in Algorithm 1.

Network Architecture. Both the generator, and the discriminator are convolutional neural networks [13], using convolutions applied with strides rather than pooling as suggested by Radford et al. [10]. In the discriminator, the image is mapped to a single scalar label, so the stride applied in the convolutional layer of the discriminator must be grater than 1. A stride of 2 is used in all convolutional layers of the discriminator. In the generator, a vector is mapped to an image, so a (positive) step size less than 1 is needed to increase the size of the image after each convolution. A stride of 0.5 is used in all convolutional layers of the generator.

Encoding Samples. Having trained both the generator and the discriminator, the discriminator can be detached from the GAN. To encode a sample, it is passed through all but the last layer of the discriminator. The discriminative network without the final layer is called the *encoder*. Both the query examples and all examples in the dataset can be encoded using the this encoder. The encoding is normalised to have unit length by dividing by the square root of the sum of squared values in the encoding.

for *Number of training iterations* **do**

    for *k iterations* **do**

        sample $p_z(z)$ to get m random samples $\{z_1...z_m\}$

        sample $p_{data}(x)$ to get m random samples $\{x_1...x_m\}$

        calculate the discriminator error:

$$J_D = -\frac{1}{2m}\left(\sum_{i=1}^{m}\log D(x_i) + \sum_{i=1}^{m}\log(1 - D(G(z_i)))\right)$$

        update θ_D using Adam [5] update rule.

    end

    sample $p_z(z)$ to get m random samples $\{z_1...z_m\}$

    calculate the generator error:

$$J_G = -\frac{1}{m}\sum_{i=1}^{m}\log(D(G(z_i)))$$

    update θ_G using Adam [5] update rule.

end

Algorithm 1. Training a GAN: After Goodfellow et al. [3] with changes to the optimisation, using Adam [5] instead of batch gradient descent. Note, m is the batch size and θ_G, θ_D are the weights of the generator, G and discriminator, D.

3.3 Retrieval

The objective is to retrieve samples that are visually similar to a query example. To retrieve examples similar to the query, similarity measures are calculated between the representation for the query and representations for all samples in the dataset. Examples with the highest similarity scores are retrieved. The focus of this paper is on learning a good representation for the data, for this reason a simple similarity measure is used, the (normalised) dot product.

4 Experiments and Results

The purpose of these experiments is to show that GANs can be used to learn a representation for our Merchant Mark dataset from only 2000 examples, that can be used to precisely retrieve visually similar marks, given a query. We compare invariance of feature representations learned and retrieval results from two different networks to show that there is some benefit to using a network designed specifically for learning representations for sketches.

4.1 GAN Architectures

Two different architectures were compared:

Sketch-GAN. We propose a novel GAN architecture inspired by Sketch-A-Net [14], a network achieving state of the art recognition on sketches. Sketch-A-Net employs larger filters in the shallower layers of the discriminative network to capture structure of sketches rather than fine details which are absent in sketches. This motivated our network design, using larger filters in the lower levels of the discriminator and the deeper levels of the generator. This network will be referred to as the *sketch-GAN*. This network has only 33k parameters.

Thin-GAN. A network similar to that proposed by Radford et al. [10] is used. This network has very small filters, consistent with most of the state-of-the-art natural image recognition networks [12]. The original network has 12.4 M parameters which would not compare fairly with the *sketch-GAN*, instead a network with 1/16th of the filters in each layer is used, this will be referred to as the *thin-GAN* and has 50 k parameters. Full details of the architecture are given in Table.1.

4.2   Details of Training

In adversarial training the generator and discriminator networks are competing against eachother in a mini-max game, where the optimal solution is a Nash Equilibrium [11]. Adversarial networks are trained iteratively alternating between the generator and discriminator using gradient descent which aims to minimise the individual cost functions of the generator and discriminator, rather than finding a Nash Equilibrium [11]. For this reason convergence, during adversarial training cannot be guaranteed [4,11]. During training we found that networks did not converge, for this reason networks were trained for a fixed number of iterations, rather than till the networks converged. The networks are trained for 2000 iterations with batch size of 128 according to Algorithm 1 [3], with $k = 1$, $dz = 2$, learning rate $= 0.002$, and $p_z(z) \sim U(0, 1)$. The networks were still able to learn features useful for retrieval despite not converging.

4.3   Feature Invariance

Merchant Marks are hand drawn, which means that the marks are likely to vary in both scale and orientation. It is therefore important to consider the rotation and scale invariance of the representations that result from training. When searching a document for Marks, one approach may be to apply a sliding box search. The step size in sliding the search box will affect the computational feasibility of the search. If a representation used for search is invariant to larger shifts, then a sliding box search can be performed with a larger step size, making the search more efficient. For this reason, shift invariance of the two representations is also compared.

Invariance to Rotation. To assess the degree of rotation invariance within the two representations, 100 samples were randomly taken from the Merchant Mark

Table 1. A summary of the network architectures used in this study. fc = fully connected layer, c = convolutional layer with stride 2, d = convolutional layer with stride 0.5, unless stated otherwise; for all cases, dz, the dimension of the random valued vector input to the generator is 2. The ReLU activation function is used in all hidden layers of all networks and the sigmoid activation is used in final layer of each network.

thin-GAN:G	thin-GAN:D
fc: $1024 \times dz$, reshape(64,4,4)	c: $8 \times 1 \times 3 \times 3$
d: $32 \times 64 \times 3 \times 3$	c: $16 \times 8 \times 3 \times 3$
batch normalisation	batch normalisation
d: $16 \times 32 \times 3 \times 3$	c: $32 \times 16 \times 3 \times 3$
batch normalisation	batch normalisation
d: $8 \times 16 \times 3 \times 3$	c: $64 \times 32 \times 3 \times 3$
batch normalisation	batch normalisation, reshape(1024)
d: $1 \times 8 \times 3 \times 3$	fc: 1×1024
sketch-GAN:G	sketch-GAN:D
fc: $128 \times dz$, reshape(8,4,4)	c: $8 \times 1 \times 9 \times 9$ (stride = 1)
d: $16 \times 8 \times 3 \times 3$	c: $16 \times 8 \times 5 \times 5$
batch normalisation	batch normalisation
d: $16 \times 16 \times 5 \times 5$	c: $16 \times 16 \times 5 \times 5$
batch normalisation	batch normalisation
d: $16 \times 16 \times 5 \times 5$	c: $16 \times 16 \times 5 \times 5$
batch normalisation	batch normalisation, reshape(1,1024)
d: $16 \times 16 \times 5 \times 5$	fc: 1×1024
batch normalisation	-
d: $1 \times 16 \times 9 \times 9$ (stride = 1)	-

dataset and rotated between the angles of $-10°$ and $10°$. At each $0.5°$ increment, the samples were encoded and the similarity score between the rotated sample and the sample at $0°$ was calculated. The similarity score used was the normalised dot product, since this was also the measure used for retrieval. The results are shown in the top left of Fig. 5. It is clear that the *sketch-GAN* encoding is more tolerant to rotation than the *thin-GAN* encoding. Note that the background of the rotated samples were set to 0 to match the background of the samples.

Invariance to Scale. A similar approach was used to assess the degree of scale invariance within the two networks. Again, 100 samples were randomly taken from the Merchant Mark dataset, and scaled by a factor between 0.5 and 1.5. At each increment of 0.05, the scaled sample was encoded and a similarity score was calculated between the scaled samples and the sample at scale 1. The results are shown in the top right of Fig. 5. Note, that when the scaling factor is <1 the scaled image is padded with zeros to preserve the 64×64 image size. When

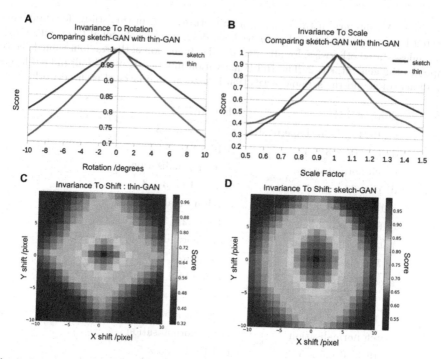

Fig. 5. Invariance: shows invariance of the *sketch-GAN* and *thin-GAN* representations to (A) rotation, (B) scale and (C, D) translation.

scaling with a factor >1, the example is scaled and cropped to be of size 64×64. The bounding box of the unscaled marks is tight, which means that at higher scaling factors parts of the marks are sometimes cropped out. Despite this, the *sketch-GAN* encoding is able to cope better with up-scaling compared to down-scaling. The *sketch-GAN* encoder generally outperforms the *thin-GAN* encoder, particularly for up-scaling.

Invariance to Shift. Finally, we compared the shift invariance of the two encoders. Sampling 100 marks from the merchant mark dataset, and applying shifts between -10 and 10 pixels in increments of 1 pixel in both the x and y directions. The results are shown as a heat map in Fig. 5, where the *sketch-GAN* encoding appears to be more invariant to shift than the *thin-GAN* encoding.

4.4   Retrieval

For the retrieval experiments, 500 queries were taken at random from the training dataset and used to query the whole dataset using features from the *sketch-GAN*. The top 9 matches were retrieved, where the first retrieval is the example itself and the rest are examples that the system thinks are similar. The results from some of these queries are shown in Fig. 6b. The same query examples were used

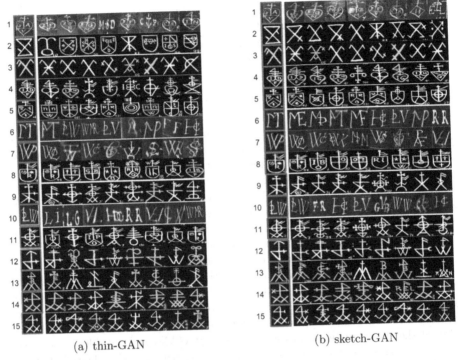

(a) thin-GAN   (b) sketch-GAN

Fig. 6. Retrieval examples using different GAN architectures. Each sub-figure shows 15 retrievals where the 1st example, in a purple box, in each row is the query and the following images on each row are the top 8 retrievals. (a) Shows retrievals using the thin-GAN encoder and (b) shows retrievals using the sketch-GAN encoder.

to query the dataset using the features from the *thin-GAN*, the results of these queries are shown in Fig. 6a.

Retrieval Results Using Trained Sketch-GAN Encoder. Results show that using the *sketch-GAN* encoder for Merchant Marks retrieval (Fig. 6b) allows retrieval of examples that have multiple similar parts for example results for queries #4, #8, #11, #14 and #15 consistently retrieve examples with at least two similar parts (Fig. 2). Specifically, most retrievals for query #15, Fig. 6b have parts 12 and 19 from Fig. 2. Exact matches are found for retrievals #4, #5, #8 and #10. Specifically, query #10 finds an exact match despite the most similar example being shifted upwards and rotated slightly. Retrievals for query #6 finds an exact match but does not rank the retrieval as high as non-exact matches, suggesting that there is still room for improvement in the representations that are learned.

Retrieval Results Using Trained Thin-GAN Encoder. On visual inspection of the retrieval results that use the *thin-GAN* encoder, it is clear that they under perform compared to the *sketch-GAN* for the same query examples, with fewer visually similar examples. The *thin-GAN* encoder fails to find exact matches for 4, 5 and 10. Failure to find a match for 10 further suggests that the *thin-GAN* is less invariant to rotation.

5   Conclusions

Convolutional networks contain, at a minimum, tens of thousands of weights. Training such networks has typically relied on the availability of large quantities of labelled data. Learning network weights that provide good image representations in the absence of class labels is an attractive proposition for many problems. One approach to training in the absence of class labels is to encourage networks to compete in coupled tasks of image synthesis and discrimination. The question is whether such Generative Adversarial Networks can learn feature representations suitable for retrieval in a way that matches human perception.

We have found that GANs can indeed be used to learn representations that are suitable for image retrieval. To demonstrate this, we compared the representation learned by GANs that were trained on Merchant Marks. We compared two related architectures, *sketch-GAN* and *thin-GAN*; *sketch-GAN* has an architectural design that is more appropriate for performing generation and discrimination of sketches. Our experiments showed that GANs are suitable for retrieval of both visually similar and exact examples. Experiments also showed that the features that were learned by the *sketch-GAN* were, on average, more robust to small image perturbations in scale, rotation and shift than the *thin-GAN*. Further, retrieval results when using the *sketch-GAN* appeared more consistent than in using *thin-GAN*.

More generally, the experiments suggest that adversarial training can be used to train convolutional networks for the purpose of learning good representations for the retrieval of perceptually similar samples; this can be achieved without the level of labelling and examples required for non-adversarial training approaches. This broadens the scope of deep networks to problems of perceptually similar retrieval in the absence of class labels, a problem that is increasingly of interest in heritage collections of images.

Acknowledgements. We would like to acknowledge Nancy Bell, Head of Collection Care at the National Archives. We would also like to acknowledge the Engineering and Physical Sciences Research Council for funding through a Doctoral Training studentship.

References

1. Crowley, E.J., Parkhi, O.M., Zisserman, A.: Face painting: querying art with photos. In: British Machine Vision Conference (2015)
2. Crowley, E.J., Zisserman, A.: In: search of art. In: Workshop on Computer Vision for Art Analysis, ECCV (2014)

3. Goodfellow, I., Pouget-Abadie, J., Mirza, M., Xu, B., Warde-Farley, D., Ozair, S., Courville, A., Bengio, Y.: Generative adversarial nets. In: Advances in Neural Information Processing Systems, pp. 2672–2680 (2014)
4. Goodfellow, I.J.: On distinguishability criteria for estimating generative models. arXiv preprint arXiv:1412.6515 (2014)
5. Kingma, D., Ba, J.: Adam: A method for stochastic optimization. arXiv preprint arXiv:1412.6980 (2014)
6. Kingma, D.P., Welling, M.: Auto-encoding variational bayes. arXiv preprint arXiv:1312.6114 (2013)
7. Krizhevsky, A., Sutskever, I., Hinton, G.E.: Imagenet classification with deep convolutional neural networks. In: Advances in Neural Information Processing Systems, pp. 1097–1105 (2012)
8. Makhzani, A., Frey, B.J.: Winner-take-all autoencoders. In: Advances in Neural Information Processing Systems, pp. 2773–2781 (2015)
9. Noh, H., Hong, S., Han, B.: Learning deconvolution network for semantic segmentation. In: Proceedings of the IEEE International Conference on Computer Vision, pp. 1520–1528 (2015)
10. Radford, A., Metz, L., Chintala, S.: Unsupervised representation learning with deep convolutional generative adversarial networks. arXiv preprint arXiv:1511.06434 (2015)
11. Salimans, T., Goodfellow, I., Zaremba, W., Cheung, V., Radford, A., Chen, X.: Improved techniques for training gans. arXiv preprint arXiv:1606.03498 (2016)
12. Simonyan, K., Zisserman, A.: Very deep convolutional networks for large-scale image recognition. arXiv preprint arXiv:1409.1556 (2014)
13. Springenberg, J.T., Dosovitskiy, A., Brox, T., Riedmiller, M.: Striving for simplicity: The all convolutional net. arXiv preprint arXiv:1412.6806 (2014)
14. Yu, Q., Yang, Y., Song, Y.Z., Xiang, T., Hospedales, T.M.: Sketch-a-net that beats humans. In: Proceedings of the British Machine Vision Conference (BMVC), pp. 7-1 (2015)
15. Zeiler, M.D., Fergus, R.: Visualizing and understanding convolutional networks. In: Fleet, D., Pajdla, T., Schiele, B., Tuytelaars, T. (eds.) ECCV 2014, Part I. LNCS, vol. 8689, pp. 818–833. Springer, Heidelberg (2014)

Convolutional Sketch Inversion

Yağmur Güçlütürk[✉], Umut Güçlü, Rob van Lier,
and Marcel A.J. van Gerven

Donders Institute for Brain, Cognition and Behaviour,
Radboud University, Nijmegen, The Netherlands
{y.gucluturk,u.guclu,r.vanlier,m.vangerven}@donders.ru.nl

Abstract. In this paper, we use deep neural networks for inverting face sketches to synthesize photorealistic face images. We first construct a semi-simulated dataset containing a very large number of computer-generated face sketches with different styles and corresponding face images by expanding existing unconstrained face data sets. We then train models achieving state-of-the-art results on both computer-generated sketches and hand-drawn sketches by leveraging recent advances in deep learning such as batch normalization, deep residual learning, perceptual losses and stochastic optimization in combination with our new dataset. We finally demonstrate potential applications of our models in fine arts and forensic arts. In contrast to existing patch-based approaches, our deep-neural-network-based approach can be used for synthesizing photorealistic face images by inverting face sketches in the wild.

Keywords: Deep neural network · Face synthesis · Face recognition · Fine arts · Forensic arts · Sketch inversion · Sketch recognition

1 Introduction

Portrait and self-portrait sketches have an important role in art. From an art historical perspective, self-portraits serve as historical records of what the artists looked like. From the perspective of an artist, self-portraits can be seen as a way to practice and improve one's skills without the need for a model to pose. Portraits of others further serve as memorabilia and a record of the person in the portrait. Artists most often are able to easily capture recognizable features of a person in their sketches. Therefore, hand-drawn sketches of people have further applications in law enforcement. Sketches of suspects drawn based on eye-witness accounts are used to identify suspects, either in person or from catalogues of mugshots (Fig. 1).

However, a challenging task that remains is photorealistic face image synthesis from face sketches in uncontrolled conditions. That is, at present, there exist no sketch inversion models that are able to perform in realistic conditions. These

Y. Güçlütürk and U. Güçlü contributed equally to this work.

G. Hua and H. Jégou (Eds.): ECCV 2016 Workshops, Part I, LNCS 9913, pp. 810–824, 2016.
DOI: 10.1007/978-3-319-46604-0_56

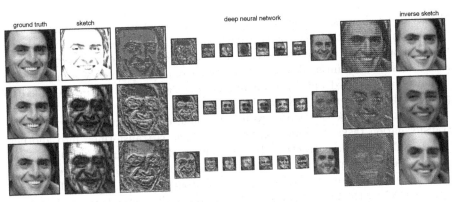

Fig. 1. Demonstration of our convolutional sketch inversion models. Our models invert face sketches to synthesize photorealistic face images. Each row shows the sketch inversion/image synthesis pipeline that transforms a different sketch of the same face to a different image of the same face via a different deep neural network. Each deep neural network layer is represented by the top three principal components of its feature maps.

conditions are characterized by changes in expression, pose, lighting condition and image quality, as well as the presence of varying amounts of background clutter and occlusions.

Here, we use DNNs to tackle the problem of inverting face sketches to synthesize photorealistic face images from different sketch styles in uncontrolled conditions. We developed three different models to handle three different types of sketch styles by training DNNs on datasets that we constructed by extending a well-known large-scale face dataset, obtained in uncontrolled conditions [21]. We test the models on another similar large-scale dataset [17], a hand-drawn sketch database [31] as well as on self-portrait sketches of famous Dutch artists. We show that our approach, which we refer to as *Convolutional Sketch Inversion* (CSI) can be used to achieve state-of-the-art results and discuss possible applications in fine arts, art history and forensics.

2   Related Work

Prior work related to face sketches in computer vision has been mostly limited to synthesis of highly controlled (i.e. having neutral expression, frontal pose, with normal lighting and without any occlusions) sketches from photographs [7, 19,26,30,34] (sketch synthesis) and photographs from sketches [7,20,30,31,33] (sketch inversion). Sketch inversion studies with controlled inputs utilized patch-based approaches and used Bayesian tensor inference [20], an embedded hidden Markov model [33], a multiscale Markov random field model [31], sparse representations [7] and transductive learning with a probabilistic graph model [30].

Few studies developed methods of sketch synthesis to handle more variation in one or more variables at a time, such as lighting [18], and lighting and pose [36]. In a recent study, Zhang et al. [35] showed that sketch synthesis by transferring the style of a single sketch could be used also in uncontrolled conditions. In [35], first an initial sketch by a sparse representation-based greedy search strategy was estimated, then candidate patches were selected from a template style sketch and the estimated initial sketch. Finally, the candidate patches were refined by a multi-feature-based optimization model and the patches were assembled to produce the final synthesized sketch.

Recently, the use of deep convolutional neural networks (DNNs) in image transformation tasks, in which one type of image is transformed into another, has gained tremendous traction. In the context of sketch analysis, DNNs were used to tackle the problems of sketch synthesis and sketch simplification. For example, [34] has used a DNN to convert photographs to sketches. They developed a DNN with six convolutional layers and a discriminative regularization term for enhancing the discriminability of the generated sketch against other sketches. Furthermore, [24] has used a DNN to simplify rough sketches. They have shown that users prefer sketches simplified by the DNN more than they do those by other applications 97 % of the time.

Some other notable image transformation problems include colorization, style transfer and super-resolution. In colorization, the task is to transform a grayscale image to a color image that accurately captures the color information. In style transfer, the task is to transform one image to another image that captures the style of a third image. In super-resolution, the task is to transform a low-resolution image to a high-resolution image with maximum quality. DNNs have been used to tackle all of these problems with state-of-the art results [3,5,6,9,13,15].

3   Semi-simulated Datasets

For training and testing our CSI model, we made use of the following datasets:

- *Large-scale CelebFaces Attributes (CelebA) dataset* [21]. The CelebA dataset contains 202,599 celebrity face images and 10,177 identities. The images were obtained from the internet and vary extensively in terms of pose, expression, lighting, image quality, background clutter and occlusion. Each image in the dataset has five landmark positions and 40 attributes. These images were used for training the networks.
- *Labeled Faces in the Wild (LFW) dataset* [17]. The LFW dataset contains 13,233 face images and 5749 identities. Similar to the CelebA dataset, images were obtained from the internet and vary extensively in terms of pose, expression, lighting, image quality, background clutter and occlusion. A subset of these images (11,990) were used for testing the networks.
- *CUHK Face Sketch (CUFS) database* [31]. The CUFS database contains photographs and their corresponding hand-drawn sketches of 606 individuals. The dataset was formed by combining face photographs from three other databases and producing hand-drawn sketches of these photographs. Concretely, it consists of 188 face photographs from the Chinese University of Hong Kong

(CUHK) student database [31] and their corresponding sketches, 123 face photographs from the AR Face Database [22] and their corresponding sketches, and 295 face photographs from the XM2VTS database [23] and their corresponding sketches. Only the 18 sketches that are showcased at the website of the CUFS database (six from each sub-database) were used in the current study. These images were used for testing the networks.

– *Sketches of famous Dutch artists.* We also used the following sketches: (i) Self-Portrait with Beret, Wide-Eyed by Rembrandt, 1630, etching, (ii) Two Self-portraits and Several Details by Vincent van Gogh, 1886, pencil on paper and (iii) Self-Portrait by M.C. Escher, 1929, lithograph on gray paper. These images were used for testing the networks.

3.1 Preprocessing

Similar to [4], each image was cropped and resized to 96 pixels × 96 pixels such that:

– The distance between the top of the image and the vertical center of the eyes was 38 pixels.
– The distance between the vertical center of the eyes and the vertical center of the mouth was 32 pixels.
– The distance between the vertical center of the mouth and the bottom of the image was 26 pixels.
– The horizontal center of the eyes and the mouth was at the horizontal center of the image.

3.2 Sketching

Each image in the CelebA and LFW datasets was automatically transformed to a line sketch, a grayscale sketch and a color sketch. Sketches in the CUFS database and those by the famous Dutch artists were further transformed to line sketches by using the same procedure.

Color and grayscale sketch types are produced by the same stylization algorithm [8]. To obtain the sketch images, the input image is first filtered by an edge-aware filter. This filtered image is then blended with the magnitude of the gradient of the filtered image. Then, each pixel is scaled by a normalization factor resulting in the final sketch-like image.

Line sketches which resemble pencil sketches were generated based on [2]. Line sketch conversion works by first converting the color image to grayscale. This is followed by inverting the grayscale image to obtain a negative image. Next, a Gaussian blur is applied. Finally, using color dodge, the resulting image is blended with the grayscale version of the original image.

It should be noted that synthesizing face images from color or grayscale sketches is a more difficult problem than doing so from line sketches since many details of the faces are preserved by line sketches while they are lost for other sketch types.

4   Models

We developed one DNN for each of the three sketch styles based on the style transfer architecture in [15]. Each of the three DNNs was based on the same architecture except for the first layer where the number of input channels were either one or three depending on the number of color channels of the sketches. The architecture comprised three convolutional layers, five residual blocks [12], two deconvolutional layers and another convolutional layer. Each of the five residual blocks comprised two convolutional layers. All of the layers except for the last layer were followed by batch normalization [14] and rectified linear units. The last layer was followed by batch normalization and hyperbolic tangent units. All models were implemented in the Chainer framework [27]. Table 1 shows the details of the architecture.

Table 1. Deep neural network architectures. BN; batch normalization with decay = 0.9, $\epsilon = 1e-5$, ReLU; rectified linear unit, con.; convolution, dec.; deconvolution, res.; residual block, tanh; hyperbolic tangent unit. Outputs of the hyperbolic tangent units are scaled to $[0, 255]$. x/y indicates the parameters of the first and second layers of a residual block. +x indicates that the input and output of a block are summed and no activation function is used.

Layer	Type	in_channels	out_channels	ksize	Stride	Pad	Normalization	Activation
1	con.	1 or 3	32	9	1	4	BN	ReLU
2	con.	32	64	3	2	1	BN	ReLU
3	con.	64	128	3	2	1	BN	ReLU
4	res.	128/128	128/128	3/3	1/1	1/1	BN/BN	ReLU/+x
5	res.	128/128	128/128	3/3	1/1	1/1	BN/BN	ReLU/+x
6	res.	128/128	128/128	3/3	1/1	1/1	BN/BN	ReLU/+x
7	res.	128/128	128/128	3/3	1/1	1/1	BN/BN	ReLU/+x
8	res.	128/128	128/128	3/3	1/1	1/1	BN/BN	ReLU/+x
9	dec.	128	64	3	2	1	BN	ReLU
10	dec.	64	32	3	2	1	BN	ReLU
11	con.	32	3	9	1	4	BN	tanh

4.1   Estimation

For model optimization we used Adam [16] with parameters $\alpha = 0.001$, $\beta_1 = 0.9$, $\beta_2 = 0.999$, $\epsilon = 10^{-8}$ and mini-batch size = 4. We trained the models by iteratively minimizing the loss function for 200,000 iterations. The loss function comprised three components. The first component is the standard Euclidean loss for the targets and the predictions (pixel loss; ℓ_p). The second component is the Euclidean loss for the feature-transformed targets and the feature-transformed predictions (feature loss) [15]:

$$\ell_f = \frac{1}{n} \sum_{i,j,k} \left(\phi(t)_{i,j,k} - \phi(y)_{i,j,k} \right)^2 \tag{1}$$

where n is the total number of features, $\phi(t)_{i,j,k}$ is a feature of the targets and $\phi(y)_{i,j,k}$ is a feature of the predictions. Similar to [15], we used the outputs of the fourth layer of a 16-layer DNN (relu_2_2 outputs of the VGG-16 pretrained model) [25] to feature transform the targets and the predictions. The third component is the total variation loss for the predictions:

$$\ell_{tv} = \sum_{i,j} \left((y_{i+1,j} - y_{i,j})^2 + (y_{i,j+1} - y_{i,j})^2 \right)^{0.5} \tag{2}$$

where $y_{i,j}$ is a pixel of the predictions. A weighted combination of these components resulted in the following loss function:

$$\ell = \lambda_p \ell_p + \lambda_f \ell_f + \lambda_{tv} \ell_{tv} \tag{3}$$

where we set $\lambda_p = \lambda_f = 1$ and $\lambda_{tv} = 0.00001$.

The use of the feature loss to train models for image transformation tasks was recently proposed by [15]. In the context of super-resolution, [15] found that replacing pixel loss with feature loss gives visually pleasing results at the expanse of image quality because of the artefacts introduced by the feature loss.

In the context of sketch inversion, our preliminary experiments showed that combining feature loss and pixel loss increases image quality while maintaining visual pleasantness. Furthermore, we observed that a small amount of total variation loss further removes the artefacts that are introduced by the feature loss. Therefore, we used the combination of the three losses in the final experiments. The quantitative results of the preliminary experiments in which the models were trained by using only the feature loss are provided in the Appendix (Tables 4 and 5).

4.2   Validation

First, we qualitatively tested the models by visual inspection of the synthesized face images (Fig. 2). Synthesized face images matched the ground truth photographs closely and persons in the images were easily recognizable in most cases. Among the three styles of sketch models, the line sketch model (Fig. 2, first column) captured the highest level of detail in terms of the face structure, whereas the synthesized inverse sketches of the color sketch model (Fig. 2, third column) had less structural detail but was able to better reproduce the color information in the ground truth images compared to the inverted sketches of the line sketch model. Sketches synthesized by the grayscale model (Fig. 2, second column) were less detailed than those synthesized by the line sketch model. Furthermore, the color content was less accurate in sketches synthesized by the grayscale model than those synthesized by both the color sketch and the line sketch models. We found that the line model performed impressively in terms of

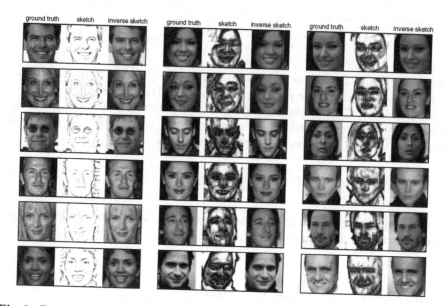

Fig. 2. Examples of the synthesized inverse sketches from the LFW dataset. Each distinct column shows examples from different sketch styles models, i.e. line sketch model (column 1), grayscale sketch model (column 2) and colour sketch model (column 3). First image in each column is the ground truth, the second image is the generated sketch and the third one is the synthesized inverse sketch.

matching the hair and skin color of the individuals even when the line sketches did not contain any color information. This may indicate that along with taking advantage of the luminance differences in the sketches to infer coloring, the model was able to learn color properties often associated with high-level face features of different ethnicities.

Then, we quantitatively tested the models by comparison of the peak signal to noise ratio (PSNR), structural similarity (SSIM) and standard Pearson product-moment correlation coefficient R of the synthesized face images [32] (Table 2). PSNR measures the physical quality of an image. It is defined as the ratio between the peak power of the image and the power of the noise in the image (Euclidean distance between the image and the reference image):

$$PSNR = \frac{1}{3} \sum_k 10 \log_{10} \frac{\max DR^2}{\frac{1}{m} \sum_{i,j} (t_{i,j,k} - y_{i,j,k})^2} \tag{4}$$

where DR is the dynamic range, and m is the total number of pixels in each of the three color channels. SSIM measures the perceptual quality of an image. It is defined as the multiplicative combination of the similarities between the image and the reference image in terms of contrast, luminance and structure:

$$\text{SSIM} = \frac{1}{3} \sum_k \frac{1}{m} \sum_{i,j} \frac{\left(2\mu\left(t_{i,j,k}\right)\mu\left(y_{i,j,k}\right) + C_1\right)\left(2\sigma\left(t_{i,j,k}, y_{i,j,k}\right) C_2\right)}{\left(\mu\left(t_{i,j,k}\right)^2 \mu\left(y_{i,j,k}\right)^2 + C_1\right)\left(2\sigma\left(t_{i,j,k}\right)^2 \sigma\left(y_{i,j,k}\right)^2 C_2\right)}$$

(5)

where $\mu\left(t_{i,j,k}\right)$, $\mu\left(y_{i,j,k}\right)$, $\sigma\left(t_{i,j,k}\right)$, $\sigma\left(y_{i,j,k}\right)$ and $\sigma\left(t_{i,j,k}, y_{i,j,k}\right)$ are means, standard deviations and cross-covariances of windows centered around i and j. Furthermore, $C_1 = (0.01 \max \text{DR})^2$ and $C_2 = (0.03 \max \text{DR})^2$. Quality of a dataset is defined as the mean quality over the images in the dataset.

Table 2. Comparison of physical (PSNR), perceptual (SSIM) and cor relational (R) quality measures for the inverse sketches synthesized by the line, grayscale and color sketch-style models. $x \pm m$ shows the mean $\pm$ the bootstrap estimate of the standard error of the mean.

	PSNR	SSIM	R
Line	**20.1158 ± 0.0231**	**0.8583 ± 0.0003**	**0.9298 ± 0.0005**
Grayscale	17.6567 ± 0.0263	0.6529 ± 0.0008	0.7458 ± 0.0020
Color	19.2029 ± 0.0293	0.7154 ± 0.0008	0.8087 ± 0.0017

The inversion of the line sketches resulted in the highest quality face images for all three measures (20.12 for PSNR, 0.86 for SSIM and 0.93 for R). In contrast the inversion of the grayscale sketches resulted in the lowest quality face images for all measures (17.65 for PSNR, 0.65 for SSIM and 0.75 for R). This shows that both the physical and the perceptual quality of the inverted sketch images produced by the line sketch network was superior than those by the other sketch styles.

Finally, we tested how well the line sketch inversion model can be transferred to the task of synthesizing face images from sketches that are hand-drawn and not generated using the same methods that were used to train the model. We considered only the line sketch model since the contents of the hand-drawn sketch database that we used [31] were most similar to the line sketches.

We found that the line sketch inversion model can solve this inductive transfer task almost as good as it can solve the task that it was trained on (Fig. 3). Once again, the model synthesized photorealistic face images. While color was not always synthesized accurately, other elements such as form, shape, line, space and texture were often synthesized well. Furthermore hair texture and style, which posed a problem in most previous studies, was very well handled by our CSI model. We observed that the dark-edged pencil strokes in the hand-drawn sketches that were not accompanied by shading resulted in less realistic inversions (compare e.g. nose areas of sketches in the first and second rows with those in the third row in Fig. 3). This can be explained by the lack of such features in the training data of the line sketch model, and can be easily overcome by including training examples more closely resembling the drawing style of the sketch artists.

For all the samples from the CUFS database, the PSNR, the SSIM index and the R of the synthesized face images were 13.42, 0.52, and 0.67, respectively

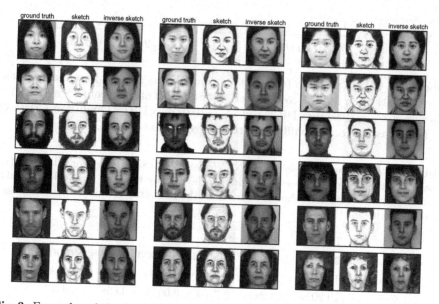

Fig. 3. Examples of the synthesized inverse sketches from the CUFS database. First image in each column is the ground truth, the second image is the sketch hand-drawn by an artist and the third one is the inverse sketch that was synthesized by the line sketch model.

(Table 3). Among the three sub-databases of the CUFS database, the quality of the synthesized images from the CUHK dataset was the highest in terms of the PSNR (15.07) and R (0.83). While the PSNR and R values for the AR dataset was lower than those of the CUHK dataset, SSIM did not differ between the two datasets. The lowest quality inverted sketches were produced from the sample sketches of the XM2GTS database (with 13.42 for PSNR, 0.42 for SSIM and 0.41 for R).

Additional results on both computer-generated sketches and hand-drawn sketches are provided at https://github.com/yagguc/CSI due to space limitations.

Table 3. Comparison of physical (PSNR), perceptual (SSIM) and correlational (R) quality measures for the inverse sketches synthesized from the sketches in the CUFS database and its sub-databases. $x \pm m$ shows the mean $\pm$ the bootstrap estimate of the standard error of the mean.

	PSNR	SSIM	R
CUHK (6)	**15.0675 ± 0.3958**	0.5658 ± 0.0099	**0.8264 ± 0.0269**
AR (6)	13.8687 ± 0.7009	**0.5684 ± 0.0277**	0.7667 ± 0.0314
XM2GTS (6)	11.3293 ± 1.2156	0.4231 ± 0.0272	0.4138 ± 0.1130
All (18)	13.4218 ± 0.6123	0.5191 ± 0.0207	0.6690 ± 0.0591

5   Applications

5.1   Fine Arts

In many cases self-portrait studies allow us a glimpse of what famous artists looked like through the artists' own perspective. Since there are no photographic records of many artists (in particular of those who lived before the 19th century during which the photography was invented and became widespread) self-portrait sketches and paintings are the only visual records that we have of many artists. Converting the sketches of the artists into photographs using a DNN that was trained on tens of thousands of face sketch-photograph pairs results in very interesting end-products.

Here we used our DNN-based approach to synthesize photographs of famous Dutch artists Rembrandt, Vincent van Gogh and M.C. Escher from their self-portrait sketches[1] (Fig. 4). To the best of our knowledge, the synthesized photorealistic images of these artists are the first of their kind.

Fig. 4. Self-portrait sketches and synthesized inverse sketches along with a reference painting or photograph of famous Dutch artists: Rembrandt (top), Vincent van Gogh (middle) and M.C. Escher (bottom). Sketches: (i) Self-Portrait with Beret, Wide-Eyed by Rembrandt, 1630, etching. (ii) Two Self-portraits and Several Details by Vincent van Gogh, 1886, pencil on paper. (iii) Self-Portrait by M.C. Escher, 1929, lithograph on gray paper. Reference paintings: (i) Self-Portrait by Rembrandt, 1630, oil painting on copper. (ii) Self-Portrait with Straw Hat by Vincent van Gogh, 1887, oil painting on canvas.

---

[1] For simplicity, although different methods were used to produce these artworks, we refer to them as sketches.

Our qualitative assesment revealed that, the inverted sketch of Rembrandt synthesized from his 1630 sketch indeed resembles himself in his paintings (particulary his self-portrait painting from 1630), and Escher's to his photographs. We found that the inverted sketch of van Gogh synthesized from his 1886 sketch was the most realistic synthesized photograph among those of the three artists, albeit not closely matching his self-portrait paintings of a distinct post-impressionist style.

Although we do not have a quantitative way to measure the accuracy of the results in this case, results demonstrate that the artistic style of the input sketches influence the quality of the produced photorealistic images. Generating new training sketch data to match more closely to the sketch style of a specific artist of interest (e.g. by using the method proposed by [35]), and training the network with these sketches would overcome this limitation.

Sketching is one of the most important training methods that artist use to develop their skills. Converting sketches into photorealistic images would allow the artists in training to see and evaluate the accuracy of their sketches clearly and easily which can in turn become an efficient training tool. Furthermore, sketching is often much faster than producing a painting. When for example the sketch is based on imagination rather than a photograph, deep sketch inversion can provide a photorealistic guideline (or even an end-product, if digital art is being produced) and can speed up the production process of artists. Figure 3, which shows the inverted sketches by contemporary artists that produced the sketches in the CUFS database, further demonstrates this type of application. The current method can be developed into a smartphone/tablet or computer application for common use.

5.2 Forensic Arts

In cases where no other representation of a suspect exists, sketches drawn by forensic artists based on eye-witness accounts are frequently used by the law enforcement. However, direct use of sketches for automatically identifying suspects from databases containing photographs does not work well because these two face representations are too different to allow a direct comparison [29]. Inverting a sketch to a photograph makes this task much easier by reducing the difference between these two alternative representations, enabling a direct automatized comparison [31].

To evaluate the potential use of our system for forensic applications, we performed an identification analysis (Fig. 5). In this analysis, we evaluated the accuracy of identifying a target face image in a very large set of candidate face images (LFW dataset containing over 11,000 images) from an (inverse) face sketch. The identification accuracies for the synthesized faces were always significantly higher than those for the corresponding sketched faces ($p \ll 0.05$, binomial test). While the identification accuracies for the color and grayscale sketches were very low (2.38 % and 1.42 %, respectively), those for the synthesized color and grayscale inverse sketches were relatively high (82.29 % and 73.81 %, respectively). On the other hand, identification accuracy of line sketches was already high, at 81.14 %

before inversion. Synthesizing inverse sketches from line sketches raised the identification accuracy to an almost perfect level (99.79 %).

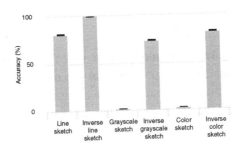

Fig. 5. Identification accuracies for line, grayscale and color sketches, and for inverse sketches synthesized by the corresponding models. Error bars show the bootstrap estimates of the standard errors.

6   Conclusions

In this study we developed sketch datasets, complementing well known unconstrained benchmarking datasets [17, 21], developed DNN models that can synthesize face images from sketches with state-of-the-art performance and proposed applications of our CSI model in fine arts, art history and forensics. We foresee further computer vision applications of the developed methods for non-face images and various other sketch-like representations, as well as cognitive neuroscience applications for the study of cognitive phenomena such as perceptual filling in [1, 28] and the neural representation of complex stimuli [10, 11].

Appendix

Table 4. Comparison of physical (PSNR), perceptual (SSIM) and correlational (R) quality measures for the inverse sketches synthesized by the line, grayscale and color sketch-style models trained using feature loss alone. $x \pm m$ shows the mean $\pm$ the bootstrap estimate of the standard error of the mean.

	PSNR	SSIM	R
Line	14.8956 ± 0.0207	0.5931 ± 0.0006	0.6023 ± 0.0017
Grayscale	17.1654 ± 0.0277	0.6301 ± 0.0008	0.7175 ± 0.0022
Color	**18.9884 ± 0.0296**	**0.7072 ± 0.0008**	**0.7976 ± 0.0019**

Table 5. Comparison of physical (PSNR), perceptual (SSIM) and correlational (R) quality measures for the inverse sketches synthesized from the sketches in the CUFS database and its sub-databases with the line sketch model trained using feature loss alone. $x \pm m$ shows the mean $\pm$ the bootstrap estimate of the standard error of the mean.

	PSNR	SSIM	R
CUHK (6)	**14.6213 ± 0.4061**	0.5358 ± 0.0216	**0.8295 ± 0.0200**
AR (6)	14.1721 ± 0.4127	**0.5608 ± 0.0232**	0.7811 ± 0.0217
XM2GTS (6)	11.7158 ± 1.3050	0.4096 ± 0.0258	0.3817 ± 0.1341
All (18)	13.5030 ± 0.5639	0.5021 ± 0.0205	0.6641 ± 0.0658

References

1. Anstis, S., Vergeer, M., Lier, R.V.: Looking at two paintings at once: luminance edges can gate colors. i-Perception **3**(8), 515–518 (2012). http://dx.doi.org/10.1068/i0537sas
2. Beyeler, M.: OpenCV with Python Blueprints. Packt Publishing, Birmingham (2015)
3. Cheng, Z., Yang, Q., Sheng, B.: Deep colorization. In: International Conference on Computer Vision. Institute of Electrical and Electronics Engineers (IEEE), December 2015. http://dx.doi.org/10.1109/ICCV.2015.55
4. Cowen, A.S., Chun, M.M., Kuhl, B.A.: Neural portraits of perception: reconstructing face images from evoked brain activity. NeuroImage **94**, 12–22 (2014). http://dx.doi.org/10.1016/j.neuroimage.2014.03.018
5. Dong, C., Loy, C.C., He, K., Tang, X.: Learning a deep convolutional network for image super-resolution. In: European Conference on Computer Vision (2014)
6. Dong, C., Loy, C.C., He, K., Tang, X.: Image super-resolution using deep convolutional networks. IEEE Trans. Pattern Anal. Mach. Intell. **38**(2), 295–307 (2016). http://dx.doi.org/10.1109/TPAMI.2015.2439281
7. Gao, X., Wang, N., Tao, D., Li, X.: Face sketch-photo synthesis and retrieval using sparse representation. IEEE Trans. Circ. Syst. Video Technol. **22**(8), 1213–1226 (2012). http://dx.doi.org/10.1109/TCSVT.2012.2198090
8. Gastal, E.S.L., Oliveira, M.M.: Domain transform for edge-aware image and video processing. ACM Trans. Graph. **30**(4), 1 (2011). http://dx.doi.org/10.1145/2010324.1964964
9. Gatys, L.A., Ecker, A.S., Bethge, M.: A neural algorithm of artistic style. CoRR abs/1508.06576 (2015)
10. Güçlü, U., van Gerven, M.A.J.: Deep neural networks reveal a gradient in the complexity of neural representations across the ventral stream. J. Neurosci. **35**(27), 10005–10014 (2015). http://dx.doi.org/10.1523/JNEUROSCI.5023-14.2015
11. Güçlü, U., van Gerven, M.A.J.: Increasingly complex representations of natural movies across the dorsal stream are shared between subjects. NeuroImage (2015). http://dx.doi.org/10.1016/j.neuroimage.2015.12.036
12. He, K., Zhang, X., Ren, S., Sun, J.: Deep residual learning for image recognition. CoRR abs/1512.03385 (2015)
13. Iizuka, S., Simo-Serra, E., Ishikawa, H.: Let there be color! Joint end-to-end learning of global and local image priors for automatic image colorization with simultaneous classification. ACM Trans. Graph. **35**(4), 110 (2016)

14. Ioffe, S., Szegedy, C.: Batch normalization: accelerating deep network training by reducing internal covariate shift. CoRR abs/1502.03167 (2015)
15. Johnson, J., Alahi, A., Fei-Fei, L.: Perceptual losses for real-time style transfer and super-resolution. CoRR abs/1603.08155 (2016)
16. Kingma, D., Ba, J.: Adam: a method for stochastic optimization. CoRR abs/1412.6980 (2014)
17. Learned-Miller, E., Huang, G.B., RoyChowdhury, A., Li, H., Hua, G.: Labeled faces in the wild: a survey. In: Kawulok, M., Celebi, M.E., Smolka, B. (eds.) Advances in Face Detection and Facial Image Analysis, pp. 189–248. Springer, Heidelberg (2016). http://dx.doi.org/10.1007/978-3-319-25958-1_8
18. Li, Y.h., Savvides, M., Bhagavatula, V.: Illumination tolerant face recognition using a novel face from sketch synthesis approach and advanced correlation filters. In: International Conference on Acoustics, Speech, and Signal Processing. Institute of Electrical and Electronics Engineers (IEEE) (2006). http://dx.doi.org/10.1109/ICASSP.2006.1660353
19. Liu, Q., Tang, X., Jin, H., Lu, H., Ma, S.: A nonlinear approach for face sketch synthesis and recognition. In: Conference on Computer Vision and Pattern Recognition. Institute of Electrical and Electronics Engineers (IEEE) (2005). http://dx.doi.org/10.1109/CVPR.2005.39
20. Liu, W., Tang, X., Liu, J.: Bayesian tensor inference for sketch-based facial photo hallucination. In: International Joint Conference on Artificial Intelligence (2007)
21. Liu, Z., Luo, P., Wang, X., Tang, X.: Deep learning face attributes in the wild. In: International Conference on Computer Vision (2015)
22. Martinez, A.M., Benavente, R.: The AR-face database. CVC Technical report 24 (1998)
23. Messer, K., Matas, J., Kittler, J., Jonsson, K.: XM2VTSDB: The extended M2VTS database. In: Audio and Video-based Biometric Person Authentication (1999)
24. Simo-Serra, E., Iizuka, S., Sasaki, K., Ishikawa, H.: Learning to simplify: fully convolutional networks for rough sketch cleanup. ACM Trans. Graph. **35**(4), 121 (2016)
25. Simonyan, K., Zisserman, A.: Very deep convolutional networks for large-scale image recognition. CoRR abs/1409.1556 (2014)
26. Tang, X., Wang, X.: Face sketch synthesis and recognition. In: International Conference on Computer Vision. Institute of Electrical and Electronics Engineers (IEEE) (2003). http://dx.doi.org/10.1109/ICCV.2003.1238414
27. Tokui, S., Oono, K., Hido, S., Clayton, J.: Chainer: a next-generation open source framework for deep learning. In: Workshop on Machine Learning Systems at Neural Information Processing Systems (2015)
28. Vergeer, M., Anstis, S., van Lier, R.: Flexible color perception depending on the shape and positioning of achromatic contours. Front. Psychol. **6** (2015). http://dx.doi.org/10.3389/fpsyg.2015.00620
29. Wang, N., Tao, D., Gao, X., Li, X., Li, J.: A comprehensive survey to face hallucination. Int. J. Comput. Vis. **106**(1), 9–30 (2013). http://dx.doi.org/10.1007/s11263-013-0645-9
30. Wang, N., Tao, D., Gao, X., Li, X., Li, J.: Transductive face sketch-photo synthesis. IEEE Trans. Neural Netw. Learn. Syst. **24**(9), 1364–1376 (2013). http://dx.doi.org/10.1109/TNNLS.2013.2258174
31. Wang, X., Tang, X.: Face photo-sketch synthesis and recognition. IEEE Trans. Pattern Anal. Mach. Intell. **31**(11), 1955–1967 (2009). http://dx.doi.org/10.1109/TPAMI.2008.222

32. Wang, Z., Bovik, A., Sheikh, H., Simoncelli, E.: Image quality assessment: from error visibility to structural similarity. IEEE Trans. Image Process. **13**(4), 600–612 (2004). http://dx.doi.org/10.1109/TIP.2003.819861

33. Xiao, B., Gao, X., Tao, D., Li, X.: A new approach for face recognition by sketches in photos. Sig. Process. **89**(8), 1576–1588 (2009). http://dx.doi.org/10.1016/j.sigpro.2009.02.008

34. Zhang, L., Lin, L., Wu, X., Ding, S., Zhang, L.: End-to-end photo-sketch generation via fully convolutional representation learning. In: International Conference on Multimedia Retrieval. Association for Computing Machinery (ACM) (2015). http://dx.doi.org/10.1145/2671188.2749321

35. Zhang, S., Gao, X., Wang, N., Li, J.: Robust face sketch style synthesis. IEEE Trans. Image Process. **25**(1), 220–232 (2016). http://dx.doi.org/10.1109/TIP.2015.2501755

36. Zhang, W., Wang, X., Tang, X.: Lighting and pose robust face sketch synthesis. In: European Conference on Computer Vision (2010)

Detecting People in Artwork with CNNs

Nicholas Westlake[1(✉)], Hongping Cai[2], and Peter Hall[1]

[1] Department of Computer Science, Unversity of Bath, Bath, UK
{n.westlake,p.m.hall}@bath.ac.uk
[2] Department of Computer Science, University of Bristol, Bristol, UK
hongping.cai@bristol.ac.uk

Abstract. CNNs have massively improved performance in object detection in photographs. However research into object detection in artwork remains limited. We show state-of-the-art performance on a challenging dataset, *People-Art*, which contains people from photos, cartoons and 41 different artwork movements. We achieve this high performance by fine-tuning a CNN for this task, thus also demonstrating that training CNNs on photos results in overfitting for photos: only the first three or four layers transfer from photos to artwork. Although the CNN's performance is the highest yet, it remains less than 60 % AP, suggesting further work is needed for the cross-depiction problem.

Keywords: CNNs · Cross-depiction problem · Object recognition

1 Introduction

Object detection has improved significantly in recent years, especially as a result of the resurgence of convolutional neural networks (CNNs) and the increase in performance and memory of GPUs. However, in spite of the successes in photo-based recognition and detection, research into recognition within styles of images other than natural images (photos) remains limited [1]. We refer to this as the *cross-depiction problem*: detecting objects regardless of how they are depicted (photographed, painted, drawn, etc.).

We believe that cross-depiction recognition is an interesting and open problem. It is interesting because it forces researchers to look beyond the surface appearance of object classes. By analogy, just as a person retains their identity no matter what clothes they wear, so an object retains its class identity no matter how it is depicted: a dog is a dog whether photographed, painted in oils, or drawn with a stick in the sand.

Cross-depiction is a practical problem too: an example is an image search. The world contains images in all sorts of depictions. Any recognition solution that does not generalise across these depictions is of limited power. Yet most current computer vision methods tacitly assume a photographic input, either by design or training. Any model premised on a single depictive style e.g. photos will lack sufficient descriptive power for cross-depiction recognition. Therefore, an image search using methods will limit its results to photos and photo-like depictions.

© Springer International Publishing Switzerland 2016
G. Hua and H. Jégou (Eds.): ECCV 2016 Workshops, Part I, LNCS 9913, pp. 825–841, 2016.
DOI: 10.1007/978-3-319-46604-0_57

Fig. 1. Detecting people across different depictive styles a challenge: here we show some successful detections.

In our paper, we talk about natural images (photos) and non-natural images (artwork) as a linguistic convenience. We would argue that this is a false dichotomy: the universe of all images includes images in all possible depictive styles, and there is no particular reason to privilege any one style. Nevertheless, we acknowledge that the distribution of styles is not uniform: photos may be more abundant and certainly are in computer vision datasets such as ImageNet [2]. This creates problems for generalisation: training a detector on photos alone constrains it not only in terms its ability to handle denotational varieties, but projective and pose varieties too, as we discuss later.

We present a new dataset, *People-Art*, which contains photos, cartoons and images from 41 different artwork movements. Unlike the *Photo-Art* dataset [3], which had 50 classes, this dataset has a single class: people. We labelled people since we observe that people occur far more frequently across the wide spectrum of depictive styles than other classes, thus allowing a far greater variety. Detecting people within this dataset is a challenging task because of the huge range of ways artists depict people: from Picasso's cubism to Disney's Sleeping Beauty. The best performance on a pre-release of the dataset is 45 % precision (AP), from a CNN that was neither trained nor fine-tuned for this task. By fine-tuning a state-of-the-art CNN for this task [4], we achieved 58 % AP, a substantial improvement.

As well as achieving state-of-art performance on our *People-Art* dataset, we make the following contributions, in order of strength:

1. We show that a simple tweak for "Fast Region-based Convolutional Network" method (Fast R-CNN) [4], changing the criteria for negative training exemplars compared to default configuration, is key to higher performance on artwork.
2. We show the extent to which fine-tuning a CNN on artwork improves performance when detecting people in artwork on our dataset (Sect. 5.2) and the *Picasso* dataset [5] (Sect. 5.4). We show that this alone is not a solution: the performance is still less than 60 % AP after fine tuning, suggesting the need for further work.
3. Consistent with earlier work [6], we show that the lower convolutional layers of a CNN generalise to artwork: others benefit from fine-tuning (Sect. 5.1).

We begin by presenting related work and our *People-Art* dataset.

Fig. 2. Our *People-Art* dataset contain images from 43 different styles of depiction: here we show one example for depiction style.

2   Related Work

We use a state-of-the-art CNN to improve performance on a cross-depiction dataset, thereby contributing towards cross-depiction object recognition. We first explore related work on deep learning for object detection and localisation (largely in photos), followed by previous work on the cross-depiction problem.

2.1   Deep Learning for Object Detection and Localisation

Deep learning has been around for a few decades [7–9]. After a period of limited use within computer vision, Krizhevsky et al. (2012) [10] demonstrated a vast performance improvement for image classification over previous state-of-the-art methods, using a deep CNN. As a result, the use of CNNs surged within computer vision.

Early CNN based approaches for object localisation [11–14] used the same sliding-window approach used by previous state-of-the-art detection systems [15,16]. As CNNs became larger, and with an increased number of layers, this approach became intractable. However, Sermanet et al. (2014) [17] demonstrated that few windows are required, provided the CNN is fully convolutional. Furthermore, as the size of their receptive fields increased, CNNs either became or were trained to be less sensitive to precise location and scale the input. As a result, obtaining a precise bounding box using sliding window and non-maximal suppression became difficult. One early approach attempted to solve this issue by training a separate CNN for precise localisation [18].

Szegedy et al. (2013) [19] modified the architecture of Krizhevsky et al. (2012) [10] for localisation by replacing the final layer of the CNN with a regression layer. This layer produces a binary mask indicating whether a given pixel lies within the bounding box of an object. Schulz and Behnke (2011) [20] previously used a similar approach with a much smaller network for object segmentation.

Girshick et al. (2014) [21] introduced "regions with CNN features" (R-CNN), which surpassed previous approaches. The authors used selective search [22], a hierarchical segmentation method, to generate region proposals: possible object locations within an image. Next, a CNN obtains features from each region and a support vector machine (SVM) classifies each region. In addition, they used a regression model to improve the accuracy of the bounding box output by learning bounding box adjustments for each class-agnostic region proposal. He et al. (2015) [23] improved the run-time performance by introducing SPP-net, which uses a spatial pyramid pooling (SPP) [24,25] layer after the final convolutional layer. The convolutional layers operate on the whole image, while the SPP layer pools based on the region proposal to obtain a fixed length feature vector for the fully connected layers.

Girshick (2015) [4] later introduced Fast R-CNN which improves upon R-CNN and SPP-net and allows the CNN to output a location of the bounding box (relative to the region proposal) directly, along with class detection score, thus replacing the SVM. Furthermore, this work enables end-to-end training of the whole CNN for both detection and bounding box regression. We use this approach to achieve state-of-the-art performance on our *People-Art* dataset and detail the method in Sect. 4.

To make Fast R-CNN even faster and less dependent on selective search [22], Lenc and Vedaldi (2015) [26] used a static set of region proposals. Ren et al. (2015) [27] instead used the output of the existing convolutional layers plus additional convolutional layers to predict regions, resulting in a further increase in accuracy and efficiency.

Redmon et al. (2015) [28] proposed "You Only Look Once" (YOLO), which operates quicker though with less accuracy than other state-of-art approaches. A single CNN operates on an entire image, divided in a grid of rectangular cells, without region proposals. Each cell outputs bounding box predictions and class probabilities; unlike previous work, this occurs simultaneously. Huang et al. (2015) [29] proposed a similar system, introducing up-sampling layers to ensure the model performs better with very small and overlapping objects.

2.2 Cross-Depiction Detection and Matching

Early work relating to non-photographic images focused on matching hand-drawn sketches. Jacobs et al. (1995) [30] used wavelet decomposition of image colour channels to allow matching between a rough colour image sketch and a more detailed colour image. Funkhouser et al. (2003) [31] used a distance transform of a binary line drawing, followed by fourier analysis of the distance transforms at fixed radii from the centre of the drawing, to match 2D sketches and 3D projections, with limited performance. Hu and Collomosse (2013) [32] used a modified version of Histograms of Oriented Gradients (HOG) [15] to extract descriptors at interest-points in the image: for photographs, these are at Canny edges [33] pixels; for sketches, these are sketch strokes. Wang et al. (2015) [34] used a siamese CNN configuration to match sketches and 3D model projections, optimising the CNN to minimise the distances between sketches and 3D model projections of the same class.

Another cross-depiction matching approach, by Crowley et al. (2015) [35], uses CNN generated features to match faces between photos and artwork. This relies on the success of a general face detector [36], which succeeds on artwork which is "largely photo-realistic in nature" but has not been verified on more abstract artwork styles such as cubism.

Other work has sought to use self-similarity to detect patterns across different depictions such as Shechtman and Irani (2007) [37] and Chatfield et al. (2009) [38] who used self-similarity descriptors formed by convolving small regions within in image over a larger region. This approach is not suitable for identifying (most) objects as a whole: for example, the results show effective matching of people forming a very specific pose, not of matching people as an object class in general.

Recent work has focused on cross-depiction object classification and detection. Wu et al. (2014) [3] improved upon Felzenszwalb et al.'s Deformable Part-based Model (DPM) [16] to perform cross-depiction matching between photographs and "artwork", (including "clip-art", cartoons and paintings). Instead of using root and part-based filters and a latent SVM, the authors learnt a fully connected graph to better model object structure between depictions, using the structured support vector machine (SSVM) formulation of Cho et al. (2013) [39]. In addition, each model has separate "attributes" for photographs and "artwork": at test-time, the detector uses the maximum response from either of "attribute" set, to achieve depiction invariance. This work improved performance for detecting objects in artwork, but depended on a high performing DPM to bootstrap the model. Our dataset is more challenging than the one used, leading to a low accuracy using DPM and hence this is approach is also not suitable.

Zissermann et al. (2014) [40] evaluate the performance of CNNs learnt on photos for classifying objects in paintings, showing strong performance in spite of the different domain. Their evaluation excludes people as a class, as people appear frequently in their paintings without labels. Our *People-Art* dataset addresses this issue: all people are labelled and hence we provide a new benchmark. We also believe our dataset contains more variety in terms of artwork styles and presents a more challenging problem. Furthermore, we advance their findings: we show the performance improvement when a CNN is fine-tuned for this task rather than simply fine-tuned on photos.

3   The *People-Art* Dataset and Its Challenges

Our *People-Art* dataset[1] contains images divided into 43 depiction styles. Images from 41 of these styles came from *WikiArt.org* while the photos came from PASCAL VOC 2012 [41] and the cartoons from google searches. We labelled people since, according to our empirical observations, people are drawn or painted more often than other objects. Consequently, this increases the total number of individual instances and thus the range of depictive styles represented. Figure 2 shows one painting from each style represented in our *People-Art* dataset.

The 41 depictive styles from *WikiArt.org* are catagorised based on art movements. These depiction styles cover the full range of projective and denotational styles, as defined by Willats [42]. In addition, we propose that these styles cover many poses, a factor which Willats did not consider.

We believe that our dataset is challenging for the following reasons:

Range of denotational styles. This is the style with which primitive marks are made (brush strokes, pencil lines, etc.) [42]. We consider photos to be a depictive style in its own right.

Range of projective style. This includes linear camera projection, orthogonal projection, inverse perspective, and in fact a range of ad-hoc projections [42]. An extreme form is shown in cubism, in which it is common for the view of a person from many different viewpoints to be drawn or painted on the 2D canvas [5].

Range of poses. Though pose is handled by previous computer vision algorithms [16], we have observed that artwork, in general, exhibits a wider variety of poses than photos.

---

[1] https://github.com/BathVisArtData/PeopleArt

Overlapping, occluded and truncated people. This occurs in artwork as in photos, and perhaps to a greater extent.

4   CNN Architecture

We use the same architecture as Fast R-CNN [4], which is built around a modified version of the Caffe library [43]. The CNN has two inputs: an image and a set of class-agnostic rectangular region proposals. Many algorithms exist for generating region proposals; we use selective search [22] with the default configuration.

The first stage of the CNN operates on the entire image (having been resized to a fixed dimension while preserving aspect ratio). This stage consists of convolutional layers, rectified linear units (ReLUs) [10,44], max-pooling layers and, in some cases, local response normalisation layers [10]. The final layer is a region of interest (ROI) pooling layer which is novel to Fast R-CNN: as well as the input from the previous convolutional or ReLU layer, this layer receives another input, a region proposal or ROI; the output is a fixed-length feature vector formed by max-pooling of the convolution features. In order to preserve information about the global structure of the ROI, i.e. at a scale within an order of magnitude of the ROI size, the max-pooling happens over a uniformly spaced rectangular grid,

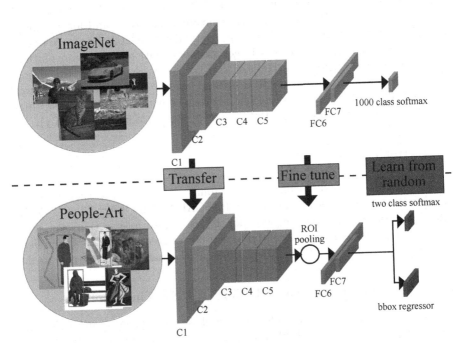

Fig. 3. We use a network pre-trained on ImageNet and fine-tuned on our *People-Art* dataset (training and validation sets): we fix the weights for the first F layers, selected by validation.

size $H \times W$. As a result, the layer outputs feature vector with CHW dimensions where C is the number of channels of the previous convolutional layer.

This feature vector is the input to the second stage of the CNN, which is fully connected. It consists of inner product and ReLU layers, as well as dropout layers (training only) aimed at preventing overfitting [45]. The output for each class is a score and a set of four co-ordinate which indicate the bounding box co-ordinates relative to the ROI. We modified the final layer to output a score and bounding box prediction for only one class: person.

We use the same approach for training as Fast R-CNN, which uses stochastic gradient descent (SGD) with momentum [10], initialising the network with weights from the pre-trained models, in our case, trained on ImageNet [2,10]. We fix the weights of the first F convolutional layers to those in the pre-trained model; this parameter is selected by validation. We experiment with different criteria for the region proposals to use as training ROI, as detailed in Sect. 5.1. Since the final inner product layers have a different size output as we only detect one class, we use random (Gaussian) initialisation. Figure 3 shows our network architecture in detail.

We fine-tune the models (pre-trained on ImageNet) using our *People-Art* dataset (training and validation sets). We test three different models: CaffeNet, which is a reproduction of AlexNet [10] with some minor changes, Oxford VGG's "CNN M 1024" (VGG1024) [46] and Oxford VGG's "Net D" (VGG16) [47]. Both CaffeNet and VGG1024 have five convolutional layers and local response normalisation layers and vary slightly: in particular VGG1024 has more weights and channels. VGG16 is much a larger network, with thirteen convolutional layers and no local response normalisation. Except for the number of dimensions, all three networks have the same ROI pooling layer and fully connected network structure: each CNN's fully connected network structure consists of two inner product layers, each followed by ReLU and dropout layers (training only).

5   Experiments

For both validation and testing, our benchmark is average precision (AP): we calculate this using the same method as PASCAL Visual Object Classes (VOC) detection task [48]. A positive detection is one whose intersection over union (IoU) overlap with a ground-truth bounding box is greater than 50 %; duplicate detections are considered false. Annotations marked as difficult are excluded.

5.1   ROI Selection and Layer Fixing for CNN Fine-Tuning

Although we used the default selective search settings to generate region proposals, we experimented with different criteria to specify which region proposals to use in training. The default configuration of Fast-RCNN [4] defines positive ROI be region proposals whose IoU overlap with a ground-truth bounding box is at least 0.5, and defines negative ROI to be those whose overlap lies in the interval [0.1, 0.5]. The cutoff between positive and negative ROI matches the

Table 1. Validation performance using different criteria for positive and negative ROI: we use CNNs pre-trained on ImageNet, fine-tune on the training set and then test on the validation set; we select the best configuration for each CNN (bold).

CNN	Configuration	ROI IoU		Fixed layers (F)	AP
		Negative	Positive		
CaffeNet	default	$[0.1, 0.5)$	≥ 0.5	2	33.7 %
CaffeNet	gap	$[0.1, 0.4)$	≥ 0.6	2	33.5 %
CaffeNet	**all-neg**	$[0.0, 0.5)$	≥ 0.5	0	**42.5 %**
CaffeNet	gap+all-neg	$[0.0, 0.4)$	≥ 0.6	1	42.2 %
VGG1024	default	$[0.1, 0.5)$	≥ 0.5	1	38.4 %
VGG1024	gap	$[0.1, 0.4)$	≥ 0.6	3	35.8 %
VGG1024	**all-neg**	$[0.0, 0.5)$	≥ 0.5	1	**42.6 %**
VGG1024	gap+all-neg	$[0.0, 0.4)$	≥ 0.6	1	42.0 %
VGG16	default	$[0.1, 0.5)$	≥ 0.5	1	43.9 %
VGG16	gap	$[0.1, 0.4)$	≥ 0.6	2	39.0 %
VGG16	all-neg	$[0.0, 0.5)$	≥ 0.5	3	50.0 %
VGG16	**gap+all-neg**	$[0.0, 0.4)$	≥ 0.6	3	**50.1 %**

definition of positive detection according the VOC detection task [48]. Girshick (2015) states that the lower cut-off (0.1) for negative ROI appears to act as a heuristic to mine hard examples [4,16].

We experimented with two alternative configurations for fine tuning:

gap. We discarded ROI whose IoU overlap with a ground-truth bounding box lies in the interval [0.4, 0.6): we hypothesised that ROI lying in this interval are ambiguous and hamper training performance.

all-neg. We removed the lower bound for negative ROI. We hypothesised that this would improve performance on our *People-Art* dataset for two reasons:

1. This results in the inclusion of ROI containing classes which appear similar to people, for example animals with faces.
2. This permits the inclusion of more artwork examples, for example images without any people present. We hypothesised that this would make the CNN better able to discern between features caused by the presence of people and features resulting from a particular depiction style.

We fixed all other hyper-parameters of the CNN except for F, the number of convolutional layers whose weights we fix to those learnt from ImageNet, which we select based validation performance.

Table 1 shows the validation performance for the different criteria, i.e. from testing on the validation set after fine-tuning on the *People-Art* training set. Removing the lower bound on negative ROI (all-neg) results in a significant increase in performance, around a 9 % point increase in average precision in the best performing case. Indeed, it appears that what is *not* a person is as important as what *is* a person for training. Discarding ROI with an IoU overlap in the interval $[0.4, 0.6)$ yields mixed results: it was marginally beneficial in one case, and detrimental in all others.

We note that the optimal number of convolutional layers for which to fix weights to the pre-trained model, F, varies across the different training configurations, even for the same CNN. The variation in performance could be explained by stochastic variation caused by the use of SGD. The performance falls rapidly for $F \geq 5$; we therefore conclude that the first three or four convolutional layers transfer well from photos to artwork. Fine-tuning these layers yields no significant improvement nor detriment in performance. In this respect, we show similar results to Yosinski et al. (2014) [6] for our task: i.e. the first three or four convolutional layers are more transferable than later layers, in our case from photos to artwork.

For all later experiments, including the performance benchmarks, we select the configuration which maximises performance on the *validation set* (bold in Table 1) and re-train (fine-tune) using the combined *train and validation sets*.

5.2   Performance Benchmarks on the People-Art Dataset

Table 2 shows how each CNN model and other methods perform on the *People-Art test set*. The best performing CNN, VGG16, scores 58 % AP, an improvement of 13 percentage points on the best previous result 45 % [28]. The results demonstrate the benefits of fine-tuning the CNN (on the *training and validation sets* of *People-Art*) for the task. We also conclude that training and fine-tuning a CNN on photos yields a model which overfits to photographic images.

As noted in Sect. 4, Fast R-CNN (unlike YOLO) relies on an external algorithm, here selective search [22], to generate region proposals. We used the default settings, which are tuned to photos. Selective search achieves a recall rate of 98 % on the *People-Art test set*. As such, this does not appear to be a limiting factor for the performance.

Table 2. Performance of different methods on the test set of our *People-Art* dataset: the best performance is achieved using a CNN (Fast R-CNN) fine-tuned on *People-Art*

Method	Datasets		Average precision
	Pre-train	Fine tuning	
Fast R-CNN (CaffeNet)	ImageNet	People-Art (train+val)	46 %
Fast R-CNN (VGG1024)	ImageNet	People-Art (train+val)	51 %
Fast R-CNN (VGG16)	ImageNet	People-Art (train+val)	58 %
Fast R-CNN (CaffeNet)	ImageNet	VOC 2007	36 %
Fast R-CNN (VGG1024)	ImageNet	VOC 2007	36 %
Fast R-CNN (VGG16)	ImageNet	VOC 2007	43 %
DPM [16]	People-Art	N/A	33 %
YOLO [28]	ImageNet	VOC 2010	45 %

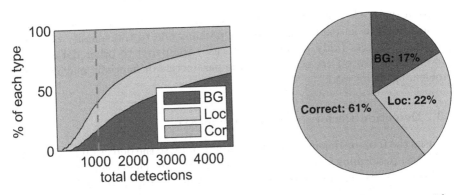

Fig. 4. Left: The proportion of detections by type as the threshold decreases: either correct, a background region (BG) or poor localisation (LOC); Right: the proportion for D=1088, the actual number of people, marked as a grey dashed line on the left plot

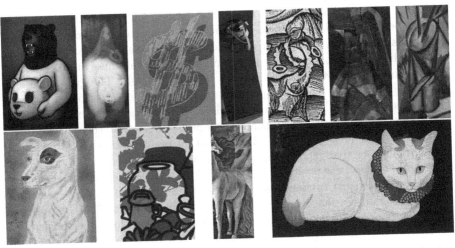

Fig. 5. False positive detections on background regions from the best performing CNN

Fig. 6. False positive detections due to poor localisation from the best performing CNN

We attempted to fine-tune YOLO [28] on *People-Art*. The default configuration results in an exploding gradient, perhaps due to the sparsity of regions containing objects (only people in this case) compared to other datasets. We expect that a brute-force search over the parameters or heuristic may solve this problem in future work.

5.3   Detection Performance on People-Art

We used the tools of Hoiem et al. (2012) [49] to analyse the detection performance of the best performing CNN. Since we only have a single class (person), detections have three types based on their IoU with a ground truth labelling:

Cor correct i.e. $IoU \geq 0.5$
Loc false positive caused by poor localisation, $0.1 \leq IoU < 0.5$
BG a background region, $IoU < 0.1$

Figure 4 shows the detection trend: the proportion of detection types as the number of detections increases, i.e. from reducing the threshold. At higher thresholds, the majority of incorrect detections are caused by poor localisation; at lower thresholds, background regions dominate. In total, there are 1088 people labelled in the test set, and that are not labelled difficult. The graph in Fig. 4 shows a grey dashed line corresponding to this number detections and Fig. 4 shows a separate pie chart for this threshold. This threshold corresponding to this number of detections is significant: with perfect detection, there would be no false positives or false negatives. This shows that poor localisation is the bigger cause of false positives, though only slightly more so than background regions.

Figure 5 shows false positives caused by background regions. Some are caused by mammals which is understandable given these, like people, have faces and bodies. Others detections have less clear causes. Figure 6 show the false positives caused by poor localisation. In some of the cases, the poor localisation is caused by the presence of more than one person, which leads to the bounding box covering multiple people. In other cases, the bounding box does not cover the full extent of the person, i.e. it misses limbs or the lower torso. We believe that this shows the extent to which the range of poses makes detecting people in artwork a challenging problem.

5.4   Performance Benchmarks on the Picasso Dataset

In addition to the results on *People-Art*, we show results on the *Picasso Dataset* [5]. The dataset contains a set of Picasso paintings and labellings for people which are based on the median of the labellings given by multiple human participants. Table 3 shows how each CNN and other methods perform. As before, each CNN performed better if it was fine-tuned on *People-Art* rather than *VOC 2007*; moreover, DPM performs better than CNNs fine-tuned on *VOC 2007* but worse than those fine-tuned on *People-Art*. This confirms our earlier findings:

Table 3. Performance of different methods on the *Picasso* dataset

Method	Training	Fine tuning	Average precision
Fast R-CNN (CaffeNet)	ImageNet	People-Art	45 %
Fast R-CNN (VGG1024)	ImageNet	People-Art	44 %
Fast R-CNN (VGG16)	ImageNet	People-Art	44 %
Fast R-CNN (CaffeNet)	ImageNet	VOC 2007	29 %
Fast R-CNN (VGG1024)	ImageNet	VOC 2007	37 %
Fast R-CNN (VGG16)	ImageNet	VOC 2007	33 %
DPM [16]	VOC 2007	N/A	38 %
YOLO [28]	ImageNet	VOC 2012	53 %

CNNs fine-tuned on photos overfit to photo. In addition, we show that our fine-tuning results in a model which is not just better for *People-Art* but a dataset containing artwork which we did not train on.

Interestingly, the best performing CNN is the smallest (CaffeNet), suggesting that the CNNs may still be overfitting to less abstract artwork. Furthermore, the best performing method is YOLO despite being fine-tuned on photos (*VOC 2012*). Selective Search achieved a recall rate of 99 % on the *Picasso Dataset*, so this is unlikely to be the reason that Fast R-CNN performs worse than YOLO. We therefore believe that YOLO's design is more robust to abstract forms of art.

5.5 The Importance of Global Structure

Earlier work [3,50,51] suggests that structure is invariant across depictive styles, and therefore useful for cross-depiction detection. As described in Sect. 4, Fast R-CNN includes an ROI pooling layer, which carries out max-pooling over $H \times W$ uniformly spaced rectangular grid. Therefore, the ROI pooling layer captures the global structure of the person, while earlier convolutional layers only pick up the local structure.

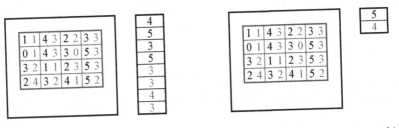

Fig. 7. Two pooling layers and their resulting feature vectors from a two channel input; Left: An ROI pooling layer (red grid) takes the maximum for each channel in each cell of an ROI (blue grid) resulting in an 8 dimensional vector; Right: A global max-pooling layer simply takes the maximum yielding a 2 dimensional vector (Color figure online)

Table 4. Replacing the ROI pooling layer (default) with a single cell max-pooling layer yields a performance drop greater than not fine tuning *People-Art*

Fine-tuning	People-Art		VOC 2007
ROI Pooling	Default	Single cell	Default
CaffeNet	46 %	34 %	36 %
VGG1024	51 %	35 %	36 %
VGG16	58 %	40 %	43 %

To test whether the *global structure* is useful for detecting and localising people in artwork, we replaced the ROI pooling layer replaced with a single cell max-pooling layer. This is equivalent to setting $W = 1$ and $H = 1$ for the ROI pooling layer (see Fig. 7). This is similar to "bag of visual word" algorithms: with $W = H = 1$, the fully connected layers have no information about the location the previous layer's output. We fine-tuned as before.

Table 4 shows the results. In all cases, replacing the default ROI pooling layer with a single cell max-pooling layer results in worse performance. On top of this, the performance is worse than when fine-tuned on *VOC 2007* with the default configuration. This supports the claim of earlier work, that structure is invariant across depictive styles.

6   Conclusion

We have demonstrated state-of-the-art cross-depiction detection performance on our challenge dataset, *People-Art*, by fine-tuning a CNN for this task. In doing so, we have shown that a CNN trained on photograph alone overfits to photos, while fine-turning on artwork allows the CNN to better generalise to other styles of artwork. We have also made other observations, including the importance of negative exemplars from artwork.

The performance on our *People-Art* dataset, though the best so far, is still less than 60 % AP. We have demonstrated that the CNN often detects other mammals instead of people or makes other spurious detections and often fails to localise people correctly. We propose further work to address these issues.

In addition, the dataset only covers a subset of possible images containing people. Our dataset does not include African, Babylonian, Chinese or Egyptian art, the Bayeux Tapestry, stained glass windows, photos of sculptures and all kinds of other possibilities. Therefore, we are only beginning to examine the cross-depiction problem, which provides a huge scope for further research.

Acknowledgements. This research was funded in part by EPSRC grant reference EP/K015966/1. This research made use of the Balena High Performance Computing Service at the University of Bath.

References

1. Hall, P., Cai, H., Wu, Q., Corradi, T.: Cross-depiction problem: recognition and synthesis of photographs and artwork. Comput. Vis. Media **1**(2), 91–103 (2015)
2. Deng, J., Dong, W., Socher, R., Li, L.J., Li, K., Fei-Fei, L.: Imagenet: A large-scale hierarchical image database. In: IEEE Conference on Computer Vision and Pattern Recognition, 2009, CVPR 2009, pp. 248–255. IEEE (2009)
3. Wu, Q., Cai, H., Hall, P.: Learning graphs to model visual objects across different depictive styles. In: Fleet, D., Pajdla, T., Schiele, B., Tuytelaars, T. (eds.) ECCV 2014, Part VII. LNCS, vol. 8695, pp. 313–328. Springer, Heidelberg (2014)
4. Girshick, R.: Fast R-CNN. In: Proceedings of the IEEE International Conference on Computer Vision, pp. 1440–1448 (2015)
5. Ginosar, S., Haas, D., Brown, T., Malik, J.: Detecting people in cubist art. In: Agapito, L., Bronstein, M.M., Rother, C. (eds.) ECCV 2014, Part I. LNCS, vol. 8925, pp. 101–116. Springer, Heidelberg (2015). doi:10.1007/978-3-319-16178-5_7
6. Yosinski, J., Clune, J., Bengio, Y., Lipson, H.: How transferable are features in deep neural networks? In: Advances in Neural Information Processing Systems, pp. 3320–3328 (2014)
7. Fukushima, K.: Neocognitron: a self-organizing neural network model for a mechanism of pattern recognition unaffected by shift in position. Biological Cybern. **36**(4), 193–202 (1980)
8. Giebel, H.: Feature extraction and recognition of handwritten characters by homogeneous layers. In: Grüsser, O.-J., Klinke, R. (eds.) Zeichenerkennung durch biologische und technische Systeme/Pattern Recognition in Biological and Technical Systems, pp. 162–169. Springer, Heidelberg (1971)
9. LeCun, Y., Boser, B., Denker, J.S., Henderson, D., Howard, R.E., Hubbard, W., Jackel, L.D.: Backpropagation applied to handwritten zip code recognition. Neural Comput. **1**(4), 541–551 (1989)
10. Krizhevsky, A., Sutskever, I., Hinton, G.E.: Imagenet classification with deep convolutional neural networks. In: Advances in Neural Information Processing Systems, pp. 1097–1105 (2012)
11. Matan, O., Baird, H.S., Bromley, J., Burges, C.J., Denker, J.S., Jackel, L.D., Cun, Y., Pednault, E.P., Satterfield, W.D., Stenard, C.E., et al.: Reading handwritten digits: a zip code recognition system. Computer **25**(7), 59–63 (1992)
12. Nowlan, S.J., Platt, J.C.: A convolutional neural network hand tracker. In: Advances in Neural Information Processing Systems, pp. 901–908 (1995)
13. Rowley, H.A., Baluja, S., Kanade, T.: Neural network-based face detection. IEEE Trans. Pattern Anal. Mach. Intell. **20**(1), 23–38 (1998)
14. Sermanet, P., Kavukcuoglu, K., Chintala, S., LeCun, Y.: Pedestrian detection with unsupervised multi-stage feature learning. In: Proceedings of the IEEE Conference on Computer Vision and Pattern Recognition, pp. 3626–3633 (2013)
15. Dalal, N., Triggs, B.: Histograms of oriented gradients for human detection. In: IEEE Computer Society Conference on Computer Vision and Pattern Recognition, CVPR 2005, vol. 1, pp. 886–893. IEEE (2005)
16. Felzenszwalb, P.F., Girshick, R.B., McAllester, D., Ramanan, D.: Object detection with discriminatively trained part-based models. IEEE Trans. Pattern Anal. Mach. Intell. **32**(9), 1627–1645 (2010)
17. Sermanet, P., Eigen, D., Zhang, X., Mathieu, M., Fergus, R., LeCun, Y.: Overfeat: Integrated recognition, localization and detection using convolutional networks. In: ICLR (2014)

18. Vaillant, R., Monrocq, C., Le Cun, Y.: Original approach for the localisation of objects in images. IEE Proceedings-Vision, Image and Signal Processing **141**(4), 245–250 (1994)
19. Szegedy, C., Toshev, A., Erhan, D.: Deep neural networks for object detection. In: Advances in Neural Information Processing Systems, pp. 2553–2561 (2013)
20. Schulz, H., Behnke, S.: Object-class segmentation using deep convolutional neural networks. In: Proceedings of the DAGM Workshop on New Challenges in Neural Computation, Citeseer pp. 58–61 (2011)
21. Girshick, R., Donahue, J., Darrell, T., Malik, J.: Rich feature hierarchies for accurate object detection and semantic segmentation. In: Proceedings of the IEEE Conference on Computer Vision and Pattern Recognition, pp. 580–587 (2014)
22. Uijlings, J.R., van de Sande, K.E., Gevers, T., Smeulders, A.W.: Selective search for object recognition. Int. J. Comput. Vis. **104**(2), 154–171 (2013)
23. He, K., Zhang, X., Ren, S., Sun, J.: Spatial pyramid pooling in deep convolutional networks for visual recognition. IEEE Trans. Pattern Anal. Mach. Intell. **37**(9), 1904–1916 (2015)
24. Grauman, K., Darrell, T.: The pyramid match kernel: discriminative classification with sets of image features. In: Tenth IEEE International Conference on Computer Vision, ICCV 2005, vol. 2, pp. 1458–1465. IEEE (2005)
25. Lazebnik, S., Schmid, C., Ponce, J.: Beyond bags of features: spatial pyramid matching for recognizing natural scene categories. In: 2006 IEEE Computer Society Conference on Computer Vision and Pattern Recognition, vol. 2, pp. 2169–2178. IEEE (2006)
26. Lenc, K., Vedaldi, A.: R-cnn minus r. arXiv preprint arXiv:1506.06981 (2015)
27. Ren, S., He, K., Girshick, R., Sun, J.: Faster r-cnn: Towards real-time object detection with region proposal networks. In: Advances in Neural Information Processing Systems, pp. 91–99 (2015)
28. Redmon, J., Divvala, S., Girshick, R., Farhadi, A.: You only look once: Unified, real-time object detection. arXiv preprint arXiv:1506.02640 (2015)
29. Huang, L., Yang, Y., Deng, Y., Yu, Y.: Densebox: Unifying landmark localization with end to end object detection. arXiv preprint arXiv:1509.04874 (2015)
30. Jacobs, C.E., Finkelstein, A., Salesin, D.H.: Fast multiresolution image querying. In: Proceedings of the 22nd Annual Conference on Computer Graphics and Interactive Techniques, pp. 277–286. ACM (1995)
31. Funkhouser, T., Min, P., Kazhdan, M., Chen, J., Halderman, A., Dobkin, D., Jacobs, D.: A search engine for 3d models. ACM Trans. Graph. (TOG) **22**(1), 83–105 (2003)
32. Hu, R., Collomosse, J.: A performance evaluation of gradient field hog descriptor for sketch based image retrieval. Comput. Vis. Image Underst. **117**(7), 790–806 (2013)
33. Canny, J.: A computational approach to edge detection. IEEE Trans. Pattern Anal. Mach. Intell. (6) 679–698 (1986)
34. Wang, F., Kang, L., Li, Y.: Sketch-based 3d shape retrieval using convolutional neural networks. arXiv preprint arXiv:1504.03504 (2015)
35. Crowley, E.J., Parkhi, O.M., Zisserman, A.: Face painting: querying art with photos. In: British Machine Vision Conference (2015)
36. Parkhi, O.M., Vedaldi, A., Zisserman, A.: Deep face recognition. In: British Machine Vision Conference, vol. 1. 6 (2015)
37. Shechtman, E., Irani, M.: Matching local self-similarities across images and videos. In: IEEE Conference on Computer Vision and Pattern Recognition, CVPR 2007, pp. 1–8. IEEE (2007)

38. Chatfield, K., Philbin, J., Zisserman, A.: Efficient retrieval of deformable shape classes using local self-similarities. In: 2009 IEEE 12th International Conference on Computer Vision Workshops (ICCV Workshops), pp. 264–271. IEEE (2009)

39. Cho, M., Alahari, K., Ponce, J.: Learning graphs to match. In: Proceedings of the IEEE International Conference on Computer Vision, pp. 25–32 (2013)

40. Crowley, E.J., Zisserman, A.: In search of art. In: Agapito, L., Bronstein, M.M., Rother, C. (eds.) ECCV 2014. LNCS, vol. 8925, pp. 54–70. Springer, Heidelberg (2015). doi:10.1007/978-3-319-16178-5_4

41. Everingham, M., Van Gool, L., Williams, C.K.I., Winn, J., Zisserman, A.: The pascal visual object classes (voc) challenge. Int. J. Comput. Vis. **88**(2), 303–338 (2010)

42. Willats, J.: Art and Representation: New Principles in the Analysis of Pictures. Princeton University Press, Princeton (1997)

43. Jia, Y., Shelhamer, E., Donahue, J., Karayev, S., Long, J., Girshick, R., Guadarrama, S., Darrell, T.: Caffe: Convolutional architecture for fast feature embedding. arXiv preprint arXiv:1408.5093 (2014)

44. Nair, V., Hinton, G.E.: Rectified linear units improve restricted boltzmann machines. In: Proceedings ofs the 27th International Conference on Machine Learning (ICML 2010), pp. 807–814 (2010)

45. Srivastava, N., Hinton, G., Krizhevsky, A., Sutskever, I., Salakhutdinov, R.: Dropout: a simple way to prevent neural networks from overfitting. J. Mach. Learn. Res. **15**(1), 1929–1958 (2014)

46. Chatfield, K., Simonyan, K., Vedaldi, A., Zisserman, A.:Return of the devil in the details: Delving deep into convolutionalnets. arXiv preprint arXiv:1405.3531 (2014)

47. Simonyan, K., Zisserman, A.:Very deep convolutional networks for large-scale image recognition.arXiv preprint arXiv:1409.1556 (2014)

48. Everingham, M., Winn, J.:The pascal visual object classes challenge 2007 (voc2007) developmentkit. University of Leeds, Technical report (2007)

49. Hoiem, D., Chodpathumwan, Y., Dai, Q.: Diagnosing error in object detectors. In: Fitzgibbon, A., Lazebnik, S., Perona, P., Sato, Y., Schmid, C. (eds.) ECCV 2012. LNCS, vol. 7574, pp. 340–353. Springer, Heidelberg (2012). doi:10.1007/978-3-642-33712-3_25

50. Xiao, B., Song, Y.Z., Balika, A., Hall, P.M.: Structure is a visual class invariant. In: da Vitoria Lobo, N., Kasparis, T., Roli, F., Kwok, J.T., Georgiopoulos, M., Anagnostopoulos, G.C., Loog, M. (eds.) SSPR&SPR 2008. LNCS, vol. 5342, pp. 329–338. Springer, Heidelberg (2008)

51. Xiao, B., Yi-Zhe, S., Hall, P.:Learning invariant structure for object identification by using graphmethods. Comput. Vis. Image Underst. **115**(7), 1023–1031 (2011)

Transferring Neural Representations for Low-Dimensional Indexing of Maya Hieroglyphic Art

Edgar Roman-Rangel[1]([⊠]), Gulcan Can[2,3], Stephane Marchand-Maillet[1],
Rui Hu[2,3], Carlos Pallán Gayol[5], Guido Krempel[6], Jakub Spotak[4],
Jean-Marc Odobez[2,3], and Daniel Gatica-Perez[2,3]

[1] Department of Computer Science, University of Geneva, Geneva, Switzerland
{edgar.romanrangel,stephane.marchand-maillet}@unige.ch
[2] Idiap Research Institute, Martigny, Switzerland
{gcan,rhu,odobez,gatica}@idiap.ch
[3] École Polytechnique Fédérale de Lausanne (EPFL), Lausanne, Switzerland
[4] Comenius University, Bratislava, Slovakia
spotak.jakub@gmail.com
[5] University of Bonn, Bonn, Germany
pallan.carlos@gmail.com
[6] Bonn, Germany
tilalhix@googlemail.com

Abstract. We analyze the performance of deep neural architectures for extracting shape representations of binary images, and for generating low-dimensional representations of them. In particular, we focus on indexing binary images exhibiting compounds of Maya hieroglyphic signs, referred to as glyph-blocks, which constitute a very challenging dataset of arts given their visual complexity and large stylistic variety. More precisely, we demonstrate empirically that intermediate outputs of convolutional neural networks can be used as representations for complex shapes, even when their parameters are trained on gray-scale images, and that these representations can be more robust than traditional hand-crafted features. We also show that it is possible to compress such representations up to only three dimensions without harming much of their discriminative structure, such that effective visualization of Maya hieroglyphs can be rendered for subsequent epigraphic analysis.

Keywords: Shape retrieval · Neural networks · Dimensionality reduction

1 Introduction

Deep Learning has become the standard technique to face many problems in visual recognition [12], where its potential for dealing with shape images has mainly focused on recognizing numeral instances [7], generic shapes [21], and 3D

© Springer International Publishing Switzerland 2016
G. Hua and H. Jégou (Eds.): ECCV 2016 Workshops, Part I, LNCS 9913, pp. 842–855, 2016.
DOI: 10.1007/978-3-319-46604-0_58

Fig. 1. Three glyph-blocks with 2, 3, and 3 individual glyph-signs, respectively: T0267, T0613; T0001, T0671, T0671; and T0115, T0667, T0024.

shapes [22]. However, more challenging scenarios remain to be explored, like the case of ancient inscriptions [8].

Such is the case of the ancient Mayan languages, which were recorded by means of a highly sophisticated system of hieroglyphic writing, comprising several thousand hieroglyphic signs, which has left us with an exceptionally rich artistic legacy. Maya hieroglyphs constitute a collection of signs highly rich in terms of style as reflected by their intricate visual structures and variations. Therefore, enabling effective retrieval of visually similar hieroglyphs can help epigraphers understand the structure of ancient languages and scribal practices. Also, given a visual language model, it can help them recognize ambiguous instances. However, these are very challenging tasks because of the highly visual complexity of the hieroglyphic signs, including visual variations of them. Figure 1 shows three examples of Maya hieroglyphs.

Following the successful trend of deep learning to analyze shapes [21,22], we propose: (1) to index shapes of Maya hieroglyphs by using representations extracted from intermediate layers of Convolutional Neural Networks (CNN), namely the Vgg-m network [19]; and (2) to use advanced dimensionality reduction methods for enabling effective visualization of them. In particular, we focus on binary images containing glyph-blocks from the ancient Maya culture. This is, groups of individual hieroglyphic-signs, which are combined to form coherent sentences, and whose combinations may vary arbitrarily in location and scale, according to scribal styles and practices.

More precisely, we use the output of intermediate layers of Vgg-m as the representation of the glyph-blocks. However, given the relative small size of our dataset, a constraint for effectively training the parameters of the network is imposed. Therefore, we kept the network parameters as learned from the Imagenet dataset [12] instead of training it with the shapes of Maya hieroglyphs. This approach has proven effective in previous works [16,23], and in this work we demonstrate experimentally that it can be exploited to the extreme of representing binary images with parameters learned on images of different nature, i.e., gray-scale images. We compare the CNN intermediate representations with the Histogram of Orientations Shape Context (HOOSC) [17], a handcrafted local shape descriptors which has proven robust for dealing with complex shapes. Our evaluation shows that representations extracted from intermediate layers of the Vgg-m net outperform the retrieval precision of HOOSC.

In turn, we also investigate the potential of deep learning methods for generating low-dimensional shape representations, which could allow us to visualize glyph-blocks for further epigraphic/palaeographic analysis. Namely, we use supervised autoencoders and t-SNE [19] to map our data onto very short representations [11,14]. Autoencoders have been used to learn local descriptors and found to be competitive with respect to handcrafted descriptors [3]. An early use of autoencoders for image retrieval proposed a binary representation for hashing-based retrieval, which proved to be highly effective [11]. A thorough review of representation learning techniques and details about autoencoders can be found in [1]. Our results show that these techniques provide more robust short representations with respect to traditional PCA [10]. Namely, t-SNE obtained slightly improved retrieval performance with respect to the use of autoencoders.

The remaining of this paper is organized as follows. Section 2 discusses work related to description and indexing of Maya hieroglyphs. Section 3 details our methodology. Section 4 explains the dataset we used. Section 5 presents our experimental protocol and results. And Sect. 6 lists our conclusions.

2   Related Work

Binary shapes have been previously described by using autoencoders with logistic transfer functions [7]. Specifically, the work in [7] gives a detailed description of the architecture of autoencoders, and discusses their potential for processing faces and digits with visualization purposes. However, the dataset of digits is far less challenging that the Maya hieroglyphs we process in this work.

In a related direction, shapes of generic object (i.e., manual sketches) were successfully described by using convolutional neural networks (CNN) to perform sketch-based 3D shape retrieval [21]. In particular, that work proposes a methodology for cross-modal retrieval based on the use of siamese convolutional networks, which work well for shapes of generic objects.

The VGG-m net [19] is a deep CNN proposed to address the problem of classifying large datasets of images. It has been evaluated varying its architecture and parameters, and it was shown that deep CNN are suitable for extracting visual patterns from images at different levels of abstraction. Thus, we use two of its intermediate layers to compute shape representations in this work.

Later, it has been shown that it is possible to use convolutional neural networks off-the-shelf [16]. This is, to use the parameters of a network as learned on a training dataset of different nature than the test dataset. Variations of this approach might use such parameters as initial solution and then perform a fine tuning of them on a training set of similar nature than the test dataset. We, however, use the VGG-m network parameters off-the-shelf as learned on the Imagenet dataset i.e., with no fine tuning. The reason for this is that our dataset is not large enough for conducting an adequate training of the network. Nevertheless, off-the-shelf parameters work well in practice, as shown by our results.

Regarding the processing of Maya hieroglyphs, a retrieval system encoding glyph context information was proposed in [9], where glyphs within a block were converted into a first-order Markov chain, statistical glyph co-occurrence model and shape representation were combined for glyph retrieval. HOOSC [17] descriptor with Bag-of-Words pipeline was used to represent shape feature of glyphs. The proposed system was further evaluated in [8], where two statistical glyph co-occurrence language models extracted from diverse data sources were tested on two different Maya glyph datasets extracted from codices and monuments separately.

In [3], two types of shape representations were studied in a bag-of-words based pipeline to recognize Maya glyphs. The first was a knowledge-driven HOOSC representation, and the second was a data-driven representation obtained by applying an unsupervised Sparse Autoencoder (SA). In addition to the glyph data, the generalization ability of the descriptors was investigated on the larger-scale sketch dataset [5]. From their experiments, the data-driven representation performed overall in par with hand-designed representation for similar locality sizes for which the descriptor was computed. It is also observed that a larger number of hidden units, the use of average pooling, and a larger training data size in the SA representation improved the descriptor performance. Additionally, it is noted that the characteristics of the data and stroke size played an important role in the learned representation.

A limitation of the work presented in [3] was that a single layer autoencoder was used. We expect deeper autoencoders to provide better overall shape representations. In our paper, we designed an autoencoder with 3 hidden layers. Furthermore, we use the learned hidden representations for dimensionality reduction and visualization purposes instead of using them as convolutional filters. This is why the deepest layer in our autoencoder model has only 3 units. Another different aspect of this work and our work is training separate autoencoders for each class. This brings supervision to our overall model.

3   Approach

This section explains the preprocessing steps used for description, the supervised autoencoder model and its training, and the procedures for dimensionality reduction.

3.1   Preprocessing

In this work, we face the problem of describing shapes of very high visual complexity. This problem has been faced previously using local shapes descriptors [17], which reported high success rates. Therefore, we also rely on local shape descriptors, both for the baseline method and the proposed approach.

Binarization. Following the state-of-the-art on document binarization, we first applied a robust segmentation procedure to the images. We found that the graph-based segmentation strategy [6] applied on the image filtered by mean-shift over a combination of its HSV components added with spatial localisation, provides robust segmentation results. In particular, this segmentation is robust to small noisy artifact found in the pictures. We then simply computed average gray-scale color for every region and applied a fixed threshold to obtain the binary mask.

Description. We computed robust descriptors for the glyph-blocks using 3 approaches:

- BoW: We sampled, uniformly, 15 % of points from the medial axis of the shape, and used them as points of interest on which to compute Histograms of Orientations Shape Context (HOOSC) [17]. On average, this sampling rate resulted in 804.6 ± 417.4 points per glyph-block. To produce final representations for subsequent actions, we quantized the sets of HOOSC descriptors to generate bag representations. In particular, it has been shown that a visual vocabulary of 2000 words works well for the HOOSC descriptor [17]. Therefore, we used a randomly selected set of HOOSC's to compute $k = 2000$ visual words using k-means clustering [13]. Compared to other methods for shape description, HOOSC has obtained higher retrieval results dealing with individual hieroglyphs and generic shapes [17], as well as localizing specific shapes within large images [18].
- conv5: We used the output of the fifth convolutional layer of the Vgg-m network [19] as shape representation.
- fc7: This is the last fully-connected layer of the Vgg-m network.

The VGG-m network is inspired from Zeiler and Fergus's network (ZFnet) [24] for ImageNet data. ZFnet builts upon AlexNet [12] (8-layer network with 5-convolutional and 3 fully-connected layers) with few differences: smaller stride and receptive field sizes in the first convolutional layer and larger stride in conv2 layer. As the only difference of the VGG-m network with respect to the ZFnet, the conv4 layer has half number of filters (512 vs. 1024). In both cases, conv5 and fc7, the network parameters are kept as learned from the Imagenet data [12]. We decided to use the output of these layers as they are shown to be competitive as global image descriptors, especially fc7-layer activations outperform the shallow handcrafted representationsfor many computer vision tasks [16]. As pointed out in [24], the activations from early layers learn primitive edge and color structures, and each next layer learns more complex combinations of the previous layer activations, i.e., edges, object parts, and in the end, object templates. Furthermore, the experiments in [23] show that layers towards the end of the network are more dataset-specific, whereas the output of middle layers has better generalization for different datasets.

Table 1 shows the dimensionality of each of the three shape representations previously described.

Table 1. Number of features of each of the three shape representations.

Representation	BoW	conv5	fc7
Number of features	2,000	86,528	4,096

3.2 Model Training

Following previous works for dimensionality reduction with autoencoders [7,11], we trained several 7-layer fully connected autoencoders, one per visual class in our datasets. Here, the input layer contains as many units as the dimensionality of the shape representation, i.e., 2000 for HOOSC, 86528 for conv5, and 4096 for fc7. We decided to use 3 units for the 4-th layer, which is the deepest layer of the encoding phase, as we are interested in producing output representations that are suitable for visualization purposes. The number of units in the two intermediate layers, 500 and 100 units, was chosen after trying several combinations, such that it minimized the reconstruction error. Also, we used a fully connected architecture between consecutive layers, and a Logistic function in all units of the autoencoder. Figure 2 shows the architecture of the supervised autoencoder used in this work and the definition of its units.

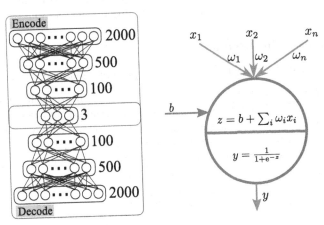

Fig. 2. Architecture of the supervised autoencoders used in this work, and detail of a single unit in it.

For training the autoencoders, we relied on standard gradient descent and back-propagation algorithms [7], which iteratively minimize the reconstruction square error e between m input training representations and their corresponding reconstructed outputs. This is,

$$e = \frac{1}{2} \cdot \frac{1}{m} \sum_{j=1}^{m} \sum_{i=1}^{n} \left(I_i^j - O_i^j \right)^2, \tag{1}$$

where j is the index of the training example, and the dimensionality of the input I^j and its respective output O^j are indexed from $i = 1, \dots, n$.

We trained all autoencoders during 1000 epochs, and used an auxiliary criterion for early stopping. Namely, training finished when one of the three following conditions was met:

- The maximum number of epochs was reached.
- The average sum of the square reconstruction error e was less than or equal to 10^{-3} in the last epoch.
- The average error e_t, of the t-th epoch, is very close to the average historic error h_t, which we computed using exponential smoothing as,

$$h_t = \alpha h_{t-1} + (1 - \alpha) e_t, \qquad (2)$$

where, α is a parameter to control the amount of history that is tracked (we set $\alpha = 0.15$ in this work). Thus, we stopped training if $\Delta(e) \leq 10^{-6}$, where,

$$\Delta(e) = |h_{t-1} - e_t|, \qquad (3)$$

where, $|\cdot|$ denotes absolute difference.

Although training itself is conducted without supervision, we refer to these autoencoders as "supervised" since the set of instances for training each autoencoder is defined under supervision, i.e., one autoencoder per class.

3.3 Dimensionality Reduction

Once the autoencoders are trained, shape representations are reduced by:

1. *Filter:* This step consists of passing a shape representation through both the encoder and the decoder to generate a reconstructed representation, which is expected to be a cleaned version of itself. In our case we consider one autoencoder per class, and we assume unawareness of the class of the test instance. Therefore, we pass its representation I through all autoencoders and generate a set $\{O^f\}$ of F different *filtered* outputs, as

$$O^f = g^f(I), \qquad (4)$$

where, $g^f(\cdot)$ denotes the full sequence of encoding and decoding performed by the f-th autoencoder.

2. *Max-pooling:* This consists of choosing the best candidate among the outputs generated by the set of autoencoders to be the final cleaned version. More precisely, we choose the output with the lowest reconstruction error with respect to the input representation. This is,

$$O^* = arg \min_{O^f} \|I - O^f\|_2^2. \qquad (5)$$

Finally, we choose the autoencoder that attains the lowest reconstruction error for a given input, and then use only its encoding phase to produce a short representation s. Mathematically,

$$s = \eth^*(I), \qquad (6)$$

where $\eth^*$ denotes the encoding phase of the autoencoder that produces O^*, which is chosen by Eq. (5).

Note that such short representations are suitable for both indexing and retrieval, as we will show in Sect. 5.

4   Hieroglyphic Shapes

The dataset used in this work is a subset of a larger collection currently under compilation by joint efforts of epigraphers and computer scientists. It comprises manually segmented and annotated glyph-blocks, among several more sign compounds of different granularity, which have been extracted from the extant Maya codices (folded bark-paper books) produced by the ancient Maya civilization within the Yucatan peninsula during the postclassic period (ca. 1100–1520 C.E). Although several thousand Maya hieroglyphic texts recorded on different media have been documented by explorers, archaeologists and researchers, the paramount importance of the codices lies in part in their extreme rarity, as the majority were destroyed by Spanish clerical authorities during colonial times, and only three of undisputed authenticity are preserved today at libraries at Dresden, Paris, and Madrid. The database is planned to be accessible to scholars as part of a future project publication.

Each record in the dataset consists of a single annotated glyph-block, which is a compound of several individual glyph-signs (glyph-blocks are often composed by one to six glyphs signs), which numbers and arrangement possibilities within the block can take a myriad different configurations that we are systematically investigating for Digital Palaeography and Sign-Encoding purposes. In turn, each individual sign is indicated by a unique code. The most commonly used catalog of glyph-signs is the Thomson catalog [20], where each glyph-sign is referred to by a consecutive number preceded by the letter 'T', e.g., T0024, T0106, etc.

Given that glyph-blocks are conformed by individual glyph-signs, we annotated them by the sequence of their constituting "members". For instance, T0759b-T0025-T0181 and T0024-T1047a define two different classes, the former with 3 glyph-signs, and the later with 2. Note that, although the order of signs suggests by itself a sequential visual placement of the individual signs [8], there is not certitude of their actual location, and of whether they have been subject to scale or affine transformations. Nevertheless, our methodology is able to decode such visual variations, and produce accurate retrieval results. Furthermore, this definition of class poses two potential scenarios for partial matching: two classes with same individual glyph-signs in different order; and one class being a subclass of another one. However, we did not investigate partial matching cases in this work.

To produce the data used in this work, epigraphers in our team manually cropped glyph-block from the three Maya codices. For this work, a subset of glyph-blocks was chosen so that the percentage of images with visual noise was kept as in the complete dataset. Overall we defined two datasets: training and testing, both of them with the same 12 classes.

Regarding the training set, it corresponds to 102 instances manually cropped and cleaned by epigraphers. The test set, whose instances were only cropped but not cleaned, is formed by 780 glyph-blocks. Figure 3 shows the same glyph-block in both the training and test dataset, i.e., with and without the manual cleaning procedure.

Fig. 3. Glyph-block with two glyph-signs: T0668 top and T0102 bottom. The same block is in both the training and test dataset, respectively, i.e., without and with the manual cleaning procedure.

Table 2. Total number of instances (glyph-blocks) in each dataset. Also, the minimum and maximum number of instances per class, and the respective average.

Dataset	Num. classes	Num. instances	Minimum	Average	Maximum
Train	12	102	5	8.5 ± 3.6	16
Test	12	780	8	65 ± 44.6	144

As shown in Table 2, the datasets are not totally balanced. However, the amount of instances per class remains within the same order, i.e., minimum and maximum within the same dataset. As small as these datasets might seem, epigraphers conducted a largely time consuming process to produce them. In fact, one long term objective of this work is to ameliorate such process.

5 Experimental Results

To assess the impact that the trained supervised autoencoders have on the shape representations, we computed the average intra-class variation that the three different shape representations produce on the training set, both before and after using the autoencoders. Namely, we computed this average intra-class variation as the average of the pairwise distance (Euclidean) between all elements within each class, and then averaged them across classes.

As shown in Table 3, the use of autoencoders helps producing representations with higher similarity within a visual class. In particular, the intra-class variation of the BoW representations does not change largely, while the neural representations conv5 and fc7 produce much lower intra-class variations after using the autoencoders.

We compared the retrieval performance obtained by:

- Raw: these are the three shape representations: BoW, conv5, and fc7.

Table 3. Average intra-class variation in the training dataset before and after cleaning the shape representations with the supervised autoencoders.

Method	Before (raw)	After (clean)
BoW	9.11×10^{-2}	3.03×10^{-3}
conv5	3.87×10^{3}	1.32×10^{1}
fc7	1.21×10^{2}	5.22×10^{-5}

- PCA: this consists in applying PCA to the input shape representations. For visualization purposes we chose the 3 principal components as output representations.
- AE3D: it results from applying dimensionality reduction by using only the encoding phase of the autoencoder, i.e., using Eq. (6). Thus a 3-dimensional vector.
- t-SNE: this is a dimensionality reduction method based on minimizing the Kullback-Leibler divergence between the distributions of representations in their original and reduced space [15]. We chose 3 components to make it comparable with PCA and AE3D.

Note that the dimensionality of Raw varies depending on the representation method, while PCA, AE3D, and t-SNE are the shortest representations with only 3 dimensions each.

We report our results as training and testing. For training, we used all elements in the training set as queries, one at a time, and compared them against all remaining instances also in the training set. This is done by using the L2 distance between pairs of shape representations. We proceed likewise for the elements in the test set, comparing them against all elements in the test set only. However, both the estimation of the visual vocabulary and the training of autoencoders were conducted using only the training set. We report the mean of the average precision computed using the 10 most similar glyph-blocks as retrieved by each of the methods (mAP@10).

Table 4 show the retrieval performance of the three shape representations before applying the dimensionality reduction techniques. As seen in Table 4, the neural-based representations work well for shape images, even when their parameters were learned using gray-scale images from the Imagenet. In particular, in the case of noisy data (the test set), off-the-shelf CNN representations from the conv5 layer outperform the other representations by a large margin ($\approx 26-49\%$).

As mentioned before, one of our goals is that of generating short representations that facilitate the visualization of the glyph-blocks for epigraphic analysis. Table 5 shows the mAP@10 results obtained after using the dimensionality reduction techniques listed at the beginning of this section. We used the training set here to learn the parameters of the autoencoder (AE3D). However, these results correspond to the test set only.

Table 5 shows that the use of t-SNE, with only 3 dimensions, improves the retrieval performance of the BoW approach, i.e., from 0.412 to 0.567; and that it produces retrieval results that are only slightly below for the neural-based

Table 4. Mean Average Precision before dimensionality reduction, i.e., using the 3 raw representations. These results were computed using the 10 most similar glyph-blocks as retrieved by each three shape representations (mAP@10).

	Training	Test
BoW	0.757	0.412
conv5	0.895	0.904
fc7	0.805	0.672

Table 5. Mean Average Precision (mAP@10) using dimensionality reduction techniques on the test set. Best result for each representation in bold.

	PCA	AE3D	t-SNE
BoW	0.390	0.515	**0.567**
conv5	0.569	0.564	**0.898**
fc7	0.346	0.256	**0.601**

representations, i.e., from 0.904 to 0.898 and from 0.672 to 0.601 respectively. Note that in general, t-SNE with 3 dimensions achieves higher retrieval performance than the other 3-dimensional approaches, i.e., PCA and AE3D. Namely, the t-SNE representations also have smooth transitions, e.g., erosion, among samples of a given class as reported in [2].

Regarding the performance attained with AE3D, one can see that this is an adequate approach to deal with bags of local descriptors. However, it results rather harmful for the case of neural representations. This behavior remains to be confirmed in a neural architecture that could include such compression layer, such that its training could happen during the classification-based training of the whole network, and not separately as we did here. In [4], the dimensionality of the last layer was decreased from 4096 to 128 with a small decrease in the performance (about 2 %) for the VGG-m net. As a future study, these encouraging results can motivate to add a dimensionality reduction layer at the end of the network structure and learn its parameters together with other parameters.

Also, an evaluation conducted using shallow autoencoders, of only one hidden layer of 3 units, resulted in very low performance, i.e., only 0.16 for the conv5 representation. Likewise, an attempt to use a single autoencoder for all classes produced very poor performance. This is due to fact that 3 dimensions are not enough for encoding enough information in a single model, which is the motivation for evaluating the performance of supervised autoencoders.

Figure 4 shows the average retrieval precision as a function of the standard recall for the three raw shape representations, and for their respective short representations obtained using t-SNE. These curves correspond to the generalization case, i.e., when the models are learned on the training dataset and then applied to the test data. Note that in general they are consistent with the results shown in Tables 4 and 5.

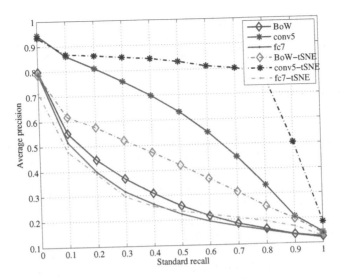

Fig. 4. Average retrieval precision of each method as a function of the standard recall.

The most relevant results from this experimentation are that: (1) complex shapes can be effectively indexed by neural representations (i.e., intermediate outputs of a convolutional neural network), even if they are trained on different datasets; and that (2) their dimensionality can be reduced up to 3 dimensions without too much harm to the retrieval performance, thus allowing for effective visualization of the complex shapes.

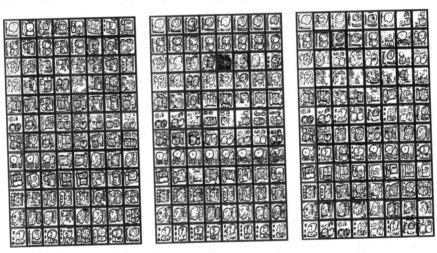

Fig. 5. Examples of retrieval results obtained on the Maya glyph-blocks with the three shape representations and the dimensionality reduction technique. From left to right: BoW-tSNE, conv5-tSNE, and fc7-tSNE. First column shows queries. Then from left to right are the most similar elements in descending order. The blue frame denotes a glyph-bock relevant to the query.

Finally, Fig. 5 shows examples of retrieval results obtained using the three shape representations and t-SNE. As seen in Fig. 5, more relevant glyph-blocks are retrieved by conv5-tSNE in comparison with the other two representations.

6   Conclusions

We proposed the use of neural representations of complex shapes, and the use of dimensionality reduction techniques for indexing Maya hieroglyphs, this with purposes of retrieval and visualization. Namely, we compared the retrieval performance obtained using the outputs of intermediate layers from a convolutional neural network, trained on the Imagenet dataset, and bag representations constructed from handcrafted robust local shape descriptors.

Our results show that this methodology is suitable to produce improved shape representations of very low dimensionality, i.e., up to 3 dimensions. In particular, the use of autoencoders is able to improve bag representations built upon handcrafted descriptors, although it does not have positive impact on the neural representations. Also, both bag and neural representations can be *compressed* to 3 dimensions with only a negligible drop in retrieval performance.

Two aspects of this work stand out. First, the successful use of neural-based representations learned on different datasets, which was important as the dataset of interest in this work is relatively small, thus resulting on the over-parametrization of the networks with respect to the dataset. Second, different from classical learning approaches, where evaluation is performed on datasets of considerably smaller size with respect to the training sets, we were able to achieve good performance with handcrafted features using a training set of about half the size of the evaluation set.

Finally, our methodology can be used for proposing known instances of Mayan glyphs, as candidates for deciphering new examples where visual noise hampers the decision of epigraphers.

Acknowledgments. This work was supported by the Swiss-NSF MAAYA project (SNSF–144238).

References

1. Bengio, Y., Courville, A., Vincent, P.: Representation learning: a review and new perspectives. IEEE Trans. Pattern Anal. Mach. Intell. **35**(8), 1798–1828 (2013)
2. Can, G., Odobez, J.M., Gayol, C.P., Gatica-Perez, D.: Ancient Maya writings as high-dimensional data: a visualization approach. In: Digital Humanities (DH) (2016)
3. Can, G., Odobez, J.M., Gatica-Perez, D.: Evaluating shape representations for Maya glyph classification. ACM J. Comput. Cult. Heritage (JOCCH) (2016, accepted for publication)
4. Chatfield, K., Simonyan, K., Vedaldi, A., Zisserman, A.: Return of the devil in the details: delving deep into convolutional nets. In: British Machine Vision Conference (2014)

5. Eitz, M., Hays, J., Alexa, M.: How do humans sketch objects? ACM Trans. Graph. **31**(4), 44:1–44:44 (2012)
6. Felzenszwalb, P., Huttenlocher, D.: Efficient graph-based image segmentation. Int. J. Comput. Vis. **59**(2), 167–181 (2004)
7. Hinton, G., Salakhutdinov, R.: Reducing the dimensionality of data with neural networks. Science **313**(5786), 504–507 (2006)
8. Hu, R., Can, G., Gayol, C.P., Krempel, G., Spotak, J., Vail, G., Marchand-Maillet, S., Odobez, J.M., Gatica-Perez, D.: Multimedia analysis and access of ancient Maya epigraphy: tools to support scholars on maya hieroglyphics. IEEE Sig. Process. **32**(4), 75–84 (2015)
9. Hu, R., Pallan-Gayol, C., Krempel, G., Odobez, J.M., Gatica-Perez, D.: Automatic Maya hieroglyph retrieval using shape and context information. In: Proceedings of the ACM International Conference on Multimedia (ACM-MM) (2014)
10. Jolliffe, I.: Principal Component Analysis. Springer, New York (1986)
11. Krizhevsky, A., Hinton, G.: Using very deep autoencoders for content-based image retrieval. In: Proceedings of The European Symposium on Artificial Neural Networks (ESANN) (2011)
12. Krizhevsky, A., Sutskever, I., Hinton, G.E.: ImageNet classification with deep convolutional neural networks. In: Advances in Neural Information Processing Systems (NIPS) (2012)
13. Lloyd, S.: Least squares quantization in PCM. IEEE Trans. Inf. Theor. **28**(2), 129–137 (2006)
14. Lu, S., Chen, Z., Xu, B.: Learning new semi-supervised deep auto-encoder features for statistical machine translation. In: Proceedings of the 52nd Annual Meeting of the Association for Computational Linguistics (2014)
15. van der Maaten, L., Hinton, G.: Visualizing high-dimensional data using t-SNE. J. Mach. Learn. Res. **9**, 2579–2605 (2008)
16. Razavian, A.S., Azizpour, H., Sullivan, J., Carlsson, S.: CNN features off-the-shelf: an astounding baseline for recognition. In: Proceedings of the IEEE Conference on Computer Vision and Pattern Recognition (CVPR) (2014)
17. Roman-Rangel, E., Pallan, C., Odobez, J.M., Gatica-Perez, D.: Analyzing ancient Maya glyph collections with contextual shape descriptors. Int. J. Comput. Vis. **94**(1), 101–117 (2011)
18. Roman-Rangel, E., Wang, C., Marchand-Maillet, S.: SimMap: similarity maps for scale invariant local shape descriptors. Neurocomputing **175**(B), 888–898 (2016)
19. Simonyan, K., Zisserman, A.: Very deep convolutional networks for large-scale image recognition. CoRR abs/1409.1556 (2014)
20. Thompson, J.E.S.: A Catalog of Maya Hieroglyphs. University of Oklahoma Press, Norman (1962)
21. Wang, F., Kang, L., Li, Y.: Sketch-based 3D shape retrieval using convolutional neural networks. In: Proceedings of the IEEE Conference on Computer Vision and Pattern Recognition (CVPR) (2015)
22. Wu, Z., Song, S., Khosla, A., Yu, F., Zhang, L., Tang, X., Xiao, J.: 3D ShapeNets: a deep representation for volumetric shapes. In: Proceedings of the IEEE Conference on Computer Vision and Pattern Recognition (CVPR) (2015)
23. Yosinski, J., Clune, J., Bengio, Y., Lipson, H.: How transferable are features in deep neural networks? In: Advances in Neural Information Processing Systems (NIPS) (2014)
24. Zeiler, M.D., Fergus, R.: Visualizing and understanding convolutional networks. In: Fleet, D., Pajdla, T., Schiele, B., Tuytelaars, T. (eds.) ECCV 2014, Part I. LNCS, vol. 8689, pp. 818–833. Springer, Heidelberg (2014)

Dynamic Narratives for Heritage Tour

Anurag Ghosh[✉], Yash Patel, Mohak Sukhwani, and C.V. Jawahar

CVIT, IIIT Hyderabad, Hyderabad, India
anurag.ghosh@research.iiit.ac.in

Abstract. We present a dynamic story generation approach for the egocentric videos from the heritage sites. Given a short video clip of a 'heritage-tour' our method selects a series of short descriptions from the collection of pre-curated text and create a larger narrative. Unlike in the past, these narratives are not merely monotonic static versions from simple retrievals. We propose a method to generate on the fly dynamic narratives of the tour. The series of the text messages selected are optimised over length, relevance, cohesion and information simultaneously. This results in 'tour guide' like narratives which are seasoned and adapted to the participants selection of the tour path. We simultaneously use visual and GPS cues for precision localization on the heritage site which is conceptually formulated as a graph. The efficacy of the approach is demonstrated on a heritage site, Golconda Fort, situated in Hyderabad, India. We validate our approach on two hours of data collected over multiple runs across the site for our experiments.

Keywords: Storytelling · Digital heritage · Egocentric perception

1 Introduction

Heritage sites are the places of interest commemorating people, places or events. These sites could be standalone structures or an agglomeration of multiple structures built across a large area. Spread across the site are the tales describing life and events over the centuries. Such tales are referred to as narratives in our present work. Digitalization and preservation attempts for heritage sites have ranged from methods dealing with restoration [1] to virtual reality based 3D re-constructions [2]. For the first time we attempt enhancing cultural diversity of heritage sites tour via a medium of text narration generation. We propose a method to create contextually aware, richer and multi-facet long descriptions instead of small 'tags'. Describing an area as "Built in twelfth century, this gate serves as an entrance to the main site. Accompanying eleven other gates, it is most remarkable of all and is located on the eastern..." is far more apt and relevant than a static annotation – 'Site entrance'.

In recent past, we have witnessed an increased interest in the use of computer vision and localization algorithms [3] to create digital representations for each

---

A. Ghosh and Y. Patel—Equal Contribution.

© Springer International Publishing Switzerland 2016
G. Hua and H. Jégou (Eds.): ECCV 2016 Workshops, Part I, LNCS 9913, pp. 856–870, 2016.
DOI: 10.1007/978-3-319-46604-0_59

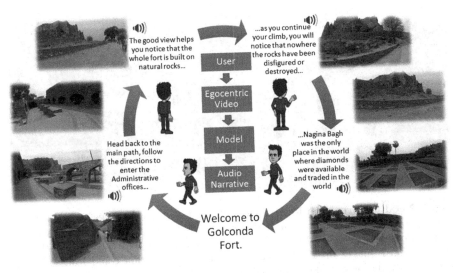

Fig. 1. Dynamic Narration generation for tour videos: Narrative generation using both vision cues and GPS tags while user walks across the site. Unlike past, the site specific audio narrations are detailed and optimized over the various parameters such as relevance and content.

of the aspects of cultural heritage sites [2,4]. Use of mobile based applications [5] to identify monuments on the fly by taking images have also gained significant traction. Story driven visual localization and summarization have also been attempted on egocentric videos [6]. We propose a method to generate text based summary for a given input egocentric tour video. Existing design selections for such vision based assistive technology are all centred around the utility for differentially abled people [7–11]. We propose a new use case which not (necessarily) caters to visually impaired users but in general to all. We suggest a new exemplar for vision based assistive technology with its use ranging from entertainment to educational purposes.

Accurrate localization is elusive in many situations. GPS based localization using mobile devices has proven unreliable in cases of short range distances [12]. Indoor environments where satellite signals find difficult to penetrate are also dead zones for GPS tags. People have used additional cues such as wi-fi signal strength [13], special purpose hardwares, blue-tooth [14] and probabilistic framework formulations over GPS to improve localization tags. Schroth et al. [15] use mobile recordings as a visual cue of the environment and match them to a geo-referenced database to provide pose information. In this work, we use combination of GPS and vision based localization to determine participants present location (Fig. 2). We use these location awareness cues to retrieve (from corpus of text describing the heritage area) the most relevant story of nearest heritage monument. Our stories comprise of details about the monument, its historical importance, events occurred and even includes the details of nearby structures.

Fig. 2. Need for precision localization: (best viewed in color) GPS signal in its raw form is noisy. Precise localization at GPS deadzones (and otherwise too) are achieved using vision cues. Such localization is achieved by matching current image with a set of GPS tagged images in the database. Inaccurate localization could lead to invalid semantic associations. (Color figure online)

Such a method of narrative generation imparts freedom to participants movement across the site and has potential to contribute to their learning.

The ability to create human like narratives to depict immersive and holistic heritage representations remains a challenging task. The proposed method needs to adapt to various external conditions simultaneously. The suggested localization scheme should be precise enough to generate valid semantic associations. Vision based multimedia retrieval methods must be real time and prone to illumination variations. Weather changes, pollution and other environmental degradations pose a direct threat to heritage monuments. The recognition module must be susceptible to ever changing (degrading) heritage structures. This requires a massive manual effort to map the full heritage area with relevant images (for localization) and text (for narration generation). Every monument needs to be tagged with multiple images from varied view-points and perspectives. We even need to have huge curated text corpus with site-specific information. Extensions of such kind to other monuments would thus require manual mapping of the whole site. This makes it extremely taxing to attempt a problem of this kind at such a scale.

Dynamic acquisition of narratives for heritage sites involves both content selection and ordering to create a seamless immersive experience for the participant. We use both vision cues and GPS measurements to design a method that generates narratives for heritage-site videos. The proposed solution generates narratives simultaneously optimized over content, coherence and relevance. This enables the generated narratives to be informative and dynamic in nature, i.e. it coexists with participants interaction and exploration of the space. We use the term 'relevant' to portray the applicability of the text with respect to the surrounding and the word 'informative' describes the 'comprehensive' nature of the selected narrative text. This paper is organized as follows: we describe the

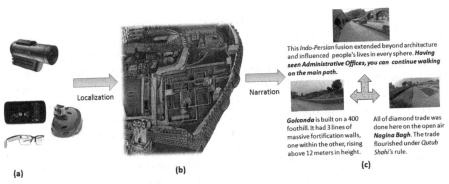

This *Indo-Persian* fusion extended beyond architecture and influenced people's lives in every sphere. *Having seen Administrative Offices, you can continue walking on the main path.*

Golconda is built on a 400 foothill. It had 3 lines of massive fortification walls, one within the other, rising above 12 meters in height.

All of diamond trade was done here on the open air *Nagina Bagh*. The trade flourished under *Qutub Shahi's* rule.

(a)   (b)   (c)

Fig. 3. Overview of the approach: (a) During training time, the site is mapped using images and high precision GPS sensors. At test instance, the participant can use any video capture device. (b) The heritage site is conceptualized as a graph and the user is localized on it using both vision and GPS cues. (c) The narrative generated are dynamic in nature and varied path selection lead to different narratives.

intricacies of narration generation task and discuss associated motivations in Sect. 2. User localization using visual cues are outlined in Sect. 3.1. The challenges associated with combining vision and natural language based processing are explicitly discussed in Sects. 3.2 and 3.3. The penultimate section describes the experiments on captured two hours of egocentric video of the tour.

2   Problem Statement

Storytelling using vision based approaches is still in the nascent stages. Majority of the work in this domain is focused on creation of visual storyline graphs of images summarizing series of events that have chronological relationship. Using methods described in [16,17] one can create such structural stories using collection of images, [16] uses friendship graphs to generate better stories. Similar to [18] we focus on creating interactive narrative systems in which details of heritage sites is unfolded steadily. While participants stroll around the site, the narrations adapt according to the participant's position. Dynamic story generation involves both content selection and ordering of the summaries depending participants present position and his overall tour path. The path selected and the speed of the trek determine the text selection. Thus, the variability is scripted at design time depending on user's preference. Figure 1 depicts one such use case – given an egocentric video of the stroll around the heritage site, we generate relevant narratives of the tour. Recent attempts for caption generation [19–21] do not bind variabilities at run time – participant's speed and pathway selection. Once trained these methods [19,20] resolve video details by learning temporal structure in the input sequence and associate these details to text. Deep learning based approaches [21] directly map videos to full sentences and can handle variable-length input videos but they do not scale to long tour videos described using mutliline text outputs.

Our problem can be stated as dynamic narration generation, i.e. given an egocentric video feed of the visitor we form a sequence of summaries aligned with the sequence of heritage sites that are being visited. Narrations in our case are the amalgamation of basic monument details – its historical importance and the details about nearby structures and form an integral part of cultural tourism of heritage sites. The ego-centric video frames are prone to camera motions which makes the inference of the heritage site or the location from the video frames an extremely challenging task. Factors like environmental and lighting conditions along with the crowd makes the problem even harder. GPS data in its raw form are error prone until explicit corrections are applied on measurements, as we can see in Fig. 2. We aim to generate an aligned set of relevant and cohesive narratives to maintain the engagement levels of participants high. The method is expected to operate at real time and within the computational and storage capacities of the device. Also, the method should be independent of GPS signal obtained from the visitors device as they are not very accurate in indoors and other GPS dead zones. The readers should note that the focus of the approach is to retrieve the best narrations linked to a particular GPS signal from the pre-curated text collection. We assume that sentences in the text collection are both grammatically and syntactically well formed.

Fig. 4. Visual localization qualitative results: (best viewed in color) (a) The GPS estimate for a tour computed via the proposed method is shown in the 'blue' and the baseline in 'yellow' while the ground truth is overlayed in 'pink'. The estimates closely match the ground truth. (b) Frames from an egocentric viewpoint are taken as a query to find the top matches in the visual index. (c) From the query frame in sub-figure:b, the obtained top matches for the query are re-ranked by computing the most similar affine pair of the matches. The top matches are visually similar to the 'query frame'. (Color figure online)

3   Approach

Creating compelling narratives to highlight artistic and cultural significance of the heritage monument is formulated as an optimization problem. We propose a two-fold approach, we first identify participant's location using vision cues and later craft the most appropriate story linked to that location. The proposed solution primarily focuses on (1) use of vision cues over standalone GPS for accurate localization. (2) narrative generation for the localized structures as an optimization problem over a constructed graph. The overview of our approach is illustrated in the Fig. 3.

For a given heritage site, we first identify the major locations within a site ('interest points'). We conceptualize the heritage site as a graph where every interest point represents a vertex and an edge between any two interest points denotes a possible traversable trail between them. Every edge in a graph has following associations: (a) ground truth GPS tags, (b) relevant (hand curated) summaries linking both the interest points and (c) 'glue' sentences (which assist in connecting two selected summaries coherently).

Multiple egocentric tours are recorded along with loosely correlated GPS tags. The videos are partitioned as training and validation tours. The training set along with the embedded GPS tag are used to create frame level inverted index. For a test video of a tour, whose GPS tags are not known, the localization is achieved using a two-staged approach – (1) search similar frames using the inverted index (2) estimate GPS tags of a query frame by linearly interpolating location from the matched image pairs in the set of retrieved images. The computed GPS tags are associated to the (nearest) appropriate edge. The narrative generation is then formulated as an optimization problem over the constructed graph and other associations to obtain a sequence of summaries and 'glue' sentences. During training and inverted index creation, high precision GPS sensors are used. At test time we use vision based precise localization.

3.1   Localization

The images are represented by their corresponding bag-of-features representation, d. We use RootSIFT descriptors [22,23] and build a visual vocabulary using approximate nearest neighbor [24]. For fast image querying, we use inverted index data structure for our experiments. For every query point(q), the top-k visually similar images are retrieved, E_k. The retrieved image list is re-ranked using geometric verification of the estimated affine transformations using RANSAC [24]. To assure that image pairs share visual content and can be meaningfully used to estimate the GPS tag, the pairs are restricted by to *a unit graph distance* [3]. We instead employ the pairing of the top-k retrieved list of the images to achieve the same result.

The best matching pair (from E_k) is obtained by locating the most similar affine combination [3] in retrieved set of top-k similar images. The least affine similarity among the pairs is computed by minimizing the following:

$$s_1, s_2 = \underset{(i,j) \in E_k}{\operatorname{argmin}} \frac{(d_j - d_i)^T (q - d_i)}{\|d_j - d_i\|^2} \tag{1}$$

The location of q is expressed as an affine combination of the most similar affine pair s_1 and s_2. The relative similarity of q with d_{s_1} and d_{s_2} is computed as,

$$\beta = \frac{q^T d_{s_1}}{q^T d_{s_1} + q^T d_{s_2}} \tag{2}$$

We consider the following linear localization function to estimate the location (the location for a point p is represented as x_p):

$$x_q = x_{s_1} + (a_0 + a_1 \beta)(x_{s_2} - x_{s_1}), \tag{3}$$

where, a_0 and a_1 are the regression parameters estimated from representative set, R, of randomly sampled GPS tags (details in Sect. 4.1). We thus obtain the estimated location from the linear combination of the most similar affines.

3.2   From Locations to Edges

A heritage area can be viewed as a culmination of prominent 'sites' and the 'pathways' joining these sites. In a conceptual framework, this can be represented by a graph $G = (V, E)$, with the sites being vertices V and the pathways being the edges E. Edges, e_i are represented as set of linear splines between the associated GPS points. Extended kalman filter [25,26] is used to smooth the input GPS signal, x. For each computed GPS coordinate, we assign the weights to every edge of the graph [27]. Each weight correspond to the shortest (euclidean) distance of the point from the edge. Starting from the first input coordinate to the last, each GPS tag is greedily assigned an edge label corresponding to the least weight, Algorithm 1. To suppress the errors in the labels assigned to GPS tags, which arise due to abrupt changes in the edge assignment, we smoothen the assigned labels and eliminate the infrequent ones. The smoothing is performed by considering sliding window of various sizes, say b. The effects of such varied window size selections are discussed in Sect. 4.3.

3.3   Forming Narratives

We associate text of various lengths to each edge of the graph G (Sect. 3.2), $S = [s_i^j \| e_i \in E]$ where j denotes the jth summary (each summary is of a different length) and i represents the index of the edge. We also associate multiple glue sentences with an edge, $H = [h_{x,y}^k \| e_x, e_y \in E]$, where k is the kth glue sentence and (x, y) represent indices of the two edges. These glue sentences are used to bind adjacent edge summaries together. We define a function L which computes the length of a summary. The optimal length of an edge, l_i^* depends on the participant's pace along the known length of an edge and is computed by

Algorithm 1. GPS to Edge classification: Each GPS tag is assigned an edge for narrative generation.

```
1: procedure LOCATIONCLASSIFIER(x, E, b)                    ▷ x - GPS time signal
2:     x ← ExtendedKalmanFilter(x)                          ▷ E - edge set
3:     y ← argmin_e EuclideanDistance(x, E)                 ▷ y - classified points to edges
4:     for i in 1..length(y) do
5:         if y[i] ≠ y[i + 1] then
6:             current, next ← y[i], y[i + 1]
7:             hit ← 0
8:             for j in i..i + b do                         ▷ b - window size
9:                 if y[j] = next then
10:                    hit = hit + 1
11:                end if
12:            end for
13:            if hit ≠ b then
14:                y[i + 1] ← current
15:            end if
16:        end if
17:    end for
18:    return y
19: end procedure
```

counting number of GPS locations belonging to a particular edge. All values are scaled and centered to have the same units. The length (function, $L()$) of the summary is estimated by multiplying the number of words in a summary with average time taken to speak one word by the Text to Speech Engine.

Our problem is reduced to the selection of a sequence of summaries and glue sentences for a known path and speed such that it forms a narrative which is relevant, cohesive and informative. We maximize the following function,

$$R(l, l') = \sum_i \left(\sum_j \alpha_i^j L(s_i^j) + \sum_k \beta_{i,i+1}^k L(h_{i,i+1}^k) \right)$$

subject to the following constraints,

$$\sum_j \alpha_i^j = 1 \quad \forall\, i \tag{4}$$

$$\sum_k \beta_{i,i+1}^k = 1 \quad \forall\, i \tag{5}$$

$$\alpha_i^j L(s_i^j) + \beta_{i,i+1}^k L(h_{i,i+1}^k) \leq l_i^* \quad \forall\quad i, j, k \tag{6}$$

The objective function represents the selection of the most informative summaries and glue sentences. Equation 6 represents the constraints imposed to keep the summaries relevant to the localization. The glue sentence selection makes the narrative cohesive.

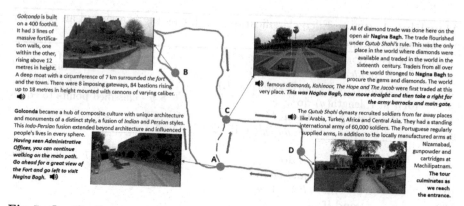

Fig. 5. Qualitative results: (best viewed in color) The narratives generated and spoken by a text-to-speech engine are not only site specific and encapsulate the details of the nearby sites. Although the participant does not walk via the dotted (red) path from site A, yet the narrative generated are comprehensive in nature and assimilate the details of site C and vice-versa. (Color figure online)

4 Experiments and Results

In this section, we present quantitative and qualitative results for each of the building blocks described in Sect. 3. We begin by describing the dataset that we formulate our model. Moving further we discuss the results of visual localization, edge classification and narrative generation modules.

4.1 Dataset

We demonstrate the application of the proposed framework on a dataset that is created by visiting a region inside a world heritage site. Built in distinctive style of Pathan, Hindu and Persian architecture the site is spread across an area of 20,000 sq.m. We capture 2 h of 'tour' videos tagged with GPS values. We used a Contour Plus2 camera to capture multiple tour videos around 6 distinct sites in the same region. 8 tour videos are taped at 30 fps with GPS frequency of 1 Hz. 6 videos are used for training and 2 for validation and testing. The associated GPS tags act as a ground truth for localization. To bestow maximum lighting and occlusion variations in the video dataset, we record videos at varied times of day with varying crowd densities. While taking 'tour' videos we avoid following a standard and fixed pathways across the sites and take varied paths for every tour to capture the variabilities involved with participants path selection.

We sample GPS-annotated frames from the 'tour' videos at a *sampling rate* [3], $\triangle = 15$ and use them for training. In all we have 5952 images and corresponding GPS tags in our training set, M. To create validation set, T, we sample GPS annotated frames at $\triangle = 30$ to obtain 915 images. A representative set, R, of 124 GPS annotated images is randomly sampled from our training videos to estimate the regression parameters a_0 and a_1 (discussed in Sect. 3.1).

The narration corpus comprises of hand-crafted summaries of the site collected from various open descriptions available both on-line and off-line tour books. Multiple versions of different lengths are created for each site. The summaries describe historical importance of a site, accompanied by anecdotes and other details. Summaries of different length capture the essence of a site at various levels: the longest summary includes the maximum details while the shorter ones include only the most important details. In brief, our dataset is comprised of tour videos, associated GPS tags and associated narrations text.

4.2   Visual Localization

We evaluate the localization accuracy of the model on our validation set. We train a Bag of Visual Words model for a vocabulary size of $500K$ words using video training set. The localization performance is measured by calculating the percentage of query frames localized within d meters from their ground truth GPS location, loc_d [3]. The localization error is calculated using Harversine formula.

Baseline: We baseline the visual localization by comparing our results with the nearest neighbor (NN) [3] approach in Table 1

Table 1. Frame localization: The percentage of correctly localized frames sharply increases with the increase in the radius. The visual localization method (marginally) leads the baseline for different values of k. Here, k represents top-k retrieval

Measure	Our method			
	NN	$k = 2$	$k = 3$	$k = 5$
loc_5	48.1400	48.2495	49.1247	46.8271
loc_{10}	80.3063	81.9475	82.7133	83.1510
loc_{15}	90.4814	92.1225	93.3260	95.9519

Visual localization performs better than the nearest neighbour baseline (Table 1). The larger value of k improves the accuracy for loc_{15} as it considers more viewpoints which are sparsely represented but we lose out on the accuracy in loc_5 (where the location is densely represented). Thus we choose $k = 3$ as an optimal value our subsequent experiments. The qualitative results are depicted in Fig. 4 where we can see that an estimated tour closely matches the ground truth.

4.3   Edge Classification from Localization

We evaluate the edge classification accuracy on our validation set by manually labelling every GPS coordinate with an edge. The classification error is calculated as the percentage of coordinates which are misclassified by our algorithm while varying the window size.

Table 2. Edge classification: No smoothing or small window size indicates that aberrations cannot be removed without smoothing across an appropriate sized neighbourhood. Large window size indicates that a higher window size leads to loss of information instead of decreasing ambiguity.

Window size	0	5	10	15	20	25
Error percentage	7.6	5.4	4.3	4.3	4.3	10.41

The smoothing performed to eliminate aberrations in the GPS signal is tested over various window sizes and the best window size is selected. The results in Table 2 indicate that the window size of 15 yields the best results and we use this value for subsequent experiments. The error is due to the precision of the GPS signal and subsequent visual localization estimate which forms our input signal, thus coordinates close to two edges are classified ambiguously at times, resulting in abrupt aberrations. The suggested approach classifies each coordinate to an edge and then smoothens the resultant signal in the window.

4.4 Narrative Generation

The optimization problem is solved as an Binary Integer Programming Problem using PuLP python library [28]. The error for each edge, E_{e_i} is computed as the difference between the optimal time and spoken summary time.

$$E_{e_i} = l_i^* - (L(s_i^j) + L(h_{i,i+1}^k)) \tag{7}$$

where i denotes the index of the edge, j denotes the jth summary selected for the edge from the set of all summaries associated with the edge and k denotes the kth glue sentence selected from the set of all glue sentence associated for the two edges in order (e_i and e_{i+1}).

Table 3. Narrative generation: The overall tour percentage error of both baseline and the proposed approach are similar. The suggested approach being more robust performs marginally better than the baseline. Both the methods are comparable to the actual ground truth as can be seen for the tours in the validation set. The last two rows (Tour 3 and 4) correspond to videos in test set.

Tour	Our method	Nearest neighbour	Ground truth
Tour 1	7.85	7.14	5.50
Tour 2	5.39	6.19	5.37
Tour 3	6.12	6.32	–
Tour 4	10.20	17.63	–

The percentage error for a tour is calculated as the sum of the error components E_{e_i} divided by the sum of the optimal time for each edge. Say p is the walk followed, then percentage error is given by,

$$E_p = \frac{\sum_p E_{e_p}}{\sum_p l_p^*} \qquad (8)$$

Baseline: We present our results for two video tours in the validation and test set. The best performing results, $k = 3$ (Sect. 4.2), of our method are compared with Nearest Neighbour (NN) baseline. The proposed method is marginally better than the NN baseline, Table 3. The errors in themselves are very marginal and it shows that our model is synchronous and relevant with respect to the entire tour.

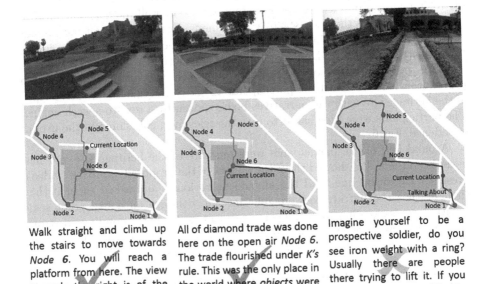

Walk straight and climb up the stairs to move towards *Node 6*. You will reach a platform from here. The view towards the right is of the *heritage site* and on the left you can see different kinds of flowers.

All of diamond trade was done here on the open air *Node 6*. The trade flourished under *K's* rule. This was the only place in the world where *objects* were available and traded in the world in the sixteenth century.

Imagine yourself to be a prospective soldier, do you see iron weight with a ring? Usually there are people there trying to lift it. If you can lift it, you are qualified to be recruited into the army.

Fig. 6. Human evaluation test bench: The participants were shown narrations linked output videos and were asked to rate the experience. For every video snippet we show the 'current location' on the map and other nearby sites. The narrations generated should have information of the present location and other nearby sites. The last row exhibits the narration (spoken by a text-to-speech engine) generated by the system for the present location. The third instance shows a 'negative' case where the text generated does not imbibe the details of the present location and other nearby sites.

Fig. 7. Human evaluation: Qualitative assessment for 35 participants. The proposed approach garners an average score (shown by a straight line on the graph) of 3.97 for the relevance with respective to the surrounding, 3.4 for cohesion between narration sentences and 3.6 for participants overall experience.

4.5 Human Evaluation

Human perception can be highly non-linear and unstructured. Multiple facets of any human-computer interacting system need to be well thought out, profiled and tested to make them satisfactory to humans. In the context of the present scenario, we need to evaluate if the sequence of the text selected is relevant to the current location? Due to paucity of any formal evaluation scheme to measure the effectiveness of the proposed approach, we contrive an evaluation procedure where we asked the participants to watch a dynamic narrative video of the heritage site with the narratives being spoken by a text-to-speech engine. The participants were then asked to rate the relevance, cohesion and the overall experience, Fig. 6.

Around half of the participants were unaware of the heritage site and had never been there. We showed them the output of the proposed approach (videos, present location on map and the aligned narrations), and asked them if they thought that the narrations were relevant and cohesive on a five point scale – with 1 corresponding to strong disagreement and 5 corresponding to strong agreement. The same scale was used to ask if they were comfortable with the accent of the speaker and if the narration improved the overall experience of the tour.

A visualization of the human evaluation results can be seen in Fig. 7, with the vertical axis representing the five point scale and the horizontal axis representing the participants. Majority of the participants agree that the narrations were relevant while not as many believe that the narrations were cohesive in nature. The overall experience is even more varied. This can be attributed to the low scores (average score was 2.6) given for the accent of the narration as many participants found it slightly difficult to understand what was being said.

5 Conclusion

We suggest an approach to harness location based technology and text summarization methods to engage audiences in an unstructured environment. The proposed approach demystifies the details imbibed in the egocentric tour videos to generate a text based narration. We solve the adverse effects of inaccurate and unreliable GPS signals using vision cues for robust localization. The dynamic narratives generated on fly are simultaneously optimised over content, length and relevance thus creating 'digital tour guide' like experience. Museums, heritage parks, public places and other similar sites can reap the benefits of such approach for both entertainment and educational purposes. Generating seamless denser stories and descriptions for diverse audiences over larger regions are some of the identified areas of future work.

References

1. Ikeuchi, K., Oishi, T., Takamatsu, J., Sagawa, R., Nakazawa, A., Kurazume, R., Nishino, K., Kamakura, M., Okamoto, Y.: The great buddha project: digitally archiving, restoring, and analyzing cultural heritage objects. In: IJCV (2007)
2. Adabala, N., Datha, N., Joy, J., Kulkarni, C., Manchepalli, A., Sankar, A., Walton, R.: An interactive multimedia framework for digital heritage narratives. In: ACMMM (2010)
3. Torii, A., Sivic, J., Pajdla, T.: Visual localization by linear combination of image descriptors. In: ICCV Workshop (2011)
4. Van Aart, C., Wielinga, B., Van Hage, W.R.: Mobile cultural heritage guide: location-aware semantic search. In: Knowledge Engineering and Management by the Masses (2010)
5. Panda, J., Brown, M.S., Jawahar, C.V.: Offline mobile instance retrieval with a small memory footprint. In: ICCV (2013)
6. Lu, Z., Grauman, K.: Story-driven summarization for egocentric video. In: CVPR (2013)
7. Chen, X., Yuille, A.L.: A time-efficient cascade for real-time object detection: with applications for the visually impaired. In: CVPR (2005)
8. Ezaki, N., Bulacu, M., Schomaker, L.: Text detection from natural scene images: towards a system for visually impaired persons. In: ICPR (2004)
9. Schwarze, T., Lauer, M., Schwaab, M., Romanovas, M., Bohm, S., Jurgensohn, T.: An intuitive mobility aid for visually impaired people based on stereo vision. In: ICCV Workshops (2015)
10. Rodríguez, A., Yebes, J.J., Alcantarilla, P.F., Bergasa, L.M., Almazán, J., Cela, A.: Assisting the visually impaired: obstacle detection and warning system by acoustic feedback. In: Sensors (2012)
11. Pradeep, V., Medioni, G., Weiland, J.: Robot vision for the visually impaired. In: CVPR (2010)
12. Lin, T.Y., Belongie, S., Hays, J.: Cross-view image geolocalization. In: CVPR (2013)
13. Martin, E., Vinyals, O., Friedland, G., Bajcsy, R.: Precise indoor localization using smart phones. In: ACMMM (2010)
14. Bay, H., Fasel, B., Gool, L.V.: Interactive museum guide. In: UBICOMP Workshop (2005)
15. Schroth, G., Huitl, R., Chen, D., Abu-Alqumsan, M., Al-Nuaimi, A., Steinbach, E.: Mobile visual location recognition. Signal Process. Mag. **28**(4), 77–89 (2011)
16. Kim, G., Xing, E.P.: Reconstructing storyline graphs for image recommendation from web community photos. In: CVPR (2014)
17. Wang, D., Li, T., Ogihara, M.: Generating pictorial storylines via minimum-weight connected dominating set approximation in multi-view graphs. In: AAAI (2012)

18. Riedl, M.O., Young, R.M.: From linear story generation to branching story graphs. IEEE Comput. Graph. Appl. **26**(3), 23–31 (2006)
19. Yao, L., Torabi, A., Cho, K., Ballas, N., Pal, C., Larochelle, H., Courville, A.: Describing videos by exploiting temporal structure. In: ICCV (2015)
20. Rohrbach, M., Qiu, W., Titov, I., Thater, S., Pinkal, M., Schiele, B.: Translating video content to natural language descriptions. In: ICCV (2013)
21. Venugopalan, S., Rohrbach, M., Donahue, J., Mooney, R., Darrell, T., Saenko, K.: Sequence to sequence-video to text. In: ICCV (2015)
22. Arandjelović, R., Zisserman, A.: Three things everyone should know to improve object retrieval. In: CVPR (2012)
23. Lowe, D.G.: Distinctive image features from scale-invariant keypoints. In: IJCV (2004)
24. Philbin, J., Chum, O., Isard, M., Sivic, J., Zisserman, A.: Object retrieval with large vocabularies and fast spatial matching. In: CVPR (2007)
25. Hu, C., Chen, W., Chen, Y., Liu, D.: Adaptive Kalman filtering for vehicle navigation. Positioning **1**(04) (2009)
26. Tolman, B.W.: GPS precise absolute positioning via Kalman filtering. Ionosphere **2**(L1), L2 (2008)
27. Marchal, F., Hackney, J., Axhausen, K.: Efficient map-matching of large GPS data sets-tests on a speed monitoring experiment in Zurich. Arbeitsbericht Verkehrs-und Raumplanung (2004)
28. Mitchell, S., OSullivan, M., Dunning, I.: PuLP: a linear programming toolkit for python. The University of Auckland, New Zealand (2011)

Convolutional Neural Networks as a Computational Model for the Underlying Processes of Aesthetics Perception

Joachim Denzler[✉], Erik Rodner, and Marcel Simon

Computer Vision Group, Friedrich Schiller University Jena, Jena, Germany
{joachim.denzler,erik.rodner,marcel.simon}@uni-jena.de
http://www.inf-cv.uni-jena.de

Abstract. Understanding the underlying processes of aesthetic perception is one of the ultimate goals in empirical aesthetics. While deep learning and convolutional neural networks (CNN) already arrived in the area of aesthetic rating of art and photographs, only little attempts have been made to apply CNNs as the underlying model for aesthetic perception. The information processing architecture of CNNs shows a strong match with the visual processing pipeline in the human visual system. Thus, it seems reasonable to exploit such models to gain better insight into the universal processes that drives aesthetic perception. This work shows first results supporting this claim by analyzing already known common statistical properties of visual art, like sparsity and self-similarity, with the help of CNNs. We report about observed differences in the responses of individual layers between art and non-art images, both in forward and backward (simulation) processing, that might open new directions of research in empirical aesthetics.

Keywords: Aesthetic perception · Empirical aesthetics · Convolutional neural networks

1 Introduction

Today, researchers from a variety of disciplines, for example, psychology, neuroscience, sociology, museology, art history, philosophy, and recently mathematicians and computer scientists, are active in the area of understanding, modeling, or identifying processes related to aesthetic and aesthetic perception. The reason for such a still increasing interest in aesthetics arises from several questions:

1. How do artists create artwork? What are the underlying processes during such an artistic creativity?
2. What are the underlying processes in our brain leading to an aesthetic perception of specific images, text, sounds, etc.?
3. Can we compute a universal aesthetic value for art not being biased by cultural or educational background?

© Springer International Publishing Switzerland 2016
G. Hua and H. Jégou (Eds.): ECCV 2016 Workshops, Part I, LNCS 9913, pp. 871–887, 2016.
DOI: 10.1007/978-3-319-46604-0_60

4. Are we able to optimize creation of art? Can we even support users of cameras to optimize the artistic value of the images and videos they record?

The first two questions resides more in neuroscience and psychology, with the goal to *propose* and *verify* models for the underlying processes, and to explain certain observations in aesthetic perception. The third question seems to be a machine learning problem. However, training a discriminative classifier from data will always suffer from the possible bias in the training set. The forth question would benefit from an available *generative model* that allows the creation or modification of images with certain aesthetic properties. Besides commercial interest, artificial creation of visual art with specific aesthetic values, will be helpful for psychological studies as well to verify answers for the first question.

Our observation is that a computational framework to *model* aesthetic perception is still missing, although the joint efforts in the intersection of experimental aesthetics, computer vision, and machine learning lead to numerous interesting findings. While researchers from computer vision and machine learning are satisfied with accurate prediction of aesthetic value or beauty of images, researchers from empirical aesthetics hunt for findings and interesting properties that allow differentiation of art from non-art. However, the connecting element, a *computational model* is still missing that would be of significant help towards answering at least three of the four questions from above.

In this study, we want to show perspectives towards model building in empirical aesthetics. The main motivation of our work arises from recent progress of and insight in deep learning methods and convolutional neural networks (CNN). CNNs are multi-layer neural networks with convolutional, pooling, and fully connected layers. Currently, these methods define state-of-the-art in many different computer vision and machine learning tasks, like object detection and classification. More details can be found in Sect. 3. Due to parallels of the processing architecture of CNN and that of the visual cortex [1], such models might be an ideal basis for further investigation of properties of visual art, as well as using CNNs models to verify hypotheses of empirical aesthetics. In addition to the arrival of CNNs, also recently various rated datasets of visual art have become publicly available and enabled further research in the field. Examples are the AVA dataset [2], the JenAesthetics dataset [3], and - although without rating - the Google Art Project [4].

2   Progress in Computational and Empirical Aesthetics

One area of research is computational aesthetics. According to encyclopedia britannica [5], computational aesthetics, is

"a subfield of artificial intelligence (AI) concerned with the computational assessment of beauty in domains of human creative expression such as music, visual art, poetry, and chess problems. Typically, mathematical formulas that represent aesthetic features or principles are used in conjunction with specialized algorithms and statistical techniques to provide numerical aesthetic assessments. Those assessments, ideally, can be shown to correlate well with domain-

competent or expert human assessment. That can be useful, for example, when willing human assessors are difficult to find or prohibitively expensive or when there are too many objects to be evaluated. Such technology can be more reliable and consistent than human assessment, which is often subjective and prone to personal biases. Computational aesthetics may also improve understanding of human aesthetic perception".

Obviously, understanding of human aesthetic perception is not in the main focus. Successful results from this area of research are measuring aesthetic quality of photography [6–9] and paintings [10,11], quality enhancement of photos [12,13], analysis of photographic composition [14–16], classification of style [17–19], and composition [20,21], and painter [22]. Most recently, related work has been published for videos as well [23–26].

Some works present results for automatic creation of art [27,28], for measuring emotional effects of artwork on humans [29–31], and for improving and quantifying quality of art restoration [32]. Commercial use of those results for building intelligent cameras can be found in [33,34]. Systems that provide a (web-based) rating tool of photographs are [35,36].

The second main area of research related to aesthetics is empirical aesthetics. The aim of empirical aesthetics is to develop and apply methods to explain the psychological, neuronal, and socio-cultural basis of aesthetic perceptions and judgments. Compared to computational aesthetics, the aim is more understanding of the processes in aesthetic perception, i.e. why do people perceive music and visual art as varying in their beauty, based on factors such as culture, society, historical period, and individual taste. Some researchers are also interested in general principles of aesthetic perception independent from the so called cultural or educational filter [37].

While computational aesthetics can be interpreted as an application-driven procedure, like a discriminative classifier, empirical aesthetics aims more at observation and verification of hypothesis, i.e. parallels can be drawn to generative classifiers. A lot of findings have been reported about, for example, common statistical properties of visual art and natural scenes [38,39], certain unique properties of art work, like anisotropy in the Fourier domain [40] or self-similarity in the spatial domain [41], verified for different artwork, like faces/portraits [42], text/artistic writing [43], print advertisement/architecture [44], as well as cartoons/comics/mangas. However, the main shortcoming of most of the work from empirical aesthetics is the observation-driven approach without succeeding model building. Although we have observed and identified that there is a difference between images of visual art and arbitrary images, we do not know how this differences leads to aesthetic perception in humans. This finding would be a preliminary to finally understand the process of art creation. In other words, it is necessary to come up with an initial mathematical and computational model of aesthetic perception that can be verified and tested. As in many other disciplines such a model can be used to iteratively gain more insight into the involved processes, to verify hypotheses, to adapt and improve the model itself, and to even synthesize artwork as feedback for human raters in psychological studies.

To the best of our knowledge, there exists no (mathematical or computer) model for aesthetic perception capable to match with findings from empirical aesthetics, i.e. more effort must be put into developing such a model that can be used to explain known, unique properties of visual art and to relate those properties to processing principles in our visual cortex/brain.

In this study, we investigate the potentials of CNNs with respect to model building for aesthetic perception by asking the following questions:

- Is there any difference in the representation of images of artwork in CNNs compared to standard images (Sect. 6)?
- Which representation level (layer) of a CNN shows the most prominent differences (Sect. 6)?
- Is there any difference in the findings, if the CNN is trained with images from natural scenes compared to one that is trained on ImageNet? Can we confirm the hypothesis that the human visual system is adapted to process natural scenes more efficiently and that this adaptation builds the basis for aesthetic visual perception (Sect. 6)?
- Can we confirm some of the hypotheses from prior work in terms of sparse coding/processing for art, natural scenes, and general images (Sect. 7)?
- Can CNNs serve as a computational model to generate or modify images with certain universal aesthetic properties (Sect. 8)?

3   Convolutional Neural Networks

Convolutional neural networks are parameterized models for a transformation of an image to a given output vector. They are extensively used for classification [45], where the output vector consists of classification probabilities for each class, and detection problems [46,47], where the output vector may additionally contain the position of certain objects [47]. The model itself is comprised of a concatenation of simple operations, the so called layers.

The number of parameters of such a model in typically used architectures is often in the order of millions. Thus, training from a large-scale dataset is required. The interesting aspect that motivated our research is that there is strong evidence that such models can indeed learn very typical structural elements of natural images and objects. This was shown for example in the works of [48] for a CNN learned from ImageNet, which is the common "birthplace" of CNNs in vision currently. Furthermore, there has been further empirical evidence that these models are better suited for modeling the visual processing of human vision. Agrawal et al. [49], for example, investigates CNNs for neuroscience studies, where human brain activity is predicted directly from features extracted from the visual stimulus. In addition, Ramakrishnan et al. [50] compares CNNs with other layered vision models in an fMRI study.

Let's walk through a sample architecture, which is sketched in Fig. 1. The input for our network is in our case a single image. The first layer is a convolutional layer, which convolves the image with multiple learned filter masks. Afterwards, the outputs at neighboring locations are optionally combined by

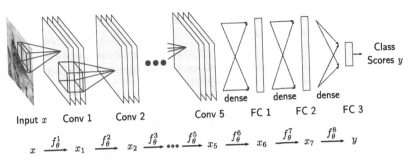

Fig. 1. Example of a convolutional neural network architecture.

applying a maximum operation in a spatial window applied to the result of each convolution, which is known as max-pooling layer. This is followed by an element-wise non-linear activation function, such as the rectified linear unit used in [45]. The last layers are fully connected layers which multiply the input with a matrix of learned parameters followed again by a non-linear activation function. The output of the network are scores for each of the learned categories. We do not provide a detailed explanation of the layers, since there is a wide range of papers and tutorials available already [45]. In summary, we can think about a CNN as one huge model that maps an image through different layers to a semantically meaningful output. The model is parameterized, which includes the weights in the fully connected layers as well as the weights of the convolution masks. All parameters of the CNN are learned by minimizing the error of the network output for an training example compared to the given ground-truth label.

Interestingly, many parts of the model can be directly related to models used in neuroscience [51] for modeling the V1-layer for example.

4   Dataset

We use all images of the JenAesthetics dataset [3], which is a well established dataset in the area of computational aesthetics. The dataset contains images of 1625 different oil paintings by 410 artist from 11 different art periods/styles.

The content or subject matter of a painting plays a crucial role in how an observer will perceive and assess a painting. 16 different keywords identify the most of the common subject matters. The subject matters are: abstract, nearly abstract, landscapes, scenes with person(s), still life, flowers or vegetation, animals, seascape, port or coast, sky, portrait (one person), portrait (many person), nudes, urban scene, building, interior scene, and other subject matters. 425 paintings have 3 and 1047 paintings have 2 subject matter keywords.

These images will serve as a representative sample of the category "art". Images not related to art paintings ("non-art") show various semantic concepts like plants, vegetation, buildings etc. Specifically, we used 175 photographs of building facades, 528 photographs of entire buildings, mostly without the ground floors to avoid the inclusion of cars and people, 225 photographs of urban scenes. We also included an additional dataset [52] with 289 photographs of large-vista natural scenes, 289 photographs of vegetation taken from a distance of about 5–50 m, and 316 close-up photographs of one type of plant. A detailed description of the used data can be found in [42,52,53].

5 Analyzed Models and Experimental Setup

Learning convolutional neural networks is done in a supervised fashion with pairs of images and the corresponding category labels [45]. Relating this to the processing in the brain, supervised learning of networks can be seen as teaching with different visual stimuli towards the goal of categorization in a specific task.

To study visual processing for different types of stimuli in the teaching phase, we train CNNs with a common architecture from three different datasets. We make use of the AlexNet [45] architecture. The first model is trained on roughly 1.5 million images and 1000 common object categories of the ImageNet Large Scale Visual Recognition Challenge 2012 [54] dataset, and is denoted by imagenet_CNN [45]. Second is the places_CNN [55], which is trained on over 7 million images divided into 205 scene categories including indoor and outdoor scenes, comprised by natural and man-made scenes. Third and last is a CNN trained on 125.000 images showing 128 categories of natural scenes. These images were taken from ImageNet and the categories were manually selected. We refer to this network as natural_CNN and it achieves an accuracy of almost 70 % on the 1280 held-out test images of the natural scene categories. The reason we added this network to our analysis is that it allows us to study a model completely learned with natural non-human-made visual stimuli. In addition, we also experiment with the deeper architecture VGG19 proposed by [55].

In the layer names used in the following, the prefix conv refers to the output of convolutional layers and fc correspond to the output of a fully connected layer.

6 Separation of Art vs. Non-art at Different Layers

In the beginning, we asked whether there is any difference in the representation of images (art vs. non-art) over the individual layers, i.e. at which level of the abstraction of an input image do we observe the largest difference. We also want to test whether there are differences in processing art images, if we initially train the CNNs on different datasets. With this experiment we want to verify whether the adaptation of the visual system of humans during evolution towards natural scenes plays a role for the underlying processes of aesthetic perception.

Measuring the differences is a non-trivial task since the output of a layer is high-dimensional. Therefore, we decided to use a classification approach, where we estimate the differences between both categories (artwork and all other images) over the individual layers by classification performance. The idea is, if the feature representations of the two categories are similar, the classifier would not be able to separate the two classes. In particular, we learn a linear support vector machine classifier using the layer outputs for each image of the two categories. The classifier is learned on 25 % of the data and the classification performance is measured using the remaining 75 %. As a performance measure we use the area under the ROC curve, which is well suited for binary classification problems, since it's value is invariant with respect to the distribution of the categories in the test dataset. To increase the robustness of our estimates, we also sample 5 different splits of the data into training and testing subset. The SVM hyperparameter is tuned using cross-validation for each run of the experiments. We restrict our analysis to linear layers, i.e. fully connected and convolutional layers.

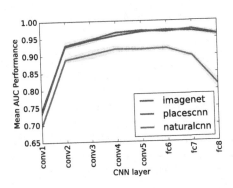

Fig. 2. Which layers of a CNN show the highest differences between artwork and all other images? We evaluate the separation ability of (1) `imagenet_CNN` (2) `natural_CNN` and (3) `places_CNN`.

The results of our analysis are given in Fig. 2 for all three of our networks. Regarding the maximum absolute performance, the `imagenet_CNN` showed the best performance. For `imagenet_CNN` and `places_CNN`, the differences between artwork and non-artwork increase up to the `conv4` layer and stay constant for later layers, which is not the case for `natural_CNN`. Interestingly, `natural_CNN` shows the worst performance, i.e. the statistics of images from natural scenes are not as well suited for separation of art and non-art images later on. This observation seems to be contradictory to the hypotheses that the adaption of the visual system toward natural scenes during evolution plays some role in explaining aesthetic perception. However, a more technical explanation is more likely. Since the art images under investigation show basically objects and scenes that are also present in ImageNet and Places data set, the representational power of those CNNs are superior to the one trained solely on natural scenes.

7 Are Artworks Characterized by Sparse Representations?

Next, we asked whether hypotheses from [37] and findings from [38] can be verified for representations in CNNs as well. One hypotheses is that a universal

878   J. Denzler et al.

model of aesthetic perception is based on sparse, i.e. efficient coding, of sensory input [37, Chap. 4]. If activities in the visual cortex can be coded with sparse representations, they allow for efficient processing with minimal energy. Comparing statistics of natural scenes and visual art showed that these two categories of images share a common property related to sparsity in the representation [38, 39]. Hence, we analyze next the sparsity of the output representations in different layers of a CNN. Sparse CNN representations of visual stimuli correspond to only a few activated neurons with non-zero output for which we first need to define a mathematical measure.

Sparsity measure. As a sparsity measure for a representation, we use the ℓ_1/ℓ_2 value given in [56], which we additionally normalize as follows to compare values of this measure also for vectors of different dimensionality. Let $x \in \mathbb{R}^D$ be a vector of size D, our sparsity is therefore defined as follows:

$$\text{sparsity}(x) = \frac{1}{\sqrt{D}} \frac{\|x\|_1}{\|x_2\|_2} = \frac{\sum_{k=1}^{D} |x_k|}{\sqrt{D \cdot \sum_{k=1}^{D} x_k^2}} \leq 1 . \tag{1}$$

This sparsity measure is small for sparse vectors, e.g. $\text{sparsity}([1, 0, \ldots, 0]) = \frac{1}{\sqrt{D}}$, and high for non-sparse vectors, e.g. $\text{sparsity}([1, \ldots, 1]) = 1$. In contrast to the standard ℓ_0 sparsity measure, where simply non-zero components are counted, our sparsity measure has the advantage of being smooth and taking into account approximate sparseness, e.g. with vectors having values close to zero relative to the overall magnitude.

Sparsity values for art and non-art images and different CNNs. Figure 3 shows the distribution of sparsity values for pairs of layers and different networks. The figures reflect our results obtained in Sect. 6: the discrimination ability increases for imagenet_CNN and places_CNN in later layers. It is indeed interesting that this is reflected in the sparsity values as well. Art images show more sparse representations at layer fc6 than non-art images. The lower representational power of the natural_CNN is confirmed in this analysis as well. Images from art and non-art show no significant difference in terms of sparsity over the individual layers. However, the representation in the intermediate layers (see conv1 vs. conv5) is systematically more sparse for natural_CNN, ranging from values 0.09 to 0.14 compared to values from 0.14 to 0.28 for the other two CNNs. So far, no conclusion seems be to directly possible. However, this experiment shows that there are differences in sparsity between layers and networks when comparing art and non-art images.

8 CNN as Generative Model: Transferring the Statistics of Artworks

In the following, we analyze the change of intrinsic statistics of images, when we apply methods that allow for optimizing common images towards being "art-like". This includes the texture transfer method of [57] as well as the method of

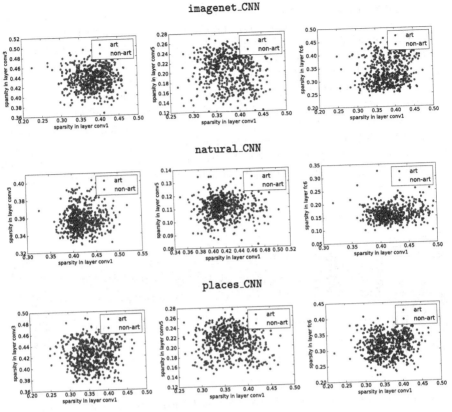

Fig. 3. Distribution of sparsity scores for art and non-art images computed for the outputs of two layers. Columns: conv1 vs. conv3, conv1 vs. conv5, conv1 vs. fc6. Rows correspond to different networks: imagenet_CNN, natural_CNN, and places_CNN. Smaller values correspond to higher sparsity. Best viewed in color. (Color figure online)

[58], which we modified to maximizing the probability of the image for belonging to the "art category". We can indeed show that transferring images towards art-like also transfers intrinsic statistical properties, like self-similarity or sparsity, towards art-like.

8.1 Texture Transfer

The work of [57] presented an approach for transferring the style from a painting to a different image. In this section, we will use this idea to visualize and understand the type of style information encoded in each layer of the CNN. It will turn out that each layer captures a fundamentally different aspect of the style, which can also be connected to the observations concerning sparsity of the previous sections.

The style transfer approach of [57] takes two images as input. One image provides the content and the second one the style, as shown in Fig. 4. Starting from a white noise image, we now try to find a new image, which matches the content of the first and the style of the second image. This is done by changing the image step-by-step such that the neural activations at selected layers match the content and the style image, respectively. For the style image, the entries of the Gram matrix $G^l = \sum_{i,j}(x^l_{i,j}) \cdot (x^l_{i,j})^T$ of the style layer should match instead of the activations itself. Here, $x^l_{i,j} = (x^l_{i,j,k})_k$ denote the feature descriptor at position (i, j) of layer l. As an example, for the first output image in Fig. 4, the white noise image is optimized such that the activations of layer conv4_2 match the content image and the Gram matrix of the activations of layer conv1_1 match the style image.

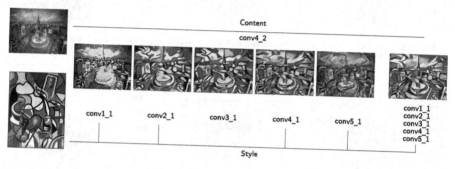

Fig. 4. Texture transfer for the content image shown on the top left and the style given by the image on the bottom left. The content was defined by the activations of the layer conv4_2 for all images. The style was defined by the bilinear activations of different layers as annotated below each image. Best viewed in color. (Color figure online)

How does self-similarity change? With the above technique, we analyze the process of transforming an image into a more artistic image by transferring a mean style of artworks to images. We use all images of the JenAesthetics database, compute their mean Gram matrix and use it as the definition of "style" in the above algorithm.

Self-similarity is a well-known measure used in computational aesthetics to characterize an image [41,42]. The question arises how the values of this measure change while optimizing a regular image towards an artwork. The results are given in Fig. 5, where we refer to the image after the texture transfer as "Art-transfer image". For all the images shown in the Fig. 5, we observe a significant increase in self-similarity after applying the texture transfer technique. It is worth noting that the self-similarity values after texture transfer are in the range of artwork for not-art images as well. Even art images show an increase of self-similarity (second row, first image). Please also observe the "generation" of a synthetic art image in the last row. In this case, no content image was constraining the generation process. As in the other cases, we started with a white noise image and modified it such that the style matches the mean art feature.

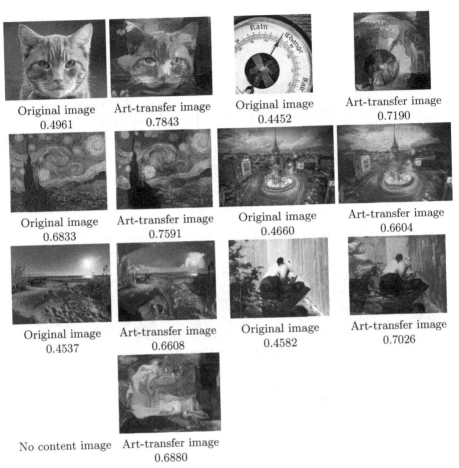

Original image   Art-transfer image   Original image   Art-transfer image
0.4961   0.7843   0.4452   0.7190

Original image   Art-transfer image   Original image   Art-transfer image
0.6833   0.7591   0.4660   0.6604

Original image   Art-transfer image   Original image   Art-transfer image
0.4537   0.6608   0.4582   0.7026

No content image   Art-transfer image
0.6880

Fig. 5. Self-similarity changes when optimizing regular images towards artworks. We use the texture transfer technique of [57] in this case. The numbers below the images show the self-similarity scores from [42].

A second investigation concerns the change of the self-similarity score over time during the texture transfer. Figure 6 depicts the progress for three examples. For each example, the plot is shown above the content as well as the final image. The first plot combines the input image with the style of the painting "Transverse Line" by Kandinsky and the second one with the painting "Clin d'oeil à Picasso" by Bochaton. The self-similarity score of the generated image is shown in blue. As shown already in the previous figure, the self-similarity changes when transferring style to a new image. The change, however, is not monotonic but shows in the first ten iterations a dramatic increase from 0.5335 to 0.8056 and 0.8427, respectively, and thus surpasses the self-similarity score of the target style image depicted in green. After the initial overshoot, the score gets closer the one of the painting, but converges at a higher level of 0.7581 and 0.7363,

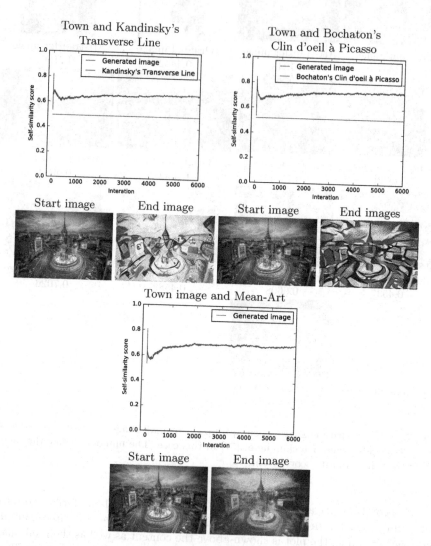

Fig. 6. Change of the self-similarity score over time during the texture transfer given an input image and a painting. We depict the change for two different styles transferred to the input image shown on the left. The plots show the self-similarity score of the image after iteration k in blue and the self-similarity score of the painting in green. (Color figure online)

respectively. The third subplot depicts the change over time for an optimization towards the mean art style. Similarly, there is an initial overshoot, followed by a short descent and a strong increase towards the final value of 0.7155.

We belief that these initial experiments with the texture transfer method indicate that CNNs are capable as a generative model in empirical aesthetics and can be exploited to generate images with specific, statistical properties related to an aesthetic value of the image.

8.2   Maximizing Art Probability

Adapting DeepDream towards optimizing art category probability. Instead of indirectly optimizing images towards artworks by transferring the texture as done in the previous section, we can also perform the optimization directly.

First, we fine-tune a convolutional neural network to solve the binary classification task artworks vs. non-artworks. The original DeepDream technique of [58] tries to modify the image such that the L_2-norm of the activations of a certain layer is maximized. We modify this objective, such that the class probability for the artworks category is optimized. The algorithm for the optimization is still a gradient-descent algorithm as in [58] using gradients computed with back-propagation.

Details about the fine-tuning. Fine-tuning is done with a pre-trained `imagenet_CNN` model. In particular, we set the learning rate to 0.001 and the batch size to 20 and perform optimization with the common tricks-of-the-trade: (1) momentum with $\mu = 0.9$, (2) weight decay of 0.0005 and (3) dropout with $p = 0.5$ applied after the first and second fully connected layers.

How does the self-similarity score change? Figure 7 shows quantitative results of our analysis, where we compared the self-similarity scores before and after the optimization towards the artwork and the non-artwork category. As can be seen, the self-similarity scores increase in both cases for a large number of images. This is not the expected result when considering the findings of the texture transfer technique. So far, optimizing towards category probabilities seems not to be a reasonable method for enforcing certain statistical properties of art or non-art images. However, this is not a surprise, considering the amount of information contained in category probabilities compared to the target image style represented by the Gram matrix.

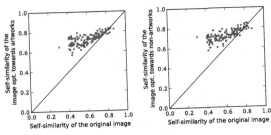

Fig. 7. Self-similarity scores before and after the optimization with respect to the artwork and the non-artwork category.

9   Conclusions

This work started with the observation that a computational model is missing in empirical aesthetic research. Such an initial model would allow the verification of hypotheses, to generate and modify images for psychological studies, to refine hypotheses as well as the model, and to initiate succeeding experiments and investigations along the way to understand the underlying processes in aesthetic perception.

We started to investigate the potentials of CNNs in this area, extending its previous use as pure classifier. The main goal was to figure out whether already known statistical properties of visual art, like sparsity and self-similarity, are reflected in the representation of images by CNNs as well. In addition, we analyzed two methods to use CNNs for generating new images with specific category properties (DeepDream) or style properties (texture transfer).

Our results indicate that there are statistical differences in the representation over the hierarchies of layers in CNNs. Those differences not only arise from the input image being processed, but also from the underlying training data of the CNN. The main finding is that sparsity of activations in individual layers is one property to be further investigated. This is in accordance with previous findings.

In addition, we applied CNNs as a generative model using techniques from literature. Interestingly, the method of texture transfer is able to modify self-similarity in images, a property that has been previously used to characterize art work. Hence, generating images with aesthetic properties seems to be possible as well.

So far, we only started the investigation. There are several aspects not considered so far, for example, different network architectures, different other statistical properties of aesthetic images, like fractality or anisotropy, and how such properties can be mapped to arbitrary images. These aspects are subject to future work.

References

1. Cadieu, C.F., Hong, H., Yamins, D.L., Pinto, N., Ardila, D., Solomon, E.A., Majaj, N.J., DiCarlo, J.J.: Deep neural networks rival the representation of primate it cortex for core visual object recognition. PLoS Comput. Biol. **10**(12), e1003963 (2014)
2. Murray, N., Marchesotti, L., Perronnin, F.: Ava: a large-scale database for aesthetic visual analysis. In: 2012 IEEE Conference on Computer Vision and Pattern Recognition (CVPR), pp. 2408–2415. IEEE (2012)
3. Amirshahi, S.A., Hayn-Leichsenring, G.U., Denzler, J., Redies, C.: JenAesthetics subjective dataset: analyzing paintings by subjective scores. In: Agapito, L., Bronstein, M.M., Rother, C. (eds.) ECCV 2014. LNCS, vol. 8925, pp. 3–19. Springer, Heidelberg (2015). doi:10.1007/978-3-319-16178-5_1
4. Proctor, N.: The google art project: a new generation of museums on the web? Curator Museum J. **54**(2), 215–221 (2011)
5. Goetz, P.W., McHenry, R., Hoiberg, D. (eds.): Encyclopedia Britannica, vol. 9. Encyclopaedia Britannica Inc., Chicago (2010)

6. Ravi, F., Battiato, S.: A novel computational tool for aesthetic scoring of digital photography. In: Conference on Colour in Graphics, Imaging, and Vision, Society for Imaging Science and Technology, pp. 349–354 (2012)
7. Datta, R., Joshi, D., Li, J., Wang, J.Z.: Studying aesthetics in photographic images using a computational approach. In: Leonardis, A., Bischof, H., Pinz, A. (eds.) ECCV 2006. LNCS, vol. 3953, pp. 288–301. Springer, Heidelberg (2006)
8. Romero, J., Machado, P., Carballal, A., Osorio, O.: Aesthetic classification and sorting based on image compression. In: Chio, C., et al. (eds.) EvoApplications 2011. LNCS, vol. 6625, pp. 394–403. Springer, Heidelberg (2011). doi:10.1007/978-3-642-20520-0_40
9. Wu, Y., Bauckhage, C., Thurau, C.: The good, the bad, and the ugly: predicting aesthetic image labels. In: 2010 20th International Conference on Pattern Recognition (ICPR), pp. 1586–1589. IEEE (2010)
10. Wickramasinghe, W.A.P., Dharmaratne, A.T., Kodikara, N.D.: A tool for ranking and enhancing aesthetic quality of paintings. In: Kim, T., Adeli, H., Ramos, C., Kang, B.-H. (eds.) SIP 2011. CCIS, vol. 260, pp. 254–260. Springer, Heidelberg (2011). doi:10.1007/978-3-642-27183-0_27
11. Li, C., Chen, T.: Aesthetic visual quality assessment of paintings. IEEE J. Sel. Top. Sign. Process. **3**(2), 236–252 (2009)
12. Bhattacharya, S., Sukthankar, R., Shah, M.: A framework for photo-quality assessment and enhancement based on visual aesthetics. In: Proceedings of the International Conference on Multimedia, pp. 271–280. ACM (2010)
13. Zhang, F.L., Wang, M., Hu, S.M.: Aesthetic image enhancement by dependence-aware object re-composition. IEEE Trans. Multimedia **15**(7), 1480–1490 (2013)
14. Escoffery, D.: A framework for learning photographic composition preferences from gameplay data (2012)
15. Jin, Y., Wu, Q., Liu, L.: Aesthetic photo composition by optimal crop-and-warp. Comput. Graph. **36**(8), 955–965 (2012)
16. Gallea, R., Ardizzone, E., Pirrone, R.: Automatic aesthetic photo composition. In: Petrosino, A. (ed.) ICIAP 2013, Part II. LNCS, vol. 8157, pp. 21–30. Springer, Heidelberg (2013)
17. Wallraven, C., Fleming, R., Cunningham, D., Rigau, J., Feixas, M., Sbert, M.: Categorizing art: comparing humans and computers. Comput. Graph. **33**(4), 484–495 (2009)
18. Condorovici, R.G., Florea, C., Vrânceanu, R., Vertan, C.: Perceptually-inspired artistic genre identification system in digitized painting collections. In: Kämäräinen, J.-K., Koskela, M. (eds.) SCIA 2013. LNCS, vol. 7944, pp. 687–696. Springer, Heidelberg (2013)
19. Karayev, S., Hertzmann, A., Winnemoeller, H., Agarwala, A., Darrell, T.: Recognizing image style. arXiv preprint arXiv:1311.3715 (2013)
20. Yao, L.: Automated analysis of composition and style of photographs and paintings. Ph.D. thesis. The Pennsylvania State University (2013)
21. Obrador, P., Schmidt-Hackenberg, L., Oliver, N.: The role of image composition in image aesthetics. In: 2010 17th IEEE International Conference on Image Processing (ICIP), pp. 3185–3188. IEEE (2010)
22. Cetinic, E., Grgic, S.: Automated painter recognition based on image feature extraction. In: 2013 55th International Symposium ELMAR, pp. 19–22. IEEE (2013)
23. Wang, Y., Dai, Q., Feng, R., Jiang, Y.G.: Beauty is here: evaluating aesthetics in videos using multimodal features and free training data. In: Proceedings of the 21st ACM International Conference on Multimedia, pp. 369–372. ACM (2013)

24. Chung, S., Sammartino, J., Bai, J., Barsky, B.A.: Can motion features inform video aesthetic preferences. University of California at Berkeley Technical report No. UCB/EECS-2012-172, 29 June 2012

25. Bhattacharya, S., Nojavanasghari, B., Chen, T., Liu, D., Chang, S.F., Shah, M.: Towards a comprehensive computational model for aesthetic assessment of videos. In: Proceedings of the 21st ACM International Conference on Multimedia, pp. 361–364. ACM (2013)

26. Moorthy, A.K., Obrador, P., Oliver, N.: Towards computational models of the visual aesthetic appeal of consumer videos. In: Daniilidis, K., Maragos, P., Paragios, N. (eds.) ECCV 2010, Part V. LNCS, vol. 6315, pp. 1–14. Springer, Heidelberg (2010)

27. Galanter, P.: Computational aesthetic evaluation: steps towards machine creativity. In: ACM SIGGRAPH 2012 Courses, p. 14. ACM (2012)

28. Zhang, K., Harrell, S., Ji, X.: Computational aesthetics: on the complexity of computer-generated paintings. Leonardo 45(3), 243–248 (2012)

29. Zhang, H., Augilius, E., Honkela, T., Laaksonen, J., Gamper, H., Alene, H.: Analyzing emotional semantics of abstract art using low-level image features. In: Gama, J., Bradley, E., Hollmén, J. (eds.) IDA 2011. LNCS, vol. 7014, pp. 413–423. Springer, Heidelberg (2011)

30. Joshi, D., Datta, R., Fedorovskaya, E., Luong, Q.T., Wang, J.Z., Li, J., Luo, J.: Aesthetics and emotions in images. Sign. Process. Mag. 28(5), 94–115 (2011). IEEE

31. Bertola, F., Patti, V.: Emotional responses to artworks in online collections. In: Proceedings of PATCH (2013)

32. Oncu, A.I., Deger, F., Hardeberg, J.Y.: Evaluation of digital inpainting quality in the context of artwork restoration. In: Fusiello, A., Murino, V., Cucchiara, R. (eds.) ECCV 2012. LNCS, vol. 7583, pp. 561–570. Springer, Heidelberg (2012). doi:10.1007/978-3-642-33863-2_58

33. Lo, K.-Y., Liu, K.-H., Chen, C.-S.: Intelligent photographing interface with on-device aesthetic quality assessment. In: Park, J.-I., Kim, J. (eds.) ACCV Workshops 2012, Part II. LNCS, vol. 7729, pp. 533–544. Springer, Heidelberg (2013)

34. Mitarai, H., Itamiya, Y., Yoshitaka, A.: Interactive photographic shooting assistance based on composition and saliency. In: Murgante, B., Misra, S., Carlini, M., Torre, C.M., Nguyen, H.-Q., Taniar, D., Apduhan, B.O., Gervasi, O. (eds.) ICCSA 2013, Part V. LNCS, vol. 7975, pp. 348–363. Springer, Heidelberg (2013)

35. Yao, L., Suryanarayan, P., Qiao, M., Wang, J.Z., Li, J.: Oscar: on-site composition and aesthetics feedback through exemplars for photographers. Int. J. Comput. Vis. 96(3), 353–383 (2012)

36. Datta, R., Wang, J.Z.: Acquine: aesthetic quality inference engine-real-time automatic rating of photo aesthetics. In: Proceedings of the International Conference on Multimedia Information Retrieval, pp. 421–424. ACM (2010)

37. Redies, C.: A universal model of esthetic perception based on the sensory coding of natural stimuli. Spat. Vis. 21(1), 97–117 (2007)

38. Redies, C., Hasenstein, J., Denzler, J.: Fractal-like image statistics in visual art: similarity to natural scenes. Spat. Vis. 21(1–2), 97–117 (2007)

39. Redies, C., Haenisch, J., Blickhan, M., Denzler, J.: Artists portray human faces with the fourier statistics of complex natural scenes. Netw. Comput. Neural Syst. 18(3), 235–248 (2007)

40. Koch, M., Denzler, J., Redies, C.: $1/f^2$ characteristics and isotropy in the fourier power spectra of visual art, cartoons, comics, mangas, and different categories of photographs. PLoS ONE 5(8), e12268 (2010)

41. Amirshahi, S.A., Koch, M., J.D., Redies, C. : PHOG analysis of self-similarity in aesthetic images. In: IST/SPIE Electronic Imaging (2012)
42. Amirshahi, S.A., Redies, C., Denzler, J.: How self-similar are artworks at different levels of spatial resolution? In: Computational Aesthetics (2013)
43. Melmer, T., Amirshahi, S.A., Koch, M., Denzler, J., Redies, C.: From regular text to artistic writing and artworks: fourier statistics of images with low and high aesthetic appeal. Front. Hum. Neurosci. 7(00106) (2013)
44. Braun, J., Amirshahi, S.A., Redies, J.D.: Statistical image properties of print advertisements, visual artworks and images of architecture. Front. Psychol. 4, 808 (2013)
45. Krizhevsky, A., Sutskever, I., Hinton, G.E.: Imagenet classification with deep convolutional neural networks. In: Advances in Neural Information Processing Systems, pp. 1097–1105 (2012)
46. Girshick, R., Donahue, J., Darrell, T., Malik, J.: Rich feature hierarchies for accurate object detection and semantic segmentation. In: Proceedings of the IEEE Conference on Computer Vision and Pattern Recognition, pp. 580–587 (2014)
47. Redmon, J., Divvala, S., Girshick, R., Farhadi, A.: You only look once: unified, real-time object detection. arXiv preprint arXiv:1506.02640 (2015)
48. Zeiler, M.D., Fergus, R.: Visualizing and understanding convolutional networks. In: Fleet, D., Pajdla, T., Schiele, B., Tuytelaars, T. (eds.) ECCV 2014. LNCS, vol. 8689, pp. 818–833. Springer, Heidelberg (2014). doi:10.1007/978-3-319-10590-1_53
49. Agrawal, P., Stansbury, D., Malik, J., Gallant, J.L.: Pixels to voxels: modeling visual representation in the human brain. arXiv preprint arXiv:1407.5104 (2014)
50. Ramakrishnan, K., Scholte, S., Lamme, V., Smeulders, A., Ghebreab, S.: Convolutional neural networks in the brain: an FMRI study. J. Vis. 15(12), 371–371 (2015)
51. Pinto, N., Cox, D.D., DiCarlo, J.J.: Why is real-world visual object recognition hard? PLoS Comput. Biol. 4(1), e27 (2008)
52. Redies, C., Amirshahi, S.A., Koch, M., Denzler, J.: PHOG-derived aesthetic measures applied to color photographs of artworks, natural scenes and objects. In: Fusiello, A., Murino, V., Cucchiara, R. (eds.) ECCV 2012. LNCS, vol. 7583, pp. 522–531. Springer, Heidelberg (2012). doi:10.1007/978-3-642-33863-2_54
53. Amirshahi, S.A., Denzler, J., Redies, C.: Jenaesthetics–a public dataset of paintings for aesthetic research. Technical report, Computer Vision Group. Friedrich-Schiller-University Jena (2013)
54. Russakovsky, O., Deng, J., Su, H., Krause, J., Satheesh, S., Ma, S., Huang, Z., Karpathy, A., Khosla, A., Bernstein, M., et al.: Imagenet large scale visual recognition challenge. Int. J. Comput. Vis. 115(3), 1–42 (2014)
55. Zhou, B., Lapedriza, A., Xiao, J., Torralba, A., Oliva, A.: Learning deep features for scene recognition using places database. In: Advances in Neural Information Processing Systems. pp. 487–495 (2014)
56. Hurley, N., Rickard, S.: Comparing measures of sparsity. IEEE Trans. Inf. Theor. 55(10), 4723–4741 (2009)
57. Gatys, L.A., Ecker, A.S., Bethge, M.: A neural algorithm of artistic style. arXiv preprint arXiv:1508.06576 (2015)
58. Mordvintsev, A., Tyka, M., Olah, C.: Inceptionism: going deeper into neural networks, google research blog. Accessed 17 June 2015

Pose and Pathosformel in Aby Warburg's Bilderatlas

Leonardo Impett[✉] and Sabine Süsstrunk

School of Computer and Communication Sciences,
École Fédérale Polytechnique de Lausanne, Lausanne, Switzerland
leonardo.impett@epfl.ch

Abstract. look at Aby Warburg's concept of Pathosformel, the repeatable formula for the expression of emotion, through the depiction of human pose in art. Using crowdsourcing, we annotate 2D human pose in one-third of the panels of Warburg's atlas of art, and perform some exploratory data analysis. Concentrating only on the relative angles of limbs, we find meaningful clusters of related poses, explore the structure using a hierarchical model, and describe a novel method for visualising salient characteristics of the cluster. We find characteristic pose-clusters which correspond to *Pathosformeln*, and investigate their historical distribution; at the same time, we find morphologically similar poses can represent wildly different emotions. We hypothesise that this ambiguity comes from the static nature of our encoding, and conclude with some remarks about static and dynamic representations of human pose in art.

Keywords: Pose · Pathos · Emotion · Pathosformel · Bilderatlas · Warburg

1   Introduction

Aby Warburg's *Bilderatlas*, an unfinished atlas of the history of art, consists of 1230 photographs of various kinds (styles, periods and media) of art, arranged in 63 panels. Warburg wrote little explicitly about the Bilderatlas (and he died before it could be completed); but we do understand that Warburg was interested in two key concepts, *Pathosformel* (formulas that express emotion), and the *Nachleben der Antike*. The panels of the Bilderatlas have been studied extensively by art-historians and iconographers, often cross-referencing the seemingly ambiguous panels with Warburg's extensive previous work (see e.g. [1]). Excellent introductions to Warburg and to the Bilderatlas exist elsewhere (see eg. Foster's preface in [2,3]); here, we content ourselves with a brief introduction of two key Warburgian concepts mentioned above.

1.1   The Pathosformel

The *Pathosformel* (plural *Pathosformeln*), or formula of pathos (emotion), is a key Warburgian concept. On the most basic level, it describes the portrayal or

© Springer International Publishing Switzerland 2016
G. Hua and H. Jégou (Eds.): ECCV 2016 Workshops, Part I, LNCS 9913, pp. 888–902, 2016.
DOI: 10.1007/978-3-319-46604-0_61

communication of emotion, movement and passion, through a repeatable visual paradigm or formula. Salvatore Settis describes it as: "the oxymoronic word, in that it merges in the same term the movement of pathos and the rigidity of the formula-schema" [4, p. 167]. Freedberg [5] notes the intuitive nature of the Pathosformel - asking "How does a picture or sculpture engage the body, and what are the emotional responses that may ensue?... Not only do the gestures ring humanly true, one also knows immediately how often one has seen them in art".

We understand these *Pathosformeln* specifically as body poses, neglecting other portrayals of emotion (such as accessory items, facial expression and hand gestures) - as human pose is both a formally quantifiable aspect of a work of art, and a primary expression of emotion (as further described in Sect. 2.2).

1.2 Nachleben der Antike

Warburg theorised that classical Pagan formulae (from Greek and Roman times), particularly in the portrayal of elementary impulses, were reborn in the Italian Renaissance. He called this the *Nachleben der Antike*, the after-life of classical antiquity [2].

Warburg's collaborator and assistant, G. Bing, noted in particular the emotional strength of art in antiquity: "The gestures of classical art, in their first formulations, come from a period in which the reality of myths was a ritual reality... These gestures are still capable of provoking a suitable reaction"[1].

These antique formulae were not *rediscovered* in an archeological sense, but rather preserved in common cultural memory. They fell out of favour during the medieval period, as the "expression of elementary impulses" [2] was prohibited for religious reasons. When Pathosformeln are renewed in the Renaissance, the emotion or meaning attributed to a certain formula often changes - the so-called 'antithetical' principle (see [2, p. 38]).

We will seek to describe formally the *Nachleben* of *Pathosformeln* through the Bilderatlas. Indeed, the entire Bilderatlas has been described as "a means to chart the afterlife of ancient forms through time to his present day" [6].

2 Emotion as Pose

2.1 Within Art History

Human form has long been part of art-historical analysis, particularly in sculpture - see for example Argan's comparison of syntactic (each human body separately) and paratactic (the relationship between bodies) analysis of pose [7, p. 49]. Analysis of classical sculpture includes such concepts as the *contrapposto*, where the weight of the statue is supported by one foot - twisting the axis of the hips and legs [7]. More recently, Robin Osborne's monograph [8] has

---

[1] All translations by the author.

attempted to describe social and historical aspects of the history of art through the depiction of bodies in Greek antiquity.

David Freedberg, an art historian and current director of the Warburg Institute, makes three specific claims that are relevant to our analysis [5]:

1. We can draw connections between art (as images) and the perception of art on the level of emotions, feeling and empathy
2. Emotions *might be* classifiable (as suggested by Ekman [9])
3. It is impossible to consider emotions as separate from the body, or indeed from the *movement* of the body.

The first two claims form good art-historical assumptions for our study of Pathosformeln through human pose; the third, hinting at movement, lies at the base of our proposed future work. Warburg's interest in motion within images has recently been explored in detail by Philippe-Alain Michaud [3].

2.2 Psychological and Psychophysical Evidence

Most experimental evidence for the emotional perception of pose follows the Light Spots Model of Johansson (1973) [10]. Instead of a whole video or image of a person, only some bright spots are shown (lights fixed to the body), describing the position of the main joints of the body. Johansson found that between 10 and 12 such spots are adequate for 'a compelling impression of human walking, running, dancing etc.'. These Light Spots are therefore a compelling analogue of our own reduced pose model for paintings (our own analysis, described subsequently, uses 12 points to describe a human figure).

The most important results from the psychological literature seem to focus on the difference between *static* pose (photographs) and *dynamic* pose (videos). Recently, it has been shown that dynamic pose conveys qualitative ('which emotion?') as well as quantitative ('how intense?') information [11]. This echos the much more recent results found in action classification for computer vision, which - although not concerned with emotion recognition - can classify actions much more successfully with dynamic data [12].

Static pose, when seen as a single frame of a dynamic sequence, leads to emotional ambiguities. Indeed Atkinson found that, if we reverse the time-direction of Light Spots videos of actors, the percieved emotion changes. This, it is argued, is evidence that static form (pose) and dynamics give distinct contributions to the perception of emotions [13]. This inherent ambiguity in static pose may not be inconsistent with Warburg's own writings on the antithetical nature of the Nachleben.

From this, it could be suggested that artists use visual cues of movement to disambiguate between the different possible emotive implications of the same pose. In the analysis presented in the rest of this report, we focus only on static pose - whilst being conscious of the additional ambiguities presented by this reduction.

Our study explicitly ignores facial expressions, which are well-studied by psychologists; it has been suggested [14], however, that body cues play the major role in the perception of emotions from photographs, substantially informing our interpretation of facial expressions.

3   Collecting a Dataset

In keeping with our understanding of the Pathosformel as human pose, we have started to create a dataset of the pose of every figure in the Bilderatlas. Although our dataset is created with an analysis of Nachleben and Pathosformel in mind, it is also intended to serve as the basis for a future training dataset for automatic pose detection in paintings, currently an unsolved problem (see for example [15,16]).

3.1   Digitising the Bilderatlas

As the panels of the Bilderatlas no longer exist, our only primary digital sources are high-resolution[2] scans of the 1920s black-and-white photographs of the Bilderatlas. Unfortunately, even high-resolution scans of Panels are frequently not of high enough quality to be able to discern smaller individual bodies clearly.

For this reason, colour photographs of the original artwork were sourced for 21 of the Bilderatlas' 63 panels. The originals were mainly collected from museum websites and open-access art collections. Images that clearly contained no human figures (such as unillustrated manuscript pages) were not sourced. 9 % of the images were either not found, or contained no human bodies. We have 318 images for our 21 panels from this process, which is 26 % of the total number of works in the Bilderatlas (1230).

3.2   Two-Stage Annotation

We crowdsourced the annotation of poses in our images using the CrowdFlower platform [17]. This platform uses its own workers, as well as those of other services (such as Amazon Mechanical Turk and SamaSource) - see [18] for a detailed comparison with Amazon Mechanical Turk.

After a series of preliminary experiments on crowdsourced pose annotation, we designed a two-stage system for the annotation of poses in paintings. In particular, we found that when asked to annotate poses directly (given a whole painting):

1. Individual bodies are often too small to be annotated accurately on-screen
2. We often find groups of people standing close to one another in paintings; these can make the pose annotation of each body difficult and confusing
3. When paid per painting, the worker has an economic motivation to not annotate all the bodies
4. If users decide to annotate a different subset of the people in a painting, annotations cannot be aggregated.

---

[2] Some of the panels are digitsed to size 3000 × 4030 pixels.

We therefore split the pose annotation task into two stages (see Fig. 1):

1. Individual bodies are segmented from the paintings
2. Each pose is annotated separately from a cropped figure of that body.

By giving a smaller, cropped figure containing the relevant body, annotation becomes clearer and more explicit for the user, and pose is more easily aggregated.

We should acknowledge at this point that some paintings will have many tens of figures (such as battle scenes); others will have just one. Our decision to annotate all figures in each painting gives a bias in our dataset towards those paintings with more figures.

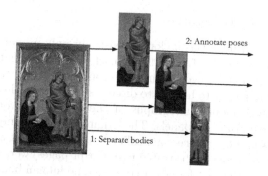

Fig. 1. A diagram of our two-stage pose annotation process

3.3   Aggregation Algorithms

Extracting Bodies. In order to extract bodies from the paintings, crowd workers were asked to draw a line from the face to the foot of each figure. This gives an indication of both position and size of the body within the painting. Whilst the annotation of feet varies widely (for instance, when the feet of a figure are spread), the annotation of the head is precise, and gives us an explicit 2D point for matching separate annotations.

Each painting was annotated separately by three annotators - giving three separate sets of annotations. Aggregation was performed on the annotations in the following way:

1. Pick the set of annotations with the most lines (i.e., the most bodies)
2. Keep the annotations that agree with at least one other set (where the heads are within a 50 pixel radius)
3. Construct circles around the annotations, using the head-foot lines as tangents (giving an area for the body, even where the lines are horizontal)
4. Crop 1.5× the width and height of this area.

Note that we never average the aggregation, only compare agreement - it was found that averaging between clustered annotations can give artefacts (eg. where heads of different bodies are close together). Failure cases include non-human bodies being reliably annotated (Fig. 2d), and incomplete bodies (where pose is not fully defined) (Fig. 2e) - both cases are rare.

We often find that more than one body is included in the final crop - for this reason, we also display the labelled points of the head and foot of the relevant body (see Fig. 2b).

In total, we extract 1,772 figures of individual bodies, from our 318 original images.

Single Human Pose. Once figures of individual bodies had been produced, the pose of each body was annotated - again using three separate annotations. This task involved drawing twelve lines (implying 24 points), corresponding to the twelve limbs of the figure (see Fig. 3a). Compared to datasets on photographic pose estimation (such as the Leeds Sports dataset [19]), we omit the hips, as they were often visually ambiguous in the paintings and (in our preliminary experiments) frequently omitted by workers.

Due to the fact that we sometimes have more than one figure in the cropped image (see Fig. 2b), we eliminate cases where the pose of the wrong person seems to have been annotated. We reject annotations where the average of all limb co-ordinates (the centre of mass of the body) is more than one spine-length away from the average of all the other annotations.

We then take the average skeleton. The standard deviation of the individual (non-rejected) annotations around the average, when normalised by the spine length of each body (to compare bodies of different size), is 0.23. Overall, 1665 aggregate annotations were produced from our 1773 skeletons (94 %) - with the remaining 6 % of figures not having any accepted annotations (eg. due to the failure cases shown in Fig. 2d and e).

4   Data Analysis

After annotating and aggregating our human poses, we perform a series of normalisations on the data before our unsupervised learning models:

1. All limb lengths are ignored, and only the *angles* of limbs are conserved
2. All bodies are rotated such that their spine is vertical
3. Poses are mirrored such that their highest arm is on the right
4. The angles of the lower body are multiplied, such that the sum of the variances in upper and lower body angles is equal (due to anatomical constraints, variance in lower body angles is always smaller than that in the upper).

Our 12 2-dimensional co-ordinates (for each pose) thus become an 11-dimensional angular vector.

(a) A set of annotations for Adolf Furtwängler's copy of a 5th century BC Puglian vase - Figure 1 from Panel 2 of the Bilderatlas. The coloured arrows show three complete sets of annotations (red, blue and green).

(b) Successful segmentation from (a)

(c) Successful segmentation from (a)

(d) Failure case; non-human body

(e) Failure case; incomplete body

Fig. 2. Finding bodies in images - annotations (a), successful segmentations (b–c) and failure cases (d–e). Note in (a)–(c) how the green annotator has identified all bodies correctly; the blue missed a few, and the red has only indicated a single body. This variance in the number of bodies annotated is a good reason to split pose annotation into two parts; to make sure the same poses are annotated each time. (Color figure online)

4.1 Unsupervised Learning

Hierarchical Clustering. In order to compare human poses in the Bilderatlas morphologically, we seek to build hierarchical trees of poses from our dataset.

Hierarchical clustering works well in non-Euclidian spaces, as it requires only a point-to-point distance metric. For our purposes, we define the distance between pose i and j as:

$$D(P_i, P_j) = \sum_{k=1}^{11} ||\theta_{i,k} - \theta_{j,k}||_2$$

(a) The twelve lines of our pose annotation - used in the instructions for crowdworkers

(b) An example aggregate body pose (in red), showing individual annotations (in green)

Fig. 3. Body pose annotation - our second-stage crowdsourcing

We use *agglomerative* hierarchical clustering - each data-point starts in its own cluster, and we merge the two clusters with the smallest pairwise distance D, until all the data is in one cluster. The order of these merging operations gives us a hierarchical tree, which we can represent in a dendrogram (see Fig. 4).

Two-Stage Clustering. Hierarchical clustering can give us a good impression of morphological structure between similar poses, such as those in Fig. 4. The higher-level structure, however, is less meaningful - groups of completely separate poses (running, sitting, walking) have no intuitive hierarchical relationship between them.

For this reason, we attempt first to cluster general types of poses. We use a two-stage clustering technique:

1. Different pose-types are defined using K-means clustering
2. Within each pose-type, variations and structure is investigated using hierarchical clustering.

K-Means with Stereographic Projections. Unlike hierarchical clustering, K-means cannot be applied naïvely to angular data - it cannot encode angle wraparound. Although appropriate variations of K-means exist, we follow Dortet and Berdanet [20] in simplifying the problem using *stereographic projection*. Here, for each person i, we map each angle θ_k to Cartesian form (x_k, y_k). It can be shown that the mean in stereographic space is equivalent to the circular mean in angular space.

We apply a K-means algorithm (with 50 replicates) to our pose-data in stereographic space. After manual inspection of the cluster means, original figures and associated in-cluster variances for a range of K from 2 to 50, we choose to learn $K = 16$ clusters.

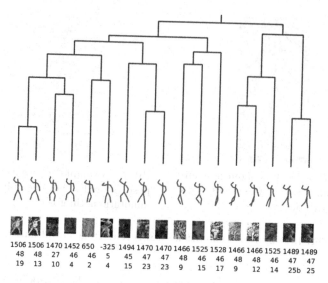

Fig. 4. A detail from a dendrogram of poses from our dataset, showing the pose, original image, year, panel number and image index for each pose.

4.2   Visualisation

For an art-historical interpretation of the clusters, intutive and accurate visualisations are required. Plotting the cluster mean is uninformative of the variance of each cluster - and can also lead to an uncharacteristically static pose (when compared with the cluster dendrograms).

We therefore model each cluster (in stereographic space) as a Gaussian, with mean μ and covariance Σ. To visualise the range of skeletons, we then take 10 samples from a narrower Gaussian: $\theta \sim N(\mu, 0.1 \times \Sigma)$.

Figure 5 shows the result of this Gaussian-sample visualisation. The range of each limb gives a qualitative, relative impression of the variance in each angle, whilst the silhouette of the figure gives an impression of the mean. We can immediately spot clusters with a very large variance (such as Cluster 10), as well as much narrower ones (Cluster 1).

4.3   Ideal-Type

Weber and the Ideal-Type. Although our Gaussian-sample visualisations give an idea as to the range of poses present in each cluster, it is interesting (from an art-historical perspective) to ask a subtly different question: what are the *defining characteristics* of each cluster? For instance, Christopher Johnson - in analysis of the figure of the Nymph - notes that [21, p.105] "The nymph is the paradigm of which individual nymphs are the exemplars". For each cluster, we seek to identify this paradigm.

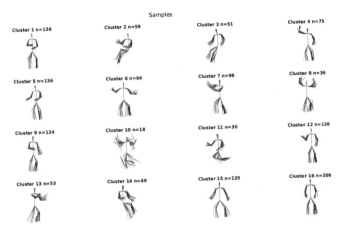

Fig. 5. A visualisation of 10 Gaussian samples taken from each cluster, showing the relative variance of each limb, for each cluster.

We interpret this set of defining characteristics as a Weberian[3] ideal-type[4]: the goal of ideal-type concept-construction is always to make clearly explicit not the class or average character but rather the unique individual character of cultural phenomena [23, p. 101–102].

We understand this ideal-type as a frequentist hypothesis-testing paradigm, where we test the hypothesis that each angle θ is differently-distributed for a *single* cluster than it is for the whole dataset. A detailed discussion on the deeper parallels between Weberian ideal-types and hypothesis-testing scientific models is provided elsewhere [24].

Frequentist Interpretation. In order to identify the *defining characteristics* of each cluster, we apply a two-sample Kolmogorov-Smirnov test for the distributions of each angle k, for each cluster i. The null hypothesis of this test is that samples were generated from the same distribution. Under our understanding of the ideal-type, if we can reject the null hypothesis, we can define the angle k as a *defining characteristic* of cluster i. In other words, if the distribution of $_{i,k}$ is significantly different to $_k$ (for all i), then the limb k is a defining characteristic of cluster i.

The Kolmogorov-Smirnov statistic between two samples, θ_1 and θ_2, is defined as:

$$D = \max_x(|F_1(x) - F_2(x)|)$$

---

[3] Weber and Warburg knew and respected each other's work [22, p. 68–69].
[4] Note that Weberian ideal-types are explicitly not 'ideal' in a value-judgement sense.

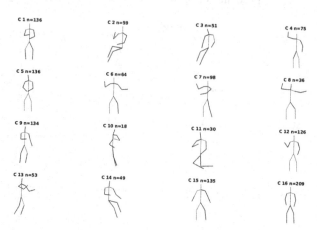

Fig. 6. Our frequentist ideal-type visualisation - limbs which compromise *defining characteristics* are coloured in red. (Color figure online)

where $F_1(x)$ is the proportion of θ_1 values that are less than x. We reject the null hypothesis (two samples are drawn from the same distribution) when:

$$D > c(\alpha)\frac{n + n'}{nn'}$$

at some confidence level α - we use a lookup table to calculate $c(\alpha)$. We use a 95 % confidence test: $\alpha = 0.05$.

Once we have calculated the defining limbs of each cluster, we can visualise them, as in Fig. 6. The visualisation is produced by taking the cluster means, and colouring the defining limbs in red. It should be noted that a defining limb can, in this sense, be very close to the mean - but with a different distribution around it. The legs of Cluster 16, for instance, are almost exactly at the mean, but with an atypically narrow distribution.

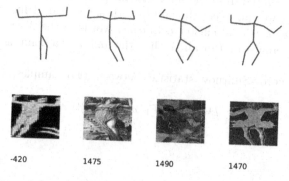

Fig. 7. A selection of the dendrogram of cluster 8, showing related poses (and years) from antiquity and the Renaissance.

Such an ideal-type visualisation as Fig. 6, combined with the Gaussian-sample visualisation in Fig. 5, can aid us in identifying the characteristic poses which constitute what Warburg describes as a Pathosformel - that is, a formula for the expression of emotion. One possible such instance, the cluster of figures with two raised arms, is shown in Fig. 7.

In particular, we note the antithetical nature of the first two images - very similar poses, one from antiquity and one from the Renaissance, but with different emotional implications. The first shows a personified star being chased away by the sun. Rather than fleeing, the boy looks towards the sun defiantly, with open arms (see Fig. 2a for the whole image). The second also represents a chased figure - Daphne, pursued by a desiring Apollo. After a long pursuit, Daphne prays to her father to destroy her beauty; and is turned into a tree. We thus see two morphologically similar poses but corresponding to two completely different notions of Pathos, defiance and desperation.

4.4   Nachleben

Having identified and investigated typical poses, we now turn our attention to Warburg's concept of Nachleben (see Sect. 1.2). In particular, we seek to identify some characteristic poses which are present in classical antiquity and in the Renaissance, and contrast them with those that seem to be novel inventions of the Renaissance.

We can see from Fig. 8 that some forms seem to be present in antiquity (specifically, before 250 A.D) and experience a Nachleben (rebirth) in the

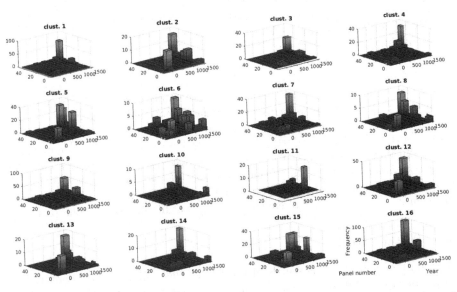

Fig. 8. 3D histograms showing the distribution through time (x-axis), and through panels (y-axis), of our 16 typical poses. Each time-period corresponds to 250 years.

Renaissance (after around 1250 A.D) - such as clusters 5, 12 and 15. Others (1, 4, 10, 11) appear to be inventions of the Renaissance, without a classical precedent.

Unfortunately, our dataset comprises only one-third of the panels of the Bilderatlas, so we cannot make strong claims as to what is *not* present. However, it is surprising that we find no historical pattern of Nachleben for the Nymph (cluster 4). She is regarded by Warburg as one of the key figures of the Nachleben, who described her as a "pagan [i.e. pre-Christian] goddess in exile" [25]. Despite this, she seems quite rare in classical antiquity in our dataset; where the pose does appear, it generally relates to soldiers holding spears and shields, and not to female Nymphs.

5   Conclusions

We have presented a methodology for extracting poses from a set of artwork of various styles, and for clustering and classifying these poses in 2D. From an art-historical point of view, we have given evidence to support some basic Warburgian notions: the presence of Pathosformeln, and their renewal from antiquity (the Nachleben). We have also made some more controversial suggestions: namely, that Pathosformeln can sometimes be characterised entirely by body pose (at least in the case of the Nymph), and that the Nymph does not seem to display an obvious Nachleben - at least, for our one-third subset of the Bilderatlas.

A clear limitation of our characterisation of the Pathosformel in terms of static poses is Warburg's own principle of antithesis - that similar poses are used for completely different actions. Whilst this static pose characterisation allows us to link similar antique and Renaissance forms together, we clearly ignore the inherent emotional ambiguity of static pose.

Indeed, we can propose a verifiable art-historical hypothesis based on Warburg's principle of antithesis. Artists might use visual cues for *motion* to give a static (image, not video) impression of dynamic pose. These visual movement cues might therefore suggest more precise emotional information.

Visual movement cues can be compared to Warburg's *accessory forms* [3]. In Warburg's discussion of Botticelli's *Birth of Venus* and *Spring*, he notes that Botticelli allows the Nymph to escape the emotional context of her classical legacy by manipulating "the surface mobility of inanimate accessory forms, draperies and hair" - after noting (in the same text) that the "most difficult problem in all art...is that of capturing images of life in motion" [26, p. 47].

5.1   Further Work

With only one-third of the panels of the Bilderatlas digitised and annotated, a clear priority for future work is to annotate the remaining two-thirds - particularly because our most polemical claim (about the lack of Nachleben of the Nymph) refers to what is *not* present in our data (so far).

If the remaining two-thirds of the panels contain the same number of human bodies, we should finish with a set of 5,000 figures from painting and sculpture, each annotated with 2D human pose. This dataset would be of interest to the computer vision community (which currently lacks a large-scale pose dataset comparable to [19]).

The Art Historian David Freedberg claims that emotions are inseparable from the movement of the body [5] - following our hypothesis above on accessory forms as visual cues for movement (and therefore emotion), we might seek to investigate whether motion cues are already encoded in 2D pose, and in what way other visual cues for motion disambiguate the emotional implications of a pose.

Acknowledgments. The authors would like to thank Isabella di Lenardo, Robin Osborne and John Robb, for their help and insights on the history of art and the body. Most of all, we are indebted to Franco Moretti, for his constant and wise guidance on this project.

References

1. Angel, S.: The mnemosyne atlas and the meaning of panel 79 in Aby Warburg's Oeuvre as a distributed object. Leonardo **44**(3), 266–267 (2011)
2. Warburg, A., Forster, K.W., Britt, D.: The Renewal of Pagan Antiquity: Contributions to the Cultural History of the European Renaissance. Getty Research Institute, Los Angeles (1999)
3. Michaud, P.: Aby Warburg and the Image in Motion. Hawkes Zone Books, New York (2004)
4. Forster, K., Mazzucco, K.: Introduzione ad Aby Warburg e all'Atlante della memoria. Bruno Mondadori (2002)
5. Freedberg, D.: Empathy, motion and emotion. Emotionen in Nahsicht f, Wie sich Gefuehle Ausdruck verschaffen, pp. 17–51 (2007)
6. Becker, C.: Aby Warburg's Pathosformel as methodological paradigm. J. Art Historiography (2013)
7. Argan, G.C.: Storia dell'arte italiana, vol. 1. 2nd edn. Sansoni, Florence (1971)
8. Osborne, R.: The History Written on the Classical Greek Body. Cambridge University Press, Cambridge (2011)
9. Ekman, P.: An argument for basic emotions. Cogn. Emotion **6**(3–4), 169–200 (1999)
10. Johansson, G.: Visual perception of biological motion and a model for its analysis. Percept. Psychophy. **14**(2), 201–211 (1973)
11. Atkinson, A.P., Dittrich, W.H., Gemmell, A.J., Young, A.W.: Emotion perception from dynamic and static body expressions in point-light and full-light displays. Perception **33**(6), 717–746 (2004)
12. Poppe, R.: A survey on vision-based human action recognition. Image and Vision Computing **28**(6), 976–990 (2010)
13. Atkinson, A.P., Tunstall, M.L., Dittrich, W.H.: Evidence for distinct contributions of form and motion information to the recognition of emotions from body gestures. Cognition **104**(1), 59–72 (2007)
14. Aviezer, H., Trope, Y., Todorov, A.: Body cues, not facial expressions, discriminate between intense positive and negative emotions. Science **338**(6111), 1225–1229 (2012)

15. Ginosar, S., Haas, D., Brown, T., Malik, J.: Detecting people in Cubist art. Computer Vision-ECCV 2014 (2014)
16. Carneiro, G., da Silva, N.: Artistic image classification: an analysis on the printart database. In: Computer Vision-ECCV 2014 Workshops (2014)
17. Pelt, C., Sorokin, A.: Designing a scalable crowdsourcing platform. In: Proceedings of the 2012 International Conference on Management of Data - SIGMOD 2012, New York, USA, p. 765. ACM Press, New York (2012)
18. Finin, T., Murnane, W., Karandikar, A., Keller, N., Martineau, J., Dredze, M.: Annotating named entities in Twitter data with crowdsourcing. In: Proceedings of the NAACL HLT 2010 Workshop on Creating Speech and Language Data with Amazon's Mechanical Turk, Association for Computational Linguistics, pp. 80–88, June 2010
19. Johnson, S., Everingham, M.: Clustered pose and nonlinear appearance models for human pose estimation. In: BMVC (2010)
20. Dortet-Bernadet, J., Wicker, N.: Model-based clustering on the unit sphere with an illustration using gene expression profiles. Science $9(1)$, 66–80 (2008)
21. Johnson, C.: Metaphor Lost and Found in Mnemosyne, pp. 70–109. Cornell University Press, New York (2012)
22. Schoell-Glass, C.: Aby Warburg and Anti-Semitism: Political Perspectives on Images and Culture. Wayne State University Press, Detroit (2008)
23. Weber, M.: Objectivity in social science and social policy. Methodol. Soc. Sci. **78**, 50–112 (1949)
24. Weinert, F.: Weber's ideal types as models in the social sciences. Science **41**, 73–93 (2010)
25. Agamben, G., Cuspinero, A.: Ninfas. Pre-textos (2010)
26. Johnson, C.D.: Memory, Metaphor, and Aby Warburg's Atlas of Images. Cornell University Press, New York (2012)

A New Database and Protocol for Image Reuse Detection

Furkan Isikdogan[1,2], İlhan Adıyaman[2], Alkım Almila Akdağ Salah[3],
and Albert Ali Salah[2(✉)]

[1] Department of Electrical and Computer Engineering,
The University of Texas at Austin, Austin, TX, USA
isikdogan@utexas.edu

[2] Department of Computer Engineering, Boğaziçi University, Istanbul, Turkey
ilhan.adiyaman@boun.edu.tr, salah@boun.edu.tr

[3] College of Communication, İstanbul Şehir University, Istanbul, Turkey
almilasalah@sehir.edu.tr

Abstract. The use of visual elements of an existing image while creating new ones is a commonly observed phenomenon in digital artworks. The practice, which is referred to as image reuse, is not an easy one to detect even with the human eye, less so using computational methods. In this paper, we study the automatic image reuse detection in digital artworks as an image retrieval problem. First, we introduce a new digital art database (BODAIR) that consists of a set of digital artworks that re-use stock images. Then, we evaluate a set of existing image descriptors for image reuse detection, providing a baseline for the detection of image reuse in digital artworks. Finally, we propose an image retrieval method tailored for reuse detection, by combining saliency maps with the image descriptors.

Keywords: Image database · Digital art · Image retrieval · Feature extraction · DeviantArt · Image reuse · BODAIR

1 Introduction

One of the main focus of art historical research is the detection of stylistic similarities between works of art. As early as 1915, Heinrich Wöllflin, who is deemed by many as the "father" of art history as a discipline, introduced the notion of comparing artworks to define the style of a period [1]. Art historians, connoisseurs, and art critics are trained to detect whether certain features of an artwork are apparent in another one, and whether two artworks belong to the same artist or not. The experts not only use their visual understanding for such detection, but also rely heavily on historical records and archival information, which are not always sufficiently clear or available. Hence, for decades, art historical research has applied scientific methods such as infrared and x-ray photographic techniques (among others) to help in different instances where the

© Springer International Publishing Switzerland 2016
G. Hua and H. Jégou (Eds.): ECCV 2016 Workshops, Part I, LNCS 9913, pp. 903–916, 2016.
DOI: 10.1007/978-3-319-46604-0_62

trained eye faltered. Using computational approaches in detecting stylistic traditions of artworks is a relatively new addition to the field [2]. In this paper, we introduce a new digital image database that consists of original artworks that are re-used to create new artworks. We use this database to examine approaches for image reuse detection. In the long run, trying to detect which image is reused with computational methods will help in detecting stylistic similarities between artworks in general [3].

In Western tradition, artists learned their trade by joining ateliers of masters as apprentices. With the introduction of printing press and the wider availability of paper, and especially due to the replacement of etchings on woodblocks with engravings on metal proliferated the art education in ateliers. Metal engravings started to be widely used to teach apprentices drawing, by copying known forms and designs. Novices used these models as the basis of their new artworks, and in that sense, these designs might be the first ones that were massively re-used in visual art. Today, a similar tendency is to use the so called "stock-images" for the same purpose: to help facilitate the design of a new artwork. These images are made freely available online, and can be found in repositories and dedicated websites. With the help of multimedia technologies and digital drawing tools, as well as the availability of free stock images, it has become a common approach in digital image creation to reuse existing images. The digital re-use scenarios are on the one hand quite different than their forefathers from centuries ago: they heavily rely on photo manipulation tools to generate a desired effect or design. On the other hand, certain photo manipulation tools offer the same (basic) design changes that were commonly used centuries ago. Unlike early archives with erroneous and missing data, today, we may have access to precise information about who has reused which image for which artwork. Social networks and online communities for digital artworks, such as DeviantArt[1], and 500px[2], help us to follow the interaction between artists to minute detail, and build a reliable database of artworks which have re-used other images.

Image reuse detection in digital art is a high-level semantic task, which can be challenging even for humans. Despite the advances in image retrieval and image copy detection techniques, automatic detection of image reuse remains a challenge due to the lack of annotated data and specific tools designed for the analysis of reuse in digital artworks. Image reuse detection differs from general-purpose image retrieval in its scale and amount of the reused pictorial elements. A small object in an artwork can constitute a major part in another composition. An image can be featured in another image in a variety of forms. Developing a global method that addresses all types of image reuse is challenging, as the types of image reuse and modifications vary greatly among different artists and genres of digital art. Another challenge in reuse detection is that the images can have similar content without actually reusing parts from each other. For example, a famous architectural structure can be depicted by several artists. An ideal image reuse detection system should be able to detect even a small amount

---

[1] http://www.deviantart.com.
[2] http://www.500px.com.

Fig. 1. Example images from the BODAIR database in the animal, food, nature, place, plant, and premade background categories.

of reuse without retrieving false positive images. To develop a robust framework for image reuse detection, it is essential to develop tools and datasets that are designed for the task.

The prolific expansion in the reuse of pictorial elements introduces problems related to the detection and analysis of image reuse. Automatic detection of image reuse would be useful for numerous tasks, including source image location, similar image retrieval [4,5], popularity and influence analysis [6], image manipulation and forgery detection [7–9], and copyright violation detection [8,10,11]. Information about the sources of elements in an image could be used in image search as a semantic variable in addition to low-level image features. Furthermore, such information would be useful for image influence analysis, for discovering the relationships between different genres of (digital) artworks, measuring the popularity of a specific piece of art, and detecting possible copyright violations.

In this paper, we first introduce a novel database called BODAIR (Bogazici-DeviantArt Image Reuse Database[3]). The BODAIR database is open for research use under a license agreement. To annotate BODAIR, we introduce a taxonomy in image re-use types and techniques. Next, we evaluate a set of baseline image retrieval methods on this database, discussing their strengths and weaknesses. Finally, we propose a saliency-based image retrieval approach to detect reuse on images.

The rest of the paper is organized as follows: Sect. 2 introduces the BODAIR database. Section 3 describes the methods that we employ in reuse detection and Sect. 4 presents the experimental results. Finally, Sect. 5 summarizes our contributions and conclusions.

2   The Bogazici-DeviantArt Image Reuse Database Database

DeviantArt[4] is a social network for artists and art enthusiasts with more than 38 million registered users. DeviantArt members post over 160,000 images every day. Images posted under the *stock image* category are usually published under an open license and are free to use by others. Using these images, we built an image reuse database. Being artistic creations, the images in our database pose a real challenge for reuse detection.

---

[3] Available from http://www.cmpe.boun.edu.tr/~salah/bodair.html.

[4] http://www.deviantart.com.

(a) Partial reuse   (b) Remake/inspiration

(c) Direct reuse   (d) Use as a background

Fig. 2. Examples to the types of reuse: Source images (left), destination images (right).

The etiquette of DeviantArt requires members to leave each other comments if they reuse an image. This tradition helped us to track down which stock images are used in which new works, by performing link and text analysis on the stock image comments. We used regular expressions in the comments to detect any reference to another artwork and crawled more than 16,000 images in the following six subcategories of stock images: animals, food, nature, places, plants, and premade backgrounds (e.g., Fig. 1). Our image crawler used a depth limited recursive search to download the reused images (children images) and related the images to their source images (parent images). In addition to the automatically extracted parent-children relationships between images, we manually annotated a total of 1,200 images for four reuse types and nine manipulation types:

Reuse Types

Partial reuse: superimposition of a selected area in an image on another one.
Direct reuse: use of an image as a whole, such as insertion or removal of objects, addition of frames or captions, color and texture filters, and background manipulations.
Remake: remake or inspirational use of an image, such as paintings, sketches, and comics based on another artwork.
Use as a background: use of an artwork as a part of the background in another image.

Manipulation Types

Color manipulations: brightness and contrast change, color replacement, hue and saturation shift, tint and shades, and color balance change.
Translation: moving the visual elements in an image.

Texture manipulations: altering the texture of the image, such as excessive blurring/sharpening, overlaying a texture, or tiling a pattern.
Text overlay: image captions, motivational posters, and flyer designs.
Rotation: rotation of elements in an image.
Aspect ratio change: non-proportional scaling of images.
Alpha Blending: partially transparent overlay of visual elements.
Mirroring: horizontal or vertical flipping of images.
Duplicative use: using a visual element more than one time.

Each image in the database has an ID and a reference to the ID of the original work if the image is a reused one. The manually annotated images also include the information about the aforementioned types of reuse and manipulation. The manually annotated images include 200 original images, selected among the most popular posts, and their derivatives in each of the six subcategories. The distribution of the partial reuse, direct reuse, use as a background, and remake/inspiration among the manually annotated images are 27 %, 47 %, 44 %, and 6 %, respectively. The direct reuse and background categories have a considerable overlap, since the background images are generally used as a whole without excessive cropping. In this classification, only the direct and partial reuse categories are considered to be mutually exclusive.

Examples of the types of reuse are shown in Fig. 2. Figure 3 shows the overlaps between different categories of image reuse in the database. The matrix is symmetric, and the diagonals show the total number of images annotated with a given reuse or manipulation category. Only *remake* is not included in this figure. There are 75 exemplars of *remake*, and since they are very different than the original stock images, they are not annotated with any manipulations. Subsequently, the *remake* category has no overlaps with other categories. Manipulation examples are shown in Fig. 4.

	Partial reuse	Direct reuse	Background	Color Manipulation	Translation	Texture Manipulation	Text Overlay	Rotation	Aspect Ratio Chg.	Alpha Blending	Mirroring	Duplication
Partial reuse	**323**	0	37	235	308	74	28	62	29	43	26	34
Direct reuse	0	**568**	400	409	246	165	142	7	33	4	13	11
Background	37	400	**526**	395	283	157	116	11	37	15	21	4
Color Manipulation	235	409	395	**717**	471	229	105	51	51	38	33	32
Translation	308	246	283	471	**628**	163	88	71	63	48	46	46
Texture Manipulation	74	165	157	229	163	**264**	38	21	10	14	6	8
Text Overlay	28	142	116	105	88	38	**180**	5	5	6	8	3
Rotation	62	7	11	51	71	21	5	**74**	10	7	4	13
Aspect ratio chg.	29	33	37	51	63	10	5	10	**70**	2	2	3
Alpha Blending	43	4	15	38	48	14	6	7	2	**50**	3	8
Mirroring	26	13	21	33	46	6	8	4	2	3	**47**	4
Duplication	34	11	4	32	46	8	3	13	3	8	4	**46**

Fig. 3. Overlaps between reuse types in the BODAIR database.

3   Methods

In this section, we describe the methods we apply for image reuse detection. We first summarize several image description methods that are used in matching-based tasks in computer vision, such as content-based image retrieval, image

(a) Aspect Ratio Change, Color Manipulation and Translation

(b) Rotation, Color and Texture Manipulations

(c) Mirroring and Translation

(d) Alpha Blending and Translation

(e) Translation

(f) Text Overlay and Color Manipulation

Fig. 4. Examples of manipulations.

copy detection, and object recognition. Then, we discuss how saliency maps could be combined with image descriptors to improve matching accuracy and reduce computation time in image reuse detection.

Representing an image by its most discriminant properties is an important factor to achieve higher accuracies. Different feature descriptors extract different features from the images to achieve invariance to certain conditions such as color, illumination or viewpoint changes. Traditional image recognition methods usually involve sampling keypoints, computing descriptors from the keypoints, and matching the descriptors [12]. The image descriptors can also be computed over the entire image without sampling keypoints. However, these global features usually perform poorly in detecting partial correspondences between images where a small portion of an image constitutes a major part of another image. Local descriptors, such as SIFT [13] and its color variants CSIFT [14], Opponent-SIFT [14], on the other hand, are more robust in the detection of partial matches. Although the local descriptors usually perform better than global approaches, computation of local descriptors can be computationally expensive as they usually produce a high-dimensional representation of the image which may create a bottleneck in large-scale image retrieval tasks. As suggested by Bosch et al. [12], Bag-of-visual-words (BoW) methods reduce the high-dimensional representation to a fixed-size feature vector, sacrificing some accuracy [14].

More recent approaches make use of convolutional neural networks (CNNs) to learn powerful models from the data itself [15–18]. Training these models usually requires a large dataset, such as the ImageNet [19] which consists of over 15 million images in more than 22,000 categories. However, it has been shown that the models trained on a set of natural images can be generalized to other datasets [20], and the features learned by a model can be transferred to another model with another task [21].

In this work, we evaluate five image descriptors that are commonly used in image matching and content-based image retrieval problems for image reuse detection: color histograms, Histogram of Oriented Gradients (HOG) [22], Scale Invariant Feature Transform (SIFT) [13], and the SIFT-variants OpponentSIFT and C-SIFT, which are shown to have a better overall performance than the original SIFT and many other color descriptors [14]. In addition, we also use a CNN model [15] pretrained on the ImageNet [19] as a feature extractor, using the fully connected layer outputs (FC6 and FC7) as feature vectors.

Different strategies in image description can lead to a fixed or variable size description of an image. A fixed-size vector representation of images allows the use of vector distance metrics, such as the Euclidean distance, to measure image similarity. As the color histograms and HOG features produce fixed-size image descriptions, candidate matches for a query image can be ranked in order of ascending standardized Euclidean distance. On the other hand, the local descriptors, SIFT and its variants, can extract features from a different number of keypoints on each image, resulting in a variable-size representation. Variable-size representations of images usually require computation-intensive pairwise matching processes. Such a matching process can be improved using an inlier selection algorithm, such as RANSAC, which selects random feature pairs and keep the largest set of inliers to find corresponding image matches [23].

Image saliency can help narrow down the areas of interest in image reuse detection. In our earlier work [24], we showed the effectiveness of using saliency maps in image description for image reuse detection. The purpose of the saliency map is to represent the conspicuity or *saliency* at every spatial location in the visual field by a scalar quantity and to guide the selection of attended locations [25]. Many stock images feature a foreground object that is more likely to be used in other artworks. Therefore, features can be extracted only from the salient regions, which will reduce the processing time and improve the matching

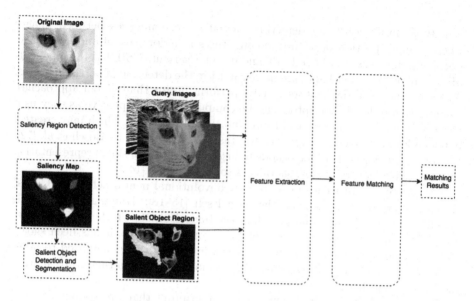

Fig. 5. Proposed framework for image reuse detection.

accuracy. We use the saliency maps only in the stock images, assuming that each stock image provides such a region of interest to the composition images. We extract features from the query images as a whole, as the use of saliency maps could exclude some references completely.

The overall proposed framework (see Fig. 5) consists of four modules: salient region detection, salient object segmentation, feature extraction, and feature matching. For saliency map estimation, we use a recently proposed Boolean Map based Saliency (BMS) model [26], which is an efficient and simple-to-implement estimator of saliency. Despite its simplicity, BMS achieved state-of-the-art performance on five eye tracking datasets. To segment salient objects, we threshold the saliency maps at their mean intensity to create a binary segmentation mask.

4   Experimental Results

To assess the feature descriptors for detecting image reuse, we designed several experiments. In the experiments, we divided the BODAIR database into a gallery containing a set of stock images and a query set with images that reuse stock images in the gallery. In each experiment, we evaluated the usefulness of the descriptors with a retrieval paradigm. Given a query image I, we ranked the images in the gallery in descending order of probability that the stock image is used in the query image.

4.1   Tuning the Model Parameters

We chose the keypoint sampling strategy and the number of visual words experimentally. For 144 stock and 1,056 query images in the database, we ran the SIFT

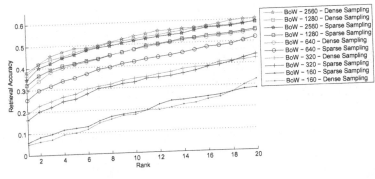

Fig. 6. Cumulative matching accuracies for BoW model with different parameters.

descriptor with two sampling strategies: sparse salient keypoint detection, and dense sampling. For sparse sampling, we used the default keypoint detector of SIFT, and for dense sampling, we sampled every 8th pixel. Then, we generated a BoW codebook with different vocabulary sizes. We selected the number of clusters for the BoW model as 160, 320, 640, 1,280, and 2,560. The first 20 rank retrieval accuracies for the above-mentioned parameters are shown in Fig. 6.

When the BoW framework is used, dense sampling worked better, as also shown in Nowak et al.'s work on the evaluation of sampling strategies [27]. Thus, we selected uniform dense sampling as our default sampling strategy for the BoW methods. However, in the experiments where we use SIFT with RANSAC without the BoW framework, we selected sparse sampling as our default sampling strategy after some preliminary experiments. Dense sampling increases the outliers in the matching results, which furthermore increases the complexity of finding inliers using RANSAC. Furthermore, sparse sampling results in a smaller set of features, reducing the computational cost.

The accuracy increased parallel to an increase in the number of clusters, i.e. visual words. Increasing the number of clusters did not improve the performance significantly after a point of saturation (Fig. 6). Therefore, we selected the number of visual words as 1,280 in the rest of the experiments.

4.2   Evaluation of the Methods

We ran experiments on the BODAIR database to evaluate the image description methods for image reuse detection. We compared the methods for all four types of reuse and nine types of manipulations. We calculated and compared Top-1 and Top-5 retrieval accuracies for all of the methods.

Figures 7 and 8 show the Top-1 and Top-5 retrieval accuracies, respectively, for the four types of reuse. As the figures show, methods using sparse sampling outperformed dense sampling methods for SIFT with RANSAC on all types of reuse, except *remake*, in the BODAIR database. In the *direct reuse* category, SIFT-based methods produced the best retrieval results. This is in line with

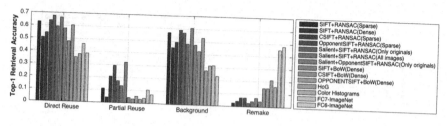

Fig. 7. Top-1 retrieval accuracies on the BODAIR database for the four types of reuse.

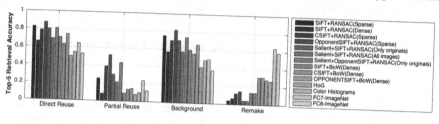

Fig. 8. Top-5 retrieval accuracies on the BODAIR database for the four types of reuse.

Mikolajczyk and Schmid's earlier results on the use of SIFT for object recognition [28]. The methods that rely on the BoW framework failed to outperform the RANSAC-based methods. Color-based variants of SIFT descriptors gave better results than standard SIFT descriptor. In the *partial reuse* category, the local descriptors produced the most accurate results. Using saliency to reduce the matched area in the gallery image also marginally improved the performance in the SIFT approach with RANSAC. Figure 9 shows an example RANSAC matching. In this example, the query image partially reuses the stock image with *color manipulation* and *translation*.

The *remake* category is relatively less restricted, therefore more challenging, than the other types of reuse. Images in this category can be similar to their source images in color, texture, edge distribution, or another aspect. None of the compared methods provided a holistic approach that could recognize all types of artistic remake. Therefore, all of the methods performed poorly on remade images.

We also evaluated these methods and how they perform when it comes to the nine classified image manipulation types: color manipulation, translation, texture manipulation, text overlay, rotation, aspect ratio change, alpha blending, mirroring, and duplication. Overall, the use of saliency maps improved the Top-1 accuracies, although it caused a small decrease in the Top-5 accuracies. HOG features showed poor performance on cropped and translated images, since HOG is not robust to translations when computed globally. All descriptors seem to have a poor performance on images involving rotations, alpha blending, mirroring, and duplication. However, these types of manipulations are frequently observed in tandem with other manipulations in our database. Therefore, the performance of the descriptors is likely to be affected by more than a single type

(a) Stock Image   (b) Query Image

(c) Tentative Matches   (d) Inliner Matches Only

Fig. 9. Examples of matching with RANSAC. (Color figure online)

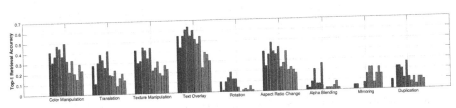

Fig. 10. Top-1 retrieval accuracies on the BODAIR database for nine different types of manipulations.

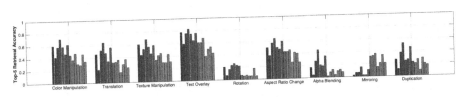

Fig. 11. Top-5 retrieval accuracies on the BODAIR database for nine different types of manipulations.

of manipulation. Experimental results for each of the nine types of manipulations are shown in Figs. 10 and 11.

Overall, SIFT and its color-based variants resulted in a higher accuracy without using the BoW framework. Saliency-based approaches provided a better Top-1 retrieval accuracy almost in all types of reuse and manipulations, when they are applied to the original images only. Even though CNN-based approaches failed to outperform SIFT and its color-based variants, the results are promising. With its overall high performance, we recommend using the Opponent SIFT descriptors with RANSAC as a baseline model for the future use of the BODAIR database.

To investigate the poor performance on the *rotation* manipulations, we took 12 rotated versions of each query image, extracted SIFT descriptors, and used them in comparisons with the gallery. We took the best matching rotation for each gallery image. The Top-1 accuracy showed some slight improvement (from 0.09 to 0.11), but the Top-5 accuracy did not change. The reason, we figure, is that *rotation* is often used together with other manipulation and reuse types. The database contains 74 images with *rotation*, of which 71 contain a *translation*, 62 contain *partial reuse*, and 51 contain *color manipulation*.

5   Conclusions

In this work, we focused on how to detect image reuse in digitally created artworks. To that end, we first collected stock images from DeviantArt, a website where digital artworks are posted by users, and built the BODAIR database. Using automatic link and text analysis in the images' comment sections, as well as manual labeling, we made available a database that has two sets of images: stock images, and images that reuse those stock images. We furthermore made the distinction between "type of reuse" and "type of manipulation", i.e. we highlighted the difference between the contextual approach, and technical approach in reuse. We have detected four type of reuse scenarios, and nine ways of manipulations. We evaluated methods for image reuse detection that are widely used in related tasks, such as image retrieval and object recognition. Lastly, we improved the performance of these methods by using saliency maps. The methods we evaluated provide a baseline for the future research on image reuse detection.

References

1. Wölfflin, H.: Kunstgeschichtliche Grundbegriffe: das Problem der Stilentwicklung in der neueren Kunst. Münich, Hugo Bruckmann (1915)
2. Stork, D.G.: Computer vision and computer graphics analysis of paintings and drawings: an introduction to the literature. In: Jiang, X., Petkov, N. (eds.) CAIP 2009. LNCS, vol. 5702, pp. 9–24. Springer, Heidelberg (2009). doi:10.1007/ 978-3-642-03767-2_2
3. Akdag Salah, A.A., Salah, A.A.: Flow of innovation in deviantart: following artists on an online social network site. Mind Soc. 12(1), 137–149 (2013)
4. Smeulders, A., Worring, M., Santini, S., Gupta, A., Jain, R.: Content-based image retrieval at the end of the early years. IEEE Trans. Pattern Anal. Mach. Intell. 22(12), 1349–1380 (2000)
5. Liu, Y., Zhang, D., Lu, G., Ma, W.Y.: A survey of content-based image retrieval with high-level semantics. Pattern Recogn. 40(1), 262–282 (2007)
6. Buter, B., Dijkshoorn, N., Modolo, D., Nguyen, Q., van Noort, S., van der Poel, B., Akdag Salah, A.A., Salah, A.A.: Explorative visualization and analysis of a social network for arts: the case of deviantART. J. Convergence 2(2), 87–94 (2011)
7. Bayram, S., Avcibas, I., Sankur, B., Memon, N.: Image manipulation detection. J. Electron. Imaging 15(4), 041102 (2006)
8. Ke, Y., Sukthankar, R., Huston, L., Ke, Y., Sukthankar, R.: Efficient near-duplicate detection and sub-image retrieval. In: ACM Multimedia, pp. 869–876 (2004)
9. Fridrich, A.J., Soukal, B.D., Lukáš, A.J.: Detection of copy-move forgery in digital images. In: in Proceedings of Digital Forensic Research Workshop, Citeseer (2003)
10. Kim, C.: Content-based image copy detection. Signal Process. Image Commun. 18(3), 169–184 (2003)
11. Zhao, W.L., Ngo, C.W.: Scale-rotation invariant pattern entropy for keypoint-based near-duplicate detection. IEEE Trans. Image Process. 18(2), 412–423 (2009)
12. Bosch, A., Muoz, X., Mart, R.: Which is the best way to organize/classify images by content? Image Vis. Comput. 25(6), 778–791 (2007)
13. Lowe, D.: Distinctive image features from scale-invariant keypoints. Int. J. Comput. Vis. 60(2), 91–110 (2004)
14. Van De Sande, K., Gevers, T., Snoek, C.: Evaluating color descriptors for object and scene recognition. IEEE Trans. Pattern Anal. Mach. Intell. 32(9), 1582–1596 (2010)
15. Krizhevsky, A., Sutskever, I., Hinton, G.E.: Imagenet classification with deep convolutional neural networks. In: Advances in Neural Information Processing Systems (2012)
16. He, K., Zhang, X., Ren, S., Sun, J.: Deep residual learning for image recognition. In: Proceedings of IEEE CVPR, pp. 770–778 (2016)
17. Simonyan, K., Zisserman, A.: Very deep convolutional networks for large-scale image recognition. arXiv preprint arXiv:1409.1556 (2014)
18. Szegedy, C., Liu, W., Jia, Y., Sermanet, P., Reed, S., Anguelov, D., Erhan, D., Vanhoucke, V., Rabinovich, A.: Going deeper with convolutions. In: Proceedings of the IEEE Conference on Computer Vision and Pattern Recognition, pp. 1–9 (2015)
19. Russakovsky, O., Deng, J., Su, H., Krause, J., Satheesh, S., Ma, S., Huang, Z., Karpathy, A., Khosla, A., Bernstein, M., Berg, A.C., Fei-Fei, L.: ImageNet large scale visual recognition challenge. Int. J. Comput. Vis. (IJCV) 115(3), 211–252 (2015)

20. Zeiler, M.D., Fergus, R.: Visualizing and understanding convolutional networks. In: Fleet, D., Pajdla, T., Schiele, B., Tuytelaars, T. (eds.) ECCV 2014. LNCS, vol. 8689, pp. 818–833. Springer, Heidelberg (2014). doi:10.1007/978-3-319-10590-1_53
21. Yosinski, J., Clune, J., Bengio, Y., Lipson, H.: How transferable are features in deep neural networks? In: Advances in neural information processing systems, pp. 3320–3328 (2014)
22. Dalal, N., Triggs, B.: Histograms of oriented gradients for human detection. In: IEEE Computer Society Conference on Computer Vision and Pattern Recognition, CVpPR 2005, vol. 1, pp. 886–893. IEEE (2005)
23. Fischler, M.A., Bolles, R.C.: Random sample consensus: a paradigm for model fitting with applications to image analysis and automated cartography. Commun. ACM 24(6), 381–395 (1981)
24. Isikdogan, F., Salah, A.: Affine invariant salient patch descriptors for image retrieval. In: International Workshop on Image and Audio Analysis for Multimedia Interactive Services, Paris, France (2013)
25. Itti, L., Koch, C., Niebur, E.: A model of saliency-based visual attention for rapid scene analysis. IEEE Trans. Pattern Anal. Mach. Intell. 20(11), 1254–1259 (1998)
26. Zhang, J., Sclaroff, S.: Saliency detection: a Boolean map approach. In: Proceedings of the IEEE International Conference on Computer Vision, pp. 153–160 (2013)
27. Nowak, E., Jurie, F., Triggs, B.: Sampling strategies for bag-of-features image classification. In: Leonardis, A., Bischof, H., Pinz, A. (eds.) ECCV 2006. LNCS, vol. 3954, pp. 490–503. Springer, Heidelberg (2006). doi:10.1007/11744085_38
28. Mikolajczyk, K., Schmid, C.: A performance evaluation of local descriptors. IEEE Trans. Pattern Anal. Mach. Intell. 27(10), 1615–1630 (2005)

Author Index